The Reviewers Say

"Shtern is the first to uncover the techniques of writing software that is maintainable. For programmers of all levels, it's insightful, easy-to-read, and packed with sensible advice and helpful examples."

—Daniel F. Costello
Senior Software Engineer
GE Marquette Medical Systems, Inc.

"A great book for either the novice or experienced C programmer wishing to gain a solid understanding of the C++ language as well as basic object-oriented concepts."

—Steve Glass
Senior Software Engineer
Motorola

CORE C++

A Software Engineering Approach

ISBN 0-13-085729-7

90000

9 780130 857293

PRENTICE HALL PTR
CORE SERIES

* Sun Microsystems Press titles.

CORE C++
A Software Engineering Approach

VICTOR SHTERN

Prentice Hall PTR, Upper Saddle River, NJ 07458
www.phptr.com

Library of Congress Cataloging-in-Publication Data

Shtern, Victor.
   Core C++: a software engineering approach / Victor Shtern.
      p. cm.
   Includes bibliographical references and index.
   ISBN 0-13-085729-7
   1. C++ (Computer programming language) I. Title.

   QA76.73.C153 S48 2000
   005.13'3--dc21   00-027507

Editorial/Production Supervision: *Jan H. Schwartz*
Acquisitions Editor: *Tim Moore*
Editorial Assistant: *Julie Okulicz*
Development Editor: *Jim Markham*
Marketing Manager: *Bryan Gambrel*
Buyer: *Maura Goldstaub*
Cover Design: *Talar Agasyan*
Cover Design Direction: *Jerry Votta*
Art Director: *Gail Cocker-Bogusz*
Series Interior Design: *Meg Van Arsdale*
Compositor: *MetroVoice Publishing Services*

© 2000 Prentice Hall PTR
Prentice-Hall, Inc.
Upper Saddle River, NJ 07458

Prentice Hall books are widely used by corporations and government agencies for training, marketing, and resale.

The publisher offers discounts on this book when ordered in bulk quantities.
For more information, contact Corporate Sales Department, phone: 800-382-3419;
fax: 201-236-7141; e-mail: corpsales@prenhall.com
Or write: Prentice Hall PTR
         Corporate Sales Department
         One Lake Street
         Upper Saddle River, NJ 07458

Printed in the United States of America
10 9 8 7 6 5 4 3 2 1

ISBN 0-13-085729-7

Prentice-Hall International (UK) Limited, **London**
Prentice-Hall of Australia Pty. Limited, **Sydney**
Prentice-Hall Canada Inc., **Toronto**
Prentice-Hall Hispanoamericana, S.A., **Mexico**
Prentice-Hall of India Private Limited, **New Delhi**
Prentice-Hall of Japan, Inc., **Tokyo**
Pearson Education Asia Pte. Ltd.
Editora Prentice-Hall do Brasil, Ltda., **Rio de Janeiro**

To Ludmila

Contents

PART 2

OBJECT-ORIENTED PROGRAMMING WITH C++ .. 361

7   PROGRAMMING WITH C++ FUNCTIONS 363

PART 3

OBJECT-ORIENTED PROGRAMMING
WITH AGGREGATION AND INHERITANCE . . 693

12   COMPOSITE CLASSES: PITFALLS AND ADVANTAGES. . . 695

PART 4

Preface

Congratulations! You have opened one of the most useful C++ books on the market! It will teach you the strengths and weaknesses of C++, and it will do this better than any other book I have seen. And I have seen a lot of C++ books.

How Is This Different from Other C++ Books?

Of course, any author can claim that his or her book is one of the best on the market. What sets this book apart is its software engineering and maintenance perspective on writing C++ code. Very few C++ books (if any) do that.

Why is the software engineering and maintenance approach important? The point is that C++ changed not only the way we *write* computer programs, it also changed the way we *learn* programming languages. In the "good old days," you would spend a day or two looking at the basic syntax of the language, then you would try your hand at simple programming problems. Then you would learn more-complex syntax and would tackle more-complex problems. In a week or two (or in three or four weeks for a really complex language), you would have seen it "all" and could pose as an "expert."

It's different with C++; a very large and very complex language. Granted, it is a superset of C, and you can learn to write simple C programs (and, hence, C++ programs) very quickly. But things are different for complex programs. If the programmer does not know C++ well, a complex C++ program will not be portable; its code will be difficult to reuse, and it will be difficult to maintain.

C++ is a great language—it was created as a general-purpose engineering language, and its design is a clear success. Today, C++ is a language of choice for business, engineering, and even real-time applications. Significant effort was spent on the design of the language, to ensure that C++ programs provide great performance, that they support dynamic memory management, and that different parts of programs could be made relatively independent. Yet in all three areas, things can potentially go wrong even with a syntactically correct and thoroughly tested C++ program:

1. It can be slow—much slower—than a comparable C program.

2. It can contain memory management errors that affect the program only when memory usage changes (e.g., another program is installed); these errors might crash the program or quietly produce incorrect results.

3. It can contain dependencies between different parts of the program so that the maintainer has a hard time understanding the intent of the designer; a poorly written C++ program can be harder to maintain and reuse than a non-object-oriented program.

How important is this? If you are writing a small program that will be used only for a short time, then execution speed, memory management, maintainability, and reusability may not be of great importance. All that counts is your ability to quickly produce a solution. If this solution is not satisfactory, you can cut your losses by throwing the program away and writing another one. For this, any C++ book would do (but hey, you can still buy this one and enjoy its informal style and original insights into the language and its usage).

However, if you are working in a group, creating large applications that cannot be easily discarded and will be maintained for a long time, everything matters. The software engineering and maintenance approach I am advancing in this book is very useful and quite unique. Most books on the market do not mention these issues at all. (Just check their indexes and see for yourself.)

When they do, they fail to spell out the techniques that can remedy a tough situation.

Another important characteristic of this book is its approach to the presentation of the material. There are many books on the market that do a good job enumerating the features of the language but do a mediocre job teaching you how to use the language. This is similar to learning a natural language. If you read a French grammar book, will it enable you to speak French? I did not study French, but I did study English, and I know—reading grammar books does not help to develop language fluency. In this book, I will show you how to use and how not to use the language, especially from the point of view of reusability and future maintenance.

Another teaching issue is that C++ features are so intertwined that it is hard to present C++ in a linear fashion, from simple to more complex. Many C++ authors do not even try. They say that these efforts "offend the intelligence of the reader." As a result, they might mention in Chapter 3 a concept that is explained only in Chapter 8, leaving the reader intimidated and frustrated.

My approach to teaching C++ is different. I introduce topics cyclically, first as a general overview and then again at a greater depth, with bells and whistles, and nowhere will your understanding depend on material in later chapters.

I developed my approach through years of teaching working software professionals. At Boston University Metropolitan College, most of my students hold professional jobs and come to classes in the evening in search of professional growth. I also taught numerous professional development seminars and on-site training courses. I developed great empathy for the students and their struggle with language concepts and programming techniques, and I translated this experience into a well-thought-out sequence of topics, examples, counterexamples, and recommendations. I think that my approach to teaching C++ is fairly unique, and you will benefit from it.

Who This Book Is For

This book is written for professionals who are looking for a no-nonsense presentation of practical details combined with a deep understanding of C++ subtleties.

This book is written for you if you are looking for practical details of new technologies with a thorough discussion of their use.

It is written for you if you have experience in other languages and are moving to C++. If you are an experienced C++ programmer, you will find this book useful and sometimes an eye-opener. If this is your first programming book (and this is perfectly all right if it is), you will be well rewarded for the effort spent on reading it.

How This Book Is Organized

I decided not to follow other authors who give you a detailed tour of their books, explaining what is covered and where. Unfamiliar terms, concepts and techniques will not make much sense to you now and will probably be quite boring. This is why I put the summary of the book into its final chapter, Chapter 19, "What We Have Learned," and you can read it if you are interested. It makes more sense there.

Instead, let me tell you what parts of the book might be of interest to you, depending on your background and experience.

- If you are experienced in C++, Parts 3 and 4 will be most useful to you with their coverage of C++ power and programming pitfalls. If, in your initial study of C++, you were rushed to objects without building your muscle in procedural programming, memory management, and creating maintainable code, a review of Parts 1 and 2 will also be helpful (and interesting).

- If you are an experienced C programmer who wants to move on to C++, Parts 2, 3, and 4 are written for you. If you briefly review Part 1, you might find the discussion of C from the software engineering and maintenance perspective interesting.

- If you a programmer with experience in high-level languages other than C, C++, or Java, you should probably start with Part 1.

- If you are looking for an introduction to programming, you should skip Chapter 1, "Object-Oriented Approach: What's So Good About It?": It will be too abstract for you at this stage. Study the other chapters of Part 1 first, then go back to Chapter 1, and then continue with Parts 2, 3, and 4.

Conventions Used in This Book

All the code presented in the numbered listings in this book has been thoroughly debugged and tested using several compilers, including Microsoft Visual C++, Borland, and GNU compilers. This code can be run without any modifications. The code snippets outside of the listings have also been debugged and tested. They are runnable, but they require a harness to be run.

Throughout the book, the code listings and snippets are presented in a monospace font. The same is true of C++ terms in the text of the book. If, for example, I am discussing a C++ class whose name is "Account," I will write it as `Account`, the way it would be written in program code. When I talk about private data members, I will use the regular font for the word "private" and the monospace font for the keyword `private`.

Icons denote statements that are particularly useful or need your special attention. They are notes, tips, and alerts.

Note

This icon flags information that deserves special attention, such as an interesting fact about the topic at hand or one that the reader may want to keep in mind while programming.

Alert

This icon flags information that, while useful, may cause unexpected results or serious frustration.

Tip

This icon flags particularly useful information that will save the reader time, highlight a valuable programming tip, or offer specific advice on increasing productivity.

Accessing the Source Code

It is important to practice when you learn a language. Studying C++ without practicing it is as effective as taking a driver education course without driving: You'll learn a lot of useful things about driving, but you will not be able to drive. I strongly recommend that you experiment with the programs discussed in this book. The source code for all the listings can be found at the following site:

```
ftp://ftp.prenhall.com/pub/ptr/c++programming.w-050/corec++
```

Feedback

This book was thoroughly reviewed, carefully edited, and meticulously proofread. Still, some errors might remain.

In my drive to produce a unique book, I might have made statements that are groundless, unjustified, or plain erroneous. Or, they could be controversial and you might want to debate them.

Please do not hesitate to contact me at the following e-mail address:

```
shtern@bu.edu.
```

For each typo or error that is pointed out to me or for each valid point regarding a discussion in the book, I promise to mention the names of the first two people who do so in the next edition of this book.

Acknowledgments

Many people helped me to make this book a reality and I am grateful to all of them. First, I would like to thank Bjarne Stroustrup for designing this wonderful and powerful programming language. We owe it all to him.

Next, I would like to thank Timothy Budd, Tom Cargill, Jim Coplien, Cay Horstmann, Ivor Horton, Bertrand Meyer, Scott Meyers, and Stephen Prata. They wrote programming books that have helped me to develop my own vision of C++ programming.

I am indebted to my students at Boston University and to participants in professional development seminars and on-site training courses that I have taught. Their questions and concerns helped me understand what works and what does not work in teaching C++.

At Boston University, my sincere thanks go to Tanya (Stoyanka) Zlateva, Jay Halfond, and Dennis Berkey. I am grateful for their faith in this project. By giving me the time to complete it, they made this book possible.

I would like to acknowledge the work of technical reviewers Steve Glass, Dan Costello, and C. L. Tondo. Their efforts purged the book of many embarrassing mistakes that I myself did not notice.

At Prentice Hall, I would like to thank the book's development editor, Jim Markham, for his help and encouragement. It was Jim who first told me that my writing was of good quality despite the fact that English is not my first language. He also prodded me not to go off on tangents of soul searching but to stick to the schedule instead. He almost succeeded.

I would also like to thank Jan Schwartz, the Prentice Hall production editor, and her copyediting staff who patiently struggled with my Russian way of using articles and prepositions and made the book sound like English.

Most and foremost, I would like to thank Tim Moore, my Prentice Hall acquisitions editor. He found time to listen to my proposal, had imagination to believe me, and had enthusiasm to tell everybody in sight that this was going to be a great book. If it were not for Tim, this book would never have happened. Thanks, Tim, your efforts are very much appreciated!

I am grateful to my family who encouraged me, admired me, and let me do my writing without distracting me too much *with* the mundane needs of running the household. The last detail is particularly important: While I was writing this book, my wife was writing hers. I also encouraged her, admired her, and let her do her writing without distracting her too much *from* the mundane needs of running the household.

Last, but not least, I would like to acknowledge the late Senator Henry M. Jackson (D, Washington) and Representative Charles Vanik (D, Ohio), the authors of the Jackson-Vanik amendment that linked human rights with foreign trade benefits, which is under fire from many quarters. I am one of the fortunate people whose life was affected by this linkage. Because of this, the difference between freedom and bondage is an immediate personal experience for me rather than a nice, but abstract, concept. And for that I am very grateful.

CORE C++
A Software Engineering Approach

Part 1

INTRODUCTION TO PROGRAMMING WITH C++

The first part of this book is about foundations of programming with C++. As everybody knows, C++ is an object-oriented language. But what does this mean? Why is using an object-oriented programming language better than using a traditional non-object-oriented language? What should you pay attention to while programming so that you reap the benefits of object orientation? Often, people take the object-oriented approach for granted, and this reduces the effectiveness of its use.

The first chapter answers these questions. It is all about breaking the program into parts. A large program has to be written as a collection of relatively independent, but communicating and cooperating, components. If, however, you break apart what should be kept together, you introduce excessive communications and dependencies between parts of the program, and the code becomes more difficult to reuse and maintain. If you leave together, in the same component, what can and should be broken into separate pieces, you wind up with complex and confusing code which is—guess what—difficult to reuse and maintain.

There is no magic in using objects. Using them in and of themselves brings no benefits. However, thinking about your program in terms of objects helps you to avoid these two dangers: breaking apart what should belong together and keeping together what should be put into separate parts. Chapter 1, "Object-Oriented Approach: What's So Good About It?" discusses these issues—it shows which problems should be solved with the use of the object-oriented approach and how the object-oriented approach solves these problems.

Chapter 2, "Getting Started Quickly: A Brief Overview of C++," gives you a brief introduction to the language, including objects. The introduction is high level only. (You have to read other chapters of the book to see the details.) Nevertheless, this chapter covers enough to enable you to write simple C++ programs and prepares you for the detailed study of the strong and weak features of C++.

Other chapters in Part 1 present the basic non-object-oriented features of the language. According to the promise I made in Chapter 1, I pay particular attention to writing reusable and maintainable code. For each C++ construct, I explain how to use and how not to use it. Even though I do not discuss objects yet, the presentation becomes quite complex, especially in Chapter 6, "Memory Management: The Stack and The Heap." After all, C++ is a complex language. Skip topics that you find obscure and come back to them later, when you have more time to concentrate on coding details.

OBJECT-ORIENTED APPROACH: WHAT'S SO GOOD ABOUT IT?

Topics in this Chapter

Chapter 1

The object-oriented approach is sweeping all areas of software development. It opens new horizons and offers new benefits. Many developers take it for granted that these benefits exist and that they are substantial. But what are they? Do they come automatically, just because your program uses objects rather than functions?

In this chapter, I will first describe why we need the object-oriented approach. Those of you who are experienced software professionals, can skip this description and go on directly to the explanation of why the object-oriented approach to software construction is so good.

Those of you who are relatively new to the profession should read the discussion of the software crisis and its remedies to make sure you understand the context of the programming techniques I am going to advocate in this book. It should give you a better understanding of what patterns of C++ coding contribute to the quality of your program, what patterns inhibit quality, and why.

Given the abundance of low quality C++ code in industry, this is very important. Many programmers take it for granted that using C++ and its classes delivers all the advantages, whatever they are, automatically. This is not right. Unfortunately, most C++ books support this incorrect perception by concentrating on C++ syntax and avoiding any discussion of the quality of C++ code. When developers do not know what to aim for in C++ code, they wind up with object-oriented programs that are built the old way. These programs are no better than traditional C, PL/I (or whatever—insert your favorite language) programs and are as difficult to maintain.

The Origins of the Software Crisis

The object-oriented approach is yet another way to fight the so-called software crisis in industry: frequent cost overruns, late or canceled projects, incomplete system functionality, and software errors. The negative consequences of errors in software range from simple user inconvenience to not-so-simple economic losses from incorrectly recorded transactions. Ultimately, software errors pose dangers to human lives and cause mission failures. Correction of errors is expensive and often results in skyrocketing software costs.

Many experts believe that the reason for software crisis is the lack of standard methodology: The industry is still too young. Other engineering professions are much older and have established techniques, methodologies, and standards.

Consider, for example, the construction industry. In construction, standards and building codes are in wide use. Detailed instructions are available for every stage of the design and building process. Every participant knows what the expectations are and how to demonstrate whether or not the quality criteria have been met. Warranties exist and are verifiable and enforceable. Consumer protection laws protect the consumer from unscrupulous or inept operators.

The same is true of newer industries, like the automobile industry or electrical engineering. In all these areas of human endeavor we find industry-wide standards, commonly accepted development and construction methodologies, manufacturer warranties, and consumer protection laws. Another important characteristic of these established industries is that the products are assembled from ready-made components. These components are standardized, thoroughly tested, and mass-produced.

Compare this with the state of the software industry. There are no standards to speak of. Of course, professional organizations are trying to do their best, coming up with standards ranging from specification writing to software testing to user-computer interfaces. But these standards only scratch the surface—there are no software development processes and methodologies that would be universally accepted, enforced, and followed. Mass-market software warranties are a joke: The consumer is lucky if the manufacturer is responsible for the cost of distribution medium. Return policies are nonexistent: If you open the box, you forfeit your right to ever get your money back.

The products are crafted by hand. There are no ready-made, off-the-shelf components. There is no universally accepted agreement what the components and the products should do. In its legal suit against Microsoft, the United States government got into an argument over the definition of the *operating system* and its components—whether the browser is part of the operating system or just another application, like a word processor, spreadsheet, or appointment scheduler. The operating system is as important to the computer as the ignition system to the car (probably even more so). But could you imagine a legal argument over the composition of the ignition system? We all know that when the technology required it, a carburetor was part of the ignition system. When technology changed, it was eliminated without public discussion.

The young age of the software industry has definitely contributed to the situation. Hopefully, some elements of this dismal picture will disappear in the future. However, this young age did not prevent software industry from becoming a multibillion dollar one that plays a crucial role in the economy. The Internet changed the way we do commerce and search for information. It also changed the stock market landscape beyond recognition.

Doomsayers heralded the Year 2000 problem as a major menace to the economy. It is not important for the purposes of this discussion whether or not those fears were justified. What *is* important is that the software industry has matured enough in terms of sheer power. If a software problem can potentially disrupt the very fabric of the Western society, it means that the industry plays an important role in the society. However, its technology lagging behind other industries, mostly because of the nature of the software development process.

Very few software systems are so simple that one person can specify it, build it according to the specification, use it for its intended purpose, and maintain it when the requirements change or errors are discovered. These simple systems have a limited purpose and a relatively short time span. It is easy to throw them away and start from scratch, if necessary; the investment of time and money is relatively small and can easily be written off.

Most software programs exhibit quite different characteristics. They are complex and cannot be implemented by one person. Several people (often, many people) have to participate in the development process and coordinate their efforts. When the job is divided among several people, we try to make these parts of the software system independent from each other, so that the developers can work on their individual pieces independently.

For example, we could break the functions of the software system into separate operations (place an order, add a customer, delete a customer, etc.). If those operations are too complex, implementing them by an individual programmer would take too long. So, we divide each operation into steps and substeps (verify customer, enter order data, verify customer credit rating, etc.) and assign each piece to an individual programmer for implementation (Figure 1–1).

The intent is to make system components independent from each other so that they can be developed by people working individually. But in practice, these separate pieces are not independent. After all, they are parts of the same system; so, they have to call each other, or work on shared data structures, or implement different steps of the same algorithm. Since the parts that different developers work on are not independent, the individual developers have to cooperate with each other: they write memos, produce design documents, send e-mail messages and participate in meetings, design reviews, or code walkthroughs. This is where the errors creep in—something gets misunderstood, something gets omitted, and something is not updated when related decisions are changed.

These complex systems are designed, developed, and tested over a long time. They are expensive. Some are very expensive. Many users depend on their operations. When requirements change, or errors or missing requirements are discovered, such systems cannot be replaced and thrown away—they often represent an investment too significant to be discarded.

Figure 1–1   Breaking the system into components.

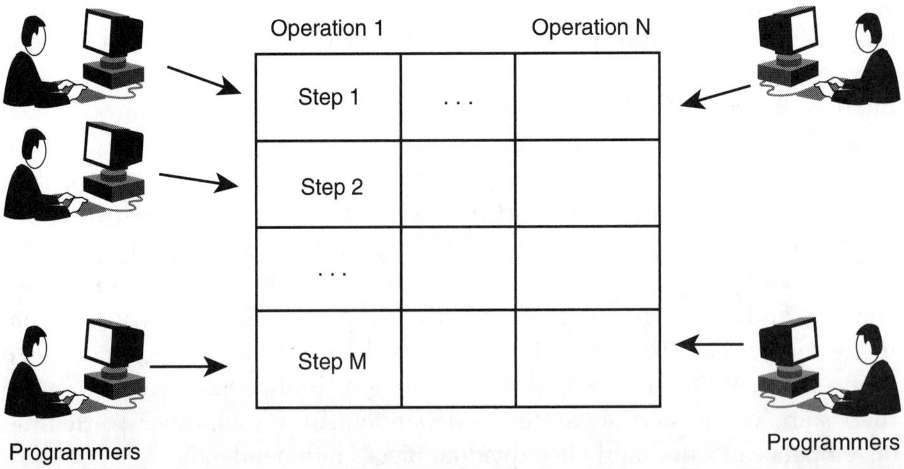

These systems have to be maintained, and their code has to be changed. Changes made in one place in the code often cause repercussions in another place, and this requires more changes. If these dependencies are not noticed (and they *are* missed sometimes), the system will work incorrectly until the code is changed again (with further repercussions in other parts of the code). Since these systems represent a significant investment, they are maintained for a long time, even though the maintenance of these complex systems is also expensive and error-prone.

Again, the Year 2000 problem comes to mind. Many people are astonished by the fact that the programmers used only two last digits to represent the year. "In what world do these programmers live?" asks the public. "Don't they understand the implications of the switch from year 1999 to year 2000?" Yes, this is astonishing. But it is not the shortsightedness of the programmers that is astonishing, rather it is the longevity of the systems designed in the 1970s and 1980s. The programmers understood the implications of Year 2000 as well as any Y2K expert (or better). What they could not imagine in the 1970s and 1980s was that somebody would still be using their programs by the year 2000.

Yes, many organizations today pour exorbitant amounts of money into maintaining old software as if they are competing with others in throwing money away. The reason for this is that these systems are so complex that rebuilding them from scratch might be more expensive than continuing to maintain them.

This complexity is the most essential characteristic of most software systems. The problem domains are complex, managing the development process is complex, and the techniques of building software out of individual pieces manually are not adequate for this complexity.

The complexity of system tasks (this is what we call "the problem domain"), be it an engineering problem, a business operation, mass-marketed shrink-wrapped software, or an Internet application, makes it difficult and tedious to describe what the system should do for the users. The potential system users (or the marketing specialists) find it difficult to express their needs in a form that software developers can understand. The requirements presented by users that belong to different departments or categories of users often contradict each other. Discovering and reconciling these discrepancies is a difficult task. In addition, the needs of the users and marketers evolve with time, sometimes even in the process of formulating requirements, when the discussion of the details of system operations brings forth new ideas. This is why programmers often say that the users (and marketing specialists) do not know what they want. There are still few tools for capturing system requirements. This is why the requirements are usually produced as large volumes of text with drawings; this text is often poorly structured and is hard to comprehend; many statements in such requirements are vague, incomplete, contradictory, or open to interpretation.

The complexity of managing the development process stems from the need to coordinate activities of a large number of professionals, especially when the teams working on different parts of the system are geographically dispersed, and these parts exchange information or work on the same data. For example, if one part of the system produced data expressed in yards, the part of the system that uses this data should not assume that the data is expressed in meters. These consistency stipulations are simple, but numerous, and keeping them in mind is hard. This is why adding more people to a project does not always help. New people have to take over some of the tasks that the existing staff has been working on. Usually, the newcomers either take over some parts of the project that existing staff was supposed to work on later, or the parts of the project are further subdivided into subparts and are assigned to the newcomers.

The newcomers cannot become productive immediately. They have to learn about the decisions already made by the existing staff. The existing staff also slows down, because the only way for the newcomers to learn about the project is by talking to the existing staff and hence by distracting this staff from productive work.

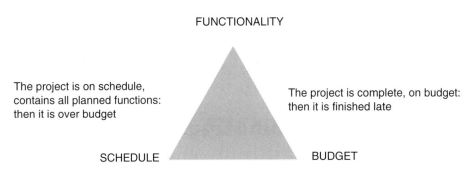

FUNCTIONALITY

The project is on schedule,
contains all planned functions:
then it is over budget

The project is complete, on budget:
then it is finished late

SCHEDULE   BUDGET

The project is on budget and schedule:
then it fails to implement all functions
that were promised at its inception

Figure 1–2   The mystery triangle of software projects.

Building software from individual pieces by hand adds to the problem: it is time consuming and prone to error. Testing is arduous, manual, and unreliable.

When I came to United States, my boss, John Convey, explained to me the situation in the following way. He drew a triangle where the vertices represented such project characteristics as schedule, budget, and system functionality (Figure 1–2). He said, "We cannot pull out all three. Something has to give in. If you implement all the system functionality on the budget, you will not be able to complete work on time, and you will ask for an extension. If you implement all functionality on schedule, chances are you will go over budget and will have to ask for more resources. If you implement the system on budget and on schedule (that does not happen often, but it is possible), well, then you will have to cut corners and implement only part of what you promised."

The problems shown in the triangle have plagued the software industry for a long time. Initial complaints about the software crisis were voiced in 1968. The industry developed several approaches to the problem. Let us take a brief look at a list of potential remedies.

Remedy 1: Eliminating Programmers

In the past, hardware costs dominated the cost of computer systems; software costs were relatively small. The bottleneck in system development seemed to be in communication between the programmers and software users, who tried to explain to the programmers what their business or engineering applications had to accomplish.

The programmers just could not get it right because they were trained as mathematicians, not in business, engineering, and so forth. They did not know business and engineering terminology. On the other hand, business and engineering managers did not know design and programming terminology; hence, when the programmers tried to explain what they understood about the requirements, communication breakdown would occur.

Figure 1-3   Communication breakdown between the user and the developer.

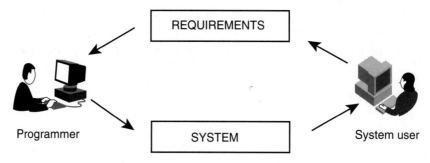

Similarly, the programmers often misunderstood the users' objectives, assumptions, and constraints. As a result, the users were getting not exactly what they wanted.

A good solution to the software crisis at that time seemed to be to get rid of programmers. Let the business and engineering managers write applications directly, without using programmers as intermediaries. However, the programmers at that time were using machine and assembly languages. These languages required intimate familiarity with the computer architecture and with the instruction set and were too difficult for managers and engineers who were not trained as programmers.

To implement this solution, it was necessary to design programming languages that would make writing software faster and easier. These languages should be simple to use, so that engineers, scientists, and business managers would be able to write programs themselves instead of explaining to the programmers what should be done.

FORTRAN and COBOL are the languages that were initially designed so that scientists, engineers, and business managers could write programs without communicating with the programmers.

This approach worked fine. Many scientists, engineers, and business managers learned how to program and wrote their programs successfully. Some experts predicted that the programming profession would disappear soon. But this approach worked fine only for small programs that could be specified, designed, implemented, documented, used, and maintained by one person. It worked for programs that did not require cooperation of several (or many) developers and did not have to live through years of maintenance. The development of such programs did not require cooperation of developers working on different parts of the program.

Actually, Figure 1–3 is correct for small programs only. For larger programs, the picture is rather like Figure 1–4. Yes, communication problems between the user and the developers are important, but the communication problems between developers are much more important. It is communication between developers that cause misunderstandings, incompatibilities and errors regardless of who these developers are—professional programmers, professional engineers, scientists, or managers.

Even Figure 1–4 is an oversimplification. It shows only a few users, who specify the requirements and evaluate the effectiveness of the system. For most software projects, there are many users (marketing representative, sales-people) who specify the system, and more than one person who evaluates it (often, this is not the same person). Inconsistencies and gaps in specifying what the system should do (and in evaluating how well it does it) add to the communication problems among developers. This is especially true when a new system should perform some of its functions similarly to an existing system. This often leads to different interpretations among developers.

Another attempt to get rid of programmers was based on the idea of using *superprogrammers*. The idea is very simple. If ordinary programmers cannot create parts of the program so that these parts fit together without errors, let us find a capable individual who is so bright that he (or she) can develop the program alone. The superprogrammers' salaries have to be higher than the salaries of ordinary programmers, but they would be worth it. When the same

Figure 1–4   Communication breakdown between program developers.

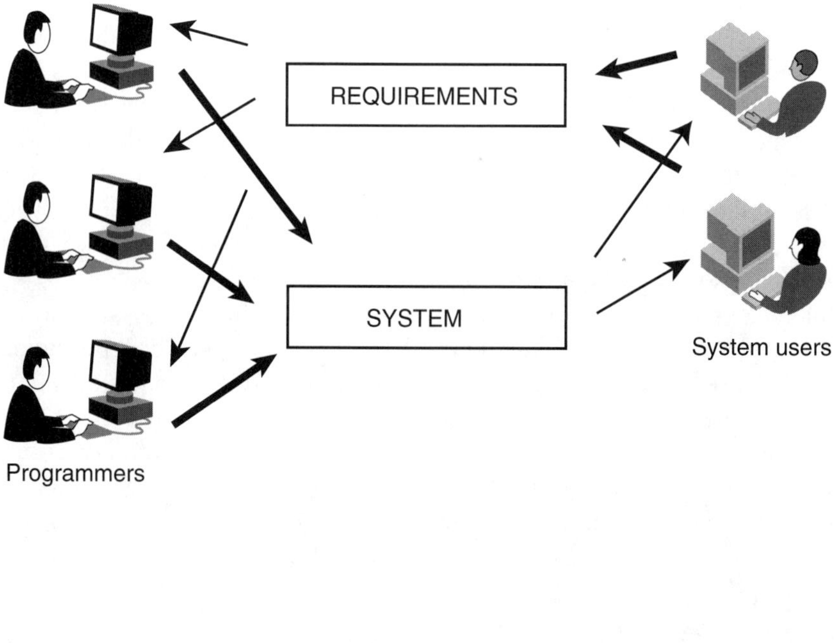

person creates different parts of the same program, compatibility problems are less likely, and errors are less frequent and can be corrected quicker.

In reality, the superprogrammer could not work alone—there was too much mundane work that could be performed by ordinary people with smaller salaries. So, the superprogrammers had to be supported by technicians, librarians, testers, technical writers, and so on.

This approach met with limited success. Actually, each development project was an unqualified success—produced on schedule, under budget, and with complete functionality despite that pessimistic model on Figure 1–2. However, communication between the superprogrammer and the supporting cast was limited by the ordinary human capabilities of the supporting cast.

Also, the superprogrammers were not available for long-term maintenance; they either moved on to other projects, were promoted to managerial positions and stopped coding, or they moved on to other organizations in search of other challenges. When ordinary maintenance programmers were maintaining the code created by a superprogrammer, they had as much trouble as with the maintenance of code written by ordinary programmers, or even more trouble because superprogrammers tend to produce terse documentation: to a superprogrammer, even a complex system is relatively simple, and hence it is a waste to provide it with a lengthy description.

Nowadays, very few people promise that we will learn how to produce software systems without programmers. The industry turned to the search for the techniques that would produce high-quality programs with the use of people with ordinary capabilities. It found the solution in the use of management techniques.

Remedy 2: Improved Management Techniques

Since hardware costs continue to plummet, it is the cost of software development and maintenance that dominates the cost of computer systems rather than hardware cost. An expensive software system represents a significant investment that cannot be discarded easily and rewritten from scratch. Hence, expensive systems are maintained longer even though they are more expensive to maintain.

Continuing increase in hardware power opens new horizons; this entails further increases in code complexity and software costs (both for development and for maintenance).

This changes priorities in the software development process. Since the hopes for resolving this problem with the help of a few exceptionally bright individuals were dashed, the industry turned to methods of managing communication among ordinary individuals—users and developers and, especially, managing developers working on different parts of the project.

To facilitate the communications between users and developers, the industry employed the following two management techniques:

- the *waterfall* method (partitioning the development process into separate distinct stages)
- *rapid prototyping* (partial implementation for users' earlier feedback)

The Waterfall Method

There are several variations of the waterfall approach used in managing programming projects. They all include breaking the development process into sequential stages. A typical sequence of stages might include requirement definition, systems analysis, architectural design, detailed design, implementation and unit testing, integration testing, acceptance testing, and maintenance. Usually, a separate specialized team of developers performs each stage. After a period of trial use and the review of utility of the system, a new (or amended) set of requirements could be defined, and the sequence of steps might be repeated.

Transitions between stages are reflected in the project schedule as milestones related to a production of specific documents. The documents developed during each stage are ideally used for two purposes: for feedback from the previous stage to evaluate correctness of the development decisions and as an input document for the next stage of the project. This can be done either informally, by circulating the document among interested parties, or formally, by running design reviews and walkthrough meetings with representatives of each development team and the users.

For example, the requirement definition process produces the requirements document used as a feedback to the project originators or user representatives and as an input document for the systems analysts. Similarly, the systems analysis stage produces the detailed system specification used as a feedback to the users and as an input document for the design stages. This is the ideal. In practice, people who should provide the feedback might have other pressing responsibilities and might devote only limited time to providing the feedback. This undermines the whole idea of quality control built into the process.

In addition, the further the project proceeds, the more difficult it becomes to get meaningful feedback from the users : The vocabulary becomes more and more computer oriented, the charts and diagrams use notation that is unfamiliar to the users, and design reviews often degenerate into a rubber stamp.

The advantage of this approach is its well-defined structure with clearly defined roles of each developer and specific deliverables at each milestone. A number of methods and tools exist for project planning and evaluating the duration and cost of different stages. This is especially important for large projects when we want to ensure that the project is moving in the right direction. The experience accumulated in one project helps in planning for subsequent similar projects.

The disadvantage is its excessive formalism, the possibility to hide from personal responsibility behind the group process, inefficiency, and the time lag of the feedback mechanism.

Rapid Prototyping

The rapid prototyping method takes the opposite approach. It eliminates the formal stages in favor of facilitating the feedback from the users. Instead of producing the formal specification for the system, the developers produce a system prototype that can be demonstrated to the users. The users try the prototype and provide the developers with much earlier and more specific feedback than in the waterfall approach. This sounds great, but is not easy to do for a large system—producing a rapid prototype might not be rapid at all and could easily approach the complexity and expense of producing the whole system. The users who should try the prototype might be burdened with other, more direct responsibility. They might lack skills in operating the system, they might lack skills in systematic testing, and they might lack skills (or time) in providing the feedback to the developers.

This approach is most effective for defining system user interface: menus, dialog boxes, text fields, control buttons, and other components of the human-computer interactions. Often, organizations try to combine both approaches. This works; often, it works well, but it does not eliminate the problem of communication among developers working on different parts of the system.

To improve communication among developers, a number of formal "structured" techniques were developed and tried with different degrees of success.

For writing system requirements and specifications, structured English (or whatever language is spoken by the developers) is used to facilitate understanding of the problem description and identification of the parts of the problem. For defining the general architecture and specific components of the system, structured design became popular with conjunction with such techniques as data flow diagrams and state transition diagrams. For low-level design, different forms of flowcharts and structured pseudocode were developed to facilitate understanding of algorithms and interconnections among parts of the program. For implementation, the principles of structured programming were used. Structured programming limited the use of jumps within the program code and significantly contributed to the ease of understanding code (or at least significantly decreased the complexity of understanding code).

It is not necessary to describe each of these techniques here. These formal management and documentation techniques are very helpful. Without them, the situation would be worse. However, they are not capable of eliminating the crisis. Software components are still crafted by hand, and they are connected through multiple interconnections and dependencies. The developers have difficulties documenting these interconnections so that those who work on other parts of the system would understand the mutual expectations and constraints. The maintenance programmers also have difficulties understanding complex (and poorly documented) interconnections.

As a result, the industry turned to techniques that alleviate the effects of interconnections. We are currently witnessing a shift from methodologies that allow us to write software faster and easier to methodologies that support writing understandable software. This is not a paradox—it is a shift in attitude toward program quality.

Remedy 3: Designing a Complex and Verbose Language

Earlier programming languages, such as FORTRAN, COBOL, APL, Basic, or even C were designed to facilitate the work of writing code. These programming languages were relatively small, terse, and easy to learn. Beating around the bush in writing code was frowned on, while succinct programming expressions were viewed as a manifestation of superb programming skills.

Lately, there's been a clear shift in programming language design. Modern languages, such as Ada, C++, and Java use the opposite approach. These languages are huge and difficult to learn. Programs written in these languages are invariably longer than similar programs written in more traditional languages. The programmers are burdened with definitions, declarations, and other descriptive elements of code.

This verboseness contributes to code consistency. If the programmer uses inconsistent code in different parts of the program, the compiler discovers that and forces the programmer to eliminate the inconsistency. With older languages, the compiler would assume that inconsistency was introduced intentionally to achieve some purpose known to the programmer. Language designers and compiler writers liked to say that "We do not want to second-guess the programmer." With such permissible languages, finding an error often required elaborate run-time testing and might result in errors escaping the hunt altogether. Modern languages treat code inconsistency as a syntax error and force the programmer to eliminate it even before the program has a chance to run. This is an important advantage, but it makes writing code much more difficult.

Another advantage of this verboseness is that code expresses the intent of the programmer better. With traditional languages, the maintenance programmer often had to guess what the code designer meant. Detailed comments in source code were needed to help the code reader, but the code designers often did not have the time (or skills) to comment code adequately. Modern languages allow the code designer to make the code more self-documented. "Redundant" declarations reduce the need for comments in code and make it easier for the maintenance programmer to understand the intent of the code. This is a new tendency in industry, and we will see specific coding examples that support this approach.

These modern languages are both huge and complex; they are, of course, too large and too complex for managers or scientists or engineers to use. These languages are designed for professional programmers who are trained in the art of partitioning the software system into cooperating parts without excessive interconnections among parts (and excessive shared knowledge among developers). The basic unit of modularization in older languages was a function. They provided no means to indicate in the program code that certain functions were logically closer to each other than to other functions. New languages also use functions as units of program modularization, but they also give the programmer the means to aggregate functions together. In Ada, this means of aggregation is called *package*. Ada package can contain data, and package functions can operate on that data, but there is only one instance of that data in the Ada program. C++ and Java make the next step: their unit of aggregation, class, allows the programmer to combine functions and data so that the program can use any number of data instances, objects.

However, the use of modern programming languages does not create any advantages in and of itself. Using these languages, you can write programs that are as bad as programs written in any traditional language, with multiple links between parts of the program, with obscure code that needs extensive documentation, so that the maintainer's focus of attention is spread over different levels of computations. This is where the object-oriented approach comes into play. In the next section, I will discuss why the object-oriented approach is so good.

The Object-Oriented Approach: Are We Getting Something for Nothing?

Everybody is excited about the object-oriented approach (well, almost everybody). Almost everybody knows that this approach is better than what preceded it (even though not everybody knows why). Those who are not excited about the object-oriented approach do not really doubt its effectiveness. They doubt whether the organizational changes are worth the trouble: expense of training the developers and the users; efforts to produce new standards, guidelines, and documentation; project delays due to learning; and assimilation of new technology with all related mistakes and false starts.

The risks are significant, but so are the rewards (or so we think). The major boost for the object-oriented approach comes from the availability and broad acceptance of languages that support objects; C++ is without a doubt the most significant factor here.

Is the object-oriented approach just a new buzzword? Will it be replaced by something else in due time? Does it have real advantages? Are there any drawbacks or tradeoffs to be made?

Let us be frank: There is no reason why the object-oriented approach (and the use of classes in C++) is advantageous for writing small programs. The advantages of the object-oriented approach outweigh drawbacks for large complex programs only.

There are two components to the program complexity:

- the complexity of the application itself (what the application does for its users)
- the complexity of the program implementation (introduced by the decisions made by designers and programmers while implementing the program)

We cannot control the complexity of application—it is defined by the goal of the program. We cannot expect that in future applications that complexity will somewhat decrease; if anything, it is going to increase with further increase in hardware power that puts more and more complex tasks within our reach.

It is the second component of complexity that we should control. Every time we decide that part of the work should be done in one unit of the program and another part of the work should be done in another unit of the program, we introduce additional complexity of cooperation, coordination, and communications among these units. This risk is particularly high when we tear apart the actions that should belong together and put them in different units of the program. Doing that creates significant additional complexity in the program.

Why would one want to tear apart what should belong together? Nobody does this intentionally or maliciously. However, often it is not easy to recognize which things belong together and which do not. To recognize these situations, we have to learn how to evaluate the quality of design. And, by the way, what is design?

What Does the Designer Do?

Many software professionals think that design is about deciding what the program should do, what functions it should perform for the user, what data it has to produce, what data it needs to do the job. Others add such tasks as deciding what algorithms should be used to do the job, what the user interface should look like, what performance and reliability should we expect, and so on. This is not design. This is analysis.

Design comes later, when we already know what functions the program should perform for the user, its input and output data, data transformation algorithms, user interface, and so on. Design, in general, is a set of the following decisions:

- What units a program will consist of. When you design a software program, this decision produces a set of functions, classes, files, or other units the program might consist of.
- How these units will be related to each other (who uses whom). This design decision describes which unit calls the services of which other unit and what data these units exchange to support the services.

- What the responsibility of each individual unit is going to be. It is while making this set of design decisions that one could go wrong and break apart what should belong together. But this observation is too general to be useful in practice. You need specific design techniques catered to specific units of modularity.

Come to think of it, this is true not only of software design, but of any creative activity. Be it a musical composition, a book, a letter to a friend, or a painting, we have to decide what components the product should have, how these components are related to each other, and what the role of each component in achieving the common goal is. The more complex the task, the more important design is for the quality of the result. A simple e-mail message does not need careful planning. A software user manual does.

Structured design uses functions as units of modularity. The designer identifies the tasks that the program should perform, partitions these tasks into subtasks, steps, substeps, and so on, until these steps are small enough; after that, each step is implemented as a separate, presumably independent function.

Data-centered design assigns modules so that each module is responsible for processing a specific element of input or output data. The designer identifies the data that the program uses as its input and the data that the program produces as its output. Then the designer breaks complex data into components until processes that are needed to produce output data from input data are small enough. After that, each data transformation process is implemented as a separate, presumably independent, function.

There are numerous variations of these techniques catered toward different types of applications: database applications, interactive applications, real-time, and so on.

All high-level programming languages provide functions, procedures, subroutines, or other similar units of modularity (e.g., COBOL paragraphs) and support these modular design techniques. These methodologies are useful, but they do not eliminate the problem of design complexity: The number of interconnections between program modules remains high, because the modules are linked through data. References to data make the module code obscure. The designers (and then maintainers) have too many factors to consider, and they make errors that are hard to find and correct.

Software designers use several criteria that allow them to minimize complexity and mutual dependencies between cooperating parts of the code. Traditional software quality criteria are cohesion and coupling. Modern object-oriented criteria are information hiding and encapsulation.

Design Quality: Cohesion

Cohesion describes relatedness of the steps that the designer puts into the same module. When a function performs one task over one computational object, or several related steps directed toward a specific goal, we say that this function has good cohesion. When a function performs several unrelated tasks over one object, or even several tasks over several objects, we say that the function has poor, weak, low cohesion.

High-cohesion functions are easy to name; we usually use composite terms that contain one active verb for the action and one noun for the object of the action, for example, `insertItem`, `findAccount` (if the name is honest, which is not always the case). For low-cohesion functions, we use several verbs or nouns, for example, `findOrInsertItem` (unless, of course, we want to hide the designer's failure and we just call the function `findItem` that finds the item in a collection or inserts the item if it is not found).

The remedy for poor cohesion (as for any design flaw) is redesign. Redesign means changing the list of parts (functions) and their responsibilities. In the case of poor cohesion, it means breaking the function with weak cohesion into several cohesive functions.

This approach works most of the time but should not be taken to the extreme. Otherwise, it will result in too many small functions, and the designer (and the maintainer) winds up with a larger number of things to remember (function names and their interfaces).

This is why cohesion is not used alone; it is not a very strong criterion. It needs other criteria to complement it. Make sure, however, that you consider it when you evaluate design alternatives.

Design Quality: Coupling

The second traditional criterion, coupling, describes the interface between a function (a server, a called function) and the calling functions (server's clients). The clients supply the server function with input data values. For example, the function `processTransaction` (a client) might call the function `findItem` (a server) and pass the item ID and the text of an error message as input data to `findItem`. The server depends on the correctness of its input data to produce correct results (e.g., find the item, display the right error message).

The clients depend on results produced by the server. For example, the function `findItem` might produce for its client (`processTransaction`) the flag that says whether the item was found or not and the index of the item if it was found. This represents the server output. The total number of elements in server input and output represents the measure of coupling. We try to minimize coupling by reducing the number of elements in the function interface.

The criterion of *coupling* is more powerful than cohesion is. It is very sensitive to design decisions when the designer tears apart operations that should belong together. Almost invariably, these design decisions result in extra communication among modules and in additional coupling. For example, transaction error processing should be done in one place and should not be torn between `processTransaction` and `findItem`.

The solution to excessive coupling is, of course, redesign: reconsidering the decisions as to what function does what. If part of the operation on data is done in one function, and another part of the operation is performed in another function, the designer should consider allocating both parts to the same function. This decreases complexity of design without increasing the number of functions in the program. For example, moving error processing from `findItem` to `processTransaction` eliminates the need for passing the text of error message to `findItem` and passing the flag back to `processTransaction`.

Note

Cohesion and coupling are discussed in more details later when we look at specific coding examples in Chapter 9, "C++ Class as a Unit of Modularization."

At this stage I would like to make sure that when you look at C++ source code, you analyze it from the point of view of cohesion, coupling, and tearing apart what should belong together.

Design Quality: Binding Together Data and Functions

What contributions does the object-oriented approach make to these quality criteria? Remember, improving software quality does not mean making code aesthetically nicer, because aesthetics does not reduce complexity of code. Improving quality means making program modules more independent, making code more self-documented, and the intent of the designer easily understood.

The object-oriented approach is based on binding together data and operations. We will spend a good deal of time discussing the syntax for doing that. It is important, however, before we look at the object syntax, to understand what this syntax tries to accomplish and why it is so expedient to use this syntax.

Why is binding together data and operations beneficial? The problem with the functional approach to the program design is that the "independent" functions are connected with other functions through data. For example, one function can set a value of a variable, and another function might use its value (findItem sets the value of the index, and processTransaction uses that index). This creates interdependencies between these two functions (and probably between other functions, too).

One solution to this problem is to merge these two functions. When it works, this solution has to be used. But it does not work all the time. Often, we call the server function repeatedly, and probably from different client functions. Eliminating the server function (findItem) does not make sense.

In addition, some other functions might set and use that value (the item index might be used in functions deleteItem, updateItem, and so on). In a small program, it is not difficult to trace all instances of accessing and modifying the value of a variable and find the source of the problem if something is done incorrectly. In a large program, this is more difficult, especially for the maintainer who does not completely understand the intent of the designer. Even the original designer, who returns to the program after several weeks or months of interruption, often feels at a loss in understanding the program and locating the functions that use a particular value.

It would be beneficial to indicate the set of functions that access and modify a particular variable by placing functions together in the source code. This would help the maintainer (and the designer when he or she returns to the program) to understand the intent of the designer at the time of writing the program. Many software designers do that because they understand the importance of the self-documenting characteristics of the code.

However, this is often hard to do. Functions are often placed in the source code so that they are easy to locate, in alphabetical order. Even when they are grouped according to the variables they access, there is no assurance that all relevant functions are indeed grouped together. When the designer (or the maintainer) needs a quick fix to some problem and adds a function that accesses this variable at some other place in the program, this is not a syntax error. The compiler will accept the program. The execution results will be correct. And the future maintainer might never notice that additional function. With functional programming, it is not easy to make sure that all functions that access or modify particular data are listed in the same place.

The object-oriented approach resolves this problem by binding together data values and functions that access and modify these values. C++ combines data and operations in larger units called *classes*. We do not tear related things apart, we put them together, reducing the number of things to remember about other parts of the program. Data can be made private, assuring that only the functions that belong to the class can access these particular values. Hence, the knowledge of the designer (that is, the list of functions that access data) is expressed explicitly in the syntactic unit: class description. The maintenance programmer is assured that no other function accesses or modifies these values.

Figure 1–5 shows a relationship between two objects, a server and a client object. Each object consists of data, methods, and the border. Everything that is inside the border is private and is not available to other parts of the program. Everything that is outside of the border is public and is available to other parts of the program. Data are inside the border and are invisible from outside. Methods (functions) are partially inside and partially outside of the border. The outside part represents the method interface known to the clients. The inside part represents the code implementation hidden from the client code.

Figure 1–5   The relationship between server and client objects.

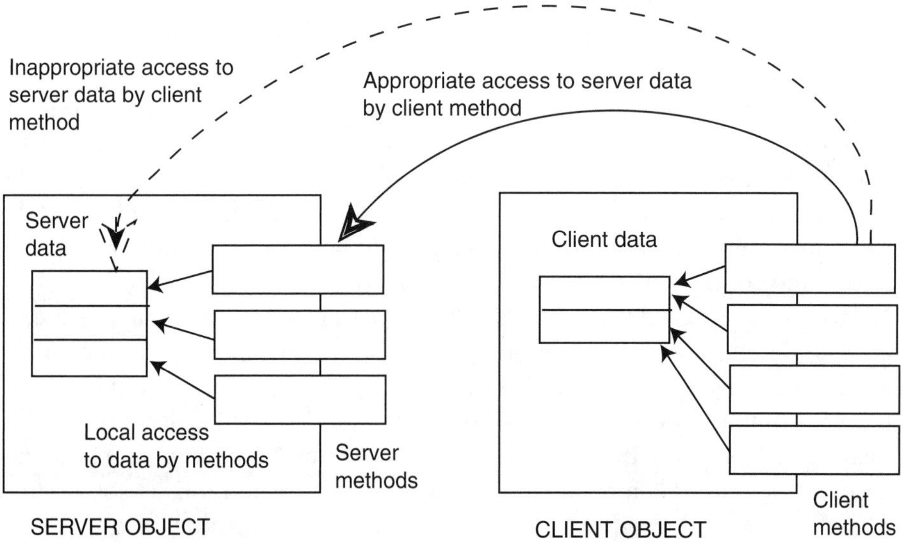

Note

This notation was developed by Booch for design and programming with Ada. It proved to be very useful for any object-oriented programming and design. When the client method needs the server data to do its job, it does not specify the names of server data, because that data is private and is not available outside of the server class. Instead, the client method calls the server method that accesses the server data. Since the server method implementation is inside the server, it has no difficulty accessing private server data.

Design Quality: Information Hiding and Encapsulation

When we decide what data and functions should belong together, we should choose among a large number of alternatives. Some alternatives are clearly not good, while some others are better. Choosing which one to implement can be a chore.

The criterion of encapsulation requires us to combine data and operations so that the client code would be able to do its job by calling server functions without explicitly mentioning the names of server data components.

The major advantage of this approach is that the list of functions that access server data is immediately available to the maintainer in the form of class description.

Another advantage is that the client code contains less data-related manipulation and hence becomes self-documented. Let us say that the application has to set the variables describing a customer—first and last name, middle initial, street address, city, state, zipcode, social security number, and so on—16 values in all. If the client code is written using the traditional approach, the designer writes the client code with 16 assignment statements. Now the maintainer has to decide:

- whether or not all components of the customer description are assigned values
- whether or not the values assigned here, only to components of the customer description or some other data, are also handled

It might take some time and effort to answer both questions, and this contributes to complexity.

If this code is written using the object-oriented approach, the data is private, and the client code cannot mention the names of variables describing the customer—name, address, and so on. Instead, the client code calls an access function such as `setCustomerData`. This passes the designer's intent to the maintainer immediately.

The criterion of information hiding requires us to combine data and operations and distribute responsibilities among operations so that the client code will be independent from the data design.

For example, we might not need to check the validity of the state and zip code values and check whether they are consistent. It is appropriate to push this job down to the server rather than to the client. If the assignment of zip codes to states changes, or if a city secedes from the state and becomes a separate state, we will have to change only the server and not the client code. Had we assigned this responsibility to clients, we would have to change each place zip code is used.

The important advantage of the object-oriented approach over the traditional approach is the narrow scope of modification changes. Let us say that we switch from a five-digit zip code to a nine-digit zip code. With the traditional approach, all client code has to be inspected, because the customer data can be handled anywhere. If in some places you miss adding the code that handles additional digits, it is not a syntax error, and it has to be discovered during regression testing.

With the object-oriented approach, you have to change the functions that handle customer zip code, and the client code that calls these functions is not affected. So, the major advantages of encapsulation and information hiding are:

- There is a clear indication what functions access specified data by binding together data and functions in class descriptions.
- The meaning of client code is clear from function names, not from the interpretation of a large number of low-level computations and assignments.
- When the data representation changes, the class access functions change, but the range of changes in the client code is narrow.

Design Issue: Name Conflicts

Less crucial but still very important is the issue of name conflicts in a large program. The names of the functions must be unique in a C++ program. If one designer chose the function name findItem, no other designer can use this name for another function in the same program. At first glance it looks like a simple problem. So, anybody who wants to use this name will use a slightly modified name, for example, findInventoryItem or findAccountingItem.

For many developers, the need to come up with unique names is an annoying restriction. But this is not just a problem of creativity in naming. This is the problem of excessive communication between developers.

Let us say you are a member of a 20-person development team, and you want to name the function you are working on findItem. Let us say there are three other developers on the team that write client code that will call this function. With the object-oriented approach, only these three developers should know that you are writing a findItem function. All others do not have to learn about that and can concentrate on other things.

With the traditional approach, all 20 developers have to be notified about your decision. Of course, they will not devote all their working time to learning the name of your function. But still, all of them will have to know the names of your functions and the functions designed by all other developers. Notice that you also have to learn (or keep handy) the list of all function names that all other developers are designing, even though you do not use them. Many organizations develop sophisticated standards for function names to avoid name conflicts and spend significant resources training developers to use these standards, enforcing compliance, and managing change when the standards have to evolve.

This can easily become a chore that channels human attention from other issues. After all, the power of our attention is limited, and the thinner it is spread, the higher is the likelihood of errors. The object-oriented approach alleviates this problem. It allows you to use the same function name for as many functions as you want if these functions belong to different classes. Hence, only those developers who actually call your functions should know about your names. All others can devote their energy to other issues.

Design Issue: Object Initialization

Another less crucial but still important issue is object initialization. In the traditional approach, computational objects are initialized explicitly in the client code. For example, the client code must explicitly initialize the components of the customer description. With the object-oriented approach, a call to setCustomerData takes care of that. Still, the client code has to call this function. If this function is not called, this is not a syntax error but a semantic error, and it has to be discovered at run time during testing. If customer processing requires system resources (files, dynamic memory, etc.), these resources also have to be returned by the client code explicitly, for example, by calling the appropriate function.

The object-oriented approach allows us to do these operations implicitly. When the client code creates an object by passing the necessary initializing data (we will see the syntax for doing that later), there is no need to explicitly call initializing functions. At the end of computations, resources allocated to the object can be returned without explicit action of the client code.

Note

This discussion is quite general. Later in the book, I will spare no effort trying to indicate the features of C++ that contribute to these characteristics of the object-oriented approach. When reading the rest of the book, please come back to this chapter often to make sure that the trees of syntax do not hide from your view a beautiful forest of object-oriented programming.

What Is an Object, Anyway?

In object-oriented programming, we design a program as a set of cooperating objects rather than as a set of cooperating functions. An *object* is a combination of data and behavior. As a programmer, you might be familiar with other terms for data, such as data fields, data members, or attributes. We often refer to object behavior using such terms as functions, member functions, methods, or operations.

Data characterizes the state of an object. When similar objects can be described in the terms of the same data and operations, we generalize the idea of the object in the concept of the class. A class is not an object. A class is a description of common properties (data and operations) of objects that belong to that class. A class does not live in the memory of the computer during program execution. An object does. Every object of a specific class has all the data fields defined for the class. For example, each InventoryItem might have an i.d. number, item description, quantity on hand, purchase price, retail price, and so on. We describe these common properties in the definition of class `InventoryItem`. During the program execution, objects of the class `InventoryItem` are created and allocated memory for their data fields. These objects can change independently of each other. When the values of data fields change we say that the state of the object changes.

All objects of the same class are characterized by the same behavior. Object operations (functions, methods, or operations) are described in the class definition together with data. Each object of a specific class can perform the same set of operations. These operations are performed on behalf of other objects in the program. Usually, these are operations over object data; these operations can retrieve the values of data fields, or they can assign new values to data fields, or compare values, print values and so on. For example, an inventory item object can have, among others, such functions that set retail price to a given value or compare the item's i.d. number with the given number.

A computer program can have more than one object of the same kind. The term object is used to describe each such object instance because an object is an instance of a class. Some people also use the term object to describe the group of objects of the same kind. More often, however, it is the term class that is used to describe the set of potential object instances of the same kind. Each object of the same class has its own set of data fields, but the corresponding fields in different objects have the same names. For example, two inventory item objects might have the same (or different) values of retail price; the i.d. number will probably be different for different inventory item objects. All objects of the same class can perform the same operations, that is, they respond to the same function calls. All objects of the same kind have the same properties (data and operations). When we call an object function that changes the state of the object or retrieves information about the state of the object, we say that we are sending a message to the object.

This is a very important detail. In a C++ program, a function call usually involves two objects. One object sends a message (calls the function), another object receives the message (sometimes we say it is a target of the message). We will call the object that sends the message the *client object*; we will call the target of the message the *server object*; although this terminology sounds similar to the client-server terminology used for the client-server computer system architecture, it means different things. Actually, these terms were used in object-oriented programming much earlier than the first client-server systems became popular. We are going to spend a lot of time talking about client-server relationships among objects in a C++ program.

As you are going to see later, the objects in a C++ program look syntactically very much like ordinary variables—integers, characters, and floating point numbers. They are allocated memory pretty much the way ordinary variables are: allocated on the stack or on the heap (again, we will see the details later). A C++ class is a syntactic extension of what other languages call structures or records that combine data components together. The C++ class includes both data declarations and function declarations.

So, when the client code needs to use the object, like comparing an item i.d. number with a given value or setting the value of the item retail price, it does not mention the names of the object data fields. Instead, it calls the functions provided by the object and these functions do the job for the client; they compare item i.d. numbers and set the value of the retail price.

Advantages of Using Objects

Although it does not sound like a big deal—the client code mentions the names of object functions rather than the names of object data fields—the difference is significant. Experience shows that the design of data structures is more volatile and amenable to change than is the design of operations. By using the names of functions rather than the names of data fields, we insulate the client code from potential changes in the server object design. By doing so, we improve the maintainability of the program, and this is one of the important goals of the object-oriented approach.

Also, when the client code calls a server function, for example, `compareID`, the intent of the client designer is immediately clear to the maintainer. When the client code retrieves and manipulates IDs of the objects, the meaning of the code has to be deduced from the meaning of elementary operations rather than from function names.

In summary, the goal of the object-oriented approach is the same as for other software development methodologies: to improve software quality as perceived by the ultimate user (program functionality and total development and maintenance costs).

Proponents of the object-oriented technology hope that the object-oriented approach allows us to reduce complexity of program code. With less complexity to deal with, we hope to decrease the number of errors in software and to increase productivity during development and maintenance.

Software complexity can be reduced by partitioning programs into relatively independent parts that can be understood in isolation, with few references to other parts of the program. When we use classes as program units, we have a chance to decrease interconnections between the parts. We pay for that by increasing interconnections between parts of the class; class member functions operate on the same data. But this is fine—a class is usually developed by the same person, and it is interpersonal communication that is prone to omissions, inconsistencies, and misunderstanding. Reduced dependencies between classes reduce coordination among team members assigned to these classes, and the number of errors.

Unlike interconnected parts, independent classes can be easier to reuse in other contexts; this improves productivity during development of the system and possibly productivity during development of other software systems.

Interconnected parts have to be studied together, which is slow and prone to error. Independent classes can be easier to understand: This improves productivity during program maintenance.

The object-oriented technology is not without its risks and costs. Developers, users, and managers—all have to be trained, and training costs are significant. Object-oriented projects seem to take longer than traditional projects do, especially during the first phases of the project, analysis and design. Object-oriented programs contain more lines of code than do traditional programs. (Do not be scared—I am talking about lines of source code, not about the size of object code—the size of executable code really does not depend on the development methodology.) Most important, the languages that support object-oriented programming (especially C++) are complex. Using them entails certain risk that the benefits will not be realized, that the object-oriented program will be larger, more complex, slower, and more difficult to maintain than the traditional program. Hopefully, this book will teach you not only how to use C++ but also what to avoid. The proper use of this powerful and stimulating language will help you realize the promise of the object-oriented technology.

Characteristics of the C++ Programming Language

C++ is a superset of the C programming language. C itself is a descendant of several generations of early languages; it was created and implemented with conflicting goals in mind. This is why C++ contains features that are inconsistent and sometimes irritating. In this section, I will briefly review the major characteristics of C and then will show how C++ uses this "inheritance" to achieve its goals.

C Objectives: Performance, Readability, Beauty, and Portability

The first goal of C was to give software developers a performance-oriented systems programming language. This is why C and C++ do not support run-time checking for errors that could cause incorrect program behavior but could be found by the programmer during testing. This is why C and C++ contain low-level operators that emulate assembly language instructions and allow the programmer to control computer's resources, such as registers, ports, and flag masks.

Note

If you do not know what registers, ports, and masks mean, do not worry; this will not prevent you from mastering C++; just rest assured that fate has spared you hundreds of hours of debugging anguish of assembly language programming.

The second goal of C was to give software developers a high-level language suitable for implementing complex algorithms and sophisticated data structures. This is why C and C++ allow the programmer to use loops, conditional statements, functions, and procedures. This is why C and C++ support processing of different data types, arrays, structures, and dynamic memory management. (If you are not comfortable with these terms, do not worry; this will not prevent you from mastering C++ using this book.) These features support code readability and maintainability.

The third goal of C was to allow software developers to write source code that is elegant and aesthetically pleasing. It is not exactly clear what "elegant" and "aesthetically pleasing" meant; it probably meant different things to different people, but the consensus was that if the program is succinct, terse, and puts a lot of processing into a few lines of well-designed code than it is elegant and aesthetically pleasing. As a consequence of this approach, the language affords the programmers significant "freedom" in writing code without flagging this code as syntactically incorrect. We are going to see more of this issue later.

The fourth goal of C was to support program portability at the level of the source code; this is why C and C++ executable object code is not expected to run under different operating systems or on different hardware platforms. However, the source code is expected to be compiled by different compilers or for different platforms without changes, and it should run exactly the same way without modifications.

The first three goals were achieved reasonably well, even though they were somewhat conflicting. C was used for the development of the UNIX operating system, which gradually became very popular and was implemented on a large number of hardware platforms, including multiuser environments (mainframes, minicomputers, PC servers) and single-user environments (PCs). C was also used for implementing system utilities, database systems, word processors, spreadsheets, editors, and numerous applications.

The conflict between readability and succinct expressiveness (programming aesthetics) was not resolved. Those developers who valued readability learned how to use C to produce readable code. Those developers who valued expressiveness learned how to use C to produce succinct code and even had competitions for writing the most obscure and expressive code.

The fourth goal, the portability of C code was also met, but with significant reservations. That is, the language itself is portable: If the language statements are compiled under different operating systems or on different hardware platforms, the program will execute in exactly the same way. The catch is that any real C program contains much more than C language statements: it contains numerous calls to library functions.

The implicit goal of the C language design was to create a small language. Initially, it had only 30 keywords. If you compare it with COBOL or PL/I, the difference is staggering. As a result, the language is very small. It does not have the exponentiation operation, it cannot compare or copy text, and it does not include input or output operations. However, you can do all of that (and much more) using library functions that come with the compiler. The language designers felt that it was up to compiler vendors to decide what library functions should be used to compare or copy text, to perform input or output operations, and so on.

This was not a good idea. It was at odds with the idea of source code portability. If different compilers and different platforms were using different library functions, then the program could not be ported to a different platform without modifications to library function calls. It could not even be recompiled on the same platform using a different compiler. Also, this approach was at odds with the idea of "programmer portability." A programmer who learned one library had to be retrained to be able to use another library.

This is no small matter, and vendors of compilers for different platforms recognized its importance and developed the "standard" library that programmers could use on different machines without making too many modifications to program code. "Too many" means that some modifications had to be made. Because of the lack of one strong center for standardization, several versions of UNIX were developed, and libraries of different compiler vendors behaved somewhat differently on different machines under different operating systems.

American National Standards Institute (ANSI) spearheaded the standardization effort and codified ANSI C in 1983–1989 with the goal of promoting portability. The ANSI version of the language also incorporates some new ideas, but does it with backward compatibility, so that the legacy C code could be recompiled by new compilers.

Today, even though C source code is mostly portable, problems do exist, and porting a program to a different machine or operating system might require changes. Skills of C programmers are also mostly portable; and programmers can move from one development environment to another with little retraining (but some training might be needed).

The C designers also did not see the "catch" in introducing diverse libraries. We pay for that "flexibility" with increased costs of code porting and programmer retraining. The experience that the industry accumulated dealing with these issues is one of the reasons why Java designers pay so much attention to enforcing uniform standards. The Java language is extremely unforgiving and flags many C idioms as syntax errors. The issue of backward compatibility with C has a relatively low priority in Java design. Clearly, Java designers did not want to sign on that dotted line.

C++ Objectives: Classes with Backward Compatibility with C

One C++ design goal was to expand the power of C by supporting the object-oriented approach to programming. Here, "expand" should be taken literally. C++ is designed for 100% backward compatibility with C: Every legal C program is a legal C++ program. (Actually, there are some exceptions, but they are not important.) Hence, C++ shares with C all its design features, good or bad (until death do us part).

Similar to C, C++ is token oriented and case sensitive. The compiler breaks the source code into component words regardless of their position on the line, and elements of the program code should not be in specific columns (e.g., they have to be in FORTRAN or COBOL). The C++ compiler ignores all white space between tokens, and the programmers can use white space to format code for readability. Case sensitivity helps avoid name conflicts but can result in errors if the programmer (or the maintainer) does not pay (or does not have time to pay) attention to subtle differences in capitalization.

Similar to C, C++ only has a few basic numeric data types, fewer than in other modern languages. To add insult to injury, some of these basic data types have different ranges on different machines. To make matters even more confusing, the programmers can use so-called modifiers that change the legal range of values acceptable on a given machine. This has implications both for software portability and maintainability.

To compensate for the scarcity of built-in data types, C++ supports data aggregation into composite types: arrays, structures, unions, and enumerations; data aggregates can be combined to form other aggregates. This feature is also borrowed from C.

C++ supports a standard set of flow control constructs: sequential execution of statements and function calls, iterative execution of statements and blocks of statements (for, while, do loops), decision-making (if, switch constructs), jumps (break, continue, and, yes, there is the goto statement too). This set of control constructs is the same as in C, but there are some differences in the use of for loops.

Similar to C, C++ is a block-structured language: Unnamed blocks of code can be nested to any depth, and variables defined in inner blocks are not visible to the outer blocks. This allows programmers who write the inner blocks to use any names for local variables without the fear of conflict (and need for coordination) with the names defined by the programmers who write the outer blocks.

On the other hand, a C (and C++) function (i.e., a named block) cannot be nested inside another function, and the function names must be unique in the program. This is a serious limitation. It increases pressure on coordination among programmers during development and makes maintenance more difficult. C++ partially corrects this problem by introducing the class scope. Class methods (that is, functions defined inside the class) have to be unique within the class only, not within the program.

C++ functions can be called recursively in exactly the same way as C functions can. Older languages did not support recursion because recursive algorithms represent a miniscule fraction of all algorithms. Naïve use of recursion can waste both time and space during execution. However, a few algorithms where recursion is useful really benefit from it, and recursion is a standard feature in modern programming languages (but not in scripts).

Exactly as in C, C++ functions can be placed in one file or in several source files. These files can be compiled and debugged separately, thus enabling different programmers to work on different parts of the project independently. Compiled object files can be linked together later to produce an executable object file. This is important for labor division in large projects.

Very much like C, C++ is a strongly typed language: It is an error to use a value of one type where a value of another type is expected, for example, in expressions or in passing arguments to a function. Today, this is a common principle of programming language design. Many data type errors that would manifest themselves at run time can be flagged at compile time. It saves the time spent on testing and debugging.

Even more than C, C++ is a weakly typed language (yes, it is both a strongly typed and weakly typed language). Conversions among numeric types are done silently both in expressions and in parameter passing. This is an important departure from modern language design and prone with errors that cannot be discovered at compile time. In addition, C++ supports conversions between related classes. On the one hand, this allows us to use a nice programming technique called polymorphism. On the other hand, this feature prevents the compiler from catching substitutions made inadvertently.

C++ inherits from C support for the use of pointers for three purposes: a) passing parameters from a calling function to a called function, b) dynamic memory allocation from the computer heap (for dynamic data structures), and c) manipulating arrays and array components. All techniques for using pointers are prone to error; these errors are particularly difficult to discover, localize, and correct.

Very much like C, C++ is designed for efficiency: Array bounds are checked neither at compile time nor at run time. It is up to the programmer to maintain program integrity and avoid corruption of memory if an invalid index is used. This is a popular source of errors in C/C++ programs.

Similar to C, C++ is designed for writing succinct and terse code: It gives a special meaning to punctuation and operator characters such as asterisks, plus signs, equal signs, braces, brackets, commas, and so forth. These symbols can have more than one meaning in a C++ program: The meaning depends on context, and this makes learning and using C++ more difficult than learning and using other languages.

C++ adds a number of new features to C. The most important feature is support for objects. C++ expands C structures to classes; they bind together data and functions as a unit of code. Classes encourage information hiding by localizing data representation within their borders so that the data components are not available outside of the class. Classes support encapsulation by providing access functions (methods) that are called by client code. The use of class scope reduces name conflicts in C++ programs.

Classes facilitate hierarchical approach to design so that higher-level classes reuse lower-level classes. Class composition and class inheritance allow the programmers to implement complex models of the real world and manipulate program components easily.

There are a number of other features in the language that help the designer express code intent in the code itself, not in comments.

However, the C++ language, similar to C, was designed for an experienced programmer. The compiler does not try to second-guess the programmer, assuming that he or she knows what he or she is doing. (And we do not always, do we?) It is important to know what we are doing. If the developer is not careful, a C++ program can be quite complex and intimidating to a reader and difficult to modify and maintain. Type conversions, pointer manipulation, array processing, and parameter passing are also frequent sources of obscure errors in C++ programs.

Hopefully, sound software engineering practices recommended in this book will help you to understand what you are doing and to avoid pitfalls of unnecessary complexity.

Summary

In this chapter, we looked at different solutions to the software crisis. The use of object-oriented languages seems to be the most effective way of avoiding budget overruns, missed deadlines, and scaled-down releases. However, writing programs in object-oriented languages is more difficult than writing them in traditional procedural languages. Used correctly, object-oriented languages facilitate the reading of a program, not the writing of it. Actually, this is very good. After all, we write source code only once, when we type it in. We read code many, many times over—when we debug it, test it, and maintain it.

As an object-oriented language, C++ allows you to bind together data and functions in a new syntactic unit, class, which extends the concept of type. Using C++ classes, you write the program as a set of cooperating objects rather than as a set of cooperating functions. Using classes promotes modularization, and code design with high cohesion and low coupling. Classes support encapsulation, class composition, and inheritance. This contributes to code reuse and maintainability. The use of classes eliminates naming conflicts and contributes to understanding code.

It is important to learn how to use C++ correctly. The indiscriminate use of the features that C++ inherited from C could easily eliminate all advantages of object-oriented programming. Our discussion of these features was by necessity cursory and introductory. Later in the book, I will try to do my best to show you how to make the best use of C++ features. This presentation will be full of specific technical details. As I mentioned earlier, I think it is a good idea to come back to this chapter from time to time to make sure that you do not lose sight of powerful object-oriented ideas behind low-level syntactical details.

In the next chapter, we will start our road toward the correct use of C++ by reviewing its basic program structure and most important programming constructs.

GETTING STARTED QUICKLY: A BRIEF OVERVIEW OF C++

Topics in this Chapter

- The Basic Program Structure
- Preprocessor Directives
- Comments
- Declarations and Definitions
- Statements and Expressions
- Functions and Function Calls
- Classes
- Dealing with Program Development Tools
- Summary

Chapter 2

In this chapter, I will briefly preview the basic programming constructs of the C++ language before going on to discuss them in more depth in the chapters that follow. Because C++ is a large language, anything that is "brief" is not going to cover much of the language, and anything that indeed reviews the most important features of the language is not going to be "brief." I will try to strike a reasonable compromise.

Studying a language like C++ feature by feature cannot give you a general picture that would connect different features into a cohesive whole. Many features are intertwined and cannot be discussed separately. This is why you need this preview. It will give you the first look at the most important concepts and constructs of the C++ language, will enable you to write your first C++ programs, and will prepare you for studying these concepts and techniques in depth and in breadth.

The programs in this book are written using the ISO/ANSI standard C++. This version of the language adds new features and also changes the syntax of some existing features. There are still many compilers in use in industry that implement only some features of the new language. There are too many different vendors and too many different compiler versions to discuss their differences in implementing standard C++ in detail. Eventually, older compilers will be replaced by newer versions. However, the industry will have to deal with the code written in prestandard C++ for many years to come. This old code will be supported by newer compilers as well, because backward compatibility is one of the important goals of C++ design, and standard C++ adds new features without making old features illegal. As a rule, I will cover new standard C++ syntax without mentioning that explicitly. Where necessary, I will make reference to older ways of writing code to make sure you can deal with legacy code with confidence.

The Basic Program Structure

Listing 2.1 shows the source code for your first C++ program. It welcomes you to the world of C++ (as most first programs in programming language books do). In addition, just to demonstrate more features than a canonical "Hello World" program does, it makes some simple computations and prints the result of raising the value of pi (3.1415926) to the power of two.

Listing 2.1   Your first C++ program.

```cpp
#include <iostream>                              // preprocessor directive
#include <cmath>                                 // preprocessor directive
using namespace std;                             // compiler directive
const double PI = 3.1415926;                     // definition of a constant
int main(void)                                   // function returns integer
{
  double x=PI, y=1, z;                           // definitions of variables
  cout << "Welcome to the C++ world!" << endl;   // function call
  z = y + 1;                                     // assignment statement
  y = pow(x,z);                                  // function call
  cout << "In that world, pi square is " << y << endl;
  cout << "Have a nice day!" << endl;
  return 0;                                      // return statement
}                                                // end of the function block
```

Do not worry if this program looks obscure. By the end of this chapter, you will understand every detail here (and more).

Similar to other modern programming languages, C++ allows us to write instructions to the computer in the form of human-readable source code. The C++ compiler translates the source code into machine-readable object code. During program execution, machine language instructions are executed one after another and produce the results.

Most computations are performed over values that are stored in computer memory. For our purposes, we can think of computer memory as an array of locations with values. Locations cannot be referred to by the values that are stored in them. They can be referred to either by their numeric addresses (in the object code) or by their symbolic names (in the source code). For example, our first C++ program contains the statement:

```
z = y + 1;
```

It instructs the computer to fetch the value that is stored at the location named y, increment that value (without changing the contents at location y), and put the result into the location labeled z. The real addresses of locations named y and z are specified in the executable code but not in the source code; the programmer makes up these symbolic names but has no interest in what memory addresses are assigned by the compiler to each name.

In real memory, integers, floating point numbers, and characters (text) are allocated different numbers of bits and bytes, and their bit patterns are handled differently at run time. To generate executable code correctly, the compiler has to understand the programmer's intent. This is why before the statement z = y + 1; can be executed, the compiler has to be told that y and z are indeed symbolic names for locations in memory (and not for other things, e.g., functions) and that the values stored in memory under these names are of the type double (one of C++ designations for numbers with fractional parts).

So, most of the source code that the programmer writes either defines the objects that the program manipulates (here, their names are x, y, z and others specified in #include and #define directives) or describes what should be done with these objects (add, assign, pass as a parameter to a function).

The source code for a C++ program can be an ordinary text file created by a text editor, like Emacs or Vi on Unix, Edt on VMS, or by an Integrated Development Environment (IDE) on PC or Mac. Here we save it as a file on the hard disk.

Usually, you give your source code files the names you see fit, but you are limited as to what file name extension to use. Depending on the compiler, source files should be saved with file name extension .cc, .cpp, or .cxx. Using other extensions is possible but less convenient. When standard extensions are used, only the name of the source file has to be specified, and the development tools append the extension automatically. Nonstandard extensions are allowed (and frowned on) but they have to be specified explicitly.

The source file can define several functions (our first C++ program has only one; its name is main). The program can consist of several source files (this program has only one). Each source file has to be compiled, producing the object file. Most environments require that the compiled program (object files) be linked before it can be executed. (You will learn more about that later in the chapter.) Figure 2–1 shows the output of execution of our first C++ program.

This output was produced by the executable file generated by the Microsoft Visual C++ compiler, Professional Edition version 6.0. It is a part of Microsoft Development Studio, which integrates several development tools in the same package. The program was called by the Development Studio. The last line of the output is generated by the compiler, not by the program. Otherwise, the window would be removed from the screen immediately after program termination, and the user would not be able to inspect the program output. Older versions of the Microsoft compiler do not add this message, but they do not remove the window from the screen either—the user has to do that. The program can also be run as a stand-alone application directly from the DOS prompt. In that case, the last line does not appear. Figure 2–2 shows the result of running this program from the DOS prompt.

The numeric output on different machines might be somewhat different as well. This depends on the default setting for the number of digits in the output. C++ allows the programmer to explicitly specify the format of the output, so that it does not depend on the compiler settings, but it is rather complex and does not belong to this preview. You will see the examples of doing that later.

Figure 2–1 Output of our first C++ program produced by a Microsoft compiler.

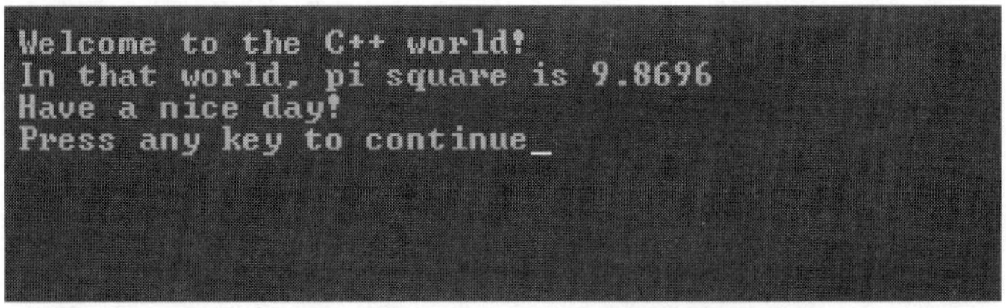

```
Welcome to the C++ world!
In that world, pi square is 9.8696
Have a nice day!
Press any key to continue_
```

Figure 2–2 Output of our first C++ program run from the DOS command prompt.

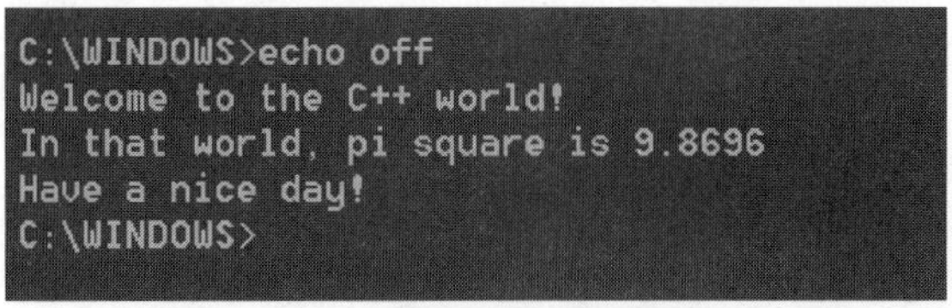

```
C:\WINDOWS>echo off
Welcome to the C++ world!
In that world, pi square is 9.8696
Have a nice day!
C:\WINDOWS>
```

Our first C++ program demonstrates the following components that should be present in any C++ program:

- preprocessor directives
- comments
- declarations and definitions
- statements and expressions
- functions and function calls

In the following sections I'll discuss the use of each kind of program component in more detail.

Preprocessor Directives

In most other languages, what you write in the source file is what the compiler sees during compilation. This is not the case in C++. The compiler is not the first tool that deals with the source code on its way to becoming an executable program. The first tool that processes the source code is the preprocessor. What is this? Well, it is an interesting invention that C++ inherited from C. Its goal is to decrease the amount of source code that the programmer writes during development (or reads during debugging or maintenance).

The preprocessor processes the source file and passes the results of processing to the compiler for compilation. Most of the program statements are ignored by the preprocessor and are passed to the compiler unmodified. The preprocessor pays attention only to preprocessor directives (and to statements that are related to them).

The preprocessor directives start with a '#' and take up the whole line. You cannot put more than one directive on a single source line. If the directive does not fit into one source line, it can be continued on the next line, but the previous line should be ended by a special continuation character, the escape character '\'. The pound sign '#' should be the first character on the line. What about the free format of C++ source code? In the previous chapter, I told you that you can format C++ code the way you (and not the compiler) see fit. Well, formally, preprocessor directives are not part of the C++ (or C) language, and the preprocessor is not part of the compiler.

In practice, of course, you cannot write even a simple C++ program without using preprocessor directives, but in theory, these directives are not part of the language! In practice, it is the compiler vendors that supply the pre-processors, but in theory, compilers and preprocessors are not related. Lately, compiler vendors have relaxed the rule: The '#' does not have to be the first character on the line, but it should be the first nonblank character.

Listing 2.1 uses two #include preprocessor directives. The #include directive causes direct text substitution: The preprocessor fetches the whole file whose name is specified as the directive argument and replaces the directive by the contents of the file taken verbatim. This can be used to combine several source files into one source file that is then compiled as a whole. The most popular use of this directive is to include function headers that describe functions used by the source code.

The names of these header files are put in the angle brackets to indicate to the preprocessor that it has to search for this file in the standard directory where the compiler stores its header files. For example, the #include directives used in the first program specify two header files. The first one is needed for using the function pow(), the second one is needed for using the operator << and the object cout. We will learn more about functions, operators, and objects later. This is just one of the examples of the complexity of C++—it is impossible to discuss even a simple program without using components that cannot be understood without learning much more than a simple program.

```
#include <iostream>
#include <math>
using namespace std;
```

The last line in this code segment from our first program is the using namespace directive. It is not a preprocessor directive. It instructs the compiler to recognize the code brought in by the header files. This is a new language feature. If you are using an older compiler, it might reject these three lines. For such a compiler, the using namespace directive should not be used. The names of the header file used in older code should have extension .h. Hence, the first three lines of the program in Listing 2.1 should be replaced with the following two lines.

```
#include <iostream.h>
#include <math.h>
```

The preprocessor directives direct the preprocessor to search the compiler directory for the include files (function pow() that computes powers of floating point numbers, object cout that represents the standard output, i.e., the screen, and operator << that displays the values on the monitor screen).

Other header files could describe functions that are not part of the standard library. They are usually written by the programmers working on the project. When the names of these files are used in the #include directives, they are enclosed in double quotes, for example,

```
#include "c:\work\mydef.h"
```

This directive directs the preprocessor to copy into the source file the contents of the file mydef.h from directory c:\work. In this example, I am using the absolute path in the file name. This is convenient if the source file is moved to one directory and the header file stays in another directory. In this case, the directive does not have to be modified. Often, however, the whole directory tree for a project is moved to another directory. When the location of the header file changes, the source file that uses that header file has to be modified. To avoid this, programmers use relative paths in the #include directives.

After being processed by the preprocessor, the #include directive itself disappears from the source file and is not passed on to the compiler.

The #include directives are extremely important: The program will not compile without them. However, they are not very sophisticated: All you have to know is what function requires what header file. The compiler help facility will assist you with that.

The definition of a constant in Listing 2.1 initializes the variable with a symbolic name PI to the value of 3.1415926. (It is customary to use capital letters for symbolic constants to distinguish them from variables whose values can change during program execution.) Later, the compiler will process this line of code:

```
double x=PI, y=1, z;       // definitions of variables
```

The executable code will copy the value allocated at the address PI the location at the address x. An alternative method to introduce the constant PI is to use the #define directive. The #define directive is also used for text substitution: Its first argument specifies the text to be substituted, and the second argument specifies the text to be used as the substitute. When the preprocessor finds in the further text of the source file the symbol that corresponds to the first directive argument, it replaces that symbol with the second directive argument. This is an example from our first C++ program:

```
#define  PI 3.14159266
```

This directive directs the preprocessor to replace every occurrence of PI with 3.1415926. When the preprocessor processes this line of code,

```
{ double x=PI, y=1, z;                    // definitions of variables
```

it passes to the compiler the following line.

```
{ double x=3.1415926, y=1, z;
```

Notice that the preprocessor removes the comments so that the compiler does not see them either. (We will discuss comments in the next section.)

The #define directive can be used to define macros, that is, sequences of computations that are inserted in the source code rather than a simple symbol as in the above example. Logically, they are used in the code in the same way as functions, combining a number of operations under a single name. Macros are faster than functions, and they are very popular in C. In C++, we use inline functions instead of macros. This is why I will not discuss macros in further detail, even though a few years ago you had to know how to write macros to pass as a C programmer. Macros are great fun, but they are a source of errors that are difficult to debug.

Another important set of preprocessor directives controls conditional computations. The #ifdef directive includes the code that follows it if the symbol used with this directive is defined. The scope of this directive is limited by the #endif directive. For example, the following code is included in the compilation if the symbol CPLUSPLUS is defined; otherwise, the preprocessor hides this code from the compiler because it is not needed when the program is compiled as a C program.

```
#ifdef CPLUSPLUS
    . . . whatever is needed when the program is written in C++
#endif
```

Notice that the symbol does not have to have a value; the use of the symbol in a #define directive is enough for the symbol to be defined for the purposes of the #ifdef directive. Also notice that the symbolic names are in uppercase. It is not necessary, but it is a common programming convention. Another popular convention is to use lowercase, but start the symbol name with two underscore characters:

```
#define __cplusplus
    #ifdef __cplusplus
    . . . whatever is needed when the program is written in C++
#endif
```

Another method to indicate the scope of the #ifdef directive is to use the #else directive. The code that follows the #else directive (until the #endif directive is found) is not included in the computation when the code that follows the #ifdef directive is included, and vice versa. For example,

```
#define MT
   #ifdef MT
   #define NFILE   40
   #else
   #define NFILE   20
#endif
```

This code is similar to what you find in the header files; if the symbol MT is defined, the limit for the number of files is 40; if we remove its definition from the source file, the limit will be 20.

The #ifndef directive is opposite to the #ifdef directive. It includes the source code that follows it (until the #else or #endif directive) only if the symbol used in that directive is not defined. If the symbol is defined, the code that follows the #ifndef directive is skipped; if the #else directive is present, the code that follows it (until the #endif directive) is passed on to the compiler. The next example is again borrowed from a header file:

```
#ifndef NULL
   #define NULL   0
#endif
```

This is a very popular technique to make sure that the symbol is defined and defined only once even though it is repeated in several files. If this definition is found in another file again, it will be silently ignored.

The preprocessor directives for conditional compilations are often used to support program portability. If the application should work in several environments, and the code for the application is basically the same for each environment with the exception of localized segments, you put these segments inside the conditional compilation directives. When the system is ported from one environment to another, all that it takes is to replace the #define directive for one symbol with the #define directive for another symbol.

This sounds simple and effective. The reality is somewhat more complex, and the preprocessor directives can be easily abused. This is why it is important to limit the use of preprocessor directives to simple #include directives for header files. Use other directives when you become more comfortable with the language.

Comments

C++ has two types of comments: block comments and end-of-line comments. Block comments start with a two-character symbol '/*' and end with a two-character symbol '*/'; end-of-line comments start with a two-character symbol '//' and end at—yes, you've guessed it—the end of line; that is, at a next newline character in the source file. The two-character symbols are quite common in C++. Most of them are inherited from C. Using the two-character symbols for operators and in other contexts instead of additional keywords was one of the ways the designers of C managed to design the language with only 30 keywords (and persuaded everyone that C was indeed a very small language).

The characters of two-character symbols (all two-character symbols in C++, not just comments) have to be typed next to each other. They cannot be separated by white space (or, for that matter, by any other character).

Text within comments of either type is equivalent to white space and hence is logically invisible to the compiler; actually, it is invisible to the compiler because the preprocessor removes the comments before the text of the source code is compiled. Here is an example of a block comment:

```
/* Comments are directed to a human, not to a compiler.
   Any symbol could be in a comment, including tabs, new
   lines, //, /*. We can format comments nicely, so that
   the structure of the text is clear to the reader. */
```

Many programmers use block comments as a preface to functions or significant segments of the algorithm. In these comments, they describe the purpose of the algorithm, input data used for processing, output data that is the result of computations, and other functions that are called to accomplish the task. Often, the update history is documented as well: the initial author and the date of the first version, authors and dates of updates, and the purpose of each update. The exact format of these block comments varies from organization to organization. It is, of course, important to stick to an uniform format. Even more important is to stick to the habit and provide the comments. Can anything be more important than providing comments? Sure: updating the comments when the code changes. There are few things more detrimental to maintenance than comments that are incorrect.

Note

In C, only block comments are available. If the programmer wants to comment on individual lines of code, the block comments are used for individual lines similar to the way I did it for our first C++ program. I think that the designers of C felt that the programmers will not be bothered by the need to finish each line comment with a two-character symbol '/'.*

Listing 2.2 shows our first C++ program written for an older compiler: I use the .h extension for library header file, the #define directive instead of const, and the C-type block comments.

Listing 2.2   Your first C++ program with block comments.

```
#include <iostream.h>                                 /* preprocessor directives */
#include <math.h>
#define  PI  3.1415926
int main(void)                                        /* function returns integer */
{
  double x=PI, y=1, z;                                /* definitions of variables */
  cout << "Welcome to the C++ world!" << endl;        /* function call */
  z = y + 1;                                          /* assignment statement */
  y = pow(x,z);                                       /* function call */
  cout << "In that world, pi square is " << y << endl;
  cout << "Have a nice day!" << endl;
  return 0;                                           /* return statement */
}                                                     /* end of the function block */
```

To avoid typing useless characters, C++ designers added the end-of-line comments to the language, which work the same way as block comments: Everything between the two-character symbol '//' and the next end of line is invisible to the compiler.

There are two differences between the two types of comments in C++. The first one is obvious: end-of-line comments cannot span several lines, whereas block comments can; this is why block comments were introduced into the language to begin with. This difference is significantly mitigated (or even rendered irrelevant) by the fact that an end-of-line comment can take the whole line.

```
// Comments are directed to a human, not to a compiler.
// Any symbol could be in a comment, including tabs, new
// lines, //, /*. We can format comments nicely, so that
// the structure of the text is clear to the reader.
```

The second difference is more subtle. The end-of-line comment can contain any character, including other comment symbols. Its delimiter is the new line character (ASCII code 12). The block comment can contain any character, including other comment symbols, with the exception of the end-of-block comment symbol '*/'. In other words, block comments cannot be nested. The preprocessor misses the nested opening symbol '/*' because it is just part of the comment; when it finds the nested closing symbol '*/', it accepts it as the end of comment and passes the rest of the comment (including the second closing symbol '*/') on to the compiler; the compiler gets confused and generates misleading error messages.

```
/* Here, the second opening symbol /* is invisible */
    and the compiler thinks the last line is no comment */
```

This is a manifestation of the age-old tension between programmers and compiler (and preprocessor) designers, or rather between the size of the tools we use and their intelligence. The C language (and its successor C++) favors tool designers. After all, every programmer is told that nesting of block comments is not allowed. So, when the error occurs, the programmer should be able to figure out what is going on easily.

Why do programmers want to use nested comments? Often, we would like to experiment with some alternative version of the code, especially when we are not sure how it works. Let us look at our first C++ program as an example. What should we do if we want to see how it works without three lines in the middle? The simplest way to achieve that is to comment this code out. Listing 2.3 shows how our example looks now:

Listing 2.3   Your first C++ program with code blocked out.

```
#include <iostream.h>                                  /* preprocessor directives */
#include <math.h>
#define   PI   3.1415926
int main(void)                                         /* function returns integer */
{
   double x=PI, y=1, z;                                /* definitions of variables */
   cout << "Welcome to the C++ world!" << endl;   /* function call */
/* beginning of the block to be cut out
   z = y + 1;                                          /* assignment statement */
   y = pow(x,z);                                       /* function call */
   cout << "In that world, pi square is " << y << endl;
*/                                                     // end of the block to be cut out
   cout << "Have a nice day!" << endl;
   return 0;                                           /* return statement */
}                                                      /* end of the function block */
```

The preprocessor comments out the first line (z = y + 1;) correctly, but it perceives the '*/' symbol at the end of that line as the end of comment. Then the preprocessor passes the second and the third lines to the compiler against our wishes. Finally it passes the solitary symbol '*/' at the end-of-block comment to the compiler, and the compiler chokes on it and gives an error message like this (different compilers can produce very different error messages):

```
Compiling...

c:\data\ch02.cpp
c:\data\ch02.cpp(11) : warning C4138: '*/' found outside of comment
c:\data\ch02.cpp(11) : error C2059: syntax error : '/'

DEMO.EXE - 1 error(s), 1 warning(s)
```

This is yet another reason why it is better to use end-of-line comments as line comments. If I used the end-of-line comments in this example, the block comment would work correctly. Of course, we can use conditional compilations described in the previous section. But they are more complex than block comments are, prone to name conflicts, and are used for porting the finished program to different environments rather than for experiments in the process of writing the program.

One more comment about comments. In C++, strings are represented as sequences of characters in double quotes. Within double quotes, comment symbols are interpreted literally, not as comment delimiters. In other words, comments do not work within strings in double quotes. Consider, for example, the following statement

```
cout << "Hello /* there */ world" << endl;
```

This statement does not print `Hello world` but `Hello /* there */ world`.

Alert

Block comments do not work inside strings in double quotes. You have to cut the text out rather than comment it out.

Tip

Blank lines could be (and should be) used for readability, to separate logically distinct code segments. This should not be overdone, because it can result in excessive spreading of code vertically.

Declarations and Definitions

When the programmer designs the logical flow of computations, the results of one step of computation are often used as data for another step. Hence, these results should be stored in memory and retrieved when needed again. In our first C++ program, one is added to the value denoted as y, and the result is used as the second argument in a call to function pow (it raises its first argument to the power of its second argument). To be able to store the value in memory and quickly access it for further use, the value should have a physical address in the computer memory. Since we do not want to use physical addresses in our source code, the value should have a symbolic name that the programmer will use in the program.

In Listing 2.1 and Listing 2.2, the sum of the value stored at location y and 1 is stored at a location that I called z. How the address and the name are connected is not a concern for the programmer; this is a problem for the compiler designer. The task of the programmer is to decide what values should be stored in memory and what names to use to denote these values. The technical term for the name that a programmer gives to a memory location is *identifier*. Actually, the programmer has to invent identifiers not only for variables, but also for such program components as constants, functions, data types, and labels (more about these components later).

The syntactic rules for identifiers are simple: they can start with a letter or an underscore '_' character only, not with a digit or any other special character. Other characters of an identifier can be capital letters A-Z, lowercase letters a-z, digits 0-9, or underscores. Theoretically, the total number of characters in an identifier is not limited. In practice, the compiler might not distinguish among identifiers if they are identical in their first 31 characters (the old limit on the identifier length). If this is not enough for you, look for a way to make the names shorter.

With the exception of the underscore, no other special symbol ($, #, etc.) is allowed. Embedded spaces are not allowed either.

Even though it is legal to start an identifier with the underscore character, it is better to avoid it because system-defined identifiers may begin with an '_' or '__', and that might result in unexpected name conflicts. Use the underscore only in the middle of an identifier to separate identifier name components (sum_of_squares). Another popular technique is to capitalize the first letter of each identifier component, (SumOfSquares).

Good taste and programming prudence require that we use mnemonic names for identifiers. *Mnemonic* here means that the name of the identifier is somehow connected to the purpose for which its value is used by the program. From that point of view, the names I used in the first C++ program (x, y, and z) are not particularly good. They can be used only if the values are used only a few times, in relatively simple computations, and there is no ground for confusion. The name PI is better—it conveys the meaning of the value (at least for those in the know).

Note

> C++ is a case-sensitive language. This means that if the program uses two identifiers that are different in capitalization only, the compiler will distinguish between them. For example, cnt, Cnt, and CNT are all different names for the C++ compiler. This is a common cause of errors for programmers with experience in other languages that do not distinguish between upper- and lowercase.

As I mentioned in the previous section, the constants defined by the program are often in uppercase to distinguish them from program objects whose values can change during program execution (PI in the first C++ program).

C/C++ keywords are reserved words that cannot be used as programmer-defined identifiers; they are all in lowercase. Here is the list of keywords that are common both to C and C++, sorted alphabetically:

```
auto    break   case    char    const   continue  default  do    double
else    enum    extern  float   for     goto      if       int   long
register return  short   signed  sizeof  static
struct  switch  typedef  union   unsigned void     volatile while
```

Here is the list of keywords that are reserved words in C++ but not in C:

```
asm   bool   catch   class   const_cast   delete
dynamic_cast  explicit  export  false  friend  inline  mutable
namespace  new  operator  private  protected  public
reinterpret_cast  static_cast  template  this  throw
true  try  typeid  typename  using  virtual  wchar_t
```

I do not think you should try to remember all of these keywords now. They will be discussed in due time. Moreover, if you use these keywords as identifiers for your variables, the compiler will tell you that you should not do it. So, the goal of this list is not to prevent you from using these keywords but to explain to you why the compiler complains if you use these keywords as identifiers.

In other, more-permissive languages, if the programmer feels that a value has to be stored in memory, the programmer may invent an appropriate identifier and use it on the left-hand side of the assignment without much ado:

```
sum_of_squares = 0;
```

Not so in C++. If you do that in a C++ program, the compiler will tell you that `sum_of_squares` is an undeclared identifier, and this is a syntax error in C++. Before the identifier is used as a name for a variable in a C++ the program, it has to be defined.

The names of variables denote locations (addresses) in computer memory that hold typed values. These values can change during program execution.

This is different from the name `PI` used in our first C++ program. In Listing 2.1, it is defined as a constant; any attempt to change its value (for example, `PI = 0;`) will be flagged as a syntax error. In Listing 2.2, it is also a constant specified with the `#define` preprocessor directive. After the preprocessor substitutes its value, it becomes a constant value that cannot be changed. For example, the statement `PI = 0;` will be converted to 3.1415926 = 0; this is a syntax error.

Variables in memory hold *typed* values, meaning that the programmer must make a commitment to the type of value that is going to be stored in these variables. The type of the variable describes the range of values permissible for that type and the operations allowed over values of this type. The definition establishes an association between the identifier and its type; each definition ends with a semicolon as follows:

```
int num;
double sum_of_squares;
char letter;
```

The first definition using the keyword `int` says that the identifier `num` is used for an integer variable. Its size is four bytes (32 bits), its range of values is from –2147483648 to +2147483647. (As you will see later, the sizes of types are machine dependent.)

Operations specific to this type are the four arithmetic operations, modulo operation (finding a remainder), comparisons, shifts left or right, logical operations, and increment and decrement (more about this in Chapter 3, "Working with C++ Data and Expressions.")

The second definition using the keyword `double` says that the identifier `sum_of_squares` is used for a double floating point variable. Its size is eight bytes, its absolute value (positive or negative) can reach 1.79769313486231158e+308 (here, e+308 denotes 10 to the power of 308—a rather large number). Operations specific to this type include the four arithmetic operations, increment and decrement, and comparisons.

The third definition using the keyword `char` says that the identifier letter is used for a character variable. Its size is one byte and it can contain the values that represent characters according to ASCII coding conventions. As far as operations over characters are concerned, C++ treats characters as small integers.

Integer values are used for counting and math computations. The operations over integers are the fastest available on each specific machine. This is why integer values are used in all cases where their range and precision are sufficient. Floating-point values have a fractional part; they are used in business and scientific calculations where whole numbers do not provide sufficient precision (or the range of two trillion is not enough).

The concept of type is fundamental to both functional and object-oriented programming. Every value handled by a C++ program must have a type. If the type is used incorrectly, the compiler flags this usage as a syntax error. This might happen when a value of one type is used where a value of another type is expected. Concern about using the values of the correct type is always at the focus of attention of the C++ programmer.

C++ has only few built-in data types, that is, data types that are immediately available from the language. They are integers (65), floating point numbers (65.0), or characters ('a').

All these types are *primitive* (or scalar) types that is, the values of these types cannot be decomposed into components that could be manipulated by the program. For example, the double floating point value has as its components an integer part and a fractional part (and also an exponent part), but the C++ language does not allow the programmer to access these parts directly. We can access the whole value only. Hence, C++ types are an abstraction tool: They allow us to concentrate on *what* can be done to a value rather than on *how* the individual components of the value are manipulated.

C++ partially makes up for the scarcity of fundamental types by introducing some variations of integers and floating point types of other sizes, ranges, and precision. This does not change the situation much. More important, C++ supports techniques for combining individual primitive values into aggregates—arrays, structures, and classes. The values of these aggregate types are composite values; they consist of several components, and C++ supports techniques for accessing the individual components of these aggregates.

When the definition of a variable is elaborated (or executed) at run time, space is allocated for that variable, whether this variable is of primitive or of aggregate type; after that, the variable can be used to store and to retrieve the values of its declared type. There is nothing special about this; all modern strongly typed languages work this way.

Some programmers use a separate source code line for each definition, so that each one stands out for easier review. Others say that the large number of separate short lines makes reviewing definitions difficult; they put several definitions on the same line:

```
int num;   double sum_of_squares;
```

When the variables are of the same type, they can be defined separately; each definition includes the type name and ends with a semicolon, such as:

```
int a;   int b;   int c;
```

It is perfectly OK to combine these definitions; the name of the type is used only once, and the names of the variables are separated by commas; the definition ends with a semicolon, for example:

```
int a, b, c;              // acceptable shorthand
```

In other words, the scope of the type name (in this case, `int`) includes the names of all variables found between the type name and the next semicolon; variables a, b, and c are all integers. These two styles of definitions are equivalent, but you should not confuse the two. For example, this definition is a syntax error:

```
int a, b, int c;          // syntax error     *
```

On the other hand, these definitions are perfectly all right:

```
int a, b;   int c;        // no syntax error
```

The difference is small but important. The C++ programmer should always be cognizant about differences of this kind.

For a C++ programmer, the difference between a comma and a semicolon is crucial. Make sure you do not confuse the two.

Most programmers define variables at the beginning of a function block or a file. This is what I did in our first C++ program. This is the only way to define variables in C. C++, however, allows the programmer to define variables in the middle of code closer to their first use. Listing 2.4 shows how Listing 2.1 *could* look like if I used a more flexible way to define variables:

Listing 2.4 Your first C++ program with definitions in the middle of the code.

```cpp
#include <iostream>                              // preprocessor directive
#include <cmath>                                 // preprocessor directive
using namespace std;                             // compiler directive
const double PI = 3.1415926;                     // definition of a constant
int main(void)                                   // function returns integer
{
   cout << "Welcome to the C++ world!" << endl;  // function call
   double y=1, z;                                // definitions of variables
   z = y + 1;                                    // assignment statement
   double x=PI;                                  // definition of variable
   y = pow(x,z);                                 // function call
   cout << "In that world, pi square is " << y << endl;
   cout << "Have a nice day!" << endl;
   return 0;                                     // return statement
}                                                // end of the function block
```

For program execution, it does not make any difference how far in advance the variable is defined. The output of this version of the program is the same as we discussed on Figure 2–1. Presumably, the distance between the definition and the use of a variable in the source code makes a difference for a human reader, especially if the variable is used once or twice without much interruption. If the next use of the variable is separated from the first one, and the maintainer wants to check the definition of this variable, it might be more convenient to find the definition at the start of the function rather than in the middle.

Another term that you should be familiar with is *declaration*. In other languages, declarations and definitions are synonyms. C++ inherited from C a subtle distinction between the two. While definitions associate the name of the variable with its type and allocate the space for the variable, declarations only associate the name and the type, because the space for the variable is allocated elsewhere. This happens, for example, in a multifile program when a variable is defined in one file and is also used in another file. In the file that uses this variable, the variable is defined as external using the keyword extern:

```cpp
extern int count;
```

Now we can use the variable count in the source code of this file. All references to the variable count in this file will be translated into the address of the variable count that is defined in another file.

Another difference between definitions and declarations is that the definitions must be unique in the program; declarations can be repeated as many times as you want. For example, these definitions are not allowed (even if you wanted to do this):

```
int a;   int a;                              // syntax error
```

On the other hand, these declarations are acceptable:

```
extern int count;   extern int count;   // this is OK
```

This does not look smart either, but there are situations where you might want to do something like this. And if you do it by mistake, the compiler will not tell you that this is an error. The point I am making here is a fundamental one, and we will see it generalized for functions and for types.

Alert

A definition must be unique, but a declaration might be repeated.

After the variables are defined (or declared), they can be manipulated by the program. Before their values are used by the program, they have to receive these values. Failure to do so represents the use of uninitialized variables, a common cause of errors in programs.

There are two ways for a variable to receive a value: assignment statement and initialization. In this example, I am using assignment statements (each statement ends with a semicolon):

```
double x, y, z;
x = PI;   y = 1;
```

As you probably noticed, in the first C++ program I used initialization for variables x and y (but not for z).

```
double x = PI, y = 1, z;
```

The result is exactly the same: the variable x receives the value 3.1415926536, variable y receives the value 1, and z remains uninitialized. While we are dealing with variables of primitive types, the difference between assignment and initialization is not important from a practical point of view. When we start dealing with programmer-defined objects, the difference will become crucial. I think I will tell you the story about the bagel and cream cheese once again when we discuss initialization of objects.

Variables can be initialized only at definition and not at declaration. For example, the variable count can be initialized only in the file where it is defined (where the space for this variable is allocated). In the file where the variable is declared (as an external variable) the variable can be assigned and accessed without limitations, but it cannot be initialized. This attempt, for example, will be flagged as an error:

```
extern int count = 0;    // syntax error
```

This is only an introduction to the topic of C++ data types. Chapter 3 discusses C++ types in more detail along with operations available on the values of these types.

Statements and Expressions

A *statement* is a program unit that is executed as a logical whole so that its component steps are hidden from the programmer, and the details of these steps should not attract the programmer's attention (at least, not at the moment). A program statement is an abstraction tool: It allows us to concentrate on *what* is being done rather than on *how* this is done.

For example, declarations and definitions that we discussed in the previous section are statements. We are not interested in the details of memory allocation, such as whether variable a is next to variable b or to variable c, whether the address of variable a is greater than variable c, whether the word starts with the senior byte, and so on. All that we want is to be sure that memory for three integer variables is allocated:

```
int a, b, c;
```

The assignments we saw in the previous section represent the second type of statement. The target of the assignment (the variable that receives the value) is on the left-hand side of the assignment; the expression that specifies the value sent to the target is found on the right-hand side of the assignment statement. In our first C++ program, we had the following assignment:

```
z = y + 1;
```

When this statement is executed, the value stored in the variable denoted y is added to 1 and the result 2 is stored in the location that corresponds to the variable z. The value stored in variable y is not affected by its usage. It changes only when the name of the variable appears on the left-hand side of the assignment statement, as a target of the assignment.

Let me repeat that the definitions at the beginning of Listing 2.1 contain initializations and not assignments. Even though the syntax is similar, different functions are called for C++ objects:

```
double x=PI, y=1, z;    // x and y are initialized, not assigned
```

Expressions that are found on the right-hand side of assignment statements are, well, expressions. They consist of operators and operands. *Operands* are either variables or literal numbers or smaller expressions. In the first C++ program, the expression that was used to set the value of variable z contained the operands y and 1. If necessary, parentheses can be used to structure complex expressions, for example,

```
z = (y + 1) * (y - 1);   // expression with subexpressions
```

Here, the operands y + 1 and y - 1 are smaller expressions. Every expression returns a typed value that can be used in an assignment statement or in another expression.

Expressions can be formed using 55 different C++ operators, including arithmetic operations '+', '-', '*', '/', comparisons '<', '>' and others. 55 is a large number of operators to learn. Since there are not enough special symbols to denote all these operators, two-symbol operators are common in C++ (for example, comparison for equality is denoted as '=='). Operators are organized into 18 levels of precedence. This is also a lot to learn. Many programmers prefer to use parentheses to indicate the order of computations rather than rely on the precedence of operators. We are going to see more details in the next chapter.

There is an important difference between components of the left-hand side and the right-hand side of the assignment. We can mix both names of variables and literal values in C++ expressions. When the name of the variable is specified (y), the expression uses not the address denoted by the name but the value that is stored in that location. When the value is specified (1) the expression again uses the value directly, even though this value is also stored at some specific address. As the target of the assignment, we can use only names of the variables. Well, this is not that simple, but the main fact is: A literal value cannot appear on the left-hand side of the assignment. For example, this looks like a nice equation, but this is not legal C++ code:

```
1 = z - y;              // impossible in C++
```

The third type of statement is a function call. A function call specifies the name of the function to be executed, the arguments that it should use (when it has arguments), and the value it returns (if it returns a value).

Our first C++ program consists of one function (main). It uses (calls) the function pow. There is a common convention among programmers and technical writers to distinguish between function names and all other names when writing about C++ code. We do that by appending empty parentheses to the function name regardless of the number of arguments, for example, main() and pow(), similar to the way it is done in code.

The library function pow() uses two arguments, the base value and the power to raise the base to. It returns the result of raising the value stored in the first argument to the power specified by the second argument. The returned value can be used as a component of an expression. This is why this function is called using the following syntax:

```
y = pow(x,z);
```

When the first argument is 3.1415926 and the second argument is 2, the return value is 9.869604. (As in other languages, computations on nonintegers are approximate.)

When the function is called during the program execution, the execution of the calling function is suspended and the called function executes its code. When the called function terminates (returns), the execution of the calling function is resumed. If the calling function calls another function, the process repeats itself.

The C++ input/output library calls are much more difficult to explain than other library calls are. They use predefined classes, objects, and overloaded operators that we will discuss in detail much, much later. Let us give it a try. We use library objects cout (for output) and cin (for input) together with two kinds of two-symbol operators. The insertion operator '<<' is used with the library object cout and sends output to the computer screen using the names of variables that should be displayed. Literal numeric values and strings in double quotes can be used too. The extraction operator '>>' is used with the library object cin and accepts input from the keyboard into variables whose names are specified as operands.

It sounds sophisticated, but basic input/output is very simple. Since each input or output statement has to specify its own object (cin or cout), they are not intermixed. Hence, input and ouput operators '>>' and '<<' are not intermixed in the same statement. Listing 2.5 shows an example that accepts two integer numbers from the keyboard and displays their sum.

Listing 2.5   An interactive program with input and output statements.

```
#include <iostream>
using namespace std;
int main(void)
{
    int a, b, c;                                  // definitions of variables
    cout << "Type two integers, press Enter ";
    cin >> a >> b;                                // two function calls: extraction
    c = a + b;
    cout << "Their sum is " << c << endl;
    return 0;
}
```

The output of this program is represented in Figure 2–3.

Each use of the operators << and >> represents a function call. The endl library component represents a so-called manipulator. Each element of output, including strings in double quotes (and characters in single quotes), literals (numeric values), variables, or expressions has to have its own operator. The same applies to each element of input. Using commas or spaces to separate input/output components is incorrect; for example, this is in error:

```
cout << "Their sum is ", c  endl;          // typical errors: a comma, a space
```

To add insult to injury, the compiler often is unable to correctly diagnose the source of the problem. In error messages, you are going to read about missing semicolons, missing arguments, mismatch in parameters, and other interesting problems. This is yet another indication that you should not spend too much effort trying to decipher compiler messages. Use this message mostly as an indication that the code has a problem and rely on your logic to identify that problem.

Figure 2–3   Output of the program with interactive I/O.

```
Type two integers, press Enter: 22 33
Their sum is 55
```

Alert

Each component of input and output has to have its own >> operator or << operator. Using commas or spaces to separate components is not allowed. Mixing input and output operations in the same statement is not allowed either.

The iostream library is powerful and flexible. You will find, however, the code for formatted output with the use of this library is verbose. C++ also supports another set of "standard" library functions: printf(), scanf(), and their variations. They come from C and are quite common in legacy C and C++ code. To use them, you should include the header file stdio.h. It is easier to write code for formatted output with the use of these functions than with the use of iostream functions. However, the stdio.h functions are more prone to error. The iostream library is more popular than these older functions are—they are not "standard" anymore. Unfortunately, we cannot just forget about the stdio.h library and switch completely to the iostream library because the stdio.h functions are often used for Windows and GUI programming and in string processing.

Similar to other types of statements, a function is an abstraction tool. In the client source code (e.g., in our first C++ program) it specifies *what* has to be done without clouding the picture with the details as to *how* it is done.

We looked at three most popular types of statements: definitions (and declarations), assignments, and function calls. The fourth type of statement is a *type definition*. Type definitions combine the components into aggregate type such as structures or classes that can be manipulated as a whole. We are going to have the first brief look at type definitions in the section "Functions and Function Calls," and most of the book will be devoted to programming with classes.

The last type of statement is a *compound statement*, or a *statement block*. It is a sequence of statements enclosed in braces. The compound statement can appear everywhere where a single statement can (including another compound statement). For example, in our first C++ program we can combine the last three statements in a statement block, as shown in Listing 2.6.

Listing 2.6 Your first C++ program with a nested statement block.

```
#include <iostream>                        // preprocessor directives
#include <cmath>
using namespace std;
const double PI = 3.1415926;               // definition of a constant
int main(void)
{
   double x=PI, y=1, z;                    // definitions of variables
   cout << "Welcome to the C++ world!" << endl;
   z = y + 1;
   y = pow(x,z);
   {                                       // start of statement block
     cout << "In that world, pi square is " << y << endl;
     cout << "Have a nice day!" << endl;
     return 0;
   }                                       // end of statement block
}                                          // end of the function block
```

Here, it does not buy us much: The program executes exactly as before. However, there are many language constructs in C++ (for example, conditional and loop constructs) that have a slot for one C++ statement only. If the logic of computations cannot be squeezed into one statement, we have a problem. The use of a statement block resolves this problem.

The one-character block delimiters '{' and '}' should be paired; it is a syntax error if they do not match. They open and close a scope, that is, a structural element of a program. You see that the main() function is also delimited by braces; the source code of every function is. The difference between a compound statement and a function body is that the compound statement does not have a name (it is an unnamed statement block), and the function body is a named block.

Statements in a C++ program are executed one after another, from top down. Ideally, each statement is placed on a separate line and indented so that the control structure is evident to the reader. For example, in Listing 2.6 the statements in the main() function are indented to the right relative to the preprocessor directives and the main() function header; statements in the nested statement block are indented farther to the right relative to other statements in the main() function.

It is OK to put several statements on the same line if they are consecutive steps to achieving the same goal:

```
z = y + 1;  y = pow(x,z);        // two substeps of the algorithm
```

Statements on the same line are executed from left to right. How many statements should we put on the same line of code? The answer is related to the issue of minimizing the eye movements when reading source code. When each statement is allocated a separate line, the coding segments become too long. As the result, the eye has to travel long distances through the code so that at the bottom of the page we do not remember exactly what we saw on the top of the page or two pages earlier. Packing several statements on the same line alleviates this problem—we can see more code at a glance—but now the eye travels more in horizontal direction, and there is a danger that we will overlook an action packed in the middle of some line among other statements. To a large extent, it is a matter of taste. In any case, statements that you put on the same line should be directed toward a common goal.

In C++, each statement has to be terminated by a semicolon. In some other languages, the semicolon separates statements, so that the last statement in the sequence does not have it. In C++ every statement ends with a semicolon. Well, not quite so. Compound statements do not end with a semicolon. Notice that in our first C++ program, both right braces (for the unnamed block and for the `main()` function) are not followed by a semicolon.

Actually, the semicolon can turn any expression into a statement. For example, this is legal in C++:

```
y + 1;
```

This, of course, is totally useless. No other language would allow this. But it is legal in C and hence it is legal in C++. Why should you worry whether a senseless thing is legal or not? You are not going to write it, right? Wrong. This is not as harmless as it looks. If you did this by mistake, for example, by accidentally erasing the target of the assignment, the compiler does not stand by to guard you against the error. What should have been a syntax error (and is an error in other, less-permissive languages) is not discovered immediately. It becomes a run-time error that can be discovered only by hard labor during debugging.

Flow control constructs also can be viewed as a kind of statement. They modify sequential flow of execution of statements. There are three kinds of flow control statements:

- conditional statements
- loops
- function calls

Note

In this section, we will look only at a small set of control constructs. You will find a more detailed treatment in Chapter 4, "C++ Control Flow."

The simplest conditional statement is the `if` statement. Its general form is

```
if (expression) statement_to_execute;
```

Syntactically, the `if` statement is a single statement. When the `statement_to_execute` is a simple statement, it ends with a semicolon. For a compound statement, no semicolon is used after the closing brace. Parentheses around the conditional expression are mandatory, not optional.

The `statement_to_execute` that follows the conditional expression is executed if the expression is true; if the expression is false, the statement is skipped. Indentation is often used to stress the flow of control. The next segment of code checks whether the temperature in Fahrenheit is above the freezing point and displays an encouraging message if it is or keeps silent if it is not:

```
if (fahr > 32)                    // expression is commonly on a separate line
   cout << "Do not worry about starting your car" << endl;
```

The second form of conditional statement has two branches: One is executed when the condition is true, another is executed when the condition is false. Each branch can contain one statement (terminated by a semicolon) or a compound block (without a semicolon); for example,

```
if (fahr > 32)                    // no "then" keyword in C++
   cout << "Do not worry about starting your car" << endl;
else
   cout << "Be careful in the morning" << endl;
```

There is no `then` keyword in C++; it is implied. The `else` keyword has to be used. Notice the indentation that stresses the flow of control.

The simplest loop statement is a `while` statement:

```
while (expression) statement_to_execute;
```

Syntactically, the loop body is a single statement; for a simple `statement_to_execute`, it ends with a semicolon. When the loop body is a compound statement, no semicolon is needed after the closing right brace at the end of the statement. Parentheses around the expression are mandatory.

The loop body, `statement_to_execute`, is executed if the expression is true. Then the loop expression is tested again; if it is true, the next iteration through the loop body takes place and the loop expression is tested again. The loop body is skipped if the expression is (becomes) false, and the next statement (whatever it is) is executed.

In Listing 2.7, the program computes the squares of numbers 8, 9, 10, and 11, and displays the numbers and their squares in the form of a table (the output is shown in Figure 2–4). It first prints the table header and a blank line, and then it uses the variable num as the loop variable. Before the loop, it initializes num to 8; this value is used in the first pass through the loop. In the body of the loop it increments num by 1; in the loop condition, it checks whether the value of num is still less than 12; if yes, the body of the loop (in braces) is executed, and the value of num is incremented again. The loop execution continues until the value of num becomes 12: The loop condition becomes false, the loop body is skipped, and the last statement of the program is executed.

Listing 2.7 An example of a loop with formatted output.

```
#include <iostream>
#include <iomanip>
using namespace std;
int main (void)
{
  int num = 8, square;                      // num is initialized before loop
  cout << "Numbers Their Squares" << endl << endl;
  while (num < 12)                          // num is used as a loop variable
    { square = num * num;                   // num is used in the body
      cout << "   " << num << "      " << square << endl;
      num = num + 1;                        // it is modified at loop end
                  }                         // no ';' at end of the block
  cout << endl <<"Have a nice day." << endl;
  return 0;
}
```

When the operator << sends the characters to the screen using the object cout, it displays characters next to each other without intervening spaces. When it finishes the conversion of one value (e.g., num) from binary form to characters and starts converting another value (e.g., square), it also does not insert intervening spaces. This unformatted output is, of course, ineligible. For quick and dirty output, blank spaces can be inserted between output components: This is what the cout statement does in the loop in Listing 2.7.

```
Numbers Their Squares
   8         64
   9         81
  10        100
  11        121

Have a nice day.
```

Figure 2–4
Output of the loop computing the squares of numbers.

This method of formatting is rarely satisfactory. When different passes through the loop produce values with different number of characters, the columns get out of alignment, as they do in Figure 2–4. This can be corrected by using a manipulator setw that specifies the number of output positions (width of the output) allocated for the next output component. The setw manipulator has to be inserted into the output stream with the operator << the same as any other output component. For example, inserting setw(4) allocates four output positions for the next component. If you want to format several components, each one has to be preceded by its own setw manipulator, even when the width of the output is the same for each component.

Let us replace the loop cout statement in Listing 2.7 with the following statement:

```
cout << setw(4) << num << setw(10) << square << endl;
```

For this scheme to work, the program has to include the iomanip header file (see Listing 2.7). The output of this version of the program is shown in Figure 2–5. For numeric values, the output is aligned to the right in the specified width; for character strings, it is aligned to the left. If the output value does not fit into the specified width, the cout object takes as many positions on the screen as necessary and pushes the rest of the output to the right. The output is never truncated because of its excessive width.

Make sure that you are comfortable with the elements of loop design and with tracing the loop iterations. A correctly designed while loop should contain the following:

- initialization of the current value of the loop variable before the loop started
- the use of the current value of the loop variable in the body of the loop
- change (increment) of the current value in the loop body (often, at the end of the loop body)

```
Numbers Their Squares

    8        64
    9        81
   10       100
   11       121

Have a nice day.
```

Figure 2-5
Output of the loop with the width specified
for each output value.

In our example in Listing 2.7, the variable num is used as the loop variable. It is initialized when it is defined, before the loop. Its value is used in the body of the loop. It is incremented in the body of the loop (at its end). Its value is used to decide whether it is time to terminate the loop.

Functions and Function Calls

Functional modularization allows us to divide the job of software implementation among programmers: We put groups of functions in different source files, assign a programmer to each file, and let the programmers work in parallel. Obviously, a programmer can work on several functions or several files, but several programmers cannot work simultaneously on the same function. If the function is so large that several programmers should work on it, it should be broken into several functions.

Other advantages of using functions include:

- caller's code is expressed in terms of function calls (whose names should reflect the meaning of the operations) that is more readable than lower-level computations

- size of the source (and object) code can decrease if the same operations are done in different parts of source code—it is the shorter function calls that are repeated in the source (and object) code rather than longer low-level operations

- using standard libraries (and placing project-specific functions into project libraries) improves source code reusability within the project and from one project to the next project

Breaking the program into separate functions changes the structure of the program but does not change its output (if it is done correctly). However, the quality of the program might be quite different for different modularization decisions: Independent functions make programs easier to understand and to maintain.

Let us take a look at different possible implementations of Listing 2.1. Since this program is tiny, these examples will not demonstrate advantages related to readability, program size, and reusability. However, these examples will allow us to demonstrate the syntax and semantics (meaning) of using functions.

In the first redesign (see Listing 2.8), I implement the initial greeting as a separate function with a long name `displayInitialGreeting()`. This function is called from `main()`. Hence, `main()` is its client, and the function itself is a server of `main()`.

Listing 2.8 Your first C++ program with one server function.

```
#include <iostream>
#include <cmath>
using namespace std;
const double  PI = 3.1415926;

void displayInitialGreeting()                       // function header
{
    cout << "Welcome to the C++ world!" << endl;    // its body
}                                                   // end of the function block

int main(void)
{
  double x=PI, y=1, z;
  displayInitialGreeting();                         // function call
  z = y + 1;
  y = pow(x,z);
//  cout << "In that world, pi square is " << y << endl;
//  cout << "Have a nice day!" << endl;
  return 0;
    }                                               // end of the function block
```

Of course, `displayInitialGreeting()` is rather a silly function because it consists of only one statement. However, even such a silly function demonstrates that using functions in C++ requires coordination of three elements of the program:

- function header
- function body
- function call

The function header specifies the function interface: its return type, function name, parameter list (in parentheses) with types and names of formal parameters (if any). If the function uses no parameters, the parameter list in parentheses is empty; if the function returns no value, the return type is `void`.

Its name describes the meaning of processing and follows a popular convention of combining an active verb that describes the action (`display`) and a noun that describes the object of the action (`InitialGreeting`). Following the popular programming convention, we put the first word of the function name in lowercase; the first letters of other words (if any) are capitalized.

We see that the `displayInitialGreeting()` function does not return any value (it has void return type). This is why it needs no return statement. If you want, you can use it, but it should not return any value. The function also uses no parameters (it has an empty parameter list). Parentheses in the header are used even if there are no parameters. The keyword `void` can be used to indicate the absence of formal parameters:

```
void displayInitialGreeting(void)                 // void in parameter list
{
   cout << "Welcome to the C++ world!" << endl    // function body
   return;                                        // avoid unnecessary code
   }
```

The function body is a sequence of statements enclosed in matching braces; it is a statement block (a compound statement). Each statement is terminated by a semicolon, but the block itself does not have a terminating semicolon. If necessary, the function body can have definitions and declarations of variables that are necessary to support the computations within the function. Each function body has its separate name space (scope). This means that the names of the variables defined within the function (local variables) do not conflict with the names of variables defined within other functions, and the function designer does not have to coordinate the names of local variables with other designers.

Similar to C, function definitions in C++ cannot be nested; hence, function names are global within the program and have to be unique. The function designer has to coordinate the function name with other designers regardless of whether they need to call this function or not.

The `displayInitialGreeting()` function does not define any local variables. To emphasize the limits of the function body, both the opening brace and closing braces are allocated separate source code lines. Some programmers feel that this extends the vertical dimension of the source code without the benefit of readability; they would not allocate separate lines for the braces. However, they would leave an empty line between functions:

```
void displayInitialGreeting()      // function header
{ cout << "Welcome to the C++ world!" << endl; }
                                   // function body
```

The third element of using the function, the function call, consists of the function name followed by the list of actual arguments in parentheses. If there are no arguments, parentheses are still used. Unlike in the function header, the keyword `void` cannot be used in the function call.

```
displayInitialGreeting(void);      // incorrect function call
```

This is yet another feature that C++ inherited from C we are left to wonder about. For the designers of the C language, the simplicity of design was never a priority. After all, does it take much to remember that you can use `void` in the function header but not in the function call? Not really. At least not for them. They discounted the fact that accumulation of such features could lead to confusion for programmers.

Actually, a real C expert knows the answer to this question and probably will even call this answer simple. But it is not. I have taught C++ seminars to a very large number of C programmers; most of them were good programmers, some of them were excellent C programmers, but it was very infrequent that any seminar participants came up with the answer, and only after much prodding and hints. I will tell you this answer when we accumulate more knowledge about the language.

When a function is called, the calling function (client function) suspends its execution, and control passes to the called function (server function). Its statements are executed sequentially. When the execution reaches the closing brace of the server function body, the server function terminates, and control returns to the calling function (this is why the function termination is called `return`). After that, the client function resumes its execution.

Next, let us take a look at a function with parameters. Listing 2.9 shows yet another version of our first C++ program; it has a function `displayResults()` that implements the functionality of the local block in the previous version. The function accepts a value of type `double` as a parameter and displays it on the screen with additional messages to the user.

Listing 2.9 Your first C++ program with two server functions.

```
#include <iostream>
#include <cmath>
using namespace std;
const double PI = 3.1415926;

void displayInitialGreeting()                    // function header
{ cout << "Welcome to the C++ world!" << endl; }  // its body

void displayResults(double y)                    // function header
{ cout << "In that world, pi square is " << y << endl;
  cout << "Have a nice day!" << endl; }          // its body

int main(void)
{
   double x=PI, y=1, z;
   displayInitialGreeting();                      // function call
   z = y + 1;
   y = pow(x,z);
   displayResults(y);                             // another function call
   return 0;
   }
```

The function `displayResults()` does not return any value to its caller (it has the `void` return type), but its parameter list is not empty. You see that the parameter definition is similar to definitions of variables: The programmer chooses a name for the parameter and specifies its type. The result of this definition at execution time is similar to the results of variable definition: When the function is called, memory for the parameter of the appropriate type is allocated. This location is used when the parameter name is mentioned in the function body (e.g., a reference to the variable `y` in the first `cout` statement). The value of the parameter is initialized to the value of the actual argument in the function call.

The function call specifies the name of the function and the list of actual arguments in parentheses. Here, the list contains only one argument (its name is the same as the name of the formal parameter, but this is just a coincidence). Notice that the actual argument is an expression, not a definition of a variable: You specify its type in the function header but not in the function call. This form of the function call would be incorrect:

```
displayResult(double y);              // error
```

Next, let us look at a function with a non-void return type and several parameters. Listing 2.10 shows yet another version of our first C++ program. (Indeed, there are many ways to skin the cat.) It has a function computeSquare() with two parameters of type double; the function returns a value of type double.

Listing 2.10 Your first C++ program with three server functions.

```
#include <iostream>
#include <cmath>
using namespace std;
const double PI = 3.1415926;

void displayInitialGreeting()                   // void return type
{ cout << "Welcome to the C++ world!" << endl; }

double computeSquare(double x, double y)        // non-void return
{ double z;                                     // a local variable
  z = y + 1;
  y = pow(x,z);
  return y; }                                   // mandatory return statement

void displayResults(double y)                   // function header
{ cout << "In that world, pi square is " << y << endl;
  cout << "Have a nice day!" << endl; }         // function body

int main(void)
{
  double x=PI, y=1;
  displayInitialGreeting();                     // function call
  y = computeSquare(x,y);                       // another function call
  displayResults(y);                            // yet another call
  return 0;
    }
```

Notice that there are no limitations on the types of parameters and return values; the fact that they are all `double` in this example is again a pure coincidence.

Notice that each parameter is specified by its type and name, pretty much like in a definition of a variable; even when parameters are of the same type, each parameter should be described separately; we cannot use the comma-separated definitions similar to definitions of variables. Remember that story about the herring? The parameter list in this function definition is incorrect:

```
double computeSquare(double x, y)    // syntax error
{ double z;
  z = y + 1;
  y = pow(x,z);
  return y; }
```

Note

Parameters and return values can be of any type. The type of each parameter has to be specified separately, even if they are all the same.

Since the header of the function `computeSquare()` specifies a non-void return value (in this case, `double`), the function body must contain a `return` statement. The keyword `return` is used, and a value of type `double` is specified as its argument. Some programmers put the return value in parentheses, but this is not necessary. The body of the function `computeSquare()` defines a local variable z, assigns it a value, computes the value of variable y, and returns this value to the caller. (There are several subtleties in this code that we will discuss in more detail in Chapter 5, "Aggregation with Programmer-Defined Data Types.") When the client code calls this function, it passes to it the values of arguments, and these values are used inside the function. Since the function returns a value, its return value can be used by the client code in an expression as if it were a value of that type (in this example, `double`).

```
  y = pow(x,z);
```

Make sure that you distinguish between the terms parameter and argument. A *parameter* is a variable defined within a function header and used within the body of the function; an *argument* is a variable defined in the client function and used in the function call. Often, we use terms formal parameters and actual arguments.

For simplicity of the example, I used the same names both for formal parameters and for corresponding actual arguments for the function `computeSquare()`. This does not happen often in real life. In a large program, the client function is developed by one programmer, and the server function is developed by another programmer. There is no need to coordinate the names of parameters. It is enough for the client programmer to learn the types of parameters and return values.

Often, the server function is developed earlier than the client function is; it is put into the library, and its source code is not available. Even if it is available, it is an extra burden on the client programmer to research the server source code and to learn the names of formal parameters. Fortunately, there is no need for that. The names of actual arguments do not have anything to do with the names of formal parameters. Here is yet another version of function `computeSquare()` that could be used in Listing 2.10 with nothing else changed that stresses this independence.

```
double computeSquare(double base, double exponent)
{ double power = exponent + 1;              // a local variable
  return pow(base,power); }                  // return statement
```

In all these examples, I put the definitions of server functions before the calls to these functions in the client function. This is similar to the situation with ordinary variables—the definition lexically precedes the use of the variable. What happens if I place these functions in the source file in a different order? Here we again bump into a limitation that C++ inherited from C: If the definition of the function does not lexically precede the function call, the compiler will play dumb and tell you it does not know what the identifier `displayInitialGreeting()` and others are. Listing 2.11 shows an incorrect version of our program.

```
┌─────────────────────────────────────────────────────────────────────────┐
│ Listing 2.11  Incorrect C++ program with functions following the function calls. │
└─────────────────────────────────────────────────────────────────────────┘
```

```cpp
#include <iostream>
#include <cmath>
using namespace std;
const double PI = 3.1415926;

int main(void)
{
   double x=PI, y=1;
   displayInitialGreeting();                     // syntax error
   y = computeSquare(x,y);                        // another syntax error
   displayResults(y);                             // and another syntax error
   return 0;
     }

void displayInitialGreeting()                     // function definition
{ cout << "Welcome to the C++ world!" << endl; }  // body

double computeSquare(double base, double exponent)
{ double power = exponent + 1;                    // a local variable
   return pow(base,power); }                      // return statement

void displayResults(double y)
{ cout << "In that world, pi square is " << y << endl;
   cout << "Have a nice day!" << endl; }          // function body
```

My compiler tried to give me "helpful" information about terms and functions being redefined:

```
Compiling...
c:\data\ch02.cpp
c:\data\ch02.cpp(7) : error C2065: 'displayInitialGreeting' : undeclared identifier
c:\data\ch02.cpp(7) : error C2064: term does not evaluate to a function
c:\data\ch02.cpp(8) : error C2065: 'computeSquare' : undeclared identifier
c:\data\ch02.cpp(8) : error C2064: term does not evaluate to a function
c:\data\ch02.cpp(9) : error C2065: 'displayResults' : undeclared identifier
c:\data\ch02.cpp(9) : error C2064: term does not evaluate to a function
c:\data\ch02.cpp(13) : error C2371: 'displayInitialGreeting' : redefinition;
    different basic types
c:\data\ch02.cpp(17) : error C2371: 'computeSquare' : redefinition;
    different basic types
c:\data\ch02.cpp(23) : error C2371: 'displayResults' : redefinition;
    different basic types
DEMO.EXE - 9 error(s), 0 warning(s)
```

Your compiler might produce somewhat different messages, but this is not the point. Usually, the initial reaction of a beginning C++ programmer is that of disbelief: "What do you mean the identifier is not defined? It is defined, right here, before your eyes! Hey, compiler, are you blind?" The compiler is not blind. It is the same tradeoff between the interests of the compiler designer and the compiler user. The compiler user loses to the general rule: Everything that is used in the code has to be defined before it is used. "Everything" means *everything*, including the names of the variables and the function names.

The purpose of applying this requirement to the function calls is obvious: It is important that the compiler check whether the function name is spelled right, the function is called with the correct number of arguments, and the arguments are of the correct types. The error messages, of course, could be more helpful. And, of course, this check could be achieved without asking the programmer to do something about it. The second pass through the source code (as in some older languages) would eliminate the problem altogether.

In C++, the programmer is asked to resolve this problem by using function prototypes. A function prototype has the same syntactic form as the function header. The only difference is that the prototype has to be terminated by a semicolon. There are no limitations on the placing of the prototypes with the exception that it should lexically precede the first call to this function. It is a common convention to put prototypes at the beginning of the source file with client functions.

The relationship between function definitions and function prototypes is a generalization of the relationship between definitions and declarations of variables. A function prototype is a declaration of the function, and it can be repeated as many times as needed. A function definition can be found in the program only once.

The added benefit of using function prototypes is that now there is no need to put the function definitions in the same file as the client function. The prototypes are enough to satisfy the compiler. Listing 2.12 is a corrected version of Listing 2.11 with server function prototypes at the top of the file and the function definitions moved elsewhere.

Listing 2.12   Corrected C++ program with prototypes preceding the function calls.

```
const double PI = 3.1415926;

void displayInitialGreeting();          // function prototypes
double computeSquare(double x, double y);
void displayResults(double y);

int main(void)
{
    double x=PI, y=1;
    displayInitialGreeting();          // function calls
    y = computeSquare(x,y);
    displayResults(y);
    return 0;
                                       // end of the function block
}
```

Even for this tiny example, we can see the advantages of using functions. The code of the `main()` function is purged of details of *how* things are done. It only says *what* is being done. To know the details of how it is being done, the maintainer can turn to the source code of the server functions in different files. Since each function is in a separate file, the attention of the maintainer will not be distracted by irrelevant details. The programmer even does not have to mention the names of the source files with server functions. The object code for these functions, however, has to be linked with the object code for `main()`. The `#include` files are also gone. They are included in the source code of the server functions that call the library functions. The client programmer does not have to know what services its server uses.

If a server function is used by different client functions in several files, the prototype of this server function should be included in each file. Often, programmers put prototypes into separate header files and include them in the files where client functions are implemented. The difference between including standard library files like `iostream` and programmer-defined header files is the use of path names and double quotes. Listing 2.13 is our program where the prototypes are moved to the file `c:\data\cppbook\ch02\display.h`:

Listing 2.13 Your first C++ program with prototypes in a separate file.

```
const double PI = 3.1415926;
#include "c:\data\cppbook\ch02\display.h"   // prototypes

int main(void)
{
   double x=PI, y=1;
   displayInitialGreeting();                 // function calls
   y = computeSquare(x,y);
   displayResults(y);
   return 0;
}                                            // end of the function block
```

The use of parameter names in function prototypes is optional. The compiler does not use them for checking the correctness of function calls; only the types of the arguments are used. The parameter names could be useful for documentation purposes. If the parameter names are not used, the c:\data\cppbook\ch02\display.h file could look this way:

```
   void displayInitialGreeting();
   double computeSquare(double, double);    // no parameter names
   void displayResults(double);
```

Classes

My next task is to describe the syntax for combining functions with data into an aggregate data type. C++ supports this by providing the struct and class keywords and the rules for merging components into an aggregate that can be handled as a whole. In the class definition, you specify the types and the names of the data members (data fields) and the headers or the bodies of member functions (that access these data fields). The class name can be used by client code as a type name. This means that we can define variables of this type (objects), pass them as parameters to functions, and so on.

Let us consider representing time of day as a combination of hours and minutes. We want to have an object that can store time data and display the time stored in it. The client code might request the military time representation (18:45), or conventional representation (6:45 P.M.)

Here, I create a class description with two integer data fields, hours and minutes, which can be accessed from outside of the class. It describes the composition of class objects (instances and variables) that will be defined and manipulated later in the program:

```
struct TimeOfDay          // keyword struct is used
  {
int hours;                // one data member: an integer
int minutes;              // another data member: also an integer
  } ;
```

A common convention for class names is to capitalize the first letter of each component of the name. The opening and closing braces denote the class scope—the boundary that separates everything within the class from what is outside. Unlike in other cases of using scope braces, the semicolon after the closing brace is mandatory. Just to make sure you do not think that C++ is straightforward and boring.

The definitions of class data fields are similar to definitions of variables. They associate the type and the name of the field. When an object (instance or variable) of class TimeOfDay is created, memory is allocated for each field according to its type.

```
TimeOfDay time1, time2;     // two objects are allocated
```

When the fields are of the same type, you can use only one type name for several data fields with the comma separator between field names. This is again similar to definitions of variables of built-in C++ types.

```
struct TimeOfDay
  {
    int hours, minutes;     // two integer data members
  } ;
```

Again, you can use this syntax for defining variables and class data fields but not for function parameters.

Notice that data fields should be private. They should not be accessed from outside of the class. My next step is to provide member functions (methods) that access the class data fields on behalf of the client code. These access functions should be public so that the client code can use them to set and display time in the military and conventional formats. For example, I can implement functions setTime(), displayMilitaryTime(), and displayTime(). The function setTime() should have two parameters: one for hours and one for minutes. Other functions have no parameters. They display the values stored in the object. Listing 2.14 shows the syntax for the class definition with data members and member functions.

Listing 2.14   Your first C++ class that combines data and functions.

```
#include <iostream>
using namespace std;
class TimeOfDay {                          // keyword class is used
  private:                                 // keyword private makes data hidden
    int hours, minutes;
  public:
    void setTime(int hrs, int min)
      { hours = hrs;  minutes = min; }
    void displayMilitaryTime(void)
      { cout << hours << ":" << minutes; }
    void displayTime(void)
      { if (hours > 12)
          cout << hours-12<<":"<<minutes<<"P.M.";
        else
          cout << hours <<":"<<minutes<<"A.M."; }
} ;
```

The function setTime() copies the values of parameters into the data fields of the object. The function displayMilitaryTime() displays hours and minutes. The function displayTime() checks whether hours (in military representation) exceeds 12; if yes, it subtracts 12 from hours and displays the difference with minutes and the P.M. label; if not, it displays hours with minutes and the A.M. label. The C++ iostream library is used in this example.

These member functions are inside the class and hence handle class data without limitations: They can set and access data values as appropriate for the goals of the client code. Their very existence is related to the needs of the client code, not to the needs of the class itself. This is why these member functions are defined as public: They can be called by the client code. To call these functions, the client code has to define class objects using the standard syntax for defining C++ variables; in these definitions, the client code connects the type name (TimeOfDay) and the names of the variables (e.g., time1, time2).

I saved the class definition in a header file c:\data\cppbook\ch02\time.h. To be able to use this class, the source file with the client code has to include this header file. Otherwise, the compiler will complain that TimeOfDay is not defined. Listing 2.15 shows an example of the client code that defines TimeOfDay objects, analyzes the return value of the class functions, and formats its output accordingly. (It has to include the class header file.)

Listing 2.15   Client code for your first C++ class that combines data
               and functions.

```
#include <iostream>
using namespace std;
#include "c:\data\cppbook\ch02\time.h"

int main(void)
{
  TimeOfDay time1, time2;             // class instances
  int hours = 19, minutes = 15;       // integer variables
  time1.setTime(7,35);
  time2.setTime(hours, minutes);      // initialize objects
  cout << "First time: ";
  time1.displayMilitaryTime();        // message to first object
  cout << endl << "First time: ";
  time1.displayTime();
  cout << endl << "Second time: ";
  time2.displayMilitaryTime();        // message to second object
  cout << endl << "Second time: ";
  time2.displayTime();
  return 0;
}
```

Here, the variables time1 and time2 are of type TimeOfDay. They are
defined similar to variables of a built-in type. In essence, the class definition
expands the set of types available in C++ and adds to it our modest contribution: the TimeOfDay type. Although the contribution is modest, the class
facility is very significant. It opens enormous opportunities for extending the
power of the language. The relationship between client code and class code
is shown in Figure 2–6. When the client code needs access to private parts (to
set time or display time), it does not access the data directly (the dashed line
in Figure 2–6). Instead, it calls the member functions setTime(),
displayTime(), and displayMilitaryTime() (solid lines in Figure 2–6),
and these functions access private data on behalf of the client code.

A call to a member function is called a message to the object. Notice the
message syntax: When a member function is called, you should specify on
what object we want that function to operate (using the dot selector operator). When the target object is time1, it is the hours and minutes data fields
of object time1 that get displayed. When the target object is time2, it is the
field values inside time2 that are displayed. Figure 2–7 shows the output of
the program.

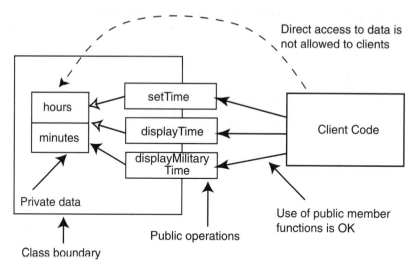

Figure 2-6   Client code uses access functions instead of accessing data directly.

```
First time:   7:35
First time:   7:35A.M.
Second time:  19:15
Second time:  7:15P.M.
```

Figure 2-7
Output of the `TimeOfDay` access functions.

Unlike other functions we saw earlier, member functions cannot be called by just using the function name (and supplying arguments if necessary):

```
displayTime();                         // syntax error
```

Come to think of it: What time do I want to display? Of what object? I did not specify that, and the compiler has no means of figuring out what I meant. This is why this function call is an error. The target of the message must be specified. However, this target must be of the same type as the member function being called; a variable of another type cannot be used as the target. For example, this is also incorrect.

```
hours.displayTime();                   // syntax error
```

The variable `hours` is of type `int`. You can add, subtract, and do other operations over an integer value, but `displayTime()` is not among these operations. This is why this statement is an error too. The target has to be of the correct type.

The potential for extending the C++ language with classes is supported by using class composition and class inheritance. I could have given here simple examples of class composition and inheritance, but this will make the preview too long. Even without examples of composition and inheritance, the preview did its job—you have had your first glimpse of C++. You can write simple C++ programs—not elegant yet, but robust and working. Most importantly, you can now study C++ building on this firm foundation.

Before you go on to discuss the details of the language, you should consider the issues related to linking and execution of C++ programs.

Dealing with Program Development Tools

As I mentioned earlier, you should use a text editor to create C++ source code. This code is compiled by a C++ compiler that will generate error messages if your source code has syntactic errors and will enable you to run your program if there are no syntax errors. In this section, we will look at more sophisticated tools that you can use for creating and running a C++ program. I will explain the role of each tool and the way to use these tools most effectively. Of course, the specifics depend on whether you use command-line assorted tools (e.g., the GNU compiler under UNIX) or an Integrated Development Environment (the Microsoft IDE under Windows).

Many development environments require (or suggest) that in addition to saving your source files, you also add your files to a project (the project can have several source files). Treated as a unit, the project files can be used to collect information about your program that is helpful for program analysis and debugging. Also, the vendors of integrated environments often provide the capability of generating a multifile framework for you so that you add your application code to class and function skeletons generated by the tool. This might be useful for an experienced programmer, but it can be a hindrance while you are studying the language. Instead of concentrating on specific language topics, you have to study the code generated for you by the tool, and this code can use language features you are not familiar with.

Tip

To avoid unnecessary complexity and to simplify the extraneous tasks of project management, it is a good idea to stay with one-file programs while you are experimenting with the language. Some integrated environments create a default project for you whether you like it or not. Go along and accept it, but try to avoid using the environment-generated code for your first explorations in C++. This will make your life simpler.

Saving your files after editing and before testing the program is a good idea. If you do not and your program contains run-time errors that crash the system, you lose the changes that you introduced. Only a few people today write code changes on paper before typing them in, and one can lose a significant amount of work as the result of a crash. Saving the file to disk (under a different name) before compiling reduces this danger. To help you to know the status of your source file, some editors display the indication of the status of the screen. If the code is changed but the file is not saved yet, the editor puts an asterisk next to the file name at the top of the editor window or displays a message at the bottom of the editor window. After the file is saved, the asterisk (or the message) disappears.

Yet other integrated environments do not trust your common sense and save your source file when you ask to compile it, even when your changes are experimental and you are not sure whether you want to keep them or roll them back.

If the source file does not contain syntactic errors, the compiler produces an object file that has the same name as the source file does. Depending on the system, the file name extension for object fields is .o or .obj. If the code contains syntactic errors, the object file is not created. Instead, the compiler generates error messages that tell you on what line in your source code the error(s) occurred and what kind of error it is. With older tools, you had to count the lines in your source file or rely on the line numbers displayed by the editor. Newer tools eliminate the need for tracing line numbers even though they also tell you the line number in error. When you click on the error message in the message window, the tool moves the focus to the editor window with the cursor on the line that the error message indicated. This is a very useful feature.

When you become comfortable with the language, you will find compiler error messages both understandable and helpful. Well, at least some of them. Until that time of bliss, please make yourself a rule: Never take compiler error messages literally, never analyze them, or at least stop at the very first difficulty. Do not persist. Do not hang on. Do not persevere. Do not do anything that is so commendable in our society of people who never give up. It is a wasted effort with error messages. It is never worth the trouble.

At least 90% of error messages are incomprehensible to a beginner. Are there any exceptions? Sure there are exceptions. About 10% of error messages are relatively easy to understand. But you see, it is exactly those cases where you could understand what the error is as soon as you glance at the line of code that contains the error, and you do not need any error messages to help you. This is why I recommend that you do not waste your time, energy, and emotions on error messages. Later on, when you become used to their terminology, you might benefit from that information, and it will be worth your while to look at the message and decide what direction you want to take. But at initial stages of studying the language, reading error messages will do you more harm than good.

The reason for this situation is that the compiler designers want to be most helpful to you and give you the most detailed analysis of the situation. Small wonder that their error messages use advanced C++ terminology that the beginner should not understand. Often, the problem can be caused by different kinds of errors, and the compiler has neither the time nor the knowledge to do detailed analysis and to correctly pinpoint the cause of the error. So the error message that sounds so technical and specific often has little to do with the error you actually made.

I will be frank with you: Do not expect much help from compiler error messages. Rely on your own wits instead. The only reliable piece of information that the error messages provide is the place where the error originated. And even that information is not always correct. Sometimes, the error originates on the previous line. So, when you get that error message (yes, you will, no doubt about that), do not concentrate only on the line indicated in the message; check the previous line too.

Often, the compiler generates more than one error message. Many programmers, when in doubt of what caused the first message, start analyzing the second, third, and other messages if they seem to make more sense.

Do not follow this logic. Do not analyze the second error if you do not understand the first one. After correcting the first error, do not start correcting the next error immediately. This is not right. It is a holdover from the old days, when the turnaround of the compilation was several minutes or even several hours. With turnaround time that long, it made sense to spend more human time on analysis of compiler error messages (even if some of them were spurious) and eliminate as many errors at once as possible.

Today a compilation takes only a few seconds. It is very inexpensive. The time that you spend analyzing the second and the third error is often wasted: After you correct the first error, other errors either change or disappear. They are generated not because you made mistakes, but because the compiler lost the track of flow of your source code after the first error. Your time is more expensive than the compilation time, and hunting phantom errors rarely pays. With experience, you will learn to distinguish spurious errors from real ones; then you will be able to correct several errors at once. Until that time, use the extension of the rule of not trusting the compiler: analyze only one error, then recompile.

Following is another version of Listing 2.1 with a small single error in it. The compiler generated three error messages with line numbers and causes of all three errors spelled out for you.

```
#include <cmath>                                    // preprocessor directive
#include <iostream>                                 // preprocessor directives
using namespace std;                               // compiler directive
const double PI = 3.1415926;                        // definition of a constant
int main(void)                                     // function returns integer
{
  double x=PI, y=1, z,                              // definitions of variables
  cout << "Welcome to the C++ world!" << endl;     // function call
  z = y + 1;                                       // assignment statement
  y = pow(x,z);                                    // function call
  cout << "In that world, pi square is " << y << endl;
  cout << "Have a nice day!" << endl;
  return 0;                                         // return statement
}                                                  // end of the function block


Compiling...
ch02.cpp
C:\Data\ch02.cpp(7) : error C2143: syntax error : missing ';' before '<<'
C:\Data\ch02.cpp(7) : error C2143: syntax error : missing ';' before '<<'
C:\Data\ch02.cpp(10) : error C2296: '<<' : illegal, left operand has type 'double'
C:\Data\ch02.cpp(10) : error C2297: '<<' : illegal, right operand has type 'char [29]'
C:\Data\ch02.cpp(11) : error C2296: '<<' : illegal, left operand has type 'double'
C:\Data\ch02.cpp(11) : error C2297: '<<' : illegal, right operand has type 'char [17]'
Error executing cl.exe.

ch02.exe - 6 error(s), 0 warning(s)
```

All this intelligent looking activity is totally in vain, much like trying to save your loafers by crawling in the mud in search of rubber shoes lost at another corner. You can spend hours chasing your tail and trying to add semicolons before operators << on line 7 or hunting for help types of operands on lines 10 and 11. All that is taking place at a wrong corner. Lines 7, 10, and 11 contain no errors no matter what the compiler says. Line 5 does. It looks like I fell asleep at the keyboard and pressed the comma key instead of the semicolon.

And one more comment about compiler errors. Programmers make errors of this kind quite often. These are small, simple, and we do not expect them. Combined with misleading error messages, they are hard to find. Often, we suspect other statements, especially when we have some misgivings about their syntax. We might start changing these statements. This makes them incorrect and generates more error messages. We analyze them, try something else, make things worse, and so on. After spending much time (and emotion) and finally resolving the problem we say: "How could I make such a stupid error? And how was I able to look at the code without seeing it when it is so obvious? How could I be so dumb?"

I want to expand my advice on not taking compiler error messages literally. Do not evaluate yourself on the basis of these errors. After all, you found them and corrected them. The time that you spend on that is not very important. It is important, but not very important. Your confidence in your skills is much more important. And frequent self-criticism can undermine your confidence. In addition, this blame is utterly unfair; it comes at the moment when you deserve a pat on the back—you just resolved that elusive problem! Please do not blame yourself. Develop the feeling of self-confidence and competence.

Sometimes the compiler generates warning messages. When you get enough experience, it is a good idea to analyze them similarly to error messages because these warnings often reflect real errors. Until that time, disregard the warnings. They are often misleading. They do not prevent the compiler from generating object code and from running and debugging your code. Hence, you can test your code at run time. But later on, do make a point of understanding warnings and eliminating them.

The next step after the successful compilation is linking (or "building" under some tools). When the program consists of several source files, each file can be (and should be) compiled separately while it is being developed. When the source code contains declarations of identifiers (variables or functions) that are defined in another file, the compiler has a problem—it does not know address-es of these identifiers because the compiler compiles one file at a time. The linking stage takes place when all source files are successfully compiled. The linker goes over all object files and resolves external references to identifiers defined in other files.

During linking, the linker adds more precompiled code to your object code which comes with C++ libraries. Although the library source code is usually available, it is not recompiled each time one of your functions calls pow(), operator, <<, or another library function. The library functions are compiled in advance, and the linker resolves these external references in the same way as any others.

The result of the linking stage is an executable program file. For a single file program, its name is the same as the name of your source file. For a multifile program, the name of the executable file is the same as the name of the project (the programmer usually can choose any name). The extension is usually .exe.

Linking errors are not frequent. When they occur, they are caused either by misspelled function names or by incorrect manipulation of the project.

The executable file can be run. Most IDEs give you a choice of running the program in the debugging mode or in production mode. Debugging mode is fine, but I recommend you do not use the debugger. During your first steps with C++, you will be busy learning the language, the editor, the compiler, and the linker—you cannot avoid that. Learning the debugger is a major undertaking. The return on the time you would invest in it is small, at least until you start writing complex C++ programs. Until then, inspection of program output (and adding extra print statements when necessary) is sufficient.

Here, another warning is appropriate. It is all too often that the programmer looks at the output of the program and does not see that the output is incorrect. I have no good explanation, but this is a fact. This is probably related to the human capacity of self-deception and denial, but I am not sure. Whatever the reason, we often miss run-time errors.

Some programmers try to avoid that by writing expected output down before the program is run. This is helpful but does not give the total assurance.

Make sure you are always vigilant when you check the test results.

Summary

Congratulations! You have reviewed the most important components of the C++ programming language. You know what preprocessor directives to use, how to define variables and functions, how to control the flow of execution with conditional statements and loops, how to comment your code, and how to disregard misleading compiler messages. You even saw how to define and use a C++ class. Very good!

Actually, this is enough for writing most of the C++ code you want to write. This is similar to learning natural language. Pidgin English is much smaller and simpler than English, but it is amazing how much you can express using only a fraction of language facilities available to an experienced native speaker. This is probably yet another manifestation of the rule that 80% of all work is done by 20% of contributors.

However, we should not limit ourselves to these 20% of the language. It is time to move on and start learning language facilities available to an experienced programmer.

WORKING WITH C++ DATA AND EXPRESSIONS

Chapter 3

In this chapter, we will study how to work with C++ data: what data types are available, what operations over values of these data types are supported, and what pitfalls the C++ programmer should be aware of. As with many other aspects of the language, C++ combines opposites. Its set of numeric data types is very small, and differences between existing types are not that drastic, so that the choice between them is not always clear-cut. Its set of operators is very large. Some C++ operators are quite complex; others have unusual notation. What is common to both C++ data types and operators is potential for portability problems. Things very often do not work the same way on different machines.

C++ inherits from C exceptional flexibility for converting the values from one type to another and for combining them into sophisticated expressions. Let us take a look at what is available.

Values and Their Types

In C++, every value, at every moment in its lifetime (during program execution), is characterized by its type. C++ variables are associated with their types at the time of definition. The type describes three characteristics of the value:

- the size of the values of that type in computer memory
- the set of values that are legal for the type (the method of interpretation of the bit pattern that represents the value of that type)
- the set of operations that are legal on the values of that type

For example, the values of type int on my machine are allocated four bytes, and the set of legal values ranges from –2,147,483,648 to +2,147,483,647. The set of legal operations includes assignment, comparisons, shifts, arithmetic operations, and some others. The values of the type TimeOfDay that I defined in the section "Classes," in Chapter 2, "Getting Started Quickly: A Brief Overview of C++," are allocated the size of two int values (unless the compiler adds more space to align values in memory for faster access). The set of TimeOfDay legal values is any combination of values for the first integer (from 0 to 23) and for the second integer (from 0 to 59). The set of TimeOfDay legal operations includes setTime(), displayTime(), and displayMilitaryTime(); it includes assignment but not comparisons. Sure, TimeOfDay components can be compared (they are integers, and the rules of int apply to them) but not the TimeOfDay values: You should distinguish between properties of the type and properties of its components. If the client code has to compare TimeOfDay values, class TimeOfDay has to support this by implementing functions such as isLater() or compareTime() or something like that. (Again, notice the client-server terminology I am using here.)

Every C++ variable has to be defined by specifying the type of its values. In addition, type also characterizes the values of constants, functions, and expressions. This means that you can combine typed values into expressions that give other typed values as results, and these values can be used in other expressions and so on.

In most cases, the type is denoted by an identifier, that is, the type has a name (e.g., int or TimeOfDay). This is common and natural, but this is not the only way to define types. C++ allows so-called anonymous types that do not have specific names. These types are not common.

Type names of built-in C++ types are reserved words: int, char, bool, float, double, and void (actually, this is it, this is the whole list). In this list void denotes the absence of the value that can be manipulated in an expression. We use it to indicate that further use of the value in other expressions is not appropriate. For example, the function computeSquare() in the section "Functions and Function Calls," in Chapter 2, returns the value that can be used in expressions, and the function displayResults() in the same section cannot be used this way: It returns no value. If you try to use it incorrectly, the compiler will tell you that this is an error.

```
int a, b;
a = computeSquare(x,y) * 5;        // this is legal C++
b = displayResults(PI*PI) * 5;     // this is an error
```

Other languages do not have this special "type" because they distinguish between functions (that return values) and procedures (that do not return values). C++ inherited from C the function syntax that doubles both as a function and as a procedure. Logically, the absence of the specified return type should be interpreted as the absence of the return value; not so in C. To add insult to injury, the absence of type specification in C denotes the integer type and requires a `return` statement that returns an integer value. C++ implements a compromise. If you do not specify the return type, the compiler does not go after you and does not demand that the function return an integer value (as the C compiler does); the new C++ compiler assumes that you want the `void` return type.

```
displayResults(double y)                   // C++ it is void
{
  cout << "In that world, pi square is " << y << endl;
  cout << "Have a nice day!" << endl;        // no error in C++
  }
```

However, if you use this function as an operand in an expression, C++ assumes that you are using an old C convention and want to return an integer. At run time, `displayResults()` silently returns junk. As they say, the compiler "does not second-guess the programmer" and removes compile time protection.

```
b = displayResults(PI*PI) * 5;     // not a syntax error
```

If you supply the `return` statement, the function with no return type is treated as if it returns an integer value.

```
displayResults(double y)           // C++ assumes it is int
{
  cout << "In that world, pi square is " << y << endl;
  cout << "Have a nice day!" << endl;
  return 0;                        // no syntax error
  }
```

The client code can use the return value as it sees fit.

```
b = displayResults(PI*PI) * 5;     // this is legitimate
```

The use of int as a default return type goes back to the days when most C functions were designed to return values and saving the programmer three keystrokes was viewed as a nontrivial advantage. Avoid this practice. If the return type is integer, say int. If a function returns no value, denote return type as void.

Alert

Always specify the return type of a function. If the function returns no value, specify type void. Do not rely on C++ default.

The types defined by the program in addition to built-in C++ types are called user-defined types. I do not like this terminology, because users do not define types. A user is a person or an organization that uses the implemented system to achieve the stated objectives. It is the programmer who defines the type composition and the name of the type, similar to the type TimeOfDay in the section "Classes," in Chapter 2. This is why I prefer to call these types programmer-defined types.

Although different types in C++ are of different sizes, there is nothing unusual for values of different types to have the same size in memory. For different types, it is the interpretation of the bit pattern that distinguishes the values. For example, the bit pattern 01000001 is interpreted as value 65 if it is stored in an integer variable; the same bit pattern is interpreted as A if it is stored in a variable of character type.

In the old days, programmers had to know how to read binary numbers, octal numbers, hexadecimal numbers, ASCII codes, EBCDIC codes, remember by heart the powers of 2 to the 16th power (sometimes to the 20th or even 32nd power), understand one-complement and two-complement representation for negative numbers and whatnot. Today, most programmers do not need that. Still, the computer hardware is built in sizes that are increments of 8 bits. A byte has 8 bits, a half-word has 16 bits, a word has 32 bits. On some machines, it is a word that has 16 bits, and a double word has 32 bits. This is why it is a good idea to know at least the ranges of values that can be stored in memory of different sizes.

So, 4 bits can represent 16 different combinations of bits (one hexadecimal digit). Usually, these 16 combinations are assigned to integer numbers from zero to 15. Similarly, 8 bits can represent 256 values (2 to the power of 8). These 256 bit combinations are assigned to integer numbers from zero to 255. What if we want to represent both positive and negative numbers, not just positive? We still have only 256 bit combinations at our disposal. The range from –128 to +128 would not do because this range has 257 values, not 256. The common solution is to represent numbers from –128 to +127.

Two bytes (16 bits) can represent 65,536 bit combinations (this magic number is 2 to the power of 16). For positive numbers, the range is from zero to 65,535. For `signed` values (positive and negative numbers) the range is from –32,768 (2 to the power of 15) to +32,767 (2 to the power of 15 minus 1). Similarly, 32 bits (four bytes) can represent 4,294,967,296 values. For `signed` numbers, four bytes cover the range from –2,147,483,648 (2 to the power of 31) to +2,147,483,647. This is probably all that you should know about binary numbers.

Integral Types

On all computer architectures, the C++ integer type represents the most basic type. What does "basic" mean? It simply means that the values of this type are always the fastest to operate on the given platform. The keyword `int` is used to denote this type.

```
int cnt;
```

The size of `int` defines the range of values available for representation (2 to the power of the number of bits). The industry is now shifting from 16-bit architectures to 32-bit architectures, but both architectures are going to be used for some time. Most stationary installations will use 32-bit computers, but embedded systems and communications systems will continue to use 16-bit computers, and the number of these systems is going to grow as computers find their way into cars, major appliances, or even toasters.

This means that programs written for one architecture might not run exactly the same way on another architecture.

What happens if the value that can be stored in an integer does not fit? The answer is: nothing much. There is no such thing as arithmetic overflow in C++. You want to add 1 to 32,767 on a 16-bit machine? Go ahead and do it. The result will be –32,768. You want to add another one? Go ahead and do it. The result will be –32,767.

Listing 3.1 shows a program that I ran on a 16-bit platform (it was a 32-bit machine with a 16-bit compiler). The `limit` header file contains library constants for implementation-dependent numeric values for the given platform. The constant `INT_MAX` is one such value (32767). In this example, I am using the `while` loop similar to one discussed in Chapter 2, and the `iostream` library. The output of this program is presented on Figure 3–1. The variable num happily goes around the clock and assumes negative values. Each element in the cout statement has its own output operator <<; even the separator (in double quotes) between the printed values of variables cnt and num.

Listing 3.1   Demonstration of integer overflow.

```
#include <limits>
#include <iostream>
using namespace std;

int main(void)
{
  int num = INT_MAX - 2;
  int cnt = 0;
  cout << "Integer overflow in C++:" endl;
  cout << "Incrementing from " << num << endl;
  while (cnt < 5)
  { num = num + 1;
    cnt = cnt + 1;
    cout << cnt << "     " << num << endl; }
  cout << "Thank you for worrying about integer limits" << endl;
  return 0;
    }
```

Earlier versions of C++ (and C) did not allow run-time values to be used to initialize variables; they had to be computed at compile time. However, you could always initialize variables not only to a specific value, but also to an expression (for example, INT_MAX-2 in Listing 3.1). In modern C++, the initializing expression can be of arbitrary complexity. It can even include the run-time return values of function calls. For example, this is legal in C++:

```
int a = computeSquare(x,y) * 5;      // this is legal C++
```

Figure 3–1   Integer overflow does not terminate the program; it silently produces incorrect results.

This is quite a feat from the point of view of compiler design. This is why older C and C++ compilers do not support this feature. Now see if you think that I am repeating myself. Did I not say in the section, "Values and Their Types," that you can use the return value of a function in computations?

```
a = computeSquare(x,y) * 5;     // legal in C and C++
```

Make sure you see the difference. The example from the section, "Values and Their Types" demonstrates assignment. It is always possible in C++, C, or any other language. The example from this section demonstrates initialization. Although the code is quite similar, they mean two different things. Initialization allocates memory and sets its value. Assignment deals with the object (variable) that is already allocated, has its address in memory (and probably some initial value at that address), and the value at this address is being replaced. I mentioned that difference in Chapter 2, and you will see further implications later.

Despite this progress in compiler writing, C++ does not expect its compilers to be two-pass compilers. They are all one-pass compilers and have no ability to see forward. This is why they cannot use a value that is not defined yet even if it is defined on the next line. For example, this is an error:

```
int a = b, b(5);                // error in C++
```

Here, variable b cannot be used to initialize variable a. The inverse order is legitimate. (Notice the syntax for initialization that is similar to a function call: It is not allowed in C but is acceptable in C++.)

```
int b(5), a = b;                // this is acceptable
```

Integer Type Qualifiers

C++ inherits from C a technique for fine-tuning integer ranges: the use of qualifiers. These are keywords that change either the size of memory allocated for integers or the interpretation of the bit pattern: signed, unsigned, short, and long.

The signed qualifier we have been using all along is a default, and it does not have to be specified. This definition for the variable cnt means exactly the same thing as the previous one:

```
signed int cnt;                 // signed is default
```

The unsigned qualifier can be used for variables that cannot take on negative values (indices, counters, tallies, inventory quantities, etc.). This qualifier does not change the size of the memory allocated for the value (16 bits or 32 bits) but it changes the interpretation of the bit pattern. The legal range of unsigned integers is not from –32,768 to +32,767 but from zero to 65,535 on a 16-bit machine, and from zero to 4,294,967,295 on 32-bit machine. Listing 3.2 shows the previous example where an unsigned integer is used instead of signed. The output of this version is presented in Figure 3–2. We see that the problem disappears. Well, it disappears at this stage. Of course, it will manifest itself at the upper range of unsigned integers, but it will manifest itself differently. When the unsigned number overflows, its value silently goes back to zero rather than to a large negative value. I am not sure this is much better.

Listing 3.2 Demonstration of unsigned int type.

```cpp
#include <limits>
#include <iostream>
using namespace std;

int main(void)
{
   int unsigned num = INT_MAX - 2;
   int cnt = 0;
   cout << "Integer overflow in C++:" << endl;
   cout << "Incrementing from " << num << endl;
   while (cnt < 5)
   { num = num + 1;
     cnt = cnt + 1;
     cout << cnt << "    " << num << endl; }
   cout << "Thank you for worrying about integer limits" << endl;
   return 0;
   }
```

Figure 3-2 For unsigned integer values, the overflow happens at larger values than for plain integers with the same memory size.

```
Integer overflow in C++:
Incrementing from 32765
1    32766
2    32767
3    32768
4    32769
5    32770
Thank you for worrying about integer limits
```

Using unsigned numbers is a nice idea (not so much for extending the range of the values but for passing on to the maintainer the knowledge of the designer) that the value of the particular variable cannot be negative. On the other hand, if this intent will somehow get lost on the maintainer, and the unsigned variable will be used for negative values, the results will be quite disastrous. Listing 3.3 shows the previous version of the program where the variable num is initialized to 2 and is unwittingly decremented in a loop. The output of the program is shown in Figure 3–3.

Listing 3.3 Negative values in an unsigned variable.

```
#include <iostream>
using namespace std;
int main(void)
{
  int unsigned num = 2;
  int cnt = 0;
  cout << "Negative values in an unsigned variable" << endl;
  cout << "Count down starting with +1" << endl;
  while (cnt < 5)
  { num = num - 1;
    cnt = cnt + 1;
    cout << cnt << "    " << num << endl; }
  cout << "Thank you for worrying about integer limits" << endl;
return 0;
    }
```

Two qualifiers that control the amount of memory allocated to an integer are long and short:

```
    int cnt;   short int short_cnt;   long int long_cnt;
```

Figure 3–3 Unsigned variables cannot hold negative values; when decremented, they assume large positive values without warning.

```
Negative values in an unsigned variable
Count down starting with +1
1   1
2   0
3   65535
4   65534
5   65533
Thank you for worrying about integer limits
```

The goal here is not only to provide a larger range for integers, but also to save space where it can be saved. C++ programmers are supposed to be concerned with performance, both in terms of execution time and in terms of space. Using `signed` integers (without qualifiers) provides the fastest data type, using `long` integers protects from overflow at the expense of memory, and using `short` integers allows the programmer to avoid wasting memory. For example, the variable `cnt` in the previous examples changes from 0 to 5. Why should it be allocated 32 bits on a modern machine? Actually, a byte would be more than enough. Using the `short` integer data type for this variable might sound like a good option for a machine with scarce memory.

How important is it to use the `short` qualifier to save memory and the `long` qualifier to expand the range of values? These size qualifiers make the program more complex. Many programmers use them only if they do know that the problem of overflow (or memory scarcity) exists and they know that the use of qualifiers resolves the problem (often neither one is the case). Otherwise, most programmers use regular integers without qualifiers and do not worry about these issues. This is especially true on modern 32-bit machines. The use of four bytes for regular integers protects the program from early overflow. The abundance of memory makes savings from using `short` integer irrelevant.

As is often the case with C++ features inherited from C, the situation is not exactly what you think. Logically, a `short` integer should be allocated less memory than an integer, and a `long` integer should be allocated more memory than an integer. The C (and C++) standard, however, requires from the compiler designers only that the `short int` not be longer than the regular `int` and that the `long int` not be shorter than the regular `int`. This is not as confusing as it sounds. On 16-bit machines, both `short int` and `int` variables are allocated the same amount of memory, 16 bits, and `long int` variables are allocated 32 bits. On 32-bit machines, this is quite the opposite. How is it opposite? Simple: `short int` values are allocated 16 bits, and both `int` and `long int` are allocated 32 bits.

C++ has the `sizeof` operator that can be used to compute the size of data in bytes; its argument can be either a variable name or a type name. For any platform, the following relation between returned values of the `sizeof` operator holds.

```
sizeof(short int) <= sizeof(int) <= sizeof(long int)
```

There is an interesting consequence of this design: `short int` and `long int` are always of the same size no matter whether the machine is 16 bits or 32 bits. On any architecture, `short int` is always 16 bits, and `long int` is always 32 bits. This is why those programmers who are concerned with the issues of portability do not use plain vanilla integers. They use `short int` for relatively small values and `long int` for all other values that might not fit into `short int`. These are usually the programmers who design embedded and communications systems. In these systems, computer memory is often at a premium because of size and price limitations, and the same code should be able to run on multiple hardware platforms.

Tip

Integers are either 16 bits or 32 bits depending on the hardware; short integers are always 16 bits, and long integers are always 32 bits. Their use eliminates the portability issue.

Is it possible to combine the `unsigned` qualifier with the `short` and `long` qualifiers, as in these examples?

```
unsigned short int short_cnt;   long unsigned int long_cnt;
```

Yes, it is possible. (Notice that the order of qualifiers does not matter.) This can be found, for example, in hard disk controllers, where the size of the file or the number of cylinders requires large integers that can never be negative. Still, for most applications, it is a good idea to avoid extra complexity and use regular integers.

One more comment. At the beginning of this chapter, I mentioned the old rule that when the type name is omitted the default type is integer. This rule applies to this situation too. When you use `long` and `short` data types, there is no need to specify the keyword `int`.

```
int cnt;   short short_cnt;   long long_cnt;        // same meaning
```

Integer literal values can be represented as decimal, octal, values and hexadecimal values. For example, decimal 64 can be represented as octal 100 or as hexadecimal 40. To avoid confusion, the integer literal starts with 0 to denote the octal system and with 0x (or 0X) to denote the hexadecimal system. So, 100 means 100 (decimal), but 0100 is octal and means 64 in decimal, and 0x100 is hexadecimal and means 256 in decimal.

Literal values are allocated memory pretty much in the same way as variables are; the only difference is that we cannot manipulate their addresses and hence cannot change the values that are stored there. So, 63 can be allocated two bytes as a `short` literal and four bytes as a `long` literal. To indicate the difference, we can denote `short` and `long` constants using qualifiers in upper- or in lowercase: 63s, 63S, 63l, 63L. The same is true for `unsigned` values: 63u, 63U, or 63us or 63UL. This is rarely of practical importance.

Characters

The character type is treated by C++ as just another kind of integer. Its size is 1 byte (8 bits). It can represent any ASCII symbol: a letter, a digit, or a nonprintable control character. Here are examples of definitions for character variables.

```
char c, ch;   char first, last;
```

There are no `short` and `long` qualifiers for characters. However, `signed` or `unsigned` qualifiers are allowed for characters. Unfortunately, the default is not standardized; on some machines, the type `char` means `unsigned char`; on other machines, the type `char` means `signed char`.

Why do you care? Usually, you do not, and this is why it has not been standardized. The difference becomes important, however, when you treat `char` values as integers in computations. For example, a `signed char` can contain the "end-of-file" library constant `EOF` whose value is defined as –1; `unsigned char` can contain positive values only. So, if you try to put –1 into an `unsigned char`, you will find there the code for 255, not –1. Since the `char` type can be `signed` or `unsigned` implicitly, this can introduce portability issues.

As any variable, a `char` variable can be initialized at definition or assigned a value later. Small integers can be used for initialization and assignment, and their values will be interpreted as character codes. Character literals are enclosed in single quotes and can be characters, octal or hexadecimal numeric values, or escape sequences. It is important not to confuse single quotes and double quotes. Single quotes are used to denote character literals; double quotes are used to denote string literals (sequences or arrays of characters).

```
char c = 'A',  ch = 65;        // both c and ch contain 'A'
```

This is an example of using a character literal in quotes and using a decimal literal number. Other character representations start with the escape character '\'. The escape character is not treated as an ordinary character; it is a signal to the compiler to treat what follows in a special way, for example, as an octal or a hexadecimal value.

```
c = '\0101';  ch = '\0x41';    // octal and hex values for 'A'
```

Here, the quotes and the escape characters are not really necessary. You can use octal and hex values directly, similar to the way the decimal value 65 was used above, by starting an octal literal with a 0 and a hexadecimal literal with a 0x (or 0X).

```
c = 0101;  ch = 0x41;          // octal and hex values for 'A'
```

The escape characters are necessary only if these values are embedded in a string. Also, the use of the escape character indicates to the maintenance programmer that we are dealing with characters and not with numbers. The most common escape sequence is the new line character '\n'. Other escape sequences are '\r' (carriage return), '\f' (form feed or new page), '\t' (tab character), '\v' (vertical tab character), and '\a' (sound bell).

Since single and double quotes have a special significance in C++, we have to use the escape character to represent them too, '\'' and '\"'. The same is true of the escape character itself. If you need to display it, two escape characters in a row are used: '\\'.

There are two more escape sequences: '\b' and '\0'. The first denotes a backspace. The second denotes numerical zero. It is not a printable character (a printable '0' has numeric value 48), but it is an important character. At the end of every string, a C++ compiler inserts this character, and it is used to find the end of the string. For example, the string literal "Hello" contains not five but six characters; the last character is that zero code inserted by the compiler. Since we have not discussed arrays yet, we cannot discuss strings in more detail now, but later on we will see a lot of them.

C++ treats characters as small integers. Hence, you can perform arithmetic operations and comparisons on character values. Listing 3.4 shows an example of this kind of character manipulation: The program first prints the alphabet in capital letters and then prints the alphabet in lowercase. It also shows the use of an escape character to output a single quote, a double quote, and the escape character itself. The output of the program is shown in Figure 3–4.

Listing 3.4   An example of manipulating character values.

```
#include <iostream>
using namespace std;
int main(void)
{ char ch;   int cnt;
  ch = 65; cnt = 0;                  // ch contains 'A'
  while (cnt < 26)
    { cout << ch;
      ch = ch + 1; cnt = cnt + 1; }
  cout << endl;
  ch = 'a' - 1;                      // ch contains character '`'
  while (ch < 'z')
    { ch = ch + 1;                   // ch contains 'a', 'b', ... 'z'
      cout << ch; }
  cout << endl;
  cout << "Single \' and double \" quotes are special\n";
                                     // new line: same as endl
  cout << "And so is the escape character \\" << endl;
  return 0;
  }
```

Figure 3–4   Output of the program (Listing 3.4) that performs arithmetic operations on character variables.

```
ABCDEFGHIJKLMNOPQRSTUVWXYZ
abcdefghijklmnopqrstuvwxyz
Single ' and double " quotes are special
And so is the escape character \
```

Performing arithmetic operations on characters is not a nice practice because it can confuse a maintenance programmer. Another problem is that it works only on computers with contiguous character sets (e.g., ASCII). The code in Listing 3.4 would produce nonprintable results if it were used on a machine with a noncontiguous character set (e.g., EBCDIC). However, character arithmetic is done quite often because it produces the code that is aesthetically pleasing.

Character variables are allocated one byte. This means that the character type can support character sets with only 256 characters (including control and nonprintable characters). This is more than enough for the English language but leaves almost everyone else in the cold to invent their own non-ASCII character sets. The Unicode character set tries to standardize these efforts so that English, French, Russian, Chinese, and Japanese characters fit into the same 16-bit character set.

C++ supports this effort by providing a wide character type, wchar_t, which can represent extended character sets. The amount of memory allocated for this type is based on one of the integer types, for example, int or short int. To represent the literal values for wide characters, the prefix L is used. (It must be in uppercase.)

```
wchar_t wc = L'a';
```

C++ allows the programmer to use any character set. For portability, ASCII is probably the best option.

Boolean Values

Most modern programming languages support boolean values that can take values true and false only. These values are useful for computing logical expressions and for choosing execution paths through the program code.

C does not support the boolean type. Instead, C treats any nonzero value as true and the zero value as false. C allows you to perform logical operations on these values (again, any nonzero result is interpreted as true, and any zero result is interpreted as false). This is sufficient for handling logical expressions. As you are going to see later, this also allows us to make errors that are not identified by the compiler. Initially, C++ inherited the same approach. The new standard, however, tries to rectify the situation somewhat by introducing the type bool with two values, true and false.

```
bool flag = false, result = true;
```

I am saying "somewhat rectify" rather than "rectify" because the use of the boolean type does not eliminate the error-prone features inherited from C. They are still used as legitimate C++ idioms. The boolean values themselves are treated as small integers. If you try to print the values flag and result defined above, the first one will be printed as zero (not as false), and the second one will be printed as one (not as true).

The boolean values take only one byte of memory. Since the boolean type has only two different values, boolean variables could take even less memory than one byte. One bit would be enough; that is, the compiler could pack eight boolean values in one byte. This, however, would require additional code for packing and unpacking these values, because modern computers cannot directly address a unit of memory that is less than one byte. Actually, many computers cannot directly address units of memory that are less than two bytes. As far as the speed of execution is concerned, modern computers are the fastest when they access units of memory in four byte chunks. This is why integers are allocated four bytes on many modern machines.

You are going to see more of these boolean values later when you start working with relational and logical operators.

Floating Point Types

Integers and characters are integral types: the values of these types are separated from each other by values that are multiples of one. They cannot contain fractional parts. Or, rather, whatever bit pattern they contain, that bit pattern cannot be interpreted by the C++ compiler as a fraction. Other types are used if the fractional part is needed.

C++ does not have fixed point numbers that would give the programmer control over the number of digits after the decimal point. Instead, the programmer can use floating point values that consist of a mantissa (with whole and fractional parts) and an exponent. The exponent is expressed in literal numbers as a power of ten, but in the computer memory it is, of course, expressed as a power of two.

There are three floating point types in C++: float, double, and long double. There is no such thing as short double: The type float does this job. The size of these types is machine dependent. Usually, type float is allocated four bytes, type double is allocated eight bytes, and type long double is allocated 10 bytes (or just eight bytes, the same as for double).

The number of mantissa digits that can be represented by a floating point number is also machine dependent. Usually, type float values have seven digits; double values have 15 digits, and long double values have 19 digits.

The range of values depends on the number of bits allocated for the exponent part of the value. For float values, the exponents are in the range of –38 to 38. For double values, the range is from –611 to 611. For long double, it is from –4932 to 4932, more than enough to represent all cosmic data.

Here are examples of defining floating point variables:

```
float pi;  double r;  long double d;
```

The goal of the hierarchy of the floating point types is the same as for integer types: to give the programmer the choice of making a tradeoff between the memory size and the precision and magnitude of values that can be handled by a variable. For the applications where the precision of calculations does not matter but the space is scarce (most real-time embedded systems), float type could be used. For the applications where the precision of calculations is vital (navigation), long double could be used, even though these values take more space and computations are performed slower. For all others, double would do.

It is probably fair to say that for most applications, float is too short and long double is too costly in terms of time and space; unless there are strong indications to the contrary, type double should be used. All functions in the C++ math library expect double arguments and return double values (the function pow() that I used for our first C++ program in Chapter 2).

Floating points data types have fixed precision: for type double, both very large and very small numbers have the same number of digits on a given platform. As I mentioned, C++ has no fixed decimal point data type (with a given number of digits after the decimal point).

Floating point literal values can be in radix notation (with a decimal point) or in scientific notation (E or e denotes the exponent).

```
double r=5.3; long double d=530.0e-2;
```

These two numbers represent the same value. Ten to the power of –2 is one divided by 10 to the power of +2, that is, divided by 100.

In this case, scientific notation has no advantage over normal (radix) notation. Scientific notation is convenient for compact representation of very large or very small values.

Most floating point literals have all three components of the mantissa: integer part, decimal point (only one, of course), and fractional part. Not all three components need to be present in all the cases.

However, it is important to use the representation that distinguishes a floating point value from an integer. Hence, it is OK to miss the integer part if the decimal point and the fractional part are both present. It is also OK to omit the fractional part if both the integer part and the decimal point are present.

```
double small = .09, large = 5.;
```

It is even OK to skip both the decimal point and the fractional part if the exponent is present to distinguish the value from an integer.

```
double big = 500e2;
```

In scientific notation, the exponent has to be an integer. Even though mathematically it can be anything, C++ accepts only integer exponents. The exponent can be optionally signed even when it is positive.

```
double big = 500e+2;             // big = 500e+2.2; is no good
```

Similar to integer literal values, C++ allows us to distinguish between literals of different types by using qualifiers that can be appended to the value. The qualifier 'f' or 'F' denotes a float floating point value, and the qualifier 'l' or 'L' denotes a long double value. You might assume that the qualifier 'd' or 'D' denotes a double floating point value, but that would be, although logical, an incorrect conclusion. All floating point literals without a qualifier are double values by default.

```
float pi = 3.14f;   double r = 5.3;   long double d = 5.3 L;
```

Working with C++ Expressions

Expressions consist of operands and operators. Operands are anything that have a typed value, that is, variables, function return values, or expressions, which in turn consist of operators and operands. Operators are symbols whose meaning is reserved in C++. Application of an operator to operand(s) results in a value that can be used in another expression. White space is useful for readability but is not required.

```
x = (a + b) * (a + 2*b) * (a+3*b);    // space is optional
```

Two operator attributes affect the order of evaluation: operator precedence level (higher level operators are performed first), and operator associativity (operators of the same precedence are evaluated either from left to right or from right to left).

There are 56 operators in C++: 18 levels of priority to learn (or to struggle with). Table 3.1 lists C++ operators. Obviously, it is not possible to learn this table by reading it. I put it here for your reference, not for memorizing. You will learn it gradually by using these operators. When in doubt about the precedence of operators, use parentheses. After all, even if you remember all precedences by heart, the maintenance programmer who comes after you might not know this table so well and might confuse the order of evaluation.

Table 3.1   C++ Operators

Category	Operators	Associativity
Scope resolution	::	left to right
Primary	() [] -> typeid dynamic_cast static_cast reinterpret_cast const_cast	left to right
Secondary	++ — ~ ! + - ° & Sizeof new delete (type)	right to left right to left
Member selection	->° .°	left to right
Multiplicative	° / %	left to right
Additive	+ -	left to right
Shifts	<< >>	left to right
Relational	< <= > >=	left to right
Equality	== !=	left to right
Bitwise AND	&	left to right
Exclusive OR	^	left to right
Inclusive OR	|	left to right
Logical AND	&&	left to right
Logical OR	||	left to right
Assignment	= °= /= %= += -= <<= >>= &= |= ^=	right to left
Conditional	?:	right to left
Throw	throw	
Comma	,	left to right

High-Priority Operators

At the top of the table, at the highest priority, we see operators that bind their operands more strongly than other operators (which is just another way of saying that they are of the highest priority). For example, parentheses are high-priority operators. No matter what other operators you use in the expression, subexpressions in parentheses are going to be evaluated first.

Two other operators that we can discuss now are plus '+' and minus '–' operators. As unary operators, they take only one operand, for example, +2.0, –2.0. You might ask what the difference is, between a unary plus or minus and the addition and subtraction operator we are all familiar with and that are of lower priority. Well, the difference is that the unary plus or minus takes only one operator and the addition or subtraction operator takes two. This distinction allows us to write mixed expressions with unary operators that do not require extra parentheses for evaluation, for example, 2.5- -0.25. Since the unary minus is an operator, it can be separated from its operand by any number of blanks, for example, 2.5- -0.25. This does not interfere with the evaluation of the expression. Of course, if you want to be appreciated by the maintenance programmer, you will write this expression as 2.5-(-0.25) without worrying about these subtleties.

The `sizeof` operator was discussed earlier in the chapter. This is the only C++ operator that can operate both on a type identifier and on the name of the variable.

```
int x = sizeof(int);   int y = sizeof(x);      // same values
```

Here, x gets the number of bytes allocated to any integer; y gets the number of bytes allocated to a particular variable x (which happens to be an integer). As any unary operator, `sizeof` can be used without parentheses around the operand when the operand is the name of a variable.

```
int x = sizeof(int);   int y = sizeof x;       // same results
```

You might think that the same is allowed when the operand is the type name, but this is not the case: the parentheses here are mandatory.

```
int x = sizeof int;   int y = sizeof x;            // not OK
```

Unfortunately, that is all that can be said about high-priority operators now. We will see more of them later.

The same is true of member selection operators at the next level of priority and the `throw` operator near the end of the table. The type operator (cast) will be discussed later in the chapter.

Arithmetic Operators

At the fifth and sixth levels of priority in Table 3.1, we come to the multiplicative and additive operators that can be discussed, but there is little to be discussed. Multiplication and division are of higher priority than addition and subtraction. When we need to change the order of evaluation, we use parentheses.

```
x = (a + b) * (a + 2*b) * (a+3*b);    // buyers beware
```

C++ does not raise any exception in case of overflow, and it is the responsibility of the programmer to prove that overflow is not possible no matter what input data the program processes.

Arithmetic operations are legal both on integers and floating point values. Even though the same division operator '/' can be applied to integers and floating point values, it behaves differently. On floating point values, it results in a floating point value computed with appropriate precision. On integers, it results in an integer that is truncated towards zero. For example, 7/3 is 2.333333 for floating point operands and two for integer operands.

The modulo operator '%' returns the remainder of integer division. It is valid for integral types only (integers, characters), not for floating point values. For example, 7 divided by 3 is 2 with 1 remaining. Hence, 7 modulo 3 is 1. Similarly, 8 divided by 3 is 2 with 2 remaining. Hence, 8 modulo 3 is 2. Since 9 divided by 3 is 3 with no remainder, 9 modulo 3 is zero.

```
int x1=7, x2=8, x3=9;  int r1, r2, r3;
r1 = x1 % 3; r2 = x2 % 3;  r3 = x3 % 3;        // r1 is 1, r2 is 2, r3 is 0
```

The same holds when the first operand is smaller than the second. For example, 5 divided by 7 is zero with 5 remaining. Hence, 5 modulo 7 is 5. Similarly, 6 divided by 7 is zero with 6 remaining. Hence, 6 modulo 7 is 6. Since 7 divided by 7 is 1 with no remainder, 7 modulo 7 is zero.

```
int a1=5, a2=6, a3=7;  int r1, r2, r3;
r1 = a1 % 7; r2 = a2 % 7;  r3 = a3 % 7;        // r1 is 5, r2 is 6, r3 is 0
```

This is rather straightforward for positive operands. For negative operands, the results are machine dependent. Fortunately, you never have to use the modulo operator for negative operands. The most common use of this operator is when trying to decide whether there is free space at the end of the container or we already filled it with data (and have to go back to the beginning of the container). The length of container and the position of the next item within the container are never negative.

Left-to-right associativity means that when several operators of the same priority are used in the same expression, they are evaluated from left to right. This is not important for multiplication and addition but is important for subtraction and division. It is all the same whether we evaluate a + b + c as (a + b) + c or as a + (b + c). It is important to make sure that we evaluate a - b - c as (a - b) - c and not as a - (b - c). Similarly, a/b/c means (a/b)/c and not a/(b/c).

The increment operator '++'and decrement operator '--' are trademarks of C/C++ programming. They are addition and subtraction operators with one operand equal to 1. Hence, they need only one operand to be specified. They implement assembly language-type processing: one is added or subtracted as an uninterrupted high-priority operation. In a sense, these operators create a side effect on their operands.

```
int x = 6, y = 10;   x++;   y-;        // now x is 7, y is 9
```

In their basic form these operators are very simple. The increment operator increments its operand by 1; the decrement operator decrements its operand by 1. This example is exactly equivalent to the following code:

```
int x = 6, y = 10;   x = x + 1;   y = y - 1;        // now x is 7, y is 9
```

Programmers who come to C++ from languages other than C often wonder why they should use the increment and decrement operators if they are exactly equivalent to conventional addition and subtraction. In old days, the answer was that the object code generated by the compiler for decrement and increment operations was more efficient than the object code generated for conventional addition and subtraction. This is not valid anymore. With modern techniques of compiler design and object code optimization, there is no difference in performance.

Today, the issue is mostly a matter of style. Of course, you do not have to use the increment and decrement operators. You can use conventional addition and subtraction, and your program will be every bit as elegant, correct, and fast as the program written with the increment and decrement operators. It is just that your boss (and probably your peers) will have some lingering doubts whether you are really as expert at C++ as you seem to be.

Actually, the increment and decrement operators are quite versatile. They are not limited to integral values. Floating point values are allowed too.

```
float small = 0.09;   small++;        // now small is 1.09
```

Also, there are two types of increment and decrement operators: prefix and postfix operators. What I used in previous examples were postfix operators:

the operator followed the operand that was modified by the operator. The prefix operator is the operator that precedes its operand. This is an example of using the prefix operators:

```
int x = 6, y = 10;   ++x;   --y;        // now x is 7, y is 9
```

You probably want to know what is the difference. The results seem to be the same as for the postfix operators. Indeed, the use of prefix operators in this context is equivalent to the following code:

```
int x = 6, y = 10;   x = x + 1;   y = y - 1;        // now x is 7, y is 9
```

As you see, it is exactly the same as before. The difference between the prefix and postfix operators is how they are used in expressions. You see, the result of these operations (as any other operation in C++, and this is a very important principle) is a value. In our examples, both x++ and ++x return value 7, and both y-- and --y return value 9. These values can be used in any other expression where an integer value is acceptable. And it is here where the prefix and postfix operators behave differently.

When a prefix operator is used, the value of the operand is first incremented (or decremented), and then the resulting value is used in the expression.

```
int x=6, y=10, a, b;   a = 5 + ++x; b = 5 + --y;        // a is 12, b is 14
```

Notice spaces preceding the prefix operators; they are useful to avoid confusion. The compiler (and the maintainer) might be confused over 5+++x, even though neither the compiler nor the maintainer is going to be confused over 5+--y.

When a postfix operator is used, the value of the operand is first used in the expression, and only then is the variable incremented or decremented.

```
int x=6, y=10, a, b;   a = 5 + x++; b = 5 + y--;        // a is 11, b is 15
```

You probably feel that it is not too difficult to write confusing code using the increment and decrement operators. You are probably right. However, these operators are immensely popular in their simplest form, when a counter or an index has to be incremented or decremented at each iteration of a loop. Look at Listing 3.1 (or other loops in earlier in the chapter). No experienced C++ programmer would write this code without using the increment operators (see Listing 3.5; its output is, of course, the same as for Listing 3.1).

Listing 3.5 Demonstration of the increment operator.

```
#include <limits>
#include <iostream>
using namespace std;
int main(void)
{
  int num = INT_MAX - 2;
  int cnt = 0;
  cout << "Integer overflow in C++:" << endl;
  cout << "Incrementing from " << num << endl;
  while (cnt < 5)
  { num++;  cnt++;                          // increment operators
    cout << cnt << "    " << num << endl; }
  cout << "Thank you for worrying about integer limits" << endl;
  return 0;
    }
```

You will probably come to love the increment and decrement operators very soon. If you are not comfortable with them now, no problem—use the same arithmetic operators as in other languages. However, if you avoid increment and decrement operators altogether, your boss might suspect that you are not as fluent in C++ as you try to suggest. Make sure that from time to time you do what everybody else does.

The next two subsections, "Shift Operators" and "Bitwise Logical Operators," can be skipped to make your first reading easier.

Shift Operators

Next in the table of C++ operators, we see the shift operators '<<' and '>>'. Wait a minute! These are not shift operators! These are the insertion and extraction operators that we used with the output object cout and the input object cin. This is right. Here we are dealing with the design technique called *operator overloading*. The shift operators were used in C from time immemorial. When C++ was designed, its designers decided to apply the existing operators to a new context. That is, instead of learning new operators (or new keywords), you learn new meanings for the existing operators.

I am not sure what is easier, but the technique of overloading operators is not really new. For example, how many meanings does the operator '+' have in plain C++? It is used a) as a unary plus, b) for adding integer numbers, c) for adding floating point numbers (and these operations are implemented differently from each other and from integer addition), d) as part of prefix and postfix increment operators—and we have not finished the discussion of operators yet.

The shift operators shift bits of an integral value of its left operand to the left or to the right; the second operand specifies the number of bits to shift the first operator. Actually, this is not as bad as it sounds. Let us consider the right shift first.

```
int x=5, y=1, result;   result = x >> y;      // result is 2
```

The operator shifts the bit pattern of its left operand (in this case, x that contains 5) to the right the number of positions specified by the right operand (in this case, y that contains 1). The binary representation of integer 5 is 101. When we shift this bit pattern one position to the right, we wind up with the bit pattern 10; it corresponds to integer 2. In this form, the shift right represents a fast method of dividing integers by 2 (or by a power of two specified by the second operand).

The left shift operator moves the bits in the opposite direction. Here, the bit pattern 101 becomes 1010, which corresponds to decimal 10.

```
int x=5, y=1, result;   result = x << y;      // result is 10
```

When bits are shifted to the left, the bits that shifted out from the first operand are lost; the right bits of the operand are filled with zeros (as in the last example). Similarly, when bits are shifted to the right, the bits that are shifted out are lost, but what happens on the left end of the operand is machine dependent.

The left-most bit of the signed integer value is the sign bit; if it is zero, the value is positive; if it is 1, the value is negative. When the number is positive, there is no problem: the zero in the sign bit is shifted to the right, and the zeros are shifted in from the left into the sign bit. If the value is negative, the one from the sign bit is shifted to the right, and here the portability problem arises. On some machines, ones are shifted into the sign bit (and propagate further as appropriate); this is called the *arithmetic shift*. On other machines, zeros are shifted into the sign bit (and propagate further to the right); this is called the *logical shift*.

Bitwise Logical Operators

The bitwise logical operators include the bitwise AND operator '&', the bitwise exclusive OR operator '^', the bitwise inclusive OR operator '|' and the higher-priority bitwise complement (negation) operator '~'. The first three operators are binary, and the last operator is a unary operator (it needs only one operand).

Similar to shift operators, logical operators work on bit patterns. They operate on each bit of the two operands individually. Each individual operation on two corresponding bits of operands contributes to the corresponding bit of the result.

The bitwise AND operator sets the result bit to 1 if both corresponding operand bits are 1; it sets the result bit to 0 if at least one operand bit (or both) is 0. In the examples that follow, I consider only four bits of operands and the result assuming that all other bits are set to zero. To illustrate the AND operator, let us assume that the first operand is 12 (its binary code is 1100) and the second operand is 10 (the binary code 1010). Comparing each individual bit in the first operand with the corresponding bit in the second operand, you see that only for the senior bit of the result are both operand bits 1; for all other bits, either one operand or both has a 0; hence the value of the result is 1000 (decimal 8): 1100 & 1010 is 1000.

The bitwise inclusive OR operator sets the result bit to 1 if one or both operand bits are 1; the result bit is set to 0 only if both operand bits are 0. For the operand values 12 (binary 1100) and 10 (binary 1010), all bits of the result with the exception of the right-most one will be set to 1, giving the binary code 1110 (decimal 14): 1100 | 1010 is 1110.

The bitwise exclusive OR operator sets the result bit to 1 if only one operand bit is 1; it sets the result bit to 0 if both operand bits are the same (both are 1 or both are 0). For our example, the first and last bits of the operands are the same, and the second and the third bits are different, giving the binary code 0110 (decimal 6): 1100 ^ 1010 is 0110.

The bitwise complement operator sets the result bits to the inverse of the operand bits; if the operand bit is 1, the result bit is zero, if the operand bit is zero, the result bit is one. For example, complementing 12 (binary 1100) results in binary code 0011 (decimal 3), that is, ~1100 is 0011.

These operators are often used when the application deals with a large amount of status information: the communication channel might be on or off, the device might be ready or not ready, the wire might have high voltage or low voltage, the customer might be eligible for a senior discount, have good credit rating, and so on. On a large machine, we can afford to allocate an integer for each of these values, even though we will be using only one bit, setting it either to 0 or to 1. On a smaller machine, we can use a set of boolean values, allocating one byte for each of these values. On a small machine, both approaches are wasteful. This is why these kinds of information are often packed into status words so that each bit (*flag*) in the bit patterns has its own meaning. To extract the value of a specific bit from the status word or to set the value of individual bits, we use shifts and logical operators with constants with specific bit patterns (*masks*).

Let's say that the third bit from the right in the status word (whose name, for example, is flags) means that a device is turned on. When the device is turned on, the program should set this bit to 1.

To be able to set this bit to 1, you should have a variable (whose name, for example, is onMask) whose third bit is set to one. If you apply the inclusive OR operator to the third bit of variables flags and onMask, the third bit of the result will be set to one no matter what the state of the third bit in flags is. This is faster than checking what the third bit in flags is and then deciding whether to go ahead with inclusive OR. The problem is that you cannot apply logical operators to individual bits—they are applied to all bits of the operands simultaneously. This means that all other bits in the variable onMask (with the exception of the third bit) should have a value such that it does not change the value of other bits of the variable flags. For the inclusive OR operation, this value is 0.

This is exactly how you design masks to handle packed bits: you set selected bits to the values that assure the required state, and you set the other bits to the values that do not change the existing state. In this example, the variable onMask should have the third bit set to 1 and all other bits set to 0. For a 4-bit representation, this gives the bit pattern 0100 or decimal 4:

```
int flags, onMask = 4;
flags = flags | onMask;        // this sets the 3rd bit to 1
```

When the device is turned off, this should be reflected by resetting the third bit to 0 and leaving the other bits unchanged. You need another mask (whose name is, for example, offMask) that has the third bit set to 0 so that the logical AND operator with any value would produce 0. To leave other flag bits unchanged, you should set other bits of the mask to 1. Hence, the variable offMask should have the bit pattern 1011, or decimal 11.

There is a catch, however. This bit pattern is 11 only when its size is 4 bits. For 8 bits, the bit pattern should be 11111011, and its decimal value is 244. For 16 and 32 bits, you need yet other value. This is a typical example of the portability problem. The solution here is a simple one. All these bit patterns represent the negation of the bit pattern 0100 for different word sizes. Hence, the portable method of initializing the variable offMask is to use the bit pattern that is the inverse of the bit pattern 0100:

```
int offMask = ~onMask;
flags = flags & offMask;            // this resets the 3rd bit to 0
```

To check whether or not the third bit is on, you can AND the mask `onMask` with the variable `flags`. This operation will set all the bits in the result to 0 with the exception of the third bit (because all the bits in `onMask` are zeros with the exception of the third bit). If the third bit in `flags` is 0 (the device is off), the result is 0 (`false`). If the third bit in `flags` is one (the device is on), the result is non-zero (`true`). Another method to access the bit value is to shift the flags pattern two positions to the right and AND the result with the mask that has all zeros except for the right-most bit. If the result is 1, the bit was set, if the result is 0, the bit was 0 (We will talk about the equality operator shortly.):

```
if (((flags >> 2)&1)==1) cout << "3rd bit ON\n";        // test it
```

Those of you who are not going to develop embedded and communications systems are not going to shift the values around much, and you can pay little attention to this material. Those of you who are will have to practice more because shifts and logical operations are quite common in these systems.

Relational and Equality Operators

The relational operators are used in all applications. C++ supports four relational operators: less than '<', less than or equal '<=', greater than '>', and greater than or equal '>='. The symbols in two-character operators have to be next to each other as with any other two-symbol C++ operator. These operators are mostly used in comparisons in conditional statements and in loops. For example, in Listing 3.1 the loop condition checks whether `cnt` < 5. If this is the case (during first iterations), the loop body is executed. If the value of `cnt` increases so that it becomes 5, the condition 5 < 5 is not true, and the loop is terminated. What can be simpler than that? Well, this is yet another thing inherited from C that is not as simple as it looks.

C++ has no built-in boolean type with values that are independent from integers. The boolean type we discussed earlier is implemented as a small integer: `true` is 1, and `false` is 0. That is, the result of comparison in C++ is not just `true` or `false` (as in all other programming languages), but numbers 1 and 0. The size of this integer is only 1 byte, but it can be converted to an integer of a larger size if necessary.

Hence, the value of $x > y$ is 1 if x is greater than y; otherwise it is 0; the value of $x < y$ is 1 if x is less than y; otherwise it is 0. Similarly, $x >= y$ is 1 if x is not less than y, and 0 if x is less than y. The value of $x <= y$ is 1 if x is not greater than y, and 0 if x is greater than y.

This does not change the form of simple comparisons and the way they work. But the use of logical values as numbers creates an enormous potential for abuse. For example, what is the value of x > y > z? In most programming languages (there are some exceptions though), this is just a syntax error and the end of the story.

In C++, it is a perfectly valid expression. Since relational operators associate from left to right, we compare x and y first. If x is greater than y, the result is 1, and we compare 1 with z; if 1 is greater than z, the value of the expression is 1; otherwise it is 0. If, however, x is not greater than y, the result is 0, and we compare 0 with z; if 0 is greater than z, the value of the expression is 1; otherwise it is 0. I doubt that anybody who could write this expression meant anything like that.

Next in the table we find equality operators. C++ supports two operators: the equality operator '==' and the inequality operator '!='. Again, the symbols in these operators should not be separated. When the comparison is true, the operator returns 1; when the comparison is false, the operator returns 0.

So, the value of x == y is 1 if x is equal to y; otherwise it is 0; the value of x != y evaluates to 1 if x is not equal to y; otherwise it returns 0.

Let us assume that you want to set the value of z to 10 if x is equal to y and to 9 if x and y have different values. In all programming languages (including C and C++) you can write something simple and straightforward:

```
if (x == y)          // set z to 10, or to 9
   z = 10;
else
   z = 9;
```

In C++, you can proudly write:

```
z = 9 + (x == y);
```

It is more difficult to understand, but it is definitely more concise and elegant.

The situation is aggravated by the fact that any value, not just 1, is equivalent to the true value and can be used instead. In addition, in C++, everything returns a value, including the assignment operator. For example, this assignment statement sets the variable x to the value of y and returns this value for further use in expressions if necessary.

```
x = y;
```

This means that if you accidentally misspell the equality operator '==' as the assignment operator '=', you are on your own. This misspelling of the equality operator is not a syntax error (as it should have been); it is a perfectly valid C++ expression.

Let's assume, for example, that in the example above the value of x is 1 and the value of y also is 1. This means that the expressions should set the value of z to 10. Now let us assume that we misspelled the first expression as:

```
if (x = y)
   z = 10;
else
   z = 9;
```

This statement sets the value of x to y (which does not change the value of x because both x and y have the same value 1 in this example), returns this value to the if statement, interprets it as true (because it is not 0), and sets z to 10. Everything is fine.

With a little testing, you can easily persuade yourself that the code works correctly. If you are diligent enough and test for a different set of values, say, x is 1 and y is 2, it will take some vigilance to discover that the value of z is still 10 and not 9 (again, the assignment x = y will return a value of 2 here and this is again true because it is not 0).

Now let us assume that we misspelled the second expression as

```
z = 9 + (x = y);
```

The assignment will return the new value of x that is changed to the value of y and this new value will be added to 9 to be used in setting the value of z. The variable z will be set neither to 9 nor to 10 but to 11.

If you see this for the first time, you might think that it is not a big deal, because the difference between the assignment operator '=' and the equality operator '==' is not that small and can be easily spotted. Sure. I am not saying that the difference is small. I am simply stating that whatever the explanation is, we all collectively in the software industry waste an enormous amount of time, energy, money, and emotion hunting these errors when we misspell '==' as '=', and we do that too often.

Please always check whether you spelled it right, both in assignments and in comparisons! I am putting here just one exclamation point because I do not want to look too emotional, but I would really like to attract your attention to this issue.

Alert

Misspelling the equality operator '==' as the assignment '=' is not a syntax error. It results in a legitimate C++ expression and the compiler silently produces incorrect code. Always check all your conditions for this error.

Logical Operators

The next set of operators includes logical operators: logical AND operator '&&', logical OR operator '||' (inclusive), and logical negation operator '!'. Similar to bitwise operators, the AND and the OR operators are binary operators (they require two operands), and the negation operator is a unary operator. There is no exclusive OR among logical operators.

Logical operators are immensely popular. They are as important as relational operators. You can hardly find a program where these operators are not used. Why then is their notation a derivative of the bitwise operators, almost as an afterthought? Because C++ inherited these operators from C, and in C, these operators are indeed secondary to the bitwise operators.

Unlike bitwise operators, logical operators treat each of their operators as the whole; if the value is 0, it is considered to be `false`; if the value is nonzero, whatever it is, it is considered to be `true`.

The logical AND operator '&&' returns 1 (of the size of `bool`) only if its operands are both nonzero; otherwise, it returns 0.

```
if (x < y && y < z) cout << "y is between x and z\n";
```

The logical OR operator '||' returns 1 if any of its two operands is nonzero; it returns 0 only if its both operands are 0.

```
if (x > 0 || y > 0) cout << "At least one is positive\n";
```

The logical negation operator '!' returns 0 if its operand is nonzero; it returns 1 if the operand is 0. You can always avoid using this operator by rearranging other conditions appropriately. Sometimes it is simpler to use the negation. For example, consider a program that grants a discount to senior citizens (`age >= 65`) with good credit rating (`rating == 2`). It is not too difficult to negate these conditions for somebody who is not eligible for a discount, but the programmer might find it simpler to write

```
if (!(age >= 65 && rating == 2)) cout << "No discount\n";
```

Both integer and floating point objects can be used as logical operands: Any nonzero value evaluates to `true`, and any 0 value evaluates to `false`. Notice that there is no need for operands of logical operations to be in parentheses. However, the logical expression of the `if` statement (and of the `while` statement) has to be in parentheses; this is why there are two sets of parentheses in the last example.

As in other languages, the logical operators evaluate from left to right; unlike in other languages, the '`&&`' operator binds tighter than the '`||`' operator. This allows you to write complex logical expressions without using parentheses. For example, the same discount of 10% might be offered to senior citizens with credit rating 2 and to first-time customers with an order of $200 or more. This can be expressed in the following form.

```
if (age>=65 && rating==2 || first_time == true && total_order>200.0) discount = 0.1;
```

This is not always a better way to write complex logical expressions. In a complex expression, it might be a good idea to use parentheses to indicate to the maintenance programmer what the components of the expression are.

```
if ((age>=65 && rating==2) || (first_time == true && total_order>200.0)) discount = 0.1;
```

In this example, parentheses around logical subexpressions are optional. Sometimes they are mandatory. For example, senior citizens might be eligible for a discount if their credit rating is either 1 or 2. The logical expression without parentheses is incorrect.

```
if (age>=65 && rating==1 || rating==2) discount = 0.1;   // incorrect logical expression
```

This statement gives the discount to senior citizens with rating 1 and to all customers with rating 2, not to senior citizens only (remember, the AND operator '`&&`' is of higher priority than the OR operator '`||`'). The use of parentheses corrects the problem.

```
if (age>=65 && (rating==1 || rating==2)) discount = 0.1;   // correct logical expression
```

Note

The logical operator AND '`&&`' is of higher priority than is the logical operator OR '`||`'. Use parentheses to help the maintainer to understand the meaning of complex logical expressions.

The C++ logical operators are a short circuit. This means that the first operand is evaluated first, and the second operand is not evaluated if the result is determined by the first evaluation. In the next example, if x is not less than y, it makes no sense to check whether y is less than z: we will not be able to conclude that y is between x and z; in this case, the second condition will not be evaluated.

```
if (x < y && y < z) cout << "y is between x and z\n";
```

In this example, you save a few microseconds; this is not a big deal; later on, we will see examples where this property allows you to protect the integrity of your code.

Assignment Operators

The assignment operator (and its variants) is of low precedence. This is appropriate because it has to be performed after all other operations in the expression are complete; the fact that the assignment is an operator opens some exciting syntactic possibilities and also creates some dangers. Anything that has an address in memory can be used as a target of the assignment, and its value can be used directly in other expressions.

The technical term associated with having an address in memory is *lvalue*. It means just that—that the expression can be used on the left-hand side of the assignment operator. It has an address, and the value at this address is modified when it is used as the target of the assignment. So far we have seen only one kind of lvalue: the name of a variable. There are other lvalues in C++, and we will see them later. Notice that being an lvalue does not prevent the value from being used on the right-hand side of the assignment.

The other kind of C++ value is *rvalue*. It has a value but has no address in memory available for the program for changing the value. Examples of rvalues are literal values, return values of functions, results of binary operations. Rvalues can be used on the right-hand side of the expression only and cannot be used as a target of the assignment. Here are examples of incorrect attempts to use an rvalue as an lvalue. They are all flagged as syntax errors.

```
5 = foo();          // a literal should not be used as an lvalue
foo() = 5;          // return value should not be used as an lvalue
score * 2 = 5;      // result of operation should not be used as an lvalue
```

Unlike in other languages, the C++ assignment is a binary operator that has an rvalue that can be used; this allows for chained assignments.

```
int x, y, z;    x = y = z = 0;
```

Assignment associates from right to left: x = y = z = 0; means x = (y = (z = 0)); and not (((x = y) = z) = 0); since x = y is not an lvalue, it cannot be assigned to. This feature can be easily abused.

```
x = (a = b*c)*4;    // this is legal in C/C++
x = a = b*c*4;      // this has a different meaning
x = 4*a = b*c;      // syntax error: there is no lvalue for 4*a
```

In addition to the traditional assignment operator, C++ has a number of variants—arithmetic assignment operators. Their goal is to shorten arithmetic expressions. For example, instead of saying x = x + y; we can say x + = y; The result is the same. These assignment operators are available for all binary operators ('+=', '-=', '*=', '/=', '%=', '&=', '|=', '^=', '<<=', and '>>='). They are almost as popular as the increment and decrement operators and are used for the same purposes. Here is an example of a segment of code that computes the sum of squares of first 100 integers.

```
double sum = 0.0;    int i = 0;
while (i++ < 100)
    sum += i*i;   // arithmetic assignment
cout << "The sum of first 100 numbers is " << sum << endl;
```

Here is the same segment of code that uses more traditional operators:

```
double sum = 0.0;    int i = 0;
while (i < 100)
    { i = i + 1;
      sum = sum + i*i; }
cout << "The sum of first 100 numbers is " << sum << endl;
```

As I mentioned earlier, the object code generated by the compiler is the same in both cases. The difference is purely aesthetic, and every C++ programmer has to learn to appreciate the expressiveness of shorthand operators.

Conditional Operator

The next operator in the hierarchy of C++ operators is the conditional operator. It is the only C++ operator that is a ternary operator: it has three operands. The operator itself consists of two symbols, '?' and ':', but unlike all other two-symbol operators, these symbols are separated by the second operand. This is the general syntactic form of the conditional operator:

```
operand1 ? operand2 : operand3      // evaluate operand2 if operand1 is true
```

Here, operand1 is the test expression; it can be of any scalar type (simple, with no program accessible components), including float. This operand is always evaluated first. If the result of evaluation of the first operand is true (nonzero), then operand2 is evaluated and operand3 is skipped. If the result of evaluation of the first operand is false (0), then operand2 is skipped and operand3 is evaluated. The value that is returned for the further use is either the value of operand2 or the value of operand3; the choice is done on the basis of the value of operand1.

Do not be misled by the use of true and false in this description. The expression operand1 can of course be a boolean expression, but it does not have to be. C++ allows you to use any type that can assume 0 and nonzero values.

In the next example, I set the value of variable a to the smallest of the values of variable y and variable z. The operand1 here is the expression y < z; if this expression is true, the operand2 (in this case, variable y) is evaluated and its value is returned as the value of the expression; if the expression y < z is not true, the value of operand3 (in this case, variable z) is returned. In case of a tie, it is the value of z again, but it does not matter.

```
a = y < z ? y : z;      // a is set to minimum of y, z
```

Notice that, unlike in all other cases of using logical expressions, operand1 does not have to be in parentheses. (It is probably easier to read if you use parentheses.) The conditional operator is concise and elegant, but it might be hard to read, especially if the result is used in other expressions. In this example, the same purpose can be achieved by using the if statement

```
if (y < z)
   a = y;                // a is set to minimum of y, z
else
   a = z;
```

Here is another example that demonstrates the advantages of the conditional operator; its return value here is used as part of another expression (the output statement). If the score of the applicant is greater than 80, the statement prints "Your application has been approved." Otherwise, it prints "Your application has not been approved."

```
cout << "Your application has" << (score > 80 ? "" : " not")
    << " been approved.\n";
```

The traditional approach is more verbose but may be easier to read:

```
if (score > 80)
    cout << "Your application has been approved.\n";
else
    cout << "Your application has not been approved.\n";
```

Comma Operator

Other languages do not treat the comma as an operator. C++ does. It connects operands that are evaluated from left to right and returns the right-most expression for further use. It is convenient if you need to evaluate several expressions in the place where C++ syntax allows a single expression only.

```
expr1, expr2, expr3,  ...  , exprN
```

Each expression is evaluated starting with the left-most one; since the comma has the lowest priority, it is executed last; the value of the last expression is the value returned. It is often used as the side effect of the left-most expressions. Here is our previous example, where I wanted to get rid of block delimiters.

```
double sum = 0.0;  int i = 0;
while (i < 100)
    i = i+1,  sum = sum + i*i; // no block delimiters are needed
cout << "The sum of first 100 numbers is " << sum << endl;
```

This is not a good idea, but treating the comma as an operator makes it legitimate. This is an example of an intentional abuse, and it is relatively harmless. The use of the comma as an operator is more dangerous when it happens unintentionally, and results in incorrect code but is not flagged as a syntax error because the code does not violate C++ syntactic rules. Consider, for example, the first example of the loop that computes the sum of squares.

```
double sum = 0.0;  int i = 0;
while (i++ < 100)
    sum += i*i,  // arithmetic assignment
cout << "The sum of first 100 numbers is " << sum << endl;
```

The only difference between the first version and this version is that I put a comma at the end of the loop body instead of the semicolon. Unfortunately, this error did not render the code syntactically incorrect. It compiles and runs—and runs incorrectly. It prints the results 100 times rather than once. This is an error that is easy to spot. But if the statement after the loop did something less conspicuous, the existence of the error would be harder to discover. Beware of the comma operator that shows up in the wrong places in the disguise of a legitimate C++ operator.

Alert

> Erroneous use of the comma might not be reported by the compiler since the comma is a legitimate C++ operator.

Mixed Expressions: Hidden Dangers

C++ is a strongly typed language. This means that if the context requires a value of one type, it is a syntax error to use a value of another type instead. This is an important principle that allows the programmers to weed out errors with less effort: Instead of hunting the errors down in the laborious process of run-time testing, the programmer is told by the compiler that the code is incorrect.

Consider, for example, the TimeOfDay type that I used in Chapter 2. It is a composite type (not a scalar) with two integer components. Notation exists for setting the field values and for accessing them, and that is all. You cannot add 2 to a TimeOfDay variable or compare it with another TimeOfDay variable (at least not with what we have seen of C++ yet). This is why the following segment of code is syntactically incorrect:

```
TimeOfDay x, y;
x.setTime(20,15); y.setTime(22,40);    // this is OK: legitimate operations
x += 4;                                // syntax error: incorrect operand type
if (x < y)                             // syntax error: incorrect operand type
   x = y - 1;                          // syntax error: incorrect operand type
```

However, C++ is weakly typed when it comes to numeric types. The last three lines in the example above would be syntactically correct if x and y were of type int. However, they would also be correct for any other numeric type: unsigned int, short, unsigned short, long, unsigned long, signed char, unsigned char, bool, float, double, long double. Moreover, these three lines would be syntactically correct even if the variables x and y belonged to different numeric types. The operations would be correctly performed at run time despite the fact that these variables would have different sizes and their bit patterns would be interpreted differently.

This is quite different from other strongly typed languages. For example, the following code is acceptable (and quite common) in C++.

```
double sum;
    . . .
sum = 1;                    // no syntax error
```

From the point of view of modern strongly typed languages, this is a clear example of programmer's inconsistency that would be flagged at compile time. In one place—the program, the programmer says that the variable sum is of type double. In another place (and this place can be separated from the first place by large number of lines of code), the programmer treats this variable as an integer. If this code is flagged as a syntax error, the programmer has an opportunity to think about it and decide how to eliminate this inconsistency: Either define the variable sum as integer or replace the last line of code with

```
sum = 1.0;
```

In modern strongly typed languages, the arithmetic operations must be performed on the operands of exactly the same type. For a C++ programmer, the whole issue is moot: both versions of this statement are acceptable and generate very little discussion.

Ideally, of course, all operands of an expression should be of the exact same type according to the principle of strong typing. However, this rule is relaxed somewhat for numeric types. C++ allows us to mix values of different numeric types in the same expression.

At the object code level, C++ follows the same rule as other modern languages do: All binary operations are performed over operands of exactly the same type. It is only at the source code level that we can mix different types. When expressions are evaluated, values of numeric types could be (and often are) changed into values of other numeric types so that the operations are actually performed over operands of exactly the same types.

This is done for your convenience, so that you could write mixed-type expressions without making them syntactically incorrect. But we pay for that. We pay for that by learning the rules of conversion among types and then worrying whether the results of the conversions are correct.

There are three kinds of type changes in mixed-type expressions:

- integral promotions
- implicit conversions
- explicit conversions (casts)

Integral promotions (widening) are applied to "small" integer types to convert their values into "natural" integer size. These promotions are applied to `bool`, `signed` char, and `short int` values; after they are retrieved from memory, they are always promoted to `int` for use in expressions. These conversions always preserve the value being promoted because the size of `int` is sufficient for representing any value of these "smaller" types. In this example, two `short` values are added and the result and its size are printed out:

```
short int x = 1, y = 3;
cout <<"The sum is " << x + y <<" its size is " <<sizeof(x+y)<<endl;
                                             // it prints 4 and 4
```

The computations are not performed on `short` values. They are performed on corresponding integer values. The conversion is rather simple. On a 16-bit machine, it is trivial because the `short` and `int` types are of the same size. On a 32-bit machine, two more bytes are added to the `short` value and are filled with the value of the sign bit (zero for positive, 1 for negative numbers). These promotions preserve the value being promoted.

Similarly, `unsigned char` and `unsigned short int` are promoted to `int`. This can cause no problem on a 32-bit machine, because the range of integers on these machines is larger than the range of `short` values is even when they are unsigned. The situation is different on a 16-bit machine. The maximum `unsigned short` value on these machines is 65,535, and this is larger than the maximum `int` value (32,767). Still, there is no reason to worry. If the value does not fit into the integer range, the compiler expands it to `unsigned int`. Again, the promotion is transparent to the programmer.

The floating point promotions are similar to integral promotions. They promote `float` values to `double`. No computation is performed on `float`. When a `float` value is retrieved from memory, it is promoted to `double`.

The integral and floating point promotions are dry, technical, and boring. You should know about them because they take time, and that might be important for time-critical applications. For example, when processing a large number of characters in a communications application, the programmer might choose to keep the characters in memory as integers to avoid promoting them implicitly each time a character value is retrieved from memory.

This is a typical case of the time-space tradeoff that is common in programming. The good news, however, is that integral promotions are not going to hurt you from the point of view of correctness of the program. Other conversions can.

Implicit conversions are generated by the compiler in:

- expressions with mixed types of operands and
- assignments (according to the target type).

When an expression contains operands of numeric types of different sizes, widening conversions are performed over the "shorter" operand, converting its value into a value of a "larger" type. After that, the operation is done over the two operands of the same, "larger" type. If the expression contains more than one operator, the expression is evaluated according to the operators' associativity (usually from left to right), and the conversions are performed at each step as appropriate. This is the hierarchy of sizes for conversions in expressions:

```
int --> unsigned int --> long --> unsigned long --> float --> double --> long double
```

Similar to promotions, these implicit conversions preserve the value of the operand being promoted. However, it is up to the programmer to make sure that the necessary conversion takes place. Failure to do that might result in the loss of accuracy (see Listing 3.6 and Listing 3.7).

Assignment conversions change the type on the right-hand side of the assignment to the data type of the assignment target on the left-hand side; again, the operation itself (the assignment) is always performed over operands of exactly the same type. If truncation takes place, a loss of precision is possible, but this is not a syntax error. Many compilers in their infinite goodness would issue a warning about the possible loss of precision, but the operation is legal in C++. If this is what you want, this is what you get. Or, in other words, the C++ programmer has all the right to shoot himself (or herself) in the foot.

In addition to loss of precision, there are two other possible implications of implicit conversion: execution speed and correctness of the results.

Consider the code in Listing 3.6 for converting the temperature measurements from Celsius to Fahrenheit. The sample output of this program is shown in Figure 3–5.

```
Please enter the value is Celsius: 20
Value in Fahrenheit is 68
```

Figure 3–5   Code in Listing 3.6 produces correct results
with implicit conversions to `double`.

Listing 3.6   Demonstration of implicit type conversions.

```cpp
#include <iostream>
using namespace std;
int main()
  {
    float fahr, celsius;
    cout << "Please enter the value is Celsius: ";
    cin >> celsius;
    fahr = 1.8 * celsius + 32;                      // conversions ?
    cout << "Value in Fahrenheit is " << fahr << endl;
    return 0;
    }
```

The type of the literal 1.8 is `double`. The variable `celsius` of type `float` is
converted to `double` before multiplication; since the type of the literal 32 is
`int`, it is converted to `double` before addition to make sure that the addition
is performed on the operands of the same type. The result of the computation
is of type `double`. Since the variable `fahr` is of type `float`, the result of computation is converted again before the assignment takes place. Of course, three
conversions are not much. But if these computations have to be repeated
many times, this can impair the performance of your program. And a C++ programmer should always be concerned about performance or at least be ready
to discuss the issues related to performance.

A remedy of this kind for a problem could be either using explicit type suffixes or doing computations in `double`.

Here is the example of using explicit type suffixes.

```cpp
float fahr, celsius; . . .
fahr = 1.8f * celsius + 32f;      // floats are promoted to double
```

Here is the example of doing computations in `double`.

```cpp
double fahr, celsius; . . .
fahr = 1.8 * celsius + 32.0;      // no conversions
```

Even if you are not concerned with performance (and yes, often we are not concerned with performance) and design your code for readability, you should remember the issues related to implicit conversions. For example, the standard conversion from Celsius to Fahrenheit uses the coefficient 9/5. I converted 9/5 to 1.8 just for the sake of example. Normally, I would not want to risk errors by doing manual computations and I would implement the program as in Listing 3.7. After all, in an interactive program, the execution time is spent waiting for the user to input data or displaying data for the user, and a few extra conversions are not going to change much. The sample output of this program is shown in Figure 3–6.

Listing 3.7 Example of the loss of precision in integer computations.

```
#include <iostream>
using namespace std;
int main()
  {
    double fahr, celsius;
    cout << "Please enter the value is Celsius: ";
    cin >> celsius;
    fahr = 9 / 5 * celsius + 32;            // accuracy ?
    cout << "Value in Fahrenheit is " << fahr << endl;
    return 0;
    }
```

The reason for the incorrect output is that, despite my expectations, no conversion from integer to double took place. Since binary operators associate from left to right, it is integer 9 that is divided by integer 5, and the result is 1. Even. The result would be different had I coded this line of code as

```
    fahr = celsius * 9 / 5 + 32;            // accuracy ?
```

Here, the variable celsius is of type double, and all computations are performed in type double.

As you see, the programmer needs a tool for making sure that the desired conversion takes place. C++ provides the programmer with casts, the means to explicitly control conversions between numeric types. A cast is a unary

Figure 3–6 Code in Listing 3.7 produces incorrect results after delayed conversion to double.

```
Please enter the value is Celsius: 20
Value in Fahrenheit is 52
```

operator of high priority. It consists of the type name in parentheses, which is placed before the value to be converted to the type indicated in the cast. For example, (double) 9 converts integer 9 into double 9.0; similarly, (int)1.8 converts double 1.8 into integer 1. Well, let me take that back. This is how programmers describe the casts (converting 9 to double and so on). In reality, 9 is not converted; that is, it remains an integer. A new value is produced of type double, which is numerically equivalent to integer 9.

Note

We say that casts convert values. In reality, the cast produces a value of the target type and initializes it using the numeric value of the cast operand.

The offending line in Listing 3.7 could be coded with explicit casts as:

```
fahr = (double)9 / (double)5 * celsius + (double)32;
```

Actually, to avoid the truncation problem, it would be enough to say

```
fahr = (double)9 / 5 * celsius + 32;
```

This would convert integer 9 to double 9.0, and hence the integer value 5 would be converted implicitly to double 5.0.

This form of the cast is inherited by C++ from C. C++ also supports another form of the cast that is similar to the syntax of the function call: The type name is used without parentheses, but the operand is used in parentheses. Using the C++ cast, the computation from Listing 3.7 will look this way.

```
fahr = double(9) / 5 * celsius + 32;
```

In addition, C++ supports four more types of casts: dynamic_cast, static_cast, reinterpret_cast, and const_cast. These casts will be discussed later. Some programmers use explicit conversions (casts) to a type that is appropriate for the expression to indicate to the maintenance programmer what their intent was at the time of design. Some programmers feel that casts clog the source code and make the task of a maintenance programmer more difficult. Some do not use casts because they do not want to do extra typing.

One more comment about expression evaluation. On several occasions, I mentioned that operands are executed from left to right, and that could create an impression that the components of the expression are also evaluated from left to right. This is incorrect. C++ makes no commitment to the order of evaluation of expression components, only to the order of executing the operators in an expression.

This is a subtle distinction that often escapes the attention of programmers. Often, it does not matter. For example, in the expression that converts Celsius to Fahrenheit, the operators are evaluated from left to right, and it does not matter in what order the values of 9, 5, `celsius`, and 32 are evaluated. They are independent from each other. It matters when you use the operators with side effects within another expression. What, for example, is the result of this code?

```
int num = 5, total;
total = num + num++;                        // 10 or 11?
cout << "The sum is " << total << endl;
```

Since I am using a postfix operator here, the value of `num` is used in the expression before it is incremented, so that the value of `total` equals 10. But this assumes that the components of the expression are evaluated from left to right. If they are evaluated from right to left, then `num++` is evaluated first, the value 5 is saved for use in computations, and the value of `num` becomes 6; then the left operand `num` is evaluated, but its value is already 6, so the value of `total` becomes 11, not 10.

On my machine the result is 10. On your machine the result might be also 10. This does not mean anything. C++ explicitly outlaws any program that relies on the left-to-right order of evaluation of expression components. What is the remedy? Do not use side effects in expressions. You want the result to be 10 on all machines? Do the following:

```
int num = 5, total;
total = num + num;                        // 10, not 11 num++;
cout << "The sum is " << total << endl;
```

Do you want the result to be 11 on all machines? This is not difficult either:

```
int num = 5, total;
int old_num = num;   num++;
total = num + old_num;                    // 11, not 10
cout << "The sum is " << total << endl;
```

It is always possible to say explicitly what you mean. Try to do it.

Summary

All right, this is enough on C++ types and expression evaluation. As you see, it is always a good idea to think about the ranges of types you are using. This is important both from the point of view of portability and from the point of view of correctness of the results. Unless you have specific reasons to do otherwise (like your boss tells you to), use types int and double, but make sure that they work correctly for you.

We covered a lot of ground in this chapter, and it might take some time for the material to settle down. Experiment with the examples, and rely on the material covered in Chapter 2 as the foundation of your work in C++. Do not use advanced features too much, too soon.

Mix numeric types in expressions freely as you see fit, but think about conversions and their effects on performance and correctness. Use explicit casts moderately, do not use expressions with side effects as part of another expression. Avoid unnecessary complexity: It will confuse your compiler, your maintainer, and yourself too.

Make sure you know what you are doing.

C++ CONTROL FLOW

Chapter 4

In the previous chapter, we discussed the cornerstone of C++ programming: data types and operators that combine typed values into expressions and statements. In this chapter, we will look into the next level of programming—putting statements together to implement algorithms capable of decision making and executing different segments of code depending on external circumstances.

The proper use of control constructs is one of the most important factors that define the quality of code. When the flow of execution is sequential and the statements are executed one after another in fixed order, it is relatively easy for the maintainer to understand the code. For each segment of code, there exists only one set of initial conditions and hence only one result of the computations. But sequential programs are too primitive; they cannot do much. Every real-life program executes some segments of code for some conditions and other segments of code for other conditions. Control should be transferred from one segment of code to another. The more flexible the programming language is from the point of view of control structures, the more power it places in the programmer's hands.

When a segment of code can be executed either after one segment or after another segment, there exists more than one set of initial conditions and hence more than one possible result of the computations. Keeping in mind all alternatives becomes difficult. Programmers make errors writing the code, maintainers make mistakes reading the code and making changes. This is why modern programming languages try to limit what the programmer can do when transferring flow of control from one segment of code to another. This approach is known as *structured programming*. The programmer uses only a small set of disciplined control constructs (loops and conditional statements) so that each segment of code has one (or two) entry and one (or two) exit.

C++ takes the middle approach. It comes with a rich set of control constructs that change the flow of control in the program. These constructs are flexible and powerful enough to support complex decision making in the program. At the same time, they are disciplined enough to discourage convoluted designs that would be difficult to understand and to maintain.

Statements and Expressions

In C++, unlike in other languages, the difference between an expression and an executable statement is quite small: Any expression can be converted to a statement by appending it with a semicolon. Here are some examples of expressions and executable statements.

```
x * y          // valid expression that can be used in other expressions
x * y;         // valid statement in C++, but quite  useless
a = x * y      // valid expression that can be used in others (do it with caution)
a = x * y;     // valid C++ statement, useful and common
x++            // valid expression that can be used in others (do it with caution)
x++;           // valid C++ statement, common and useful
foo()          // call to a function returning a value (a valid expression)
foo();         // call to a function with return value unused (a valid statement)
;              // null statement, valid but confusing
```

As in other languages, C++ statements are executed sequentially, in order of their occurrence in the source code. Logically, each statement is a unit that is executed as a whole, without interruption.

Executable statements can be grouped into blocks (compound statements). Blocks should be delimited by curly braces. Syntactically, a block of statements is treated as a single statement and can be used anywhere a single statement is expected. Each statement in a block has to be terminated by a semicolon, but the closing brace of the block should not be followed by a semicolon.

Merging statements into a block has two important advantages. First, you can use the block with several statements in the place where syntactically only one statement is allowed. Second, you can define local variables within a block. The names of these variables will not conflict with the names of variables defined elsewhere. The first property is crucial for writing control statements. Without it, no realistic program could be written. The second property is important for writing functions. Again, without it no realistic program could be written. Here is a general syntactic form of a compound statement.

```
{ local definitions and declarations (if any);
  statements terminated by semicolons; }          // no ; at the end
```

Compound statements can be used as function bodies, nested blocks within functions, and as control statement bodies. If you forget the rule of not putting the semicolon after the compound statement and put it there, in most cases it wouldn't hurt— you would wind up with a useless null statement that generates no object code. Sometimes, however, it can change the meaning of the code. It is better not to use the semicolon after the closing brace (you will have to remember the exceptions where the semicolon is necessary, like in a class definition and in a few other cases).

Compound statements are evaluated as a single statement, after the previous one and before the next one; inside the block, the normal flow of control is again sequential, in order of lexical occurrence.

C++ provides a standard set of control statements that can change sequential flow of execution in the program. These control statements include:

conditional statements: `if`, `if-else` statements

loops: `while`, `do-while`, `for` statements

jumps: `goto`, `break`, `continue`, `return` statements

multientry code: `switch` statements with `case` branches

In a conditional construct, the statement it controls can be either evaluated once or skipped depending on a boolean expression of the conditional. In a loop, its statement can be evaluated once, several times, or skipped depending on the loop boolean expression. The boolean expression is an expression that returns `true` or `false`. It is often called a logical expression, a conditional expression, or just an expression. In C++, any expression can be used as a boolean expression, and this expands the flexibility of C++ conditional statements and loops. In other languages, using a non-boolean expression where a boolean expression is expected results in a syntax error.

In a switch, an appropriate case branch (out of several branches) is selected depending on the evaluation of an integral expression. Jumps unconditionally change the flow of control. Often, they are used in conjunction with some other control construct (a conditional statement, a loop, or a switch).

In summary, for all control constructs, the scope of the action is only a single statement. When the logic of the algorithm requires that several statements are executed as the result of testing the logical expression, a compound statement in braces can be used instead. No semicolon should be used after the closing brace, but each statement in the block (including the last) should be followed by a semicolon.

In the rest of this chapter, we will look at each type of C++ flow control statements in detail, with examples and specific recommendations of what to do and what not to do while using these control statements for writing C++ code.

Conditional Statements

Conditional statements are probably the most ubiquitous control construct in C++ programs. You can hardly write a few statements of code without bumping into the need to do something only in the case when some condition holds; otherwise, you would do a different thing.

There are several forms of conditional statements that you can choose from while writing C++ code. Complex forms of conditional statements require diligent testing, but they often provide opportunities for making source code more concise and more elegant.

Standard Forms of Conditional Statements

The C++ conditional statement in its most general form has two branches, the True branch and the False branch. Only one of these branches can be executed when the conditional statement is executed.

Here is the general form of the conditional statement in context, between a statement that precedes it and a statement that follows it.

```
previous_statement;
if (expression)              // no 'then' keyword is used in C++
   true_statement;           // notice the semicolon before 'else'
else
   false_statement;          // notice optional indentation
next_statement;
```

The `if` and `else` keywords must be in lowercase. There is no 'then' keyword in C++. The expression must be in parentheses.

After the `previous_statement` is executed (it can be anything, including one of the control constructs), the expression in parentheses is evaluated. Logically, it is a boolean expression; we want to know whether the condition is `true` or `false`. When this conditional expression is `true`, the `true_statement` is executed, and the `false_statement` is skipped. When the condition is `false`, the `false_statement` is executed, and the `true_statement` is skipped. Since we are studying C++ and not Pascal, Basic, Java, or PL/I, the conditional expression does not have to be boolean. It can be any expression of any complexity. Its value is evaluated, and any nonzero value (it does not even have to be integer) is processed as true, and the 0 value is processed as false.

After one of these two statements, `true_statement` or `false_statement`, is executed, the `next_statement` is executed unconditionally. Again, it can be anything, including one of control constructs.

Listing 4.1 shows a program that prompts the user to enter the temperature measurement in Celsius, accepts the data, and then tells the user whether the temperature is valid (above absolute 0). In case you are not sure what the value of absolute 0 is, especially in Celsius, it is 273 degrees below the freezing point; or –273°C.

Notice the uses of the new line escape sequence both at the beginning and at the end of the strings in double quotes that are printed by the `cout` object. Also notice the use of the `endl` manipulator at the end of the program. If your operating system does not use buffering output, there is no difference between the new line escape character '\n' and the `endl` manipulator. With buffering, `endl` sends the output to the buffer and "flushes" the buffer, that is, performs the actual output from the buffer, whereas '\n' only sends the output to the buffer and flushes it only when the buffer becomes full. This sometimes improves program performance, but many programmers do not worry about the difference.

The output of the program is shown on Figure 4–1.

Listing 4.1 A conditional statement.

```
#include <iostream>
using namespace std;

int main ()
{
  int cels;
  cout << "\nEnter temperature in Celsius: ";
  cin >> cels;
  cout << "\nYou entered the value " << cels << endl;
```

```
if (cels < -273)
  cout <<"\nThe value " <<cels <<" is invalid\n" // no ;
       <<"It is below absolute zero\n";          // one statement
else
  cout <<cels<<" is a valid temperature\n";
cout << "Thank you for using this program" <<endl;
return 0;
}
```

Notice the indentation I used in the general example of the conditional statement above and in Listing 4.1. It is customary to indent the keywords if and else at the same level as the previous and the next statements. It is customary to indent both the true_statement and the false_statement a few spaces to the right. This makes the flow of control clearer to the maintenance programmer (and to the code designer at the time of debugging). How much to indent is a matter of taste. I feel that two spaces are enough. If you indent more, you will shorten the line, especially when you use nested control constructs, when either the true_statement or the false_statement (or both) are themselves conditional statements, or loops, or switch statements.

Notice that when the input temperature is invalid, the program displays two output lines. Normally, the code for doing that would look this way.

```
cout <<"\nThe value " <<cels <<"is invalid\n";   // ; at end
cout <<"It is below absolute zero\n";             // two statements
```

Written this way, these two statements have to be placed within the braces of the compound statement. The reason for that is when the code is part of a conditional statement, each branch of a conditional statement has the space for one statement only, not for two.

Listing 4.1 uses a different technique. The cout statement can be arbitrarily long and can span any number of source code lines, provided the line breaks are between statement components, not in the middle of a token. This means that it is incorrect to break the line in the middle of the string. It is all right, however, to break the string in two if needed.

```
Enter temperature in Celsius: 20

You entered the value 20
20 is a valid temperature
Thank you for using this program
```

Figure 4-1
Output of the program from
Listing 4.1.

The `false_statement` is optional. It can be omitted if some action has to be performed only if the boolean expression evaluates to `true`. Here is a general form of a conditional statement without the `false_statement`:

```
previous_statement;
if (expression)
   true_statement;
next_statement;
```

This conditional statement has neither `then` nor `else` as a keyword. Listing 4.2 shows a "scaled-down" version of the program in Listing 4.1. The user is warned when the input data is invalid (that is, the temperature is below absolute 0), but the program proceeds to do its job. (For simplicity's sake, the "job" is omitted here, and only the concluding statement is displayed.) The results of the run are shown in Figure 4–2.

Listing 4.2   A conditional statement without the `else` part.

```
#include <iostream>
using namespace std;
#define ABSOLUTE_ZERO -273

int main ()
{
  int cels;
  cout << "\nEnter temperature in Celsius: ";
  cin >> cels;
  cout << "\nYou entered the value " << cels << endl;
  if (cels < ABSOLUTE_ZERO)
    cout <<"\nThe value " <<cels <<" is invalid\n"
        <<"It is below absolute zero\n";              // one statement
  cout << "Thank you for using this program" <<endl;
  return 0;
}
```

Like the previous listing, the keyword `if` is indented at the same level as the previous and the next statements; the code in the `true` clause is indented to the right to indicate the control structure.

```
Enter temperature in Celsius: 20

You entered the value 20
Thank you for using this program
```

Figure 4–2
Output of the program from Listing 4.2.

Notice the use of a named constant for absolute 0 instead of a literal value that I used in Listing 4.1. It is considered good programming practice to use named constants for each literal value and put their definitions together in the program. This makes maintenance easier: The maintainer knows where to find the value, and one change is effective for every occurrence of the value in the program. This is much better than chasing each occurrence of the literal in code and introducing bugs by overlooking changes. In this small example, –273 is the only numeric value used in the program, and it is used only once. If you want to change this value, it is all the same in what place in the program you change it (and after all, how many times are you going to change the value of the absolute 0 during program maintenance?). Hence, it is all the same whether you use a constant or a literal here. However, the use of symbolic constants is a good practice.

Note

The `true_statement` *and* `false_statement` *in conditionals can be compound statements if necessary.*

Listing 4.3 shows a modified program from Listing 4.1. I use two statements in the `true` branch, and I also use two statements in the `false` branch. Notice the use of the `const` keyword. As I mentioned earlier, this is a more-popular technique in C++ than using the `#define` preprocessor directive. The output of the program is shown in Figure 4.3.

Listing 4.3 A conditional statement with compound branches.

```
#include <iostream>
using namespace std;
const int ABSOLUTE_ZERO = -273;

int main ()
{
  int cels;
  cout << "\nEnter temperature in Celsius: ";
  cin >> cels;
  cout << "\nYou entered the value " << cels << endl;
  if (cels < ABSOLUTE_ZERO)
    { cout <<"\nThe value " <<cels <<" is invalid\n";
      cout <<"It is below absolute zero\n"; }          // a block
  else
    { cout <<cels<<" is a valid temperature\n";         // a block
      cout << "You can proceed with calculations\n"; }
  cout << "Thank you for using this program" <<endl;
  return 0;
}
```

```
Enter temperature in Celsius: 20

You entered the value 20
20 is a valid temperature
You can proceed with calculations
Thank you for using this program
```

Figure 4-3
Output of the program from
Listing 4.3.

Compound statements must use the opening and closing braces. The statements in each compound statement are indented more to the right to indicate that they are executed sequentially. This helps the maintainer to understand the intent of the designer of the code at the time of implementation. Some programmers put the opening and the closing brace of each compound statement on lines by themselves. They feel that this helps to underline the structure of code. I am not sure whether each brace deserves this treatment. Doing so expands the code listing vertically and that makes it more difficult to grasp the general meaning of code (especially when you work with the screen display rather than with the hard copy printout). This is why I use the vertical white space sparingly.

Common Errors in Conditional Statements

Conditional statements add to the complexity of code. Errors in conditional statements are often hard to find. If we are lucky, the errors render the code syntactically incorrect. Often, the errors result in incorrect execution. Since not all parts of the conditional statement are executed every time, it takes additional planning and additional test runs to discover these errors.

Errors often happen in transmitting the intent and knowledge of the program designer to the maintainer. They manifest themselves in incorrect indentation or in incorrect use of braces delimiting compound statements.

Missing braces is a common error in control structures. Let us assume that I wrote the conditional statement in Listing 4.3 in the following way:

```
if (cels < ABSOLUTE_ZERO)
  { cout <<"\nThe value " <<cels <<" is invalid\n";
    cout <<"It is below absolute zero\n"; }          // a block
else
    cout <<cels<<" is a valid temperature\n";          // no braces
    cout << "You can proceed with calculations\n";
```

```
Enter temperature in Celsius: -300

You entered the value -300

The value -300 is invalid
It is below absolute zero
You can proceed with calculations
Thank you for using this program
```

Figure 4-4
Output of the modified program
from Listing 4.3.

This version of the program looks fine. It compiles fine. It runs fine. At least, when the input data is 20, the program output is exactly the same as in Figure 4–3. However, if you run this program using the value –300 as input, the output will look as shown in Figure 4–4.

I hope you see that this output is incorrect. The reason is that indentation is visible to the human reader only, not to the compiler. Despite the indentation that shows that both cout statements belong to the else branch, the compiler sees it differently. Without the braces, the compiler thinks that the second cout statement is the next_statement rather than part of the false_statement. This is what the compiler thinks I wrote:

```
if (cels < ABSOLUTE_ZERO)
  { cout <<"\nThe value " <<cels <<" is invalid\n";
    cout <<"It is below absolute zero\n"; }        // a block
else
     cout <<cels<<" is a valid temperature\n";     // no braces
cout << "You can proceed with calculations\n";     // next_statement
```

Fortunately, a similar error in the true branch of an if statement will result in a syntax error:

```
if (cels < ABSOLUTE_ZERO)
  cout <<"\nThe value " <<cels <<" is invalid\n";
  cout <<"It is below absolute zero\n";            // this is nonsense
else
  { cout <<cels<<" is a valid temperature\n";      // a block
    cout << "You can proceed with calculations\n"; }
```

Here, the compiler accuses me of misplacing the else keyword because the compiler sees the following code:

```
if (cels < ABSOLUTE_ZERO)                              // an 'if' without an 'else' is ok
  cout <<"\nThe value " <<cels <<" is invalid\n";
cout <<"It is below absolute zero\n";                  // this is nonsense
else                                                   // this 'else' does not have the 'if'
 { cout <<cels<<" is a valid temperature\n";           // a block
   cout << "You can proceed with calculations\n"; }
```

The compiler thinks that the first `cout` statement belongs to an `if` statement without the `else` clause, and this is perfectly legitimate. The compiler thinks that the second `cout` statement is the `next_statement`, and this is also OK. Then the compiler finds the `else` keyword and gives up.

A related issue is the use of a semicolon at the end of C++ statements. As I have mentioned earlier, the absence of a semicolon after a C++ statement leads to trouble. Beginning C++ programmers often struggle with this rule. Some programmers become so anxious about this issue that they start putting a semicolon at the end of each line whether or not it is needed there. When you use an extra semicolon in your source code, you wind up with a null statement that does not do anything and is mostly harmless. (This is an observation, not a quote from a travel book.)

However, an extra semicolon is not always harmless. Let us assume that I wrote the #define directive in Listing 4.2 this way:

```
#define ABSOLUTE_ZERO -273;      // incorrect #define
```

This is, of course, incorrect: There should be no semicolon here (but yes, there should be a semicolon at the end of the `const` definition in Listing 4.3). However, the compiler does not tell me that this line is in error. Instead, the compiler accuses me of writing the conditional statement incorrectly. The reason for that is that the #define directive works as literal substitution. Every time the preprocessor finds the identifier `ABSOLUTE_ZERO` in the program, the preprocessor substitutes its value into the source code. And its value now is –273; and not –273. This is perfectly legitimate for the preprocessor, but the compiler gets from the preprocessor the following conditional statement to deal with:

```
if (cels < -273;)                          // semicolon in expression: error
  cout <<"\nThe value " <<cels <<"is invalid\n"
       <<"It is below absolute zero\n";   // one statement
```

A semicolon at the end of an expression turns the expression into a statement. The compiler tells you that the expression `cels<ABSOLUTE_ZERO` contains an extra semicolon. You see with your own eyes (Listing 4.2) that this expression contains no semicolon. You think the error is caused by something else, and you start changing everything around this line that is suspicious. The more you have to suspect, the worse things go. The distance between the place where the error is made (the `#define` directive) and where it manifests itself (the conditional statgement) makes the analysis of the situation difficult. This is one reason why the use of the `const` keyword is encouraged over the use of `#define` directives.

Sometimes one might put a semicolon at the end of the line with the conditional expression. Let us assume that I wrote the conditional statement from Listing 4.3 this way:

```
if (cels < ABSOLUTE_ZERO);                        // the true branch
  { cout <<"\nThe value " <<cels <<" is invalid\n";  // next_statement
    cout <<"It is below absolute zero\n"; }          // a block
else                                                 // nonsense for the compiler
  { cout <<cels<<" is a valid temperature\n";
    cout << "You can proceed with calculations\n"; }
```

This is a syntax error. As happens all too often, the compiler is not able to direct you to the offending line; instead, it tells you that you misplaced the `else` keyword. For the compiler, the extra semicolon after the conditional expression makes it into a perfectly valid statement. It does not do much, but this is not a problem in C++. This is what the compiler thinks I wanted this code to look like:

```
if (cels < ABSOLUTE_ZERO)
  ;                                              // it does not do much
{ cout <<"\nThe value " <<cels <<"is invalid\n";
  cout <<"It is below absolute zero\n"; }        // next statements
else                                             // misplaced 'else'
  { cout <<cels<<" is a valid temperature\n";
    cout << "You can proceed with calculations\n"; }
```

The compiler sees the conditional statement without the `else`, a block with two statements that follows the conditional statement and then the `else` keyword that comes out of the blue, and it flags this line as in error, not the line where the error is made. Make sure that if you make an error like that you do not spend too much time understanding the compiler error message or rearranging the structure of your code.

Next, let us assume that I put an extra semicolon after the logical expression in the version of the program shown in Listing 4.2. The conditional statement from Listing 4.2 will look this way:

```
if (cels < ABSOLUTE_ZERO);              // this is definitely harmful
  cout << "\nThe value " <<cels <<" is invalid\n"
       << "It is below absolute zero\n";
```

This conditional statement has no `else` clause. The misplaced `else` is not an issue here, and this version of the program compiles without any problem. The compiler fails to notify you about the error, and you are left to fend for yourself during debugging and testing. When I run this version of the code using the value 20 as input data, the results are different from what you see in Figure 4–2. The output of the modified program is shown in Figure 4–5.

This is the kind of error that is psychologically hard to catch during debugging. When the program produces voluminous correct output, a little extra line can easily escape the programmer's attention. Make sure you watch your semicolons as relentlessly as you watch your braces.

Using control constructs raises a new issue, the issue of program testing. Actually, it is not a new issue, but for control statements it requires more planning, skills, and yes, vigilance. When testing sequential programs, it is usually sufficient to run the program once. If the program is correct, the results are correct, and additional testing will not bring any extra return on additional time, effort, and expense. If the program is incorrect, the results will be incorrect. This will be obvious from the first run unless, of course, the programmer is dozing off or thinking about something else or simply is in a hurry to move on to other things.

```
Enter temperature in Celsius: 20

You entered the value 20

The value 20 is invalid
It is below absolute zero
Thank you for using this program
```

Figure 4–5
Output of the modified program from Listing 4.2.

Note

All listings in previous chapters were sequential programs with only one path of execution. This is why they had only one screen shot as evidence of program correctness.

Even for sequential programs, running the program only once is not always sufficient. It is important to run them for at least two sets of data. The reason for this is the possibility of accidental correctness. To illustrate this point, consider the example of conversion from Celsius to Fahrenheit implemented in Listing 3.7. As you remember, the statement I used to implement the computations was incorrect:

```
fahr = 9 / 5 * celsius + 32;          // accuracy ?
```

When the programmer designs input test data, the important consideration is the simplicity of manual computations. This is quite reasonable, because often the algorithms are so complex that manual computations for a general case are hard to do correctly. In this case, it is quite realistic to expect that the programmer would test the program in Listing 3.7 by entering 0 as input data. The results are shown on Figure 4–6. As you can see, they are correct. This is why one set of data is not sufficient, even for sequential segments of code.

Let us go back to the example in Listing 4.1. Is running the program for the input data 20 (as in Figure 4–1) sufficient? Obviously not, because there are statements in the program that have never been executed during that program run. What if these statements transfer money to the programmer's account? Launch an intercontinental missile? Crash the program? Or just silently produce incorrect output? The first principle of testing is that the set of test data should exercise each statement in the program at least once (or more, if you want to protect the program from errors that are hidden behind accidental correctness). Hence, the program from Listing 4.1 needs the second test run in addition to the one on Figure 4–1.

Figure 4–6   Output of the program from Listing 3.7.

```
Please enter the value is Celsius: 0
Value in Fahrenheit is 32
```

Figure 4.7 shows the second test run of the program in Listing 4.1. We see that the results are correct, and that increases our confidence in the correctness of the program. The output confirms that both branches of the conditional statement are indeed there, and they do the right thing.

Is this testing sufficient? Probably not. If the value of absolute 0 was typed incorrectly, for example, as –263 instead of –273, the results of both tests would still be correct. This leads us to the second principle of testing: The set of test data should exercise the boundaries of conditional expressions. This means using –273 as input data. If absolute 0 were entered as –263, the program would incorrectly print that the temperature –273 is invalid. Hence, using –273 as input would discover the error that the input value 0 on Figure 4–2 is not capable of discovering.

But this is not the end of the story. What if the value of absolute 0 is typed as –283 instead of –273? Using –273 as input would not find this error: The condition –273 < –283 will evaluate to `false`, and the program will print (correctly) that this is a valid temperature. This leads us to the third principle of testing: The boundaries of conditional expressions have to be exercised for both `true` and `false` outcomes.

In the case of integer data, this means using the value –274 as input. In the case of floating point data, the programmer has to choose some small increment over the boundary, like –273.001 or any other value that makes sense in the context of the application.

In general, if the code contains the condition x < y, it has to be tested with two test cases, one for x equals y (the result should be `false`) and another for x equals y - 1 for integers or equals y minus a small value for floating point data (the result should be `true`).

Similarly, if the code contains the condition x > y, it also has to be tested with two test cases, one for x equals y (the result should be `false`) and another for x equals y + 1 for integers or equals y plus a small value for floating point data (the result should be `true`).

```
Enter temperature in Celsius: -300

You entered the value -300

The value -300 is invalid
It is below absolute zero
Thank you for using this program
```

Figure 4-7
The second run of the program from Listing 4.1.

Unfortunately, this is not all. These guidelines do not work for conditions that include equality. If the code contains the condition x <= y, the test case x equals y will return true, not false as in the case of x < y. To test for the false result, the code should be tested for x equals y + 1 (or y + a small number). Similarly, if the code contains the condition x >= y, the test case x equals y should return true rather than false, and the second test case should be for x equals y - 1 (or y - small number).

This makes things quite complex. Each condition in the program has to be tested separately, with two test cases for each condition, and that makes the number of test cases large. Some programmers just do not have the patience to analyze, design, run, and inspect numerous test cases. They limit themselves to visual code inspection. This is unfortunate. The code inspection is useful but not a reliable tool for finding errors.

When the numbers are tested for equality (or inequality), the situation becomes even more complex. Listing 4.4 shows the program that prompts the user for a nonzero integer, accepts the input value and then checks whether this number is 0 (to protect itself against division by 0). If the number is not 0, the user is praised for correct behavior, and the program computes the inverse and the square of the input value. If the input value is 0, the program criticizes the user for not following the instructions. Of course, it is a rather trivial example, but it demonstrates the issues involved without making things too complicated.

Listing 4.4 Checking values for inequality (incorrect version).

```
#include <iostream>
using namespace std;

int main ()
{
  int num;
  cout << "\nPlease enter a non-zero integer: ";
  cin >> num;
  if (num > 0)                              // it should be (num != 0)
    { cout <<"\nYou followed the instructions correctly";
      cout <<"\nThe inverse of this value is " << 1.0/num;
      cout <<"\nThe square of this value is " << num * num; }
  else
      cout <<"\nYou did not follow the instructions";
  cout << "\nThank you for using this program" <<endl;
  return 0;
}
```

Notice that if I were to say `1/num` instead of `1.0/num`, the output would be incorrect because integer division truncates the results. Figure 4–8 shows that the program passes the test for input value 20: It displays correct output.

Since one test case is not enough, I test the program with the input data that violates the program instructions to make sure I exercise the `else` branch of the `if` statement. As you see from Figure 4–9, the program passes this test, too: It reprimands the user for not following the instructions.

But wait, this program is incorrect! I did make a typo while working on the program: Instead of `num != 0`, I typed `num > 0`. By the way, mistyping a relational operator is quite a common mistake. When writing number-crunching applications, programmers sometimes forget to correctly implement and test behavior that corresponds to negative numbers. To demonstrate this error, I have to test the program a third time, using a negative input number, as in Figure 4–10.

You can see that the program admonishes the user for the error instead of accepting the input. You can also see the corrected version of this program in Listing 4.5.

```
Please enter a non-zero integer: 20

You followed the instructions correctly
The inverse of this value is 0.05
The square of this value is 400
Thank you for using this program
```

Figure 4–8
Output of the first test for Listing 4.4.

```
Please enter a non-zero integer: 0

You did not follow the instructions
Thank you for using this program
```

Figure 4–9
Output of the second test for Listing 4.4.

```
Please enter a non-zero integer: -20

You did not follow the instructions
Thank you for using this program
```

Figure 4–10
Output of the third test for Listing 4.4.

> ## Listing 4.5 Checking values for inequality (correct version).

```
#include <iostream>
using namespace std;

int main ()
{
  int num;
  cout << "\nPlease enter a non-zero integer: ";
  cin >> num;
  if (num != 0)                               // now this is correct
    { cout <<"\nYou followed the instructions correctly";
      cout <<"\nThe inverse of this value is " << 1.0/num;
      cout <<"\nThe square of this value is " << num * num; }
  else
      cout <<"\nYou did not follow the instructions";
  cout << "\nThank you for using this program" <<endl;
  return 0;
}
```

This leads us to yet another principle of testing. For conditional expressions with the equality operator, three tests should be used: one test for equality (it should return `true`) and two tests for inequality on each side of the boundary (these tests should return `false`). The same is true for conditional expressions with the inequality operator: The test for equality should return `false`, and two tests for inequality should return `true`.

Tip

For if statements with relational operators, use test values on the border and next to the border; using test values that are far from the border could miss an error.

I summarize these principles in Table 4.1. The condition is represented as x op y, where operator op can be either '<', '>', '<=', '>=', '==', '!='. For each operator, the table lists the test cases and the expected value of the conditional expression. The values of x and y are assumed to be integers. For floating point numbers, a small increment should be used instead of 1. For equality and inequality tests of nonnumeric data, two tests will be sufficient rather than three.

Table 4.1   Test Cases for Testing Simple Conditional Expressions

Expression	Test	Outcome
x < y	x equals y	False
	x equals y – 1	True
x >= y	x equals y	True
	x equals y – 1	False
x > y	x equals y	False
	x equals y + 1	True
x <= y	x equals y	True
	x equals y + 1	False
x == y	x equals y	True
	x equals y + 1	False
	x equals y – 1	False
x != y	x equals y	False
	x equals y + 1	True
	x equals y – 1	True

You see that test cases for x < y and for x >= y are the same, but the outcomes are exactly the opposite. Test cases for x > y and for x <= y are again the same, but the outcomes are inverse from each other. Similarly, test cases for x == y and for x != y are the same with inverse results. This means that x < y and x >= y are negations of each other. Every condition that uses x < y can be rewritten as !(x >= y) and vice versa, and every condition that uses x >= y can be rewritten as !(x < y). When one condition is true, the second condition is false, and vice versa.

Similarly, conditions x > y and x <= y are negations of each other. So are conditions x == y and x != y. When one condition in each pair is true, the second one is false.

It is an important programming skill to be fluent in negating logical conditions. For the conditional statement, it is a matter of formatting the code properly. For example, if the true branch takes many complex statements and the false branch takes only one or two, the false branch might be lost in the code. Some programmers prefer to put a shorter sequence of statements as the true branch of the conditional statement. For example, the conditional statement in Listing 4.5 could be written this way:

```
if (num == 0)                          // negation of (num != 0)
  cout <<"\nYou did not follow the instructions";
else
  { cout <<"\nYou followed the instructions correctly";
    cout <<"\nThe inverse of this value is " << 1.0/num;
    cout <<"\nThe square of this value is " << num * num; }
```

As I mentioned earlier, it is important not to mistype the operator '==' as the operator '='. This is also a common source of errors that are hard to find. For example, the conditional statement above could easily be written as

```
if (num = 0)                           // this is perfectly valid in C++
  cout <<"\nYou did not follow the instructions";
else
  { cout <<"\nYou followed the instructions correctly";
    cout <<"\nThe inverse of this value is " << 1.0/num;
    cout <<"\nThe square of this value is " << num * num; }
```

This code raises no syntax or run-time errors. Some compilers might issue a warning, but it is a totally legitimate C++ idiom. Some programmers are so annoyed at the prospect of this kind of an error that they put the literal on the left-hand side of comparison and the variable on the right-hand side, for example,

```
if (0 == num)              // you will not use a constant as lvalue
  cout <<"\nYou did not follow the instructions";
else
  { cout <<"\nYou followed the instructions correctly";
    cout <<"\nThe inverse of this value is " << 1.0/num;
    cout <<"\nThe square of this value is " << num * num; }
```

If you misspell this comparison as the assignment 0 = num, the compiler will flag this as an error, because C++ literal values, although they are saved in memory like anything else, do not have the address that can be manipulated by the program (they are rvalues). It is a common tendency in programming language design to push as many errors as possible from the category of run-time errors into the category of compile-time errors. It was not always this way. I remember once I was working in FORTRAN on PDP-11, and somehow I managed to set the value of constant 1 to 2. So every time my source code was saying 1, the compiler was using the value 2. All my loops went berserk, and I could not figure out why.

Another common technique for writing logical conditions is to use the fact that in C++ any nonzero evaluates to true, and 0 evaluates to false. For example, many programmers would write the conditional statement in Listing 4.5 this way:

```
if (num)                       // a popular C++ idiom, same as if (num!=0)
  { cout <<"\nYou followed the instructions correctly";
    cout <<"\nThe inverse of this value is " << 1.0/num;
    cout <<"\nThe square of this value is " << num * num; }
else                           // the 'else' should be closer to the 'if'
    cout <<"\nYou did not follow the instructions";
```

Make sure that you are comfortable with this C++ idiom. It is very popular. If the inverse of this logical condition is used (that is, num == 0), many programmers would write this conditional statement this way:

```
if (!num)               // a popular C++ idiom, same as: if (num == 0)
   cout <<"\nYou did not follow the instructions";
else                    // the 'else' should be closer to the 'if'
{ cout <<"\nYou followed the instructions correctly";
  cout <<"\nThe inverse of this value is " << 1.0/num;
  cout <<"\nThe square of this value is " << num * num; }
```

Notice that if ! (num) ... is incorrect: the logical condition must be in parentheses. It is easy to overuse this feature and write code that the maintainer will have a hard time understanding.

The examples that we have discussed so far were relatively simple. To implement more complex processing tasks, we can use compound conditions and nested conditional statements. In compound conditions, the testing should exercise not only the true and false outcome of the compound condition, but also each possible reason for the true and false outcome. Consider, for example, the following conditional statement where processOrder() is a function defined elsewhere.

```
if (age > 16 && age < 65)
processOrder();
else
cout << "Customer is not eligible\n";
```

We can test the true branch of this conditional in only one way: by setting both age > 16 and age < 65 to true. We can test the false branch in two ways: by setting age < 65 to false (e.g., when age is 65) or by setting age > 16 to false (when age is 15). Which one to choose? If you only use the first way, you will not display an error if the first condition is set to true incorrectly, for example, if age > 0. If you only choose the second way, you will not find the error if the second condition is true but is incorrect, for example, if age < 250. This is why both ways of traversing the false branch of the conditional statement should be tested. This is more testing than for a simple conditional statement, but this is natural. The design of test cases for setting individual conditions to true or false should be done according to Table 4.1.

Notice that we do not test for the third way of traversing the `false` branch, when both `age > 16` and `age < 65` are `false`. Some programmers justify skipping this combination because these conditions are related: their truth value depends on the value of the same variable `age`. Depending on the value stored in the variable `age`, these conditions can both be `true` (the middle of the range of values), either of them can be `false` (the lower and the higher ranges of values), but they cannot both be `false`: The value cannot belong both to the lower and to the higher ranges of values. This is not the issue, however. For the AND operation, we test the `false` values of these conditions individually; testing them together is a waste of time and money.

Similar considerations apply to the test of OR compound conditions. Consider the following example which compares two floating point values:

```
if (amt1 < amt2 - 0.01 || amt1 > amt2 + 0.01)      // is difference more than 1 cent?
  cout << "Different amounts\n";
else
  cout << "Same amount\n";
```

We can test the `false` branch of this statement in only one way: by setting both conditions to `false`. We can test the `true` branch in two ways: either by setting the first condition to `true` or by setting the second condition to `true`. Which one to choose? The answer is the same as in the case of the AND operator: We have to test both to make sure that both conditions are tested adequately according to the guidelines in Table 4.1.

The good news is that we do not have to make up test cases for the third way to traverse the `true` branch, where both conditions are `true`. These conditions are related (they both depend on the values of variables `amt1` and `amt2`), and they cannot be made `true` simultaneously. Even if the conditions were not related, this test would be redundant.

Table 4.2 shows what test cases have to be included in the test design for compound conditions.

Table 4.2   Test Design for Compound Conditions

Operation	First Condition	Second Condition	Outcome
AND	True	True	True
	True	False	False
	False	True	False
OR	True	False	True
	False	True	True
	False	False	False

As I mentioned, the fact that the conditions in compound statements are related does not affect the testing strategy much. Consider, for example, the following conditional statement with independent conditions. Here, the functions `processPreferredOrder()` and `processNormalOrder()` are defined elsewhere and are called in different branches of the conditional statement. The customer gets preferential treatment if the previous business exceeds $1,500, and the current purchase amount reached $200.

```
if (amount > 200 && previous_total > 1500)
  processPreferredOrder();
else
  precessNormalOrder();
```

To test this code we have to design three test cases. One test case should traverse the true branch, when both `amount > 200` and `previous_total > 1500` are true (e.g., `amount = 200.01, previous_total = 1500.01`). Two test cases should traverse the `false` branch. One test case should set the condition `amount > 200` to true but `previous_total > 1500` to false (e.g., `amount = 200.01, previous_total = 1500.00`). The second test should set `amount > 200` to false but `previous_total > 1500` to true (e.g., `amount = 200.00, previous_total = 1500.01`). Each test case should be designed at the boundary conditions according to Table 4.1. These conditions are independent, and we can set both `amount > 200` and `previous_total > 1500` to `false` (`amount = 200.00, previous_total = 1500.00`). However, this test would not weed out any errors not discovered by the previous tests and would not increase our confidence in the correctness of the code.

Similarly to the AND operation, the OR operation over independent conditions has to be tested for three test cases: when the first condition is `true` and the second is `false`, when the first condition is `false` and the second condition is `true`, and when both conditions are `false`. Consider the following example, where `displayRelaxationPackage()` and `displayActivePackage()` are functions defined elsewhere.

```
if (age > 65 || previous_history == 1)
  displayRelaxationPackage();
else
  displayActivePackage();
```

The test cases for this code should cover three situations:

- `age > 65` is true and `previous_history == 1` is false
- `age > 65` is false and `previous_history == 1` is true
- both `age > 65` and `previous_history == 1` are false

The first two test cases traverse the `true` branch of the conditional state-ment, and the last test case covers the `false` branch. Since the conditions in the logical operation are independent, they can be set to `true` simultaneous-ly. However, there is no need to test for the case where both `age > 65` and `previous_history == 1` are `true` because this test does not weed out errors that would not be displayed by three previous tests.

Tip

For the `&&` operation, test it for three cases: first condition is `false`, second condition is `false`, both conditions are `true`. For the `||` operation, test it for three cases: first condition is `true`, second condition is `true`, both con-ditions are `false`.

Nested Conditionals and Their Optimization

Nested conditional statements are very popular. Putting conditional state-ments in the branches of a conditional statement is not very different from using other kinds of statements. Indentation to the right displays the structure of the code and helps the maintainer understand the intent of the code designer. If there is a need to put more than one statement in the branch, braces are used for the compound statement. The only caveat with using nest-ed conditional statements is matching `if`s and `else`s. Each `else` should be matched with the closest `if`:

```
if (condition)
   if (condition1)
      true_statement1;
   else                  // this belongs to the if with condition1
      false_statement1;
else                     // belongs to if (condition)
   if (condition2)
      true_statement2;
   else                  // this belongs to the if with condition2
      false_statement2;
```

This is a no-brainer, where each conditional statement is a complete state-ment with both `true_statement` and `false_statement` present. The situa-tion might become more complex if one of these statements were missing. This might happen when the programmer finds similarities in conditions or in statements and tries to optimize the source code, that is, to make it more concise and expressive.

Let us consider a section from the mail order processing system that evaluates the size of the order and customer status. If the order amount exceeds the size of a small order (e.g., $20), there is no service charge; in addition, preferred customers get a discount (10%), and the customer savings are displayed. For small orders, there is no discount for any customer; in addition, regular (but not preferred) customers are charged a service charge ($2 per order). As you see, the description of the processing rambles somewhat. This is often the case because writers of requirements are only human, and human language is not always precise and terse. Come to think about it, some redundancy in requirements might actually be helpful because it prevents misunderstanding when the programmer tries to interpret text that is too concise.

Listing 4.6 shows one possible interpretation of the requirements. Despite the fact that there are three conditional statements in this code, in effect, there are only two checks (the size of the order and the status of the customer). Since these conditions are independent, we need two test cases for each condition (small order, large order, preferred status, and regular status). The results of the runs of the program are shown on four screen shots in Figures 4–11 through 4–14.

Listing 4.6   Nested conditional statements.

```cpp
#include <iostream>
using namespace std;

int main ()
{
  const double DISCOUNT = 0.1, SMALL_ORDER = 20;
  const double SERVICE_CHARGE = 2.0;
  double orderAmt, totalAmt; int preferred;
  cout << "\nPlease enter the order amount: ";
  cin >> orderAmt;
  cout << "Enter 1 if preferred customer, 0 otherwise: ";
  cin >> preferred;
  if (orderAmt > SMALL_ORDER)
    if (preferred == 1)
    { cout <<"Discount earned " <<orderAmt*DISCOUNT<<endl;
      totalAmt = orderAmt * (1 - DISCOUNT); }
    else
      totalAmt = orderAmt;
  else
    if (preferred == 0)
      totalAmt = orderAmt + SERVICE_CHARGE;
```

```
    else
        totalAmt = orderAmt;
    cout << "Total amount: " << totalAmt << endl;
    return 0;
}
```

The implementation in Listing 4.6 maps back onto the requirements fairly well, but its redundancy will leave many programmers uneasy. There are related tests in different branches (preferred == 1 and preferred == 0)

```
Please enter the order amount: 20
Enter 1 if preferred customer, 0 otherwise: 1
Total amount: 20
```

Figure 4-11   Output for Listing 4.6 (small amount, preferred customer).

```
Please enter the order amount: 20.01
Enter 1 if preferred customer, 0 otherwise: 1
Discount earned 2.001
Total amount: 18.009
```

Figure 4-12   Output for Listing 4.6 (large amount, preferred customer).

```
Please enter the order amount: 20
Enter 1 if preferred customer, 0 otherwise: 0
Total amount: 22
```

Figure 4-13   Output for Listing 4.6 (small amount, regular customer).

```
Please enter the order amount: 20.01
Enter 1 if preferred customer, 0 otherwise: 0
Total amount: 20.01
```

Figure 4-14   Output for Listing 4.6 (large amount, regular customer).

that beg for optimization. There is similar processing in different branches (totalAmt = orderAmt) that beg for the same thing. One of the ways to optimize this code is to start with the assignment totalAmt = orderAmt and then check whether it has to be modified because of the discount for large orders by preferred customers or because of the service charge for small orders by regular customers.

This technique often allows one to eliminate the else clause. Our first solution in Listing 4.6 can be described by the following pseudocode:

```
if (some_condition_holds_true)
  do_processing_the_first_way;
else
  do_processing_the_second_way;
```

The optimized solution I am going to implement starts with doing the processing the second way and then either modifying it or leaving the result alone. Its pseudocode looks like the following:

```
do_processing_the_second_way;
if (some_condition_holds_true)
  do_processing_the_first_way;
```

This optimized implementation is shown in Listing 4.7. The results of the first two test cases are exactly the same as shown in Figures 4–11 and 4–12. The tests for regular customers, however, give the results shown in Figures 4–15 and 4–16. They are different from the results shown in Figures 4–13 and 4–14. Why is that so?

Figure 4–15 Output for Listing 4.7 (small amount, regular customer).

```
Please enter the order amount: 20
Enter 1 if preferred customer, 0 otherwise: 0
Total amount: 20
```

Figure 4–16 Output for Listing 4.7 (large amount, regular customer).

```
Please enter the order amount: 20.01
Enter 1 if preferred customer, 0 otherwise: 0
Total amount: 22.01
```

Listing 4.7   An optimized nested conditional statement.

```cpp
#include <iostream>
using namespace std;

int main ()
{
  const double DISCOUNT = 0.1, SMALL_ORDER = 20;
  const double SERVICE_CHARGE = 2.0;
  double orderAmt, totalAmt; int preferred;
  cout << "\nPlease enter the order amount: ";
  cin >> orderAmt;
  cout << "Enter 1 if preferred customer, 0 otherwise: ";
  cin >> preferred;
  totalAmt = orderAmt;                   // do it the second way
  if (orderAmt > SMALL_ORDER)            // change totalAmt if not a small order
    if (preferred == 1)
      { cout <<"Discount earned " <<orderAmt*DISCOUNT<<endl;
        totalAmt = orderAmt * (1 - DISCOUNT); }
  else                                   // this is an optical illusion
    if (preferred == 0)                  // for small order, check customer status
      totalAmt = orderAmt + SERVICE_CHARGE;
  cout << "Total amount: " << totalAmt << endl;
  return 0;
}
```

This implementation shows us an optical illusion: The indentation has to convey to the maintainer (and to the tester) the intent of the original designer. However, it is different from how the compiler understands the code. According to the rule of matching the `else` keyword, the compiler sees the conditional statement as:

```cpp
totalAmt = orderAmt;                   // do it the second way
if (orderAmt > SMALL_ORDER)            // change totalAmt if not a small order
  if (preferred == 1)
    { cout <<"Discount earned " <<orderAmt*DISCOUNT<<endl;
      totalAmt = orderAmt * (1 - DISCOUNT); }
  else
    if (preferred == 0)
      totalAmt = orderAmt + SERVICE_CHARGE;   // no processing for small orders
```

In this solution, small orders are not processed, no matter what kind of customer is making the order. (The correctness of results for small order and preferred customers is accidental.) For large orders, it imposes the service charge incorrectly. Human understanding and compiler understanding go their separate ways and do not intersect; they only pretend to describe the same thing.

In this case, it is not too difficult to establish a common point of view and eliminate pretending. All it takes is to put the branches of the conditional statement within braces. After all, a compound statement does not have to be one that consists of several statements. It can contain a single statement only. What makes a statement a compound statement is not the number of statements bound together but the braces that denote the block. The conditional statement in Listing 4.7 should look this way.

```
totalAmt = orderAmt;                 // do it the second way
if (orderAmt > SMALL_ORDER)          // modify totalAmt if not a small order
  { if (preferred == 1)
    { cout <<"Discount earned " <<orderAmt*DISCOUNT<<endl;
      totalAmt = orderAmt * (1 - DISCOUNT); } }
else
  if (preferred == 0)                // for small order, check customer status
    { totalAmt = orderAmt + SERVICE_CHARGE; }
```

Many programmers find this coding style effective, and they use braces each time they design a conditional statement (or any other control construct, for that matter). This helps to avoid another common problem: Often, we start with one statement in a branch of a conditional statement and hence do not use braces. Then, we find we have to add another statement. We add it, and sometimes forget to add the braces, especially if the change is made by the maintainer. Putting the braces around each branch of a conditional statement reduces the number of things the maintainer has to think about when making changes. And this is a very important advantage. So, the canonical for the conditional statement should look this way:

```
if (expression)
  { true_statement; }       // ready for future expansion
else
  { false_statement; }      // ready for future expansion
```

Another good example of nested conditional statements and their optimization is the leap year problem. Generally, a leap year is a year that can be divided by 4 evenly, without a remainder. This is where the modulo operator can be put to good use. As part of the implementation, we could write something like this:

```
if (year%4 != 0)      // if the year cannot by divided by 4, it is not a leap year
  { cout <<"Year " <<year <<" is not a leap year" <<endl; }
else
  { cout << "Year " << year << " is a leap year" << endl; }
```

Actually, for an algorithm that is that simple, it is surprisingly accurate. It accumulates 1 day error approximately every 130 years. This is why when this algorithm was finally replaced by a more accurate algorithm after being about 1700 years in operation, the calendar correction was only 14 days.

So the more-accurate rule is that if the year is divisible by 4, it is a leap year, but if it is divisible by 100, it is not a leap year. Our code could look something like this:

```
if (year % 4 != 0)              // if year is not divisible by 4, it is not a leap year
  { cout <<"Year " <<year <<" is not a leap year" <<endl; }
else                            // when it is divisible by 4, it is a leap year
  if (year % 100 == 0)          // unless it is divisible by 100
    { cout <<"Year " <<year <<" is not a leap year" <<endl; }
  else
    { cout << "Year " << year << " is a leap year" << endl; }
```

This is, as they say, the truth and only the truth, but it is not the *whole* truth. This rule shaves away one day every hundred years, and this is too much. So, the correct rule is that if the year is divisible by 100 it is *not* a leap year unless the year *is* divisible by 400. Then it is a leap year again. "Unless" is difficult to translate from requirements into code. The logical operator AND (&&) or a nested conditional is often used. Listing 4.8 gives a solution to this problem. If the year is not divisible by 4, it is not a leap year, period. If it is divisible by 4 and is divisible by 100, it is still not a leap year unless it is divisible by 400—then it is a leap year. If the year is divisible by 4 but is not divisible by 100, it is a leap year. Systems analysis is not easy. Imagine doing it every day for a living.

Listing 4.8 A solution to the leap year problem.

```
#include <iostream>
using namespace std;

int main ()
{
  int year;
  cout << "Please enter year: ";
  cin >> year;
  if (year % 4 != 0)                        // not divisible by 4, period
    cout <<"Year " << year <<" is not a leap year" << endl;
  else
    if (year % 100 == 0)
```

```
  if (year/%/400 == 0)              // divisible by 400 (hence, by 100)
    cout <<"Year " << year <<" is a leap year" << endl;
  else                              // divisible by 4 and by 100 but not by 400
    cout <<"Year "<<year<<" is not a leap year" <<endl;
  else                              // divisible by 4 but not divisible by 400
  cout << "Year " << year << " is a leap year" << endl;
  return 0;
}
```

There are three conditional expressions here, so the worst case scenario might involve six test cases. However, the expressions are related. There are only four branches to exercise, and we can get away with only four test cases. We need to cover the following cases:

- year % 4 != 0 is true (e.g., 1999)
- year % 4 != 0 is false (that is, year % 4 == 0 is true), year % 100 == 0 is true, and year % 400 == 0 (e.g., 2000)
- year % 4 == 0 and year % 100 == 0 are both true, but year % 400 == 0 is false (e.g., 1900)
- year % 4 == 0 is true but year % 100 == 0 is false (e.g., 2004)

Figure 4–17 shows the results of the execution of this code for the year 2000. There are a number of problems with this code that have little to do with its correctness but are directly related to its aesthetic attributes. There are three levels of nesting, and this clearly calls for merging of conditions. The case where year % 4 == 0 is true has two branches for the leap year, and

```
Please enter year: 2000
Year 2000 is a leap year
```

Figure 4–17
Output for Listing 4.8 (year is divisible by 4, 100, and 400).

they also should be combined. How to do that? First, experiment with negating conditions so that similar branches are brought closer to each other, for example,

```
if (year % 4 != 0)           // not divisible by 4, end of story
  cout <<"Year " << year <<" is not a leap year" << endl;
else
  if (year % 100 == 0)
    if (year % 400 != 0)     // divisible by 100 but not by 400)
      cout <<"Year "<<year<<" is not a leap year" <<endl;
    else                     // divisible by 4, by 100 and by 400
      cout <<"Year " << year <<" is a leap year" << endl;
  else                       // divisible by 4 but not divisible by 100
    cout << "Year " << year << " is a leap year" << endl;
```

Now you can combine the two conditions that follow each other using the AND operation, and the last two clauses for a leap year can be combined, too. That gives a more concise solution:

```
if (year % 4 != 0)                   // not divisible by 4, period
  cout <<"Year " << year <<" is not a leap year" << endl;
else
  if (year % 100==0 && year % 400!=0)   // by 100 but not by 400
    cout <<"Year "<<year<<" is not a leap year" <<endl;
  else                               // divisible by 4 but not divisible by 100
    cout << "Year " << year << " is a leap year" << endl;
```

Isn't this nice? There are only two levels of nesting, and this is quite acceptable. But the same processing related to non-leap year is repeated, and this is not good enough for a C++ programmer. The year is not a leap year when the year is not divisible by four or when the condition (year % 100 == 0 and year % 400 != 0) is true. This calls for the OR operation, right? Listing 4.9 gives us the answer that is not only correct and efficient, but also is concise and elegant.

Listing 4.9 An optimized solution to the leap year problem.

```
#include <iostream>
using namespace std;

int main ()
{
  int year;
  cout << "Please enter year: ";
  cin >> year;
  if (year % 4 != 0 || year % 100 == 0 && year % 400 != 0)
    cout <<"Year " << year << " is not a leap year" <<endl;
  else
    cout << "Year " << year << " is a leap year" << endl;
  return 0;
}
```

Running this program with the test cases just discussed produces the same results as for Listing 4.8 (Figure 4–17).

There is no question that the program in Listing 4.9 is better than the program in Listing 4.8. Whether or not the time spent on eliminating six extra lines of code (and proving that it was done correctly) is well spent is debatable.

Sometimes, when I spend a few hours trying to optimize complex conditional statements, I feel proud of the results. Whether these efforts bring more than just the use of boiled water and whether such use of time is economically justifiable is not clear. See for yourself.

Iteration

Conditional statements play a very important role in programming. They are the workhorse of every program. But they cannot do the job alone. In every program, we deal with the situation when we have to repeat the same sequence of statements, for different customers, transactions, online clients, and so on. These tasks require iteration.

For repeated actions, C++ provides three iterative statements: `while` loops, `do-while` loops, and `for` loops. Each kind of C++ loop controls the repetition of a single statement (which ends with a semicolon) or a compound statement (block) enclosed in braces (and there is no semicolon after the closing brace of the block). To control iterations, all types of loops use logical expressions similar to logical expressions used in conditional statements. These logical conditions evaluate to `true` or `false` (nonzero or 0). They are tested for each loop repetition. When the loop condition becomes `false`, the iterations are terminated. If the condition is `true`, the body of the loop (the statement or the block) is repeated. Notice that I said "for each loop repetition" and not "before each loop repetition" because the loops differ in the way in which the loop conditions are tested. No matter what the loop design, the loop body has to do something that affects the loop condition. If that does not happen, the loop condition might stay `true` forever—a serious menace for every program that uses loops.

The `while` loop tests the loop condition before each iteration through the loop body and stops the iterations when the loop condition becomes `false`. The loop expression is tested before the first iteration too. Hence, zero repetitions of the body is possible if the loop condition is `false` when the loop is first entered.

The `do-while` loop tests the loop condition after each iteration and stops looping when the condition becomes `false`. Since the condition is tested the first time only after the first iteration and not before it, the loop always results in at least one repetition.

The `for` loop is often designed to produce a predefined fixed number of repetitions.

Usually, the same algorithm could be designed using any loop format, and the choice is a matter of taste. Sometimes, one of the formats fits better than other forms: it takes fewer statements, or the statements fit together better.

The Use of the WHILE Loop

The `while` loop is executed as a single statement; the difference between other statements and the loop is that the loop body can be executed repeatedly depending on the value of the logical condition of the loop.

The `while` loop has the following logical structure:

```
previous_statement;
while (expression)        // this is the loop expression
  statement;              // this is the loop body
next_statement;
```

The control construct repeats the loop body while its logical condition (expression) is `true`. Eventually (or even before the first pass) the condition becomes `false`. When this happens, the loop statement is skipped and `next_statement` is executed. When the loop controls several statements, block scope delimiters (braces) are used.

```
while (expression)
  { statement;            // notice the indentation
  . . .
    statement; }          // end of loop body
```

It is a common error to try to design a loop so that the body does not change the value of the expression to `false`; the execution continues in an "infinite loop" and the program has to be terminated with the help of the operating system.

Usually, loop design revolves around the concept that can be called current data. We process some data items repeatedly. This means that the data item has to be initialized, evaluated, processed (printed, used in computations, saved, or whatever the algorithm needs). Then it has to be modified for the next iteration and evaluated again and processed again, and so on until the last item is processed. The processing steps could be folded into the `while` loop format using the following pattern:

```
initialize_current_data;
while (evaluate_current_data)     // decision point
  { process_current_data;         // main goal of this code
    change_current_data; }        // do not forget this step!
```

Let us consider an example of transaction processing. For simplicity sake, let's assume that the program enters and adds up five amounts (I will make it more realistic soon). Since I know the total number of transactions, I can have a variable that counts the number of transactions already processed. This is part of current data: It has to be initialized to 0 and incremented by 1 after each transaction. Another element of current data is the total of the amount entered. It also has to be initialized to 0, and the transaction amount is added to the total at each iteration. However, the total cannot be used to check whether or not the loop should be terminated. The count of transactions can. Hence, the components of the loop are as follows:

- `initialize_current_data`: set count to 1, total to 0
- `evaluate_current_data`: test if count of transactions does not exceed 5
- `process_current_data`: enter next transaction amount, add it to total
- `change_current_data`: increment transaction count by 1, go test it

Listing 4.10 shows an implementation of this design. This design is hardly practical. It is unlikely that the application is written for the specific size of the data set.

Listing 4.10   A `while` loop with an infinite number of iterations.

```
#include <iostream>
using namespace std;

int main ()
{
  double total, amount; int count;
  total = 0.0; count = 1;                 // initialize current data
  while (count <= 5)                      // evaluate current data
    { cout << "Enter the amount: ";
      cin >> amount;                      // enter current data
      total += amount; }                  // process current data
  cout<< "\nTotal of 5 transactions is "<<total << endl;
  return 0;
}
```

This is a typical example of a programming error. The loop executes as long as count does not exceed 5. When count reaches the value 6, the loop should terminate. The problem is that count will never reach 6 (or any other value) because the loop body does not change the value of count. To correct the situation, the loop body should increment the value of count by 1 during each iteration. Doing it at the bottom of loop body is appropriate.

```
while (count <= 5)          // evaluate current data
  { cout << "Enter the amount: ";
    cin >> amount;          // enter current data
    total += amount;        // process current data
    count++; }              // change current data: do not forget it!
```

We would like to be able to write applications where a segment of code (e.g., processing a transaction) is applied as many times as needed for each element of input data, and the size of the data set is different for different runs of the program. Hard-coding the size of the data set as in Listing 4.10 is not appropriate. The program has to know when the last element of the data set is processed. One of the ways to solve this problem is to ask the user directly how many items there are to process and use this value as the limit in the loop condition. However, the user is not always available. Input data, for example, can come through a communications line from a remote computer. In this case, the first item of data is often the count of data items that follow. But the size of the data set might not be known in advance, or it might be too large: It is one thing to count five items and another thing to count several hundred or several thousand items.

A more common approach to iterative processing is to enter data items one by one, while they are available, and ask the user (or the input file or a communication line) whether there is yet another item to process.

There are two ways to do this. One is to have separate variables to store the transaction data and the user response to the question whether there are more data. After entering each transaction, the user answers the question whether there are more entries to process. The second way is to enter a special value (called the sentinel value) that tells the application that the data set is finished. A sentinel is a special value that is not valid as normal data and is used only to indicate the end of valid data, like a negative or 0 value for transaction amounts. When the data arrive through communications lines, the sentinel value is the last value in the data set.

For transaction amounts, such a special value could be 0 or a negative value. Listing 4.11 shows the implementation of the loop with a negative or 0 sentinel value.

Listing 4.11   Implementing the `while` loop with a negative or zero sentinel value.

```
#include <iostream>
using namespace std;

int main ()
{
  double total, amount; int count;
  total = 0.0; count = 0;              // different initialization
  amount = 1.0;                        // an artificial trick: why 1 and not 10?
  while (amount > 0)                   // evaluate current data
    { cout << "Enter amount (negative or zero to end): ";
      cin >> amount;                   // enter current data
      total += amount;                 // process current data
      count++; }
  cout << "\nTotal of " << count << " transactions is "
     << total << endl;
  return 0;
}
```

In Listing 4.10, the loop continued as long as `count` did not exceed 5. Before the first pass through the loop, count was 1, before the second pass it was two, before the fifth pass it was 5, and after the fifth pass, when `count <= 5` became `false`, it was 6. This is no good for Listing 4.11, where at the end of the run we want the value in `count` to reflect the number of items processed. This is why count is initialized to 0 in Listing 4.11 rather than to one.

This is the concern that a C++ programmer (actually, any programmer) should always think about when building the loops. Are my initial values correct? Do they assure correct terminating values? This is why I used such a small value of items in this example: to make sure I can trace the loop iterations easily. The output of a sample run for Listing 4.11 is shown in Figure 4–18.

Figure 4–18   Output for Listing 4.11 with a negative or zero sentinel value.

```
Enter amount (negative or zero to end): 22
Enter amount (negative or zero to end): 33
Enter amount (negative or zero to end): 44
Enter amount (negative or zero to end): -1

Total of 4 transactions is 98
```

But wait a minute—the number of transactions is incorrect! Before the user entered –1.0, the value of count was 3, and it was correct. After the user entered –1.0, it became 4, and this was not correct. To add insult to injury, this negative amount was also added to total, and the value of total was not correct either.

There are a number of solutions to these technical problems. We can initialize count to –1. Or we can decrement count after the loop. The same can be done to the total amount. The code after the loop could look this way:

```
count--; total -= amount;          // after-loop correction
cout << "\nTotal of " << count << " transactions is "
     << total << endl;
```

This solution is not elegant, but it works. Another solution is to add a conditional statement in the middle of the loop and change the values of total and count only if the value of amount is not a sentinel value:

```
while (amount > 0)                 // evaluate current data
  { cout << "Enter amount (negative or zero to end): ";
    cin >> amount;                 // enter current data
    if (amount > 0)                // test for end of data
      { total += amount;           // process current data
        count++; } }
```

You see that all these fixes eliminate the problems by contributing to the complexity of code. They are not elegant. Often (but not always) this is a manifestation of a conceptual problem. And indeed, there is another problem with the solution in Listing 4.11, and this problem is not technical. It is conceptual. It is the issue of the first pass through the loop. When memory for C++ variables is allocated, it contains random values (which is not the whole truth, and we will talk about that later). This random value in some runs of the program might be 0. This means that the program will terminate without processing input data. To prevent that, I initialize amount to some value just to prevent the loop from terminating prematurely.

This is not correct from the software engineering point of view. I am using the value 1.0 that has no semantic meaning in the context of the application. If it were 2.0, the result would be the same. This value sends no message from the designer to the maintenance programmer and hence clogs the channel of communication between them. The maintainer will spend some time figuring out what this 1.0 means before he or she realizes that it means nothing. Granted, this doesn't take a long time. However, it is from these kinds of glitches that the complexity of applications increases above what it should be.

Another problem with this loop is that it does not treat the sentinel value correctly. When the user enters the negative amount (or a negative amount arrives as the end of transmission through a communications line), this value is first added to `total` and only after that is used to terminate the loop.

A good solution to these problems is to change the structure of the loop body. In Listing 4.11, the body of the loop first accepts `amount` (it might be a sentinel) and then processes it. What I suggest here is to first process `amount` that has been entered earlier, during the previous iteration, and only at the end of the loop body accept `amount` for the next iteration. The loop structure should look like this:

```
while (amount > 0)                    // evaluate current data
  { total += amount;                  // process current data
    count++;
    cout << "Enter amount (negative or zero to end): ";
    cin >> amount; }                  // change current data
```

But what about the very first iteration through the loop? The value 1.0 that I used in Listing 4.11 is not appropriate. Should I initialize the variable `amount` to 0? When 0 is added to `total`, no harm is done. This is possible, but it will terminate the loop on the first test—the condition `amount > 0` will evaluate to `false`. Also, this solution would not work if we needed to print the amount that was entered or process it in some other nontrivial way.

A good solution here is what is known as a *prime read* technique. You accept the first value before the loop, process that value at the top of the loop, and then accept the next value at the bottom of the loop and process it at the top of the loop during next iteration. You can see this solution on Listing 4.12, and the results of the test run on Figure 4–19.

Listing 4.12 Implementing the `while` loop with the prime read.

```
#include <iostream>
using namespace std;

int main ()
{
  double total, amount; int count;
  total = 0.0; count = 0;                   // different initialization
  cout << "Enter amount (negative or zero to end): ";
  cin >> amount;                            // enter current data (first time)
  while (amount > 0)                        // evaluate current data
  { total += amount;                        // process current data
    count++;
    cout << "Enter amount (negative or zero to end): ";
```

```
   cin >> amount; }                    // change current data
 cout << "\nTotal of " << count << " transactions is "
      << total << endl;
 return 0;
}
```

All our problems (and their complex fixes) are gone. The variables `count` and `total` are initialized to their logical initial value (0). The variable `amount` is not initialized at all because whatever value we would want to put there will not be used—it will be overwritten by the input operation. There is no postprocessing after the loop that adjusts the values modified incorrectly by the loop.

The drawback of this solution is that the input statements are coded twice. In real life, it is not a big deal because entering and verifying input data takes more than two statements and will probably be encapsulated in a function. So, we will have two calls to that input function, and we can live with that. But no, nothing is perfect.

Before I go on to discuss the `do-while` loops, I would like to illustrate some other issues of the `while` loop design. I will use processing of a stream of characters as an example. For simplicity of the example, I will just echo the characters, count their total, and also count the number of spaces, if any. The processing should continue until the user presses the `Enter` key (the character '\n'). I will use the loop structure with the prime read. The first character is entered before the `while` loop; at the top of the loop I echo the character that has been entered before; count the number of characters; and check whether it is a blank character. At the bottom of the loop, the next character is read. The loop condition checks whether or not this next character is the newline character. If it is *not* (the loop condition is `true`), processing continues, the top of the loop echoes the character and counts it, and then the bottom of the loop accepts the next character. If it *is* the newline character, the loop condition evaluates to `false`, and the loop terminates.

Figure 4–19 Output for Listing 4.12 with the prime read.

```
Enter amount (negative or zero to end): 22
Enter amount (negative or zero to end): 33
Enter amount (negative or zero to end): 44
Enter amount (negative or zero to end): -1

Total of 3 transactions is 99
```

To enter the character, I use the `get()` function from the `iostream` library, which I send as a message to the `cin` object. You already saw the message syntax in the section, "Classes" in Chapter 2, and it is nice to continue using it. Actually, all that you should know to use it correctly is that the function call `cin.get()` returns the next character from the input buffer.

Listing 4.13 shows the solution to this problem, and Figure 4–20 demonstrates the results of the test run.

Listing 4.13   The `while` loop with the prime read for reading characters.

```
#include <iostream>
using namespace std;

int main ()
{
  char ch; int count = 0, spaces = 0;      // initialize counters
  cout << "\nType a sentence, press Enter\n";
  ch = cin.get();                          // prime read for the loop
  while (ch != '\n')                       // no semicolon after the condition
    { cout << ch;                          // process data: echo, check, count
      if (ch == ' ')
        spaces++;
      count++;
      ch = cin.get(); }                    // change current data
  cout << "\nTotal number of characters " << count << endl;
  cout << "Number of spaces is " << spaces << endl;
  return 0;
}
```

Here again we bump into the difference between how things look and what they are in reality. The code indicates that the first character the user entered is displayed before the user entered the second character, and the second character is displayed before the user enters the third character, and so on. If you run this program, you will see that the characters are not displayed at all until you press the Enter key. After that they are displayed all at once. The reason is that the call `cin.get()` reads not from the keyboard but

Figure 4–20 Run results for Listing 4.13 (processing input characters).

```
Type a sentence, press Enter
This is a test.
This is a test.
Total number of characters 15
Number of spaces is 3
```

from an internal buffer in computer memory. When the user presses key-board keys, the data are sent to the buffer but become available to the program only after the user presses the Enter key or when the buffer becomes full. The use of buffers can improve program performance when the program needs frequent file I/O operations, each for small amount of data. With buffering, the slow external file I/O is done only once for a larger amount of data. (It takes almost the same time, independent of the amount of data.) After that, multiple I/O operations are directed to the buffer in memory much faster. (it does not do much for this program.) So, do not be surprised if you do not see the output while you are typing data.

Notice that the loop condition while (ch != \n) is tested immediately after the statement ch = cin.get(); the first time around it is the statement before the loop; at all other times it is the statement at the bottom of the loop body. This code structure invites the use of popular C++ idiom: combining the assignment and testing of the condition. Listing 4.14 shows this important idiom.

Listing 4.14   The while loop with the assignment in the loop condition.

```cpp
#include <iostream>
using namespace std;

int main ()
{
  char ch; int count = 0, spaces = 0;       // initialize counters
  cout << "\nType a sentence, press Enter\n";
  while ((ch = cin.get()) != '\n')          // change current data
  { cout << ch;                             // process next symbol
    if (ch == ' ') spaces++;                // OK for a single line
    count++; }
  cout << "\nTotal number of characters " << count << endl;
  cout << "Number of spaces is " << spaces << endl;
  return 0;
}
```

This is a very popular C++ idiom. You could not use it in the program in Listing 4.12 because the input statement there (cin >> amount;) does not return the value entered by the user. Actually, it does return a value, but this is the value of the cin object, not the value entered by the user. The input statement in Listing 4.13 (ch = cin.get();) does return the character value and can be used in the loop condition here, in Listing 4.14.

Notice the parentheses around the input statement in Listing 4.14. Omitting them is not a syntax error, but it changes the meaning of the code.

```
cout << "\nType a sentence, press Enter\n";
while (ch = cin.get() != '\n')          // no parentheses around input statement
{ cout << ch;
  if (ch == ' ')
    spaces++;                           // process next symbol
  count++;  }
```

Priority of operators is important here. The assignment operator is of lower priority than is the comparison for inequality. This means that the compiler sees this code as

```
    while (ch = (cin.get() != '\n'))      // quite a different story
```

The character is entered and then is compared with the newline character. For all characters (except the very last character in the input) the result of comparison is true (they are not newline characters), and the variable ch gets the value 1 (it is not a printable code). The characters are displayed incorrectly, and the number of spaces is reported as 0.

Do not complain about C++ operations performed in the wrong order. Know that order, and avoid problems. Use parentheses if in doubt (and even if you are not in doubt).

Iterations with the DO-WHILE Loop

The do-while loop is very similar to the while loop. Often, they can be used interchangeably. The major difference is that the do-while loop tests its condition at the bottom of the loop body, after each iteration, whereas the while loop tests its condition at the top of the body, before each iteration.

Similar to the `while` loop, the `do-while` loop controls the repeated execution of the body consisting of a single statement (or a statement block in braces). The `do-while` loop has the following general structure:

```
previous_statement;
do
  statement;                     // or { statements }
while (expression);
next_statement;
```

After the `previous_statement` is executed, the loop body following the `do` keyword is executed. After that, the loop expression is evaluated. If it evaluates to `true`, the loop body is executed again. If the expression evaluates to `false`, the iterations are terminated and the `next_statement` is executed.

Because of this structure, the loop body is guaranteed to be executed at least once. The loop body must change the loop expression eventually for the loop to terminate and to avoid the infinite iterations.

To prevent confusion, programmers often use braces, even for a loop body with a single statement, like the following:

```
do
  { statement; }
while (expression);
```

In the `do-while` loop, it is necessary to put the semicolon after the loop expression to avoid a syntax error. This is just the opposite of the situation with the `while` loop, where you do not put the semicolon after the loop condition. Make sure you see that putting a semicolon after the loop expression in the `while` loop does not confuse the compiler enough to generate a syntax error, but confuses it enough to generate incorrect code (a semantic error). To indicate to the maintenance programmer that this `while` keyword is special and hence the semicolon should be used at the end of the line, some programmers put the closing brace on the same line as the `while` keyword.

```
do
  { statement;
} while (expression);        // the brace warns about the presence of the semicolon
```

The strategy for the loop body design is similar to that of the `while` loop.

```
initialize_current_data;
do { change_current_data;
     process_current_data;
     } while (evaluate_current_data);
```

For the example of transaction processing and computing the total amount, components of this structure should perform the following operations:

```
initialize_current_data:  set total and count to zero
change_current_data:      enter new value of amount
process_current_data:     if positive, increment total and count
evaluate_current_data:    test if the amount is a sentinel
```

Listing 4.15 shows this version of the program. The output of this version is of course the same as on Figure 4–19 for Listing 4.12.

Listing 4.15   The do-while loop without the prime read.

```cpp
#include <iostream>
using namespace std;

int main ()
{
  double total, amount; int count;
  total = 0.0; count = 0;              // initialize current data
do {
  cout << "Enter amount (negative or zero to end): ";
  cin >> amount;                       // enter (change) current data
  if (amount > 0)                      // check for end of data
  { total += amount;                   // process current data
    count++; }
  } while (amount > 0);                // evaluate current data
  cout << "\nTotal of " << count << " transactions is "
       << total << endl;
  return 0;
}
```

You can see that the do-while loop simplifies initialization and eliminates the need for the prime read (compare with Listing 4.12). On the other hand, it requires an extra conditional statement in the middle of the loop body to avoid erroneous treatment of the sentinel value as a legitimate input value.

Counting space characters in an input line can be done in a do-while loop as in Listing 4.16. The use of do-while loop eliminates the need for the prime read. Similar to the previous example in Listing 4.15, this structure requires checking the body of the loop for whether the sentinel value has arrived. Hence, evaluation of current data is done twice—first time in the body of the loop and the second time in the loop logical condition.

Listing 4.16   The do-while **loop for character input.**

```cpp
#include <iostream>
using namespace std;

int main ()
{
  char ch; int count = 0, spaces = 0;      // initialize data
  cout << "\nType a sentence, press Enter\n";
do {
    ch = cin.get();                        // change current data
    if (ch != '\n')                        // check for end of data
    { cout << ch;
      if (ch == ' ') spaces++;             // process current data
      count++; }
    } while (ch != '\n');                  // evaluate current data
  cout << "\nTotal number of characters " << count << endl;
  cout << "Number of spaces is " << spaces << endl;
  return 0;
}
```

Here, the value of character ch is set by the assignment and is soon tested in the conditional statements. This opens the opportunity to combine the assignment and the test in one statement, as in Listing 4.17.

Listing 4.17   The do-while **loop with assignment within a conditional statement.**

```cpp
#include <iostream>
using namespace std;

int main ()
{
  char ch; int count = 0, spaces = 0;      // initialize data
  cout << "\nType a sentence, press Enter\n";
  do {
    if ((ch = cin.get())!= '\n')           // change current data
    { cout << ch;
      if (ch == ' ') spaces++;             // process current data
      count++; }
    } while (ch != '\n');                  // evaluate current data
  cout << "\nTotal number of characters " << count << endl;
  cout << "Number of spaces is " << spaces << endl;
  return 0;
}
```

Again, this optimization does not change program performance or correctness, but it makes code more concise and elegant.

Iterations with the FOR Loop

The for loop is usually considered an appropriate loop when the number of repetitions is known in advance, before the loop starts. This is not an important factor. This form of iteration visually brings together the three most important elements of the loop design: initialization of the current value before the first iteration, evaluation of the current value before the start of next iteration, and change of the current value after the iteration (before the next iteration). In other loops, these elements are spread through different places in the loop.

The for statement has the following standard form, where we combine three expressions that control the execution of the loop body in parentheses (initialization of current data, its evaluation, and its modification). Just to make sure that learning C++ is never dull, these expressions are separated by semicolons. They are separated, not terminated (as statements are). This is why the last expression does not have a semicolon before the closing parenthesis.

```
previous_statement;
for (InitialExpr; ContinuingExpr; IncrementExpr)
  statement;                      // compound statement in braces is OK
next_statement;
```

InitialExpr is evaluated only once, before the first iteration; this is a convenient place to initialize values for the loop setup: index, count of items, total amount, and so on.

IncrementExpr is evaluated at the end of each iteration, immediately after the loop body is executed. This is a convenient place to change current data, increment indexes, counts, tallies, and so on.

ContinuingExpr is evaluated before the first iteration and before each succeeding iteration. This expression evaluates the need for the next loop iteration. If this expression evaluates to true, the loop statement is executed, and immediately after that IncrementExpr is executed; after that, ContinuingExpr is evaluated again to decide the need for the next iteration. If this expression evaluates to false, the loop is terminated.

Make sure you see that the for loop is equivalent to the following while loop:

```
previous_statement;
InitialExpr;
while (ContinuingExpr)
  { statement;                    // or a sequence of statements
    IncrementExpr; }
next_statement;
```

Listing 4.18 shows the implementation of the transaction processing example using the `for` loop. The initialization includes setting `count` to 0; the test for continuation includes the test for the sentinel value (this is why the prime read is still needed); the increment includes incrementing the variable `count`.

Listing 4.18   Implementing transaction processing in a `for` loop.

```cpp
#include <iostream>
using namespace std;

int main ()
{
  double total, amount; int count;
  total = 0.0;                           // different initialization
  cout << "Enter amount (negative or zero to end): ";
  cin >> amount;                         // enter current data
  for (count=0; amount>0; count++)       // three expressions
  { total += amount;                     // process current data
    cout << "Enter amount (negative or zero to end): ";
    cin >> amount; }                     // change current data
  cout << "\nTotal of " << count << " transactions is "
       << total << endl;
  return 0;
}
```

Each of three expressions in the `for` loop is an expression. This "profound" observation means that a sequence of expressions separated by commas can be used for each of these expressions. Remember, a comma is a full-fledged operator in C++: it evaluates its operands (expressions) from left to right and returns the rightmost value. In the `for` loop, return values are of no importance—they are discarded. The only exception is the `ContinuingExpr` that defines whether the next iteration should take place. This means that we can expand the `InitialExpr` as in Listing 4.19.

Listing 4.19   A `for` loop with comma operator in its initial expressions.

```cpp
#include <iostream>
using namespace std;

int main ()
{
  double total, amount; int count;            // no initialization
  cout << "Enter amount (negative or zero to end): ";
  cin >> amount;                              // enter current data
  for (total=0.0, count=0; amount>0; count++)
  { total+=amount;
```

```
    cout << "Enter amount (negative or zero to end): ";
    cin >> amount; }                           // change current data
  cout << "\nTotal of " << count << " transactions is "
       << total << endl;
  return 0;
}
```

An even more interesting representation is possible for the character processing example as shown in Listing 4.20. Here, the comma-separated expressions are used in the initial expression, and the assignment is used as a part of
comparison in the continuing expression (compare this version with Listing
4.13 and Listing 4.16).

Listing 4.20 The for loop with assignment in its ContinuingExpr.

```
#include <iostream>
using namespace std;

int main ()
{
  char ch; int count, spaces;            // no initialization
  cout << "\nType a sentence, press Enter\n";
  for (count=0, spaces=0; (ch=cin.get())!='\n'; count++)
    { cout << ch;                        // process next input symbol
      if (ch == ' ') spaces++; }
  cout << "\nTotal number of characters " << count << endl;
  cout << "Number of spaces is " << spaces << endl;
  return 0;
}
```

The next interesting thing that we can do in a for loop is to define variables within the loop, in its InitialExpr. Consider, for example, Listing
4.21. The program adds up the squares of first natural numbers. The number
of squares to add is entered by the user. The for loop initializes the variable
n to 1, tests whether the value of n reached the limit num, and increments n
after each iteration. Since variable n is used in the loop only, there is no need
to define it in the broader scope. This is why this variable is defined in the for
statement rather than in the main() function. This is a popular C++ idiom.
The test run of the program is shown in Figure 4–21.

Listing 4.21 Computing sum of squares using the `for` loop.

```cpp
#include <iostream>
using namespace std;

int main ()
{
  int sum=0, num;
  cout << "\nEnter the number of squares to add: ";
  cin >> num;
  for (int n = 1; n <= num; n++)
    { sum += n * n; }
  cout << "Total of squares is " << sum << endl;
  return 0;
}
```

As we saw in Listing 4.19 and Listing 4.20, C++ allows the programmer to initialize several variables in the initial expression of the `for` loop. C++ also allows you to define several variables in the initial expression provided they are all of the same type. In Listing 4.22, both variable n and variable sum are defined in the loop. In addition, the variable sum is updated in the continuing expression using the comma operator as a tool. The output of this version is the same as for Listing 4.21. As you see, the loop body degenerates into an empty statement.

Listing 4.22 A `for` loop that degenerates to an empty statement.

```cpp
#include <iostream>
using namespace std;

int main ()
{
  int num;
  cout << "\nEnter the number of squares to add: ";
  cin >> num;
  for (int sum = 0, n = 1; n <= num; sum+=n*n, n++);     // !!
  cout << "Total of squares is " << sum << endl;
  return 0;
}
```

```
Enter the number of squares to add: 4
Total of squares is 30
```

Figure 4-21
Run results for Listing 4.21 (adding squares of natural numbers).

Many programmers do not like to use a semicolon at the end of the loop statement. It is not a common place for the semicolon, and it can confuse the maintenance programmer. To pass the designer's knowledge to the maintainer, these programmers put the semicolon on a separate line, for example,

```
for (int sum = 0, n = 1; n <= num; sum+=n*n, n++)
    ;                                            // !!
```

Some programmers stay away from empty statements altogether because they are too confusing, using instead the structure similar to Listing 4.21, with at least one statement in the body of the loop. The biggest problem with Listing 4.21 is that of portability. The variable sum is defined within the loop, but it is used after the loop terminates. The original C++ allowed that. However, the new standard C++ treats it as a syntax error; you can define in the loop only those variables that are not used outside of the loop. Most compilers compile this code, but it should not be used. It is probably a good idea not to optimize for loops too much.

C++ Jump Statements

The conditional and the loop statements are indispensable tools of programming. We cannot write even the simplest program without using them. They are an essential necessity. Other control statements are useful but not necessary. They represent syntactic fluff that makes our programs more concise and aesthetically appealing.

These other C++ control statements are different sorts of jumps. Program designers love jumps because they allow them to transfer control to any place in the program source code effectively and efficiently. However, the program that uses jumps is more difficult to analyze than the program that does not use jumps. To understand the results of the execution of a program statement when the flow of control is sequential, the maintainer has to understand only those statements that precede immediately the one being analyzed. When the program control can jump to that statement from different places in the program, all these places can affect how this statement works. This makes the task of the maintainer more difficult. This is why jumps have a bad reputation in programming.

C++ tries to strike a compromise. It does allow jumps so that the programmers are able to write concise and powerful code. On the other hand, it restricts the jumps so that the maintenance programmer does not have too difficult a task to do.

The BREAK Statement

The break statement is used for immediate exit from a loop; after executing this statement, control flow jumps to the statement that follows the loop. It can be used with the while, for, and do-while loops. Abandoning a loop in the middle, however drastic, does not make the flow of control too confusing. However, the break statement cannot be used to get out of a branch of an if statement: this would result in too convoluted a flow of control. Later in this section, you will see the use of the break statement within switch statements.

It does not make much sense to execute the break statement unconditionally. That would mean that the loop is not executed at all. The break statement is usually executed in a conditional statement; the logical expression of this conditional specifies the condition for terminating the loop. Often, this simplifies the loop condition; for example, the loop might be set up to go "forever".

Consider, for example, Listing 4.12 with a loop that processes input data until a sentinel value appears. The loop condition uses the value of the variable amount. Hence, this variable has to be initialized before the loop, and this is the job that the prime read does.

```
cout << "Enter amount (negative or zero to end): ";
cin >> amount;                              // enter current data
while (amount > 0)                          // evaluate current data
{ total += amount;                          // process current data
  count++;
  cout << "Enter amount (negative or zero to end): ";
  cin >> amount; }                          // change current data
```

Using the break statement allows me to replace the loop condition with something that does not change, for example, while(1 == 1). Since this condition is always true, there is less chance to make a mistake writing this expression. Since this condition does not use the value of amount, there is no need to initialize this value. Hence, the need for prime read is eliminated, and the new value of amount can be accepted at the top of the loop, not at the bottom. The problem with this loop structure is how to terminate the loop when the sentinel value appears. The break statement provides the solution. I want to continue iterations when amount > 0. Hence, the loop termination condition is the negation of this one, that is, amount <= 0.0. When this (negated) condition holds true, the break statement is executed and control flow leaves the loop and jumps to the next statement.

```
while (1 == 1)                                // loop forever
{ cout << "Enter amount (negative or zero to end): ";
  cin >> amount;                              // change current data
  if (amount <= 0.0) break;                   // explicit break
  total += amount;                            // process current data
  count++; }
```

One might argue that moving the test amount > 0 from the loop expression to the break statement does not change code complexity much. But it allows me to eliminate the prime read.

The do-while version of this algorithm (see Listing 4.15) does not use the prime read, but it has to check twice whether the next input value is a legal value, in the middle of the loop and in the loop condition:

```
do {
  cout << "Enter amount (negative or zero to end): ";
  cin >> amount;                    // enter (change) current data
  if (amount > 0)                   // evaluate current data
  { total += amount;                // process current data
    count++; }
  } while (amount > 0);             // evaluate current data again
```

The use of the break statement allows me to replace the loop condition with the trivial condition that is always true (like, 1==1 or even 1). To terminate the loop when the sentinel value appears, the condition amount > 0 has to be negated similar to the previous example. When amount <= 0, the break statement transfers control to the statement that follows the loop. The structure of the loop is simplified somewhat; there is no need for the local compound statement with its braces. Notice that the loop while(1) is a legitimate alternative to while(1 == 1) since a nonzero value is true in C++.

```
do {
  cout << "Enter amount (negative or zero to end): ";
  cin >> amount;               // enter (change) current data
  if (amount <= 0) break;      // evaluate current data
  total += amount;             // process current data
  count++;                     // no need for compound statement
} while (1);                   // no need to evaluate current data here
```

Yet another example of the use of the break statement is range checking, which is often used for input validation. Let us assume that the user has to enter the response, for example, in the range from 1 to 5. If the user makes a mistake, the input has to be repeated until a legal value is entered. In Listing 4.23, the do-while loop is used because its body has to be executed at least once. The variable error_flag is set to 1 if the input value is invalid and to 0 if it is within the range.

Listing 4.23   Using the `do-while` loop for input validation.

```cpp
#include <iostream>
using namespace std;
const int N = 5;

int main ()
{
  int num, error_flag;
  do {
    cout << "Enter number between 1 and " << N << ": ";
    cin >> num;
    if (num < 1 || num > N)
      { cout << "This is incorrect; please repeat.\n";
        error_flag = 1; }
    else
      error_flag = 0;
  } while (error_flag == 1);
  cout << "Your input is " << num << endl;
  return 0;
}
```

This is a popular technique for communication between different parts of the program. In one part of the program (the loop condition), we have to know what happened in another part of the program (the body of the loop). To make it possible, in one part of the program we test the variable that is set in another part of the program.

Some programmers do not like proliferation of flags and other control variables whose only goal is to carry information from one part of the program to another. This increases coupling and complexity of the code. Another way to implement this algorithm is to repeat the test in the loop condition instead of using the error flag.

```cpp
do {
  cout << "Enter number between 1 and " << N << ": ";
  cin >> num;
  if (num < 1 || num > N)
    cout << "This is incorrect; please repeat.\n";
} while (num < 1 || num > N);
```

This is a more concise solution. Yet another approach is to use the infinite loop and break it when the value is legitimate. Since I continue the loop with request for data when either n < 1 or num > N, I terminate the loop when this condition becomes `false`.

```
do {
  cout << "Enter number between 1 and " << N << ": ";
  cin >> num;
  if (!(num < 1 || num > N)) break;
  cout << "This is incorrect; please repeat.\n";
  } while (true);
```

Notice here the third form of the "forever" loop, with the `true` literal value as the condition for continuation.

Many programmers prefer to negate the compound condition explicitly. To do that, we replace each `&&` operator with the `||` operator, each `||` operator with the `&&` operator, and negate each individual condition. Consider, for example, the expression `a1 && (~a2) || a3` where `a1`, `a2`, and `a3` are boolean expressions. Its negation is `(~a1) || a2 && (~a3)`. In our case, negation of `num < 1` is `num >= 1` and negation of `num > N` is `num <= N`. The condition for breaking the loop now is as follows:

```
do {
  cout << "Enter number between 1 and " << N << " : ";
  cin >> num;
  if (num >= 1 && num <=N) break;              // nice and simple
  cout << "This is incorrect; please repeat.\n";
  } while (true);
```

Some programmers feel uncomfortable negating compound conditions, but this is a very useful skill and has to be practiced as much as possible.

The `break` statement is one of the tame and effective jumps in C++. Other jumps are either more dangerous or not as effective.

The CONTINUE Statement

The `continue` statement is a tamer modification of the `break` statement. Similar to `break`, it is also used within the loop constructs. It skips the remainder of the loop body between the `continue` statement and the end of the loop body.

The `continue` statement can be used for `while`, `do-while`, and `for` loops. In the `while` and `do-while` loops, it jumps and returns to the bottom or to the top of the loop to test the loop condition. In a `for` loop, the `continue` statement does not bypass the increment expression; it only jumps over the remainder of the loop body.

Consider, for example, Listing 4.11 (without the prime read) and its modification that solves these problems by updating current data only if the sentinel value is not entered yet:

```
while (amount > 0)                              // evaluate current data
  { cout << "Enter amount (negative or zero to end): ";
    cin >> amount;                              // change current data
    if (amount > 0)                             // test validity of data
      { total += amount;                        // process current data
        count++; } }
```

Instead of using a block in the conditional statement, I can negate its condition and use the continue statement.

```
while (amount > 0)                              // evaluate current data
  { cout << "Enter amount (negative or zero to end): ";
    cin >> amount;                              // change current data
    if (amount <= 0) continue;                  // test validity of data
    total += amount;                            // process current data
    count++; }
```

The improvement is not really very spectacular. As I mentioned, the continue statement is tame. It can always be replaced by a conditional statement. It is not that often that you see the use of the continue statement that significantly improves code. Actually, I saw such an example once, and I thought that it was good use of continue and I had to write it down. But I did not write it down because something distracted me, and now I cannot tell you what that example was.

The GOTO Statement

The goto statement is a queen of jumps. It is the use of unrestricted goto statements that caused so much discussion whether the jumps are actually harmful and why they should be outlawed. And indeed, many modern languages ban unrestricted jumps. So does C++.

In C++, goto jumps are allowed within the single function scope only. This means that both the goto statement and its target (the statement the flow of control jumps to) have to be within the same function. In addition, no jumps are allowed over definitions. This is quite restrictive relative to a conventional jump. This is why the C++ goto statement is less harmful than in older languages. This is what a C++ goto statement looks like:

```
void foo
{ ...
  goto label1;          // no colon after the label name
  int x;                // a jump over a definition: syntax error
  ...
  label1: statement;    // a colon after the label name
  ...
  goto label1; }        // no jumps over definitions: OK
```

A label is an identifier; it is put in front of the statement that assumes control and also at the end of the goto statement. The programmer makes up label names. Unlike identifiers for names of variables, functions, and types, labels do not have to be defined before they are used. They are just used. The label identifiers have their own name space. This means that their names do not conflict with other identifiers: names of variables, functions, or types.

A colon should follow the label that is used as the target of a jump. No colon should follow the label that is used in the goto statement; the semicolon is used instead.

Listing 4.24 shows the transaction processing example implemented without loops, with conditional statements and jumps only. Isn't it nice?

Listing 4.24   Transaction processing with goto jumps.

```
#include <iostream>
using namespace std;
int main ()
{
  double total=0.0, amount; int count=0;       // initialize
start:
  cout << "Enter amount (negative or zero to end): ";
  cin >> amount;                               // enter (change) current data
  if (amount <= 0) goto finish;                // evaluate current data
  total += amount;                             // process current data
  count++;
  goto start;                                  // go back to the start of loop
finish:
  cout << "\nTotal of " << count << " transactions is " << total << endl;
  return 0;
}
```

Some programmers, especially those that plan their code using flowcharts, like this style of programming. For a small example like this it probably does not matter whether you use jumps or loops. It is a good idea, however, to avoid using goto statements. Use them only if their use gives obvious (and important) performance advantage.

The RETURN and EXIT Jumps

The return statement represents a jump that terminates the execution of a function that executes the return. If this function is the main() function, the program is terminated. If this function is some other function that is called from `main()` directly or indirectly, that function is terminated and control is returned to the function that called the terminated function.

If the function return type is non-void, the function must have a `return` statement. If the function return type is `void`, the `return` statement is optional.

The `return` statement might or might not have arguments. If the function is defined as a `void` function, its `return` statement must not have an argument. The original C++ inherited two forms of `main()` from C: the one with the `int` return type and another with the `void` return type. The new standard C++ favors the first form of `main()`, but you will see a lot of legacy C++ code with the `main()` function that does not have a return type; hence, these functions did not use the `return` statement. If a `void main()` function were to use the optional `return` statement, it would look this way.

```
void main(void)
{ . . .
  return; }              // no argument, no parentheses
```

When the `return` statement is used in a `void` function, it must have no argument and no parentheses: `return 0` is an error; `return()` is an error.

In previous examples, I used the `main()` function that returns an integer value. As any non-void function, this `main()` function must have a `return` statement, and that statement must return an integer value (or a value that can be converted into an integer). This `main()` function looks like this:

```
int main(void)
{ . . .
  return 0; }            // argument mandatory, parentheses optional
```

Actually, C++ compilers must accept (grudgingly) this form of the `main()` function:

```
main(void)               // default return type is integer
{ . . .
  return (0); }          // optional parentheses
```

As I mentioned earlier, the missing return type information in C++ does not mean the absence of the return value (`void`). It means `int`. This is in keeping with the philosophy inherited from C that a concise program is better than a program that is not so concise, and the programmer who wants to write concise programs (by omitting the return type) should be encouraged to do so and supported them with appropriate language features.

Recently, this philosophy is being supplanted by the opinion that concise programs force the maintenance programmer to spend more time and effort understanding the program. That means that the concise program looks more complex to the maintainer than a program that is not so concise. The programmer who wants to write concise programs should be asked to please think more about readability and understandability of code—thinking especially about the maintenance programmer, who may not be well trained and as experienced as the original programmer is.

The `return` statement makes the return value available to the calling function. For example, the `cin.get()` function calls that I used in the previous examples made a character value available to the algorithms we have discussed. This means that within that function `get()`, there is some statement like `return c`; here, c is the name of some variable (the name could be different) of type `char`.

When the `main()` function returns a value, it is the operating system that accepts this value and makes a judgment about normal or abnormal termination of the program. Many platforms disregard the program return value.

This does not mean that you can omit a `return` statement if the function you are writing (including the `main()` function) returns a typed value. You made a commitment (non-void return type), and you have to live up to it: If the function's return value is not defined as `void`; the function should have a `return` statement that returns the value (expression) of the appropriate type. Parentheses around the return expression are optional (but used).

There are no limits on how many `return` statements a function could have. If a `return` is executed in the middle of the function, the rest of the function body is not executed.

Let us consider a simplified example of a primitive calculator that asks the user to enter two operands and an operator and displays the result of the operation (Listing 4.25). For the sake of the example, I am using here the `main()` function that does not return a value. A sample of the program run is shown on Figure 4–22.

Listing 4.25 A simplified primitive calculator.

```cpp
#include <iostream>
using namespace std;
void main(void)

{
  double op1, op2; char ch;
  cout << "Enter operand, operator, another operand: ";
  cin >> op1 >> ch >> op2;
  if (ch == '+')
    cout << "Result is " << op1 + op2 << endl;
  else
    if (ch == '*')
      cout << "Result is " << op1 * op2 << endl;
    else
      if (ch == '-')
        cout << "Result is " << op1 - op2 << endl;
      else
        if (ch == '/')
          if (op2 != 0.0)
            cout << "Result is " << op1 / op2 << endl;
          else
            cout << "Division by zero" << endl;
        else
          cout << "Illegal operator" << endl;
}
```

I called this calculator program primitive because it performs only four arithmetic operations and does not remember results. It has enough functionality for this discussion, however. I called this calculator simplified because it does not do what a real program should do to validate its input. The discussion of input validation would take us too far from our topic.

First, I would like to discuss formatting. The code represents a deeply nested conditional statement, and I wrote it indenting to the right a couple of spaces for each level of nesting. This formatting describes what this code made of (nested conditional statements) well. However, it does not stress for the maintainer what this code does.

```
Enter operand, operator, another operand: 22/0
Division by zero
```

Figure 4-22 Run results for Listing 4.25 (division by zero).

This code chooses one of five alternatives (addition, multiplication, subtraction, division, illegal operation) but the structure of the code does not pass the designer's knowledge and intent on to the maintainer of the program.

Below is a different version of the conditional statement that reflects the logic of processing.

```
if (ch == '+')                          // first case
  cout << "Result is " << op1 + op2 << endl;
else if (ch == '*')                     // second case
  cout << "Result is " << op1 * op2 << endl;
else if (ch == '-')                     // third case
  cout << "Result is " << op1 - op2 << endl;
else if (ch == '/')                     // fourth case: more complex
  { if (op2 != 0.0)
      cout << "Result is " << op1 / op2 << endl;
    else
      cout << "Division by zero" << endl; }
else                                    // fifth case
  cout << "Illegal operator" << endl;
```

Return statements can turn the different branches of processing into independent conditional statements that follow each other without intervening `else` keywords.

```
if (ch == '+')                          // first case
  { cout << "Result is " << op1 + op2 << endl; return; }
if (ch == '*')                          // second case
  { cout << "Result is " << op1 * op2 << endl; return; }
if (ch == '-')                          // third case
  { cout << "Result is " << op1 - op2 << endl; return; }
if (ch == '/')                          // fourth case: more complex
  { if (op2 != 0.0)
      cout << "Result is " << op1 / op2 << endl;
    else
      cout << "Division by zero" << endl;
    return; }
cout << "Illegal operator" << endl;
```

Another popular termination technique is a call to the function `exit()` from the standard library file `stdlib.h`. While the `return` statement terminates only the function (if it is the `main()` function, the program is terminated), a call to `exit()` terminates the program no matter what function makes this call. The function `exit()` is called with one integer argument; according to a popular convention, 0 indicates normal termination, 1 indicates abnormal termination. Using these values, the program passes on to the operating system the information about the way it terminates (see the earlier story about the Russian psychiatrist).

To protect the programs that want to communicate this way with the operating system from future changes in conventions, the file stdlib.h (or, according to the new standard, cstdlib) defines two symbolic literal constants, EXIT_SUCCESS and EXIT_FAILURE. These constants are recommended for the instead of literal values 0 and 1. Listing 4.26 shows the primitive calculator program using these constants.

Listing 4.26 Calls to the library function exit().

```cpp
#include <iostream>
#include <cstdlib>
using namespace std;

void main(void)
{
  double op1, op2; char ch;
  cout << "Enter operand, operator, another operand: ";
  cin >> op1 >> ch >> op2;
  if (ch == '+')                          // first case
    cout << "Result is " << op1 + op2 << endl;
  else if (ch == '*')                     // second case
    cout << "Result is " << op1 * op2 << endl;
  else if (ch == '-')                     // third case
    cout << "Result is " << op1 - op2 << endl;
  else if (ch == '/')                     // fourth case: more complex
    { if (op2 != 0.0)
        cout << "Result is " << op1 / op2 << endl;
      else
        cout << "Division by zero" << endl; }
  else                                    // fifth case: error
    { cout << "Illegal operator" << endl;
      exit(EXIT_FAILURE); }               // tell them we are bust
  exit(EXIT_SUCCESS);                     // tell them we are OK
}
```

Actually, the values of these library constants are currently 0 and 1. The idea behind using the constants is that some day, for some reason, the operating system will expect a different set of values from the C++ program, then the programs that use literal values 0 and 1 will be in trouble—operating systems will misunderstand them. The values of the library constants, EXIT_SUCCESS and EXIT_FAILURE, can be modified in the library, and the programs that rely on these names will always be able to communicate with the operating system correctly. I find this logic somewhat forced, but many programmers use these constants.

The SWITCH Statement

The switch statement is a tool for making multiway decisions in a program. It provides alternative execution paths based on the value of an integral expression. The expression in parentheses follows the keyword switch. The rest of the statement consists of branches that are placed within the braces. (The opening and the closing braces are mandatory.)

Each branch consists of the keyword case, a value of the same type as the switch expression, a colon, and a set of one or more statements terminated by semicolons. The closing brace of the switch statement is not followed by a semicolon. Here is the general form of the switch statement:

```
switch(expression) {                     // braces are mandatory
  case ConstantExpr1: statements;        // first branch
  case ConstantExpr2: statements;        // other branches
  . . . . .
  default: statements;                   // default branch
}                                        // semicolon after the closing brace
```

The switch expression can be only of type char, short, int, or long (integral types). Floating point types (float, double, or long double) are not allowed. Neither are programmer-defined types: arrays, structures, or classes.

The case labels must be constant expressions, that is, compile-time constants. They should be of the same type as the switch expression.

For example, the simplified primitive calculator from Listings 4.25 and 4.26 can be implemented using the switch statement with the operator as the switch expression. Listing 4.27 shows the implementation of the calculator.

Listing 4.27 Calculator with the switch statement (bad program).

```cpp
#include <iostream>
#include <cstdlib>
using namespace std;

void main(void)
{
  double op1, op2; char ch;
  cout << "Enter operand, operator, another operand: ";
  cin >> op1 >> ch >> op2;
  switch(ch) {                                  // mandatory braces
    case '+': cout << "Result is " << op1 + op2 << endl;
    case '*': cout << "Result is " << op1 * op2 << endl;
    case '-': cout << "Result is " << op1 - op2 << endl;
    case '/': if (op2 != 0.0)
```

```
              cout << "Result is " << op1 / op2 << endl;
          else
              cout << "Division by zero" << endl;
  default: cout << "Illegal operator" << endl;
          exit(EXIT_FAILURE); }                 // mandatory braces
  exit(EXIT_SUCCESS);                            // next statement
}
```

The literal labels in the `case` branches are not variables. They are compile-time constants (here, '+', '*', and so on). In the same `switch` statement, no two `case` labels can have the same value. (It is OK if they are in different switches.)

During the execution, the value of the `switch` expression (in this case, variable `ch`) is compared (top-down) with the case literals. If the expression value matches a label, execution continues with the statements that follow the label, until the end of the `switch` statement.

If no literal matches the `switch` expression, it is not an error. In this case, the statements that follow the `default` keyword are executed. The `default` label is optional. Usually, it is the last label in the `switch` statement, but it can be put in the middle. If it is absent and no label matches the value of the `switch` expression, all the statements in the switch construct are skipped and the next statement executed. Notice that the statements of the `switch` cases do not have to be taken into block braces. The braces do not change the order of execution: All the statements are executed sequentially.

An example of the execution for Listing 4.27 is shown on Figure 4–23. We see that the C++ `switch` statement is not a multibranch construct. It is a multientry construct. If a multibranch construct is needed, it can be built from a `switch` statement using a `break`, `goto`, or `return` statement to terminate each branch. Listing 4.28 shows a better design for our `switch` statement. The results of the program run are the same as in Figure 4–22.

```
Enter operand, operator, another operand: 22+2
Result is 24
Result is 44
Result is 20
Result is 11
Illegal operator
```

Figure 4–23   Run results for Listing 4.27 (incorrect program).

Listing 4.28 Calculator with the `switch` statement (better program).

```
#include <iostream>
#include <cstdlib>
using namespace std;

void main(void)
{
  double op1, op2; char ch;
  cout << "Enter operand, operator, another operand: ";
  cin >> op1 >> ch >> op2;
  switch(ch) {                                  // mandatory braces
    case '+': cout << "Result is " << op1 + op2 << endl;
              break;
    case '*': cout << "Result is " << op1 * op2 << endl;
              break;
    case '-': cout << "Result is " << op1 - op2 << endl;
              break;
    case '/': if (op2 != 0.0)
                  cout << "Result is " << op1 / op2 << endl;
              else
                  cout << "Division by zero" << endl;
              break;
  default: cout << "Illegal operator" << endl;
              break; }                          // break is optional here
  exit(EXIT_SUCCESS);                           // next statement
}
```

The `break` statement within the `switch` transfers control to the next statement that follows the closing brace of the `switch`. The `exit()` statement terminates the function as before.

The `goto` statement can be used to transfer control out of the `switch` branches, but for most cases, the `break` statement is sufficient. Some programmers put the `break` statement even before the closing brace of the `switch`. The `break` statement here is useless, but it might prevent errors if further branches are added to the `switch` statement and the `break` statement were not inserted. This is not an important issue, but it is definitely a good way to make the job of the maintainer easier.

The fact that the `switch` statement is a multientry statement rather than a multibranch statement can be used to avoid repeating code if more than one branch require the same processing. Consider, for example, the variable response that contains the user response to the application prompt. Let us say that I want to do one thing when the user enters either `'y'` or `'Y'` and another thing when the user enters either `'n'` or `'N'` and yet another thing if the response is different. The `switch` statement for processing user response could look this way:

```
switch (response) {
  case 'y': case 'Y':
    cout << "Thank you for confirmation\n"; break;
  case 'n': case 'N':
    cout << "Request is canceled\n"; break;
  default: cout << "Incorrect response\n"; }
```

When the response is, for example, `'y'`, the implicit null statement between `case 'y':` and `case 'Y':` is executed and then the statement following the next label (in this case, `'Y'`) is executed.

Of course, a series of conditional statements could do the same job, but the `switch` statement does it better—it is easy to read and its execution is easy to trace. It is a very powerful tool.

Summary

There is lot to say about C++ control flow constructs. C++ has all the traditional conditional and loop statements that allow the programmer to express complex algorithms. What is unique to C++ is the ability to put assignment statements within the logical expressions in conditional statements and in the loop. Combined with C++ capability to treat any nonzero value as a `true` boolean value gives in the hands of a C++ programmer a powerful tool for writing concise and forceful code.

For beginning programmers, it might be difficult to understand this kind of code. In your study of C++, it is important to allocate enough time for mastering these features. All too often, C++ programmers concentrate on studying classes and objects and neglect the skills that represent the foundation for writing professional C++ code.

Other C++ control constructs, jumps and switches, are not as indispensable for writing C++ code as are conditional statements and loop statements. You can write robust C++ code without using them. However, they are indispensable as tools of your professional skills. Without using these statements and using them correctly, your code cannot be considered professional C++ code. Make sure you allocate enough time to study and practice these elements of the C++ language.

AGGREGATION WITH PROGRAMMER-DEFINED DATA TYPES

Topics in this Chapter

- Arrays as Homogeneous Aggregates
- Structures as Heterogeneous Aggregates
- Unions, Enumerations, and Bit Fields
- Summary

Chapter 5

In the previous chapter, we studied the tools for implementing algorithms
in C++. Conditional statements, loops, and jumps are the language constructs you use to indicate how computations should be performed and in
what sequence. In this chapter, you will take the next step toward learning
how to implement well-designed C++ programs. We will discover how to
expand the set of data types that comes with the language.

C++ allows the programmer to define collections of data: arrays (homogeneous collections), structures (heterogeneous collections), and derived data
types. As I mentioned earlier, they are sometimes called user-defined data
types. This is the compiler writer's point of view rather than the programmer's. For the compiler writer, it is the programmer who is the user. For the
programmer, the user is a person who runs the program (or uses its results).
This is why I call the types that the programmer defines for the program *programmer-defined data types*.

You can define variables of programmer-defined data types (they are also
called computational objects, or just objects) as if these programmer-defined
data types were built-in types—integers, characters, and so on.

The C++ syntax for defining the variables is the same, and the rules of
handling variables are the same. In effect, you expand the meager set of C++
data types by adding to it programmer-defined data types. Programmer-
defined data types can also be used as building blocks for defining other,
more-complex programmer-defined types. In this chapter, I will concentrate

on the discussion of arrays, structures, and their variations: unions, bit fields and enumerations.

C++ classes as collections of data and functions can be discussed only after we discuss C++ functions in greater detail. The coverage of functions presented in Chapter 2, "Getting Started Quickly: A Brief Overview of C++," is sufficient for understanding the basic concepts about functions, but not for understanding classes and different ways to build them.

I am going to cover a lot of ground in this chapter, and the material I discuss is going to be diverse and complex. You may want to make your road to learning classes easier and skip those parts of this chapter that are not direct prerequisites for understanding classes. If this is the case, concentrate on arrays (one-dimensional only) and structures (but not on hierarchical structures). Unions and bit fields are programming techniques that have little to do with classes. I do not mean to say that they are not important. You can come back to this chapter when you feel you want to expand the breadth of your programming skills.

I am not so sure about enumerations. Formally, you do not need enumerations to understand classes, but C++ programmers often use enumerations to define sizes of class components. When you study Chapter 9, "C++ Class as a Unit of Modularization," you will see some enumerations used. These are quite intuitive, but if you feel you need more discussion of enumeration type, come back to this chapter and look it up.

Arrays as Homogeneous Aggregates

An *array* is a set of elements of the same data type. One can visualize an array as a set of contiguous memory locations. These locations are all of the same size and represent components of the same type. We can define arrays of integers, or floating point values, or characters, or any programmer-defined type as long as this type is known at the place in the source code where the array is being defined.

Arrays as Vectors of Values

The ordinary variables we studied in Chapter 3, "Working with C++ Data and Expressions," are called scalars or atomic variables (simple variables).

They are characterized by a single value. Sometimes you might want to distinguish between different components of the value, for example, between the whole part and the fractional part of a floating point number. However, the language does not support this distinction. It treats these variables as having no components. This is why these variables are called scalar or atomic variables. To extract the fractional part of a floating point number, you have to invent some C++ code to do that. This is not too difficult (library functions are available), but there is no language-defined, built-in way to do that.

```
fraction = x - floor(x);          // get fractional part of x
```

Here, x and fraction are double floating point numbers, and floor() is a function defined in the math.h (or cmath) library header file that returns the largest integer (converted to double) that does not exceed its argument. The language itself, however, treats the values of built-in types as atomic.

Arrays are vectors—their state is characterized by a set of values, not by a single value. Each component value is available immediately by using native C++ notation (the subscript operator).

Arrays are useful when each array element undergoes the same processing by the program. This is why arrays have to be homogeneous: All elements of the array have to be of the same type. Then the program can go over the elements of the array, performing the same operations over each element. This is why array components are usually processed in a loop. The fact that the array components are of the same type is important. This prevents any problem that might arise if an operation can be applied to one array component but cannot be applied to another.

Arrays are ordered collections of data. This means that each element of the array has the previous element and the next element. There are two obvious exceptions: the first array element does not have the previous element, and the last element of the array does not have the next element. The array has a name, but individual array elements do not have individual names. The program accesses them using the name of the array appended with the subscript (or index), the position of this element in the ordered collection.

Arrays are finite. The number of elements in the array has to be known at compile time and cannot be changed during program execution. The programmer has to decide how many elements will be stored in the array, make a commitment at the time of writing the program, and stick to this commitment for good and for bad.

This is a serious limitation. If the programmer allocates too much space for program arrays, this space will be wasted, and the program might not have enough memory for other purposes. If the programmer does not allocate enough space, the program corrupts memory during execution time, and the application can crash or produce incorrect results. If the programmer wants to change the size of the array, this can be done only through editing the program source code, recompiling, and relinking it. This is simple for a small program, but very difficult for a complex production program or for a program distributed to thousands of customers.

Sometimes, the size of the array is known exactly. For example, an array with the hours worked for different days of the week should have seven components (unless you expect a day or two to be added to the week in the near future). The same is true for the array whose components contain the number of days in a month (unless the number of months in the year changes). The same is true for an array whose components represent the chessboard. In most cases, however, we try to find a "reasonable" compromise, allocating more elements than we think we are going to need but not too many (twice the amount). The compromise is "reasonable" if this decision is supported by the code that checks for array overflow and takes a "reasonable" action when it occurs. For some people, "reasonable" might mean program termination. For others it means termination of input with notification of the user.

Sometimes, the position of an element in the array has an application-related meaning. For example, the name of the doctor running the hospital ward on a given day is related to the day of the week. When data come in, it does not necessarily come for the first element first and for the second element next. Some array elements might not have valid data at all. When arrays are used in this way, we have to design a way for the program to tell the difference between the elements that have valid data from the elements that do not. These arrays are called sparse arrays.

Most arrays are used as contiguous arrays. The first data item to be stored in the array is stored in the first element. The next data item is stored in the next element. Here, we also need to distinguish between elements that contain valid data and the elements that do not. The advantage of this approach is that there is no need to mark each array element as valid or unused. All array elements up to a specific location are used; all array elements after that location are unused.

There are two ways to implement contiguous arrays. One is to keep count of valid values inserted into the array. Then the loops that process valid elements of the array could use this count to terminate iterations. Another way to implement contiguous arrays is to have a special value that is inserted after the last valid element of the array. Then the loops that process valid array elements would stop when they find this special value. This special value is called a sentinel (it is similar to the sentinels I used to determine the end of input in Chapter 4, "C++ Control Flow"). It should be different from the values that a valid array element can assume.

Defining C++ Arrays

As any C++ variable, an array variable has to be defined before it can be used. The array definition connects the name of the array with the type of the array elements and with the number of elements in the array. As any definition, array definitions cause memory for the array to be allocated during execution time. As any definition, array definitions end with a semicolon. You can define each array on a separate line, or you can combine several definitions on the same line, for example:

```
int hours[7]; char grade[35]; double amount[20];
```

This line defines three arrays: array `hours[]` of 7 integer components, array `grade[]` of 35 character components, and array `amount[]` of 20 double floating point components. Notice empty square brackets attached to the name of the array in this paragraph. This notation indicates that the variable we are discussing is a vector with several values rather than a scalar with a single value.

For arrays of different types, as in the previous examples, each array has to be defined separately, ending its definition with the semicolon. For arrays of the same type, it is all right to define several arrays separating the definitions with commas (and ending the last definition with a semicolon). Actually, one can combine definitions of arrays and scalar variables if their type is the same, for example:

```
int category[7], i, num, scores[35], n;
```

Some programmers choose the names for their arrays using plural. When an array is passed as a parameter to a function, it is more appropriate to indicate that the function gets a set of scores rather than an individual score, for example, `sum(scores)`. Others choose array names using singular. When an individual element of the array is referred to using its index, for example, `category[i]`, it is more appropriate to indicate that it is a single category that is manipulated rather than a set of categories. In the broader scheme of things, this issue is not very important.

Although the array size should be known at compile time, it does not have to be a literal value. It can be a #defined symbolic literal, an integer constant, or an integer expression of any complexity. The only requirement is that this expression could be evaluated at compile time, not at run time. For example:

```
#define MAX_RATES 35          // array size as a #defined value
int const NUM_ITEMS = 10;     // array size as a constant
int rates [MAX_RATES]; double amount[2*NUM_ITEMS];
```

An array can be initialized at definition just like any other C++ variable. The programmer supplies initial values similar to initializing scalar variables. These initial values are specified in a comma-separated list of values delimited by braces. Since commas are separators and not terminators, the last initializer before the closing brace does not have a comma after it.

```
int hours[7] = { 8, 8, 12, 8, 4, 0, 0 };        // 7 values
int side[5] = { 40,35,41 } ;                     // other array elements are 0's
char option[2] = { 'Y', 'N', 'y', 'n' };         // syntax error
int week[52] = { , , 40, 48 };                   // syntax error
```

The first initial value initializes the first component of the array, the second initializer goes to the second component, and so on. Initial values should be of the same type as the array type or, if the types are different, conversion between the values of the two types should be allowed. These conversions are the same as the conversions discussed in Chapter 3 for mixed numeric types in expressions. (For example, it is OK to initialize an array of components of type double using integer initial values.)

In these examples, I supplied values for each component of the array hours[]. It is all right to supply fewer values than there are components, as for array side[]: The components are initialized starting with the first one until all initial values are exhausted. Those components that are left without values are initialized to zero of the appropriate type. It is not all right to supply more initial values than there are components in the array, as I did for array option[]. And it is not allowed to skip some components by using commas, as I did for array week[]. Job Control Language (JCL) allows this syntax, but C++ is not JCL.

Similar to scalar variables, an array variable defined in one file might be used in algorithms that are implemented in another file. To make it possible, that other file has to declare the array variable using the same name. The major difference between the array definition and declaration is that the declaration does not specify the size of the array. Array declarations do not allocate memory for the array. (This is the task for array definitions.) Although C++ declarations and definitions are similar, the programmer has to distinguish between them.

For example, some other file might need the values of components of array hours[], or it might compute the values that these components have to be assigned to. In that file, array hours[] would be declared this way:

```
extern int hours[];            // declaration: no memory allocated
```

For this declaration to be valid, the original definition of the array hours[] should be placed outside of any function as a global variable.

Similar to declarations of scalar variables, array declarations are used to establish the address of the array in memory. Now the code in this file can access elements of array `hours[]` as if the array were defined in this file. Since array declarations (as any other declarations) do not allocate memory, they do not support initialization.

C++, however, allows the programmer to use the declaration syntax for defining arrays. This is done when the size of the array is specified by the number of initializers rather than by an explicit compile-time constant, for example,

```
double rates[] = { 1.0, 1.2, 1.4 };          // three elements
```

Here, despite the declaration notation for array `rates[]`, three elements of the array are allocated and initialized. This definition is equivalent to the following definition.

```
double rates[3] = { 1.0, 1.2, 1.4 };          // explicit count
```

The advantage of the first definition is that one saves keystrokes for the size of the array. On the other hand, the first definition forgoes the opportunity to define a constant for the size of the array, and such a constant could come in handy in the algorithms for array processing.

One of the ways to resolve this problem is to compute the number of array components using the `sizeof` operator you saw in Chapter 3. Dividing the size of the array by the size of one component, you get the number of array components.

```
int num = sizeof(rates) / sizeof(double);
```

Notice the sequence of topics that the discussion of C++ arrays goes through. It is similar to the discussion of other data definition facilities. Each time, we discuss the meaning of the new C++ facility to be introduced (variables in Chapter 3, arrays in this chapter, then structures, classes, composite classes, and derived classes), the syntax of the definitions (and declarations if appropriate), and then we discuss the initialization issues. This sequence of discussion is no accident. Initialization is extremely important in C++, and we will be studying the methods of initialization related to each kind of memory usage in C++.

Operations over Arrays

The discussion of initialization is invariably followed by the discussion of array operations. What can we do with arrays? C++ is very limited in this regard. You cannot assign one array variable to another, and you cannot compare two arrays, add two arrays, multiply them, and so on. The only thing that you can do to an array is to pass it as an argument to a function. This is why when we want to assign one array to another, or compare two arrays, and so on, we write our own code or use library functions if they are available.

All operations can be performed over individual array elements only. When we copy one array to another, we copy each array element individually. When we compare arrays, we compare corresponding array elements individually. In these operations, we refer to individual array elements by using the subscript operator and the index (also called subscript) value.

For example, `side[2]` denotes the element of array `side` at index 2. For all intents and purposes, `side[2]` is an ordinary scalar integer variable. Since array `side[]` is an array of integers, you can do to `side[2]` all you can do to any integer variable as an lvalue or as an rvalue. It is just the name that is different— instead of the identifier that we use for an integer variable, we use the array name plus the index and the subscript operator.

```
side[2] = 40;               // use as lvalue
num = side[2] * 2;          // use as rvalue
```

On the first line, `side[2]` gets the value 40 to store at its location. On the second line, the value stored at location `side[2]` is multiplied by 2 and the result is stored in variable `num` (it has to be numeric). As we see, individual array elements do not have individual names. Their names are composed from the name of the array and the value of the subscript (index).

The C++ notation for array elements is quite conventional. What is unusual is that C++ treats the square brackets as the operator rather than just an element of notation. And if you look at Table 3.1 in Chapter 3, you will see that this operator is of high priority, on the top of the C++ operator table. As any operator, the subscript operator has operands. What are they? It is the name of the array and the value of the subscript. The operator is applied to name `side` and value 2, the result of the operation is `side[2]`, the name of the array component.

I know this sounds pretty abstract and remote from practice. What difference does it make whether it is an operator or special notation? At this point it makes no difference. Later on, we will use this operator in some interesting contexts.

The subscript does not have to be a literal value or even a compile-time value. Any run-time numeric expression can be used as a subscript. If the expression is a floating point, character, `short`, or `long` value, it is converted to an integer. Here, for example, the function `foo()` is called at run time, and its return value is used to compute the subscript.

```
side[3*foo()] = 40;                    // is this legal?
```

For this to be legal, the function `foo()` should be defined and its return value (the value of subscript) should be within the range of legal indices. If only part of the array elements is assigned values, the index has to be the index of one of these elements. If all array elements are assigned values, the index has to be within the first and last components. Indices that are outside of this range refer to locations in memory that do not belong to the array and hence should not be referred to as components of the array.

Index Validity Checking

Now brace yourself, fasten the seat belt, and get ready for a bombshell. The programmer cannot choose the range of index values for an array arbitrarily: It is fixed for all C++ arrays. This is unpleasant because often we want to assign some meaning to the index. For example, we might have an array `revenue[]` that stores revenue data from 1997 to 2006; it would be convenient to have the range from 1997 to 2006 as the range of array indices. Other languages allow programmers to choose subscript ranges, but C++ does not: In this case, the interests of compiler writers got precedence over the interests of application programmers. In C++, the range is fixed. More over, it starts with 0.

Yes, the index of the first array component for any C++ array is 0 and not 1, and this is very important.

For example, if the array `side[]` has five components, the legal array components are `side[0]`, `side[1]`, `side[2]`, `side[3]`, and `side[4]`. Notice that `side[5]` is not a legal component of this array.

What happens if you make a mistake and refer to `side[-1]`, or `side[6]`, or even to `side[5]`? Does the compiler tell you that you made a mistake? No. A subscript value can be a run-time value, not known at compilation time, and the compiler writers give up on checking. Even when the index is a compile-time literal value that can be easily checked, the compiler does not check the index validity.

C++ skips this validity check with the air of deference to the programmer. If you say `side[-1]` in your code, you obviously meant something, and it is not the job of the compiler to second-guess you and tell you that you are wrong. No, there is no built-in compile-time validity check for indices.

Is there a run-time check? After all, some other languages validate every reference to array components against the legal range of indices. Not C++. Index or subscript validation at run time would affect performance, and this is a sacred cow in C++. And what if you do not have a performance problem in your program? What if you want to check the validity of the index at run time? No problem. Do it yourself; check the value of the index against its legal limits. No, there is no built-in run-time validity check for indices.

Of course, the underlying assumption for this kind of language design is that the programmer knows what he or she is doing at every moment and does not need any help from the compiler or the run-time system. Needless to say, this assumption is totally baseless, and errors in handling subscripts are a common source of errors and worries for C++ programmers.

The reason for this rigidity (inherited from C) is that the array name is used as the address of the first element of the array. The displacement of the first element from the beginning is zero. The displacement of the second element is one length of the element (depending on its type). The displacement of the third element is two lengths of the element. The compiler knows the size of the element, and it is simpler to compute the address of the element using its displacement than using its position in the array.

When the index value is invalid, the compiler still uses this index as displacement to compute the address of the component in memory, and the program corrupts its memory. However, if this address is not used for something useful, you can get away with that.

Alert

There is no compile-time index validity check in C++. There is no run-time index validity check in C++. The computer memory can be corrupted by your program. Watch out!

Let us look at some consequences of errors in handling indices. Listing 5.1 shows a program that correctly assigns values to the sides of a polygon, but prints them incorrectly: The first value of the index is 1, the last value of the index is 5. The program output is shown on Figure 5–1.

Listing 5.1 Erroneous scan over the array.

```cpp
#include <iostream>                    // or #include <iostream.h>
using namespace std;

int main()
{
  int size[5] = { 39, 40, 41, 42, 43 };
  for (int i = 1; i <= 5; i++)         // bad start, bad end
    cout << " " << size[i]; cout << endl;
  return 0;
}
```

In this case, inspection of the output tells you that there is an error in the code. Often, however, if the programmer is consistent in making errors, inspection of the output shows no sign of error. Listing 5.2 shows the program that assigns the sides of a polygon incorrectly and prints them incorrectly. The program does not use the location side[0] that belongs to the array. Instead, it used the memory location side[5] that does not belong to the array. As Figure 5–2 shows, the output is correct although the program corrupts the memory location it refers to as side[5].

Figure 5–1
Output reveals the error in code.

Figure 5–2
Correct output hides errors in array handling.

Listing 5.2   Error is hidden by correct output.

```
#include <iostream>                              // or #include <iostream.h>
using namespace std;

int main()
{
  int size[5];
  size[1]=39; size[2]=40; size[3]=41; size[4]=42; size[5]=43;
  for (int i = 1; i <= 5; i++)                  // bad start, bad end
    cout << " " << size[i]; cout << endl;
  return 0;
}
```

How dangerous is corruption of memory? If the memory that this code corrupts is not allocated for anything useful (and there are plenty of machines around with huge memories that are not allocated for anything useful), this is not a problem. If the corrupted memory is used by the program, the error is difficult to find. As Listing 5.2 shows, it is even difficult to realize that the program is incorrect and where to start looking for the error. Listing 5.3 expands this example. As you can see from Figure 5–3, the value in a[0] is incorrect: It changes from 11 to 43 even though there is no second assignment to a[0]. It is quite unlikely that in a real-life setting one would suspect that handling the array side[] might change the values in array a[]. On your machine, this program might corrupt memory in a different way. Despite whatever it does, this innocent-looking little program is incorrect.

Listing 5.3   Error in one place corrupts memory in another.

```
#include <iostream.h>
void main()
{ int a[3]; int size[5];
  a[1]=11; a[2]=12; a[3]=13;                    // a victim of corruption
  size[1]=39; size[2]=40; size[3]=41; size[4]=42; size[5]=43;
    for (int i = 1; i <= 5; i++)                // bad start, bad end
      cout << " " << size[i];
    cout << endl;
    for (i = 0; i < 3; i++)                     // correct start, end
      cout << " " << a[i];
    cout << endl; }
```

Correct iteration over array components should start with 0, not with 1. Iteration should end one value short of the array size. If array size is 5, the correct form of the test is $i < 5$; if array size is 3, the correct form of the test is $i < 3$. In general, if the number of valid array elements is in variable NUM, the correct

```
39  40  41  42  43
43  11  12
```

Figure 5-3
Array a[] is corrupted by handling of array side[].

form of the continuation test is i < NUM. The loop over array a[] in Listing 5.3 is designed correctly. Notice that index i is defined in the first loop, not at the beginning of the program. Its name is known until the end of the function. Hence, the second loop does not define this variable but uses it as if it were defined at the beginning of the function. My compiler (Microsoft Visual C++ version 6.0) does not implement standard C++ correctly—the scope of index variable i should be the first loop only, not throughout the function.

Validity of indices is something a C++ programmer has to think about all the time. When you iterate over all elements of the array, you should start the iteration with index 0. You should end the iteration with index one less than the number of elements. This is a very simple rule. It is not difficult to remember. It is not difficult to use. And most of the time we get it right. But at one time or another, every programmer makes mistakes in accessing array components, and these mistakes are very costly, especially when they are made at the time of maintenance. If you add together all the time, effort and, frustration that the software industry has wasted on errors in handling array subscripts, the result would be staggering. This is why C++ programmers should think about the validity of indices all the time.

Tip

Start iterations over the array with the index set to 0. Continue while the index value is less than the number of valid array elements.

Multidimensional Arrays

C++ supports multidimensional arrays. Theoretically, there is no limit to the number of array dimensions. When defining a multidimensional array, you specify the type of array components, the name of the array, and, in separate brackets, the number of elements in the first direction, number of elements in the second direction, and so on. For example, a two-dimensional

array of two rows and three columns (let us keep it simple) of integers would
be defined as

```
int m[2][3];              // 2 rows of arrays, 3 elements each
```

Multidimensional arrays can be initialized using syntax similar to initialization of one-dimensional arrays: The initial values are listed in a block with comma separators.

```
int m[2][3] = { 10, 20, 30, 40, 50, 60 };
```

Here, the first three values go to the first row of the matrix, and the last three values go to the second row. For larger arrays, you can indicate the group of values that belongs to the same row by using the scope braces. Row initializers are separated by commas. This will help the maintenance programmer to identify data for each row easier.

```
int m[2][3] = { { 10, 20, 30 }, { 40, 50, 60 } };
```

Similar to one-dimensional arrays, you can specify fewer initial values than there are elements in each row. The remaining elements will be assigned the zero value. For example,

```
int m[2][3] = { { 10, 20 }, {30, 40 } };
```

This is equivalent to the following explicit definition where the first three values go to the first row, and the last three values go to the second row.

```
int m[2][3] = { 10, 20, 0, 30, 40, 0 };
```

Similar to one-dimensional arrays, you cannot specify more initial values than there are slots in a row. This is a syntax error.

```
int m[2][3] = { { 10,20,30,40 }, { 50,60 } };        // error
```

The method of defining the size of the array by specifying initial values is available for multidimensional arrays as well, but only partially. You can omit the number of rows, but you must supply the number of columns, and the compiler will count the number of initial values and will figure out the number of rows.

```
int m[][3] = { { 10, 20, 30 }, { 40, 50, 60 } };
```

You cannot omit the number of columns, whether or not you specify the number of rows. This is an error.

```
int m[2][] = { { 10,20,30 }, { 40,50,60 } };        // error
```

The compiler could count the row groups and figure out the structure of the matrix, but it does not do it. It is probably better to specify the array dimensions explicitly anyway.

Access to an element of the multidimensional array requires several indices, one for each dimension. Similar to one-dimensional arrays, each index represents a displacement of the element and hence starts with 0 and ends at the value one less than the number of elements in each dimension. For example, the first element of the second row in the matrix m[][] is denoted as m[1][0]. This notation can be used both as an rvalue (as an operand in an expression) and as an lvalue (as a target of an assignment).

When traversing the elements of a multidimensional array, nested loops should be used. In the nested loops for multidimensional arrays, the inner loop ends all its iterations first for one iteration of the outer loop, then for the next iteration of the outer loop, and so on.

Listing 5.4 shows the nested loop that displays each element of matrix m[][] row-wise. The inner loop changes index j from 0 to 2 for each value of the outer loop index i (which changes from 0 to 1). The output of the program is shown in Figure 5–4.

Listing 5.4   Example of manipulating a two-dimensional array.

```
#include <iostream.h>
void main()
{ const int ROWS = 2, COLS = 3;
  int m[ROWS][COLS] = { { 10, 20, 30 }, { 40, 50, 60 } };
  for (int i=0; i < ROWS; i++)              // done once for each row
    { for (int j=0; j<COLS; j++)            // done for each index i
        cout << " " << m[i][j];
      cout << endl; }                       // end of row: once for each index i
}
```

Those programmers who switch to C++ from other languages find this notation for multidimensional array elements somewhat difficult (or just new). They sometimes use only one set of brackets and separate indices by commas. For example, instead of m[1][0], the programmer might use m[1,0]. Unfortunately, the compiler does not stand by to tell you that you

---

```
10  20  30
40  50  60
```

Figure 5–4
A two-dimensional array is displayed row-wise.

made an error. Instead, the compiler quietly accepts this comma expression for indices and leaves it to chance and to your ingenuity to notice that the program is incorrect. Figure 5–5 shows the output of the program in Listing 5.4 where `m[i][j]` was mistakenly written as `m[i,j]`.

There are two reasons for this mishap, both of which are inherited from C. One is that the comma is a full-fledged C++ operator. When the compiler evaluates the comma-separated index expression `[i,j]`, it first evaluates `i` (or 1), then finds the comma, drops the value of `i` and evaluates the next expression, `j` (e.g., 0). Then the compiler returns this value as the index. For all intents and purposes, `m[i,j]` could have been written as `m[j]`. The second reason is that `m[j]`, with one index only, is a legal notation for a row at displacement `j`—not all indices are required for multidimensional arrays.

Note

To refer to a component of a two-dimensional array, use the form with two sets of brackets: `a[i][j]`. Do not use the comma: `a[i,j]` leads to trouble.

Multidimensional arrays are supported in C++ as syntactic fluff, only for the convenience of the programmer. Under the hood, they are implemented as one-dimensional arrays. Some programmers prefer to use a one-dimensional array with `ROWS*COLS` components and compute the index for element in the `i`th row and `j`th column as `i*COLS+j`. (Do not forget: indices start with 0 and end with `ROWS*COLS-1`.) Listing 5.5 shows the same program as in Listing 5.4, where the array is explicitly treated as a one-dimensional array. The output of this program is the same as in Figure 5–4.

```
0x34C4   0x34CA   0x34D0
0x34C4   0x34CA   0x34D0
```

Figure 5–5
Listing 5.4 output with `m[i][j]` spelled as `m[i,j]`.

Listing 5.5 Using a one-dimensional array to implement a matrix.

```
#include <iostream>
using namespace std;

int main()
{
  const int ROWS = 2, COLS = 3;
  int m[ROWS * COLS] = { 10, 20, 30, 40, 50, 60 };    // same size
  for (int i=0; i < ROWS; i++)
    { for (int j=0; j < COLS; j++)
        cout << " " << m[i*COLS + j];                 // do it hard way
      cout << endl; }                                 // end of row: done once for each i
  return 0;
}
```

Which way of handling indices is better? It might depend on the application and on personal preference, so it is hard to recommend one over another.

Often, when you choose the array representation, it does not matter whether you use a one-dimensional or multidimensional array, whether you use one index or several indices. Just make sure you are ready to handle index manipulations.(Bring your car with you if it makes you feel more confident.)

Defining Character Arrays

The significance of character arrays is based on the fact that text is represented in C++ as arrays of characters (they are often called *strings*). All that was said in this chapter about arrays (one- and multidimensional) applies to arrays of characters as well.

Whatever you do with any arrays—printing, saving to file, copying into another array, comparing with another array, and so on—you have to know where the array ends. Often, the array definition is not available for reference. Even when available, the definition is useless, because the size of the array should be larger than any set of elements that is stored in the array. This is why the actual number of elements in the array is often smaller than the size of the array.

As I mentioned earlier, there are two approaches to dealing with this problem: one is to keep the count of elements in the array and the other is to use a sentinel value at the end of the array. For noncharacter arrays, either method could be used. For character arrays, C++ uses the second method. The sentinel value for character arrays that C++ uses is the numeric 0, because 0 is a special code that is different from any legal character code. (It is often called the *zero terminator* character or just the *terminator.*)

To distinguish this code from the character '0' (in ASCII, 48 in decimal, 0x30 in hex), the sentinel character is often represented as the escape sequence '\0' (0 in decimal, 0x0 in hex).

When an array of characters or a literal string is passed as an argument to any of the C+ library functions, the functions expect the text to be appended with this sentinel character. Whenever a function generates a character array, it appends the sentinel character to the end of the text in the array so that the array can be used by other library functions.

```
char t[4] = { 'H','i','!','\0' };         // four array elements
cout << t << endl;                        // It displays "Hi!"
```

Here, the array `t[]` is initialized using the standard syntax for one-dimensional arrays and then is passed to the operator function `<<` as an argument. This function keeps printing the string characters one after another until it finds the zero code; then it stops.

The escape character representation is mandatory only when this value is part of a string literal. In many contexts, the numeric 0 can be used. Here, for example, it is OK to use the zero (0) code instead of the escape zero character (`'\0'`). Some programmers prefer to use the character notation.

```
char t[4] = { 'H', 'i', '!', 0 };          // some prefer '\0'
```

This notation is inconvenient for initializing long character arrays. Recognizing this practical need, C++ allows a special dispensation: You have the right to use a string literal instead of a set of character initial values. The compiler will understand what you mean, will put each character into its position in the array, and will add the zero terminator at the end.

```
char t[4]="Hi!";                      // t[0] is 'H', t[1] is 'i', etc.
char u[]="Today is a nice day.";      // 21 characters with terminating 0
```

The string literal `"Hi!"` has four characters, the fourth being the code 0. The string literal `"Today is a nice day."` has 21 characters including the code 0; hence, array `u[]` has 21 components, not 20. The sentinel character needs an extra array element to be stored there. Failure to provide the space for this extra element could cause problems. This, for example, is a syntax error.

```
char v[3]="Hi!";              // Four initial values for 3 elements
```

It is all right to define a character array with more space than there are initializing characters. It is OK to define a character array and leave its contents undefined.

```
char last[30]="Jones", first[30];        // space is available
```

Access to individual string components is, of course, similar to ordinary arrays. Each array component is of type `char`. The first index is 0.

```
t[0] = 'N'; t[1] = 'o';           // t[] contains "No!" now, not "Hi!"
```

When dealing with character and string literals, it is important to remember which one requires single quotes, and which one needs double quotes. For example, `'o'` above is a character literal, but `"o"` is a string literal. It consists of two characters: character `'o'` and character `'\0'`.

Operations on Character Arrays

Individual characters can be assigned to each other or compared with other characters. They can be shifted, added, and so on. None of these operations is available for strings (character arrays). Fortunately, the C++ library comes with a large number of functions that operate on string arrays. As an argument to a function, the array name is used without a subscript.

Function `strcpy()` implements assignment for character arrays. It takes two arrays as arguments and copies the components of the second argument into the corresponding components of the first one. Copying takes place until the zero code in the second argument is found. The zero terminator is copied too, making the target array a well-formed array that can be used as an argument to other functions.

```
strcpy(u,t);            // Now u[] contains "No!", too
```

Because no function is going to look at the string contents beyond the sentinel, there is no need to clean up the rest of the string. Before this function call, the string `u[]` had the contents `"Today is a good day.\0"` where "\0" is the sentinel character. After the function call, it has `"No!\0y is a good day.\0"` but nothing after the first "`\0`" is relevant anymore. (Here, the use of the escape character is mandatory.) For all intents and purposes, the contents of this string is `"No!"`.

There is no problem with passing a string literal as argument to a function that expects a character array because every string literal has the zero terminator at the end. The only requirement is that the function not change the state of the array because the literal is a constant and its contents cannot be changed by the function.

```
strcpy(t,"Yes");          // Now t[] contains "Yes" plus zero
strcpy("Yes",t);          // No, you cannot do that: syntax error
```

Function `strcat()` implements the operation `+=` for character arrays. It also takes two character arrays as its arguments and copies the second argument into the first one. Unlike `strcpy()`, it does not replace the contents of the first parameter with the new contents but rather appends it to the current contents. The result is *concatenation* of two strings.

```
strcat(u," means No!");    // u[] contains "No! means No!"
```

The appended characters start from the position where the null terminator used to be before concatenation and overwrites it and other characters that might be in the array. The null terminator is inserted after the appended characters so that the contents of array `u[]` now is `"No! means No!\0e day.\0"` Since no C++ function looks beyond the terminator, the string contains `"No! means No!"` for all intents and purposes.

Function `strcmp()` implements the comparison operation for its two character arrays arguments. It compares the corresponding characters one after another until it either finds two different characters at the same displacement or reaches the sentinels. If the function finds two different characters, it compares their lexicographical order, that is, which one precedes another in the table of ASCII codes. If the strings are ordered and the character in the first argument precedes the character in the second argument, `strcmp()` returns –1. If the strings are out of order and the character in the second argument precedes the character in the first argument, the function returns 1. If the function reaches both sentinels at the same displacement, it returns 0 and the strings are considered the same.

For example, `strcmp("Hi","Hello")` returns 1: The strings are out of order. On the other hand, `strcmp("Handler","Hello")` returns –1, and so does `strcmp("Hell","Hello")` because the sentinel in the first string is compared with character 'o' in the second string. Since lowercase letters follow uppercase letters in the ASCII table, `strcmp("hello","Hello")` returns 1, and the `true` branch of this conditional statement is executed.

```
if (strcmp("hello","Hello")) cout << "Not ordered\n";
```

Note

All C++ library functions stop processing the string when they find a terminating zero. Symbols that follow the zero are not available to library functions. Use `strlen()` *to evaluate the number of symbols preceding the terminating zero.*

Another useful library function is `strlen()`, which accepts a character array as an argument and returns the number of characters in the string that *precedes* the zero terminator. For example, `strlen("Hello")` returns 5, and `strlen(t)` returns 3 (it contains `"Hi!"`). All library functions stop looking at the string contents as soon as they find the sentinel character.

String Functions and Memory Corruption

None of these functions will check whether there is enough space to do the operation. The formal reason is that no C++ function knows the total number of elements in the array it receives as its argument, whether it is a character array or any other type. But the real reason is that this check might affect program performance, and this is why a C++ programmer should think about the available space (along with other issues) all the time and make sure that enough space is available.

In addition, these functions give "undefined results" if two arrays are overlapping in memory. This means that the results might be correct or incorrect, but there is no assurance either way.

Listing 5.6 shows a program that deals with the available space recklessly. What can be simpler than reading two items of data and echoing them back? The program passes the arrays `first[]` and `last[]` to the extraction function `>>` that fills the arrays with input characters and appends them with the zero terminators.

The program output is shown in Figure 5–6. When the data are short enough, there is no problem. When data are longer, the problem (in this trivial example) becomes evident. One can say those six characters for the first or the last name are not much. Moreover, there are only five slots available because the sixth one is taken by the terminating null. Do you think that 20 characters is enough? My friend Galina Beloselskaya-Belozerskaya would have a problem and overflow that array—her name contains 33 characters including the blank and the terminating zero.

And what if the key stuck on the user's keyboard? The user will notice and correct this obviously erroneous entry, but other memory locations might be silently damaged.

Listing 5.6   A simple example of array overflow.

```
#include <iostream>
using namespace std;
int main()
{
  char first[6], last[6];                // are not these arrays too short?
  cout << "Enter first name: ";          // I enter "John\0" (5 symbols)
  cin >> first;                          // no protection against overflow
  cout << "Enter last name: ";           // I enter "Johnson\0" (8 symbols)
  cin >> last;                           // no protection against overflow
  cout << first << " " << last << endl;  // just to check results
  return 0;
}
```

Here, array `first[]` contains the string `"John\0"` (the last two symbols, `'\0'` represent one memory location whose contents is 0). Array `last[]` contains `"Johnson\0"` (eight symbols including the terminating zero). However, array `last[]` has space available for only six symbols. Where do the two symbols `"n\0"` go? On my machine, array `first[]` actually follows array `last[]` in memory. Why that is so, is not important. What is certain is that these two characters have to go somewhere. After entering the last name, the array `first[]`contains these two characters `"n\0"` plus whatever is left from `"John\0"`, that is, `"n\0hn\0"`. When I print the array `first[]` with `cout`, printing stops when the first `'\0'` is found, immediately after printing 'n'.

How do you like it? This is quite interesting; and quite dangerous. On your machine it might work somewhat differently. Some compilers allocate space in 4-byte chunks, so that the arrays will actually contain eight characters each rather than six, and you have to use a longer name to see memory corruption. Some compilers do not place array `first[]` after array `last[]`. Whatever the case, the important fact is that string processing is prone to memory corruption.

```
Enter first name: John
Enter last name: Johnson
n Johnson
```

Figure 5–6
Array overflow on input silently damages other data.

Dynamic memory management is a good solution to this problem, but we do not have the necessary tools yet. Another practical solution is to limit the number of characters that can be put into an array. This could be done by using the input function get() which allows the programmer to specify the upper limit on the number of characters read as input.

```
cin.get(first,6);          // read up to 5 characters + null
```

If function get() finds the newline character before the number of characters reaches the limit minus one, it stops input, and the newline character '\n' remains in the input buffer as the first character to be read next time. Another null character is appended to the array, and everything is fine.

If the user keeps typing away without pressing the Enter key, the input is terminated when the number of characters read reaches the limit minus one. The terminating null is appended so that the string is well formed. When the user finally presses the Enter key, the extra characters remain in the input buffer terminated by the new line character. They will be read by the next input statement (if there is one).

The use of function get() poses two problems. Let us say that the first name contains only three characters (e.g., "Amy"). Next, the last name is entered.

```
cin.get(last,6);          // it stops when it finds new line
```

The first thing that this statement finds in the input buffer is the newline character leftover from the previous call to get() that read "Amy". This call to get() reads this character and terminates. As a result, the empty string is read into array last[]. Get it? Whatever the user types does not get into the array last[] and is left in the input buffer. If the first input was too long ("Vladimir"), only five characters were put into array first[] with the terminating zero. The rest of the input ("mir") is left in the input buffer waiting for the next input request. Whatever the user types for the last name does not get into array last[]. The program will read characters from the input buffer ("mir") and will stop at the newline character in the buffer (leaving it there).

We see that function get() cannot do this job alone. It needs function ignore() that reads input characters and throws them away. It expects you to specify the upper limit on the number of characters to throw out and the delimiter character that stops throwing characters out. (Here, we will use the newline character.)

Listing 5.7 shows this solution to the problem of input data overflow. It also demonstrates the next problem, this time related to copying and concatenation. The program forms the customer name out of the last name, comma, space, and the first name. If the number of characters copied into array

name[] exceeds the size of the array, the characters are still copied into whatever memory space happens to be adjacent to the array. Figure 5–7 shows the
results of execution. Even though array name[] contains "correct" data, array
last[] is silently damaged, even though no program statement explicitly
changes its contents.

Listing 5.7 An example of array overflow in concatenation.

```cpp
#include <iostream>                              // or #include <iostream.h>
#include <cstring>                               // or #include <string.h>
using namespace std;
int main()
{
  char first[6], last[6]; char name[10];         // name = last, first
  cout << "Enter first name: ";
  cin.get(first,6); cin.ignore(2000,'\n');       // has to remove CR
  cout << "Enter last name: ";
  cin.get(last,6); cin.ignore(2000,'\n');        // it stops at first CR
  cout << first << " " << last << endl;
  strcpy(name,last);                             // copy last[] into name[]
  strcat(name,", ");                             // append a comma and a space
  strcat(name,first);                            // append first[] to name[]
  cout << "Customer: " << name << endl;
  cout << first << " " << last << endl;          // "just in case"
  return 0;
}
```

Here, array first[] contains "John" and array last[] contains "Smith";
these arrays are protected from overflow on input. Then I concatenate the
name component in array name[] as "Smith, John"; this string contains 12
characters including terminating zero. Since array name[] has only 10 characters, two last characters, "n\0", go elsewhere. On my machine, they go into
array last[]. As the result, array last[] contains these two characters and
whatever was left from "Smith", that is, "n\0ith\0". When the last cout
statement of the program prints the first name, it prints correctly; when it
prints the last name, it prints "n" and stops.

```
Enter first name: John
Enter last name: Smith
John Smith
Customer: Smith, John
John n
```

Figure 5–7
Array overflow on concatenation silently
damages other data.

To deal with this problem, the C++ library `string.h` offers functions `strncpy()` and `strncat()`, which are similar to `strcpy()` and `strcat()` but have a third argument that specifies the limit of the number of characters to be copied.

Their use is shown in Listing 5.8. Function `strncat()` terminates copying when the specified number of characters is copied (or the end of the second argument is reached) and appends the null terminator. It is safe. Function `strncpy()` appends the null terminator only if the length of the second string is shorter than the specified limit. When the limit is reached, it terminates copying but does not append the sentinel character. Hence, `strncpy()` does not always create a well-formed string. It is not safe to use. Figure 5–8 shows that the use of `strncat()` does protect the target array from overflow. The target array `name[]` contains truncated data (`"Smith, Joh"` instead `"Smith, John"`), but this data are well formed.

Listing 5.8 An example of preventing array overflow in concatenation.

```
#include <iostream>
#include <cstring>                        // notice a new header file
using namespace std;
int main()
{
  char first[6], last[6], name[10];
  cout << "Enter first name: ";
  cin.get(first,6); cin.ignore(200,'\n');  // it has to remove CR
  cout << "Enter last name: ";
  cin.get(last,6); cin.ignore(200,'\n');   // it stops at first CR
  cout << first << " " << last << endl;
// strncpy(name,last,4);                    // no null if length>=count
  strcpy(name,last);
  cout << "After copy: " << name << endl;
  strcat(name,", ");
  strncat(name,first,3);
  cout << "Customer: " << name << endl;
  cout << first << " " << last << endl;    // "just in case"
  return 0;
}
```

```
Enter first name: John
Enter last name: Smith
John Smith
After copy: Smith
Customer: Smith, Joh
John
```

Figure 5–8
Truncation of data to prevent memory corruption.

Or is it? I calculated my truncation strategy incorrectly. Array `name[]` contains 10 characters, and the string `"Smith,  Joh"` contains 11 characters, including the zero terminator. Where does this zero go? On my machine it wound up as the first character in array `last[]`, corrupting its contents as `"\0mith"` instead of `"Smith"`. When the last `cout` was printing the array `last[]`, it found the zero as the first character and did not print anything.

Tip

For all operations on strings, make sure that long input data do not overflow character arrays and do not damage unrelated program data. These errors are hard to find because they are unrelated data that are damaged.

Did I scare you? If I did, that was my intent. C++ programmers exercise tremendous influence. They write programs that affect lives of many people. The language they use is powerful and beautiful. It is dangerous in inexperienced hands—pretty much like a handgun or an automobile. Make sure that you make all the effort necessary to use this potent language correctly.

Two-Dimensional Character Arrays

A character array can contain more than one word. For many text processing applications, the text has to be broken into separate words and organized into arrays of words for processing. An array of character arrays is, of course, a two-dimensional array of type `char`. Let us, for example, consider an array of days of the week. We want to search this array to check whether input data in array `day[]` contains the days of the week `"Sunday"` or `"Monday"` or `"Tuesday"` and so on. Even if these words are of different lengths, we represent these data as a two-dimensional array of characters that has seven rows for seven days of the week. The rows have to be the same length. The maximum length has the word `"Wednesday"` that has nine characters. With yet another position for the terminating zero, the array has to have ten columns.

```
char days[7][10], day[10];
```

If we want to check whether or not array `day[]` contains a legal day of the week, we compare this array with each row of array `days[][]`. We can do that the hard way, comparing each element in the `i`th row (`i` changes from 0 to 6). If the characters of array `day[]` are the same as the characters in the `i`th row of array `days[][]`, we stop the iterations of index `i` because the input data are found in the array. Hence, in the outer loop we should know what happens in the inner loop. This is usually done using a control flag (e.g., variable `found`). Before the inner loop starts, we set it to 1 (`true`); if different characters are discovered by the inner loop, the inner loop sets this variable to 0 (`false`), indicating to the outer loop that the word was not found. If all the characters in array `day[]` and in the `i`th row of array `day[][]` are the same, the assignment `found = 0;` is never executed, flag value remains 1, and the `break` statement terminates the outer loop.

```
for (i = 0; i < NUM; i++)
{ found = 1; j = 0;
  do {
    if (day[j] != days[i][j])        // word is not found
    { found = 0; break; }            // stop, do it for next i
      j++;
      } while (day[j] != '\0');
  if (found == 1) break; }           // break outer loop
```

Some C++ programmers would code the last four lines more concisely.

```
do
{ if (day[j]!=days[i][j++])          // compare and increment
    { found = 0; break; }            // stop, do it for next i
    } while (day[j]!='\0');          // no need for separate j++
    if (found) break; }              // any nonzero value is true
```

Using the concise form of the conditional statement is safe and appropriate. Combining comparison and increment is reckless. Here, `j` is used in two subexpressions, and as I told you in Chapter 3, we do not know in what order they are evaluated. On my machine, this code executed incorrectly. On your machine, it might execute correctly. It does not matter: A prudent C++ programmer has to be aware of the issue and avoid this style of coding.

Often, we simplify this kind of processing by using the `strcmp()` library function. Listing 5.9 shows the program that prompts the user for the day of the week, searches the two-dimensional array of characters, and displays the number of the day that was found. Notice that after the search loop is terminated, the program must decide why the loop was terminated: either because the word was found or because we ran out of array elements without finding a match. There are several ways to do this. Here, I check the value of index `i`. If it is equal to the number of elements in the array, this means that the search was unsuccessful. If it is less than the number of elements, the loop was terminated by the `break` statement. Figure 5–9 shows the results of the run. I did not test all possible legal input values, and this is not prudent: `"Friday"` is misspelled in the array initialization.

Listing 5.9   Using a two-dimensional array of characters for search.

```
#include <iostream>
#include <cstring>
using namespace std;
#define NUM 7                              // do we expect the week length to change?

int main(void)
{
  int i; char day[10];
  char days[NUM][10] = { "Sunday","Monday","Tuesday",
      "Wednesday","Thursday","friday","Saturday" };
  do {                                     // do until the user enters "end"
    cout << "Enter day of the week or 'end' to finish: ";
    cin.get(day,10); cin.ignore(2000,'\n');      // this is prudent
    cout << "Your input: " << day << endl;
    if (strcmp(day,"end")==0) break;
    for (i = 0; i < NUM; i++)
      if (strcmp(day,days[i])==0) break;         // stop search if found
    if (i == NUM)                               // check why we got here
    cout << "Input \"" << day << "\" is incorrect\n";
  else
    cout << day << " is day no. " << i+1 << endl;
  } while (1==1);                              // go on forever
  cout << "Thank you for using this program" << endl;
  return 0;
}
```

Figure 5–9   Cutting corners in testing is asking for trouble.

```
Enter day of the week or 'end' to finish: Sunday
Your input: Sunday
Sunday is day no. 1
Enter day of the week or 'end' to finish: Thursday
Your input: Thursday
Thursday is day no. 5
Enter day of the week or 'end' to finish: saturday
Your input: saturday
Input "saturday" is incorrect
Enter day of the week or 'end' to finish: end
Your input: end
Thank you for using this program
```

Array Overflow in Insertion Algorithms

The algorithm in Listing 5.9 used the array of data (days of the week) for searching only, and the issue of array overflow did not come up. The size of the array was the same as the number of valid elements in the array. Usually, arrays have to be filled with data before they can be used for further processing. The data take the first part of the array, and each new element is appended after the current last element. At each moment, the part of the array used for data is a contiguous set of elements, and the second part of the array contains locations that are available for use but do not contain valid data.

Further processing should be done, not over each element of the array but over each element in the contiguous part filled with valid data. This is why it is often necessary to keep track of how many valid data elements there are in the array. The algorithms that append (or insert) elements in the array must worry about array overflow.

Listing 5.10 shows the algorithm that enters transaction data. This is an extension of examples discussed in Chapter 4. Those examples used a bogus negative value to indicate the end of input. Here, we want to do that in a more-civilized way, by asking the user to terminate the input by typing "end." (Hitting the Enter key to indicate the end of input is not a bad idea, but it can be done accidentally.) To be able to treat input data both as text and as numbers, the program enters data into array `buff[]` and checks whether it is the `"end"` sentinel. If it is not the sentinel, the program converts the string into a floating point number calling a library function `atof()` defined in the header file `cstdlib` (or `stdlib.h`). In this function name, `'a'` stands for ASCII, `'to'` stands for "to" and `'f'` stands for ... well, I wish I could say for float, but I have to be frank with you: This function returns `double`. There are also functions `atoi()` (ASCII to integer) and `atol()` (ASCII to long), but there is no `atod()` function. These functions can convert up to 100 characters, so a 20-character buffer is OK. If the buffer does not contain numeric data, `atof()` returns 0, and the program warns the user. A better strategy is to check whether the input data contain anything in addition to a number, but that would require functions `strtod()` and `strtol()` (string to `double` and to `long`) and the use of pointers, and we are not ready to do that yet.

Otherwise, the program accumulates the value of `total`, saves the input value in the array, and increments the index. At the end of input, variable `count` will contain the number of valid values in the array. This is why further processing (printing the transaction values) uses a loop that iterates until the index reaches `count` and not the number of array elements `NUM`. Notice the use of the library function `width()`, which specifies the minimum number of positions in output that are allocated for the next value. The default width is zero: The value takes only as many output positions as it needs. If the number of characters in the output value is less than the requested width, the rest is filled with spaces (numbers are right aligned, strings are left aligned). If the number of characters to display is greater than the width requested, the width is disregarded and the value takes as many positions as it needs.

Notice also debugging statements that display the input data and the data converted to numeric form. Things often go wrong when the program interprets input data incorrectly but we do not know about it. It is always a good idea to check what the program actually gets as input. The example of the program run is shown on Figure 5–10.

Listing 5.10 Filling the contiguous array with transaction data.

```cpp
#include <iostream>
#include <cstring>
#include <cstdlib>
using namespace std;

int main ()
{
  const int NUM = 100;                        // the size can of course change
  double total, amount, data[NUM]; int count;
  char buff[20];
  total = 0.0; count = 0;                      // initialize current data
do {                                          // do until the user enters "end"
  cout << "Enter amount (or 'end' to finish): ";
  cin.get(buff,20); cin.ignore(2000,'\n');
// cout << "You entered '" << buff << "'" << endl;  // debugging
  if (strcmp(buff,"end")==0) break;
  amount = atof(buff);                        // convert to double up to 100 chars
// cout << "Amount: " << amount << endl;      // debugging aid
  if (amount <= 0)                            // zero if non-numeric input
    cout << "This value is discarded as incorrect.\n"
         << "Please reenter it correctly.\n";
  else
  { total += amount;                          // process current data
    data[count] = amount;
    count++; }
  } while (1 == 1);
cout << "\nTotal of " << count << " values is "
     << total << endl;
  if (count == 0) return 0;
cout << "\nTran no. Amount\n\n";
  for (int i = 0; i < count; i++)
  { cout.width(4); cout << i+1;
    cout.width(11); cout << data[i] << endl; }
  return 0;
}
```

```
Enter amount (or 'end' to finish): 22
Enter amount (or 'end' to finish): 33
Enter amount (or 'end' to finish): 44
Enter amount (or 'end' to finish): 55
Enter amount (or 'end' to finish): end

Total of 4 values is 154

Tran no.   Amount

   1          22
   2          33
   3          44
   4          55
```

Figure 5-10   Using contiguous array for storing input data.

The program in Listing 5.10 does a good job using the contiguous set of array elements to store data. The second loop does not display all available array elements, only those that the first loop put into the array. However, the program does not prevent array overflow if the number of input values exceeds the array length.

To prevent array overflow and corruption of memory, the first loop should test whether index count points to a legal array element. Remember, the first illegal index value is NUM, the number of elements in the array. So, as long as count is less than NUM, the value could be saved in the array. Otherwise, the input should be terminated.

Real-life programs contain long arrays, and to test the protection from overflow, one has to supply hundreds or thousands of values. This is time consuming and prone to error. Listing 5.11 shows the version of the program in Listing 5.10 that implements protection against overflow. To avoid using large sets of data, the size of the array is decreased to 3. This is a good debugging technique.

In the example in the previous section, the character array was not modified, and the index value was a reliable indicator of why the loop was terminated. If the index value was less than the number of elements, it meant that the item was found. Otherwise, the loop tested all array elements unsuccessfully. In this example, this approach is not 100 percent reliable, because count could reach NUM when the user entered exactly NUM values. This is a very rare occurrence for very large arrays, extremely rare. This is why some programmers do not account for it in code. This is not right. Listing 5.11 tests whether the user entered "end"—if not, the loop was terminated because of array overflow. Figure 5–11 shows the results of execution.

This version of the code also shows the use of the const keyword with array LAST[]. This allows the maintenance programmer to easily change the terminator to "finish" or an empty string or anything else, without chasing all occurrences of "end" in the source code. The same is true of the symbolic literal NUM. Changing a constant literal is much better than global editing. Once, I wanted to change the size of my array from 100 to 300, and I did that using the global replace command. This was a financial application that counted on the fact that each dollar contained exactly 100 cents. After this global replacement, one dollar in my program was worth 300 cents, and my boss did not like that.

Listing 5.11 Entering input data in the array with overflow protection.

```cpp
#include <iostream>
#include <cstring>
#include <cstdlib>                          // to support atof()
using namespace std;

int main ()
// { const int NUM = 100;                   // the size can of course change
{
  const int NUM = 3;                        // for debugging only
  const char LAST[] = "end";                // literal for termination
  double amount, total, data[NUM];
  char buff[20]; int count;
  total = 0.0; count = 0;                    // initialize current data
do {                                         // do until the user enters "end"
  cout << "Enter amount (or '" << LAST << "' to finish): ";
  cin.get(buff,20); cin.ignore(2000,'\n');
  if (strcmp(buff,LAST)==0) break;          // end of input data
  amount = atof(buff);                      // convert to double up to 100 chars
  if (amount <= 0)                          // zero if non-numeric input
  cout << "This value is discarded as incorrect.\n"
       << "Please reenter it correctly.\n";
  else if (count < NUM)
  { total += amount;                        // process current data
    data[count] = amount;
    count++; }
  else
  { cout << "Out of memory: input is terminated\n";
    break; }
  } while (1 == 1);
  if (strcmp(buff,"end") != 0)
      cout << "The value " << amount << " is not saved\n";
```

```
cout << "\nTotal of " << count << " values is "
     << total << endl;
if (count == 0) return 0;
cout << "\nTran no. Amount\n\n";
for (int i = 0; i < count; i++)
  { cout.width(4); cout << i+1;
    cout.width(11); cout << data[i] << endl; }
return 0;
}
```

Notice that if you do not include the cstdlib (or stdlib.h) header file, the compiler will flag a call atof()as a syntax error, telling you that it does not know what that atof() function is. Let us call a lie a lie. The compiler knows what the library functions are and where they are. What do you do if you do not remember what header file atof() needs? You ask the compiler. Under UNIX, you type man atof. Under Windows, you highlight atof in your source code and hit F1 for Help. Immediately the Help page is displayed, which tells you all there is to be known about atof(), including the name of its header file.

Figure 5-11 Using a very short array to test for overflow protection.

```
Enter amount (or 'end' to finish): 22
Enter amount (or 'end' to finish): 33
Enter amount (or 'end' to finish): 44
Enter amount (or 'end' to finish): 55
Out of memory: intput is terminated
The value 55 is not saved

Total of 3 values is 99

Tran no.  Amount

   1         22
   2         33
   3         44
```

Defining Array Types

In all previous examples in this chapter, the arrays we used were array variables rather than array types. If we needed another array with the same structure as a given array (that is, with the same type and number of components), we had to define another array from scratch.

```
double data[NUM];
double tax[NUM];
```

If these definitions are in different places in the program, it would take extra effort on the part of the maintainer (or the fellow designer) to understand that these two computational objects have the same structure. Again, the issue here is writing code in such a way that the knowledge of the designer (in this case, that two arrays have the same structure) is passed on to the maintenance programmer.

A good way to convey that knowledge would be to define a type, like SalesData, for arrays of NUM components of type double, and use this type name to define any number of variables of that type,

```
SalesData data;
SalesData tax;
```

This is exactly the way we use built-in scalar types to define variables of this type. C++ allows us to do that by using the typedef keyword. In general, typedef is a facility to define new names, including the type names, on the basis of other names known to the compiler. Its general form is a statement that connects the known type and the new name that is equivalent to the known type.

```
typedef known_type new_type_name;
```

After this statement (terminated by the semicolon), the program can use both known_type and new_type_name as synonyms.

A simple example of the use of typedef would be the following segment of code that processes inventory information.

```
int idx, quant, const MAX=30, qty[MAX];
for (idx = 0; idx < MAX; idx++)
  { cin >> quant;
    qty[idx] = quant; }
```

Here, variables `idx`, `quant`, `MAX`, and elements of array `qty[]` are all integers. However, they are integers of a different nature: one is the index of the array, and others describe quantities of inventory items. Statements like `qty[idx] = quant;` make sense. Statements like `idx = quant;` do not make sense; you cannot mix apples and oranges in computations. As far as C++ rules are concerned, both kinds of statements are legitimate. One way to stress their different nature is to introduce two new type names.

```
typedef int Index;              // one kind of integers
Index idx;
const Index MAX=30;
typedef int Stock;
Stock quant, qty[MAX];          // another kind of integers
for (idx = 0; idx < MAX; idx++) // comparison between the same type
  { cin >> quant;
    qty[idx] = quant; }         // assignment between the same type
```

Here, `idx` and `MAX` are of the same type, `Index`; small wonder: Their comparison is legitimate. Variables `quant` and `qty[idx]` are of the same type, `Stock`, and the assignment is appropriate. If the programmer had said, for example, `idx = quant;` this assignment would be suspect because these variables are of different types.

In this example, the `typedef` facility is used to define a new name for the existing type, `int`, and not to introduce a new type. It is only for the programmer that these types are different. For the compiler, `Index` and `Stock` are aliases for the same type name.

For defining an array type, we use a somewhat different form of `typedef` that defines a new type.

```
int const MAX = 30;
typedef double SalesData[MAX];
```

In this definition, the keyword `typedef` precedes a syntactically complete definition of an array. If it were not for `typedef`, this definition would introduce a new name, `SalesData`, defined through type `double` and constant `MAX`, as the name of an array variable. Since `typedef` is present, this definition introduces the new name, `SalesData`, as the name of a new type. According to what follows `typedef`, this type defines an array of `MAX` components of type `double`. (Of course, `MAX` can be any compile time constant, including a literal integer value.)

Now we can use this type name to define variables of this type. Each variable is an array of `MAX` components of type `double`, even though the definition of the variable includes only the type name and the name of the variable. Each of these two array definitions allocates memory for `MAX` components of type `double`.

```
SalesData data;
SalesData tax;
```

Variables `data` and `tax` can be used as any array variables by using the same notation for array components as ordinary array variables do.

```
for (int idx = 0; idx < MAX; idx++)
  { tax[idx] = data[idx] * 0.05; }
```

Although the form of `typedef` that we used for defining types `Index` and `Stock` is different from the form used for defining type `SalesData`, they work in the same way. They define as a new type name the only element of `typedef` that is not yet defined in the `typedef` statement (`Index` and `Stock` in the first case, `SalesData` in the second case).

We will see more on the use of `typedef` in the next section.

Structures as Heterogeneous Aggregates

The next programmer-defined aggregate data types on our agenda are structures. C++ structures are a powerful aggregation tool for combining related components. There is more than one method to define a structure in C++, and we will discuss the most popular ones. All methods allow the programmer to define structure components (fields, or data members), that is, to list the types and names of the components.

Defining Structures as Programmer-Defined Types

The structure definition starts with the keyword `struct` followed by the programmer-defined name that will be used as a type name to define variables in the program. The structure fields are declared within scope curly braces followed by a semicolon. Each field declaration is similar to a declaration of a variable: It includes the type and the programmer-defined name but cannot include initialization.

```
struct Account {              // 'Account' is a type name now
  long number;                // 'number' is a field name
  double balance;
  double overdue; } ;         // semicolon follows the brace
```

Each field declaration ends with a semicolon. If the fields that follow each other in the structure definition are of the same type, they can be declared using only one type name and commas as separators. This structure definition defines exactly the same type as the previous one—no difference.

```
struct Account {              // 'Account' is a type name now
  long number;                // 'number' is a field name
  double balance, overdue; } ;
```

C++ supports yet another syntax for defining a structure that it inherited from C: using `typedef` to define a new type.

```
typedef struct tagAccount {
  long number;
  double balance, overdue; } Account;
```

This is the same use of `typedef` that we saw in the previous section for integers.

```
typedef known_type new_type_name;
```

Here, `known_type` is represented by the definition of `struct tagAccount`, and `Account` is `new_type_name` (similar to all previous examples of using `typedef`, the name `Account` is the only name that is not defined yet). Actually, `struct tagAccount` is also a type name and can be used anywhere type `Account` is used, but this name is less convenient, because the keyword `struct` makes this type name different in form from the names of built-in types. This form of defining the structure type name is very popular in C, but it is not needed in C++.

Creating and Initializing Structure Variables

The structure definition does not allocate any memory. It defines a template for future memory allocations: how much memory to allocate, how to interpret that memory, and what names to use to access values in that memory. When the structure name is used in definitions of variables, it is used in the same way as are built-in primitive types `int`, `double`, and so on.

```
Account a1, a2;        // memory for two Account variables
```

Two variables of type `Account` are created here. Each one has fields with names `number`, `balance`, and `overdue`. The total size of each `Account` variable is the total size of one `long` and two `double` values plus some alignment space (in case a value cannot start at an arbitrary address and must be aligned at an address divisible by 4 or 8).

The braces in the structure type definitions in the previous section should be taken seriously. They denote a block with its separate scope similar to the other scopes (more on that in the next chapter). The names that are defined within that scope are not known outside of the scope. Since `number` is a `long` data member, not a `long variable`, we cannot use its name without any qualification.

```
number = 800123456L;              // there is no such thing as number
```

This is nonsense because it does not specify to what account this `number` belongs. The C++ dot operator, or selector operator (of high priority), selects fields of structure variables. Similar to array components accessed by indices, structure fields can be accessed uniformly as lvalues and as rvalues using the same dot notation.

```
a1.number = 800123456L;           // field is used as lvalue
if (a1.number == 800123456L)      // field is used as rvalue
  a2.number = a1.number;          // both lvalue and rvalue
```

Similar to arrays, the number of elements in a structure should be specified at compile time. Array components are of the same type; they do not have individual names, but they are ordered. Array components can be referred to using the name of the array variable and the element's subscript. The result is a value of the type specified in the array definition. Structure components are not ordered. They have individual names and can be of different types. They can be referred to using the name of the structure variable and the name of the component. The result is the value of the type specified for that component in the structure definition.

Again, structure fields are not ordered. The definition of the `Account` field could be done in any order, and that should not change anything in the program that uses this structure.

When structure variables are created, their fields do not contain useful values. C++ supports the initialization syntax similar to that for arrays, where a value of appropriate type is specified for each structure component.

```
Account a1 = { 800123456L, 532.84, 0 } ;
```

This syntax is valid for structures with public fields only, the structures whose fields can be accessed by client code, (and structures we discuss in this chapter all have public fields). We will learn later how to use constructors to initialize structure and class variables with nonpublic fields.

Similar to nonaggregate variables, it is OK to initialize a structure variable from another structure variable that was defined earlier.

```
Account a3=a1;          // it has 800123456, 532.84, 0 in fields
```

Hierarchical Structures and Their Components

The goal of using C++ structures is to support data abstraction and encapsulation. Structure fields represent attributes of objects relevant to the application: for example, personnel data, medical records, inventory data, and customer data. They also represent related pieces of information that are often used together: task control block, parser symbol table, font metrics structure, communication packet, and so on. Structures are popular both in systems programming and in application programming.

Each structure variable represents a single composite object whose components can be used either individually or as a whole. Structure variables can be handled as a unit, then they are passed to functions. Inside functions, these components can be handled individually. Structure variables can be further combined into arrays, linked lists, queues, and so on.

```
Account cards[500];        // array of 500 structures
```

When we access the fields that belong to the elements of this array, we have to use hierarchical notation. The subscript operator and the dot selector operators are of the same priority and associate from left to right. This is how you access the `number` field of the component at index 75 of array `cards`. (You read the code from right to the left.)

```
cards[75].number = 800123456L;
```

And, of course, we can use structures as components of other structures. For example, we can combine the customer name, address, and account data into a new type.

```
struct Customer
  {
    char name[30]
    char address[70];
    Account acct;
  } ;
```

This format gives to each brace and each field a line of its own to indicate the composition of the structure. Other programmers prefer a more-succinct format.

```
struct Customer
  { char name[30], address[70];
    Account acct; } ;
```

When a `Customer` variable is created, its memory includes two character arrays and an `Account` variable, which in turn consists of a `long` field and two `double` fields. Again, hierarchical notation is used for elements of arrays and for elements of `Account`.

```
Customer c;
strcpy(c.name,"Doe, John");                      // c.name is of type char[]
strcpy(c.address,"72 Main, Anytown, MA");
c.acct.number = 800123456L;                       // type long int
c.acct.balance = 532.84; c.acct.overdue = 0;      // type double
```

Again, dot selector operators associate from left to right and are read from right to left, so that, for example, `c.acct.balance` is the `balance` field (of type `double`) of the field `acct` (of type `Account`) that belongs to the structure variable `c` (of type `Customer`).

You see that it can easily become quite verbose and unwieldy. One of the ways to deal with this problem is to write access functions that simplify the code that handles aggregate variables. We will see numerous examples of access functions in later chapters.

Operations on Structure Variables

Structure variables can be assigned to each other if they are of the same type. The field values of the source variable are copied bitwise into the fields of the target variable.

```
    a2 = a1; c.acct = a1;          // same type (Account)
```

This is equivalent to the following set of assignment operations.

```
a2.number = a1.number;
a2.balance = a2.balance; a2.overdue = a1.overdue;
c.acct.number = a1.number; c.acct.balance = a1.balance;
c.acct.overdue = a1.overdue;
```

Here the C++ strong typing properties come shining through. No conversions are allowed between different structure types. The type name must be the same.

```
c = a1; a1 = c;          // no, they are of different types
a1 = 800123456L;         // do not even think about it!
```

It is the type name rather than the structure composition that is the issue here. Let us say we have a structure with the same composition as `Account`.

```
struct FrozenAcct
{ long number;                    // same structure as Account
  double balance, overdue; } ;
```

Still, a `FrozenAcct` structure cannot be assigned to an `Account` structure and vice versa.

```
    FrozenAcct fa; fa = a1;        // no, type names are different
```

There is no structure comparison in C++ because C++ does not know what fields to use for comparisons and how to do it. You have to write your own code to satisfy the application requirements if you need to compare structure variables.

```
if (a1.number > a2.number)         // swap accounts to order numbers
  { a3 = a1; a1 = a2; a2 = a3; }   // a3 holds data temporarily
```

The next example shows some graphical computations. Since the drawing functions are not portable, I do not want to draw on the screen in my examples. Instead, I ask the user to enter coordinates of endpoints of two lines, AB and CD. Then I compute the length of each line and the angle between each line and the x-axis.

Listing 5.12 shows the source code for this example that uses two data types, `Point` and `Line`. The program requests input data in pixels (integers), uses the data to initialize points, uses these points to initialize the lines, and then computes the line lengths and angles. Functions `sqrt()` and `atan2()` come from the `math.h` library header file. They compute the square root and arctangent of their `double` parameters. Because their actual arguments are defined as `int`, they are converted implicitly to `double`. Since line length is also expressed in pixels as integers, the result of computing the square root is cast implicitly. To avoid truncation, 0.5 is added to the length to achieve proper rounding. Variable `coeff` converts angles from radians to degrees. Figure 5–12 shows the results of the execution of the program.

Listing 5.12 Using #include directive for programmer-defined types.

```
#include <iostream>
#include <cmath>                         // to support sqrt() and atan2()
#include "point.h"                       // to make type Point known to compiler
#include "line.h"                        // to make type Line known to compiler
using namespace std;

int main ()
{
  const double coeff = 180/3.1415926536;
  Point p1, p2; Line line1, line2;       // programmer-defined types
  int diffX, diffY, length1, length2;
  double angle1, angle2;
  cout << "Enter x and y coordinates of point A: ";
  cin >> p1.x >> p1.y;
  cout << "Enter x and y coordinates of point B: ";
  cin >> p2.x >> p2.y;
  line1.start = p1; line1.end = p2;
  cout << "Enter x and y coordinates of point C: ";
  cin >> p1.x >> p1.y;
  cout << "Enter x and y coordinates of point D: ";
  cin >> p2.x >> p2.y;
  line2.start = p1; line2.end = p2;
  diffX = line1.end.x - line1.start.x;   // ugly notation
  diffY = line1.end.y - line1.start.y;
  length1 = sqrt(diffX*diffX + diffY*diffY) + 0.5;
  angle1 = atan2(diffY,diffX) * coeff;
  cout << "Length AB is " << length1 << " at angle "
       << angle1 << " degrees\n";
  diffX = line2.end.x - line2.start.x;
  diffY = line2.end.y - line2.start.y;
  length2 = sqrt(diffX*diffX + diffY*diffY) + 0.5;
  angle2 = atan2(diffY,diffX) * coeff;
  cout << "Length CD is " << length2 << " at angle "
       << angle2 << " degrees\n";
  return 0;
}
```

Figure 5-12 Execution example for program in Listing 5.12.

```
Enter x and y coordinates of point A: 20 20
Enter x and y coordinates of point B: 80 80
Enter x and y coordinates of point C: 20 20
Enter x and y coordinates of point D: 160 80
Length AB is 84 at angle 45 degrees
Length CD is 152 at angle 23.1986 degrees
```

Defining Structures in Multifile Programs

For a small example like Listing 5.12, it is perfectly reasonable to include the structure definitions in the source code. Programmer-defined types must be unique in the program name space; therefore, a multifile program might present a problem if a programmer-defined type has to be used in several files. Actually, you do not even like to repeat the type definition in several files. If these definitions are ever updated during maintenance, they might easily become inconsistent.

The solution is to put each type definition in a separate header file and include these files in all source files that use this type. This is what I did for types Point and Line in Listing 5.12. Notice the double quotes in file names instead of angle brackets. It is common to use the same name for the header file as for the type defined in the file. Since all type names must be unique in a C++ program, this should not lead to name conflicts when the header files are kept in the same directory. Often, header files are kept in a separate directory that is different from the directory where the program executable file is. In this case, the #include directives should specify the full path name.

A common practice to avoid repeated compilation of the same programmer-defined data type in a multifile program with several source files is the use of conditional compilations. Listings 5.13 and 5.14 show the contents of the header files.

Listing 5.13 The header file `"point.h"`.

```
#ifndef _POINT
#define _POINT
struct Point
{ int x, y; } ;
#endif
```

Listing 5.14 The header file `"line.h"`.

```
#ifndef _LINE
#define _LINE
#include "point.h"
struct Line
{ Point start, end; } ;
#endif
```

When we include these files in several source files, the very first definitions processed by the compiler will define the names _POINT and _LINE. When other files are compiled, the conditional directives in these files will exclude the type definitions from being compiled. It is customary to use the same name for the symbolic constant as the type name, capitalize it, and prefix (and/or append) it with the underscore character to avoid accidental name conflicts.

Notice that the file `"line.h"` has to include file `"point.h"`. Otherwise, the compiler might not know what the type name `Point` in file `"line.h"` means.

This is all that you need to know about structures to use them intelligently. The main point about using structures is that we put in each structure only related information. Try to avoid including structure fields that do not belong together with other fields. Another important thing is that each structure variable has a full complement of the fields that can be accessed using dot notation and the names declared in the structure definition. Last, each field (expressed in the dot notation) is for all intents and purposes a variable of the type specified for that field in the structure definition.

Unions, Enumerations, and Bit Fields

This section is going to be relatively short. It discusses three ideas related to naming program entities for the programmer's convenience. The first idea is to define a variable that can be used to store information of more than one type, for example, an integer and a floating point number. This is the idea of a *union*. The second idea is to define symbolic names for related constants without getting into details of assigning numerical values to these symbolic constants. This is the idea of *enumeration*. The third idea is naming parts of the word so that they can be manipulated separately from the rest of the word. This is the idea of *bit fields*.

C++ implements these ideas in a similar manner to defining a structure. The programmer uses a keyword (union, enum, or struct) at the beginning of the type definition. Then the programmer introduces the name chosen for this new type and then describes the type composition (within the braces terminated by a semicolon). After that, the programmer-defined name can be used as a type name by the program.

Unions

Let us consider an array of structures of type Number with some kind of arbitrary numeric information.

```
Number num[6];
```

Since any numeric value is a valid value, we should use a nonnumeric sentinel, for example, a string "end" or something else. Strong typing supported by C++ does not allow us to store text information in a numeric field. One solution to this problem is to define a structure with two fields, one for the numeric value, and another for the text. The following definition will do.

```
struct Number
{ double value;
  char text[4]; } ;
```

Now we can use the elements of this type in an array, keeping numeric information in the field value and using the field text for a sentinel, like "end" to indicate the end of valid data in the array. However, for each array element only one field is used; the element is either a valid numeric entry or a text sentinel. C++ allows us to avoid wasting memory space by defining a *union*. The keyword union is used in C++ to provide for two or more different interpretations of the same area in memory. The keyword union defines a new type using the same syntax as structure definitions. The fields of the union are defined similarly to the fields of a structure. If there are several fields, they represent alternative representations of the same area in memory. This is how the union definition will look in this example.

```
union Number            // yet another C++ keyword
{ double value;         // any number of fields can be defined
  char text[4]; } ;     // do not forget the semicolon!
```

This definition introduces type Number. We can define variables of this type, and each variable will have two fields. Unlike structures, these fields do not exist simultaneously. Rather, they represent different interpretations of the same area in memory. When a union variable is defined, it is allocated enough memory to accommodate the longest interpretation. The programmer can choose which interpretation to use, floating point or a character array. If one makes a mistake and saves data as one type and then retrieves it as another type, the result is garbage. As usual, the C++ compiler is not going to watch over the programmer's shoulder, checking whether or not the programmer is consistent in the use of memory.

In this sample code, I put a numeric value in union variable n1 and a string in union variable n2. But then I display the contents of n1 as text and the contents of n2 as a numeric value. This is no good, but the compiler knows that this is a free country, after all. This example also shows that you can legitimately store text in the place where a numeric value used to be stored and vice versa.

```
Number n1, n2;
n1.value = 5.0; strcpy(n2.text,"no");        // making a commitment
cout << n1.value << " " << n2.text << endl;   // this is OK
cout << n1.text << " " << n2.value << endl;   // this is a disaster
strcpy(n1.text,"yes"); n2.value = 25.0;       // old contents disappears
cout << n1.text << " " << n2.value << endl;    // now this is OK
```

This example shows that when we use union variables, the notation is similar to the notation we use for structures. Listing 5.15 shows a short program written to illustrate this point. It looks as if the text fields of the first three components of array num[] are not initialized and that the value field of the last used component is not initialized. In reality, the same space is used for both interpretations. (The compiler allocates the same amount of space for each element—enough to accommodate the largest interpretation.) The output of the program is shown in Figure 5–13.

Listing 5.15   Using union to store values of different types in a variable.

```
#include <iostream>
#include "number.h"                          // to make type Number known to compiler
#include <cstring>
using namespace std;

int main ()
{
  Number num[6]; int i = 0;                  // array of union variables
  num[0].value = 11.0; num[1].value = 21.0;  // initialization
  num[2].value = 31.0; strcpy(num[3].text,"end");
  while(strcmp(num[i].text, "end") != 0)     // iteration
    cout << num[i++].value << endl;
  cout << num[i].text << endl;               // for illustration purposes
  cout << "Text as double: " << num[i].value << endl;

  return 0;
}
```

Make sure you are not intimidated by notation like num[0].value; array num[] contains components of type Number; hence, num[0] is of type Number and has the fields whose names are value and text. When field text is used,

```
11
21
31
end
Text as double: 3.57452e-031
```

Figure 5-13
Output for program in Listing 5.15.

it is a character array, hence you can pass `num[i].text` as an argument to the `strcmp()` function. Incrementing the index while printing a field value (as in `num[i++].value`) is both legitimate and expedient. Since index `i` is used only once here, there is no danger related to the order of evaluation.

The last two lines of the program show how the same value looks when interpreted differently. Erroneous use of unions can easily produce garbage. Notice, that once in a while, the value 3.57452e-031 might be a legitimate floating point value in the application; it will be interpreted as `"end"` and will terminate the iteration.

To avoid errors of interpretation, some programmers use so-called tag fields for unions whose values indicate how to use the union value. This tag field cannot be a member of the union, so the union and the tag field have to be parts of a larger structure. For example, the address might contain three lines, and the second line might be either the street address or post office box number. Listing 5.16 shows an illustration program that defines the address structure with a union field, `second`, and a tag field, `kind`. When the tag field is 0, the second line is interpreted as street address; when the tag field is 1, the second line is interpreted as P.O.B. number. This code sticks to this convention when data are set (by setting the value of `kind` to 0 or 1) and when data is used (by testing the value of the `kind` field). The output of the program is shown on Figure 5–14.

Listing 5.16 Using `union` with a tag field to enforce access integrity.

```cpp
#include <iostream>
#include <cstring>
using namespace std;

union StreetOrPOB
  { char street[30];          // alternative interpretations
    long int POB; } ;

struct Address
{ char first[30];
  int kind;                   // 0: street address; 1: P.O.B.
```

```
  StreetOrPOB second;                         // either one or another meaning
  char third[30]; } ;

int main ()
{
  Address a1, a2;
  strcpy(a1.first,"Doe, John");                // address with street
  strcpy(a1.second.street,"15 Oak Street"); a1.kind = 0;
  strcpy(a1.third,"Anytown, MA 02445");
  strcpy(a2.first,"King, Amy");
  a2.second.POB = 761; a2.kind = 1;            // address with POB
strcpy(a2.third,"Anytown, MA 02445");
  cout << a1.first << endl;
  if (a1.kind == 0)                            // check data interpretation
    cout << a1.second.street << endl;
  else
    cout << "P.O.B. " << a1.second.POB << endl;
  cout << a1.third << endl;
  cout << endl;
  cout << a2.first << endl;
  if (a2.kind == 0)                            // check data interpretation
    cout << a2.second.street << endl;
  else
    cout << "P.O.B. " << a2.second.POB << endl;
  cout << a2.third << endl;
  return 0;
}
```

This is nice, but it introduces yet another level into the hierarchical structure of types. As a result, the programmer has to use names like a1.second.street, and this is no fun. Meanwhile, the only use of type StreetOrPOB in the program is with type Address. To remedy this, C++ supports anonymous unions. They have no name, and no variable of this type can be defined; however, their fields can be used without any qualification. For example, we can define type Address without using type StreetOrPOB but using an anonymous union instead.

```
Doe, John
15 Oak Street
Anytown, MA 02445

King, Amy
P.O.B. 761
Anytown, MA 02445
```

Figure 5-14
Output for program in Listing 5.14.

```
struct Address
{ char first[30];
  int kind;                    // 0: street address; 1: P.O.B.
  union
  { char street[30];
    long int POB; } ;          // no 'second' field of type StreetOrPOB
  char third[30]; } ;
```

The union type is gone, but type Address now has two alternative fields,
street[] and POB, and they can be referred to by name as in any other field.
Of course, it remains the responsibility of the programmer to know which one
is which. Remember the story about the bagel and cream cheese? Data must
be retrieved consistently with the way they were set. But the extra level of
hierarchical notation is not needed anymore.

```
if (a1.kind == 0)              // check data interpretation
  cout << a1.street << endl;   // use one interpretation
else
  cout << "P.O.B. "<< a1.POB << endl;   // or use another one
```

This is a powerful programming style. However, the maintenance programmer has to spend extra time and effort to understand the code. There
are extra conditional statements that increase the complexity of code.
Presumably, the use of inheritance with virtual functions is good competition
for this programming technique. We will discuss it later.

Enumerations

Enumeration types allow the programmer to define variables that accept values only from a defined set of identifiers. Usually, we introduce integer symbolic constants (using either #define or const definitions) and set up
conventions for using them. For example, to emulate the behavior of a traffic
light, we need the values that denote the red, green, and yellow colors of the
light. Similar to the example with the days of the week, we can introduce
character arrays "red", "green", and "yellow" and do assignments and
comparisons using string manipulation library functions.

```
char light[7] = { "green" };         // it is green initially
if (strcmp(light, "green") == 0)     // next it is yellow
  strcpy(light, "yellow");           // and so on
```

This is nice and clear, and the maintenance programmer will have little
trouble understanding the intent of the code designer, but these string operations are unnecessarily slow. You do not want to move a lot of characters

around (searching for the terminator inside the library functions) just to trace the state of the traffic light. Another drawback of this solution is the lack of protection. If somebody wants to make the light pink or magenta, there is no way to stop the programmer from doing so.

Another solution is to use integers to denote colors with numbers. I can assign 0 to green, 1 to red, and 2 to yellow. Notice how I introduced these values—0, 1, and 2, not 1, 2, and 3. This is what dealing with C++ arrays and indices does to the way people think. When a C (or C++) programmer counts people in the room, he or she says: "Zero, one, two, three, four, five, six, seven, eight, nine; OK, there are ten people in the room."

With this approach you avoid using the string manipulation functions.

```
int light = 0;          // it is green initially
if (light == 0)         // next it is yellow
    light = 2;          // and so on
```

The advantage of this approach is speed. This is the only advantage. This type of coding always requires comments, especially for complex algorithms with more-complicated systems of states and transitions between the states. If the comments are too cryptic or somewhat obsolete, the transmission of the designer's knowledge to the maintainer is not facilitated, to say the least.

One of the ways to make code more readable while keeping it fast is the use of symbolic constants. We can define symbolic constants whose names are appropriate for the application, for example, RED, GREEN, and YELLOW, and assign a special integer value to each constant.

```
const int RED=0, GREEN=1, YELLOW=2;        // color constants
```

Now you can rewrite the example above using these constants. The code is as fast as in the previous example and as clear as the original version with character strings.

```
int light = GREEN;              // it is green initially
if (light == GREEN)             // next it is yellow
  light = YELLOW;               // and so on
```

This solution does protect your steak from falling on the floor to begin with. But it does not protect your code from deterioration in the course of maintenance. If maintainers (or the original designer in the crunch) want to use numbers instead of symbolic constants, it is not a syntax error. If they assign to variable light a value that is outside of the agreed upon range of color values (e.g., light = 42;), it is not a syntax error either. You can add these values (e.g., RED + GREEN), and do all kinds of things you do not actually do to colors.

The enumerations are introduced into the language to deal with these kinds of problems. The programmer can define a programmer-defined type and explicitly enumerate all legal values that a variable of that type is allowed to assume. The keyword enum is used to introduce the programmer-defined type name (e.g., Color) similar to the way the keyword struct (or union) introduces programmer-defined types. The braces (followed by the semicolon) follow the type name, again, similar to struct or union. In the braces, the designer lists all values allowed for the type being defined. Often, the programmers use uppercase (similar to constants introduced by #define and by const), but this is not mandatory. For our example, we can define type Color as the enum type.

```
enum Color { RED, GREEN, YELLOW } ;        // Color is a type
```

Now we can use type Color to define variables that can only accept values RED, GREEN, and YELLOW. These values are enumeration constants—they can be used as rvalues only and cannot be changed.

```
Color light = GREEN;            // it is green initially
if (light == GREEN)             // next it is yellow
  light = YELLOW;               // and so on
```

This solution removes the thumb from your steak. The only operations that are defined on values of enumeration type are assignment and relational operators. You cannot add them or do input or output, but you can compare them for equality or inequality and you can check whether one value is greater (or less) than another.

```
if (light > RED) cout << "True\n";        // this prints 'True'
```

The reason is that under the hood, enumeration values are implemented as integers. The first value in the enumeration list is 0 (no surprise, as this is how we count things in C++), the next is 1, and so on. The program can access these values by casting enumeration values to integers.

```
cout << (int) light << endl;           // this prints 0, 1, or 2
```

If the programmer wants to change this value to another value, one can do that explicitly in the enumeration list.

```
enum Color { RED, GREEN=8, YELLOW } ;     // YELLOW is 9 now
```

After that, the assignment of values resumes (YELLOW is 9, and so on). If for some reason you want to set GREEN to 0, this is OK with the compiler, but the program will not be able to distinguish between RED and GREEN (not a big problem unless it tries to control traffic).

This technique is useful when the enumeration values are going to be used as masks for bitwise operations and hence have to represent powers of two.

```
enum Status { CLEAR = 2, FULL = 8, EMPTY = 64 } ;
```

Many programmers enthusiastically embrace this facility and use it for defining integer compile time constants.

```
enum { SIZE = 80 } ;                  // use it to define arrays etc.
```

Notice that this enumeration is anonymous (similar to anonymous union). It does not have a name and hence you cannot define variables of this type, but this is not a big loss because all we need is the symbolic constant SIZE. The result is the same as defining the constant explicitly.

```
const int SIZE = 80;                      // same thing
```

It is a matter of personal taste (yours or your boss's) what method of defining constants to use.

Bit Fields

Similar to our discussion of unions and enumerations, we will start with examples of practical problems that can be solved using additional C++ user-defined types.

The smallest object that can be allocated and addressed in a C++ program is a character. Sometimes a program might need a value that is too small, and using a full-size integer to store it looks like a waste. Often, we do not pay attention to the opportunity to save memory. When memory is scarce, we would like to pack small values together. Often, external data formats and hardware device interfaces force us to process word elements.

For example, a disk controller might manipulate memory addresses and their components: a page number (from 0 to 15) and the offset of the memory location on the page (from 0 to 4095). The algorithm might require manipulation of the page number (4 bits), offset (12 bits), and the total address (unsigned 16 bits), be able to combine the page number and offset into the address, and extract the page number and offset from the address.

Another example might be an input/output port where specific bits are associated with specific conditions and operations. Bit 1 of the port might be set if the device is in the clear to send condition, bit 3 might be set if the receiving buffer is full, and bit 6 might be set if the transmit buffer is empty. The algorithm might require setting each bit in the status word individually and retrieving the state of each bit individually. Each of these computational tasks requires bit manipulation and the use of bitwise logical operations.

Combining the page number and the offset into the memory address requires shifting the memory address 12 positions to the left and performing the bitwise OR operation on the result of the shift and the address.

```
unsigned int address, temp;      // they must be unsigned
int page, offset;                // sign bit is never set to one
temp = page << 12;               // make four bits most senior
address = temp | offset;         // assume no extra bits there
```

Retrieving the page number and offset from the memory address is more complex. To get the page number, we shift the address right 12 positions to throw away the bits of the offset and move the page number into the least significant bits of the word. To get the address, we use the bitwise AND operation with the mask 0x0FFF that has each of 12 least significant bits set to 1.

```
page = address >> 12;            // strip offset bits, get page bits
offset = address & 0x0FFF;       // strip page bits from address
```

To set individual bits to 1, we use three masks: each mask has only 1 bit set to 1 and all other bits set to 0. By using the bitwise OR operation on the status word, we set the corresponding bit to 1 if it was 0 or leave all the bits in the same state if it was already set to 1. The constants CLEAR, FULL, and EMPTY defined in the previous section are the masks that have only 1 bit set to 1 and other bits set to 0. The constant CLEAR has bit 1 set to 1, FULL has bit 3 set to 1, EMPTY has bit 6 set to 1.

```
unsigned status=0;      // assume it is initialized properly
status |= CLEAR;        // set bit 1 to 1 (if it is zero)
status |= FULL;         // set bit 3 to 1 (if it is zero)
status |= EMPTY;        // set bit 6 to 1 (if it is zero)
```

To reset individual bits to 0, we need masks with all bits set to 1 with the exception of 1 bit. Using the bitwise AND operation will leave all bits in the status word unchanged and will reset the bit that is 0 in the mask. To reset bit 1, we need a mask that has bit 1 reset to 0. To reset bit 3, we need a mask that has bit 3 reset to 0. To reset bit 6, we need a mask that has bit 6 reset to 0 and all other bits should be set to 1. These masks are difficult to express as decimal or even hexadecimal constants. Also, on different platforms we might need the masks of different sizes, and that affects code portability. It is common to invert (negate) the constants' use to set these bits to 1 and use the result of negation to reset these bits to zero in the AND operation.

```
status &= ~CLEAR;       // reset bit 1 to 0 (if it is 1)
status &= ~FULL;        // reset bit 3 to 0 (if it is 1)
status &= ~EMPTY;       // reset bit 6 to 0 (if it is 1)
```

To access the value of individual bits, we use the AND operation with the masks that have all the bits reset to 0 with the exception of 1 bit that is being accessed. If this bit's status is set, the result of the operation is not 0 (true). If this bit's status is reset to 0, the result of the operation is 0 (false). The masks that will work in these operations are exactly the same as those we used to set and reset status bits.

```
int clear, full, empty; // to test for True or False
clear = status & CLEAR; // True if bit 1 is set to one
full = status & FULL;   // True if bit 3 is set to one
empty = status & EMPTY; // True if bit 6 is set to one
```

These low-level operations for packing and unpacking sequences of bits (addressing example) or individual bits (status example) are complex, counterintuitive, and prone to error. C++ allows us to give names to segment bits of different sizes. This is done using conventional structure definitions. For each field, the number of bits allocated to it (field width) is specified using a nonnegative constant after the column.

```
struct Address {
  int page : 4;
  int offset : 12; } ;        // it is not large enough for 12 bits
```

Field members are packed into machine integers. One has to be careful with signed integers: One bit is usually allocated for the sign. If you want to use all the bits allocated for the field, the field has to be unsigned, as in this example.

```
struct Address {
  unsigned int page : 4;
  unsigned int offset : 12; } ;        // place for 12 bits
```

The bit field may not straddle a word boundary. If it does not fit into the machine word, it is allocated to the next word and the remaining bits are left unused. It is a syntax error if the width of the field exceeds the size of the basis type on the given platform (which can be different for different machines).

Fields might save data space: There is no need to allocate a byte or a word for each value; however, the size of the code, which manipulates these values, increases because of the need to extract the bits. The end result is not clear.

The variables are defined in the same way as structure variables are. Access to bit fields is the same as for regular structure fields.

```
Address a; unsigned address;        // make sure that a is initialized
address = (a.page << 12) | a.offset;
```

If you want to allocate 1 bit for a flag, make sure the field is unsigned rather than signed. Fields do not have to have names; unnamed fields are used for padding. (We still have to specify the type, colon, and width.)

```
struct Status {
  unsigned : 1;                    // bit 0
  unsigned Clear : 1;              // bit 1
  unsigned : 1;                    // bit 2
  unsigned Full : 1;               // bit 3
  unsigned : 2;                    // bits 4 and 5
  unsigned Empty : 1; } ;          // bit 6
```

The code for manipulating the status variables is very simple. Under the hood, it is implemented through shifts and bitwise logical operations similar to the examples we discussed at the beginning of this section.

```
Status stat;                             // make sure it is initialized
int clear, full, empty;                  // for testing for True or False
stat.Clear = stat.Full = stat.Empty = 1; // set bit to one
stat.Clear = stat.Full = stat.Empty = 0; // reset bits to zero
clear = stat.Clear;                      // the values can be tested
full = stat.Full;
empty = stat.Empty;
```

The width of zero is allowed; it is the signal to the compiler to align the next field at the next integer boundary. It is allowed to mix data of different integral types. Switching from the type of one size to the type of another size allocates the next field at the word boundary. Careless use of bit fields might not decrease the allocated space, as the next (contrived) example demonstrates. (This code is written for a 16-bit machine where integers are allocated two bytes.)

```
struct Waste {
  long first : 2 ;          // this allocates all 4 bytes
  unsigned second : 2;      // this adds two more
  char third : 1;           // short starts on even address
  short fourth : 1; } ;     // and this: 10 bytes total
```

On some machines, fields are assigned left to right, and on others they are assigned right to left (so-called little endiens and big endiens).

This is not a problem for internally defined data structures; however, this is significant for mapping externally defined data, for example, device I/O buffers. When external data come in one format and the computer uses another, the data in the bit fields might be saved incorrectly.

Before you decide to use bit fields, evaluate the alternatives. Remember that accessing a character or an integer is always faster than accessing a bit field and takes less code.

Summary

In this chapter, we looked at major program-building tools that the programmer has for creating large complex programs. Most of these tools deal with aggregation of data into larger units: homogeneous containers (arrays) and heterogeneous objects (structures). These aggregate data types do not have operations of their own with the exception of the assignment for structures. All operations over aggregate objects have to be programmed in terms of operations over individual elements.

Since structure fields are accessed using individual field names; they are relatively safe. Array components are accessed using subscripts, and C++ provides neither compile-time nor run-time protection against illegal values of indices. This can easily lead to incorrect results or to memory corruption and is a source of concern for a C++ programmer. This is especially true for character arrays where the end of valid data is specified by the zero terminator.

We also looked at such programmer-defined types as unions, enumerations, and bit fields. Unlike arrays and structures, they are not really necessary. Any program can be written without using these structures. Often, however, they simplify the appearance of the source code, convey more information to the maintainer about the designer's intent, and make the job of the maintainer (and the designer) easier.

MEMORY MANAGEMENT: THE STACK AND THE HEAP

Topics in this Chapter

- Name Scope as a Tool for Cooperation
- Memory Management: Storage Classes
- Memory Management: Using Heap
- Input and Output with Disk Files
- Summary

Chapter 6

In the previous chapter, we studied the tools for implementing programmer-defined data structures. Arrays and structures are the basic programming tools that allow the designers to express complex ideas about the application in a concise and manageable form—both for the designers themselves and also for maintenance programmers. Unions, enumerations and bit fields help the designer to represent code in the most understandable way.

All variables, of built-in and of programmer-defined types alike, that were used in the previous coding examples, were named variables. The programmer has to choose the name and the place of the definition in source code. When the program needs memory for named variables, it is allocated and deallocated without further programmer participation, according to the language rules, in the area of memory called *stack*. We pay for this simplicity with the lack of flexibility: The size of each data item is defined at compile time.

For flexible sizes of data structures, C++ allows the programmer to build dynamic arrays and linked data structures. We pay for this flexibility with the complexity of using pointers. When the program needs more space for dynamic unnamed variables, the memory is allocated from the area called *heap*. Dynamic variables do not have names, and we refer to them indirectly, through pointers. We pay for this flexibility with the complexity of dynamic memory management.

In this chapter, we will study C++ techniques for managing the stack and the heap and will learn the basic techniques of such methods as using name scope, name extent, and dynamic memory management with pointers. These techniques are the key to the efficient use of system resources. In inexperienced hands, however, dynamic memory management can lead to system crashes, memory corruption, and memory leaks (when the system runs out of memory). Some programmers love the power and the thrill of dynamic memory management. Others prefer to use pointers as little as possible. Whatever your personal preferences, make sure that you understand the principles of name management and memory management supported by C++.

Before discussing the issues of dynamic memory management, I'll introduce the concepts of name scopes and storage classes that are important for the understanding of memory management issues in C++. After discussing the issues of dynamic memory management, I discuss the techniques of using external storage—disk files. Storing data in a disk file enables the program to handle infinitely large sets of data.

Note

Take a deep breath. This is a large chapter. It contains a mixture of important concepts and practical coding techniques. You cannot become a skillful C++ programmer without mastering concepts and techniques of memory management and file I/O. However, you can learn the rest of C++ without becoming an expert in these areas. If you are overloaded with the size and complexity of this material, move on to the next chapter and come back to this one when you feel you are ready to learn more.

Name Scope as a Tool for Cooperation

Each programmer-defined name, or identifier, has its lexical scope in the C++ program (often called just scope).

It is called lexical because it refers to a source code segment where the name is known and can be used. It is called scope because outside of this code segment the name is either not known or refers to a different entity. The entities whose names have scopes are the names of programmer-defined data types, functions, parameters, variables, and labels. The possible uses of the names known within the scope include definitions, expressions, and function calls.

C++ Lexical Scopes

Lexical scope is a static name characteristic. This means that the scope is defined by the lexical structure of the program at compile time rather than by program behavior at run time. There are four scopes in C++:

- block scope
- function scope
- file scope
- the scope of the whole program
- class scope
- namespace scope.

In this chapter, I will discuss the first four scopes. The other two scopes will be discussed in later chapters, after the concepts of class and namespace are explained in more detail. The opening and closing curly braces delimit the block scope. The function scope is also delimited by the opening and closing curly braces. The difference between the block and the function scope is that the function has parameters (and their names are known within the scope) and the name. The function scope is entered during execution when the function is called. The block scope is not called. The block is executed after the statement that precedes it (if any) is executed. For example, during each iteration through this `for` loop, the scope of its unnamed block between braces is entered. When function `getBalance()` is called (using its name), the scope of its block is entered. (You will see this function later in Listing 6.1.)

```
for (i = 0; i < count; i++)
{ total += getBalance(a[i]); }                 // accumulate total
```

The file scope is delimited by the physical boundaries of the file. It can contain type definitions, definitions and declarations of variables, and definitions and declarations of functions. Each program listing I used in previous chapters was a listing of a source file delimited by file boundaries.

The program scope has no delimiters. Anything belonging to any source file that is part of the program is within the program scope.

Name Conflicts Within the Same Scope

Name conflicts within a scope are not allowed in C++. A name should be unique within the scope where the name is declared. In C, programmer-defined types used to form a separate space. It means that if a name was used for a type, it could be used for a variable in the same scope. The compiler (and the maintainer) would figure out from the context whether the name means the type or the variable.

C++ takes a more-stringent position. All programmer-defined names form a single name space. If a name is declared in a scope for any purpose, it should be unique in that scope among all the names declared in the same scope for any purpose. This means that if, for example, count is a name of a variable, then no type, function, parameter, or another variable can be named count in the same scope where the variable count is declared.

Similar to most software engineering ideas in language design, this idea aims to improve readability rather than the ease of writing the program. When the designer (or the maintainer) finds the name count in the source code, there is no need to figure out which one of the possible meanings this one has: It has only one meaning within the scope. When the designer (or the maintainer) wants to add variable count to a scope, he or she has to find out whether this name is already used in this scope.

The only exception from this rule is label names. They do not conflict with names of variables, parameters, or types declared or known in the same scope. Since labels are not used that often in C++ code, this does not result in deterioration of readability. Still, do not use this special dispensation too much.

The converse of this principle of uniqueness is that the same name can be used in different scopes without a conflict. This principle decreases the amount of coordination between designers. Different programmers can work on different parts of the program (different files) and choose names independently, without communications among team members. Even for the same file, the need to coordinate names defined in different scopes in the same file would make the job of the designer (and the maintainer) harder.

Lexical scopes of different program entities (data types, functions, parameters, variables, and labels) are somewhat different. Type names can be declared in a block, function, or file. They are known within that block, function, or file from the place of definition until the end of the scope. They are not known outside of the scope of that block, function, or file. The same is true about the names of variables. They can be declared in a block, function, or file. They are known from the place of the definition until the end of the scope.

Parameters can be defined in a function only. They are known from the opening brace of the function scope until the closing brace of the function. Labels can be defined either in a block or in a function, but their names are known in the whole function that uses the label and are not known outside the function.

C++ function names can be defined in a file, but not in a block and not in another function. Function names have the program scope; that is, the function name should be unique in the project. This potential for project-wide name conflicts often makes coordination in the development teams a headache. The same is true of expanding an existing program during maintenance: Adding new function names might result in conflicts. Another potential source of trouble related to function names is integration into the project several libraries that come from different vendors (or from past projects). Often, the problem might not surface until the files developed separately by different programmers are linked together quite late in the development cycle.

Listing 6.1 shows a simple example that loads account data, displays data, and computes total of account balances. For simplicity of the example, I do not load the data set from the keyboard, an external file, or a database. (We will do that later.) Instead, I use two arrays, `num[]` and `amounts[]`, which supply the values of account numbers and account balances. The data is loaded in the infinite `while` loop until the sentinel value (–1) is found for the account number; then the second loop prints account numbers, the third loop prints account balances, and the fourth loop computes the total of account balances. I use two programmer-defined types, structure `Account` and integer synonym `Index` and function `getBalance()`, not because they are really needed, but to illustrate the interaction of scopes. For simplicity's sake, keep the size of the data set very small. The output of the program is shown on Figure 6–1.

Listing 6.1 Demonstration of lexical scope for types, parameters, variables.

```
#include <iostream>
using namespace std;

struct Account {                    // global type definition
  long num;
  double bal; } ;

double getBalance(Account a)
{ double total = a.bal;             // total in independent scopes
  return total; }                   // return a.bal; is better
```

```
int main()
{
  typedef int Index;                               // local type definition
  Index const MAX = 5;
  Index i, count = 0;                              // integers in disguise
  Account a[MAX]; double total = 0;               // data set, its total
  while (true)                                     // break on the sentinel
  { long num[MAX] = { 800123456, 800123123, 800123333, -1 } ;
    double amounts[MAX] = { 1200, 1500, 1800 } ;   // data to load
    if (num[count] == -1) break;                   // sentinel is found
    a[count].num = num[count];                     // loading data
    a[count].bal = amounts[count];
    count++; }
    cout << " Data is loaded\n\n";
  for (i = 0; i < count; i++)
  { long temp = a[i].num;                          // temp in independent scopes
    cout << temp << endl; }                        // display account numbers
  for (i = 0; i < count; i++)
  { double temp = a[i].bal;                        // temp in independent scopes
    cout << temp << endl; }                        // display account balances
  for (i = 0; i < count; i++)
  { total += getBalance(a[i]); }                   // accumulate total for balances
  cout << endl << "Total of balances $" << total << endl;
  return 0;
}
```

```
  Data is loaded

  800123456
  800123123
  800123333
  1200
  1500
  1800

  Total of balances $4500
```

Figure 6-1
Output of code in Listing 6.1.

Note

This program was compiled by the latest version of a 32-bit compiler. This is why there is no need to indicate that value 800123456 and others are of type long. This program will not compile by an older 16-bit compiler. In similar code examples in Chapter 5, "Aggregation with Programmer-Defined Data Types," I used these values with the L suffix (800123456L and so on); these examples will compile with any compiler. C++ programmers should always think about portability issues. Failure to do so can cause errors. Finding and correcting these errors is frustrating and costly.

Here, type `Account` has the file scope and is known from the place of its definition to the end of the source file. Variables of type `Account` can be defined anywhere in this scope. The use of name `Account` for any other purpose in this scope, for example, as the name of an integer, is incorrect.

```
int Account = 5;              // incorrect use of the name Account
```

Type `Index` has the function scope and is known from the place of its definition until the closing brace of the `main()` function. Variables of type `Index` can be defined in `main()` but not in another scope, for example, in function `getBalance()`.

```
double getBalance(Account a)
{ Index z;                    // syntax error: name Index is unknown here
  return a.bal; }
```

Function `getBalance()` has the program scope. No other object in the program scope can be called `getBalance`.

Lexical scope of variable names is most diverse. C++ variables can be defined as:

- Block variables: defined after the opening brace of a block (or in the middle of the block) and are visible from the place of definition until the end of the block. In Listing 6.1, block variables are arrays `amounts[]` and `num[]` defined in the first loop in `main()`, variable `temp` defined in the second loop in `main()`, and variable `temp` defined in the third loop in `main()`.

- Function variables: similar to the block variables but their scope is a named function rather than an unnamed block. They are defined in the function body (after the opening brace or if in the middle) and are visible from the place of definition until the closing brace of the function. In Listing 6.1, function variables are i, count, MAX, a[], and total defined in main() and variable total defined in getBalance().

- Function formal parameters: defined in the function header and are visible everywhere in the function body. This means that the parameter name would conflict with a variable defined in this function. There is only one formal parameter, a, in function getBalance() in Listing 6.1.

- Global variables: have the file scope—they are defined in a file outside any function and are valid from the definition to the end of file. There are no global variables in Listing 6.1; I will discuss them in the next example.

The names of structure fields are local to the block of the structure definition. This means that they can be referenced (without further qualifiers) outside of this scope. In Listing 6.1, the field names num and bal are known only within the definition of structure Account. Hence, bal = 0; in main() is incorrect, because bal is not known in main(). On the other hand, these fields can be referenced (using the selector operator) anywhere where variables of type Account are in scope (known, visible). In Listing 6,1, it is the scope of function main() (where the array a[] of type Account is defined) and the scope of function getBalance() (where the parameter a of type Account is defined). Since C++ allows the programmer to define variables in any place within a scope, it is important to make sure that the name is not used in the scope before it is defined. In Listing 6.1, the constant MAX should lexically precede the definition of the arrays a[], amounts[], and num[] in function main().

Using Same Names in Independent Scopes

When names are defined in different scopes they do not conflict with each other (well, with some exceptions).

The term "different" in the previous paragraph actually needs some clarification. How should the scopes be related to each other so that the same name could be used in each for different purposes?

Two blocks whose scopes do not intersect (do not have common statements) are different. Moreover, they are independent from each other. For example, two unnamed blocks that follow each other (directly or indirectly) in the file or in the function scope are independent and can define and then use the same name for totally different purposes. The names defined in independent scopes will not conflict with each other.

In Listing 6.1, the name `temp` is used in two loops in function `main()`. Actually, there is no need to use local variables in these loops: The fields of array elements could be displayed directly. However, using these variables illustrates the concept of scope well. Since each of these loops has its own set of scope braces, these uses of name `temp` refer to different variables, do not conflict with each other, and do not require coordination of their use.

The same is true about function blocks that define variables or parameters using the same name. For example, variable `total` is defined both in `getBalance()` and in `main()`. Again, function `getBalance()` could do its job without using a local variable, but its use illustrates the concept of scope.

Similarly, the name `a` is used as a parameter in function `getBalance()` and as an array in function `main()`. Again, when the names are defined in independent scopes, each name is known within its own scope only; and there is no need to coordinate their use.

Using Same Name in Nested Scopes

The next type of different scopes is related to the concept of nesting. C++ is a block-structured language. This means that its scopes can be lexically nested within each other, that is, the braces of one scope can be totally inside braces of another scope. Notice that different scopes can be either independent (one scope ends before another starts) or nested (one scope is inside another), but they cannot intersect.

Most C++ programs use nested scopes. An unnamed block can be nested in another unnamed block or in a function. An unnamed block cannot be nested in the file scope directly because control would not be able to reach it—it needs the function header. A function can be nested in the file scope only; it cannot be nested in another function. For example, in the design below I try to hide function `getBalance()` inside `main()` so that its name would not be in the file scope and hence would cause no conflict if some other use of the name `getBalance`. No such luck: This function is totally nested within function `main()`, and hence this design is illegal in C++.

```
int main()
{ double getBalance(Account a)                  // idea is illegal in C++
  { double total = a.bal;
    return total; }

  . . . .

  for (i = 0; i < count; i++)
  { total += getBalance(a[i]); }                // accumulate total
  cout << endl << "Total of balances $" << total << endl;
  return 0; }
```

In Listing 6.1, the loop bodies are implemented as unnamed blocks. They are nested within the scope of function main(); the scopes of functions main() and getBalance() are nested within the source file scope. In a sense, the file scope is nested in the program scope.

The introduction of nested scopes does not change the rules of visibility for variables or types defined in the outer scope. They are visible in nested scopes. For example, variable count is known from the place of its definition to the end of function main() regardless of whether function main() has any nested scopes. Hence, when the unnamed nested block in the first loop in main() refers to variable count, it is the variable defined in the outer block that is referenced. Similarly, the elements of array a[] are referenced in nested blocks in all three loops. Variable total is defined in main() and is referenced in the nested block of the third loop.

On the other hand, variables defined in the nested scope cannot be referenced in the outer scope. For example, arrays num[] and amounts[] are defined in the block of the first loop in main() and cannot be used by main() outside of that block. It would be incorrect to write the second loop in Listing 6.1 in the following way, referring to num[] in the outer scope.

```
for (i = 0; i < count; i++)
   cout << num[i] << endl;                    // num[] is not known
```

C++ allows a nested scope to define a variable whose name is also defined in an encompassing scope. This results in the interaction of the names defined in nested scopes. In this case, the entity defined in the encompassing scope becomes unavailable in the nested scope. When the name is used inside the nested scope, it refers to the entity defined in this nested scope. Outside of the nested scope this name would still refer to the entity (variable, type, or parameter) defined in the outer scope.

To demonstrate the effects of nesting, let us consider Listing 6.2 that shows a modified version of the code presented in Listing 6.1. Useless code, both local variables temp in the loop bodies in main() and function getBalance(), is gone. Other useless changes are done for the sake of the example: variables MAX (actually, it is a constant), count, and array of Account a[] became global in the file scope, the function printAccounts() was added that prints both account number and account balance for each account (on a separate line) in array a[]. The indices are defined within the loops in main(), not in main() itself. The total of balances is displayed and then the program searches for a particular account number and displays its balance if found. The output of this version is shown in Figure 6–2.

Listing 6.2 Demonstration of nesting scopes and name overriding.

```
#include <iostream>
using namespace std;

struct Account {
  long num;
  double bal; } ;

const int MAX = 5;                              // maximum size of the data set
int count = 0;                                  // number of elements in data set
Account a[MAX];                                 // global data to be processed

void printAccounts()
{ for (int i = 0; i < count; i++)               // global count
  { double count = a[i].bal;                    // local count
    cout << a[i].num << " " << count << endl; } }

int main()
{
  typedef int Index;
  long num[MAX] = { 800123456, 800123123, 800123333, -1 } ;
  long number = 800123123; double total = 0;    // outer scope
  while (true)                                  // break it in the sentinel
  { double amounts[MAX] = { 1200, 1500, 1800 } ; // data to load
    if (num[count] == -1) break;                // sentinel is found
    double number = amounts[count];             // number hides outer number
    a[count].num = num[count];                  // loading data
    a[count].bal = number;
    count++; }
  cout << " Data is loaded\n\n";
  printAccounts();
  for (Index i = 0; i < count; i++)             // global count
    { double count = a[i].bal;                  // local count
      total += count;                           // global count
      if (i == ::count - 1)
        cout << "Total of balances $" << total << endl; }
  for (Index j = 0; j < count; j++)
    if (a[j].num == number)                     // outer number, global array
  cout <<"Account "<< number <<" has: $" << a[j].bal << endl;
  return 0;
}
```

```
Data is loaded

800123456    1200
800123123    1500
800123333    1800
Total of balances $4500
Account 800123123 has: $1500
```

Figure 6–2
Output of code in Listing 6.2.

The scope of global variables is the file where they are defined. Any function in that file can reference that name (unless the name is hidden), and all these references will refer to the same global variable. For example, array a[] and variable count in Listing 6.2 are referenced only in function printAccounts() and in main(), constant MAX is used only in main(). There is no need to define these names in printAccounts() and in main() to use them. The global definitions are enough.

In a sense, the scope of global variables is the program scope rather than the file scope. If you define the name MAX, count, a, or num as a global name in another file in the same program, the compiler will compile each file individually because the compiler does not check the contents of other files during the compilation. However, the linker will report duplicate definitions regardless whether these names are used for the same or for a totally different purpose. For example, a[] and num[] could be defined as scalar variables in another file rather than arrays—still, this duplicate usage is an error. This is true of global definitions only and applies neither to declarations nor to non-global definitions. We will see examples in a moment.

Other C++ scopes (function or block scopes) defined in a particular source file are nested in that global file scope. Hence, global names are visible in functions within the file as are any outer names visible in nested scopes. If functions have nested scopes themselves, the names of global variables are still visible in these nested scopes. In Listing 6.2, global arrays a[] and num[] and index count are all used in the body of the first loop nested in the scope of main(). Again, existence of nested scopes (of any depth) does not change the visibility of names defined in encompassing scopes.)

Nested scopes can define variables using the names defined in enclosing scopes (and hence already known in the nested scopes). When this name is used in the local nested scope (a function in a file, or a block in a function or another block), the meaning of this reference is the local name. When this name is used in the enclosing scope, the meaning of the reference is the meaning defined in the enclosing scope (because the local name cannot be known outside of its scope).

In Listing 6.2, function `printAccounts()` uses the name `count` in the loop continuing condition. This name refers to the global variable `count`. Within the loop, however, the name `count` refers to the variable defined in the loop body, not in the global scope. The nested name overrides the global name. In addition to overriding names in nested scopes, other terms are name hiding and name redefining. Notice that the nested name does not have to define a variable of the same type. It can be anything.

It is not difficult to write function `printAccounts()` without using the variable `count`. I introduced it only to illustrate the concepts of the name scope on a relatively simple example. Actually, it is impossible to make up an example where reusing a global name is really a necessity. You can always come up with a local name different from the name in the encompassing scope. The beauty of the name scope concept is that you do not have to come up with a different name. You use the name you like, and this name is known in this scope no matter what names are known in encompassing scopes.

When the nested scope redefines the name defined in an encompassing scope (global or nested in another scope), the name defined in the encompassing scope becomes unavailable in the nested scope. Redefining the name from the outer scope signals to the maintainer the intent of the designer not to use the global name in the local scope.

In Listing 6.2, the body of the first loop in `main()` defines variable `number` using the same name that is defined in the scope of `main()` itself. This means that when the loop body says `number`, it refers to the local variable of type `double` rather than to the outer variable of type `int` because the nested name redefines the outer name. Outside of the nested loop, however, the name `number` again refers to the variable defined in `main()` itself, for example, on the line before last in Listing 6.2.

Similarly, the body of the second loop in `main()` in Listing 6.2 defines variable `count` of type `double` that redefines the global variable `count` of type `int`. References to name `count` within that loop are resolved by the compiler as references to the local variable of type `double`, even though the loop continuing condition refers to the global variable `count` of type `int`.

If the nested scope needs to access the global name too, it can use the C++ global scope operator, '`::`', to access the global name. In Listing 6.2, for example, the total of balances is printed inside the second loop rather than after the loop (which would be simpler and more natural). So, the loop has to compare its index `i` with the number of valid elements in the data set. In this context, `::count` in the second loop in `main()` refers to the global object `count` rather than to the local object `count`.

Hidden global objects should not be accessed lightly. If the nested scope needs the global name, the global name should not be overridden. After all, the nested scope is free to come up with any name to avoid name conflict. However, the need to use this scope operator might arise in the course of maintenance when new requirements call for the use of the global name that was overridden because this need was not anticipated during the original design.

Alert

The global scope operator :: overrides scope rules. For the maintainer, it is easier to assume that the scope rules stand than to search for the scope operator. Name your variables to minimize the need for the scope operator.

Notice that the scope operator accesses the global variables only. C++ provides no mechanism for the nested scope to access a variable from the enclosing scope that is redefined in the nested scope.

In Listing 6.2, the body of the first loop defines the variable number that hides the variable `number` defined in `main()`. This means that all references to `number` in that loop are references to the local variable. The variable `number` defined in `main()` can be accessed only outside of the body of this loop (e.g., in the last loop in Listing 6.2).

Note

The scope operator accesses the global name. If a nested scope redefines a name defined by an outer block, the nested scope forfeits the ability to refer to the name defined by the outer block. If the nested block needs that outer name, do not redefine it in the nested block.

Scope of Loop Variables

Defining loop variables in the header of the loop is modeled after a similar facility in Ada, but C++ implements it differently, and different compilers do it differently. When the loop variable name is the same as the name defined in encompassing scopes, some compilers flag it as an error, whereas others do not. When the loop variable is used outside of the loop body, some compilers flag it as an error, and others do not. The new C++ standard limits the scope of loop variables to the body of the loop. Hence, it should not be used outside the loop. When another loop in the same scope uses the same name for another loop variable, some compilers flag it as an error, and others do not, even though the new standard allows that. Listing 6.2 shows examples of prudent and portable use of this facility: Loop variables do not redefine names defined in encompassing scopes, they are not used outside of the loop bodies, and they are not redefined in other loops in the same scope.

In general, lexical scope is an important tool: Names can be simply reused (without conflict) in independent scopes and redefined (with hiding of outer names) in nested scopes; when scopes of objects with the same name are nested, the most recently defined name hides less recently defined names.

Scope rules help us avoid name conflicts and excessive communications among programmers.

Memory Management: Storage Classes

The lexical scope discussed in the previous section is a compile-time characteristic of the program. It defines the segments of the program source code where a particular name is known. However, it does not define when memory is allocated for a particular variable during execution and when this memory is taken away and made available for other uses. The rules of memory allocation at run time depend on another characteristic of programmer-defined names: their storage class (or extent).

Storage class refers to a span of execution time when the association between a name of a variable and its location in memory is valid, that is, when the storage is allocated for that variable. Unlike lexical scope, storage class is a run-time feature of program behavior.

Program execution in C++ always starts with main(); the first executable statement in main() is usually the first statement executed by the program. Function main() calls other program functions, and these functions call yet other functions. When a server function finishes its execution (it executes a return statement, or its execution reaches the closing brace of the function body), control returns to the client function that called it. When the last function called from main() terminates and execution of main() reaches its closing brace (or a return statement) the program terminates.

So far we saw two versions of function main(), one with the int return type and another is a void function. When the return type is not present, the compiler assumes that it is int (which is, of course, unfortunate). Each form of main() can be used with optional parameters.

```
void main(int argc, char* argv[])       // command line arguments
{ for (int i = 0; i < argc; i++)        // start of program execution
  cout << "Argument " << i << ": " << argv[i] << endl;
. . . . . }                             // end of program execution
```

The parameters are passed to `main()` from the operating system when `main()` is called. They contain information about command line arguments printed by the user during program invocation (if any). These parameters are defined as the count of command line arguments (`argc`) and the array (vector) of strings (`argv[]`), where each string contains one of the command line arguments. (We will talk about the pointer notation for arrays later.)

Often, these strings are file names typed on the command line. In the example above, function `main()` uses the count of command line arguments to go over each of the arguments. In this case it just displays each argument. The name of the program executable file is included in the list of command line arguments. Its index in the array of strings is of course 0. For example, if the name of the executable file is `copy`, then the command line

```
c:\>copy account.cpp c:\data
```

will print the following lines

```
Argument 0: copy
Argument 1: account.cpp
Argument 2: c:\data
```

In the process of program execution, program variables (objects) can be allocated in three areas of memory reserved for the program: fixed memory, stack memory, and heap memory. For the purposes of this discussion, it is not important to know how the specific computer architecture manages these areas of memory. Whether it is a scalar variable, an array, a structure or class variable, or a union or enumeration variable, it will wind up in one of these memory areas during program execution depending on its storage class.

The concept of the storage class further refines the concept of the name scope. Variables defined as global in the file scope are placed in the fixed area. Variables defined as local to a function or block are placed on the stack. In addition, C++ supports dynamic variables. They are not defined as global or local and hence they have no names. Instead, they are allocated explicit program statements (operator `new`). Dynamic variables are allocated on the program heap.

In definitions of variables, C++ storage classes can be specified using the following keywords.

- `auto`: default for variables defined as local in a block scope or in a function scope (automatic variables)
- `extern`: can be applied to variables that are global in file scope
- `static`: can be used for global variables in a file scope or for local variables defined in a block or in a function scope
- `register`: used for variables kept in high-speed registers rather than in random-access memory

For objects (variables) of these classes, the language rules define allocation and deallocation: `extern` and `static` variables are allocated in the fixed data memory of the program, `auto` variables are allocated on the program stack, and `register` variables are allocated in registers if possible. If there are not enough registers available, these variables are allocated either in the fixed area (for global variables) or on the program stack (for local variables).

Automatic Variables

Automatic variables are local variables defined in functions or in blocks. The `auto` specifier is default and is not often used. For example, function `printAccounts()` in Listing 6.2 could have been written in the following way.

```
void printAccounts()
{ for (auto int i = 0; i < count; i++)          // global count
  { auto double count = getBalance(a[i]);        // local count
    cout << a[i].num << " " << count << endl; } }
```

Since C++ programmers dislike making extra keystrokes if there is no good reason for doing so, they prefer to omit these default specifiers.

Storage for automatic variables is allocated from the stack when execution enters the opening brace of the function or the block. If the definition includes initialization (as in the previous `printAccounts()` example), the storage allocated for the variable is initialized. If no initial value is specified in the definition, the value of the variable is undefined. Most likely, it is a value left from the previous use of the memory location allocated for the variable. At any rate, it is not a good idea to try to figure out what that undefined value is and use it in the program. The word "undefined" is not a C++ keyword, but you should take it very seriously. If you need a specific value, initialize the variable and use it, but do not rely on undefined values. They can be anything, and they can be different from one program execution to another, even if your experiments confirm that they are always the same. Please do not trust these experiments.

Automatic objects exist in memory only after the scope where they are defined is entered in the course of program execution. They are allocated on the program stack (and can be referred to by name) until the closing brace of the scope is reached during execution. At this moment, their memory is returned to the stack and can be reused for other purposes.

This is a great technique for memory management. It relieves the programmer from the responsibility of allocating and deallocating memory for individual computational objects. For some tasks, this technique is not sufficient, and dynamic memory management is used instead. As you are going to see later in this chapter, dynamic memory management is more complex and error-prone. This is why automatic variables should be used (and are used) as much as possible.

Memory allocated for an automatic variable in another call to the same function (or for another iteration of the same loop) might not be at the same stack location with the same contents. Hence, automatic variables cannot pass data between consecutive calls to the function or between consecutive iterations of the loop. If the variable is not initialized, it has undefined value at each allocation. If the definition of the variable includes initialization, this initialization is repeated every time when the scope is entered. In the example of `printAccounts()`, storage for local `count` is allocated, initialized, and deallocated for each iteration through the loop. Storage for `i` is allocated, initialized, and deallocated for each call to `printAccounts()`.

When the program has sufficient memory and execution speed, you should not try to optimize the memory management for local variables. When resources are scarce, it is important to understand the consequences of a design decision. For example, in Listing 6.2 I define array `num[]` as a local variable in function `main()` and array `amounts[]` as a local variable in the body of the first loop. Both these arrays contain data for loading values into global array `a[]`. Defining arrays `num[]` and `amounts[]` in different places in the program represents an example of tearing apart what should belong together.

This decision also might have performance implications. Array `num[]` is allocated only once, at the beginning of the function `main()` execution. Array `amounts[]` is allocated, initialized, and deallocated as many times as the loop body is executed. Array allocation and deallocation does not take much execution time (it involves manipulating the stack pointer), but copying values into array elements for initialization takes about as much time as does copying data from array `amounts[]` into array `a[]`. It would be nice to allocate arrays `num[]` and `amounts[]` in the same place, and where it is done only once during program execution.

```
int main()
{ typedef int Index;
  long num[MAX] = { 800123456, 800123123, 800123333, -1 } ;
  double amounts[MAX] = { 1200, 1500, 1800 } ;        // data to load
  long number = 800123123; double total = 0;          // outer scope
  while (true)
  { if (num[count] == -1) break;
    . . . . . } }                                     // end of main()
```

The names of automatic variables are invisible outside their scope. This is why they can be reused in other scopes; there is no connection between the memory locations for names in different scopes. This is great from the point of view of reducing coordination among developers. When a global variable is used in different scopes, the same location is referred to in each scope. This is why its use in each function has to be studied to figure out whether the same location can indeed be used for several purposes or different variables had to be introduced. The use of automatic variables simplifies the job for the designer and the maintainer alike.

A name can be reused for another object in a nested block according to the scope rules. A new object with the same name is allocated on the stack at a location that is different from the location of the variable defined in the outer scope. The name in the nested scope hides the object that has been allocated on the stack earlier (and is still alive). In Listing 6.2, for example, variable number is defined in function main() and is redefined in the body of the first loop in main(). The second variable number is allocated on the stack at the start of each loop iteration and is deallocated at the end of each iteration. It is a totally different location (actually, it might be different for each loop iteration) and it has nothing to do with the stack location allocated for number at the beginning of main(). This is why when the third loop in main() needs the value that was assigned to number at the beginning of main(), this value is still intact and is used again without any difficulty after the nested scope of the first loop terminates.

Similarly, when the main() calls printAccounts(), memory for variable count is allocated from the stack for each loop iteration in printAccounts(). These locations can be different for different iterations, and none of them has anything to do with the location of the global variable count in the fixed data area.

If the nested scope does not hide the variable that has been defined in the encompassing scope, the name of that variable is available in the nested scope. In Listing 6.2, variable total is allocated at the beginning of main() and is not redefined in its nested scopes. When the second loop refers to total in its body, this reference is to the variable defined in the encompassing scope.

Function formal parameters are treated as automatic variables defined in the function scope; they are initialized with the values of actual arguments in the function call. For example, in the first version of the example program (in Listing 6.1) function `getBalance()` initializes its parameter a with the value of `a[i]` in `main()`. Memory for parameters is allocated on the stack when the function execution starts and is deallocated when the execution reaches its closing brace.

In general, it is a good idea to define a variable as deep in the nested structure of blocks as possible. Doing this provides the following advantages.

- It minimizes the scope of the program where the name is known and hence minimizes the potential for name conflicts with other objects.

- It ties up memory for this variable during the shortest period of time; outside of this time period the memory can be reused for other purposes.

The tradeoffs to consider are accessibility of the object in other parts of the program and the negative impact on performance because of repeated memory allocation, initialization, and deallocation. Another tradeoff is the danger of running out of stack space: The total memory needs depend on the sequence of function invocations, and neither the compiler not the programmer is able to predict it accurately. This is especially important when arrays are defined as local variables in functions and nested blocks, for example, array `amounts[]` in Listing 6.2.

External Variables

External or global variables are variables that are defined outside any function. As I mentioned in the section, "Name Scope as a Tool for Cooperation," their scope is the file they are declared in, from the place of definition until the end of file. Hence, it cannot be used in another file to refer to the same variable—the name is not visible in another file. (Actually, this can be done with some effort.) However, this name cannot be used in another file to define another external variable. In that sense, the names of global variables have the program scope, similar to names of C++ functions.

Memory for global variables is allocated differently from automatic variables. The space is allocated from the fixed data area. It is allocated at the beginning of the program execution, just before the first statement of the `main()` function is executed. The memory location is kept associated with the name of the variable until the program terminates and is released just after the last statement of `main()` is executed.

Definitions of global variables may be initialized. If initialization is not present, the variable is initialized to the zero value of the appropriate type. This is an important difference from automatic variables, which do not have default initial values and whose initial state is undefined (programmers often call it junk or garbage).

In Listing 6.2, variables `MAX`, `count`, and `a[]` are defined as global variables.

The total amount of memory needed for all global variables in the program is easy to evaluate. The compiler compiles each file individually and tallies the space required for global variables by adding up the sizes of all global objects. (This would not make sense for automatic objects because not all of them exist in memory at the same time.) Another advantage of using global variables is speed. Since each global variable is allocated and deallocated only once rather than each time the scope is entered, this operation cannot slow down the program (of course, for many applications this is not important).

Yet another advantage of using global variables is less demand on the program stack. The size of the stack that is required for the program cannot be estimated accurately, and the possibility of running out of stack memory always exists. This is why it is important not to increase demand for stack space without a good reason. For example, array `amounts[]` in Listing 6.2 is defined as local, while array `num[]` is defined as global. Not only do I tear apart what logically belongs together, not only do I allocate and initialize this array on each loop iteration, I also allocate array `amounts[]` on the stack. The first two operations require time. The third operation requires additional memory. Making this array global would eliminate all three drawbacks. In this example, the array is only three elements long, and it is not going to break the stack. But many programmers allocate large arrays on the stack without realizing the implications for the stack size.

Yet another advantage, at least for some programmers, of using global variables is the opportunity to avoid using function parameters. Since the scope of a global variable is the file it is defined in, the code of any function defined in the same file after the definition of that global variable can access the variable directly. For example, function `printAccounts()` in Listing 6.2 directly accesses global variables `count` and `a[]` without the complexity (and time overhead) of parameter passing. Other programmers view direct access to global variables as a failure to convey to the maintenance programmer what the function interface is. To recognize which variables the function uses and which variables the function modifies, it is necessary to inspect each code line of the function. As we will see later, parameters can document the function interface directly, without the need to inspect each line of code.

The negative side of spreading the life span of a global variable over the whole time of program execution is that reverting its memory to other uses within the program becomes more difficult. For example, variables count and a[] are used throughout the whole program in Listing 6.2. On the other hand, arrays num[] and amounts[] are needed only in the body of the first loop in main(). After that, their space can be reverted to other uses. This is what happens to array amounts[] allocated on the stack. Array num[], however, is kept around, and reusing it for some other purpose requires careful planning during development and might become a nightmare during maintenance. This is why we do not define all program variables as global variables.

The name of a variable defined as global in a source code file is known in any scope nested within that file. You can access a global variable from any place in the file. In Listing 6.2, for example, count is used in main() as the loop limit, MAX is used to define arrays a[], num[], and amounts[]. Global array num[] is referenced in main(), and global array a[] is referenced in function main() and in function printAccounts().

As I mentioned earlier, a nested scope can redefine (hide, override) the global name. The space for this redefinition is allocated from the stack, not from the fixed area, and this name in the nested scope will refer to the local automatic variable, not to the global variable. In Listing 6.2, function printAccounts() uses the name count for an automatic variable, and so does the second loop in main(). When the scope operator ':: ' is used with the redefined name, it refers to the memory location in the fixed data memory rather than to the memory location on the stack (::count in Listing 6.2).

If another file in the program in Listing 6.2 defines a local variable count in one of its functions, it will cause no problem because these scopes are independent. This function will refer to a memory location on the stack. If, however, another file defines a global variable count (and this should be a popular name and short and expressive), the program will not link. The use of global variables requires additional coordination among programmers working on different files in the program.

However, a global variable defined in one file can be referenced from other files in the application. This is yet another reason for using global variables.

The extern keyword is used to make a global variable defined in one file known in another file. This is not about reusing the name of the global variable for other purposes. This is about referring to the same memory location using the same name.

Let us say that the program in Listing 6.2 evolves, and is partitioned into more functions. These functions should be placed into different files so that more programmers can work on the program. Let us say that instead of searching for a particular account at the end of `main()`, we want to call function `printAverage()`, which uses the sum of account balances computed in `main()` as its parameter and prints the average balance. Instead of using a literal value in the `cout` statement, I want to have a variable `caption[]`, which contains the text `"Average balance is $"` (a common technique to facilitate internationalization of the program), and I want function `printAverage()` to call function `printCaption()`, which uses the variable `caption[]`. Again, I am using very small examples so that they are relatively easy to understand, but I introduce additional functions to discuss the issues important for development of large programs.

To implement `printAverage()` and `printCaption()` in another source file, you need to make sure that two things happen:

- The source file that calls the function `printAverage()`, that is, file with `main()`, knows that `printAverage` is the name of a function defined in some other file.

- The file where `printAverage()` and `printCaption()` are implemented knows about global variables `count` and `caption[]` defined in some other file.

Listing 6.3 shows the modified Listing 6.2 that solves this problem. Function `printAccounts()` is simplified, type `Index` is eliminated, array `amounts[]` is defined next to array `num[]` (as I said earlier, the two should belong together), function `printAverage()` is called at the end of `main()`. A global array `caption[]` is added, which contains the caption to be printed with the average balance. Listing 6.4 shows the second file where functions `printAverage()` and `printCaption()` are implemented. The output of the program is shown in Figure 6–3.

```
Data is loaded

800123456    1200
800123123    1500
800123333    1800

Data is processed

Average balance is $1500
```

Figure 6–3
Output of code in Listing 6.3 and Listing 6.4.

We see in Listing 6.3 that the first problem is resolved by adding to the source file the prototype for `printAverage()` preceded by the keyword `extern`.

```
extern void printAverage(double);        // it is defined elsewhere
```

If the keyword `extern` is omitted in the function declaration, both the compiler and linker will figure out the function interface anyway. Some C++ programmers prefer to use the keyword to prevent portability issues.

```
void printAverage(double);        // still, it is defined elsewhere
```

When used for variables, the keyword `extern` has two meanings: First, it denotes that the global variable defined in this file can be seen in another file; second, it denotes a variable defined in another file and is declared in this file so that it can be seen by functions in this file. In the first meaning, the use of `extern` is optional; in the second meaning it is mandatory.

Sounds complex? Do not worry, this is simple: `extern` is optional in definitions and is mandatory in declarations. Let's look at the examples of external variables in Listing 6.3. Global variables in Listing 6.3 are all definitions. Hence, they are external variables implicitly: They can be seen in another file, and there is no need to use the `extern` keyword. When used, it does not do any harm if the variable initialized.

```
    extern int count = 0;        // OK: this is a definition
```

The presence of initialization tells the compiler that this is a definition, not a declaration. If initialization is omitted, then the definition without initialization becomes a declaration, and the linker would complain about the lack of definition for `count`.

```
    extern int count;        // this is a declaration
```

Meanwhile, the absence of both initialization and the keyword `extern` makes it again a definition (the value, of course, should be initialized elsewhere), and the variable can be accessed from another file (Listing 6.4, wich defines `printAverage[]`).

```
    int count;        // OK: this is a definition
```

Alert

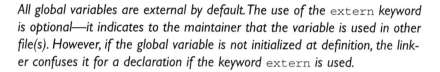

All global variables are external by default. The use of the extern *keyword is optional—it indicates to the maintainer that the variable is used in other file(s). However, if the global variable is not initialized at definition, the linker confuses it for a declaration if the keyword* extern *is used.*

The array caption[] in Listing 6.3 is initialized. Hence, this is a definition (the memory is allocated for the array in fixed area), and the array is extern by default and can be used in another file, Listing 6.4, which defines printCaption[]. Arrays num[] and amounts[] are also global and can be used in other files. They are not (and should not, because they just contain initialization data for the program). The fact that caption[] is used in other files but num[] and amounts[] are not is not immediately evident to the maintainer from this design. I will correct this failure by introducing the static storage class soon.

Listing 6.3 Communicating with another file through external declarations (Part 1).

```
#include <iostream>
using namespace std;

struct Account {                        // global type definition
  long num;
  double bal; } ;

extern void printAverage(double total);   // defined elsewhere

const int MAX = 5;
Account a[MAX];                         // global data to be processed
int count = 0;                         // number of elements in data set
char caption[] = "Average balance is $";  // caption to print

long num[MAX] = { 800123456, 800123123, 800123333, -1 } ;
double amounts[MAX] = { 1200, 1500, 1800 } ;   // data set to load

void printAccounts()
{ for (int i = 0; i < count; i++)       // global count
  cout << a[i].num << " " << a[i].bal << endl; }

int main()
{
  double total = 0;
  while (true)                         // break on sentinel
  { if (num[count] == -1) break;
```

```
   a[count].num = num[count];              // global a[], num[], amounts[]
   a[count].bal = amounts[count++]; }      // load data
cout << " Data is loaded\n\n";
printAccounts();                           // local function
cout << "\n Data is processed\n\n";
for (int i = 0; i < count; i++)
  { total += a[i].bal; }
printAverage(total);                       // global in another file
return 0;
}
```

Listing 6.4 shows function `printCaption()`. It is called by `printAverage()` from this file and uses array `caption[]` defined in the file in Listing 6.3. To make this possible, array `caption[]` is defined as `extern` in Listing 6.4. Variable `count` is also defined as `extern` without initialization. This makes it a declaration. Omitting the keyword would turn it into a definition, and the linker would flag the two definitions of `count` as errors (even if the types were different). The compiler, however, compiles source files individually and will miss the issue. The use of keyword `extern` allows one file to access data and functions defined in other files, but it does not tell the maintainer which global variables and functions are used in other files, like `printAverage()`, and which ones are not, like `printCaption()`. Again, the use of `static` keyword will solve this problem.

Listing 6.4 Communicating with another file through external declarations (Part 2).

```
#include <iostream>
using namespace std;
extern count;                       // defined and initialized elsewhere
extern char caption[];              // defined and initialized elsewhere

void printCaption()                 // called from this file only
{ cout << caption; }

void printAverage(double sum)       // called from another file
{ if (count == 0) return;
  printCaption();
  cout << sum/count << endl;
}
```

Also notice that the declaration of the array (`caption[]`) does not require the size of the array because declarations do not allocate memory: They indicate the existence of a definition for this object elsewhere. Similarly, you should not initialize `extern` objects; this would turn a declaration into a definition (and create a name conflict).

Unlike definitions, external declarations can be repeated in different files or even in the same file. With these declarations, the code in that file can use the global names as if the variables were defined in this file. For example, in Listing 6.4, function `printAverage()` refers to `count`, and function `printCaption()` refers to `caption[]`, which are defined in another file (Listing 6.3).

External variables provide a good communication tool between functions defined in different files in large programs. Make sure you use them only when the advantages of spreading these functions among different files outweigh the advantages of keeping these functions in the same file. Listing 6.3 and Listing 6.4 represent a glaring example of excessive communications between files. Putting together things that should belong together eliminates the need for communication between files, eliminates the need for `extern` declarations, simplifies the tasks of design and maintenance, and decreases the likelihood of errors.

Static Variables

The keyword `static` in C++ has five meanings. There are some common features for all static variables. (They are all allocated in the fixed memory rather than on the stack.) However, the differences between different meanings are significant, and the use of the same keyword in different context might become confusing. The following C++ entities can be defined as `static`.

- global variables that should be accessed by the code only in the same file where the variables are defined but not by the code in other files

- local variables defined in a function (or in an unnamed block) so that their values should survive from one function call to another (or from one scope execution to another)

- structure (or class) fields that should refer to the single memory locations for all variables (or objects) of this type

- class member functions that access only parameters, global variables, and class static variables but do not access nonstatic class fields

- global (nonmember) functions that are accessible to the client code only in the same file they are defined in but not in other files

This is more than we can comfortably discuss now. This is why I will discuss only the first two and the last meanings here. Two other meanings will be discussed in Chapter 8, "Object-Oriented Programming with Functions."

The first use of the static keyword, for global variables, represents a powerful tool for making variables private to a file, so that no other file can access these variables by defining them as extern. For example, Listing 6.3 defines global variables MAX, a[], count, caption[], num[], and amounts[] but it does not specify which variables are accessed from other files. To indicate that only count can be accessed from another file but that all functions accessing other global variables are in the same file (and to make sure that no other file can access these global variables), Listing 6.3 should define other global variables as static.

```
int count = 0;                // it can be made extern elsewhere
static const int MAX=5;       // it cannot be made extern elsewhere
static Account a[MAX];        // no access from code in other files
static long num[MAX]={ 800123456, 800123123, 800123333, -1 } ;
static double amounts[MAX] = { 1200, 1500, 1800 } ;
```

By adding the static keyword to a definition of a global variable, we change neither the place in memory where it is allocated (fixed storage) nor its life span (from the beginning to the end of the program execution). The only result of this addition is that the variable cannot be defined as extern in other source files and thus accessed from other files in the program. This programming technique is highly recommended.

Notice that array caption[] is not among these global variables. Since it is used only by function printCaption[] (in Listing 6.4), it should not be torn away from this function and put into Listing 6.3 where no function accesses it. It should be moved to Listing 6.4. Since functions defined in other files do not access this array, it can (and should) be declared in Listing 6.4 as static. This is how the top of Listing 6.4 should look.

```
extern count;                 // defined elsewhere
static char caption[]         // no extern, defined and init here
 = "Average balance is $";    // used locally, not in other files
```

Some programmers believe that this is primarily a security measure. Using static variables of this kind eliminates errors by preventing accidental or unauthorized changes from other parts of the program. This is true, but these kinds of errors are very few and far between. What I am after is more common and more important. The real value of this technique is elimination of communication between programmers. By defining global variables as static, it becomes possible for other designers to use such nonspecific and popular names as MAX, a, num, amounts, and caption in any file in the program without coordinating the choice of names.

In general, the use of global variables should be limited. When they are used for communication between functions in the same file, they should be made static to decrease interference with programmers working on other files. Leave them nonstatic only when there is a pressing need to access them from other files (but check whether you are tearing apart what should belong together). Of course, when a global variable is defined as static, it cannot be accessed from another file. If it is not made static (as count is in Listing 6.3), there is no guarantee that it is indeed accessed from other files, or the programmer neglected to pass on to the maintainer his or her knowledge that this variable is accessed from one file only. This is why we have to make an effort to be meticulous in using this keyword for global static variables.

This technique of defining global variables as static is very important in C. This is how the object-oriented approach was first used in that language. Data and functions were bound together in the same file (like array caption[] and function printCaption() after moving the array to Listing 6.4), data were defined as static and hence invisible from outside, and functions in that file would be called from other files and access data on behalf of the client functions.

In C++, data and functions are bound together in classes. This weakens the pressure to use global variables. Namespaces further reduce the need for global variables. Hence, the importance of this technique in C++ is less than in C. Still, when you define variables as global, do not forget to define them as static to eliminate interference with other designers, and to pass your knowledge about communication between functions to the maintenance programmer.

The second meaning of keyword static is different. When applied to a local variable defined in a function or in a block (remember, by default these variables are automatic), this keyword moves the variable from the stack to the fixed area of memory. The life span of this memory location is now not from the start to the end of the function or block (as for automatic variables) but from the start of the program to the end of its execution. This means that the value at this location that was set at one execution of the scope becomes available when the scope is entered again. As far as the name of the variable is concerned, it is still governed by the scope rules as discussed in the first section in this chapter. The name is not known outside of the braces where the variable is defined. Hence, other independent scopes, even in the same file, can use this name for other purposes. Moreover, several variables in different scopes can be defined as static using the same name. This will not cause name conflict, even though all these variables are allocated in the fixed area. Since they are in different scopes, the names are known at different moments of program execution.

For example, function `printAccounts()` in Listing 6.3 might be modified to print one account only. To do this, I could define a global variable, `i`, and use it as an index within `printAccounts()`.

```
const int MAX = 5;
Account a[MAX];              // global data to be processed
int count = 0;              // number of elements in data set
int i;                       // global index
. . .
void printAccounts()
{ cout << a[i].num << " " << a[i].bal << endl;
  i++; }                    // increment index after use
```

In `main()`, I would call `printAccounts()` in a loop.

```
for (int j = 0; j < count; j++)
  printAccounts();
```

The language allows me to use index `i` in the loop too, but the current version of my compiler does not let me do that. (The last loop in Listing 6.3 defines `i`.) The drawback of this design is the use of more global variables (polluting the global space). To avoid that, I can move the definition of the index `i` in `printAccounts()` to avoid potential conflicts with other uses of this name.

```
void printAccounts()
{ int i = 0;
  cout << a[i].num << " " << a[i].bal << endl;
  i++; }                    // increment index after use
```

This does not fly because now the index is an automatic variable, and it gets new space on the stack each time `printAccounts()` is called from `main()`. Hence it cannot remember the index value from the previous invocation. Also, the index is set to 0 each time the function is called. The keyword `static` resolves both problems.

```
void printAccounts()
{ static int i = 0;
  cout << a[i].num << " " << a[i].bal << endl;
  i++; }                    // increment index after use
```

At first glance this does not make sense. How is the index going to be incremented if the value of `i` is reset to 0 at every invocation? But it is not what you think it is.

In the previous version of printAccounts(), the initial value was assigned to i at each call. In this version, since i is static, it is assigned only once, despite the appearance of doing this at each call. Actually, it is not done at the first invocation of printAccounts(). It is done when all global variables are allocated, before the first statement of main() is executed. When printAccounts() is called, the initialization statement is skipped, and the previous value of this local variable is used in the next statement.

```
void printAccounts()
{ static int i = 0;                    // executed only once
  cout << a[i].num << " " << a[i].bal << endl;
  i++; }                               // executed in each call
```

In this case, explicit initialization is not even necessary. Static variables are implicitly initialized to 0, and this version of printAccounts() is perfectly legitimate.

```
void printAccounts()
{ static int i;               // implicit initialization to zero
  cout << a[i].num << " " << a[i].bal << endl;
  i++; }                      // executed at each function call
```

However, the maintainer should think several extra seconds to figure out why this function updates a variable that has never been explicitly initialized. The previous version is less concise but it conveys the intent of the designer better.

Using local static variables is not a good programming practice. It requires too much coordination between the client and server functions and too much effort to understand the code. And it is rarely necessary. In most cases, it is not hard to find a solution that does not require the use of static local variables. For example, the way the accounts were printed in Listing 6.3 (and in previous versions of the program) is simple and does not require static local variables.

Static global functions are similar to static global variables in the sense that they cannot be called outside of the file where they are defined because the name of a static function is invisible in other files. This means that the name can be used in other files for any other purpose without name conflicts and related interference. If a function is called only by the functions that are in the same file where it is defined, it is a good idea to explicitly define the function as static and make it visible in that file only, not in the whole program. In Listing 6.3, function printAccounts() should be made static.

```
static void printAccounts()
{ static int i = 0;
  cout << a[i].num << " " << a[i].bal << endl;
  i++; }                              // increment index after use
```

Similarly, function `printCaption()` in Listing 6.4 should be defined as static.

```
static void printCaption()         // called from this file only
{ cout << caption; }
```

Similar to static global variables, the issue here is name conflicts and communicating with the maintainer. By putting server functions in the same file with their callers and by defining them as `static` global functions, you allow the programmers that work on other files to use these function names without coordination with you. In addition, it explicitly says to the maintainer that there are no other functions in other files that depend on this one. Putting server and client functions in the same file is not always possible or desirable. When it is done, it should be documented by defining the server functions as `static`.

There is yet another twist in using the `static` storage class for functions that are bound to classes. They can access only static fields of the class. We will see more on `static` functions and `static` fields later.

Memory Management: Using Heap

Scope rules and the variety of storage classes in C++ go a long way toward helping programmers to manage memory for program objects. However, these tools do not solve the problem of implementing dynamic data structures adequately.

Array implementations of dynamic data structures with a sentinel or a count of valid entries are powerful and simple. When the number of elements in the data set grows or shrinks, these implementations can add or remove components. Yet they need the maximum size of the data set known at compile time. Any choice of the maximum size might entail either a danger of overflow or wasted space.

Dynamic memory management resolves this problem by allocating and reallocating memory dynamically. When the data set fills all available space in the array, we allocate a larger array dynamically, copy data into the new array, and release the old array. When the data set shrinks so that too much space becomes wasted, we allocate a smaller array, copy data into the new array, and release the larger array. This technique eliminates both the danger of overflow and of excessive wasted space.

Another problem with contiguous arrays is that they are efficient only when new elements are added at the end of the array. If you need to add a new element at the start or in the middle of the array, you have to shift remaining array elements toward the end of the array to make room.

Similarly, when an element is deleted from the middle of the array rather than from the end, you have to shift remaining elements toward the start of the array to close the gap. This requires additional time. Another approach is not to close the gap but to introduce yet another sentinel value to denote deleted elements. This eliminates the shift during deletion but requires additional testing of each element for validity during search. If the array is short, or insertions and deletions in the middle are not frequent, these drawbacks are not important. For long arrays and frequent insertions and deletions, these techniques might negatively affect performance.

One of possible solutions to these problems is to eliminate the array as a mechanism for allocating memory for many elements at once. Instead, we allocate memory for an element only when it has to be inserted into the data set. We link the elements using pointers that contain addresses of these dynamically allocated elements. Manipulating pointers, we can insert an element into the data set without spending time shifting other elements. When the element has to be deleted, its memory is deallocated for other uses. Here, too, pointer manipulation allows us to close the gap without shifting other elements and without marking the element as deleted.

Using pointers for dynamic arrays and linked data structures is both useful and popular. However, it is more complex than using fixed-size arrays, which we discussed earlier. Errors in handling pointers are run-time errors rather than compile-time errors and often are difficult to discover. Frequent allocation and deallocation of memory might affect performance.

In many languages, like Lisp, Eiffel, and Java, memory management is considered to be too vital for program integrity to be trusted to the fallible programmer. These languages use so-called automatic garbage collection that evaluates the use of memory by the program and reclaims the locations that the programmer should have returned to the memory pool. Naturally, these algorithms are relatively slow, complex, and inexact.

In C++, the opposite approach is taken—but for a similar reason! In C++, memory management is considered to be too vital for program performance to be trusted to a general (and often inefficient) algorithm. In C++, the programmer is given full control of memory allocation and deallocation. If the programmer makes mistakes, they can result in memory corruption or memory leaks and program crashes. This is bad, but good programmers do not make too many mistakes. The algorithms for dynamic memory management are simple. Implemented diligently, they are safe. Also, standard libraries provide appropriate data structures and functions that help the programmer to avoid errors.

The segment of program memory for storing dynamic data allocated on explicit demand is called the *heap*. The name comes from how this storage gets organized after multiple allocations and deallocations. The heap structure facilitates the search for a free piece of memory of appropriate size to satisfy the next memory request.

The size of the fixed data segment for global and static variables is computed during compilation and linking. The size of the stack and the heap cannot be computed exactly. Usually, the stack and the heap grow toward each other to avoid premature overflow.

There are two differences between variables allocated on the heap and conventional variables I have discussed so far.

- Conventional variables (allocated on the stack and the fixed data area) are allocated according to language rules; heap variables are allocated by explicit operations specified by the programmer.

- Conventional variables have names that are aliases (used as mnemonic references) for their memory locations; variables allocated on the heap do not have names; they are referred to through pointers.

C++ Pointers as Typed Variables

A pointer is a variable that contains an address of another variable, which can be a conventional (named) stack variable. However, pointers usually point to variables allocated on the heap (unnamed variables). Pointers themselves, however, are commonly allocated either in the fixed data section (as global or static) or on the stack (as auto). It is very unusual to allocate a pointer on the heap. Pointers are ordinary named variables.

In C++, pointers are usually used for the following:

- dynamic allocation of arrays of size specified at run-time size
- building dynamic data structures composed of noncontiguous linked nodes
- passing parameters to functions

In this chapter, I will discuss the general syntax and semantics of pointers and will give examples of the first two uses of pointers. Passing parameters to functions will be discussed in the next chapter.

To create a pointer variable, you specify, first, that it is a pointer, and, second, the type of a variable the pointer can point to. A C++ pointer can point (in other words, provide indirect reference) to a variable of one type only; the type is specified when the pointer variable is defined. When you study more advanced aspects of C++ such as inheritance and polymorphism (sorry for using the buzzwords that are not meaningful yet), you will see that this rule has some interesting exceptions. But at the moment, it is a very good idea to remember that a pointer defined as a pointer to an integer should point to an integer value and not to a double. Similarly, a pointer defined as a pointer to a double should point to a double value and not to an integer.

To indicate that the variable is a pointer variable, you use the asterisk * notation after the type name or before the name of the variable; spaces (or lack of spaces) surrounding the operator are not significant.

```
int * pi; char* pc; double*pd;        // any spacing is OK
```

Notice that the asterisk here is not even an operator, it is just notation. It denotes that the variable is a pointer to the type specified to the left of the asterisk. You read pointer declarations from right to left. For example, `pi` is a pointer to an `int` variable, or `pc` is a pointer to a `char` variable, and so on. Or you could say that `pi` is of type `int*`, or `pc` is of type `char*`, and so on. Later on you will find it useful to say that `*pi` is of type `int`, or `*pc` is of type `char`, and so on.

However, in these expressions the asterisk is not just notation, it is an operator that is applied to a pointer variable (`pi`, `pc`, and so on) to get the value of the basic type. This is the value at the location pointed to by the pointer variable. The name of the asterisk operator that retrieves the value pointed to by the pointer is the dereference operator (or indirection operator).

If getting the address of the value is called pointing, then getting the value from the address could be called depointing, not dereferencing. But C++ borrows this terminology from C, and C was designed as a high-level language for assembly language programmers, and assembly language programmers call the things the way they like, not the way other mere mortals would call them.

The scope of the asterisk pointer notation is just one pointer variable: It applies to the identifier that follows the asterisk, not to the type name that precedes it. This is different from the way other definitions and declarations work. For example, here it is only `pc` that is a pointer to `char`, and `pchar` is of type `char`, not `char*`.

```
char* pc, pchar;        // pchar is of type char, not char*
```

This is quite a common mistake. To indicate that pchar is also a pointer, you could say

```
char* pc, *pchar;          // both pc and pchar are pointers
```

Again, pointer variables are regular named variables, automatic or global; they are allocated sufficient space for holding an address of a specific type. Often, the size of the pointer is the same as the size of the integer, but you should not count on that. The sizeof operator can tell you whether this is the case on your machine, but it is definitely not a good idea to write code that relies on the pointer size. This code will not be portable.

Alert

Pointer variables (addresses) are often of the size of integers regardless of the type of the values they point to. Do not use the pointer size in your code because it can render your program nonportable.

At definition, similar to other variables, pointers have no useful value (zero if global, undefined if automatic). Pointers may contain addresses of objects of

- built-in types (e.g., char* pc)
- programmer-defined types (e.g., Account* pa)
- arrays of built-in or programmer-defined types (notation is the same as for variables, e.g., char* pc or Account* pa)
- functions (it is too early to describe pointer functions here)
- other pointers (e.g., char** pcc can be used as a pointer to a character pointer, such as pc above; again, I just want to mention that this is possible, but you should not rush to use it in your code)

To access the value of the object that the pointer points to, you apply the dereferencing operator (asterisk *) to the pointer as a prefix unary operator (to the left of the pointer name). In other words, you dereference the pointer. For example, here I move 5.0 to a double variable pointed to by pointer pd, move 20 to an int variable pointed to by pointer pi, and move 'a' to a character variable pointed to by pc if the double value pointed to by pd is positive (and it is positive).

```
*pd = 5.0; *pi = 20; if (*pd > 0) *pc = 'a';          // not ok
```

As I mentioned above, if `pi` is a pointer to an `int`, then `*pi` is of type `int`; similarly, `*pd` is a `double`. From the point of view of value types, this example is OK. However, I never initialized these pointers, and dereferencing noninitialized pointers is illegal.

When a global pointer is not initialized, it contains 0. Dereferencing a null pointer immediately terminates the program.

```
pd = NULL; *pd = 5.0;          // null pointer exception
```

When a local pointer (automatic variable) is not initialized, it contains a random bit pattern as any other automatic variable. This pattern can be interpreted as an address, but this address can be anywhere in memory. Reading from this location returns garbage; writing to this location corrupts computer memory. It might crash the operating system, cause run-time memory protection exception, produce incorrect results, or even produce correct results (if the location pointed to by the pointer is not used by the program). Using noninitialized pointers is a common error, and it is hard to diagnose because they can point to any area in memory.

Noninitialized pointers can take you to any location in memory, and this can result in memory corruption or incorrect results. In C++, these errors of dereferencing noninitialized pointers are run-time errors, not compile-time ones. This is unfortunate: If you make this error, the friendly compiler does not stand by telling you to correct it. Instead, you have to surmise the very existence of the error through run-time testing.

Pointers can be initialized to point to named variables with the use of address-of operator (reference operator `&`). Listing 6.5 shows some examples of pointer manipulation. Its `main()` function defines two automatic variables, of type `int` and `char`. It also defines two pointers, to `int` and to `char`, initializes the character pointer to point to the character variable, and assigns the integer pointer to point to the integer. After that it assigns a new value to the integer using the dereferenced pointer. Then it checks the value of the integer using the dereferenced pointer and assigns the character value using the dereferenced character pointer. At the end, it sets the character pointer to point to the integer value.

Most compilers would disallow direct assignment `pc = &i`; indeed, `pc` is of type `char*` and `&i` is of type `int*`. C++ is also strict—it allows implicit conversions between numeric types but not between pointers of different types. For pointer assignment to be valid, the pointers must be of exactly the same type. However, explicit conversions between pointers (casts) of different types are allowed without limitations. The assumption is that you, the programmer, know what you are doing. Pointer casting is a dangerous practice. By dereferencing the character pointer I can now access and change parts of the integer bit pattern. Figure 6–4 shows that dereferencing of two pointers pointing to the same integer variable gives different results depending on the type of the pointer.

Listing 6.5 Using pointers with ordinary named variables.

```cpp
#include <iostream>
using namespace std;

int main()
{
  int i; int pi; char *pc;          // noninitialized pointers
  pi = &i;                          // this turns pointer to i
  *pi = 502;                        // this is ok, but so is i = 502;
  if (*pi>0) *pc = 28791;           // same as if(i>0) i=28791
  pc = (char*) &i;                  // some compilers don't need it
  int a1 = *pi;                     // access to i through pointer
  int a2 = *pc;                     // access to i through pointer
  cout << " i as decimal: " << i << endl
       << " i as hex: " << hex << i << endl;
  cout << " i through int pointer: " << dec << a1 << endl;
  cout << " i through char pointer: " << a2 << endl;
  cout << "i through char pointer in hex: " << hex << a2 << endl;
  return 0;
}
```

Figure 6–4   Output of code in Listing 6.5 (notice incorrect access to int).

```
i as decimal: 28791
i as hex: 7077
i through int pointer:    28791
i through char pointer:   119
i through char pointer in hex: 77
```

In Listing 6.5, the terms hex and dec are called *manipulators*. They indicate to the cout object the base to be used for computing output values (decimal or hex). Similar to the endl manipulator, they are inserted in the output stream and change its characteristics. As you see from Figure 6–4, the value retrieved by the pointer pi is correct (28791). But the value retrieved by the character pointer pc is incorrect. As output in hex shows in Figure 6–4, the character pointer retrieves only part of the bit pattern (77 in hex) of the value of i (7077 in hex). In a sense, the integer pointer can see the whole integer, but the character pointer can see only one byte. Neither of them is capable of fetching, for example, a double value correctly. This is why it is so important to make sure that you dereference pointers of correct types.

Tip

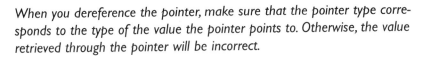

When you dereference the pointer, make sure that the pointer type corresponds to the type of the value the pointer points to. Otherwise, the value retrieved through the pointer will be incorrect.

Operations on pointers are not very intuitive. It is hard to follow pointer manipulation by reading code. This is why it is important to help your intuition by drawing pictures. There are two kinds of pictures you could draw: One type indicates whether the variables are allocated on the stack or on the heap (Figure 6–5a), another type stresses what pointers point to what values (Figure 6–5b).

Figure 6–5a shows integer i, integer pointer pi, and character pointer pc allocated on the stack. Even though their real size might be the same, it is common to show pointers as smaller rectangles. I show the value that integer i contains. Pointers pi and pc contain the address of i, but I do not know (and do not want to use) this address. Instead of the address, I use arrows to indicate that the pointers point to the same location. Even though the arrows point to somewhat different places, this is acceptable approximation. I do not know whether the pointer contains the address of the most significant byte, or the least significant byte, or anything in between. I indicate only that pointers point to the value, and dereferencing these pointers can retrieve that value (provided that the type of the pointer is correct).

Figure 6–5b shows the same configuration without specifying whether the variables i, pi, and pc are allocated on the stack or on the heap. The working assumption might be that if the names of the variables are specified, they are allocated on the stack; if the names are not specified, the variables are allocated on the heap. Again, the arrows indicate that the pointers contain the

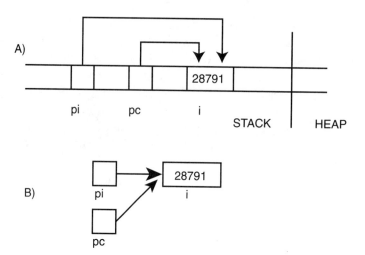

Figure 6–5   Integer pointer and character pointer pointing to a named integer variable `i` allocated on the stack.

addresses of variables that the arrows are pointing to; hence, the pointers can be used for access to these variables.

As you see, using pointers for operations over named variables is not very useful. Using pointers for this kind of data manipulation is no better than directly using variables (in this example, `i`) pointed to by these pointers. Setting pointers to point to values of inappropriate types leads to complexity and errors. Some programmers use similar techniques in function calls to avoid the use of address-of operator (we will see that in the next chapter). But this is not what the pointers are for. They are for allocating space on the heap.

Allocating Memory on the Heap

C++ operators are mostly simple symbols. Since C++ has more operators than there are special symbols on the standard keyboard, C++ uses two-symbol operators and even one three-symbol operator. Still this is not enough, and C++ uses some reserved words as operators. Two of these reserved words used as operators are `new` and `delete`. They are both unary operators taking one operand only. These operators are used for memory management on the heap. Heap here is just another piece of terminology. The programmer does not have to know where the heap is located. What is the heap? The heap is the area of memory where operators `new` and `delete` allocate and deallocate memory. All that you should know is that the memory that has been allocated should be deallocated at the proper time.

The operator new takes the name of a type as its operator; it asks the operating system to allocate the amount of memory necessary to accommodate the value of the type specified as the operand. If the allocation is successful, the operator new returns the address of the memory location on the heap allocated by the operating system. This address value is usually assigned to a pointer of the appropriate type, and this pointer can be used to manipulate the allocated unnamed memory. If the system runs out of memory, the new operator returns 0 instead of the address of a heap location, and the program can test this returned value to decide what to do next (for example, print a message and terminate).

The operator delete takes the name of a pointer as its operator. It finds the area on the heap pointed to by its operand pointer and asks the operating system to mark this location (of the size defined by the type in the pointer definition) as unused. It is of paramount importance that for any use of the new operator allocating memory that the program contains a symmetric delete operator returning that memory to avoid memory leak.

Listing 6.6 shows examples of using these operators. Its main() function defines two pointers, pi to type int and pc to type char, and initializes them by using the operator new. After that, it tests whether the space allocation was successful. If not, the program has to terminate because it cannot do what it is supposed to do. Often, some recovery measures should be taken to let the program terminate gracefully (save data). Sometimes, the program might try to release some memory to proceed in a special mode with limited functionality. As Figure 6–6 shows, the memory allocation is successful, and the pointers set and then retrieve the values (integer 28791 and character 'a') correctly.

Listing 6.6 Using pointers with unnamed heap variables.

```
#include <iostream>
using namespace std;

int main()
{
  int *pi; char* pc;                          // noninitialized pointers
  pi = new int;                               // get unnamed space, point to it
  if (pi == NULL)                             // if new fails, it returns zero
    { cout << "Out of memory\n"; return 0; }  // or try to recover
  pc = new char;                              // get unnamed space, point to it
  if (pc == 0)                                // necessary precaution
    { cout << "Out of memory\n"; return 0; }  // or try to recover
  *pi = 28791;
```

```
if (*pi > 0) *pc = 'a';                         // manipulate unnamed objects
cout << " integer on the heap: " << *pi << endl;
cout << " character on the heap: " << *pc << endl;
delete pi; delete pc;                           // part of heap memory life cycle
cout << " (after delete) int: " <<*pi <<" char: " <<*pc <<endl;
return 0;
}
```

In this example, NULL is a library constant. Many programmers prefer to use this constant rather than numeric 0 to indicate that the source code is dealing with pointers. Others use the numeric 0. The result is the same. It is important to remember that any use of the operator new should be followed by the test for success of memory allocation.

Operator delete returns the space allocated by operator new back to the heap. It is intelligent enough to know the type of its pointer operand and release exactly as much memory as new allocated. If you forget to use delete, your program will work. With time, it might deplete the heap memory, and the next use of new will return 0, especially if the application works around the clock. It is an important part of programming skills to be able to release all the heap memory that the program requested.

When you read the code that contains the delete operators, you just read it aloud. You say "delete pi, delete pc." This is fine. Make sure that you do not talk yourself into believing that you indeed delete pointers. You delete unnamed heap memory (of the appropriate size) pointed to by pointers pi and pc. Pointers here are named stack variables, and they are allocated according to the scope rules discussed earlier in this chapter. They are allocated when their definition is executed (here, at the beginning of the main() function), and they are deallocated when they go out of scope, that is, when execution reaches the closing brace of the scope they are allocated in (here, at the main() closing brace).

You delete unnamed heap variables only. It is not a good idea to delete named stack variables, for example, variable i in Listing 6.5 above (either through pointer pi or though pointer pc or directly without pointers).

Figure 6-6 Output of code in Listing 6.6.

```
integer on the heap:    28791
character on the heap: a
(after delete) int: -572662307 char: ▌
```

After you delete the heap variable pointed to by a pointer, the pointer becomes noninitialized again and should not be used for dereferencing. At the end of Listing 6.6, I try to retrieve the values pointed to by pointers pi and pc. As Figure 6–6 shows, these pointers now point to whatever locations they want, not where you thought they should be pointing. Just like the Soviet Union choosing with which countries to have common borders. Notice that the compiler did not tell me that I was making a mistake. The operating system also did not prevent me from doing so, although it could have, and probably should have. Just like with the expansion of the Soviet Union.

One final touch about the delete operator. You should not use this operator on a noninitialized pointer, only on a pointer that points to heap memory allocated to by the operator new. For example, deleting memory twice is a run-time error (not a compile-time error).

```
delete pi; delete pi;          // this code is incorrect
```

This code is incorrect in the sense that its behavior is undefined. It could crash, produce incorrect results, or even produce correct results—it could do whatever it wants. Make sure you watch what you do with memory management, especially in loops. Do not use delete on the same pointer twice. Deleting on a NULL pointer is allowed and has no effect.

Figure 6–7 shows the memory pictures for Listing 6.6. Figure 6–7a shows that pointers pc and pi are allocated on the stack, and the unnamed integer

Figure 6–7 Integer pointer and character pointer pointing to an unnamed integer variable and unnamed character variables allocated on the heap.

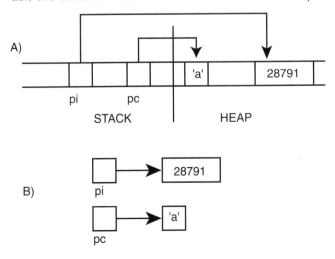

value and character value are allocated on the heap. Figure 6–7b shows the
same relationships. The pointers are named (allocated on the stack), and the
integer and the character are not named (allocated on the heap). I try to represent roughly that integers and characters are of different sizes, but I do not
try to do that for a pointer. Pointers are drawn smaller than values they point
to even when they take more memory.

Operators new and delete are available in C++ but not in C. In C, dynamic
memory allocation is done with calls to the library function malloc(). Memory
is returned with calls to the library function free(). Function malloc() is less
intelligent than the operator new. It does not know the sizes of data types, and it
needs the number of bytes requested as its argument. Also, it returns a generic,
so-called void pointer that cannot be dereferenced. The pointer returned by
malloc() has to be converted to the appropriate type by using the cast operator. If the allocation fails, malloc() returns the NULL pointer, and the program
can check whether the memory requested is indeed available. Since C++ is
backward compatible with C, malloc() is supported in C++. It is defined in the
cstdlib (or stdlib.h) standard library.

```cpp
pi = (int*) malloc(sizeof(int));        // get unnamed heap space
```

Function free() takes a pointer as its argument. It is intelligent enough to
know how many bytes to release.

```cpp
free(pi);                    // return heap memory for other uses
```

Listing 6.7 shows the same operations that were implemented in Listing
6.5 but with the use of malloc() and free(). Notice the stdlib.h header
file. The output of this program is the same as in Figure 6–5.

Listing 6.7 Using malloc() and free() for memory management.

```cpp
#include <iostream>
#include <cstdlib>                          // header for malloc() and free()
using namespace std;

int main()
{
  int *pi; char* pc;                        // noninitialized pointers
  pi = (int*) malloc(sizeof(int));          // get unnamed space
  if (pi == NULL)                           // if malloc() fails, it returns zero
    { cout << "Out of memory\n"; return 0; }  // or try to recover
  pc = (char*) malloc(sizeof(char));        // get unnamed space
  if (pc == NULL)                           // necessary precaution
    { cout << "Out of memory\n"; return 0; }  // or try to recover
  *pi = 28791;
```

```
if (*pi > 0) *pc = 'a';              // manipulate unnamed objects
cout << " integer on the heap: " << *pi << endl;
cout << " character on the heap: " << *pc << endl;
free(pi); free(pc);
cout << " (after delete) int: " <<*pi <<" char: " <<*pc <<endl;
return 0;
}
```

Many C++ compilers actually implement operators new and delete in terms of functions malloc() and free(). However, in C++ new and delete are used much more often than malloc() and free(). They are simpler. Also, when they are used to manage memory for class objects, they can call special functions, constructors and destructors, implicitly. Functions malloc() and free() do not do that. There is one catch, however. These operators and library functions have to be used in pairs. If memory is allocated with new, it cannot be returned with free(). If memory is allocated with malloc(), it cannot be returned with delete. Again, the compiler cannot catch this type of error. Run-time testing is also useless. To avoid errors, many C+ programmers use operators new and delete only and avoid the use of malloc() and free().

However, there is a significant body of legacy C (and C++ code) that uses malloc() and free(). Judging from the longevity of programs that caused the Y2K problem, you should be ready to deal with these function calls for many years to come.

As you see, using heap for dynamic memory management of the values of built-in types is interesting but not very useful. We can achieve all that dynamic memory management provides using named variables on the stack instead.

Some programmers do allocate individual values on the heap. This is not an error in and of itself. The program compiles and executes correctly. It is just more complex than it should be. Dynamic memory management of individual variables forces us to worry about proper time for memory allocation and release. It adds to the program complexity of pointer definition, initializing, and dereferencing. And all that for nothing—there are no advantages. Avoid this practice. Use heap memory only for dynamic arrays and dynamic data structures.

Arrays and Pointers

The need to specify the array length at compile time is a major C++ feature aimed at efficient use of memory and run-time performance. As we saw, it also introduces the problems of array overflow or memory waste because in many applications the sizes of data sets to process become known at run time rather than at compile time. Meanwhile, C++ syntax rejects anything as the array size that is not a run-time constant. It is in these situations that the dynamic memory allocation is useful.

To be able to use dynamically allocated arrays, you should learn the relation between C++ arrays and pointers. This relation is based on yet another unique C++ feature: The name of an array (used without brackets or other modifiers) means the same thing as does the address of the starting array element. Hence, the name of the array can be used to initialize a pointer of the appropriate type (i.e., the same type as the array element). The pointer content becomes the address of the first array element. Dereferencing the pointer will retrieve (or change) the first element of the array. This opens a possibility to use a pointer as a synonym for the array name in function calls and with array indices.

In the next example, I allocate two short character arrays, `buf[]` and `data[]`, and define two character pointers, `p` and `q`. I initialize the pointers by using the address of the starting array element. The example shows that it could be done either explicitly, by using the address notation (`p = &buf[0];`) or implicitly, by using the array name (`q = data;`).

```
char buf[6], data[6], *p, *q;      // arrays and pointers
int i;
p = &buf[0];                       // explicit syntax for address of first element
q = data;                          // implicit syntax for address of first element
for (i=0; i < 6; i++)              // assign array components
  { p[i] = 'A'+i;                  // uppercase letters "ABCDEF"
    q[i] = 'a'+i; }                // lowercase letters
```

The only difference between a pointer and the array name is that the pointer can be reassigned to point to another location (using the address-of operator `&`, or pointer assignment), but the array name is a constant and hence cannot be reassigned to contain another address. In the next coding example, the first part of array `data[]` (lowercase characters) is copied into the second part of array `buf[]` so that array `buf[]` contains letters "ABCabc" rather than "ABCDEF."

```
p = &buf[3];                       // turn it to point to second half of the array
for (i=0; i < 3; i++)              // replace last 3 components
  p[i] = q[i];                     // same as buf[i+3]=data[i];
```

In both of these coding segments, pointer names are used as array names. Everywhere where I said `q[i]`, I could have said `data[i]`. This is nice but not very practical, because it does not allow you to do anything new. But this is only part of what you could do to arrays using pointers.

Another unique C++ feature is that the arithmetic operations over pointers take into account the type and the size of the memory element pointed to by the pointer. If, for example, `ptr` is a pointer to a `double` located at address 2000, then `ptr+1` points to the `double` value that is next to the location pointed to by `ptr`, at address 2008, not to the location at address 2001.

This is especially handy when the pointer points to an element of the array. Incrementing the pointer by 1 is not what you would think. It does not add 1 to the contents of the pointer variable as arithmetic operators over numeric types do. It turns the pointer to point to the next element of the array! Dereferencing the pointer retrieves (or changes) the value of the next array element! Incrementing the pointer by 2 moves the pointer two elements up. In the next coding example, the first part of array `data[]` (the same lowercase characters "abc") is copied into the first part of array `buf[]` so that its contents becomes "abcabc."

```
p = buf;                    // point to start of the array again
for (i=0; i < 3; i++)       // replace the first half of array
  *(p+i) = *(q+i);          // again, same as buf[i]=data[i];
```

Notice that the dereference operator is of higher priority than the arithmetic operators. This is why, `*p+i` should not be used here. It means `p[0]+i` and not `p[i]`.

Even more concise code can be written applying increment (or decrement) operators to pointers. In all the cases adding 1 to a pointer actually means adding the size of the type to the address stored in the pointer and moving the pointer to point to the next array element. Listing 6.8 summarizes the preceding examples. In the first loop, it sets and displays the contents of array `buf[]` (ABCDEF) using `p[i]` instead of `buf[i]`. In the second loop, it modifies the second half of the array; in that loop, `p[i]` means not `buf[i]` but `buf[i+3]`. The third loop displays the array `buf[]` (ABCabc) using conventional notation. Then the pointer `p` is set back to the start of `buf[]`, and the fourth loop replaces the first half of the `buf[]`. The result is displayed using the increment operator over the pointer. The output of the program is shown in Figure 6–8.

Listing 6.8   Using pointers for array processing.

```
#include <iostream>
using namespace std;

int main()
 {
    char buf[6], data[6], *p, *q;      // arrays and pointers
    int i;                             // array index
    p = &buf[0];                       // explicit syntax for address
    q = data;                          // implicit syntax for address
    cout << "Initial buffer: ";
    for (i=0; i < 6; i++)              // assign array components
      { p[i] = 'A'+i;                  // upper case letters
        cout << p[i];                  // display ABCDEF
        q[i] = 'a'+i; }                // q and data are synonyms
    p = &buf[3];                       // point to second half
    for (i=0; i < 3; i++)              // replace last 3 components
      p[i] = q[i];                     // same as buf[i+3]=data[i];
    cout << endl << "Replaced second half: ";
    for (i=0; i < 6; i++)
      cout << buf[i];                  // display ABCabc
    p = buf;                           // point to start of array
    for (i=0; i < 3; i++)              // replace the first half of array
      *(p+i) = *(q+i);                 // same as buf[i]=data[i];
    cout << endl << "Replaced first part: ";
    while (p - buf < 6)                // incremented pointer
      cout << *p++;                    // do not overuse this feature
    cout << endl;
    return 0;
 }
```

When the increment and dereferencing operators are used in the same expression, like *p++, their priority is the same, and they are evaluated from right to left, not from left to right as the majority of C++ operators are (see Table 3.1 in Chapter 3, "Working with C++ Data and Expressions"). However, the postfix operator passes on the value of the pointer before incrementing it. Hence, the meaning of *p++ is: save the old pointer, increment the pointer to point to the next element of the array, and return the value at

Figure 6–8   Output of code in Listing 6.8.

```
Initial buffer:       ABCDEF
Replaced second half:  ABCabc
Replaced first part:   abcabc
```

the address pointed to by the old pointer. In other words, if `temp` is a character pointer, `*p++` is equivalent to:

```
(temp = p, p++, *temp)
```

Again, pointers and array names are equivalent in all regards with the exception of one: The pointer can be incremented or reassigned but the array name cannot. For example, at the end of Listing 6.8 it would be a mistake to print the array `buf[]` once again as

```
while (p - buf < 6)        // displacement in array elements
  cout << *buf++;          // syntax error
```

It would be no problem to use another pointer for that purpose.

```
q = buf;
while (p - q != 0)         // displacement in array elements
  cout << *q++;            // do not overuse this feature
```

Notice that pointer `p` here is used as a sentinel. At the end of Listing 6.8, pointer `p` was incremented to point past the last element of the array `buf[]`. This is why the loop above terminates when pointer `q` ends its run over the elements of array `buf[]` and points past the last element, that is, to the same location as pointer `p`.

Of course, it is important to understand the connection between the pointer notation and array notation. There is a lot of legacy C and C++ code that uses this feature. However, pointer notation is not intuitive and can easily confuse the inexperienced. This is why it is better to increment indices rather than pointers. For many, however, incrementing pointers instead of indices is a sign of programming maturity because arithmetic operations over pointers look so nice.

In the "good old days," the operations over pointers not only looked nice, but also resulted in faster executable code. With modern compilers, this is not true anymore. Both techniques generate the same code.

Dynamic Arrays

So far I have discussed several uses of pointers—as pointers to named stack variables, as pointers to unnamed heap variables, and as pointers to named stack arrays. These techniques make your code unnecessarily complex without giving any advantages. Even using pointers to point to named arrays (as in the examples above) is not very useful. Using named arrays is simpler than using pointers.

Now let us look at the examples where the utilization of pointers is beneficial and appropriate. Pointers can help you manage memory dynamically and avoid the curse of specifying the size of the arrays at compile time. You achieve that by using dynamically allocated arrays.

Listing 6.9 shows a simplified version of the program shown in Listing 5.11 in Chapter 5 that processes transaction amounts entered from the keyboard.

The technique I used back in Chapter 5, Listing 5.11 (a character sentinel value at the end of data input) is a good solution for interactive input. In Listing 6.9 I use the zero sentinel. I break the reading loop when the zero amount is entered. I also break the loop if the count of data values entered by the user exceeds the size of the array data[].

So, the reading loop can be broken for two reasons: the end of input and array overflow. If the behavior of the program has to be different for different cases of the loop termination, the program has to check what the reason was. In this example, the program prints the message warning the user about array overflow. Checking whether count == NUM is not reliable here because the input data set might contain exactly as many entries as there are elements in the array data. For real programs that process hundreds and probably thousands of entries, this is not likely to happen often. However, it is a common programming blunder to assume that if this is rare then there is no need to check for that. Sooner or later, the unlikely event happens. Not checking for a rare event is asking for trouble.

In Listing 6.9, I test whether the sentinel was found (amount was zero) when the loop was terminated. If it was not, I conclude that the reason for loop termination is array overflow. If the sentinel was found, I assume that all data have been read.

The output of this program with only three entries in the array is shown on Figure 6–9.

Listing 6.9 Reading transaction data with protection against array overflow.

```
#include <iostream>
#include <iomanip>
using namespace std;

int main ()
{
  const int NUM = 3;                         // for debugging: it should be larger
  double amount, total = 0, data[NUM];
  int count = 0;                             // initialize current data
do {                                         // do until EOF or array overflow
  cout << "Enter amount (or 0 to finish): ";
  cin >> amount;                             // get next double from the file
```

```
   if (count==NUM || amount==0) break;          // overflow or sentinel
   total += amount;                             // process current valid data
   data[count++] = amount;                      // and get next input line
   } while (true);
   if (amount != 0)                             // was all data read in?
    { cout << "Out of memory: input was terminated\n";
      cout << "The value " << amount << " is not saved" << endl; }
   cout << "\nTotal of " << count << " values is "
       << total << endl;
   if (count == 0) return 0;                    // no results if no input
   cout << "\nTran no. Amount\n\n";             // print the table header
   cout.setf(ios::fixed);                       // set up fixed format for double
   cout.precision(2);                           // total digits if NO ios::fixed
   for (int i = 0; i < count; i++)              // go over the data again
    { cout << setw(4); cout << i+1;             // tran number
      cout << setw(11); cout << data[i] << endl; }  // tran value
   return 0;
}
```

Formatted data output here is different from Listing 5.11 in Chapter 5. The setf() function sets control flags of the cout object. It uses the flag ios::fixed as the argument that tells the display to use fixed-point notation with the decimal point rather than scientific notation with the mantissa and exponent. The precision() function takes the number of digits as its argument. If the ios::fixed flag is not set, this number means the total number of meaningful digits that should be used to display a value. When the ios::fixed flag is set, this number means the number of digits displayed after the decimal point. Make sure that you do not confuse these two meanings of the precision() function.

Figure 6–9   Output of code in Listing 6.9 (input is truncated).

```
Enter amount (or 0 to finish): 22
Enter amount (or 0 to finish): 33
Enter amount (or 0 to finish): 44
Enter amount (or 0 to finish): 55
Out of memory: intput was terminated
The value 55 is not saved

Total of 3 values is 99

Tran no.  Amount

   1       22.00
   2       33.00
   3       44.00
```

Alert

The meaning of the argument to function `precision()` *depends on the* `ios::fixed` *flag. When the flag is set, the argument denotes the number of digits after the decimal point. When the flag is not set, it is the total number of meaningful digits.*

In the example in Listing 5.11, the function `width()` specifies the minimum number of positions that the next output value will take on the display. If the value needs more positions to be displayed, the additional positions are used (thus destroying formatting). Other formatting functions, `setf()` and `precision()`, affect the format until these functions are called again with a different argument. The `width()` function has the scope of one output value only. After the next value is output, the display reverts to the default width (zero), that is, to the absence of any formatting of output data. This is why the `width()` function should be called before outputting each value.

In Listing 6.9, I use the manipulator `setw()`, which is inserted into the output stream similar to manipulators `endl`, `dec`, and `hex` that were discussed earlier. Similar to function `width()`, the scope of this manipulator is one output value only. This is why the `setw()` manipulator has to be inserted before each value even if the width of the field should remain the same. Notice that the code in Listing 6.9 uses the header file `iomanip`. Earlier examples used manipulators (at least, `endl`) but they did not need this header file. Only manipulators that use arguments, as `setw()` does, need this header file. If you forget to include it, the code will not compile. It is unfortunate that the design of manipulators and formatters is inconsistent. It is, of course, unfortunate that you should worry about header files at all.

Alert

When you use formatting functions (for example, `width()`*) or manipulators without arguments (for example,* `endl`*), there is no need to include the* `iomanip` *header file. When you use manipulators with arguments (for example,* `setw()`*), you should include the* `iomanip` *header file.*

Listing 6.10 shows the program that implements the same functionality as the program in Listing 6.9 but the program in Listing 6.10 does it by a dynamically allocated array. This is where the use of pointers comes shining through, combining program integrity with efficiency of execution.

Listing 6.10 Reading data into an array allocated on the heap.

```
#include <iostream>
#include <iomanip>
using namespace std;

int main ()
{
  const int NUM = 3;                        // for debugging:it should be more
  double amount, total = 0, *data;
  int count = 0, size = NUM;                // initialize current data
  data = new double[size];                  // initial array on the heap
do {                                        // do until zero is entered
  cout << " Enter amount (or 0 to finish): ";
cin >> amount;                              // get next double value
  if (amount == 0) break;                   // stop when sentinel appears
  if (count == size)                        // out of space, ask for more
   { size = size * 2;                       // make it conspicuous
     double *q = new double[size];          // double array size
     if (q == 0)
       { cout <<" Out of heap memory: input was terminated" <<endl;
         break; }
     else {
       cout << "More memory allocated: size = " << size << endl;
       for (int i=0; i < count; i++)        // copy old data
         q[i] = data[i];                    // use subscript notation
       delete [] data;                      // do not forget to free old data
       data = q; }                          // hook up main pointer
total += amount;                            // process current valid data
data[count++] = amount;                     // and get next input value
 } while (true);
  if (amount != 0)                          // and what is this for?
   { cout << "Out of memory: input was terminated\n";
     cout << "The value " << amount << " is not saved" << endl; }
  cout << "\n Total of " << count << " values is "
       << total << endl;
  if (count == 0) return 0;                 // no results if no input
  cout << "\n Tran no. Amount\n\n";         // print the table header
  cout.setf(ios::fixed);                    // set up fixed format for double
  cout.precision(2);                        // total digits if NO ios::fixed
  for (int i = 0; i < count; i++)           // go over the data again
   { cout << setw(4); cout << i+1;          // tran number
     cout << setw(11); cout << data[i] << endl; } // tran value
  return 0;
}
```

Instead of allocating the array `data[]` on the stack using a predefined compile-time constant (in this example, 3), the program allocates the array of the same size on the heap using the variable `size` to specify the size of the array. This variable has a run-time value rather than a compile-time value. Notice that the dynamic array does not have a name and is accessed through the character pointer `data` only. When pointers were used to point to named arrays (see Listing 6.8), I had a choice between using the pointer name (e.g., `p[i]`) or the array name (e.g., `buf[i]`). Here, I do not have a choice. The heap array does not have a name, and I am forced to use the pointer name to access the elements the array.

If the next amount read by the program fits into the array, that is, the condition `count == size` is still false, the value is saved in the array. Notice the use of the pointer `data` as the array name. The statement `data[count++] = amount;` is the same both in Listing 6.10 and in Listing 6.9, but its meaning is different. In Listing 6.9, `data` is the name of a stack array; in Listing 6.10 `data` is the name of the pointer pointing to an unnamed heap array.

Things become interesting when all slots in the dynamic array are taken and the condition `count == size` becomes true. In Listing 6.9, I issued an error message and truncated further input of data. In Listing 6.10, I have an opportunity to recover from the array overflow by allocating more memory on the heap and copying existing data into a new heap array.

The program cannot use the same pointer, `data`, to allocate more memory. When `data` receives the address of the new chunk of memory, it loses the address of existing data. This is why I need another local pointer, `q`, to allocate another array on the heap, twice the size of the existing heap array. Doubling the size of memory is a common heap management strategy, but other increments could be used too.

```
double q = new double[size*=2];      // get more heap memory
```

Modifying `size` in the statement that allocates memory is not a good practice. The maintainer can easily overlook this action. It is better to do that explicitly before using the operator `new`.

```
size = size * 2;
double *q = new double[size];      // double array size
if (q == NULL)
  { cout << "Out of heap memory \n"; return; }
else
  /* copying data into array pointed to by q */
```

Notice that the same pointer type, `double*`, is used to point to a single value of the type `double` and to an array of values of the type `double`. This is a general observation. Looking at the type of the pointer, you cannot tell whether it points to an array or to a single value. You just remember that. This makes it more difficult to pass to the maintainer the designer's knowledge.

It is a good idea to always check whether the memory allocation is successful. Running out of memory is rare, and programmers are often complacent and do not check whether the operator new returns 0. While copying the existing array into the first part of the new array, the pointer names can be used as array names, thus avoiding computations over pointers.

```
for (int i=0; i < count; i++)
  q[i] = data[i];           // copy old data into the first half of new data
```

Some programmers would organize this loop using pointer arithmetic with the index, for example, the following way

```
for (int i=0; i < count; i++)      // copy old data
  *(q+i) = *(data+i);
```

Others would use the following loop incrementing pointers to point to the next location in the heap array.

```
for (double *p=q,*r=data; p-q < count; p++, r++)      // is it nice?
  *p = *r;
```

Yet others would use the following form.

```
double *p = q, *r = data; int i = 0;
while (i++ < count)
  *p++ = *r++;                         // real nice?
```

My personal taste is to stay as close as possible to array notation and avoid pointer arithmetic. But other forms of the loops are legitimate C++ idioms too. You will see them in legacy C/C++ code.

Back to dynamic memory allocation. After the existing data are copied into the new array, the existing array has to be deleted, and the pointer to the existing array should be turned to the new array, making it the next version of the existing array. Both the steps and their sequence are important. If we do not delete the existing array, there will be memory leak in the program. If we first turn the pointer to the new array, we will not be able to delete the existing array.

The results of the run of this program in Listing 6.10 are shown on Figure 6–10.

There are a number of little problems in the program in Listing 6.10. Notice that there is only one way to leave the loop: when the operator >> fails to read next amount. So what is the if statement doing there after the end of the loop? This is a common programming blunder: to leave in the source code the statements that are not used anymore. After all, how long does it take for the maintenance programmer to figure out what this test means?

```
Enter amount (or 0 to finish): 22
Enter amount (or 0 to finish): 33
Enter amount (or 0 to finish): 44
Enter amount (or 0 to finish): 55
More memory allocated: size = 6
Enter amount (or 0 to finish): 66
Enter amount (or 0 to finish): 0

Total of 5 values is 220

Tran No. Amount

   1       22.00
   2       33.00
   3       44.00
   4       55.00
   5       66.00
```

Figure 6–10   Output of code in Listing 6.10 (with debugging messages).

Actually, the maintenance programmer has to figure out that this test does not mean anything, and it always takes longer to conclude that there is no meaning than it does to find meaning if one exists.

Another example of programming sloppiness is the place where the variable amount is defined. To avoid name conflicts, especially during maintenance, and to facilitate the understanding of the code by the maintainer, it is important to define variables as deep in the nested block structure as possible. This is why pointer q is defined in the local block of the if statement. We cannot do the same to variables total, data, count—they are needed outside of the input loop. But the variable amount could be defined inside the input loop. It does not look like a major issue because the program is so small, but finding a proper place for definitions is an important skill and it should be developed, as any skill, by practicing it.

When the program terminates, I do not return the remaining memory to the heap. In this case it is probably not dangerous because the operating system will do the cleanup, but it is not a good programming style. And it is not good to rely on the kindness of operating system designers.

It is not even a good idea to discuss whether it is dangerous to have memory leak. It should be an automatic habit: You allocated memory on the heap—find a place to return it to the heap. In this case, the main() should do it immediately before the return statement.

```
delete [] data;        // array (but not the pointer) is deleted
```

Notice brackets in the delete statement when the array is deallocated. The delete operator is not intelligent enough to figure out whether the pointer points to an array or to an individual value, and it does need the brackets to indicate that it is an array that is deleted rather than a single variable. Again, in the tradeoff between the interests of the programmer and the compiler writer, C++ makes the life of the compiler writer easier.

When I copy the existing array into the new array before releasing the existing array, I use `count` as the loop limit rather than `size`, even though this segment of code started with the test `count == size`. This equality does not hold at the time of copying because I incremented `size` before I allocated the new array. It is probably better to do change `size` after copying is over.

```
if (count == size)                          // out of space, ask for more
  { double *q = new double[2*size];          // double array size
    cout << "More memory allocated: size = " << size << endl;
    for (int i=0; i < size; i++)             // copy old data
      q[i] = data[i];
    size *= 2;                               // double the limit for next test
    delete [] data;                          // do not forget to free old data
    data = q; }                              // hook up main pointer
```

Figure 6–11 summarizes the operations for recovery from array overflow. Figure 6–11a shows the heap array `data[]` and stack variables `amount`, `size`, and `count` when the overflow has been detected (when I say `data[]`, I mean

Figure 6–11   Sequence of actions to recover from the heap array overflow.

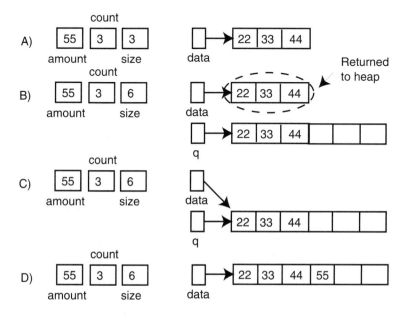

the heap array pointed to by pointer data). Figure 6–11b shows the heap array q[] after copying values from array data[] and array data[] after it was returned to the heap. Figure 6–11c shows both pointers, data and q, pointing to the new heap array. Figure 6–11d shows the array when pointer q is deleted according to the scope rules.

The next example of a useful dynamic array is related to entering text. When the program expects the input of character data, for example, customer name or address and the like, it is hard to imagine that the program needs an array of more than 30–50 characters to accommodate the input. But what do we do if a key is stuck on the keyboard (because of spilled coffee or for any other good or not so good reason)? The input data will overflow this short array and corrupt memory. Also, when we read from a file or from a telecommunications line, there is no guarantee that the size of the input line will be limited by any specific value. The risk of memory corruption is always there, no matter how large an array of fixed size the program allocates.

Listing 6.11 shows a solution to this problem. The idea is to enter data into a relatively short named array allocated on the stack (buf[]) and copy data into a heap array (pointed to by pointer data). If data keep coming, read it into the stack array again (over the data that have been already copied into the heap array), allocate a larger heap array (pointed to by pointer temp), copy into this array the data from the previous heap array (pointed to by data), and then append the data from the stack array buf[].

Listing 6.11   Using a dynamic array to accommodate infinite input string.

```
#include <iostream>

using namespace std;

int main(void)
 {
  const int LEN = 8; int len=1;                    // short array for debugging
  char buf[LEN], *data = 0;                        // init to zero for first pass
  cout << " Type text, press Enter: \n";
  do {
    cin.get(buf,LEN);                              // data goes into a stack array
    len += strlen(buf);                            // total length of old data
    char *temp = new char[len];                    // request new heap array
    if (temp == 0)                                 // test for allocation success
      { cout << " Out of memory: program terminated\n";
        return 0; }                                // no luck, give up
    if (data == 0)
      strcpy(temp,buf); }                          // copy data from input buffer
    else
    {strcpy(temp,data); strcat(temp,buf); }        // copy data
```

```
    delete [] data;                              // delete existing array
    data = temp;                                 // point to the new array
    cout << " Total: " << len << " added: " << buf << endl;
    cout << " Dynamic buffer: " << data << endl;    // debug

  char ch = cin.peek();                          // what is left in the buffer?
  if (ch == '\n')                                // quit if it is new line
   { ch = cin.get(); break; }
  } while (true);                                // or keep going until EOF
  cout << "\n You entered the following line: \n\n";
  cout << data << endl;                          // same syntax as for arrays
  delete [] data;
  return 0;
}
```

In Listing 6.11, the user enters data into a stack array buf[] whose size is made artificially short (LEN = 8 characters) to demonstrate how the algorithm works. The get() function reads until it either reads LEN - 1 characters or finds the newline character in the input stream. It does not remove the newline character from the input stream. (It has to be removed by other means, e.g., calling function get() that reads exactly one character.)

In either case, get() adds a terminating zero to the string in buf[]. Next, the code will allocate len characters from the heap to accommodate characters read into buf[]. The first time around, it is len = len + strlen(buf), since len is initialized to 1, and strlen() counts the number of characters without the terminating zero. If the allocation was not successful (pointer temp is set to 0), the program terminates.

If this is the first pass through the loop (pointer data is still initialized to null), this is the end of the story: The program copies the input data from buf[] into the array pointed to by temp. Here equivalency between pointer and array notation comes in very handy: You pass pointer temp to the function strcpy(), and it copies characters from buf[] into the array pointed to by temp.

If this is not the first pass through the loop (pointer data is not 0; it points to the array previously allocated from the heap) things are more complex. First, the program copies the previous data into a newly allocated array using strcpy(), and then it appends the characters from buf[] to the end of the previous data using strcat().

Now pointer temp points to updated input string, and pointer data points to the previous data. Next, the program deletes previous data and sets pointer data to point to the updated input string.

The next task is to figure out what happened during the call to get(): Was input terminated because the newline character was found (and left in the input stream) or because LEN - 1 characters were input and array buf[]

became full? To decide which was the case, the program looks at the next input character by calling the `peek()` function; if the next character is indeed the newline character (and it will be the newline character for a short input line), the program removes it by calling another `get()` that reads one character only and terminates the loop.

If the input line does not fit into the buffer, the function `get()` at the top of the `do` loop will terminate input after reading `LEN - 1` characters and will still append the null terminator to the end of array `buf[]`. The `peek()` function will return the next character that is not the newline character. Hence, it is not a good idea to remove this character from the input stream: It will be the first character read by the next call to `get()`.

During the next iteration through the `do` loop, the `get()` statement at the top of the loop will read the next batch of characters into array `buf[]`; during this iteration, we have to copy the data from `buf[]` into a dynamically allocated array.

This time around, the array pointed to by the character pointer `data` already exists. Its length (including the zero terminator) is in variable `len`. The program uses the local pointer `temp` to allocate another array on the heap asking for enough memory to accommodate for the existing heap array (pointed to by `data`) and newly entered characters in `buf[]`. This is where the expression `len += strlen(buf)` comes from. The program populates the newly allocated array by copying into it the array pointed to by `data` and concatenating it with the result of the contents of the array `buf[]`. After that the program deletes the existing array pointed to by `data` and sets `data` to point to the newly allocated array (pointed to by `temp`). The iterations continue until finally the next call to `peek()` discovers the newline character or the end of file is found.

The results of the execution of the program are shown in Figure 6–12.

Figure 6–12 Output of code in Listing 6.11 (with debugging messages).

```
Type text, press Enter:
Hello World!
Total: 8 added: Hello W
Dynamic buffer: Hello W
Total: 13 added: orld!
Dynamic buffer: Hello World!

You entered the following line:

Hello World!
```

Here again, the arrays allocated on the heap do not have names. They are referred to through pointers that are allocated on the stack. (Hence, these pointers have names temp and data.) The program uses these pointers as if they were arrays allocated on the stack. For example, pointers temp and data are passed to the functions strcpy(), strcat(), and strlen() in exactly the same way as the ordinary array buf[]. The same is true for the insertion operator << at the end of Listing 6.11: The pointer data is used as if it were an array name. The difference is that the memory for named arrays is returned according to the language rules, at the end of their scope, and dynamic arrays are returned using the explicit delete operator (notice the brackets in the delete statements).

Figure 6–13 shows the memory management operations for input data in Figure 6–12. Figure 6–13a shows that array buf[] is full with "Hello W" and pointer data is 0 (the grounding notation is used). Figure 6–13b shows that variable len contains 8, temp points to a heap array of 8 characters, and data points to the same array. (Notice that the delete operator over a null pointer has no effect.) Figure 6–13c shows array buf[] after entering "orld!". Figure 6–13d shows that len contains 13, temp points to the array that contains "Hello World!", the array pointed to by data is deleted, and data points to the same array as temp.

Figure 6–13   The pointer diagram for input data in Figure 6–12.

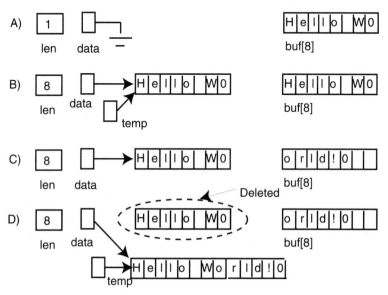

Note

It is illegal to apply the delete *operator to the same pointer twice without initializing the pointer after the first* delete. *It is, however, perfectly legitimate to apply the* delete *operator to a pointer that is set to 0. This operation has no effect.*

I am not sure how much time you should spend on this topic during the first reading. If you feel that things are becoming too complex, do not bang your head against the wall; skip this material. With experience, memory management will seem simpler to you. Experience, however, should include running simple exercises, drawing diagrams similar to those you saw in this chapter, and developing your intuition and debugging skills.

If you feel comfortable with this material, go on. The previous example dealt with entering one line of input data of arbitrary length. This is no small feat for a language like C++ with its fixed-size stack arrays. Similar techniques could be used in many real-life applications.

The next example will build on the previous one—it accepts any number of lines of arbitrary length. Of course, it does not make much sense to read data from the keyboard just to drop it on the floor. You will see the techniques for writing to a disk file in the next section in this chapter.

Listing 6.12 uses the algorithm implemented in Listing 6.11 as an inner loop. The outer loop continues reading input data until the user presses the Enter key without typing any characters on the line. This empty line serves as a sentinel value that terminates input.

Listing 6.12   Using a dynamic array to read an arbitrary set of lines.

```
#include <iostream>

using namespace std;

int main(void)
  {
    const int LEN = 8; char buf[LEN];
    int cnt = 0;
    cout << "Enter data (or press Return to end): \n";
do {                                       // start of outer loop for input lines
    char *data = new char[1]; data[0] = 0; // initially, it is empty
    int len = 0;                           // initial size is zero
    do {                                   // start of inner loop for line segments
      cin.get(buf,LEN);                    // get next line segment
      len += strlen(buf);                  // update total string length
```

```
      char *temp = new char[len+1];
      strcpy(temp,data); strcat(temp,buf);
      delete data;
      data = temp;                          // expand the long line
      cout <<"Allocated " << len+1 <<": " <<data <<endl;
      char ch = cin.peek();                 // what is left in the buffer?
        if (ch == '\n' || ch == EOF)        // quit if if new line
          { ch = cin.get();                 // but first remove it from input
           break; }
  } while (true);
      if (len == 0) break;                  // end on empty string
      cout << " line " << ++cnt << ": " << data << endl;
      delete [ ] data;
      } while (true);                       // continue until break on empty line
      return 0;
  }
```

There are several interesting differences between programs in Listing 6.11 and Listing 6.12. In Listing 6.11, variable `len` denotes the size of the array allocated on the heap. In Listing 6.12, variable `len` denotes the number of characters to be copied in the heap array; the size of the array is one more to accommodate the zero terminator.

These two programs also treat the first read differently. There are two differences between the first read into `buf[]` and all other reads. During the first read, the heap array does not yet exist. This is why the size of the memory to request is one more than the number of characters read into `buf[]`, not the sum of the characters in the heap array and in `buf[]`. This means the use of the `if` statement.

```
if (data == 0)
  len = strlen(buf) + 1;      // first time copy from but[] only
else                          // otherwise copy from data[] and buf[]
  sen = strlen(data)+strlen(buf)+1;
```

Also, during the first read the heap array accepts data from `buf[]` only; during other iterations, the newly allocated heap array copies data from the existing heap array and from array `buf[]`. This is why Listing 6.11 contains this `if` statement.

```
if (data == 0)
  strcpy(temp,buf);           // first time copy from buf[] only
else                          // otherwise copy from data[] and buf[]
  { strcpy(temp,data); strcat(temp,buf); }
```

However, Listing 6.11 does not contain the first `if` statements. Programmers often feel that extra tests make code harder to understand, and they try to avoid these extra tests by clever use of data that works for different cases. In Listing

6.11, I initialized data to 0 and len to 1. Hence, I was able to use for both cases the following statement.

```
len = len + strlen(buf);        // works for first and for next read
```

I did that, I tested the program, everything works, but I still feel some embarrassment. This statement needs an explanation (and careful testing). The if statement above is self-explanatory. What should you prefer: verbose self-explanatory code or concise code that needs explanation? In the preceding chapters I was telling one thing, but here I'm doing another.

Well, in Listing 6.12, I did yet another thing. The pointer data initially points to a heap array of size 1 whose first (and only) character contains the zero terminator—this is commonly known as an empty string. Variable len is initialized to 0—the length of this empty string.

```
int len = 0;                            // initial length of data
char *data = new char[1]; data[0] = '\0';   // empty string
```

Now there is no difference between the first iteration and all other iterations: I add the length of buf[] to the length of data[], copy data[] into the new heap array (the first time around it is an empty string), and append to it the contents of buf[].

```
do {                                    // start of inner loop for line segments
  cin.get(buf,LEN);                     // get next line segment
  len += strlen(buf);                   // update total string length
  char *temp = new char[len+1];         // allocate new heap array
  strcpy(temp,data); strcat(temp,buf);  // merge data there
```

I think I like this code, but let me be frank with you—the version with two if statements is more self-explanatory.

Another issue is program termination. If the user hits the Return key, the program in Listing 6.12 should terminate. Presumably, that enters the newline character '\n' (ASCII code 10) and the peek() call retrieves it and terminates the inner loop. The test for len == 0 breaks the outer loop. Well, not on my machine. When I enter characters and press Return, the newline character is entered. But when I press Return without entering any character, it is the "end of file" marker that is entered. This is why Listing 6.12 tests both for the newline and for EOF (the constant whose value is –1).

```
if (ch == '\n' || ch == EOF)        // quit if it is new line or EOF
  { ch = cin.get(); break; }        // but first remove it from input
```

By the way, the program in Listing 6.11 does not do that. This means that if you hit Return instead of typing a long string, the program goes into the infinite loop—there is no newline character to satisfy that `if` statement. Such a nice program—and has such an ugly bug in it. What a pity!

But the program in Listing 6.12 is not much better. Well, it is better—it works, and it does not go into an infinite loop, or so I think. But it defines the type of variable `ch` as `char`, and then it compares this variable with `EOF`, and `EOF` is negative. This will work only if `char` is signed by default. What gives me the right to think that the type `char` is signed? On my machine this is so, but on your machine, this might not be. To see what happens in this case, replace the definition of `ch` with

```
unsigned char ch = cin.peek();      // on end of file, it is 255
```

Run the program in Listing 6.12, and you will see that it indeed goes into an infinite loop.

This is a common portability problem. A good solution is to use type `int`.

```
int ch = cin.peek();                // on end of file, it is -1
```

All right, this is enough for the program in Listing 6.12. The run of the program is demonstrated on Figure 6–14.

Again, these examples are becoming more and more complex, and I think it is time to talk about other techniques of memory management. If you feel that it is already too complex, go directly to Chapter 7, "Programming with C Functions," and have fun with C++ functions. But do not forget to come back later and learn about dynamic structures.

```
Enter data (or press Return to end):
First line
Allocated 8: First 1
Allocated 11: First line
  line 1: First line
This is the last line
Allocated 8: This is
Allocated 15: This is the la
Allocated 22: This is the last line
  line 2: This is the last line

Allocated 1:
```

Figure 6-14 Output of code in Listing 6.12 (with debugging messages).

Dynamic Structures

In the previous section, we looked at using heap memory for allocating arrays at run time rather than defining their sizes at compile time. This technique of using pointers is much more useful than are the techniques discussed at the beginning of this chapter: pointing at named variables allocated on the stack or allocating individual unnamed heap variables.

Using dynamic arrays eliminates the dangers of both memory corruption and wasted space. The tradeoff to consider is some additional complexity and the danger of memory leak if the programmer does not manage heap memory correctly. Another effect to consider is on program performance. Heap management takes time. For most applications, the performance impact of dynamic array management is not significant, but it is still possible to slow the program down by making it allocate and deallocate memory too often.

The common limitation of all arrays, fixed size and dynamic arrays alike, is that the additions and removals of elements are fast and simple only when they are done at the last valid element of the array. When the elements have to be inserted or deleted in the middle of the array, things become both complex and slow. Dynamically allocated structures are a good alternative to using arrays with frequent insertions and removals in the middle.

Programmer-defined structures can be allocated as individual nodes and connected into linked lists or nets of nodes. To be included in a linked list, the node has to be a structure with at least two components: an information item and the address of the next node (a pointer to the next node in the linked list). The information item can be a single value or a structure with as many fields as necessary to support the needs of the application. To be able to concentrate on programming issues rather than on application details, we will consider a very simple structure: the information item should contain only one value, such as the transaction amount.

In defining the node type, we have free choice in naming the field that contains the address of the next node. Let us say we call it next. There is no free choice in deciding what the type of this field is.

```
struct Node {
  double amount;          // information item
  Node* next; } ;         // link to next Node
```

Whatever the name of the type we use for the node, the name of the type for the next field is the same with the addition of the pointer notation, because the next field is a pointer to a structure of the Node type. It is also nice to be able to use the same node type for different contexts, changing the type of the information field as appropriate. One way to do that is to introduce yet another type, Item, and define it using the typedef facility. (Another way to do that is to use C++ templates; they are more flexible and more complex.)

```
typedef double Item;      // Item is synonym for double
struct Node {
  Item item;              // information item
  Node* next; } ;         // link to next node
```

You can allocate nodes on the heap at any time. The idea of using nodes is to allocate a node only when the program needs to store information for a new item (after reading data from the keyboard, file, or net). Hence, there is no need to reserve memory for more than one item in advance; that is, there is no need to use arrays. Hence, there is no danger of array overflow to put up with no wasted space, shift elements up for insertions, or shift them down for deletion.

Dynamic memory management with linked nodes is more complex than using dynamic arrays. It is an important programming skill. Pointers that are used for node manipulations are named variables; they are allocated on the stack as global variables or local to some scope (function or block scope). Pointers should be a) properly defined, b) properly initialized, and c) properly managed.

Programmers are rarely interested in the value of the address itself. You use the pointer not to figure out the address that is stored there, but to access the object pointed to by the pointer, using the name of the pointer and without using the object name (because the object allocated on the heap does not have any).

This segment of code shows a typical programming error: It defines two pointer variables correctly but dereferences the pointer that is not initialized.

```
Node *p,*q;              // the scope of the * is one name
q->item = amount;        // it damages location pointed to by q
```

A pointer that is not initialized points to wherever it wants. If your program does not use this area of memory, the results might be correct. If this area is used by the operating system of another program, expect trouble unannounced.

Make sure that you are not confused by terminology or notation. This is a new type of intuition for the programmer. So far, you have dealt only with rvalues that needed initialization. In this coding segment with integers, it is clear that variable x has to be initialized before it is used in the assignment (as an rvalue), but variable y does not have to be initialized prior to its use because it is used as an lvalue.

```
int x; int y;            // definitions of noninitialized variables
y = x;                   // x needs initialization, but y does not
```

In the example above, q->item is used as an lvalue and does not have to be initialized in advance. However, q is used as an rvalue, and it must have a legitimate value before it is used to access the item field.

When a pointer, for example, q, is properly initialized, its content is the memory address of a structure of the type Node. We do not know whether pointer q contains the address of field item or field next, the beginning of the structure, its end, or anything in between. And it is not a good idea to find out and use the results to optimize your program. The pointer address is and should remain an abstraction of the address. Whatever the contents of q, *q is the value pointed to by this pointer, in this case, an unnamed structure of type Node. Accessing that value is called *dereferencing the pointer*. Similarly, q->item is the value of the field item in the structure pointed to by pointer q, and q->next is the value of the field next in the same structure. Accessing the fields of an unnamed structure through a pointer pointing to this structure (q->item and q->next) is also called dereferencing the pointer.

Some programmers dislike dealing with two selection operators, the arrow and the dot. It is all right to use the uniform notation, (*q).item for q->item and (*q).next for q->next. Parentheses here are necessary because the selection operator is of higher priority than the dereferencing operator. Hence, *q.item means *(q.next) and this is a syntax error because the dot selector operator can be applied to a structure variable only (named or unnamed), not to a pointer.

So, the program should not dereference a pointer that is not initialized. If this pointer is global, its default value is NULL, and dereferencing a NULL pointer is a run-time error; usually, it terminates the program. If this pointer is local, its value is junk. Being interpreted as an address, this value can point to any place in memory (heap or no heap). Make sure that you avoid corruption of memory or retrieval of incorrect values.

There are several ways to set the value of a pointer. One of them is to assign to the pointer the address of a named variable using the address-of operator, q=&count. This is not very useful. That leaves us with two other ways to set the value of the pointer:

- allocate a new unnamed variable on the heap and set the pointer to the value returned by the operator new (and yes, we do not know whether it points to the beginning or end of the allocated memory)
- find the pointer that is already pointing to the area of memory we are interested in and use it as the source in the assignment; this pointer might be either a) a stack variable or b) a field of a heap variable

That's all to the pointer initialization and assignment. This is the segment of code that uses both methods of pointer initialization.

```
Node *p,*q = new Node;    // q is initialized, but p is not
q->item = amount;         // it saves value of amount in heap memory
q->next = NULL;           // popular sentinel for linked lists
p = q;                    // p now points to the same node as q
```

In many algorithms, you need to traverse a linked structure, that is, visit each node and perform some operation (retrieving the item value, checking whether the last node is reached, and so on). One way to do that is to use the count of nodes similar to array traversal. Another way to do that is to traverse the nodes until a sentinel value is found in the list. A standard way to use a sentinel is to set the next field of the last node in the data set to NULL. The advantage of this approach is that this value cannot be confused with other values possible for a pointer. As I mentioned earlier, a regular 0 would do, but many programmers prefer the library-defined value NULL to indicate that the program deals with pointers.

C++ does not allow the address of one type of variable to be assigned to the pointer of another type. In that sense, C++ is a strongly typed language. In this sample of code, the programmer tries to print the contents of each byte of the Node variable (pointed to by pointer q) as ASCII characters. Notice that not all codes found in the binary representation of the Node fields are codes of printable characters. This is exactly the kind of abuse that strong typing seeks to prevent.

```
char *c = q;                              // no, this is a syntax error
for (int i = 0; i < sizeof(Node); i++)    // go over each byte
  cout << *c++ << ' ';                     // print each byte as a character
```

However, C++ allows the programmer to do that if the programmer feels that this is what should be done. This is a free country, after all. If you want to print every byte of the structure, do it—just tell the compiler (and the maintainer) that you are using the different pointer type and that you know what you are doing. The C++ mechanism for telling the compiler (and the maintainer) that you know what you are doing is casting. This is how you do that.

```
char *c = (char*) q;                      // now this is NOT a syntax error
for (int i = 0; i < sizeof(Node); i++)    // go over each byte
  cout << (int)(*c++) << ' ';             // print each byte as an integer
```

Notice that the char type and Node type are incompatible. The value of one type cannot be converted into a value of another type even with the use of casting. This is an example of C++ support for strong typing. The values of pointers of different types cannot be assigned to each other directly but they can be converted using the explicit cast. Make sure you see the difference. Also, make sure that you do not abuse the pointer conversion feature.

When the program is building a linked structure (in a loop), each node is created on the heap, filled with data (from keyboard of file), and attached to the linked structure. There are several kinds of linked structures. I will consider a simple linked list where a new node is appended to the end of the list.

With the linked list structure, the program can access each node in turn by starting with the first node of the list, going to the next node, and so on until the node that contains the sentinel value in the next field is found. The problem, however, is how to get to the end of the list when inserting new nodes. Traversing each node from the beginning in search of the sentinel node is unnecessary complexity. Also, it might become too expensive in terms of the execution time if the list grows long.

One solution to this problem is to maintain a pointer to the last node of the list. When a new node is created, it is attached to the list without visiting each node in the list. What does "attach" mean? It means that the next field of the last node (the one that contains the NULL address) will be set to point to the new node. Hence, we need to find the names for the next field of the last node (the lvalue of the assignment) and the address of the new node (the rvalue of the assignment). But both nodes are allocated on the heap—they do not have names! This means we have to find pointers that point to these two nodes (the last node and the new node). In the following code segment, the name of the pointer that points to the last node is last. The name of the pointer that points to the new node is q. Hence the assignment that attaches the new node to the end of the linked list is last->next = q; In context, it looks this way.

```
Node *last;              // pointer to the last node
do {                     // do until EOF causes failure
  . . .                  // read value of amount from file
  Node* q = new Node;    // create new node on the heap
  if (q == 0)            // test for success of request
    { cout << "Out of memory: input terminated" << endl;
      break; }           // gracefully terminate if not
  q->item = amount;      // fill node with program data
  q->next = NULL;        // sentinel value for list end
  last->next = q;        // attach as last node in list
  . . . .                // whatever else is needed to be done
} while (true);
```

This is a nice solution. It shows how to attach the new node to the linked list quickly, without traversing through all existing nodes in the list. It just does not specify two important things: how to start and how to finish. How to start means how to attach the very first node to an empty list. How to finish means how to make sure that during the next iteration through the loop the pointer last does indeed point to the last node in the list and not to the former last node (that now precedes the newly inserted node).

When the very first node is being inserted into the list, the expression last>next does not make sense because there are no nodes in the list and hence next cannot belong to any previously allocated node. This means that when the first node is inserted into the list, you should not do this assignment and must do something else instead. This "something else" is attaching the first node to the head of the list.

Usually the head of the list is yet another pointer. Let us call it data. One way to tell that there are no nodes attached to the list is to keep the count of nodes in the list. When the count is 0, the new node should be attached to the list pointer data. When the count is not 0, the new node should be attached to the end of the list, to list->next.

```
Node *last, *data; int count=0;    // last/first pointer, node count
do {                               // do until until end of data
  . . .                            // read the value of amount
  Node* q = new Node;              // create new node on the heap
  if (q == 0)                      // test for success of request
    { cout << "Out of memory: input terminated" << endl;
      break; }                     // gracefully terminate if not
  q->item = amount;                // fill node with program data
  q->next = NULL;                  // sentinel value for list end
```

```
if (count == 0)          // for the first node only
   data = q;             // attach as the first node in list
else
   last->next = q;       // attach as last node in list
   . . . .               // whatever else is needed to be done
} while (true);
```

Remember the conditional operator? This is the situation where this operator comes in handy. This expression returns either `data` or `last->next` depending on the value of `count`, and then `q` is assigned either to `data` or to `last->next`.

```
(count == 0 ? data : last->next) = q;        // nice code
```

Another way to start the list is to initialize the list pointer `data` to `NULL`. In the loop, after a new node is allocated and initialized, you test whether the list pointer is still `NULL`. If it is, the new node is the first node and should be attached to `data`. If it is not `NULL` anymore, this means that the new node is not the first node, and it should be attached to `list->next`.

```
if (data == NULL)        // this means that there are no nodes yet
   data = q;             // point the list pointer to the first node
else
   last->next = q;       // attach new node to the last list node
```

If you like the conditional operator, it can be used here too.

```
(data == 0 ? data : last->next) = q;         // concise code
```

Figure 6–15 illustrates this discussion. Figure 6–15a shows the initial state of the list, pointer `data` that is initialized to 0 and pointer `last` that can point (for now) wherever it wants. Figure 6–15b shows the state of the list after the insertion of the first node (with the `amount` value of 22): The new node is initialized, is pointed to by pointer `q`, and pointers `data` and `last` are set to point to the new node. Notice that the field `next` is drawn of the same size as pointers `data` and `last` because they all have the same type `Node*`. Figure 6–15c shows the list with yet another node allocated for insertion: It is pointed to by pointer `q`. Figure 6–15d shows the first step of insertion at end: The `next` field of the last node (`last->next`) is set to point to the new node (pointed to by `q`). Figure 6–15e shows the second step of insertion: pointer `last` is turned to point to the new node.

You see that after the new node is attached to the end of the list, you should move the pointer `last` because now it points to the node preceding the last node, and the assignment to `last->next` during next iteration would be incorrect. To move the pointer `last` means to design an assignment state-

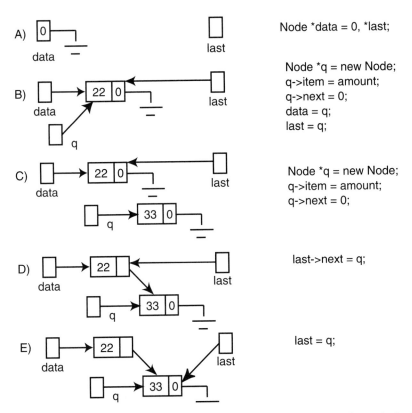

A)

Node *data = 0, *last;

B)

Node *q = new Node;
q->item = amount;
q->next = 0;
data = q;
last = q;

C)

Node *q = new Node;
q->item = amount;
q->next = 0;

D)

last->next = q;

E)

last = q;

Figure 6–15 The pointer diagrams for inserting a new node at the end of a linked list.

ment where the pointer `last` is on the left-hand side. What should be on the right-hand side of that assignment? To answer this question, you should find a pointer that already points to the node you want the target of the assignment to point to, that is, a pointer to the new node.

Look at Figure 6–15d. Are there any pointers that point to the newly attached node? Sure. Actually, there are two pointers pointing to that node. One is pointer `q` that was used to allocate the new node. Another is pointer `last->next` that was used to attach that node to the list. Either would do.

```
last = q;        // divert the pointer back to the last node
```

Using the second pointer pointing to the new node, you get the following.

```
last = last->next;    // move pointer to next list node
```

This second form of moving the pointer last is actually a general technique for moving a traversing pointer to point to the next node in the linked list. This technique is very popular in list processing algorithms. It is equivalent to the statement, i++ in the array traversal that moves the index to the next element in the array.

Listing 6.13 shows the program similar to ones shown in Listing 6.9 and Listing 6.10. Transaction data is read from the keyboard. Instead of allocating a fixed array on the stack (as in Listing 6.9) or allocating a dynamic array on the heap (as in Listing 6.10), this program allocates an individual node for each value that is read. The node is then appended to the end of the linked list.

Listing 6.13   Using a linked list of heap nodes.

```cpp
#include <iostream>
#include <iomanip>
using namespace std;
typedef double Item;
struct Node {
  Item item;
  Node* next; } ;

int main ()
{ int count = 0;                      // count of amounts
 Node *data=0, *last;                 // pointers to start and end of list

do {                                  // do until EOF causes failure
  double amount;                      // local variable for input
  cout << " Enter amount (or 0 to finish): ";
  if (amount == 0) break;
  cin >> amount;                      // get next double from user
  if (amount==0) break;               // stop input on no more data
  Node* q = new Node;                 // create new node on the heap
  if (q == 0)                         // test for success of request
    { cout << "Out of heap memory" << endl;  break; }
  q->item = amount;                   // fill node with program data
  q->next = NULL;                     // sentinel value for list end
  (data == 0 ? data : last->next) = q;
  last = q;                           // last=last->next; is ok, too
  count++;                            // increment count
    } while (true);
  cout << "\nTotal of " << count << " values are loaded\n";
  if (count == 0) return 0;           // no output if no file input
  cout << "\nNumber Amount Subtotal\n\n";  // print header
  cout.setf(ios::fixed);              // fixed format for double
  cout.precision(2);                  // digits after decimal point
  double total = 0;                   // total for input amounts
  Node *q = data;                     // start at start of the list
```

```
for (int i = 0; i < count; i++)      // go over list data
  { total += q->item;                 // accumulate total
    cout.width(3); cout << i+1;        // transaction number
    cout.width(10); cout << q->item;   // transaction value
    cout.width(11); cout << total << endl;       // running total
    q = q->next; }                     // idiom to pointing pointer to next node
  Node *p = data, *r = data;           // initialize traversing pointers
  while (p != NULL)                    // go on until it runs off the list
    { p = p->next;                     // prevent next node from hanging
      delete r; r = p; }               // delete node, catch up with next
  return 0;
}
```

After all the data were read in, the program traverses the linked list. For each node, it prints the amount of each transaction and running subtotal of transactions. The output of the program is shown in Figure 6–16.

The code for traversing the linked list initializes the local pointer q to point to the start of list (q = data;). Then it makes count steps through the list. At each step, it accesses the node pointed to by q (in this case, it accumulates the total, prints the transaction Number, Amount, and Subtotal). Then it traverses to the next node by setting q to q->next. When q becomes NULL, it means that it was pointing to the last node (whose next field is NULL), and the loop can terminate.

Figure 6–16 Output of code in Listing 6.13.

```
Enter amount (or 0 to finish): 22
Enter amount (or 0 to finish): 33
Enter amount (or 0 to finish): 44
Enter amount (or 0 to finish): 55
Enter amount (or 0 to finish): 66
Enter amount (or 0 to finish): 0

Total of 5 values are loaded

Number  Amount   Subtotal

   1    22.00      22.00
   2    33.00      55.00
   3    44.00      99.00
   4    55.00     154.00
   5    66.00     220.00
```

Another form of this loop manipulates the traversing pointer in the header of the `for` loop.

```
double total = 0;                         // total for input amounts
int i = 0;                                // start at start of the list
for (Node* q=data; q!=NULL; q=q->next)    // go over list data
  { total += q->item;                     // accumulate total
    cout.width(3); cout << i+1;           // transaction number
    cout.width(10); cout << q->item;      // transaction value
    cout.width(11); cout << total << endl; // running total
    i++; }                                // increment the count of nodes processed
```

Notice that the name `q` was used earlier in the program code. It was made local in the input loop. Because of that, it can be reused in the rest of the program without any analysis of its use. Had it been defined in the scope of the `main()` function, similar to `data`, its further use in the program would require analysis of how this pointer is used and whether it can be used for other purposes or a different name should be invented instead. This is yet another example of how the correct use of scope reduces dependencies between parts of the program. This reduces complexity of both design and maintenance.

The last loop of the program in Listing 6.13 shows yet another form of list traversal. Its goal is to return the list nodes to the heap to avoid memory leak. For this simple example, where the program allocates nodes, traverses them once, and terminates, this is not vital. The operating system will take care about the heap memory. This is vital for programs that allocate and deallocate nodes many times during execution, sometimes around the clock. For these programs, failure to release the nodes that are no longer needed is asking for trouble.

I included this loop in the program because I wanted to show you yet another way to traverse the linked list. The loop should go over each node of the loop and delete it. Again, a pointer should be initialized to point to the first list node and move to the next node. After the pointer points to the last node, the move to the next node makes this pointer NULL. A popular solution for the loop traversal uses the `for` loop.

```
for (Node *q = data; q != NULL; q = q->next)  // visit each node
  { delete q; }                               // release its heap memory
```

This is a nice loop; its header is almost standard and can be used in many contexts. The problem with this loop here is that the increment expression `q = q->next` is executed after the body of the loop, before the test for loop termination. Meanwhile, the body of the loop releases memory pointed to by pointer `q`. This memory can be used for other purposes and should not be referred to by this program anymore. The next thing that this loop does after `delete q;` is that it refers to `q->next`!

By the way, it does not mean that the program executes incorrectly. On one of my machines, it executed correctly because the memory pointed to by pointer `q` was only marked as available but was not actually reused yet for other purposes. So the expression `q->next` indeed retrieved the address of the next node correctly. But this should not be taken as license to refer to somebody else's memory. On my other machine, this program crashed. Correct results of a C++ program do not necessarily mean that the program is correct.

The program in Listing 6.13 uses a more-complex but more-robust form of the loop. Pointers `p` and `r` point to the same node. Then `p` moves to point to the next node, and the node pointed to by `r` is deleted. After that, `p` and `r` point again to the same node.

```
Node *p = data, *r = data;    // initialize traversing pointers
while (p != NULL)
  { p = p->next;              // move it to point to the rest of list
    delete r;                 // delete node, make pointer invalid
    r = p; }                  // catch up with the rest of list
```

Notice that I read "delete `r`" as "the node pointed to by `r` is deleted" rather than "`r` is deleted." I am afraid that some programmers might believe that this statement deletes the pointer. Nothing can be further from the truth. This pointer has a name, hence it is allocated on the stack, hence it is deleted according to the language rules at the closing brace of the scope where this variable is defined. The `delete` operator deletes only unnamed variables allocated on the heap.

And the last warning. When the program handles linked nodes allocated on the heap, the fact that the program compiles and executes correctly for all sets of test data does not mean that the program is correct. Algorithms that do not use heap memory are free of this menace. Make sure that you do not use a solution that is more complex than the application warrants.

Input and Output with Disk Files

In all previous examples, the code read input data from the keyboard and sent output data to the screen. This was nice because it allowed you to concentrate on one thing at a time. For real-life applications, this would not do. You should be able to read data produced by other applications and save the results for future use. In this section, we will briefly look at files as yet another technique for handling large sets of data.

C++, similar to other modern languages, does not have built-in input and output operations. What you use for I/O belongs to a library rather than to the language itself. C++ programs can use two libraries, the standard I/O library `stdio` inherited from C and the newer `iostream` library designed specifically for C++.

Both libraries support file input and output. The C library is complex and prone to error. Its knowledge is important for programmers who maintain legacy C code. The C++ library is less error-prone but is complex and cumbersome. Often, there are many ways to do the same thing. To understand how the C++ library works, one has to know how to use C++ classes, inheritance, multiple inheritance, and other concepts I have not discussed yet. This is why in this section I will discuss bare-bones facilities that will enable you to write and read data to and from disk files.

Output to File

Let us start with writing to a file because it is somewhat simpler than reading from the file.

Actually, writing data to a disk file is similar to writing data to the monitor screen, but instead of the predefined object `cout` you should use a programmer-defined object of the library class `ofstream` (output file stream). This class is defined in the library header file `fstream` that has to be included in the source code.

As you recall from Chapter 2, "Getting Started Quickly: Brief Overview of C++," an object is an instance of a class that combines data and behavior, that is, a structure whose members include functions. The library class `ofstream` is designed in such a way that all the functions available for the predefined object `cout` are available for programmer-defined objects of the `ofstream` class.

This is very convenient. All you have to do to channel the program output to a disk file rather than to the screen is to define an object of class `ofstream` and substitute that object for `cout` in your program. The output statements (including formatting statements) do the same job as for the object `cout`— they will convert the bit patterns in program variables into sequences of characters to write, but writing is done to a file rather than to the screen.

In Listing 6.14, I reimplement the program from Listing 6.12. The program reads an arbitrarily long set of input lines and saves the data to file `data.out`. The changes are minimal.

Listing 6.14   Using a dynamic array to read an arbitrary set of lines and write it to a disk file.

```
#include <iostream>
#include <fstream>                        // for ifstream, ofstream objects
using namespace std;

int main(void)
 {
   const int LEN = 8; char buf[LEN];      // short buffer for input
   int cnt = 0;                           // line count
   ofstream f("data.out");                // new: output file object
   cout << "Enter data (or press Return to end):\n";
do {                                      // start of outer loop for input lines
   int len = 0;                           // initial length of data
   char *data = new char[1]; data[0] = '\0';
   do {                                   // start of inner loop for line segments
      cin.get(buf,LEN);                   // get next line segment
   len += strlen(buf);                    // update total string length
   char *temp = new char[len+1];
   strcpy(temp,data); strcat(temp,buf);
   delete [] data; data = temp;           // expand the long line
   int ch = cin.peek();                   // what is left in the buffer?
   if (ch == '\n' || ch == EOF)           // quit if it is new line or EOF
      { ch = cin.get(); break; }          // but first remove it from input
   } while (true);                        // continue until break on new line
   if (len == 0) break;                   // quit if the input line is empty
   cout << " line " << ++cnt << ": " << data << endl;
   f << data << endl;                     // save data to the file
   delete [] data;                        // avoid memory leak
   } while (true);                        // continue until break on empty line
   cout << " Data is saved in file data.out" << endl;
   return 0;
}
```

As you see, I define an object that I named f of class `ofstream`. The name of the physical disk file to be used as the output file is specified as an argument when the `ofstream` file object is created.

```
ofstream f("data.out");        // open output file
```

This statement associates object f with the physical file `data.out` in the same directory as the executable program file. If you need a file in a different directory, the corresponding path name should be used (remember to use '\\' to denote the escape character in file paths). If the disk file with this name does not exist, it is created. If the file with this name exists, it is silently deleted and a new empty file with the same name is created. (Operating systems that support file versions create a next version of the file.)

What if the disk is full or write-protected? The creation operation fails silently—there is no run-time error generated.

One way to deal with this problem is to call the member function `fail()` that returns `true` if the previous I/O operation fails (for any reason) and `false` if it is successfully completed.

```
ofstream f("data.out");            // open output file dat.out
if (f.fail())                      // test for success, give up if not
   { cout << "Cannot open file" << endl; return 0; }
```

Many programmers think that a full or write-protected disk is a rarity and it is safe to disregard this possibility. I disagree because the program that disregards this is not portable. But you see, I disregarded this in Listing 6.14, and I feel bad about it.

After the `ofstream` file object is created successfully, it can handle the values for storing in the physical file similar to the way that the `cout` object handles the values for display. This means that when the insertion operator `<<` is called, the numerical bit pattern in computer memory is converted into a sequence of characters representing data. For character data, this transformation is trivial.

```
f << data << endl;        // write array to output file, not to cout
```

As you see, the syntax of access to data is the same as for object `cout`. Can an output operation fail? Many programmers feel that if the file is opened successfully, there is no need to check each individual operation. This is not right. Remember, we are discussing storing large amounts of data. Even though modern disks have huge capacities relative to those of the recent past, they can become full. And it is not difficult at all to overflow a floppy or even a Zip disk. This is why you need to test for success after each I/O operation.

```
f << data << endl;                    // save data to the file
if (f.fail())                         // test for success of operation
   { cout << "Disk is full, output terminated" << endl; break; }
```

Note

It is reckless to assume that the I/O operation will not fail. Creation of file objects and messages to file objects should always be followed by a test whether the operation was indeed successful.

```
Enter data (or press Return to end):
First line
  line 1: First line
Second line
  line 2: Second line
This is the last line of text
  line 3: This is the last line of text

Data is saved in file data.out
```

Figure 6-17

Example of the execution of code in Listing 6.14.

Figure 6–17 shows the example of the run of the program in Listing 6.14. For input data in Figure 6–17, the output file data.out contains the following lines.

```
First line
Second line
This is the last line of text
```

When the ofstream file object goes out of scope (in Listing 6.14, at the end of main() function), it is destroyed. This breaks the association between the file object and the physical file, and the physical file is closed. The disappearance of the ofstream file object does not cause the physical file to disappear.

Input from File

Now let us look at the examples where the program uses the data generated by another program, text editor, or communication line. A simple way to do this is to define an object of class ifstream (input file stream) that represents the input file streams.

Similar to class ofstream, class ifstream is defined in the header file fstream, which should be included in the source file. Again, similar to class ofstream, the name of the physical disk file is used as a parameter for the object.

```
ifstream f("amounts.dat");      // open file amounts.dat for input
```

What if the specified file is not found? Or it cannot be opened because it is being used by another application? Similar to ofstream, the ifstream object is still created, but it cannot be used for input. Any attempt to create an ifstream object should be followed by a test for success.

```
ifstream f("amounts.dat");          // open file amounts.dat for input
if (f.fail())                       // test for success
  { cout << "Cannot open file" << endl; return 0; }
```

When the file object of type `ifstream` is defined successfully, the name of the object is associated with the name of the physical disk file. After that, you can use the extraction operator `>>` to read data into the program variables. Instead of object `cin` that represents the keyboard, you will use the programmer-defined file object `f`. The syntax of access to data is the same as for the `cin` object. All other input functions, `get()`, `getline()`, `setf()`, and `precision()`, are available along with manipulators and are used in exactly the same way.

Let me remind you that when the extraction operator is used, the sequence of characters is read and converted to the bit pattern of the designated type (if this conversion is possible): integer, double, character, and so on. The extraction operator skips the leading white space (including the newline character) until it finds the characters to convert, stopping when it finds anything that cannot be part of the value (e.g., the newline character). It is also possible to read data from the file in the binary form rather than as a sequence of characters. The binary form is more compact but it cannot be read by text editors or displayed on the screen in a readable form.

Can an input operation fail? Of course it can. Moreover, when you read data from an input file, you expect the operation to eventually fail when the program reaches the end of file. To check whether the end of data is reached, you can use the member function `eof()`, which returns `true` if the end of file is reached and `false` otherwise.

```
do {                        // do until EOF causes failure
  double amount;            // local variable for input
  f >> amount;              // get next double from file
  if (f.eof()) break;       // stop input on no more data
```

Notice that the previous statement is somewhat vague. What is "the end of file is reached?" There are two possible interpretations, and you should know the difference. When the program reads from a file, the end of file condition can be raised immediately after the program reads the last entry in the file. Another possibility is that it is only when the program tries to read past the last entry in the file that the end of file condition is raised.

Ada and Pascal use the first interpretation. In these languages, a `do` loop that reads data from an external file would look the following way (I am using C++ syntax).

```
do {                        // Ada or Pascal loop structure
  if (f.eof()) break;       // stop input on no more data
  double amount;            // local variable for input
  f >> amount;              // get next double from file
  . . . . . }               // process the amount read
```

COBOL, C++, and Java use the second interpretation: the end of file condition is raised only after the program tries to read past the end of data in the file. In these languages, the structure of a do loop that reads data from an external file should be different.

```
do {                            // C++ or Java loop structure
  double amount;                // local variable for input
  f >> amount;                  // get next double from file
  if (f.eof()) break;           // stop input on no more data
  . . . . . }                   // the rest of the loop
```

What happens if you make a mistake and use the first loop structure instead of the second one in a C++ program? The last value will be read from the file and processed by the rest of the loop. In the next iteration, eof() will return false, and the statement f >> amount; will be executed again. When there are no data, the end of file condition will be raised, but the value of amount in memory will be left the same (on most systems). Since the program is not notified that there are no more data, the rest of the loop will process the last value the second time as if it were repeated in the input file. In the next iteration, the end of file condition will be raised and the loop terminates.

Alert

> In C++, the end of file condition is not raised when the program reads the last item from the file. It is raised on the next read, when the program tries to read past the last file item. Avoid using the last file item twice.

Listing 6.15 shows the version of the program from Listing 6.13 that reads data from a file rather than from the keyboard. To make the comparison easier, I commented out the statements that read from the keyboard rather than cut them out. As you see, switching from reading from the keyboard to reading from a file is not difficult. Figure 6–18 shows the results of the program execution.

Listing 6.15 Using a linked list of heap nodes for data read from a disk file.

```
#include <iostream>
#include <iomanip>
#include <fstream>                              // for ifstream class
using namespace std;

typedef double Item;

struct node {
Item item;
Node* next; } ;

int main ()
{
  int count = 0;                               // count of amounts
  Node *data=0, *last;                         // pointers to start and end
  ifstream f("amounts.dat");                   // file to read data from
  if (f.fail())
  { cout << "Cannot open file" << endl; return 0; }
do {                                           // do until EOF causes failure
  double amount;                               // local variable for input
// cout << " Enter amount (or 0 to finish): ";
// cin >> amount;                              // get next double from user
// if (amount == 0) break;
 f >> amount;                                  // get next double from file
 if (f.eof()) break;                           // stop input if no more data
  Node* q = new Node;                          // create new node on the heap
  if (q == 0)                                  // test for success of request
    { cout << "Out of heap memory" << endl; break; }
  q->item = amount; q->next = NULL;            // fill node with data
  (data == 0 ? data : last->next) = q;
  last = q;                                    // last=last->next; is ok, too
  count++;                                     // increment count
  } while (true);
  cout << "\nTotal of " << count << " values are loaded\n";
  if (count == 0) return 0;                    // no output if no file input
  cout << "\nNumber Amount Subtotal\n\n";      // print table header
  cout.setf(ios::fixed);                       // fixed format for double
  cout.precision(2);                           // digits after decimal point
  double total = 0;                            // total for input amounts
  int i = 0;
  for (Node *q = data; q != NULL; q = q->next) // OK
    { total += q->item;                        // accumulate total
      cout << setw(3) << ++i;                  // transaction number
      cout << setw(10) << q->item;             // transaction value
      cout << setw(11) << total << endl;       // running total
    }
  Node *p = data, *r = data;
  while (p != 0)
  { p = p->next;                               // return heap memory
    delete r; r = p; }
  return 0;
}
```

```
Total of 4 values are loaded

Number  Amount   Subtotal

  1     330.16    330.16
  2      76.33    406.49
  3      50.00    456.49
  4     120.00    576.49
```

Figure 6–18

Example of the execution of code in Listing 6.15.

The file `amount.dat` that I used to produce Figure 6–18 contains the following lines.

```
330.16
76.33
50
120
```

Many programmers are satisfied with this use of the `eof()` function. This, however, leaves your program vulnerable to the errors in the input file formatting.

Let us say, that while typing 50 on the third line of the input file, I pressed the 'o' key instead of 0. When the statement `f >> amount;` reads that line, it finds 5 and then 'o'. The program concludes that the input value is 5, leaves the 'o' character in the input stream and executes the next statement. During the next iteration, the statement `f >> amount;` finds the 'o' in the input stream, concludes that this is the end of the input value and terminates. The next statement is executed, and the hapless program gets into an infinite loop.

Of course, input errors of that type are more likely from keyboard input than from file input, because the file can be proofread before the execution. Still, they are not impossible. Some programmers avoid using the operator `>>` because it is too vulnerable to input format errors—infinite loops are as unpleasant for keyboard input as they are for file input. Instead, they use functions `get()` and `getline()` described earlier to read data as characters. When the input line is in memory, the program can analyze the data and generate an intelligent error message if the data are incorrect.

Another source of vulnerability is the way the file ends. In the example above, the newline character was typed after each value, including the last value, 120. When the last entry in the file is followed by the newline character at the end of file, the extraction function `>>` stops before that newline character when it reads that entry. In this case, the end of file condition is raised only when the program reads past the last entry.

What happens if the last newline character is not added? Or all values are typed on a single line without the terminating newline character? If the newline character does not follow the last file entry, the extraction function reads the end of file marker and raises the end of file condition. The eof() function (which is called after the statement f >> amount;) returns true, and the loop terminates without ever processing the last value.

This is not right. The code should be written in such a way that its behavior does not change, whether or not the data entry person (or telecommunications software) put the newline character after the last entry in the input file. To eliminate this problem, some programmers avoid using the eof() function altogether. Instead, they use your old friend fail().

```
do {                            // C++ or Java loop structure
  double amount;                // local variable for input
  f >> amount;                  // get next double from file
  if (f.fail()) break;          // stop input on no more data
  . . . . . }                   // the rest of the loop
```

The function fail() returns true when the operation fails for any reason, including reaching the end of file. When I type 5o instead of 50, 5 is read, and 'o' is found in the input stream during the next loop iteration. The statement f >> amount; does not read anything, and the fail() function returns true. The input loop terminates. First, earlier termination is better than an infinite loop. Second, the program can analyze the situation after the loop terminates and generate a message if the loop terminates prematurely.

In the second example, when the value 120 is not followed by a newline character, the end of file condition is raised, but the fail() function returns false because the value 120 was read by the statement f>>amount; correctly. It is only on the next pass through the loop, when the program tries to read past the value 120, that this function returns true. Hence, the last value in the file is processed correctly.

Input/Output File Objects

In addition to ifstream and ofstream, the C++ iostream library defines a very large number of other classes. For 99 percent of your work, you do not need to know about these classes. I will mention only one stream class, fstream, because it combines the characteristics of ifstream and ofstream classes.

When you create objects of type ifstream and ofstream, you do not specify in what mode you want to open them—ifstream is created by default for reading, ofstream is created by default for writing. For objects of class fstream, you can specify the mode of opening by providing the second argument when creating an object.

```
fstream of("data.out",ios::out);           // output file
fstream inf("amounts.dat",ios::in);        // input file
```

The input mode is default—it might be omitted. Other available modes of opening include `ios::app` (file is open for appending data to its end), `ios::binary` (file is open in binary rather than text format), and some others. These modes are implemented as binary flags. If necessary, they can be combined using the bitwise inclusive or operator '`|`'.

```
fstream mystream("archive.dat",ios::in|ios::out);   // input/output
```

As is common in C++, there is more than one way to check whether a file operation has succeeded or failed. In addition to function `fail()` described above, you can use function `good()`.

```
fstream inf("amounts.dat",ios::in);        // input file
if (!inf.good())                           // another way to do things
  { cout << "Cannot open file" << endl; return 0; }
```

You can even treat the file object as a numeric value. When the operation fails, the value is 0. When the operation succeeds, the value is nonzero. This is yet another example of testing whether the file has opened successfully.

```
fstream inf("amounts.dat",ios::in);        // input file
if (!inf)                                  // yet another way to do it
  { cout << "Cannot open file" << endl; return 0; }
```

The same syntax can be used for testing success of reading and writing operations. For example, you can count the number of characters in the file using the `get()` function with a one-character parameter. When the reading operation fails (because the end of file marker was reached or for any other reason), it returns 0, and this value can be used to terminate a `while` loop.

```
int count = 0; char ch;
while (inf.get(ch))               // stop when the object is no good
  count++;                        // increment count of characters
cout << "Total characters: " << count << endl;
```

Normally, you do not close the files, because they are closed when the file object that is associated with the file is destroyed at the end of its scope. Sometimes you need to close the file explicitly using the function—what else—`close()`.

```
  inf.close();                     // close the file
```

You need to do that when you want to close the file before its file object goes out of scope, for example, when you have opened several files, and the next file fails to open. In this situation it is prudent to explicitly close all open files before the program terminates or tries to recover. You can also close the file when you do not want to keep several files open, for example, when you read from one file, process data in memory, and then write the results to another file to be used later.

Listing 6.16 shows the modified program from Listing 6.15. In addition to sending the results to the screen, it also saves the report in file `amounts.rep`. Testing for success of I/O operations is done through comparing the file objects to 0. This is a common C++ idiom. The input file is closed at the end of input.

Listing 6.16 Reading from file and writing to screen and to output file.

```cpp
#include <iostream>
#include <iomanip>
#include <fstream>
using namespace std;

typedef double Item;
struct Node {
  Item item;
  Node* next; } ;

int main ()
{
    int count = 0;                          // count of amounts
    Node *data=0, *last;                     // pointers to start and end of list
    fstream inf("amounts.dat",ios::in);      // file to read data from
    if (!inf) { cout << "Cannot open file" << endl; return 0; }
do {                                        // do until end of data
  double amount;                            // local variable for input
  inf >> amount;                            // get next double from file
  if (!inf) break;                          // stop input on no more data
    Node* q = new Node;                     // create new node on the heap
    if (q == 0) { cout << "Out of heap memory" << endl; break; }
    q->item = amount; q->next = NULL;       // fill node with data
    (data == 0 ? data : last->next) = q;
    last = q; count++;                      // set last, increment count
    } while (true);
  inf.close();                              // file is not needed anymore
  fstream of("amounts.rep",ios::out);       // file to write data to
  if (!of) { cout << "Cannot open output file" << endl; }
  cout << "\nTotal of " << count << " values are loaded\n";
  of << "\nTotal of " << count << " values are loaded\n";
  if (count == 0) return 0;                 // no output if no file input
  cout << "\nNumber Amount Subtotal\n\n";   // print table header
```

```
of << "\nNumber Amount Subtotal\n\n";              // print table header
cout.setf(ios::fixed); cout.precision(2);          // precision for screen
of.setf(ios::fixed); of.precision(2);              // precision for file
double total = 0; int i = 0;                       // subtotal, line count
for (Node *q = data; q != NULL; q = q->next)       // OK
  { total += q->item;                              // accumulate total
    cout << setw(3) << i;                          // transaction number
    cout << setw(10) << q->item;                   // transaction value
    cout << setw(11) << total << endl;             // running total
    of << setw(3) << ++i << setw(10) << q->item;   // transaction
    of << setw(11) << total << endl; }             // running total
Node *p = data, *r = data;
while (p != 0)
{ p = p->next;                                     // return heap memory
  delete r; r = p; }
  return 0;
}
```

As you can see, the statements for formatting data in the output file are the same as the statements for formatting data on the screen. For input data in Figure 6–18, the output file created by the code in Listing 6.16 contains the following data.

```
Total of 4 values are loaded

Number   Amount   Subtotal

   1     330.16    330.16
   2      76.33    406.49
   3      50.00    456.49
   4     120.00    576.49
```

All right, this is all that you should know about working with files using the iostream library. The library contains much more than I described, but it is not nice to describe it in detail before you have studied classes and inheritance. Actually, I am not sure that even after you have studied classes and inheritance you will need to know more than I have told you. The iostream library provides you with multiple ways to do the same thing, and you do not have to learn all these ways at once. Instead, pay attention to basic language facilities and make sure that you understand the concepts behind these basic facilities. This will prepare you for dealing with other library facilities when you encounter them in somebody else's code.

Summary

This chapter deals with rather complex material. You looked at several uses of pointers in C++. The first one was to use pointers to point to ordinary variables allocated on the stack and to provide an alternative technique of accessing these variables through aliasing. With the exception of passing parameters by pointer (which I will discuss in the next chapter) this technique is useless. However, some programmers believe that this technique makes their code easier to understand. Make sure you are ready to deal with this kind of pointer manipulation in legacy code.

The second use of pointers is allocating individual variables on the stack rather than on the heap. The heap variables do not have names, and the use of pointers provides the only way to access their contents. However, the use of heap variables instead of ordinary stack variables gives no practical advantages and should be avoided. Some programmers believe that this technique decreases the possibility of stack overflow. Again, make sure that you are ready to deal with this kind of pointer manipulation in legacy code.

Two other uses of pointers are legitimate, useful, and quite common in C++ programs. Unnamed dynamic arrays represent an excellent alternative to C++ named arrays whose size is defined at compile time. Dynamic arrays eliminate the danger of array overflow and wasted space. They are fast and not very complex. When defining dynamic arrays, make sure you do not wind up allocating and deallocating the array repeatedly. Look for the place to define such an array so that it does not impair program performance.

The second valuable use of pointers is for linked structures. It is the most flexible technique of memory allocation, because it does not reserve memory in advance but only on an as-needed basis. It is also the most complex technique. The operations over pointers for node insertion and removal are complex and counterintuitive. The same is true for traversal operations. Errors in pointer manipulation are hard to find. They do not always manifest themselves in incorrect program behavior. Allocation and deallocation of memory in a piecemeal fashion, individually for each node rather than for several elements at once, might negatively affect program performance.

When you feel you should use a linked implementation, consider alternatives. One alternative is the use of dynamic arrays. Another reasonable alternative is the use of the standard template library that provides implementations of such data structures as lists, stacks, queues, trees, and so on. The use of libraries allows you to combine the flexibility of dynamic memory management with simplicity of use. That is, you can have your cake and eat it too.

The last topic of this chapter also deals with sequences of data whose length is not predefined: physical files. I showed you the ways to define library objects that allow you to use the same operations that you use for input from the keyboard and output to the screen. Using files expands the program storage indefinitely and supports data persistence. After saving data to a file, the data survive normal program termination, crash, or power outage. More important, the data can be used by another program at a different time (and probably at a different place). This significantly expands the flexibility of computer information systems.

This chapter ends the discussion of non-object-oriented features of C++. In the following chapters, you will start the detailed study of C++ functions and classes and will learn how to create object-oriented programs. This is a very exciting subject! As I mentioned earlier, the object-oriented approach is probably the only approach that helps the designer create the program from relatively independent pieces and to transmit his or her knowledge about the program to the maintainer directly in the code of the program. This skill does not come automatically, just in the process of learning the language. I hope that studying the rest of this book will help you to master this important skill.

Part 2

OBJECT-ORIENTED PROGRAMMING WITH C++

This part of the book provides you with basic tools of object-oriented programming with C++. Object-oriented programming is first and foremost about using functions because each operation on an object should be implemented as a function call. C++ functions are complex, and Chapter 7, "Programming with C++ Functions," tells you all you should know about the syntax of C++ functions. Passing parameters in C++ has a reputation for difficulty, and I hope that this chapter does a good job helping you to master this essential C++ skill.

Chapter 8, "Object-Oriented Programming with Functions," continues the discussion of C++ functions by explaining how to use functions. It introduces the criteria of cohesion, coupling, encapsulation, and information hiding and discusses the principle of readability and independence of program functions. It shows that most of the benefits of object-oriented programming can be achieved without using C++ objects, by designing access functions that the client code calls (instead of accessing structure fields directly). It also demonstrates the limitations of object-oriented programming with functions and lists the goals that the use of C++ classes has to achieve. This chapter is very important for developing the right intuition about object-oriented programming.

Chapter 9, "C++ Class as a Unit of Modularization," introduces the jewel of C++ programming: C++ classes. It describes the syntax of C++ class definition and discusses data members, member functions, control of access to class members, object initialization and destruction, returning objects from functions, and other technical details of using objects. The chapter contains a lot of complex details—there is no way around this: C++ classes are sophisticated. Make sure that these technical details do not hide from you the main goal of using classes: suppressing minute details when the maintenance programmer needs to understand the general meaning of processing and data flows between the functions.

Chapter 10, "Operator Functions: Another Good Idea," describes operator functions, a nice part of C++ syntax. Operator functions are introduced into the language to support the philosophical concept that a program should be able to do to class objects everything that it can do to numerical variables—add, subtract, and so on. This concept is not very important from the point of view of software engineering principles, but it gives a nice syntactic touch to C++ source code.

Chapter 11, "Constructors and Destructors: Potential Trouble," discusses the dangers of naïve use of C++ constructors and destructors and explains how to recognize these dangers. It offers several techniques for avoiding memory corruption and memory leaks. It is a very important chapter—an inexperienced C++ programmer can do a lot of damage by handling object initialization incorrectly.

PROGRAMMING WITH C++ FUNCTIONS

Topics in this Chapter

- C++ Functions as Modularization Tools
- Argument Promotions and Conversions
- Parameter Passing in C++
- Inline Functions
- Parameters with Default Values
- Function Name Overloading
- Summary

Chapter 7

In the previous chapters, we looked at the basics of the C++ language that allow us to implement any complex requirements a computer system might face.

The C++ built-in data types allow the programmer to cater computational objects to the task at hand. They provide the necessary choices for numeric ranges and precision. The C++ operators allow the programmer to combine input values into powerful and flexible expressions to compute required output values. The C++ control structures allow the programmer to organize computations into proper sequences, change the flow of computation when some conditions become true or false, and repeat computations iteratively if necessary.

We also looked at the C++ features that support aggregation of components. We discussed programmer-defined data types. They let the programmer combine individual data values that logically belong together. Combining individual values into aggregates allows us to handle them as a unit and helps the designer to pass on to the maintainer the designer's knowledge that these components belong together. We also discussed arrays. They let the programmer combine related components that undergo similar processing in the program. Finally, we discussed dynamic memory management and file management. They expand the power and flexibility of ordinary arrays and allow us to overcome their limitations.

Next, you are going to look at yet another C++ aggregation and modularization tool: functions. Combining individual statements into functions allows the programmer to treat them as a single logical unit. Breaking the program's functionality into separate functions is a powerful tool of labor division: Different programmers develop different functions in parallel.

In this chapter, you will study the techniques for writing C++ functions. The main emphasis is going to be on function communications: how functions exchange data. You will learn various techniques of passing parameters and returning values from functions. These techniques differ depending on whether the function arguments are modified by the function or keep the value they had before the function call was made. These techniques also vary depending on whether the function parameter is of a built-in C++ type, an array, or a programmer-defined structure (or class).

You will also learn other techniques of function design directed toward alleviating the restrictions on function names, such as default parameter values and function name overloading. These techniques significantly expand the set of choices that a C++ programmer has to use in his or her implementation decisions. In addition, you will learn how to eliminate the performance overhead of function calls using inline functions. You will also see what happens when actual arguments supplied in the function call are not of exactly the same type as the formal parameters defined in the function header.

This is an ambitious program. C++ functions are flexible and powerful, and they leave the programmer with an almost bewildering array of choices of how to go about implementation. We will try to make some sense out of it.

All the material in this chapter is vitally important for mastering C++ classes. Do not give up, type in the chapter examples, experiment with them, and you will see that it is not that hard.

C++ Functions as Modularization Tools

In C++, as in other languages, the programmer hides the complexity of computer algorithms in relatively small units of modularity: *functions*. Each function is a collection of language statements directed toward achieving a specific goal. These statements can be simple assignments, complex control constructs, or calls to other functions. These other functions can be standard library functions that come with the compiler, specific library functions that come from previous projects, or programmer-defined functions that are custom-made for this particular project.

From the programmer's point of view, the difference between different kinds of functions is that the implementation code of custom-made project functions is available for inspection. As far as library functions are concerned, the programmer who uses these functions as servers for the function he or she is writing does not know their implementation. What the programmer knows is the description of the server function interface: what parameters the caller should supply, what values the function computes, how the output values are computed from the input values, and what restrictions and exceptions apply.

It is not that the code for library functions is a trade secret. Sometimes it is, but often it is freely available. It is that limiting the programmer's knowledge to the function interface and excluding the function code is beneficial; this decreases the code complexity that the programmer faces. Studying function code is justifiable only if the function might contain errors that have to be corrected. This is the case with the programmer-defined functions that are custom made for this particular project. Even for these functions, the task of analysis of function cooperation should be limited to studying function interfaces rather than function implementations.

This is how we are going to evaluate different methods of function communications. Those methods that allow the maintainer (or another designer) to study the function interface only, without reading the function code, will be considered superior to those methods that require inspection of the function code as well.

The callers (client functions) handle the called function (a server function) as a single unit. In the function call, the caller specifies the function name and the actual arguments (if any). The caller of the function does not know *how* the function (the server) does its job. The client knows only *what* job the server function does and what the interface specification is. Hence, using function calls streamlines the client code. It is directed toward its own goal by removing detailed steps and abstracting them in the form of the function call.

A function is the smallest unit of modularization; using functions allows the designers to organize a large program into smaller, more-manageable units. Different functions can be assigned to different programmers to speed up development of a large application.

If an algorithm is needed in several places in the program, implementing it as a function allows the designers to call it from different places in the program instead of reproducing all the details in the client code. This makes object code smaller and contributes to code reuse. During maintenance, smaller functions are easier to understand and manage than is a huge monolithic program.

Functions used as modular units for organizing program code can be put into a library; their use by other applications also improves the amount of code reuse.

Good functional design is crucial for code readability, for independence of program parts, and hence for reducing the application complexity. However, function communications add to program complexity. When using functions, the programmer has to coordinate code in three different places in the program.

- function declaration (function prototype) including the function name, its return type, and types of its parameters
- function definition, including the function header and the implementation of the function body
- the function call, including the function name and the names (or values) of actual arguments

These three elements have to coordinate. This probably does not sound like much, because it is only three elements and no more. And indeed most programmers most of the time get it right. The problem is that the cases when the programmers do not get it right, however rare as a percentage of the total, are numerous enough to cause serious problems.

Function Declarations

C++ requires that the compiler see either a function declaration or function definition before it processes a function call. Hence, the source file where a function is called has to declare (or define) this function before it is called. This is why the issue of supplying necessary function prototypes is an important component of C++ programming.

In the function declaration, the types of parameters and the function return value (if any) should be described along with the function name. If the function is called in several files, the function must be declared in each file.

```
returnType functionName(type1 param1, type2 param2, ...);
```

If the function returns no value, the return type is specified as void rather than just omitted. If return type is omitted, it is still not a syntax error. The compiler assumes that you wanted to make it int rather than void. Omitting the return type used to be popular in C programming. This is why it is allowed in C++. However, it is confusing, and the maintenance programmer has to spend extra effort to figure out what is going on. If the return type is int, the code has to say that the return type is int. This is why omitting the return type is frowned on in C++ programming, and some compilers might issue a warning that this style of function definition is obsolete.

```
add(int x, int y);              // int return value: bad style
void PutValues(int val, int cnt);  // no return value: void type
```

A function can return only one value. If the client code needs more than one value from the function, the function can return a structure variable, although this slows down program execution. A function can also modify any number of global variables that are defined outside of any function in the file. As we are going to see, neither of these techniques is a good software engineering practice: They are prone to error. The function can also modify the values of its arguments. As we are going to see, these techniques are complex. Do not feel depressed yet. All this is doable.

Function Definitions

In the function definition, the function algorithm is implemented in C++ code. The function definition starts with a header line that specifies the return value type, the function name (a programmer-defined identifier), and the types and names of parameters in a comma-separated argument list. The difference between the function header and the function prototype is that the prototype ends with a semicolon, and the header does not. Another difference is that the parameter names are optional in prototypes but mandatory in the function headers. Actually, if the parameter is not used in the function body, its name is optional in the header, too, but I hope you will never write such a poorly designed function.

The function body is a block with its own scope. As in any C++ code, the statements in the function body are executed sequentially unless control constructs or function calls are used.

```
void PutValues(int val, int cnt)
{ cout << "Value " << val << " is found ";
  cout << cnt << " times" << endl;
  return; }              // optional; no return value in a void function

int add (int x, int y)
{ count++;               // global variable is modified
  return x+y;  }         // return statement and return value are mandatory
```

For a `void` function, `return` statements are optional. They can be used any place in the code but are not allowed to return a value. The execution of any `return` statement terminates the execution of the function and returns control to the caller. For a non-void function, at least one `return` statement is mandatory; more than one `return` statement can be used. Each `return` statement must return a value of the type specified in the function header (or of the type that can be converted to the `return` type).

Function Calls

Pascal, Ada, and other modern languages distinguish between procedures and functions. Procedures in these languages do not return values but are allowed to have side effects in their arguments and global variables. In the client code, they can be used as separate statements only, not as part of another expression. Functions in these languages return values but can have no side effects. In the client code, they cannot be used as separate statements but must be used as part of an expression (or as an rvalue in the assignment).

```
a = add(b,c) * 2;        // the use of return value in expression
PutValues(a,5);          // function call as a statement
b = PutValues(a,5)*2;    // nonsence: there is no value to return
```

C++ does not distinguish between procedures and functions. C++ functions can both provide return values and have side effects. A returned type can be of any built-in or programmer-defined type, but arrays are not allowed as returned values. If the function is `void`, it works as a procedure and returns no value to the caller, it cannot be used in an expression. Such a function should be called in a separate statement in the caller code.

Unlike Pascal or Ada, C++ allows the client to ignore a return value in a function call and use a function call as a procedure call. This means that a non-void C++ function can be used as a part of an expression and as a separate statement. When the caller uses such a function as a statement, the only purpose of the function call is its side effects on global variables.

```
add(b,c);        // correct syntax even if it makes no sense
```

This is not a good programming practice. If a function returns a value, it should be used in the client code. However, there are many C++ library functions that have non-void return values that are rarely used, e.g., `strcpy()` and `strcat()`, among others.

The function body in braces specifies actions performed when the body is evaluated during the function call. We say that the call operator `()` is applied to the function name with comma-separated arguments of the call.

```
PutValues(17,14);        // the call operator is applied
```

Most of us do not think of a function call in terms of applying a call operator. It is sufficient to think about the list of arguments in parentheses. In advanced C++ programming, however, it is important to remember that in C++ a function call is the use of the call operator. Moreover, we can use this operator in other contexts, giving it a different meaning.

If a definition of the server function appears lexically before the definition of the client function, then the compiler has already seen the definition of the server before compiling the function call. In these cases, the server definition can also serve as its declaration. Most programmers do not rely on the lexical order of functions in source code and use prototypes as a matter of habit.

A function may be defined only once in a program. Function prototypes can be repeated as many times as needed (or more). Function prototypes are often placed in header files in a separate project directory. These files are included in the source files that call these functions. Often, programmers include header files and functions that are not used in the file; this is simpler than studying who calls whom and in what file. This is OK for the compiler, because it ignores extra prototypes. Header files cannot and should not, however, be ignored by maintenance programmers. Indiscriminate use of prototypes makes the understanding of mutual dependencies between different parts of the program more difficult.

C++ allows us to omit parameter names in function prototypes. They are really needed in function definitions only. Many programmers omit the names of parameters because the compiler does not need them.

```
void PutValues(int, int);        // what do parameters do?
```

This is adequate when the types of the parameters are different, the roles of the parameters are well understood by the designer and maintainer (e.g., in a library function that is used frequently), and the prototype is hidden away in the header file. For a programmer-defined function, using parameter names might provide a helpful hint about their roles.

Some programmers declare prototypes in client code not at the start of the file, but immediately inside the client function that makes the call, as a documentation aid. This clearly tells the maintainer that it is this function (as opposed to many other functions in the same file) that uses the server function. Do not be distracted by the simplicity of the examples that I use to illustrate these points. This is a serious software engineering issue.

```
void Client(void)
{ void PutValues(int value, int count);        // list of dependencies
  int val, cnt;
  cout << "Please enter the value and its count: ";
  cin >> val >> cnt;
  PutValues(val, cnt); }
```

If a function has no parameters, its prototype and its definition can use either empty parentheses or the keyword void between parentheses.

```
int foo();  int f(void);    // functions with no parameters
```

In a function call, however, only the empty parentheses are used to indicate the function call operator.

```
foo();  f();                // parentheses are allowed and mandatory
```

Why is the keyword void allowed in the function definition and the function declaration but not in a function call? This is done to make the life of the compiler writer easier. If the keyword void were allowed in the function call, this could mislead the compiler into thinking that this is a prototype of a function in the middle of the client code.

```
f(void);                    // this is not a call, it is a prototype
```

But there is no return type—why would the compiler think this is a prototype? Because it thinks that the programmer just omitted the integer return type: It is not a good programming practice but is still allowed. By the way, to make sure that you know that I keep my word when I make a promise, this is the answer to the question I promised to answer in Chapter 2, "Getting Started Quickly: A Brief Overview of C++."

Argument Promotions and Conversions

Since C++ is a strongly typed language, a C++ function call should use correct types and the number of actual arguments for each of the function formal parameters. Within the function body, the values of actual arguments are used as the values of corresponding formal parameters. If the number or the order of arguments does not match the number or order of formal parameters, it is a syntax error—no questions asked.

```
PutValues(25);              // one argument is missing: error
```

If the number and the order of the arguments is correct, but the types are incompatible with corresponding parameter types, matching between arguments and parameters results in a syntax error. Types are called incompatible if a conversion between their values does not make sense. For example, if one of the types is a programmer-defined type (structure or class) and another is either a simple built-in type, an array, or another programmer-defined type, one value cannot be used instead of another.

For example, let us assume that `a1` is of a programmer-defined type `Account` (a structure), and `a2` is an array (it does not matter what type). Then this function call represents two syntax errors.

```
PutValues(a1,a2);              // incompatible types: two errors
```

The reason why C++ takes such a harsh point of view is that inside the `PutValues()` function code deals with integer parameters. The operations that are legal for integers are not legal for `Account` objects or for arrays. A structure or an array variable cannot do what a number can (being added, multiplied, compared, etc.). Their individual components can, but this is a different story.

Similarly, let us consider a function that draws a square using a parameter of some programmer-defined type `Square`.

```
void draw(Square);
```

It does not matter what composition or properties the type `Square` has. This client code is incorrect.

```
draw(5);                       // incompatible types: syntax error
```

Again, this is understandable. A number cannot do what a structure can (access a component through the dot selector operator). Here, the stand taken by C++ is firm and uncompromising, similar to other modern languages.

However, if there is only a mismatch between a declared and an actual type, not incompatibility as described above, promotions and conversions can be applied. A mismatch means that the types are different, but they have common operations, and hence the values of one type can be used instead of values of another type. These types are viewed as compatible types.

Promotions from "smaller" to "larger" numeric types are performed implicitly for some types before any computations are done. Arguments of `enum` types are promoted to `int`, and types `char`, `unsigned char`, and `short` are promoted to type `int`. Similarly, the `unsigned short` type is promoted to `int` (or to `unsigned int` on a machine where an `int` is not larger than a `short`). Arguments of type `float` are promoted to type `double`. These argument promotions are "safe"—there is no danger of the loss of accuracy or danger of applying an operation that is not defined on a "smaller" type.

If after promotion the argument type does not match the formal parameter type, or the argument is not eligible for promotion (of type `int`, `long`, or `double`), then implicit conversions are used: Any numeric type (including unsigned) can be converted to any other numeric type. This is done even if the conversion results in a potential loss of accuracy (e.g., conversions from double to int). The actual argument *zero* can be converted to a formal parameter of any numeric type or to a pointer type even when a loss of accuracy is possible.

Consider, for example, the function PutValues() again. What happens if you pass arguments of type double rather then int? They are silently converted to int. Some compilers could issue a warning, but this is legal C++.

```
double x = 20, y = 5;       // integers are converted to double
PutValues(x,y);             // double are converted to integers
```

How can you tell the compiler that this mismatch is not an oversight and that you know what you are doing? A common way to say that is to use an explicit cast that converts the value of one type into a value of another type.

```
PutValues((int)x,(int)y);    // explicit cast for compiler, maintainer
```

Another way to do that is to use the function-like syntax for the cast.

```
PutValues(int(x),int(y));    // alternative syntax for explicit cast
```

Notice that the explicit cast passes the designer's intent not only to the compiler but to the maintainer as well. There is no need to figure out what is going on.

The same rules of conversions apply if there is a mismatch between the declared return type and the type of the actual return value. If the actual return type is "smaller" than the declared return type, the actual value is promoted to the declared type. If the actual return type is not "smaller" or the promotion cannot be applied (the actual value is of type int, long, or double), then the actual value is converted to the declared return type.

These argument promotions and conversions are the same as promotions and conversions that C++ uses in expression evaluation. The goal is to make them as legal as possible. Here, C++ takes a softer stand than other modern languages do. Moreover, the use of inheritance, constructors, and overloaded conversion operators (described later) makes C++ even more lenient about argument conversions. This is great if these conversions are exactly what the designer had in mind. This is not so great if the designer made a mistake and the compiler does not stand by, telling the designer about the error. In all the cases, the use of implicit conversions makes the life of the maintenance programmer more difficult.

It is a good idea to match arguments and return values exactly or to use explicit casts to help the maintenance programmer to understand what is going on.

Parameter Passing in C++

There are three parameter-passing modes in C++: by value, by pointer, and by reference.

When a parameter is passed by value, the changes made to the parameter within the function do not affect the value of the actual argument used in the function call. When a parameter is passed by pointer or by reference, changes made to the parameter do affect the actual arguments in the client space. In addition, there is a special mode of passing array parameters.

We will consider different modes of parameter passing, their syntax, and their semantics, and we will try to formulate guidelines for the use of C++ parameter-passing modes that provide the best performance and the best transmission of designer ideas to the maintenance programmer.

Calling by Value

When a function is called, argument values can be specified as variables (or symbolic constants), expressions, or literal values of appropriate types

```
int n = 22, cnt = 20;
PutValues(n,cnt);            // arguments as variables
PutValues(2*n,cnt-11);       // arguments as expressions
PutValues(18,14);            // arguments as literal values
```

During execution, function parameters are treated as local variables whose scope is the function body. The name of a parameter is known to the compiler and refers to a specific memory location between the opening and the closing braces of the function. Outside of the function scope, this name is not known. Even if the name itself can be defined outside of the function for some other purpose, it never refers to the same memory location as the function parameter.

Parameters are defined (allocated and initialized) when the function is invoked. The space for parameters is allocated from the program stack and initialized with the values of actual arguments. The formal parameters are the separate copies of the values of actual arguments. These copies are destroyed when the function terminates (when it executes a `return` statement or reaches the closing brace). Consider, for example, the following primitive function that returns the sum of its arguments.

```
int add (int x, int y)      // x, y are created/initialized
{ return x+y;  }            // x, y are destroyed
```

Since the parameters (the copies of actual arguments) are in the scope of the called function, they can be modified by the function code.

```
int add (int x, int y)
{ x = x+y;       // awkward but legitimate: x is modified
   return x;     // the new value is copied into the client variable
  }              // the modified copy of argument is destroyed
```

The actual arguments are not in the scope of the called function: The values move in one direction only, from the calling function to the called function. If parameters are modified by the called function, the changes are not passed back to the caller's space when the parameters are destroyed. Consider the client code:

```
int a = 2, b = 3, c;   . . . .
c = add(a,b);    // variable 'a' does not change in client space
```

"Call by value" is a "native" mode for parameter passing in C++. In this parameter mode, the values of actual arguments (variables, expressions, literal values) are copied into temporary variables representing function parameters. After that, the arguments in the client space are not related to these copies: Copies are manipulated by the function and destroyed upon exit. Changes that are made to the copies inside the function do not affect client argument values.

This is understandable. When parameters are passed by value, the actual arguments can be any rvalues, for example, expressions or literals. These rvalues cannot and should not be modified in the function code. In this call, for example, it should be guaranteed that the first argument does not change in the function call.

```
c = add(2*5,b);     // passing an rvalue 2*5 to a function
```

For side effects, C++ provides passing parameters by pointer and by reference. These modes of parameter passing are more complex than passing parameters by value. Using these modes incorrectly makes program maintenance more difficult. Using them correctly contributes both to program performance and to program readability.

Calling by Pointer

A pointer variable contains a memory address of another variable; this is why they are called pointers; they point to some other program entity. You can manipulate program variables using pointers with addresses of these variables pretty much the same way as you manipulate variables using their own names. In Chapter 6, "Memory Management: The Stack and the Heap," you learned how to use pointers for dynamic memory management. In this section, you will study the concepts related to the use of pointers for parameter passing.

Pointers are a powerful and flexible programming tool; it is a dangerous tool too. This is why C++ tries to limit the power of pointers: A pointer cannot point to variables of arbitrary types. When the pointer is defined, you make a commitment: You decide whether this pointer is going to point to variables of type int, double, Account, or Square. This is not different from the commitment that has to be made when you define non-pointer variables.

In all other regards, pointers are ordinary variables. They have a type, they are given programmer-defined names, they can be initialized, and operators can be applied to them. Pointer variables are eventually destroyed according to C++ scope rules. In the definition of a pointer variable, the fact that it is a pointer is expressed by adding the asterisk * to the left of the pointer name. When the pointer is created, it does not contain a valid value. As any other variable, the pointer has to be initialized or assigned a value.

```
int v1, v2;          // two integer variables; they contain junk yet
int *p1, *p2, *p3;   // pointers to integers; they point nowhere yet
```

Operations available for pointers are assignment, comparisons, and dereference operations. Pointers can be assigned the following values:

- the value NULL
- a value contained in another pointer variable of the same type (It can be incremented or decremented by an integer.)
- an address of a variable of the appropriate type (The C++ address operator & is applied to the left of the name of the variable whose address is assigned to the pointer.)

```
v1 = 123;  v2 = 456;   // variables are assigned integer values
p1 = &v1;              // pointer is assigned the address of variable v1
p2 = p1;               // pointer is assigned a value from another pointer
p3 = NULL;             // pointer is assigned the value NULL
```

The symbolic constant NULL is defined in the header file stdlib.h and in many other library files, including iostream.h. It the same thing as 0. Some C++ programmers prefer to use NULL because it clearly indicates that the code is dealing with pointers. Other programmers use 0, and this is OK too. Usually, C programmers use NULL and C++ programmers use 0.

Both p1 and p2 now point to variable v1. The syntax for pointer comparison is the same as for any other numeric comparison.

```
if (p1 == p2) cout << "The same address, not value\n";
if (p3 == 0) cout << "This is a null pointer\n";
if (p1 != 0) cout << "We can start working\n";
```

The last operator, the dereferencing operator, is denoted as the asterisk *. When applied to a pointer, it denotes the value that the pointer points to. This value is of the type that was used for pointer definition. For example, p1 points to integer v1 that contains 123. Hence, *p1 means 123. It is an integer. The same asterisk was used for the pointer definition: int *p1; this is no accident: It says that p1 is a pointer to an integer, but it also says that *p1 is an integer. This is why the scope of this asterisk is only one name. When you define integers (or variables of other built-in types), the type name covers any number of variables; for example, I defined variables v1 and v2 above using only one keyword int. This does not work for pointers. This, for example, defines one pointer and two integers:

```
int* pt1, pt2, pt3;      // pt1 is a pointer, pt2 and pt3 - integers
```

Let us go back to this business of dereferencing. The dereferenced pointer is the synonym of the variable it is pointing to.

```
*p1 = 42;   // v1 is not 123 anymore; it is 42
*p2 = 180;  // v1 is not 42 anymore; it is 180
*p3 = 42;   // do not dereference NULL pointers; this causes crash
```

In this example, p1 points to v1; hence, *p1 and v1 are synonyms for all intents and purposes. They are not synonyms forever, but until the pointer gets another assignment.

```
p1 = &v2;  // p1 now points to v2, not to v1; now *p1 means 456
if (*p1 == 456) *p1 = 42;   // v2 is not 456 anymore; it is 42
```

If the dereferenced pointer and the variable it points to are synonyms, why should we worry about pointers that are not related to dynamic memory management? The answer is that we will use pointer parameters to change the values of actual arguments in the client space. If a pointer variable is passed to a function, the function can change the value pointed to (the actual argument), using the syntax of dereferencing.

Consider, for example, the following modification of the add() function. Similar to the previous version, it computes the sum of its two arguments; instead of returning the result, it assigns it to the dereferenced pointer, that is, to the value pointed to by the pointer parameter.

```
void add (int x, int y, int *z)    // z is a pointer to an integer
{ *z = x + y; }                    // location pointed to by pointer z is modified
```

How does the client code call this function add()? Well, the first two arguments should be the integer values we want to add up. And the third argument? Remember that business with strong typing? It cannot be a double, a short, or even an int. It must be a pointer to an integer. How do you get a value that could be assigned to a pointer? It must be either NULL (useless in this case), or another pointer (probably in some other examples but not here), an address of an integer—that's it, this is what we need! You pass as the third argument the address of the variable you want to contain the sum. For the address operator, you use the & sign. This is how a call by a pointer should be done in client code.

```
int a = 2, b = 3, c;
add(a, b, &c);              // and c does change after the call!
```

Remember I told you that the call by value is the native mode of parameter passing in C++? This is true even when parameters are passed by pointer. It is the pointer that is passed by value, not the value in the client space. It is a local copy of the pointer that is made, initialized, used, and destroyed in the server space, as with any passing by value.

Since it is the address of the actual argument that is passed to the function, you have to dereference the pointer within the body of the function when the function accesses the value of the actual argument. If a new value is assigned to the dereferenced variable within the function, it persists in the client space.

If this logic seems somewhat convoluted, don't worry. You will get used to it. Just remember this simple checklist: Passing parameters by pointer, you have to specify:

- the address-of operator for the actual argument in the call
- the pointer type for the parameter in the function header
- the dereference operator for the parameter in the function body

Do not resist this logic—follow it, and you will be safe. Any deviation from this checklist, and something will go wrong—it is not worth the trouble.

Let us consider another popular example: swapping parameter values. If the first parameter is greater than the second parameter, you swap them so that they become ordered in ascending sequence. To swap parameters a1 and a2, you save the first parameter value in the temporary variable temp so that you can use location a1 to store a different value. Then you copy the value of a2 into a1. After that, you move the value stored away in temporary variable temp into a2, and bingo! What used to be in a2 is now in a1, and what used to be in a1 is now in a2. Listing 7.1 shows the implementation of the function swap() and its client function main(). For debugging purposes I also included display statements for the values before the swap, after the swap, and after the call. The results of the executions are shown on Figure 7–1.

Listing 7.1   Passing parameters for side effects (bad version).

```
#include <iostream>
using namespace std;

void swap (int a1, int a2)          // wrong parameter mode
{ int temp;
  if (a1 > a2)
  { cout << "Before swap: a1=" << a1 << " a2=" << a2 << endl;
    temp = a1;   a1 = a2;   a2 = temp;
    cout << "After swap:  a1=" << a1 << " a2=" << a2 << endl; } }

int main ()
{
  int x = 84, y = 42;               // values are out of order
  swap(x,y);                        // bad parameter mode; it should not work
  cout << "After call:  x=" << x << " y=" << y << endl;
  return 0;
  }
```

Figure 7-1   Output for program in Listing 7.1.

```
Before swap: a1=84 a2=42
After swap:  a1=42 a2=84
After call:  x=84 y=42
```

As you might expect, the parameter values within the function are swapped correctly. But the change does not stick in the client space: The values of the actual arguments are not swapped. Passing parameters by pointer should help. This is how the next version of the function swap() looks.

```
void swap (int *a1, int *a2)               // correct parameter mode
{ int temp;
   if (a1 > a2)
   { cout << "Before swap: a1=" << a1 << " a2=" << a2 << endl;
      temp = a1;   a1 = a2;   a2 = temp;
      cout << "After swap:  a1=" << a1 << " a2=" << a2 << endl; } }
```

This looks nice, but it does not fly either. The statement temp = a1; is incorrect. Variable temp is of type int. Variable a1 is not (variable a1 is a pointer to int). You can assign one integer to another. You can assign one integer pointer to another integer pointer. You cannot assign values of different types. Do not let your experience with numeric types mislead you. Different numeric types are compatible. They can be converted to one another. Pointer values are incompatible types. They cannot be converted to values of a non-pointer type.

When you get that compiler message, do not despair, but figure out what should be on the right-hand side of that assignment. Variable a1 is not an integer. What related variable is an integer? Look at the parameter list. What does it say is integer? It says int *a1—hence, it is *a1 that is an integer. This assignment should say temp = *a1; this is actually not very difficult; however, making changes in the body of the function is quite tedious and prone to error. You have to make sure that you do dereference a1 and a2 but do not use dereferencing on temp.

```
void swap (int *a1, int *a2)                   // correct parameter mode
{ int temp;
   if (a1 > a2) {
      cout << "Before swap: *a1=" << *a1 << " *a2=" << *a2 << endl;
      temp = *a1; *a1 = *a2;   *a2 = temp;       // correct dereferencing
      cout <<"After swap:  *a1=" <<*a1 <<" *a2=" <<*a2 <<endl; } }
```

For the version of the `swap()` function in Listing 7.1, the compiler shot at me complaining about the call `swap(x,y);` indeed, variable x is of type integer, but the function `swap()` expects a pointer to integer, that is, an address of an integer variable. Does this make sense? Listing 7.2 shows the corrected version of the program. The output is shown on Figure 7–2.

Listing 7.2   Passing parameters by pointer (parameter modes are correct).

```
#include <iostream>
using namespace std;

void swap (int *a1, int *a2)                // correct parameter mode
{ int temp;
  if (a1 > a2) {
    cout << "Before swap: *a1=" << *a1 << " *a2=" << *a2 << endl;
    temp = *a1; *a1 = *a2;  *a2 = temp;    // correct dereferencing
    cout << "After swap:  *a1=" <<*a1 <<" *a2=" <<*a2 << endl; } }

int main ()
{
  int x = 82, y = 42;                       // values are out of order
  swap(&x,&y);                              // correct parameter mode; it should work
  cout << "After call:  x=" << x << " y=" << y << endl;
  return 0;
  }
```

Figure 7–2 Output for program in Listing 7.2.

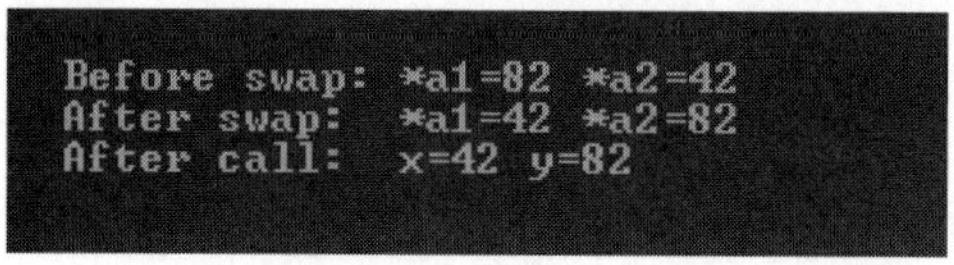

```
Before swap: *a1=82 *a2=42
After swap:  *a1=42 *a2=82
After call:  x=42 y=82
```

A good mnemonic rule for passing parameters is… Wait a minute. Did I do what I had to do to test this program? It contains a conditional statement, but I ran it only once. This is a simple little program, and if I waste my time on thorough testing of everything that is as clear as day, I will never get anything done. Still, with parameter passing you are never sure (you know, step to the left, step to the right). So I changed the `main()` function this way, just to make sure that when the argument values are ordered, the function `swap()` does not swap them.

```
int main ()
//{ int x = 82, y = 42;        // values are out of order
{ int x = 42, y = 84;          // values are ordered
  swap(&x,&y);                  // no swapping for ordered arguments
  cout << "After call:  x=" << x << " y=" << y << endl;
  return 0; }
```

The result of this run is shown in Figure 7–3. Now, I have two questions to ask. Question number one: Do you see the problem with the output? Make sure you do. It is all too often that we look at output and do not see the error because we did not write the answer in advance. Here, the code seems to swap the arguments unconditionally even though there is the `if` statement in the function `swap()`. This probably means that this statement does not compare the values of parameters but compares something else instead. Question number two: Do you see the problem with code on Listing 7.2? This is more difficult because there is no methodology to follow to find this error.

There are 10 asterisk operators in function `swap()`, but I missed two more. When I compare `a1` and `a2`, the compiler does not object because these two variables are of the same type. If I want to compare two addresses, I have the right to do so, and if the first address is larger than the second, the program swaps the arguments whether or not their values are ordered. This is what it means that the compiler does not try to second-guess the programmer. Sometimes I prefer that shot without warning. At least it tells me that I have a problem. The corrected version of the program is shown in Listing 7.3.

Figure 7–3 Output for program in Listing 7.2 with modified `main()`.

```
Before swap:  *a1=42  *a2=84
After swap:   *a1=84  *a2=42
After call:   x=84 y=42
```

Listing 7.3   Passing parameters by pointer (corrected dereferencing).

```
#include <iostream>
using namespace std;

void swap (int *a1, int *a2)                // correct parameter mode
{ int temp;
  if (*a1 > *a2) {                          // Oh, boy
    cout << "Before swap: *a1=" << *a1 << " *a2=" << *a2 << endl;
    temp = *a1; *a1 = *a2;  *a2 = temp;  // correct dereferencing
    cout << "After swap:   *a1=" <<*a1 <<" *a2=" <<*a2 << endl; } }

int main ()
//{ int x = 82, y = 42;                     // values are out of order
{ int x = 42, y = 84;                       // values are ordered
  swap(&x,&y);                              // correct parameter mode; it should work
  cout << "After call:   x=" << x << " y=" << y << endl;
  return 0;
  }
```

By the way, this is not a contrived example. This is a scaled-down version of what happened to me in real life. I made the situation easier to review by removing extraneous details.

So, where were we? Oh yes. A good mnemonic rule for passing parameters by pointer is: When you choose the name for a parameter, you must start this name with the asterisk and remember to use this asterisk as part of the name on all occasions. The trouble with my first version of swap() (and alas, with the second version too) was that I thought that the parameter names were a1 and a2. This was not productive. Had I thought from the very beginning that their names were *a1 and *a2 throughout, writing this function as in Listing 7.3 would have been a breeze, including the use of *a1 > *a2 in the conditional statement.

Still, this is much more complex than passing parameters by value. You have to:

- use the pointer notation in the function header (and the prototype)
- dereference parameters inside the body of the function
- use the address-of operator outside of the function, in the client code. As your reward, changes made to parameters are reflected in actual arguments in the client code

Everybody makes mistakes in passing parameters by pointer. The only difference between experienced and inexperienced programmers is that experienced programmers make these errors less often and correct them faster. As for the anguish and self-criticism… Well, I told you that you should never criticize yourself. After all, it was not you who invented these rules.

Some programmers try to simplify passing parameters by pointer by eliminating the use of the address-of operator in the function call. Instead, they use a pointer that they have set up to point to the actual argument. For example, they would write the call to swap() in the following way.

```
int main ()
{ int x = 82, y = 42;             // values are out of order
   int *p1 = &x, *p2 = &y;         // set pointers to point to values
   swap(p1,p2);                    // no address-of operator
   cout << "After call:  x=" << x << " y=" << y << endl;
   return 0; }
```

This works. The values in arguments pointed to by pointers p1 and p2 are swapped correctly. However, you should introduce additional program elements, pointers, and set them using the same address-of operator. Additional manipulations mean additional possibility for error and additional effort in understanding what the code does. I am not sure it is simpler than biting the bullet and using the address-of operators in the function call directly. But if you like this technique, use it. It works.

Since the values of actual arguments change in the call by pointer, only lvalues that can be manipulated through their addresses are allowed as actual arguments. You cannot use rvalues—expressions, literal values or constants. For example, this function call to swap() is incorrect.

```
swap(&5, &(x+y));    // no good: no address-of operator for rvalues
```

Another issue related to passing parameters by pointer is type conversions. For all intents and purposes, they are not allowed. What I described earlier is relevant to conversions of values, not pointers. Consider the following code that tries to use the `swap()` function to order `double` values.

```
int main ()
{ double x = 82, y = 42;    // double values are out of order
  swap(&x,&y);              // no conversion from double* to int*
  cout << "After call:  x=" << x << " y=" << y << endl;
  return 0; }
```

You can talk the compiler into accepting these arguments by using an explicit cast to `int*` like in this function call.

```
swap((int*)&x, (int*)&y);    // it swaps integers, not double values
```

Here, the function call compiles, but it compares and swaps (if it does) only that part of a `double` value that has the size of the integer. The compiler accepted this call because I told it, "I know what I am doing." But, what I was doing was incorrect. Make sure that when your program compiles, you check whether what the compiler accepted really makes sense.

Since C++ had an explicit goal to support the C legacy code, passing parameters by pointers is a valid C++ technique. However, C++ added yet another mode of passing parameters, passing by reference, that eliminates some of the drawbacks of passing by pointer. We will try to use passing by pointer as little as possible. Unfortunately, you cannot just forget about it. In addition to legacy C code, there are C++ library functions that pass parameters by pointer. Dynamic memory management also requires dealing with pointers. Make sure you are not intimidated by the complexity of pointers.

Parameter Passing in C++: Calling by Reference

In addition to pointers, C++ provides reference types that are not available for programmers who use C. Like a pointer variable, a reference refers to another location: It contains the memory address of another variable. Similar to pointers, when you define a reference, you specify the type of the value this reference is going to point to. Similar to pointers, you can define a reference to any type, built-in or programmer-defined. Similar to pointers, reference variables are just ordinary variables that can be defined, allocated memory, initialized, manipulated, and destroyed.

Unlike a pointer, a reference variable can point to only one location. This location should be of the same type as the reference itself. The reference variable cannot abandon the location it is pointing to and start pointing to another location. This is why, unlike pointers, references must be initialized at definition. If you do not do that, you lose your chance to point the reference variable anywhere, and it will remain useless. To indicate that a variable is a reference rather than a pointer, you use the ampersand & to the left of the programmer-defined name rather than the asterisk *. When a reference is initialized, no operator has to be applied to the variable that the reference is going to point to. This change in notation is very clever. It is one of the reasons why references were introduced in C++.

```
int v1=123,v2=456;        // integer variables; optional initialization
int *p1=&v1, *p2=&v2;     // pointers to int; initialization is optional
int &r1=v1, &r2=v2;       // references: always initialized, no operator
```

For pointers, it is *p1 and v1 that are synonyms: We need a dereference operator *. For references, it is r1 and v1 that are synonyms; no operator is needed. There is no dereference operator for references in C++, and this is the second reason why references were introduced in C++.

```
if (p1 != p2) cout << "Different addresses\n";        // sure, &v1 != &v2
if (*p1 != *p2) cout << "Different values\n";         // sure, 123 != 456
if (r1 != r2) cout << "Different values\n";           // sure, 123 != 456
```

With pointers, it is all the same whether you access the value using the dereferenced pointer (e.g., *p1) or the name of the variable (e.g., v1). With references, it is all the same, whether you access the value using the name of the reference (e.g., r1) without any operator or the name of the variable (e.g., v1): They are synonyms.

```
*p1 = 42;        // v1 (and r1) is not 123 anymore; it is 42
r1 = 180;        // v1 (and *p1) is not 42 anymore; it is 180
v1 = 42;         // r1 (and *p1) is again 42
```

This might sound somewhat confusing: you "dereference" pointers, not "depointer" them. On the other hand, you do not dereference references. This is not done to confuse you—there is no malice in this design. It happened for purely a historical reason. In pre-ANSI C community, pointers were often called references because they "referred" to variables. Pass by pointer was often called pass by reference, and the term "dereferencing" was always used instead of "depointering" (or "depointing"?). Actually, the latter terms did not exist.

This terminology survived the ANSI standardization effort. When C++ was designed, a new term was needed to convey the idea of pointing, referring, directing, aiming, accessing, training, signing, indicating, or denoting.

The term "reference" won in the selection process, and now we are derefer-encing pointers but not references. This is OK.

Unlike a pointer, a reference cannot be changed to refer to another vari-able (memory location) after it was initialized. There is no way to do that: They are together until death do them part, that is, until they go out of scope. The assignment to reference changes the data, not the address of the data, because the reference provides an alias for the variable.

```
p1 = &v2;               // p1 abandons v1, points to v2 instead
p1 = p2;                // another way to do the same thing
r1 = v2;                // r1 still points to v1 that now contains 456
r1 = r2;                // another way to move data from v2 to v1
if (r1==v2) r1 = 42;    // comparison holds, and v1 becomes 42
```

All right, this is all you have to know about references, their terminology, and their notation to use them for parameter passing. This is how our little function add() looks when you pass the third parameter by reference rather than by pointer.

```
void add (int x, int y, int &z)    // z is a reference to an integer
{ z = x + y; }                     // location pointed to by z is modified
```

Here, variable z is a reference to an integer. When the function is called and this parameter is allocated memory, it is initialized with the address of the actual argument. (We will see in a moment how this is done.) The assignment to z modifies the location this reference is pointing to, that is, the actual argu-ment. We see that the function body looks exactly as if the parameter z were passed by value; unlike with passing parameters by pointer, no dereferencing is needed. The function header has the reference operator & as the indicator of the pass by reference. In the function call, you have to initialize the refer-ence with the address of the location it is going to refer to. How do we do that? According to the syntax of reference initialization, you use the name of the variable with no operators. Hence, the function call in the client code should look this way.

```
int a = 2, b = 3, c;
add(a, b, c);                   // and c does change after the call!
```

Hence, in passing parameters by reference we specify:

- argument names without address operators in the call
- reference type for parameters in the function header (and the prototype)
- names of parameters without dereferencing in the function body

You see that a call by reference is quite similar to a call by value. Parameters are not dereferenced in the server function body, and no address-of operator is used in the function call in the client code, but side effects are available because of the reference operator in the server function header.

In a sense, this language design is similar to Pascal where the keyword var plays the same role as the reference operator & in C++: It indicates that the changes made to the formal parameter in the function body are visible in the value of the actual argument in the client code. The keyword is probably easier to learn than the operator.

Now let us implement the swapping function using pass by reference. Listing 7.4 shows the source code. The changes are straightforward; the code is much simpler than using pass by pointer. There is less opportunity for error. The results of the run are shown in Figure 7–4.

Listing 7.4   Passing parameters by reference (robust method).

```
#include <iostream>
using namespace std;

void swap (int &a1, int &a2)                    // correct parameter mode
{ int temp;
   if (a1 > a2) {                               // no dereference operator
      cout << "Before swap: a1=" << a1 << " a2=" << a2 << endl;
      temp = a1; a1 = a2;   a2 = temp;          // no dereferencing
      cout << "After swap:  a1=" << a1 << " a2=" << a2 << endl; } }

int main ()
{ int x = 82, y = 42;                           // values are out of order
//{ int x = 42, y = 84;                         // values are ordered
   swap(x,y);                                   // this is beautiful!
   cout << "After call:  x=" << x << " y=" << y << endl;
   return 0;
}
```

I summarized the rules for parameter passing in Table 7.1. Here the term var (with operators where applicable) denotes the name of the variable used as an argument in the function call, as a parameter in the function header (and prototype), and in the function body.

Figure 7–4 Output for program in Listing 7.4.

```
Before swap: a1=82 a2=42
After swap:  a1=42 a2=82
After call:  x=42 y=82
```

The table shows that pass by value is the simplest—no operators are applied to the argument or to the parameter in the function body. Pass by pointer is the most complex: Operators have to be used in all three code elements—in the argument, the parameter, and the function body. The pass by reference is similar to pass by value: The only difference is the reference operator in the function header.

Pass by reference lacks complexity of pass by pointer but supports side effects to actual arguments in the client space. If the parameter is not changed within the body of the function, it should be passed by value. This would indicate to the maintenance programmer that the designer wanted to keep the actual argument the same.

Table 7.1 Summary of Parameter Passing for Simple Variables			
Code Element	*By Value*	*By Pointer*	*By Reference*
Function call	var	&var	var
Function header	var	*var	&var
Function body	var	*var	var

When parameters are passed by reference and modified inside the function, the same limitations apply that apply to pass by pointer. You can use lvalues only as actual arguments, and they should be of exactly the same type because C++ supports no implicit conversions between references of different types. Explicit conversions are possible but they are useless—a reference variable can access only the value of the type used in its definition. The use of expressions, literals, and constants is not allowed.

Tip

When the function does not change the values of its parameters of C++ built-in types, pass parameters by value. When the function has to change the values of its parameters of built-in types, pass parameters by reference. Avoid passing parameters by pointer.

Structures

Structures (and class objects) could be passed by value, by pointer, or by reference. If a structure variable is used by the function as input for its operation and is not modified by the function, it can be passed by value. If a structure is used by the function as output (delivering values to the client function), that is, when the structure fields are modified by the function, it should be passed by pointer or by reference. Otherwise, the changes are not effective in the client space.

The rules formulated in the previous sections for individual variables stand for structure variables too. Additional rules for structures as arguments are related to the access to structure components in the function body.

To keep examples simple, let us consider a simplified type `Account`.

```
struct Account {
    long num;                 // just two fields for simplicity sake
    double bal; } ;
```

Its access function `printAccounts()` accepts two `Account` variables as parameters and prints the values of account number and balance. These `Account` objects are input variables for `printAccounts()`: Their values have to be set by the client code before the call because the `printAccounts()` function needs the `Account` values to be set by the client to do its job properly.

```
void printAccounts(Account a1, Account a2)        //server code
{ cout << "First account:  No. " << a1.num
       << "  balance " << a1.bal << endl;
  cout << "Second account: No. " << a2.num
       << "  balance " << a2.bal << endl; }
```

The client code creates `Account` objects, initializes their fields, and calls the server function `printAccounts()` to print the state of accounts.

```
Account x, y;                          // client code
x.num = 800123456;   x.bal = 1200;
y.num = 800123123;   y.bal = 1500;
printAccounts(x,y);
```

Since this discussion concentrates on parameter passing, I ignore such issues as whether it is a good idea to have access functions to such a trivial structure or it is better to access structure fields from the client code directly. I need these simple function examples to illustrate the issues related to communication between functions.

The basic rules of parameter passing stand here, that is, the programmer has to coordinate code in three different places: the function call, the function header, and the function body. According to the rules for parameter passing by value, you use the name of the variable without any operators in the function call, in the function header, and in the function body. When the function code needs to access the structure fields, it uses the same dot selector operator as the client code uses. This is the simplest mode of parameter passing. (Compare notation for `a1.bal` in `printAccount()` and for `x.bal` in the client code.)

Next consider another access function, `swapAccounts()`, that compares the account numbers of its two parameters and swaps the parameters if the account numbers are out of order. Since the values of actual arguments have to change, passing parameters by value would not be appropriate. This function passes its parameters by pointer.

```
void swapAccounts (Account *a1, Account *a2)      // pass by pointer
{ Account temp;
   if (a1->num > a2->num)                          // operator
   { temp = *a1;   *a1 = *a2;   *a2 = temp; } }
```

When the client code calls this function, it passes to the function the addresses of the actual arguments.

```
swapAccounts(&x,&y);
```

You see that the basic rules of pass by pointer hold here. In the function call the client code uses the address-of operator `&`. In the function header the server code uses the asterisk `*`. In the function body the server code uses the dereferencing operator `*`. When the server code has to access the fields of the structure, the two-character arrow selector operator `->` is used instead of the dot selector operator.

This is a general rule and is not limited to parameter passing. The dot selector operator selects a field when its left operand is the name of a structure variable. The arrow selector operator is used when its left operand is a pointer to a structure variable. You should not confuse the two. Often, programmers are oblivious to this distinction. When a pointer is used, it does not matter whether it points to a named stack variable or to an unnamed heap variable. A pointer needs an arrow selector operator. If you use one operator in the context where another operator is required, an error message (sometimes obscure) is generated.

Some programmers try to use naming conventions to give themselves visual cues when a variable is a pointer rather than a value. These programmers start the names of pointer parameters with `p` or `ptr`. This is how `swapAccounts()` looks when this naming convention is used.

```
void swapAccounts (Account *ptrA1, Account *ptrA2)
{ Account temp;
   if (ptrA1->num > ptrA2->num)
   { temp = *ptrA1;   *ptrA1 = *ptrA2;   *ptrA2 = temp; } }
```

I feel more comfortable with the previous version because I think that the names of parameters (of type `Account`) are `*a1` and `*a2` (for me, the name of the parameter starts with an asterisk), and the `ptr` component in the name distracts me. But this is a common technique, and you should use it if the parameter name reminds you that you are dealing with the pointer.

For some programmers, the need to decide whether to use one or another selector operator represents an additional burden. You could use the dot selector operator with a pointer if you dereference the pointer first. Here is the `swapAccounts()` function that uses this technique.

```
void swapAccounts (Account *a1, Account *a2)        // pass by pointer
{ Account temp;
   if ((*a1).num > (*a2).num)                        // no arrow selector
   { temp = *a1;   *a1 = *a2;   *a2 = temp; } }
```

Parentheses here are important because the selector operator is of higher priority than the dereference operator. The expression without parentheses, for example, `*a1.num`, is understood by the compiler not as `(*a1).bal` but as `*(a1.bal)`, which makes no sense. First, the expression `a1.bal` is not legal because pointer `a1` cannot work with the dot selector operator; it needs the arrow operator. Second, even if `a1.bal` were legal, the type of field `bal` is `double`, and you cannot dereference a `double` value; it should be a pointer.

Using dereference and the dot selector is a legitimate technique, but most programmers grow to feel comfortable switching from one selector operator to another and do not strive for operator uniformity. If you avoid using the arrow operator all the time, your boss might suspect that you do not know C++ as well as you say you do.

In `swapAccounts()`, the structures are passed by pointer and not by value because the actual arguments have to change as the result of a swap. However, some C++ programmers, especially with good experience in C, dislike passing structures by value so much that they pass structures by pointer even when they are input variables and are not changed by the function. This is how `printAccounts()` would look if it were written by such a programmer: The parameters are passed by pointer and not by value, and the structure fields are accessed using the arrow selector operator.

```
void printAccounts(Account *a1, Account *a2)        // misleading
{ cout << "First account:  No. " << a1->num
       << "  balance " << a1->bal << endl;
  cout << "Second account: No. " << a2->num
       << "  balance " << a2->bal << endl; }
```

The reason that you might want to pass structure parameters by pointer rather than by value is program performance. Of course, the `Account` structure in my examples is small, but we often deal with structure objects that take hundreds or thousands of bytes each. Copying these structures while passing them by value takes both execution time and stack memory, often significant for program performance. The drawback of this technique is greater complexity of the pass by pointer and, some programmers feel, the danger of unauthorized change of actual arguments or accidental damage to their data. When parameters are passed by value, even if the server function tries to change them, these changes do not affect actual arguments. When parameters are passed by pointer, changes made within the server function propagate to the client space.

I do not think that data integrity is a serious issue here. After all, if the server function tries to change its parameters incorrectly, this has to be discovered and corrected, not swept under the rug by passing parameters by value.

The real tradeoff here is the transmission of the designer's intent to the maintainer. The designer does not want to change the arguments of `printAccounts()`. However, the designer hides this knowledge from the maintainer because the function header clearly says that the change is possible—the parameters are passed by pointer. The same distorted message is transmitted to the maintainer by the function call that passes arguments by pointer because it uses the address-of operator in the function call.

```
printAccounts(&x,&y);        // clearly, arguments can change!
```

In this case, it does not take long to inspect four lines of code to figure out what is taking place. But there might be many lines of code to inspect, and these lines of code could do something quite obscure. When parameters are passed by value, there is no need to inspect the body of the function at all. This is an important issue.

On the other hand, performance is often important. This is where passing parameters by reference allows you to have your cake and eat it too: You can avoid complexity of pass by pointer, you can avoid performance penalty of pass by value, and you can convey the intent of the designer to the maintenance programmer.

How come? Listing 7.5 shows the example program that implements both server functions, `printAccounts()` and `swapAccounts()`, passing parameters by reference. The output of the program is shown in Figure 7–5.

Listing 7.5	Passing structures as reference parameters.

```
#include <iostream>
using namespace std;

struct Account {
   long num;
   double bal; } ;

void printAccounts(const Account &a1, const Account &a2)   // header
{ cout << "First account:  No. " << a1.num                 // body
       << "  balance " << a1.bal << endl;
   cout << "Second account: No. " << a2.num
       << "  balance " << a2.bal << endl; }

void swapAccounts (Account &a1, Account &a2)               // header
{ Account temp;                                           // body
   if (a1.num > a2.num)
   { temp = a1;   a1 = a2;   a2 = temp; } }

int main()
{
   Account x, y;
   x.num = 800123456;   x.bal = 1200;
   y.num = 800123123;   y.bal = 1500;
   cout << "Before swap\n";
   printAccounts(x,y);                                    // call
   swapAccounts(x,y);                                     // call
   cout << "After swap\n";
   printAccounts(x,y);
   return 0;
   }
```

Function `swapAccounts()` is straightforward. The name of the structure is used in the function call, the reference notation is used in the function header, and the name of the structure is used in the function body. The parameter fields in the function body are accessed using the dot selector opera-

Figure 7-5   Output for program in Listing 7.5.

```
Before swap
First account:  No. 800123456  balance 1200
Second account: No. 800123123  balance 1500
After swap
First account:  No. 800123123  balance 1500
Second account: No. 800123456  balance 1200
```

tor, which makes the issue of choosing the correct selector operator moot. You see that passing structure parameters by reference simplifies notation relative to passing parameters by pointers.

Function `printAccounts()` is also straightforward. Its function call uses the name of the structure variable as in pass by value, the function body uses the names of the parameters, and access to their fields is called exactly as in pass by value. The two differences are in the function header: It uses the reference notation with the parameter names, and it uses the `const` keyword before the parameter types. The first difference eliminates copying of actual arguments: Their addresses rather than the copies of the fields are passed to the function. The second difference prevents the changes to the values of parameters within the function and clearly tells the maintenance programmer that the parameters are not modified. That's a promise. There is no need to inspect the function body to discover or to confirm that.

The use of the `const` modifier is similar to its use for defining variables. This modifier can be used with values, pointers, and references. When it is used with values, it says that the value can be changed neither through direct assignment nor through pointer or reference.

```
const int val = 10;       // initialization is mandatory
val = 20;                 // syntax error: assignment is not allowed
int *p = &val;            // illegal so as to prevent indirect change *p = 20;
int &r = val;             // illegal so as to prevent indirect change r = 20;
```

When the `const` modifier is used with pointers and references, it has two meanings, depending on its position. If it is used before the type name, it means that the value pointed to by the pointer or reference cannot be modified by dereferencing the pointer or through the reference.

```
const int val = 10;
const int *constp = &val;    // OK, but *constp=20 is a syntax error
const int &constr = val;     // OK, but constr=20 is a syntax error
```

Notice that the direct modification of variable `val`, for example, `val = 20;` is illegal because this variable is defined as constant. However, indirect modification is illegal here as well, not because the variable `val` is constant but because the pointer (and the reference) variable is defined as a pointer to a `const`. For a pointer (or reference) to a constant, indirect modification is illegal, even when it points to a nonconstant value. Make sure you see the difference.

```
int value = 10;              // this variable can be modified
const int *constp = &value;  // *constp=20 is still a syntax error
const int &constr = value;   // constr=20 is still a syntax error
```

When the `const` modifier is between the type name and the name of the pointer, it means that the pointer is a constant. It can be dereferenced, and the value pointed to by the pointer can be changed, but the pointer cannot be redirected to point to another variable. Although its initialization is not mandatory, it is necessary. If the constant pointer is not initialized at definition, it is quite useless—it cannot be assigned later.

```
int value = 10;              // it is not const in this example
int* const pconst = &value;  // they are married for life
*pconst = 20;                // this is OK, value is not const
pconst = NULL;               // syntax error: pointer is constant
```

You cannot declare a reference constant because all references are constant in C++ by default. They are initialized at definition and cannot point to another location. The notation that we use in parameter passing says that not only the reference cannot be turned to another location, but also the location the reference points to cannot change its value. This reference is initialized by the value of the actual argument at the time of the function call.

What happens if the designer becomes tired of analyzing all these subtleties and passes structures by reference without using the `const` modifier? What happens? Nothing much. Here is function `printAccounts()` simplified.

```
void printAccounts(Account &a1, Account &a2)     // can they change?
{ cout << "First account:  No. " << a1.num
       << "  balance " << a1.bal << endl;
  cout << "Second account: No. " << a2.num
       << "  balance " << a2.bal << endl; }
```

Is this function correct? Yes, it is. And even if it does not promise to change its parameters, it does not change them. Still, this is a clear contribution to software crisis. The designer fails to tell the maintainer what the designer knows at the time of design—that he or she has no intention of changing the values of parameters in the body of the function.

Some programmers say that using the `const` modifier is useful because it protects the arguments from unauthorized changes by the function. This is not the issue. Errors do not happen every time you call a function. But every time you inspect the code of a function, you want to know what it does to its parameters, and using the `const` modifier is a sure way to tell that the parameter is used as input. Similarly, the absence of the `const` modifier should tell you that the function changes the parameter, not that the programmer became tired of analyzing all these subtleties.

Please make it your firm rule: If a structure parameter is changed by the function you write, pass it by reference and do not use `const`; if a structure parameter is not changed, pass it by reference and do use `const`.

Similarly, the absence of the `const` modifier should clearly tell the maintainer that the parameter changes within the function, not that the designer was sloppy and absent-minded. Yes, I know, this sounds somewhat convoluted, but in C++ we do not have a better way to distinguish between input and output reference parameters.

Tip

To avoid impact on performance, avoid passing structures by value. To avoid unnecessary complexity, avoid passing structures by pointer. Always pass structures by reference. When the parameter is not modified by the function, indicate that it is by using `const`. *When the parameter is modified by the function, indicate it is by not using* `const`.

Passing structure by references has advantages over pass by value and over pass by pointer. It is both fast (no copying) and simple (no address-of operators in the call and no dereferencing in the function body). Used correctly, it conveys the intent of the designer to the maintainer. Pass by reference is very popular in C++. Please use it correctly.

Arrays

Arrays are always passed in the special array mode, similar to passing by pointer. Although the notation is similar to the pass by pointer, it is not exactly the same. If the server function makes changes to the components of the array parameter, these changes to components are visible in the client space in the argument array.

This is the only mode of passing arrays as parameters available in C++. We have to use this mode both for input parameters and for output parameters. Similar to other cases of parameter passing, we have to coordinate code written for the function call, the function header, and the function body.

Here is an example of a function that copies the contents of its second array argument into its first array argument; since the function does not know the size of the arrays, the number of components to copy is specified by the third parameter.

```
void Copy(double dest[], double src[], int size)
  { for (int i=0;  i < size;  i++)            // classic array loop
    dest[i] = src[i]; }
```

It is, of course, the responsibility of the caller to make sure that the arrays have enough components for this operation. C++ gives the programmer no protection against corruption of memory. This is an example of the client code.

```
double x[100], y[100];   int n=0;
do {
   cout << "Enter data value (0 to terminate): ";
   cin >> y[n++];               // fill array y[], assign n
   . . . } while (true);
Copy(x,y,n);                    // copy n components of y[] into x[]
```

As this example shows, while passing arrays as parameters we specify:

- the array name without brackets in the function call
- empty brackets after the array name in the function header
- array components (or name without brackets) in the body

Unlike with passing parameters by pointer, there is no address-of operator in the function call in the client code, and there is no pointer notation in the function header. The programmers who like to stress the similarity between arrays and pointers would code this function this way.

```
void Copy(double *dest, double *src, int size)
   { for (int i=0;  i < size;  i++)          // classic array loop
     dest[i] = src[i]; }
```

You can also dereference the address of array components similar (but not identical) to passing parameters by pointer.

```
void Copy(double *dest, double *src, int size)
   { for (int i=0;  i < size;  i++)          // classic array loop
      *(dest+i) = *(src+i); }               // or *dest++ = *src++;
```

This notation is closer to pass by pointer—the pointer notation is used in the function header. Still, it is not the parameter that is dereferenced in the function body; it is the sum of the parameter and the index. The programmers who like to stress the similarity between arrays and pointers would use the address of the first component of the array in the function call.

```
double x[100], y[100];   int n;   // fill array y[], assign n
Copy(&x[0],&y[0],n);             // copy n components of y[] into x[]
```

Still, it is an address of the first component of the array, not the address of the actual argument.

Whatever syntax we use, neither the function call nor the function header can indicate the role of array parameters as input or output parameters. In this example, array src[] is an input parameter; the values of its components are used by the function to do its job and do not change as the result of the call. Array dest[] is an output parameter: Whatever values its components had before the call are not used within the function, and the content of these components changes as the result of the call. However, notation for both arrays is the same in all three places (the function call, the function header, and the function body). This is not right. When the code designer does not intend to change the array within the function, it is a good idea to use the const modifier to indicate that to the maintenance programmer.

```
void Copy(double dest[], const double src[], int size)
   { for (int i=0;  i < size;  i++)
     dest[i] = src[i]; }       // src[i] = dest[i]; is a syntax error
```

Similar to passing structure parameters, it is of paramount importance to use the const modifiers when passing array parameters and do that consistently. They prevent the function from modifying input variables. More important, they indicate the code intent for the maintenance programmer.

If the parameter is labeled const, it can accept the actual argument either labeled as const or even not labeled as const. This is considered safe: A non-

`const` argument can be changed, but the function does not change it, and that is all right. It is not OK to pass a `const` variable as an actual argument for a parameter that does not have the `const` modifier.

```
const double c[] = { 1.1, 1.2, 1.3, 1.3 } ;
Copy(x,c,4); Copy(y,a,4);    // ok: c[] and src[] are const arrays
Copy(c,x,4);                 // syntax error: c[] is a const array, dest[] is not
```

Sometimes, the use of `const` modifiers makes the life of the designer more difficult. Do not give up. Use them. As I told you earlier, modern languages make writing code more difficult to make reading code easier. Just make sure that the action and its declared intent coincide and that you are consistent in passing parameters through to server functions.

Here is an example of difficulty. Some time ago I wrote this simple function that computes the sum of a given number of array components.

```
double sum (double a[], int n)
{ double total = 0.0;             // initialize the tally
   for (int i = 0;  i < n;  i++)  // another classic loop
     total += a[i];               // accumulate total
   return total; }
```

Later, I had to compute the average of valid array elements. For that, I had to compute the total and divide it by the number of elements. It would not be difficult to do that from scratch, but since I already had the `sum()` function, I decided to use it.

```
double avg (const double a[], int n)
   { return sum(a,n)/n; }         // syntax error
```

This is an example of passing the parameter through to another server function `sum()`. Previous examples demonstrated that for the elements of the parameter arrays we use the name of the array and the index in subscript brackets. This example shows how to use the name of the array in the body of the function without brackets.

But the main point of this example is that the compiler did not like it. This is the logic of the compiler: array `a[]` is declared `const` in the header of the function `avg()`; hence, it will not be modified within `avg()`. However, the body of `avg()` passes `a[]` as an argument to function `sum()`; but this latter function makes no commitment to keep its parameter constant and hence it might change it, violating the promise made by `avg()`.

The compiler will not check whether function `sum()` in fact changes the array. Remember that story? If there is no copper wire, it is evidence of the use of cellular phones. Following this archeological logic, the compiler would flag the function call to sum() as a syntax error.

This sounds rather bureaucratic. It would be better if the compiler checked what function sum() actually does to its parameter. But do not forget that function sum() might be in a different file, and the compiler sees only its prototype. And even if this function is in the same file as function avg(), the compiler does not bother to analyze the flow of values in the program.

To correct the situation, I have to put my money where my mouth is and define all the parameters that do not change as const. The code intent must be reflected in the server interface.

```
double sum (const double a[], int n)      // array is input
   { double total = 0.0;
     for (int i=0;  i<n;  i++)
       total += a[i];
     return total; }
```

The function prototype for a function with array parameters follows the rules for other function prototypes: It is a function header terminated by the semicolon.

```
double sum (const double a[], int n);     // function prototype
```

The names of parameters are optional in prototypes. How does it look for arrays? It looks funny, but the compiler understands this notation. Make sure it does not confuse you.

```
double sum (const double[], int);     // parameter names are optional
```

If you use the pointer notation for arrays, the prototype will look this way.

```
double sum (const double*, int);      // no change to value pointed to
```

Tip

There is only one way to pass arrays as parameters in C++. To distinguish between input arrays and output arrays, use the const *modifier for input arrays (that are not modified by the function).*

Passing arrays as parameters is efficient in C++. No copying of array date is involved, and that saves both execution time and stack space. Similar to passing structures as parameters, make sure that the absence of the const modifier is clear evidence that the components of the array are changed within the function. This will be your contribution to the fight against the software crisis.

More on Type Conversions

As I mentioned in the section on promotions and conversions, C++ takes a firm stand on parameter passing: If a scalar value is expected as a parameter, no structure or array can be used as the actual argument.

This rule is extended to structures: If a structure (or class) instance of a specific type is expected as a parameter, no scalar value, array, or structure of a different type can be used as the actual argument. It is a syntax error; no excuses are accepted. Even if that structure of a different type has exactly the same composition as the type that is expected by the function, it does not help. Even if the fields in both types have the same order and the same types and the same names—the compiler expects the argument of the type whose name is the same as the type name of the formal parameter, and does not do any additional analysis.

All this is true of passing structures by value. It is somewhat different for passing structures by pointer and by reference and for passing arrays.

In the section on passing structures as parameters we discussed the type `Account` and the function `swapAccounts()`, which passed its `Account` parameters by pointer.

```
struct Account {
    long num;                    // just two fields for simplicity sake
    double bal; } ;

void swapAccounts (Account *a1, Account *a2)    //account is needed
{ Account temp;
    if ((*a1).num > (*a2).num)
    { temp = *a1;   *a1 = *a2;   *a2 = temp; } }
```

Now, let us consider another type, `Transaction`, and try to pass a variable of this type to `swapAccounts()`. The compiler rejects this attempt as a syntax error.

```
struct Transaction {
    long num;                    // same name and the same type as in Account
    double amt; } ;             // different name but the same type

Transaction tran1, tran2;    ...  // client code
swapAccounts(&tran1,&tran2);      // error: wrong argument type
```

But wait a minute—these are really the same structures, and I would like to use `swapAccounts()` for swapping transactions rather than to write yet another function `swapTransactions()`. I know what I am doing, and I would like the compiler to accept this code rather than to flag it as an error. C++ gives us the means to tell the compiler that we know what we are doing: casting, or explicit type conversions. All I have to do is to cast the `Transaction` pointer to the `Account` pointer, and the compiler will accept this code.

```
swapAccounts((Account*)&tran1,(Account*)&tran2);    // no syntax error
```

This is pretty ugly, but it works—it supports my right to tell the compiler that I know what I am doing. Other programmers would say that it is the right to shoot myself in the foot. Indeed, in the process of maintenance, either type `Account` or type `Transaction` (or both) might change, and then God help us. It is probably safer to write this little function `swapTransactions()` after all.

The same is true for passing structures by reference. In Listing 7.5, we discussed the function `printAccounts()`, which expects `Account` arguments passed by reference. If I pass `Transaction` variables as actual arguments, the compiler in its rightful indignation will flag this code as a syntax error.

```
Transaction tran1, tran2;  ...  // transaction objects
printAccounts(tran1,tran2);      // syntax error: wrong argument type
```

If I insist on my right to do that, I can tell the compiler that I know what I am doing by casting `Transaction` references to `Account` references.

```
printAccounts((Account&)tran1,(Account&)tran2);    // no syntax error
```

Again, this is not good software engineering, but this is what C++ lets you do. Notice that casts clearly tell the maintenance programmer what I had in mind at the time of designing this code (that I reused an existing function for a new purpose instead of writing a new function).

A similar situation exists with arrays because the array name without modifiers is equivalent to the pointer to the first array element.

If the function has an array of a specific type as its formal parameter, and you use a scalar variable, a structure variable, or an array of a different type as an actual argument, it is a syntax error. C++ lives up to its reputation as a strongly typed language.

Consider, for example, function `copyAccounts()`, which copies one array of type `Account` into another array.

```
void copyAccounts(Account dest[], const Account src[], int size)
  { for (int i=0;  i < size;  i++)
    dest[i] = src[i]; }                    // same code as for Copy()
```

If I try to use this function to copy an array of `Transaction` objects or an array of integers, the compiler will pour its rightful wrath on me.

```
Transaction tran1[5], tran2[5];   ...      // transaction arrays
int data1[20], data2[20];    ...           // arrays of integers
copyAccounts(tran1,tran2,5);    // syntax error: wrong argument type
copyAccounts(data1,data2,20);   // syntax error: wrong argument type
```

Using casting, I can talk the compiler into accepting these function calls.

```
copyAccounts((Account*)tran1,(Account*)tran2,5);      // no error
copyAccounts((Account*)data1, (Account*)data2,20);    // no error?
```

Since the variables of type `Transaction` are of the same size as objects of type `Account`, the first function call has a chance to do something reasonable. The second function call does not. It will copy 20 chunks of memory of the `Account` size rather than `int`, corrupting computer memory.

The same applies to the case of passing arrays of built-in scalar types. The function `Copy()` in the previous section expects `double` arrays as its arguments. If I pass an array of `int` instead, the compiler will generate an error message. If I cast the actual argument to `(double*)`, the compiler will generate object code that will copy memory in chunks of `double`, not `int`.

Fortunately, you cannot get into situations like that by mistake—it takes an explicit cast to force the compiler to accept this code.

Returning a Value from a Function

In all previous examples, the return types I used were either `void` or a built-in scalar type such as `int`. The values are returned from C++ functions, well, by value. This means that a copy of the return value in the function space is made and assigned to the variable in the caller space.

C++ allows you to return a structure from a function if the return type of that function is defined as the type of the structure. In the examples below I use a modified version of the function `swapAccounts()`. As in the previous version, it compares the account numbers of its two `Account` arguments and swaps the arguments if the numbers are out of order. (That is, the number of the first argument is greater than the number of the second argument.) Unlike in the previous version, the function returns the `Account` variable that has a greater value in the account number (parameter `a2`).

```
Account swapAccounts (Account &a1, Account &a2)   // new return type
{ Account temp = a1;
  if (a1.num > a2.num)
  { a1 = a2;   a2 = temp; }
  return a2.num; }                      // bad return type: no conversion from long
```

The rules of strong typing apply: If the return type is defined as a structure (in this case, `Account`), the same type should be used in two other places, for the returned expression in the function and for the variable in the caller space. Neither the expression, nor the caller variable can be of a built-in type, of another structure type, or an array: No conversion between these types is possible.

```
Account ac1,ac2,ac3;   long acc_num; ...   // value in caller space
acc_num = swapAccounts(ac1,ac2);           // error: no conversion
```

Similar to parameter passing, returning from functions requires that you coordinate the code that we write in three places: a) return type, b) return expression, and c) variable in the caller space. Using the same type in all three places is legitimate.

```
Account swapAccounts (Account &a1, Account &a2)
{ Account temp = a1;                  // initialize temp to a1
  if (a1.num > a2.num)                // check if numbers are out of order
  { a1 = a2;   a2 = temp; }           // swap arguments if out of order
  return a2; }                        // correct type of return expression

ac3 = swapAccounts(ac1,ac2);          // correct use of return value
```

This is legitimate but could be slow for large structures (when the function is called often). This is why most functions are designed as either `void` or as returning an integer or boolean value that indicates for the caller success or failure of the function call.

C++ does not allow a function to return an array. However, C++ allows a function to return a pointer or a reference. This can be used to eliminate the problem of copying the return value. In the following example, the function `swapAccounts()` compares the `num` fields of its two `Account` arguments, swaps them if they are out of order, and returns the pointer to the `Account` variable that has a greater value of the account number.

```
Account* swapAccounts (Account &a1, Account &a2)   // return pointer
{ Account temp = a1;
  if (a1.num > a2.num)
  { a1 = a2;   a2 = temp; }
  return &a2; }                       // return the address of actual argument
```

Again, the types should be compatible in all three places: a) the declared function return type, b) the type of the expression returned by the function, and c) the type of the variable in the caller space.

```
Account ac1, ac2, ac3, *ac4;         . . .
ac4 = swapAccounts(ac1,ac2);   // ac4 is a pointer, not an Account
ac4->num = 0;                  // it affects ac1 or ac2 that are not mentioned here
*ac4 = ac3;                    // copying ac3 into structure with larger number
```

As you see, returning a pointer allows us to use rather obscure coding patterns in the client code, such as ac4->num = 0; this might refer either to ac1 or to ac2, and the maintainer has to study the implementation of the server function, for example, swapAccounts(), to find out. The server function could be quite obscure, and any need to study other segments of code adds to the complexity of the maintenance task and increases the likelihood of errors. Returning pointers allows you to use even more fancy syntax in the client space: I could set the larger number to 0 using the following code.

```
swapAccounts(ac1,ac2)->num = 0;    // is not this nice?
```

If I want to copy variable ac3 into the structure with greater balance, I could use the following code.

```
*swapAccounts(ac1,ac2) = ac3;    // actually, this is not very nice
```

This code is correct, but it does not convey the intent of the designer well. The maintainer has to spend extra time trying to grasp the meaning of the code. If this coding pattern is undesirable, the designer of swapAccounts() can express that by defining the return value as a pointer to a const object.

```
const Account* swapAccounts (Account &a1, Account &a2)   // new idea
{ Account temp = a1;
  if (a1.num > a2.num)
  { a1 = a2;   a2 = temp; }
  return &a2; }              // return the address of actual argument
```

This means that the return address cannot be used to modify the variable it is pointing to. With swapAccounts() defined this way, this code becomes a syntax error.

```
*swapAccounts(ac1,ac2)=ac3;        // error: no changes to a const object
swapAccounts(ac1,ac2)->num = 0;    // error: no change to a const
```

The use of such a return value becomes quite limited. It cannot be assigned to an arbitrary pointer of the correct type because the pointer could be used to change the value it is pointing to.

```
Account *ac5 = swapAccounts(ac1,ac2);    // syntax error
ac5->num = 0;                            // hence this code will never compile
```

This return value can be used only to access the members of the object or assigned to a pointer to a `const` object.

```
const Account *ac5 = swapAccounts(ac1,ac2); // this is OK now
ac5->num = 0;                            // this code still does not compile
```

One has to be careful to return a pointer to something that continues to exist in the caller space after the server function terminates. This is why it is not a good idea to return a pointer to a variable that is defined only in the server function scope. In the previous example, I was careful to return a pointer to a function parameter that actually was a pointer to an actual argument that continued to exist in the client space after the call. Hence, the address returned by the function remained valid. But this is not always the case. Consider, for example, the following implementation of `swapAccounts()`, which returns a pointer to the structure that winds up holding the account number from parameter a1.

```
Account* swapAccounts (Account &a1, Account &a2)    // return pointer
{ Account temp = a1;               // temp holds data from a1
  if (a1.num > a2.num)
  { a1=a2; a2=temp; }              // a1 might change, but temp holds its data
  return &temp; }                 // whose address is this, anyway?
```

When the execution reaches the closing brace of this function scope, variable temp is destroyed. Hence, pointer ac4 in our client code winds up not with the address of the structure that holds the data from variable ac1, but with the value that points to the memory location that no longer belongs to the program. This is called a "dangling pointer": a pointer that points to an object that has already disappeared.

Not every run-time environment is sophisticated enough to catch this memory access violation, but some are. Moreover, the location used for temp might not be used for other purposes for some time, and the client code using its address will produce correct results.

Time and again, we bump into situations where acceptance of the code by the compiler and correct run-time results of executing all branches of the program cannot be used as sufficient evidence that the program is correct.

Returning pointers to local variables is not safe. It is safe to return pointers to the heap memory or to variables in the client space. Here is an example of returning a pointer to variables in the client space that solves the problem of a dangling pointer.

```
Account* swapAccounts (Account &a1, Account &a2)   // return pointer
{ Account temp = a1;                   // temp holds data from a1
  if (a1.num > a2.num)
  { a1=a2; a2=temp;
    return &a2; }                      // data from a1 is now in a2
  return &a1; }                        // data from a1 remains in a1
```

When returning pointers to variables in the client space, one should know whether these variables are constants or not. Consider an example of a function that compares the `bal` fields of two `Account` variables and returns a pointer to the object with the larger balance value.

```
Account* largerBalance (const Account &a1, const Account &a2)      //no!
{ return (a1.bal>a2.bal) ? &a1:&a2; }       // pointer to actual argument
```

This is a good example of dealing with constant objects. The function does not change the state of its parameters; it only accesses them as the input values in its computations. This is why the `const` modifier is used in the function header. However, this function does not compile. Why? Because it returns a pointer that is not defined as a pointer to a constant object. This function promises not to change the state of its actual arguments, but the pointer it returns points to one of the actual arguments and hence can modify its fields. By flagging this code as a syntax error, the compiler prevents me from writing this type of client code, which compiles but modifies the object that is defined as constant.

```
const Account acc1 = {325,1000.0}, acc2 = {370,100.0};   // immutable
Account *p = largerBalance(acc1,acc2);   // valid syntax but dangerous
p->bal = 0;              // valid syntax but modifies a constant object
```

That seems to be overkill. Even though the function `largerBalance()` defines its parameters as `const`, it might be passed arguments that are not constants.

```
Account acc1 = {325,1000.0}, acc2 = {370,100.0};   // mutable objects
Account *p = largerBalance(acc1,acc2);     // valid syntax but dangerous
p->bal = 0;            // OK for non-const but not OK for const objects
```

However, the compiler is not intelligent enough to distinguish between constant and nonconstant objects passed to this function. As sometimes happens in other areas of human affairs, the solution is to forbid all related activities. Here, C++ requires that the `const` modifier be used in the return type. (Notice that I do not suggest removing the `const` modifiers from the function header.)

```
const Account* largerBalance (const Account &a1, const Account &a2)
{ return (a1.bal>a2.bal) ? &a1 : &a2; }        // this code compiles
```

This code compiles. How does it prevent the client code from modifying a
constant object? Very simple. Now this code does not compile.

```
const Account acc1 = {325,1000.0}, acc2 = {370,100.0};    // immutable
Account *p = largerBalance(acc1,acc2);    // now this is a syntax error
p->bal = 0;        // no syntax error, but compiler wants to prevent this
```

The compiler wants to prevent the assignment p->bal = 0: Since it is a syntactically correct operation, the compiler flags the assignment to pointer p
because it did not pledge to refrain from modifying the object it points to. The
compiler pushes me to be consistent, to define pointer p as a pointer to a constant object.

```
const Account acc1 = {325,1000.0}, acc2 = {370,100.0};  // immutable
const Account *p = largerBalance(acc1,acc2);  // OK: no syntax error
p->bal = 0;                          // now this is a syntax error!
```

It is still overkill in the case where the Account objects are not defined as
immutable. Even in this case, pointer p cannot be used to modify them. But
this is the price you pay for the safety of the constant objects (and for the
unwillingness of compiler designers to do data flow analysis in the program).

The safest use of return addresses is for dynamic memory management.
The server function allocates heap memory and returns the pointer to that
memory to the client code to use. (Some other function should delete that
heap memory later.) In this example, the function allocateAccounts() allocates the dynamic array of Account objects; the size of the array is passed as
an argument.

```
Account* allocateAccounts(int size)    // pointer to non-const
   { if (size <= 0) return 0;          // test argument validity
     Account *p = new Account[size];
     if (p == 0)                       // simple but too crude
       cout << "Out of memory in allocateAccounts()\n";
     return p; }                       // NULL if anything went wrong
```

If anything goes wrong, this function returns the NULL value. It is the
responsibility of the client code to test whether the memory allocation was
successful.

Returning a reference is another alternative to returning a structure value
that avoids copying the values at run time. Conceptually, it is similar to returning a pointer to a structure value. Practically, it is quite different because in
C++ references are constant by default. Let us consider a version of

swapAccounts(), which returns a reference to the actual argument with the greatest account number.

```
Account& swapAccounts (Account &a1, Account &a2)
{ Account temp = a1;
  if (a1.num > a2.num)
  { a1 = a2;  a2 = temp; }
  return a2; }                        // wrong type if return &a2;
```

Notice that it is almost the same as the version that returns the structure by value. The only difference is the reference operator & in the return type. It would be incorrect to return &a2 rather than a2; a2 is of type Account and can be used to initialize an Account reference; &a2 is an Account pointer and cannot be used to initialize an Account reference. These two types are incompatible in C++.

The client code, however, could easily run into problems.

```
Account ac1,ac2,a3, &ac4; ...     // this time around, it is reference
ac4 = swapAccounts(ac1,ac2);      // this is a pipe dream, not real code
```

This code is incorrect. It assigns the return value of swapAccounts() to the reference variable ac4, but this is too late. References have to be initialized at definition, and the segment of code above fails to do so. The only way to assign this return value is to use it for initialization.

```
Account ac1,ac2,a3; ...
Account &ac4 = swapAccounts(ac1,ac2);   // this time it is OK
ac4.num = 0;                      // it affects ac1 or ac2 that are not mentioned
ac4 = a3;                         // copying a3 into structure with larger number
```

Since ac4 is a synonym for either ac1 or ac2, the results of this code are somewhat obscure. Since the return value of swapAccounts() is a reference, the fancy syntax I showed for returning a pointer is available—and with gusto.

```
largerBalance(ac1,ac2).num = 0; // is not this nice?
largerBalance(ac1,ac2) = a3;    // actually, this is not nice at all
```

All languages, including plain C, disallow this kind of syntax: A returned value of the function cannot be used as an lvalue. C++ allows it. It is probably better to render the algorithm in terms that do not require these types of computations.

In the preceding example, I was careful to define ac4 as a reference, not as a structure variable. If I use a structure variable to accept the value that is returned from a function by reference, copying takes place exactly as it takes place when the value is returned from a function by value.

```
ac3 = largerBalance(ac1,ac2);   // ac3 is an Account, not a reference
```

Since ac3 is an ordinary structure object, all advantages of returning the value by reference go down the tubes.

This discussion was quite complex, with many ideas flying around in complex relationships. Reading and understanding the code that returns structure values, pointers, and references is not trivial at all. Is the convenience or performance worth the trouble? Are there other, simpler ways to achieve the same result?

It is probably a good idea to return from C++ functions only logical flags that indicate the success or failure of the function call. Sometimes, especially when dynamic memory management is involved, returning a pointer makes sense. Each time you return a pointer or a reference, make sure that you test whether a) performance benefits are indeed there and b) the integrity of the program is not violated.

Inline Functions

Another useful technique associated with program modularization with C++ functions is the use of inline functions. As you saw earlier, argument copying and context switching during the function call might affect the size of the stack memory that the program needs and its performance. These are important issues. When a function is small and is called often from functions with a large number of local variables, it is a pity to waste time and stack memory for saving the caller environment for the sake of executing a few lines of code.

Consider, for example, the function that computes tax by using a constant coefficient.

```
double tax(double gross)
{ return gross * 0.05; }
```

When the client code calls this function, the "context" of the client function (its parameters and local variables including local arrays) is saved on the stack. When the function terminates, the context is restored.

```
double sales, state;    ...
state = tax(sales);                 // function call
```

It would be nice to avoid the overhead of the function call for such a small function. C solves this problem by providing macros for literal code substitution and for simulating a function call.

```
#define  tax(x)   x * 0.05
```

Hence, client code `state = tax(sales);` is expanded to `state = sales*0.05;`— the overhead of the function call is avoided.

C++ supports exactly the same macro capabilities as C. But macros are expanded by the preprocessor, not translated by the compiler. A macro is not a function. It cannot have local variables, it provides no parameter type checking, and it is invisible to a debugger.

It is awkward to span macros over several code lines. When the expanded code contains syntax errors, the compiler provides the line number for the source code where the macro is called, not where the macro is defined. If the macro contains several lines, it is very hard to figure out what causes the error message.

Macros do not know about priority of C++ operations. They just do literal text substitution without regard to the real intent of the code. Consider, for example, this client code.

```
state = tax(sales+20.0);        // expression as the actual argument
```

For the programmer, this code means

```
state = (sales + 20.0) * 0.05;   // desired interpretation
```

Instead, the preprocessor will evaluate it using literal substitution of the macro code as

```
state = sales + 20.0 * 0.05;     // preprocessor interpretation
```

There are, of course, means to deal with this problem (e.g., using parentheses in the macro definition), but this example shows that macros have pitfalls that are better to avoid. C++ allows the programmer to declare a function as an inline expanded function. It is a macro-like facility without the drawbacks of the `#define` preprocessor statement.

If a function has the `inline` modifier, any call to this function is replaced with the statements of the function definition: There is no function call overhead and no use of stack space.

```
inline double tax(double gross)
{ return gross * 0.05; }
```

At the same time, an `inline` function is a function. It can span multiple lines without any difficulty, define nested blocks, and have local variables. As a C++ function, an `inline` function permits parameter type checking and debugging operations.

This facility provides the advantages of modularization without an overhead of context switching (at the beginning and the end of a function call).

The function body is inserted into the client code at every call. There are as many copies of the `inline` function in the compiled object code as there are calls to the function.

Inline functions improve performance, but this improvement might be small if the function call overhead for functions declared as `inline` is not a major component of execution time. Inline functions increase the size of the executable program, and this might cause additional swapping and actually decrease the speed of execution.

The `inline` modifier is not a nonconditional command to the compiler; it is only a suggestion. The compiler can ignore this suggestion if the function is too long or too complex in the opinion of the compiler designer.

Some compilers do not accept any control constructs in inline functions. Others accept one or two `if` statements but ignore functions that contain loops. Use this facility for simple functions only.

For many functions, making them `inline` does not improve program performance. Make sure that you use this modifier for those functions whose function calls do affect program performance. Profile your programs to identify bottlenecks, if any.

In Chapter 2, I mentioned two ways of defining functions that are members of a class (structure). One is to implement these functions within the boundaries of class specification. Another is to specify in the class specification function prototypes only and to implement the functions themselves elsewhere. Member functions that are defined in the class specification are inline by default, implicitly; no `inline` modifier is necessary:

```
struct Counter {
private:
    int cnt;
  public:
    void InitCnt(int Value)
    { cnt = Value; }                // inline by default
    void UpCnt()
    { cnt++; }
    void DnCnt()
    { cnt-; }
    int  GetCnt()
    { return cnt; } } ;
```

It is common to specify in the class specification function prototypes only, not their implementation.

```
struct Counter {
private:
    int cnt;
  public:
    void InitCnt(int);      // prototypes only
    void UpCnt();           // no indication how it is implemented
    void DnCnt();
    int GetCnt(); } ;
```

If a member function is implemented outside the class braces, it is not inline by default, but it can be defined as inline using the `inline` keyword.

```
void Counter::InitCnt(int Value)
   { cnt = Value; }
inline void Counter::UpCnt()
   { cnt++; }
inline void Counter::DnCnt()
   { cnt-; }
inline int Counter::GetCnt()
   { return cnt; }
```

We will discuss classes in more detail in the following chapters.

Parameters with Default Values

This is a new language facility (not available in C) whose goal is a further improvement in code readability and modifiability. When declaring a function, you can specify default values for one or more parameters in the parameter list.

Here is a declaration for a function `sum()` that computes the sum of given number of components of an array of `double` values. This declaration uses the initialization syntax for the second formal parameter to specify the default value 25.

```
double sum (const double a[], int n=25);        // a prototype
```

This initialization syntax directs the compiler to use the default value specified in the prototype when no actual value is specified in the call in the client code.

```
double total;  double x[100];  int n;  ...      // whatever
total = sum(x);                // add up 25 components of array x[]
```

The client code can, of course, override the default value by providing an explicit actual argument value.

```
total = sum(x,n);              // add up n components of array
```

At first glance, this does not look like much. After all, if I want to add up 25 components, why can't I be explicit about that? Indeed, using default parameter values entails some subtle details that increase the complexity of the code. In some cases it can simplify client code when a function with a large number of parameters is called mostly for the same values of arguments and only seldomly for other argument values. For example, the istream.h function getline() has the following prototype.

```
istream& getline(char buf[], int count, char delimiter = '\n' );
```

Most of the time it is called with two parameters only: the character array to read data in and the maximum number of characters to save (including the zero terminator) if the newline delimiter is not found in the input stream. This function also allows the programmer to use arbitrary delimiters, such as, a dollar sign, a pound sign, or whatever is appropriate. The use of the default value in this case relieves the programmer from specifying the standard '\n' delimiter each time the function is called with the newline as input delimiter.

Notice that the default values for parameters with default values should be specified in the prototype, not in the function definition. The function definition cannot contain the default value.

```
double sum(const double a[],int n)   // no default value is not used
  { double total = 0.0;
    for (int i=0;  i<n;  i++)
      total += a[i];
    return total; }
```

This means that the function designer might not even know that the client code uses default values. Different functions implemented in different files could declare prototypes with different default values for the same parameter without coordinating their use.

Only one default value for a given parameter can be used in the same file. If the function is defined in the same file where it is used, the default value can be specified in the function definition itself if the prototype of this function is not used in the same file. If both the prototype and the function definition are placed in the same file where the function is used, only one of them can contain the default value. If two prototypes of the same function are placed in the same file, only one of them can specify the default value. Even if both prototypes specify the same default value, it is a syntax error. The compiler does not compare the default values but accuses you of redefining the default value instead.

Since parameter names are optional in function prototypes, it is perfectly all right to "initialize" the type name to the default value instead of the parameter name.

```
double sum (const double a[], int=25);    // assign to int?
```

Do we really assign 25 to the type `int`? Of course not! This is not an assignment. It is just a notation whose purpose is to notify the compiler (and the maintainer) about the existence of the default value.

This is a typical C++ language design decision. The language expands C significantly. It is big, and it needs many new keywords and operators. But the number of operator symbols is limited, and even C already uses some two-symbol operators. C++ adds some more two-symbol operators, but the number of reasonable symbol combinations is not very large. C++ also adds some keywords, but the need to learn many more keywords would create the impression that the language is large. Since C++ is a superset of C, it tries to pose as a small language that is easy to learn and use. This is why C++ adds new keywords very sparingly (good examples are `new`, `delete`, `class`, `public`, `private`, and `protected`). And this is why, when the need arises, C++ allows the reuse of operators and keywords for other purposes. We already saw the address-of operator `&` that was reused as a reference operator. In our `sum()` function prototype, C++ reuses the assignment operator for a new purpose: specifying a default parameter value.

Actually, this design strategy is not that bad. It decreases the number of symbols and keywords you should learn and master. On the other hand, for each reused operator, you need to learn its different uses, and that might result in confusion. The reuse of the operator `&` is one such example. It does create confusion, especially for the inexperienced.

C++ allows default values for right-most parameters only; it does not allow default values in the middle of the parameter list.

```
int foo(int a=0,int b=2,double d1,double d2=1.2);     // no
```

Either the left-most default values (for both `int` parameters) should be removed, or the first `double` parameter should receive a default value.

This is not a severe limitation. After all, the default value can always be overridden explicitly.

The reuse of the assignment operator as the default value operator could create problems if it is confused with the ordinary assignment operator. Consider, for example, a function that creates a new node (of type `Node`) dynamically and initializes its information field (of type Item) and the link to the next node in the linked structure (of type Node*).

```
Node* createNode(Item item, Node* next)
{ Node *p = new Node;                   // allocate heap memory
  p->item = item;  p->next = next;      // initialize node fields
  return p; }                           // pointer for client use
```

In many applications, the new node is appended to the end of the linked list, and its next field is set to NULL to indicate the last node in the list. Hence, the client code would call createNode() with the value of 0 (or NULL) as the second actual argument.

```
tail->next=createNode(item,0);      // append node to list end
tail = tail->next;                  // point to new last node
```

Making it the client's responsibility to specify the zero value every time the function createNode() is used as a server is probably not right. This responsibility should be pushed down to the server so that the client code can look this way.

```
tail->next=createNode(item);        // append node to list end
tail = tail->next;                  // point to new last node
```

Using the default value for the second parameter is one of the possible solutions to this problem.

```
Node* createNode(Item item, Node* next=0);       // prototype
```

However, omitting parameter names in the prototype unexpectedly creates a new problem.

```
Node* createNode(Item, Node*=0);    // what does this mean?
```

This is a syntax error: The compiler jumps on you because it thinks that you are using the operator *= here. You are not, but you get chastised anyway. The only way to placate the compiler is to add a space between the asterisk and the equal sign.

```
Node* createNode(Item, Node* =0);  // this is better
```

Remember, I told you that C++, similar to C, is space blind? Yes, C is totally space blind, and C++ lives up to its promise by being space blind—with some exceptions. These exceptions are caused by the use of the same operator for different purposes.

Default parameter values are useful in applications where the same function is often called with the same values of variables describing the context of its use. If specific values of parameters are used only in special circumstances, the use of default parameter values is justified. This is typical, for example, in Windows programming.

Indiscriminate use of default parameter values will make the client code harder to understand and should be avoided.

In some cases, default parameter values might facilitate program evolution by adding new code instead of changing existing code.

Let us consider a simple function, `registerEvent()`, used in a real-time control system.

```
inline void registerEvent()
{ count++;   span = 20; }      // increment event count, set time span
```

Actually, the function did much more than that, but I cleaned it up to eliminate irrelevant detail, keeping only the count of events and starting its time span using global variables. Let us say, it is a large and complex system, and you wrote about 400 pages of code that contain calls to this function.

```
registerEvent();               // server call in client code
```

At the time of system evolution and maintenance, the unavoidable happened. The system should deal with other kind of events, and for these events you have to set up the time span individually. The 400 pages of code do not require changes, because the main event is processed exactly as before, but we have to write about 10 pages of code dealing both with the main event and with new events.

One way to deal with this problem is to write another function that would do the job: `regEvent()`.

```
inline void regEvent(int duration)    // another server function
{ count++;   span = duration; }       // increment event count
```

This is a viable solution, but a mixture of function calls to `registerEvent()` and `regEvent()` might be somewhat confusing. Also, you need an extra function name, and that is always an issue during maintenance. Finally, it would be nice to have the same function name for similar actions. If you want to draw a shape or set the drawing context, the name of the function for all shapes should be `draw()` and `setContext()`, not `draw1()` or `setContext1()` or something like that.

So, it looks like we have to change `registerEvent()` by giving it an additional parameter and by changing its body to adapt it to new requirements.

```
inline void registerEvent(int duration)    // we change the header
{ count++;   span = duration; }            // we butcher the body, too
```

Now, we write 10 pages of code with the calls to `registerEvent()` with different values of the actual argument.

```
registerEvent(50); registerEvent(20);     // new client code
```

In addition, the calls to `registerEvent()` in the existing 400 pages of code have to be changed.

```
registerEvent(20);          // modified server call in client code
```

This solution requires the following:

1. adding new client code
2. changing the existing server header
3. changing the existing server body
4. changing the existing client code

When the code has to be coordinated in four places, chances are good that things will fall between the cracks. This is especially true about the last activity. The use of a default parameter value provides a viable alternative. We do change the existing server function: We modify its header and butcher its body.

```
inline void registerEvent(int duration)    // we change the header
{ count++;   span = duration; }            // we butcher the body, too
```

But the function prototype in the new client code and in the existing client code should look this way.

```
inline void registerEvent(int duration=20);      // prototype
```

This eliminates the need for the most burdensome activity on our list: changing existing code as the result of changes elsewhere (in this case, changes to the server function). This is probably the most unpleasant part of maintenance. The issue here is not the labor involved in making changes. The issue is making sure that all the places that have to be changed are in fact changed (and no change is made in the places that do not have to be changed). Also, regression testing needed to establish that these changes are done correctly is difficult to plan, arduous to implement, and almost impossible to document.

Granted, not all maintenance can be reduced to the use of default parameter values. Make sure, however, that you do not miss the opportunity to use it when it can be used. It is a serious improvement over the traditional technology of maintenance.

In the next section, we will consider yet another C++ programming technique that can be used as an alternative to default parameter values—function name overloading.

Function Name Overloading

Function name overloading is yet another important improvement in the area of program modularization in C++.

Most languages connect each name with a unique object within a scope (block, function, class, file, and program). This is true of type names, names of variables, and names of functions.

In C, there are no nested scopes for functions within other functions, and their names must be unique within the program scope, not just within the file scope. Two function definitions with the same name in a source file is a syntax error. Two function definitions with the same name in two different files is a link error. C does not take into account parameter types or return values. It is only the function name that matters, and it should be unique within the project (including libraries).

In C++, each class has a separate scope; hence, the same name can be used for a member function and for a global function. Also, the same function name can be used for member functions in different classes. Notice that the use of the same name in different scopes does not require any difference in the number of parameters or in their types. They could be the same or they could be different; it does not matter. As soon as two functions are defined in two different scopes (the global scope and a class scope or two class scopes), the issue of name conflicts is moot.

This innovation is really a great improvement in the state of software development. The C requirement that all function names have to be unique is too restrictive, especially for large projects. A proliferation of names makes project management difficult. For large projects, coordination between teams working on separate parts of the program becomes too complex. Introduction of class scope in C++ eliminates most of these problems. Most, but not all.

The C++ scope rules are the same as in C: The programmer-defined names must be unique within a scope where these names are defined (class or file scope for type names and names of variables, project scope for function names). It would be convenient to use the same name for different functions in the same scope, not just in different scopes.

C++ provides yet another significant improvement in this area; it allows the overloading of function names. The meaning of a function name in C++ depends on the number of parameters that the function has and on the types of these parameters. The use of the same function name for different functions with a different number or type of parameter is called function name overloading. The compiler will distinguish among overloaded functions.

Here is the example of using the same function name, add(), for two different functions. The number of parameters is different: One function has two parameters, another function has three parameters.

```
int add(int x, int y)              // two parameters
{ return x + y; }

int add(int x, int y, int z)       // three parameters
{ return x + y + z; }
```

If the parameter lists for several functions are different, the C++ compiler treats them as different functions even if they have the same programmer-defined name. When the function is called by the client code, the parameter list that is passed by the client to the function causes the compiler to choose the proper function definition.

```
int a = 2, b = 3, c, d;    ...     // whatever
c = add(a,b);       // call to:  int add(int x, int y);
d = add(a,b,c);     // call to:  int add(int x, int y, int z);
```

If the number of parameters is the same but the types are different, so that the two lists can be distinguished from each other, name overloading is also possible.

```
void add(int *x, int y)            // also two parameters
{ *x += y; }
```

This function add() also has two parameters, but the first parameter is of a different type: It is a pointer to int rather than int. This is sufficient for the compiler to tell one function from another because the function calls in the client code are different.

```
int a = 2, b = 3, c, d;    ...     // whatever
c = add(a,b);       // call to:  int add(int x, int y);
d = add(a,b,c);     // call to:  int add(int x, int y, int z);
add(&a,b);          // call to:  void add(int *x, int y);
```

We see that in C++ the meaning of the function call depends on its context: the types of the actual arguments supplied by the client code. For resolving ambiguities, the C++ compiler uses the function signature. Another term for the function signature is the public interface of the function. It is based on the number and type of function arguments. Different order of parameter types is sufficient.

Argument names are, of course, irrelevant for distinguishing among overloaded functions.

The `return` value is not taken into account when distinguishing overloaded function names: The functions must differ in either the type of parameters or in the number of parameters.

```
double add(int x, int y)      // signature is the same: syntax error
{ double a = (double)x,  b = (double)y;
   return a + b; }            // return type is different: not enough
```

The C++ compiler is not able to distinguish this function from the first function `add()` that returns `int`.

```
int a = 2, b = 3, c, d;  double e;    ...        // whatever
c = add(a,b);            // call ambiguity: which function?
e = add(a,b);            // call ambiguity: which function?
```

Here, the fact that the first call is used to set the value of an integer variable and the second call sets the value of a double variable might be sufficient for a human reader to make the choice but not for the compiler.

If these two functions `add()` are defined in different files but are called from the same file with client code, the compiler flags the second prototype as an attempt to redefine the function that has already been defined.

```
int add(int x, int y);       // a legitimate prototype
double add(int x, int y);    // function redefinition: syntax error
```

Notice that if the return types match, the compiler accepts the second prototype as a simple redeclaration of the function.

```
int add(int x, int y);       // a legitimate prototype
int add(int x, int y);       // function redeclaration: no problem
```

The differences in function code do not count either; it is the responsibility of the programmer to make sure that overloaded functions perform semantically similar operations (as their common name implies). For example, the programmer could write yet another function `add()` with four parameters that returns the maximum value of its actual arguments.

```
int add(int a, int b, int c, int d)    // yet another overloaded add()
{ int x = a>b?a:b, y = c>d?c:d;        // bad use of conditional operator
  return x>y ? x : y; }                 // return maximum value
```

As far as the C++ compiler is concerned, it is perfectly legal, and it will distinguish between this function and other add() functions on the basis of their interfaces. As far as your boss is concerned (or for that matter, the maintainer), well, you know what they will think.

The use of function overloading eliminates the need for devising unique names for different but related functions.

```
int addPair (int, int);       // instead of int add(int x, int y);
int addThree (int,int,int);   // instead of int add(int,int,int);
void addTo (int *, int);      // instead of void add(int *, int);
```

Neither the compiler nor the maintainer will have any difficulty deciding which function is called by the client code.

If the compiler cannot match actual arguments with any set of formal parameters available for the given function name, it is a syntax error. If an exact match is not possible, the compiler uses promotion and conversion. In this example, I assume that type Item is a structure not compatible with type int.

```
int c;   Item x;    ...        // whatever
c = add(5,x);                  // no match: syntax error
c = add(5,'a');                // no error: promotion
c = add(5,20.0);               // no error: conversion
```

Using a character where an integer is expected for computations does not make much sense. It should have been made illegal, but it was not; try not to use these kinds of promotion/conversions unless there are some tangible benefits of doing so. (Frankly, I could not think of any, but I did not want to sound too dogmatic by saying "never.")

Note

For class arguments, the C++ compiler applies programmer-defined conversions if conversion operators and/or conversion constructors are defined for the class. (I will discuss this in more detail later.)

When two overloaded functions have the same number of parameters but the types of parameters allow conversion between them, it is better to supply actual arguments of exact type to avoid ambiguities of conversion. Let us say we have two functions max(), one with integer parameters and another with double parameters.

```
long max(long x, long y)          // return the maximum value
{ return x>y ? x : y; }

double max(double x, double y)    // it is different from long
{ return x>y ? x : y; }
```

When argument types match the types of formal parameters exactly, the C++ compiler has no difficulty finding the right function for the call in client code.

```
long a=2, b=3, c;
double x=2.0, y=3.0, z;
c = max(a,b);      // no call ambiguity: long max(long, long);
z = max(x,y);      // no call ambiguity: double max(double, double);
z = max(a,y);      // ambiguity: which function?
```

In the last function call here, the first actual argument is of type `long`, and the second is of type `double`. Even though the return value is of type `double`, the compiler refuses to make the decision as to what function to call. You can instruct the compiler by explicitly casting the argument to the appropriate type.

```
z = max((double)a,y);   // no ambiguity: double max(double,double);
```

In the next example, I will try to pass an argument of type `int`. Obviously, the conversion from `int` to `long` is more natural than is the conversion from `int` to `double`, right? Wrong. It is natural for a human being, but not for the C++ compiler. There is no such concept as affinity of types in C++. A conversion is a conversion is a conversion.

```
int k=2, m=3, n;
n = max(k,m);            // ambiguity: which function? long? double?
```

It is all the same for the compiler whether to convert `int` to `long` or `int` to `double`. Since it is all the same, the compiler flags this call as ambiguous.

You see that using such a nice feature as function name overloading entails significant complexity under the hood of the program. Come to think of it, using two functions, `maxLong()` and `maxDouble()`, might not be such a bad idea. Especially because this is not the end. Let us consider two other overloaded functions.

```
int min (int x, int y)           // return the minimum value
{ return x>y ? x : y; }

double min(double x, double y)   // it is different from int
{ return x>y ? x : y; }
```

Now let us play the same game of ambiguity. You know the answer—it is all the same for the compiler whether to convert from `long` to `int` or from `long` to `double`. Hence, this function call is a syntax error.

```
long k=2, m=3, n;
n = min(k,m);            // ambiguity: which function? int? double?
```

Now let us do the same thing for `short` and `float` actual arguments. One would expect the same response from the compiler: ambiguous function calls. Not at all—the compiler compiles this code without any objections.

```
short a=2, b=3, c;
float x=2.0f, y=3.0f, z;
c = min(a,b);            // no call ambiguity: int max(int, int);
z = min(x,y);            // no call ambiguity: double max(double, double);
```

The reason that the compiler is so tolerant is that there is no conversion here. The values of type `short` are *promoted* to `int`, not *converted*. Similarly, the values of type `float` are promoted to type `double`, not converted. After promotion, the compiler is able to match the argument types with the types of parameters exactly. Hence, there is no ambiguity.

When arguments are passed by value, the `const` specifier is considered superfluous or trivial. Hence, it cannot distinguish among overloaded functions. For example, this function cannot be distinguished from `int min(int,int)`.

```
int min (const int x, const int y)      // return the minimum value
{ return x>y ? x : y; }
```

Similarly, a conversion from a type to a reference is trivial. It cannot be used to distinguish among overloaded functions because function calls to these functions look the same. For example, the compiler cannot distinguish this function from the function `int min(int,int)`.

```
int min (int &x, int &y)                // return the minimum value
{ return x>y ? x : y; }
```

On the other hand, the compiler has no difficulty distinguishing between pointers and pointed types, for example, between `int*` and `int`. It also distinguishes between constant and nonconstant pointers and references. As an illustration, let us consider two other little silly functions.

```
void printChar (char ch)        // value parameter
{ cout << ch; }

void printChar (char* ch)       // pointer parameter
{ cout << *ch; }
```

The function calls in the client code look different, and both the compiler and the human maintainer can distinguish between them when a regular character (nonconstant) is used as an argument in the first two function calls.

```
char c = 'A';  const char cc = 'A';
printChar(c);          // ok: void printChar(char);
printChar(&c);         // ok: void printChar(char*);
printChar (cc);        // const can be passed to void printChar(char);
printChar(&cc);        // const cannot be used in printChar(char*);
```

The third function call is also acceptable because a const argument can be passed where a nonconstant value is expected. If the function changes the value of its parameter, this change will not propagate to the client space and will not change the value of the const argument. The fourth function call is a syntax error. If the function changes its parameter (passed to it by pointer), this change will propagate to the client space; since the actual argument is declared const, it cannot be used in this function call.

Are you tired yet? Let us add yet another overloaded function to this set of functions. In this function, the header reflects what the function body does; the actual argument is not changed by the function.

```
void printChar (const char* ch)      // pointer, but value is const
{ cout << *ch; }
```

Now all four function calls above compile and execute correctly. Notice that if the second function (void printChar(char*);) disappears, the second function call will still compile; it will call void printChar(const char*);—it is quite appropriate (and safe) to pass a nonconstant value where a const value is expected.

Also notice that all string literals in double quotes are of type char* rather than const char*. This is why you can set regular pointers to point to them and then change them through these pointers.

```
char *p = "day"; p[0] = 'p';       // now it says "pay"
```

Function overloading can be used for functions of the same class in the same way as it is used for functions in the same file: If the number (or the types) of parameters must be different, then the use of the same name for different functions is legal. When member function names are overloaded in the same class, their semantics should be similar. (Of course, no compiler checks if this is the case.) Class constructors are often overloaded. This overloading provides client code with options for object initialization in different contexts. (We will see more detail in the next chapter.)

Even though the examples I used to illustrate function name overloading were quite rudimental, they demonstrate that the use of overloading might make client code difficult to understand. Deciding which function to call might be hard, even for the C++ compiler. It can confuse a human reader too. In C++, too often too much takes place behind the scenes. This feature should be used sparingly.

Function name overloading could be used for program evolution similarly to function default parameters. When the program functionality evolves, we change existing functions to accommodate new requirements. Often, this approach requires changes in both the function interfaces and in function bodies as well as in the client code that calls these functions. This process is complex, error-prone, and expensive.

In some cases, function name overloading allows us only to add new server functions rather than to edit existing server functions and client function calls. Let us go back to that simple function, registerEvent(), that I used to illustrate default parameter values.

```
inline void registerEvent()
{ count++;  span = 20; }     // increment event count, set time span
```

Again, I assume that it is a large and complex system that contains about 400 pages of code with calls to this function.

```
registerEvent();              // server call in client code
```

Now I want to add about 10 pages of code where we set the time span individually for each event. The 400 pages of code do not require changes, because the time span there remains the same.

Of course, writing another function, for example, regEvent(), to serve these 10 pages is always a viable option.

```
inline void regEvent(int duration)     // another server function
{ count++;  span = duration; }         // increment event count
```

Again, this is a small example, and it is not difficult to write this tiny function from scratch. In real life, functions are long and complex, and the pull to adapt existing functions to new conditions is always strong. Let's change the existing function registerEvent() by giving it an additional parameter and by changing its body accordingly.

```
inline void registerEvent(int duration)   // we change the header
{ count++;  span = duration; }            // we butcher the body, too
```

As I indicated in the previous section, this solution requires the following:

1. adding new client code (new 10 pages)
2. changing the existing server header (add a new parameter)
3. changing the existing server body (use the new parameter)
4. changing the existing client code (all 400 pages)

Using default parameter values eliminates the need to change existing client code but still requires editing existing server code and its interfaces. With function overloading, you do not change the existing `registerEvent()` function. You write another `registerEvent()` function. (It looks exactly like the last function.)

```
inline void registerEvent(int duration)   // new function header
{ count++;  span = duration; }            // new function body
```

The agenda for the change now looks the like this.

1. adding new client code (new 10 pages)
2. adding new server function

Not only changes to the existing client code but also changes to the existing server function are eliminated. This is great! Again, not every maintenance task is amenable to this technique. But if it is, make sure that you do not miss this opportunity. It is the most serious improvement in the traditional technology of maintenance.

Summary

In this chapter we looked at C++ functions as a major program-building tool. C++, as a descendant of C, is unique among modern programming languages, by requiring the programmer to provide prototypes of the functions used in each source code file. This rule supports separate compilation and hence the management of large projects but creates additional problems for the designer and for the maintainer.

Parameter passing is a complex skill in C++. The programmer has to coordinate the code that is written for the function in four places: in the client code (in the function call itself), in the server function header, in its prototype, and in the body of the server function. Often this is much too much, and something goes wrong in one of these places, causing all kinds of aggravation.

Passing parameters by value is actually relatively simple, but it does not support modification of actual arguments. Passing parameters by pointer supports side effects in the client code but is complex and error-prone. C++ inherited these two parameter modes from C. To reduce the frequency of errors, C++ tries to make the use of passing by pointer less frequent. This is achieved by making yet another parameter mode available—passing by reference. This looks like a good compromise, even though this parameter mode introduces some terminological and notational confusion.

For structures, pass by value has yet another drawback: Additional time and space are required for copying actual arguments into the stack space allocated for the function parameter. Pass by reference eliminates copying without additional complexity inherent in pass by pointer. However, pass by reference makes it difficult to convey to the maintenance programmer the intent of the code designer: what parameters are modified by the function and what parameters are not. Using `const` specifiers solves this problem. This is an extremely useful technique.

For arrays, only one parameter mode is available, and the syntax is the same for both input and output parameters. Again, that makes it difficult for the maintenance programmer to understand the data flow in the program: what parameters are modified by the function and what parameters retain their values.

Using `const` specifiers allows the code designer to pass to the maintainer the information about the arrays that are not modified as the result of the function call. Making the assumption that the array that does not have the `const` specifier is indeed modified by the function is not always safe, and it is up to the designer to make sure that the maintainer benefits from this technique.

We also looked at argument promotions and conversions. When the argument type and parameter types are incompatible, none of that is allowed. The types are incompatible when they belong to different categories defined as scalar value, pointer, structure, and array. There are no conversions among these categories. There are no conversions among structures of different types. Here, C++ enforces strong typing. However, C++ allows implicit conversions between scalar numeric types—no questions asked. In addition, C++ allows explicit conversions (casts) between pointers of different types or among arrays of different types. These conversions provide the programmer with greater flexibility, but they are prone to error and might be confusing to the maintainer.

We also looked at inline functions, which eliminate the performance overhead of the function call. Used correctly, inline functions can improve program performance. Used incorrectly, they might increase the size of the object code and even cause deterioration of performance because of extra swapping.

In addition, we discussed default parameter values and function name overloading. These are great language features that decrease the pressure on the namespace in C++ programming projects. They also open new avenues for program maintenance by eliminating the need to change existing client code when the functions called from this code require changes. However, these features should be used sparingly. They are complex, and too much is going on under the hood of a C++ program. Reckless use of these features can easily confuse not only the compiler but also the human maintainer.

The techniques of functional programming represent the backbone of C++ programming. Without fluency in using C++ functions, it is impossible to create high-quality object-oriented programs. Actually, it is impossible to create any high-quality programs, object-oriented or not. In the next chapter we will start our study of object-oriented programming—the most powerful way of creating high-quality programs.

OBJECT-ORIENTED PROGRAMMING WITH FUNCTIONS

Topics in this Chapter

- Cohesion
- Coupling
- Data Encapsulation
- Information Hiding
- A Larger Example of Encapsulation
- Shortcomings of Encapsulation with Functions
- Summary

Chapter 8

In this chapter, I start a discussion of principles and techniques of object-oriented programming. Some of them are common programming knowledge, others I formulated and adapted for use with C++. These principles and techniques are rarely discussed in other C++ books. This is why I suggest that you do not skip this chapter even if you are an experienced C++ programmer.

In the previous chapters, I concentrated on C++ language rules that define what is syntactically legal in a C++ program and what is not. Similar to natural languages, illegal constructs should be ruled out, not because of bad taste or ambiguity, but because the compiler will not be able to convert them into object code. As for legal constructs, there exists a large variety of ways to "say the same thing." In the previous chapters, I compared different ways of using legal constructs, often from the point of view of program correctness, performance, and, yes, bad taste. But my major concern was with program maintainability, making sure that the maintenance programmer does not spend extra effort trying to understand what the code designer had in mind when the source code was written.

In this chapter (and in the chapters that follow), understandability of code will be my major concern. However, the focus of the discussion will shift from writing control constructs in a segment of code to a higher level of programming: breaking the program into cooperating pieces (functions and, later, classes).

I will not get into systems analysis, that is, deciding what functions should be in the program to support the goals of the application. That would make the scope of this book too broad. So I will assume that whatever functions are necessary for achieving the goal of the program are already there. Instead, I will concentrate on the ways in which additional functions should be used to make the program more maintainable and reusable.

There is always more than one way of dividing the job between client functions that cooperate with each other to achieve the program goal. There is always more than one way of designing the server functions that handle data and operations on behalf of their client functions. Assuming that all versions are equivalent from the point of view of program correctness, how do you decide which one is better?

In the past, most programmers would use program performance as the major criterion. Hardware progress made this criterion irrelevant for many applications, especially for interactive applications. For those applications where performance is still important, it is the choice of algorithms and data structures that affects performance, not the way work is allocated between client and server functions.

Another important criterion is the ease of writing code. It is still a relevant criterion for small programs that are developed by a few people, are used for short periods of time, and then are either discarded or replaced by totally new code. For large systems that are designed by many cooperating developers and are maintained for long periods of time, the economics of software development suggests a different answer. The best version of the program is the one whose parts are easier to reuse (providing savings during development of the application or its future releases) or easier to maintain (providing savings during program evolution).

These two characteristics—maintainability and reusability—are *the* most important characteristics of software quality. However, these characteristics are too general. Indeed, it is not obvious how to decide which version of the code is less expensive to maintain and which version of the code is less expensive to reuse.

Reusability is related to the independence of program parts. Among several versions of C++ code, the version that has fewer links with other segments of the program is more reusable in other contexts. Maintainability is also related to independence of program parts. Among several versions of C++ code, the version that takes less time to understand, preferably without studying other segments of the program, is easier to change without side effects to other parts of code.

This is why the need to refer to other segments of the program is evidence of poor quality of the code. This is why the potential to understand the code in isolation, without referring to other code segments, is evidence of good quality of the code. I will often say that this version of the code is better than another one if this version can be understood with less effort or with fewer lookups in other parts of the code.

This is nice but is still not specific enough for the practicing programmer. The concepts of code understandability and independence should be supported by more-specific technical criteria that are easier to recognize and to use. In this chapter, I will offer you several technical criteria. Two criteria, cohesion and coupling, are relatively old. Two other criteria, encapsulation and information hiding, are relatively new, and the industry has not accumulated enough experience in using them. In addition to encapsulation and information hiding, I will use several varieties of criteria related to code understandability and independence:

- pushing responsibility down to server function from client functions
- limiting knowledge shared by server and client functions
- separation of concerns for client and server functions
- avoiding tearing apart what should belong together
- passing developer's knowledge to the maintainer in code rather than in comments

I did not find one all-embracing term for these principles ("principle of maximum independence"? "Shtern principle"? "sharing knowledge on the-need-to-know basis"? "principle of self-explanatory code"?). As you are going to see, these principles somewhat overlap with each other and with the criteria of cohesion, coupling, information hiding, and encapsulation. I think that practicing programmers should be familiar with all of these principles. Their major advantage is that they are operational: They show the programmer the directions to go in search of a better design. Using them will help you to understand how to improve your coding practices.

The idea behind these criteria or principles is that the functions in a program cooperate doing parts of the same job. For any division of responsibilities among them, these functions have to share some knowledge, have common concerns, partition parts of the same job, and do it in different functions. After all, these functions are parts of the same program. To make these functions reusable and understandable, you should assign the responsibilities between functions (design the system) in such a way that these dependencies among functions are minimized.

As it is often the case with high-quality programming, writing a better program requires more programming time and results in more source code lines than writing a lower quality program does. Some programmers (and managers) might be disappointed by this increase in the amount of work to do. I would like to persuade these programmers (and managers) with an analogy about traffic rules.

When I sit waiting at a red light, I sometimes think that without restrictive traffic rules we all could get to our destinations faster. And this is probably true, at least for some destinations and for some drivers. But not for all destinations and not for all drivers. Driving without rules causes more traffic accidents and more congestion. Those drivers that avoid accidents will indeed get to their destinations faster without the rules. But many more drivers will be delayed either by accidents or by congestion caused by accidents. Traffic rules force us to make the investment of time up front to save time in the long run.

Similarly, ignoring rules of maintainability and reusability will let you write programs faster, at least for some applications and for some programmers. But not for all applications and not for all programmers. The time saved by writing programs that are hard to understand will be more than offset by the time spent trying to understand what the code designers were striving to achieve when they were writing code (and where they went wrong).

This is why the software industry pays so much attention to writing comments. Comments are an investment that we make up front so that it pays off in the long run (when they are clear, complete, and up-to-date). Often, line comments are obscure, incomplete, or do not reflect changes made after the code was written. Investing in writing self-explanatory code is better than investing in comments.

If you are writing a small program, the rules for writing self-explanatory quality code are not very important. If you are developing a large application, investing up front in writing quality code is crucial for reaping the benefits in the long run.

Cohesion

Cohesion describes the relatedness of the steps that the designer puts into the same segment of code, for example, a function.

When a function has good cohesion (high cohesion), it performs one task over one computational object or data structure; when cohesion is poor (weak cohesion), the function performs several tasks over one object or even several tasks over several objects. When the function exhibits poor cohesion, it contains diverse unrelated computations over unrelated computational objects. This means that these objects belong elsewhere: The designer tore apart things that should have belonged with something else and instead put them into the same function.

High-cohesion functions are easy to name. Usually, one uses a verb-plus-noun combination. The active verb is used for the action that the function performs, and the noun is used for the object (or the subject) of the action. For example, `insertItem()`, `findAccount()`, and so on (if the function name is honest, which is not always the case).

For low-cohesion functions, one has to use several verbs or nouns, for example, `findOrInsertItem()`.

Here is an example, however awkward. (All good examples of poor cohesion are awkward because they describe poorly designed functions.)

```
void initializeGlobalObjects ()
{ numaccts = 0;                      // one computational object
  fstream inf("trans.dat",ios::in);  // transaction file
  numtrans = 0;                      // another computational object
  if (inf==NULL) exit(1); }          // transaction file again
```

In this example, `numaccts` should be initialized where accounts are processed—it belongs with account processing. Similarly, `numtrans` should be initialized where transactions are processed—it belongs with transaction processing, not with account initialization. In this function, I tore apart what belongs with other steps of processing and put them together into a function of weak cohesion.

The remedy is to redesign. As I mentioned in Chapter 1, "Object-Oriented Approach: What's So Good About It?" redesign means changing the list of parts (functions) and their responsibilities. In the case of poor cohesion, redesign usually means breaking the function with poor cohesion into several cohesive functions. The tradeoff is that you can wind up with too many small functions. Besides potential impact on performance, this imposes on the maintenance programmer a larger number of things to remember (function names and their interfaces). For a small function like `initializeGlobalObjects()` above, breaking up does not make sense. Such a function probably should be eliminated.

Cohesion is not a very strong criterion; the decision to redesign by breaking up functions should not be made lightly. In case of doubt, cohesion needs other criteria to complement it. However, cohesion is important for evaluating designs. Make sure you use it when you evaluate design alternatives—the distribution of work between functions.

Coupling

Coupling is a much stronger and useful criterion than cohesion. It describes the interface, or flow of data values, between a called function (a server function) and a calling function (a client function).

Coupling can be implicit, with functions communicating through global variables, or explicit, when the client and server functions communicate through parameters. Implicit coupling is higher—it results in a higher degree of dependency between the client and server functions. Explicit coupling is lower: When functions communicate through parameters, it is easier to understand, reuse, and modify them.

The intensity of coupling is described by the number of values that flow from the client function to the server function and back. A large number of values means strong coupling: a high degree of dependency between functions. A small number of values means weak coupling: a low degree of dependency between the client and server functions.

Implicit Coupling

The client function supplies the server function with input data for computations and depends on the results computed by the server function (server output). Coupling is implicit when the functions communicate through global variables that are not listed in the server function interface.

Consider, for example, an interactive program that prompts the user to enter the year and prints whether it is a leap year.

```cpp
int year, remainder;  bool leap;         // program data
cout << "Enter the year:   ";            // prompt the user
cin >> year;                             // accept user input
remainder = year % 4;
if (remainder != 0)                      // it is not divisible by 4
    leap = false;                        // hence, it is not a leap year
else
   { if (year%100 == 0 && year%400 != 0)
       leap = false;                     // divisible by 100 but not by 400
     else
       leap = true; }                    // otherwise, it is a leap year
if (leap)
   cout << year << " is a leap year\n";  // print results
else
   cout << year << " is not a leap year\n";
}
```

This program is similar to the code I discussed in Chapter 4, "C++ Control Flow," (Listings 4.8 and 4.9). This is a small program and, in truth, it does not need any modularization. On the other hand, a program that benefits the most from modularization should be fairly large. Studying program details and comparing different alternatives would become a task in itself and would distract you from the discussion of the principles of modularization, which I would like you to concentrate on. It is these principles you will apply in real life, not the details of examples.

This is why I would like you to pretend that this is a very large and complex program and follow me through several cycles of its redesign by breaking it into cooperating functions.

So, this is a large monolithic program that I would like to break into manageable components. Again, for simplicity's sake, let us break it into only two functions, main() which is responsible for the user interface and the general flow of computations, and isLeap(), which uses the values of year and remainder to compute the value of leap that is used by main() to print the results.

```
void isLeap()
    { if (remainder != 0)          // it is not divisible by 4
        leap = false;              // hence, it is not a leap year
      else if (year%100==0 && year%400!=0)
        leap = false;              // divisible by 100 but not by 400
      else
        leap = true; }             // otherwise, it is a leap year
```

There is one technical problem here that is related to the concept of scope discussed in Chapter 6, "Memory Management: The Stack and the Heap." The values of year and remainder that the function isLeap() uses are set in main(). The value of leap that the function isLeap() computes is used by main(). However, if I define these variables in main(), they will be visible only in main(): The C++ scope rules would prevent them from being visible in any other function, and isLeap() will not be able to manipulate these variables. If I define these variables in isLeap(), they would be visible only in isLeap(). The C++ scope rules would prevent these variables from being visible in main(). To make these variables visible both in main() and isLeap(), I have to define them as global to both of these functions.

Listing 8.1 demonstrates this solution. A sample run of this program is shown in Figure 8–1.

Listing 8.1   Example of implicit coupling through global variables.

```cpp
#include <iostream>
using namespace std;

int year, remainder;              // global input variables
bool leap;                        // global output variable

void isLeap()                     // inputs: year, remainder; output: leap
   { if (remainder != 0)          // access three global variables
       leap = false;              // if not divisible by 4, it is not leap
     else if (year%100==0 && year%400!=0)    // access global variables
       leap = false;              // divisible by 100 but not by 400: not leap
     else
       leap = true; }             // otherwise, it is a leap year

int main()
{ cout << "Enter the year:   ";
  cin >> year;                    // prompt the user, enter data
  remainder = year % 4;           // access global variables
  isLeap();                       // define whether it is a leap year
  if (leap)
    cout << year << " is a leap year\n";      // print results
  else
    cout << year << " is not a leap year\n";
  return 0;
  }
```

In this program, function `main()` calls function `isLeap()`. Function `main()` is a client that gets its job done by calling other functions. Function `isLeap()` is a server that does some job for a client that calls it. This relationship between the two functions is shown in a structure chart in Figure 8–2. The structure chart also shows the data flow between the functions. Variables `year` and `remainder` are set in `main()` and are used by `isLeap()` as its input values to compute its results. The value of variable `leap` is produced by function `isLeap()` as its output and is used by `main()` after the call to `isLeap()`.

Figure 8–1   Output for program in Listing 8.1.

```
Enter the year:  1999
1999 is not a leap year
```

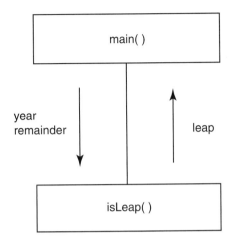

Figure 8-2
A structure chart for the program
in Listing 8.1.

Notice that input variables year and remainder must have legitimate values before the function isLeap() is called by main(). It is the responsibility of the client function to make sure that these variables are properly initialized: The server isLeap() does not make any checks of validity; it assumes that the client main() lives up to its obligations.

Similarly, the output variables (in this case the variable leap) do not have to have a legitimate value before the call to the server function. It is the responsibility of the server isLeap() to set the output value, and the client main() uses this value after (but not before) the call.

It is important to understand the data flow between the functions. If I know that variables year and remainder are input variables for isLeap(), I would expect that the server function uses these values but does not change them. It would be quite odd to expect that function isLeap() does something like that.

```
void isLeap()
   { remainder = 4; year = 2000;   . . .      // unexpected nonsense!
```

Similarly, if I know that variable leap is an output variable for function isLeap(), I would not expect the client main() to initialize this variable before main() calls isLeap() (or, for that matter, change its value immediately after the call without first using it for some purpose).

```
int main()
{ cout << "Enter the year:   ";
  cin >> year;                    // prompt the user, enter data
  remainder = year % 4;           // access global variables
  leap = false;                   // misleading initialization before call
  isLeap();                       // define whether it is a leap year
  leap = true;                    // misleading (and incorrect) if done after call
  . . .
```

What will the maintainer assume reading the main() function above? After establishing the goal of the assignment to remainder (it is used in isLeap() for computing the value of variable leap), the maintainer will study isLeap() again, trying to figure out the purpose of the assignment to leap. For a small function, it will only take a few seconds to figure out that the value assigned in client main() to leap is not used in the server isLeap() or even in client main(). But this is true only for a small function. For a large program, this will require more time, and the maintainer might become confused and come to a wrong conclusion.

True, some programmers dislike noninitialized variables so much that they initialize variables even when initialization is not needed. They say that this is helpful when the server function for some reason fails to assign the value. But isLeap() is not one of those functions! Neither are the majority of the functions you have written or will ever write. If programmers understood the data flow between functions, the functions would never fail to assign values to their output variables.

You see that this innocent-looking "defensive" programming technique results in code that requires more time to understand. From the point of view of quality criteria (readability and independence of program parts), this technique invariably results in inferior code; that is, it contributes to the software crisis we all would like to eliminate. Avoid this practice. Instead of initializing everything in sight, tell the maintainer what values will be used as server input (by initializing them in the client) and what values are server output variables (by not initializing them in the client).

I hope that you follow this discussion and see the importance of passing to the maintainer the knowledge the developer has about the data flow between the functions. Let us go back to the discussion of coupling.

Coupling describes how much one has to study to understand the data flow between the functions. Often it requires one to study the pattern of data handling by the client and the server functions. In Listing 8.1, for example, I notice that main() assigns values to variables year and remainder and that isLeap() uses these values. I also notice that main() does not initialize leap, isLeap() assigns to leap a value, and main() uses this value after the call to isLeap(). That's that.

However, to establish these simple dependencies, I have to study both the client and server functions in their entirety. It is easy to do for this trivial example I am discussing, but it takes more time for any function of realistic size and complexity. Can one improve this labor-intensive and error-prone technique? Sure. The way to do that is to use explicit coupling instead of implicit coupling.

Explicit Coupling

Explicit coupling is through function parameters, when all input and output variables used by the server function are included in the server function parameters, and no global variables are used in the data flow between the client and the server. Listing 8.2 shows the same example as in Listing 8.1 where explicit parameters replace the use of implicit data flows through global variables. This program executes in the same way as the program in Listing 8.1.

Listing 8.2   Example of explicit coupling through parameters.

```cpp
#include <iostream>
using namespace std;

void isLeap(int year, int remainder, bool &leap)    // parameters
// inputs: year, remainder; output: leap
  { if (remainder != 0)
       leap = false;
    else if (year%100==0 && year%400!=0)
       leap = false;
    else
       leap = true; }
int main()
{ int year, remainder;                    // local input variables
  bool leap;                              // local output variable
  cout << "Enter the year:   ";
  cin >> year;                            // input variables are set
  remainder = year % 4;
  isLeap(year,remainder,leap);            // output variable is set
  if (leap)                               // output variable is used
     cout << year << " is a leap year\n";
  else
     cout << year << " is not a leap year\n";
  return 0;
  }
```

In Listing 8.2, the server function `isLeap()` has three parameters. There are no global variables. Variables `year`, `remainder`, and `leap` are defined as local in the client function `main()`. Why is this possible? Because they do not have to be known in the scope of function `isLeap()` as they do in Listing 8.1. Instead, function `isLeap()` accesses these variables as actual arguments that are passed from the client function in the call to function `isLeap()`.

This is a general observation: When two functions communicate through data, the components of the data flow should be either declared as global to both functions, or they can be defined in the scope of the client function and passed as parameters to the server function.

As in the previous example, variables `year` and `remainder` are input variables for `isLeap()` and variable `leap` is an output variable. How do I know? I study the header (or the prototype—whatever is available) of the function `isLeap()` rather than the body of the function.

```
void isLeap(int year, int remainder, bool &leap)          // parameters
{ . . . }
```

Can you tell without studying the function code what the role of each parameter is? Sure. Parameters `year` and `remainder` are passed by value. Hence, they cannot be output parameters. You do not expect function `isLeap()` to set their values.

```
void isLeap(int year, int remainder, bool &leap)     // parameters
{ remainder=4; year=2000; . . .                      // useless for value parameters
```

Hence, you conclude that these two are input parameters. The values of the actual arguments should be set by the client code before the function call, and these values will be used by the server function in its computations.

Similarly, parameter `leap` is passed by reference. This means that it is an output parameter. Actually, it also can be an input/output parameter; that is, the client function might set its value initially, and then the server function might update that value. But the main point is that function `isLeap()` changes the value of parameter `leap`.

How much should I study to arrive at these conclusions? Not very much, just the header of the function. The structure chart for the program in Listing 8.2 is shown in Figure 8–2. It is the same as for the program in Listing 8.1, but explicit data flows of global variables are replaced by explicit data flows of parameters. Does the amount of time I spend depend on the size or complexity of the client function? No. Does the amount of time depend on the size or complexity of the server function? No again! The switch from implicit coupling to explicit coupling results in a drastic decrease in the code complexity for the maintainer and developer alike.

This example illustrates why you should avoid global variables. It has been about 30 years since the industry was first arguing about the use of global variables, but many programmers still are not sure what the problem is. I often ask my students in college courses and attendees in training seminars if they know why global variables are to be avoided. They say that any function in the file (or even in the program) can accidentally (or even maliciously) change the value of a global variable, and it would be difficult to find the source of the error. Some add that the core of the problem is that the list of functions accessing a global variable is not evident. This means that the problem can come from any place in the program.

All that might be true (I have some doubts about the importance of unauthorized access), but the main harm from global variables comes in the form of implicit coupling. Using global variables forces the developer and maintainer to study large segments of code to understand the data flow in the program—what functions set the values of the variables and what functions use these values. Using explicit coupling through parameters allows you to understand data flow by studying only server function headers (or prototypes). This makes a big difference.

Tip

Avoid implicit coupling through global variables. Use explicit coupling with parameters, so that the maintainer (and the client programmer who calls this function) can understand the function interface by studying only its header, not the whole code of the function and its caller(s).

However, this decrease in complexity does not come automatically just because you use explicit coupling through parameters instead of global variables. You should choose parameter modes correctly. Consider, for example, the following version of the server function isLeap().

```
void isLeap(int &year, int &remainder, bool &leap)     // parameters
  { if (remainder != 0)
      leap = false;
    else if (year%100==0 && year%400!=0)
      leap = false;
    else
      leap = true; }
```

Is this function syntactically correct? Yes, it is. Is this function semantically correct? Yes, it is. If I use this function instead of the one I use in Listing 8.2 will the results of execution be the same? Absolutely. The results are the same for both functions for any set of input data.

Is this function any good from the point of view of the software quality? No. All its parameters are passed by reference, and this misleads the maintainer into thinking that all three parameters are set by this function and are used in its client. To discover the truth, the maintainer has to study the entire server function. This is better than studying both the server and client code as was necessary in the case of using only global variables. Still, it is a far cry from only studying the server interface, as in Listing 8.2.

By passing all parameters by reference in this version of the function, the developer of this function failed to express the knowledge he or she had at the time of design. The developer knew that the parameter `leap` was the only output variable but did not pass that knowledge in the code itself.

The maintainer should believe that the pass by reference is evidence that the parameter is changed by the server function (unless there is the `const` modifier), and the pass by value is evidence that the parameter is not changed. Otherwise, the maintainer is back to studying both the server and client in all details instead of studying the parameter list of the server, and the advantages of explicit coupling go down the tubes.

This is why the rules for parameter passing that I formulated in Chapter 7, "Programming with C++ Functions," are so important. Using them consistently describes the function interface for the maintenance programmer, eliminates the need to study several functions at once, and decreases the volume of code to study. Use the joke about the copper wire to choose parameter modes correctly. The presence of the `const` modifier is evidence that the parameter is an input parameter. The absence of the `const` modifier is evidence that the parameter is changed by the function (similar to the absence of copper wire being evidence of cellular phones). Make sure you do not forego this powerful method of improving software quality.

If using parameters is so much better than using global variables, why do programmers still use global variables? There are three reasons for that.

The first reason is program performance. Functions that use parameters spend time for memory allocation and deallocation of parameters and copying their values (or the values of their addresses). Functions that use global variables save that time. When you use global variables for that purpose, make sure that you establish two things in advance. First, you should know that your program does have a performance problem. Second, you should know that using global variables instead of parameters resolves this performance problem. I emphasize that you should *know* that you have a problem and that global variables resolve it rather than *think* that the use of global variables will speed up your application.

Using global variables for functions that are called infrequently will not speed up your program. Using global variables for functions that do external input or output will not speed up your program. Using global variables for short and simple functions will speed up these functions but might not speed up the program because these functions do not affect the overall program performance. I am not telling you that you should never use global variables. I am telling you that you should know whether their use speeds up your program.

The second reason for using global variables is a developer's performance. It is easier and faster to write a server function that uses global variables rather than parameters. When you use parameters, as in Listing 8.2, you might wind up with extra parameters you do not actually need, or you might need some additional parameters so that you have to go back and rewrite the function. Writing a function with parameters requires more investment of time in preliminary planning.

In Listing 8.1, you define variables as global and use whatever you need for the function, without preliminary planning. In the earlier days of computing, this was considered an important advantage. We believed that speeding up the writing of code was beneficial. Today we do not believe that making code *writing* easier saves time and money. It is making code *reading* easier that saves time and money, and modern languages, like C++, induce you to spend more time on writing to make code more readable.

The third reason for the use of global variables for function communication is the lack of awareness among developers. They do not think much about the complexity of using global variables within server functions; they just use them. They increase the amount of interaction with other developers, but again they do not think that these interactions are going to affect the program quality.

The issues that I am explaining here are rarely discussed in programming books. Some of these topics are covered in software engineering books, but these books usually only present general principles rather than specific coding patterns in a specific language. I hope that this discussion along with the presentation in Chapter 7 will persuade you that it is a good idea to:

- use parameters rather than global variables
- pass simple input parameters by value and output parameters by reference
- pass structure and class parameters by reference using the const modifier for input parameters
- pass input arrays using const (and output arrays without const)

Alert

Pass parameters using the guidelines presented in this book. Deviation from these guidelines makes writing code easier; however, it hides from the maintainer what you knew at the time of writing the function code, that is, which parameters you used as input to the function and which parameters you used as output.

How to Reduce the Intensity of Coupling

The number of values in the data flow between the client and the server defines intensity of coupling. The larger the number of these values, the more the client and server function depend on each other, and the more difficult it is to study one function without studying another.

How do we go about reducing the data flow between functions? This is not a simple task. The only way to decrease the number of dependencies among functions is to redesign, that is, to change the division of responsibilities among functions. All other approaches are futile.

Some programmers, for example, believe that the number of parameters can be decreased by combining them into a structure. They have a point. This indeed reduces the number of parameters. However, it does not necessarily reduce coupling. Listing 8.3 shows the version of the `isLeap()` function where three parameters are combined.

Listing 8.3   Example of merging parameters into a structure.

```
#include <iostream>
using namespace std;
struct YearData
{ int year, remainder;
  bool leap; } ;

void isLeap(YearData &data)                    // one parameter only
   { if (data.remainder != 0)
      data.leap = false;
    else if (data.year%100==0 && data.year%400!=0)
      data.leap = false;
    else
      data.leap = true; }
```

```
int main()
{ YearData data;                                // local variable
  cout << "Enter the year:   ";
  cin >> data.year;                             // input fields are set
  data.remainder = data.year % 4;
  isLeap(data);                                 // output field is set
  if (data.leap)                                // output field is used
        cout << data.year << " is a leap year\n";
  else
        cout << data.year << " is not a leap year\n";
  return 0;
}
```

Indeed, the number of parameters here is less than in Listing 8.2. Did data flow between functions decrease? Figure 8–3 shows the data flow for this version of the program. You see that there are still two input values, data.year and data.remainder, and one output value, data.leap.

One can even argue that this version of the program is more difficult to write. It is definitely more difficult to understand and more difficult to reuse, because this version of isLeap() cannot be used without the type YearData. At any rate, the main point of this example is that in the program version in Listing 8.3, coupling between isLeap() and its client did not decrease. This is natural. To arrive at this version, I did not do any redesign—this version of the program uses the same distribution of responsibilities between main() and isLeap() as does the version in Listing 8.2. Hence, data flows between the functions are the same.

Some programmers try to decrease coupling by shunning output parameters. They say that the use of output function parameters is inferior to the use

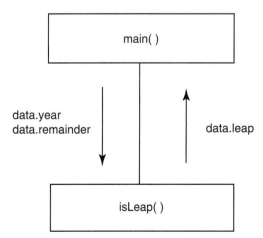

Figure 8-3
A structure chart and data flow for the program in Listing 8.3.

of return values. They also have a point here. Listing 8.4 shows another version of this program, where function isLeap() returns a value rather than setting the value of the output parameter leap.

Listing 8.4   Example of using a return value rather than an output parameter.

```
#include <iostream>
 using namespace std;
bool isLeap(int year, int remainder)          // fewer parameters
   { if (remainder != 0)
       return false;
     else if (year%100==0 && year%400!=0)
       return false;
     else
       return true; }

int main()
{ int year, remainder;                         // local input variables
  bool leap;                                   // local output variable
  cout << "Enter the year:   ";
  cin >> year;                                 // input variables are set
  remainder = year % 4;
  leap = isLeap(year,remainder);               // output variable is set
  if (leap)                                    // output variable is used
        cout << year << " is a leap year\n";
  else
        cout << year << " is not a leap year\n";
  return 0;
  }
```

Again, the number of parameters in the data flow here is less than in Listing 8.2. The function isLeap() here is easier to write; there is no need to struggle with the reference parameter. It is somewhat easier to use, too. For example, you can eliminate variable leap altogether by directly using the return value of isLeap() in the if statement in main() rather than setting the value of a local variable first.

```
int main()
{ int year, remainder;                         // no variable leap
  cout << "Enter the year:   ";
  cin >> year;                                 // input variables are set
  remainder = year % 4;
  if (isLeap(year,remainder)==true)            // output value is used
    cout << year << " is a leap year\n";
  else
    cout << year << " is not a leap year\n";
  return 0; }
```

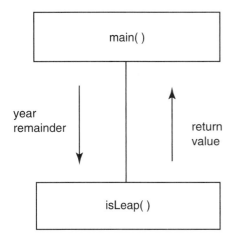

Figure 8–4
A structure chart and data flow for the program in Listing 8.4.

Did data flow between `main()` and `isLeap()` decrease? Not really. Figure 8–4 shows the data flow for this version of the program. You see that there are still two input values, `year` and `remainder`, and one output value represented by the function return value.

Again, coupling did not decrease because I did not do any redesign: This program distributes the responsibilities between `main()` and `isLeap()` in the same way as does the version in Listing 8.2.

To decrease coupling, you should analyze the distribution of computational responsibilities and apply the principles listed at the beginning of this chapter. One of the ways to accomplish this is by identifying the components of data flow that are due to tearing apart what should belong together. Tearing apart computations that should belong together in the same function usually results in the need for those torn apart computations to communicate with each other. When these computations are implemented in different functions, communications manifest themselves in the form of excessive data flow. By bringing together in the same function what has been torn apart, you eliminate the need for communication among functions.

One giveaway of tearing apart what should belong together is the situation where the meaning of the parameter is not clear from the study of the server function code without studying the client code as well. For example, in Listing 8.4, the meaning of parameter `remainder` cannot be deduced from studying function `isLeap()` alone. The maintainer has to study its client `main()` to figure out that this variable represents the remainder of dividing the year by 4. This value is used in `main()` only as a parameter to `isLeap()`. This is why it makes sense to combine the computation of `remainder` and its use in the same function, in this case, `isLeap()`.

Listing 8.5 shows the version of the program where responsibility for the computation of remainder is moved from function main() to its server isLeap(). Figure 8–5 shows the data flow between two functions.

Indeed, isLeap() now needs only one value from main(); it computes the remainder itself, without bothering its client with the demands of doing it before the call.

Listing 8.5   Example of pushing responsibility from client to server.

```cpp
#include <iostream>
using namespace std;

bool isLeap(int year)                   // even fewer parameters
    { int remainder=year%4;             // do not separate what belongs together
      if (remainder != 0)
        return false;
      else if (year%100==0 && year%400!=0)
        return false;
      else
        return true; }

int main()
{ int year; // local data - no remainder
  cout << "Enter the year:   ";
  cin >> year;                          // input variable is set
  if (isLeap(year))                     // output variable is used
    cout << year << " is a leap year\n";
  else
    cout << year << " is not a leap year\n";
  return 0;
  }
```

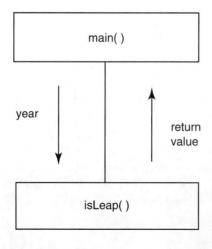

year

return
value

main( )

isLeap( )

Figure 8–5

A structure chart and data flow for the program in Listing 8.5.

Moving the computation of the remainder from one function to another is redesign: I change the distribution of responsibilities among functions. Notice that I merged what had been torn apart by moving responsibility from the client function to the server function. This is an example of pushing responsibilities down to servers. It is not always beneficial, but it often is.

This is a very powerful technique. Decreasing communication among functions expedites maintenance, facilitates reuse, and decreases communication among programmers when the functions are written by different people (or by the same person at different periods of time). Make sure that you always check whether you have torn apart the pieces of code that should belong together.

Also, you should always think about the danger of excessive communications between functions. The best way to decrease coupling is to eliminate the need for communications by bringing together what should belong together.

How far should you go? Does it make sense to move the prompt and the definition of variable `year` in `isLeap()`? That would further decrease data flow between the functions. However, it would require communication among programmers about the user interface—what function is responsible for what part of the user interface. This would manifest itself in reduced cohesion of function `isLeap()`: it would combine computations with input/output.

In Listing 8.5, `main()` is responsible for user interface, and `isLeap()` is responsible for computations. Tearing user interface apart is as detrimental as tearing apart computations. Make sure that the area of responsibility of each function is clearly defined.

Further improvements to this example might include the elimination of variable `remainder` along the lines discussed in Chapter 4.

```
bool isLeap(int year)
   { if (year % 4 || year%100==0 && year%400!=0)
        return false;
     else
        return true; }
```

If you like really tight code, you can implement it in the following way.

```
bool isLeap(int year)
   { return (year % 4 || year%100==0 && year%400) }
```

As I mentioned in Chapter 4 (see the appropriate Russian joke there), I am not sure whether these improvements are worth the trouble. At any rate, they do not affect coupling because they do not change the division of jobs among the functions.

Alert

Often, coupling is increased when developers put in different functions; the operations that should be implemented in the same function. This increases communication among developers and impedes maintenance and reuse. Make sure that you think about this danger all the time.

Data Encapsulation

In C++, as in other languages, the programmers hide the complexity of computer algorithms in functions. Each function is a collection of statements directed toward achieving a specific goal. The name of the function usually reflects this goal. It is common to compose the function name using two components, an active verb that describes the action and the noun that describes the object (or is it the subject?) of the action, for example, `processTransaction()`, `acceptInput()`, and so on. When the object of the action is clear from the context (e.g., when it is passed to the function as a parameter), only a verb can be used, for example, `add()`, `delete()`, and so on.

The collection of statements in the function can contain simple assignments, complex control constructs, or calls to other functions. These other functions can be either library functions or programmer-defined functions that are custom-made for this particular project.

From the programmer's point of view, the difference between these two kinds of functions is that the implementation source code of programmer-defined functions is available for inspection and the source code of library functions is not. Even when the library source code is available, the client programmer does not want to expand his or her scope of attention by studying it. What the client programmer wants to know is the description of the server function interface: what parameters the caller code should supply, what values the function computes, how the output values are related to the input values, and what restrictions and exceptions apply. This enables the programmer to select the appropriate library function and use it correctly.

The programmer-defined functions are usually designed, not selected. The source code for these functions is often modified to better suit the needs of the client functions. These functions are not as well tested as library functions are. When a problem arises, it can be either in a client function or in any of the server functions. Hence, the client programmer (and maintainer) has to study the source code of related functions—clients and servers—together. This makes the task of the client programmer (and maintainer) more complex than when using library functions. It is desirable to design programmer-defined functions so that this component of program complexity is minimized. The concept of data encapsulation is one of the concepts that help the programmer to achieve this task. After the server functions are sufficiently tested, they are treated by the client programmer (and maintainer) similarly to library functions, as black boxes with a specified interface.

Let us consider a simple example: a part of a graphics package that deals with geometric shapes, for example, cylinders. For simplicity of the example, let us assume that each cylinder object can be characterized by two `double` values only, radius and height of the cylinder.

```
struct Cylinder {
  double radius, height; } ;
```

The program prompts the user to enter the dimensions of two cylinders. If the volume of the first cylinder is less than the volume of the second cylinder, the program scales the first cylinder up by increasing each of its dimensions by 20% and prints the final dimensions of the first cylinder. In real life, this code could be part of a program that uses cylinder objects to describe heat exchange in a chemical reactor, to study the flow of electric current in a microchip, or to analyze a steel building framework. Listing 8.6 shows the source code, Figure 8–6 gives an example of the program run.

Listing 8.6   Example of direct access to underlying data representation.

```
#include <iostream>                          // no encapsulation yet
using namespace std;

struct Cylinder {                            // data structure to access
  double radius, height; } ;

int main()
{
  Cylinder c1, c2;                           // program data
  cout << "Enter radius and height of the first cylinder:  ";
  cin >> c1.radius >> c1.height;             // initialize first cylinder
  cout << "Enter radius and height of the second cylinder: ";
  cin >> c2.radius >> c2.height;             // initialize second cylinder
  if (c1.height*c1.radius*c1.radius*3.141593     // compare volumes
    < c2.height*c2.radius*c2.radius*3.141593)
  { c1.radius *= 1.2;  c1.height *= 1.2;     // scale it up and
    cout << "\nFirst cylinder changed size\n";   // print new size
    cout <<"radius: "<<c1.radius<<" height: "<<c1.height<<endl; }
  else                                       // otherwise do nothing
    cout << "\nNo change in first cylinder size" << endl;
  return 0;
}
```

Here, the `main()` function accesses `Cylinder` data representation directly, without the help of any server functions. In doing so, it mixes access to data (e.g., `c1.radius` in the source code) with data manipulation (e.g., computing volume, scaling size, or printing cylinder data). As the result, the maintenance programmer has to figure out the meaning of operations in the code rather than recognize it from the names of server functions.

Figure 8–6   Output for program in Listing 8.6.

```
Enter radius and height of the first cylinder:  50 40
Enter radius and height of the second cylinder: 70 40

First cylinder changed size
radius: 60 height: 48
```

Of course, the code designer can supply comments that explain the meaning of the code, similar to what I did in Listing 8.6. However, the comments that somebody else made are often not clear enough for the reader. Or they are missing. Or, worse yet, the designer did not have time to update the comments when the source code changed.

A solution to this problem is to find a set of server functions that access the fields of the Cylinder structure on behalf of the client code. By "pushing the responsibility" for doing computations "down to server functions," you purge the client code from the low-level details of the computations. The high-level meaning of computations, however, is preserved in the names of the server functions that are called by the client code. As a result, the client code becomes self-explanatory: The reader of the client code understands *what* is being done by the client function, even if it is not clear exactly *how* this is done by the server functions.

```
int main()                              // pushing responsibility to servers
{
  Cylinder c1, c2;                      // program data
  enterData(c1,"first");                // initialize first cylinder
  enterData(c2,"second");               // initialize second cylinder
  if (getVolume(c1) < getVolume(c2))    // compare volumes
    { scaleCylinder(c1,1.2);            // scale it up and
      printCylinder(c1); }              // print new size
  else                                  // otherwise do nothing
      cout << "No change in first cylinder size" << endl;
  return 0;
  }
```

To understand the meaning of this version of main(), it is not really important to understand how the server functions enterData(), getVolume(), scaleCylinder(), and printCylinder() do their job. The line comments in this version of the client code are the same as in Listing 8.6 that did not use the access functions. Unlike in Listing 8.6, in this version of the client code, these line comments are not helpful at all. They just repeat what the names of the server functions say when they are called from the client code. This is one of the important advantages of "pushing responsibility from client code down to the server functions," an important principle that I formulated at the beginning of this chapter.

With the traditional approach to programming, line comments are important. If the code does not have line comments, the programmer should be asked to go back and add them. With data encapsulation, when details of the computations are pushed into the server functions, the client code does not need line comments: The meaning of processing is clear from the names of the server functions used in the function calls. If the client code is still obscure without line comments, that means that the server functions are not designed well—the programmer should be asked to go back and redesign the code (not to add comments).

Another problem with the coding style that mixes access to data with computations over data values is that data validation is obscure and awkward. Often it is omitted. For example, the first version of the code (Listing 8.6) did not do any data validation. In this example, the input data comes from the user, and the program has to be protected from user errors. In real life, the input data might come from an external file or from a communication line, and these sources of data are as likely to produce corrupt data as a human user is. But even the crudest form of error recovery, for example, setting the cylinder fields to default values, obscures the client code.

```
int main()
{ Cylinder c1, c2;                                   // program data
  cout << "Enter radius and height of the first cylinder:  ";
  cin >> c1.radius >> c1.height;                     // initialize first cylinder
  if (c1.radius < 0) c1.radius = 10;                 // defaults for corrupted data
  if (c1.height < 0) c1.height = 20;
  cout << "Enter radius and height of the second cylinder: ";
  cin >> c2.radius >> c2.height;                     // initialize second cylinder
  if (c2.radius < 0) c2.radius = 10;                 // defaults for corrupted data
  if (c2.height < 0) c2.height = 20;
  if (c1.height*c1.radius*c1.radius*3.141593         // compare volumes
     < c2.height*c2.radius*c2.radius*3.141593)
  { c1.radius *= 1.2;   c1.height *= 1.2;            // scale it up and
    cout << "\nFirst cylinder changed size\n";       // print new size
    cout <<"radius: "<<c1.radius<<" height: "<<c1.height<<endl; }
  else                                               // otherwise do nothing
    cout << "\nNo change in first cylinder size" << endl;
  return 0;
}
```

Using access functions allows you to eliminate this low-level data validation from the client code. This could be done by using, for example, a function validateCylinder( ), which sets the cylinder fields to default values if the input values are negative. Listing 8.7 shows this version of the program. The output of this program is the same as the version in Listing 8.6.

Listing 8.7 **Example of using access functions to insulate client code from the names of data fields.**

```cpp
#include <iostream>                    // encapsulation with server functions
using namespace std;

struct Cylinder {                      // data structure to access
    double radius, height; } ;

void enterData(Cylinder &c, char number[])
{ cout << "Enter radius and height of the ";
  cout << number << " cylinder:  ";
  cin >> c.radius >> c.height; }       // initialize cylinder

void validateCylinder(Cylinder c)
{ if (c.radius < 0) c.radius = 10;     // defaults for corrupted data
  if (c.height < 0) c.height = 20; }

double getVolume(const Cylinder& c)    // compute volume
{ return c.height * c.radius * c.radius * 3.141593; }

void scaleCylinder(Cylinder &c, double factor)
{ c.radius *= factor;  c.height *= factor; }     // scale dimensions

void printCylinder(const Cylinder &c)    // print object state
{ cout << "radius: " <<c.radius << " height: " <<c.height <<endl; }

int main()                             // pushing responsibility to server functions
{
   Cylinder c1, c2;                    // program data
   enterData(c1,"first");              // initialize first cylinder
   validateCylinder(c1);               // defaults for corrupted data
   enterData(c2,"second");             // initialize second cylinder
   validateCylinder(c2);               // defaults for corrupted data
   if (getVolume(c1) < getVolume(c2))  // compare volumes
     { scaleCylinder(c1,1.2);          // scale it up and
       cout << "\nFirst cylinder changed size\n";      // print size
     printCylinder(c1); }
   else                                // otherwise do nothing
     cout << "No change in first cylinder size" << endl;
   return 0;
   }
```

You see that indeed this new method of programming results in more source code. For real-time systems, additional function calls can affect performance. Using inline functions eliminates this problem.

The advantage of this approach is two distinct areas of attention, one related to the design of the programmer-defined type Cylinder and its access functions and another related to the client code that uses `Cylinder` objects and calls `Cylinder` access functions. With traditional programming (as in Listing 8.6), distinct areas of attention do not exist. If the names of fields of the programmer-defined type `Cylinder` structure change, the whole code has to be inspected, because these names can be used any place in the program. With new programming (as in Listing 8.7), the change in `Cylinder` field names will affect the access functions only—a well-defined set of functions. The rest of the program, however large the program may be, is not affected. Figure 8–7 illustrates this relationship between the client and the server code in the form of the structure chart. The client `main()` calls its server functions that access the fields of `Cylinder` objects. These server functions encapsulate the client function from the `Cylinder` design.

Data encapsulation is a relatively new concept and it is not yet well understood. Many programmers think that data encapsulation is about using functions to protect data from erroneous or unauthorized changes. Without data encapsulation, client code can change the data at will and inconspicuously, accessing data fields directly by name. With data encapsulation, client code calls the access functions, for example, `scaleCylinder()`, and it is these access functions that change the data fields.

This concern for data protection is similar to the concern about the harm from using global variables: If global names are available to the whole program, someone could set the values of these variables incorrectly and hurt other parts of the program. Similarly, if the names of data fields are available to the whole program, the same thing could happen. Passing parameters protects global variables. Encapsulation protects data fields.

These ideas about data protection are passed from one generation of programmers to another because they sound simple and reasonable and it is easier to accept them than to go against the consensus. I would like to voice my

Figure 8–7   Structure chart for program in Listing 8.7.

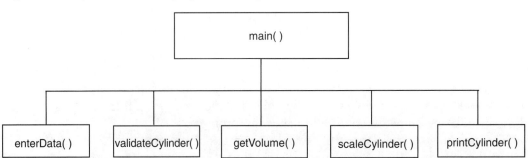

objections. While data protection is indeed a part of the story, it is a minor part. Data encapsulation is more about readability and independence of program components, that is, about the major theme of this chapter.

Indeed, passing parameters does not protect variables. If somebody erroneously thinks that a variable has to be set to a new value, it can be set using direct assignment (if it is a global variable) or as an assignment to a parameter (if it is passed as a reference or a pointer parameter). Similarly, if somebody erroneously thinks that `c1.radius` should get a new value, this can be done using direct assignment (if encapsulation is not used) or calling an access function, for example, `setCylinder()`, if encapsulation is used. There is no difference.

The real explanation is in the principle of the separation of concerns that I formulated in the beginning of this chapter. During maintenance, this separation of concerns for client code and for access functions is important for both global variables and for data fields. If you need to change the use or the name of a global variable, you have to search all program files for possible dependencies, because any file could use or change the global value. There is no clearly defined and relatively small area of concern—the span of a maintainer's attention is the whole program. This is labor intensive and prone to error.

Similarly, if you change the name or the type of a data field in a program that does not encapsulate its data, you have to search all program files for possible dependencies, because any file could use or change the field values. Again, there is no clearly defined and relatively small area of concern—the span of a maintainer's attention is the whole program.

Notice that I am not complaining that making changes in the code is too much work. After all, how much time do we spend writing or changing code? It is always the easiest and shortest part of the development effort. I am complaining that there are no clearly labeled parts of the program that you can inspect for changes when the design of the cylinder (or any other data structure) changes. It is finding all the places that have to be changed, and making sure that unintended side effects are not introduced, that makes maintenance so error prone and expensive.

When we use encapsulation, it is the set of access functions that has to be changed when we change the name or the type of a data field. All other parts of the program are not affected. Those parts of the program that call access functions have to be recompiled, but their source code does not change. Hence, the scope of attention of the maintainer is relatively narrow—it is limited to code that is concerned with the names of data fields. This is the real advantage of encapsulation: by not using the names of data fields directly, the client code avoids developing dependencies on data design.

It is important to learn to think about code design in terms of data encapsulation. When you do that, you create two separate areas of concern: segments of code that do and do not use the names of data fields.

But using access functions in and of itself does not necessarily improve readability and independence of code components. This is why you need yet another criterion to judge the quality of code—information hiding.

Information Hiding

The concept of information hiding is also related to the principle of separation of concerns. Normally, without information hiding, the programmer who writes the code (or the person who maintains the code) has to keep in mind two sets of design decisions, or two sets of knowledge, simultaneously. One set of knowledge and concerns is about the design of data (e.g., type `Cylinder`), and another set of knowledge is about the application-related manipulation of data (setting fields, comparing volumes, scaling sizes, etc.).

With information hiding, the areas of concern are separate. The programmer who writes (or maintains) the client code is concerned only with application-related manipulations of data, not with data design. The programmer who writes (or maintains) the data access functions is concerned only with data design, not with application-related manipulations of data.

If this sounds similar to the concept of data encapsulation, you have it right. I have to admit that most definitions of information hiding I have read are vague and nonoperational; they do not explain how to distinguish information hiding from encapsulation, how to recognize the lack of information hiding, or how to implement information hiding. Most people tacitly assume that information hiding is the same as encapsulation.

The concept of encapsulation is narrower—we want the names and types of data fields to be encapsulated from the client code so that the client code will not explicitly mention the names of underlying data fields. In our example, it will mean that the client code shall not mention `c1.radius`, `c1.height`, and so on explicitly, as I did in the snippet of code above. Encapsulation through the use of access functions improves the quality of code: its readability and independence of components.

How is information hiding different from encapsulation? Before I answer this question, let us consider an example of encapsulation that is not very effective. Try to implement encapsulation by introducing server functions that perform operations on a `Cylinder` object, for example, returning the values of `Cylinder` fields or setting the `Cylinder` dimensions. These server functions are also called access functions because they access cylinder data on behalf of their client code. The term "access" does not distinguish between different types of access—these functions can either retrieve field values or modify them.

```
void setRadius(Cylinder &c, double r)      // modifier function
{ c.radius = r; }

void setHeight(Cylinder &c, double h)      // modifier function
{ c.height = h; }

double getRadius(const Cylinder& c)        // selector function
{ return c.radius; }

double getHeight(const Cylinder& c)        // selector function
{ return c.height; }
```

The `main()` function does not have to use the names of cylinder components; if they change, it is the functions `setRadius()`, `setHeight()`, `getRadius()`, and `getHeight()` that have to change, not `main()` or any other client of `Cylinder`. Listing 8.8 shows the use of these access functions. The output of this program is the same as the output of the code in Listing 8.6—I changed the design of the code but not its functionality.

Listing 8.8   Example of ineffective encapsulation.

```
#include <iostream>                        // awkward encapsulation
using namespace std;

struct Cylinder {                          // data structure to access
    double radius, height; } ;

void setRadius(Cylinder &c, double r)      // modifier
{ c.radius = r; }

void setHeight(Cylinder &c, double h)      // modifier
{ c.height = h; }

double getRadius(const Cylinder& c)        // accessor
{ return c.radius; }

double getHeight(const Cylinder& c)        // accessor
{ return c.height; }

int main()
{
```

```
Cylinder c1, c2;   double radius, height;          // program data
cout << "Enter radius and height of the first cylinder:  ";
cin >> radius >> height;                            // initialize data
setRadius(c1,radius); setHeight(c1,height);
if (getRadius(c1)<0) setRadius(c1,10);             // verify data
if (getHeight(c1)<0) setHeight(c1,20);
cout << "Enter radius and height of the second cylinder: ";
cin >> radius >> height;                            // initialize data
setRadius(c2,radius); setHeight(c2,height);
if (getRadius(c2)<0) setRadius(c2,10);             // verify data
if (getHeight(c2)<0) setHeight(c2,20);
if (getHeight(c1)*getRadius(c1)*getRadius(c1)*3.141593
  < getHeight(c2)*getRadius(c2)*getRadius(c2)*3.141593)
{ setRadius(c1,getRadius(c1)*1.2);
  setHeight(c1,getHeight(c1)*1.2);                  // scale up
  cout << "\nFirst cylinder changed size\n";        // print new size
  cout <<"radius: "<<c1.radius<<" height: "<<c1.height<<endl; }
else                                                // otherwise do nothing
  cout << "No change in first cylinder size" << endl;
return 0;
}
```

You see that indeed the `main()` function is encapsulated from `Cylinder` data field names. If these names change in the process of redesign, there is a limited and easily identified set of access functions that have to be changed. No other place in the program, even if the program is very large, has to be modified or even inspected. It has to be recompiled, but this is a different story. Figure 8–8 shows the object diagram for this design. Similar to the object diagram that I introduced in Chapter 1, "Object-Oriented Approach: What's So Good About It?" (Figure 1–7), this diagram demon-

Figure 8–8   Object diagram for program in Listing 8.8.

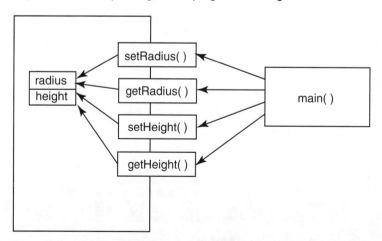

strates that server functions `setRadius()`, `setHeight()`, `getRadius()`, and `getHeight()` conceptually belong together. They access `Cylinder` fields `radius` and `height` on behalf of the client code. The client code accesses server data only through calls to the server access functions, not directly.

However, the encapsulation here is awkward. Actually, it is useless. The design principles listed at the beginning of this chapter are not used. The access functions do little for achieving the goals of the client code: The responsibility for data manipulation is not pushed to the server functions, it remains with the client. Despite the use of access functions, the `main()` client code mixes access to data, for example, calls to `getRadius()` with data manipulation, so that the meaning of computations (computing volume, scaling the size) is not easy to grasp. If the number of fields of the programmer-defined type `Cylinder` changes, the number of access functions will change, too, and the client code has to be modified as well.

To correctly choose the set of access server functions, you have to take into account the responsibilities of the client code. In this example, the client code is responsible for initializing cylinder objects, validating object data, computing cylinder volume, scaling cylinder size, and displaying cylinder attributes. Let us design access functions that do exactly that: `setCylinder()`, `validateCylinder()`, `getVolume()`, `scaleCylinder()`, and `printCylinder()`.

With these access functions, you push responsibility down from the client code to the server code. It is the server functions that set cylinder fields, validate cylinder data, compute volume, change size, and display cylinder data. The client code only requests these operations. As a result, the operations in `main()` are expressed in terms of function calls to servers.

The mix of access to data with data manipulation disappears. The client code specifies *what* should be done (set data fields, compute volume, etc.) The server code specifies *how* this is done. The `Cylinder` data representation is encapsulated: If the field names change, the client code is not affected. If you add more fields to the `Cylinder` design, the client code is not affected. (Well, for that to be entirely true, the input operations have to be encapsulated as well.)

The knowledge shared by client designers and server designers is limited to the names and interfaces of server functions. The areas of concern for client programmers and server programmers are separate: one encompasses high-level application-related operations, another is limited to data field names and low-level computations.

Even for this tiny example, you see the advantages of using access functions. The client code is expressed in terms of meaningful application-related operations. What does `c1.height*c1.radius*c1.radius*3.141593` mean in

Listing 8.6? The maintenance programmer has to figure that out. The same is true about the statements `c1.radius* = 1.2;` and `c1.height* = 1.2`—do all dimensions of the cylinder change? Is the factor the same for all dimensions? In printing statements, are all cylinder dimensions displayed or only some? When the access to data and the application-related operations are intermixed, it is more difficult to figure out the meaning of processing.

Using access functions also makes validation of user input easier—the `main()` function is not cluttered by details of validation. If the data representation (cylinder design or just field names) changes, it is the server functions that have to change. As I mentioned earlier, this is not just a matter of labor needed for maintenance. It is a matter of attention span. Without access function, the potential area of change is the whole program. (Cylinders could be used anywhere.) With access functions, the potential area of change is well defined—it includes functions that access the cylinder data representation.

This approach promotes reusability. Without access functions, any algorithm that uses cylinder objects has to be written and verified from scratch. With access functions, new algorithms can be written in terms of function calls to them. Each of these operations has to be verified only once.

The drawback of this approach is that you have to write and test more source code. One can argue, however, that this is actually an additional advantage. In the total balance of time, typing code takes a small fraction. All other development steps require reading the code—debugging, testing, integration, and maintenance. Writing client code in terms of function calls to access functions (which are already written and tested) makes these steps easier, less error prone, and less expensive.

So, what does the criterion of information hiding add to data encapsulation? Let us look again at the server functions `validateCylinder()` and `getVolume()`. The first function encapsulates the validation operations, default values, and the like. This is good, because the client code does not need to know the details of validation; it is enough to know that validation is done. The second function encapsulates the geometrical computations. This is also good, because the client code need not be concerned with the rules of geometry; it is enough for it to know that the cylinder volume is computed.

Both of these functions are no good from the point of view of information hiding. They expand the client designer's knowledge about the design of the server, enlarge the client designer's attention span, and bring information to the client code for manipulation instead of manipulating it in the server code.

The first function, `validateCylinder()`, betrays the need for data validation—it should not be within the span of attention of the client code designer and maintainer. This can be eliminated by redesign, that is, by changing the list of functions and their responsibilities. A good solution to this problem is to merge functions `validateCylinder()` and `enterData()`.

```
void enterData(Cylinder &c, char number[])
{ cout << "Enter radius and height of the ";
  cout << number << " cylinder:   ";
  cin >> c.radius >> c.height;           // initialize cylinder
  if (c.radius < 0) c.radius = 10;       // defaults for corrupted data
  if (c.height < 0) c.height = 20; }
```

As you see again and again, the criteria of cohesion, coupling, encapsulation, and information hiding are not operational. They signal the existence of a design drawback, but they do not indicate in what directions you should change the design to eliminate the drawback. The principles listed at the beginning of this chapter are operational: They indicate how to change the design. In this example, information hiding is improved by pushing responsibility to server functions. Instead of forcing the client code to call two server functions, `enterData()` and `validateCylinder()`, this design requires the client code to call only one access function.

The function `getVolume()` violates the principle of pushing responsibilities to server functions by giving the client code more information than it needs. The client code needs to know whether one cylinder is larger than another. Instead of serving this client need, the server code returns the computed value of the volume of the cylinder and lets the client code do with this value whatever the client likes. Information about the cylinder volume should be hidden from the client code. To serve this client need, I should change the design, introducing, for example, function `firstIsSmaller()`.

```
bool firstIsSmaller(const Cylinder& c1, const Cylinder& c2)
{ if (c1.height*c1.radius*c1.radius*3.141593       // compare volumes
    < c2.height*c2.radius*c2.radius*3.141593)
    return true;
  else
    return false; }
```

Listing 8.9 shows the version of the source code that combines proper encapsulation with information hiding. Notice that the functionality of the code remained the same for all versions of the program. It is the design that I changed, and it is the design that affects the quality of the code. The output of the program is the same as the output of the program in Listing 8.6.

Listing 8.9   Combining encapsulation and information hiding.

```
#include <iostream>
using namespace std;

struct Cylinder {                                // data structure to access
    double radius, height; } ;

void enterData(Cylinder &c, char number[])
{ cout << "Enter radius and height of the ";
  cout << number << " cylinder:   ";
  cin >> c.radius >> c.height;                   // initialize cylinder
  if (c.radius < 0) c.radius = 10;               // defaults for corrupted data
  if (c.height < 0) c.height = 20; }

bool firstIsSmaller(const Cylinder& c1, const Cylinder& c2)
{ if (c1.height*c1.radius*c1.radius*3.141593     // compare volumes
      < c2.height*c2.radius*c2.radius*3.141593)
    return true;
  else
    return false; }

void scaleCylinder(Cylinder &c, double factor)
{ c.radius *= factor;  c.height *= factor; }     // scale dimensions

void printCylinder(const Cylinder &c)            // print object state
{ cout << "radius: " <<c.radius << " height: " <<c.height <<endl; }

int main()                          // pushing responsibility to server functions
{
  Cylinder c1, c2;                               // program data
  enterData(c1,"first");                         // initialize first cylinder
  enterData(c2,"second");                        // initialize second cylinder
  if (firstIsSmaller(c1,c2))
    { scaleCylinder(c1,1.2);                     // scale it up and
      cout << "\nFirst cylinder changed size\n"; // print new size
      printCylinder(c1); }
  else                                           // otherwise do nothing
      cout << "\nNo change in first cylinder size" << endl;
  return 0;
  }
```

Figure 8–9 shows the object diagram for this design. Similar to the previous figure, it shows that functions enterData(), firstIsSmaller(), scaleCylinder(), and printCylinder() belong together. Here, the server serves the client code better because the access functions do the work for the client code rather than bring information to the client for further manipulation.

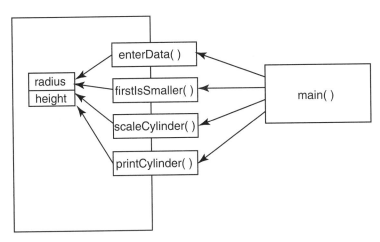

Figure 8-9   Object diagram for program in Listing 8.9.

A Larger Example of Encapsulation

The next example is input expression verification. Again, for simplicity sake, I will limit the functionality of the example to verifying whether parentheses and brackets in the input expression properly match each other. Let us consider a function `checkParen()` that scans the characters of the expression in a null-terminated array one-by-one until it either finds the terminating null (end of expression) or it discovers a parenthesis or a bracket that does not have a match. For example, the expression `a = (x[i] + 5)*y` should be recognized as a valid expression, and the expression `a = (x[i] + 5]*y` should be declared invalid.

The example will use two global arrays, `buffer[ ]` and `store[ ]`. Index `i` retrieves a character from array `buffer[ ]`, and index `idx` retrieves a character from array `store[ ]`. The flag `valid` will be returned by the code. It is initially set to 1 (true). If in the process of verification the expression will prove invalid, this flag will be set to 0 (false). In a loop, the code will inspect the next character in array `buffer[ ]`. If it is a left symbol (a parenthesis or a bracket), the decision should be deferred until the matching right symbol is found; so the code will save the character in array `store[ ]` (and will adjust array index `idx`).

```
char buffer[81];  char store[81];
bool checkParen ()
{ char c, sym; int i, idx; bool valid;
   i = 0; idx = 0; valid = true;          // initialize data
   while (buffer[i] != '\0' && valid)     // end of data or error?
     { c = buffer[i];                     // get next symbol
       if (c=='(' || c=='[')              // is next symbol left?
         { store[idx] = c;  idx++; }      // then save it away
// THE REST OF THE CODE
   return valid; }
```

If the next character in array `buffer[ ]` is a right symbol (a parenthesis or a bracket), the code will retrieve the last symbol stored in the array `store[ ]` (again, adjusting array index `idx`). At this moment, the program can check whether the two symbols match. That is, if the symbol in array `buffer[ ]` is a right parenthesis, the symbol in array `store[ ]` should be a left parenthesis, not a left bracket; similarly, if the symbol in array `buffer[ ]` is a right bracket, the symbol in array `store[ ]` should be a left bracket, not a left parenthesis. If the two symbols match, there is nothing to do; the code will go to the next character in array `buffer[ ]`. If the two symbols do not match, the expression is invalid: The code will set the flag `valid` to `false`; this will terminate the loop, and the zero value will be returned to the client code.

```
char buffer[81];  char store[81];
bool checkParen ()
{ char c, sym; int i, idx; bool valid;
   i = 0; idx = 0; valid = 1;             // initialize data
   while (buffer[i] != '\0' && valid)     // end of data or error?
     { c = buffer[i];                     // get next symbol
        if (c=='(' || c=='[')             // is next symbol left?
          { store[idx] = c;  idx++; }     // then save it away
        else if (c==')' || c==']')        // is next symbol right?
          { idx--;  sym = store[idx];     // get the last symbol
            if (!((sym=='(' && c==')') ||
                  (sym=='[' && c==']')))   // if they do not match
              valid = false; }            // then it is an error
// THE REST OF THE CODE
   return valid; }
```

Of course, this approach is too simplistic. How does the code know that there is always a symbol in array `store[]` for matching the right symbol found in array `buffer[ ]`? If the input expression has several right parentheses that are not matched by preceding left parentheses, array `store[ ]` will be depleted, its index `idx` will become negative, and we should declare the expression invalid.

```
char buffer[81];  char store[81];
int checkParen ()
{ char c, sym; int i, idx; bool valid;
   i = 0; idx = 0; valid = 1;           // initialize data
   while (buffer[i] != '\0' && valid != 0)  // end of data or error?
   { c = buffer[i];                     // get next symbol
      if (c=='(' || c=='[')             // is next symbol left?
         { store[idx] = c;  idx++; }    // then save it away
      else if (c==')' || c==']')        // is next symbol right?
         if (idx > 0)                   // does saved symbol exist?
            { idx--;  sym = store[idx]; // get the last symbol
               if (!((sym=='(' && c==')') ||
                   (sym=='[' && c==']')))  // if they do not match
                  valid = 0; }          // then it is an error
         else
            valid = 0;        // if no saved symbol to match, it is an error
// THE REST OF THE CODE
   return valid; }                      // return the error status
```

We are almost there. We decided what to do if the next character in the array buffer[ ] is a left symbol, and what to do if it is a right symbol; if it is neither a right nor a left symbol, we should simply go to the next character in array buffer[ ], that is, just to increment its index i.

```
char buffer[81];  char store[81];
bool checkParen ()
{ char c, sym; int i, idx; bool valid;
   i = 0; idx = 0; valid = true;        // initialize data
   while (buffer[i] != '\0' && valid)   // end of data or error?
   { c = buffer[i];                     // get next symbol
      if (c=='(' || c=='[')             // is next symbol left?
         { store[idx] = c;  idx++; }    // then save it away
      else if (c==')' || c==']')        // is next symbol right?
         if (idx > 0)                   // does saved symbol exist?
            { idx--;  sym = store[idx]; // get the last symbol
               if (!((sym=='(' && c==')') ||
                   (sym=='[' && c==']')))  // if they do not match
                  valid = false; }      // then it is an error
         else
            valid = false;         // an error if no saved symbol to match
i++; }                                  // go get next symbol
// SOMETHING TO WORRY ABOUT AFTER THE END OF THE LOOP
   return valid; }                      // return the error status
```

There is one more thing to take care of in this code. If at the end of the loop the flag valid is set to false, this value should be returned to the caller, no questions asked—the input expression is invalid. If, however, the flag remains true, the program should not hurry to pass the good news on to the caller. First, it should check whether there are any extra symbols left in array store[ ] that were not matched by right symbols in the expression. If this is the case (idx > 0), the expression is invalid and the flag valid should be set to false.

The checkParen() function along with its test driver is found in Listing 8.10. The number of if statements in this example is fairly large. It means that the function should be called more than once to demonstrate its correctness, and it pays to design a test harness that stands between the test driver and the function. The test harness checkParenTest() calls the function checkParen(), and prints the input expression and the result of the function execution. Figure 8–10 shows an example of program execution.

Listing 8.10   Example of direct access to underlying data representation.

```cpp
#include <iostream>                      // No encapsulation yet
#include <cstring>
using namespace std;

char buffer[81];   char store[81];       // global data

bool checkParen ()
{ char c, sym; int i, idx; bool valid;
  i = 0; idx = 0; valid = true;          // initialize data
  while (buffer[i] != '\0' && valid)     // end of data or error?
  { c = buffer[i];                       // get next symbol
    if (c=='(' || c=='[')                // is next symbol left?
      { store[idx] = c;  idx++; }        // then save it away
    else if (c==')' || c==']')           // is next symbol right?
      if (idx > 0)                       // does saved symbol exist?
      { idx--;   sym = store[idx];       // get the last symbol
        if (!((sym=='(' && c==')') ||
             (sym=='[' && c==']')))      // if they do not match
              valid = false; }           // then it is an error
      else
        valid = false;                   // error if no symbol to match
    i++; } // go get next symbol
  if (idx > 0) valid = false;            // unmatched left symbols: an error
  return valid; }                        // return the error status

void checkParenTest(char expression[])   // test harness
{ strcpy(buffer,expression);
  cout << "Expression " << buffer << endl; // print the expression
  if (checkParen())                      // validate it
    cout << "is valid\n";                // print the result
  else
    cout << "is not valid\n";
}
```

```
int main()                              // test driver
{ checkParenTest("a=(x[i]+5)*y;");      // first test run: valid
  checkParenTest("a=(x[i)+5]*y;");      // second test run: invalid
  return 0;
  }
```

Similar to the earlier examples in this chapter, I will try to encapsulate the code in `checkParen()` from the symbol representation. The algorithm for checking symbols does not depend on the specific symbols. For example, if the code should handle braces, the algorithm should be exactly the same. However, `checkParen()` has to be modified (along with other functions in the application) if the expressions processed by the application are to include braces (or other paired symbols). It will probably require a different name, since it will check more than parentheses.

The server functions have to encapsulate the client code from the details of how the left and the right symbols look and what the rules are for matching symbols. Here is an example of three access functions that do that job. I pass the index in the character array `buffer[ ]` to functions `isLeft()` and `isRight()` and they return true or false depending on what symbol is found under that index. For function `symbolsMatch()`, I pass two indices, to array `buffer[ ]` and to array `store[ ]`, and the function returns `true` or `false` depending on whether the symbols under these indices match.

```
bool isLeft (int i)
{ char c = buffer[i];                   // get symbol from buffer
   return (c=='(' || c=='['); }         // check if it is a left symbol

bool isRight (int i)
{ char c = buffer[i];                   // get symbol from buffer
   return (c==')' || c==']'); }         // check if it is a right symbol

bool symbolsMatch (int idx, int i)
{ char sym = store[idx], c = buffer[i]; // get two symbols to match
   return (sym=='('&&c==')')||(sym=='['&&c==']');} // do they match?
```

Listing 8.11 shows the version of the code that uses these access functions. If the application has to handle braces, it is access functions `isLeft()`, `isRight()` and `symbolsMatch()` that will change, not `checkParen()` or

```
Expression a=(x[i]+5)*y;
is valid
Expression a=(x[i)+5]*y;
is not valid
```

Figure 8–10
Output for program in Listing 8.10.

other client code. The output of this version of the program is the same as the output of the code in Listing 8.11.

Listing 8.11   Example of encapsulation with shared knowledge.

```
#include <iostream>                          // Bad distribution of knowledge
#include <cstring>
using namespace std;

char buffer[81];  char store[81];

bool isLeft (int i)
{ char c = buffer[i];                        // get symbol from buffer
  return (c=='(' || c=='['); }               // check if it is a left symbol

bool isRight (int i)
{ char c = buffer[i];                        // get symbol from buffer
  return (c==')' || c==']'); }               // check if it is a right symbol

bool symbolsMatch (int idx, int i)
{ char sym = store[idx], c = buffer[i];   // get two symbols to match
  return (sym=='('&&c==')')||(sym=='['&&c==']');}        // do they match?

bool checkParen ()
{ char c; int i, idx; bool valid;
  i = 0; idx = 0; valid = true;              // initialize data
  while (buffer[i] != '\0' && valid)         // end of data or error?
  { c = buffer[i];                           // get next symbol
    if (isLeft(i))                           // is next symbol left?
      { store[idx] = c;  idx++; }            // then save it away
    else if (isRight(i))                     // is next symbol right?
      if (idx > 0)                           // does saved symbol exist?
      { idx--;                               // get the last symbol
        if (!symbolsMatch(idx,i))            // if they do not match
            valid = false; }                 // then it is an error
      else
        valid = false;                       // error if no saved symbol to match
  i++; }                                      // go get next symbol
  if (idx > 0) valid = false;                // unmatched left symbols: an error
  return valid; }                            // return the error status

void checkParenTest(char expression[])       // test harness
{ strcpy(buffer,expression);
  cout << "Expression " << buffer << endl;   // print the expression
  if (checkParen())                          // validate it
    cout << "is valid\n";                    // print the result
  else
    cout << "is not valid\n"; }
```

```
int main()                              // test driver
{
  checkParenTest("a=(x[i]+5)*y;");      // first test run: valid
  checkParenTest("a=(x[i]+5]*y;");      // second test run: invalid
  return 0;
}
```

Is this good encapsulation? Not too good. Symbol representation is indeed hidden from the client code, but the server functions know more than the symbol representation and the rules for matching. They share with the client code the knowledge about array `buffer[ ]` and array `store[ ]`. The scopes of attention for client and for servers are not separate. There is no good reason for sharing this knowledge—it should belong to the client code only. As is commonly the case with shared knowledge, when the design changes, both groups of functions should be changed too. If I change the names of these arrays or switch from an array to a linked list representation, it is only `checkParen()` that should be affected. With this design, the symbol access functions have to be changed. If I decide that using a global array is not appropriate, even the interface of the symbol access functions will change—I will have to pass these arrays as parameters.

This is a relatively rare form of violation of information hiding. Usually, it is the client code that is exposed to excessive knowledge. As this example shows, the server code also can be exposed to excessive knowledge. The server functions should know about only one data structure, and hide this knowledge from everybody else.

To assure the quality of the C++ code you write, you should constantly think about shared knowledge. I know I told you that on another occasion, and I am going to do it again later.

To eliminate this drawback of shared knowledge, I redesign the program again, changing the distribution of responsibilities. I hide the array indices from server functions by passing to these functions the symbols themselves, not their indices. In this version, shown in Listing 8.12, the symbol access functions `isLeft()`, `isRight()`, and `symbolsMatch()` only know about the symbols, not about the way the client code stores these symbols. It is only the client code that knows about the arrays.

Listing 8.12   A better example of encapsulation.

```
#include <iostream>                              // Better distribution of knowledge
#include <cstring>
using namespace std;

bool isLeft (char c)
{ return (c=='(' || c=='['); }                   // check if it is a left symbol

bool isRight (char c)
{ return (c==')' || c==']'); }                   // check if it is a left symbol

bool symbolsMatch (char c, char sym)
{ return (sym=='('&&c==')')||(sym=='['&&c==']');}    // do they match?

bool checkParen (char buffer[])                  // expression in parameter
{ char store[81];                                // local array
  char c,sym; int i, idx; bool valid;
  i = 0; idx = 0; valid = true;                  // initialize data
  while (buffer[i] != '\0' && valid)             // end of data or error?
  { c = buffer[i];                               // get next symbol
    if (isLeft(c))                               // is next symbol left?
       { store[idx] = c;  idx++; }               // then save it away
    else if (isRight(c))                         // is next symbol right?
       if (idx > 0)                              // does saved symbol exist?
          { sym = store[-idx];                   // get the last symbol
             if (!symbolsMatch(c,sym))           // if they do not match
                   valid = false; }              // then it is an error
     else                                        
       valid = false;                            // error if no saved symbol to match
  i++; }                                         // go get next symbol
  if (idx > 0) valid = false;                    // unmatched left symbols: an error
  return valid; }                                // return error status

void checkParenTest(char expression[])
{ cout << "Expression " << expression << endl;   // print expression
  if (checkParen(expression))                    // validate it
          cout << "is valid\n";                  // print the result
  else
          cout << "is not valid\n"; }

int main()
{
  checkParenTest("a=(x[i]+5)*y;");               // first test run: valid
  checkParenTest("a=(x[i]+5]*y;");               // second test run: invalid;
  checkParenTest("a=(x(i]+5]*y;");               // third test run: invalid;
  return 0;
  }
```

In this version of the program, encapsulation is much better, and separation of concerns is more consistent. The client code knows about arrays and indices, and server functions know about symbols and rules for matching them.

The knowledge about one of the arrays, buffer[ ], is natural in the client code: this is the array that checkParen() processes, and encapsulating this array does not make much sense. If expression processing is done in stages, then this function checkParen() is one of the expression access functions that does expression validation and evaluation.

However, checkParen() uses another array, store[ ], and this array adds complexity to the client code. The programmer has to decide whether to initialize index idx to zero, one, or some other value. When a symbol is saved in the array, the programmer has to decide whether to save the symbol first and then to increment the index, or the other way around. When the symbol is retrieved from the array, the programmer again has to decide whether to get the symbol first and then to decrement the index or the other way around. (Notice that the answer to the last two questions is different.) Also, when checkParen() checks whether any unmatched symbols are left in array store[ ], the programmer has to decide whether the index should be compared to zero, one, or some other value.

These questions are not difficult to answer, because the example is small. Combined with other similar questions, they accumulate complexity and increase the possibility of an error at the development phase and, especially, at the maintenance phase. Most important, these issues have little to do with the algorithm that checkParen() implements—scanning symbols, saving left symbols and retrieving them back when right symbols are found. Each function should deal with only one nonencapsulated data structure, and this data structure for checkParen() is the array buffer[ ], not store[ ].

This is why the next step in the design of this example should be encapsulating array store[ ] and its index idx in a separate structure and providing access functions that can be used by checkParen() to access the components of this structure.

```
struct Store {
   char a[81];                 // array for temporary storage
   int idx; } ;                // index to first available slot

void initStore (Store &s)
   { s.idx = 0; }              // initialize the empty store

bool isEmpty (const Store& s)
   { return (s.idx == 0); }    // check whether the store is empty
```

```
void saveSymbol (Store &s, char x)
{ s.a[s.idx] = x;               // save the symbol in the store
  s.idx++; }

char getLast(Store &s)
{  s.idx-;                      // get back the last symbol saved
   return s.a[s.idx]; }
```

Experienced readers probably recognize this structure as a common stack implemented with a fixed-size array. If you are not familiar with this data structure, do not worry. This is not important. What is important is that the access functions insulate the client code from all details of data representation and allow it to express its algorithm in terms of function calls (see Listing 8.13).

Listing 8.13   Encapsulating temporary storage `store[ ]`.

```
#include <iostream>                    // Encapsulation with info hiding
#include <cstring>
using namespace std;

struct Store {
  char a[81];                          // array for temporary storage
  int idx; } ;                         // index to first available slot

void initStore (Store &s)
  { s.idx = 0; }                       // initialize the empty store

bool isEmpty (const Store& s)
  { return (s.idx == 0); }             // check whether the store is empty

void saveSymbol (Store &s, char x)
{ s.a[s.idx++] = x; }                  // save the symbol in the store

char getLast(Store &s)
{ return s.a[-s.idx]; }                // get back the last symbol saved

bool isLeft (char c)
{ return (c=='(' || c=='['); }         // check if it is a left symbol

bool isRight (char c)
{ return (c==')' || c==']'); }         // check if it is a left symbol

bool symbolsMatch (char c, char sym)
{ return (sym=='('&&c==')')||(sym=='['&&c==']');}     // do they match?
```

```
bool checkParen (char buffer[])              // expression in parameter
{ Store store;                               // array is encapsulated
  char c,sym; int i; bool valid;
  i = 0; initStore(store); valid = true;     // initialize data
  while (buffer[i] != '\0' && valid)         // end of data or error?
  { c = buffer[i];                           // get next symbol
    if (isLeft(c))                           // is next symbol left?
        { saveSymbol(store,c); }             // then save it away
    else if (isRight(c))                     // is next symbol right?
      if (!isEmpty(store))                   // does saved symbol exist?
      { sym = getLast(store);                // get the last symbol
        if (!symbolsMatch(c,sym))            // if they do not match
              valid = false; }               // then it is an error
      else
        valid = false;                       // error if no saved symbol to match
    i++; } // go get next symbol
    if (store.idx>0) valid=false;            // error: unmatched left symbols
    return valid; }                          // return the error status

void checkParenTest(char expression[])
{ cout << "Expression " << expression << endl;     // print expression
  if (checkParen(expression))                // validate it
          cout << "is valid\n";              // print the result
  else
          cout << "is not valid\n"; }

int main()
{ cout << endl << endl;
  checkParenTest("a=(x[i]+5)*y;");           // first test run: valid
  checkParenTest("a=(x[i)+5]*y;");           // second test run: invalid;
  checkParenTest("a=(x(i]+5]*y;");           // third test run: invalid;
  cout << endl << endl;
  return 0;
  }
```

When developing this example, I was trying to keep the line comments the same. What I would like you to do now is to go back to Listing 8.10 (the first version of this example) and compare that version with Listing 8.13. You will see that in the first, nonencapsulated version, the line comments are useful. They explain what the meaning of manipulating the data representation is. In the last, encapsulated version, the comments are useless. They just repeat what the code says. The meaning of the code is expressed in the names of the server function calls.

In this version of the code, there are no details of data manipulation to interfere with that meaning and to siphon away the attention of the developers and the maintainer. The scope of attention is divided into three narrow zones. No knowledge of data structures is shared between the client code and the server code. Responsibility for access to data is pushed to the server functions.

Shortcomings of Encapsulation with Functions

This is a great way to write software. However, there are a number of short-comings in implementing encapsulation and information hiding with functions only. It is these drawbacks that C++ tries to eliminate with the introduction of classes.

One drawback is that access functions do not indicate to the maintainer what the designer knows, that these functions belong together and access the same data structure. In the examples in this chapter, I was putting the server functions together into the same listing for everyone to see. A better solution is to put functions `isLeft()`, `isRight()`, and `symbolsMatch()` into one file (functions accessing symbols), and the functions `initStore()`, `isEmpty()`, `saveSymbol()`, and `getLast()` into another file (functions accessing tempo-rary storage).

In real life, functions accessing one data structure are often mixed with functions accessing other data structures, they are placed in alphabetical order by their names, and the relationship between the data structure and its access functions becomes dim. Even when the related functions are put together in a separate file without any extraneous functions, this solution is a managerial solution, not a language-supported solution. In C (and in other earlier languages), there is no language mechanism for indicating that some functions logically belong together but not with other functions. C++ offers an excellent solution—binding together the data and its related access func-tions within the boundary (curly braces) of the class. The very boundaries of the class indicate what functions and data belong together. The functions that belong together cannot be scattered among other nonrelated functions.

The second drawback of encapsulation with access functions is that encap-sulation is voluntary. The client programmer (or the maintainer) can use the access functions or can disregard access functions and directly access the struc-ture fields. The language rules do not prevent that. For example, at the end of `checkParen()` in Listing 8.13, I check whether any opening symbols were left on the store that were not matched during the call to `checkParen()`. The cor-rect way to do that is to use the access function `isEmpty()`.

```
if (!isEmpty(store)) valid=false;   // error: unmatched left symbols
```

Instead, I made a shortcut and used the name of the field `idx` of the structure of the programmer-defined type `Store`.

```
if (store.idx>0) valid=false;        // error: unmatched left symbols
```

All advantages of encapsulation went down the tubes. The meaning of the client code is not self-explanatory and has to be deduced from the comments and the context. The task of the maintainer is complicated by the need to deal with the mix of access to data and manipulation of the data. If the name of the data field `idx` were to change, for example, to `top` (a better and more commonly used name), the client code should be modified too. These dependencies between the client and the server code make the code more complex. This is why it is not nice to depend on the kindness of the programmer to provide data encapsulation. C++ resolves this problem by providing the code designer with the `private` access qualifier to make breaking encapsulation impossible.

The third drawback is that the access functions are global functions. Their names are part of the global name space and can conflict with other function names. Hence the programmers working on different parts of the program have to coordinate their actions to avoid name conflicts, and that forces the programmers to know more about other parts of the program than is necessary.

C++ resolves this problem by introducing the class scope in addition to the block, function, file, and program scope. Every name defined as a member of the class, be it a data member or a member function, is defined within the scope of the class. This eliminates name conflicts. The programmers do not have to know about the names used in other parts of the program if they do not have to use these names. This decreases the amount of coordination among programmers.

Yet another drawback is that many data structures have to be initialized explicitly by the client code. For example, the store variable in Listing 8.13 is initialized by an explicit call to function `initStore()`. This expands the scope of attention of the client maintainer and creates a possibility that data will be used without proper initialization.

C++ resolves this problem by pushing responsibilities from client code to server code with special functions: constructors. They are called implicitly every time an object of the class is created. In this function, the designer of the server class specifies how the class object will be initialized. In the division of responsibilities between a client programmer and a server programmer, this pushes the work down to the server programmer, making the server programmer responsible for initialization. This responsibility is thus removed from the designer of the client code. C++ also provides another type of special function, destructors, which are called implicitly when the class object is destroyed. These functions return dynamic memory and other resources that the object might acquire and remove the burden of returning resources from the client programmer.

There are also a number of other ways that C++ classes promote binding together data and operations, encapsulating the names of the server fields, hiding server design from client code, pushing responsibility from clients down to servers, and avoiding dependencies between client and server code.

C++ classes have a great potential for improving software quality, and they will be discussed in detail in the following chapters.

Summary

In this chapter, we looked at the use of C++ functions as a major program-building tool. For a given functionality of the program, there exist numerous ways of implementing that functionality in C++ code.

The goal of allocating jobs to functions is to arrive at a program whose functions can be understood and maintained in isolation from other functions and are easy to reuse in other contexts. Everything that requires the client designer (or maintainer) to read the code in several places for understanding and modification, impedes reuse and maintenance.

The criteria of readability and component independence are too general. For a practicing programmer, these criteria have to be supplemented by more-specific technical criteria. In this chapter, I discussed traditional criteria of cohesion and coupling and object-oriented criteria of encapsulation and information hiding. I also discussed new criteria, such as pushing job responsibilities from client functions to server functions, avoiding breaking apart the parts of functionality that should belong together in the same piece of code, the separation of concerns and limiting common knowledge between components, and passing the knowledge of the developer to the maintainer in code rather than in comments.

Cohesion describes how well the elements of the function belong together. Functions that exhibit good cohesion do one thing over one object. Functions with weak cohesion do several things. The remedy for weak cohesion is redesign: putting things that do not belong together into different functions instead of in the same function. Cohesion is not a sharp criterion and should be used as a supplement to other criteria.

Coupling describes the interface between a server function and its client functions. Loose coupling means that the functions are relatively independent. The strongest form of coupling is the use of global variables. They require coordination among developers who write client and server functions. The same names of global variables are used when functions are moved for reuse in other contexts. To analyze data flow between these functions, one has to study the whole code of both the client and the server functions.

Functions that communicate through parameters are easier to reuse. The developers have to coordinate the number and type of parameters but not parameter names. Data flow can be understood from the study of the function interface only, not the whole code. To reap the benefits of this approach, developers should use the guidelines for parameter passing presented in this and in previous chapters.

To reduce coupling, you reallocate jobs among functions so that the operations performed in different functions are moved to the same functions. This eliminates the reasons for additional communications between functions. Developers have to always keep an eye on checking what communications are needed and what communications could be avoided. This is a very important tool in the programmer's tool bag.

Encapsulation is a method of programming that insulates client functions from the names of data fields these client functions need. These fields are accessed by server functions on behalf of client functions. The code in client functions is expressed in terms of function calls to server functions, not in terms of data fields. Using this approach enhances maintainability because it creates two independent areas in the program. When the data design changes, access functions change and client functions stay the same. When the application functionality changes, the client functions change and the access functions stay the same. If encapsulation is not provided, every place in the code should be inspected for possible changes.

Information hiding is a method of programming that further insulates client functions from data representation. Access functions are chosen so that they do the work on behalf of the client functions. The client code is expressed in terms of calls to server functions, whose names describe the client code algorithm. This approach further enhances program maintainability and reusability.

When these techniques are used consistently, the client code becomes object oriented because it is expressed in terms of operations over data structures. However, object-oriented programming with functions leaves some issues unresolved. There is no language-level indication that the data and their access functions belong together; the maintainer has to figure out that relationship through code inspection. The names of access functions are global to the program scope, and name conflicts are possible. Encapsulation is voluntary and is based on a developer's discipline. If the developers of client functions use the names of data fields in client functions, the advantages of encapsulation disappear.

C++ resolves these issues by adding the class construct to the language. The class boundaries indicate that the data and functions belong together. Each class has its own separate scope, and access functions with the same name but in different classes do not conflict with each other. The class developer can indicate that data (and functions) are private and prevent direct access from the client functions.

This is very exciting! Using classes opens new horizons for writing high-quality programs. Starting with the next chapter, we will focus on C++ classes.

C++ CLASS
AS A UNIT OF
MODULARIZATION

Topics in this Chapter

Chapter

9

In the previous chapter, I formulated the basic principles of object-oriented programming using functions as program building blocks. With the
object-oriented approach to building programs, client code calls server
access functions instead of accessing and modifying data fields directly. Server
functions provide operations directed toward achieving the client code goals.
Responsibilities are allocated among functions so that client functions do not
know about data representation, and server functions do not know about
client code algorithms.

This creates independent areas of concern. When changing access functions, the maintainer does not have to introduce corresponding changes into
client functions (if the server interface does not change). When changing
client functions, the maintainer does not have to consider the details of data
processing in server functions—they will not require changes. The client code
is expressed in terms of function calls to server functions, not in terms of data
manipulation. Putting together what should belong together (instead of tearing it apart) makes functions independent from each other and further facilitates maintenance and reuse. The object diagrams I drew for the previous
chapter indicated that server functions logically belong with each other and
with the data they access.

I also admitted that using functions for implementing the object-oriented
approach relies on the voluntary efforts of the programmers. Server functions
can be placed in unrelated places in the source code, and the maintainer

might fail to notice that they are related to each other and to the data representation. Client functions can fail to use encapsulation; instead, they can access the data representation directly and create links and dependencies between different parts of the program.

Under time pressure or because of the narrow span of human attention, programmers can introduce dependencies among functions. Functions with mutual dependencies are difficult to develop because different programmers who work on different interdependent functions have to coordinate their activities, and it is the coordination of human activities that breaks down so often and so miserably.

Interdependent functions become more difficult to maintain because they require the maintainer to study these dependencies before making changes. These functions are more difficult to reuse, because they cannot be moved to another application alone; they need data and other functions to accompany them. This is why a programmer needs all the help from the programming language that she or he can master to avoid these pitfalls. To help the programmers to create better code, C++ offers a wonderful language construct, *class*, which physically binds together data representation and operations (functions) over that data that are otherwise bound together only conceptually, in the mind of the designer. This binding data and operations together supports the concepts of data encapsulation and information hiding.

In this chapter, I will take a close look at C++ classes. You will see class syntax and semantics and will learn how to define class members, both data members and member functions. I will explain how to specify access rights to class members; how to implement classes in one-file and multifile programs; how to define objects (class instances); and how to manipulate the objects, that is, how to send messages, pass them as parameters, and return them from functions.

I will also discuss special member functions, constructors and destructors, which are often misunderstood. I will further discuss the use of the `const` modifier discussed earlier in Chapter 7, "Programming with C++ Functions," to help the developer to pass on his or her knowledge at the time of design to the maintainer at the time of modification. Another special kind of data members and member functions is static data members and functions. Static members and functions help the designer to describe class characteristics that are common to all objects of the class.

This is an ambitious program. By the end of this chapter, you should feel comfortable using larger units of modularization (classes), instead of smaller units of modularization (functions). But you might also feel overwhelmed by the immense amount of technical detail you have to assimilate. This is natural. C++ is a large and complex language, and it takes time to get used to its concepts, practical details, and pitfalls. Anybody who promises you an easy way to learn C++ is either lying or does not realize the complexity of this task. If you feel overwhelmed and confused, do not dig your heels in—try the incremental approach to learning. Skip some parts of this chapter, read the next chapters, come back to this chapter for repeated reading. Modify its coding examples, experiment with different ways to say the same thing in C++ code, and you will see that there is a beautiful internal logic connecting different elements of C++ programming, and it is not difficult to use after all. But this feeling of ease will come only after extended practice.

It is important to come back to master the C++ basics of using classes. Many programmers jump over this phase and move on to more complex issues such as inheritance and polymorphism too quickly, without having a good foundation. They become confused even more and wind up writing programs that are hard to understand, maintain, and reuse. After all, C++ offers you only a set of tools. These tools might be misused (similar to guns, automobiles, or computers). Using these tools does not automatically guarantee good results. It is up to you, the programmer, to use this set of tools effectively. Good luck.

Basic Class Syntax

The goal of introducing classes in C++ is to render support to the practices of object-oriented programming and eliminate the drawbacks caused by using smaller units of modularity: functions.

The first primary goal of the class construct is to bind together data and operations into one syntactical unit, and to indicate that these coding elements belong together. The next primary goal is to eliminate name conflicts so that data and functions in different classes can use the same names without clashes. The third important goal of the class construct is to allow the server designer to control access to class elements from the outside (from the client code). The fourth goal is to support encapsulation, information hiding, pushing responsibilities from client code down to the server code, creating separate areas of concern and eliminating overlapping knowledge and coordination among programmers working on different parts of the program.

These goals are a natural extension of the practice of using functions for object-oriented programming. If you view C++ classes as yet another syntactic construct, not related to these four goals I described, the use of classes will not improve the quality of your code. Make sure that you pay sufficient attention to these four goals and try to achieve them every time you add a class to your program.

The class is the center of C++ and object-oriented programming. It gives a programmer the tools to create new data types that more closely match the behavior of real-world objects than functional programs do. Some experts say that it is the use of inheritance and polymorphism that is central to object-oriented programming. I disagree. There are many programs that do not benefit from the use of inheritance and polymorphism. However, every large C++ program benefits from the use of C++ classes if these classes are used correctly and achieve the four goals just outlined. A correctly designed C++ program is a combination of components (modules) that cooperate in performing their common task but are independent enough to be separately maintainable.

Binding Together Data and Operations

Structures also support the concept of binding by combining data fields. They allow you to combine different components into a composite data object. These composite objects can be manipulated as a whole, for example, sent as a parameter to a function, or they can provide access to their components individually.

A structure definition, however, models only a set of data but not their behavior. The server programmer provides the tools to manipulate the data, that is, a set of access functions to access and manipulate data on behalf of client functions. In "functional" or "procedural" programming, data and algorithms are syntactically separated. They are related together only in the mind of the programmer, not in code. In the examples that I discussed in Chapter 8, "Object-Oriented Programming with Functions," I used object diagrams to indicate that functions and data logically belong together.

When programs consist of functions, connections among different functions in the program are not evident; every function can access every piece of data in the program. That makes development and, especially, maintenance and reuse more difficult.

The only way to indicate that data are related to the code that works with the data is to put the data items and the function prototypes into the same header file or in a separately compiled source file. But a disk file is a hardware (or operating system) concept and not part of the language. This is why C++ expands the `struct` facility by binding together data members that contain values and member functions that operate on these values.

Resulting objects represent larger units of modularity. Client programmers focus on data and on related functions, not on stand-alone functions whose connections are not evident.

In a well-designed C++ program, class data is accessed by functions that belong only to that class. Client code is expressed in terms of operations rather than in access to data. This narrows the horizon of client designers and maintainers.

Formally, when you put together fields in a `struct` definition, you actually create a C++ class.

```
struct Cylinder {               // programmer-defined type (class)
   double radius, height;  } ;   // end of class scope
```

In C++, the keywords `struct` and `class` are synonymous (well, almost). For class `Cylinder` just defined, you can define objects (or instances or variables) of this class. You can set the values of object fields. You can either handle an object as a single entity (e.g., pass it as a function argument or store on a disk file) or use its individual parts in computations.

In the example that follows, the `main()` function defines two `Cylinder` objects (variables and instances), initializes them, and compares their volumes. If the volume of the first `Cylinder` object is less than the volume of the second `Cylinder` object, the first `Cylinder` is scaled up by 20%, and the new dimensions of the first `Cylinder` are printed. This is similar to the example I discussed at the beginning of Chapter 8.

```
int main()
{ Cylinder c1, c2;                               // program data
  c1.radius = 10; c1.height = 30; c2.radius = 20; c2.height = 30;
  cout << "\nInitial size of first cylinder\n";
  cout <<"radius: " <<c1.radius <<" height: " <<c1.height <<endl;
  if (c1.height*c1.radius*c1.radius*3.141593        // compare volumes
     < c2.height*c2.radius*c2.radius*3.141593)
  { c1.radius *= 1.2;  c1.height *= 1.2;            // scale it up and
    cout << "\nFirst cylinder changed size\n";      // print new size
    cout <<"radius: " <<c1.radius <<" height: " <<c1.height <<endl; }
  else                                             // otherwise do nothing
    cout << "\nNo change in first cylinder size" << endl;
  return 0; }
```

In this code, the names of data fields are used explicitly. The client code accesses the field values and does whatever is necessary (computing volumes, scaling size, printing). Changes to the `Cylinder` design affect not only the `Cylinder` structure, but the client code as well. The maintenance programmer has to deduce the meaning of processing (again, computing volumes, scaling size, printing) from following each step of computations. To check whether all dimensions of the object are initialized or scaled up or printed, one has to refer to the class `Cylinder` definition. The reuse of these operations (computing volumes, scaling size, printing) for the same or for another project is difficult because they are tied to the client code context.

These drawbacks can be eliminated by using access functions that encapsulate operations over structure fields: `setCylinder()`, `printCylinder()`, `getVolume()`, and `scaleCylinder()`. Listing 9.1 shows this version of the client code and server code. The results of the program run are shown in Figure 9–1.

Listing 9.1   Example of using access function on behalf of the client code.

```
#include <iostream>
using namespace std;

struct Cylinder {                                   // data structure to access
   double radius, height; } ;

void setCylinder(Cylinder& c, double r, double h)
{ c.radius = r;   c.height = h; }

double getVolume(const Cylinder& c)                 // compute volume
{ return c.height * c.radius * c.radius * 3.141593; }

void scaleCylinder(Cylinder &c, double factor)
{ c.radius ^= factor;   c.height ^= factor; }        // scale dimensions

void printCylinder(const Cylinder &c)               // print object state
{ cout << "radius: " <<c.radius << " height: " <<c.height <<endl; }

int main()                          // pushing responsibility to server functions
{ Cylinder c1, c2;                                  // program data
  setCylinder(c1,10,30); setCylinder(c2,20,30);     // set cylinders
  cout << "\nInitial size of first cylinder\n";
  printCylinder(c1);
  if (getVolume(c1) < getVolume(c2))                // compare volumes
  { scaleCylinder(c1,1.2);                          // scale it up and
    cout << "\nFirst cylinder changed size\n";      // print new size
    printCylinder(c1); }
  else // otherwise do nothing
    cout << "\nNo change in first cylinder size" << endl;
  return 0;
  }
```

```
Initial size of first cylinder
radius: 10 height: 30

First cylinder changed size
radius: 12 height: 36
```

Figure 9-1   Output for program in Listing 9.1.

This example is similar to the one in Listing 8.7, and what I demonstrated so far does not go beyond the capabilities of an ordinary structure. Let us make the next step: combine data fields and functions within the same class. In the following example, the syntactic boundaries of the class `Cylinder` are denoted by the opening and the closing braces and by the closing semicolon.

This class contains two fields, or data members: `radius` and `height`. In addition to data members, the class contains four member functions. (Another term for member functions is method; it comes from Smalltalk and artificial intelligence.) Member functions have the same syntax as global non-member functions: They can have parameters and return values, and each function has its own scope for its local variables. Unlike global functions, member functions are defined inside class boundaries (braces). Now everyone can see that these functions, `setCylinder()`, `getVolume()`, `scaleCylinder()`, and `printCylinder()`, belong together and with data fields `radius` and `height`.

```
struct Cylinder {                              // start of class scope
  double radius, height;                       // class data members
void setCylinder(double r, double h)           // class member functions
{ radius = r;   height = h; }                  // set field values
double getVolume()
{ return height * radius * radius * 3.141593; }     // compute volume
void scaleCylinder(double factor)
{ radius *= factor;   height *= factor; }      // scale dimensions
void printCylinder()                           // print object state
{ cout << "radius: " <<radius << " height: " <<height <<endl; }
} ;                                            // end of class scope
```

Adding member functions does not change the basic property of a structure; it is a template that is capable of defining objects of this class.

```
Cylinder c1, c2;      // space for two object instances is allocated
```

When you discuss object-oriented designs and programs, you naturally use the term "object." Unfortunately, this term has more than one meaning. Some people use this term to denote an abstract concept important for the application, such as customer, account, or transaction objects. Other people use this term to denote individual objects, such as an account that belongs to a particular customer. Yet other people do not really know what they mean when they use this term but still somehow expect other people to figure that out. I do not want to press you to make your choice right away, but please do not get into this third category.

In this book, I use the terms variables, instances, class instances, class objects, and object instances as synonyms. They all denote a program entity that is allocated memory (on the stack or on the heap) for some period during program execution; they belong to a specific storage class and are subject to scope rules. I try to avoid using the term "object" altogether. If push comes to shove and I do use the term, I use it in the sense of a program variable. In most cases, it will be a variable of a programmer-defined type, but I have no qualms about using this term "object" for variables of built-in types as well. This is the programming meaning of the term.

In object-oriented analysis and design, the term "object" is often used to denote a set of potential instances with the same properties. This usage is closer to the concept of the class (programmer-defined type) than to the concept of the object instance. I do not want to get into an argument as to which usage is correct. But because of this ambiguity, it is a good idea not to use the term "object" without describing the meaning of the term.

This might sound funny that in a book devoted to object-oriented programming, I argue against using the term "object," but the indiscriminate use of the term does cloud its meaning. When you use this term, always make sure to be clear what you mean—a single instance in the computer memory that exists during program execution or a generalized description of these potential instances, a C++ class that will be used to create specific instances during program execution.

The presence of member functions expands the size of the structure definition but does not expand the size of structure instances: It is still the sum of sizes of individual fields (with possible additional space for alignment). In this case, each `Cylinder` instance is allocated the space sufficient for holding two `double` values.

Elimination of Name Conflicts

Class opening and closing braces (and the closing semicolon) form the class scope pretty much in the same way as an ordinary structure forms a separate scope for its fields. This class scope, which is nested within the file scope, is similar to the scope of an ordinary structure. The difference is that the class scope can nest function scopes.

Nonmember functions (e.g., access functions in Listing 9.1) are global functions, and their names must be unique in the program (unless they are made static in the file scope, but only a small minority of functions can be made static in the file scope; more on static functions can be found in Chapter 6, "Memory Management. The Stack and The Heap," and later in this chapter). Normally, only those team members that use class Cylinder should learn about these function names because they are going to call this functions. In practice, every team member should learn about these names to avoid accidental name conflicts. This information obstructs the channels of communication among programmers.

When functions are implemented as class member functions (as in Listing 9.2 later), their names are local to the class scope. As a result, you cannot call member functions (or, for that matter, access data members) using their names, for example, radius or setCylinder(). You have to indicate whose Cylinder instance this radius belongs to or for what Cylinder variable to call the function setCylinder().

```
c1.radius = 10;                    // radius of c1
c2.setCylinder(20,30);             // setCylinder() for c2
```

In this example, it is radius of Cylinder variable c1 that is set to 10, and it is Cylinder variable c2 that is used to call setCylinder().

If the application uses another class, for example, Circle, which needs a data member radius, it does not result in name conflicts.

```
struct Circle {
    double radius;                 // it can be integer or anything
. . . } ;
```

To access the radius field of class Circle, the application has to define Circle object instances and use their names to access the radius field.

```
Circle cir1;  cir1.radius = 10;    // no ambiguity: Circle, not Cylinder
```

All class members (data members and member functions) are in the same scope within the class braces. Hence, they can access each other by name, without qualifying references (scope operators) to the class name or to the object name. For example, function setCylinder() sets the values of fields (data members) radius and height.

```
void setCylinder(double r, double h)      // set field values
{ radius = r;   height = h; }
```

Whose radius and height are these? They are the fields of some Cylinder object (class instance). When a member function, for example, setCylinder(), is called in the client code, this is called sending a message to an object. Client code (which is outside of the class braces) identifies the target of the message (the object whose fields are used inside the member function) by explicitly using the object name, the name of the member function, and the dot selector operator between the two.

```
Cylinder c1, c2;                          // potential targets of messages
c1.setCylinder(10,30); c2.setCylinder(20,30);    // messages to c1, c2
```

The message applies to an instance of an object of that class. When the first message executes, it is radius and height of object c1 that are used inside setCylinder(). When the second message executes, it is radius and height of object c2 that are used inside setCylinder(). This is true not only when the values of the fields are changed during message execution, but also when they are merely used in computations.

```
if (c1.getVolume() < c2.getVolume())       // compare volumes
   { c1.scaleCylinder(1.2);   . . .        // scale it up
```

In the first message, it is the fields of variable c1 that are used in the computation of the volume (whatever these computations are); in the second message, it is the fields of instance c2 that are used for computing volume. In all the cases, you use the name of the object, the dot selector operator, and the name of the message (member function). The message syntax is the same as the syntax for accessing (or changing) the fields of the structure. For a field, you use the name of the object, the dot selector operator, and the name of the field.

```
c1.radius = 40.0;   c1.height = 50.0;      // variable c1 is used
```

Listing 9.2 shows the version of the client code and server code that uses class Cylinder where data fields are bound together with member functions. Since functionality of the program is the same as in Listing 9.1 and it is the implementation only that has changed, the output of this program is the same as that in Listing 9.1.

Listing 9.2   Example of binding data and functions in a class with its own scope.

```
#include <iostream>
using namespace std;

struct Cylinder {                          // start of the class scope
   double radius, height;                  // data fields to access

void setCylinder(double r, double h)       // set cylinder data
{ radius = r;   height = h; }
```

```
double getVolume()                              // compute volume
{ return height * radius * radius * 3.141593; }

void scaleCylinder(double factor)               // scale dimensions
{ radius *= factor;  height *= factor; }

void printCylinder()                            // print object state
{ cout << "radius: " <<radius << " height: " <<height <<endl; }
} ;                                             // end of class scope

int main()                        // pushing responsibility to server functions
{ Cylinder c1, c2;                              // define program data
  c1.setCylinder(10,30); c2.setCylinder(20,30);    // set cylinders
  cout << "\nInitial size of first cylinder\n";
  c1.printCylinder();
  if (c1.getVolume() < c2.getVolume())          // compare volumes
  { c1.scaleCylinder(1.2);                      // scale it up and
    cout << "\nFirst cylinder changed size\n";  // print new size
    c1.printCylinder(); }
  else                                          // otherwise do nothing
    cout << "\nNo change in first cylinder size" << endl;
  return 0;
  }
```

Compare Listing 9.2 with Listing 9.1 and make sure you see the difference between using stand-alone global functions, as in Listing 9.1, and functions bound with the data, as in Listing 9.2. With stand-alone access functions, the object variable whose data is to be used within the function is passed as a parameter.

```
void setCylinder(Cylinder& c, double r, double h)   // access function
{ c.radius = r;  c.height = h; }                    // Cylinder is a parameter
```

The appropriate object instance should be used in the function call as the actual argument.

```
setCylinder(c1,10,30); setCylinder(c2,20,30);
```

Without using classes, it would be utterly incorrect to implement setCylinder() function without a Cylinder parameter and call this function without passing the actual object to operate on.

```
void setCylinder(double r, double h)     // nonsense: what Cylinder?
{ c.radius = r;  c.height = h; }

setCylinder(10,30); setCylinder(20,30);  // nonsense: what Cylinder?
```

When you design a function as a class member function, there is no need to pass the object to be used as a parameter.

```
void setCylinder(double r, double h) // method: no Cylinder parameter!
{ radius = r;   height = h; }        // data members, not parameter fields!
```

Instead, the appropriate object instance is specified as a target of the message during the function call.

```
c1.setCylinder(10,30);                // object c1 as a message target
c2.setCylinder(20,30);                // object c2 as a message target
```

Many beginning C++ programmers try to have it both ways. When they design class member functions, they also pass the object to be operated on as a parameter.

```
void setCylinder(Cylinder& c, double r, double h)    // bad method
{ c.radius = r;   c.height = h; }

c1.setCylinder(c1,10,30); c2.setCylinder(c2,20,30);  // bad messages
```

I am not sure what attracts programmers to these C++ idioms, but I see them quite often. Is this code syntactically correct? Sure, otherwise the programmers would not be able to use it. Is this coding idiom semantically correct? Sure, otherwise the programmers would have done something about it. Still, it is an ugly design.

Notice that exactly the same results could be achieved using different message targets.

```
c2.setCylinder(c1,10,30); c1.setCylinder(c2,20,30);    // still bad
```

It seems that I am sending the first message to variable c2 and the second message to variable c1. But it is not what you think. The first message still sets the fields of variable c1, and the second message sets the fields of variable c2, as in the previous example. But it takes a few extra seconds to figure out that the target of the message has nothing to do with the message itself!

This awkward design is just an example of how easy it is in C++ to write code that is not doing what it seems to be doing and is using program components that have nothing to do with what is going on. This kind of design always increases the complexity of the code and coupling between the client and server code.

Moving from writing stand-alone functions to writing classes requires a paradigm shift. Make sure you make this shift and feel comfortable in both paradigms.

Implementing Member Functions Outside of Class

Notice that these member functions are correct only when they are implemented inside the class scope, that is, within the class braces, as in Listing 9.2. If they are implemented outside the class scope, different syntax should be used. This syntax is used when the relationship between member functions and data members of the class is established using function prototypes within the class declaration (specification) instead of the complete implementations, as in Listing 9.2.

```
struct Cylinder {                        // start of class scope
   double radius, height;                // data fields to access
void setCylinder(double r, double h);    // set Cylinder fields
double getVolume();                      // compute volume
void scaleCylinder(double factor);       // scale dimensions
void printCylinder();                    // print object state
} ;                                      // end of class scope
```

This means that the function definitions (function bodies) are to be implemented separately. Usually, the class specification is in a header file with the extension .h, and the function implementations are in a source file with extensions .cpp or .cxx, depending on the compiler.

Function prototypes in the class declaration look exactly like function prototypes of stand-alone global functions. The only difference is that they are defined within the class scope. Please take the class scope borders seriously. Programmers rarely forget to specify the starting and ending braces. But forgetting the ending semicolon is a common programming mistake. Unfortunately, the compiler rarely tells you that you forgot the semicolon at the end of the class specification. Usually, the compiler accuses you of doing something bad on the next line of code. Make sure that when the line in error follows the class specification, you check whether the semicolon is missing.

Alert

Programmers sometimes forget to place the semicolon after the closing class brace. Often, the compiler will refer you to the following line, not to the line where the semicolon is missing.

When the member functions are implemented outside of the class specification, you have to indicate the name of the class to which these member functions belong. This is natural, because each class has its own scope, and each class might have a member function, for example, `getVolume()`. I first wanted to say that each class might have member functions, for example, `setCylinder()` or `printCylinder()`, but then I realized that the likelihood of using these function names in classes like `Cube`, `Circle`, or `Account` is not very high. For these classes, the programmers would use names such as `setCube()`, `setAccount()`, `printAccount()`, and so on. But the name `getVolume()` can be used for classes `Cylinder`, `Cube`, or even `Circle` (the result would be zero).

Names like `setCylinder()` and `setAccount()` used to be the only reasonable option before the advent of C++, because C did not distinguish between functions with different signatures. C++ distinguishes between functions with the same name but with different signatures (see Chapter 7 for a discussion of function name overloading). Hence, in C++ it is possible to use the name `set()` instead of `setCylinder()` and `setAccount()` because the first function `set()` would have a `Cylinder` parameter, and the second function `set()` would have an `Account` parameter.

With class scope added to C++, name conflicts for member functions cease to be a serious problem. Hence, I could use the name `set()` instead of `setCylinder()`, `print()` instead of `printCylinder()`, and so on.

```
c1.set(10,30); c2.set(20,30);    // Cylinder objects as message targets
```

When the compiler processes a message, it identifies the name of the target object and searches for the definition (or declaration) of this object to identify its type. In this case, the compiler will easily establish that object instances c1 and c2 are of type `Cylinder`. Then the compiler searches for the definition (or declaration) of this type and searches whether a member function with the name of the message is defined there. If the member function `set()` is found, the compiler checks the function interface: the number and type of arguments. If the number of arguments matches but there is a type mismatch for an argument, the compiler is looking for a possibility of a conversion. If this process results in a match, the compiler generates object code; if not, the compiler generates an error message.

This is nice, but the compiler has no difficulty in establishing the type of the target object. It just searches the source code (or rather, the tables that the compiler has created processing the declarations of variables). Not so for a human maintenance programmer. A human has to search the code, and this might become difficult, time consuming, and error prone. From this point of view, a longer function name could give the maintainer the cue to avoid the search for the message target definition.

```
c1.setCylinder(10,30);        // objects are Cylinders, right?
c2.setCylinder(20,30);
```

All right, back to the discussion of implementing the member functions when the class specification contains member function prototypes only. The implementation is exactly the same as when the functions are implemented within the class boundaries. The only difference is in function names—they have to be qualified by the class name. To do so, you use the scope operator between the class name and the function name.

```
inline void Cylinder::setCylinder(double r, double h)
{ radius = r;  height = h; }                  // set data fields

inline double Cylinder::getVolume()
{ return height * radius * radius * 3.141593; }   // compute volume

inline void Cylinder::scaleCylinder(double factor)
{ radius *= factor;  height *= factor; }          // scale dimensions

inline void Cylinder::printCylinder()             // print object state
{ cout << "radius: " <<radius << " height: " <<height <<endl; }
```

In human terms, the real name of the member function setCylinder() is not just setCylinder() but rather setCylinder() of class Cylinder. In syntactic terms, you denote this as Cylinder::setCylinder().

This two-part class definition (specification with prototypes and separate implementations) defines exactly the same class Cylinder as before. Notice that when a member function is implemented within the class specification, it is inline by default; when it is implemented separately, it is not inline by default, but it can be made inline explicitly.

As I mentioned, the class specification with prototypes is usually placed in a header file and function implementations are placed in a separate source file. It is okay, however, to implement all or some of the member functions in the header file. The header file has to be included in every file where the name of the class is mentioned, for example, in the client source file, and even in the source file where the member functions are implemented (because the class name is used in the class scope operator).

Since the linker should not see a function definition more than once, class specifications should be bracketed by preprocessor directives for conditional compilations (see other examples in Chapters 2, "Getting Started Quickly: A Brief Overview of C++," and 5, "Aggregation and Programmer-Defined Data Types"). For example, the header file for class `Cylinder` could look the following way.

```
#ifndef CYLINDER_H                          // common convention for symbol name
#define CYLINDER_H
#include <iostream>
using namespace std;

struct Cylinder {                           // start of the class scope
   double radius, height;                   // data fields to access
void setCylinder(double r, double h)        // set cylinder data
{ radius = r;   height = h; }
double getVolume()                          // compute volume
{ return height * radius * radius * 3.141593; }
void scaleCylinder(double factor)           // scale dimensions
{ radius *= factor;   height *= factor; }
void printCylinder()                        // print object state
{ cout << "radius: " <<radius << " height: " <<height <<endl; }
} ;                                         // end of class scope
#endif
```

It is a common convention to put this code in file `Cylinder.h` and use the symbol name for conditional compilation `CYLINDER_H`. Implementation of member functions in a separate file is an important contribution to program modularity. Logically, member functions, for example, `Cylinder::setCylinder()`, are defined within the class braces, whether they are within the class braces or not. This is why these functions do not need a qualifier (scope operator) to access the radius and height data members.

In separate implementation, the function name qualifier is mandatory. Without it, function `setCylinder()` would refer to global variables `radius` and `height`, not to class data members `radius` and `height`.

```
inline void setCylinder(double r,double h)     // class scope operator is missing
{ radius = r;   height = h; }                   // are these data members or what?

inline double Cylinder::getVolume()             // compute volume
{ return height * radius * radius * 3.141593; }

inline void Cylinder::scaleCylinder(double factor)
{ radius *= factor;   height *= factor; }        // scale dimensions

inline void Cylinder::printCylinder()            // print object state
{ cout << "radius: " <<radius << " height: " <<height <<endl; }
```

The compiler will accept a global function definition with no problem; it is legal in C++. If no variables `radius` and `height` are declared in this file scope, the compiler will complain about undefined variables `radius` and `height`, not about the missing scope operator. Thus, it will produce a misleading error message. Your first reaction will probably be that of disbelief. Doesn't the compiler see that `radius` and `height` are defined right here, in the class specification? It must be yet another bug in this compiler! But the compiler has no way of knowing that you forgot to use the scope operator to define global variables. By the way, if variables with these names are defined in this scope for some other purpose, the compiler will silently generate code that refers to these global variables, not to class data members.

Alert

Programmers sometimes forget to place the scope operator before the member function name. The compiler assumes that you want to implement a global function and accuses you of using undefined variables with the names of class data members used in the function.

Defining Class Objects of Different Storage Classes

Class scope includes all its data and function members. It is nested within the file (or another class, function, or even a block) where the class is declared, along with other functions and/or classes. The components of the class can be accessed only when a class object is in scope.

As for variables of any type, class objects (instances, variables) in C++ can be defined as automatic, global, static, or dynamic variables. (See Chapter 6 for a discussion of storage classes.)

For automatic and global (`extern` or `static`) variables, the space is allocated implicitly as a result of the object definition. All the previous examples of defining class instances were examples of automatic variables. They are created when program execution reached their definitions. For example, variables c1 and c2 in Listing 9.2 are created when execution reaches the line in `main()` where these variables are defined.

If a class variable is defined as global, the space for this object is allocated before the `main()` function starts execution. The same is true when a class variable is defined as static (either as global in a file or as local in some function scope).

What is common to all these object instances is that they can be referred to through their names. For access to data fields and member functions of these objects (and references to them), the object name with the dot notation can be used by the client code when the client code needs to access class members.

```
Cylinder x;
x.setCylinder(50,80);
double volume = x.getVolume();   x.radius = 100;
```

For dynamic variables, space is allocated explicitly using the operator `new`. The object is not defined by name; it can be accessed using a pointer only. The client function will use the pointer name (not the object name, because the object instance does not have a name) with the arrow notation to access data and function members of the object. Here, a named pointer to `Cylinder` objects is created, and then an unnamed object of class `Cylinder` is created and manipulated.

```
Cylinder* p;                        // no object is created yet
p = new Cylinder;                   // no object name exists
p->setCylinder(50,80);              // unnamed object is accessed
double volume = p->getVolume();     // same notation
p->radius = 100;
```

If you want to avoid the arrow selection operator, you can use the dereference operator with the dot selection operator.

```
(*p).setCylinder(50,80);             // same as p->setCylinder(50,80);
```

Similarly, when an object is passed to a client function by pointer (rather than by value or by reference), the arrow notation (rather than the dot notation) is used.

```
void CopyData(Cylinder *to, const Cylinder &from)      // copy Cylinder
{ to->radius=from.radius;  to->height=from.height; }  // arrow notation

Cylinder x,y;  x.radius=3.0;  x.height=7.0;    // client for CopyData()
CopyData(&y,x);                                // passing object by pointer
```

Automatic variables are destroyed when they go out of scope where they are defined. The programmer should not do anything to return their memory to the system for reuse. The same is true for global and static variables. They are destroyed when they go out of scope, that is, immediately after `main()` terminates. No programming action is necessary.

Dynamic variables are different. They have to be deleted explicitly, since the system does not know when the programmer wants to return dynamic memory.

```
Cylinder* p = new Cylinder;             // unnamed object is created
p->setCylinder(50,80);                  // unnamed object is accessed
cout << "Volume: " << p->getVolume() << endl;   // arrow operator
delete p;              // unnamed Cylinder is destroyed, pointer is not
```

As with variables of any type, client access to class instances and to their members depends on the scope rules: They can be accessed only when the class instance is in scope. In addition, C++ allows the class designer to establish additional limitations for other parts of the program.

Controlling Access to Class Members

In the previous section, I designed class `Cylinder` that binds together its data members and member functions in a syntactic unit. This syntax repairs two problems with using global functions for object-oriented programming.

First, using global functions for access to data does not force the indication that data and operations belong together. Hence, it is possible to tear apart the functions that belong together and spread them throughout different places in the source code (making the code more difficult for the maintainer to understand and modify). Second, global function names are global. To avoid potential name conflicts, programmers have to coordinate their activities even when parts of the program they are working on are not immediately related. The class syntax clearly indicates that data and functions belong together. The class scope eliminates the potential for function name conflicts.

At the beginning of this chapter I mentioned two other goals of adding the class facility to C++: pushing responsibility from client code to the server functions and control of access to class members.

Pushing responsibilities down from the client code to the server class is accomplished by the right choice of member functions. (Sometimes, the choice of data members is also important.) In Chapter 8, I discussed the example (see Listing 8.8) where the choice of member functions `setRadius()`, `getRadius()`, `setHeight()`, and `getHeight()`, forced the client code to do the work rather than asking the servers to do the work for it. From that point of view, the choice of member functions in Listing 9.2 is better—instead of getting the values of `radius` and `height` for scaling, printing, or computing volume, the client code asks the objects of class `Cylinder` to scale and print themselves or compute their volume.

Pushing responsibility down to the servers is an important concept. What is sufficient and what is not is often subjective. I brushed aside the design in Listing 8.8, but it might be quite useful if the class is used as a library utility that has to serve the largest number of users. For some users, the design in Listing 9.2 might be too restrictive—they might want to compute the surface of the cylinder, scale it using different factors in different directions, and so on. Yet, for other users, the design in Listing 9.2 might be too general—these users might not need the numerical value of cylinder volume, but they might be interested in finding out whether the first cylinder object is smaller than the second (see Listing 8.9 for comparison).

Pushing responsibilities down to server classes will pop up often during the further discussions of class design. In this section, I will discuss the techniques that allow the class designer to control access to class data members and member functions.

Figure 9–2 describes the class `Cylinder` and its relationship with its client `main()`. Here the class has three components: data, functions, and the border that separates everything inside the class from everything outside the class. It shows that data are inside the class. Functions are partially inside the class (their implementation) and outside the class (their interfaces that are known to the client).

The picture also shows that when the client code needs the values of cylinder fields (e.g., for computing cylinder volume, scaling, printing, or setting the field values), the client code uses member functions `getVolume()`, `scaleCylinder()`, and so on rather than accessing the values of fields `radius` and `height`. This is what the dashed line means. It shows that the direct access to data is ruled out.

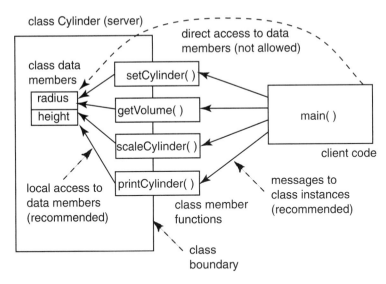

Figure 9-2   Class `Cylinder` and its relationship with its client `main()`.

There are two motivations for barring access to data members. The first objective is to limit the extent of changes to the program when data design changes. If the interfaces of member functions stay the same (and usually it is not difficult to keep them the same when the data design changes), then it is member function implementations that have to change, not the client code. This is important for maintenance. The set of functions that have to change is well defined—they are all listed in the class definition, and there is no need to inspect the rest of the program for possible implications.

The second reason for barring direct client access to data members is that the client code expressed in terms of calls to member functions is easier to understand than is the code expressed in terms of detailed computations over field values (provided that the responsibility is pushed to the member functions and they do the work for the client, not just retrieve and set the values of the fields, as is the case with the `getHeight()` and `setHeight()` functions).

To achieve these advantages, everything inside the class should be private to the class, not accessible from outside the class, leaving only function interfaces public, accessible from the outside of the class. This would prevent the client code from creating *dependencies* on server class data. Remember that the word *dependency* is the dirtiest word in programming. Dependencies between different parts of program code denote:

- the need for cooperation among programmers during program development
- the need to study and change more code during program maintenance than is necessary
- difficulties in reusing code in the same or similar project

Meanwhile, the class design in Listing 9.2 does not enforce any protection against access to data. The client code can access the fields of the `Cylinder` object instances, developing dependencies on the `Cylinder` data design, and foregoing essential advantages of using classes.

```
Cylinder c1, c2;                              // define program data
c1.setCylinder(10,30); c2.setCylinder(20,30); // use access function
c1.radius = 10; c1.height = 20;  . . .         // this is still ok!
```

C++ allows the class designer to use fine control over access rights to class components. You can indicate access rights to each class component (data or function) by using the keywords `public`, `private`, and `protected`. Here is another version of class `Cylinder`.

```
struct Cylinder {                       // start of class scope
   private:
      double radius, height;            // data is private
   public:                              // operations are public
      void setCylinder(double r, double h);
      double getVolume();               // compute volume
      void scaleCylinder(double factor);
      void printCylinder();             // print object state
} ;                                     // end of class scope
```

The keywords divide the class scope into segments. All data members or function members following the keyword, for example, `private`, have the same private access mode. In our example, data members `radius` and `height` are `private`, and all member functions are `public`.

There might be any number of `public`, `protected`, and `private` segments in any order you want. In this example, I define the `radius` data member as `private`, then two member functions as `public`, then the `height` data member as `private`, then two more member functions as `public`.

```
struct Cylinder {                       // start of class scope
   private:
      double radius;                    // data is private
   public:                              // operations are public
      void setCylinder(double r, double h);
      double getVolume();
```

```
private:
   double height;                          // data is private
public:                                    // operations are public
   void scaleCylinder(double factor);
   void printCylinder();                   // print object state
} ;                                        // end of class scope
```

This is a nice element of flexibility, but usually programmers group all class components with the same access rights in the same segment.

In general, class members (either data members or member functions) in `public` segments are available to the rest of the program as in the previous examples.

Class members (again, both data and functions) in `private` segments are available to the class member functions only (and to functions with access rights of a `friend`; I will discuss `friends` later, in Chapter 10, "Operator Functions: Another Good Idea."). Using the name of a private class member outside of the class (or friend) scope is a syntax error.

Notice that these rules do not prevent you from making data private and making functions public. However, in traditional C++ class design, data members are made private, and member functions are made public.

Class members in `protected` segments are available to the class member functions and to member functions of classes that inherit from this one (directly or indirectly). Discussing inheritance now will take us too far from the topic of class syntax; I will do that later.

Client functions (global functions or member functions of other classes) can access `private` class members only through the functions (if any) in the public part.

```
Cylinder c1, c2;                           // define program data
   c1.setCylinder(10,30); c2.setCylinder(20,30);   // use access function
// c1.radius = 10; c1.height = 20;         // this is now a syntax error
   if (c1.getVolume() < c2.getVolume())    // another access function
      c1.scaleCylinder(1.2);               // scale it up
```

It is the duty of the class designer to provide necessary access to its data to support class clients and to avoid excessive access. If the client code uses the class feature it does not have to use, it develops extra dependencies. Should this feature change, the client code is affected as well. Also, the more features of the class that are made public, the more knowledge the client programmer and maintainer have to acquire to use the class instances productively.

With the use of private access to class data members, the implementation details of the class `Cylinder` are now hidden; if the names or types of `Cylinder` fields change, the client code is not affected as long as the

`Cylinder` class interface remains the same. The client code is prevented from developing dependencies on class `Cylinder` data design. The client programmer (and maintainer) is excused from the need to learn class `Cylinder` data design.

Usually, it is the data part that is likely to evolve. This is why, in a typical class, data members are `private` and member functions are `public`. This enhances modifiability of the program and reusability of class design. Notice that class member functions (whether `public` or `private`) can access any data member of the same class, whether `public` or `private`.

This is why any group of functions that accesses the same set of data should be bound together as class member functions, and calls to these functions should be used as messages to class instances in the client code. This enhances reusability.

The class is isolated from other parts of the program. Its private parts are outside the reach of other code (similar to local variables in a function or a block).

This property decreases the amount of coordination among design team members and reduces the likelihood of human miscommunication. This enhances program quality.

In all previous examples, I used the keyword `struct` to define a C++ class. C++ also allows you to use the keyword `class` for that purpose. Here is an example of class `Cylinder` that uses the keyword `class` rather than `struct`.

```
class Cylinder {                        // change from 'struct' to 'class' keyword
    private:
        double radius, height;          // data is still private
    public:                             // operations are public
        void setCylinder(double r, double h);
        double getVolume();
        void scaleCylinder(double factor);
        void printCylinder();
} ;                                     // end of class scope
```

What is the difference between this class definition and the previous class definition? There is none. This class specification defines exactly the same class. The objects of these classes are exactly the same—there is no difference at all. There are only two differences between the keywords `struct` and `class` in C++. One difference is that the keyword `struct` has only one meaning in C++: It is used for one purpose only (to introduce a programmer-defined type into the program the way I did in the previous examples). Another difference between the keywords `struct` and `class` in C++ is in default access rights. In `struct` (and in `union`), default access is `public`. In `class`, default access is `private`. That is all.

Using default access rights allows you to structure the sequence of data fields and member functions differently. In the next version I am responding to the criticism of some programmers who say that class examples that describe data rather than functions first (as I did in previous examples) are hypocritical. The purpose of the class construct is to hide data design from the client code, and it is not a good idea to open the class specification with the description of the so-called "hidden" data. The client code uses public member functions; hence, it is appropriate if they are listed first in the class specification.

```
struct Cylinder {          // some prefer to list public members first
    void setCylinder(double r, double h);  // operations are public
    double getVolume();
    void scaleCylinder(double factor);
    void printCylinder();
  private:
    double radius, height;                  // data is private
  } ;                                       // end of class scope
```

Others feel that understanding data is important for understanding what member functions do. Hence, there is nothing wrong with describing data first. After all, data "hiding" is not about military-type classified information or KGB-like secrecy, where information should be prevented from being *known*. In programming, information hiding and encapsulation is about preventing the client code from *using* the information in the client design, not about knowing this information. In this case, if you want to use default access rights, the class keyword is better than struct.

```
class Cylinder {               // some prefer to list data first
    double radius, height;     // data is still private
  public:                      // operations are public
    void setCylinder(double r, double h);
    double getVolume();
    void scaleCylinder(double factor);
    void printCylinder();
  } ;                          // end of class scope
```

Some programmers say that the keyword `struct` is inferior to the keyword `class`, because if you define the class using the default access rights, data will not be protected against use by the client code, and that will defeat encapsulation.

```
struct Cylinder {                          // default access rights are used
    double radius, height;                 // data is not protected from client access
  void setCylinder(double r, double h);    // methods are public
  double getVolume();
  void scaleCylinder(double factor);
  void printCylinder();
} ;                                        // end of class scope
```

Yes, this class design does defeat encapsulation. But hey, this does not prove that the keyword `struct` is inferior to the keyword `class`. If you replace `struct` with `class` in this design, the result will be even worse than with the keyword `struct`. Do you see why?

```
class Cylinder {                           // default access rights are used
    double radius, height;                 // data is protected from client access
  void setCylinder(double r, double h);    // methods are not accessible
  double getVolume();
  void scaleCylinder(double factor);
  void printCylinder();
} ;                                        // end of class scope
```

This class is not usable at all. Yes, the data fields are now private (and this is fine), but so are member functions, and the client code cannot access them. This is not a very good design.

It is probably better not to rely on defaults and instead specify access rights explicitly. Let us call a spade a spade.

Initialization of Object Instances

When the compiler processes a definition of a variable, it uses its type definition to allocate the required amount of memory, either from the heap (for `static` and `extern` variables or for dynamic variables) or from the stack (for local automatic variables).

This is true for simple variables, arrays, structures, and classes with member functions. If the code later assigns a value to a variable, the variable does not need initialization at its definition. If the algorithm uses the variable as an rvalue, it needs initial values for its data members.

```
Cylinder c1;                    // data members are not initialized
double vol = c1.getVolume();    // no, this is no good
```

This coding pattern, however, might be appropriate if some default values could be used in computations. However, C++ initializes only static and global variables. (Default values are zeros of a suitable type.) Dynamic variables and automatic variables are left without initial values.

Sometimes you would like to specify default initial values. It would be nice to initialize data members at their definition, similar to regular variables, but in C++, a data member definition cannot contain an initializer.

```
class Cylinder {
   double radius = 100, height = 0; ...   // no, this is illegal in C++
```

The class could provide a member function for the client code to call to specify the object's initial state.

```
class Cylinder {
   double radius, height;
public:
   void setCylinder(double r, double h);  ... } ;
```

Using this function, client code would send the `setCylinder()` message to `Cylinder` objects.

```
Cylinder c1;
c1.SetCylinder(100.0,0.0);      // set radius to 100, height to zero
```

This is, of course, overkill. This code allows you to specify any initial values rather than specified default values. This is where constructors become useful.

Constructors as Member Functions

Class objects can be initialized implicitly, using a constructor. A constructor is a class member function, but its syntax is more rigid than it is for other member functions. It cannot have an arbitrary name; you should give the constructor function the same name as the class. The constructor interface cannot specify a return type, not even `void`. It cannot return values even if it contains a `return` statement.

```
class Cylinder {
  double radius, height;
public:
  Cylinder ()                     // same name as class, no return type
    { radius=1.0;  height=0.0; }  // no return statement
    ... } ;
```

When client code creates an object, the default constructor is called.

```
Cylinder c1;                // default constructor: no parameters
```

It is called a default constructor because it has no parameters. I know, this is a strange reason, but that's the way it is.

A constructor cannot be called explicitly at will, as can any other member function.

```
c1.Cylinder();    // syntax error: no explicit calls to constructors
```

The constructor can be called only when an object is created, not later. The compiler generates code that implicitly calls the constructor immediately after the instance of the object is created. This is why constructors are usually placed in the public section of the class specification. Otherwise, an attempt to create a class instance would generate an error as does any access to a private class member.

In general, an instance of the object can be created in the following ways:

- at the beginning of the program (`extern` and `static` objects)
- at entry into the scope with the object definition (automatic objects)

- when a variable is passed to a function (or returned from a function) by value
- when a variable is created dynamically using the operator `new` (but not `malloc`)

Now you see why constructors have no return values: Constructors are called implicitly by the code generated by the compiler, and there is nobody around to use this return value.

As member functions, constructors can have parameters; hence, constructors can be overloaded. If necessary, constructor parameters can have default values. When a class has more than one constructor, each one could be called when an object is created. Which constructor is called depends on the context, that is, on a set of arguments supplied by the client code at the time of object creation (the number and type of arguments).

Supplying constructors in the class means providing services to class clients: Client programmers do not have to call initializing functions explicitly anymore. However, they should worry about supplying the arguments for the constructor. Here is an example of a constructor with two parameters.

```
class Cylinder {
    double radius, height;          // initialized in constructors
public:
    Cylinder(double r, double h);   // member function prototype
    void setCylinder(double r, double h);
    . . . . . } ;

Cylinder::Cylinder(double r, double h)    // scope operator
    { radius = r;   height = h; }
```

Notice the name of the constructor implemented outside the class boundaries. The first `Cylinder` denotes the class to which the member function belongs. The second `Cylinder` denotes the name of the member function (the same as the name of the class). Constructors that have fewer than two parameters have special names. (You will see them shortly.) Constructors with two or more parameters do not have special names—they are just general constructors.

This constructor with two parameters does the same thing as `setCylinder()`: It sets the values of data members to the values of the arguments supplied by the client. The difference is that `setCylinder()` can be called many times for the same object instance in the client code. The constructor is called only once—when the object is created.

Here are a few examples of constructor invocations in client code. These different syntactic forms call the same general constructor with two parameters. Notice that an assignment operator in the second statement does not mean that an assignment operation is performed. Despite the appearance of using an assignment, this is not what you think (quite a common situation in C++. Remember that story about the crocodile?): There is no assignment there. It is just a different syntactic form for a constructor call.

```
Cylinder c1(3.0,5.0);       // a constructor call for a named object
Cylinder c2 = Cylinder(3,5);      // it is still a constructor call
Cylinder *r = new Cylinder(3.0,5.0);      // unnamed object
```

Notice the syntax for a variable with arguments. This is a new syntax. One of the implicit ambitions of C++ language design is the uniform treatment of variables of built-in and programmer-defined types. For built-in types, we used the assignment operator for initialization. With the advent of programmer-defined types, you can use the syntax with arguments for variables of built-in types as well as class objects.

```
int x1(20);                       // same as int x1=20
```

When an object is allocated with a call to `malloc()`, no constructor is called. Hence, the client code has to initialize class objects explicitly.

```
Cylinder *p = (Cylinder*)malloc(sizeof(Cylinder));       // no constructor call
p->setCylinder(3,5);                              // object fields are assigned values
```

A call to `malloc()` is the only way in C++ to create an object without a constructor call. Creation of all other objects, named objects and dynamic objects, is followed by a call to a constructor. Without any fanfare, we crossed a point of no return. From now on, there will be no situation where you just create an object instance and give it a chunk of memory. Any creation of an object will be accompanied by a function call—a call to a constructor. Again, this requires a change in thinking. Every time you see an object instance created (remember that story about the brick?), you should remind yourself: "OK, this means that a constructor is called. Which constructor?"

Default Constructors

Many classes do not need constructors because class objects do not need default initialization. When the class designer does not add any constructors to the class, the system provides a default constructor (which does nothing) for the class.

```
class Cylinder {                   // OK if no constructors/destructors
    double radius, height;   // data is protected from client access
public:
  void setCylinder(double r, double h);    // methods are accessible
  double getVolume();
  void scaleCylinder(double factor);
  void printCylinder();
} ;                                        // end of class scope
```

All of the versions of class Cylinder that I discussed in the previous section were using the system-supplied default constructor. I did not mention it to avoid unnecessary complication of the discussion. When the client code creates a Cylinder object, this default constructor is called.

```
Cylinder c1;    // default constructor is called, no initialization
```

Why should you know about this? After all, this constructor does not do anything. What you should know, however, is that if a class defines a nondefault constructor (constructor with parameters), then the system no longer supplies the default constructor.

Why should you know about that? Because syntactic errors occur if the client designer defines class variables and arrays that need the default constructor.

This last version of class Cylinder did not have programmer-defined constructors. Hence, the system gave this class Cylinder the default constructor that did nothing. When variable c1 was created, that constructor was called. How do I know that? Well, *some* constructor must be called. (There is no such thing anymore as object creation without a constructor call.) Which constructor? That depends on the number of arguments supplied. The variable c1 does not have any arguments supplied. This is evidence that a constructor without arguments is called (remember that joke about copper wire?). A constructor without arguments is a default constructor. Does the class provide the default constructor? No. Does the class provide any constructor? No. Hence, the default constructor is supplied by the system. It does nothing. Everything is fine.

Let us look at a version of class Cylinder that provides a general programmer-defined constructor. This means that the system takes the default constructor away.

```
class Cylinder {
    double radius, height;
  public:
    Cylinder(double r, double h)          // this is not enough
    { radius = r;   height = h; }
    . . . } ;
```

When the client code tries to create `Cylinder` objects, trouble follows.

```
Cylinder c1(3.0,5.0);          // this is OK
Cylinder c2, c[1000];          // 1001 syntax errors
Cylinder *p = new Cylinder;    // one syntax error
```

Here, I create 1001 `Cylinder` object instances without supplying arguments. Recall that there is no creation of an object without constructor calls? So the compiler tries to generate code for 1001 constructor calls. Which constructor? Since I did not specify any arguments, the compiler is trying to call a constructor with no arguments, that is, a default constructor `Cylinder::Cylinder()`. But this version of class `Cylinder` does not define a default constructor. Since it defines a general constructor, the system takes the default constructor away. What happens when the client code calls a member function 1001 times to initialize 1001 `Cylinder` objects? Since this function is not found in the `Cylinder` class specification, the compiler generates a syntax error. Make sure that you learn to rush through this logical derivation quickly.

The problem can be resolved by supporting the client code with a programmer-defined default constructor. This default constructor could do nothing, similar to the system-supplied default constructor, or it could initialize object data members to some reasonable values.

```
class Cylinder {
    double radius, height;
    public:
        Cylinder ()                 // programmer-supplied default constructor
        { radius = 100.0; height = 0.0; }    // reasonable values
        Cylinder(double r, double h)         // general constructor
        { radius = r;   height = h; }
        . . . } ;
```

Client code:

```
Cylinder c1(3.0,5.0);          // this is OK
Cylinder c2, c[1000];          // now this is OK, too
Cylinder *p = new Cylinder;    // no syntax error
```

Notice that the creation of each object is accompanied by at least one function call; here, constructors are inline functions; still, this can have performance implications. There is no such thing in C++ as the creation of an object without a function call.

Note

Creation of objects in C++ is always followed by a constructor call. If the class defines no constructor, creation of objects is followed by a call to a default constructor supplied by the system. If the class defines any constructor, the system does not supply the default constructor. In this case, you cannot create arrays of objects or objects without arguments. The system gives, the system takes away.

Copy Constructors

One of the important ideas underlining C++ philosophy about objects is that classes are types. Defining classes for your program extends the system of built-in C++ types. C++ wants to treat built-in types as objects. C++ also wants to treat programmer-defined types as built-in types.

For example, you can define variables of built-in types without specifying their initial values. Hence, you are able to do that for object variables.

```
int x; Cylinder c1;            // noninitialized variables
```

The syntax is the same, but the meaning is different. The definition of a variable of a built-in type just allocates memory for this variable. The definition of a variable of a programmer-defined class allocates memory for this variable and then calls the default constructor. If class does not define constructors, this default constructor is supplied by the system and does nothing. If class defines constructors, the definition of the class variable is a syntax error unless the class also defines a default constructor. This constructor could do nothing, or it could initialize the fields of the object to default values.

Similarly, one might want to initialize a nonclass variable of a built-in type with another variable of the same type. C++ supports a similar syntax that allows the client code to initialize one class object with the values of another object of the same class.

```
int x(20); Cylinder c1(50,70);  // objects are created, initialized
int y=x; Cylinder c2=c1;     // initialization from existing objects
```

Do not be misled by the assignment operators on the second line. There is no assignment in these statements. The assignment operator is reused here to denote initialization. Remember, when the name of the type is present next to the name of the variable, you are dealing with initialization. When the name of the type is absent and the name of the variable appears alone, you are dealing with assignment. Why should you care? As you are going to see later, different functions are called in each case.

What function is called in this case? The answer is simple. Since the object is created and initialized, it is a constructor that is called here. What constructor? As I said earlier, it depends on context, that is, on the number and types of actual arguments supplied when the object is created.

In this example, there is one argument that is used to initialize object c2, namely, object c1. The type of this object is Cylinder. Hence, the constructor that is called has one parameter of type Cylinder. Is this derivation clear? You should do something like that each time you analyze object creation statements.

The special name for a constructor with one parameter of the same type as the class is a copy constructor. The reason for this name is that it copies the values from the fields of the existing source object into the fields of the target object just created. As you can see, the last version of class Cylinder does not have a constructor with one parameter of type Cylinder. It has a general constructor with two double parameters and a default constructor with no parameters. Does it mean that the statements above are in error, similar to the situation when I introduced the concept of the default constructor? No, and this is yet another confirmation that life is never dull while you are learning C++.

If the class defines no constructors, C++ supplies its own copy constructor. This copy constructor copies data members bitwise from the source object into the target object. Unlike the system-supplied default constructor, this system-supplied copy constructor is not taken away even if the class defines other constructors. Hence, you can always count on its existence.

For a class like Cylinder, it does not make much sense to define its own programmer-defined copy constructors. All you could do in such a constructor is to copy the radius and height fields of the parameter. But this is exactly what the system-supplied copy constructor does. The only reason you would use a programmer-defined copy constructor is for debugging purposes.

```
class Cylinder {
  double radius, height;
public:
    Cylinder (const Cylinder &c)
    { radius = c.radius;   height = c.height;
      cout << "Copy constructor: " << radius << ", "
. . . . } ; << height << endl; }
```

Notice that the parameter should be a reference to a variable of the given type rather than a value of the given type. What happens if the parameter to the copy constructor is passed by value?

```
Cylinder (Cylinder c)                // incorrect constructor interface
   { radius = c.radius;   height = c.height;
     cout <<"Copy constructor: "<< radius <<", " <<height <<endl; }
```

When this constructor is called, a copy of the actual argument is made—the space for a `Cylinder` variable is allocated and is initialized by the values of the fields of the actual argument. But wait a minute! There is no such thing as creation of an object in C++ without a constructor call! "The space for a `Cylinder` variable is allocated and is initialized by the values of the fields of the actual argument" means that the copy constructor is called for the parameter of the copy constructor. When this second version of the copy constructor is called, the copy of its actual argument is made, and the constructor is called again. This process of recursive invocation continues until either the user loses patience or the machine runs out of stack space.

If you do not have much experience with recursion and this explanation sounds too obscure, just try passing a copy constructor parameter by a value, and I am sure you won't want to do it again. Still, let me post an alert to that effect.

Alert

> The copy constructor has one parameter of the type of the class to which the constructor belongs. Make sure that you pass this parameter by `const` reference and not by value. Passing the copy constructor parameter by value results in an infinite sequence of copy constructor calls.

One more comment about the copy constructor. Since it is a function call, you can call it using the standard syntax for a function call to a general constructor.

```
int x = 20; Cylinder c1(50,70); // objects are created, initialized
int y=x; Cylinder c2(c1);       // call to Cylinder copy constructor
```

But C++ wants to treat objects and variables of built-in types in the same manner. This means that the initialization syntax of the constructor call is extended backwards to built-in variables, even though no constructor can be called for variables of these types. This syntax is available in C++ only, not in C.

```
int x(20);              // object is created and initialized
int y(x);               // variable y is created and initialized
```

One more general comment about constructor invocations. For all constructors, with the exception of the default constructor, the syntax of the function call (with its parentheses) is available. Here are examples of a general constructor and a copy constructor, for named variables and for dynamic variables.

```
Cylinder c1(50,70);             // general constructor is called
Cylinder c2=c1;                 // copy constructor is called
Cylinder *p = new Cylinder(50,70); // general constructor is called
Cylinder *q = new Cylinder(*p);   // copy constructor is called
```

For default constructors, this syntax is not available. It is a syntax error to use parentheses when the client code calls a default constructor.

```
Cylinder c1();                  // syntax error
Cylinder c2;                    // default constructor is called
Cylinder *p = new Cylinder();   // syntax error: parentheses
Cylinder *q = new Cylinder;     // default constructor is called
```

Why this inconsistency? To make compiler writing easier. Look at the first line of this last code. How do you know that this is supposed to be a constructor call and not a prototype of a function whose name is `c1()` and whose return type is `Cylinder`? You do not know. Neither does the compiler writer. One way to avoid this ambiguity is to prohibit the use of prototype everywhere but at the start of the source code file. This is reasonable because that is where prototypes usually are. However, C allows the prototypes to be used everywhere, and C++ design values backward compatibility too much to make it a syntax error. Java did not have the goal of backward compatibility with C, and its syntax for default constructor invocation in the client code is consistent with its syntax for calling all other constructors.

Conversion Constructors

A constructor with one parameter of some other type, not the same type as the class, is called a conversion constructor. Often, it is the type of one of the data members of the class. The conversion constructor is useful when the client code wants to specify only one individual value for creation of each object and use the same default values for other fields of each object.

For example, in a modeling program you might want to create `Cylinder` objects using different values of their radius. Initially, all objects should have height zero, and then they will grow to reflect the process being modeled (growth or arteries, connecting electronic components, heat exchange through the pipe walls, etc.).

```
Cylinder c1(50.0);        // conversion constructor is called
Cylinder c2 = 30.0;       // conversion constructor is called
```

Again, despite different syntax, both statements have the same meaning—a call to a conversion constructor.

Unlike default and copy constructors, conversion constructors are not supplied by the system. Unless a conversion constructor with one double parameter is defined in the class, both statements above are in error. The conversion constructor specifies what to do with the only value provided as a parameter and what default values to use for other fields of the object. In the next example, class `Cylinder` defines four constructors: default constructor, copy constructor, conversion constructor, and a general constructor with two parameters.

```
class Cylinder {
    double radius, height;
  public:
  Cylinder ()                  // programmer-supplied default constructor
     { radius = 1.0; height = 0.0; }
  Cylinder (const Cylinder &c)        // copy constructor
     { radius = c.radius;  height = c.height; }
  Cylinder(double r, double h)
     { radius = r;  height = h; }      // general constructor
  Cylinder (double r)
     { radius = r;  height = 0.0; }  // conversion constructor
  . . . } ;
```

The conversion constructor deals the first blow to the system of strong typing in C++. As I mentioned earlier, all modern languages support strong typing. If a value of one type is expected in a specific context, it is a syntax error to provide a value of another type. Consider, for example, the statement:

```
Cylinder c2 = 30.0;       // conversion constructor is called
```

If `Cylinder` is a simple C structure, it is a syntax error: You are told that you made a mistake and you have a chance to think about it and decide what you want to do. If `Cylinder` is a C++ class without a conversion constructor, it is a syntax error: Again, you do not have to run the program and analyze the program output to know about that. If `Cylinder` is a C++ class with a conversion constructor, it is not a syntax error. If you did it on purpose, fine. If you made a mistake, the friendly compiler does not stand by protecting you from your mistake. The system of strong typing is weakened.

As another example, consider function `CopyData()` from this chapter (again assuming that the radius and height data members are public).

```
void CopyData(Cylinder *to, const Cylinder &from)        // copy Cylinder data
   { to->radius=from.radius;   to->height=from.height; }   // arrow notation
```

Again, for a simple C structure or for a C++ class without a conversion constructor, this function call in the client code is a syntax error:

```
CopyData(&c2,70.0);             // the FROM Cylinder is missing here
```

If the conversion constructor is available, the compiler will generate code that creates a temporary unnamed `Cylinder` object, calls the conversion constructor (with actual argument 70.0) for that temporary object, and passes that temporary unnamed object to `CopyData()` as the second argument.

If the client code uses a numeric type value that is different from `double`, this is not a problem. The compiler generates code that converts this numeric value to `double` and then passes that converted value to the conversion constructor as the actual argument.

```
Cylinder c2 = 30;          // 30 is converted to double
CopyData(&c2,70);          // 70 is converted to double
```

Of course, if this client code is exactly what you want to write, it is a good thing that C++ provides you with the flexibility to implement your intent. If you wrote this code by mistake, it is a pity that the compiler does not tell you about the error so that you could correct it before the program has a chance to run.

Destructors

A C++ object is destroyed either at the end of program execution (for `extern` and `static` objects), at the exit from the closing brace of a scope (for automatic objects), when the operator `delete` is executed (for dynamic objects allocated with `new`), or when the library function `free()` is called (for objects allocated with `malloc()`).

Whenever a class object is destroyed (with the exception of the call to `free()`), the class destructor is called immediately before the destruction; if the class defines no destructor, the system-supplied default destructor is called (similar to default constructor, it does nothing).

A programmer-supplied destructor, similar to a constructor, is a class member function. Destructor syntax is even more rigid than constructor syntax is. No return type is allowed in the function interface, and no return statement is allowed in the function body. The destructor has the same name as the class name preceded by a tilde (~), for example, ~Cylinder(). Unlike constructors, destructors cannot have parameters.

Both constructors and destructors are good places to put debugging print statements.

```
class Cylinder {
  double radius, height;
public:
  ~Cylinder ( )        // programmer-defined destructor: no return type
  { cout << "Cylinder (" << radius << ", " << height
      << ") is destroyed" << endl; }     // no return value
  . . . . } ;
```

When a destructor is implemented outside of the class scope, the scope operator is used. Notice that the tilde is part of the function name, not of the scope operator.

```
Cylinder::~Cylinder ( )          // class destructor: no return type
{ cout << "Cylinder (" << radius << ", " << height
    << ") is destroyed" << endl; }      // no return value
```

Since destructors cannot have parameters, they cannot be overloaded, because overloaded functions must be different in their parameter lists. Hence, each class can have, at the most, one destructor.

A programmer-defined destructor is needed if the object uses dynamic memory or other resources (files, database locks, etc.); the destructor should return these resources to the system to avoid resource leaks. Destructor functions are complements of constructors for such sequences as memory allocation and deallocation, file opening and closing, and so on.

Let us consider an example of a class where the destructor could be useful. Class Name accommodates a string of characters that contains a person's name. The constructor initializes an array of characters. (It is a conversion constructor since it has one parameter of a type that is different from Name.) For simplicity's sake, I am making data public and supplying only one method, show_name(), which displays the object's contents on the screen.

```
struct Name {
    char contents[30];      // fixed size object, public data
  Name (char* name);        // or Name(char name []);
  void show_name();
  } ;                       // destructor is not needed yet

Name::Name(char* name)      // conversion constructor
{ strcpy(contents, name); } // standard action: copy argument data

void Name::show_name()
{ cout << contents << "\n"; }
```

The client code can define objects of this type and display their contents on the screen.

```
Name n1("Jones");                    // conversion constructor is called
Name *p = new Name("Smith");         // conversion constructor is called
n1.show_name();  p->show_name();
delete p;                            // unnamed object is deleted
```

This design allocates the same amount of memory no matter how large the name contents is. This is wasteful when the name is short, and this is prone to memory corruption when the name is too long.

Dynamic memory management is a popular solution to this problem. Instead of a fixed-size array as a data member, the class defines only a character pointer. The amount of heap memory depends on the length of the name that the client code supplies. In the constructor, `strlen()` is called to compute the amount of memory to allocate on the heap (the extra character is for the terminating zero), the memory is allocated, and `strcpy()` is called to initialize the heap memory.

```
struct Name {
    char *contents;                  // pointer to dynamic memory: still public
  Name (char* name);                 // or Name(char name []);
  void show_name();
     } ;  // destructor is needed now

Name::Name(char* name)               // conversion constructor
{ int len = strlen(name);            // number of characters in argument
  contents = new char[len+1];        // allocate heap memory for argument data
  if (contents == NULL)              // 'new' was not successful
     { cout << "Out of memory\n";  exit(1); }    // then give up
  strcpy(contents, name); }          // success: copy argument data

void Name::show_name()
{ cout <<contents << "\n"; }
```

I put the client code in a global function, `Client()`, to be able to discuss what happens when the new version of class `Name` is used.

```
void Client()
{ Name n1("Jones");                  // conversion constructor is called
  Name *p = new Name("Smith");       // conversion constructor is called
  n1.show_name();  p->show_name();
  delete p;                          // destructor for object pointer by p is called
  }                        // p is deleted, destructor for object n1 is called
```

When the delete p; statement is executed in the function Client(), memory pointed to by pointer p is deleted. This memory consists of pointer contents only. The memory pointed to by pointer contents is not deleted and becomes inaccessible. It is memory leak. Notice that the statement delete p; does not delete pointer p, it deletes what p points to. Pointer p is deleted according to the scope rules, when the scope where it is defined terminates. This happens when the execution of function Client() reaches its terminating brace.

Similarly, when function Client() terminates, its local object n1 is destroyed, and its pointer contents is returned to the stack. Memory pointed to by pointer contents is not returned to the system and represents memory leak.

It is for these types of classes, which manage their resources dynamically, that the use of destructors is vital. Destructors are needed to maintain the integrity of a C++ program. The destructor is called every time an object is destroyed by scope rules or by operator delete (but not by a function call to free()). Hence, the destructor is a good place to release memory (and other resources) acquired by the object during its lifetime (mostly, in its constructor, but other member functions can allocate dynamic memory as well).

For class Name, the destructor is very simple. Listing 9.3 shows class Name with the destructor that returns the heap memory. Figure 9–3 shows the result of the execution of the program with the output from debugging statements in the constructor and in the destructor.

Listing 9.3   **Example of using the destructor to return heap memory allocated to named and unnamed objects.**

```
#include <iostream>
using namespace std;

struct Name {
    char *contents;                    // public pointer to dynamic memory
    Name (char* name);                 // or Name (char name []);
    void show_name();
    ~Name(); } ;                       // destructor eliminates memory leak

Name::Name(char* name)                 // conversion constructor
{ int len = strlen(name);              // number of characters
    contents = new char[len+1];        // allocate dynamic memory
    if (contents == NULL)              // 'new' was not successful
      { cout << "Out of memory\n";  exit(1); }    // give up
    strcpy(contents, name);            // standard set of actions
    cout << "object created: " << contents << endl; }    // debugging
```

```
void Name::show_name()
{ cout <<contents << "\n"; }

Name::~Name()                         // destructor
{ cout << "object destroyed: " << contents << endl;     // debugging
  delete contents; }                  // delete heap memory, not pointer 'contents'

void Client()
{ Name n1("Jones");                   // conversion constructor is called
  Name *p = new Name("Smith");        // conversion constructor is called
  n1.show_name();   p->show_name();
  delete p;                   // destructor for object pointed to by p is called
  }                           // p is deleted, destructor for object n1 is called

int main()                            // pushing responsibility to server functions
{ Client();
  return 0;
  }
```

When function `Client()` executes `delete p;` the class `Name` destructor is called and executes the statement `delete contents`. When function `Client()` destroys object n1, the destructor is called and executes statement `delete contents`. This eliminates memory leak.

Figure 9–4 shows the memory use by function `Client()`. Figure 9–4(A) shows the state of memory after the named object n1 and the unnamed object pointed to by pointer p are created. The numbers show that stack space for n1 is allocated first (by scope rules), heap space for "Jones" is allocated next (by the constructor), then stack space for pointer p (by scope rules), space for the unnamed object (pointed to by p) on the heap, and finally heap space for "Smith" is allocated.

Figure 9–4(B) and (C) demonstrate the destruction of objects. Figure 9–4(B) shows that the heap space for "Smith" is returned first (by the destructor), and then the unnamed heap object is deleted (by the `delete` operator). Pointer p stays because the `delete` operator does not delete the pointer; it deletes the heap memory pointed to by the pointer.

Figure 9–4(C) shows that the scope rules deallocate the stack space for pointer p and for the named object n1. The demise of the pointer does not

Figure 9–3
Output of the program from Listing 9.3.

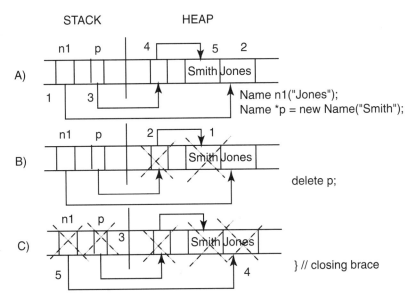

Figure 9-4 Memory management map for the client function `Client()` in Listing 9.3.

lead to any events. The destruction of object n1 causes a call to the Name constructor, deletion of heap memory allocated to `"Jones"` (by the constructor),
and then the destruction of stack space allocated to n1.

Make sure that you spend enough time working with this figure and experimenting with your own code. Some programmers find heap memory
(`"Smith"` and `"Jones"` in these examples) easier to analyze if they view it as
part of Name object instances. I find it more convenient to think only about
data members as parts of object instances: Heap memory is an additional
resource that is allocated to each object instance and is later returned. From
that point of view, the space allocated to the object itself is the size defined
by its data members, not by arguments to its constructor. But this is a matter
of taste.

Notice that if function `Client()` fails to execute `delete p;` then the
object pointed to by pointer p (its pointer `contents` and memory pointed to
by `contents`) is never returned to the system. It is the responsibility of the
client programmer to preserve the integrity of the program. There is no such
requirement for objects controlled by scope rules. For example, object n1 is
deleted automatically when execution reaches the closing brace of `Client()`.
The client programmer does not lift a finger to make it happen. All that is
required for memory management is that the server programmer include the
destructor in the design of class Name.

Timing of Constructor and Destructor Invocations

The term "constructor" implies that this member function constructs the object. The term "destructor" implies that this member function destroys the object. Do not fall into this trap. These terms describe the tasks performed by constructors and destructors incorrectly.

In the previous discussion, I was careful to point out that the constructor is called *after* the object is constructed, and the destructor is called *before* the object is destroyed. Often, C++ books do not pay attention to this difference and state that constructors and destructors are called *when* the objects are constructed and destroyed. This is unfortunate, because it makes programmers think that constructors construct objects and destructors destroy objects.

This is not the case. It is scope rules (for named objects) and operators `new` and `delete` (for unnamed objects) that construct and destroy objects. Constructors only initialize object fields after these fields have been constructed and allocate additional resources, for example, heap memory. Destructors only return resources that objects acquired during their lifetime; for example, heap memory in constructors and in other functions.

Constructors do not construct, and destructors do not destruct.

Class Scope and the Overriding of Names in Nested Scopes

The actual times of constructor/destructor invocations depend on the scope and storage class of the object instances.

Scope defines the accessibility of variables and objects for different parts of the program code. Storage class defines the lifetime of variables and objects from their creation to their destruction. This section extends the discussion of scope and storage class from Chapter 6. If you feel that it is too complex, you can skip it during the first reading. (I hope there will be a second reading.) This material is important, but it can wait until you accumulate more experience with writing and reading C++ code.

Since a global variable can be defined anywhere in the file, even after some function definitions, it is not accessible from the functions that are defined earlier in the file than the variable declaration is.

```
Cylinder Cglobal;              // available everywhere in the file

int main ()
{ Cylinder c;                  // scope is limited to main()
   . . . . }

int y;                         // not visible in main(), visible in foo()

void foo()                     // cannot be called from main() if no prototype
{ y = 0;                       // access to global variable
   Cylinder Clocal;
   Clocal.setCylinder(10,30);  // public members are visible
   Cglobal.setCylinder(5,20); }  // public members are visible
   . . . .                     // Cglobal, y, foo() are visible here
```

This is legal C++, but it is not a good programming style.

Since a local variable can be defined anywhere in a block (a function block or an unnamed block), it is not accessible in the code in this block that precedes this variable. If a local name is the same as a global name, the local name is used in the block where it is defined, and the global name is used outside the local block.

To these two scopes (described in detail in Chapter 6), C++ adds yet another scope: class scope. Each name defined in the class scope (a data member or a member function, a public or a private member) is known within the whole class scope. The rules of one-pass compilation for global and local scopes do not apply to the class scope. This is why in all of our examples of `Cylinder` class, `Cylinder` data members are accessible in `Cylinder` member functions for any order of member definitions.

If a name defined in class scope is the same as a global name, then all references to this name within the class scope are to the name defined in the class scope; outside the class scope (that is, outside the class member functions), the references to that name are to the global name.

If a name defined in the class scope is the same as a local name defined in one of its member functions, then the local name is used within that member function, and the name defined in the class scope is used in other member functions.

In short, a local scope name can hide both class scope names and global names; a class scope name can hide a global name. These rules of name hiding can be overridden by the global scope operator `::` (for global names) and by the class scope operator (for the class scope name).

In the next example, the name `radius` is used for a global variable, for the `Cylinder` data member, and as a local name in the `Cylinder` member function `setCylinder()`.

```
double radius = 100;                  // global name

struct Cylinder {                     // start of the class scope
    double radius, height;            // member radius hides global radius

void setCylinder(double r, double h)
{ double radius;
   radius = r;  height = h;           // local radius hides data member radius
   Cylinder::radius = radius; }       // class scope operator overrides the rule

void scaleCylinder(double factor)
{ radius  = ::radius;                 // global scope operator overrides the rule
   height *= factor; }
   . . . } ;                          // end of class scope
```

When parameter r in setCylinder() is assigned to radius, it is a local variable that is assigned, not the Cylinder data member. To assign a value to the data member radius, the class scope operator should be used. In member function scaleCylinder(), radius means the class data member; to get the value of the global variable radius, the global scope operator should be used.

Sometimes programmers use the same name for a method parameter as for a data member. For example, this version of setCylinder() function is incorrect.

```
void Cylinder::setCylinder(double radius, double h)      // incorrect function
{ radius = radius;  height = h; }      // parameter is local, hides data member
```

This function compiles and runs without any problems. However, the designer and the compiler understand the assignment radius = radius; differently. For the designer, the left-hand side radius means the data member radius, and the right-hand side radius means the parameter. For the compiler both sides mean the parameter. Assigning the parameter to itself is not very useful, but this is one of the examples where the compiler refuses to second-guess the programmer. You want to assign the parameter to itself? Fine, it is legal C++.

Storage class refers to the scope of the life cycle of a variable: when they are created and when destroyed (automatic, external, static).

Local automatic variables are allocated on the stack when the execution reaches their definitions (different space for different execution of the scope). If the same name is used in different scopes, it refers to different locations in memory. If there is no initialization, the contents of memory are undefined. For an object, a constructor is called immediately after the space is allocated.

Automatic variables are destroyed when the execution reaches the end of the block where it is defined. For an object, the destructor is called immediately before the space is returned to the system.

For external or static (local or global) variables, space is allocated and initialized in fixed memory before the program starts to run. If no explicit initial value is specified, memory is initialized to zero. For an object, constructor code is executed (and all functions that the constructor might call) after the space is allocated, before the start of `main()`. The order of invocation of constructors for different objects is undefined.

External and static (local or global) variables are destroyed when `main()` terminates (reaches its closing brace or terminates in other ways); for objects, the destructor is called immediately before the object is destroyed.

This is a big change relative to our discussion of storage classes in Chapter 6. If the program does not use global variables of programmer-defined classes, the order of code execution is well defined. It starts with the first line of `main()` and ends with the last line of `main()`.

Dynamic variables are allocated and deallocated explicitly. Usually, the calls to operators `new` and `delete` or to functions `malloc()` and `free()` do not happen in the same function (scope). Often, a dynamic variable is allocated in one function, attached to a dynamic structure (stack, queue, linked list, etc.), and then deallocated in another function. (These functions should probably belong to the same client class.)

Memory Management with Operators and Function Calls

In this section, I compare the use of operators `new` and `delete` with the use of functions `malloc()` and `free()`. Similar to the previous section, you can skip this section if you feel it is too technical. Make sure you come back to this section for two things: a) the recommendation to use `new` and `delete` over `malloc()` and `free()`, and b) the criticism of my example for not abiding by the principles of object-oriented programming.

Notice that the constructor is called only after the class object is created by the scope rules or by the operator `new`. It is not called after a `malloc()` call. Similarly, the destructor is called only before the object is destroyed by the scope rules or by the operator `delete`. A call to `free()` does not call the destructor.

When `malloc()` and `free()` are used, it is the responsibility of the client programmer to ensure that objects have the necessary heap memory and this memory is returned when not needed. The client code has to allocate dynamic memory from the heap and later deallocate it, returning it to the heap. Violation of this responsibility results in memory corruption and memory leaks. It is also important to distinguish dynamic management of class objects from dynamic management of object memory, where a class data member is a pointer that points to dynamic memory.

Listing 9.4 shows an example similar to Listing 9.3, but instead of new, malloc() is used to allocate the object space pointed to dynamically by pointer p. Obviously, memory management here is more complex than in Listing 9.3: The client code allocates the heap memory for an unnamed object and then for the dynamic memory that contains dynamic memory of the object (with contents "Smith"). The output of this example is the same as for Listing 9.3. (I turned off the debugging statements in the constructor and the destructor.)

Listing 9.4   Memory management by client code rather than by server object.

```
#include <iostream>
using namespace std;

struct Name {
     char *contents;              // public pointer to dynamic memory
   Name (char* name);             // or Name (char name []);
   void show_name();
   ~Name(); } ;                   // destructor eliminates memory leak

Name::Name(char* name)           // conversion constructor
{ int len = strlen(name);        // number of characters
   contents = new char[len+1];   // allocate dynamic memory
   if (contents -- NULL)         // 'new' was not successful
     { cout << "Out of memory\n";  exit(1); }    // give up
   strcpy(contents, name); }     // standard set of actions

void Name::show_name()
{ cout <<contents << "\n"; }

Name::~Name()                    // destructor
{ delete contents; }             // it deletes heap memory, not the pointer

void Client()
{ Name n1("Jones");                          // conversion constructor is called
   Name *p=(Name*)malloc(sizeof(Name));      // no constructor is called
   p->contents = new char[strlen("Smith")+1];     // allocate memory
   if (p->contents == NULL)                  // 'new' was not successful
     { cout << "Out of memory\n";  exit(1); }     // give up
   strcpy(p->contents, "Smith");             // 'new' was successful
   n1.show_name();   p->show_name();   // use the objects
   delete p->contents;                 // avoid memory leak
   free (p); // notice the sequence of actions
   }                      // p is deleted, destructor for object n1 is called
```

```
int main()              // pushing responsibility to server functions
{ Client();
  return 0;
  }
```

In this example, the object n1 is created by scope rules, and its constructor properly allocates and initializes the heap memory for it. The unnamed object pointed to by pointer p is allocated by malloc(), and the constructor is not called. The call to malloc() only allocates object memory, that is, the pointer p->contents. It does not allocate additional heap memory needed to store the name information. Hence, the client code allocates and initializes heap memory pointed to by p->contents.

When the function Client() terminates, no care should be exercised to delete object n1 and return its heap memory. The scope rules destroy this object, and the destructor returns its heap memory. It is different for the unnamed object pointed to by pointer p. Not only does the object have to be destroyed by the client code, but the object's heap memory has to be returned by the client code.

In this little example, I use classes, objects, messages, dynamic memory management, constructors, and destructors—all of the impressive arsenal of C++ programming. Nevertheless, I managed to violate all the principles of object-oriented programming. The only redeeming feature is that I did it on purpose. Often, programmers do it without noticing. Let us run through the list again.

I violated the principle of encapsulation: client code uses the name of object field contents, thus creating the dependency; if the name of this field of class Name changes, function Client() has to be changed too.

I violated the principle of information hiding (in the sense discussed in Chapter 8): The client code knows that class Name uses heap memory rather than a fixed-size character array; if the design of class Name changes, function Client() will be affected as well.

These dependencies created the need for human coordination: I have to ask the designer of class Name about details such as field names, dynamic memory management, and who knows what else instead of just learning the interface of the public member functions, as is possible in the case of using variable n1.

The code of function Client() is not expressed in terms of the function calls to class Name member functions; instead, it is cluttered with access to data and data manipulation so that the maintainer has to spend extra time trying to understand what I wanted to achieve.

Worst of all, I did not push the responsibility to the server class, even though all necessary services are there; I did memory allocation and dealloca- tion in the client code rather then using the server object.

The result is dismal. The client code is much more complex than it needs to be. Also, it is error prone. A little change in function `Client()`, and it falls apart. In this version, I free the object pointed to by pointer p first, and then I try to delete heap memory. When the program is run, the operating system accuses the program of memory violation and aborts it. This is reasonable, because when the object pointed to by p disappears, pointer p->contents disappears as well. Not every operating system can afford the luxury of check- ing every memory access at the expense of the execution speed, and on many platforms this flaw would go unnoticed.

```
void Client()
{ Name n1("Jones");                                // conversion constructor is called
  Name *p=(Name*)malloc(unsigned(sizeof(Name))); // no constructor is called
  p->contents = new char[strlen("Smith")+1];      // allocate dynamic memory
  if (p->contents == NULL)                         // 'new' was not successful
    { cout << "Out of memory\n";  exit(1); }       // give up
  strcpy(p->contents, "Smith");                    // 'new' was successful
  n1.show_name();  p->show_name();                 // use the objects
  free (p);                                        // wrong sequence of actions !
  delete p->contents;                              // there is nothing to delete here!
  }                          // p is deleted, destructor for object n1 is called
```

In addition, if the object is allocated with `new`, it should be deallocated with `delete`; it is a semantic error (!) to use `free()`. Similarly, it is a semantic error (!) to use `delete` to return memory allocated by `malloc()`.

I am using these exclamation points to alert you that a semantic error is dif- ferent than a syntactic error, run-time abort, or incorrect result of execution (which can be discovered by observing test results). The concept of "seman- tically incorrect program" is an unfortunate contribution of C++ to software engineering. The results of an incorrect sequence of calls are "undefined," and you are left to fend for yourself to make sure that the program does not contain that time bomb waiting to wreak havoc.

These two characteristics of functions `malloc()` and `free()`—no calls to constructors and destructors and the danger of incorrect program when mixed with the operators `new` and `delete`—are troubling. This is why using `malloc()` and `free()` for dynamic memory management is not popular in C++. However, they are very popular in C (there are no `new` and `delete` operators in C), and legacy systems often use these functions. They are also used when the applica- tion that dynamically handles a lot of memory scrambles to improve its perfor- mance. Functions `malloc()` and `free()` can be used for creating customized operators `new` and `delete` for selected classes. This is an advanced use of operators that will be discussed later.

The version presented in Listing 9.3 is better than the version in Listing 9.4: It does not defeat encapsulation, violate information hiding, or create the need for additional human cooperation. It expresses its algorithm in terms of messages to the server object. However, it burdens the client code with the responsibility of allocating and deallocating the `Name` object pointed to by pointer `p`. Programmers often use dynamic memory management where it is not very useful. This is the case here. This object has to be allocated and deallocated using scope rules rather than by using explicit memory management.

```
void Client()
{ Name n1("Jones");    // conversion constructor is called
  Name n2("Smith");    // no dynamic allocation/deallocation
  n1.show_name();   n2.show_name();
  }                      // destructor for objects n1 and n2 is called
```

Make sure that you do not make your C++ programs more complex than they have to be.

Using Returned Objects in Client Code

C++ functions can return built-in values, pointers, references, and objects. They cannot return arrays, but returning pointers allows you to simulate returning arrays. Built-in values can be used as rvalues only. Other return types (pointers, references, and objects) can be used as lvalues. This opens the door to quite interesting idioms in the source code. These idioms contribute to the expressiveness of C++ programs but sometimes make the source code more difficult to understand.

The material in this section can be easily skipped in the first reading, even though the programming idioms I am discussing here are quite common.

Returning Pointers and References

I will start with the discussion of simple (noncomposite) built-in return types. The values of these atomic types are used as rvalues, but the pointers and references can be used as both rvalues and lvalues.

Consider the following version of class `Point`. Its `setPoint()` member function modifies the state of the target `Point` object. Its `getX()` and `getY()` member functions return integer values; `getPtr()` returns a pointer to data member x, and `getRef()` returns a reference to data member x. I am not providing functions that return a pointer and a reference to data member y because functions `getPtr()` and `getRef()` are sufficient to illustrate the related issues, including modification of the object state.

```
class Point
{ int x, y;                        // private data
  public:
    void setPoint(int a,  int b)
    { x = a;   y = b; }
    int getX()                     // return a value
     { return x; }
    int getY()
     {return y; }
    int* getPtr()                  // return a pointer to the value
     { return &x; }                // the address operator is needed
    int& getRef()                  // return a reference to a value
     { return x; } } ;             // no address operator for reference
```

In deciding whether the address-of operator should or should not be used, you rely on the same logic as for assignment or for parameter passing. Function `getPtr()` returns a pointer; hence, to return a value of x would be a type mismatch, a syntax error. Function `getRef()` returns a reference, and the reference could (and should) be initialized by the value to which it is going to point for the rest of its life. Hence, using &x would be a type mismatch, a syntax error—it is an address, not an `int` value.

When a value is returned from a function, it can be used as rvalue only, on the right-hand side of assignments or in comparisons (or as input parameters in function calls). In this example, client code manipulates the value returned by the function. The value changes, but the object whose value was returned by the function does not change, because return by value makes a copy of the original value, pretty much like passing parameters by value.

```
Point pt;   pt.setPoint(20,40);
int a = pt.getX(), b = 2* pt.getY() + 4;      // ok, use as rvalue
a += 10;                              // 'a' changes, but pt.x does not
```

When a pointer or a reference is returned from a function, it can be used both as rvalue and also as lvalue, on the left-hand side of the assignment, or as an output parameter in a function call. In the next example, the first line treats the values returned by `getPtr()` and `getRef()` as rvalue—nothing unusual. The second line modifies the values pointed to by pointer `ptr` and reference `ref`. Notice that they both point inside the variable `pt` to its data member `pt.x`. This data member is private, but the client code is able to change it without using access functions. The third line uses the function call as an lvalue, and it also modifies the state of variable `pt`. Notice that there is no need for parentheses in the expression `*pt.getPtr()`; the selector operator is of higher priority than the dereference operator, which here dereferences the value returned by the method, not a pointer pointing to the target object. (`pt` is not a pointer, it is the name of a `Point` object.)

```
int *ptr = pt.getPtr(); int &ref = pt.getRef();    // ok, use as rvalue
*ptr += 10; ref += 10;   // private data is changed through aliasing
*pt.getPtr()=50; pt.getRef()=100;         // private data is changed
```

First, this syntax of using a function call as an lvalue is unusual. Second, this practice, as some say, "breaks encapsulation and information hiding": It changes the private data that should not be accessible to client code. But hey, who says that information hiding is about not changing private data? A call to `setPoint()` does change private data, and it does not break information hiding. Neither does a call to `getRef()`. Encapsulation and information hiding are about avoiding dependencies between classes, not about avoiding changes to private data members.

From a software engineering point of view, the major problem with this example is that it uses aliasing—it refers to data member `x` but uses other names instead: `ptr`, `ref`, `getPtr()`, and `getRef()`. These names, especially `getPtr()` and `getRef()`, give no indication that they refer to data member `x`. Hence, this coding idiom forces the maintainer to spend additional effort to understand the meaning of the code. Use this technique with caution, if at all. It is legal C++, but it is dangerous. It is more harmful than using global variables.

Returning pointers and references requires that the address passed to the caller remain valid after the function terminates. In the previous example, `getPtr()` and `getRef()` return a pointer to `pt.x`, and `pt.x` remains in scope after the function returns. Sometimes, this is not the case. In the next example, functions `getDistPtr()` and `getDistRef()` compute the distance between the target `Point` object and the point of origin. They return the pointer and the reference to the computed value of the distance. This is a regrettable blunder!

```
class Point
{ int x, y;
public:
   . . .                     // setPoint(), getX(), getY(), getPtr(), getRef()
   int* getDistPtr()
   { int dist = (int)sqrt(x*x + y*y);
     return &dist; }          // no copying, but dist disappears
   int& getDistRef()
   { int dist = (int)sqrt(x*x + y*y);
     return dist; }  } ;      // different syntax, same problem
```

The local variable dist disappears after getDistPtr() and getDistRef()
terminate. The use of its address might produce correct results if its memory
location is not used for something else, or it can silently result in incorrect
computations. Some compilers might produce a warning, others won't. At any
rate, this version of Point code above and client code below are both syntactically correct.

```
Point pt;  pt.setPoint(20,40);
int * ptr = pt.getDistPtr();                              // invalid pointer
cout << " Pointer to distance : " << *ptr << endl;        // okay
int &ref = pt.getDistRef();                               // invalid reference
cout << " Reference to distance : " << ref << endl;       // okay
cout << " Pointer to distance : " << *ptr << endl;        // bad
cout << " Reference to distance : " << ref << endl;       // bad
```

The results of running this example on my machine are shown on Figure
9–5. I got away with the first use of invalid pointer and invalid reference: Both
output values 44 are correct even if neither the pointer nor the reference is
valid. The attempt to print these values again gave incorrect results. This
means that any other use of these values is incorrect. This is likely to go unnoticed. After all, I have just tested the values of ref and *ptr, saw the correct
results, and have no reason to expect that they will change! My vigilance will
likely be directed toward other issues. What about yours?

After all, we all take correct results of the execution as evidence of program
accuracy. You might want to test the program on another set of test data to
cover additional paths through the program, but it is counterintuitive (and
counterproductive) to repeat the tests for the same input data. The results
should be the same. They are in other programming languages. They are in
C++, too, but only if you know what you are doing.

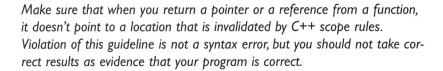

```
Pointer to distance : 44
Reference to distance : 44
Pointer to distance : 4198928
Reference to distance : 4198928
```

Figure 9–5   Correct and incorrect results of returning a pointer and a reference.

Alert

Make sure that when you return a pointer or a reference from a function, it doesn't point to a location that is invalidated by C++ scope rules. Violation of this guideline is not a syntax error, but you should not take correct results as evidence that your program is correct.

In general, it is a good idea to limit return values to boolean flags that report back to the client code on success or failure of a function call. However, the aesthetic allure of functions such as getX() and getY() is too strong, and programmers will always use them. Make sure you are not too excited by the power of C++ and do not return pointers and references, especially to values that soon become invalid. The compiler will not stand by to prevent you from making a mistake.

Returning Objects

In the next example, I am adding to class Point three more member functions: closestPointVal(), closestPointPtr(), and closestPointRef(). Each function accepts a reference to a Point object as a parameter and computes the distance to the point of origin for the parameter and for the target of the message. If the parameter is closer to the point of origin, the function returns the parameter object. If the target of the message is closer to the point of origin, the function returns the target object (as a dereferenced pointer this that points to the target object).

The first function returns the closest object itself, the second function returns the pointer to the closest object, and the third function returns the reference to the closest object. The advantage of this interface is that it makes possible the chain message notation, where the return value of one function call is used as the target for another function call. The use of both as an rvalue or even as an lvalue is possible for all three kinds of return values: objects, pointers, and references.

```
class Point
{ int x, y;
public:
    . . .                        // setPoint(), getX(), getY(), getPtr(), getRef()
    . . .                            // getDistPtr(), getDistRef()
    Point closestPointVal(Point& pt)
    { if (x*x + y*y < pt.x *pt.x + pt.y * pt.y)
         return *this;               // object value: copying to temp object
      else
         return pt; }                // object value: copying to temp object
    Point* closestPointPtr(Point& p)       // returns pointer: no copy
    { return (x*x + y*y < p.x*p.x + p.y*p.y) ? this : &p; }
    Point& closestPointRef(Point& p)        // returns reference: no copy
    { return (x*x + y*y < p.x*p.x + p.y*p.y) ? *this : p; } } ;
```

Here, this is a keyword that denotes a pointer to the target object of the message; in the following example, it is object p1. The first function uses longhand (two return statements), the last two functions use shorthand (the conditional operator).

Notice how addressing modes play themselves in returning object values. Function closestPointVal() returns a Point object (by value). When the target object is returned, the this pointer (which points to the target) has to be dereferenced, and the fields of the target object (object p1) are copied into the fields of the receiving object (object pt). When the parameter object is returned, reference pt is used. This reference is a synonym for the object it is pointing to (object p2), and the fields of this object are copied into the receiving object (object pt).

```
Point p1,p2;  p1.setPoint(20,40);  p2.setPoint(30,50);     // set Point objects
Point pt = p1.closestPointVal(p2);      // fields of the closest point are copied
```

Function closestPointPtr() returns a pointer to the closest Point object. When the target object is closer than the parameter object is, the this pointer (which points to the target, e.g., p1) is returned. In the next example, the pointer value is copied in the receiving pointer (pointer p). When the parameter object is closer, its reference p is used. Since this reference is a synonym for the object it is pointing to (and not for the address of this object), the value of &p is copied into the receiving pointer. This pointer can be used to access the members of the closest object (p1 or p2).

```
Point *p = p1.closestPointPtr(p2);      // pointer is returned: fast
p->setPoint(0,0);            // move p1 or p2 to the point of origin
```

You see that returning the object value is potentially slow, and that returning the object pointer avoids copying the object fields. When an object reference is returned, the situation is not clear-cut. Function `closestPointRef()` returns a reference to the closest `Point` object. When the target object is closer, the `this` pointer should be used. Since you cannot assign a pointer to a reference, you should use notation for the target value, `*this`. Keep in mind, however, that this does not mean that the copy of the target object is created. It is only notation. Similar to passing parameters by reference, it is only the address (reference) that is copied, not the object fields. When the parameter object is closer, its reference `p` is used directly with the same result: only the reference is copied, not the fields.

```
Point &r =p1.closestPointRef(p2);      // reference is returned: fast
r.setPoint(0,0);                 // move p1 or p2 to the point of origin
```

If, however, the receiving variable in the client code is of the object type rather than of the reference type, copying does take place.

```
Point pt = p1.closestPointRef(p2);     // p1 or p2 is copied into pt
```

You see that returning an object reference does not necessarily eliminate a potential performance problem.

The major stimulus for returning an object (whether it is returned by value, pointer, or reference) is the possibility of the chain notation for messages: sending a message to an object that is returned by a function.

```
Point p1, p2;  p1.setPoint(20,40);  p2.setPoint(30,50);
int a = p1.closestPointVal(p2).getX();         // might be slow
int b = (*p1.closestPointPtr(p2)).getX();      // fast and elegant
int c = p1.closestPointRef(p2).getX();         // fast and elegant
```

The object returned by `closestPointVal()` above is a temporary unnamed `Point` object that is held long enough to be sent the `getX()` message. After that, the unnamed object disappears. In two other function calls, both the pointer and the reference are pointing to one of the objects defined in the client space, and the issue of the target life span is moot—it is there.

In the previous example, the message sent to a returned object did not change the state of that object. The chain notation might also be used with messages that change the state of the target object.

```
p1.closestPointRef(p2).setPoint(15,35);    // what is set here? p1? p2?
p1.closestPointPtr(p2)->setPoint(10,30);   // and what is set here?
```

In the example above, client code changes either object `p1` or object `p2`, but the change sticks. In the next example, it is a temporary unnamed object that is changed and then immediately destroyed! This operation is not very useful, but it is definitely legal C++.

```
p1.closestPointVal(p2).setPoint(0,0);    // create, set, destroy object
```

Make sure that you use returned objects with caution; often, the gain in performance and convenience in notation are not worth integrity risks and confusion about results of the operation. Also, creation and destruction of unnamed objects takes time, both for memory management of the heap and for constructor and destructor calls.

More on the `const` **Keyword**

This section is very important. It reviews the multiple meanings of the keyword `const` and shows how to use this keyword for one of the most important tasks of the software developer—transmitting the developer's knowledge about properties of program components to the maintenance programmer. Failure to do so is one of the simplest (and most common) ways to contribute to software crisis.

As you saw earlier (Chapters 4, "C++ Control Flow," and 7), the `const` keyword has several meanings in C++; the meaning depends on the context. When the keyword precedes the type name of the variable, it specifies that the value of the variable will remain constant. The variable has to be initialized at definition, and any attempt to assign to it a different (or even the same) value will be flagged as a syntax error.

```
const int x = 5;    // x will not (and cannot) change
x = 20;             // syntax error: it prevents changes to x
int *y = &x;        // syntax error: it prevents future changes to x
```

When a pointer has to point to a constant variable (no pun is intended; it is called a variable, but it does not change), it has to be labeled as a pointer to constant by using the `const` keyword before the type name. Then, any subsequent attempt to use this dereferenced pointer as an lvalue will be flagged as a syntax error.

```
const int *p1 = &x;    // ok: *p1 will not be used to change x
*p1 = 0;               // syntax error: *p1 cannot be an lvalue
int a = 5;             // an ordinary variable: it can be changed
p1 = &a;    *p1 = 0;   // syntax error: 'a' cannot change through *p1
```

When a reference has to point to a constant variable, it has to be labeled as a reference to constant by using the `const` keyword before the type name. Then, any subsequent attempt to use this reference as an lvalue will be flagged as a syntax error.

```
int &r1 = x;              // syntax error: x should not change through r1
const int &r2 = x;        // ok: reference to a constant, x will not change
r2 = 0;                   // syntax error: r2 is a reference to a constant
const int &r3 = a;        // 'a' can change but not through r3
r3 = 0;                   // syntax error: 'a' cannot change through r3
```

When the keyword const follows the pointer operator, it means that it is a constant pointer: It has to point to the same location and cannot be diverted to point to another location, but no promise is made to keep the value pointed to by this pointer the same.

```
int* const p2 = &a;       // p2 will point to 'a' only, not elsewhere
*p2 = 0;                  // ok: no promises were made to keep it const
int b = 5;  p2 = &b;      // syntax error: breach of promise
```

There is no need to define a special notation to indicate that a reference is constant. All references are constant by default in C++ and cannot be turned to refer to another location. As with pointers, no promise is made to keep the value referred to by the reference the same.

```
int& r4 = a;              // r4 points to 'a' only, no const is needed for pledge
r4 = b;                   // no syntax error; just r is not diverted
```

The use of const in function interfaces is similar to its use with values and pointers: It states that the actual argument (or the pointer) does not change as the result of the call.

```
void f1(const int& x);    // x is not changed by the function
void f2(const int x);     // redundant: x is passed by value anyway
void f3(int* const y);    // redundant: y is passed by value
void f4(int * const *y);  // ok, pointer is passed by pointer
void f4(const int *&y);   // ok: pointer is passed by reference
```

Using const objects in function interfaces can make it more difficult for a function to return a pointer or a reference to the parameter object. Allowing it to do so would make it possible for the client code to change that object through aliasing, similar to examples discussed earlier in this chapter.

In case you skipped that section let me repeat that three functions, closestPointVal(), closestPointPtr(), and closestPointRef() do the same job. Each function compares the distance between the target object and the point of origin and between the parameter object and the point of origin. If the target object is closer to the point of origin, each function returns the target object. If the parameter object is closer, each function returns the parameter object. The difference is that closestPointVal() returns the object itself, closestPointPtr() returns the pointer to the object, and `closestPointRef()` returns a reference to the object. In the section, *Using Returned Objects in Client Code*, I did not use the `const` keyword for the function parameter. In this next example, I am adding this keyword.

```
class Point
{ int x, y;                              // private data
public:                                  // public operations
   . . .                                 // setPoint(), getX(), getY(), getPtr(), getRef()
   . . .                                 // getDistPtr(), getDistRef()
   Point closestPointVal(const Point& pt)  // irrelevant: data is copied
   { if (x*x + y*y < pt.x *pt.x + pt.y * pt.y)
        return *this;                    // object value: copying to temp object
     else
        return pt; }                     // object value: copying to temp object
   Point* closestPointPtr(const Point& p)  // parameter is const
   { return (x*x + y*y < p.x*p.x + p.y*p.y) ? this : &p; }       // error
   Point& closestPointRef(const Point& p)  // parameter is const
   { return (x*x + y*y < p.x*p.x + p.y*p.y) ? *this : p; } } ;   // error
```

Function `closestPointVal()` returns either the target object or the parameter object, but in either case it is a copy of the `Point` object. Hence, the `const` keyword for the function parameter does not limit the use of the function. If the client code changes the returned object, this change will be made to a copy of the actual argument, not to the object that is promised to be kept constant.

```
Point p1,p2;
p1.setPoint(20,40);   p2.setPoint(30,50);   // set Point objects
Point pt = p1.closestPointVal(p2);
pt.setPoint(0,0);                            // no breach of pledge
p1.closestPointVal(p2).setPoint(0,0); // not useful, and not harmful
```

Function `closestPointPtr()` can return a pointer to its `Point` argument. This pointer can then be used by the client code to change the state of the argument object. Similarly, function `closestPointRef()` can return a reference to its `Point` argument. This reference also can then be used to change the state of the argument object.

```
Point *p = p1.closestPointPtr(p2);       // p2 should not be changed
p->setPoint(0,0);           // p2 could be changed - breach of promise
Point &r =p1.closestPointRef(p2);        // p2 should not be changed
r.setPoint(10,10);          // p2 could be changed - breach of promise
```

In this example, the object p2 does not really change because all three functions return the object p1 that is closer to the point of origin than is object p2. Even if it was the object p2 that is modified, it is modified outside of functions `closestPointPtr()` and `closestPointRef()`! Never mind; C++ does not allow such use of constant objects. However, it is too difficult for the compiler to discover this offense when it analyzes the client code (note that it is not easy for a human being either). So, the compiler declares both functions to be in error.

The formal reason for doing this is that the parameter object, for example, in function closestPointPtr(), has the const keyword, but the return type does not.

```
Point* closestPointPtr(const Point& p)          // inconsistency: damage to const
{ return (x*x + y*y < p.x*p.x + p.y*p.y) ? this : &p; }          // syntax error
```

C++ provides you with three ways of handling the situation. One is to give up and eliminate the const keyword from the function interface. The second way to avoid the syntax error is to use the const_cast operator to suppress the constant property inside the member functions. The third way is to use the const keyword in yet two other ways.

Eliminating the const keyword from the function interface is for the faint-hearted and fearful. The real programmer never forfeits the opportunity to pass on to the client code programmer and to the maintenance programmer what the class designer had in mind during design. The function does not change its parameter object, and hence the const keyword should be there.

The second technique is more complex. The const_cast operator converts its constant argument to the same type with protection against changes removed. The type is specified in angle brackets between the const_cast operator and the argument. For example, const_cast<valueType>(constValue) casts constValue of type valueType to a value of the same type valueType with protection against changes removed. For class Point, I am converting the pointer to a constant Point object into a pointer to a nonconstant Point object using const_cast<Point*>(&p).

Here is the version of the Point class that removes the constant property of the argument when the value is returned from the member functions.

```
class Point
{ int x, y;
public:
    . . .                        // setPoint(), getX(), getY(), getPtr(), getRef()
    . . .                        // getDistPtr(), getDistRef(),closestPointVal()
    Point* closestPointPtr(const Point& p)              // prevents damage to p
    { return (x*x + y*y < p.x*p.x + p.y*p.y) ? this : const_cast<Point*>(&p); }
    Point& closestPointRef(const Point& p)              // prevents damage to p
{ return (x*x+y*y < p.x*p.x+p.y*p.y) ? *this : const_cast<Point&>(p);
    } } ;
```

Now the client code that changes the returned objects becomes valid. This is a brute-force solution. I do not like it, and I discuss it here only for completeness, not to recommend it. It is somewhat better than removing the const keyword from the function parameter because removing the const keyword removes protection from any use of the parameter inside the function. Using the const_cast keyword removes protection only for this specific operation (in this example, returning the value), not in general. But it is awkward and not well understood.

The best way to make closestPointPtr() and closestPointRef() compile is to promise not to change their return object by making it constant. To do that you put the const keyword in front of the function return value. This is the third meaning of the const keyword (with the fourth meaning coming shortly). Used with the return value of the function, it prevents the caller from modifying the return value of the function. This means that the returned value can be used as an rvalue only but not as an lvalue.

```
class Point
{ int x, y;
public:
// . . .  setPoint(), getX(), getY() and so on
const Point* closestPointPtr(const Point& p)
    { return (x*x + y*y < p.x*p.x + p.y*p.y) ? this : &p; }    // okay
const Point& closestPointRef(const Point& p)
    { return (x*x+y*y < p.x*p.x+p.y*p.y) ? *this : p; } } ;    // okay
```

Now the client code is restricted in its use of point objects.

```
Point p1,p2;  p1.setPoint(20,40);  p2.setPoint(30,50);
Point *ptr = p1.closestPointPtr(p2);         // syntax error: should be const
Point &ref = p1.closestPointRef(p2);         // syntax error: should be const
const Point *p = p1.closestPointPtr(p2);     // *p is an rvalue
p->setPoint(0,0);                            // syntax error: no change to object
const Point &r =p1.closestPointRef(p2);      // r cannot be an lvalue
r.setPoint(10,10);                           // syntax error: no change to object
```

So, what are this pointer p and reference r good for? The answer should be obvious—they cannot call functions like setPoint() that modify the target object, but they should be able to call functions like getX() that do not modify the target object. Something like that.

```
int x1 = p->getX();          // p points to a constant Point
int x2 = r.getX();           // r refers to a constant Point
```

If you like chain notation, you could dispense with the pointer and the reference and get the coordinate of the closest point this way.

```
x1=(p1.closestPointPtr(p2)).getX();     // syntax error
x2=p1.closestPointRef(p2).getX();       // syntax error
```

I hope that even though you are not yet fluent in the details of syntax, you follow the general sense of the discussion. C++ provides you with the const keyword that is used by the compiler and the maintainer to indicate whether an entity changes during execution. We looked at the way to prevent changes to a value, pointer, function parameter, parameter pointer, and return value of a function that returns a pointer or a reference.

Naturally, a pointer or a reference to a constant object cannot be used to call such functions as setPoint() because setPoint() changes the state of the object pointed to by the pointer or the reference. But what is wrong with calling such an innocent function as getX()? It does not change the state of the object pointed to by the pointer of the reference—or does it?

This brings us back to the fundamental ideological issue that I discussed in Chapter 7 relative to function parameters. How do we know whether the function changes its parameter or leaves it the same? We do not want to study the code of the function. We look at the function header. If the header says that the parameter is const, we know that it does not change. If the header does not say that the parameter is const, we say that it does change, no matter what the function actually does. Remember that story about archeologists who thought that if copper wire is good evidence that the ancients used phones, then the absence of copper wire is good evidence that the ancients used cell phones?

The C++ compiler uses the same logic. It is smart enough to look up the const keyword in the header and flag changes to that parameter as a syntax error. But it is not smart enough to go through the code of the function and make an independent conclusions about changes to parameters. It assumes that if the const keyword is absent, then the parameter changes.

Now let us go back to the two functions setPoint() and getX(). So, how do you know that the first one changes the object and the second one does not? Aha! You just know it— you looked up the code, you trust the title; this is obvious, isn't it? Not for the C++ compiler. It flags a call to setPoint(), not because it knows that setPoint() changes the object, but because it does not see evidence that setPoint() does not change the object. For the compiler, getX() is no better than setPoint(). If there is no evidence that getX() leaves the object the same, the compiler concludes that getX() changes the state of the object.

This is where C++ uses the const keyword with yet another meaning. The keyword is inserted between the closing parenthesis of the parameter list and the opening brace of the function body. In a prototype, it is inserted between the closing parenthesis and the semicolon. Here class Point explicitly states what its member functions do to (a) function parameters, (b) function return values, and (c) target object data members.

```
class Point
{ int x, y;
public:
  void setPoint(int a,int b)   // it modifies fields, right?
    { x = a;   y = b; }
  int getX() const    // it does not modify fields: see the evidence?
    { return x; }
  int getY() const    // it does not modify fields: see the evidence?
    { return y; }
const Point& closestPointRef(const Point& p) const // isn't it nice?
    { return (x*x+y*y < p.x*p.x+p.y*p.y) ? *this : p; } } ;
```

Isn't this really nice? I know, this discussion was convoluted, but what can I do if the keyword const has so many meanings in C++! There is at least one more meaning to discuss in the next section. But make sure that you take this keyword seriously. When you write server code, it is your major tool for passing on your knowledge at the time of design to others. When you read code, it is your major tool for understanding the intent of the designer. Use the const keyword wherever possible; it is a serious error not to pass your knowledge about class member functions on to the client programmer and to the maintenance programmer.

Tip

Use the const *keyword to denote that a value (or a pointer) does not change after being initialized; use it to denote that a function parameter (or a pointer) does not change during function execution; use it to denote that a return function value (returned by pointer or reference) is not changed by the client code; use it to denote that a member function does not change the state of the target object during the message call. When you study C++ code, study the use of the* const *keyword as well. Do not be oblivious.*

As you can see, I worry about paying attention to the const keyword as much as I worry about putting it into C++ code to begin with.

Static Class Members

In this section, I will generalize the notion of a class data member. Conceptually, a class is a blueprint for objects. The class specification describes what each object of that class has: data and functions.

This is why when you create an instance of a class object, a separate set of data members is created for that object. This happens no matter how you create the object, either through a definition of an object as a local or a global named variable, with the `new` operator as an unnamed dynamic variable, passing an object by value as a function parameter, or returning an object from a function by value. Each object instance has its own set of data member values: private, public, or protected.

There is no need to create a separate set of member functions for each object. The object code for each member function is generated only once. In addition to parameters designed by the programmer, each member function has an implicit parameter, a pointer to the target object. When a member function is called with a particular object as a target, the `this` pointer to the target object is passed to that function, and the function operates the data members of the target object.

Using Global Variables as Class Characteristics

Sometimes it is more memory efficient and logically appropriate to provide only one common copy of a data member for all the objects of the class rather than maintain individual copies in each class object.

For example, the application might need a count of class object instances. Consider, for example, class `Point`, which includes the `count` data member. Logically, this data member belongs to the class as much as any other data member.

```
class Point {
    int x, y;          // individual for each Point object
    int count;         // common for all Point objects
   . . . } ;
```

Practically, there are a number of problems. You need only one count of points. If the application instantiates a thousand `Point` objects, it makes no sense to allocate a thousand `count` data fields and maintain the same value in each data field. Also, how do you maintain this count? You increment it every time a new `Point` object is created. This means that the `Point` constructor is a good place for doing that. Similarly, the destructor is a good place for decrementing the count of objects.

```
Point::Point (int a, int b)        // general constructor
   { x = a;  y = b;  count++; }    // increment the count of objects
```

But this is not a good solution. It increments only one count, in the new object being created, and does not increment the data members that belong to other objects. Also, the `count` data field in the object being created has not been initialized to the previous value of the `count` data field in objects created earlier. Hence, this constructor increments a value that has not been initialized. No, this is not a good solution.

A global variable would do the job. It can be initialized to zero at the beginning of the program run and then incremented (in the constructor) when the next object is created and decremented (in the destructor) when an object is destroyed.

For example, a global variable could count the number of points instantiated: A constructor would increment the count, and the destructor would decrement the count. Listing 9.5 shows the implementation of class `Point` that uses this approach. The `Point` constructor can be used as a default constructor (client supplies no arguments), a conversion constructor (client code supplies one argument), and a general constructor (client code supplies two arguments for point coordinates). For illustration purposes, I include statements in the constructor and the destructor so that you can trace the order of function calls. Function `quantity()` returns the `count` value so that the client code will not change if the name of the global variable changes. Variable `count` is explicitly initialized to zero. According to C++ language rules, it can be initialized to zero implicitly, but explicit initialization is better.

Listing 9.5   Using a global variable to count object instances.

```
#include <iostream>
using namespace std;

int count = 0;           // does maintainer know it belongs to Point?

class Point {
    int x, y;                      // private coordinates
  public:
    Point (int a=0, int b=0)       // general constructor
       { x = a;   y = b;   count++;
          cout << " Point created: x=" << x << " y=" << y << endl; }
    void set (int a, int b)        // modifier function
       { x = a;   y = b; }
    void get (int& a, int& b) const      // selector function
       { a = x;   b = y; }
    void move (int a, int b)       // modifier function
       { x += a;   y += b; }
    ~Point()                       // destructor
       { count-;
          cout << " Point destroyed: x=" << x << " y=" << y << endl; }
} ;

int quantity()                     // access to global variable
   { return count; }

int main()
{ cout << "Number of points: " << quantity() << endl;
   Point *p = new Point(80,90);    // dynamically allocated object
   Point p1, p2(30), p3(50,70);    // origin, x-axis, general point
   cout << "Number of points: " << quantity() << endl;
   return 0;                // dynamic object is not properly deleted
   }
```

The results of the program run are shown on Figure 9–6. You see that I start with creating an unnamed `Point` object. The first named point to be created (`p1`) is initialized with the default constructor, the next one (`p2`) is initialized with the conversion constructor, the third one (`p3`) is initialized with the general constructor. These named `Point` variables are destroyed in the inverse order. Notice that I failed to delete the unnamed dynamic `Point` object properly, and you do not see the output message that documents its destruction.

This design works, but it has a number of drawbacks when you scale it up to a large program. Any place in client code could access or modify the variable `count`; this introduces dependencies between parts of the program. The name

```
Number of points: 0
  Point created: x=80 y=90
  Point created: x=0 y=0
  Point created: x=30 y=0
  Point created: x=50 y=70
Number of points: 4
  Point destroyed: x=50 y=70
  Point destroyed: x=30 y=0
  Point destroyed: x=0 y=0
```

Figure 9-6   Output for program in Listing 9.6.

of the global variable might clash with other global names in the project or in a library. Every team member has to be notified about this name even though most team members do not have to know about class Point. This extends the scope of the knowledge the programmers have about other parts of the project and increases complexity of the project for the developers and for the maintainer.

The major problem with this solution, however, is that it fails to transmit to the maintenance programmer the knowledge that the developer had at the time of design. When I was defining the variable count, I knew that this variable had to count the number of Point objects, not the number of Rectangle objects or anything else. But there is no syntactic indication that this variable is associated with a particular class. The maintainer has to figure that out either by reading my comments (and if they are hard to understand, obsolete, or absent) or by studying large segments of source code.

The Fourth Meaning of the static Keyword

In C++, you can resolve this problem by reusing the static keyword for yet another purpose. In Chapter 6, you saw three meanings of this keyword.

In its first meaning, it denotes a global variable that is visible only to functions defined in the same file—this variable cannot be made visible to functions in another file by making it extern in another file.

In its second meaning, the keyword is applied to a variable that is local to a function. It means that the value of this variable does not disappear when the function terminates (as the values of other local variables do) but is saved by the system and used to initialize the value of this variable if the function is called again. In its third meaning, the keyword applies to a function that can only be called from the same file.

In this section, the keyword static is applied to a class data member. It means exactly what we need—that there is only one instance of that data member for all objects of the class. It is common to all objects of the class type.

Static data members are ordinary data members in other regards. They can be defined as public, private, or protected as necessary. The syntax of defining and accessing a static data member is the same as for any other class data member. The only difference is that the keyword `static` is used.

```
class Point {
    int x, y;                       // private coordinates
    static int count;               // another meaning of the keyword
  public:
    Point (int a=0, int b=0)        // versatile constructor
      { x = a;  y = b;  count++; }
    void set (int a, int b)         // modifier function
      { x = a;  y = b; }
    void get (int& a, int& b) const // selector function
      { a = x;  b = y; }
    void move (int a, int b)        // modifier function
      { x += a;  y += b; }
    ~Point()                        // destructor
      { count--;  } } ;
```

Here a data member `count` is a single shared value accessible to all instances of class `Point` objects. This data member is in scope whenever the class definition is in scope (accessible).

Initialization of Static Data Members

Similar to nonmember global variables, a static data member is initialized outside of the class specification. Unlike the global variable `count`, the static data member `count` is a class data member and must be initialized explicitly—there is no implicit initialization for data members, static or not static. Similar to using any class member name outside of the class braces, the class scope operator should be used to indicate to what class the data member belongs.

```
int Point::count  = 0;   // this is not an assignment (see the type name here?)
```

On several occasions, I have referred to the difference between assignment and initialization in C++. Often, the assignment operator can denote either assignment or initialization. The initialization is recognized by the presence of the type name next to the name of the variable. The assignment in recognized by the absence of the type name next to the name of the variable. Here the difference between initialization and assignment is important. The initialization is legal and has the same syntax for public and nonpublic static data members. The assignment is illegal for nonpublic static data members.

```
Point::count  = 0;        // assignment (illegal for private 'count')
```

Only one initialization statement for a static data member is allowed. Hence, this statement should be placed in the implementation .cpp file together with the definitions of the member functions and not in the class header file.

Access to a static class member is identical to access to a nonstatic member. Nonmember functions (e.g., quantity()), cannot access private static data members directly. To avoid this problem, I can make function quantity() a class member.

```
class Point {
    int x, y;                      // private coordinates
    static int count;              // another meaning of keyword
  public:
    Point (int a=0, int b=0)       // versatile constructor
    { x = a;   y = b;   count++; }
    int quantity() const           // no change to object state
    { return count; }
  . . . } ;
```

Notice that the previous (global) version of quantity() did not have the const modifier. Only a member function can promise not to change the data member of its target object; global functions have no target object.

A static data member cannot be a member of a union. It cannot be a class bit field. Both unions and bit fields indicate a special use of memory that belongs to a particular object. Static data members belong not to a particular object but to the class as a whole. You probably are not going to use union fields and bit fields much or define them as static, so this restriction is not going to hurt you.

Static Member Functions

We are almost done, but before this chapter ends, I would like to introduce the fifth meaning of the keyword static in C++. This keyword can be applied as a modifier to a class member function that does not access nonstatic data members. This means that a static member function can access only its parameters, class static data member, and (oh, horror) global variables.

A good candidate for becoming a static member function is function quantity(). It does not have any parameters, it accesses the static data member count, and it does not access any nonstatic data members.

```
class Point {
    int x, y;                       // private coordinates
    static int count;               // private count of objects
  public:
    Point (int a=0, int b=0)        // versatile constructor
    { x = a;   y = b;   count++; }
    static int quantity()           // it cannot be const
    { return count; }
    . . . } ;
```

A static member function cannot be declared const even if it does not change the values that it accesses. The values that a static function accesses are parameters, static data members, and global variables; these values are not part of the object state. The const keyword applied to a member function claims that it does not change the target object data member that this function accesses. Since a static function does not access nonstatic data members, there is nothing to promise.

I know, it sounds somewhat similar to, "When did you stop beating your wife?" but there is a more sound logic behind this. I started this series of examples with function quantity() implemented as a global nonmember function that accesses a global variable count. Then I made the global count a static class data member. Function quantity() followed the variable count and became a class Point member function. As a nonstatic member function, it was defined as const to indicate that it does not change nonstatic class data members. Finally, I turned this function into a static member function, and the const modifier became irrelevant.

Similar to static data members, a static member function may be invoked through a target class object (or a pointer to a class object) in the same way a nonstatic member function is invoked. It can also be invoked directly, using the class scope operator, even if no class object has been created.

```
int main()
{ cout << "\nNumber of points " << Point::quantity();   // it prints 0
  Point p1(20,40);
  cout << "\nNumber of points " << p1.quantity();        // it prints 1
  cout << "\nNumber of points " << Point::quantity();    // it prints 1
... }
```

Listing 9.6 shows class Point with the static data member count. It is initialized outside the class definition even though it is private. Function quantity() is defined as static and can be accessed using the class scope operator (the first call) and a target object (the second call).

Listing 9.6   Using static data members and member functions.

```cpp
#include <iostream>
using namespace std;


class Point {
    int x, y;                            // private coordinates
    static int count;
  public:
    Point (int a=0, int b=0)             // general constructor
       { x = a;  y = b;   count++;
         cout << " Point created: x=" << x << " y=" << y << endl; }
       static int quantity()             // const is not allowed
             { return count; }
       void set (int a, int b)           // modifier function
       { x = a;  y = b; }
       void get (int& a, int& b) const   // selector function
       { a = x;  b = y; }
       void move (int a, int b)          // modifier function
       { x += a;  y += b; }
       ~Point()                          // destructor
       { count--;
         cout << " Point destroyed: x=" << x << " y=" << y << endl; }
 } ;

int Point::count = 0;

int main()
{ cout << " Number of points: " << Point::quantity() << endl;
  Point p1, p2(30), p3(50,70);          // point of origin, x-axis, general point
  cout << " Number of points: " << p1.quantity() << endl;
  return 0;
  }
```

The results of the program run are shown in Figure 9–7.

Figure 9-7   Output for program in Listing 9.7.

```
Point created: x=640 y=0
Number of points: 1
Point created: x=0 y=0
Point created: x=30 y=0
Point created: x=50 y=70
Number of points: 4
Point destroyed: x=50 y=70
Point destroyed: x=30 y=0
Point destroyed: x=0 y=0
```

Let us consider yet another version of class `Point` that has a member function that compares the coordinates of its two `Point` parameters and returns true if the coordinates are the same.

```
class Point {
    int x, y;                          // private coordinates
    static int count;                  // private count of objects
  public:
    Point (int a=0, int b=0)           // versatile constructor
      { x = a;   y = b;   count++; }
    static int quantity()              // it cannot be const
    { return count; }
    bool samePoints (const Point &p1, const Point &p2)
      { return p1.x == p2.x && p1.y == p2.y; }
    . . . } ;
```

Did I pass to the maintainer the knowledge that I had at the time of design? No, I did not. An obvious rebuke is that I did not reflect on the fact that the function `samePoints()` does not change the state of the target object and hence should be defined as const. But this is not the whole story. What I have to tell the maintainer is that this function operates only on its parameters. It can be a global function because it does not need the target `Point` object data members—it operates on data members of its parameters. But it is made a class `Point` member function to indicate that it logically belongs to class `Point`: it deals with objects of class `Point` and not with objects of class `Rectangle`, `Circle`, and whatnot. This is why it should be defined as static.

To illustrate the issue, let us see how you can call this function. There are several ways to do that. Here is an example.

```
Point p1, p2(30), p3(50,70);
if (p1.samePoints(p2,p3)==true) cout << "Same points\n";
```

What does object p1 have to do with comparing objects p2 and p3? Remember that story about the crocodile and the monkey? This is ugly. Another way to do this is to use object p2 twice.

```
Point p1, p2(30), p3(50,70);
if (p2.samePoints(p2,p3)==true) cout << "Same points\n";
```

It is still ugly. The object should be used only once. Let us define this function as static.

```
class Point {
    int x, y;                          // private coordinates
    static int count;                  // private count of objects
  public:
    Point (int a=0, int b=0)           // versatile constructor
      { x = a;  y = b;  count++; }
    static int quantity()              // it cannot be const
    { return count; }
    static bool samePoints (const Point &p1, const Point &p2)
      { return p1.x == p2.x && p1.y == p2.y; }
    . . . } ;
```

Now I can call this function using the class scope operator.

```
Point p1, p2(30), p3(50,70);
if (Point::samePoints(p2,p3)==true) cout << "Same points\n";
```

This is beautiful!

So, when do you use static data members and static functions? You define data members as static to indicate that global data logically belong to the class (for example, count). You define member functions as static to indicate that global functions logically belong to the class and operate on static data, global data, or parameters, but not on nonstatic data members (e.g., quantity(), samePoints()).

Using static data and functions is not your first priority when you are learning C++. Make sure, however, that you understand the underlying issues and use them to pass your knowledge on at the time of development to the client code programmers and to the maintainers.

Summary

In this chapter, we looked at the use of C++ classes as a program-building tool. The use of classes eliminates the drawbacks of using global functions as the tools of object-oriented programming.

The first drawback of using global functions is that it does not necessarily indicate to the maintainer what the designer knows at the time of coding, that the functions accessing the same data structure logically belong together.

If, for example, the program uses Point and Rectangle data structures, and the designer puts all Point access functions together and all Rectangle access functions together, fine. If the access functions are separate, the compiler is not going to complain, but the maintainer is going to be confused. Hence, the discipline of the programmer is important.

The second drawback is that encapsulation with global functions is voluntary. The programmer can disregard access functions and directly access the structure fields. The language rules do not prevent that. Again, this approach is based on the discipline of the programmer.

The third drawback is that all the functions are global, and their names are part of the global name space and can conflict with other function names. Hence, to avoid conflicts, the programmers have to know about all function names used in the project, and this increases the complexity of the system for the programmers.

C++ classes eliminate these drawbacks. By binding together data and operations we eliminate the first drawback; by controlling access to data fields, we eliminate the second; by using the class scope, we eliminate the third.

Classes have great potential for improving software quality.

OPERATOR FUNCTIONS: ANOTHER GOOD IDEA

Topics in this Chapter

- Overloading of Operators
- Limitations on Operator Overloading
- Overloaded Operators as Class Members
- Case Study: Rational Numbers
- Mixed Types as Parameters
- Friend Functions
- Summary

Chapter 10

The previous chapter discussed the syntax and semantics of C++ classes. C++ was not the first programming language to support the class concept, but it was the first language that did it on a large industrial scale and that did it successfully.

Initial acceptance of C++ was slow because the industry was apprehensive about C++ efficiency and robustness. Misgivings about efficiency were mostly without foundation. Most C++ programs take as much memory as equivalent C programs and no more. Most C++ programs execute as fast as equivalent C programs and not slower. Granted, there are some exceptions related to the use of the iostream library, virtual functions, and templates. (They will be discussed in later chapters.) But the tremendous progress in hardware power resulted in a dramatic increase in the size of computer memory and in the execution speed of most computers. This placated whatever anxiety was remaining about C++ memory requirements and run-time performance. Experience with C++ clearly demonstrated that programming with classes can be efficient. Any new programming language that will be developed in the near future is expected to support classes.

Misgivings about robustness were not placated at all. Just the other way around: Industrial experience confirmed the dangers and pitfalls that programmers should be aware of. Strangely, this did not prevent C++ from becoming a major programming language for a broad spectrum of applications. The complexity of the language is the major contributing factor to the failure to achieve robustness. In the previous chapter, you saw that the idea behind C++ classes is simple. C++ classes had to help the programmers

- to bind together object data and operations
- to control access to class elements from the outside of the class
- to introduce additional scope for avoiding name conflicts and
- to push responsibilities from clients to servers

The previous chapter also showed you that C++ designer Bjarne Stroustrup put into C++ classes much more than this list of four items requires. Constructors and destructors help class objects manage their resources, mostly dynamically allocated memory. The availability of these member functions puts a burden on the class programmer (server designer) to provide a variety of constructors to support client code in a variety of contexts. They also put some additional burden on client programmers for supplying data for object initialization, but this is considered a minor side effect.

Using composite objects results in additional complications. The designer of the container class should facilitate initialization of component objects. The member initialization list provides a new syntax for doing that. The idea of composite classes requires incorporation of such additional details as constant components, reference components, pointer components, and recursive components. The concept of class attributes leads to other extensions of this idea such as static data members and static functions that characterize the class as a whole rather than as individual object instances of the class.

I also mentioned that C++ has yet another design goal: treating the class instances in the same way as the variables of built-in types. In the previous chapter, this principle manifested itself in the form of the uniform syntax for initialization for both objects and variables. In this chapter, I will discuss yet another manifestation of the same idea: extending it to C++ operators so that the same expression syntax with operators can be applied to class objects in the same way as it is applied to variables of built-in types in conventional C++ expressions.

As usual, C++ supports more than one way to do that. I will discuss different techniques for implementing overloaded operator functions. These techniques will help you become more proficient in using C++ and in understanding what is going on under the hood of a C++ program.

Overloading of Operators

In C++, the concept of programmer-defined types (classes) is an extension of the concept of built-in numeric types. You can define variables of programmer-defined types using the same syntax as for simple numeric variables. Similar to built-in types, you can use object instances of programmer-defined types as array elements or as data members of even more-complex types. You can pass objects of programmer-defined types as parameters and return them from functions. You can set pointers and references to programmer-defined values using the same syntax as for built-in values. You can define pointers as constant pointers. You can define pointers and references as pointers and references to constant values using the same syntax as for built-in types.

These similarities are not accidental. One of the important C++ goals was to treat programmer-defined types in the same way as it treats built-in types. This goal has nothing to do with object-oriented programming, improving productivity of development, enhancing efficiency of maintenance, or any other software engineering consideration. This is a purely aesthetic goal. And this is legitimate. Computer programming, as any creative human activity, has an essential aesthetic component. Although programming books rarely discuss this issue, the programs we write should be as elegant as they should be readable, portable, and maintainable.

Of course, many programs, especially large programs, are not elegant. Neither are they readable, portable, or maintainable, but the language is designed to help the programmer achieve these goals.

There is, however, a big gap in treating classes and numeric types in the same way. C++ programmer-defined types are not exactly like native numeric types. The biggest difference is that you cannot apply C++ operators to objects of programmer-defined types—addition, subtraction, comparisons for equality, inequality, and so on. You can write your own functions to implement these operations, and notation might often be somewhat awkward.

Let us consider a simple example: complex numbers that are characterized by values of the real and imaginary components. Those of you who are not familiar with complex numbers could think of them as points on the plane where the real component corresponds to the x-coordinate, and the imaginary component corresponds to the y-coordinate. When you add (or subtract) complex numbers, the result is yet another complex number; its real component is the result of adding (or subtracting) the real components of the two operands, and its imaginary component is the result of adding (or subtracting) the imaginary components of the two operands. Multiplication and division are more complicated, but they also are carried as operations over components of the operands.

Let us represent complex numbers as a class with two data members, `real` and `imag`. For simplicity of the discussion, I will leave both data members public (they will become private in the next version of the class).

```
struct Complex {
    double real, imag; } ;                // public data members
```

Listing 10.1 shows an example of the code that defines object instances of type `Complex`, initializes them, and then performs some arithmetic operations over these objects.

Note

This is not a good example of C++ code. Most C++ books avoid showing bad C++ code. As a result, the reader never learns how to see the difference between bad and good C++ code. This is pretty much like learning painting by going to great museums rather than taking art lessons. Similar to painting, C++ programming is always a struggle to find a solution that is better than a competing solution is. Instead of showing you a reasonable solution, I prefer to show you an inferior solution, explain what is wrong with it and how it could be improved, and then show you a better solution and explain why this solution is better.

In Listing 10.1, the client code performs computations over complex numbers by using direct access to public object components: The client code specifies the names of data members `real` and `imag` instead of using access functions. As a result, the client code represents the mix of access to data fields and the computations over data field values. The meaning of these computations is not expressed in the function calls and has to be deduced by the maintainer from the analysis of low-level details of computations. The responsibility for low-level operations is not pushed down to server functions, and the developer has to keep in mind several levels of the algorithm simultaneously: the high-level goal of the computation and its low-level details. There are no separate areas of concern, and changes to the design of class `Complex` will affect the client code as well. The use of the keyword `struct` instead of `class` is appropriate here since all data members are public.

Listing 10.1   Example of operations over objects of class `Complex`.

```cpp
#include <iostream>
using namespace std;

struct Complex {                           // programmer-defined type
    double real, imag; } ;

int main()
{  Complex x, y, z1, z2;                    // objects of type Complex
    x.real = 20; x.imag = 40;              // initialization
    y.real = 30; y.imag = 50;
    cout << " First value:   ";
    cout << "(" << x.real << ", " << x.imag << ")" << endl;
    cout << " Second value: ";
    cout << "(" << y.real << ", " << y.imag << ")" << endl;
    z1.real = x.real + y.real;             // add real components into z1
    z1.imag = x.imag + y.imag;             // add imaginary components
    cout << " Sum of two values:       ";
    cout << "(" << z1.real << ", " << z1.imag << ")" << endl;
    z2.real = x.real + y.real;             // add real components into z2
    z2.imag = x.imag + y.imag;             // add imaginary components
    z1.real = z1.real + x.real;            // add to the real component of z1
    z1.imag = z1.imag + x.imag;            // add to the imag component of z1
    cout << " Add first value to z1: ";
    cout << "(" << z1.real << ", " << z1.imag << ")" << endl;
    z2.real += 30.0;                       // add to real component of z2
    cout << " Add 30 to sum:          ";
    cout << "(" << z2.real << ", " << z2.imag << ")" << endl;
    return 0;
}
```

The output of the run of this program is shown in Figure 10–1.

Although this is not a good example of object-oriented programming, it is a good starting point for the discussion of operator function overloading. Also, I'd like to take the opportunity to repeat the list of drawbacks of poor use of C++. This list is very important: Repeatedly using it for the evaluation

```
First value:   (20, 40)
Second value: (30, 50)
Sum of two values:    (50, 90)
Add first value to sum: (70, 130)
Add 30 to sum:        (80, 90)
```

Figure 10–1   Output for program in Listing 10.1.

of your code is the best way to learn how to use C++ correctly and how to improve the quality of your C++ code.

To encapsulate the client code from the details of data design, you have to write access functions that would manipulate the objects of type `Complex` to serve the needs of client code. For example, if you want to add variables of this type, you have to write a function that accepts two parameters of type `Complex`, performs necessary computations over components of these two objects, and returns the result as a value of the same type. This means that the interface of this function named, for example, `addComplex()`, will look this way:

```
Complex addComplex(const Complex &a, const Complex &b);
```

As I mentioned earlier, adding two complex values requires adding their real components and adding their imaginary components.

```
Complex addComplex(const Complex &a, const Complex &b)
{ Complex c;                        // local object
  c.real = a.real + b.real;         // add real components
  c.imag = a.imag + b.imag;         // add imaginary components
  return c; }
```

To use this function, the client code defines and initializes variables of type `Complex`, passes them as parameters to this function, and uses its return value as a value of type `Complex`.

```
Complex x, y, z1, z2;               // objects of type Complex
x.real = 20; x.imag = 40;           // initialization
y.real = 30; y.imag - 50;
z1 = addComplex(x,y);               // use in the function call
```

This is very nice (and trivial). Most programmers are used to this functional style of programming and do not feel that using function names like `addComplex()` makes their programs ugly or unreadable. A real C++ programmer, however, feels uncomfortable (to say the least) that C++ does not support (at least, not yet), writing the client code in the following way.

```
Complex x, y, z1, z2;               // objects of type Complex
x.real = 20; x.imag = 40;           // initialization
y.real = 30; y.imag = 50;
z2 = x + y;                         // use in expression
```

If you do this, the compiler will tell you that the operation of addition is not defined, C++ ambitions for equal treatment of types notwithstanding. Since you cannot use built-in operations on programmer-defined data types, you have to invent new function names like `addComplex()` and implement them to perform necessary operations. This disparity between programmer-defined types and built-in types is painful for every real C++ programmer.

As a remedy, C++ offers you a break or, rather, a contract. You, as a programmer, limit yourself to special function names that include the keyword `operator` and the sign for the operation you would like to use in your code, for example, +. You design and implement that function, `operator+()`, in exactly the same way you design and implement any function with the name of your free choice, for example, `addComplex()`. C++, as a supporting programming language, allows you to call this function using the operator notation that corresponds to the sign of the operator you included in the name of the function. If you called the function `operator+()`, then you can call this function using the same notation as that for built-in numeric types.

```
z = x + y;          // under the hood, this is z = operator+(x,y);
```

Isn't that nice? You associate services provided by the function with a built-in C++ operation. This is marvelous!

Actually, this is not that unique. In C++, the same function name in the same scope can represent different algorithms provided their signatures are different (see Chapter 7, "Programming with C++ Functions," for more discussion on function name overloading). When the client code calls the function, the compiler matches the actual argument types with function declarations available in that scope and decides which one, if any, to use to implement the function call.

This is true of any C++ function name. As far as arithmetic operators are concerned, operator overloading is used in every programming language, not only in C++. Operator overloading means giving multiple interpretations to the same symbol. Consider, for example, the addition operator.

```
int a,b,c;
float d,e,f;
a = 20; b = 30;   d = 40.0; e = 50.0;
c = a + b;   f = d + e;       // different operations, same operator
```

In C++ (and in other languages), the + operator is used to add integer or floating point values. These operations are very different. For integers, each bit of the first operand is added with each bit of the second operand and with the carry bit from the lower order bit.

For floating point values, the binary representation consists of the mantissa and the exponent. To avoid the complexity of binary (or hex) values, I will illustrate this issue using the example in the decimal system. In the mantissa-exponent representation, for example, 3000.0 is $3*10^3$ and 300.0 is $3*10^2$.

(Here, I use the operator ^ to denote exponentiation, even though C++ does not have an exponentiation operator.) When adding floating point values, the mantissa of the smaller operator is shifted to the right so that the exponents of the two operands became the same (when adding 3000 and 300, 300 would be shifted three decimal positions to the right to be represented as $0.3 \cdot 10^{\wedge}3$). After that the bits of the mantissa (not all bits as for integers) are added up (when adding 3000 and 300, the result would be $3.3 \cdot 10^{\wedge}3$).

Whatever the details of floating point addition are, it is clear that they are different from the details of integer addition. At the assembly language level, these operations are represented by two different operation codes. In high-level programming languages, we do not force the programmers to learn separate notation for integer addition and for floating point addition.

I hope that you recognize in this discussion the concepts of information hiding and pushing responsibilities down from client code to server code. In this case, the server is the addition operator, and the client is the high-level code that contains expressions with the addition operator. The programmer who writes the expression with the addition operator does not want to know the details of addition—this programmer concentrates on the higher goals of the expression and on related issues. It is the programmer who implements the addition operator that is aware of details of addition for each type and implements each operator accordingly.

C++ takes this idea of having different operators denoted with the same symbol to the next level and extends this capability to programmer-defined data types. If you write your functions in agreement with C++ rules, you can apply any operator (well, with few exceptions) to any programmer-defined type!

Here is the `operator+()` function implemented for parameters of the type `Complex`.

```
Complex operator+(const Complex &a, const Complex &b)    // magic name
{ Complex c;                                             // local object
  c.real = a.real + b.real;                              // add real components
  c.imag = a.imag + b.imag;                              // add imag components
  return c; }
```

How did I write this function? I copied the `addComplex()` function presented earlier, kept the body of the function, return type and the parameter list without changes, cut out the function name `addComplex`, and moved in the magic function name `operator+`. Bingo! I did my part of the deal. Now C++ will do its part of the deal: it will accept the addition operator with operands of `Complex` type and will not print the syntax error message that says that the addition operator is not defined for the type `Complex`. This operator is now defined.

```
Complex x, y, z;                  // objects of type Complex
x.real = 20; x.imag = 40;         // initialization
y.real = 30; y.imag = 50;
z = x + y;                        // use in expression
```

When I say that the compiler "will accept the addition operator with operands of Complex type," what does this actually mean? What code will the compiler generate? The compiler will call the overloaded function operator+() that I wrote. It will use the left operand of the expression as the first actual argument of the function, and the right operand as the second argument of the function. The code that the compiler will generate for the code snippet above will be exactly the same as for the following client code.

```
Complex x, y, z;                  // objects of type Complex
x.real = 20; x.imag = 40;         // initialization
y.real = 30; y.imag = 50;
z = operator+(x,y);               // this is absolutely legitimate
```

If the function name includes the keyword operator and the symbol of the operator, the compiler accepts either the function call syntax or the operator syntax and will generate exactly the same code. If you use the function call syntax z=operator+(x,y); the compiler matches the actual argument types with parameter types as for any other function call. If you use the operator syntax z=x+y; the compiler discovers that the operands are of a programmer-defined type and searches for a function whose name contains the keyword operator and the operator sign used in the client code. If this function is found, the compiler checks whether its parameters match the number and the types of operands in the client expression.

As a result, the responsibility is pushed down to the server classes, and the client code is purged from the details of server design. The client programmer uses the same syntax for adding integers, floating point values, objects of type Complex or whatever other programmer-defined type you would like to use with this syntax.

This is a very flexible and powerful mechanism. As with many things in C++, it gives you more than you bargained for. We started with the goal of using the objects of programmer-defined types in the same way as the variables of built-in types and wound up with something much more potent. Now you can do to the objects of your type what you could not even dream of doing to built-in numeric types because the language does not limit you in what you can do in the privacy of your own overloaded operator function. You are limited only in the function interface—the function name and the number of parameters. These cannot be chosen arbitrarily; they have to emulate the built-in operator you are overloading.

Listing 10.2 illustrates the use of operator function overloading. In addition to the overloaded addition operator, it also shows the use of `operator+=()` that adds one `Complex` object to another. It also demonstrates the use of `operator+=()` that adds a floating-point number to the real part of the `Complex` object. Although the names of these two operator functions are the same, their parameter lists are different. This is a legitimate use of function name overloading (see Chapter 7 for more details on function name overloading in C++).

Listing 10.2 Example of operator function overloading.

```
#include <iostream>
using namespace std;

struct Complex {                                    // programmer-defined type
    double real, imag; } ;

Complex operator+(const Complex &a, const Complex &b)     // magic name
{ Complex c;                                        // local object
  c.real = a.real + b.real;                         // add real components
  c.imag = a.imag + b.imag;                         // add imaginary components
  return c; }

void operator += (Complex &a, const Complex &b)     // another magic name
{ a.real = a.real + b.real;                         // add to the real component
  a.imag = a.imag + b.imag; }                       // add to the imag component

void operator += (Complex &a, double b)             // different interface
{ a.real += b; }                                    // add to real component only

void showComplex(const Complex &x)
{ cout << "(" << x.real << ", " << x.imag << ")" << endl; }

int main()
{   Complex x, y, z1, z2;                            // objects of type Complex
    x.real = 20; x.imag = 40;                        // initialization
    y.real = 30; y.imag = 50;
cout << " First value:   ";   showComplex(x);
    cout << " Second value: ";   showComplex(y);
    z1 = operator+(x,y);                             // use in the function call
    cout << " Sum as function call:   "; showComplex(z1);
    z2 = x + y;                                      // use as the operator
    cout << " Sum as the operator:    "; showComplex(z1);
    z1 += x;                                         // same as operator+=(z1,x);
    cout << " Add first value to sum: "; showComplex(z1);
    z2 += 30.0;                                      // same as operator+=(z2,30.0);
    cout << " Add 30 to sum:          "; showComplex(z2);
    return 0;
}
```

Notice the use of the `const` keyword where appropriate, in `showComplex()`, in `operator+()`, and in the first `operator+=()`. Notice the absence of the `const` keyword where appropriate: in the first `operator+=()` and in the second `operator+=()`. Notice some advantages of object-oriented programming in this example. Client code does not depend on the server design and the names of the data fields (other than for initialization), and responsibility for low-level computations is pushed down to the server functions. The meaning of high-level computations is expressed in function calls to server functions. There are different areas of concern for low-level computations (handling fields of complex numbers according to complex arithmetic) and high-level computations (handling complex numbers according to whatever the application wants to achieve). There are separate areas of change for data representation and for application algorithm: If the design of class `Complex` changes, the overloaded operators change but not the client code; if the application algorithm changes, the client code changes but not the overloaded operators.

Some advantages of object-oriented programming are absent: encapsulation is voluntary, there is no indication that data and server functions belong together, and names of functions are global. Does this sound familiar? Good. You are getting there.

The output of the run of this program is shown in Figure 10–2.

As you can see from Listing 10.2, it is all the same whether you use the spaces between the keyword `operator` and the operator sign; `operator+()` and `operator + ()` mean the same thing. If the operator sign contains two symbols, they should be placed next to each other without an intervening space.

Figure 10–2   Output for program in Listing 10.2.

```
First value:       (20, 40)
Second value:      (30, 50)
Sum as function call:    (50, 90)
Sum as the operator:     (50, 90)
Add first value to sum: (70, 130)
Add 30 to sum:          (80, 90)
```

Note

The mandatory components of the name of an overloaded operator function are the keyword "operator" and the symbol(s) for the operator. The keyword "operator" and the symbol(s) together comprise the function name. You can insert white space between the keyword and the symbol(s) if you feel that this enhances readability—breaking the function name into these two components is not a syntax error.

Keep in mind that in all the cases of the use of overloaded operators in the client space, the operation is implemented as a function call. You cannot use overloaded operators to speed up your program. It is syntactic sugar that adds to readability of your program. In all the cases of the use of overloaded operators the operator syntax can be replaced by the function call syntax. The last part of the client code in Listing 10.2 could be written this way.

```
operator+=(z1,x);                              // same as z1 += x;
cout << "Add first value to sum: " ; showComplex(z1);
operator+=(z2,30.0);                           // same as z2 += 30.0;
cout << "Add 30 to sum:          " ; showComplex(z2);
```

Of course, you do not design overloaded operator functions just to use them with the function call syntax in the client code. If you wanted to use a function call, you would call the function addComplex(), not operator+(). You go to the trouble of defining overloaded operator functions to use this special dispensation from the C++ compiler to treat the operator syntax as if it were a function call. I keep reminding you about the function call syntax to make sure that you do not forget that the operator syntax is compiled into a function call, not into arithmetic expression it pretends to be.

Limitations on Operator Overloading

As you saw in the previous section, the overloaded operators give you a powerful tool to make C++ code more beautiful by treating objects of programmer-defined types similarly to variables of built-in numeric types. There are, however, some limitations that C++ places on the use of overloaded operators. Some of these operations will not limit you much, but some are quite essential. In this section, I will discuss these limitations.

What Operators Cannot Be Overloaded

There are some limitations on operator overloading that are not very important for the practicing programmer, at least not at this stage. You cannot overload operator :: (scope), operator .* (member object selector), operator . (class object selector), and operator ?: (conditional operator or arithmetic if). I'm not sure if anybody has a good idea why one needs to overload the scope operator and the conditional operator. The same is true about member object selector and class object selector operators. (Actually, the member object selector operator has not been used here even in its initial meaning.)

The limitation that is important from the practical point of view is that you cannot make up your own operators that are not supported for C++ numeric types. The operator whose sign you append to the keyword operator in the overloaded operator function name must be a bona fide C++ operator. It is a syntax error to use a symbol that is not a C++ operator. For example, C++ has no exponentiation operator. Other languages use the double asterisk to denote exponentiation. For example, x**y means x to the power of y in FORTRAN. One might be tempted to expand the set of C++ operators and overload the double asterisk operator for this purpose.

```
Complex operator**(const Complex &a, const Complex &b);    // error
```

This is an error because C++ does not recognize the double asterisk operator as a built-in operator.

You cannot overload operators for built-in numeric types giving them new meaning. For example, your application might be interested in limiting the results of integer addition to a specific number, for example, 60 (modulo arithmetic). You might want to redefine the addition operator for integers so that the result is wrapped around the value 60.

```
int operator + (int a, int b)           // syntax error
{ return (a+b) % 60; }                  // addition modulo 60
```

It is a nice idea, but it does not fly for several reasons. The major reason is that the compiler might become confused among different additional meanings especially if the application overloads several operators. For example, in the overloaded operator for integers in the last example the addition operator is used in the body of the function. I wanted this operator to be used in the standard sense, but I have no means to tell that to the compiler. How does the compiler know that this is not a recursive function call to the new overloaded operator operator+() that I am writing?

The same difficulty emerges in the client code.

```
int a,b,c;
float d,e,f;
a = 20; b = 30; d = 40.0; e = 50.0;

// built-in operator or overloaded operator?
c = a + b;    f = d + e;
```

Here, I have no means to tell the compiler whether I want to use the built-in addition operator or the overloaded operator for integers.

This is why C++ does not allow operator overloading for built-in types. You can overload operators for programmer-defined types only. Actually, C++ generalizes this limitation by requiring that at least one parameter of the overloaded operator function is of a programmer-defined type (a class). The addition operator for integers that I tried to write violates this limitation.

Alert

You cannot expand the set of C++ operators by overloading operator symbols that are not already built-in C++ operators; you can only overload existing C+ operators. You cannot change the meaning of existing operators for built-in types by overloading them for built-in types in a different way; you can only overload operators for programmer-defined types (classes).

Notice that in all cases of overloaded operator functions you design overloaded functions, not redefine existing operators. The addition operator for Complex objects does not eliminate the addition operator for integers and floating point numbers. The overloaded operator is added to the list of operators known to the C++ compiler. Let us consider that overloaded operator again.

```
Complex operator+(const Complex &a, const Complex &b)    // magic name
{ Complex c;                                             // local object
  c.real = a.real + b.real;                              // add real components
  c.imag = a.imag + b.imag;                              // add imaginary components
  return c; }
```

The addition operator in the body of this overloaded operator function is the standard built-in operator for floating point numbers. How does the compiler know that? By looking up the types of data fields of the class Complex. Since these fields are of type double, this addition operator is not a recursive call to the overloaded operator being defined. Similar analysis applies to the client code.

```
Complex x, y, z;                    // objects of type Complex
x.real=20; x.imag=40;              // initialization
y.real=30; y.imag=50;
z = x + y;                          // use in expression
double a, b, c;                     // variables of type double
a = 20; b = 30;                     // initialization
c = a + b;                          // use in expression
```

For the first addition operator here, the compiler establishes that the operands are of the type `Complex` and calls the overloaded operator function. For the second addition operator, the compiler establishes that both operands are of the type `double` and calls the built-in addition operator.

Limitations on Return Types

Usually, overloaded operator functions return either `void`, a boolean value, or the value of the type the operator is designed to work with. Returning a value of the type of the class is common. It is especially popular for operators that compute a new value of the same type for the use in other expressions. For example, `operator+()` in the example above returns a value of type `Complex`. This allows you to use this value with the assignment operator. If the return value were `void`, that would be impossible. Moreover, returning the value allows you to support complex expressions similar to expressions over built-in values.

```
Complex a, b, c, d;                // objects of type Complex
a.real=20; a.imag=40;             // initialization
b.real=30; b.imag=50;
c.real = 0; c.imag = 20;
d = a + b + c;                     // use in expression
```

It takes some digging up to figure out what this means. C++ arithmetic operations associate from left to right. If a, b, and c were numbers, the expression a + b + c would mean (a + b) + c. Overloading operator functions does not change operator associativity. When a, b, and c are objects of the type `Complex`, the meaning of this expression is the same.

```
d = (a + b) + c;                   // use in expression
```

In terms of function syntax, this expression means the following.

```
d = operator+((a + b),c);          // use in expression
```

What remains is to represent the meaning of the expression a + b as a function call.

```
d = operator+(operator+(a,b),c);          // use in expression
```

The meaning of this code is a call to function `operator+()` with variables
a and b as actual arguments and pass the return value of this function call as
the first argument to another call to function `operator+()`.

The two overloaded operator functions `operator+=()` that I used in
Listing 10.2 have return type `void` and hence cannot be used in chain expressions that expect a value for further manipulation.

```
Complex a, b, c, d;      // objects of type Complex
a.real=20; a.imag=40;    // initialization
b.real=30; b.imag=50;
c.real = 0; c.imag = 20;
d = a + b + c;           // use in expression
a += b;                  // OK: operator+=(a,b); returns void
d = c + (b += 30.0);     // not OK: operator+=(b,30.0); returns void
```

To make it possible to use this operator in chain expressions, I had to
design it this way.

```
Complex operator += (Complex &a, double b)   // class return type
{ a.real += b;                               // add to real component
  return a; }
```

This would emulate the behavior of the built-in numeric types better, I
guess; I do not particularly like the behavior of built-in numeric types in C++.
This behavior is conducive to writing convoluted expressions instead of out-
lining the algorithms in simple sequential steps. Instead of changing the server code (the overloaded operator function) to accommodate chain operations
in the client code, I would rather keep the `void` return type and break the
client code into smaller steps that do not need the `Complex` return value.

```
Complex a, b, c, d;      // objects of type Complex
a.real=20; a.imag=40;    // initialization
b.real=30; b.imag=50;
c.real = 0; c.imag = 20;
d = a + b + c;           // use in expression
a += b;                  // OK: operator+=(a,b); returns void
b += 30.0;               // OK: operator+=(b,30.0); return value not used
d = c + b;               // OK: operator+=(c,b); returns Complex
```

But this is a matter of taste. My task here is to make sure that you see and
understand different ways of organizing the cooperation between server and
client code.

Limitations on the Number of Parameters

When you design overloaded operator functions, you should use as many arguments (usually of the same class type) as necessary for the operator (binary or unary).

You cannot change the arity of the operator, that is, the number of operands that has to be specified when the operator is used (two for binary operators, one for unary operators). The arity of the overloaded operator should be the same as the arity of the original built-in operator. You cannot define a binary operator that works on two operands and use it to create a unary operator that works with a single operand.

Here is an example of typical difficulties I had while struggling with this rule. I wanted to overload the "less than" operator < to implement the output operations over `Complex` data members I performed in function `showComplex()` in Listing 10.2.

All that I had to do was to cut out the name `showComplex` and move in the name `operator<`.

```
void operator < (const Complex &x)          // not a good idea: syntax error
{ cout << "(" << x.real << ", " << x.imag << ")" << endl; }
```

It is easy to see how to use this function in the client code using the function syntax: You call it the same way you call `showComplex()`.

```
Complex x, y, z1, z2;                 // objects of type Complex
x.real = 20; x.imag = 40;             // initialization
y.real = 30; y.imag = 50;
cout << "First value:   " ;
operator < (x);                       // same as showComplex();
cout << "Second value: " ;
operator < (y);                       // same as showComplex();
```

However, the operator "less than" is a binary operator, and the use of this function with the operator syntax requires the second operand that is missing.

```
Complex x, y, z1, z2;                 // objects of type Complex
x.real = 20; x.imag = 40;             // initialization
y.real = 30; y.imag = 50;
cout << "First value:   " ;
< x;                                  // nonsense if x is numeric
cout << "Second value: " ;
< y;                                  // nonsense if y is numeric
```

This is why my attempt fails: The operator function `operator<()` should be overloaded with two parameters, but I have only one, the `Complex` object to be printed. If I do not know what the second parameter should do, I have to find another operator that takes only one operand.

C++ has several operators that can be used either as binary or as unary operators: plus, minus, asterisk, at-sign. It is okay to overload each of those operators as either a binary or unary operator because both are available for built-in types. For example, I overloaded operator + as a binary operator. Since this operator is available as a unary plus sign, I can overload this operator using a function with only one parameter. This replacement for showComplex() is legitimate.

```
void operator + (const Complex &x)          // same as showComplex()
{ cout << "(" << x.real << ", " << x.imag << ")" << endl; }
```

There is no problem using this function with the operator syntax in the client code.

```
Complex x, y, z1, z2;        // objects of type Complex
x.real = 20; x.imag = 40;    // initialization
y.real = 30; y.imag = 50;
cout << "First value:  ";
+x;                          // operator+(x); or showComplex(x);
cout << "Second value: ";
+y;                          // same as operator+(y); or showComplex(y);
```

Limitations on Operator Precedence

Yet another limitation on operator overloading is that the precedence of overloaded operators cannot be changed.

No matter what the type of objects x and y is and the meaning of operators + and /, the division in the expression x + y/2 will be performed before the addition. If this is not what you want, you can use parentheses as usual.

Alert

When overloading operator functions, you cannot change the number of operands that the operator takes, the precedence of the operator, or its associativity. All you can do is to define the meaning of the operator for the programmer-defined type. This allows the client code to use the same expression syntax for programmer-defined classes as for standard C++ built-in numeric types.

Overloaded Operators as Class Members

As I mentioned in the previous chapter, any function related to any programmer-defined data type can be implemented either as a class member function or as a global stand-alone nonmember function. This is true of any algorithm, and this is true of overloaded operator functions. Switching from class member to nonmember implementation and back is an important programming skill. It is especially important for operator functions.

The operator can be defined as a member function of the class of its parameters. The number of parameters is one less than the arity of the operator (one for binary, none for unary). This absent parameter becomes the target of the message when the operator is used.

Replacing a Global Function with a Class Member

The rules for overloading operator functions as class members are the same as the rules for overloading operator functions as nonmember functions. You replace the name of the member function with the name that concatenates the keyword `operator` and the sign for the operator being defined.

For example, the binary `operator+()` and the binary `operator+=()` implemented as class `Complex` member functions should have only one parameter, not two like the operators implemented as global functions in Listing 10.2. The data members of the parameter that disappeared from the function interface became data members of the target of the message.

```
class Complex {                        // programmer-defined type
    double real, imag;                 // private data
public:
    Complex(double r, double i)        // general constructor
    { real =r;  imag = i; }
Complex operator+(const Complex &b)    // one parameter only
{ Complex c;                           // does it fly?
  c.real = real + b.real;              // add real components
  c.imag = imag + b.imag;              // add imag components
  return c; }
void operator += (const Complex &b)    // one parameter only
{ real = real + b.real;                // add to the real component
  imag = imag + b.imag; }              // add to the imag component
                                       // THE REST OF CLASS Complex
} ;
```

Make sure that you are comfortable with the switch from a two-parameter nonmember function to a one-parameter member function. Many programmers prefer the two-parameter implementation because it is symmetric: You add up the corresponding fields of two parameters.

```
Complex operator+(const Complex &a, const Complex &b)    // global name
{ Complex c;                                              // does it fly?

  // add components: symmetric notation
  c.real = a.real + b.real;
  c.imag = a.imag + b.imag;
  return c; }

void operator += (Complex &a, const Complex &b)          // global function
{ a.real = a.real + b.real;                              // add to the real component
  a.imag = a.imag + b.imag; }                            // add to the imag component
```

There is one problem with the first operator function when it is converted to a member function. I use a local variable of type `Complex` and do not initialize it because I do not care what the values of its data members are—these values are going to be overwritten by the function before the result is returned to the client. I used the same design in Listing 10.2 and there it was okay. I did not provide any constructors for class `Complex`, and the system supplied this class with the default constructor that did not do anything. In the design in this section, class `Complex` has a general constructor and hence the compiler takes away the general constructor and yells at me for attempting to call a nonexistent function in the first line of the operator function. You should think about constructors all the time, right?

There are two remedies. One is to give in and initialize the local object to the values I do not need.

```
Complex operator+(const Complex &b)    // one parameter only
{ Complex c(0,0);                      // a way to pacify the compiler
  c.real = real + b.real;              // add components: no symmetric notation
  c.imag = imag + b.imag;
  return c; }
```

A better way to do that is to eliminate the local object. Instead, you can create an unnamed `Complex` object, initialize it with the results of the computations, and return the value of that unnamed object from the operator function.

```
Complex operator+(const Complex &b)                      // one parameter only
{ return Complex (real + b.real, imag + b.imag); }       // nice: fast and neat
```

Note

Make sure that the class design supports not only the client code but also its own methods. The lack of necessary constructors is a common source of problems in class design.

In the client code for `Complex` objects, you can use either the function call syntax or the operator syntax. In the code snippet below, I am giving examples of both. Again, the function call syntax for the member function is different from the function call syntax for the nonmember function: one of the parameters becomes the target of the message.

```
Complex x(20,40),y(30,60),z1(0,0),z2(0,0);   // objects created
z1 = x.operator+(y);                         // use as the message to x
z2 = x + y;                                  // same as z2=x.operator+(y);
z1.operator+=(y);                            // use as the message to z1
z2 += x;                                     // same as z2.operator+=(x);
```

The operator syntax for the member function is exactly the same as the operator syntax for the nonmember function. The compiler is given a special dispensation to interpret the expressions such as the function calls to methods whose names include the keyword `operator` and the sign of the corresponding built-in operator.

```
z2 = x + y;                       // same as z2=x.operator+(y);
z2 += x;                          // same as z2.operator+=(x);
```

You can use the function call syntax for class member functions in the same way as for global functions. Few programmers do that, and I mention it here because this is the real meaning of the operator syntax in the expressions.

```
z2=x.operator+(y);                // same as z2 = x + y;
z2.operator+=(x);                 // same as z2 += y;
```

What happens if you overload both a global function and a member function for the same operator? This is not a good idea. If you call these functions using the function call syntax, the compiler will figure out what you mean. If you use the operator syntax, you will confuse the compiler. Each function could fit the bill. Both functions are of the same precedence, and the compiler will reject the expression as ambiguous.

Using Class Members for Chain Operations

Similar to nonmember implementation, the return type void for the member function precludes the use of the operator syntax in chain operations. Returning an object of the class type makes the chain expressions possible.

```
Complex a(20,40), b(30,50), c(0,20), d(0,0);      // defined and initialized
d = a + b + c;                                    // use in chain expression
```

Again, the built-in operator + associates from the left; the overloaded operator + associates from the left as well; the meaning of the chain operation is d=(a + b) + c;

The syntax of the binary operator obscures the fact that we are dealing with a message operator+() sent to an instance of an object of class type Complex. The meaning of a + b for the member function implementation is a.operator+(b). Hence, client code d=(a + b) + c; is exactly equivalent to

```
d = a.operator+(b) + c;    // message to return value of a.operator+(b);
```

Again, the operator + here represents a message sent to the object that is returned by the first function call. Hence, the meaning of the chain expression is as follows.

```
d=(a.operator+(b)).operator+(c);      //a message to the return value
```

Make sure that you feel comfortable with the interpretation of chain expressions as sequences of function calls.

Redefinition of the operator takes place only in the context of the class where the overloaded operator is defined. It is used only when a message (with a parameter of type Complex) is sent to an object of type Complex. This is why the standard meaning of the + symbol is used inside the member function definition in c.real = real + b.real; this is not a recursive call to the overloaded operator +: It is a built-in operator + applied to double values. The compiler knows that the left operand is of type double; it is not an object and cannot be a target of the operator+() message; the built-in operator + for double values is used.

Listing 10.3 shows the new version of class Complex and demonstrates the implementation of other overloaded operators as member functions. The second operator+=() function loses its Complex parameter; a Complex target object is used instead. The unary operator+() that implements the functionality of the showComplex() function now has no parameters at all. This does not contradict the rule that an overloaded operator function (implemented as a nonmember) should have at least one class parameter object—

this object is now the target of the message. Most programmers would overload the operator << rather than the operator + for the output operation. I will show you how to do that later. The output of the run of this program is shown in Figure 10–3.

Listing 10.3   Overloaded operator functions as class members.

```cpp
#include <iostream>
using namespace std;

class Complex {                           // programmer-defined type
   double real, imag;                     // private data
public:                                   // public member functions

Complex(double r, double i)               // general constructor
   { real =r;  imag = i; }

Complex operator+(const Complex &b)       // one parameter only
{ return Complex (real + b.real, imag + b.imag); }    // fast and neat

void operator += (const Complex &b)       // does target object change?
{ real = real + b.real;                   // add to the real component of the target
  imag = imag + b.imag; }                 // add to the imag component of the target

void operator += (double b)               // different parameter list
{ real += b; }                            // add to real component of the target

void operator + ()                        // it used to be showComplex(const Complex &x)
{ cout << "(" << real << ", " << imag << ")" << endl; } //

} ;                                       // end of class Complex

int main()
{  Complex x(20,40), y(30,50), z1(0,0), z2(0,0);    // objects created
   cout << " Value of x:  ";  +x;                   // same as x.operator+();
   cout << " Value of y:  ";  y.operator+();        // anything goes
   z1 = x.operator+(y);                             // use in the function call
   cout << " z1 = x + y:   ";
   +z1;                                   // display z1
   z2 = x + y;                            // same as z2=x.operator+(y);
   cout << " z2 = x + y:   ";
   +z2;                                   // display z2
   z1 += x;                               // same as z1.operator+=(x);
   cout << " Add x to z1:  ";  +z1;
   z2 += 30.0;                            // same as z2.operator+=(30.0);
   cout << " Add 30 to z2: ";  +z2;
   return 0;
   }
```

```
Value of x:    (20, 40)
Value of y:    (30, 50)
z1 = x + y:    (50, 90)
z2 = x + y:    (50, 90)
Add x to z1:   (70, 130)
Add 30 to z2:  (80, 90)
```

Figure 10–3   Output for program in Listing 10.3.

Using the const *Keyword*

The use of the const keyword for the function parameters here is the same as in Listing 10.2—there is no reason for any change. However, some parameters that you saw in Listing 10.2 are not present in Listing 10.3. This is how the global server functions from Listing 10.2 look.

```
Complex operator+(const Complex &a, const Complex &b)        // magic name
{ Complex c;                                       // local object
  c.real = a.real + b.real;                        // add real components
  c.imag = a.imag + b.imag;                        // add imaginary components
  return c; }

void operator += (Complex &a, const Complex &b)             // another magic name
{ a.real = a.real + b.real;                        // add to the real component
  a.imag = a.imag + b.imag; }                      // add to the imaginary component

void operator += (Complex &a, double &b)           // different interface
{ a.real += b; }                                   // add to real component

void showComplex(const Complex &x)                 // it is operator+() in Listing 10.3
{ cout << "(" << x.real << ", " << x.imag << ")" << endl; }
```

In Listing 10.2, the designer expressed his knowledge about the first parameter of the function operator+() in the form of the const keyword. Similarly, the first parameters of both functions operator+=() expressed the designer's knowledge in the form of the absence of the const keyword. In Listing 10.3, these parameters are gone. How should I reflect the absence (or the presence) of the const keyword for these objects? The answer that these objects are gone is not satisfactory because the objects are only gone from the function interface and not from the application. This is especially clear from the operator syntax in the client code.

```
Complex x(20,40), y(30,50), z1(0,0), z2(0,0);      // defined, initialized
z2 = x + y;                              // x and y do not change here
z1 += x;                                 // z1 changes as the result of operation
z2 += 30.0;                              // z2 changes as the result of operation
```

Whether these operators are implemented as stand-alone nonmember functions or as member functions, their right-hand side operands do not change, and their left-hand side operands change as the result of operation. This is not immediately evident from the inspection of the function call syntax for these operations. (Remember, this is the real thing; the operator syntax is just an alternative form that you are allowed to use when you comply with language limitations.)

```
Complex x(20,40), y(30,50), z1(0,0), z2(0,0);      // defined, initialized
z2 = x.operator + (y);                   // x does not change during call
z1.operator += (x);                      // z1 changes as the result of operation
z2.operator += (30.0);                   // z2 changes as the result of operation
```

So, how do you express that the data members of the object (the target of the message) do not change during the execution of the method? Right, you use the const keyword. In what position do you put it? You put it between the closing parenthesis of the parameter list and the opening brace of the function body. In the prototype, you put it between the closing parenthesis of the parameter list and the semicolon. Did I tell you that you should think about using the const keyword all the time? Yes, you should.

Listing 10.4 shows the same program as in Listing 10.3. I added the const keyword where appropriate. Also, I implemented complex member functions outside of the class braces. This forced me to use the class scope operator for function implementation. The scope operator is used with overloaded function operators in the same way as for any other member function. The const keywords are, of course, repeated in both the function prototype and the function implementation. Any difference will be flagged as a syntax error (possibly with a misleading message). The output of this program is the same as shown in Figure 10–3.

| Listing 10.4 | Overloaded operator functions implemented outside the class specification. |

```
#include <iostream>
using namespace std;

class Complex {                                // programmer-defined data type
   double real, imag;                          // private data
public:                                        // public member functions
  Complex(double r, double i);                 // general constructor
  Complex operator+(const Complex &b) const;   // no change to target
  void operator += (const Complex &b);         // target object changes
  void operator += (double b);                 // target object changes
  void operator + () const;                    // no change to target
} ;                                            // end of class Complex

Complex::Complex(double r, double i)           // general constructor
   { real =r;  imag = i; }

Complex Complex::operator+(const Complex &b) const
{ return Complex (real + b.real, imag + b.imag); }

void Complex::operator += (const Complex &b)   // target changes
{ real = real + b.real;                        // add to real component of the target
  imag = imag + b.imag; }                       // add to imag component of the target

void Complex::operator += (double b)           // target object changes
{ real += b; }                                 // add to real component of the target

void Complex::operator + () const              // no change to target
{ cout << "(" << real << ", " << imag << ")" << endl; }

int main()
{ Complex x(20,40), y(30,50), z1(0,0), z2(0,0);    // defined, initialized
   cout << " Value of x:  ";  +x;              // same as x.operator+();
   cout << " Value of y:  ";  y.operator+();   // anything goes
   z1 = x.operator+(y);                        // use in the function call
   cout << " z1 = x + y:   ";  +z1;
   z2 = x + y;                                 // same as z2=x.operator+(y);
   cout << " z2 = x + y:   ";  +z2;
   z1 += x;  // same as z1.operator+=(x);
   cout << " Add x to z1:  ";  +z1;
   z2 += 30.0;                                 // same as z2.operator+=(30.0);
   cout << " Add 30 to z2: ";  +z2;
   return 0;
 }
```

Tip

Use the `const` *keyword for parameters of overloaded operator functions that do not change the values of their parameters. When implementing overloaded operators as member functions, do not forget to use the* `const` *keyword for the target object. Make sure that the function is marked as* `const` *if the target does not change. Make sure that the absence of the* `const` *keyword is the evidence that the function changes the target object.*

Case Study: Rational Numbers

In this section, I will discuss another popular example of operator function overloading: a class that encapsulates the implementation of rational numbers (exact fractions) and implements arithmetic operations and comparisons that are supported for integers.

Rational numbers can be represented as two components, the numerator and denominator. They allow the use of operations over fractions without rounding errors, e.g., 1/4 + 3/2 = 14/8 = 7/4.

In the class implementation, the numerator and denominator should be private data members. If the application might be ported to a 16-bit machine, the data members should be of type `long`. If it will run on 32-bit machines only, data members can be either `int` or `long`—on 32-bit machines these data types represent the same range.

```
class Rational {
  long nmr;
  long dnm;                  // private data
public:
  Rational()                 // default constructor: zero values
  { nmr = 0;   dnm = 0; }    // this is not a good idea
  Rational(long n, long d)   // general constructor: fraction as n/d
{ nmr = n;   dnm = d; }
                             // THE REST OF CLASS Rational

  } ;
```

The general constructor initializes the fields of the object to the values specified by the client code. The default constructor can create noninitialized objects for further assignment of values; most programmers dislike leaving the fields of the object noninitialized, so they use some default values. If this does not affect program performance, this is all right. In this example, I initialize the object to the default value zero.

```
Rational  a(1,4), b(3,2), c, d;
c = a + b;          // 1/4+3/2 = (1*2+4*3)/(4*2)=14/8=7/4; c.nmr is 7, c.dnm is 4
```

Can the default constructor initialize both data members to zero? If the object is not used as an rvalue but only as an lvalue, similar to object c in the code snippet above, there is no harm in that. If the client programmer assumes that a noninitialized object is always initialized to null and uses this object in computations (e.g., to accumulate a total), this might result in problems.

```
Rational  a(1,4), b(3,2), c, d;
c = a + b;          // c.nmr is 7, c.dnm is 4
d += b;             // 0/0 + 3/2 = (0*2+3*0)/(0*2); d.nmr=0, d.dnm=0
```

This is why it is better to assign a nonzero value to the denominator, for example, value 1:

```
Rational::Rational()
{ nmr = 0;  dnm = 1; }       // zero value in the form 0/1
```

With this default constructor, `Rational` objects could be used both as an rvalue and an lvalue. When it is used as an lvalue (as object c below) the constructor call is wasted.

```
Rational  a(1,4), b(3,2), c, d;
c = a + b;          // c.nmr is 7, c.dnm is 4
d += b;             // 0/1 + 3/2 = (0*2+3*1)/(1*2); d.nmr=3, d.dnm=2
```

The arithmetic operators can be implemented as overloaded operator functions that follow the rules of operations over fractions. Below is the function `operator+()` that supports addition of two `Rational` objects. The comment on the first line of the function code describes the algorithm: The numerator of the result is the cross product of both operands (fractions), and the denominator of the result is the product of the denominators of both operands.

```
Rational Rational::operator + (const Rational &x) const
{ Rational temp;              // n1/d1+n2/d2 = ((n1*d2)+(n2*d1))/(d1*d2)
  temp.nmr = (nmr * x.dnm) + (x.nmr * dnm);
  temp.dnm = dnm * x.dnm;     // for example, 1/4+ 3/2 = 14/8
  return temp; }
```

The problem with this implementation is that it does not normalize the result. First, it is not convenient for the user. Second, the denominators only grow during computations, and overflow becomes likely. To avoid that, the class `Rational` should support the normalization algorithm that is called at the end of every arithmetic operation (including object construction).

```
class Rational {
  long nmr, dnm;                        // private data
public:
  Rational()                            // default constructor: zero value
  { nmr = 0;  dnm = 1; }
  Rational(long n, long d)              // general constructor: fraction as n/d
{ nmr = n;  dnm = d;
  normalize(); }
Rational operator + (const Rational &x) const   // important keyword
{ Rational temp;                        // n1/d1+n2/d2 = ((n1*d2)+(n2*d1))/(d1*d2)
  temp.nmr = (nmr * x.dnm) + (x.nmr * dnm);
  temp.dnm = dnm * x.dnm;               // for example, 1/4 + 3/2 = 14/8
  temp.normalize();
return temp; }
void normalize()                        // find the greatest common divisor
{ if (nmr == 0) { dnm = 1;  return; }   // it is zero, no work to do
  int sign = 1;                         // make it -1 if the number is negative
  if (nmr < 0) { sign = -1; nmr = -nmr; }       // make both members positive
  if (dnm < 0) { sign = -sign;  dnm = -dnm; }
  long gcd = nmr, value = dnm;          // search for greatest common divisor
  while (value != gcd) {                // stop when the GCD is found
    if (gcd > value)
      gcd = gcd - value;                // subtract smaller number from the greater
    else  value = value - gcd; }
  nmr = sign * (nmr/gcd); dnm = dnm/gcd; }      // denominator is positive
// THE REST OF CLASS Rational
  } ;
```

Those of you who are mathematically inclined can trace the details of normalization algorithm. For those of you interested in C++ programming and not in mathematics, let me take a look at the programming issues.

You see here two calls to the `normalize()` function. One, in the function `operator+()`, applies this operation to the local variable `temp`. In the example of adding 1/4 and 3/2, the result is `temp.nmr=14`, `temp.dnm=8`. Before the first pass through the `while` loop, gcd=14, value=8. In the first pass (14>8) gcd=14-8=6, value=8. In the second pass (6<=8), gcd=6, value=8-6=2. After the third pass, gcd=4, value=2. After the fourth pass, gcd=2, value=2, and the loop terminates. Well, I traced the algorithm after all.

	nmr	dnm	gcd	value	value != gcd	gcd > value
Start of algorithm:	14	8			<-(initial values of fields)	
Before the loop:			14	8	true: iterate	true: reduce gcd
After first pass:			6	8	true: iterate	false: reduce value
After second pass:			6	2	true: iterate	true: reduce gcd
After third pass:			4	2	true: iterate	true: reduce gcd
After fourth pass:			2	2	false: stop iteration	
After the loop:			2		<- (final falue of GCD)	
Before termination:	7	4			<- (final values of fields)	

Figure 10-4   Execution trace for member function normalize( ).

The second call to the `normalize()` member function is in the general constructor. It is needed in case the client code instantiates something like this:

```
Rational x(14,8);            // legitimate, but ugly
```

What is the target of this call to the `normalize()` member function? In Chapter 9, "C++ Class as a Unit of Modularization," I spent significant effort trying to persuade you that member functions look different from conventional global functions, and they are called using different syntax. (What used to be a parameter of a global function becomes the target of the message.) You see here that there is no target object, and the function is called pretty much like any global function.

When the object that should be used as the message target is not specified explicitly, it is the object that calls the function (unless the function is a global function). In this example, the target of the message is the `Rational` object x, and it is this object's nmr and dnm fields that will be used by the `normalize()` function in its algorithm.

Some C++ programmers feel uncomfortable that the calls to global functions and to member functions might look syntactically the same—without the target message. For calls to global functions, they use the global scope operator `::`; and for calls to member functions of the same class they use the object pointer `this`.

Why do these programmers dislike using the same notation for global functions and for member functions? After all, using the same notation is syntactically correct. The compiler searches the list of function members defined in the class; if the match is found, the compiler checks the interface and generates the function call; if no match is found in the class, the compiler repeats the search among global functions available in this scope.

The answer is that the human maintainer is not the compiler. It is a contribution to the quality of program code (decrease in code complexity) to directly indicate to the maintainer what the class designer knows about the nature of the functions used by the class, a member function or a global function.

Note

Always look for ways to pass your knowledge about the classes you design to the maintainer. When a function call does not have a message target, indicate whether this is a call to a class member function (by using the pointer `this` *as a target) or to a global non-member function (by using the global scope operator* `::`*).*

In the next version of the class `Rational`, I use these techniques to call `normalize()` in the general constructor and to call the global function `labs` that returns the absolute value of a `long` in the function `normalize()`. I also moved `normalize()` from the public section of the `Rational` class to its private section.

Leaving this member function in the public section of the class would indicate to the client programmer that it is okay to write algorithms that produce nonnormalized states of `Rational` objects and hence should use this member function in the client code. Meanwhile, the motivation for adding this function to the class is exactly the opposite. Its goal is to relieve the client programmer from the responsibility for normalization, to push this responsibility down to the server class to class `Rational`. Leaving this function in the public section would encourage client programmers to use it and to create dependencies on the design of this class. This is almost as bad as making data members public.

This is why it is an important task of a class designer to study the needs of potential clients and provide as much service as necessary—but not more. The set of services provided by the class is called the public interface of the class. This interface should be as narrow as possible without depriving the client code of the services that make it self-explanatory and independent on the internal design of the server class.

```
class Rational {
   long nmr, dnm;                          // private data
   void normalize()                        // private member function
   { if (nmr == 0) { dnm = 1;  return; }
     int sign = 1;
```

```
if (nmr < 0) { sign = -1; nmr = ::labs(nmr); }// to illustrate it
if (dnm < 0) { sign = -sign;  dnm = ::labs(dnm); }
long gcd = nmr, value = dnm;     // search for greatest common divisor
while (value != gcd) {           // stop when the GCD is found
   if (gcd > value)
      gcd = gcd - value;              // subtract smaller number from the greater
   else  value = value - gcd; }
nmr = sign * (nmr/gcd); dnm = dnm/gcd; }     // denominator is positive
public:
  Rational()                         // default constructor: zero values
  { nmr = 0;   dnm = 1; }
  Rational(long n, long d)           // general constructor: fraction in the n/d
  { nmr = n;   dnm = d;
    this->normalize(); }
Rational operator + (const Rational &x) const
{ return Rational(nmr*x.dnm + x.nmr*dnm, dnm*x.dnm); }
                                  // THE REST OF CLASS Rational
  } ;
```

Another important change that I made in the design of the `Rational` class is related to the `operator+()` function: I eliminated the call to `normalize()` by passing the results of computation as arguments to the `Rational` constructor. The operator function that I used in the previous version of class `Rational` was fairly expensive. Let me reproduce its code here.

```
Rational Rational::operator + (const Rational &x) const
{ Rational temp;              // n1/d1+n2/d2 = ((n1*d2)+(n2*d1))/(d1*d2)
  temp.nmr = (nmr * x.dnm) + (x.nmr * dnm);
  temp.dnm = dnm * x.dnm;     // for example, 1/4 + 3/2 = 14/8
  temp.normalize();
  return temp; }
```

For this version of the overloaded operator function, how many function calls do you see in the second line of the code snippet below?

```
Rational  a(1,4), b(3,2), c, d;
c = a + b;                         // c.nmr is 7, c.dnm is 4
```

The simple answer, "None. It is just the addition of two fractions" will not do. There is no addition operation here: we are using an overloaded operator function, and it is a function. Let me rewrite the client code with the explicit call to this function.

```
Rational  a(1,4), b(3,2), c, d;
c = a.operator + (b);              // c.nmr is 7, c.dnm is 4
```

All right, now everybody sees at least one function call. But look at the body of the function. Do you see a call to the `Rational` constructor when the object instance `temp` is created? Do you see a call to `normalize()`? That makes three function calls.

Now, when the function returns a value whose type is a programmer-defined class, a new unnamed object of the class is created, and the copy constructor is called that initializes the fields of this new object from the fields of the existing object; in this case, `temp`. Finally, the assignment operator in the expression `c=a.operator+(b);` is executed. This is also equivalent to a function call. This adds two to the count—five function calls where you see only one.

But this is not all. When the execution of the function reaches the closing brace and the function terminates, all local variables (in this case, `temp`) are going to die. What happens when an object instance is destroyed? Right, the destructor is called. And by the way, after the assignment in the client space, the unnamed object that was used for returning the value from the function (initialized with the copy constructor) will die too. That will invoke the destructor again. The total of function calls is seven.

I wish I could tell you that the new version of the operator function cuts this number to one or two. But no such luck. It eliminates the calls to the `temp` constructor and destructor, to `normalize()`, and to the copy constructor for the returned value. Instead, it introduces a call to the general constructor and, inside the constructor, to `normalize()`. So, the total count of function calls is five. The improvement does not sound like much, but things like that tend to accumulate.

Learn to see hidden function calls when you write C++ code. Two function calls here, two function calls there, and your program will be very busy doing very little. It is not for nothing that C++ programmers dislike returning objects from functions even though it is legal in C++.

Alert

Learn to see constructor and destructor calls in your C++ code. Avoid unnecessary function calls. Avoid returning objects from functions; do it only when it is needed to support required syntax in the client code.

What other services should class `Rational` provide to its clients? In addition to the `operator+()`, it should implement overloaded operator functions for the other three arithmetic operations: `operator-()`, `operator*()`, and `operator/()`. Similar to class `Complex` that I discussed earlier in this chapter, each arithmetic operator function should return the value of the class type. This result value can be either assigned to another variable of this type or used as a message target in chain notation.

Numeric algorithms often require comparisons between values, and class `Rational` is no exception. Overloaded comparison operators should return true (or 1) when the condition being tested holds or false (or 0) otherwise.

```
bool Rational::operator == (const Rational &other) const
{ return (nmr * other.dnm == dnm * other.nmr); }

bool Rational::operator < (const Rational &other) const
{ return (nmr * other.dnm < dnm * other.nmr); }

bool Rational::operator > (const Rational &other) const
{ return (nmr * other.dnm > dnm * other.nmr); }
```

Other conditional operators can be overloaded similarly. Notice that I am careful to indicate that these functions do not change the values of their parameters and do not change the values of their targets. Can you distinguish between the two? Or should I remind you of that joke about bagels and cream cheese? Or should I tell you another joke on a similar subject?

Listing 10.5 shows the implementation of class `Rational` and the test driver that demonstrates some of the operations that the class supports. It is a good example of C++ design, where the use of overloaded operator functions mirrors the way the numeric data types use the same operations.

Listing 10.5   Class `Rational` and its test driver.

```
#include <iostream>
using namespace std;

class Rational {
  long nmr, dnm;                          // private data
  void normalize();                       // private member function
public:
  Rational()                              // default constructor: zero values
  { nmr = 0;  dnm = 1; }
  Rational(long n, long d)                // general constructor: fraction as n/d
  { nmr = n;  dnm = d;
    this->normalize(); }
Rational operator + (const Rational &x) const;      // constant target
Rational operator - (const Rational &x) const;
```

```
Rational operator * (const Rational &x) const;
Rational operator / (const Rational &x) const;
  void operator += (const Rational &x);              // target changes
  void operator -= (const Rational&);
  void operator *= (const Rational&);
  void operator /= (const Rational&);
bool operator == (const Rational &other) const;      // constant target
bool operator < (const Rational &other) const;
bool operator > (const Rational &other) const;
void show() const;
  } ;                                                 // end of class specification

Rational Rational::operator + (const Rational &x) const
{ return Rational(nmr*x.dnm + x.nmr*dnm, dnm*x.dnm); }

Rational Rational::operator - (const Rational &x) const
{ return Rational(nmr*x.dnm - x.nmr*dnm, dnm*x.dnm); }

Rational Rational::operator * (const Rational &x) const
{ return Rational(nmr * x.nmr, dnm * x.dnm); }

Rational Rational::operator / (const Rational &x) const
{ return Rational(nmr * x.dnm, dnm * x.nmr); }

void Rational::operator += (const Rational &x)
{ nmr = nmr * x.dnm + x.nmr * dnm;          // 3/8+3/2=(6+24)/16=15/8
  dnm = dnm * x.dnm;                         // n1/d1+n2/d2 = (n1*d2+n2*d1)/(d1*d2)
  this->normalize(); }

void Rational::operator -= (const Rational &x)
{ nmr = nmr * x.dnm - x.nmr * dnm;          // 3/8+3/2=(6+24)/16=15/8
  dnm = dnm * x.dnm;                         // n1/d1+n2/d2 = (n1*d2-n2*d1)/(d1*d2)
  this->normalize(); }

void Rational::operator *= (const Rational &x)
{ nmr = nmr * x.nmr;  dnm =  dnm * x.dnm;
  this->normalize(); }

void Rational::operator /= (const Rational &x)
{ nmr = nmr * x.dnm;  dnm =  dnm * x.nmr;
  this->normalize(); }

bool Rational::operator == (const Rational &other) const
{ return (nmr * other.dnm == dnm * other.nmr); }

bool Rational::operator < (const Rational &other) const
{ return (nmr * other.dnm < dnm * other.nmr); }

bool Rational::operator > (const Rational &other) const
{ return (nmr * other.dnm > dnm * other.nmr); }
```

```
void Rational::normalize()                   // private member function
{ if (nmr == 0) { dnm = 1;  return; }
  int sign = 1;
  if (nmr < 0) { sign = -1; nmr = -nmr; }    // just for illustration
  if (dnm < 0) { sign = -sign;  dnm = -dnm; }
  long gcd = nmr, value = dnm;               // find greatest common divisor
  while (value != gcd) {                     // stop when the GCD is found
    if (gcd > value)
      gcd = gcd - value;                     // subtract smaller number from greater
    else  value = value - gcd; }
  nmr = sign * (nmr/gcd); dnm = dnm/gcd; }   // denominator is positive

void Rational::show() const
{ cout << " " << nmr << "/" << dnm; }

int main()
{ Rational  a(1,4), b(3,2), c, d;
  c = a + b;                                 // c.nmr is 7, c.dnm is 4
  a.show(); cout << " +"; b.show(); cout << " =";
  c.show(); cout << endl;
  d = b - a;
  b.show(); cout << " -"; a.show(); cout << " =";
  d.show(); cout << endl;
  c = a * b;                                 // c.nmr is 3, c.dnm is 8
  a.show(); cout << " *"; b.show(); cout << " =";
  c.show(); cout << endl;
  d = b / a;
  b.show(); cout << " /"; a.show(); cout << " =";
  d.show(); cout << endl;
  c.show();
  c += b;
  cout << " +="; b.show(); cout << " ="; c.show(); cout << endl;
  d.show();
  d *= b;
  cout << " *="; b.show(); cout << " ="; d.show(); cout << endl;
  if (b < c)
  { b.show(); cout << " <"; c.show(); cout << endl; }
  return 0;
  }
```

Figure 10–5   Output for program in Listing 10.5.

```
1/4 + 3/2 = 7/4
3/2 - 1/4 = 5/4
1/4 * 3/2 = 3/8
3/2 / 1/4 = 6/1
3/8 += 3/2 = 15/8
6/1 *= 3/2 = 9/1
3/2 < 15/8
```

Many designers feel that a composite class like `Rational` should provide its clients with disciplined access to its components and implement corresponding `get()` and `set()` functions.

```
long Rational::getNumer () const          // notice const
{ return nmr ; }

long Rational::getDenom () const
{ return dnm ; }

void Rational::setNumer (long n)          // no const
{ nmr = n; }

void Rational::setDenom (long d)
{ dnm = d; }
```

I do not like this addition. I think it breeds busywork for both the class designer and the client programmer. In general, you should avoid allowing the client access to the details of implementation (disciplined or otherwise). If client algorithm needs this access, well, let us bite the bullet and make data members public. After all, the structure of the rational number is not going to change, it will always contain at least two fields. Neither numerator nor denominator is going to disappear. Changes in their names are unlikely because no other name can give any additional benefits. If additional fields are to be added, they will not invalidate existing code that accesses the numerator and denominator directly.

Note

Make your data members private and your member functions public. Do not hesitate to make local functions private if they are needed only by class member functions. If the client code needs access to data members and the class design is stable and is not going to change, do not provide `set()` *and* `get()` *access functions—make the data members public.*

I feel that what I am saying runs against the most sacred principles of encapsulation, information hiding, pushing responsibilities down to servers and the like. Arguing against private data in this age means risking being laughed at. This reminds me of a Russian joke on laughing that touches popular themes of relationships between neighbors in "communal apartments" and the lack of enthusiasm for work in the workforce.

Yes, using public data often is similar to snoring at business meetings. But not always. Make sure that you know when it is appropriate. (Remember that joke about bagels and cream cheese?)

Note

For a class with a few well-established and well-understood data members, it is all right to make data members public. Examples are such geometrical and algebraic classes as `Point, Rectangle, Line, Complex, Rational.`

No matter how you design these geometrical and algebraic classes, their data members are not going to disappear, and hence the client code is not in danger of being changed. If you want to add more services by adding more member functions, this can be done easily. Of course, the indiscriminate use of public data members will make classes more difficult to modify.

Mixed Types as Parameters

Classes `Complex` and `Rational` are good examples of programmer-defined types that emulate the properties of built-in C++ numeric types. The objects of these types can be operated on by using the same set of operators as that used for an ordinary numeric variable. This supports the C++ goal of treating programmer-defined types in the same way as C++ built-in types are.

This analogy, however, is not complete. You can apply a number of operators to variables of numeric types that you cannot apply to `Complex` or `Rational` objects. Examples of such operators are modulo division, bitwise logical operators, and shifts. Of course, you can overload these operators similar to arithmetic and comparison operators, but the meaning of these operators (whatever meaning you decide to implement, the compiler will go along) will not be intuitively clear to the client programmer and to maintainer. An example of such arbitrary assignment of meaning is `Complex::operator+()` that I implemented to display the values of the data members of the `Complex` object. Intuitively, it is not clear at all what the expression +x should do to the `Complex` variable x.

Another problem with treating the objects of built-in types and programmer-defined types equally is the problem of implicit type conversions. C++ supports type conversions without reservation. For example, these expressions are syntactically and semantically correct for any numeric types.

```
c += b;        // ok for b and c of any built-in numeric types
c += 4;        // ok for c of any built-in numeric type
```

Whatever the numeric type of variable b, it is implicitly converted to the numeric type of variable c; whatever the numeric type of variable c, integer 4 is implicitly converted to that type. If variables b and c in the code snippet above are of type Rational, the second line above is in error. For this line to be syntactically correct, one of these functions should be available in the scope of the client code.

```
void Rational::operator+=(int x);      // c+=4;  is  c.operator+=(4);
void operator+=(Rational &r, int x);   // c+=4;  is  operator+=(c,4);
```

None of these functions is implemented in Listing 10.5, and that results in the syntax error in the client code. This is an example of the member function that eliminates the error.

```
void Rational::operator += (int x)     // target object changes
{ nmr = nmr + x * dnm;                 // n1/d1 + n = (n1+n*d1)/d1
   this->normalize(); }
```

Notice that if both functions are available, a member function and a global function with these interfaces, the second line in the code snippet above is still in error. This time around it is an ambiguity of the function call. Since either of these functions can foot the bill (the bill here is the interpretation of the statement c += 4;) the compiler does not know which function to call.

However, if variables b and c in the code snippet above are of type Complex, both lines in the snippet are syntactically correct. Why? Because I implemented two versions of operator+=() in Listing 10.4.

```
void Complex::operator += (const Complex &b);
void Complex::operator += (int b);
```

In the client code, the first function is called for the first line of code, and the second function is called for the second line of code.

```
c += b;      // c.Complex::operator+=(b); Complex argument
c += 4;      // c.Complex::operator+=(4); integer argument
```

This resolves the problem of using operands of mixed types in expressions. The second overloaded operator function works not only for integer arguments, but also for characters, short integers, long integers, floating point, and double floating point arguments. According to the rules of argument conversion, a value of each of these built-in types can be converted to an integer. There is no need to overload the function `operator +=()` for each of these built-in types. One function would suffice.

But do not sigh with relief yet. What about other operators such as `-=`, `*=`, `/=`? Each of these operators requires yet another overloaded operator function with a numeric parameter. And what about other arithmetic operator functions such as `operator+()`, `operator-()`, `operator*()`, and `operator/()`? Consider the following snippet for object instances of class `Rational`.

```
c = a + b;   // c = a.operator+(b);
c = a + 5;   // ?? incompatible types ??
```

Again, the second line results in a syntax error because the overloaded operator expects an object of the type `Rational` as the actual argument, not a value of a built-in numeric type. Meanwhile, all of these expressions are not a product of inflamed imagination. Numeric values are mixed with complex numbers and rational numbers in algorithms. And what about comparisons? You should be able to compare `Rational` objects with integers, and this poses yet additional problems.

The solution that I used so far is legitimate but boring. For each operator function with a `Rational` (or any other class) object as an argument, I have to write yet another operator function with a long integer value as an argument. (An integer might not be sufficient on 16-bit machines.)

Can anything be done about that? And here C++ offers you a beautiful tool that allows you to get away with only one set of operator functions (with class parameter) and force these operator functions to accept actual arguments of built-in numeric types.

What is this tool? It is a tool that allows you to cast a numeric value to a value of the class. Let us start with a very simple example.

```
Rational c = 5;              // incompatible types ??
```

It goes without saying that this line is in error. In Chapter 3, "Working with C++ Data and Expressions," I discussed the concept of the cast that converts the value of one built-in numeric type to the value of another built-in numeric type. Of course, these casts are available only between built-in types, not between built-in types and the programmer-defined type `Rational`. But if a cast between built-in types and type `Rational` existed, how would it look? Its syntax would be the same as for numeric types: the type name in parentheses. And the type name would be the name of the type to which the value is converted.

```
Rational c = (Rational)5;    // this is how the cast should look like
```

If you remember, in Chapter 3 you saw two syntactic forms for the cast, one that comes from C (the form I used in the line above) and another is the C++ function-like cast.

```
Rational c = Rational(5);    // this is how the cast could look like
```

Doesn't this line look like a constructor call? Now, what do you call the function that produces the value of the class type? Don't you call it a constructor? So this function looks like a constructor and behaves like a constructor. The conclusion is that it is a constructor.

Next question—what constructor? This is simple. In Chapter 9, we called a constructor with one parameter of nonclass type a conversion constructor. Now you should understand why this name is used. This constructor converts a value of its parameter type into the value of the class type. To make the line above syntactically correct, you have to write a constructor with one parameter.

What should this constructor do with its single parameter? If the value of the parameter is, say, 5, the value of the `Rational` object should be set to 5 or to 5/1. If the value of the parameter is 7, the value of the object should be set to 7/1. Hence, the value of the parameter should be used to initialize the numerator, and the denominator should be set to 1 for any value of the actual argument. This results in the following constructor.

```
Rational::Rational(long n)        // conversion constructor
{ nmr = n;   dnm = 1; }           // initialize to a whole number
```

This constructor is called every time that a function that expects a `Rational` parameter is called with a numeric actual argument. The class `Rational` now should look this way.

```
class Rational {
  long nmr, dnm;                          // private data
  void normalize();                       // private member function
public:
  Rational()                              // default constructor: zero value 0/1
  { nmr = 0;   dnm = 1; }
  Rational(long n)                        // conversion constructor: whole value n/1
  { nmr = n;   dnm = 1; }
  Rational(long n, long d)                // general constructor: fraction as n/d
  { nmr = n;   dnm = d;
    this->normalize(); }
Rational operator + (const Rational &x) const
{ return Rational(nmr*x.dnm + x.nmr*dnm, dnm*x.dnm); }
                                          // THE REST OF CLASS Rational
  } ;
```

Some programmers dislike writing several constructors if one constructor with default parameters can do the job. A popular constructor that can be used as general constructor, conversion constructor, and default constructor will look this way.

```
Rational(long n=0, long d=1)       // general, conversion, default constructor
  { nmr = n;   dnm = d;
    this->normalize(); }
```

Make sure that you see that this constructor is called when the client code supplies two arguments for object initialization: one argument and no arguments; default values are used instead of missing arguments when defining Rational objects.

```
Rational a(1,4);      // Rational a = Rational(1,4); - two arguments
Rational b(2);        // Rational b = Rational(2,1); - one argument
Rational c;           // Rational c = Rational(0,1); - no arguments
```

Notice that the actual arguments supplied in this example are of type int but the constructor expects arguments of type long. This is not a problem—implicit built-in conversion from int to long is available by default as it is available between all built-in numeric types. In function calls, the compiler allows not more than one built-in conversion and not more than on class-defined conversion (a conversion constructor call).

In compiling expressions with Rational operands, the compiler converts the int arguments first to long and then to Rational; after this conversion, the compiler generates the call to the appropriate operator.

```
c = a.operator+(Rational((long)5));       // real meaning of c = a + 5;
```

Now the client code above compiles without the operator
`Rational::operator+(long)`. A temporary `Rational` object is created, the
conversion constructor is then called, then the `operator+()`, and then the
`Rational` destructor.

Now you can write client code with numeric values as the second operand,
while the first operand is of type `Rational`.

```
int main()
{ Rational   a(1,4), b(3,2), c, d;
   c = a + 5;                  // c = a.operator+(Rational((long)5));
   d = b - 1;                  // d = b.operator-(Rational((long)1));
   c = a * 7;                  // c = a.operator*(Rational((long)7));
   d = b / 2;                  // d = b.operator/(Rational((long)2));
   c += 3;                     // c.operator+=(Rational((long)3));
   d *= 2;                     // d.operator*=(Rational((long)2));
   if (b < 2)                  // if (b.operator<(Rational((long)2))
      cout << "Everything works\n";
   return 0; }
```

Listing 10.6 shows a new version of class `Rational` that supports mixed types
in binary expressions. The output of the program run is shown in Figure 10–6.

Listing 10.6   Class `Rational` that supports mixed types in expressions.

```
#include <iostream>
using namespace std;

class Rational {
   long nmr, dnm;                          // private data
   void normalize();                       // private member function
public:
   Rational(long n=0, long d=1)            // general, conversion, default
   { nmr = n;   dnm = d;
     this->normalize(); }
Rational operator + (const Rational &x) const;   // const target
Rational operator - (const Rational &x) const;
Rational operator * (const Rational &x) const;
Rational operator / (const Rational &x) const;
void operator += (const Rational &x);            // target changes
void operator -= (const Rational &x);
void operator *= (const Rational &x);
void operator /= (const Rational &x);

bool operator == (const Rational &other) const;  // const target
bool operator < (const Rational &other) const;
bool operator > (const Rational &other) const;
void show() const;
   } ;                                     // end of class specification
```

```
Rational Rational::operator + (const Rational &x) const
{ return Rational(nmr*x.dnm + x.nmr*dnm, dnm*x.dnm); }
Rational Rational::operator - (const Rational &x) const
{ return Rational(nmr*x.dnm - x.nmr*dnm, dnm*x.dnm); }

Rational Rational::operator * (const Rational &x) const
{ return Rational(nmr * x.nmr, dnm * x.dnm); }

Rational Rational::operator / (const Rational &x) const
{ return Rational(nmr * x.dnm, dnm * x.nmr); }

void Rational::operator += (const Rational &x)
{ nmr = nmr * x.dnm + x.nmr * dnm;        // 3/8+3/2=(6+24)/16=15/8
  dnm = dnm * x.dnm;                       // n1/d1+n2/d2 = (n1*d2+n2*d1)/(d1*d2)
  this->normalize(); }

void Rational::operator -= (const Rational &x)
{ nmr = nmr * x.dnm - x.nmr * dnm;        // 3/8+3/2=(6+24)/16=15/8
  dnm = dnm * x.dnm;                       // n1/d1+n2/d2 = (n1*d2-n2*d1)/(d1*d2)
  this->normalize(); }

void Rational::operator *= (const Rational &x)
{ nmr = nmr * x.nmr;   dnm =  dnm * x.dnm;
  this->normalize(); }

void Rational::operator /= (const Rational &x)
{ nmr = nmr * x.dnm;   dnm =  dnm * x.nmr;
  this->normalize(); }

bool Rational::operator == (const Rational &other) const
{ return (nmr * other.dnm == dnm * other.nmr); }

bool Rational::operator < (const Rational &other) const
{ return (nmr * other.dnm < dnm * other.nmr); }

bool Rational::operator > (const Rational &other) const
{ return (nmr * other.dnm > dnm * other.nmr); }

void Rational::show() const
{ cout << " " << nmr << "/" << dnm; }

void Rational::normalize()                       // private member function
{ if (nmr == 0) { dnm = 1;  return; }
  int sign = 1;
  if (nmr < 0) { sign = -1; nmr = -nmr; }
  if (dnm < 0) { sign = -sign;  dnm = -dnm; }
  long gcd = nmr, value = dnm;             // greatest common divisor
  while (value != gcd) {                   // stop when the GCD is found
```

```
   if (gcd > value)
      gcd = gcd - value;                    // subtract smaller number from greater
   else   value = value - gcd; }
 nmr = sign * (nmr/gcd); dnm = dnm/gcd; }     // denominator is positive

int main()
{ cout   << endl << endl;
  Rational  a(1,4), b(3,2), c, d;
  c = a + 5;                                 // I'll discuss c = 5 + a; later
  a.show(); cout << " + " << 5 << " =";  c.show(); cout << endl;
  d = b - 1;
  b.show(); cout << " - " << 1 << " =";  d.show(); cout << endl;
  c = a * 7;
  a.show(); cout << " * " << 7 << " =";  c.show(); cout << endl;
  d = b / 2;
  b.show(); cout << " / " << 2 << " =";  d.show(); cout << endl;
  c.show();
  c += 3;
  cout << " += " << 3 << " =";  c.show(); cout << endl;
  d.show();
  d *= 2;
  cout << " *= " << 2 << " =";  d.show(); cout << endl;
  if (b < 2)
  { b.show(); cout << " < " << 2 << endl; }
  return 0;
  }
```

Remember that the conversions to type `Rational`, however implicit (silent), are function calls to the conversion constructor. When the function terminates, the temporary object created for this conversion is destroyed with the call to the destructor. (For this class, it is a default destructor supplied by the compiler.) Remember that story about two functions here and two functions there? (Actually, the story was about two dollars here and two dollars there.) Hence, this version of class `Rational` is somewhat slower than the version that does not rely on argument conversions and provides a separate overloaded operator for each type of the argument.

```
1/4 + 5 = 21/4
3/2 - 1 = 1/2
1/4 * 7 = 7/4
3/2 / 2 = 3/4
7/4 += 3 = 19/4
3/4 *= 2 = 3/2
3/2 < 2
```

Figure 10–6 Output for program in Listing 10.6.

This implicit use of conversion constructors is supported not only for over-loaded operators, but also for any function, member function, and global function that has object parameters. As I mentioned in Chapter 9, conversion constructors deal a blow to the C++ system of strong typing. If intentionally you use a numeric value instead of an object, fine. If you use it by mistake, the compiler does not tell you that you are making a mistake.

C++ offers a wonderful technique for preventing errors and for forcing the designer of client code to tell the maintainer what is going on. This technique consists of using the keyword `explicit` with the constructor.

```
explicit Rational(long n=0, long d=1)      // cannot be called implicitly
   { nmr = n;   dnm = d;
      this->normalize(); }
```

By declaring a constructor `explicit`, you make any implicit call to this constructor a syntax error.

```
Rational  a(1,4), b(3,2), c, d;
c = a + 5;                        // syntax error: implicit call
c = a + Rational(5);             // ok: explicit call
d = b - 1;                        // syntax error: implicit call
d = b - (Rational)1;             // ok: explicit call
if (b < 1)                        // syntax error: implicit call
if (b < Rational(2))             // ok: explicit call
   cout << "Everything is fine\n";
```

This is a very good idea because it gives the class designer a better control over the way the class objects are used by the client programmer.

Programmer-defined classes like `Complex` and `Rational` do indeed have to emulate the behavior of built-in numeric types as much as possible. Using numeric variables instead of objects in expressions is not an error but a legit-imate technique to implement computational algorithms. In the code snippet above, I marked some lines as `ok` and other lines as `syntax error`. Given a choice, every programmer would prefer to write code like in the lines marked as syntax errors. The need to spell out the casts every time a numeric operand is used is an imposition on the client programmer and results in code that is less aesthetically pleasing.

From that point of view, the use of the keyword `explicit` for the con-structors of classes like `Complex` and `Rational` is probably overkill.

Note

Do not use the keyword `explicit` *for constructors of numeric classes that implement overloaded operator functions. Utilize it for classes where using a built-in argument instead of the class object in a function call is an error, not a legitimate way of using the class.*

Friend Functions

Let us look back at the story of overloaded operator functions and see what they accomplished for us in treating programmer-defined types similar to numeric types and what remains to be done.

I started with the statement that it is highly desirable to be able to treat variables of built-in types and of programmer-defined types in exactly the same way. C++ supports this approach by entering into a deal with the programmer. You as a programmer are required to give up your freedom of choice for function names. You start your function name with the keyword `operator` and you append to this keyword the symbol (or symbols) of the C++ built-in operator that you would like to use with the objects of your class.

There are some minor limitations on what you are allowed or not allowed to do, such as using only existing C++ operators (you cannot make up your own operator that the language does not recognize); and you cannot change the relative priority of operators, their associativity, or the number of operands they take. But these are minor. If you stick to your end of the bargain, C++ sticks to its end of the bargain: It recognizes the expressions that use that operator as function calls to the function that you designed according to the rules outlined above.

C++ still allows you to call the overloaded operator functions in the same way you call other C++ functions—by using the function name (keyword `operator` plus the operator symbol), but few programmers ever do that. If you go to the trouble to call this function as a function, why bother to use the keyword `operator`? It is better to use your naming freedom and give the function a more-descriptive name, like `addComplex()` or `addToComplex()` or whatever. In the examples in this chapter, I wrote function calls using the full names of overloaded operator functions with one purpose only: to make sure you do not forget what is going on under the hood of a C++ program. Every use of the overloaded operator in an expression is in reality a function call. At least one function call. If local objects or returned objects are used, the use of operators also entails calls to constructors and destructors for these objects.

As with some bargains in real life, here you got more than you bargained for. The sky is the limit to what you can do inside the function whose header abides by the rules of overloaded operator functions. A good example is the `operator+()` function overloaded for class `Complex` in Listing 10.4. What is the meaning of this client code?

```
Complex x(20,40), y(30,50);    // defined, initialized
+x;   +y;                       // same as x.operator+(); and y.operator+();
```

If `x` and `y` were integers, the meaning of the second line would be clear: keep the sign of the value. Not a very interesting operation, but there can be no two opinions about it. With `Complex` objects, it does not mean: keep the sign of the value. It could mean anything. In this case, it means: print the contents of data members. For many classes, the operators that could be used on numbers cannot be applied to objects. Treating objects as numbers opens the way to producing code whose meaning is not intuitively clear, like using the plus sign for an output operation. (I will discuss better ways to overload operators for input and output of objects later.) This is a serious danger.

As with many bargains in real life, you also get less than you would like to. The overloaded operator functions are straightforward when they are applied to two object instances. If one operand is an object instance (the target of the message) and the second operand is of numeric type, there is a problem—the use of the operator syntax becomes a function call to the overloaded operator function with incompatible argument type.

In the previous section, I discussed two possible solutions to this problem. One is to double the number of overloaded operator functions: For each function with the parameter of the class type you write an overloaded function with the same name and the parameter of the numeric type. This is a good solution but it bloats the class design and makes it more difficult to understand.

Another solution is to overload only one function for each operator (with the parameter of the class type) and to make sure that the class has a conversion constructor. This constructor converts the value of the numeric type into the value of the class type. When the operator is used with two operands of the class type, the constructor is not called before the overloaded operator function is called. When the second operand (the function parameter) is of a numeric type, the constructor is called implicitly (or explicitly, if it is defined with the keyword `explicit`) before the call to the overloaded operator function. This solution keeps the class size manageable, but it entails the creation and destruction of a temporary class object each time a numeric value is used as the actual argument. This might affect program performance. For example, the first line in the next code snippet does not call any conversion constructor, but the second line does.

```
Rational  a(1,4), b(3,2), c;
c = a + b;           // c = a.operator+(b); - match, no constructor call
c = a + 5;           // c = a.operator+(5); - conversion constructor is called
```

But this is not the end of the story about mixed types in expressions. What about this sequence of statements in client code? The adding of two Rational objects is supported directly. Adding a Rational object and a number is supported through an additional call to the conversion constructor. But adding a number and a Rational object is not supported.

```
Rational  a(1,4), b(3,2), c;
c = a + b;           // c = a.operator+(b); - match, no constructor call
c = a + 5;           // c = a.operator+(5); - conversion constructor is called
c = 5 + a;           // syntax error: c = 5.operator+(a); is impossible
```

The expression that uses an overloaded operator member function is always a message to its left operand. Hence, this left operator must be an object instance. In the last line of the code snippet above, the left operand is a number. You cannot send a message to a number. It takes an object of a programmer-defined type to accept a message. Meanwhile, the last line in this code snippet is as legitimate as the previous line from the point of view of equal treatments of objects and numbers. Hence, it should be supported if you want to follow through with treating built-in types and programmer-defined types equally.

When you want to use the function whose interface is different from what the client code needs, one way to deal with the problem is to create a wrapper function. A wrapper function is a function with the same name you want to use and whose interface satisfies the client code and whose only purpose is to call the function you wanted to use in the client code to begin with. In the case of the operator+() for class Rational, the wrapper function should have the same name but it should be able to accept a numeric value as its first parameter.

```
Rational Rational::operator + (int i, const Rational &x) const
{ Rational temp1(i);                      // conversion constructor
  Rational temp2 = temp1.operator+(x);    // overloaded operator
  return temp2; }
```

Or better yet:

```
Rational Rational::operator + (long i, const Rational &x) const
{ Rational temp(i);          // call to the conversion constructor
  return temp + x; }         // call to operator+(const Rational&);
```

However, this function is impossible to use. There are three players here, the target of the message, the numeric parameter, and the object parameter. How do you put them together in a function call?

```
Rational  a(1,4), b(3,2), c;
c.operator+(5, b);                          // c + ???
```

The overloaded function operator is called as a message to its left operand. That means that the meaning of the last line of code is the object c plus something else. But I want to add 5 and something else, and put the result in c. Hence, this line is a syntax error. Let us try again.

```
Rational  a(1,4), b(3,2), c;
c = b.operator+(5, b);                      // c = b + ???
```

If the function name did not include the keyword `operator`, this would do. The value 5 would be converted to `Rational`, added with object b, and the result would be copied into object c. The use of the object b as the target of the message seems out of place—this object has nothing to do with the operation. But the function name does include the keyword `operator`, and this syntax is no good either. There should be only two players, not three.

Actually, it would be nice to get rid of the target object altogether and call the function with two parameters only.

```
Rational  a(1,4), b(3,2), c;
c = operator+(5, b);                        // c = 5 + b; ???
```

Remember the first overloaded operator functions that I used for class `Complex` in Listing 10.2? These functions were not class members. They were global functions. All I have to do to make the code snippet above work is to define the wrapper function as a global function.

```
Rational operator + (long i, const Rational &x)    // not a class member function
{ Rational temp(i);          // call to the conversion constructor
  return temp + x; }         // call to Rational::operator+(const Rational&);
```

Actually, I did more than just erase the class scope operator. I also eliminated the `const` modifier that specified that the function body does not change the fields of the target object. There is no target object here, and there is no need to testify that its fields do not change.

This is a good solution but it is too limited. It would be nice to use this function for other ways of writing the expression, not only for the case when the first operand is numeric. A good way to generalize this function is to eliminate the local `Rational` object and use the conversion constructor with the first parameter rather than in the body of the function.

When we use member functions to redefine a binary operator, the left argument is implicit, in the form of the pointer.

```
Rational operator + (const Rational &x, const Rational &y)
{ return x.operator+(y); }    // call to Rational::operator+(const Rational&);
```

Notice that the expression syntax in the body of this function is not appropriate. It will be interpreted as a recursive call to the global function `operator+()` I am defining here.

```
Rational operator + (const Rational &x, const Rational &y)
{ return x + y; }                // recursive call to operator+(): infinite loop
```

This is one of the few examples where an explicit call to the class member function using the function call syntax rather than the operator syntax is necessary. It allows the global function `operator+()` with two parameters to call the class member function (with one parameter).

I went through the steps of designing the interface for this global function because I felt you should trace these steps in detail. Many C++ programmers are not comfortable with writing the same algorithm as either a member function or a global function. I formulated the rules of transition in Chapter 9: The global function has one extra class parameter. The member function does not have this parameter but uses the argument object as the target of the message. Make sure you are comfortable with this transition.

Now I have to admit that this design has a flaw. I did not want to discuss it simultaneously with other issues and spread your scope of attention too thin, but now it is time to get to the problem. When the operator syntax is used in the client code, the compiler has two options for interpreting the expression: either to call the class member function with one parameter or to call the global function with two parameters. Each function provides a legitimate interpretation of the expression, be it the expression with two object instances or the one with one class instance and one operand of a built-in type (with the appropriate call to the conversion constructor). Of course, if both operands are of built-in types, there is no ambiguity—the compiler interprets the expression as a built-in operator rather than as a call to an overloaded operator function.

```
Rational  a(1,4), b(3,2), c;
c = a + b;     // ambiguity: c = a.operator+(b); or c = operator+(a,b); ??
c = a + 5;     // c=a.operator+(Rational(5)); or c=operator+(a,Rational(5));
c = 5 + a;     // no ambiguity: c=operator+(Rational(5),a); no 5.operator+(a);
c = 5 + 5;     // no ambiguity: the built-in binary addition operator
```

This is a pity because it contradicts the general algorithm of parsing the meaning of a name by the compiler as described in Chapter 9. For nonoperator functions, the compiler first looks at class member functions, and only if no match for the name is found in the class scope does it look up the name among the global functions known in this file. No such luck for operator functions.

To eliminate ambiguity for the expression where both operands are objects, I can eliminate the member operator function and implement the algorithm of the operator in the global function directly. Then the compiler will find only one way to interpret the expression.

```
Rational operator + (const Rational &x, const Rational &y)    // no Rational::
{ return Rational(y.nmr*x.dnm+x.nmr*y.dnm,y.dnm*x.dnm); }    // private data??
```

This is a nice solution, but it is too "direct"—it directly accesses the fields of its parameters, but the function itself is outside the scope of class Rational and hence has no right to do so. This means that this function will not compile.

C++ offers you an interesting workaround: the use of friend functions. A friend function is a nonmember function that has the same access rights to class members as does any member function. Notice that I am careful to say "access rights to class members" rather than just "access rights to class data" because a friend function can access private (or protected) member functions as easily as it can access private (or protected) data members.

A friend function can be either a global function or a member function of another class. Actually, there are situations where you want to allow access to class members by all member functions of another class. In this case, you will define another class as being a friend of this class. (We will discuss this situation in more detail in Chapter 12, "Composite Classes: Pitfalls and Advantages."). However, most friend functions are global functions: If you feel that you want to define a single function of another class as a friend of this class, think again; you are probably making things more complex than is necessary.

To define a function as a friend of the class, you insert the prototype of this function into the class specification (as if it were a class member), and you precede the prototype with the keyword friend. This does the trick; for all intents and purposes this function is like a member of the class.

```
class Rational {
   long nmr, dnm;                          // private data
   void normalize();                       // private member function
public:
   Rational(long n=0, long d=1)            // general, conversion, default
   { nmr = n;   dnm = d;
     this->normalize(); }
   friend Rational operator + (const Rational &x, const Rational &y);
                                           // THE REST OF CLASS Rational:
                                           // no need for operator+() functions
   } ;
```

Well, I got excited about this trick and my last statement goes too far.
There is a difference between a friend function and a member function. To
call a friend function, you do not have to specify the target object as you do
when you call a class member function. But this function can access the
Rational class members as if it were a class member function, and hence
this version of the function is now perfectly legitimate.

```
Rational operator + (const Rational &x, const Rational &y)   // no Rational::
{ return Rational(y.nmr*x.dnm+x.nmr*y.dnm,y.dnm*x.dnm); }    // yes, private data
```

Replacing the class member function with the friend function removes
ambiguity from the client code.

```
Rational  a(1,4),  b(3,2),  c;
c = a + b;    // no ambiguity: c = operator+(a,b);
c = a + 5;    // no ambiguity: c = operator+(a,Rational(5));
c = 5 + a;    // no ambiguity: c=operator+(Rational(5),a);
c = 5 + 5;    // no ambiguity: the built-in binary addition operator
```

All three forms of the expression with Rational objects are supported. If
you are concerned with calls to the Rational conversion constructor, you
can avoid them by overloading the operator function three times and defining all three functions as friends to class Rational.

```
class Rational {
   long nmr, dnm;                    // private data
   void normalize();                 // private member function
public:
   Rational(long n=0, long d=1)      // general, conversion, default
   { nmr = n;   dnm = d;
     this->normalize(); }
   friend Rational operator + (const Rational &x, const Rational &y);
   friend Rational operator + (const Rational &x, long y);
   friend Rational operator + (long x, const Rational &y);
                                  // THE REST OF CLASS Rational
   } ;
```

As I mentioned earlier, you can use the similar technique of multiple overloading with member functions. Friend functions have an advantage over member functions because member functions can support only those forms where a `Rational` object is the left operand and not the form where the left operand is a numeric variable. Since a call to an overloaded operator member function is interpreted as a message to the left operand, supporting this form would require the compiler to assign meaning to expressions like this:

```
c = 5.operator+(a);      // an integer cannot respond to Rational messages
```

Friend functions are more flexible for mixing numeric and object operands because they do not necessarily need the left operand as an object.

A similar approach can be applied to relational operators. A class member function with an object parameter supports only expressions that have object instances as its operands. If you want to support expressions with a numeric value as the right operand, you should add either a conversion operator or another overloaded operator function with the numeric parameter. Still, this does not support the expressions where the left operand is a numeric value and the right operand is an object.

```
Rational  a(1,4), b(3,2);
if (a < b) cout << "a < b\n";     // a.operator<(b);
if (a < 5) cout << "a < 5\n";     // a.operator<(5);
if (1 < b) cout << "1 < b\n";     // 1.operator<(b); is nonsense
if (1 < 5) cout << "1 < 5\n";     // built-in inequality operator
```

Adding to the program a global overloaded operator function can be used to support the fourth line of this client code.

```
bool operator < (const Rational &x, const Rational &y)
{ return x.operator<(y); }
```

Similar to the case of the arithmetic operator, using both global and member operator functions creates ambiguity for the second and the third lines of code.

```
Rational  a(1,4), b(3,2);
if (a < b) cout << "a < b\n";     // a.operator<(b); or operator<(a,b);
if (a < 5) cout << "a < 5\n";     // a.operator<(5); or operator<(a,5);
if (1 < b) cout << "1 < b\n";     // no ambiguity: operator<(1,b);
if (1 < 5) cout << "1 < 5\n";     // built-in inequality operator
```

To support all forms of relational expressions, you can replace each member operator function with the global operator function that accesses the data members of its parameters directly. To make this access legitimate, you should define this global operator function as a friend of the class.

```
class Rational {
  long nmr, dnm;                          // private data
  void normalize();                       // private member function
public:
  Rational(long n=0, long d=1)            // general, conversion, default
  { nmr = n;   dnm = d;
    this->normalize(); }
  friend Rational operator + (const Rational &x, const Rational &y);
  friend Rational operator - (const Rational &x, const Rational &y);
  friend Rational operator * (const Rational &x, const Rational &y);
  friend Rational operator / (const Rational &x, const Rational &y);
  friend bool operator < (const Rational &x, const Rational &y);
  friend bool operator > (const Rational &x, const Rational &y);
  friend bool operator == (const Rational &x, const Rational &y);
                                          // THE REST OF CLASS Rational
  } ;
```

This design eliminates ambiguities and supports all forms of relational expressions with objects as both operands, only the right operand, and only the left operand (the most difficult case).

```
Rational   a(1,4), b(3,2);
if (a < b) cout << "a < b\n";        // operator<(a,b);
if (a < 5) cout << "a < 5\n";        // operator<(a,Rational(5));
if (1 < b) cout << "1 < b\n";        // operator<(Rational(1),b);
if (1 < 5) cout << "1 < 5\n";        // built-in inequality operator
```

As you see, friend operator functions can do the same job as member operator functions do and more. The only operators that cannot be overloaded as friends are the assignment operator (operator=()), the subscript operator (operator[]()), the arrow selector operator (operator->()), and the function call or parentheses operator (operator()()). This limitation is necessary to make sure that the first operand is an lvalue (a target of the message). In all previous examples in this section, both the first operand and the second operand are rvalues.

Next, let us look at arithmetic assignment operators. The situation here is somewhat different because these operators do not return a value (return type is void). Instead, they modify the state of the target object. Since they do not return a new value of class Rational, they do not call the Rational constructor that normalizes the state of the object. Hence, the arithmetic operators have to call the Rational::normalize() function before returning.

```
void Rational::operator += (const Rational &x)          // no const
{ nmr = nmr * x.dnm + x.nmr * dnm; dnm = dnm * x.dnm;
  this->normalize(); }                                   // no constructor call
```

This operator supports the expressions where both the left and the right operands are objects (e.g., c+=b;).With the conversion constructor, this operator supports the expressions where the left operand is an object and the right one is a numeric value (e.g., c+=5;).

```
Rational  a(1,4), b(3,2), c;
c = a + b;              // c = operator+(a,b);
c += b;                 // c.operator+=(b);
c += 5;                 // c.operator+=(Rational(5));
5 += c;                 // 5.operator+=(c); is nonsense, is it not?
```

Replacing the overloaded operator member function with a global overloaded operator function does not buy you much, at least at first glance.

```
class Rational {
   long nmr, dnm;                  // private data
   void normalize();              // private member function
public:
   Rational(long n=0, long d=1)   // general, conversion, default constructor
   { nmr = n;   dnm = d;
     this->normalize(); }
   friend void operator += (Rational &x, const Rational &y);   // no const!
                              // THE REST OF CLASS Rational

   } ;
```

This operator changes the value of its first parameter. This is why this parameter does not have the const modifier.

```
void operator += (Rational &x, const Rational &y)        // no const!
{ x.nmr = x.nmr*y.dnm + y.nmr*x.dnm;   x.dnm *= y.dnm;
   x.normalize(); }                         // here, normalize() has the message target
```

Remember I told you that a friend function has access to all class members, not just to data members? This consistent treatment of class members pays off here: this operator function accessed private data members of its parameters and the private member function normalize().

This function supports the same forms of expression as the member operator function supports.

```
Rational  a(1,4), b(3,2), c;   long x = 5;
c = a + b;              // c = operator+(a,b);
c += b;                 // operator+=(c,b);
c += 5;                 // operator+=(c,Rational(5));
5 += c;                 // a constant cannot be used as an lvalue
x += c;                 // operator+=(Rational(x),c); what is this?
```

Adding anything to a numeric literal (a constant value) is a syntax error, no questions asked. Adding to a numeric variable is more complex. This variable can be changed, especially when passed to a function whose reference parameter does not have the `const` modifier.

However, this argument is not a `Rational` object, and the type conversions are required. The compiler creates a temporary object, calls the `Rational` conversion constructor to initialize it, and passes the value of x to the constructor as an argument. Now what? Modifying this temporary object within the operator function (as parameter x) is useless because this object is going to die when the function terminates, and the change will not be passed back to the variable x. A decent compiler should declare this a syntax error.

Even though in this case we cannot treat numerical types and programmer-defined types equally, this example shows that we can go a very long way toward that goal. Actually, many programmers prefer to use global friend operator functions rather than member functions, because the global operator functions are easier to write—they treat their operators symmetrically.

Listing 10.7 shows the implementation of class `Rational` with overloaded operator functions implemented as friends rather than as member functions. Figure 10–7 shows the output of the program.

Listing 10.7   Class `Rational` that uses friend functions to support mixed type expressions.

```
#include <iostream.h>

class Rational {
  long nmr, dnm;                       // private data
  void normalize();                    // private member function
public:
Rational(long n=0, long d=1)          // general, conversion, default
  { nmr = n;   dnm = d;
    this->normalize(); }
friend Rational operator + (const Rational &x, const Rational &y);
friend Rational operator - (const Rational &x, const Rational &y);
friend Rational operator * (const Rational &x, const Rational &y);
friend Rational operator / (const Rational &x, const Rational &y);
friend void operator += (Rational &x, const Rational &y);
friend void operator -= (Rational &x, const Rational &y);
friend void operator *= (Rational &x, const Rational &y);
friend void operator /= (Rational &x, const Rational &y);
friend bool operator == (const Rational &x, const Rational &y);
friend bool operator < (const Rational &x, const Rational &y);
friend bool operator > (const Rational &x, const Rational &y);
void show() const;
  } ;                                 // end of class specification
```

```
void Rational::show() const
{ cout << " " << nmr << "/" << dnm; }

void Rational::normalize()              // private member function
{ if (nmr == 0) { dnm = 1;  return; }
  int sign = 1;
  if (nmr < 0) { sign = -1; nmr = -nmr; }
  if (dnm < 0) { sign = -sign;  dnm = -dnm; }
  long gcd = nmr, value = dnm;          // search for greatest common divisor
  while (value != gcd) {                // stop when the GCD is found
    if (gcd > value)
      gcd = gcd - value;                // subtract smaller number from the greater
    else  value = value - gcd; }
  nmr = sign * (nmr/gcd); dnm = dnm/gcd; }      // denominator is always positive

Rational operator + (const Rational &x, const Rational &y)
{ return Rational(y.nmr*x.dnm + x.nmr*y.dnm, y.dnm*x.dnm); }

Rational operator - (const Rational &x, const Rational &y)
{ return Rational(x.nmr*y.dnm - y.nmr*x.dnm, x.dnm*y.dnm); }

Rational operator * (const Rational &x, const Rational &y)
{ return Rational(x.nmr * y.nmr, x.dnm * y.dnm); }

Rational operator / (const Rational &x, const Rational &y)
{ return Rational(x.nmr * y.dnm, x.dnm * y.nmr); }

void operator += (Rational &x, const Rational &y)
{ x.nmr = x.nmr * y.dnm + y.nmr * x.dnm;  x.dnm *= y.dnm;
  x.normalize(); }

void operator -= (Rational &x, const Rational &y)
{ x.nmr = x.nmr*y.dnm + y.nmr*x.dnm; x.dnm *= y.dnm;
  x.normalize(); }

void operator *= (Rational &x, const Rational &y)
{ x.nmr *= y.nmr;  x.dnm *= y.dnm;
  x.normalize(); }

void operator /= (Rational &x, const Rational &y)
{ x.nmr = x.nmr * y.dnm;  x.dnm =  x.dnm * y.nmr;
  x.normalize(); }

bool operator == (const Rational &x, const Rational &y)
{ return (x.nmr * y.dnm == x.dnm * y.nmr); }

bool operator < (const Rational &x, const Rational &y)
{ return (x.nmr * y.dnm < x.dnm * y.nmr); }

bool operator > (const Rational &x, const Rational &y)
{ return (x.nmr * y.dnm > x.dnm * y.nmr); }
```

```
int main()
{ Rational  a(1,4), b(3,2), c, d;
  c = 5 + a;
  cout << " " << 5 << " +"; a.show(); cout << " =";
  c.show(); cout << endl;
  d = 1 - b;                                    // operator-(Rational(1),b);
  cout << " 1 -"; b.show(); cout << " ="; d.show(); cout << endl;
  c = 7 * a;                                    // operator*(Rational(7),a);
  cout << " 7 *"; a.show(); cout << " ="; c.show(); cout << endl;
  d = 2 / b;                                    // operator/(Rational(2),b);
  cout << " 2 /"; b.show(); cout << " ="; d.show(); cout << endl;
  c.show();
  c += 3;                                       // operator+=(c,Rational(3));
  cout << " += " << 3 << " ="; c.show(); cout << endl;
  d.show();
  d *= 2;                                       // operator*=(d,Rational(2))
  cout << " *= " << 2 << " ="; d.show(); cout << endl;
  if (a < 5) cout << " a < 5\n";                // operator<(a,Rational(5));
  if (1 < b) cout << " 1 < b\n";                // operator<(Rational(1),b);
  if (1 < 5) cout << " 1 < 5\n";                // built-in inequality operator
  if (d * b - a == c - 1) cout << " d*b-a == c-1 ==";
  (c - 1).show();  cout << endl;
  return 0;
}
```

Many programmers struggle with implementing operators as member functions instead of using friend functions. The main reason for not using friends is the conviction that friends break encapsulation, information hiding, and all other good things that object-oriented programming promises us.

True, excessive use of friend functions makes code confusing and more difficult to maintain. There is no question about that. But what about reasonable use of friend functions? And what is reasonable and what is excessive when it comes to friends?

Figure 10-7 Output for program in Listing 10.7.

```
5 + 1/4 = 21/4
1 - 3/2 = -1/2
7 * 1/4 = 7/4
2 / 3/2 = 4/3
7/4 += 3 = 19/4
4/3 *= 2 = 8/3
a < 5
1 < b
1 < 5
d*b-a == c-1 == 15/4
```

The best way to answer this question is to recall the major goal of using classes in C++. Remember that? We need classes because when we use stand-alone global functions that access data structures, the connection between the functions and the data is only in the mind of the designer, not necessarily in the mind of the maintainer or the client programmer. Also, the encapsulation is voluntary and any function can access data directly, without using access functions. Right? Also, we wanted to have the local class scope so that the names of function and data that we use for one part of the program would not conflict with the names that we use for other parts of the program. Remember that list? I want to make sure that you hear this list of goals often enough so that you will be able to apply it to evaluation of the quality of C++ code.

With these criteria in mind, let us take a look at the design with overloaded operators implemented as member functions in Listing 10.6.

```cpp
class Rational {
  long nmr, dnm;                                   // private data
  void normalize();                                // private member function
public:
  Rational(long n=0, long d=1)                     // general, conversion, default
  { nmr = n;   dnm = d;
    this->normalize(); }
Rational operator + (const Rational &x) const;  // const target
Rational operator - (const Rational &x) const;
Rational operator * (const Rational &x) const;
Rational operator / (const Rational &x) const;
void operator += (const Rational &x);            // target changes
void operator -= (const Rational &x);
void operator *= (const Rational &x);
void operator /= (const Rational &x);
bool operator == (const Rational &other) const; // const target
bool operator < (const Rational &other) const;
bool operator > (const Rational &other) const;
void show() const;
  } ;                                              // end of class specification
```

Is the connection between data and function clear? Yes, the opening and closing braces of the class scope denote this connection. Is data protected from accessing from the functions other than member functions? Yes, data members are defined as private and cannot be accessed from the outside of the class. Is there a danger of name conflicts between members of class Rational and members of other classes? No any other class can define functions with names like operator+() and so on, and there will be no conflict.

It looks like a good design. Now let us compare it with the design that uses friend functions in Listing 10.7.

```
class Rational {
   long nmr, dnm;                     // private data
   void normalize();                  // private member function
public:
Rational(long n=0, long d=1)          // general, conversion, default
   { nmr = n;   dnm = d;
     this->normalize(); }
friend Rational operator + (const Rational &x, const Rational &y);
friend Rational operator - (const Rational &x, const Rational &y);
friend Rational operator * (const Rational &x, const Rational &y);
friend Rational operator / (const Rational &x, const Rational &y);
friend void operator += (Rational &x, const Rational &y);
friend void operator -= (Rational &x, const Rational &y);
friend void operator *= (Rational &x, const Rational &y);
friend void operator /= (Rational &x, const Rational &y);
friend bool operator == (const Rational &x, const Rational &y);
friend bool operator < (const Rational &x, const Rational &y);
friend bool operator > (const Rational &x, const Rational &y);
void show() const;
   } ;                                // end of class specification
```

Do you see what I am driving at? The list of functions connected with data is right here, between the opening and closing braces of the class scope. This list is clear not only to the class designer but also to the client programmer and the maintainer. Is data protected from access from the functions other than the functions declared between the class braces? Yes, data are declared private, and any function that needs access to data members have to be declared within class braces either as a member function or as a friend. What about name conflicts? Let us say we want to implement the overloaded operator function operator+() as a friend of class Complex. Will this function name conflict with the operator+() that is a friend of class Rational? No, the operator+() that deals with Complex objects will have a different signature.

```
Complex operator + (const Complex &x, const Complex &y);
```

So, what about friend functions that break encapsulation, information hiding, and other good things promised by object-oriented programming? This design with friend functions is every bit as good as the design with member functions. Mostly, it is a matter of taste. To my taste, friend operators are easier to code and to verify. Another important difference is that global operators support all forms of expressions, and member functions support only those forms where the left operand is an object, not a numeric value.

Tip

Do not hesitate to use friend functions when implementing overloaded operator functions. They are easier to design than member functions and they support all three forms of expression in the client code (both operands are objects, only the left operand is an object, only the right operand is an object). Do not use friend functions when they make code confusing.

Summary

In this chapter, we looked at the bells and whistles of C++: overloaded operator functions. Unlike the C++ features that were discussed in the previous chapters, overloaded operator functions are not absolutely necessary for writing high-quality C++ code.

One can even argue that, with the exception of a few classes such as Rational, Complex, and the like, the use of overloaded operators results in more confusion rather than making code easier to understand. The reason for this is that most classes are not like numeric types, and applying numeric operators is not straightforward.

For example, what do operator functions operator+() and operator<() mean for class Employee? Or for the class Transaction? Of course you can attach some meaning to these operators but this meaning is not intuitive and common. Your program might be better off if you call these functions giveRaise() and hasSeniority() or whatever is appropriate for your application.

However, the use of overloaded operators is not uncommon. They are especially popular in C++ libraries, including the Standard Template Library (STL), and you have to understand what they do and how they are implemented.

The comparison that I make between member functions and friend functions is very important. All too often we make design decisions on the basis of hearsay or arbitrary biases rather than from the point of view of goals of object-oriented programming.

Make sure that you do not treat friend functions as X-rated material. Use them if they provide more flexibility for better implementation. But do not overuse them.

CONSTRUCTORS AND DESTRUCTORS: POTENTIAL TROUBLE

Topics in this Chapter

- More on Passing Objects by Value
- Operator Overloading for Nonnumeric Classes
- More on the Copy Construction
- Overloading the Assignment Operator
- Practical Considerations: What to Implement
- Summary

Chapter 11

Overloaded operator functions give a new twist to object-oriented programming. Instead of concentrating on binding together data and operations and related ideas, we find ourselves busy with aesthetic considerations and the issues of equally treating built-in types and programmer-defined types by a C++ program.

This chapter is a direct continuation of the previous chapter. In Chapter 10, "Operator Functions: Another Good Idea," I discussed the issues that are related to the design of numeric classes, such as classes `Complex` and `Rational`. Objects of these classes are object instances in their own right. All of the issues related to dealing with objects apply to them: class declaration, control of access to class members, design of member functions, object definition, object initialization, and messages sent to objects.

The programmer-defined types discussed earlier are inherently numeric. Even though they have a more complex internal structure than integers and floating point numbers do, they can be handled by the client code similar to integers and floating point numbers: They can be added, multiplied, compared, and so on by the client code.

Notice the sloppiness of the previous statement. The first "they" at the beginning of the statement denotes programmer-defined types. What do "integers and floating point numbers" denote? Since I am comparing them to programmer-defined types, I am talking about integer and floating point types, not integer and floating point variables. It would be better to say "built-in types" instead. And what does the second "they" in the middle of the sentence mean? Probably the same thing as the first "they" in the sentence, that is, programmer-defined types. But this is not the case, because here I am talking about handling them by the client code! The client code does not handle programmer-defined types; it handles objects of programmer-defined types. It is object instances, or variables, that are multiplied, compared, and so on. I make this point because I think that you have learned enough about classes and objects to be sensitive to the loose language in object-oriented discussions and to avoid it if possible.

In other words, objects of programmer-defined numeric classes can be handled by the client code similar to variables of built-in types. This is why it makes perfect sense to support operator overloading for them. The C++ principle of treating the instances of built-in types and programmer-defined classes equally works well for these classes. In this chapter, I am going to discuss overloaded operators for classes whose objects cannot be added, multiplied, subtracted, or divided. For example, class `String` can be designed to manage text in memory. Because of the nonnumeric nature of such classes, overloaded operator functions for these classes look artificial. For example, you can implement `String` concatenation using the overloaded addition operator or `String` comparison using the overloaded equality operator. But you would be hard-pressed to come up with a reasonable interpretation of multiplication or division for `String` objects. Nevertheless, overloaded operator functions for nonnumeric classes are popular, and you should know how to deal with them.

The important distinction of these nonnumeric classes is the variable amount of data that objects of the same class can use. The objects of numeric classes always use the same amount of memory. In class `Rational`, for example, there are always two data members, one for the numerator, another for the denominator.

In class `String`, however, the amount of text that is stored in one object might be different from the amount of text stored with another object. If the class reserves for each object the same (large enough) amount of memory, the program has to deal with two unpleasant extremes—the waste of memory (when the actual amount of text is less than the reserved amount of memory) and memory overflow (when the object has to store too much text). These two dangers always haunt the designers of classes that allocate the same amount of memory to each object.

C++ resolves this problem by allocating a fixed amount of memory to each object (either to the heap or to the stack) according to the class description and then allocating additional memory to the heap as required. This additional amount of heap memory changes from one object to another. It might even change for an object during its lifetime. For example, a `String` object might receive additional heap memory to accommodate text that is concatenated to the text currently in the object.

Dynamic management of heap memory entails the use of constructors and destructors. Their unskilled use might negatively affect program performance. What is worse is that their use might result in corruption of memory and loss of program integrity that is not known in any other language but C++. Every C++ programmer should be aware of these dangers. This is why I included these issues in the title of the chapter even though this chapter continues the discussion of overloaded operator functions.

For simplicity of discussion, I will introduce necessary concepts for the fixed-sized class `Rational` that you saw in Chapter 10. In this chapter I will apply these concepts to class `String` with dynamic management of heap memory. As a result, you will hone your programming intuition about relationships between object instances in the client code. You will see that the relationships between objects are different from relationships between variables of built-in types, despite the effort to treat them equally. In other words, you are in for a big surprise.

Make sure you do not skip the material in this chapter. The dangers related to the roles of constructors and destructors in C++ are real, and you should know how to protect yourself, your boss, and the users of your code.

More on Passing Objects by Value

Earlier, in Chapter 7, "Programming with C++ Functions," I argued against passing objects to functions as value parameters or as pointer parameters and promoted passing parameters by reference instead.

I explained that pass by reference is almost as simple as pass by value, but it is faster—for input parameters that are not modified by the function. Pass by reference is as fast as pass by pointer, but its syntax is much simpler—for output parameters that are modified by the function in the course of its execution.

I also noticed that the syntax for pass by reference is exactly the same for both input and output function parameters. This is why I suggested that you use the `const` modifier for input parameters, indicating that the parameter does not change as the result of function execution. When you use no modifiers, this should indicate that the parameter changes during function execution.

I also argued against returning object values from functions unless it is necessary for sending other messages to the returned object (chain syntax in expressions).

With this approach, the pass by value should be limited to passing built-in types as input parameters to functions and returning values of built-in types from functions. Why is this acceptable for input values of built-in types? Passing them by pointer will add complexity and could mislead the reader into believing that the parameter changes within the function. Passing them by reference (with the `const` modifier) is not very difficult, but it adds a little bit of complexity. Since they are small, passing them by reference has no performance advantages. This is why the simplest way of passing parameters is appropriate for built-in types.

In the last chapter, you learned enough programming techniques to be able not only to discuss advantages and disadvantages of different modes of passing parameters but also to see the actual sequence of invocations.

Also on several occasions, I told you that initialization and assignment, even though they both use the equal sign, are treated differently. In this section, I will use debugging code to demonstrate the differences.

I will demonstrate both issues using the program in Listing 11.1, which contains a simplified (and modified) class `Rational` from the last chapter with its test driver.

Of all `Rational` functions, I left only `normalize()`, `show()`, and `operator+()`. Notice that the overloaded operator function `operator+()` is not a member function of class `Rational`; it is a friend. This is why I was careful to say at the beginning of this paragraph, "of all `Rational` functions," not "of all `Rational` member functions." I do this because I want to stress that a friend function is, for all intents and purposes, a class member function. It is implemented in the same file as are other member functions, it has the same access rights to class private members as do other member functions, and it is useless for working with objects of any class other than class `Rational`. It is only the invocation syntax that makes it different from member functions, but for overloaded operators, the operator syntax is the same for member functions and friend functions.

Listing 11.1   Example of passing object parameters by value.

```cpp
#include <iostream.h>

class Rational {
  long nmr, dnm;                          // private data
  void normalize();                       // private member function
public:
Rational(long n=0, long d=1)              // general, conversion, default
  { nmr = n; dnm = d;
    this->normalize();
    cout << " created: " << nmr << " " << dnm << endl; }
Rational(const Rational &r)               // copy constructor
  { nmr = r.nmr; dnm = r.dnm;
    cout << " copied: " << nmr << " " << dnm << endl; }
void operator = (const Rational &r)       // assignment operator
  { nmr = r.nmr; dnm = r.dnm;
    cout << " assigned: " << nmr << " " << dnm << endl; }
~Rational()                               // destructor
  { cout << " destroyed: " << nmr << " " << dnm << endl; }
friend Rational operator + (const Rational x, const Rational y);
void show() const;
  } ;                                     // end of class specification

void Rational::show() const
{ cout << " " << nmr << "/" << dnm; }

void Rational::normalize()                // private member function
{ if (nmr == 0) { dnm = 1; return; }
  int sign = 1;
  if (nmr < 0) { sign = -1; nmr = -nmr; }    // make both positive
  if (dnm < 0) { sign = -sign; dnm = -dnm; }
  long gcd = nmr, value = dnm;              // greatest common divisor
  while (value != gcd) {                    // stop when the GCD is found
    if (gcd > value)
       gcd = gcd - value;                   // subtract smaller from greater
    else value = value - gcd; }
  nmr = sign * (nmr/gcd); dnm = dnm/gcd; }   // make dnm positive

Rational operator + (const Rational x, const Rational y)
{ return Rational(y.nmr*x.dnm + x.nmr*y.dnm, y.dnm*x.dnm); }

int main()
{ Rational a(1,4), b(3,2), c;
  cout << endl;
  c = a + b;
  a.show(); cout << " +"; b.show(); cout << " ="; c.show();
  cout << endl << endl;
  return 0;
  }
```

In the general `Rational` constructor, I added the debugging printing statement. This statement should fire each time a `Rational` object is created and initialized—at the beginning of the `main()` and within the `operator+()` function.

```
Rational::Rational(long n=0, long d=1)              // default values
   { nmr = n; dnm = d;                              // initialize data
     this->normalize();
     cout << " created: " << nmr << " " << dnm << endl; }
```

I also added a copy constructor with the debugging printing statement. This statement fires when an object of class `Rational` is initialized from the data members of another `Rational` object, for example, when passing parameters by value to the `operator+()` function or when returning a `Rational` object from this function.

```
Rational::Rational(const Rational &r)       // copy constructor
   { nmr = r.nmr; dnm = r.dnm;              // copy data members
     cout << " copied: " << nmr << " " << dnm << endl; }
```

This constructor is called when `Rational` arguments are passed by value to the friend operator function `operator+()`. Despite appearances, the copy constructor is not called when `operator+()` returns the object value, since the general constructor with two arguments is called prior to returning from the `operator+()` function.

The destructor does not have a meaningful job in the `Rational` class, and I added it only for the sake of the debugging statement that fires when a `Rational` object is destroyed.

The most interesting function here is an overloaded assignment operator function. Its job is to copy the data members of one `Rational` object into the data members of another `Rational` object. How is its duty different from that of the copy constructor? The answer is that there is no difference, at least at this stage. The return type is different—the copy constructor must not have the return type, and the assignment operator, as most member functions, must have a return type. For simplicity, I return `void`.

```
void Rational::operator = (const Rational &r)       // assignment
   { nmr = r.nmr; dnm = r.dnm;                       // copy data
     cout << " assigned: " << nmr << " " << dnm << endl; }
```

The overloaded assignment operator is a binary operator. How do I know this? First, it has one parameter of the class type, and it is a member function, not a friend; as any member function with one parameter, it operates on two objects: One is the message target and the other is the parameter. The second explanation is from the syntax of the use of the assignment as an operator. The binary operator is always written between the first and the second operand. When adding two operands, write the first operand, the operator, and the second operand (e.g., `a + b`). When using the assignment, write the first operand, the operator, and the second operand (e.g., `a = b`). In the function call syntax, object `a` is the target of the message: In the assignment operator function above, `nmr` and `dnm` belong to the target object `a`. The object `b` is the argument of this function call: In the assignment operator function above, `r.nmr` and `r.dnm` belong to the actual argument `b`. Hence the function call syntax for the assignment operator is `a.operator=(b)`.

Because this operator returns `void`, it cannot support chain assignments in the client code, for example, `a = b = c`. This expression is interpreted by the compiler as `a = (b = c)`. This means that the return value of the assignment `b = c` (or `b.operator=(c)`) is used as a parameter in the assignment `a.operator=(b.operator=(c))`. For this expression to be valid, the assignment operator should return the value of the class type (here, `Rational`), Since the assignment operator was designed so that it returns `void`, the chain expression will be labeled by the compiler as a syntax error. For our first look at the assignment operator, this is not important. The chain assignment will be used later in the chapter.

The output of the program in Listing 11.1 is shown in Figure 11–1. The first three messages "created" come from creation and initialization of three `Rational` objects in `main()`. The two "copied" messages come from the data flow to the overloaded operator function `operator+()`. The next message "created" comes from the call to the `Rational` constructor in the body of the function `operator+()`.

All these calls to constructors take place at the beginning of the function execution. Next comes a series of events that takes place when the execution reaches the closing brace of the function body and local and temporary objects are destroyed. The first two "destroyed" messages occur when two local copies of actual arguments (3/2 and 1/4) are destroyed, and the destructor is called for these two objects. The object that contains the sum of parameters cannot be destroyed before it is used in the assignment operator. The next message "assigned" comes from the call to the overloaded assignment operator, and the message "destroyed" comes from the destructor for the object that was created in the body of the function `operator+()`. The last three "destroyed" messages come from the destructors that are called when the execution reaches the closing brace of `main()`, and objects a, b, and c are destroyed. Since the copy constructor is not called, the message "copied" does not appear in the output.

```
created:  1 4
created:  3 2
created:  0 1

copied:   3 2
copied:   1 4
created:  7 4
destroyed: 1 4
destroyed: 3 2
assigned:   7 4
destroyed: 7 4
1/4 + 3/2 = 7/4

destroyed: 7 4
destroyed: 3 2
destroyed: 1 4
```

Figure 11-1
Output for program in Listing 11.1.

This sequence of events plays differently if two ampersand signs are added in the interface of the operator+() function.

```
Rational operator + (const Rational &x, const Rational &y)        // references
{ return Rational(y.nmr*x.dnm + x.nmr*y.dnm, y.dnm*x.dnm); }
```

The requirement of consistency between different parts of code stands tall in C++ programming. Here, I am changing the interface of a function prototype and updating the function declaration in the class specification. (Again, it does not matter whether it is a member function or a friend function.) In this case, failure to keep related parts of code consistent is not deadly—the compiler would alert you that the code has syntax errors.

The results of the execution of program in Listing 11.1 with the operator+() above are shown in Figure 11–2. You see that four function calls are missing: Two parameter objects are not created and two parameter objects are not destroyed.

```
created:  1 4
created:  3 2
created:  0 1

created:  7 4
assigned:   7 4
destroyed: 7 4
1/4 + 3/2 = 7/4

destroyed: 7 4
destroyed: 3 2
destroyed: 1 4
```

Figure 11-2
Output for program in Listing 11.1 and passing parameters by reference.

Tip

Avoid passing object instances as value parameters. This causes unnecessary function calls. Pass parameters by reference, and label them as constant objects in the function interface (if applicable).

Next, let me demonstrate the difference between initialization and assignment. In Listing 11.1, variable c is assigned in the expression c = a + b. How do I know that it is assigned and not initialized? Because there is no type name to the left of c. Its type is defined earlier at the beginning of main(). In contrast, this version of main() creates and immediately initializes the object c to the sum of a and b rather than creating and assigning to c in separate statements.

```
int main()
{ Rational a(1,4), b(3,2), c = a + b;
  a.show(); cout << " +"; b.show(); cout << " ="; c.show();
  cout << endl << endl;
  return 0; }
```

Figure 11–3 shows the results of the execution of the program in Listing 11.1 with passing parameters by reference and this main() function. You see that the assignment operator is not called here. Neither is the copy constructor—the natural result of the switch from pass by value to pass by reference.

Later, I will use a similar technique to demonstrate the difference between initialization and assignment for the String class.

```
created: 1 4
created: 3 2
created: 7 4
1/4 + 3/2 = 7/4

destroyed: 7 4
destroyed: 3 2
destroyed: 1 4
```

Figure 11–3
Output for program in Listing 11.1, passing parameters by reference and using object initialization rather than assignment.

Tip

Distinguish between object initialization and object assignment. At initialization, a constructor is called, and the assignment operator call is bypassed. At assignment, the assignment operator is called, and the constructor call is bypassed.

These ideas about avoiding passing object parameters by value and distinguishing between initialization and assignment are very important. Make sure that you are able to read the client code and say, "Here a constructor is called, and here the assignment operator is called." Develop your intuition to enable you to perform this type of analysis.

Operator Overloading for Nonnumeric Classes

As I noted in the introduction to this chapter, the extension of built-in operators to numeric classes is natural. Overloaded operator functions for these classes are very similar to built-in operators. Misinterpretation of their meaning by the client programmer or by the maintainer is not likely. The idea of treating values of built-in types and programmer-defined types equally is a sound one that lends itself to straightforward implementation.

Operators can be applied to the objects of nonmathematical classes as well, but the meaning of addition, subtraction, and other operators might be stretched. This is similar to the story of icons for command input in the graphical user interface.

In the beginning, there was the command line interface, and users had to type long commands with parameters, keys, switches, and so on. Then there were menu bars with text entries. By selecting the entry, the user was able to enter the command to be executed without having to type the whole command. Then there were hot keys: By pressing the hot key combination, the user was able to activate commands directly, without removing the hand from the keyboard and going through several menus and submenus. Then there was the toolbar with command buttons: By clicking the toolbar button, the user was able to activate a command without needing to know the hot key combinations. The icons on the face of these command buttons were unambiguous and intuitively clear: Open, Close, Cut, Print. When more and more icons were added, they became less and less intuitive: New, Paste, Output, Execute, Go.

To help the user learn the icons, tool tip messages were added. The user interface has become more complex; applications require more disk space, memory, and programming efforts; and users are probably no better off now than they used to be with menus and hot keys. Similarly, we started with operator overloading for numeric classes, and now we are going to use operator functions for nonnumerical classes. This will require you to learn more rules, to write more code, and deal with more complexity. And the client code might be better off using old-fashioned function calls rather than modern overloaded operators.

The String Class

I will discuss a popular example of using overloaded operator functions for nonnumeric classes: using the addition operator for text concatenation.

Let us consider a `String` class with two data members: a pointer to a dynamically allocated character array and the integer with the maximum number of valid characters that can be inserted into the dynamically allocated heap memory. Actually, the C++ Standard Library contains class `string` (with the first letter in lowercase) that is designed to satisfy most requirements for text manipulation. This is a great class to use. It is much more powerful than the class that I am going to discuss here, but I cannot use class `string` for these examples because it is too complex, and details would take away from the discussion of dynamic memory management and its consequences.

The client code can create objects of the class in two ways, by specifying the maximum number of valid characters and by specifying the text contents of the string. Specifying the number of characters requires one integer parameter. Specifying the text contents also requires one parameter, a character array. The types of these parameters are different, so they have to be used in different constructors. Since each of these constructors has exactly one parameter of a nonclass type, which they convert to a class value, they are called conversion constructors.

The first conversion constructor, with the parameter for the length of the string to allocate, has the default argument value zero. If a `String` object is created using this default value (no parameters are specified), then the length of the text allocated for the object is zero. In this case, the first conversion constructor is used as a default constructor (e.g., `String s;`).

The second conversion constructor, with the character array as the parameter, does not have the default argument value. It would not be difficult to give it the default value of, say, an empty string, but then the compiler would have difficulty interpreting the function call String s;—do I want to call the first constructor with the default value of zero length, or do I want to call the second constructor with the default value of an empty string?

The current contents of the string can be modified by the client code by calling the member function modify() that specifies the new text contents of the target object. To access the contents of the String object, the member function show() can be used. This function returns the pointer to the heap memory allocated to the object. This pointer can be used by the client code to print the contents of the string, compare it with other text, and so on. Listing 11.2 shows a program that implements class String.

Listing 11.2   Class String with dynamically allocated heap memory.

```
#include <iostream>
using namespace std;

class String {
  char *str;                          // dynamically allocated char array
  int len;
public:
  String (int length=0);             // conversion/default constructor
  String(const char*);               // conversion constructor
  ~String ();                        // deallocate dynamic memory
  void modify(const char*);          // change the array contents
  char* show() const;                // return a pointer to the array
} ;

String::String(int length)
{ len = length;
  str = new char[len+1];             // default size is 1
  if (str==NULL) exit(1);            // test for success
  str[0] = 0; }                      // empty String of 0 length is ok

String::String(const char* s)
{ len = strlen(s);                   // measure length of incoming text
  str = new char[len+1];             // allocate enough heap space
  if (str==NULL) exit(1);            // test for success
  strcpy(str,s); }                   // copy text into new heap memory

String::~String()
{ delete str; }                      // return heap memory (not the pointer!)

void String::modify(const char a[])  // no memory management here
{ strncpy(str,a,len-1);              // protect from overflow
  str[len-1] = 0; }                  // terminate String properly

char* String::show() const           // not a good practice, but ok
{ return str; }
```

```
int main()
{
  String u("This is a test.");
  String v("Nothing can go wrong.");
  cout << " u = " << u.show() << endl;        // result is ok
  cout << " v = " << v.show() << endl;        // result is ok
  v.modify("Let us hope for the best.");      // input is truncated
  cout << " v = " << v.show() << endl;
  strcpy(v.show(),"Hi there");                // bad practice
  cout << " v = " << v.show() << endl;
  return 0;
}
```

Dynamic Management of Heap Memory

The first code line of the first conversion constructor sets the value of data member `len`; the second code line sets the value of data member `str` by allocating the required amount of heap memory. Then it tests for success of memory allocation, and puts zero (character `'\0'`) into the beginning of the allocated memory. For any C++ library function, this text content appears to be empty, although it has space for the number of characters specified by the client code.

If the client code defines a `String` object and does not provide arguments, this constructor is used as a default constructor that allocates one character on the heap and sets it to `'\0'` to indicate the empty string.

Figure 11–4 shows the memory diagram for the execution of each statement of the constructor for the following statement.

```
String t(20);              // 21 characters on the heap
```

Figure 11–4(a) shows the first phase of construction, and Figure 11–4(b) shows the second phase of construction. The rectangle represents the `String` object `t` with two data members, pointer `str` and integer `len`. These data members might take the same amount of memory, but I am showing the pointer as a smaller rectangle to underscore the fact that it does not contain computational data. The name of the object `t` and the names of data members `str` and `len` are drawn outside of the object rectangle.

Part A shows that after executing the statement `len = length`, the data member `len` is initialized to 20 (it contains a value) and the pointer `str` remains noninitialized (it points anywhere it wants). Part B shows that after the executing of the rest of the constructor body, the heap space (21 characters) is allocated, is pointed to by the pointer `str`, and its first character is set

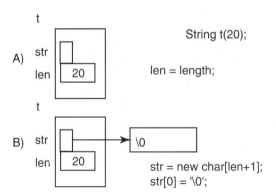

Figure 11–4   The memory diagram for the first conversion constructor in Listing 11.2.

to 0. Drawing a diagram for a simple object might seem to be overkill, but I recommend drawing these diagrams for all code that manipulates pointers and heap memory. This is the best way to develop your programming intuition for dynamic memory management.

The first line of code of the second conversion constructor measures the length of the string specified by the client code and sets the data member `len`. The second line sets the data member `str` by allocating the required amount of heap memory to be pointed to by `str` and copies the characters specified by the client code into the allocated memory. The library function `strcpy()` copies the characters from the argument array and appends the terminating zero.

Figure 11–5 shows the steps of the object initialization for the following statement.

```
String u("This is a test.");          // 15 symbols, 16 characters on the heap
```

There are three methods of dealing with the data member that keeps the size of heap memory. The first keeps the total size of heap memory allocated in the data member (the number of symbols to accommodate plus one). The second keeps the number of useful symbols as a data member and adds one to this value when characters are allocated on the heap. I use the second approach, but I would be hard-pressed to explain why it is better than the first approach. However, I do not switch because I would be equally hard-pressed to explain why the first approach is better.

The third method is not to keep the string length as a data member at all but compute the length on the fly by calling the `strlen()` function. This is an example of the time-space tradeoff. The third approach is better if you do

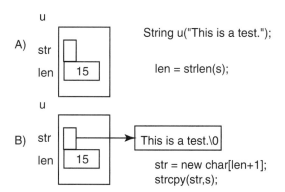

A)

u

str

len | 15

String u("This is a test.");

len = strlen(s);

B)

u

str → This is a test.\0

len | 15

str = new char[len+1];
strcpy(str,s);

Figure 11–5   The memory diagram for the second conversion constructor in Listing 11.2.

not need the length often and are loathe to allocate an extra integer for each string object.

Since heap memory is allocated for each String object individually, many programmers feel that this memory should be viewed as part of the object. With this approach, String objects appear to the client code as objects of variable length, depending on the size of the allocated heap memory. This view is valid, but it results in more confusing explanations of the workings of constructors and destructors and somewhat blurs the concept of the class itself.

I prefer the approach illustrated by the diagrams shown in Figures 11–4 and 11–5. It reflects the C++ principle that the class is a blueprint for object instances. This blueprint is the same for all String objects. According to the blueprint, each String object has two data members; the size of each String object is the same. When this statement in the client code is executed,

```
String t(20);        // two data members are allocated on the stack
```

the object t is allocated two data members on the stack; the heap memory is allocated by String member functions that execute for a particular object. Different String objects can have different amounts of heap memory or they can free memory; or acquire more memory without changing their identity.

This approach does not change as String objects themselves are allocated on the heap. Consider this example of the client code.

```
String *p;               // no String object, pointer is created on the heap
p = new String ("Hi!");  // two data members plus 4 characters on the heap
```

Here, an unnamed `String` object (pointed to by pointer `p`) gets an integer and a character pointer on the heap. After the object is created, the constructor allocates four more characters on the heap and sets the pointer `str` to point to that memory.

This approach gives me the convenience of thinking that all objects of the same class are the same size. When an object is created, there are two separate processes: creation of the object (always of the same size) and a constructor call. It initializes the object data members, including pointers that point to the heap memory.

The destructor deletes the memory allocated dynamically on the heap. It is called just before the object is going to be destroyed. When the object is destroyed, the memory allocated to its data members `str` and `len` is also destroyed and returned for further use. If the object was allocated on the stack, as object `u` and `v` in `main()` in Listing 11.2 are, this memory goes back to the stack. If the object was allocated on the heap (as the unnamed object pointed to by pointer `p`), the memory allocated for `len` and `str` goes back to the heap. But in all cases, the memory that the destructor deletes (pointed to by pointer `str`) goes back to the heap before the data members `len` and `str` disappear. Otherwise the destructor statement `delete str;` would be illegal.

Function `modify()` changes the contents of the dynamically allocated heap memory. It uses the library function `strncpy()` to make sure the memory is not corrupted, even if the client code erroneously supplies a string that is longer than the size of the dynamic memory allocated for the object. In case of overflow, `strncpy()` does not terminate the string with the null terminator. This is why I do that at the end of the function. This seems superfluous in the case when the new string is shorter than the available memory. Keep in mind that in this case, `strncpy()` fills the rest of the string with zeros anyway and doing it once more will not slow down the program.

Function `modify()` cannot expand the string over the initial length. Most `String` designs do not allow the programmer to change the contents of the `String` object. In this case, create and use another object for the different contents you need. I am implementing the compromise. Full-fledged modification facilities would require much more code and would require the discussion of many extraneous issues. This little function `modify()` is sufficient for the purposes of this discussion.

Function `show()` returns the pointer to the dynamically allocated memory. Listing 11.2 demonstrates two uses of this function by the client code in `main()`. The first use is to print the contents of the `String` object that is the target of the `show()` message. The second use is to modify the object contents by using the return value of the `show()` function as the output parameter in a call to `strcpy()` in the client code. The first use is legitimate; the second use is arrogant and written to intimidate the maintainer rather than to help the maintainer understand the intent of the code developer.

One of the first high-level computer languages, APL (A Programming Language) was very complex. It is still used, mostly for financial applications. The character set of this language is so large that it needs a special keyboard. Among other things, it includes powerful operations for array and matrix processing. APL programmers love this language. It is considered good taste to write a few lines of APL code, show it to a friend, and ask, "Guess what it means?"

I am far from suggesting that programmers with such a mindset be fired from their jobs. But they should not participate in group projects where other people have to maintain their code. Today, there is nothing to boast about if a programmer writes code that needs extra effort to understand.

```
strcpy(v.show(),"Hi there");              // bad practice
```

Notice that my indignation is directed mostly at the fact that the maintainer has to spend extra effort to understand the code. That this code does not evaluate the size of the heap memory available within the object and hence can corrupt memory is important, but it only adds insult to injury. It can be corrected by using a different division of responsibilities between the client code and the server `String`.

```
int length = strlen(v.show());            // get available space
strncpy(v.show(),"Hi there",length);      // pushes responsibility up
```

For `String` objects created with the second conversion constructor, the value of `length` is the total available space. For objects created with the first conversion constructor, the value of `length` gets the length of the last string stored, which could be less than the total available space. Most important, this method violates the principle of pushing responsibility from clients to servers and hiding details of data manipulation from the client code.

Here, it is the client code that does low-level data manipulation, even if the names of `String` data members are not used in the code. If you want to protect heap data from corruption, it is the server code that should include statements that evaluate the available size of dynamic storage. A good solution should use the name of the server function rather than manipulating server data directly and should push the responsibility for protecting heap memory to the server. Is it clear what I mean? Here is a solution that does the job well, is safe, and needs no explanation. You already saw this solution.

```
u = This is a test.
v = Nothing can go wrong.
v = Let us hope for the b
v = Hi there
```

Figure 11–6   Output for program in Listing 11.2.

```
v.modify("Hi there");        // it tests for available space
```

Figure 11–6 shows the output of the program from Listing 11.2. It demonstrates that the call to function modify() protects the dynamic memory from overflow by truncating the client code data.

The use of the pointer returned by the function show() is not protected. Here is an example of memory corruption that function String::show() makes possible.

```
char *ptr = v.show();        // reckless practice
ptr[200] = 'A';              // memory corruption
```

Or, if you like the chain notation for using objects, you can do that in only one statement.

```
v.show()[200] = 'A';         // reckless practice, memory corruption
```

This is not a good practice.

Protecting Object Heap Data from Client Code

C++ provides you with a way to protect the internals of the object from the client code that uses the pointer returned by a member function. Defining the pointer as a pointer to a constant prevents this abuse. For example, define the returned value of function show() as a pointer to a constant character rather than as a pointer to a nonconstant character, as I did in Listing 11.2.

```
const char* String::show() const    // good practice: return const
{ return str; }
```

Now, if the client code makes an attempt to change the contents of dynamic memory through the returned value of member function show(), it will be flagged as a syntax error.

```
strcpy(v.show(), "Hi there");        // error, not just bad practice
```

With this design of the server class `String`, the client code is forced to use `modify()` to change the state of the object. As a result, the client code is expressed in terms of the server function call, pushes protection operations down to the server class, and does not force the client to deal with the details of server design (limited heap space).

Overloaded Concatenation Operator

My next step is to design the overloaded operator function that concatenates two `String` objects: appending the contents of the second object to the contents of the first object. This means that client code can use this overloaded operator function in the following way.

```
String u("This is a test. ");       // left operand
String v("Nothing can go wrong.");  // right operand
u += v;                             // expression: operand, operator, operand
```

After this segment of code, the contents of the object v should be the same, and the object u will have its contents changed to "This is a test. Nothing can go wrong."

If I implement this operator function as a member function, then the object u has to be the target of the message, and the object v has to be the parameter in the function call. The real meaning of the last line in this code snippet is as follows.

```
u.operator+=(v);    // meaning of u += v; -> u is the target, v is the parameter
```

Hence the interface of this function should include the `const` modifier for the parameter and must not include the `const` modifier for the member function itself. Return type could be `void`. This will limit the use of the operator in chain expressions, but it is not a serious limitation for the client programmers.

```
void operator += (const String s);   // concatenate parameter to target object
```

I know that it is not nice to pass objects by value, but I assume that there is no performance problem here. After all, the object of type `String` has only two small data members, a character pointer and an integer. Copying these data members should not take too long.

The algorithm for `String` concatenation should include the following steps.

1. Add the length of both character arrays to define the total number of characters.
2. Allocate heap memory to accommodate the characters and the terminating zero.
3. Test for success of memory allocation; give up if the system is out of memory.
4. Copy characters from the target object into the newly allocated heap space.
5. Concatenate characters from the parameter object into the newly allocated space.
6. Set the `str` pointer of the target object to point to the newly allocated space.

Figure 11–7 shows these steps (with the exception of giving up if the system is out of heap memory) and the C++ statements that implement them. I use somewhat shorter strings in the client code to make the tracing of events simpler.

The top part of the figure shows two `String` objects, u (with contents "Hi") and v (with contents "there!"). Part A shows both objects after the field `len` of the first object was modified, heap memory was allocated, and the existing contents of object u was copied into this heap memory (steps 1–4 of the algorithm). Part B shows the state of the heap memory after step 5. Part C shows the state of the objects after the pointer `str` of the target object u was set to point to the newly allocated heap memory (step 6).

Putting it all together, you get the following server code.

```
void String::operator += (const String s)      // object parameter
{ char* p;                                      // local pointer
  len = strlen(str) + strlen(s.str);            // total length
  p = new char[len + 1];                        // allocate heap memory
  if (p==NULL) exit(1);                         // test for success
  strcpy(p,str);                                // copy the first part of result
  strcat(p,s.str);                              // concatenate the second part
  str = p; }                                    // set str to point to new memory
```

It might look like overkill to spell out the steps of this simple algorithm in such minute detail and to draw a separate picture for each small step of memory manipulation. If you feel this way, great. But you belong to a lucky minority. For most people, pointer operations are obscure and counterintuitive.

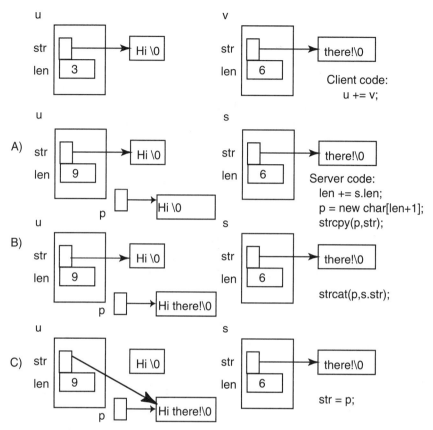

Figure 11-7   The memory diagram for the `String` concatenation operator function.

Only experienced programmers are able to notice that the heap space owned by the target object is not returned properly. The figure shows this clearly.

I think that drawing pictures is the only way to develop intuition about memory management and to discover errors. It is better to spend a few extra minutes drawing and planning than to waste hours with the debugger and other complex tools finding your way in a mire of obscure statements whose meaning is not absolutely clear to you.

The drawings are, of course, only tools. It is you who have to use the tools to make sure that you understand each statement.

Preventing Memory Leaks

As I mentioned, Figure 11–7 shows that the heap character array pointed to by the target pointer str at the beginning of the function call is not returned properly. It becomes inaccessible when pointer str is turned to point to the newly allocated segment of memory (where the local pointer p is pointing). This is memory leak—a common error in pointer manipulation and memory management. To prevent memory leak, this character array has to be returned to the heap before the pointer str is turned to point to the newly allocated array.

```
void String::operator += (const String s)    // object parameter
{ char* p;                                    // local pointer
  len = strlen(str) + strlen(s.str);          // total length
  p = new char[len + 1];                       // allocate enough heap memory
  if (p==NULL) exit(1);                        // test for success
  strcpy(p,str);                               // copy the first part of result
  strcat(p,s.str);                             // concatenate the second part
  delete str;                                  // return existing dynamic memory
  str = p; }                                   // set str to point to new memory
```

Figure 11–8 is similar to Figure 11–7. It shows that the heap character array pointed to by the target data member str disappears as a result of the delete operation. Only after that is the pointer str turned to point to the new heap array.

With memory leak taken care of, let me admit that in the discussion of this overloaded operator function I told you the truth and only the truth; but I did not tell you the whole truth. The reason is that I wanted to make sure that I took care of smaller and less difficult issues before we faced more complex and more dangerous problems. I would like to have your undivided attention.

This discussion should show you the pattern of dangerous features you have to recognize when you write your own C++ programs. The core of the problem is my favorite enemy: passing objects as value parameters.

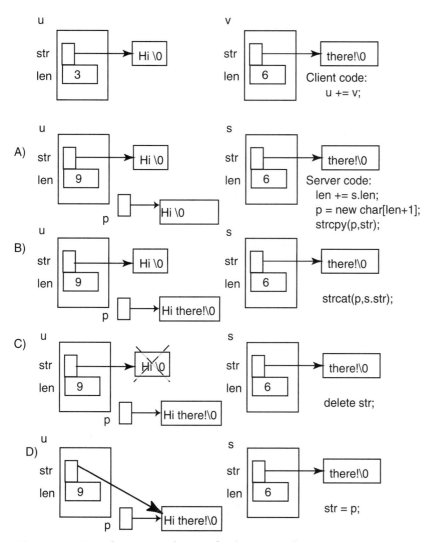

Figure 11–8 The memory diagram for the corrected String concatenation operator function.

Protecting Program Integrity

When the actual argument, object or no object, is passed by value, its value is copied into a local automatic variable on the stack. This copying is done memberwise.

648 Chapter II Constructors and Destructors

This presents no problem for arguments of built-in types but does present a minor performance nuisance for a simple class like `Rational` or `Complex`. It presents a real performance problem for larger classes whose objects require larger amounts of memory.

Most important, this presents a huge integrity problem if the class has data members that are pointers pointing to dynamically allocated heap memory. Let us look at the execution of the function with the value parameter at the crucial moments of function execution—at the beginning of the function call and at the function termination. I like to attach these moments to the opening and closing braces of the function body.

When a copy of the actual argument object is created during the pass by value, the system-supplied copy constructor is called. This constructor copies the data members of the actual argument into the corresponding data members of its local copy, the formal parameter object. When the pointer data member `str` is copied, the pointer in the formal object receives the value stored in the pointer in the actual argument object, that is, the address of heap memory allocated for the actual argument object.

As a result, pointers in both the actual argument and in its local copy point to the same section of the heap memory, and each object thinks that it has the exclusive use of this memory.

I tried to represent this situation in Figure 11–9. Actually, what I told you does not change the workings of the overloaded operator function (so far). This is why I noticed that all that I told you earlier was the truth and only the truth.

Figure 11–9, which shows the whole truth, includes a local object s whose data members are initialized to the values of the actual argument v. Figure 11–9(a) shows that this local object v and the actual argument u share the same section of the heap memory. Figure 11–9(b) shows that after the new heap memory has been allocated and initialized and replaced the existing heap memory in the target object, the local object s and the argument u continue to share the same section of the heap memory.

The whole truth should also include the termination of the function. When the function execution reaches the closing brace of its scope and the function terminates, the local copy object (`String s`) is destroyed. From the point of view of conventional programming intuition, this means that the object memory (the pointer and the integer in this case) disappear. However, there is no such thing in C++ as a destruction of the object. Each object destruction is preceded by a function call: a destructor call.

When the destructor is called, it does what the destructor code says it should do: It returns the segment of memory pointed to by the object pointer.

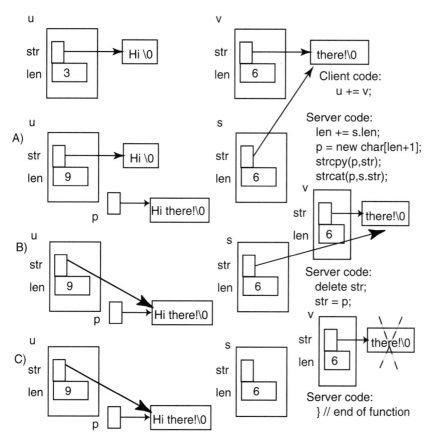

Figure 11-9   The memory diagram for passing the `String` object by value.

```
String::~String()
{ delete [] str; }          // return heap memory pointed to by pointer
```

Figure 11–9(c) shows the state of the local object s and the actual argument v after the destructor call but before the local object is destroyed. It shows that the local object loses its heap memory and so does the actual argument. (The memory pointed to by pointer `str` is deleted.) This action, of course, does not affect the state of the target object because it is not destroyed. When the overloaded operator function terminates, the target object is in exactly the same state as during the previous discussion reflected in Figure 11–8. This client code produces the correct results.

```
String u("Hi "); String v("there!");
u += v;
cout << " u = " << u.show() <<endl;    // it displays "Hi there!"
```

But the memory returned by the destructor when the formal parameter s
is destroyed did not belong to that object. It belonged (and still should
belong) to the actual argument, that is, to object v defined in the client space.
After the function call, the client object that is used as the actual argument for
the pass by value is robbed of its dynamically allocated memory. It is an error
for the client code to use it after the call.

```
String u("Hi "); String v("there!");
cout << " u = " << u.show() << endl;     // it displays "Hi "
cout << " v = " << v.show() << endl;     // it displays "there!"
u += v;
cout << " u = " << u.show() << endl;     // it displays "Hi there!"
cout << " v = " << v.show() << endl;     // displays what it wants
```

It does not look particularly smart to recheck the value of the object v that
was just printed and used as an rvalue in the function call to operator+=().
I am doing this only because I know there is a problem with this implementation. Clearly, the object has to have the same value that it had when it par-
ticipated as an operand in the expression u += v. This is the conventional
programming intuition, and it works in C++ most of the time—but not all the
time, and you should develop an alternative intuition as soon as possible. I am
telling you all that because in this innocent-looking client code, the value of
the text for the object v can be anything, and any use of this object that
assumes it is in the same state as before is reckless.

How do you like this? Sure, C++ programming is not boring. But a C++
programmer must understand what is going on under the hood of a simple
program like the snippet code in the last example.

This is not the end of the story: that takes place at yet another closing scope
brace. Always pay attention to scope braces—they do a lot of work. When the
client code reaches the closing brace of its scope and terminates, the class
destructors are called for all local objects, including that hapless object v,
which was used as the actual argument in the function call and robbed of its
dynamic memory when the call terminated. The destructor tries to deallocate
the area pointed to by the object data member str. This memory, however,
has already returned to the system. If you were designing the language, you
would have made it a "no op." No such luck. In C++, repeated use of the
delete operator on the same pointer is prohibited. It is an error.

Unfortunately, "an error" does not mean that the compiler produces a syntax error for you to correct. The compiler writer is not responsible for tracing
the flow of execution and telling you that you made an error: The code is syntactically correct. It also does not mean that the program compiles, runs, and
produces repeatable incorrect results. It simply means that the results of such

an attempt are "not defined." Actually, they are platform dependent. How the application acts depends on the operating system. The system might crash, the program might run incorrectly (quietly), or it might run correctly until some time in the future.

Listing 11.3 shows the complete program that implements this bad design. The output of the program as it appeared on my machine is shown in Figure 11–10.

Listing 11.3   Overloaded concatenation function with a value parameter.

```
#include <iostream>
using namespace std;

class String {
  char *str;                             // dynamically allocated char array
  int len;
public:
  String (int length=0);                 // conversion/default constructor
  String(const char*);                   // conversion constructor
  ~String ();                            // deallocate dynamic memory
  void operator += (const String);       // concatenate another object
  void modify(const char*);              // change the array contents
  const char* show() const;              // return a pointer to array
  } ;

String::String(int length)
{ len = length;
  str = new char[len+1];
  if (str==NULL) exit(1);
  str[0] = 0; }                          // empty String of zero length is ok

String::String(const char* s)
{ len = strlen(s);                       // measure length of incoming text
  str = new char[len+1];                 // allocate enough heap space
  if (str==NULL) exit(1);                // test for success
  strcpy(str,s); }                       // copy incoming text into heap memory

String::~String()
{ delete str; }                          // return heap memory (not the pointer!)

void String::operator += (const String s)  // pass by value
{ len = strlen(str) + strlen(s.str);     // total length
  char *p = new char[len + 1];           // allocate enough heap memory
  if (p==NULL) exit(1);                  // test for success
  strcpy(p,str);                         // copy the first part of result
  strcat(p,s.str);                       // add the second part of result
  delete str;                            // important step
  str = p; }                             // now p can disappear
```

```
const char* String::show() const          // protect data from changes
{ return str; }

void String::modify(const char a[])       // no memory management here
{ strncpy(str,a,len-1);                   // protect from overflow
  str[len-1] = 0; }                       // terminate String properly

int main()
{ String u("This is a test. ");
  String v("Nothing can go wrong.");
  cout << " u = " << u.show() << endl;     // result is ok
  cout << " v = " << v.show() << endl;     // result is ok
  u += v;   // u.operator+=(v);
  cout << " u = " << u.show() << endl;     // result is ok
  cout << " v = " << v.show() << endl;     // result is not ok
  v.modify("Let us hope for the best.");   // memory corruption
  cout << " v = " << v.show() << endl;     //  ????
  return 0;
  }
```

Notice that all these bad things happen at the function termination. The first bad thing happened when the server-overloaded function `operator+=()` was terminating, and the destructor for the formal parameter was called—the actual argument v was robbed of its heap memory. The second bad thing happened when the client function `main()` was terminating, and the object v was going out of scope—its heap memory was repeatedly deleted.

Actually, in C++, it is the repeated deleting of heap memory that is "an error." Deleting a NULL pointer is not an error. This is "no operation." Some programmers tried to fix this problem by setting the pointer to heap memory in the destructor to NULL.

```
String::~String()
{ delete str;          // return heap memory
  str = 0; }           // set to null to avoid double deletion
```

This is a nice idea, but it does not work as intended. The pointer that is set to zero belongs to the object that will be destroyed in several microseconds. It is the second pointer that is pointing to the same memory that could be set to zero, but it is not available from the destructor executing on another object. Even if it worked, it would only prevent "an error." It would not restore the memory that was incorrectly deleted.

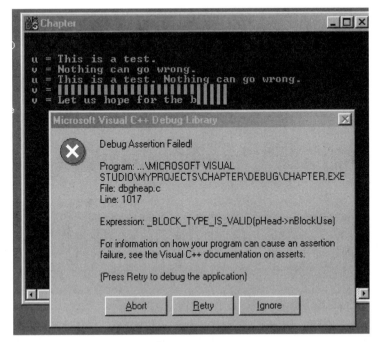

Figure 11–10   Output of the program in Listing 11.3.

How to Get There from Here

Did I scare you? If I did, this was my intent. If I did not, regardless, make sure that you always worry about dynamic memory management in your programs. Even if the programs run on your machine correctly, this is not evidence that the program is correct (add this to the list of your testing principles).

The program might run without a hitch for months and years, and then, after you install some other unrelated application or upgrade to the next version of Windows™, the use of memory changes and your program crashes. Or it produces incorrect results that may not be noticed because it has run correctly for months and even years. What do you do? Curse Microsoft because you just upgraded your operating system? But it is not Microsoft's fault! It is a fault of a C++ programmer who neglected to put one symbol, an ampersand, in the interface of the overloaded operator function operator+=().

This is how this function should look. It does not pass its object parameter by value; it passes it by reference.

```
void String::operator += (const String &s)      // reference parameter
{ len = strlen(str) + strlen(s.str);            // total length
  char *p = new char[len + 1];                  // allocate enough heap memory
  if (p==NULL) exit(1);                          // test for success
  strcpy(p,str);                                // copy the first part of result
  strcat(p,s.str);                              // add the second part of result
  delete str;                                    // important step
  str = p; }                                     // now p can disappear
```

Figure 11–11 shows the output of the program in Listing 11.3 with the concatenation function that passes its parameter by reference.

Make sure that you run this program, experiment with it, and understand the issues that may cause problems. Resist the urge to pass objects by value, unless, of course, you absolutely have to.

It is quite disheartening that adding or removing just one single character in the source code (the ampersand) can change the behavior of the program so dramatically. Notice that both versions of the code are syntactically correct—the compiler does not tell you there is any problem to worry about.

Figure 11-11   Output of the program in Listing 11.3 with the concatenation operator that passes its parameter by reference.

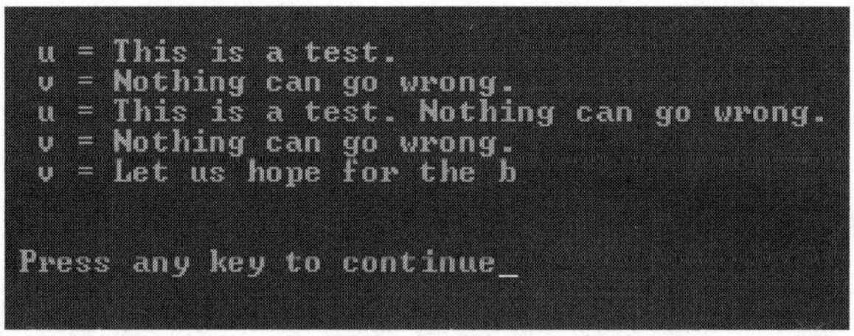

Passing object parameters by value is like driving a tank. You will get where you want to go, but you will cause a lot of indirect damage. As I said earlier, resist passing objects by value; unless, of course, you absolutely *have to*.

Alert

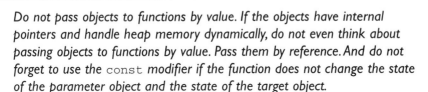

Do not pass objects to functions by value. If the objects have internal pointers and handle heap memory dynamically, do not even think about passing objects to functions by value. Pass them by reference. And do not forget to use the const *modifier if the function does not change the state of the parameter object and the state of the target object.*

More on the Copy Constructor

Let us look back at the situation. The core of the problems discussed in the previous section is copying an object whose data members are pointers to heap memory.

Each object instance is supposed to point to the area of memory that is allocated specifically for it. For example, class String has a pointer that points to the area of heap memory that contains characters associated with the individual String object.

When data members of one object are copied into data members of another object, the corresponding pointers in both objects will have the same contents. Hence, they will point to the same area of heap memory. These objects can die at different moments in time; for example, the formal value parameter of a function in Listing 11.3 disappears when the function terminates, and the actual argument continues to exist in the client space, function `main()`. When one object dies, its destructor deletes the memory pointed to by the object pointer(s), and the second object, still alive, silently loses its heap data. Any use of this object that relies on heap data is incorrect. It is "an error."

If this memory returned to the heap is not immediately reused for other purposes, this "phantom" object might behave as if the deleted memory still exists. Your testing might persuade you that the program is correct.

When the second object dies, its destructor is called. Notice that I am not saying that the destructor "is called again." The destructor was called earlier for a different object (the formal parameter), the one that was already destroyed. Now the destructor is called for the second object (the actual argument), and it tries to delete the same segment of heap memory. In C++, this results in an error. The program's behavior is undefined. This is a polite way of saying that the program can do whatever it wants.

Remedies for the Integrity Problem

There are a number of remedies one can use to avoid trouble when objects with dynamically allocated memory are passed as value parameters.

One remedy is to eliminate the destructor that returns the heap memory to the system. This is neither a good solution nor is it a good permanent solution. You might want to use it as a temporary solution when your program crashes and you need it to run so that you can debug it. Turning off the destructor will let your program run to completion.

Another remedy is to use fixed-size arrays inside objects rather than dynamically allocated memory. This is not an elegant solution, but it might do if the size of the array is allocated generously. This is especially true for programs that handle a relatively small number of objects, and the occasional truncation of data that do not fit into a fixed size is acceptable from the point of view of the integrity of the application.

For parameter passing, the best remedy is passing object parameters by reference rather than by value. It eliminates the problems created by copying objects. It also speeds up program execution by eliminating the need to create and destroy temporary objects and to call constructors and destructors.

Unfortunately, this solution is not universal. There are cases of copying one object into another object that are not related to parameter passing, where this solution cannot be applied. These are cases where one class object is initialized by another object of the same class. Consider the following segment of code, which passes the parameter to `operator+=()` by reference.

```
String u("This is a test. "), v("Nothing can go wrong.");
cout << " u = " << u.show() << endl;          // result is ok
cout << " v = " << v.show() << endl;          // result is ok
u += v;                                       // u.operator+=(v); by reference
cout << " u = " << u.show() << endl;          // result is ok
cout << " v = " << v.show() << endl;          // ok: pass by reference
v.modify("Let us hope for the best.");        // no memory corruption
String t = v;                                 // object initialization
cout << " t = " << t.show() << endl;          // ok: correct result
t.modify("Nothing can go wrong.");            // change both t and v
cout << " t = " << t.show() << endl;          // ok: correct result
cout << " v = " << v.show() << endl;          // v also changed
```

This code creates two `String` objects, u and v, initializes them with a conversion constructor, and concatenates them. Since the object argument v is passed to `operator+=()` by reference, there is no memory corruption, and the object v keeps its heap memory. When I modify object v, it is only object v that changes, not object u. Next, I create yet another `String` object t, which I set to the current state of v. When I modify the contents of object t, I expect the object of type v to remain the same. Figure 11–12 shows the expected results of the execution of this code snippet.

Things in real life, however, are not always as we expect them to be. Listing 11.4 shows the code for class `String` (with the parameter to the overloaded operator function `operator+=()` passed by reference) and the client code that implements the previous snippet of code. I modified the snippet so that object

```
u = This is a test.
v = Nothing can go wrong.
u = This is a test. Nothing can go wrong.
v = Nothing can go wrong.
t = Let us hope for the b
t = Nothing can go wrong.
v = Nothing can go wrong.
```

Figure 11–12   Expected (not real) output of the snippet of client code above.

t is created in a nested scope. When this nested code terminates and object t disappears, I can check the state of object v and verify its integrity. Figure 11–13 shows the real results of the execution of the program in Listing 11.4.

Listing 11.4   Initializing one object with data from another object.

```
#include <iostream>
using namespace std;

class String {
  char *str;                              // dynamically allocated char array
  int len;
public:
  String (int length=0);                  // conversion/default constructor
  String(const char*);                    // conversion constructor
  ~String ();                             // deallocate dynamic memory
  void operator += (const String&);       // concatenate another object
  void modify(const char*);               // change the array contents
  const char* show() const;               // return a pointer to the array
  } ;

String::String(int length)
{ len = length;
  str = new char[len+1];
  if (str==NULL) exit(1);
  str[0] = 0; }                           // empty String of zero length is ok, too

String::String(const char* s)
{ len = strlen(s);                        // measure the length of incoming text
  str = new char[len+1];                  // allocate enough heap space
  if (str==NULL) exit(1);                 // test for success
  strcpy(str,s); }                        // copy incoming text into heap memory

String::~String()
{ delete str; }                           // return heap memory (not the pointer!)

void String::operator += (const String& s) // reference parameter
{ len = strlen(str) + strlen(s.str);      // total length
  char* p = new char[len + 1];            // allocate enough heap memory
  if (p==NULL) exit(1);                   // test for success
  strcpy(p,str);                          // copy the first part of result
  strcat(p,s.str);                        // add the second part of result
  delete str;                             // important step
  str = p; }                              // now temp can disappear

const char* String::show() const          // protect data from changes
{ return str; }

void String::modify(const char a[])        // no memory management here
```

```
{ strncpy(str,a,len-1);              // protect from overflow
  str[len-1] = 0; }                  // terminate String properly

int main()
{ cout << endl << endl;
  String u("This is a test. ");
  String v("Nothing can go wrong.");
  cout << " u = " << u.show() << endl;       // result is ok
  cout << " v = " << v.show() << endl;       // result is ok
  u += v;                                    // u.operator+=(s);
  cout << " u = " << u.show() << endl;       // result is ok
  cout << " v = " << v.show() << endl;       // ok: pass by reference
  v.modify("Let us hope for the best.");     // no memory corruption
  { String t = v;                            // initialization
    cout << " t = " << t.show() << endl;     // ok: correct result
    t.modify("Nothing can go wrong.");       // change both t and v
    cout << " t = " << t.show() << endl;     // ok: correct result
    cout << " v = " << v.show() << endl; }   // v also changed
  cout << " v = " << v.show() << endl;       // t died, v is robbed
  return 0;
  }
```

Figure 11–13   Output of the program in Listing 11.4.

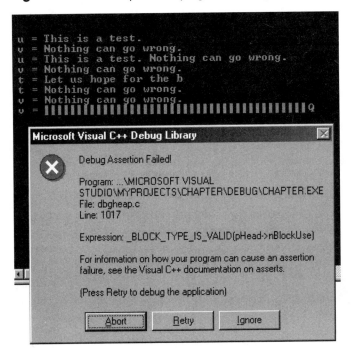

When the `String` object t is created (it is created on the stack because t is a local automatic variable), it is allocated memory enough to contain the character pointer and the integer. Next, the constructor is called. You see the assignment sign in the client code, but this is not an assignment—it is an initialization. As I said earlier, it is not a question whether a constructor is called after the object is created. It is a question of which constructor is called. The answer is that it depends on the data that the client code supplies when the object is created. In Listing 11.4, the client `main()` supplies one actual argument, existing object v. Hence, it is a constructor with one parameter that is an object of the same type to which the constructor belongs, in this case, class `String`.

What is the name of the constructor with one parameter of the class type? As you might recall from Chapter 9, "C++ Class as a Unit of Modularization," it's a copy constructor because it copies data from one object into another object. However, class `String` does not have a copy constructor. Does that mean that an attempt to call this missing copy constructor generates a syntax error? No, the compiler generates a call to the system-provided copy constructor. The compiler provides the constructor, and the compiler generates the call. This constructor copies the fields of the argument object into the fields of the object being created. For class `String`, this system-provided copy constructor looks this way:

```
String::String(const String& s)   // system-provided constructor
{ len = s.len;                     // copy the length of the object text
  str = s.str; }                   // copy the pointer to the object text
```

Figure 11–14 shows how this constructor works. When the `String` object t is created, its field `len` is set to 9, and its field `str` is set to point to the same area of heap memory that the pointer `str` of object v is pointing to.

Similar to the earlier story about parameter passing, the two objects, t and v, have only one segment of heap memory between them, not two. This segment was allocated earlier for object v, but now it is shared by object t. And each object thinks that this heap area belongs to it alone. This situation is even worse than pass by value. In pass by value, the actual argument exists in the client scope, and the formal parameter exists in the server scope. At each moment of execution, only one object is available. Here, both objects exist in the same client scope, and they both can be modified and accessed in the same scope.

Since these two objects share the same area of heap memory, they are synonyms from the point of view of client code. This is why when object t is modified by client code, object v is modified, too. Is this clear from Figure 11–14? Do you see this on the program output in Figure 11–13? From the point of

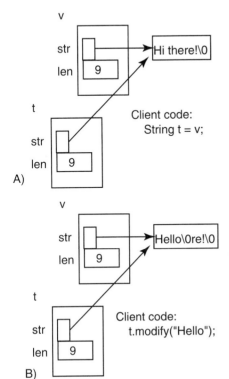

A)

Client code:
String t = v;

B)

Client code:
t.modify("Hello");

Figure 11-14
The memory diagram for initializing one
String object with data from another object.

view of common programming intuition, there is no reason why object v should change in the client code. But it does change.

Come to think of it, this is strange only from the point of view of common programming intuition. In introductory programming classes, I often meet students who have trouble with simple code dealing with integers.

```
int v = 10; int t = v; t = 20;          // what is v now?
```

For most programmers, it is obvious that v doesn't change after t has changed because t and v occupy different locations in memory. But others say, "All right, we made a commitment that these two variables, v and t, be the same. Now you are changing t. Small wonder that v also changes."

In a sense, they have a point. If the variables are synonyms, changing to one is visible through another. As you may recall, this is quite common if one variable is a regular variable, and another variable is a reference.

```
int v = 10; int& t = v; t = 20;         // what is v now?
```

In this example, common programming intuition does not work. It is the novice's logic that applies. We make a commitment for these two variables, v and t, to be the same. Small wonder that v changes after a change in t. Now v is 20. This is the logic that all C++ programmers, novices and experts alike, should become comfortable with.

Copy Semantics and Value Semantics

Actually, there are two kinds of common programming intuition that correspond to two different computer science concepts, *value semantics* and *reference semantics*. (Semantics here means the meaning of copying data.)

The more common programming intuition uses value semantics. Each computational object (e.g., a variable of a built-in type or an object of programmer-defined type) has its own separate area in memory. Equating two computational objects means repeating the bit pattern in another object's memory. In C++ (as in most other programming languages), value semantics is used for both built-in variables and objects of programmer-defined classes.

```
int v = 10; int t = v; t = 20;     // value semantics, v is 10
```

This is why this intuition is more common: From its point of view, when two objects have the same value, they have two separate bit patterns, and changing the value of one object should not affect the bit pattern already existing in the other object.

Another, less common programming intuition, uses reference semantics. When a computational object is assigned a value, it receives a reference (or a pointer) to that value. Equating computational objects means setting their references (or pointers) to point to the same location in memory. When the character array pointed to in one object changes, the second object sees the change because both pointers point to the same location. In C++, the reference semantics is used for pointers and references, in passing parameters by reference or by pointer, for arrays, and for linked data structures with pointers.

```
int v = 10; int& t = v; t = 20;    // reference semantics, v is 20
```

Small wonder that reference semantics is less common. It is used mostly for performance reasons (e.g., it eliminates copying of objects in parameter passing). Sometimes, it comes without an invitation, as in this example, and you should be ready to recognize it and to deal with it appropriately. A C++ programmer should always think about the difference between value and reference semantics.

This is not the end of trouble with the program in Listing 11.4. When the execution reaches the closing brace of the nested scope (my favorite topic of discussion during analysis of code behavior), the object t is going to disappear because it is defined in this nested scope. The object v is defined in the enclosing scope of the function main(), and it should be available for further use. In Listing 11.4, I am trying to print the value of v at the end of main(). Notice that this statement is separated from the preceding printing statement only by the closing brace of the nested scope. On the surface, no event is taking place between these two statements in the client code, and hence these two printing statements should produce the same output—but they do not. Again, traditional programming intuition is not sufficient for understanding a C++ program, and you have to develop your own intuition to help you read code segments like this.

As you see in Figure 11–14, the first statement produces a legible output. It is not what you would normally expect, but at least it is there. The second statement produces garbage. What happened between these two statements? When the closing brace of the nested scope was reached, the String destructor was called for the local object t in the nested scope. As you see from Listing 11.4 and from Figure 11–14, this destructor deleted the heap memory pointed to by the pointer str of object t. This dynamic memory actually belongs to object v, but the system does not remember that. It only remembers that the memory pointed to by pointer str should be deleted in accordance with the code of the String destructor. The object v is robbed of its dynamic memory, but nobody knows about it. The object is formally in scope and appears to be in good health. But it is only appearance: It cannot be utilized for anything useful by the client code.

This is similar to parameter passing by value, and like passing objects by value, this is not the end of the story. When the execution reaches the closing brace, the object v should disappear according to the scope rules. Before that, the destructor is called and it tries to delete the heap memory that was already deleted. The program is incorrect. It does what it wants (the program crashes).

Programmer-Defined Copy Constructor

Short of giving up dynamic memory management, this problem has only one solution—a programmer-defined copy constructor. The constructor should allocate heap space for the target object similar to the concatenation operator that was discussed in the previous section. Here is its algorithm:

1. Copy the length of the parameter's character arrays into the target's `len`.
2. Allocate heap memory; set target's pointer `str` to point to it.
3. Test for success of memory allocation; give up if the system is out of memory.
4. Copy characters from the target object into the newly allocated space.

Here is a programmer-defined copy constructor that is a solution to the problem.

```
String::String(const String& s)     // programmer-defined copy constructor
{ len = s.len;                       // length of the source text
  str = new char[len+1];             // request separate heap memory
  if (str == NULL) exit(1);          // test for success
  strcpy(str,s.str); }               // copy the source text
```

Notice that the parameter s is passed by reference. It is a reference to the actual argument object. No copy of argument data members is made in parameter passing. Instead, dynamic memory is allocated for the target object inside the constructor. Dynamic memory of the actual argument object is copied into the target's heap memory.

This is less efficient than memberwise copying in Listing 11.4. Value semantics is slower than reference semantics because it operates on values, not on references or pointers. However, value semantics is safe. Recall the client code that caused all the problems.

```
String t = v;       // no problem if copy constructor is used
```

After this code executes, the pointers `str` in two objects, t and v, are pointing to different areas in the heap memory. The integrity problem is resolved.

Note

If there are pointers among class data members, and the objects of this class handle heap memory dynamically, the class designer should decide whether the class needs value semantics or reference semantics. If you need value semantics and you initialize one object with the value of another object, make sure that the class has a programmer-defined copy constructor.

Listing 11.5 shows the program from Listing 11.4, where class String defines its own constructor that supports the value semantics for object initialization. The output of the program is shown in Figure 11–15. As you can see, the integrity problem disappears. The String objects t and v are not synonyms anymore. When object t is changed, object v remains the same. When the nested scope terminates and object t disappears, object v is alive and well and can be used by the client code without any difficulty. Trace the code and its output to make sure that you see the connection between the two.

Listing 11.5   Use of copy constructor to initialize one object with data from another.

```
#include <iostream>
using namespace std;

class String {
    char *str;                          // dynamically allocated char array
    int len;
    char* allocate(const char* s)       // private function
    { char *p = new char[len+1];        // allocate heap memory for object
      if (p==NULL) exit(1);             // test for success, quit if no luck
      strcpy(p,s);                      // copy text into heap memory
      return p; }                       // return pointer to heap memory
public:
    String (int length=0);              // conversion/default constructor
    String(const char*);                // conversion constructor
    String(const String& s);            // copy constructor
    ~String ();                         // deallocate dynamic memory
    void operator += (const String&);   // concatenate another object
    void modify(const char*);           // change the array contents
    const char* show() const;           // return a pointer to the array
    } ;

String::String(int length)
{ len = length;
  str = allocate(""); }                 // copy empty String into heap memory

String::String(const char* s)
{ len = strlen(s);                      // measure the length of incoming text
  str = allocate(s); }                  // allocate space, copy incoming text

String::String(const String& s)        // copy constructor
{ len = s.len;                          // measure length of the source text
  str = allocate(s.str); }              // allocate space, copy incoming text

String::~String()
{ delete str; }                         // return heap memory (not the pointer!)
```

```
void String::operator += (const String& s)      // reference parameter
{ len = strlen(str) + strlen(s.str);             // total length
  char* p = new char[len + 1];                   // allocate enough heap memory
  if (p==NULL) exit(1);                           // test for success
  strcpy(p,str);                                  // copy the first part of result
  strcat(p,s.str);                                // add the second part of result
  delete str;                                     // important step
  str = p; }                                      // now pointer p can disappear

const char* String::show() const                 // protect data from changes
{ return str; }

void String::modify(const char a[])              // no memory management here
{ strncpy(str,a,len-1);                           // protect from overflow
  str[len-1] = 0; }                               // terminate String properly

int main()
{ cout << endl << endl;
  String u("This is a test. ");
  String v("Nothing can go wrong.");
  cout << " u = " << u.show() << endl;           // result is ok
  cout << " v = " << v.show() << endl;           // result is ok
  u += v;                                         // u.operator+=(v);
  cout << " u = " << u.show() << endl;           // result is ok
  cout << " v = " << v.show() << endl;           // ok: pass by reference
  v.modify("Let us hope for the best.");         // no memory corruption
  { String t = v;                                 // call copy constructor
    cout << " t = " << t.show() << endl;         // ok: correct result
    t.modify("Nothing can go wrong.");           // change only t
    cout << " t = " << t.show() << endl;         // ok: correct result
    cout << " v = " << v.show() << endl; }       // v did not changed
  cout << " v = " << v.show() << endl;           // t died, v is intact
  return 0;
  }
```

Figure 11-15   Output of the program in Listing 11.5.

```
u = This is a test.
v = Nothing can go wrong.
u = This is a test. Nothing can go wrong.
v = Nothing can go wrong.
t = Let us hope for the b
t = Nothing can go wrong.
v = Let us hope for the b
v = Let us hope for the b
```

In Listing 11.5, class `String` has three constructors that do approximately the same thing: They allocate heap memory and initialize its contents. In the first conversion constructor, the initializing data is an empty string (the terminating zero). In the second conversion constructor, the initializing data is the character array supplied by the client code as the actual argument. In the copy constructor, the initializing data is a character array inside the object supplied by the client code. Since this character array is allocated on the heap, it does not have a name and is referred to through the pointer `str` pointing to this array. Since the parameter object s belongs to the same class `String` as the target object being initialized, the copy constructor has the right to access this private pointer `str` using its qualified name `s.str`.

It is only natural that different constructors use similar algorithms, because the resulting object should look much the same regardless of what constructor was called when the object is constructed. When the class has one or two constructors, it makes sense just to repeat the code verbatim. When the number of uses of this common algorithm grows (and rest assured, we have not finished yet), programmers often encapsulate it in a private function and call it from different member functions. The function should be private, because the client code is not interested in handling object memory; it is a low-level detail that should not confuse the client code algorithm and the client programmer. You can see this private function in Listing 11.5. When it copies its parameter in the heap memory it allocated, it uses the name of the pointer p that points to the heap memory because this array does not have a name.

```
char* allocate(const char* s)   // private function
{ char *p = new char[len+1];    // allocate heap memory for object
  if (p==NULL) exit(1);         // test for success, quit if no luck
  strcpy(p,s);                  // copy text into heap memory
  return p; }                   // return pointer to heap memory
```

Listing 11.5 shows that the first conversion constructor passes an empty string to function `allocate()`, the second conversion constructor passes to it its own parameter, character array; and the copy constructor passes to `allocate()` its parameter's character array `s.str`.

When one object initializes another object, a copy constructor is called. This is unavoidable. The issue is which copy constructor is called. If the class does not provide its customized copy constructor, the compiler will generate a call to the system-provided copy constructor that copies the data members of the object. If the objects of this class do not allocate heap memory, this is fine. If objects use individual segments of heap memory (value semantics), the use of the system-provided copy constructor undermines the integrity of the application. To preserve the program integrity, the class should implement its own copy constructor that will provide the target object with its own heap memory.

In the previous sentence, "the class should implement" stresses the client-server relationship between different segments of C++ code and between different areas of human concern. The client code expresses its needs by handling objects to achieve the goal of the application (e.g., initializing one object from another). The server code supports the needs of the client code by implementing member functions that the client code calls. Constructors are called implicitly, but that does not change the client-server relationship.

When the application needs copy semantics, classes with dynamic memory management might be forced to provide copy constructors for other contexts in which one object initializes another object. One such context is passing object parameters by value. With the appropriate copy constructor in place, my first version of the overloaded concatenation `operator+=()` from Listing 11.3 is perfectly fine.

```
void String::operator += (const String s)     // pass by value
{ len = strlen(str) + strlen(s.str);           // total length
  char *p = new char[len + 1];                  // allocate enough heap memory
  if (p==NULL) exit(1);                          // test for success
  strcpy(p,str);                                 // copy the first part of result
  strcat(p,s.str);                               // add the second part of result
  delete str;                                    // important step
  str = p; }                                     // now p can disappear
```

When this function is called and a copy of the actual argument is created, the programmer-defined copy constructor is called. It allocates heap memory for the formal parameter s. When this function terminates and the destructor is called for the formal parameter, its own heap memory is deleted, not the heap memory that belongs to the actual argument. The integrity problem disappears. The performance problem does not. When the parameter is passed by value, the call to the concatenation operator involves creation of the object, a call to the copy constructors, allocation of heap memory, copying characters from one object to another, a call to the destructor, and deallocation of heap memory. Call by reference does not require any of these. Reference semantics eliminates the performance overhead on unnecessary copying.

Alert

> *Do not pass objects to functions by value. If the objects have internal pointers and handle heap memory dynamically, do not pass these objects by value. But if you must pass these objects by value, define the copy constructor that eliminates the integrity problem. Make sure that copying does not impair program performance.*

Return by Value

Another context that requires value semantics is the returning of an object from a function by value. I already discussed this issue in Chapter 10 for classes that do not handle dynamic memory. Because the story for returning an object from a function is exactly the same as the story for initializing the object from another object, I will be brief.

Listing 11.6 shows another version of class String. I placed debugging statements in each constructor and added an overloaded comparison operator that was implemented as a member function. Also, I added a client function enterData() and cleaned up the main() function. The program requests the user to enter the name of the city and searches for the name in the database. For simplicity, I hard-coded the database in the main() function as an array of character arrays and used a simple sequential search to find a user's input in the database. The results of the execution are shown in Figure 11–16.

Listing 11.6   Use of copy constructor to return an object from a function.

```
#include <iostream>
using namespace std;

class String {
  char *str;                          // dynamically allocated char array
  int len;
  char* allocate(const char* s)       // private function
  { char *p = new char[len+1];        // allocate heap memory for object
    if (p==NULL) exit(1);             // test for success, quit if no luck
    strcpy(p,s);                      // copy text into heap memory
    return p; }                       // return pointer to heap memory
public:
  String (int length=0);              // conversion/default constructor
  String(const char*);                // conversion constructor
  String(const String& s);            // copy constructor
```

```
  ~String ();                                 // deallocate dynamic memory
  void operator += (const String&);           // concatenate another object
  void modify(const char*);                   // change the array contents
  bool operator == (const String&) const;     // compare contents
  const char* show() const;                   // return a pointer to the array
  } ;

String::String(int length)
{ len = length;
  str = allocate("");                         // copy empty String into heap memory
  cout << " Originate: '" << str <<"'\n"; }

String::String(const char* s)
{ len = strlen(s);                            // measure length of incoming text
  str = allocate(s);                          // allocate space, copy text
  cout << " Created: '" << str <<"'\n"; }

String::String(const String& s)               // copy constructor
{ len = s.len;                                // measure length of the source text
  str = allocate(s.str);                      // allocate space, copy text
  cout << " Copied:  '" << str <<"'\n"; }

String::~String()
{ delete str; }                               // return heap memory (not the pointer!)

void String::operator += (const String& s)    // reference parameter
{ len = strlen(str) + strlen(s.str);          // total length
  char* p = new char[len + 1];                // allocate enough heap memory
  if (p==NULL) exit(1);                       // test for success
  strcpy(p,str);                              // copy the first part of result
  strcat(p,s.str);                            // add the second part of result
  delete str;                                 // important step
  str = p; }                                  // now pointer p can disappear

bool String::operator==(const String& s) const      // compare contents
{ return strcmp(str,s.str)==0; }              // strcmp returns 0 if the same

const char* String::show() const              // protect data from changes
{ return str; }

void String::modify(const char a[])           // no memory management here
{ strncpy(str,a,len-1);                       // protect from overflow
  str[len-1] = 0; }                           // terminate String properly

String enterData()
{ cout << " Enter city to find: ";            // prompt the user
  char data[200];                             // crude solution
  cin >> data;                                // accept user input
  return String(data); }                      // call the constructor
```

```
int main()
{ enum { MAX = 4} ;
  String data[4];                        // database of objects
  char *c[4] = { "Atlanta", "Boston", "Chicago", "Denver" };
  for (int j=0; j<MAX; j++)
  { data[j] += c[j]; }                   // data[j].operator+=(c[j]);
  String u = enterData();                // crashes without copy con-
structor
  int i;
  for (i=0; i < MAX; i++)                // i is defined outside of
the loop
    { if (data[i] == u) break; }         // break if String found
  if (i == MAX)                          // how did we get here?
    cout << " City " << u.show() << " is not found\n";
  else
    cout << " City " << u.show() << " is found\n";
  return 0;
  }
```

When the array of objects is created in main(), the default String constructor (e.g., the first conversion constructor with the default value) is called for each component of the array. The constructor allocates an empty string of length zero and prints the message Originate. When the operator+=() is called to append the names of the cities to the contents of each object, the character array is passed to the comparison operator as a parameter. The overloaded operator expects a String parameter, so the second conversion constructor is called and prints the message Created for each array component.

After that, the function enterData() is called. It prompts the user, accepts the name of the city, and passes it as an argument to the String conversion constructor—you see the message Created printed by the constructor. Because the object u in main() is only created when enterData() is called, the constructor call in enterData() is used as a constructor call for object u in main(). The copy constructor is not called. Even though the

Figure 11-16   Output of the program in Listing 11.6.

String objects handle memory dynamically, the integrity of the program is preserved. The copy constructor here has nothing to do with implementing the value semantics; the conversion constructor does the job of giving the object u in main() its separate heap memory. Just like the Russian joke in Chapter 9: the crocodile plays piano, and the crocodile sings. The monkey has nothing to do with it.

To make you more comfortable with handling objects that manage memory dynamically, let us make a little change in enterData()—not much, just adding an extra local object to keep user data.

```
String enterData()
{ cout << " Enter city to find: ";           // prompt the user
   char data[200];                           // crude solution
   cin >> data;                              // accept user input
   String x = data;                          // conversion constructor
   return x; }                               // copy constructor
```

The change is small. If x were a variable of a built-in type, it would amount to nothing. For objects with dynamic memory management, this is a totally different story. The conversion constructor is called when the local object x is created. However, when the function terminates, the object u in function main() is initialized with the copy constructor. If the programmer-defined copy constructor is not implemented, the system-supplied copy constructor is used. It copies the data members of object x into data members of object u and does not allocate heap memory. The pointers str in objects u and x point to the same area of heap memory. When enterData() terminates and the object x disappears, the String destructor is called, which deletes heap memory pointed to by pointer str in object x. This means that object u is born defective—its dynamic memory was deleted when it was born.

What are the consequences? The same as before—my machine crashes, your machine might continue execution, but it is all in vain. The program is incorrect. It needs the programmer-defined copy constructor.

When the programmer-defined copy constructor is supplied, everything is fine. The sample results of the program execution are shown in Figure 11–17

The debugging output shows that after the user enters the input line, the conversion constructor is called for the local object x in enterData(), and then the copy constructor is called for the local object u in main(). The crocodile plays piano, and the monkey sings. This version is a bit slower than the previous one. But this is not important. What is important is that this version behaves differently than the previous one. What is even more important is that if x and u were variables of built-in type, this change would not affect the behavior of the program. And it is the experience with built-in types that

```
Originate:   ''
Originate:   ''
Originate:   ''
Originate:   ''
Created:   'Atlanta'
Created:   'Boston'
Created:   'Chicago'
Created:   'Denver'
Enter city to find: Moscow
Created:   'Moscow'
Copied:    'Moscow'
City Moscow is not found
```

Figure 11-17   Output of the program in Listing 11.6 with modified `enterData()` and the copy constructor.

forms our programming intuition. After all the effort, built-in and program-mer-defined types are treated differently by C++. Working with objects requires changes to the programming intuition. This is why I took the trou-ble to recount this sequence of events: I wanted to help you to develop this new intuition. Make sure you are comfortable connecting the structure of the client code with the class functions that are called implicitly.

Limits for Copy Constructor Effectiveness

We are almost there. I would like to make yet another little change to the pro-gram, this time to the client code. Instead of defining the object u in main() and initializing it immediately, I will define this object (using the default con-structor) and then assign it to what the user entered during the call to func-tion enterData().

```
int main()
{ enum { MAX = 4} ;
  // setting up the database of city names
  // String u = enterData();      // crashes without copy constructor
  String u;                       // default constructor
  u = enterData();                // It crashes! Copy constructor does not help
  // search for the city, printing the results
  return 0; }
```

After I made this change, my system crashed. I will spare you from view-ing yet another dialog box with useless information about the cause of the problem. After all, this is an example of the execution on a particular machine under a particular operating system. The important point is that the program is incorrect. Even though it compiles correctly, its behavior is undefined, and it should not be run. Since the compiler does not tell you that the program is incorrect, it is your programming intuition that should help you to understand what is going on under the hood of the program.

Overloading the Assignment Operator

On several occasions, I told you that the object initialization and object assignment are different things in C++. When you are dealing with built-in data types, this distinction is often academic. Consider, for example, the following segment of the client code.

```
int v = 5; int u = v;           // variable u is initialized
```

Compare this with the following segment of code.

```
int v = 5; int u; u = v;        // variable u is assigned
```

In the first example, variable u is initialized at definition. In the second example, variable u is assigned after definition. For built-in variables, the end result is the same. When these computational objects are objects of programmer-defined types that handle their own memory, the difference is important.

```
String v = "Hello"; String u = v;     // object u is initialized
String v = "Hello"; String u; u = v;  // object u is assigned
```

The first line of code gets you in hot water if the class lacks the copy constructor. The second line of code gets you in trouble if the class lacks the overloaded assignment operator. The copy constructor is not called for the second line.

Problems with System-Supplied Assignment Operator

If the class has the overloaded assignment operator, it is called for the second line of this client code example. If class does not supply the assignment operator, the compiler supplies its own assignment operator. This operator is very similar to the copy constructor: it copies the data fields of the object on the right-hand side of the assignment into the data members on the left-hand side of the assignment operator.

Similar to a system-provided copy constructor, this system-provided assignment operator is always available. For classes that do not do dynamic memory management (e.g., class `Complex`, `Rational`, `Rectangle`), this system-provided assignment operator is adequate. For classes that manage their memory dynamically, the system-provided assignment operator causes problems.

When the assignment is executed over `String` objects, the data members are copied memberwise. The `str` pointer of the object on the left-hand side of the assignment points to the same place in the heap memory as the `str` pointer of the object on the right-hand side of the assignment. The objects become synonyms. If you modify one object, for example, `u`, the change is seen in another object, in this case, `v`.

When one object is destroyed by scope rules or by the `delete` operator, for example, `u`, the destructor is called for that object, and the memory pointed to by the object pointer `str` is deleted. As a result, another object, in this case, `v`, is robbed of its heap memory even though it appears totally healthy in the program. Any use of this object becomes incorrect. When that object is also destroyed, the destructor is called for that object and tries to delete the heap memory pointed to by pointer `str`. But this memory is already deleted! As I explained earlier, the attempt to delete the heap memory that already has been deleted results in unpredictable behavior of the program. It is incorrect semantically, even though it is correct syntactically.

Tracing the cause of the problem is difficult because it is not immediately related to the results of program execution. And the copy constructor cannot remedy this problem because no constructor is invoked when the assignment statement is executed. In C++, assignment and initialization are not the same.

Overloaded Assignment: The First Version (Memory Leak)

The solution to this trouble is to overload the assignment operator for the class. The overloaded assignment operator has to make sure that the left-hand side and the right-hand side objects do not wind up pointing to the same area in heap memory.

The built-in C++ assignment operator is a binary operator with two operands, the left-hand side operand and the right-hand side operand. The same is true for the overloaded programmer-supplied assignment operator. Hence, the interface of the assignment operator is similar to the interface of the copy constructor: the left-hand side object is the target of the message, the right-hand side object is the parameter.

```
u = v;                    // u.operator=(v);
```

This means that the overloaded assignment operator you need for the class `String` should have the following interface.

```
void String::operator = (const String& s);    // assignment operator
```

The assignment operator should copy nonpointer data members from the parameter object into the target object, allocate enough space and copy the contents of the parameter's heap memory into the target's heap memory. These actions are similar to the actions of the copy constructor.

1. Copy the length of the parameter's character arrays into target's `len`.

2. Allocate heap memory; set target's pointer `str` to point to it.

3. Test for success of memory allocation; give up if the system is out of memory.

4. Copy characters from the parameter object into the newly allocated space.

Note

If you need to assign one object to another object, and the objects manage heap memory dynamically, make sure that the class has an overloaded assignment operator. The copy constructor is not enough.

Here is the version of the assignment operator that implements this algorithm. Although it is slower than the system-provided assignment operator, it preserves value semantics and makes the two objects independent of each other.

```
void String::operator = (const String& s)
{ len = s.len;                          // copy non-pointer data
    str = new char[len + 1];            // allocate own heap space
    if (str == NULL) exit(1);           // test for success
    strcpy(str,s.str); }                // copy heap data
```

It is a nice assignment operator, but it treats the target object exactly as the copy constructor does, as if the object were just freshly minted and did not have any previous history. This is indeed the case with the copy constructor, but this is not the case with the assignment operator. The target object u has been created earlier. This means that a constructor was called when that object was created, and during the constructor call the pointer `str` was set to point to a location in heap memory. The assignment operator disregards this heap memory. It sets the `str` pointer to point to another location in heap memory, and the memory allocated earlier to this object is lost. This assignment operator causes memory leak, the second danger to a C++ program in addition to deleting the same memory twice.

What is the remedy? Unlike the copy constructor, the assignment operator has to free the resources (memory) that the target of the assignment was using prior to the operation. It is not difficult to fix it; you just have to know that you have to fix it. This is a better version of the overloaded assignment operator:

```
void String::operator = (const String& s)
{ delete str;                    // you do not do it in the copy constructor
  len = s.len;                   // copy non-pointer data
  str = new char[len + 1];       // allocate own heap space
  if (str == NULL) exit(1);      // test for success
  strcpy(str,s.str); }           // copy heap data
```

Overloaded Assignment: The Next Version (Self-Assignment)

This assignment operator is adequate. It will serve you well in most cases. It has a problem you are not likely to encounter often: It does not support client code for assignments like this:

```
u = u; // u.operator = (u); you do not do that often, do you?
```

This is useless, but it is legal C++ for variables of built-in types. There is no good reason why it should not be legal for variables of programmer-defined types. Actually, it is legal, and the compiler does not flag this statement as a syntax error. It is just that the first statement of the `operator=()` function deletes the heap memory of the argument object. When the `strcpy()` library function executes, it copies the characters from the newly allocated string into itself. The result of copying between overlapping regions of memory is undefined (yet another headache), but even if it were defined, the contents of the object's heap memory are lost forever.

However strange, the self-assignment is not that uncommon. It often arises in sorting algorithms and in pointer manipulations. To prevent the return of the object heap memory, the operator can test whether the parameter reference points to the same address where the target object is located. The `this` pointer is a good way to access the location of the target object.

```
void String::operator = (const String& s)
{ if (&s == this) return;        // avoid memory loss on self-assignment
  delete str;                    // you do not do it in the copy constructor
  len = s.len;                   // copy non-pointer data
  str = new char[len + 1];       // allocate own heap space
  if (str == NULL) exit(1);      // test for success
  strcpy(str,s.str); }           // copy heap data
```

Of course, this test could be done in the client code before the call to the assignment operator, but this would result in pulling responsibilities up to the client code rather than pushing them down to the server code.

Another solution is to test whether the pointers str in the target object and in the parameter object point to the same area of heap memory. The test in the operator would look this way:

```
if (str == s.str) return;           // same heap memory?
```

The two remedies are equivalent, but for some reason the first one is used more often. The reason might be that the pointer this has some additional aesthetic value for C++ programmers.

Overloaded Assignment: Another Version (Chain Expression)

This overloaded assignment operator works well and should be used for all classes that handle their memory dynamically and need to support assignment. This assignment, however, does not support chain expressions that use the return value of the assignments in expressions.

```
t = u = v;          // returning void type does not support this
```

It is not clear how vital the support for chain assignment is. After all, you can always write client code using a sequence of assignments as binary operators.

```
u = v;              // binary operator: u.operator=(v);
t = u;              // binary operator: t.operator=(u);
```

But the issue here again is one of treating the built-in types and programmer-defined types equally. For variables of built-in types, the chain assignment is valid C++ code. Hence, it should be valid C++ code for variables of programmer-defined types.

The assignment operator is right associative, and the meaning of the assignment chain is as follows.

```
t = (u = v);        // t.operator = (u.operator = (v));
```

This means that the assignment operator must return a value that is suitable for being used as an actual argument for another assignment operator (or another message). This means that it should return the value of the type to which the assignment operator belongs.

```
String String::operator = (const String& s)      // return an object
{ if (&s == this) return *this;        // protection against self-assignment
  delete str;                          // you do not do it in the copy constructor
  len = s.len;                         // copy non-pointer data
  str = new char[len + 1];             // allocate own heap space
  if (str == NULL) exit(1);            // test for success
  strcpy(str,s.str);                   // copy heap data
  return *this; }
```

Listing 11.7 shows a modified program from Listing 11.6. I added the overloaded assignment operator. It calls the private function `allocate()` to request heap space and to check for success of memory allocation. To cut down the volume of debugging output, I cut out the `Originate` message from the default constructor. Instead, I added the message `Assigned` to be displayed each time the assignment operator is invoked. Also, I eliminated the call to the concatenation operator `operator+=()` in the client loop that loads the database of names and replaced it with the call to the assignment operator. The output for this program is shown in Figure 11–18.

Listing 11.7   Class `String` with the overloaded assignment operator.

```
#include <iostream>
using namespace std;

class String {
  char *str;                           // dynamically allocated char array
  int len;
  char* allocate(const char* s)        // private function
  { char *p = new char[len+1];         // allocate heap memory for object
    if (p==NULL) exit(1);              // test for success, quit if no luck
    strcpy(p,s);                       // copy text into heap memory
      return p; }                      // return pointer to heap memory
public:
  String (int length=0);               // conversion/default constructor
  String(const char*);                 // conversion constructor
  String(const String& s);             // copy constructor
  ~String ();                          // deallocate dynamic memory
```

```
void operator += (const String&);          // concatenate another object
String operator = (const String&);         // assignment operator
void modify(const char*);                  // change the array contents
bool operator == (const String&) const;    // compare contents
const char* show() const;                  // return a pointer to array
} ;

String::String(int length)
{ len = length;
  str = allocate(""); }                     // copy empty String into heap memory

String::String(const char* s)
{ len = strlen(s);                          // measure the length of incoming text
  str = allocate(s);                        // allocate space, copy incoming text
  cout << " Created: '" << str <<"'\n"; }

String::String(const String& s)             // copy constructor
{ len = s.len;                              // measure length of the source text
  str = allocate(s.str);                    // allocate space, copy incoming text
  cout << " Copied:  '" << str <<"'\n"; }

String::~String()
{ delete str; }                             // return heap memory (not the pointer!)

void String::operator += (const String& s)  // reference parameter
{ len = strlen(str) + strlen(s.str);        // total length
  char* p = new char[len + 1];              // allocate enough heap memory
  if (p==NULL) exit(1);                     // test for success
  strcpy(p,str);                            // copy the first part of result
  strcat(p,s.str);                          // add the second part of result
  delete str;                               // important step
  str = p; }                                // now p can disappear

String String::operator = (const String& s)
{ if (&s == this) return *this;             // test for self-assignment
  delete str;                               // you do not do it in copy constructor
  len = s.len;                              // copy non-pointer data
  str = allocate(s.str);                    // allocate space, copy incoming text
  cout << " Assigned: '" << str <<"'\n";    // for debugging only
  return *this; }                           // return the target object to client

bool String::operator==(const String& s) const     // compare contents
{ return strcmp(str,s.str)==0; }            // strcmp returns 0 if the same

const char* String::show() const            // protect data from changes
{ return str; }

void String::modify(const char a[])          // no memory management here
{ strncpy(str,a,len-1);                      // protect from overflow
  str[len-1] = 0; }                          // terminate String properly
```

```
String enterData()
{ cout << " Enter city to find: ";          // prompt the user
  char data[200];                            // crude solution
  cin >> data;                               // accept user input
  return String(data); }                     // conversion constructor

int main()
{ cout << endl << endl;
  enum { MAX = 4 } ;
  String data[4];                            // database of objects
  char *c[4] = { "Atlanta", "Boston", "Chicago", "Denver" };
  for (int j=0; j<MAX; j++)
  { data[j] = c[j]; }                        // assignment:
data[j].operator=(c[j]);
  String u; int i;
  u = enterData();                           // it needs assignment,
                                                no copy constructor

  for (i=0; i<MAX; i++)
  { if (data[i] == u) break; }               // if
(data[i].operator==(u))
  if (i == MAX)
    cout << " City " << u.show() << " is not found\n";
  else
    cout << " City " << u.show() << " is found\n";
  return 0;
  }
```

You see that the integrity problem went away. You can deal with String objects in exactly the same way you deal with objects of built-in numeric types. You can create them without initialization, you can initialize them from

Figure 11-18 Output of the program in Listing 11.7.

```
Created:  'Atlanta'
Assigned: 'Atlanta'
Copied:   'Atlanta'
Created:  'Boston'
Assigned: 'Boston'
Copied:   'Boston'
Created:  'Chicago'
Assigned: 'Chicago'
Copied:   'Chicago'
Created:  'Denver'
Assigned: 'Denver'
Copied:   'Denver'
Enter city to find: Denver
Created:  'Denver'
Assigned: 'Denver'
Copied:   'Denver'
City Denver is found
```

a character array, and you can initialize them from another, previously created, `String` object. You can assign one `String` object to another `String` object as if they were numbers. Notice that C++ does not allow you to do that for arrays: C++ arrays implement reference semantics, not value semantics.

You can add to the class as many arithmetic operators as you see fit (adding `String` objects to each other, subtracting, multiplying, etc.). However, keep in mind the maintenance programmer: You should not make the task of understanding your code more difficult than it has to be.

The C++ facility for overloading operators represents a significant contribution to the aesthetics of computer programming.

Performance Considerations

But this flexibility comes at a price. If you want to initialize one object from another object (at definition, passing parameters by value, or returning a value from the function), you ought to provide a copy constructor. If you want to assign one object to another object, you ought to provide an overloaded assignment operator.

The integrity problems that can arise from dynamic memory management loom so dangerous that many programmers implement the copy constructor and the assignment operator for each class that manages memory dynamically. Often, they do that even for classes that do not manage memory dynamically. After all, these functions do not require much effort to implement—let them be there, just in case.

I think that this is problem avoidance. Instead of adding numerous useless functions to the program, the developers need to study the requirements of the client code and understand the consequences of different design decisions.

There are several problems with supplying a class with more member functions than the class needs. One is bloated design. It is not a minor consequence. When the maintainer (or client programmer) browses through useless functions, attention is taken away from other, important details.

Another problem is performance. As you see from Figure 11–18, the performance problem might become quite real. For each assignment of an input string in the loop, there are two function calls plus the call to the assignment operator:

1. a call to the conversion constructor for the `operator=()` parameter

2. a call to the `operator=()` function itself

3. a call to the copy constructor for the return by value from the assignment operator

Despite all the effort, there remains a big difference between class objects and built-in values. In this loop, there is only one statement if the arrays `data[]` and `c[]` had components of built-in types. For the design of the `String` class, this is quite different: the loop body represents three function calls.

```
for (int j=0; j<MAX; j++)
{ data[j]=c[j]; }           // assign: data[j].operator=(String(c[j]));
```

Notice that each of these operations is fairly expensive. In addition to the function call itself, each entails the allocation of space on the heap, copying the parameter string into the heap space, and then, in the destructor call, returning the heap space to the system. It is unavoidable to do it once for the assignment operator that supports value semantics to keep the heap memory for its two operands separate. But to do it two more times, for the parameter of the assignment operator and for its return value, seems to be too much. To add insult to injury, the object generated by the copy constructor is not used by the client code (recall that returning the object was introduced only to support chain assignments) and is quietly dropped and eliminated after the destructor call.

First Remedy: More Overloading

There are two ways in which you can improve the performance of the overloaded assignment operator. Changing the parameter of the assignment operator from the `String` type to the character array type can eliminate the call to the conversion constructor.

```
String String::operator=(const char s[])   // array as parameter
{ delete str;                               // you do not do it in the copy constructor
  len = strlen(s);
  str = allocate(s);                        // allocate space, copy incoming text
  cout << "Assigned:   '" << str <<"'\n";   // for debugging
  return *this; }
```

If you want to support the assignment both from character arrays and `String` objects, you have to overload the assignment operator twice: for the `String` object and for the character array as its parameter type. The output of the program from Listing 11.7 with the second assignment operator added

```
Assigned:       'Atlanta'
Copied:   'Atlanta'
Assigned:       'Boston'
Copied:   'Boston'
Assigned:       'Chicago'
Copied:   'Chicago'
Assigned:       'Denver'
Copied:   'Denver'
Enter city to find: Atlanta
Created:  'Atlanta'
Assigned:  'Atlanta'
Copied:   'Atlanta'
City Atlanta is found
```

Figure 11–19 Output of the program in Listing 11.7 with the second assignment operator added.

is shown in Figure 11–19. In the debugging message of the second assignment operator, I added several spaces so that you can distinguish messages printed by the first assignment operator (with the `String` parameter), and the second assignment operator (with the character array parameter).

Second Remedy: Return by Reference

The second way to improve performance is to eliminate the redundant calls to the copy constructor. To achieve that, you should replace the return by value with a return by reference. Here is an example of doing this for the assignment operator with the character array parameter.

```
String& String::operator = (const char s[])  // return reference
{ delete str;                                 // you do not do it in the copy constructor
  len = strlen(s);
  str = allocate(s);                          // allocate space, copy incoming text
  cout << " Assigned: '" << str <<"'\n";     // for debugging
  return *this; }
```

The same should be done to the first assignment operator with the `String` parameter. When you return references from functions (more on that is discussed in Chapter 9), you should be careful to make sure that the reference still points to a valid object after the function terminates. In this case, this is safe. The reference that is returned is the reference to the object on the left-hand side of the assignment operator in the client space, for example, `data[i]` in the loop example above. It exists after the assignment operator terminates because it is defined in the client scope. Be careful with returning

```
Assigned:         'Atlanta'
Assigned:         'Boston'
Assigned:         'Chicago'
Assigned:         'Denver'
Enter city to find: Denver
Created:  'Denver'
Assigned: 'Denver'
City Denver is found
```

Figure 11-20   Output of the program in Listing 11.7 with the second assignment operator added and returning string objects from operators by reference.

references to objects defined in the server scope that disappear after the call. Many compilers only give you a warning or let you do it with impunity.

The output of the program in Listing 11.7 with two assignment operators that return object references is shown in Figure 11–20.

It looks like we beat this poor assignment operator to death, but this is not the end of it. Some purists insist that this is not enough because this design does not prevent the client programmer from doing unnecessary things such as changing the contents of the returned string object before it is destroyed. For example, this next code snippet is legal C++ for the assignment operators from Listing 11.7.

```
for (int j=0; j<MAX; j++)
  { (data[j] = c[j]).modify("A city nobody heard of"); }    // legal
```

This code assigns one object to another, returns the reference to the target object, and immediately sends a message to modify it. The assigned value is never used. This does not make much sense, and hence should be flagged as a syntax error. In order to generate a syntax error, you should make the returned reference a reference to a constant.

```
const String& String::operator = (const char s[])    // too much?
{ delete str;                           // you do not do it in the copy constructor
  len = strlen(s);
  str = allocate(s);                    // allocate space, copy incoming text
  cout << " Assigned:  '" << str <<"'\n";  // for debugging
  return *this; }
```

I am not sure I want to insist that you do that, but the purists do have a point. If something does not make sense, it should not be allowed to become a legitimate part of code.

Practical Considerations: What to Implement

Dynamic memory management has to be handled with knowledge and understanding. Step to either side and you risk either performance degradation or integrity loss.

Many programmers believe that each time you design a class that manages memory dynamically, you must provide this class with the full complement of auxiliary member functions:

- default constructor
- conversion constructor(s)
- copy constructor
- overloaded assignment operator(s)
- destructor

I am not sure you have to automatically follow this recommendation. Depending on client code requirements, you might need only part of these functions. If you supply operators with the wrong interfaces, you will eliminate the integrity problem, but you also will impair program performance for no good reason. What I am sure of is that you have to understand the issues discussed in this chapter. This understanding will let you choose member functions according to the task at hand (client requirements) and to design a class that is both efficient and correct. When you automatically supply all this machinery, the client code executes fine, but you lose your edge and forget about the distinction between the initialization and assignment. This is dangerous.

Make sure that you use the right tools for your classes. When in trouble, analyze the situation, use debugging statements, draw the pictures, but do not bloat the class with unnecessary components. Make sure that you match the tools to the job and not walk around with the nails in your hand (constructors, assignment operators, and other goodies) in search of an opposite wall. Make sure you remember that the copy constructor and the assignment operator solve different problems and cannot be used interchangeably—they hang pictures on opposite walls.

Often client code does not need to initialize one object from another object or assign one object to another object. Let us assume that the class you have to implement represents a window. For simplicity, let us consider only one data member that represents the text displayed in the window. This class `Window` is similar to class `String`. It contains the dynamically allocated character array, the destructor, and the concatenation operator that accepts a character array to be displayed in the window and adds it to the contents of the window.

```
class Window {
   char *str;                             // dynamically allocated char array
   int len;
public:
Window()
{ len = 0; str = new char; str[0]= 0 ; }  // empty String
~Window()
{ delete str; }                           // return heap memory
void operator += (const char s[])         // array parameter
{ len = strlen(str) + strlen(s);
   char* p = new char[len + 1];           // allocate enough heap memory
   if (p==NULL) exit(1);
   strcpy(p,str); strcat(p,s);            // form data from components
   delete str; str = p; }                 // hook up str to new data
const char* show() const
{ return str; } } ;                       // pointer to contents
```

For a full-fledged window, you would need more data members and member functions, but this design is sufficient to demonstrate the issues.

Of course, there are fewer objects of class `Window` in the application than there are objects of class `string`. Also, when a `Window` object is created, it is initialized to an empty contents, and the data are added during execution.

As I showed you at the beginning of this chapter, this is exactly that type of class whose objects you should not pass by value. And what if the client programmer passes the `Window` parameter by value or just missed the `&` operator and created the pass by value unintentionally?

```
void display(const Window window)          // do not do that!
{ cout << window.show(); }
```

It does not make sense to initialize one window from another or to assign one window object to another.

```
Window w1; w1 += "Welcome, Dear Customer!";    // reasonable usage
Window w2 = w1;                                 // unreasonable usage
w2 = w1;                                         // even less reasonable usage
display(w2);                                     // pass by value: slow
```

No, the second and the third lines in this code snippet do not make sense. Most people would not write this. Also, the function `display()` passes its parameter by value. Most people (especially if they read this book) would not write this. Since most people would not program this way, does it mean that one can design class `Window` without the copy constructor or the assignment operator? If someone (who did not read this book) were to write code like this snippet, it would create both an integrity problem and a performance problem—but this code is legal in C++.

Should you write a lengthy comment to your class `Window`? "Dear client programmer, please do not initialize `Window` objects from another `Window` object. Please do not assign one `Window` object to another `Window` object. And please, please, do not pass a `Window` object by value to a function or return it from a function. Your program will be in trouble." Nice pitch. It would be nice to do something more to protect client code.

One way is to add the copy constructor and the assignment operator to the class. If the client programmer writes bad code, at least the code does not cause an integrity problem.

Another way is to make bad code syntactically incorrect. This is a very interesting idea. You design your class in such a way that incorrect usage of its objects by client code becomes a syntax error. It is up to the class designer to decide what usage is incorrect. Then you do not even need this comment: "Dear client programmer."

But this is not very simple. You can take away the programmer-defined copy constructor and overloaded assignment operator. But the system will give your class its own copy constructor and assignment operator, and it is these system-provided member functions that cause the integrity problem for classes with dynamic memory management. To prevent this add to the class a programmer-defined copy constructor and an overloaded assignment operator, but do it in such a way that the client code cannot use them and that an attempt to call them would cause a syntax error.

Do you see what I am driving at? I invite you to write a function that the client code cannot call. How do you write a function that the client cannot call? One possible way is to define this function as nonpublic, to make it a private (or protected) function.

Listing 11.8 shows you this solution. The copy constructor and the assignment operators are defined as private. They do not even need to be implemented. If only a prototype of the function is given and the function is called by the client code, it is a linker error. Here, the linker does not get to see the code. The compiler complains that the last three lines in `main()` are in error. Comment out the declarations for the assignment operator and the copy constructor, and the compiler will accept the client code giving this really unreasonable code its seal of approval.

Listing 11.8   Example of private prototypes to outlaw incorrect handling of objects.

```
#include <iostream>
using namespace std;

class Window {
   char *str;                              // dynamically allocated char array
   int len;
Window(const Window& w);                   // private copy constructor
Window& operator = (const Window &w);      // private assignment
public:
Window()
{ len = 0; str = new char; str[0]= 0 ; }   // empty String
~Window()
{ delete str; }                            // return heap memory
void operator += (const char s[])          // array parameter
{ len = strlen(str) + strlen(s);
   char* p = new char[len + 1];            // allocate enough heap memory
   if (p==NULL) exit(1);
   strcpy(p,str); strcat(p,s);             // form data from components
   delete str; str = p; }                  // hook up str to new data
const char* show() const
{ return str; } } ;                        // pointer to data
```

```
void display(const Window window)          // do not pass objects by value
{ cout << window.show(); }

int main()
{ Window w1; w1 += "Welcome, Dear Customer!\n";      // reasonable
  Window w2 = w1;                                // unreasonable usage: syntax error
  w2 = w1;                                       // even less reasonable usage: syntax
error
  display(w2);                                   // pass by value: syntax error
  return 0;
  }
```

This is a great way to prevent the abuse of your classes by the client programmer. Of course, if the code labeled as unreasonable in `main()` in Listing 11.8 has to be supported (for whatever reason), and you care about performance, the class has to provide the copy constructor and the assignment operator or several assignment operators if different types of right-hand side expressions are possible. As far as the conversion operator(s) is concerned, you should provide it if the class objects have to be initialized from simple data objects, not from objects of the same type. Another good reason for adding to the class conversion operators is to avoid multiple overloaded operator functions. You decrease the number of functions in your class, but you wind up with extra constructor calls and extra memory allocation operations.

Summary

In this chapter, we looked at the dark side of C++ power. I did not want to frighten you, rather to convey to you the grave responsibility that a C++ programmer has—both for program performance and for program integrity.

I drove several more nails in the coffin of passing parameters by value, and I hope you will not compromise on that in your programs. Pass parameters by reference, and use the `const` modifier to indicate that the parameter does not change in the function.

I also argued against returning objects from functions by value. If you have to return an object, return the reference to the object, but make sure that this reference is to an object that does not disappear immediately after the function call.

If you feel strongly that the client code should not pass objects of your class by value, make the copy constructor private; that is, put the copy constructor prototype in the private section of your class. There is no need to implement the function itself.

If your class manages memory dynamically, make sure you provide the class with the destructor that returns heap memory.

If the objects of your class have to be used in the client code to initialize other objects of the class, provide the copy constructor that implements value semantics for your class and supplies each object with its own segment of heap memory.

If the objects of your class have to be assigned to each other in the client code, provide the overloaded assignment operator that implements value semantics and supplies each object with its own segment of heap memory. In the assignment operator, make sure that you prevent memory leak by returning heap memory that the object already had before being assigned a new value from the parameter object. Make sure that the memory is not deleted before you check for self-assignment. Decide whether you want to support chain assignment. Often, your clients do not need it.

The use of conversion constructors allows you to significantly relax the rules of strong typing in C++. You can pass as an actual argument data of a type different from the class required and still wind up with valid code. This is beautiful, but use this technique with caution. Extra calls to the conversion constructor are expensive, especially if you have to support value semantics.

And yes, make sure that you distinguish where the client code calls the copy constructor and where the client code calls the assignment operator. They use the same equals sign to denote the operation, but they invoke different functions in the server code. You should know which one is which.

Return to the material of this chapter often. Draw memory diagrams, experiment with its code. Always remember that dynamic memory management in C++ can easily degenerate into a joy ride around the neighborhood in a tank. It is too bad that C++ added to the traditional categories of errors, syntax errors and semantic (run-time) errors, yet another category of errors: The program is syntactically correct and is semantically correct, but still it is incorrect. No other language burdens the programmer with that much responsibility. Make sure you carry out this responsibility with respect.

Good luck to you.

Part 3

OBJECT-ORIENTED PROGRAMMING WITH AGGREGATION AND INHERITANCE

This part of the book continues the discussion of techniques of object-oriented programming. C++ adds to the programmer's toolbox such powerful techniques as class composition and class inheritance, and some programmers feel at a loss deciding which technique to use and how to avoid any unpleasant increase in program complexity.

Chapter 12, "Composite Classes: Pitfalls and Advantages," describes the syntax of using objects as members of another class, specifies the rules of access to these objects and to their data members, and explains how to initialize components of the composite object. It introduces the techniques of sharing object components through reference members and as static members and describes the use of nested classes and friend classes.

Chapter 13, "Similar Classes: How to Treat Them," introduces the techniques of using inheritance. It describes the syntax of C++ inheritance, discusses different modes of inheritance and their effect on access rights to base members in the derived object. It defines the scope rules under C++ inheritance and explains the rules of name resolution when a derived method hides the base method of the same name. It also covers the rules of construction and destruction of derived objects and the sequence of invocation of constructors and destructors.

Chapter 14, "Choosing Between Inheritance and Composition," introduces you to the Unified Modeling Language (UML), which is becoming more and more popular for describing object-oriented designs. This chapter helps you to choose between using inheritance and class composition and introduces criteria of class visibility and division of responsibilities between classes as the tools for making these design decisions. This chapter is important not only because it introduces the UML, but also because it warns you against excessive use of inheritance and the increase of program complexity that excessive use of inheritance usually leads to.

COMPOSITE CLASSES: PITFALLS AND ADVANTAGES

Topics in this Chapter

- Using Class Objects as Data Members
- Initialization of Composite Objects
- Data Members with Special Properties
- Container Classes
- Summary

Chapter 12

I n the first two parts of this book, I mostly concentrated on the rules of the C++ language. I discussed what you can and cannot do and what dangers you should be aware of to avoid loss of performance or loss of program integrity. In these parts of the book, C++ emerges as a powerful language that expects from the programmer a thorough understanding of what is happening on the surface and under the hood of the program.

The second part of the book presented basic principles of object-oriented programming related to building C++ code and to analyzing the interactions between program classes. Ideas were introduced such as:

- binding data and functions in the class to indicate that they logically belong together
- making private those class components (data and functions) whose access from outside the class would make class clients dependent on low-level details of class design
- using class scope as an additional tool to eliminate name conflicts between elements of different classes and conferring among class developers
- providing member functions to make direct access to server data field names from client code unnecessary

- pushing responsibility from client code down to server classes and member functions
- writing client code in terms of calls to server methods so that the code would not develop dependencies on server design
- providing constructors and destructors for proper object initialization, resource management, and for further pushing responsibility to server classes
- passing the server designer's knowledge about server behavior to the maintainer and to client programmers, for example, with const modifiers for data members, parameters, return values, and methods.

These ideas form the basis for programming techniques that result in self-documented object-oriented code. This code is easier to understand and to maintain. Only with the use of these ideas can you realize the full potential of C++. Without them, your code will contain highly intertwined parts that depend on each other with a large number of dependencies. Such code is difficult to understand and to modify whether it is written in C++, Java, COBOL, or FORTRAN.

In this part of the book, we will switch from considering a stand-alone C++ class to the design of programs that have several cooperating classes. You will study *class composition*, where objects of one class are used as data members, local variables, or parameters for methods of another class. This is a powerful technique of organizing cooperation among program classes. The design decisions that you implement using class composition are supported by C++ rules for constructor invocation and by C++ syntax for passing data from client code to the components of programmer-defined classes.

Another method of class cooperation is using inheritance, the method for designing classes that are similar to each other, so that one class adds to data members and methods of another class. This is a major vehicle for code reuse in C++. In addition to the design issues of deciding when inheritance is appropriate, we will discuss all the relevant sets of C++ language features that support inheritance: inheritance syntax, instantiation of objects, passing data for initialization of inherited data members, name ambiguity, and rules for resolving ambiguity.

C++ programmers love to use inheritance. Many experts say that the use of inheritance is the backbone of object-oriented programming. This is not really true. It is using C++ classes that is the backbone of object-oriented programming—binding together data and operations, controlling access to class components, and so on.

Inheritance is not the backbone of object-oriented programming. It is a technique for code and design reuse. As such, it is very important for C++ programming. Let us make sure that this important technique is used correctly.

Using Class Objects as Data Members

As was explained in Chapter 9, "C++ Class as a Unit of Modularization," the main purpose of the class construct in C++ is to let the programmer bind together those data and operations that logically belong together in the eyes of the class designer.

Almost all examples of C++ classes that appeared earlier in the book had data members of built-in types—integers, and floating point numbers. Some more complex examples had a character array as a data member. Actually, it was a pointer to a character array allocated on the heap. From the point of view of class composition, a pointer is similar to integers and floating point numbers. It has no internal structure of its own that is accessible from the outside.

However, you should not view this as an inherent limitation on class design. Class members can be more complex than values of built-in types. Rather, it is an indication of a methodical approach to the study of the language: starting from simpler features and progressing to more complex ones.

In Chapter 10, "Operator Functions: Another Good Idea," and Chapter 11, "Constructors and Destructors: Potential Trouble," you saw how much attention C++ pays to treating built-in types and programmer-defined types equally. If data members of built-in types can be used as class components, there is no good reason why a data member of a class cannot be an object of some other class that has components of its own.

C++ allows you to use class objects as components of objects of other classes. If one class has many data members, you can merge a group of related data members into a larger object, and declare this object to be a member of the class. Instead of a small number of large classes with many components, you wind up with a larger number of classes with fewer components. This facilitates the division of labor between programmers during development. Using a larger number of smaller classes also improves modularization of code and facilitates hiding unnecessary details from client code. The downside of overmodularization is that your clients can wind up with a large number of small classes, which will make learning these classes more difficult.

Classes that have objects of other classes as their data members are called *composite classes*. Almost all classes have components (data members) and hence are composite, but the term is used mostly for classes whose components have their own components. In the theory of object-oriented design, using objects of one class as components for objects of another class is called *class aggregation* or *class composition*.

As an example, consider a class `Rectangle` that contains the x and y coordinates of its top-left and bottom-right corners, respectively. This is a common convention in graphical programming.

```
class Rectangle {
  int x1, y1;                          // coordinates of the top-left point
  int x2, y2;                          // coordinates of the bottom-right point
  int thickness;                       // thickness of the rectangle border
public:
  Rectangle (int inX1, int inY1, int inX2, int inY2, int width=1);
  void move(int a, int b);             // move rectangle
  void setThickness(int width = 1);    // change thickness
  bool pointIn(int x, int y) const;    // point in rectangle?
  . . . . } ;                          // the rest of class Rectangle

Rectangle::Rectangle (int inX1, int inY1, int inX2, int inY2, int width)
{ x1 = inX1;  y1 = inY1;
  x2 = inX2;  y2 = inY2;
  thickness = width; }                 // set data members

void Rectangle::move(int a, int b)
{ x1 |= a;  y1 |= b;
  x2 += a;  y2 += b; }                 // move each corner

void Rectangle::setThickness(int width)
{ thickness = width; }                 // do the job

bool Rectangle::pointIn(int x, int y) const // is point in?
{ bool xIsBetweenBorders = (x1<x && x<x2) || (x2<x && x<x1);
  bool yIsBetweenBorders = (y>y1 && y<y2) || (y<y1 && y>y2);
  return (xIsBetweenBorders && yIsBetweenBorders); }
```

This class provides its clients with such services as moving the rectangle object around the screen, changing the thickness of the lines used to draw the rectangle on the screen, and checking whether a given point is inside the rectangle (hit test). The client code can define objects of class `Rectangle` by specifying the coordinates of their corners. It moves a point and the rectangle around the screen, trying to catch the point with the rectangle.

```
int x1=20,y1=40; int x2=70,y2=90;      // top-left/bottom-right corners
int x=100, y=120;                      // point to catch by the rectangle
Rectangle rec(x1,y1,x2,y2,4);          // create a Rectangle object
rec.setThickness();                    // line width is 1 pixel (default)
x -= 25;   y -= 15;                    // move the point around the screen
rec.move(10,20);                       // 10 pixels to right, 20 pixels down
if (rec.pointIn(x,y)) cout << "Point is in\n";      // in point in rectangle?
```

Even for this small example, I felt that the internal structure of the
Rectangle class was too complex. When I was writing this code, I made
errors, confusing x1 and y1, x1 and y2, and so on. As a client programmer, I
felt it was too much work to specify the Rectangle object (five values in the
constructor call). The reason for this unnecessary complexity of class
Rectangle and its client is the lack of implementation for a component: class
Point. Actually, the concept of point is natural here, and it is even present in
comments to both class Rectangle and its client, but this concept is not supported by a programmer-defined type.

C++ Syntax for Class Composition

Let us consider the same example, this time using a class Point that provides
the clients with a few services. Similar to previous examples, I will ask you to
imagine that this code is part of a huge program with many people working
on different parts. In this section, I will concentrate on the syntax of class
compositions and on issues related to communications among classes and
among people designing these classes.

```
class Point {
private:
    int x, y;                          // private coordinates
public:
    Point (int a, int b)               // general constructor
      { x = a;   y = b; }
    void set (int a, int b)            // modifier function
      { x = a;   y = b; }
    void move (int a, int b)           // modifier function
      { x += a;   y += b; }
    void get (int& a, int& b) const    // selector function
      { a = x;   b = y; }
    bool isOrigin () const             // predicate function
      { return x == 0 &&  y == 0; } } ;
```

I am using here common terminology for member functions. A *modifier* is
a member function that changes the state of the target object. (See that it has

no const keyword?) A *selector* is a member function that does not change the state of the target object. (See that it has the const keyword?) A *predicate* is a selector that returns a boolean value that tells something about the state of the target object (in this case, whether it is at the point of origin).

In this example, I use generic names for member functions to illustrate the fact that class scope effectively limits name conflicts in the program. When I choose the name set() for a Point member function, I do not have to notify all team members who design other classes for the application of my decision. They can use the name set() for their classes too. I will have to notify only those few team members who design classes that use my class Point as a server to do their job. One such client class is class Rectangle that I introduced at the beginning of this chapter. This version of class Rectangle has two data members of class Point to denote the top-left and the bottom-right corners of the rectangle. The data member thickness has the same meaning as before— it denotes the width of the line used to draw the rectangle on the screen.

```
class Rectangle {
  Point pt1, pt2;                             // top-left, bottom-right corner points
  int thickness;                              // thickness of the rectangle border
public:
  Rectangle (int inX1, int inY1, int inX2, int inY2, int wid=1);
  void move(int a, int b);                    // move both points
  void setThickness(int width = 1);           // change thickness
  bool pointIn(int x, int y) const;           // point in rectangle
  . . . . } ;                                 // the rest of class Rectangle

Rectangle::Rectangle (int inX1, int inY1, int inX2, int inY2, int width)
  { pt1.set(inX1,inY1);  pt2.set(inX2,inY2);// push job down
    thickness = width; }                      // set data members

void Rectangle::move(int a, int b)
  { pt1.move(a,b);  pt2.move(a,b); }          // pass buck to members

void Rectangle::setThickness(int width)
  { thickness = width; }                      // do the job

bool Rectangle::pointIn(int x, int y) const // is point in?
  { int x1,y1,x2,y2;                          // coordinates of corners
    pt1.get(x1,y1);  pt2.get(x2,y2);          // get point data
    bool xIsBetweenBorders = (x1<x && x<x2) || (x2<x && x<x1);
    bool yIsBetweenBorders = (y>y1 && y<y2) || (y<y1 && y>y2);
    return (xIsBetweenBorders && yIsBetweenBorders); }
```

You see important changes in the design of class Rectangle. I wanted to say "significant changes" but felt that it is not appropriate for such a small class. Whatever the term, these changes represent common programming idioms for class composition.

In the `Rectangle` constructor, instead of a set of low-level assignments to numerous data members of built-in types, there are two messages to component objects.

```
pt1.set(inX1,inY1); pt2.set(inX2,inY2);    // push job down
```

This is an example of insulating the client code (`Rectangle` class) from details of the design of the server code (`Point` class). The client code here is written in terms of messages to server objects; the client does not use low-level details of server design: The client code says *what* is being done instead of spelling out the details of *how* it is being done. The responsibility for the details of the operation is pushed from the `Rectangle` code to the `Point` code. This style of writing client code makes it easier to understand.

The `move()` method represents an even more interesting C++ idiom for the relationship between the composite and the component classes. When a `Rectangle` object is asked to move, the object turns back and asks its components to do the work of calling the method with the same name, `move()`. But this is not a recursive call to the same function; this second method `move()` belongs to the component class `Point`, not to the composite class `Rectangle`. This is yet another example of the tendency to treat objects of different natures equally in C++ code. In this case, the same treatment means the methods with the same name that belong to classes with similar behavior. Moving a rectangle means moving each of its points. The opportunity to write methods that pass the buck to its data members is one of the reasons why both methods are called `move()` and not `movePoint()` and `moveRectangle()`.

Access to Data Members of Class Data Members

Another important difference between this design of class `Rectangle` and the previous version is access to component's components. In the previous version, class `Rectangle` could do whatever it wanted with coordinates x and y. They were directly accessible. In the last version of class `Rectangle`, they are components of class `Point`. If the component object (in this example, of class `Point`) had public components, the composite class (class `Rectangle`) could access the data members of its object data member (in this example, x and y) using the dot selector operator. That is, if `Point` components were public, the `Rectangle` member function `Rectangle::pointIn()` could use the qualified names of `Point` components. This is how class `Rectangle` could decide whether the x parameter is between the x coordinates of `Rectangle` data members `pt1` and `pt2`.

```
bool xIsBetweenBorders = (pt1.x<x && x<pt2.x)
            || (pt2.x<x && x<pt1.x);
```

However, `Point` data members are private. And the client class (in this example, `Rectangle`) has no special privileges accessing the server (`Point`) components. Class `Rectangle` has `Point` objects as its own components. This is why its methods can access its `Point` data members (`pt1` and `pt2`). But methods of class `Rectangle` cannot access the `Point` components data members x and y. The line above is illegal. `Rectangle` methods should use `Point` public member functions, for example, `Point::get()`, to access `Point` components.

It is important not to confuse two different contexts. (How many times have I emphasized this?). The `Rectangle` class can access its own private `Point` members `pt1` and `pt2` without limitations; the `Rectangle` class cannot access private components `pt1.x`, `pt1.y`, `pt2.x`, `pt2.y` of its data members. This is why `Rectangle::pointIn()` has to use this code to retrieve data members of `Rectangle` data members `pt1` and `pt2`.

```
bool Rectangle::pointIn(int x, int y) const
{ int x1,y1,x2,y2;                          // coordinates of corners
  pt1.get(x1,y1);   pt2.get(x2,y2);         // get point data
  bool xIsBetweenBorders = (x1<x && x<x2) || (x2<x && x<x1);
  ... }                                     // and so on
```

The need to use server access functions to access components of class data members is often annoying. Because of this need, the design of the composite class methods might become quite cumbersome.

Alert

If a class has data members that belong to other classes, then the class member functions cannot access private components of these data members. This is often frustrating, but the composite class must use data member's methods to get access to components of its own components.

If you look at the design of the client code of class `Rectangle`, you will see that it does not require any changes. The client code has to supply five arguments to the `Rectangle` constructor and two arguments to the method

`Rectangle::pointIn()`. This means that introduction of the component class `Point` benefited the design of composite class `Rectangle` but did not benefit the design of client code.

```
int x1=20, y1=40; int x2=70, y2=90;      // rectangle   corners
int x=100, y=120;                        // point to catch with the rectangle
Rectangle rec(x1,y1,x2,y2,4);            // create a Rectangle object
rec.setThickness();                      // line width is 1 pixel (default)
x -= 25;   y -= 15;                       // move the point around the screen
rec.move(10,20);                         // 10 pixels to right, 20 pixels down
if (rec.pointIn(x,y)) cout << "Point is in\n";    // in point in rectangle?
```

Again, for this tiny example, the difference is not tremendous, but it is clearly here. Similar to the first version of class `Rectangle`, this client code does its processing in terms of separate entities x and y. The code does not aggregate these separate entities into a class and thus does not pass to the maintainer what the code designer knew at the time of design, that these separate entities are related and represent the coordinates of the same point. Whatever the client code needs to do with points, like moving, comparing and so on, these actions should be done over individual coordinates in the client code. The low-level individual actions clutter the client code and make it harder to grasp its meaning. Consider, for example, the client code statement `rec.move(10,20)`; it says clearly that the rectangle moves. The fact that the point at coordinates (100,120) is moved has to be deduced from the series of assignments `x -= 25; y -= 15;` This responsibility for low-level details is not pushed to the server code.

Expressing client code in terms of class `Point` objects and operations over them alleviates these problems and makes this code more object-oriented.

```
Point p1(20,40), p2(70,90);              // rectangle   corners
Point point(100,120);                    // point to catch with the rectangle
Rectangle rec(p1,p2,4);                  // see below about problems with this
rec.setThickness();                      // line width is 1 pixel (default)
point.move(-25,-15);                     // move the point around the screen
rec.move(10,20);                         // 10 pixels to right, 20 pixels down
if (rec.pointIn(point)) cout << "Point is in\n";    // is point in?
```

This code now has two servers, class `Point` and class `Rectangle`. The fact that the `Point` object `point` moves is as clear here as the fact that the `Rectangle` object `rec` moves. The responsibility for low-level details is pushed to servers, and the client code is expressed in terms of self-explanatory function calls, not in terms of individual computations.

The problem with this code is that it expects the interfaces from the class `Rectangle` that are not available. Class `Rectangle` provides the constructor with five parameters, the client code supplies only three. Class `Rectangle` expects two arguments for the function `pointIn()`, but the client code supplies only one. This problem could be resolved by changing either the function calls in the client code or by changing the function interfaces in server `Rectangle`. The smaller the program, the less difference it makes what you change.

If class `Rectangle` were a library class that you cannot change, then there is no choice. It is the client code that has to work around the limitations of the library. If class `Rectangle` is one of the cooperating classes being developed for the application, this class can change, and the decision becomes an ideological decision. From the point of view of object-oriented ideology, it is the server class (in this case, class `Rectangle`) that has to accommodate the expectations and requirements of the client code. According to this ideology, class `Rectangle` should be designed in the following way.

```
class Rectangle {
  Point pt1, pt2;                              // rectangle corners points
  int thickness;                               // thickness of the rectangle border
public:
  Rectangle (const Point& p1, const Point& p2, int width=1);
  void move(int a, int b);                     // move both points
  void setThickness(int width = 1);            // change thickness
  bool pointIn(const Point& pt) const;         // point in rectangle?
   . . . . } ;                                 // the rest of class Rectangle

  Rectangle::Rectangle (const Point& p1, const Point& p2, int width)
    { pt1 = p1;  pt2 = p2;
      thickness = width; }                     // set data members

  void Rectangle::move(int a, int b)
    { pt1.move(a,b);  pt2.move(a,b); }         // pass buck to Point

  void Rectangle::setThickness(int width)
    { thickness = width; }                     // do the job

bool Rectangle::pointIn(const Point& pt) const // is point in?
{ int x,y,x1,y1,x2,y2;                         // coordinates of pt and corners
  pt.get(x,y);                                 // get parameter's coordinates
  pt1.get(x1,y1);  pt2.get(x2,y2);             // get both corners
  bool xIsBetweenBorders = (x1<x && x<x2) || (x2<x && x<x1);
  bool yIsBetweenBorders = (y>y1 && y<y2) || (y<y1 && y>y2);
  return (xIsBetweenBorders && yIsBetweenBorders); }
```

Notice the use of the `const` keyword (and its absence) in the design of classes `Point` and `Rectangle`. They reflect the changes (and absence of changes) to the target object and to function call parameters. Since member functions in this design do not return pointers or references or objects, there is no need to use the `const` keyword for return values.

The general constructor of class `Rectangle` can be called with either two or three parameters. When it is called with two parameters, the `thickness` data member is set to its default value 1.

Access to Data Members of Method Parameters

Notice that the method parameters in C++ are treated similarly to data members of the composite class.

Member function parameters can be of any type, including class objects. There are no limitations on parameter modes for class objects: They can be passed by value, by pointer, and by reference; they can even have the `const` modifier if necessary.

Access to parameter objects in member functions follows the same rules as for any other object: It is allowed to public parts only. The parameter is available to the method, but its private components are not. If the client of the parameter (in this case, the member function) needs access to private parts of the server (its parameter), the server class member functions should be used.

This is why the `Rectangle` member function `pointIn()` uses `Point` access function `get()` to access its parameter's components `pt.x` and `pt.y`.

An important exception is made in C++ when another object being accessed is the *same* class type. This exception applies when an object is passed as a parameter to a member function of the class to which the object belongs. If the client class and the server class are both of the same type, the client object has full access rights to the parameter object components. This version of class `Point` is too simple to demonstrate this issue. Let us assume that you wish to add a member function `isSamePoint()` to class `Point`. The function should compare the coordinates of its target object and its parameter object and return true if they have the same values, false otherwise.

```
bool Point::isSamePoint(const Point& p) const     // compare data
{ return x==p.x && y==p.y; }
```

In a sense, access to another instance (in this example, `p` in `isSamePoint()`) is taking place within the class scope of the target object (of type `Point`). This is why it is allowed.

Tip

When a parameter of a class method is of a class component type, the method cannot access the parameter's private components and should use the parameter's member functions instead. When a parameter of a class method is of the same type as the class, the method can access the parameter's private components directly, without access functions. Using access functions would be syntactically correct but ugly.

To be consistent with the rule that private members are not accessible outside of the object, another object of the same class would have to use access functions. Then this function would have to be written in the following way.

```
bool Point::isSamePoint(const Point& pt) const    // compare data
  { int x1, y1;
    pt.get(x1,y1);      // overkill: access through a member function
    bool answer = (x==x1 && y==y1);
    return answer; }
```

C++ allows a small inconsistency in access rights to avoid this unnecessary, awkward code. This version of `isSamePoint()` is syntactically correct. A programmer whose productivity is measured in lines of code could write miles and miles of code like this. Whether this mileage contributes to the quality of the application is a totally different question.

Initialization of Composite Objects

The issues related to initialization play an important role in programming. Failure to initialize a computational object properly is a common source of programming errors. C++ offers the programmer a rich set of techniques for initialization of program components.

When I was describing the syntax of defining scalar variables in Chapter 3, "Working with C++ Data and Expressions," the next discussion topic was the syntax of giving initial values to these variables. When I was describing the syntax of C++ aggregates in Chapter 5, "Aggregation with Programmer-Defined Data Types,"—arrays, structures, enumerations, unions, and bit fields—the next topic for discussion was the initialization of these program components. When I described the syntax of the C++ class construct in Chapter 9, the next topic was again object initialization.

This was no accident. Initialization of C++ objects is one of the major concerns for the C++ programmer. It is an important part of the effort to push responsibility to the server class and to relieve the client code from low-level details of server design. Now that I have described the syntax of a composite class, we will discuss the initialization of composite objects. The same will happen when you study inheritance: After I discuss the syntax of inheritance, I will show you how to initialize derived objects.

As I mentioned in Chapter 9, the C++ syntax for defining program variables and the C++ syntax for defining class data members is the same. This line of code can be treated as a legitimate C++ snippet both in a function or block scope and in a class scope.

```
int x,y;        // can be in a function or block; can be in a class
```

However, the definition with initialization can be found only in executable code in a function or in a block.

```
int x=100, y=100;  // can be in a function or block, not in a class
```

Hence, you cannot initialize data members in class specifications using syntax appropriate for initialization of C++ variables. Java programmers can do that but not C++ programmers.

```
class Point {
   int x=100, y=100;        // illegal syntax for initialization
public:
   Point (int a, int b)     // appropriate means of initialization
      { x = a;  y = b; }
      . . . }  ;            // the rest of class Point
```

The syntax for defining object instances in functions and data members in composite classes is also the same. This line of code could be found both in a body of a function and in a class definition.

```
Point pt1, pt2;          // can be in a function or block or a class
```

However, supplying arguments for initialization is allowed only when defining object instances in functions or in a block scope.

```
Point pt1(20,40),pt2(70,90);    // OK in function/block, not in a class
```

Hence, data members in composite classes cannot be initialized in class specifications using the syntax appropriate for initialization of objects of the component class. In the next example, I am trying to initialize `Point` components of class `Rectangle` using the syntax appropriate for a `Point` variable. The compiler rejects this syntax.

```
class Rectangle {            // incorrect class specification
   Point pt1(20,40);         // legal in client code, illegal here
   Point pt2(70,90);         // same problem
   int thickness = 1;        // same problem
public:
   Rectangle (const Point& p1, const Point& p2, int width = 1);
   void move(int a, int b);
   . . . . } ;               // the rest of class Rectangle
```

Instead, C++ offers you two ways to initialize components of a composite class. One way to do this is to assign the values in the body of a constructor of the composite class. The constructor can assign data to appropriate data members whether they are aggregates or simple components of built-in types.

```
Rectangle::Rectangle (const Point& p1,const Point& p2,int width)
   { pt1 = p1;   pt2 = p2;      // give values to aggregate components
     thickness = width; }       // give values to built-in components
```

Another way to do it is to use a member initialization list that calls the constructor of the class components. In this example, the member initialization list calls a `Point` constructor to initialize `Point` components of class `Rectangle`.

```
Rectangle::Rectangle (const Point& p1, const Point& p2, int width)
   : pt1(p1), pt2(p2)           // call constructors for components
   { thickness = width; }       // give values to built-in components
```

Alert

The syntax for defining C++ variables and objects and the syntax for defining class members is the same. However, you cannot use the syntax for initializing C++ variables and objects when defining class members. You should either use a default constructor or a member initialization list.

I will discuss the details of the use of the constructor body first, and then I will explain the use of the member initialization list.

Using the Components' Default Constructors

In Chapter 9, I told you that when a C++ object is created, the memory is allocated to its data members. Disregarding system-specific additional space for value alignment, you can assume that the memory allocated for an object is a sum of the sizes of its data members.

I also told you that when a C++ object is created, its data members are initialized in a constructor call. I stressed that even though it might be convenient to believe that the constructor is called *while* the object is constructed, it is more correct to say that the constructor is called *after* all of the object's data members are constructed.

However, I am ready to admit that for the classes that have only noncomposite fields of built-in types, the distinction between *while* and *after* is not very important. It is similar to the distinction between initialization and assignment. For noncomposite variables of built-in types, this distinction is relatively minor. As you saw in Chapter 11, this distinction becomes very important for classes that handle heap memory dynamically. Failure to distinguish between the two might result in performance and integrity problems.

Similarly, the distinction between *while* and *after* becomes important for objects whose components are objects of programmer-defined classes. In this section, we will look at the process of building a composite object in detail.

In brief, when a C++ object is created, the memory is allocated to its data members, and then the body of a constructor is executed. It means that the constructor for an object is called only *after* all data members are created.

The important characteristic of this process is that data members are created in the order of their appearance in the class specification. When the process is over, the object of the composite type looks in memory like the total of its components.

By the way, it means that by changing the order of data members in the class, you can affect the properties of the class, but this is possible only if data members depend on each other. For example, one data member can represent the number of components in another data member. (You will see examples of dependencies later.)

When the data members are created one after another, fields of built-in types (if any) are either left noninitialized (if the object is created on the stack or on the heap) or are set to null (for objects that are created as global or static objects). If the object needs a specific value stored in a field of a built-in type, this will be taken care of later, during the constructor call. For example, the value of the field `thickness` for objects of the class `Rectangle` is set to the value specified as the constructor parameter `width`.

And what happens if the object is a composite object and some of its data members are objects of some other classes? The phrase "data members are created in the order of their appearance" three paragraphs ago should tip you off. The procedure of object creation is recursive. After a data member is created, its class constructor is called.

Recall that no C++ object can be created without a constructor call that follows the memory allocation. If a field of a composite object is of a programmer-defined type (structure or class), its constructor is called immediately after the field is allocated and before the next field is created. It is only after all the fields of the composite object are successfully created (and initialized), that the body of the composite class constructor is executed.

So, when an object of class `Rectangle` is created, events take place in the following order:

1. The data member `pt1` of class `Point` is created.
2. The data member `pt2` of class `Point` is created.
3. The data member `thickness` of type `int` is created.
4. The body of the `Rectangle` class constructor is executed.

When each of the data members of class `Point` is created in the process of the construction of the `Rectangle` object, it is done in the following order.

1. The data member `x` of type `int` is created.
2. The data member `y` of type `int` is created.
3. The body of a `Point` class constructor is executed.

You see that before the body of the `Rectangle` class constructor is executed, a class `Point` constructor is called twice: the first time to initialize fields of the data member `pt1` and the second time to initialize the fields of the data member `pt2`.

Notice that when a composite object is destroyed, the process of memory management and function calls is reversed. The composite class destructor is called first, before any memory is deallocated. When the destructor terminates, the data members are destroyed in the order opposite to the order of their creation. When each data member is destroyed, it is done recursively. First, the component destructor is called before any component memory is destroyed. After the component destructor terminates, the component data members are destroyed (from the last in the component class specification to the first).

Hence, the sequence of events for destroying the `Rectangle` object is a mirror image of events that took place when the object was created.

1. The `Rectangle` destructor is executed.
2. The `thickness` data member is destroyed.
3. The `Point` destructor is executed for data member `pt2`.
4. The data member `pt2` is destroyed (first its field `y`, then its field `x`).

5. The `Point` destructor is executed for data member `pt1`.

6. The data member `pt1` is destroyed (first its field `y`, then its field `x`).

When I was describing the process of the `Rectangle` object creation, I was rather confident when describing the call to the `Rectangle` constructor because the class `Rectangle` has only one constructor. But I was not exactly sure when I said that a `Point` class constructor was executed. What constructor is called when the `Point` data field object is created?

As with any C++ function, the answer depends on the number of arguments supplied in the constructor call by its client. A conceptual stumbling block for some programmers is that when there are no arguments supplied they do not see the constructor call take place. No, if no arguments are supplied, a constructor with no arguments is called. This means that the default constructor is called. When one argument is supplied, the constructor with the argument of that type is called, and so on. What happens if the constructor with the required signature is not available? Similar to calling any C++ function with an incorrect signature, it means that the function call (an attempt to create an object) generates a syntax error.

In this next segment of client code, we see that the code passes parameters for a call to a `Rectangle` constructor. However, there are no parameters that would pass data to the `Point` constructors.

```
Point p1(20,40), p2(70,90);    // top-left and bottom-right corners
Rectangle rec(p1,p2,4);        // this is a syntax error
```

This means that it is the default constructor of the component class that is called when the data member of the component type is created in the process of creation of the composite object.

In our example, class `Point` does not have a default constructor. This is bad news. Recall, however, that when a class does not have a default constructor, the compiler gives it one. This constructor does nothing, but it makes it possible for the client code to create objects with no arguments passed to the constructor. This is good news. Recall, however, that if the class has nondefault constructors (class `Point` has one), the compiler takes its default constructor away. This is bad news again—the definition of the composite class object generates a syntax error. This is why the last line in the code snippet above is in error.

This is an example of a link between classes (in this case, `Point` and `Rectangle`) that is often obscure to programmers. For some, the error is in the definition of the `Rectangle` class because it tries to call a constructor in the `Point` class that does not exist. However, compiling class `Point` and even compiling class `Rectangle` do not generate syntax errors.

The logical source of an error is in the design of the component class, `Point`. It is this class that does not have the default constructor. However, the logical error manifests itself as a syntax error not in the design of the component class, `Point`, and not even in the design of the composite class, `Rectangle`, but in the client code of the `Rectangle` class, during an attempt to instantiate the composite class object—in place of code far from the origin of the error. Unless the client code tries to define a `Rectangle` object, there is no syntax error in this code.

To remedy the situation, you can add a default constructor to the `Point` class. This will eliminate the syntax error in the last code snippet.

```
class Point {
    int x, y;                       // private coordinates
  public:
    Point ()
       { x=0;   y=0; }              // default constructor
    Point (int a, int b)            // general constructor
       { x = a;   y = b; }
    . . . }  ;                      // the rest of Point class
```

Another solution is to add default argument values to the general constructor so that the constructor can serve as a default constructor and a conversion constructor.

```
class Point {
    int x, y;                       // private coordinates
  public:
    Point (int a=0, int b=0)
    { x = a;   y = b; }             // default, conversion, general constructor
       . . . }  ;                   // the rest of Point class
```

To summarize, let us go through the steps of creation of the `Rectangle` object again. Figure 12–1 shows the actions of executing the following segment of client code.

```
Point p1(20,40), p2(70,90);  // top-left and bottom-right corners
Rectangle rec(p1,p2,4);       // OK if Point has default constructor
```

First, the memory for object `pt1` is allocated, and the default `Point` constructor is called, which sets `pt1.x` and `pt1.y` to zero. Next, the memory for object `pt2` is allocated, and the default `Point` constructor is called, which sets `pt2.x` and `pt2.y` to zero. After that the memory for data member `thickness` is allocated and left noninitialized. Then the `Rectangle` constructor is called.

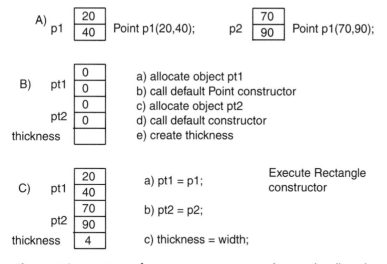

Figure 12-1 Steps of creating a `Rectangle` object with calls to the `Point` default constructor.

When its body is executing, first it copies the contents of argument p1 into data member pt1, then it copies p2 into pt2, and then it sets thickness to 4.

As a result of this sequence of events, the Rectangle object is created so that pt1.x is set to 20, pt1.y is set to 40, pt2.x is set to 70, and pt2.y is set to 90.

Do you see what happened? The values that were put into pt1 and pt2 by the Point default constructor calls were not long lived. They were written over by data from p1 and p2 during the Rectangle constructor call. The two default constructor calls for two Point data members were wasted! Do you feel this is outrageous? Are you filled with indignation about the milliseconds wasted during the creation of the Rectangle object? Yes? Good, this means that you have what it takes to know right from wrong in C++ programming.

Note

Instantiation of a C++ object always involves a function call: a call to a class constructor. Instantiation of C++ composite objects always involves more than one function call. A constructor is called immediately after each data member is created. Learn to see these function calls in any C++ code.

On many occasions I have stressed that when there is a choice between readability and performance, I favor readability. But when it comes to wasting execution time for no good reason, there is no way to have two different opinions. A C++ programmer should develop the ability to see these wasted calls when looking at C++ code. A C++ programmer should know how to avoid this waste whenever possible.

Listing 12.1 shows the implementation of the composite class `Rectangle` and the component class `Point` with the test driver. To facilitate analysis of the results, I added to class `Point` a copy constructor and the overloaded assignment operator with debugging messages to trace the process of the creation of the `Rectangle` composite object. The results of the execution of this program are shown in Figure 12–2.

Listing 12.1   Example of creation of a composite object with wasted constructor calls.

```
#include <iostream>
using namespace std;

class Point {
  private:
    int x, y;                          // private coordinates
  public:
    Point (int a=0, int b=0)           // general constructor
    { x = a;   y = b;
      cout << " Created: x= " << x << " y=" << y << endl; }
    Point (const Point& pt)            // copy constructor
    { x = pt.x;   y = pt.y;
      cout << " Copied: x= " << x << " y=" << y << endl; }
    void operator = (const Point& pt)        // assignment operator
    { x = pt.x;   y = pt.y;
      cout << " Assigned: x= " << x << " y=" << y << endl; }
    void set (int a, int b)            // modifier function
      { x = a;   y = b; }
    void move (int a, int b)           // modifier function
      { x += a;   y += b; }
    void get (int& a, int& b) const    // selector function
      { a = x;   b = y; } } ;

  class Rectangle {
    Point pt1, pt2;                    // top-left, bottom-right corner points
    int thickness;                     // thickness of the rectangle border
  public:
    Rectangle (const Point& p1, const Point& p2, int width=1);
    void move(int a, int b);           // move both points
    bool pointIn(const Point& pt) const;    // point in rectangle?
    } ;
```

```
Rectangle::Rectangle(const Point& p1,const Point& p2,int width)
  { pt1 = p1; pt2 = p2; thickness = width; }    // set data members

void Rectangle::move(int a, int b)
  { pt1.move(a,b);  pt2.move(a,b); }             // pass buck to Point

bool Rectangle::pointIn(const Point& pt) const       // is point in?
{ int x,y,x1,y1,x2,y2;                         // coordinates of pt and corners
  pt.get(x,y);                                 // get parameter's coordinates
  pt1.get(x1,y1);  pt2.get(x2,y2);             // get data from corners
  bool xIsBetweenBorders = (x1<x && x<x2) || (x2<x && x<x1);
  bool yIsBetweenBorders = (y>y1 && y<y2) || (y<y1 && y>y2);
  return (xIsBetweenBorders && yIsBetweenBorders); }

int main()
{
  Point p1(20,40), p2(70,90);                  // top-left, bottom-right corners
  Point point(100,120);                        // point to catch with the rectangle
  Rectangle rec(p1,p2,4);                      // wasted constructor calls
  point.move(-25,-15);                         // move the point around the screen
  rec.move(10,20);                             // 10 pixels to right, 20 pixels down
  if (rec.pointIn(point)) cout << " Point is in\n";     // point in?
  return 0;
  }
```

The first three Created messages in Figure 12–2 reflect the creation of Point objects p1, p2, and Point. The next two Created messages describe the creation of the Rectangle object: The first message describes the creation of data member pt1 and a call to the Point default constructor, the second message describes the creation of data member pt2 and a call to Point default constrictor. The two Assigned messages describe the execution of the Rectangle constructor after the creation of the object is finished. The first message corresponds to the first assignment in the body of the constructor, and the second message corresponds to the second assignment in the body of the constructor.

This is a typical picture of the creation of a composite object in C++. For large composite objects, the process of creation can become quite involved

```
Created: x= 20 y=40
Created: x= 70 y=90
Created: x= 100 y=120
Created: x= 0 y=0
Created: x= 0 y=0
Assigned: x= 20 y=40
Assigned: x= 70 y=90
Point is in
```

Figure 12–2
Output for program in Listing 12.1.

and wasteful. Of course, you cannot eliminate the calls for the constructors immediately after each data member is created. This is a strict law in C++—there is no creation of an object without a constructor call following immediately. But you can (and should) try to call such a constructor whose work would endure after the composite object constructor executes.

Using the Member Initialization List

C++ allows you to avoid this waste by using the *member initialization list*, or *initializer list*, in the composite class constructor. It has an unusual syntax based on the use of the space between the constructor's header and its body. This is what the member initialization list looks like.

```
class Rectangle {
   Point pt1, pt2;                              // Top-Left, Bottom-Right;
   int thickness;
public:
   Rectangle (const Point& p1, const Point& p2, int w = 1);
    . . . . } ;                                 // the rest of class Rectangle

Rectangle::Rectangle(const Point& p1,
          const Point& p2,int w)  : pt1(p1),pt2(p2)
   { thickness = w; }                           // this is much better!
```

The initializer list is placed between the closing parentheses of the constructor parameter list and the opening brace of the constructor body. The list opens with a colon and enumerates the names (not types) of data members. After each data member name, in parentheses, are listed the corresponding argument value(s) used to initialize that object data member. The list of data member names is comma separated. The list does not have a terminator; it ends when the opening brace of the constructor body is found. Each entry in the list is similar in appearance to a constructor call in a definition of a variable, for example, pt1(p1).

Notice that the initializer list syntax applies to the constructor implementation only. It does not affect the way constructor prototypes are written. Do not confuse this with default values of parameters. Default value syntax applies to prototypes only. It does not affect the way you write implementation.

The initializer list syntax forces the compiler to generate a call to the data member constructor with the appropriate number of parameters. The constructor is called after the memory for this data member is allocated and before the body of the composite class constructor is executed. Hence, component data members are already initialized by the time the composite class constructor is called. They can be used in the composite class constructor body if necessary.

Actually, any data member (including built-in types) can be initialized in the list. Here is the `Rectangle` constructor, where all data members are initialized in the initializer list.

```
Rectangle::Rectangle(const Point& p1, const Point& p2, int w)
   : thickness(w), pt1(p1), pt2(p2)        // on the line by itself
   { }                                     // empty body: a popular C++ idiom
```

As you can see, the initializer list can be on a line by itself. This is a common use of this syntax. The use of this extended initializer list results in a strange situation. By the time the constructor body is executed, there is no work left to do. This is why the constructor body is empty. It still has to be here because the function body cannot be omitted. There are no real advantages in initializing atomic data members in the initializer list. For some reason, however, the empty constructor body is popular among C++ programmers.

By the way, the initializer list above might give you the impression that the `thickness` data member is initialized before data members `pt1` and `pt2` are. This is incorrect. Despite appearances, it does not matter in what order you specify components of the initializer list. They are executed in the order in which data members appear in the class specification. Appearances lie.

Figure 12–3 shows the sequence of events for creation of the `Rectangle` object when the initializer list is used to execute this snippet of code.

```
Point p1(20,40), p2(70,90);        // top-left and bottom-right corners
Rectangle rec(p1,p2,4);            // no need for Point default constructor
```

After points `p1` and `p2` are allocated, the `Rectangle` object `rec` is constructed. First, the `Point` data member `pt1` is created; then the `Point` copy constructor is called for this data member with object `p1` as the argument. As a result, the data member `pt1` is initialized: x is 20, y is 40. Next, the point data member `pt2` is created, and the `Point` copy constructor is then called for this data member with the `Point` object `p2` as the argument. As a result, the data member `pt2` is initialized: x is 70, y is 90. After that, the data member `thickness` is created and initialized to 4. Congratulations! The wasteful calls to the `Point` default constructor have disappeared.

Listing 12.2 shows the same program as in Listing 12.1 with a different design of the composite class `Rectangle`. Instead of the conventional general constructor implemented in Listing 12.1, the program in Listing 12.2 implements the `Rectangle` constructor with the member initialization list. The results of the execution of this program are shown in Figure 12–4.

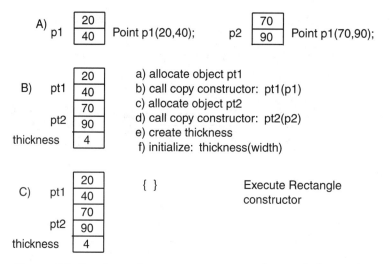

Figure 12-3   Steps of creating a `Rectangle` object with the member initialization list.

Listing 12.2   Creating a composite object without wasted constructor calls.

```
#include <iostream>
using namespace std;

class Point {
  private:
    int x, y;                        // private coordinates
  public:
    Point (int a=0, int b=0)         // general constructor
    { x = a;   y = b;
      cout << " Created: x= " << x << " y=" << y << endl; }
    Point (const Point& pt)          // copy constructor
    { x = pt.x;   y = pt.y;
      cout << " Copied: x= " << x << " y=" << y << endl; }
    void operator = (const Point& pt)  // assignment operator
    { x = pt.x;   y = pt.y;
      cout << " Assigned: x= " << x << " y=" << y << endl; }
    void set (int a, int b)          // modifier function
    { x = a;   y = b; }
    void move (int a, int b)         // modifier function
    { x += a;   y += b; }
    void get (int& a, int& b) const  // selector function
    { a = x;   b = y; } } ;

  class Rectangle {
    Point pt1, pt2;                  // top-left, bottom-right corner points
    int thickness;                   // thickness of the rectangle border
```

```
public:
  Rectangle (const Point& p1, const Point& p2, int width=1);
  void move(int a, int b);             // move both points
  bool pointIn(const Point& pt) const; // point in rectangle?
   } ;

Rectangle::Rectangle(const Point& p1, const Point& p2,int w)
 : thickness(w), pt1(p1), pt2(p2)      // initialization list
   { }                                 // empty member body

void Rectangle::move(int a, int b)
  { pt1.move(a,b);  pt2.move(a,b); }   // pass buck to Point

bool Rectangle::pointIn(const Point& pt) const      // is point in?
  { int x,y,x1,y1,x2,y2;                      // coordinates of pt and corners
    pt.get(x,y);                              // get parameter's coordinates
    pt1.get(x1,y1);  pt2.get(x2,y2);          // get data from corners
    bool xIsBetweenBorders = (x1<x && x<x2) || (x2<x && x<x1);
    bool yIsBetweenBorders = (y>y1 && y<y2) || (y<y1 && y>y2);
    return (xIsBetweenBorders && yIsBetweenBorders); }

int main()
{ Point p1(20,40), p2(70,90);          // top-left, bottom-right corners
  Point point(100,120);                // point to catch with the rectangle
  Rectangle rec(p1,p2,4);              // NO wasted constructor calls
  point.move(-25,-15);                 // move the point around the screen
  rec.move(10,20);                     // 10 pixels to right, 20 pixels down
  if (rec.pointIn(point)) cout << " Point is in\n";  // is point?
  return 0;
  }
```

The first three `Created` messages in Figure 12–4 are the same as the first three messages in Figure 12–2: They reflect the process of creation of three `Point` objects in `main()`. The next two `Copied` messages reflect the process of creation of the `Rectangle` object. The first message appears when the `Point` copy constructor is called after the data member `pt1` is created. The second message appears when the `Point` copy constructor is called after the data member `pt2` is created. As you can see, it is the `Point` copy constructor

Figure 12–4   Output for program in Listing 12.2.

```
Created: x= 20 y=40
Created: x= 70 y=90
Created: x= 100 y=120
Copied: x= 20 y=40
Copied: x= 70 y=90
Point is in
```

that is called here and not the default constructor. And its results endure—the `Point` assignment operator is not called during the `Rectangle` constructor invocation; the `Rectangle` constructor body is empty. This is very good!

In these examples, the composite class had only one constructor. If it had several constructors, the same logic would apply to each constructor. When a composite object is created, its data members are created first. What composite class constructor will be called at the end depends on the number and types of arguments that the client code supplied for the composite object. If the composite class has such a constructor, fine; if not, the object instantiation will create a syntax error. If the constructor that will be called eventually does not have the member initialization list, then the creation of each data member will be followed by a call to the default constructor for the component class. If the composite class constructor has the member initialization list, the corresponding component class constructor is called for each element on the list.

The initializer lists implemented by different constructors can be quite different. Here is another version of class `Rectangle` that overloads three constructors: the general constructor I used in previous examples, a general constructor with four parameters for coordinates of two points, and a default constructor. Each constructor has its own initialization list. They do not have to be the same.

```
class Rectangle {
    Point pt1, pt2;                      // Top-Left, Bottom-Right;
    int thickness;
public:
    Rectangle (const Point& p1, const Point& p2, int w = 1);
    Rectangle (int x1, int y1, int x2, int y2);
    Rectangle ();
    . . . . } ;                          // the rest of class Rectangle

Rectangle::Rectangle(const Point& p1, const Point& p2,int w)
    : thickness(w), pt1(p1), pt2(p2) { }

Rectangle::Rectangle (int x1, int y1, int x2, int y2)
    : pt1(x1,y1), pt2(x2,y2), thickness (1) { }

Rectangle::Rectangle () : pt1(0,0), pt2(100,100), thickness(1)
    { }
```

The first constructor demonstrates how parameters passed to the composite class constructor can be used as parameters of the component class constructors. In this example, the `Point` parameter p1 is channeled as an argument to the copy constructor to initialize the data member pt1, and the `Point` parameter p2 is channeled as an argument to the copy constructor to initialize the data member pt2. The last constructor parameter is used to initialize the integer data member.

The second constructor demonstrates that the member initialization list is not limited to the use of parameters supplied by the client code. Here, the client code supplies only the data used to call the Point general constructor. The value that initializes the data member thickness is defined as a constant literal. This is perfectly okay.

Notice that similar to default values, using literal values in the member initialization list represents a form of pushing responsibility down from client to server class. In this version of the design, it is the programmer of class Rectangle that specifies the thickness of the line to be one. I could replace the literal value with an additional parameter, such as in this version of this constructor.

```
Rectangle::Rectangle (int x1, int y1, int x2, int y2, int width)
  : pt1(x1,y1), pt2(x2,y2), thickness (width) { }
```

In this case, it would become the responsibility of the client code to specify that the thickness of the line should be one.

```
Rectangle r(20,40,70,90,1);    // responsibility is pushed up client
```

The third constructor in the class Rectangle, the default constructor, also demonstrates the use of constant literals as list arguments. When this constructor is used, each Rectangle object is initialized so that its top-left corner is at the point of origin of coordinates, and the bottom-right corner is at the point with coordinates (100,100). The default constructor does not receive any data from the client code. So, it is only natural that all objects initialized with the default constructor are initialized to the same state.

Since class Point provides a default constructor (with zero values of coordinates), the Rectangle initialization list for this constructor could be written this way.

```
Rectangle::Rectangle () : pt1(), pt2(100,100), thickness(1) { }
```

What would happen if you were to skip the initialization list entry for data member pt1? You should recall that the purpose of the member initialization list is to avoid a call to the default constructor of the component class before the call to the composite class constructor. The member initialization list replaces the call to the default constructor of the component class with the call to the constructor specified in the initialization list.

So, in this example of the Rectangle constructor, I am trying to avoid a call to the Point default constructor for member pt1 and replace it with—a call to default constructor for member pt1! It follows that the calls to default constructors in the member initialization list could be omitted. This does not change the sequence of events when the composite class object is constructed. This last version of the Rectangle constructor could be written this way.

```
Rectangle::Rectangle () : pt2(100,100), thickness(1) { }      // same
```

The initializer list syntax here is strange. It is like nothing you have seen before. Many programmers have trouble learning and using this syntax. However, it is an important part of programming with C++ classes.

Tip

Learn the initializer list syntax. It is extremely useful. It allows you to initialize components of a composite object without wasting constructor calls. It is extremely popular in C++ code. Later you will see its use for inheritance. You cannot write meaningful C++ programs without using this syntax. The sooner you learn it, the better off you will be.

You have the option of learning this syntax gradually. The use of initialization lists is optional. Their first goal is to avoid syntax errors when a component default constructor is not present. Their next goal is to avoid the negative impact on performance when the component state is reset in the composite class constructor; that is, their goal is to prevent syntax errors and improve performance. Syntax errors can be avoided by supplying the component class with the default constructor. Performance might not be so important after all.

However, use of the initialization list is mandatory for constant and reference data members.

Data Members with Special Properties

You probably never thought about using constant and reference data members before. The issue did not come up in our previous discussions of software engineering issues. When at the end of the Chapter 8, "Object-Oriented Programming with Functions," I was enumerating the issues that the introduction of C++ classes resolved, I talked about binding data and operations together, introducing class scope for data members and member function names, controlling access to class members, and pushing responsibilities from clients to servers.

All these are legitimate and internally consistent goals related to the support of object-oriented programming principles. In Chapter 9–11 I talked about other (read: unexpected) goals of using classes that also became part of the deal such as automatic initialization of objects, managing heap memory, and treating objects and built-in variables in the same way. But even then I did not mention that, in addition to other actions that C++ classes would allow you to do, you would learn about defining data members as constants or references. It comes as an unexpected bonus for accepting the whole package.

If you feel that you have had enough bonuses and interesting ideas, you can skip the rest of this section and the next one and come back when you feel you are ready for more.

Constant Data Members

The idea behind constant data members is simple. A C++ class bundles together related data members and functions. Functions provide access to data members on behalf of the client code. Often, the client code needs to change the state of the object (e.g., account balance, employee address, total number of movie rentals). Some object characteristics, however, are not intended for change (e.g., account number, employee date of hire, price paid to the vendor for the movie).

The class designer knows that the member functions of the class would not change a specific data member such as account number and so on. The maintainer has to figure that out from studying class member functions and friend functions. It would be a good idea to spare that effort and to indicate explicitly in class code what the designer knows at the time of design: The value of this data member will not be changed by any member function or friend function. This is yet another job for the const keyword.

How do you initialize such a constant data member? If you do it in the class constructor, it is somewhat too late. Recall the story that Figure 12–1 describes. The class constructor is only called after the object is already constructed. What takes place in the body of the class constructor is an assignment, not an initialization. For a constant data member, the assignment should not be allowed. A constant data member has to be initialized immediately after this data member is created. This is why C++ requires you to include the name of the constant data member in the initializer list and flags as a syntax error any assignment to this data member, even in a constructor.

A constant data member can be either a programmer-defined type or a built-in type. This does not really matter for the property I am discussing: initialization immediately after creation of the data member, before the constructor is called, not later on.

As an example of using a constant data member, let us add to the class `Rectangle` an additional data member that describes the weight of the unit of the rectangle area. Since the material the rectangle is made of remains the same during the rectangle's lifetime, this data member will not be changed after the `Rectangle` object is created. To avoid forcing the maintainer to search all class member functions and friend functions to confirm that, the `weight` data member should be defined as constant. Hence, it should be initialized in the member initialization list of `Rectangle` constructor(s).

```
class Rectangle {
   Point pt1;
   Point pt2;
   int thickness;
   const double weight;                          // weight of one unit of area
public:
   Rectangle (const Point& p1, const Point& p2, double wt, int width = 1);
   void move(int a, int b);
   void setThickness(int w=1);
   int pointIn(const Point& pt) const;
   . . . . } ;                                   // the rest of class Rectangle

Rectangle::Rectangle(const Point& p1, const Point& p2, double wt, int width)
   : pt1(p1), pt2(p2), weight(wt)                // weight is not optional here
{ thickness - width; }
```

Notice that I added the extra parameter not at the end of the parameter list but in the middle of the constructor parameter list. Remember that rule that default parameter values are allowed for rightmost parameters only? Had I added the fourth parameter at the end of the parameter list (as in the following line), I would have violated that rule.

```
Rectangle(const Point& p1, const Point& p2, int width=1, double wt);   // wrong
```

The `Rectangle` client code does not change much.

```
Point p1(20,40), p2(70,90);          // top-left, bottom-right corners
Point point(100,120);                // point to catch with the rectangle
Rectangle rec(p1,p2,0.01,4);         // supported by the initializer list
rec.setThickness();                  // line width is 1 pixel (default)
point.move(-25,-15);                 // move the point around the screen
rec.move(10,20);                     // 10 pixels to right, 20 pixels down
if (rec.pointIn(point)) cout << "Point is in\n";     // is point in?
p1.move(30,35);                      // does the rectangle object change?
```

Similar to other uses of the const keyword, the use of constant data members is directed toward making the code self-explanatory. Ideally, you should expect that if a data member does not have the const keyword, this should mean that this data member is modified during the object's lifetime by one of the functions associated with the class. It seems to me that few C++ programmers use constant data members with rigor. Hence, the absence of the const keyword in the data member definition cannot be taken as evidence that the data member changes. It might just be evidence that the programmer was busy with other aspects of class design and did not pay attention to passing as much knowledge to the maintainer as possible.

Reference Data Members

Now let us look at an example of object references used as data members of other objects. This is a good programming implementation of an association among objects where the several client objects are associated with the same server object.

In the previous examples in this chapter, each Rectangle object has its own copy of its corner points. If p1 moves, as on the last line of the previous example, the Rectangle object rec does not change. For many applications, this is exactly how objects should behave. In Chapter 11, you saw that this approach is supported by value semantics.

For other applications, it might be desirable to share points among rectangles. So, if the client code moves the corner point of a rectangle, the rectangle should change. In Chapter 11, you saw that this approach is supported by reference semantics. Many programs designed with the use of object-oriented methodology use reference semantics to implement associations among objects. For example, the account owner data (name, address, social security number, and so on) might be part of the account class. If the owner class is useful for the application, that data can be combined into a class, and an owner object can be used as a data member of the account class. If one owner can have several accounts, the application might want to use only one owner object for these accounts. Then a change to the owner data will automatically propagate to all accounts.

It is to support this kind of client code functionality that you could use reference data members. (Notice how persistently I try to promote the idea that the design of server classes is driven by the needs of the client code, not by the ideas of aesthetics, generality, or performance.) These references can point to the objects outside of the composite object. These external objects can be modified by the client code without the knowledge (or consent) of the composite object.

As I mentioned earlier, all references in C++ are constants. They cannot change after they are initialized. Hence, reference data members (similar to constant data members) must be initialized only in a member initialization list: No initialization in the body of the constructor is allowed. It is too late because the constructor is called after all data members have been constructed and their constructors were called. The new design of class `Rectangle` is very similar to the previous version. The only difference is two ampersand signs after the `Point` type in the data member definitions.

```
class Rectangle {
    Point& pt1;                      // points can be shared with other shapes
    Point& pt2;
    int thickness;
    const int weight;                // weight of one unit of area
  public:
    Rectangle (const Point& p1, const Point& p2,
                  int wid = 1, int wt = 1);
    void move(int a, int b);
    void setThickness(int w=1);
    int pointIn(const Point &pt) const;
    . . . . } ;                      // the rest of Rectangle class
```

```
Rectangle::Rectangle(const Point& p1, const Point& p2, int width, int wt)
    : pt1(p1), pt2(p2), weight(wt)   // this is not optional here
{ thickness = width; }               // same constructor as above
```

Since all references are `const`, there is no special notation for this property. In class `Rectangle`, `pt1` and `pt2` are constant references. They cannot abandon the objects they are pointing to and point to other objects instead. But the objects themselves are not constant. Their contents can change.

Similar to objects pointed to by pointers, the objects pointed to by references can be defined as constant as well. This means that not only do `pt1` and `pt2` point to the same `Point` objects and cannot be switched to other `Point` objects, but the state of these objects cannot be changed either.

```
class Rectangle {
    const Point& pt1;     // points can be shared with other shapes
    const Point& pt2;     // points cannot change their coordinates
    . . . . } ;           // the rest of Rectangle class
```

From a syntactic point of view, the requirements are the same—these data members have to be initialized in the member initialization list. From a semantic point of view, this design does not make much sense. If the corner points are constant, there are no advantages in sharing them with other `Rectangle` objects. They can be made constant members.

```
class Rectangle {
    const Point pt1;        // points are not shared with other shapes
    const Point pt2;        // points cannot change their coordinates
    . . . . } ;             // the rest of Rectangle class
```

A reference to a constant object can be used as an optimization technique. If a large number of composite objects should have the same component object, it might make sense to create only one component object and set up references to this object from all composite objects.

The process of building the object of class `Rectangle` is presented in Figure 12–5. The objects of the type `Point` are created first [Figure 12–5(a)]. Next, the object of class `Rectangle` is created [Figure 12–5(b)]: The references `pt1` and `pt2` are created. They are of different types here than in previous examples, and I am using different sizes of shapes to reflect the differences in types. The initialization list is executed and sets the references to point to `Point` objects, the constant field `weight` is created and initialized, and then the `thickness` file is created. Finally, the `Rectangle` constructor is executed [Figure 12–5(c)] and the value of the thickness field is assigned.

In this design, the references within class `Rectangle` are constants, but the `Point` objects these references are pointing to are not constants. This is why these `Point` objects can change their state, and all `Rectangle` objects

Figure 12–5   Steps for creating a `Rectangle` object with references to external `Point` objects.

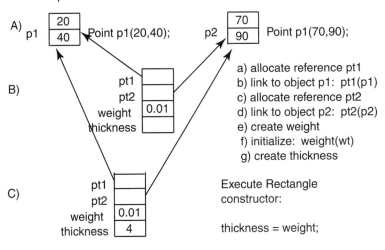

associated with these `Point` objects will change their position on the screen. Using references, however, does not allow a `Rectangle` object to abandon one `Point` object associated with it and use another `Point` object instead. This can be accomplished if the `Rectangle` class uses `Point` pointers instead of references.

```
class Rectangle {
   Point *pt1, *pt2;                // points can be shared with other shapes
   int thickness;
   const int weight;                // weight of one unit of area
public:
   Rectangle (const Point*, const Point*, int = 1, int = 1);
   void move(int a, int b);
   void setThickness(int w=1);
   int pointIn(const Point &pt) const;
   . . . . } ;                      // the rest of Rectangle class
```

```
Rectangle::Rectangle(const Point *p1, const Point *p2,
   int width, int wt)  : pt1(p1), pt2(p2), weight(wt)   // optional again
 { thickness = width; }                // same constructor as above
```

Since pointers can be changed at any point in their lifetime, using the member initialization list here is not mandatory. Still, it is a good practice.

If the objects pointed to by the pointers should remain constant throughout the `Rectangle` object's lifetime, the pointers can be declared as pointers to constant objects.

```
class Rectangle {
   const Point *pt1;        // points can be shared with other shapes
   const Point *pt2;        // point coordinates cannot change
   . . . . } ;              // the rest of Rectangle class
```

This design can provide useful optimization if a large number of `Rectangle` objects is associated with the same `Point` objects.

Do not use constant and reference data members too much. However, they are legitimate design tools wherever they reflect the properties of server objects and the needs of client code.

Using Objects as Data Members of Their Own Class

In the previous sections, I discussed the situation where an object of one class (e.g., `Point`) was used as a data member of another class (e.g., `Rectangle`). Can an object of a class be a member of its own class? For example, the application might need point coordinates that are relative to several focal points on the screen. For each point, the application might want to specify the anchor point as a characteristic of the `Point` object.

```
class Point {
    int x, y;                   // private coordinates
    Point anchor;               // this is not allowed
  public:
    Point (int a=0, int b=0)    // versatile constructor
      { x = a;   y = b; }
  . . . } ;                     // the rest of class Point
```

This is not allowed, however. Remember that story I told you at the beginning of this chapter about the sequence of events when object memory is allocated? Data members are allocated in the order of their definitions in the class specification. (Static members are allocated at the beginning of program execution.) So, when a `Point` object is created, memory for x and y is allocated first, and then memory for `anchor` is allocated. But `anchor` is of type `Point`, so memory for x and y of the `anchor` data member is allocated first, memory is allocated for its `anchor` next, and so on. This recursive process cannot end and hence is disallowed.

References to objects of the object's own class are allowed; so are pointers to objects of the same class. Both pointers and references represent an object address and do not require memory to be allocated for the whole object. Hence, memory for them can be allocated among other data members without additional difficulties.

```
class Point {
    int x, y;                   // private coordinates
    Point &anchor;              // this is reasonable
  public:
    Point (int a=0, int b=0, Point &focus)
      : anchor (focus)          // cannot be set in constructor
      { x = a;   y = b; }
  . . . } ;                     // the rest of class Point
```

As I indicated in the previous section, a reference data member cannot be initialized in the body of the class constructor. This is why I initialize it in the initializer list using a `Point` object that is passed to the constructor as the argument. The constructor parameter should not have the const modifier because the `anchor` data member is not defined as constant. Using the `anchor` reference, the `Point` object can modify the object passed to it as an argument. This is why defining the parameter as constant would be a syntax error.

Notice that here again I am making a popular error by adding a new parameter to the constructor as the rightmost parameter. This parameter does not have a default value and hence should be moved to the left of those parameters with default values.

```
class Point {
    int x, y;                           // private coordinates
    Point &anchor;                      // this is reasonable
  public:
    Point (Point &focus, int a=0, int b=0)      // better order
     : anchor (focus)                   // cannot be set in constructor
     { x = a;   y = b;   }
 . . . } ;                              // the rest of class Point
```

The client code creates the anchor point first and then passes it as an argument to the constructor of new points. The first point has to be its own anchor.

```
Point p1(p1);       // syntax error: p1 is not defined as an argument
```

This is a syntax error. When I use p1 as an argument to the constructor, this object is still in the process of construction, and therefore the reference to it is not yet defined. This is why I allocate the anchor point dynamically.

```
Point *p = new Point(*p,80,90);    // p has no value yet
Point p1(*p);                      // *p is used as the anchor
```

Here I have the same problem—when I use p as an argument to the constructor, it does not have the value yet. However, this is not an error, just a warning. I can easily avoid this warning by initializing the pointer to null before using it.

```
Point *p = 0;              // to avoid warning that pointer p has no value
p = new Point(*p,80,90);   // dynamically allocated Point object
Point p1(*p);              // it is used as the anchor
```

As you see, using a reference data member to an object of the same class sounds like a neat idea, but it creates a number of difficulties because this data structure is inherently recursive. Do not use it unless you absolutely have to.

Using a Static Data Member as a Member of Its Own Class

Using a static data member as a data member of its own class is allowed and is much simpler than using a reference data member. For example, class Point objects can have a point of origin common to all points on the plane.

Because this point of origin is common to all points in the picture, it can be represented as a static data member.

```
class Point {
     int x, y;                          // private coordinates
     static int count;
     static Point origin;               // static object is ok
  public:
     Point (int a, int b)
        { x = a;   y = b;   count++; }  . . . } ;
```

Syntax for static object initialization is the same as that for static members of built-in types. (See Chapter 9 for more discussion of static data members.) The following line of code gives an example of the static object definition and initialization. The first `Point` in this definition represents the type of data member being defined (in this case, `origin`). The second `Point` in this definition indicates that the data member being defined belongs to class `Point`. When the object is created, a constructor is called to initialize its fields. The arguments specified in this definition are passed on as constructor arguments. The number and type of arguments defined what constructor is called. In this case, it is the general `Point` constructor with two parameters.

```
Point Point::origin(640,0);       // initialization using constructor
```

This is similar to the definition of a static data member of a built-in type, for example, `count`. The type of this static field is integer, and the class scope operator indicates that it belongs to class `Point`. The initial value of this field is set to zero.

```
int Point::count = 0;
```

Similar to all other static objects, it is not exactly clear when the object is created and the constructor is called. If there are several static variables in the program, the order of their construction is undefined. Putting them in order in the source code file does not guarantee that they will be created and initialized in this order. What is guaranteed is only that all of them will be constructed before the first statement in `main()` is executed.

In the case of the `Point` class, this guarantee is not sufficient. The `Point` constructor is called not only for nonstatic `Point` objects but also for the static object `origin` that is created first. The `Point` constructor increments the value of `count`. This requires that the static data member `count` be created before the object `origin` is created.

The static nature of a static data member allows it to be used as default argument to a member function of its class, for example, a constructor. A nonstatic data member cannot be used as a default argument to a member function of its own class.

```
class Point {
   int x,y;
   static int count;
   static Point origin;              // static object is ok
   Point &anchor;                    // reference or pointer is ok
public:
   Point (Point &focus = origin, int a=0, int b=0) : anchor(focus)
         { x = a;   y = b;   count++; }
   void set (int a=x, int b)         // error: non-static data member
   { x = a;   y = b; }
      . . . . } ;                    // the rest of class Point
```

Static data members are created before the program starts execution, and access to the static members is possible even if no class objects have been created.

After Point objects are created, the count and origin data members can be accessed using any object—the result is the same because these data members are static. Unlike nonstatic data members, they can be accessed using the class name instead of the target object name.

```
int main()
{ Point p1, p2(70,90);
   cout << "Number of points: " << p1.count << endl;      // prints 2
   cout << "Number of points: " << p2.count << endl;      // prints 2
   . . . }
```

Unlike nonstatic data members, they can be accessed using the class name with the scope operator instead of the target object name with the selector operator.

```
int main()
{ Point p1, p2(70,90);
  cout << "Number of points: " << Point::count << endl;    // it also prints 2!
  . . . }
```

Moreover, this syntax is available when no class objects have been created.

```
int main()
{ cout << "Number of points " << Point::count << endl;     // it prints zero
  . . . }
```

Listing 12.3 shows class Point with two static data members, count and origin. They are initialized outside the class definition even though they are private. Function quantity() is defined as static and can be accessed using the class scope operator (the first call) and a target object (the second call).

Listing 12.3   Using static data members and a static member function.

```cpp
#include <iostream>
using namespace std;


class Point {
    int x, y;                                 // private coordinates
    static int count;
    static Point origin;
  public:
    Point (int a=0, int b=0)                  // general constructor
      { x = a;   y = b;   count++;
        cout << " Created: x=" << x << " y=" << y
             << " count=" << count << endl; }
    static int quantity()                     // const is not allowed
           { return count; }
    void set (int a, int b)                   // modifier function
      { x = a;   y = b; }
    void get (int& a, int& b) const           // selector function
      { a = x;   b = y; }
    void move (int a, int b)                  // modifier function
      { x += a;   y += b; }
  ~Point()                                    // destructor
      { count--;
        cout <<" Point destroyed: x=" <<x <<" y=" <<y <<endl; }
 } ;

int Point::count = 0;                         // initialization
Point Point::origin(640,0);                   // initialization

int main()
{ cout << " Number of points: " << Point::quantity() << endl;
  Point p1, p2(30), p3(50,70);                // point of origin, point objects
  cout << " Number of points: " << p1.quantity() << endl;
  return 0;
  }
```

The results of the program run are shown on Figure 12–6. You see that the variable count is not zero even though no Point object instances have been created explicitly. It is the static object origin that gets counted. This object is created before the first statement in main() is executed. When its constructor is called, the debugging message about its creation is printed on the top of the output. This static data member is destroyed after the program terminates. This is why you do not see the debugging message that reports its destruction.

When I swapped the definitions of variables count and origin, the output of the program did not change.

```
Created: x=640 y=0 count=1
Number of points: 1
Created: x=0 y=0 count=2
Created: x=30 y=0 count=3
Created: x=50 y=70 count=4
Number of points: 4
Point destroyed: x=50 y=70
Point destroyed: x=30 y=0
Point destroyed: x=0 y=0
```

Figure 12–6   Output for program in Listing 12.3.

```
Point Point::origin(640,0);
int Point::count = 0;
```

This means that the compiler was able to trace dependency between these variables and made sure that the variable count was available by the time the Point constructor was executing for the static object origin.

This section talked about rather complex programming techniques. Make sure that you do not use them just because you like a challenge. Have mercy on the maintenance programmer who has to work with your code for years to come.

Container Classes

The previous section discussed a number of special cases for composite class data members that you are not likely to use every day. This section discusses a number of special cases for composite class data members that you are going to use very often. Even if you will not be writing similar classes yourself, you are going to use container classes written by others. *Container classes* are a special case of composite classes, which are useful when the application needs a data type that contains a dynamic collection of values. Almost any application needs one (or more).

Even the first examples of class composition that I discussed in this chapter (e.g., class Rectangle) contained a collection of components, in this case, objects of type Point. However, this collection was not dynamic. The number of Point objects associated with the Rectangle object was always the same: two. Actually, if two Point objects were not available in the client code, it was impossible to create a Rectangle object.

Often the application needs a container or a collection class that can contain a variable number of objects. Usually, a container object is initially empty and has no components. While the application is executing, the component objects become available and are added to the container for temporary storage or for processing.

For example, the container might be the customer charge account, and the components might be customer credit card transactions that should be processed. The processing might include computing totals, taxes, printing reports, and other tasks that include accessing every component in the container in turn. Other popular tasks are testing whether a component with given data is already in the container, removing a component from the container, and making the container available for reuse.

Most of these tasks can be accomplished using a C++ array for data representation. This is a very simple and efficient data type, but it provides too few safeguards for the client code. It does not check the validity of index values. It lacks high-level operations such as appending a component, searching for a component and others. These operations have to be coded by the client code using low-level elementary operations such as assigning a value to the array component, setting the index to the next component, and checking whether the next component is a valid component.

Container classes are designed to perform these operations on behalf of the client code. The client code requests the container to add a component, find a component, and access each component in the collection; and the container object performs these operations, insulating the client code from the low-level details. As a result, responsibility is pushed down from the client code to the server code (container class).

In this section, I will give several examples of simple containers and show how they can be used by the client code.

For simplicity in the examples, I will use components of class `Sample` with only one data member, `value` of type `double`. The `Sample` objects are produced by some external process: stock exchange ticker tape, patient monitoring device, temperature or pressure observations, and so on. In the examples that follow, I will be pulling the values out of the array with pre-wired values.

```
class Sample {                      // component class
  double value;                     // no pointers among data members
public:
  Sample (double x = 0)             // default/conversion constructors
    { value = x; }
  void set (double x)               // modifier
    { value = x; }
  double show () const              // selector
    { return value; } } ;
```

When a class is used as a component in a container, it has to satisfy design requirements that will support the needs of the container object. The most common requirements are the ability to support

- default instantiation
- assignability

The requirement of default instantiation refers to the ability of an object of the component type to be created without any input data from client code. The container class might use a fixed-size array for data representation of the components.

```
Sample data[100];                      // container's data member
```

Another popular design for a container class is the use of a dynamically allocated array of components.

```
Sample *data;                          // container's data member
data = new Sample[100];                // code in container constructor
```

In either case, the component objects are allocated first and filled with data later. To support this requirement, the component class should implement the default constructor. Otherwise, defining an array of component objects results in a syntax error (or a hundred syntax errors).

Consequently, an attempt to create a composite object when the component class does not provide the default constructor results in a syntax error. The syntax error can be eliminated if the member initialization list is used in the container constructor. However, this technique works only when the number of components in the container is known in advance and is not very large. The inherent limitation of the member initialization list is that each component member of the composite class has to be listed in the initialization list, and the component name has to be explicitly mentioned.

Similar to previous examples, the `Sample` class can satisfy this requirement by providing the conversion constructor with the default value of its single parameter.

The requirement of assignability refers to the ability of an object of the component type to be assigned a new state by the client code. Since the components of the container are allocated first and filled with data later, they should support the change in the state of the component. One popular way to support this requirement is to support the assignment operator for the component class.

```
data[i] = s;                           // code in a container method
```

This works for simple classes like `Sample` because it does not have dynamic memory, but might require an overloaded assignment operator if the component class contains pointers and manages heap memory dynamically.

Another technique for supporting assignability is to provide the component class with a modifier function, which would change the state of the component object.

```
data[i].set(s);                    // code in a container method
```

Class `Sample` supports this requirement by providing the method `set()` and by allowing direct assignment without an overloaded assignment operator.

Often, the component class is expected to satisfy two more requirements, that of supporting

- copy instantiation
- total order semantics

Copy instantiation refers to the ability of the component object to be instantiated from another component object. This is supported by providing the component class with the copy constructor. This becomes necessary if the container class has to return a copy of one of its component objects to the client's code. Often, the client's needs might be satisfied with a reference to the component objects rather than with the full-fledged copy. This is why I think that the need for use of the copy constructor in containers is often exaggerated. Copy instantiation rarely occurs in container algorithms. Supporting it will invariably encourage passing object parameters by value or returning the object values from functions with all their negative consequences. I am not advocating just not providing the copy constructor and hoping for the best. This is asking for trouble, especially if the class handles heap memory dynamically. If passing objects by value or returning object values should not be allowed, I recommend the techniques of using private constructors that I described at the end of Chapter 11.

Tip

Do not be in a rush to provide each class with a copy constructor. Copy constructors make your programs slower and more complex. They encourage your clients to use passing parameters by value and returning objects by value. Instead, consider making the copy constructor private. This might eliminate a lot of trouble in the future.

Total order semantics refers to the ability of the client code to compare the component objects between themselves and also with values of built-in types. This is supported by providing the component class with overloaded comparison operators. This is a very useful capability, especially when the client code needs to implement sorting or searching algorithms. I will not implement it in the examples only because I want to limit the size of these examples to keep them understandable and manageable.

In the examples that follow, I will keep the objects of class Sample in the container object of class History. Class History keeps the Sample object in a short array (just eight components for simplicity of the example). It allows the client code to set the Sample value at a given location in the array, to print out the set of measurements, and to compute the average of measurement values.

Listing 12.4 shows the first version of the container class. The output of the program is shown in Figure 12–7.

Listing 12.4 A container class with fixed size component array (and array overflow).

```cpp
#include <iostream>
using namespace std;


class Sample {                           // component class
  double value;                          // sample value
public:
  Sample (double x = 0)                  // default and conversion constructor
    { value = x; }
  void set (double x)                    // modifier method
    { value = x; }
  double get () const                    // selector method
    { return value; } } ;

 class History {                         // container class
   enum { size = 8 };
   Sample data[size];                    // fixed-size array of samples
public:
   void set(double, int);                // modify a sample
   void print () const;                  // print history
   void average () const;                // print average
 } ;

void History::set(double s, int i)
{ data[i].set(s); }                      // or just:  data[i] = s;

void History::print () const            // print history
{ cout << "\n Measurement history:" << endl << endl;
```

```
   for (int i = 0;   i < size;   i++)                    // local index
      cout << "   " << data[i].get(); }

void History::average () const
{ cout << "\n Average value: ";                          // print average
   double sum = 0;                                        // local value
   for (int i = 0;   i < size;   i++)                     // local index
            sum += data[i].get();
   cout << sum/size << endl; }

int main()
{ double a[] = {3, 5, 7, 11, 13, 17, 19, 23, 29 } ;      // input data
   History h;                                             // default constructor
   for (int i=0; i < 9;   i++)                            // 8 slots are available
      h.set(a[i],i);                                      // set history
   h.print();                                             // print history
   h.average();                                           // compute average
   return 0;
   }
```

Notice how the design of the container class `History` implements the algorithms that require access to memory. This means that the code saves some values in memory for future use by another segment of code. Depending on how far these cooperating segments of code are located from each other, the designer winds up with different degrees of coupling between these segments of code (see Chapter 8 for the discussion of coupling and other related software engineering concepts).

In general, the class designer has the following choices for making a value or a variable available to a class method for storing or for retrieving the value:

- global variable or public data member
- method parameter
- class data member
- local variable in the method

Figure 12–7   Output for program in Listing 12.4.

```
Measurement history:

 3  5  7  11  13  17  19  23
Average value: 12.25
```

A global variable could be used when several classes have to share the information but the designer has difficulties deciding to which class this information really belongs. This method of communication between classes represents the highest degree of coupling and should be used as little as possible. A public data member could be used when the designer selects a particular class to house the information, but several other classes also need this information and it is made available to them in the form of a public data member. This degree of coupling is as high as coupling through a global variable is and should be used as infrequently.

When several program classes communicate through global variables or public data members, it should always be viewed as a reason for a design review. The designers should check the distribution of responsibilities among classes. Communications through global variables or public data members should raise suspicions that the design tears apart processing steps that could be put back together so that the need for such "long-distance" communications disappears.

In further discussion, I will concentrate on three other techniques of communications because it is the choice between these three forms of coupling that C++ programmers deal with every day.

Communications through method parameters should be used if the value or the variable must be shared between the class and its client. For example, parameters of the method `History::set()` are shared between the client code `main()` and the `History` class member function `set()`.

This is the highest form of coupling over data when two different classes share the same value. Consistent treatment of this value in two different classes requires the cooperation of the people who design these classes. If both classes are designed by the same person, they may be designed at different times, and this requires the designer to remember a larger number of concerns and limitations.

Wherever possible, this form of coupling should be reduced by merging the uses of the value and the variable within only one class thus eliminating the need to communicate between classes. This is not always possible because the object-oriented program is built as a set of cooperating classes, not totally independent classes. Hence, some communications among program classes are legitimate and helpful. However, the C++ programmer should always think about the extent of communications among classes and be on the lookout for an opportunity to eliminate excessive coupling.

Communications through class data members should be used when the variable must be shared between different methods that belong to the same class. For example, class `Sample` provides each object of the class with memory storage for the data member value. At this point of learning C++, this design decision might already look trivial to you, but keep in mind that this design supports communications between two Sample methods, set() and get(). Whatever value the sample function set() sets (e.g., in the call from set() in class History) is preserved over time. When the client code of class Sample calls the function get() later (e.g., in the methods print() or average() in class History), the function get() gets exactly the same value that was stored in this particular Sample object by its method set().

Similarly, the data member data[] in class History is used for communications among History member functions. Whatever value the History function set() sets, the functions print() and average() retrieve from the same location. This would be possible to achieve by other means. For example, array data[] could be made a local variable in main() or a global variable in the file and passed to History methods as a parameter.

Look, for example, at this version of class History: It does everything that the version in Listing 12.4 does, but it does not keep the array of Sample objects as its data member. Instead, class History receives the data it operates on from its client main().

```cpp
class History {
  enum { size = 8 };                          // size of the data set
public:
  void set(Sample[], double, int) const;      // modify a sample
  void print (const Sample[]) const;          // print history
  void average (const Sample[]) const;        // print average
 } ;

void History::set(Sample data[], double s, int i) const
{ data[i].set(s); }                           // or just:  data[i]=s;

void History::print (const Sample data[]) const    // print history
{ cout << "\n Measurement history:" << endl << endl;
  for (int i = 0;  i < size;  i++)            // local index
    cout << "   " << data[i].get(); }         // parameter data

void History::average (const Sample data[]) const
{ cout << "\n Average value: ";               // print average
  double sum = 0;                             // local value
  for (int i = 0;  i < size;  i++)            // local index
      sum += data[i].get();                   // data from parameter
  cout << sum/size << endl; }
```

However bad, this design is syntactically correct and semantically sound. Its drawback is extensive communications between the class History and its client. The client has to maintain information that in Listing 12.4 was maintained by the class `History`.

```
int main()
{ double a[] = {3, 5, 7, 11, 13, 17, 19, 23, 29 } ;     // 9 values
  Sample data[9];                          // whom should this data belong to?
  History h;                               // default constructor
  for (int i=0; i < 9;  i++)               // 8 slots are used
    h.set(data,a[i],i);                    // set history
  h.print(data);                           // print history
  h.average(data);                         // compute average
  return 0; }
```

It is small errors of this type that tend to accumulate and ruin the quality of C++ programs, turning them into a maze of dependencies between different program components. Make sure you always think about communications among classes when you look at your design.

The last mode of communication in your C++ program, through local variables in a class method, is most benign. It should be used when the member function needs to save a value for future use during the same function call. For example, function `average()` in Listing 12.4 uses the local variables `sum` and `i` to keep track of the array components processed so far and the tally of values accumulated at the particular moment of execution, used as the starting point for further accumulation of the tally for the array components.

Similar to the previous example, this design could have been implemented differently. Consider, for example, the following version of class `History` that provides specialized data members to keep track of the array components and the tally.

```
class History {                     // container class
    enum { size = 8 };
    Sample data[size];              // fixed-size array of samples
    int i;                          // index for method average()
    double sum;                     // tally for method average()
public:
    void set(double, int);          // modify a sample
    void print () const;            // print history
    void average () const;          // print average
  } ;

void History::set(double s, int i)
{ data[i].set(s); }                 // or just:  data[i] = s;

void History::print ()              // it modifies i
{ cout << "\n Measurement history:" << endl << endl;
```

```
  for (i = 0;   i < size;   i++)        // global, not local index
     cout << "   " << data[i].get(); }

void History::average ()               // it modifies sum
{ cout << "\n Average value: ";        // print average
  sum = 0;                             // global value
  for (i = 0;   i < size;   i++)       // global index
                                       sum += data[i].get();
  cout << sum/size << endl; }
```

In this version of design, the method average() accesses global variables (data members) sum and i instead of dealing with automatic variables allocated for the duration of the method execution. This, of course, has some performance implications. Since the space does not have to be allocated each time the function average() is called, this version is somewhat faster. On the other hand, this space is allocated to each History object for the duration of its lifetime and not only for the duration of the function call to average(). This version of average() is easier to write—grab available variables without going to the trouble of defining them. They can also be reused in other functions; for example, the index can be used in the function print().

The major implication is for the quality of design. This is not as bad as using global variables for communicating with other functions. The function average() uses the global variables (data members) sum and i to communicate with itself (with the next iteration through the loop), not with other functions. Still, this design is a symptom of lower quality and is to be avoided. An example of complications that might arise is the desire to reuse the global data members for other purposes (similar to the way I reused the index in function print() to avoid extra declarations), and this reuse might lead to conflicts. The software engineering mentality that C++ supports is, "Let each function define its separate local variables and use these variables how it sees fit without risk of conflict."

Make sure that you always use the lowest degree of coupling possible. If the job can be done using local variables within one member function, do not elevate these local variables to the level of class data members. If several member functions of the same class need access to the same data, implement this data as class data members, and do not pass them as parameters from the class clients. If the member function needs data defined in another class, pass it as a parameter and not as a global variable or another class public data member.

Tip

For communications between different segments of C++ code, use the lowest degree of coupling: through local variables in a method. If this is not sufficient to support data flow, use class data members. Only if this is insufficient, pass information as method parameters. In all cases, avoid the use of global variables.

Let us apply these software engineering principles to the class design in Listing 12.4. Class History is a very simple-minded container class. It does not offer any protection to the client code from overflowing the container or from referring to a nonexistent entry in the array. In this version of the container, there are only eight slots for the Sample objects to be stored in. Despite this limitation, the client code in main() puts nine values into the container. The compiler, of course, could not care less. The operating system ran the code with no visible damage even though the program was incorrect (see Figure 12–7). This is a common problem for applications that use containers. The distribution of responsibilities between the client code and the container class code might vary, but protection from container overflow must be implemented, and this should be the responsibility of the container class, not of the client code.

When a new Sample value is inserted into the container, the client code in Listing 12.4 specifies both the value to insert and the index value to be used for insertion. However, this approach goes against the software engineering principle of pushing responsibilities to the server class, in this case, the History container. For this simple algorithm this probably does not matter (all input values arrive at once, with no interfering operations over the container object), but the client code has other important responsibilities and should not have to watch how much free space the container has. Monitoring the container state should be the responsibility of the container object itself.

From the point of view of the class communication guidelines discussed earlier, this means that the coupling of the interface between the client code and `History::set()` is too high. The client code is forced to pass information about the index as an extra parameter. The next lower degree of coupling, according to the class communications guidelines, is through class data members. To improve the design, I have to keep the information about the index of the next affected `Sample` object in class `History`, not in its client. Tearing apart what must belong together results in extra communications among programmers and in extra coupling among functions.

Listing 12.5 shows a better container design. The method `History::set()` with two parameters is replaced with the method `History::add()` with only one parameter—the value to be inserted at the end of the container. The container has one extra data member, index `idx`, which monitors the memory usage by the container. The client code does not know whether the container is full; it just passes the value to be added to the method `add()`.

Since the client code now does not control the use of container memory, it is the container class which is responsible for keeping track of used and available memory and for control of overflow. Accordingly, the container knows about its memory structure and limitations. In the version of Listing 12.4, where the client code decided where the next value should go, there was no need to initialize the container object. In this version, where the container decides where the next value should go, the container has to be initialized to the empty space to ensure that the first value to arrive will go into the first slot. Accordingly, the class `History` here has a default constructor. In this constructor, the `History` class sets the index `idx` to zero. In method `add()`, the container class checks whether the array is full; if there is free space, `add()` uses yet another free slot and increments the index `idx` to point to the next free slot. If there is no free slot available for the coming data, the method `add()` does nothing and ignores the client request.

Of course, it would be nice to tell the client code whether the attempt to add a `Sample` to `History` succeeded. This would allow the client code to initiate some recovery measures or notify the user of the program. But doing so would be a waste of programmer energy. I avoid that, not because I think that the feedback to the caller is not important, but because I think that memory overflow should not be tolerated at all. All fixed-size arrays should be used for rapid prototyping only. After the algorithm is debugged, these arrays should be replaced by dynamic arrays similar to the way it was done in Chapter 6, "Memory Management: The Stack and the Heap," (unless, of course, it is a real-time system, but that is a different story).

The output of the program in Listing 12.5 is the same as the output of the program in Listing 12.4.

Listing 12.5   A container class with fixed size of component array and overflow control.

```
#include <iostream>
using namespace std;

class Sample {                          // component class
  double value;                         // sample value
public:
  Sample (double x = 0)                 // default and conversion constructor
    { value = x; }
  void set (double x)                   // modifier method
    { value = x; }
  double get () const                   // selector method
    { return value; } } ;

class History {                         // container class: set value
  enum { size = 8 };
  Sample data[size];                    // fixed-size array of samples
  int idx;                              // index of current sample
public:
  History() : idx(0) { }                // make array empty initially
  void add(double);                     // add a sample at the end
  void print () const;                  // print history
  void average () const;                // print average
 } ;

void History::add(double s)
{ if (idx < size)
    data[idx++].set(s); }               // or just:  data[idx++] = s;

void History::print () const
{ cout << "\n Measurement history:" << endl << endl;
  for (int i = 0;  i < size;  i++)      // local index
    cout << "   " << data[i].get(); }

void History::average () const
{ cout << "\n Average value: ";
  double sum = 0;                       // local tally
  for (int i = 0;  i < size;  i++)      // local index
    sum += data[i].get();
  cout << sum/size << endl; }
```

```
int main()
{ double a[] = {3, 5, 7, 11, 13, 17, 19, 23, 29 } ;     // input data
  History h;                                 // default constructor
  for (int i=0; i < 9;  i++)                 // it is protected from overflow
    h.add(a[i]);                             // add history
  h.print();                                 // print history
  h.average();                               // print average
  return 0;
  }
```

Notice the principle of minimum visibility: The container class `History` exhibits as little of its internal structure and memory limitations to its client code as possible.

One important limitation of container classes in Listings 12.4 and 12.5 is that they have to be filled to capacity before the client is allowed meaningful access to components in the container. Container methods `print()` and `average()` iterate over the container array until the end of the array. Another important limitation is that from the point of view of the client code, all operations over components are performed as a single operation. Often, the client code needs to access components individually, performing or skipping operations as appropriate for each component.

The first drawback can be eliminated by adding yet another data member, `count`, to the container class.

```
class History {                      // container class: set value
  enum { size = 8 };
  Sample data[size];                 // fixed-size array of samples
  int count;                         // number of valid elements
  int idx;                           // index of the current sample
public:
  History() : count(0), idx(0) { }   // make array empty
  void add(double);                  // add a sample at the end
  . . . } ;                          // rest of History class
```

This data member `count` is set to zero in the constructor (in the member initialization list). It should be updated each time a new component is added to the container.

```
void History::add(double s)
{ if (count < size                   // check for available space
    data[count++].set(s); }          // use next space, update count
```

Even if the container is not full, the container member functions can use `count` to process the correct number of components. Here, function `average()` uses it to limit the number of components used in the computation.

```
void History::average () const
{ cout << "\n Average value: ";
  double sum = 0;
  for (int i = 0;  i < count;  i++)
      sum += data[i].get();
  cout << sum/count << endl; }
```

The second drawback can be eliminated by providing the iterator methods, methods that allow the client code to visit each component in the container doing whatever job has to be done. Iterator methods come in a large variety of forms.

For iterations over components, I will use the existing data member `idx`, setting it to zero at the beginning of the iteration and incrementing it by one at each step of iteration. For the client code to start the iteration, I will add to the container class the method `getFirst()`:

```
void getFirst()
    { idx = 0; }                     // set to start of data set
```

For the client code to go to the next step of the iteration, I will add to the container class the method `getNext()`:

```
void getNext()
    { ++idx; }                       // move to next element in set
```

For the client code to access the current component in the container, I will add the method `getComponent()`:

```
Sample& getComponent()
    { return data[idx]; }            // get the reference, not value
```

Notice that here I do not return the current object; I return the reference to the current object. This is why I need not worry whether the component class has a copy constructor, and if the component class has the copy constructor, I need not worry whether the copying of the component will take too much time. I just circumvent the whole issue.

To stop the iterations, I have to provide a method that returns true while the iterations can be continued and false when there are no more elements in the container to iterate.

```
bool atEnd()
    { return idx < count; }          // true if there are more elements
```

Then the iteration loop in the client code would look this way.

```
for (h.getFirst();  h.atEnd();  h.getNext())      // go until end
    cout << "   " << h.getComponent().get();       // print components
```

Often, container designers merge functions `getNext()` and `atEnd()` into one function that increments the index and returns true if there are more elements to iterate.

```
bool getNext()
{ return ++idx < count; }       // move to next element in set
```

Listing 12.6 shows the version of the container class with iterator methods. I eliminated the container method `print()` and made the client code responsible for driving the iteration and accessing the state of the component elements. As a result, some of responsibilities were pulled from the container class to the client code. This is not nice, but it is a natural consequence of adding iterator capabilities to the container class.

The output of the program in Listing 12.6 is the same as the output of the program in Listings 12.4 and 12.5.

Listing 12.6   A container class with fixed size of component array and an iterator.

```
#include <iostream>
using namespace std;

class Sample {                      // component class
  double value;                     // sample value
public:
  Sample (double x = 0)             // default and conversion constructor
    { value = x; }
  void set (double x)               // modifier method
    { value = x; }
 double get () const                // selector method
    { return value; } } ;

 class History {                    // container class: set value
   enum { size = 8 };
   Sample data[size];               // fixed-size array of samples
   int count;                       // number of valid elements
   int idx;                         // index of the current sample
public:
   History() : count(0), idx(0) { } // make array empty
   void add(double);                // add a sample at the end
   Sample& getComponent()           // return reference to Sample
   { return data[idx]; }            // can be a message target
   void getFirst()
   { idx = 0; }                     // set to start of data set
   bool getNext()
   { return ++idx < count; }        // move to next element in set
   void average () const;           // print average
} ;
```

```
void History::add(double s)
{ if (count < size)
    data[count++].set(s); }                            // or just:  data[i++] = s;

void History::average () const
{ cout << "\n Average value: ";
  double sum = 0;
  for (int i = 0;  i < count;  i++)
        sum += data[i].get();
  cout << sum/count << endl; }

int main()
{ double a[] = {3, 5, 7, 11, 13, 17, 19, 23, 29 } ;    // input data
  History h;                                           // default constructor
  for (int i=0; i < 9;  i++)
    h.add(a[i]);                                       // add history
  cout << "\n Measurement history:" << endl << endl;
  h.getFirst();                                        // work is pushed up
  do {
     cout << "  " << h.getComponent().get();           // print components
     } while (h.getNext());
  h.average();
  return 0;
  }
```

Some C++ programmers prefer to bind the iterator methods into a separate iterator class and link this iterator class with the container class. I will spare you this increase in design complexity. Instead, I will eliminate the most important limitation of this container design: the limitation on the number of components that the container can contain. In the previous versions of the container, its capacity was fixed at the time the container was created. If the client tried to put into the container more elements than the container could contain, too bad; there was not much that the container class could do.

Actually, this is not too difficult. All that the container class should do is to allocate new space, copy existing data into the new space, get rid of the existing space, and use the new space until it is exhausted. A good strategy for allocating new space would be to double the size of the array.

```
void History::add(double s)
{ if (count == size)
  { size = size * 2;                                   // double size if out of space
      Sample *p = new Sample[size];
    if (p == NULL)
      { cout << " Out of memory\n";  exit(1); }        // test for success
      for (int i=0;  i < count;  i++)
        p[i] = data[i];                                // copy existing elements
      delete [ ] data;                                 // delete existing array
```

```
data = p;                                   // replace it with new array
cout << " new size: " << size << endl; }    // debugging
data[count++].set(s); }                     // use next space available
```

For this algorithm to work, the data member `data` should be a pointer to the dynamically allocated array of `Sample` objects. This requires changes to the constructor.

```
class History {                             // container class: set value
  int size, count, idx;
  Sample *data;                             // dynamic memory
public:
  History() : size(3), count(0), idx(0)     // make array empty
  { data = new Sample[size];                // allocate new space
    if (data == NULL)
      { cout << " Out of memory\n";  exit(1); } }
  . . .} ;                                   // the rest of class History
```

Listing 12.7 shows this version of the container. For simplicity of the example, I set the initial size of the container to a very small value (three components only) to demonstrate how the algorithm works. The output of the program run is shown in Figure 12–8. At the top of the screen shot, you see the debugging messages that report the increase of the size from 3 to 6 (when the fourth value is inserted in the container) and then from 6 to 12 (when the seventh value is inserted in the container.

Listing 12.7   A container class with dynamically allocated memory.

```
#include <iostream>
using namespace std;

#include <iostream>                          // dynamic container of variable size
using namespace std;

class Sample {                               // component class
  double value;                              // sample value
public:
  Sample (double x = 0)                      // default and conversion constructor
    { value = x; }
  void set (double x)                        // modifier method
    { value = x; }
  double get () const                        // selector method
    { return value; } } ;

class History {                              // container class: set value
  int size, count, idx;
  Sample *data;
```

```
public:
  History() : size(3), count(0), idx(0)        // make array empty
  { data = new Sample[size];                    // allocate new space
    if (data == NULL)
       { cout << " Out of memory\n";  exit(1); } }
  void add(double);                             // add a sample at the end
  Sample& getComponent()                        // return reference to Sample
  { return data[idx]; }                         // can be a message target
  void getFirst()
  { idx = 0; }
  bool getNext()
  { return ++idx < count; }
  void average () const;                        // print average
  ~History() { delete [ ] data; }               // return dynamic memory
} ;

void History::add(double s)
{ if (count == size)
  { size = size * 2;                            // double size if out of space
      Sample *p = new Sample[size];
    if (p == NULL)
       { cout << " Out of memory\n";  exit(1); }  // test for success
    for (int i=0;  i < count;  i++)
      p[i] = data[i];                           // copy existing elements
    delete [ ] data;                            // delete existing array
    data = p;                                   // replace it with new array
    cout << " new size: " << size << endl; }    // debugging print
   data[count++].set(s); }                      // use next space available

void History::average () const
{ cout << "\n Average value: ";
  double sum = 0;
  for (int i = 0;  i < count;  i++)
      sum += data[i].get();
  cout << sum/count << endl; }

int main()
{ double a[] = {3, 5, 7, 11, 13, 17, 19, 23, 29 } ;    // input data
  History h;
  for (int i=0; i < 9;  i++)
    h.add(a[i]);                                // add history
  cout << "\n Measurement history:" << endl << endl;
  h.getFirst();                                 // work is pushed up
  do {
    cout << "  " << h.getComponent().get();     // print each component
    } while (h.getNext());
  h.average();
  return 0;
  }
```

```
new size: 6
new size: 12

Measurement history:

  3   5   7   11   13   17   19   23   29
Average value: 14.1111
```

Figure 12-8   Output for program in Listing 12.7.

Notice that dynamic memory management requires the use of the destructor to return dynamic memory to the heap when the container object is destroyed.

More complex designs are also used: The components can be sorted, searched for, deleted, inserted, updated, and compared. Designing container classes is great fun. Using them might be fun too. A significant number of container classes are available from the Standard Template Library. This discussion will serve as a good introduction to the concepts used by the Library.

Nested Classes

Let us go back to the program in Listing 12.5. Notice that instead of adding the iterator functions, the client code in this version of the program does not use Sample objects.

```
int main()
{ double a[] = {3, 5, 7, 11, 13, 17, 19, 23, 29 } ;      // input data
  History h;                                  // default constructor
  for (int i=0; i < 9;   i++)                 // it is protected from overflow
    h.add(a[i]);                              // add history
  h.print();                                  // print history
  h.average();                                // print average
  return 0; }
```

Indeed, it is the History object that has access to class Sample. C++ allows the programmer to define a server class inside a client class so that the nested class name is not visible outside of the aggregate class.

```
class History {
  class Sample {                        // not visible outside of the client scope
    double value;                       // private data: it could be public here
  public:
    Sample (double x = 0)
      { value = x; }
    void set (double x) { value = x; }
    double show () const { return value; }
    } ;                                 // end of the nested class definition
  int size, count, idx;
  Sample *data;
public:
  History() : size(3), count(0), idx(0)   // make array empty
  { data = new Sample[size];           // allocate new space
    if (data == NULL)
      { cout << " Out of memory\n";   exit(1); } }
    . . .} ;                           // the rest of class History
```

The nested class definitions can appear in either the private or public part of a client class. In either case, the nested class is hidden from the rest of the program; the class name is known only within the scope (braces) of the composite class where the nested class is defined.

The nested classes cannot be used to declare variables of their type in other scopes outside of the composite class. We hide class definitions the same way we hide data members. Hence, if the name has to be used outside of the class where it is defined, the scope operator should be used.

```
int main()
{ double a[] = {3, 5, 7, 11, 13, 17, 19, 23, 29 } ;     // input data
  History h;                          // default constructor
  for (int i=0; i < 9;   i++)         // it is protected from overflow
    h.add(a[i]);                      // add history
    h.print();                        // print history
    h.average();                      // print average
  Sample s = 5;                       // not ok for a nested class
  History::Sample s = 5;              // scope operator resolves the problem
  return 0; }
```

To make the last statement legal, class Sample has to be defined in the public section of its client class History. Then the client code of class History would be able to use the name Sample qualified with the name of the aggregate class.

C++ allows you to combine class definition with definitions of class instances in the same statement. However, this is not a good practice because these instances are often global.

```
class Sample {                        // global in a file
   double value;
public:
   Sample (double x = 0)
     { value = x; }
   void set (double x)
     { value = x; }
   double show () const { return value; }
   } s1,s2;                           // global objects of class Sample
```

This is quite appropriate, though, to nested classes because data members are normally global within the class scope.

```
class History {
   class Sample {          // not visible outside of the client scope
      double value;
   public:
      Sample (double x = 0)
        { value = x; }
      void set (double x)
        { value = x; }
      double show () const
        { return value; }
      } *data;                 // defining data members at the end
   int size, count, idx;
public:
   History() : size(3), count(0), idx(0)    // make array empty
   { data = new Sample[size];               // allocate new space
      if (data == NULL)
        { cout << " Out of memory\n";   exit(1); } }
   . . .} ;                              // the rest of class History
```

Do not overuse this feature—it might result in obscure code.

If other classes need to use the component class as their server class, the component class should not be defined as nested. If other classes do not need the component class, nested classes do not provide any additional benefits. However, the use of nested classes allows us to avoid name conflicts where several parts of the program would like to use the same class name for totally different purposes. Then the name of the nested class does not pollute the program name space.

For example, some other class might use the name Sample to define other measurement results, with a different sensor, different type of value, and even different number of values. The class Sample above might not fit the requirements, and that part of the program might need its own class Sample. To resolve the conflict, have two different class names, for example, Sample1 and Sample2. It might be more convenient to use only one name and make it a nested class.

Class names like class Node are also popular for a component for a linked list. If the same class Node is useful for another linked structure (e.g., a stack or a binary tree), then class Node should be declared in the global name space. Often, different linked structures contain different items of information, and the same Node class cannot serve them all.

In this situation, it might be advantageous to define a Node class as a local class in each of container classes. This would eliminate potential name conflicts. Elimination of global names decreases the intensity of coordination among programming teams developing different container classes.

```
struct Node {          // a good candidate to be a nested class
  char* value;         // pointer to information contents (e.g., a word)
  Node* next; } ;      // pointer to next node
```

Friend Classes

The designer of the class should provide enough access to the class to satisfy the needs of its clients without opening it up to creating unnecessary dependencies.

Putting data members in the public section of a class is relatively rare; it provides too much access without explicitly specifying who utilizes the access. If a debugging problem arises, it is not clear which clients should be inspected; if data representation changes, the list of clients affected is not obvious.

This is why most nonmember functions (global or members of other classes) can only access the public section of a class. The use of private data and functions is possible only through public member functions.

Accessing nonpublic class members through the class member functions might make client code more cumbersome. As you saw in Chapter 11, C++ provides a mechanism to expand access to the private part of the class. When you declare a nonmember function as a friend to the class, it has the same access privileges as a member function of the class.

It does break encapsulation and should be used sparingly. On the other hand, the list of friends is an explicit part of the class definition; it is available for inspection and can be used to identify affected clients, if necessary. Since a friend function accesses private data of class objects, it is quite worthless if used outside the context of the class.

Friends are not restricted to stand-alone global functions. Friend functions can be members of another class. A member function of one class can become the friend of another.

You can declare all of the functions of one class to be friends of another class. Then the member functions of that class will be able to access private members of another class without using access functions.

It is all right to designate only some of the client's member functions as friends of the server class. (A forward declaration is needed.)

When a class is used as a server by only one client class, the design of both the client class and the server class can be simplified if the client class is made a friend of the server class, then each member function of the client class (e.g., `History`) can access nonpublic members of the server class (e.g., `Sample`). The syntax includes the use of the keyword `friend` that precedes the class name (in any section of the server class).

```
class Sample {
        friend History;            // friend declaration
    double value;
  public:
    Sample (double x = 0)
      { value = x; }
    void set (double x)
      { value = x; }
    double show () const
      { return value; }
    } ;
```

This is a syntax error unless class `History` is already defined. However, class `History` cannot be defined before class `Sample` because class `History` uses the name `Sample`.

```
class History {
    int size, count, idx;
    Sample *data;                      // circular dependency
  public:
    History() : size(3), count(0), idx(0)    // make array empty
    { data = new Sample[size];               // allocate new space
      if (data == NULL)
        { cout << " Out of memory\n";  exit(1); } }
    . . .} ;                          // the rest of class History
```

This is a typical example of circular dependency in code—class `History` uses the name `Sample` and hence needs `Sample` defined before the definition of class `History`. On the other hand, class `Sample` uses the name `History` and hence needs `History` defined before the definition of the class `Sample`.

There are two ways to tell the compiler what `History` in the definition of `Sample` means. One is to use a forward declaration, in which you specify that a name is a class name. Here, the name `History` is defined as a class name without further detail.

```
class History;                    // class is declared elsewhere

class Sample {
      friend History;             // friend declaration
    double value;
  public:
    Sample (double x = 0)
      { value = x; }
    void set (double x)
      { value = x; }
    double show () const
      { return value; }
     } ;
```

Another way to resolve this problem is to specify directly in the friend declaration itself that History is a class.

```
class Sample {
      friend class History;       // friend declaration
    double value;
  public:
    Sample (double x = 0)
      { value = x; }
    void set (double x)
      { value = x; }
    double show () const
      { return value; }
     } ;
```

It would be nice to have only one way to do things. It would be even nicer if the linker were able to resolve these cross-references.

Now the History member functions can access the Sample nonpublic data directly.

```
void History::print () const
{ for (int i = 0;  i < count;  i++)       // print valid elements only
//      cout << " " << data[i].show();
        cout << " " << data[i].value;     // no need to use methods
    cout << endl; }
```

Moreover, class Sample no longer needs to provide access member functions. Its friend History does not need them.

```
class Sample {
      friend class History;       // friend declaration
    double value;
  public:
    Sample (double x = 0)
      { value = x; }              // no need for other member functions
     } ;
```

Software engineering and programming methodologies look with suspicion at friends because friends presumably break information hiding. They do make design more complex and harder to study.

Instead of using friends, class `Sample` can be made a nested class in `History` with public fields. Since no other class but `History` can access these fields, information hiding is preserved.

```
class History {
  intsize, count, idx;
  struct Sample {                      // not visible outside of the client
scope
    double value;                      // data member IS public here
  Sample (double x = 0)
    { value = x; } } *data;            // dynamic History data
public:
  History() : size(3), count(0), idx(0)   // make array empty
  { data = new Sample[size];          // allocate new space
    if (data == NULL)
      { cout << " Out of memory\n";  exit(1); } }
    . . .} ;                           // the rest of class History
```

The implementation of `History` member functions here is as in the previous version—they have full access to `Sample` nonpublic members.

Use friends with caution; investigate other alternatives.

Summary

In this chapter, we looked at the use of C++ classes as components of a relationship: class composition. This is the way we should think of classes—not as stand-alone segments of code but as cooperating components related to each other.

The relationship of aggregation is one of the most popular relationships among classes. Using class objects as data members of other classes poses a number of technical and conceptual issues: how to define class components and how to initialize them to the appropriate state so that they can be used by their client, the component class.

We also looked at other ways to link class objects using pointers and references. This is even a more powerful technique of setting up relationships among objects, and it is very popular in practice. A detailed discussion of these programming techniques would take us too far from studying C++ syntax. But rest assured that wherever your professional programming career takes you, you will be putting objects inside other objects and you will be connecting objects with pointers and references.

We also looked at a special case of class aggregation, a container class that contains a set of component objects. This is also a very rich relationship among classes that can be implemented in a variety of ways. Again, wherever you go, you are going to build container classes or use library containers or both.

Enjoy using them.

SIMILAR CLASSES: HOW TO TREAT THEM

Chapter 13

I n this chapter, as in the previous ones, you are going to see more C++ syntax—keywords, colons, initialization lists, and the like. Make sure that this flood of syntactic details does not hide from you an important shift in the focus of your attention.

In the first part of this book, you learned computational aspects of C++. You learned about such traditional programming topics as data types, identifiers, keywords, expressions, statements, conditional statements, loops, and other control constructs. The skills of using these tools are necessary prerequisites to anything else you would like to do in any programming language, not only in C++. These skills allow you to create code that accomplishes the program goal and produces necessary results in terms of computational requirements.

Also in the first part of the book, you studied the methods of aggregation—putting data components together into arrays, structures, and other programmer-defined types, and putting statements and control constructs together into functions. Doing this in C++ is more complex than in other languages, especially when it comes to handling name scopes, passing parameters, returning values, pointers, and references. You also became familiar with the joys and perils of C++ dynamic memory management. These are the tools that are directed towards breaking the program into cooperating parts; however, the tools are directed more toward the programmers' convenience than toward achieving the computational goals of the program. The computational goals could be achieved by a variety of design alternatives, but the quality of the program (from the point of view of its maintainability) might be quite different.

The skill of combining C++ coding elements correctly and separating coding elements that should not belong together is a necessary prerequisite for writing maintainable and modifiable C++ programs.

In the second part of the book, you studied how to apply what you learned in the first part of the book to writing C++ classes. You studied class syntax, class scope, data members, member functions, access to data and functions, messages with their syntax and meaning, object initialization, different kinds of constructors and destructors, static data, and functions. You learned about operator functions, which make C++ code so much nicer but which make the design of classes so much more complex. You learned about friends. You also learned how to recognize dangerous elements of class design and how to avoid their negative consequences for your programs. Writing programs with classes makes C++ much, much more complex than other languages, but it is worth the trouble.

The skill of putting together (into the same class) related data and functions is a necessary prerequisite for writing object-oriented programs. The major difference between traditional and object-oriented programs is that traditional C++ programs are built from cooperating global functions that bind together the steps of each operation. In contrast, object-oriented programs are built from cooperating classes that bind together data and operations over that data.

However, the first two parts of the book were only a prelude to object-oriented programming. In all examples, you dealt with only one class because you were concentrating on the details of class design rather than on relationships among classes. In the third part of the book, you began studying the building of C++ programs as sets of cooperating classes. This requires implementing relationships among classes in a C++ program. In Chapter 12, "Composite Classes: Pitfalls and Advantages," you saw how one object (server object) could be used as a component of another object (its client object). The member functions of the component object provide services to the member functions of the composite class. This is the most common simple relationship among objects.

One object can also be pointed to by a pointer, which is a data member of the another object. The client object gains access to the member functions of the server object by sending messages to its pointer data member. One object can also be used as a reference data member of the client object. Syntactically, this is similar to simple class composition, but actually this is a very different relationship between the objects.

With simple class composition, the server object (a component) is a data member of the client object (a composite object). In this relationship, the client object has an exclusive use of its component object. When the server object is a reference (or a pointer) data member of the client object, the server object might be shared between several client objects; several objects can point to the same server object. The changes to the server object affect the state of the client object (or several client objects). It does not make sense to discuss which relationship is "better" in general, exclusive composition or sharing of components. For many practical situations, however, one relationship is "better" than another in the sense that it better represents the relationship between real-life entities modeled by the C++ program. It is important to choose the relationship that best models the real-life objects.

We also looked at a very popular relationship between objects, when one object is implemented as a container, and a set of objects of another class (rather than a single object) serves as a component of this container. This relationship between objects is often found in C++ programs, and you should feel comfortable arranging the objects in your application in their appropriate relationships.

In this chapter, we will continue the study of cooperation between the parts of C++ code. You will be introduced to C++ inheritance as a mechanism to represent the relationship among classes of the application. At this stage, the difference between the relationship between objects and the relationship between classes might look vague to you. By the end of this chapter you will see the difference.

Inheritance is used very often in C++ programs—and rightly so. This is a powerful mechanism for reusing C++ designs, for labor division among programmers, and for introducing modularity into C++ programs. To use inheritance correctly, you should learn its syntax, methods of instantiation of derived objects, techniques of access to components, rules for function call resolution, and much more. It is also important to learn how to decide whether to use inheritance at all or whether class composition will do the job better. For all the power and utility of inheritance, C++ programmers may sometimes overuse inheritance in situations where the use of inheritance results in creating additional relationships and dependencies that make the program harder to understand.

See for yourself.

Treating Similar Classes

Our programs model a variety of real-life objects through their data (object state) and operations (object behavior). This is a mantra of object-oriented design, but it is up to each designer to decide what to include in each class. The modeling of real-life entities should ideally reflect "common features" among real objects, for example, among inventory items, event counters, or bank accounts.

These "common features" are of course in the eye of the beholder, and C++ has different mechanisms for representing different degrees of similarity among entities.

The first mechanism that C++ offers for capturing the common features among real-life objects is the class construct itself. We use the class construct to capture commonality of objects when we believe that these objects can be characterized by the same sets of attributes and the same patterns of behavior. These objects are different in values of state attributes: The corner points of the different rectangles have different coordinates, different inventory items have different titles, and each account has its own balance and its own account owner. The common elements are that each rectangle has corner points, each item has a title, and each account has a balance and an account owner. If one account needs the interest rate to be specified and another account does not, these two accounts normally should not be viewed as objects of the same class.

Often, the situation is not clear cut. For example, each bolt in an inventory might have its own individual characteristics that make it different from all other bolts in the application. You need to design a separate class for each bolt object, give each class an individual set of data members and member functions that describe each bolt, and create a set of unique names for each class. These names might reflect the unique nature of each bolt in the application, for example, `RustyBolt`, `UglyBolt`, and `BoltFoundInPothole`. This may be complicated and make sense only if different bolts do not have common features and each bolt behaves differently.

However, if the bolts in the inventory have enough in common that you can represent each bolt using the same names for data members as for data members of other bolts in the application, this removes the need to represent each bolt as an object of a different class. You might get away with using only one class, for example, `Bolt`, and represent each bolt in your application as an object of that class, with such attributes as the date of purchase, the name of the vendor, and pitch. Similarly, you can represent all nuts in the inventory as objects of the same class, Nut, if the same set of attributes (color, material, size, etc.) sufficiently describes each nut object.

If it turns out that class Bolt, class Nut, and other inventory items use the same names for their data members, you might abandon the idea of distinguishing between nuts and bolts and use only one class, InventoryItem, to represent these diverse objects. If all the bolts are the same from the point of view of the application, you can represent them as a single object and specify the quantity of bolts among the attributes of the class. Since all the bolts are the same, the differences in pitch are not important. If pitch is important, this design cannot be used.

If all that is of interest to the application is the total cost of nuts and bolts and other inventory items, we can represent inventory as an object of type Asset, with attributes appropriate for the goals of the application.

Often, however, commonalities might exist among classes: The groups of objects might have basically similar but still somewhat different sets of attributes and operations.

For example, small bolts might have their weight specified per 100 bolts, and large bolts might have their weight specified per each bolt, and they might have an attribute for the maximum force allowed to be applied to a large bolt.

Similar, hourly employees might have their pay rate hourly and the number of hours worked during the week specified as data members. Salaried employees might have all the same attributes (name, address, date of hire, etc.), but instead of pay per hour and number of hours worked, they might have salary per year specified.

Some object groups might have somewhat different sets of operations or provide additional operations. For example, savings accounts might pay interest, and checking accounts might charge transaction fees. Simply merging all these characteristics into one class will satisfy the client code requirements but is inherently unsafe. The client code might use the object incorrectly, assuming the presence of the features that are there for other objects but that are not there for this particular object. For example, the client code might try to pay interest on the checking account and charge transaction fees on the savings account.

Still, merging all attributes and operations into one class to provide for all possible alternatives is a viable method of abstraction. It is up to the client code to make sure that each object is used according to its inherent characteristics.

Merging Subclass Features into One Class

As an example, let us consider something everyone is familiar with (or so I hope) either from first-hand experience or heard from others.

I will discuss a simplified class Account with a data member balance and member functions withdraw() and deposit(). For a checking account, the withdrawal operation should impose a charge (i.e., 20 cents). For a savings account, the daily interest is added (i.e., at the yearly rate of 6%). The values for charge and interest rate are represented as data members in the Account class. For simplicity of the example, I am not discussing the techniques for specifying and changing the numerical literals and other countless practical details such as the owner name, address, age, social security number, overdraft fee, and other grim (and cheerful) details of the banking business.

Listing 13.1 shows a program that implements the properties of both savings and checking accounts in the combined class Account. The client code defines Account objects and performs appropriate operations. This kind of client code is typical of pre-object-oriented standards of programming, which reflected our belief (often groundless) that humans always use variables correctly.

Listing 13.1   Example of combining diverse features in the same class Account.

```
#include <iostream>
using namespace std;

class Account {

   double balance;                              // for all kinds of accounts
   double rate;                                 // for savings account only
   double fee;                                  // for checking accounts only

public:

   Account(double initBalance = 0)              // for checking accounts only
   { balance = initBalance; fee = 0.2; }        // use fee but not rate

   Account (double initBalance, double initRate) // for savings
   { balance = initBalance;  rate = initRate; } // no fee here

   double getBal()
   { return balance; }                          // common for both accounts

   void withdraw(double amount)                 // common for both accounts
   { if (balance > amount)
        balance -= amount; }
```

```
  void deposit(double amount)                    // common for both accounts
  { balance += amount; }

  void payInterest()                             // for savings accounts only
  { balance += balance * rate / 365 / 100; }
  void applyFee()
   { balance -= fee; }                           // for checking accounts only
  } ;
int main()
{
  Account a1(1000), a2(1000,6.0);                // a1: checking, a2: savings
  cout << "Initial balances: " << a1.getBal()
       << " " << a2.getBal() << endl;
  a1.withdraw(100);  a2.deposit(100);            // no problem
  a2.payInterest();  a1.applyFee();              // no errors
  cout << "Ending balances: " << a1.getBal()
       << " " << a2.getBal() << endl;
  return 0;
  }
```

Today, we no longer believe in human infallibility. If something can be typed in, somebody, someplace, sometime will type it in. For example, the fifth line of the client code above could have been written this way:

```
a1.payInterest();  a2.applyFee();  // miss takes a maid (joke)
```

You cannot, of course, prevent all coding mistakes (this is why testing is needed), but you should prevent as many as possible. Or at least make sure that you are notified of errors without the need to compute the actual output. This design needs to be improved.

Notice that the client code makes an explicit comment about the nature of each account when the account is created, but nothing in this design would allow the client programmer to express this idea in code rather than comments. For this to become possible, the server class (in this case, `Account`) should support the needs of the client by assuming the responsibility to explicitly distinguish between different kinds of `Account` objects.

Pushing Responsibility for Program Integrity to the Server

To avoid the danger of incorrect use of a server object by the client code, you can add to the server class an additional attribute, a tag field, which describes what kind of account this particular object is. This means that you are introducing subclasses to the class.

When an object is created, this tag field could be set to indicate the object subclass during the object initialization. When the object is used (e.g., `payInterest()` or `applyFee()`), this field is checked to make sure that the operation is legal for this kind of object.

For example, when an `Account` object is created, I could set the tag field to zero if the object were going to be used as a checking account. If the object were going to be used as a savings account, I would set the tag field to one. This means that the constructor should somehow know what kind of `Account` object is being created.

In this example, I can make clever use of the fact that the constructors for two different kinds of accounts have a different number of parameters. Also, using numeric values for the tag field is not good software engineering practice. The designer of the code knows that zero means checking and one means savings. All others run the risk of being confused. How can the designer pass the knowledge (in this case, which tag value means checking and which tag value means savings) to the maintainer? This is what enumeration types are used for in C++. I make a field of the enumeration type `Kind` local to class `Account`. Because the type `Kind` is not going to be used outside of class `Account`, I nest the enumeration type `Kind` within class `Account`. This name does not pollute the global name space and does not prevent someone else on the project from using this name elsewhere.

```
class Account {
   enum Kind { CHECKING, SAVINGS } ;                // constants for account kind
   double balance;
   double rate, fee;
   Kind tag;                                        // tag field for object kind
public:
   Account(double initBalance = 0)                  // checking account
   { balance = initBalance;   fee = 0.2;
      tag = CHECKING;  }
   Account (double initBalance, double initRate)    // savings account
   { balance = initBalance;   rate = initRate;
      tag = SAVINGS;   }
   . . . } ;                                        // the rest of Account class
```

If it were not for this stroke of luck, the type `Kind` would be made available to the client code as well, and the client code would explicitly specify what kind of account is being created. This means that the constructor code would include a parameter for the account kind.

Let me make the example more difficult (and realistic) by assuming that the initial interest rate is the same for all savings accounts (of this kind) and hence does not have to be specified by the client code. Because of this, class `Account` needs only one constructor. Because of this, the client code has to specify the kind of account object. Because of this, the type `Kind` should be made global (and pollute the global name space, thus increasing the need for cooperation among team members). Here is how this new class `Account` looks:

```
enum Kind { CHECKING, SAVINGS } ;                    // constants for account kind

class Account {
  double balance;
  double rate, fee;
  Kind tag;                                          // tag field for object kind
public:
  Account(double initBalance, Kind kind)             // one constructor only
  { balance = initBalance;  tag = kind;              // set the tag field
    if (tag == CHECKING)
       fee = 0.2;                                     // it is checking account
    else if (tag == SAVINGS)
       rate = 6.0; }                                  // it is savings account
  . . . } ;                                           // the rest of Account class
```

Notice that I resist the temptation to use the same memory location for the interest rate if this is a savings account object and for the check cashing fee if this is a checking account object. If the application had to handle a large number of `Account` objects in memory and memory were at a premium, this could be considered too. Otherwise, it would just introduce additional dependencies to the code. Avoid alternative uses of memory.

Now the client code explicitly uses the enumeration values to specify what kind of `Account` object is being constructed. Notice that comments became redundant—they would only repeat what the code designer has now expressed in code so that the designer's knowledge is transmitted to the maintainer.

```
Account a1(1000,CHECKING);      // a1 is checking account
Account a2(1000,SAVINGS);       // a2 is savings account
```

Polluting of the name space by the enumeration type `Kind` can be avoided even when the client code needs to use the values of this type as in the example above. One way to achieve this is to make the type local in class `Account` again.

```
class Account {
  double balance;
  double rate, fee;
  Kind tag;                                          // tag field for object kind
public:
  enum Kind { CHECKING, SAVINGS };                   // constants for account kind
  Account(double initBalance, Kind kind)             // one constructor only
  { balance = initBalance;  tag = kind;              // set the tag field
```

```
        if (tag == CHECKING)
            fee = 0.2;                        // it is checking account
        else if (tag == SAVINGS)
            rate = 6.0; }                     // it is savings account
    . . .    } ;                              // the rest of Account class
```

The client code now has to use the class scope operator when using the enumeration literal values as constructor arguments.

```
Account a1(1000,Account::Kind::CHECKING);    // a1 is checking account
Account a2(1000,Account::Kind::SAVINGS);     // a2 is savings account
```

For this design to fly, the type Kind cannot be defined in the private part of class Account as I did in the first example of the Account class with two constructors. The type has to be public for its literals to be accessible in the client code. Notice that the use of this type inside the class Account (for data member tag) does not have to follow the definition of the type. Although C++ compilers are one-pass compilers, they give you a break by making two passes inside the class definition.

This is true, however, only for newer compilers. Some older compilers might give you a hard time by complaining that type Kind in the definition of the field tag is not defined. For these compilers, the definition of the type Kind should precede the definition of the field tag. To make this definition visible in the client code, it has to be placed in the public part of the class definition. To reconcile these contradicting requirements, you can have additional public and private sections in the class definition.

```
class Account {
  double balance;
  double rate, fee;
public:
  enum Kind { CHECKING, SAVINGS };           // constants for account kind
private:
  Kind tag;                                  // tag field for object kind
public:
  Account(double initBalance, Kind kind)     // one constructor only
  { balance = initBalance;   tag = kind;     // set the tag field
    if (tag == CHECKING)
        fee = 0.2;                           // it is checking account
    else if (tag == SAVINGS)
        rate = 6.0; }                        // it is savings account
  . . .    } ;                               // the rest of Account class
```

With the object tag field properly initialized in the constructor, the designer of class Account can now protect the client code from its own inconsistencies. To make sure the client programmer does not erroneously charge the fee after a call to `withdraw()` for a savings account object, the server class (class `Account`) checks the nature of the object and applies the fee to a checking account only.

```
void withdraw(double amount)          // common for both accounts
{ if (balance > amount)
    { balance -= amount;
      if (tag == CHECKING)            // for checking accounts only
          balance -= fee; } }
```

As you can see, the functionality of `applyFee()` is now provided by the member function `withdraw()` so that the client programmer does not have to remember for what kind of object it has to be called. I hope that you recognize the concepts of information hiding and pushing responsibility down to the server at work here.

Similarly, the method `payInterest()` checks whether the object that is the target of the message is a savings account. If it is, the interest for the day is paid. If the account is a checking account, a run-time error message is printed notifying the tester that the client programmer made a mistake calling this function on a wrong object, and the operation is aborted.

Notice the terminology. It is the designer of the `Account` class who does the work on behalf of the client code. In pre-object-oriented programming days, the client code had to protect itself (or make sure there were no errors). In object-oriented programming days, we push responsibility from the client code to the server class. This is a very common design approach. Make sure you feel comfortable using it.

Listing 13.2 shows the implementation of class `Account` that applies this technique to the validation of client actions. Notice that the `Kind` type is defined outside of class `Account`. The output of the program run is shown in Figure 13–1.

Listing 13.2   Example of run-time test of correctness of client code.

```
#include <iostream>
using namespace std;

enum Kind { CHECKING, SAVINGS } ;          // constants for account kind

class Account {
  double balance;
  double rate, fee;
  Kind tag;                                // tag field for object kind
```

```
public:
  Account(double initBalance, Kind kind)
  { balance = initBalance;   tag = kind;        // set the tag field
    if (tag == CHECKING)
        fee = 0.2;                              // for checking account
    else if (tag == SAVINGS)
        rate = 6.0; }                           // for savings account

  double getBal()
  { return balance; }                           // common for both accounts

  void withdraw(double amount)                  // common for both accounts
  { if (balance > amount)
      { balance -= amount;
        if (tag == CHECKING)                    // for checking accounts only
            balance -= fee; } }

  void deposit(double amount)
  { balance += amount; }

  void payInterest()                            // for savings account only
  { if (tag == SAVINGS)
      balance += balance * rate / 365 / 100;
    else if (tag == CHECKING)
      cout << " Checking account: illegal operation\n";   }
  } ;

int main()
{
  Account a1(1000,CHECKING);                     // a1 is checking account
  Account a2(1000,SAVINGS);                       // a2 is savings account
  cout << " Initial balances: " << a1.getBal()
       << "  " << a2.getBal() << endl;
  a1.withdraw(100);   a2.deposit(100);            // no problem
  a1.payInterest();   a2.payInterest();           // is this any good?
  cout << " Ending balances: " << a1.getBal()
       << "  " << a2.getBal() << endl;
  return 0;
  }
```

Figure 13–1   Output for program in Listing 13.2.

```
Initial balances: 1000  1000
Checking account: illegal operation
Ending balances: 899.8  1100.18
```

Because the type `Kind` is now global, the client code can specify the kind of the account using the identifiers `CHECKING` and `SAVINGS` only in the constructor calls.

```
Account a1(1000,CHECKING);          // a1 is checking account
Account a2(1000,SAVINGS);           // a2 is savings account
```

This, of course, is simpler than what I had to use earlier, when the type `Kind` was local (`Account::Kind::CHECKING` and `Account::Kind::SAVINGS`).

It is simpler to write. But the previous version clearly communicates to the maintainer that these enumeration literals belong to class `Account` and not to any other server class. This version is simpler to write, but the designer has to coordinate the use of global name `Kind` with other designers who might want to use this name for other purposes. As I said in Chapter 1, "Object-Oriented Approach: What's So Good About It?", the modern approach to programming favors verboseness over conciseness if conciseness were to lead to an increase in coordination and to more effort in understanding code. I am not saying that you should always prefer verbose code. I am saying that you should always weigh conciseness against increase in coordination and decrease in understandability.

With merging data and operations of different subtypes in one class, each server method enforces its legal operations; the system does not crash, and there is an opportunity for graceful degradation (or, at least, a reasonable run-time error message). However, the server class needs additional code for type analysis; each method enforces legal operations independently of others, according to the tag value for a given object. For a large system with a large number of object kinds, with a large number of methods that depend on the kind of the object, the server code becomes unwieldy.

Class `Account` knows too many unrelated things about how to treat objects of different subtypes (checking and savings accounts). The amount of information for the designer and the maintainer to maintain is too broad. If you need to add yet another kind (subtype) of the object, you have to expand each method of the existing class. When unrelated parts of code are affected, a great deal of regression testing becomes necessary.

The major problem with this approach is that client coding errors are still run-time errors, not compile-time errors. Someone has to be there to read these error messages. Someone has to see to it that the client code is changed. It would be nice to design the server class so that incorrect use of different kinds of objects would result in syntax errors, not run-time errors.

Separate Classes for Each Kind of Server Object

A good solution to this problem is to design a set of separate classes, so that each class implements a specialized class rather than all properties of all subclasses of objects. For this example, this means designing classes, for example, `CheckingAccount` and `SavingsAccount`.

Each of these classes is designed from scratch. `CheckingAccount` contains everything related to running a checking account with no attempt to include facilities related to running a savings account.

```
class CheckingAccount {
  double balance;
  double fee;                               // no interest rate
public:
  CheckingAccount(double initBalance)
  { balance = initBalance;   fee = 0.2; }   // a checking account
  double getBal()
  { return balance; }                       // common for both accounts
  void withdraw(double amount)
  { if (balance > amount)
      balance = balance - amount - fee; }   // unconditional fee
  void deposit(double amount)
  { balance += amount; }
} ;
```

Similarly, class `SavingsAccount` contains everything necessary for supporting the savings account functionality and pays no attention to the needs of clients having checking accounts.

```
class SavingsAccount {
  double balance;
  double rate;                              // no checking fee
public:
  SavingsAccount(double initBalance)
  { balance = initBalance;   rate = 6.0; }  // a savings account
  double getBal()
  { return balance; }                       // common for both accounts
  void withdraw(double amount)
  { if (balance > amount)                   // same interface, different code
      balance -= amount; }
  void deposit(double amount)
  { balance += amount; }                    // common for both accounts
  void payInterest()                        // for savings account only
  { balance += balance * rate / 365 / 100; }
} ;
```

Listing 13.3 shows the source code for the program that implements this approach. Notice that the enumeration type `Kind` is gone—it is no longer needed nor is the argument whether it should be local or global. Even though each kind of account takes the same number of parameters for initialization, the client code still does not need this enumeration type to indicate the kind of account being created. Why? Because the client code explicitly defines account objects `a1` and `a2` as objects of either class `CheckingAccount` or class `SavingsAccount`. Hence, each object definition calls the appropriate `CheckingAccount` or `SavingsAccount` constructor. The output of the program is shown in Figure 13–2.

Listing 13.3   Example of separate classes for different subtypes of objects.

```
#include <iostream>
using namespace std;

class CheckingAccount {
  double balance;
  double fee;                              // no interest rate

public:
  CheckingAccount(double initBalance)
  { balance = initBalance;   fee = 0.2; }  // a checking account

  double getBal()
  { return balance; }                      // common for both accounts

  void withdraw(double amount)
  { if (balance > amount)
      balance = balance - amount - fee; }  // unconditional fee

  void deposit(double amount)
  { balance += amount; }
} ;

class SavingsAccount {
  double balance;
  double rate;                             // no checking fee

public:
  SavingsAccount(double initBalance)
  { balance = initBalance;   rate = 6.0; } // a savings account

  double getBal()
  { return balance; }                      // common for both accounts

  void withdraw(double amount)             // common for both accounts
```

```
{ if (balance > amount)
    balance -= amount; }

void deposit(double amount)
{ balance += amount; }

void payInterest()                              // for savings account only
{ balance += balance * rate / 365 / 100; }
} ;

int main()
{
  CheckingAccount a1(1000);                      // a1: checking
  SavingsAccount a2(1000);                       // a2: savings
  cout << " Initial balances: " << a1.getBal()
       << "   " << a2.getBal() << endl;
  a1.withdraw(100);  a2.deposit(100);            // no problem
  //a1.payInterest();                            // this is a syntax error now!!
  a2.payInterest();                              // this is ok
  cout << " Ending balances: " << a1.getBal()
       << "   " << a2.getBal() << endl;
  return 0;
}
```

This design resolves the problem of erroneous client use beautifully. Instead of a run-time error, a compile-time error is generated.

```
a1.payInterest();               // syntax error: method not found
```

The only problem with this design is that it does not convey the designer's knowledge to the maintainer well. Here you see two classes that have much in common—balance data member, withdrawal and deposit operations, and access to data—but the design itself does not indicate that these two classes have anything in common. The designer of these classes knows that they have these features in common, but this knowledge is not conveyed to the maintenance programmer.

Of course, these classes have similar names, but this is not enough in a large program. In Listing 13.3, both classes are placed together on the same

Figure 13-2   Output for program in Listing 13.3.

```
Initial balances: 1000   1000
Ending balances: 899.8   1100.18
```

page (and in the same source file), but in real life they might be separated, and their similarity might elude the maintainer. When one of these classes is modified, there is no guarantee that the other class will be modified too. When the set of kinds of objects grows, the common features of these classes are not identified. In general, the knowledge of the designer is not expressed in the source code.

Using C++ Inheritance to Link Related Classes

Inheritance is another solution to this problem. You create a class, which contains the common denominator of features common to all subtypes. In terms of object-oriented analysis and design, this class represents the generalization of state and behavior of these subclasses. Then you reuse these common features for other specialized classes. Each specialized class adds specialized features to the generalized class.

For example, the concept of an account is a generalization for the specialized concepts of savings account and checking account. Instead of merging all the features of savings and checking accounts into class `Account`, class `Account` can merge only the features that are common to both kinds of accounts, `CheckingAccount` and `SavingsAccount`. These features include data member `balance`, and methods `getBal()`, `withdraw()`, `deposit()`.

```
class Account {                    // base class: common features
protected:
  double balance;
public:
  Account(double initBalance = 0)
  { balance = initBalance; }
  double getBal()
  { return balance; }              // common for all accounts
  void withdraw(double amount)     // common for all accounts
  { if (balance > amount)
  balance -= amount; }
  void deposit(double amount)
  { balance += amount; }
} ;
```

The only difference between C++ classes you have seen before and this class is that I have replaced the keyword `private` with the keyword `protected`. This keyword prevents access to class components from the outside of the class similar to the keyword `private`. There is one important difference: The keyword `protected` allows access by classes that inherit from this one.

In C++ terminology, the class that generalizes the features of other classes and combines their common characteristics is called the *base* class. It is used as a base class for further inheritance. The specialized classes that add to the common features specified in the base class are called *derived* classes. *Derivation* is the C++ term for inheritance. Java uses the term *extension* instead of derivation.

Other popular terms for the base class are superclass and *parent* class. Symmetric terms for the derived class are subclass and *child* class. In the contexts where the base class is discussed as a data type, it is appropriate to refer to the derived type as a *subtype*.

Derived classes add and sometimes replace features of a more-general base class. Additional data and methods in derived classes reflect the relationship of specialization among classes.

For example, classes `CheckingAccount` and `SavingsAccount` can be designed as separate specializations of the generalized class `Account` that implements their common features. They add capabilities related to charging fees and paying interest that the general class `Account` does not have.

The derived class `SavingsAccount` adds the data member `rate` and the member function `payInterest()` to the base class `Account`. It uses the base class data member `balance` and member functions `getBal()`, `withdraw()`, and `deposit()`, and it does not replace any of the base features. The following segment of code shows what is needed to define a derived class. You do not repeat features that the derived class inherits from the base class. The only features that need to be described in the derived class are those that the derived class adds to the base class or those that the derived class replaces with its own version. (I will discuss the syntax of inheritance in the next section.)

```
class SavingsAccount : public Account {         // derived class
   double rate;
public:
   SavingsAccount(double initBalance)
   { balance = initBalance;   rate = 6.0; }     // savings account
   void payInterest()                           // not for checking
   { balance += balance * rate / 365 / 100; } } ;
```

The derived class `CheckingAccount` adds the data member `fee` to class `Account`. It uses the base class data member `balance` and member functions `getBal()` and `deposit()`. It replaces the base class member function `withdraw()` with its own `withdraw()` function, which charges fees (unlike the member function `withdraw()` in the base class).

```
class CheckingAccount : public Account {         // derived class
  double fee;
public:
  CheckingAccount(double initBalance)
  { balance = initBalance;   fee = 0.2; }        // checking account
  void withdraw(double amount)
  { if (balance > amount)
      balance = balance - amount - fee; }        // not for savings
} ;
```

Thus, the use of inheritance becomes a tool for code and design reuse during the development phase. Instead of repeating common features of class Account in each specialized class, you define these features in the base class only once. It makes design more compact (common features do not have to be repeated) and improves developers' productivity.

In these examples, the concepts of accounts, employees, and inventory items represent an abstraction rather than real world objects, which have to be modeled by the application. After all, there are no accounts, inventory items, or employees per se. There are checking accounts, savings accounts, nuts and bolts, and salaried and hourly employees.

Often, however, there exist "natural" superclass/subclass relationships among real world entities, which could be reflected in relationships among classes that represent these entities. For example, every car is a vehicle, and every subcompact is a car. This relationship can be expressed by the use of inheritance.

Inheritance can be either direct or indirect. Vehicle is a *direct superclass* or a direct base class of car. Car is a direct superclass or a direct base class of subcompact. Vehicle is an *indirect superclass* or indirect base class of subcompact.

It is okay if a class (e.g., car) is a derived class of one class (e.g., vehicle) yet a base class of another class (e.g., subcompact).

Inheritance can also be used for further program development. As more specialized operations need to be implemented, a derived class is defined that only provides new operations; all others are provided by the base class as before.

As with any division of responsibilities among classes, inheritance can be used as a tool for division of labor in software development. One monolithic class can be developed by only one developer. The base and derived classes can be developed by different programmers or by one programmer at different times.

In addition to being a good way to enhance abstraction, the use of commonality in classes results in less code to write and in better modularization for labor division. I am not sure whether the use of inheritance actually always results in less code to write. If the base class is small, and there are only a few subtypes, the size of the source code does not decrease much, if at all. If the base class is large, and there are many varieties of subtypes, and each subtype adds only a few capabilities, then indeed the source code shrinks in size because you do not repeat the code of the base class for each subclass.

At the time of writing the code for derived classes, CheckingAccount and SavingsAccount, code for the base class Account is frozen. This is a powerful paradigm for project management. If class Account changes in the future, propagation of the change to all derived classes is automatic (which might be either good or bad, but that is a different issue).

Another popular use of inheritance is for run-time binding of methods; other terms for run-time binding are dynamic binding and polymorphism with virtual functions. Many people think that object-oriented programming is about using inheritance and polymorphism. This is not so.

Polymorphism is a special case of object-oriented programming where the program processes a set of related objects performing similar but not identical operations over different kinds of objects. The kinds of objects are so similar that they can be derived from a common base class (e.g., oval, rectangle, triangle are derived from shape). The operations are so similar that the same name can be used in each class (e.g., draw()).

Polymorphism allows you to process a list of objects, sending the same message to each object regardless of which particular class this object belongs to. The function that is actually called in each case depends on the class to which each object belongs even though formally the call looks like a call to the base class function (virtual function). Sounds confusing? Do not worry, I will not leave you out in the cold. Soon you will become an expert on polymorphism.

Syntax of C++ Inheritance

The core of using C++ inheritance is the colon that follows the name of the derived class. It denotes the place for the name of the base class and for the description of the mode of inheritance—public, private, or protected.

Listing 13.4 shows the same program as in Listing 13.3 but is implemented with the use of inheritance. The client code is the extension of the client code in Listing 13.3. This is why the output of this program (shown in Figure 13–3) is the extension of the output of the program in Listing 13.3.

Listing 13.4   Example of inheritance hierarchy for `Account` classes.

```cpp
#include <iostream>
using namespace std;

class Account {                                // base class of hierarchy
protected:
  double balance;

public:
  Account(double initBalance = 0)
  { balance = initBalance; }

  double getBal()
  { return balance; }                          // common for both accounts

  void withdraw(double amount)                 // common for both accounts
  { if (balance > amount)
  balance -= amount; }

  void deposit(double amount)
  { balance += amount; }
} ;

class CheckingAccount : public Account {        // first derived class
  double fee;

public:
  CheckingAccount(double initBalance)
  { balance = initBalance;   fee = 0.2; }       // for checking account

  void withdraw(double amount)
  { if (balance > amount)
     balance = balance - amount - fee; }        // unconditional fee
} ;

class SavingsAccount : public Account {         // second derived class
  double rate;

public:
  SavingsAccount(double initBalance)
  { balance = initBalance;   rate = 6.0; }      // savings account

  void payInterest()                            // not for checking
  { balance += balance * rate / 365 / 100; }
} ;

int main()
{
```

```
Account a(1000);                            // base class object
CheckingAccount a1(1000);                   // derived class object
SavingsAccount a2(1000);                    // derived class object
a1.withdraw(100);                           // derived class method
a2.deposit(100);                            // base class method
a1.deposit(200);                            // base class method
a2.withdraw(200);                           // base class method
a2.payInterest();                           // derived class method
a.deposit(300);                             // base class method
a.withdraw(100);                            // base class method
//a.payInterest();                          // syntax error
//a1.payInterest();                         // syntax error
cout << " Ending balances\n    account object:            "
     << a.getBal()<<endl;
cout << "    checking account object: " << a1.getBal() << endl;
cout << "    savings account object:  " << a2.getBal() << endl;
return 0;
}
```

Figure 13–3   Output for program in Listing 13.4.

```
Ending balances
   account object:         1200
   checking account object: 1099.8
   savings account object:  900.148
```

Different Modes of Derivation from the Base Class

The keywords that can be used to denote the mode of inheritance are exactly the same three keywords that denote access rights to class members: `public`, `protected`, and `private`. It is the use of these keywords (with the preceding colon) that indicates the presence of inheritance relationships among classes.

Since the keywords are the same, many C++ programmers think that each keyword means the same thing as in controlling access to class components. For example, in this snippet of code, the keyword `public` is used twice.

```
class CheckingAccount : public Account {  // Account is the base
   double fee;                            // data member added in derived class
public:                                   // start of public segment of the class
   . . . } ;                              // the rest of derived class CheckingAccount
```

Don't think that these two cases of the keyword `public` mean the same thing! They are absolutely different. The only thing that they have in common is the keyword `public` itself and the colon, and this is not much. In the access rights keyword, the colon is to the right of the keyword. It means that the class members that follow can be accessed from anywhere in the program. In the mode of inheritance keyword, the colon is to the left of the keyword, and the meaning of the keyword is that the access rights to inherited class members are exactly the same as in the base class—what is private in the base remains private in the derived class and so on (more on this in a moment).

Yes, you use the same keyword `public` to specify access rights to class data members and the mode of derivation. The keyword is the same. All the rest is different.

The use of the colon and the keyword for the mode of inheritance syntactically links the base class and the derived class. No matter where in the source code the class definitions are placed, the maintainer who is inspecting the definition of the derived class has an unambiguous visual clue. This clue establishes two things:

- the existence of another class that is used as the base for this one.
- the name of the base class

Using a Unified Modeling Language (UML) diagram, the relationship between classes is denoted by the relationship link between class icons with the hollow triangle that point to the base class. If the base class has more than one derived class, each derived class can have either an individual link to the base class with an individual triangle or a common link with only one triangle. Figure 13–4 shows two alternative ways to describe the relationship between class `Account` and its two derived classes.

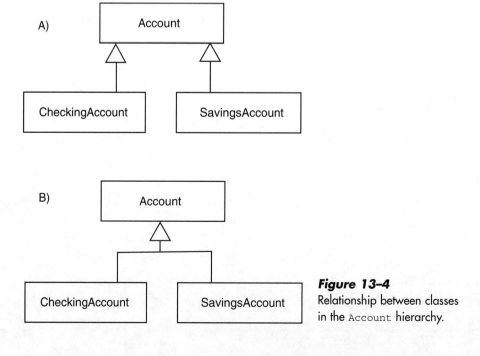

Figure 13–4
Relationship between classes in the `Account` hierarchy.

This is an example of the use of inheritance as a way to organize thinking about related application concepts. A checking account "is a kind of" an account: Every checking account is an account, but not every account is a checking account. This is a general observation about inheritance relationships. A car "is a" vehicle; every car is a vehicle, but not every vehicle is a car. A rectangle "is a kind of" a polygon: Every rectangle is a polygon, but not every polygon is a rectangle.

It is the existence of this "is a" relationship that conceptually connects classes and makes the use of inheritance appropriate. This is different from aggregation that links objects with the "has" relationship. For example, a rectangle "has" points, a history object "has" sample objects. It would be incorrect to say that the history object "is a" sample object: These two kinds of objects have entirely different data and entirely different behavior. With inheritance, data and behavior are also different for two classes, but they have a common subset that defines the base class. Class `Account` has a data member `balance` and a method `deposit()`. By virtue of inheritance, class `CheckingAccount` also has a data member `balance` and a method `deposit()` even though these components are not listed in the class definition.

This is the main thrust of inheritance. Inheritance is a relationship among classes. Class `Account` defines the data member `balance`, and class `CheckingAccount` does not need to do so. Since class `CheckingAccount` inherits from class `Account`, `CheckingAccount` objects have the data member `balance` in computer memory similar to `Account` objects. A `CheckingAccount` object is an `Account` object and has all `Account` properties and more: the properties defined in the `CheckingAccount` class definition.

Hence, inheritance does not save storage. All `Account` data is present in every `CheckingAccount` object. Inheritance helps you create smaller classes if classes become too large and indicate logical connections between these smaller classes. For example, Listing 13.4 shows that classes `CheckingAccount` and `SavingsAccount` are related—they both inherit from the class `Account`. Listing 13.3 is not capable of indicating this logical connection. Its class definitions are placed in source code together, but they do not stress the existence of common data members and common member functions—the reader has to figure that out.

Every C++ class could be used as a base class in derivation. Inheritance hierarchy is transitive. For example, class `TradingAccount` can be defined as a class derived from class `CheckingAccount`. A `TradingAccount` object would have all the capabilities of a `CheckingAccount` object. Since a `CheckingAccount` object has all the capabilities of an `Account` object, a `TradingAccount` object has all the capabilities of an `Account` object.

From this point of view, the terms superclass and subclass, often used to denote the base class and the derived class in the inheritance relationship, are not very accurate. They indicate that the base class, the superclass, is in some respect superior to the derived class, the subclass. This is not the case.

Capabilities of base classes are not lost at the bottom of the hierarchy of derived classes. `CheckingAccount` objects can do more things than can `Account` objects, and `TradingAccount` objects can do everything that `CheckingAccount` objects can do and more. It is the limitations on membership that grow toward the bottom of the hierarchy. A `CheckingAccount` class is a restricted `Account` class: There are fewer `CheckingAccount` objects in the world than there are `Account` objects, because every `CheckingAccount` object is an `Account` object. Similarly, there are fewer `TradingAccount` objects in the world because each `TradingAccount` object is a `CheckingAccount` object.

Toward the bottom of the hierarchy, you see fewer object instances in each subclass but more features available in objects of this subclass. From a mathematical point of view, the number of instances in a set might be important. From a programming point of view, it is the services that an object offers that count. Superclass offers fewer services than does subclass. This is why I am unhappy with these terms. The terms base class and derived class are better.

Inheritance enhances modularization and code reuse. A group of well-designed general-purpose classes can be organized into a library. The interface to library classes should be published, but the implementation can be encapsulated. The library classes can be customized by creating new derived classes. These classes add new data members and new member functions to the base library class. This is a common technique for creating graphical user interfaces. The application classes inherit from library classes—windows, dialogs, command buttons. Application programmers use the capabilities implemented in library classes and only add specific capabilities—how this particular window, dialog, or command button should look and behave in the application.

The base classes in the library do not need changes in the process of customization. Hence, base classes need neither editing nor recompilation.

As Listing 13.4 indicates, each derived class must explicitly specify its base class; it also may specify additional data members or member functions, but this is optional.

```
class SavingsAccount : public Account {    // syntax of derivation
    double rate;                           // additional feature
public:
    . . . } ;                              // the rest of SavingsAccount
```

The client code, however, does not have to know about derivation. If the client code is implemented in a separate file, it is only a derived class and not the base class that has to be known in this file. The base class has to be known in the files where the derived class is specified and implemented. This again confirms that inheritance is not the mechanism for serving the client better. Inheritance is the mechanism for designing the server classes (in this example, SavingsAccount and CheckingAccount). How these classes are designed, with inheritance or from scratch, makes no difference for the client code.

Defining and Using Objects of Base and Derived Classes

When the client code needs an object, it can define and use objects of the base class and the derived classes. If the client code is in a separate file, then the header files used for each class should be included (in Listing 13.4, for the base class Account and for derived classes SavingsAccount and CheckingAccount).

Which method is invoked in response to a message? The method is defined according to the declared type of the target object. The compiler finds the definition of the target object and searches the definition of the class to which the target object belongs. Listing 13.4 shows all typical situations in the client code, situations you have to be able to recognize.

```
Account a(1000);                       // base class object
CheckingAccount a1(1000);              // derived class object
SavingsAccount a2(1000);              // derived class object
a1.withdraw(100);                      // derived class method
a2.deposit(100);                       // base class method
a1.deposit(200);                       // base class method
a2.withdraw(200);                      // base class method
a2.payInterest();                      // derived class method
a.deposit(300);                        // base class method
a.withdraw(100);                       // base class method
//a.payInterest();                     // syntax error
//a1.payInterest();                    // syntax error
cout << " Ending balances\n    account object:           "
     << a.getBal() << endl;
cout << "    checking account object: " << a1.getBal() << endl;
cout << "    savings account object:  " << a2.getBal() << endl;
```

If the target object is of the base class, the compiler generates a function call to the member function that belongs to the base class.

```
a.deposit(300);                        // base class method
```

This rule holds even if the method is also defined in a derived class and is performed differently for objects of derived classes. For example, method `withdraw()` is defined differently for the derived class `CheckingAccount`. Still, when the target of the message is an object of the base class, it is the base class method `withdraw()` that is called.

```
a.withdraw(100);                       // base class method
```

In general, objects of the base class behave in the client code as if derived classes do not exist. The base class objects cannot respond to messages that derived classes define in addition to the capabilities inherited from the base class. For example, an attempt to ask an `Account` object to perform the job assigned to the derived class `SavingsAccount` is rejected by the compiler.

```
a.payInterest();                       // syntax error
```

Even though the classes `Account` and `SavingsAccount` are related to each other through the relationship of inheritance, this is not enough for the `Account` object to rise up to respond to the derived class messages. The method `payInterest()` is not in the definition of class `Account`, and this is the end of the story—the function call generates a syntax error.

The situation is somewhat different when the target of the message is an object of a derived class. Here, you should distinguish among three cases:

1. The method is inherited from the base class as is and is not redefined in the derived class.
2. The method is absent in the base class and is added to the derived class.
3. The method is present in the base class and is redefined by the derived class.

When the client code calls an inherited method, the compiler has a problem. Similar to processing other messages, the compiler finds the type of the target of the message (recall, that this is a message sent to an object of the derived class) and searches the specification of the derived class for the name of the member function.

```
a1.deposit(200);                       // base class method
```

Obviously, the member function is not there, because the inherited methods (in this case, `deposit()`) are described in the base class only, not in the derived class. It would be syntactically acceptable to describe the inherited method in the derived class too, but then it would be a redefined method, not the inherited method.

When the method is not found in the class of the target object, the compiler should alert the client programmer that a method was called that does not exist. Before doing so, the compiler checks whether the name of the class in the class specification is followed by a colon. If it is, the compiler makes the correct conclusion that this is a derived class, finds the name of the base class, and searches the definition of the base class. If the method is found, fine. If it is not there, the compiler checks whether this class has a base class and repeats the procedure until one of the two things happens. A class without a base class would be found in the inheritance chain, or the name of the member function would be found in the class specification. If the latter is the case, the compiler checks the number and the types of arguments against the function signature and generates the object code for the function call.

Notice that the use of inheritance breaks the first principle of object-oriented programming: binding data and operations together in the class definition within the boundaries of the class scope. Of course, the use of inheritance as a programming technique is very important for object-oriented programming. Hence, programmers should not be limited in their practice because of some abstract principles. C++ makes two adjustments to accommodate both the programmers and the principle, one conceptual and the other technical.

On the conceptual level, C++ claims that an object of the derived class is an object of the base class (plus more) and hence has all data and methods defined in the base class. On the technical level, C++ makes the scope of the derived class nested within the scope of the base class. According to the scope rules as we know them (for file, function, block, and class scopes), this makes the base class methods accessible from the derived class.

Sounds confusing? Yes, it is confusing. But you should not worry about these conceptual and technical problems. Just rest assured that when the compiler does not find the method in the specification of the derived class, it finds the method in the specification of the base class. Later in this chapter, I will devote a separate section to the discussion of scope rules and name resolution under inheritance.

In case 2, when an object of the derived class is the target of the method that is absent in the base class but is present in the derived class, the situation is simple. You can apply the standard rules for interpretation of a function call. The compiler finds the method in the specification of the derived class and stops. If the arguments do not match the function signature, it is a syntax error. If the arguments do match, the appropriate function call is generated.

```
a2.payInterest();                         // derived class method
```

The similar rule applies to case 3, to the methods that are redefined by the derived class. The compiler ignores the existence of the inheritance relationship. As you saw earlier, when the target of the message is an object of the base class, the compiler searches the base class for the appropriate method and ignores derived classes. When the target of the message is an object of a derived class, the compiler searches the specification of the derived class and stops when the method is found. Obviously, the method is found because it is redefined in the derived class.

```
a1.withdraw(100);                         // derived class method
```

If the number and types of the actual arguments match the method signature, the compiler generates the appropriate function call. If there is no match, it is a syntax error. The compiler does not go to the base class in search of a better match. As you will soon see, this might be a source of trouble.

Accessing Base and Derived Class Services

Normally, a derived class "is a" base class; each object of the derived class has all base class data and function members plus added and redefined data and methods.

In a sense, the derived class is a client of the base class, very much as any C++ code is a client of its server classes. The client code uses the server services: data members and member functions. The server class does not know about its client classes. It does not know even the name of its clients. This is natural because the server class or function might be from a library, written perhaps years before the client code was. The client class must know the name of its server classes and the names of its public services to be able to use them.

For example, the client code in Listing 13.4 defines an object of class Account using the class name explicitly. After that, the client code gets access to Account services using their names.

```
Account a(1000);                          // base class object
a.deposit(300);                           // base class method
cout << " Ending balances\n   account object:           "
    << a.getBal() << endl;
```

In this example, class `Account` has no idea what client code uses it. As I said, class `Account` might be designed several months (or years) earlier than its clients and by different programmers.

Similarly, the derived class uses the base class services (data and functions). The base class does not know about derived classes because the server in programming never knows the identity of its clients. The derived class must know the name of its base class, and it must know the names of its non-private services to be able to use them.

For example, the derived classes in Listing 13.4 established the inheritance relationship with the base class `Account` by specifying the name of the base class after the colon operator.

```
class SavingsAccount : public Account {      // syntax of derivation
   double rate;
public:
   . . . } ;                                  // the rest of SavingsAccount
```

There is a difference between the client-server relationships of composition (aggregation) and the derived-base relationship of inheritance. In composition, the client code must instantiate a server object to get access to services. In inheritance, the derived class does not have to instantiate a separate base object; the name of the base class in the definition of the derived class suffices.

In class composition (which I discussed in detail in the previous chapter), the container class does not provide its component's services to its own clients; it provides only its own services explicitly listed in its own interface. For example, class `Point`, which I used as a component of class `Rectangle`, has public methods `set()`, `get()`, and `move()`.

```
class Point {
   x, y;  // private coordinates
     public:
       Point (int a, int b)                  // general constructor
         { x = a;   y = b; }
       void set (int a, int b)               // modifier function
         { x = a;   y = b; }
       void move (int a, int b)              // modifier function
         { x += a;   y += b; }
       void get (int& a, int& b) const       // selector function
         { a = x;   b = y; } } ;
```

This does not mean that class `Rectangle`, which has `Point` data members as its components, is able to provide its clients with the same services. Here is an example of the client code.

```
Point p1(20,40), p2(70,90);      // top-left, bottom-right corners
Rectangle rec(p1,p2,4);          // composite object: client of Point
rec.set(30,40);                  // this does not make sense
rec.move(10,20);                 // this is ok: why the difference?
```

The difference between methods `set()` and `move()` here is that the class `Rectangle` did not bother to implement the member function `set()` but did define what the method `move()` means in the context of class `Rectangle`.

```
class Rectangle {
  Point pt1, pt2;                      // top-left, bottom-right corner points
  int thickness;                       // thickness of the rectangle border
public:
  Rectangle (const Point& p1, const Point& p2, int width=1);
  void move(int a, int b);             // move both points
  void setThickness(int width = 1);    // change thickness
  bool pointIn(const Point& pt) const; // point in rectangle?
    . . . . } ;                        // the rest of class Rectangle
```

A derived class, however, provides its clients with the services of its base class; the designer of the derived class should not lift a finger to make this possible. Consider, for example, the `SavingsAccount` class from Listing 13.4.

```
class SavingsAccount : public Account {          // another derived class
  double rate;                                   // added components
public:
  SavingsAccount(double initBalance)
  { balance = initBalance;   rate = 6.0; }       // for savings account
  void payInterest()                             // for savings account
  { balance += balance * rate / 365 / 100; } } ;
```

According to this class definition, the client code of this class can define objects of type `SavingsAccount` and send the `payInterest()` messages to these objects. That is it. If, however, you check the client code in Listing 13.4, you will see much more than sending this message.

```
SavingsAccount a2(1000);             // derived class object
a2.deposit(100);                     // base class method
a2.withdraw(200);                    // base class method
a2.payInterest();                    // derived class method
cout << "   savings account object:   " << a2.getBal() <<endl;
```

These services that the client code uses, `deposit()`, `withdraw()`, and `getBal()`, are not listed in the derived class `SavingsAccount`; they are listed in the base class `Account` only. This is not a problem for the compiler. It easily follows the chain of inheritance in class definition and finds these member functions in the base class (or in the base of the base or whatever). But what is the client programmer to do? How does the client programmer know that these services are available for the objects defined in the client code? The client programmer (and the maintainer) has to do what the compiler does: follow the chain of inheritance in class definitions.

The client programmer (and the maintainer) who uses `SavingsAccount` services has to look up the `Account` features to know that these features are available for `SavingsAccount` objects. In Listing 13.4, I conveniently put these class definitions together. For large systems and for tall inheritance hierarchies (where a derived class is used as the base for another class, and that other class is used as the base for yet another class, etc.), this is not possible. Finding the list of all capabilities that the derived class provides becomes a chore for the client programmer (and the maintainer). The description of the derived class alone is not sufficient—you should look it up elsewhere.

This increases design complexity; errors are hard to discover and even harder to correct. Again, the use of inheritance flies in the face of the principles of object-oriented programming. Inheritance is a convenience for the programmer who designs the classes in the inheritance hierarchy. It is a technique for reuse of design and for reducing the amount of code to be written.

As far as the client designer is concerned, two separate classes (`SavingsAccount` and `CheckingAccount`) represent a perfectly good engineering solution. They bind together related data and services. An attempt to send a message to a wrong class is flagged as an error by the compiler. What does inheritance add to this? Data and methods that are common to both classes have to be implemented only once, and changes to the base class propagate to all derived classes automatically. This is a convenience for the implementers of the server classes.

Inheritance makes the study of server capabilities harder for everybody else. Some C++ libraries provide their classes with a huge number of services (more than 100) and spread these services over five or more levels of inheritance. To figure out what a library window class could do for you, you have to study all these levels of inheritance, a job made more difficult because the hierarchy itself and the services available change from one release of the library to another. Hence, you have to upgrade your skills to stay current. C++ programming is never dull, especially when inheritance is used with abandon.

Unlike inherited features, redefined features are directly available in the derived class list of services. You do not have to look them up elsewhere. They usually do the same thing as the services defined in the base class do but do it either more efficiently or use somewhat different data or algorithms.

In the example of inheritance in Listing 13.4, the derived class `CheckingAccount` redefines the member function `withdraw()`, which is defined in the base class `Account`.

The redefined function does its job differently than the base function does by using the data (data member `fee`) that is available only in the derived class but not in the base class. This usually happens because other derived classes (in this example, `SavingsAccount`) have no use for this data. If they did (e.g., in our example, all derived classes use the base data member `balance`), that data member should be placed in the base class (as in the program in Listing 13.4).

The use of additional data in member functions redefined in derived classes is a popular design technique and is common but not mandatory.

Derived class objects can be viewed as a sum of the derived class parts (its private, protected, and public components) and the base class parts (its private, protected, and public components). The memory allocated for the derived class object is a sum of the memory allocated for the base part and the memory allocated for the derived part.

For example, on my machine, the size of an `Account` object is 8 bytes, and a `CheckingAccount` object and a `SavingsAccount` object are each 16 bytes. If the data types used as data members need to be aligned in memory, additional space might be added to the object to keep these object data members properly aligned.

The client of the derived object calls the public services of the base class using the derived object as if these services were a public part of the derived class itself. For example, a `CheckingAccount` object responds to messages `deposit()` and `getBal()` as if they were defined in class `CheckingAccount`; the client code does not know (and should not know) the difference.

Members of the base class have no access to features that are added or redefined in the derived classes. Base class objects do not have data members and member functions described in derived classes. For example, class `Account` does not have access to the private data member `rate` and the public member function `payInterest()` defined in class `SavingsAccount`. The following is nonsense:

```
Account a(1000);  a.payInterest();           // syntax error
```

I think that these syntactic rules make intuitive sense. They extend the notion that the derived class object is a base class object plus something else.

As far as the base class objects are concerned, they cannot know anything about another class service even if it derived from this object class. It is another class, period. The objects of the base class cannot respond to messages not described in the class specification.

Similarly, making a function or a class a friend of class `Account` does not provide this function or class with direct access to non-public elements of its derived classes `CheckingAccount` and `SavingsAccount`.

Accessing Base Components of a Derived Class Object

Now things become less intuitive and more convoluted. Members and friends of a derived class do receive access to all data members and member functions of this derived class. They also receive some access to data members and member functions of the base class. They have access to public and protected members only, not to private data members and member functions of the base class. They also do not receive access to members of other classes derived from the same base class.

One of the ways to look at this rule is that the base class has three kinds of clients (or three areas of access). In the inner area, with the greatest right to access data members and member functions, are class member functions and class friends. They can access public, protected, and private data members and member functions. They get this access by virtue of being declared within the class braces, either as a member or as a friend. In the middle area are member functions of derived classes and their friends. They can access public and protected class members but not private members. They have access by virtue of declaring this class as the base class (directly or indirectly) in the class definition.

In the outer area of access is what has been called client code throughout this book. The clients, as you know, can only access public data members and member functions of the class. The client code receives access to class services by virtue of using an object of the class as the target of a message. The object can be made available to the client code in three different ways. It can be created though the object definition, it can be created dynamically on the heap, or the object (or its reference or its pointer) can be received as a function parameter. These relationships between the class and three areas of access are shown in Figure 13–5.

Notice that it is only in the outer area of access that the client code accesses data members and member functions through a separate server object. In the two other areas, the code accesses data members and member functions of the same object: In the inner area, it is the object of the base class; in the middle area, it is the object of the derived class.

What happens in the middle area can be changed depending on the mode of derivation. Base class members can change their access status in the derived class objects. What is public in the base class might become protected or even private in the derived class object. What is protected in the base class might become private in the derived class object.

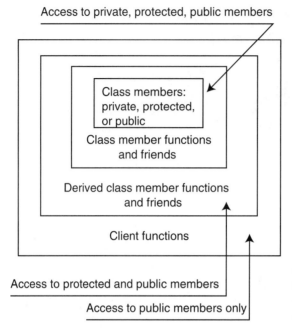

Figure 13–5
Areas of access from a class' own members and friends, from derived classes, and from client code.

Public Inheritance

Each base class can be inherited through private, protected, or public mode of inheritance. The mode defines the access status of base class elements in the derived class. With public inheritance, access status remains the same. Public, protected, and private base members remain public, protected, and private in an object of the derived class. This is the least restrictive case—nothing changes.

Hence, derived class methods can access protected and public base members of a derived object. This relationship is shown in Figure 13–6. It shows a derived class object, which consists of the base and derived parts. Each part has private, protected, and public components. It also shows the client code that uses the derived class object as its server. You see that the client code can access public base services (data and functions) along with public derived services. For the client code, the derived class object looms as the sum of public capabilities defined in the base class and in the derived class.

You also see that the derived class object can access only public and protected members inherited from the base class. To access its own private members inherited from the base class, the derived class methods should use base access functions. At the first glance, this sounds unreasonable. It is its own

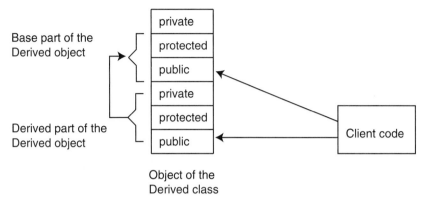

Figure 13-6   Access to services of the base and derived classes from a derived class object and from client code when the derivation mode is public.

components that the derived class object is denied access to! We did not see anything like that before!

On the other hand, the derived class is a client of the base class. The base class might have elements, especially data, whose design might change with time. Making these elements accessible to derived classes might also require changes to the derived classes. With access through non-private member functions, derived classes are protected from the repercussions of the changes to the base class. This is the same logic that suggests that we make data members private and member functions public.

Listing 13.5 shows a small abstract example that illustrates this relationship between the derived class object and its own members. Here, class Derived is derived from class Base in the public mode. The Base class has private, protected, and public members as does the Derived class. The Derived class, in its method publD(), can access its own members privD and protD (this is a no-brainer). It can also access the inherited protected and public members of the Base class, protB and publB(). It is a syntax error, however, for the Derived class to access the private member privB inherited from the Base class, even though the memory for this member is allocated within the Derived object. Class Client creates a Derived object d in its constructor and accesses the public services defined in the Derived class, publD(), and in the Base class, publD(). It cannot access non-public members of the Base and the Derived classes. Since I am trying to show access rights to the Base and Derived capabilities, the program need not produce any output. It only produces compiler error messages.

Listing 13.5   Access to `Base` and `Derived` members in a derived object for the `Derived` class and for client code under public inheritance.

```
#include <iostream>
using namespace std;

class Base {
     private: int privB;                 // accessed from Base only
     protected: int protB;               // accessed from Base and Derived
     public: void publB()                // access from Base, Derived, Client
     { privB = 0; protB = 0; } } ;       // OK to access its own data

class Derived : public Base {            // public mode of inheritance
     private:  int privD;
     protected: int protD;
     public: void publD()
     { privD = 0;   protD = 0;           // OK to access its own data
       protB = 0;                        // OK to access inherited members
//    privB = 0;                         // no access to inherited members
         } } ;

class Client {
public: Client()                         // Client class constructor
{ Derived d;                             // object of the derived class
  d.publD();                             // OK to access public services
  d.publB();                             // OK to access public Base services
  // d.privD = d.protD = 0;              // no access to non-public services
  // d.privB=d.protB=0; }                // no access non-public Base services
  } ;

int main()
{ Client c;                              // create the object, run the program
  return 0;
  }
```

Public derivation is the most natural mode of inheritance because it preserves the "is a" relationship among classes. Under public derivation, the derived class object offers all public capabilities present in a base object and adds more public services for the client. The ability for further inheritance is not limited.

Note

For public mode of derivation, inherited members of the base class retain their access status (private, protected, and public) in the objects of the derived class; all public services, those defined in the derived class and those inherited from the base class, are available for the client code. This is the most natural mode of inheritance.

Listing 13.6 shows a larger example of using inheritance. The base class `Point` offers two public services, `set()` and `get()`, to access its data members `x` and `y`. The derived class `VisiblePoint` adds to these features the data member `visible` and member functions `show()`, `hide()`, and `retrieve()`. The method `show()` sets the data member `visible` to 1 so that the point will be displayed by the graphic package. The method `hide()` sets `visible` to 0 so that the point will not be displayed. The inheritance is public. It would be better to use an enumeration type instead of numeric values for visible and hidden points, but I am watching the size of the example listing.

Listing 13.6   Access to base members in a derived object under public inheritance.

```
#include <iostream>
using namespace std;

class Point {                               // base class
  int x, y;                                 // private base data
public:
  void set (int xi, int yi)
    { x = xi;  y = yi; }
  void get (int &xp, int &yp) const         // public base methods
    { xp = x;  yp = y; } } ;

class VisiblePoint : public Point {         // colon: before public
  int visible;

public:                                     // colon: after public
  void show()
    { visible = 1; }

  void hide()
    { visible = 0; }

  void retrieve(int &xp, int &yp, int &vp) const
    { xp = x;  yp = y;                      // syntax error: comment it out!
      get(xp,yp);                           // base public method is accessed
      vp = visible; } } ;                   // derived private data: OK
```

```
int main ()
{
  VisiblePoint a,b;   int x,y,z;        // define two derived objects
  a.set(0,0);   b.set(20,40);           // call base public function
  a.hide();   b.show();                 // call derived public methods
  a.get(x,y);                           // call base public function
  b.retrieve(x,y,z);                    // call derived public method
  cout << " Point coordinates: x=" << x << "   y=" << y << endl;
  cout << " Point visibility:  visible=" << z << endl;
  return 0;
  }
```

Public base member functions `Point::set()` and `Point::get()` are accessible in the client code as are the `VisiblePoint` public methods. Any `VisiblePoint` object can provide these services to its clients.

Private data members `Point::x` and `Point::y` are not accessible in class `VisiblePoint`; an attempt to run the program as is results in a syntax error on the first line of the `retrieve()` member function. There are two remedies. One remedy is to make `Point` data members protected. Had they been protected in the `Point` class, they would be accessible in `retrieve()` in class `VisiblePoint`. Still, they would not be accessible in the client code. The second remedy is to use `Point` access functions in the `VisiblePoint` member functions to access private base data. I demonstrate the second remedy on the second line of `retrieve()`. When the first line of `retrieve()` (with the syntax error) is commented out, the program runs and produces the results shown in Figure 13–7

I like the first remedy (making base data protected rather than private) more because it requires fewer access functions in the base class and simplifies the code in the derived classes. Those who favor the use of access functions argue that direct access to protected base data from derived classes results in the same breach of encapsulation as does direct access to public data members in the client-server relationship. As I noted earlier, they definitely have a point. But the scale of the problem is much, much smaller. When you see that the scale of the problem becomes essential, make the base data private and use access functions in derived classes. Otherwise, make base data private and do not worry about encapsulation more than is necessary.

Figure 13–7   Output for program in Listing 13.6 with the syntax error removed.

```
Point coordinates: x=20  y=40
Point visibility:  visible=1
```

Note

The derived class object cannot access its inherited members that are private in the base class even though they "belong" to that derived class object. To access these members in the derived class, use base access functions or better yet, make these members protected in the base class. For the derived class, protected base members are as good (that is, accessible) as are public members. For the client code, protected is as good (that is, not accessible) as private is.

Protected Inheritance

Protected inheritance is the mechanism that limits client access to the services of the base class. Public and protected members inherited from the base class become protected in a derived class object.

These base services are available for further derivation and can be used in the derived class methods, but the client code has no access to public base services through the derived class object—they are now protected. Figure 13–8 shows the changes relative to the protected mode of inheritance. What is public in the base class became protected. The dashed line shows that access to this part of the derived class object is denied.

Figure 13–8   Access to members of the base class and the derived class from a derived class object and from client code when the derivation mode is protected.

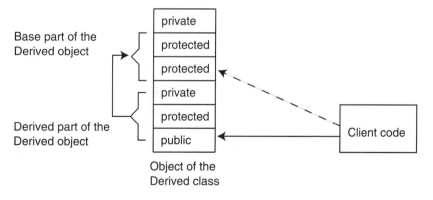

Listing 13.7 shows the small abstract example from Listing 13.5, where the public mode of inheritance is replaced by the protected mode. This example illustrates the relationship between the derived class object and its own members and also the relationship between the derived class object and its client code.

Listing 13.7   Access to `Base` and `Derived` members of the `Derived` object for the `Derived` class and the client code when the mode of derivation is protected.

```
#include <iostream>
using namespace std;

class Base {
    private: int privB;              // accessed from Base only
    protected: int protB;            // accessed from Base and Derived
    public: void publB()             // no access from Derived client
    { privB = 0; protB = 0; } } ;    // OK to access its own data

class Derived : protected Base {     // protected inheritance
    private:  int privD;
    protected: int protD;
    public: void publD()
    { privD = 0;   protD = 0;        // OK to access its own data
      protB = 0;                     // access to inherited members
//    privB = 0;                     // no access its inherited members
        } } ;

class Client {                       // Client code
public:
  Client()
{ Derived d;   Base b;               // objects of Derived, Base classes
  d.publD();                         // public part of Derived class: OK
//   d.publB();                      // no access to public Base part
//   d.privD = d.protD = 0;          // non-public Derived parts: not OK
//   d.privB=d.protB=0;              // non-public Base parts: no access
  b.publB(); }                       // Base object: public part is OK
    }

int main()
{ Client c;                          // create the object, run the program
  return 0;
  }
```

Recall that the call to the public `Base` member function `publB()` with the derived object as the target, `d.publB()`, worked in the previous version (Listing 13.5). In Listing 13.7, however, it is a syntax error. Notice that access to public `Base` members is denied only when it is made through the `Derived` class object. At the end of the `Client()` default constructor I call the publB() member function using the Base object b as the target. No problem—a public member of a class is accessible to clients of this class. It is to the clients of the Derived class that this service is not accessible.

Listing 13.8 shows the example from Listing 13.6, where the public mode of inheritance is replaced by the protected mode. The base class Point offers the same public services, set() and get(), but the client of the derived class VisiblePoint is not able to use these services—they are protected in VisiblePoint objects. An attempt to do so in the Client() constructor results in syntax errors. To resolve this problem, I add to class VisiblePoint a new service, initialize(), that accesses inherited data members x and y instead of set() and get(). Notice that the derived class now has no problem accessing the base data because I made the base data protected. In derived member function retrieve() I commented out the call to base function get() as unnecessary complexity.

Listing 13.8   Access to base members in a derived object under protected inheritance.

```
#include <iostream>
using namespace std;

class Point {                             // base class
protected:
   int x, y;                              // protected base data
public:
   void set (int xi, int yi)
      { x = xi;   y = yi; }
   void get (int &xp, int &yp) const      // public base functions
      { xp = x;   yp = y; } } ;

class VisiblePoint : protected Point {    // protected inheritance
   int visible;

public:
   void show()
      { visible = 1; }

   void hide()
      { visible = 0; }

   void retrieve(int &xp, int &yp, int &vp) const
      { xp = x;   yp = y;                  // access to protected data is OK
//       get(xp,yp);                       // no need for extra complexity
         vp = visible; }
```

```
void initialize(int xp, int yp, int vp)    // new public service
   { x = xp;  y = yp;                       // access to protected base data
     visible = vp; } } ;                    // access to derived private data

int main ()
{
  VisiblePoint a,b;   int x, y, z;          // define two derived objects
  b.initialize(20,40,1);                    // initialize derived object
// a.set(0,0);   b.set(20,40);              // now this is a syntax error
  a.hide();   b.show();                     // derived public methods: OK
// a.get(x,y);                              // and this is a syntax error
  b.retrieve(x,y,z);                        // derived public method: OK
  cout << " Point coordinates: x=" << x << "  y=" << y << endl;
  cout << " Point visibility:  visible=" << z << endl;
  return 0;
  }
```

If you comment out the two lines with syntax errors, the program runs and produces the same output as the program in Listing 13.6 (see Figure 13–7) does.

I hope you like public inheritance more than protected inheritance. Public inheritance is a technique for adding to the services provided by the base class or for replacing some of the services (without changing their name) with something more useful for the client code of the derived class. In all examples of public inheritance, the "is a" relationship holds between the derived and base objects. For the client code, a savings account object "is an" account object, with the capability to pay added interest. A visible point object "is a" point object, with the capability to show and hide added.

With protected inheritance, this is all different. It is a technique for quickly producing a class that uses non-public services of the base class (data members x and y in Listing 13.8) but does not provide to its client the public services of the base class (methods set() and get() in Listing 13.8). Instead, it provides a different set of services (method initialize() in Listing 13.8) that for some reason is more appropriate for the client code.

In Listing 13.8, a VisiblePoint object is not a Point object. Point objects provide their clients with methods set() and get() and VisiblePoint objects do not.

Another popular example of using protected inheritance is to design a stack class (providing clients with access at one end only), deriving it from an array class (that provides clients with access to any component). Using protected inheritance, the designer denies the clients the use of array methods. Instead, the stack provides methods push() and pop() that the client uses to access the top of the stack.

In the beginning of this chapter, I noted the important difference between inheritance and composition. The derived class provides its clients with all the public services of its base class. The composite class does not provide its clients with the services of its components unless these services are supported by a method of the composite class. (In my example, class `Rectangle` provided the `move()` service.)

If you wanted to take away some existing services from the client, do not use inheritance. Use class composition instead.

Listing 13.9 shows the same example as Listing 13.8, but the class `VisiblePoint` now has a data member of class `Point` rather than inheriting from `Point` in protected mode. The output of this example is the same as the output shown in Figure 13–7.

Listing 13.9   Using class composition instead of inheritance.

```
#include <iostream>
using namespace std;

class Point {                                  // component class
private:
  int x, y;                                    // private data
public:
  void set (int xi, int yi)
    { x = xi;  y = yi; }
  void get (int &xp, int &yp) const            // public method
    { xp = x;  yp = y; } } ;

class VisiblePoint {                           // no inheritance, composition
    Point pt;                                  // private component
    int visible;

public:
  void show()                                  // new service to client
    { visible = 1; }

  void hide()                                  // new service to client
    { visible = 0; }

  void retrieve(int &xp, int &yp, int &vp) const   // replace
    { pt.get(xp,yp);                           // services are hidden from client
      vp = visible; }

  void initialize(int xp, int yp, int vp)      // replace
    { pt.set(xp,yp);                           // services are hidden from client
      visible = vp; } } ;                      // just like private data are hidden

int main ()
{
```

```
VisiblePoint b;   int x, y, z;                  // define an aggregate object
b.initialize(20,40,1);                          // aggregate service
b.show();                                       // aggregate service
b.retrieve(x,y,z);                              // aggregate service
cout << " Point coordinates: x=" << x << "   y=" << y << endl;
cout << " Point visibility:  visible=" << z << endl;
return 0;
}
```

The services of the base class `Point`, `set()`, and `get()` are taken away from the client code by virtue of class composition. The `Point` data member is hidden inside the `VisiblePoint` object and is not available to the client code. As a result, the client code cannot do to a `VisiblePoint` object what it can do to a `Point` object: move the point around the screen without regard to its visibility. Instead, class `VisiblePoint` provides the client code with its own interface, member functions `initialize()` and `retrieve()`, which require that the client code deal with the visibility of the point.

The moral of this story applies to each situation when you are designing a new class to serve your clients, and you have an existing class that you want to reuse in your design. If the client needs all the services of the existing class plus more, inherit from this class publicly. The client code will use derived class objects for both inherited and added services. If it is your new class that will be using the services of the existing class and not your client, do not use inheritance and do not make it protected; use class composition instead (see Chapter 12 for more on composition).

The situation in which protected inheritance might be useful is when you are designing a class (or a family of classes) to serve your clients, and you want to build this class gradually in modular chunks using inheritance.

For example, the client code needs class `D1`, and you want to derive class `D1` from class `D`, which is derived from class `B`. Using protected inheritance to derive class `D` from class `B` and class `D1` from class `D`, you can build class `D1` using all public and protected services of class `D`. These services include all public and protected services of the base class `B`. The client code of `D1` will not use public services of classes `D` and `B`—these services are taken away from the client code because protected inheritance is being used.

In other words, protected inheritance is the way to limit client access to public services of the base class without limiting access to these services from the derived class and without limiting further inheritance.

Note

Protected inheritance takes inherited base public services away from the client code that uses the derived class object. This distorts the "is a" relationship. If this relationship is not important anyway, use class composition instead of protected inheritance. If you feel you want to use inheritance, it should be public. (This is a biased opinion, however.)

Private Inheritance

Private inheritance is a technique for limiting access to base services, not only by the clients of the derived classes but by classes derived from the derived classes as well.

When the base class is used as a private base, all public and protected base members become private members in a derived class object. They are not accessible by derived class clients. They are not accessible by methods of classes derived from the derived class. They are only accessible to the methods of the derived class if necessary.

This is an important difference between using the base class as private or as other modes of derivation. With protected and public inheritance, the access rules are transitive. If the derived class is used as a base for further derivation (protected or public), the derived class down the hierarchy has the same access rights to the base members as does the class immediately derived from the base. If, however, the derivation is private and the derived class is used for further derivation, its descendants cannot access any members of the base class. The protected and public members of the base class can be accessed only by the class immediately derived from the base. This prevents the designer of the derived class from using any of the base services for further derivation.

As with protected inheritance, the base class public interface (data and methods) is not part of the derived interface anymore—it is private for the client.

These relationships are shown in Figure 13–9. The object of a class derived from the one derived from the base (this is not a tall inheritance hierarchy) has no access to its own components inherited from the base if the base is inherited from private mode.

Listing 13.10 shows the small abstract example again; this time I am using private inheritance. As far as access rights of the derived object to its base part

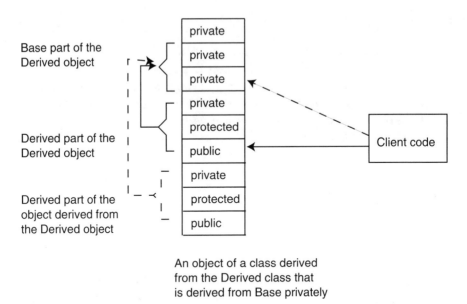

An object of a class derived
from the Derived class that
is derived from Base privately

Figure 13-9   Access to base components of a derived class object for private derivation.

are concerned, they are the same as in the previous example (with protected inheritance). In this example, I introduced yet another class, `Derived1`, which inherits from `Derived`. I made this derivation public, but it does not matter. What you are going to see are the effects of the private inheritance from the `Base` class.

I commented out the offending lines so the code could be compiled. You see that the derived class can access all non-private base members. This does not depend on the mode of inheritance. Similarly, the class `Derived1` can access all non-private members of its own "base" class (`Derived`). This again does not depend on the mode of inheritance. However, the class `Derived1` cannot access any members of the `Base` class, because its "base" class (`Derived`) inherits from the `Base` class in private mode. As far as the client code is concerned, private inheritance is similar to protected inheritance: It puts all base components of the derived object, even public components, out of reach of the client.

Listing 13.10   Access to `Base` members in the inheritance hierarchy where the `Derived` class inherits from its `Base` in private mode.

```
#include <iostream>
using namespace std;

class Base {
    private: int privB;            // accessed from Base only
    protected: int protB;          // accessed from Base and Derived
    public: void publB()           // accessed from Base and Derived
    { privB = 0; protB = 0; } } ;  // OK to access its own data

class Derived : private Base {     // private inheritance
    private:  int privD;
    protected: int protD;
    public: void publD()
    { privD = 0;   protD = 0;      // OK to access its own data
      protB = 0;                   // OK to access inherited members
 //   privB = 0;                   // not OK to access its inherited members
                              } } ;

class Derived1 : public Derived {  // class derived from derived
public: void publDD()
{ // privD = 0;                    // no access to private "base" data
  protD = 0;                       // OK to access protected "base" data
  publD();                         // OK to access public "base" data
//  protB = 0;                     // no access to any part of "private base"
//  publB();                       // no access to any part of "private base"
} } ;

class Client {
public:
  Client()
{ Derived d;   Base b;            // objects of derived and base classes
  d.publD();                      // public part of Derived class: OK
//  d.publB();                    // public Base part of Derived: not OK
//  d.privD = d.protD = 0;        // non-public part of Derived: no
//  d.privB=d.protB=0;            // non-public Base part of Derived: no
  b.publB(); }                    // public Base part of Base object: OK
  }

int main()
{ Client c;                       // create the object, run the program
  return 0;
  }
```

Private inheritance allows you to write new servers by reusing implementation. But there is no subtype relation: If you derive a class `Stack` from class `Array` privately, a `Stack` object is not an `Array` object, it does not provide `Array` services to the `Stack` clients or to classes further derived from `Stack`.

A `stack` might have an `Array` as one of its elements. The use of private or protected inheritance is not good design. It is better to use class composition.

Some experts, however, feel that this mode of derivation is useful because it forces the derived class to use base access methods to access private data, similar to all other clients of all other classes. As I said earlier, this is debatable.

Since polymorphism (to be discussed in the next chapter) is only available for public inheritance, this is probably another reason to stay only with public inheritance. Avoid protected and private inheritance.

Adjusting Access to Base Members in the Derived Class

C++ allows the programmer of the derived class to avoid these "devastating" access limitations imposed by the rules of protected and private inheritance. How does one do that? By explicitly returning to the base members in a derived object the access rights they had in a base object.

Listing 13.11 shows our skeleton example again with private inheritance from `Base` to `Derived`. In the definition of the `Derived` class, I restored the protected status of the data member `Base::protB`. I also restored the public status of the member function `Base::publB()`—notice that the syntax is the same, whether it is a data member or a member function. This does not change access rights of the `Derived` class; for any mode of inheritance, it can access all non-private members of its base class. It does change the access rights of the `Derived1` class; similar to `Derived`, it can access all non-private members of its base class. The client code also receives a break: it now has access to `Base::publB()` as if `Derived` inherited from `Base` publicly and not privately.

Listing 13.11   Example of adjusting the access rights to `Base` members in the `Derived` class (private inheritance).

```
#include <iostream>
using namespace std;

class Base {
    private: int privB;            // accessed from Base only
    protected: int protB;          // accessed from Base and Derived
    public: void publB()           // accessed from Base and Derived
    { privB = 0; protB = 0; } } ;  // OK to access its own data

class Derived : private Base {     // private inheritance
    private:  int privD;
    protected: int protD;
```

```
      protected:
         Base::protB;                      // available for further derivation
      public:
         Base::publB;                      // available for client access
         public: void publD()
         { privD = 0;   protD = 0;         // OK to access its own data
            protB = 0;                     // OK to access its inherited members
   //       privB = 0;                     // private inherited member: no access
         } } ;

class Derived1 : public Derived {          // class derived from derived
public: void publDD()
{ // privD = 0;                            // no access to private "base" data
   protD = 0;                              // OK to access protected "base" data
   publD();                                // OK to access public "base" data
   publB();                                // OK if it is made public in Derived
   protB = 0;                              // OK if it is made protected in Derived
      } } ;

class Client {
public: Client()
{ Derived d;   Base b;                     // objects of derived and base classes
   d.publD();                              // public part of Derived class: OK
   d.publB();                              // OK if it is made public in Derived
// d.privD = d.protD = 0;                  // non-public part of Derived: no
// d.privB=d.protB=0;                      // non-public Base part of Derived: no
   b.publB();                              // public Base part of Base object: OK
     } } ;

int main()
{ Client c;                                // create the object, run the program
   return 0;
   }
```

You see that by using private inheritance you can make the design quite convoluted by closing access to some components, opening access to others, making your design into a puzzle that you can proudly present to your colleagues and ask, "Guess what this does."

Actually, C++ allows you not only to adjust the access rights but also to change them to something different from what is set in the base class. The only thing that you cannot do is to make private base components non-private in the derived class by setting them to protected or public.

Default Inheritance Mode

When you define the mode of inheritance, it is nice to be explicit and say exactly what you mean. However, C++ allows you to use the default inheritance mode. In this case, you assume that the client programmer and the maintenance programmer have enough knowledge to understand what you mean, even if you do not actually say what you mean.

The default mode of inheritance for a derived C++ class is private. If you just forget to be explicit and say exactly what you mean, the compiler assumes you want the private mode of inheritance. Listing 13.12 shows the example of the skeleton program where I forgot to say what I meant. As a result, the client code cannot access the public method `publB()` inherited from `Base` through the `Derived` class target.

Listing 13.12   Example of using the default mode of inheritance for classes.

```
class Base {
   private: int privB;         // accessed from Base only
   protected: int protB;       // accessed from Base and Derived
   public: void publB()        // accessed from Base and Derived
   { privB = 0; protB = 0; } } ;  // OK to access its own data

class Derived : Base {         // it is private by default
   private:   int privD;
   protected: int protD;
   public: void publD()
   { privD = 0;  protD = 0; protB = 0; } } ;      // OK to access

int main()
{ Derived d;                   // object of the derived class
   d.publD();                  // OK to access public part of Derived class
//   d.publB();                // not OK to access public part of Base class
   return 0;
   }
```

However, this is not as simple as it looks. The default mode of inheritance is private for deriving a class defined with only the keyword `class`. The default mode of inheritance for a C++ structure is public. Recall that the keywords `class` and `struct` denote the same thing with the exception of default access rights to data members and member functions. For `class`, it is private; for `struct`, it is public. Otherwise, they are the same. You can have member functions in a structure, you can overload these member functions and set up default arguments for them, and you can have constructors and destructors, data members of other classes (and structures), member initialization lists, and all other things that distinguish object-oriented programming from procedural programming. And yes, you can inherit from a structure; and yes, you can inherit a structure from a class or a structure. All that is perfectly legal in C++. And for a derived class defined with the keyword `struct`, the default mode of derivation is public, not private.

Here is an example of the `Derived` class, which is defined using the keyword `struct`. Since it is derived from its base class using the default mode of inheritance, the mode of derivation is public.

Listing 13.13   Example of using the default mode of inheritance for structures.

```
class Base {
    private: int privB;              // accessed from Base only
    protected: int protB;            // accessed from Base and Derived
    public: void publB()             // accessed from Base and Derived
    { privB = 0; protB = 0; } } ;    // OK to access its own data

struct Derived : Base {              // it is public by default
    private:  int privD;
    protected: int protD;
    public: void publD()
    { privD = 0;  protD = 0; protB = 0; } } ;      // OK to access

int main()
{ Derived d;                         // object of the derived class
  d.publD();                         // OK to access public part of Derived class
  d.publB();                         // Hey, this is perfectly legitimate now!
  return 0;
  }
```

Please don't think that C++ made it this way just to confuse you. This is consistent with the default C++ rules for access to class members. Recall that when a class is defined using the keyword `class`, the default access rights to class members are private. When a class is defined using the keyword `struct`, the default access rights to class members are public.

Similarly, when a class is derived from another class using the keyword `class`, the inheritance mode is private. When a class is derived from another class by using the keyword `struct`, the inheritance mode is public. The difference, however, is entirely in how the derived class is defined. The base class could be defined using either keyword `class` or keyword `struct`—this does not affect the inheritance mode for the derived class.

It is not a good idea to rely on defaults. Period.

Scope Rules and Name Resolution Under Inheritance

In C++, class scope can be viewed as nested under derivation. From this point of view, the scope of a derived class is enclosed by the scope of its base class.

According to the general theory of nested scopes, whatever is defined in the inner scope is invisible in the outer, more global scope. Conversely, whatever is defined in the outer scope is visible in the inner, more local scope. In the next example, variable x is defined in the outer function scope, and variable y is defined in the inner block scope. It is appropriate to access the variable x in the inner scope. It is futile to access the variable y from the outer scope.

```
void foo()
{ int x;            // outer scope: equivalent to base class
    { int y;        // inner scope: equivalent to derived class
      x = 0; }      // ok to access the name from outer scope
  y = 0; }          // syntax error: inner scope is invisible outside
```

In this example, the outer scope plays the role of the base class and its members. The inner scope plays the role of the derived class and its members. From the derived class, you can access the members of the base class, but the members of the derived class cannot be accessed from the base class.

This means that the derived class members are invisible in the scope of the base class. This should agree with your intuition because the base class should be designed, implemented, and compiled before the derived class is written. So it is only natural that the base class member functions cannot access the derived class data members or member functions.

Conversely, base class members are in the outer scope and hence are visible in the derived class methods. Again, this concurs with your intuition because the derived class object "is a" base class object and has all member functions and data members that the base class has. From this point of view, the scope model of the relationship between the base and derived classes is not particularly helpful because it does not add much to your intuition. However, this model is very useful if the derived and base classes use the same names. Different languages use different rules to resolve these name conflicts, and the nested scope model, which is employed by C++, might be helpful in developing your intuition for writing C++ code.

The derived class scope is nested within the base class scope, which means that the derived class names hide base class names within the derived class. Similarly, the derived class names hide base class names in the derived class client code. This is a very important rule that should become part of your programming intuition: If the derived and base classes use the same name, the base class name does not have a chance, as the meaning of the derived class name will be used.

Let us clarify this rule. If a name without a scope operator is found in a derived class member function, the compiler tries to resolve the name as a name local to that member function. In the next code example, there are four variables that use the name x. All these variables are of the same type, but this is not important. They could be of different types, or some of these names could denote a function; the general rule I am discussing will stand anyway.

```cpp
int x;                          // outer scope: can be hidden by class or function
class Base {
  protected: int x;            // base name hides global names
} ;

class Derived : public Base {
  int x;                        // derived name hides base names
public:
  void foo()
  { int x;
    x = 0; } } ;               // local variable hides all other names

class Client {
public:
  Client()
  { Derived d;
    d.foo(); } } ;             // using object d as a target message

int main()
{ Client c;                     // define the object, run the program
  return 0;  }
```

In this code, you see a local variable in the member function foo() in the class Derived, a data member in the class Derived, a data member in the class Base, and a global variable in the file scope. The statement x = 0; in Derived::foo() sets the local variable x to zero. The derived data member Derived::x, the base data member Base::x, and the global name x are all hidden by this local name because the local name is defined in the most nested scope.

Comment out the definition of the variable x in the method foo(). The statement x = 0; now cannot be resolved to the local variable because this name will not be found. If the name is not found in the scope of the statement (in this case, the derived class member function), the compiler looks up the derived class scope among class data members or member functions, depending on the syntax of the reference to the name. In the above code example, if the local variable x in Derived::foo() were absent, it would be the derived data member Derived::x that would be set to zero by the statement x = 0; in the derived member function Derived::foo().

If the name mentioned in the member function is not found in the class scope either, the compiler searches the base class (and ancestor classes of the base class if they exist and if the name is not found in the base). The first name found in this search would be used to generate object code. In the code example, if both variables x in the Derived class were absent (the local variable and the data member), it would be the data member Base::x that would be set to zero by the statement x = 0; .

Finally, if the name is not found in any of the base classes, the compiler searches for the name declared in the file scope (as a global object defined in the file scope or an extern global object declared in this scope but defined elsewhere). If the name is found in this process, it is used; if not, it is a syntax error. In the code example, if neither class Derived nor class Base used the name x, the global variable x would be set to zero by the statement in Derived::foo().

Similarly, if a client of a derived class sends a message to a derived class object, the compiler searches the derived class first, and only after that does it look up the base class definition (or the base ancestor definition). If the derived class and one of its base classes use the same name, the derived class interpretation is used. The base names are not even looked up by the compiler if the name is found in the derived class. The derived class name hides the base class name, and the base name does not have a chance.

A modified example with two classes, Base and Derived, is shown next. There are two functions foo() in this example: One is a public member function of class Base, and the other is a public member function of class Derived. Similar to the previous example, the client code defines an object of the Derived class and sends the foo() message to that object. Since the Derived class defines the member function foo(), the derived member function is called. If the Derived class did not define function foo(), then the compiler would generate a call to the Base class function foo(). The Base class function has a chance only if the same name is not used by the Derived class.

```
class Base {
  protected: int x;
public:
  void foo()              // Base name is hidden by the Derived name
  { x = 0; } } ;

class Derived : public Base {
public:
  void foo()              // Derived name hides the Base name
  { x = 0; } } ;

class Client {
public:
  Client()
  { Derived d;
    d.foo(); } } ;        // call to the Derived member function

int main()
{ Client c;               // create an object, call its constructor
  return 0;   }
```

Notice that in this example I do not introduce the global scope. If neither Derived nor Base class (nor any of its ancestors) has a member function foo(), then the function call to d.foo() is a syntax error. If a function foo() were defined in the global scope, the function call d.foo() would not call this global function anyway.

```
void foo()
{ int x = 0; }
```

This global function is not hidden by the foo() member function in the Derived (or the Base) class because it has a different interface. The member functions are called with the use of a target object, and the global function is called using the function name only:

```
foo();                    // call to a global function
```

The function calls we are discussing have a different syntactic form:

```
d.foo();                  // call to a member function
```

This syntactic form cannot be satisfied by a call to a global function—it includes a target object and hence can be satisfied only by a class member function.

Name Overloading and Name Hiding

Notice that in the previous discussion, the function signature was not mentioned as a factor to consider. This is not an omission. The function signature is not a factor. The signature does not matter.

Of course I am being facetious. The function signature does matter when the compiler decides whether the actual argument matches the function's formal parameters. However, it does not matter for the resolution of nested inheritance scopes. If the name is found in the derived class, the compiler stops its search of the inheritance chain. What happens if the function found in the derived class is no good from the point of view of argument matching? Too bad—you have a syntax error. What if the base class has a better match, a function with the same name, and with the signature that matches the function call exactly? Too bad; it is too late: The base function does not stand a chance.

Unfortunately, this is quite counterintuitive for many programmers. Please try to work with these nesting rules and on the examples to make sure you hone your intuition accordingly. Next is an example from my experience. I have pruned everything not related to the issue of hiding in nested scopes and left only a small part of the code.

Listing 13.14 shows the simplified part of the hierarchy of accounting classes. I use class `Account` and class `CheckingAccount` only. The derived class overwrites the base member function `withdraw()`, but this is not going to play any role in the discussion. The client code defines `CheckingAccount` objects, sends them messages that belong to either the base class (`getBal()` and `deposit()`) or the derived class itself (`withdraw()`), and everything is fine. The output of the program run is presented in Figure 13–10.

Listing 13.14   Example of inheritance hierarchy for `Account` classes.

```
#include <iostream>
using namespace std;

class Account {                          // base class
protected:
  double balance;

public:
  Account(double initBalance = 0)
  { balance = initBalance; }

  double getBal()                        // inherited without change
  { return balance; }
```

```
  void withdraw(double amount)              // overwritten in derived class
  { if (balance > amount)
      balance -= amount; }

  void deposit(double amount)               // inherited without change
  { balance += amount; }
} ;

class CheckingAccount : public Account {    // derived class
  double fee;

public:
  CheckingAccount(double initBalance)
  { balance = initBalance;   fee = 0.2; }

  void withdraw(double amount)              // it hides base class method
  { if (balance > amount)
      balance = balance - amount - fee; }
} ;

int main()
{
  CheckingAccount a1(1000);                 // derived class object
  a1.withdraw(100);                         // derived class method
  a1.deposit(200);                          // base class method
  cout << " Ending balances\n";
  cout << "   checking account object: " << a1.getBal() <<endl;
  return 0;
  }
```

Although the client code here is only a few lines long, in real life, it was about 200 pages long. The program evolved to reflect the changes in business conditions. One of the changes required was to add to class CheckingAccount yet another function deposit(), which could be used for international wire transfers. In these transfers, a transaction fee would be imposed depending on the amount and source of the transfer. This fee could be computed by the client code and sent to the CheckingAccount class as an argument. Hence, a simple way to support this change was to write another function deposit() with two parameters.

Figure 13-10   Output for the program code in Listing 13.14.

```
Ending balances
  checking account object: 1099.8
```

```
void CheckingAccount::deposit(double amount, double fee)
  { balance = balance + amount - fee; }
```

The client code for processing international transfers and for computing the fee required only a few pages to be added to the program. Here is an example of the new client code that calls this new deposit() function.

```
a1.deposit(200,5);                        // derived class method
```

So far, so good. The change went well, the new code ran fine. There was, however, a problem during system integration. These 200 pages of code that used to work so well before the change now did not work as well. Actually, the code did not work at all and would not even compile.

Now, let me assure you that I used many languages before using C++, and I had never seen anything like this. I also suspect that whatever languages you used before C++, you never saw anything like this either. This is yet another contribution of C++ to software engineering that you should be aware of.

Of course, we all have been in situations where adding some new code breaks the existing code, which no longer works correctly. Usually this happens because the new code interferes with the data that the existing code relies upon. But the existing code always compiles. In traditional languages, when you add new code, you do not get syntax errors in existing code.

In C++, a program consists of classes that are linked to each other, not only through data but also through inheritance. Of course, the new code can make the existing code semantically incorrect by handling data incorrectly. This is possible in any language. But the new code can also make the existing code syntactically incorrect through the inheritance links! This is only possible in C++. This is why I press this point about programming intuition, needing to know the rules and developing a feel for correct and incorrect C++ code.

Let us take a look at the reason for this "innovative" kind of programming trouble. This is how my new class CheckingAccount looks.

```
class CheckingAccount : public Account {
  double fee;
public:
  CheckingAccount(double initBalance)
  { balance = initBalance;   fee = 0.2; }
  void withdraw(double amount)                       // it hides base class method
  { if (balance > amount)
      balance = balance - amount - fee; }
  void deposit(double amount, double fee)            // new method
  { balance = balance + amount - fee; }             // hides base method
} ;
```

When the compiler was processing the existing 200 pages of client code, the calls to the member function `deposit()` were aiming at the base class member function `Account::deposit()` with one parameter.

```
a1.deposit(200);                        // base class method?
```

According to the rules for the name resolution you just saw, the compiler analyzes the type of the message target, finds that the object `a1` belongs to class `CheckingAccount`, and searches the class `CheckingAccount` for a member function whose name is `deposit()`. The compiler finds this function and stops the search through the inheritance chain. The next phase is, of course, signature matching. The compiler discovers that the method `CheckingAccount::deposit()` found in the derived class has two parameters. Meanwhile, the client code (which wanted to call the base class method) supplies only one parameter. The compiler tells me in no uncertain terms that I have a syntax error.

I probably should have saved the joke about driving the tank for this discussion. It was clear to me that my code was correct and yet I found another bug in my compiler. (It does not matter what compiler it was. When learning a new language, you always find quite a few bugs in your compiler until you know the language better.)

I would have liked very much if my compiler had treated this situation as function name overloading. I had the existing `deposit()` function with one parameter in the base class. I had the new `deposit()` function with two parameters in the derived class. But the object of the derived class was also an object of the base class! It had the inherited `deposit()` function with one parameter as well. My intuition was that the derived class had two `deposit()` functions, one with one parameter and the other with two parameters. And I would have liked very much if the compiler had used the rules for function name overloading and had picked up the right function, the one with only one parameter. However, as I said before, when a base method is hidden by a derived class method, the base method does not stand a chance. The overloading applies to several functions in the same scope. Hiding takes place between functions in nested scopes. Finally, I gave up and changed my thinking. It takes time, but I am sure you will be able to do the same.

Alert

C++ supports function name overloading in the same scope only. In independent scopes, function names do not conflict, and you can use the same name with the same or different signatures. In nested scopes, the name in the nested scope hides the name in the outer scope, whether or not these names have the same signatures. If classes are related through inheritance, the function name in the derived class hides the function name in the base class. Again, the signature is not important.

Figure 13–11 shows an object of the derived class with these two functions, one coming from the base class and the other coming from the derived class. The vertical arrow from the client code shows you that the compiler starts the search in the derived class. The compiler stops as soon as the name match is found (with any signature), and no attempt is made to get to the base class using the rules for name overloading. If the concepts of nested scopes for inheritance sound too abstract to you, use this picture to remind yourself that the search stops at the first match.

Figure 13–11   How a derived class method hides a base class method in a derived class object.

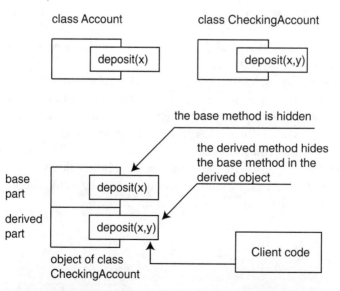

Calling a Base Method Hidden by the Derived Class

There are several remedies for this situation. One remedy is to indicate in the client code what function should be called. The scope operator does the job well.

```
int main()
{ CheckingAccount a1(1000);          // derived class object
  a1.withdraw(100);                  // derived class method
// a1.deposit(200);                  // syntax error
  a1.Account::deposit(200);          // solution to the problem
  cout << " Ending balances\n";
  cout << "    checking account object: " << a1.getBal() <<endl;
  return 0; }
```

Please make sure you do not get excited about this solution. The obvious drawback of this solution is that it requires making changes to the existing code. The advantage of the object-oriented approach is that it favors adding to the existing code rather than modifying it. This solution, however, is labor extensive and error prone. To use this solution is to ask for trouble.

From the software engineering point of view, this solution contradicts the principles of writing C++ code I discussed earlier. Which principles? Well, who bears the burden of the work in this solution? The client code. Who should carry the burden of the solution according to the principles of writing code? The server code. This solution fails to push responsibility down to the server classes. Instead, it brings responsibility up to the client code: you need to make sure that the base function is called—indicate explicitly that the base function should be called. This is a brute force solution.

Make sure that you use the criterion of pushing responsibility to the server classes in your work. It indicates in what direction you should search for a good solution. Let us look at the Account inheritance hierarchy. Our goal should be to add to these classes a method (or methods) that would make the problem go away. Why would I want to add a method? Because I do not want to change existing methods. Why would I want to add methods to the inheritance hierarchy? Because these classes serve the client code, and I want to push responsibility to the server classes.

One remedy is to overload the deposit() method in the base class rather than in the derived class. Since both functions belong to the same class and hence to the same scope, you have a case of legitimate C++ function name overloading. Both functions are inherited by the derived class and can be called through the derived class object as the message target. Here is the example of this solution.

```
class Account {                                // base class
protected:
  double balance;
public:
  Account(double initBalance = 0)
  { balance = initBalance; }
  double getBal()                              // inherited without change
  { return balance; }
  void withdraw(double amount)                 // overwritten in derived class
  { if (balance > amount)
      balance -= amount; }
  void deposit(double amount)                  // inherited without change
  { balance += amount; }
  void deposit(double amount,double fee)       // overloads deposit()
  { balance = balance + amount - fee; } } ;

class CheckingAccount : public Account {       // derived class
  double fee;
public:
  CheckingAccount(double initBalance)
  { balance = initBalance;   fee = 0.2; }
  void withdraw(double amount)                 // hides the base class method
  { if (balance > amount)
      balance = balance - amount - fee; } } ;

int main()
{ CheckingAccount a1(1000);                     // derived class object
  a1.withdraw(100);                             // derived class method
  a1.deposit(200);                              // existing client code
  a1.deposit(200,5);                            // new client code
  cout << " Ending balances\n";
  cout << "   checking account object: " << a1.getBal() << endl;
  return 0; }
```

This is a good workaround. Notice that the solution is found in the form of adding code to the server class, not in the form of modifying the client code. This solution pushes the work to the Account class, and this is good. However, this solution requires opening and changing the base class and not the derived class. This is not desirable for configuration control reasons. The higher a class is in the inheritance hierarchy, the more we want to guard this class against change because the change can affect other derived classes. The lower a class is in the inheritance hierarchy, the safer it is to open and to change.

Another problem with this solution is that the scope rules allow a base class member function to access base class data members only, not the derived class data. In my example, this is not a problem; both deposit() methods need only the base class data. Often, however, this is not so. The new method might need data that is defined in the derived class and is not available in the base class. For example, the standard withdrawal fee might be imposed on the deposit transaction as well. Then the new method `deposit()` could be implemented in the derived class only.

```
void CheckingAccount::deposit(double amount, double fee)
  { balance = balance + amount - fee - CheckingAccount::fee; }
```

However, putting the new method `deposit()` into the derived class takes us back to square one with the problem of the nested name scopes—this function hides the base class `deposit()` function and renders the existing code, with the calls to `deposit()` with one argument, syntactically incorrect.

A better remedy to this problem is to bite the bullet and place the new `deposit()` method where it belongs: in the derived class. To make the existing calls to the `deposit()` function with one legitimate parameter, you can overload the `deposit()` function in the derived class rather than in the base class. Again, the derived class is a server class for the client code, and this solution pushes responsibility to the server class.

Tip

Always look for ways to write C++ code such that the responsibility is pushed from the client code to the server code; thus the client code expresses the meaning of computations, not details of computations. This is a very general principle. It will serve you well.

Listing 13.15 shows this solution. The derived class has two member functions `deposit()` with two different signatures. Since they both belong to the same class, the rules for name overloading stand. Both new code and existing code now call the member functions of the derived class using different signatures. All that the member functions with one argument should do is call the base class member function with the same name (push the work to the server). The output of the program run is presented in Figure 13–12.

Listing 13.15   Example of inheritance hierarchy for `Account` classes.

```
#include <iostream>
using namespace std;

class Account {                              // base class
protected:
  double balance;
public:
  Account(double initBalance = 0)
  { balance = initBalance; }
  double getBal()                            // inherited without change
  { return balance; }
  void withdraw(double amount)               // overwritten in derived class
  { if (balance > amount)
      balance -= amount; }
  void deposit(double amount)                // inherited without change
  { balance += amount; }
} ;

class CheckingAccount : public Account {     // derived class
  double fee;

public:
  CheckingAccount(double initBalance)
  { balance = initBalance;   fee = 0.2; }

  void withdraw(double amount)
  { if (balance > amount)
      balance = balance - amount - fee; }

  void deposit(double amount)                // hides the base class method
  { Account::deposit(amount); }              // call to a base function

  void deposit(double amount, double fee)    // hides base method
  { balance = balance + amount - fee - CheckingAccount::fee; }
} ;

int main()
{
  CheckingAccount a1(1000);                  // derived class object
  a1.withdraw(100);                          // derived class method
  a1.deposit(200);                           // existing client code
  a1.deposit(200,5);                         // new client code
  cout << " Ending balances\n";
  cout << "    checking account object: " << a1.getBal() <<endl;
  return 0;
  }
```

```
Ending balances
  checking account object: 1294.6
```

Figure 13-12   Output for program in Listing 13.15.

Make sure that you are not intimidated by the use of scope operators in this example. The function `deposit()` with one parameter in class `CheckingAccount` could have been written this way:

```
void CheckingAccount::deposit(double amount)      // hides base method
  { deposit(amount); }                            // infinite recursive call
```

When the compiler processes the body of this function, it first looks for a match between the name `deposit()` and a name local to the function. There are no names local to the function, so the compiler looks for a match among class members. It finds the name `CheckingAccount::deposit()` and generates a call to it. As a result, the call is interpreted as an infinite recursive call.

The scope operator in Listing 13.15 directs the compiler to generate a call to the base function `Account::deposit()` and to avoid the trap of recursion. Notice that the responsibility to deal with the class hierarchy and decide to which class the `deposit()` function belongs is pushed down to the server class and not up to the client code as in my first remedy.

The function `deposit()` with two parameters in class `CheckingAccount` could have been written this way.

```
void CheckingAccount::deposit(double amount, double fee)
  { balance = balance + amount - fee - fee; }
```

When the compiler processes the body of this function, it looks for a match between the name `fee` and a name local to the function. This name is the name of the function's second parameter. Even though the class `CheckingAccount` has a data member `fee`, this data member is hidden by the name of the function parameter. To access the class data member `fee`, the code in Listing 13.15 has to use the scope operator that overrides the scope rules.

Using Inheritance for Program Evolution

Often a good way to handle this kind of program evolution is to avoid the problem and its remedies altogether. The source of my difficulties with international wire transfers in Listings 13.14 and 13.15 was that I was trying to change existing code (classes `Account` and `CheckingAccount`) to accommodate new conditions.

This is a natural way of thinking—from the traditional programming point of view. Object-oriented programming supported by C++ offers you an opportunity to think differently. Instead of looking for ways to change existing code, you could look for the ways to *inherit* from existing classes to support new requirements.

Make no mistake—I am talking about a new way of *thinking* about writing code. Using inheritance means that you are writing new code instead of changing existing code. Everyone who has ever tried to change existing code knows there is a world of difference between these two approaches. C++ offers a new approach to this little international wire transfer problem: leave the existing 200 pages alone, leave classes `Account` and `CheckingAccount` frozen, and introduce yet another derived class to support the new client code:

```cpp
class InternationalAccount : public CheckingAccount {       // great!
public:
   InternationalAccount(double initBalance)
   { balance = initBalance; }
   void deposit(double amount, double fee)                 // hides base method
   { balance = balance + amount - fee - CheckingAccount::fee; }
} ;
```

Listing 13.16 shows this solution. The classes `Account` and `CheckingAccount` are the same as in Listing 13.14. Yet another derived class, `InternationalAccount`, introduces no additional data members and only one member function, the function `deposit()`, which satisfies new client requirements. Since the objects, which are the targets of the `deposit()` messages with different numbers of parameters, belong to different classes, the issue of hiding or overloading does not arise. The object a1 is a target of the message with one parameter, and the compiler calls the function of the base class. The object a2 is a target of the message with two parameters, and the compiler calls the function of the class `InternationalAccount` derived from the class `CheckingAccount`. The output of the program run is presented in Figure 13–13.

> **Listing 13.16** Example of enhanced inheritance hierarchy for `Account` classes.

```cpp
#include <iostream>
using namespace std;

class Account {                              // base class
protected:
  double balance;
public:
  Account(double initBalance = 0)
  { balance = initBalance; }
  double getBal()                            // inherited without change
  { return balance; }
  void withdraw(double amount)               // overwritten in derived class
  { if (balance > amount)
      balance -= amount; }
  void deposit(double amount)                // inherited without change
  { balance += amount; }
} ;                                          // no changes to existing class

class CheckingAccount : public Account {     // derived class
protected:
  double fee;

public:
  CheckingAccount(double initBalance = 0)
  { balance = initBalance;  fee = 0.2; }

  void withdraw(double amount)               // hides the base class method
  { if (balance > amount)
      balance = balance - amount - fee; }
} ;                                          // no changes to existing class

class InternationalAccount : public CheckingAccount {   // great!
public:
  InternationalAccount(double initBalance)
  { balance = initBalance; }

  void deposit(double amount, double fee)    // hides base method
  { balance = balance + amount - fee - CheckingAccount::fee; }
} ;                                          // work is pushed to a new class

int main()
{
  CheckingAccount a1(1000);                  // derived class object
  a1.withdraw(100);                          // derived class method
  a1.deposit(200);                           // base class method
  InternationalAccount a2(1000);             // new server object
  a2.deposit(200,5);                         // derived class method
```

```
cout << " Ending balances\n";
cout << "    First checking account object:   "
     << a1.getBal() << endl;
cout << "    Second checking account object: "
     << a2.getBal() << endl;
return 0;
}
```

This is a very useful technique of program evolution. Instead of butchering existing classes and dealing with the dangers of invalidating existing client code, you derive another class from existing classes, which is responsible only for new program functionality. The use of C++ inheritance is the cornerstone of this new approach to software maintenance: writing new code instead of modifying existing code.

Actually, class CheckingAccount does need some modifications. The first modification is making the private data member fee protected to make sure that the new derived class, InternationalAccount, is able to access this data member. Another approach would be to add to class CheckingAccount a member function that retrieves the value of this data member; the client code (in this case, InternationalAccount) would call this function to access the base class data. As I mentioned earlier, I prefer to make a few data members accessible to one or two derived classes than to create a set of access functions that will be used only by these new derived classes (in this example, just one derived class).

Figure 13-13   Output for the program in Listing 13.16.

```
Ending balances
  First checking account object:  1099.8
  Second checking account object: 1194.8
```

Another way to avoid this modification to the existing class CheckingAccount is to exercise more foresight at the time of the class design. Why do you make class data members private? According to the principles of object-oriented programming, you do it for several reasons:

- You do not want the client code to create dependencies on server class data names.

- You do not want to complicate the client code with direct operations over data.

- You do not want the client code to know more about server design than is necessary.

- You want the client code to call server methods whose names explain the actions.

- You want the client code to push responsibility for lower level details to servers.

Notice that all these goals can be achieved by making server class data members protected rather than private. As I mentioned earlier, the protected keyword works like other access right modifiers, private and public, relative to different categories of class users. For derived classes, which are linked to the class by inheritance, the keyword protected works exactly as public works. It allows the derived classes direct access to the base class members. For client classes, which are not linked to the class by inheritance, the keyword protected works exactly as private does. There is no difference. If you think that program evolution through inheritance is possible, use protected access rights rather than private.

Tip

Always look for ways to use C++ inheritance for program evolution. Push responsibility from the client code to new derived classes. Weigh this approach against the drawbacks of creating too many small classes.

I am careful to say that the issue here is program evolution rather than initial program design. During program design, some key base classes might wind up at the top of a tall inheritance hierarchy of classes that includes many derived classes. With a large number of potential class users, the issues of data encapsulation, information hiding, pushing responsibilities to servers become important. For these key classes, you might want to use the private modifiers to force even derived classes to use access functions. For program evolution, the classes you will be using for further derivations are themselves at the bottom of the inheritance hierarchies (class CheckingAccount is a good example). They will not have a large number of derived classes dependent on them, and the issues of data encapsulation, information hiding, and pushing responsibilities to servers lose their importance with the decrease in the number of dependent classes.

The second modification is in the class CheckingAccount constructor. I added the default parameter value to avoid a syntax error in the client code when the object of the class CheckingAccount was created. This is similar to the issues I discussed for composite classes in Chapter 12. In the next section, I will discuss these issues as applied to the creation of C++ derived objects.

Constructors and Destructors for Derived Classes

When an object of a derived class is created, both its base and derived parts might need initialization. The base part of the derived class object and its derived part are created in a rigid sequence. It is important to understand this sequence to avoid potential syntactical and performance problems.

The issues of object construction under inheritance are very similar to the issues of object construction under class composition. For composition, the object data members are created (and their constructors are called) before the composite class constructor is executed. If the appropriate constructors do not exist, an attempt to create a composite object might result in a syntax error. If the appropriate constructors do exist, the creation of a composite object might result in performance penalty.

For class inheritance, the base part of the object is always created (and its constructor is called) before the derived part of the object is created and before the derived class constructor is executed. If the appropriate base constructor does not exist, an attempt to create a derived class object might result in a syntax error. If the appropriate base constructor does exist, the creation of a derived class object might result in performance penalty.

Let us consider class Point from the programs in Listings 13.6–13.9 and improve it by adding a general constructor with two parameters to this class:

```
class Point {                           // base class
   int x, y;
public:
   Point(int xi, int yi)                // general constructor
      { x = xi;   y = yi; }
   void set (int xi, int yi)
      { x = xi;   y = yi; }
   void get (int &xp, int &yp) const
      { xp = x;   yp = y; } } ;
```

The goal of this improvement is obvious: It provides for greater flexibility for the client code in creating class Point objects. The client code now has an opportunity to specify point coordinates at the time of object creation. This is better than creating an noninitialized object and later initializing it through a call to the set() member function.

As far as the class VisiblePoint from Listing 13.6 is concerned, this change in its base class does not require any adjustment: The derived class is not affected.

```
class VisiblePoint : public Point {       // public inheritance
   int visible;
public:
   void show()
      { visible = 1; }
   void hide()
      { visible = 0; }
   void retrieve(int &xp, int &yp, int &vp) const
      { get(xp,yp);                       // base public method is accessible
        vp = visible; } } ;               // derived private data is available
```

What is affected, however, is the client code of the derived class VisiblePoint. This code now contains syntax errors.

```
int main ()
{ VisiblePoint b; int x, y, z;     // define a derived object: error
   b.set(20,40);   b.show();        // base, derived public functions
   b.retrieve(x,y,z);              // call derived public function
   cout << " Point coordinates: x=" << x << "   y=" << y << endl;
   cout << " Point visibility:  visible=" << z << endl;
   return 0; }
```

As for any object, data members for the derived class object (in this case, data member visible) are allocated before the body of the derived class constructor is executed. However, even before the data described in the derived class is allocated, the base part of the derived object is created. "Created" here means that the base data members (in this case, x and y of the Point class) are allocated and a base constructor called.

Since there are no parameters passed on to the base class constructor, it is the default base constructor that is called. Since the base class `Point` provides a non-default constructor, the system-provided default constructor is taken away.

Hence, an attempt to create a derived class object results in a syntax error—a call to a function that does not exist. Notice that the client code that is in error now was perfectly all right in the programs in Listings 13.6–13.9:

```
VisiblePoint b;                 // no syntax error in previous versions
```

It is adding a general constructor to class `Point` that renders this line syntactically incorrect. Again, in traditional languages, adding new code might disrupt the operations of existing code but cannot make it syntactically incorrect. This is a new kind of link between different parts of the program that C++ adds to programming.

The remedy is of course to make sure that the base class still has a default constructor (either system-supplied or programmer-defined). This constructor is called after the base part of the derived class object is allocated.

```
class Point {                       // base class
   int x, y;
public:
   Point()
      { x = 0;  y = 0; }           // now the client code is OK
   Point(int xi,  int yi)          // general constructor
      { x = xi;  y = yi; }
   void set (int xi,  int yi)
      { x = xi;  y = yi; }
   void get (int &xp, int &yp) const
      { xp = x;  yp = y; } } ;
```

Now the client code is supported; the syntax error is gone. However, the work done by the `Point` default constructor is wasted because the client code sets the `VisiblePoint` object to the required place on the plane and either shows or hides it.

```
VisiblePoint b;                 // no syntax error
b.set(20,40);                   // write over the base part of object
b.show();                       // set the derived part of object
```

The sequence of events related to the creation of a derived class object is shown in Figure 13–14. First, the base part is created, then the base default constructor is called, the derived class is created, the derived constructor is called, and the next statements in the client code are executed.

The point of this example is that the base default constructor initializes the base data fields immediately after the base part is constructed; only after this

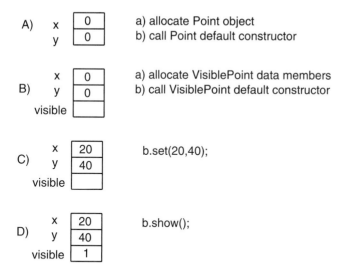

A) x [0]   a) allocate Point object
    y [0]   b) call Point default constructor

B) x [0]   a) allocate VisiblePoint data members
    y [0]   b) call VisiblePoint default constructor
    visible [   ]

C) x [20]   b.set(20,40);
    y [40]
    visible [   ]

D) x [20]   b.show();
    y [40]
    visible [1]

Figure 13-14   Steps of allocation and initialization for an object of the derived class.

is the derived part constructed and the derived class constructor executed. If the client code needs to set the base part to a specific state (rather than a default state), the calls to the base default constructor are wasted.

This design can be improved by pushing the responsibility from the derived class client to the derived class constructor. What responsibility? For initializing the derived object, including its base part. In the last code snippet this responsibility is performed by the client code by sending messages set() and show() to the derived class object. The client should be relieved from this responsibility.

The derived class might receive data for initializing its own data members and its base data in the form of parameters to the derived class constructor. These parameters can be used to explicitly set the state of the base part in the body of the derived class constructor.

```
class VisiblePoint : public Point {
  int visible;
public:
  VisiblePoint(int xi, int yi, int view)    // parameters for data
    { set(xi,yi);   visible = view; }        // set base, derived fields
    . . . . } ;                              // the rest of the VisiblePoint class
```

Now the client code does not have to explicitly call the base member function set() and its own function show() or hide(). Instead, the client code specifies additional parameters when defining derived class objects.

```
VisiblePoint b(20,40,1);      // no need to call set() or show()
```

One way to look at the call to the function `set()` in the `VisiblePoint` constructor is that the compiler first tries to find a local match within the scope of the constructor, then tries to find the match within the scope of the class `VisiblePoint`, and then tries to find the match within the scope of the base class `Point`. Another way to look at this call is that the function `set()` belongs to the base class. Since an object of a derived class "is an" object of the base class, the function `set()` belongs to the derived class as well. Hence, the call to the function `set()` does not need a target object because the derived class object (or, if you prefer, its base part) is the target of the message.

The third way to look at this call is to have pity on the reader of the code and admit that the writer of the code was interested in writing faster, not in making reading easier. When this code was written, the code writer knew to what class the function `set()` belonged. Nevertheless, it was left to the reader of the code to choose "one way to look at the call" or "another way to look at this call" and so on. This means that this code was not written according to the principles of the object-oriented approach. According to these principles, the client code (in this case, the `VisiblePoint` constructor) should be written so that the names of the function calls explain the actions. C++ supports this approach by allowing the use of the class scope operator to pass on to the reader of the code your knowledge at the time of writing the code.

```
class VisiblePoint : public Point {
  int visible;
public:
  VisiblePoint(int xi, int yi, int view)  // parameters for data
    { Point::set(xi,yi);                   // pass knowledge to maintainer
      visible = view; }
    . . . . } ;                            // the rest of the VisiblePoint class
```

Do you hear my message? I am again addressing the issue of programming intuition. Of course, traditional languages give you some means to pass the designer's knowledge on to the reader of the code. However, C++ is significantly more complex than traditional languages are. At the least, there are many more different ways to write C++ code than there are ways to write code using traditional languages. Hence, there are more ways to express the designer's knowledge in code. There is also much more need to express the designer's knowledge in code in C++ than in traditional languages. Make sure that you develop your intuition to see the opportunities to do so.

Tip

Always look for ways to pass on your knowledge at the time of code design to the client programmer and maintainer. C++ allows you to pass your knowledge in code, not in comments. Too many C++ programmers use C++ as if it were a traditional language and do not use this great opportunity to contribute to the quality of their code.

Using Initialization Lists in Derived Class Constructors

Adding a constructor to the class `VisiblePoint` pushes responsibility from the `VisiblePoint` client code to the `VisiblePoint` code. However, it does not resolve the problem of the wasted call to the constructor of the base class.

The base class default constructor is called for the base part of the derived class object anyway. This call takes place immediately after the base part of the object is allocated. Since the fields of the base part are reset in the derived class constructor when the constructor body is executed, the call to the base class default constructor is wasted.

If the base class has nondefault constructor(s), the derived class constructor can call a nondefault base constructor instead of the default base constructor. This eliminates the wasted function call.

Notice that a base class constructor is always called between the allocation of the base part and the call to the derived class constructor. The issue is only what constructor is to be called—a default constructor or a nondefault constructor.

To call a nondefault base constructor with parameters, C++ supports the initialization list syntax similar to the member initialization list syntax you used for coordination of constructor invocations in class composition.

```
class VisiblePoint : public Point {
   int visible;
public:
     VisiblePoint(int xi, int yi, int view) : Point(xi,yi)     // list
       { visible = view; }                 // no call to set()
     . . . . } ;                           // the rest of class VisiblePoint
```

The difference between these two forms of the initialization list is important. In class composition, the initialization list contains the names of object components in the form of the names of class data members. With inheritance, the initialization list contains the name of the derived object component in the form of the base class name, not the name of a data member.

The major similarity between the two forms of the initialization list is the timing of the component constructor call. In class composition, it is called immediately after the component data member is allocated. In class inheritance, it is called immediately after the base part of the derived object is allocated. In all cases, it is called before the body of the class constructor (container class or derived class) is executed. If the base part of the derived object contains components of other classes, or if the components of the composite object have base classes, this procedure is implemented recursively.

To summarize, C++ creates the base part of the derived object first, the base class constructor is then called, the derived class part is created, and the derived class constructor body is executed.

The parameters in the constructor call that follows the colon are passed to the base class constructor. They can either be parameters passed from the client code to the derived class constructor (as in the last example), literal values, or even function calls. There are no limitations.

If the base class component needs a default constructor (without parameters) for initialization of the derived class object, then it can be called either explicitly or implicitly. Say, for example, that the class `VisiblePoint` objects need their base part initialized to the origin of coordinates on the screen. Then the `VisiblePoint` constructor can be written this way:

```
class VisiblePoint : public Point {
  int visible;
public:
 VisiblePoint(int view) : Point()     // call to default constructor
 { visible = view; }                  // no call to set()
    . . . . } ;                       // the rest of class VisiblePoint
```

On the other hand, there is no need to call the base constructor explicitly. Even without the initialization list, the compiler invokes the default base class constructor automatically.

```
class VisiblePoint : public Point {
  int visible;
public:
 VisiblePoint(int view)        // implicit call to default constructor
   { visible = view; }         // no call to set()
      . . . . } ;              // the rest of class VisiblePoint
```

These two versions of the derived class constructor result in the same sequence of events when the derived class object is created: the base part of the object is allocated, the default base class constructor is called, the derived part of the object is allocated, and the derived conversion constructor is called.

You can mix both lists so that the data members of the derived class are also initialized using the member initialization syntax.

```
class VisiblePoint : public Point {
  int visible;
public:
  VisiblePoint(int xi, int yi, int view)
    : visible(view), Point(xi,yi)            // what is called first?
    { }                                      // a popular C++ idiom
    . . . . } ;                              // the rest of class VisiblePoint
```

Recall that data members are always created in the order of their appearance in the class specification. For a derived class, the base part specification is implicitly the first part of the class specification—it precedes the specification of the derived class members. Despite what it looks like in the initialization list above, the base constructor is invoked first and only then are the derived data members initialized. The derived class constructor body (if any) is always executed last.

It is quite rare that one can design a Derived class that does not have a constructor. It is rare that the initialization list is not used.

In this example, the body of the derived class constructor is empty. There are no advantages in initializing all data members of the derived class in the constructor initialization list, but it is very common. For some reason, many C++ programmers feel the satisfaction of good design if the body of the derived class constructor is empty. I do not know why.

In summary, there is no need to use an initialization list in the design of the derived class constructor(s) if:

1. the base class has no constructors (and its system-provided default constructor is called when a base part of the derived object is constructed) and

2. the base class has a programmer-defined default constructor (called when a base part of the derived object is constructed) and derived constructors (if any) that do not change the state of the base part of the derived object relative to what this default constructor does.

If the base class has a nondefault constructor, one has to distinguish between two cases:

1. The base class does not have a default constructor: Then the

derived class constructor(s) must use the initialization list syntax to invoke nondefault base constructors to avoid syntax errors at a derived object definition.

2. The base class also has a programmer-defined default constructor: The derived class constructors do not have to use initialization lists; the default `Base` constructor is called first, then the derived constructor overwrites its actions in its body. It is better to call the appropriate nondefault base constructor using the initialization list syntax.

Is it possible to have a derived class without a programmer-derived constructor? Sure. This means that neither the base part of the object nor its derived part needs any initialization. Things like that happen. However, if it happens to you, check your design again—something probably is amiss.

Destructors Under Inheritance

Next is a poor example of inheritance, but it illustrates the issues related to the use of destructors for derived classes.

I want to design a class `Address` to store people's names and e-mail addresses. Since inheritance is such a powerful mechanism for organizing classes in my program, I want to derive class `Address` from another, simpler class `Name`, which contains the name of the person to whom the e-mail address belongs. The base class `Name` has a data member, `data`, which points to a dynamically allocated character array. The class constructor dynamically allocates the object memory and copies the parameter string into the heap memory. The destructor returns the string memory to the heap before the object is destroyed. The `get()` member function returns the pointer to the name.

Listing 13.17 shows the program that implements this design. Since the goal of the example is to demonstrate the issues of dynamic memory management for base and derived classes, I have tried to keep it simple. This is why I am not implementing copy constructors and assignment operators for these classes. I do not think that potential clients should create `Name` objects: The `Name` class is needed only as the base for the `Address` class. To prevent accidental disasters, I prevent potential clients from creating `Name` objects by making the `Name` constructor protected. I cannot make it private: If I did, the `Address` objects would not be able to initialize their base part. But this is not a problem: For potential clients, `protected` works as well as `private` does. For the `Address` class, I prevent disasters by keeping both the copy constructor and the assignment operator `private`.

The output of the program is shown in Figure 13–15.

Listing 13.17   Using inheritance for classes with dynamic memory management.

```
#include <iostream>
using namespace std;

class Name {                                    // Base class
   char *name;                                  // dynamic memory management
protected:
   Name(char nm[]);                             // prevent using the objects
public:
  ~Name();                                      // return dynamic memory
   const char* get() const; } ;                 // access the contents

Name::Name(char nm[])
{ name = new char[strlen(nm)+1];                // allocate heap space
    if (name == NULL) { cout << "Out of memory\n";  exit(1); }
    strcpy(name,nm); }                          // initialize heap memory

const char* Name::get () const
{ return name; }                                // access private data

Name::~Name()
    { delete [] name; }                         // return object data

class Address : public Name {                   // Derived class
   char *email;
   Address(const Address&);                     // no value semantics
   void operator = (const Address&);
public:
   Address(char name[], char address[]);        // allocate heap space
  ~Address();
   void show() const; } ;                       // display object data

Address::Address(char nm[], char addr[]) : Name(nm)
{ email = new char[strlen(addr)+1];
    if (email == NULL) { cout << "Out of memory\n";  exit(1); }
    strcpy(email,addr); }

Address::~Address()                             // return object memory
{ delete [] email; }

void Address::show() const                      // display object data
{ cout << " Name:  " << Name::get() << endl;
    cout << " Email: " << email << endl << endl; }

int main ()
{
   Address x("Shtern", "shtern@bu.edu");        // client code
   x.show();
   return 0;
   }
```

```
Name:  Shtern
Email: shtern@bu.edu
```

Figure 13-15
Output for the program in Listing 13.17.

The class `Name` constructor (the base class constructor) allocates and copies memory for the base class; the class `Address` constructor (the derived class constructor) allocates and copies values for the derived class.

The `Address` constructor also passes the values to the `Name` constructor before the `Address` constructor code is executed. The instantiation of an object of class `Address` entails the following sequence of actions:

1. The memory for the base part of the object is allocated (pointer name).

2. The base constructor is called, and the heap memory pointed to by `name` is allocated and initialized.

3. The memory for the derived part of the object is allocated (pointer `email`).

4. The derived constructor is called, and the heap memory pointed to by `email` is allocated and initialized.

The order of destructor invocation is opposite to that of the order of constructor invocation. When a derived class object is being destroyed, the derived destructor is executed first; after that, the derived part data members are destroyed. Then the base class destructor is called, and after that the base part of the object is destroyed. Here is the list of the actions that take place.

1. The derived class destructor is called, and the heap memory pointed to by the `email` pointer is returned to the system.

2. The derived part of the object is destroyed, and its memory (pointer `email`) is returned to the system.

3. The base class destructor is called, and the heap memory pointed to by the `name` pointer is returned to the system.

4. The base part of the object is destroyed, and its memory (pointer `name`) is returned to the system.

Because a class destructor can take no parameters, the programmer does not have to coordinate destructor invocations. Just make sure that the destructors are there. Failure to implement any destructor will result in memory leak.

The base part of the object should not disappear first because it is a server of the derived part of the object. Base class data members might be necessary to preserve the integrity of the data members of the derived part of the object.

It is possible to lump dynamic memory management for both classes in the `Address` constructor and in the `Address` destructor. However, managing memory for only one class is good modularization.

Since this is a small example, the relationship between classes does not matter much. However, deriving the `Address` class from class `Name` stretches the notion of relationship. An address is not a name, but the use of inheritance suggests that. You would rather say that an address has a name. This suggests the use of the composition relationship. In the next chapter, we will look into this tradeoff in more detail.

Summary

In this chapter, we continued studying the relationships between C++ classes. The relationship of inheritance allows the use of one class as a base for another class. By virtue of doing so, the derived class inherits all data members and member functions of the base class. Usually, the derived class adds more data members and member functions to members inherited from the base class. Sometimes, the derived class redefines the capabilities inherited from the base class.

Using inheritance provides a great way to modularize the design. Instead of designing a server class in one leap, you can create and debug a base class and then add more functionality in the form of derived classes.

The use of inheritance facilitates program evolution. Instead of changing existing code, you can add new code to the client code and then support this new code, not by changing existing server classes, but by creating new derived classes that serve the needs of the new client code.

Similar to class composition, using C++ inheritance requires that you learn a host of new syntactical details. C++ implementation of inheritance is very rich and often gives you more than one way to implement your design. This means that a reckless use of inheritance can make your program much more complex than it needs to be.

Using inheritance as a design tool, you can expand your opportunities for practicing modern forms of software engineering—pushing responsibility from client code down to server classes, passing the knowledge of the code designer on to client programmers and maintainers. This is a new way to write code, and it requires a shift in intuition. Make sure that you are constantly developing your C++ programming intuition—it is a very important component of your programming skills.

In this chapter, we studied only a fraction of what there is to know about C++ inheritance. In the next chapter, we will learn other techniques for using inheritance.

Have fun.

CHOOSING
BETWEEN
INHERITANCE AND
COMPOSITION

Topics in this Chapter

- Choosing a Technique for Code Reuse
- Unified Modeling Language
- Case Study: A Rental Store
- On Class Visibility and Division of Responsibilities
- Summary

Chapter 14

In this chapter, you will see more examples of inheritance and composition. I will start with a smaller example and compare the use of inheritance with other programming techniques.

I am going to compare different design alternatives for implementing the same program. "Design" here means the same as it has in the rest of the book: deciding what parts (classes) the program should consist of and what responsibilities (data members and member functions) should be assigned to each part. In comparing different design alternatives, I will evaluate the effectiveness of the same general techniques that I formulated in Chapter 1, "Object-Oriented Approach: What's So Good About It?": pushing responsibilities from client classes to server classes, self-documented client code expressed in terms of calls to server methods, and elimination of links between classes. I will also use lower level specific criteria such as encapsulation, information hiding, coupling, and cohesion.

All of these techniques are directed toward making code easier to read. In this chapter, one of the criteria to judge the quality of design will be ease of writing. This is a major deviation from the principles proclaimed in the Chapter 1, where I stressed the ease of reading and argued that the ease of writing is usually achieved at the expense of the ease of reading and hence should be avoided. After all, we write code only once, when we type it in, and the actual typing takes only a miniscule fraction of the time that we spend reading the code when we try to debug it, test it, integrate it, reuse it, or modify it.

This shift in emphasis is unavoidable when you use inheritance because inheritance is a design technique directed toward ease of writing. The designer of the server class derives the server class from the base class, not to serve the client code better, but for the convenience of the server class implementation. Ideally, the designer of the client code should not care whether the server class is designed from scratch or is derived from some base class (as long as the server class supports the services that the client code needs).

This is the ideal but real life is different from the ideal in C++ programming, much as in other human activities. The use of inheritance (for the sake of the ease of writing the server classes) is at odds with the ease of reading, both for the client code and for the maintainer. In the next chapter, I will show you how to use inheritance to make the client code simpler as well.

For the discussion of links among classes, I will use the Unified Modeling Language (UML) notation to describe the relationships between classes in the application. Today, the use of UML is considered critical for the success of object-oriented design and implementation. Many organizations embrace it for their object-oriented projects. Anecdotal evidence of UML utility is plentiful, but there is yet no hard evidence that the use of UML makes object-oriented projects successful. UML is a product of a political and technical compromise rather than the result of a breakthrough in development. It was designed by a committee with the goal of unifying several earlier versions of object-oriented design notation and they added more features for describing object relationships in more detail. However, each member of the committee was trying to add to UML the features of their favorite notation system. As a result, the language is overblown with features and is very difficult to learn.

This is a pity. The language should be unobtrusive. It should allow the developers to communicate their ideas and understand the ideas of others with ease. If someone is a novice in the language, so that his or her statements are ambiguous or confusing, there should be a compiler that warns the designer about that. Nothing of that sort is available for UML. It tends to produce diagrams that are more complex than necessary. My experience with UML (and its predecessors) shows that it is a waste of time to learn it before you know an object-oriented language well. Also, this modeling language is so huge, and possible design variations are so broad, that one should not try to study it while learning an object-oriented language—it will not speed up the process of learning. However, the basic UML (or any of its predecessors) could and should be used to describe the object-oriented designs implemented in C++.

This is what I will try to do in this chapter: I will introduce the basic UML notation as a descriptive tool for comparing the uses of inheritance and composition. I will also use UML notation for illustrating general relationships among objects in a program. The examples I discuss in this chapter are large enough to warrant several approaches to their design and implementation, and the use of the UML will be helpful for understanding the high-level issues of program design.

Choosing a Technique for Code Reuse

In this section, I will discuss the relative advantages and disadvantages of using inheritance and composition. Both relationships are client-server relationships. A derived class is a client of the base class, and the base class is a server of the derived class. A composite class is a client of its component class, and the component class is a server of the composite class. This means that you are going to see significant similarities between C++ programs built with alternative design techniques.

The common feature of different design solutions is the division of work between the client and the server classes, be it with the use of composition or any other design techniques. This means that the server class has to be implemented before the client class can be designed. Hence, the techniques, which are discussed in this section, can be used both for program development and for program evolution.

Example of a Client-Server Relationship Between Classes

As a simple example of the client-server relationship, I will discuss an application that uses class `Circle`, with a data member for the circle radius, so that the client code can send messages to access the internal data representation in `Circle` objects.

```
Circle c1(2.5), c2(5.0);          // set the value of radius
double len = c1.getLength();      // compute circumference
double area = c2.getArea();       // access internal data
c1.set(3.0);
double diam = 2 * c1.getRadius();
```

To support this kind of client code, the class `Circle` should implement at least five public member functions:

- a constructor with one integer parameter
- a method `getLength()` that returns the circle circumference
- a method `getRadius()` that returns the circle radius
- a method `set()` that changes the circle radius
- a method `getArea()` that returns the circle area

Notice again, that it is the needs of the specific client code that define how the server class is going to look. This is not the only possible mode of C++ programming. When a high premium is put on the reuse of software components, server classes are often designed as library classes so that they can satisfy the needs of the maximum number of clients. To achieve this, the server classes offer the services that the class designer thinks will satisfy the maximum number of clients. As a result, some clients have to work harder to use these generic classes.

In this book, I do not pay much attention to the design of library classes. To design these classes well, one has to provide access to internal data representation and let the client programmers manipulate the data as they see fit.

The second mode of C++ programming, the mode of supporting the client-server relationship, is much more challenging. It requires the server programmer to recognize the client needs and implement methods that satisfy these needs rather than just bring information to the client code for manipulation.

Notice also that I send messages to the server objects to access the internal data representation. Whatever a class method does (e.g., multiplies the circle radius by two and by PI to compute the circumference), it accesses the internal data representation (in this case, radius) on behalf of the client code that does not have such access. To support the client needs in this case, class `Circle` should look this way.

```
class Circle                        // original code for reuse
{ protected:                        // inheritance is one of the options
    double radius;                  // internal data
  public:
    Circle (double r)               // support for initialization
    { radius = r; }
  double getLength () const         // compute circumference
  { return 2 * PI * radius; }
  double getArea () const           // compute area
  { return PI * radius * radius; }
```

```
double getRadius() const
{ return radius; }
void set(double r)
{ radius = r; } };                    // change size
```

Those of you who would like to avoid errors related to writing floating point numbers (and would like to have more practice in using initialization lists) could use a different version of class `Circle`.

```
class Circle                            // original code for reuse
{ protected:                            // inheritance is one of the options
    const double PI;                    // it must be initialized in the list
    double radius;                      // internal data
  public:
    Circle (double r) : PI (3.1415926536)   // initializer list
    { radius = r; }
    double getLength ()                 // compute circumference
    { return 2 * PI * radius; }
    double getArea ()                   // compute area
    { return PI * radius * radius; }
    double getRadius() const
    { return radius; }
    void set(double r)
    { radius = r; } };                  // change size
```

Notice that I quoted only one common rationale for using a constant instead of a numeric literal: the likelihood of typing errors when the same literal is typed in different places in the code. I did not use another popular rationale: convenience of changing the value at the time of maintenance. Unless there is an unexpected scientific breakthrough, the value of PI is not going to change soon. Also notice that now I multiply PI by 2 each time the method `getLength()` is called. These are not serious drawbacks, but they indicate that the real goal of defining PI as a constant in this example is to show you once again that the initializer list can contain not only constructor parameters, but also literal arguments.

Finally, notice that PI is defined as local to class `Circle`. If other classes in the application need this value, they have to either define it themselves or get it from class `Circle`. To facilitate this, this constant data member could be made public.

```
class Circle                        // original code for reuse
{ protected:                        // inheritance is one of the options
   double radius;                   // internal data
  public:
   const double PI;                 // it must be initialized in the list
  public:
   Circle (double r) : PI (3.1415926536)   // initializer list
   { radius = r; }
   . . . } ;                        // the rest of class Circle
```

You see here a popular technique for defining public data in a separate public section to make it more conspicuous. Had I defined PI in the same public section as the class member function, it might have been lost there.

All right, now class Circle is in place—but wait a minute, is it in place? In this design of class Circle, each Circle object is allocated memory for the value of PI individually. Meanwhile, this value is the same for each object. Allocating this memory for each Circle object is a waste. Programmers who work with non-object-oriented languages do not have to deal with these issues. C++ programmers deal with these issues all the time. It is important to develop the appropriate intuition to spot the potential waste. Until this intuition is developed, it is a good idea to be vigilant and scrutinize the use patterns for each data member. When a data member has the same value for each object of the class, this is a situation where the use of static data fits the bill beautifully. Here is class Circle that allocates only one value of PI for all of its objects:

```
class Circle                        // original code for reuse
{ protected:                        // inheritance is one of the options
   double radius;                   // internal data
  public:
   static const double PI;          // it must be initialized
  public:
   Circle (double r)                // initializer list
   { radius = r; }
   double getLength () const        // compute circumference
   { return 2 * PI * radius; }
   double getArea () const          // compute area
   { return PI * radius * radius; }
   double getRadius() const
   { return radius; }
   void set (double r)
   { radius = r; } };               // change size
```

```
const double Circle::PI = 3.1415926536;
```

As you see, the initialization of a static data member does not require the member initialization list. It is initialized in the definition, which is implemented in the same file as class member functions. Similar to member functions, the class scope operator specifies to which class this data member belongs. If you want to define a data member PI in another class, these names will not conflict with each other because they belong to different classes.

This example shows again that the C++ programmer should always think about different aspects of the program design. Concentrating on part of the picture only results in wrong conclusions that might lead to waste or even to errors.

Make sure that the diversity of issues you should always think about while writing C++ code does not make your vision too narrow.

All right, now that the class Circle is in place, let us consider the client code requirements of the class Cylinder that has data members describing the cylinder radius and height.

```
Cylinder cyl1(2.5,6.0), cyl2(5.0,7.5);    // initialize data
double length =cyl1.getLength();           // similar to Circle
cyl1.set(3.0);
double diam = 2 * cyl1.getRadius();        // no call to getArea()
double vol = cyl2.Volume();                // not in Circle
```

Even though classes Circle and Cylinder are different, they have similar internal structures (the radius data member) and provide services that have the same name and same interface, for example, getLength(). This is why the issue of reusing the class Circle in the design of class Cylinder is a valid one.

Although I tried to keep this example small to let you concentrate on the design issues rather than on the design details, the example shows that some of the existing Circle services should not be made available in the Cylinder objects, for example, the method getArea(). On the other hand, Cylinder clients might need services that are not available to the Circle clients, for example, the method Volume(). This is typical for most reuse contexts—some of the existing services are reused, some are suppressed or ignored, and some new services are added.

Now let us assume that the `Circle` code is available, but the class `Cylinder` is not designed yet. The similarities between classes suggest that we should try to build class `Cylinder` using class `Circle` code so that the reuse of available code is maximized and facilitated.

For many people, this similarity is a decisive argument in favor of using inheritance. This is too simplistic. Inheritance is used too much in industry. It should not be your first choice in reuse, or at least it should be chosen as the result of comparisons with other techniques of code reuse. How do you choose one technique over another?

The amount and convenience of code reuse should be your first criterion. The next two criteria should be the amount of new code that should be written and the extent of testing. This example is very small, so the differences are not going to be essential, but they will show you what to pay attention to while deciding which way to go.

In general, there are four approaches to code reuse: reuse of human intelligence (i.e., writing code from scratch); writing a new class so that its methods are using (buying) methods (services) of the existing class; writing a new class so that it inherits from the existing class, and its objects provide their clients with the base services; and using inheritance with redefinition of some methods. For this example, the agenda for each approach should include:

1. Human intelligence: Write new code for `Cylinder` from scratch, using the editor to copy the `Circle` code for `radius`, `getLength()`, and other member functions into class `Cylinder` and adding new `Cylinder` code to do the job that class `Circle` does not provide.

2. Buy services: Using the assumption that each cylinder "has a" circle object inside it, you design the `Cylinder` class as a composite class. An object of the `Circle` type is used as a data member in class `Cylinder`, and the `Cylinder` methods (e.g., `getLength()`), send messages with the same name to the `Circle` component.

3. Inherit from the existing class as a base class: Using the assumption that each cylinder object "is a" circle (plus some more and probably minus some), you design the `Cylinder` class as a class derived from `Circle`; there is no need to implement code for inherited methods, for example, `getLength()` because each `Cylinder` object can respond to these messages inherited from its `Circle` base.

4. Inherit but redefine some methods: This approach supports a new way to do existing operations; for example, the area of a cylinder should be computed differently from the area of a circle.

In the following sections, I will implement the class Cylinder using each of these techniques and will discuss relative advantages and disadvantages of each approach.

Reuse Through Human Intelligence: Just Do It Again

Reuse through human intelligence is very common in non-object-oriented programming. It seems that in object-oriented languages, the programmers are so excited about using inheritance and composition that they look down on such a low-tech method of code reuse.

In this approach, you draw on your past. If you have experience in similar tasks, you reproduce the code you wrote earlier and edit as is appropriate to satisfy the new requirements. In this case, assume that you wrote and tested class Circle recently, and now your task is to write class Cylinder. I call this approach reuse through human intelligence because you reuse the knowledge that you accumulated by working on similar code.

Listing 14.1 shows the design of class Cylinder, which uses the design of class Circle. You reproduce the data part of the class Circle (in this case, the radius data member) and add whatever the class Cylinder requires (the height data member). You reproduce the constructor and add the parameter and code to initialize the height data member. You copy the methods that can be reused verbatim (in this case, the method getLength() and others). You bite the bullet and implement the Cylinder methods that the class Circle lacks (in this case, the Volume() method). And you do not pay attention to the Circle methods that are not needed in the class Cylinder (in this case, the getArea() method). The results of program execution are shown in Figure 14–1.

Listing 14.1   Example of code reuse through human intelligence.

```
#include <iostream>
using namespace std;

class Cylinder                              // new class Cylinder
{ protected:
    static const double PI;                 // from class Circle
    double radius;                          // from class Circle
    double height;                          // new code

  public:
    Cylinder (double r, double h)           // from Circle plus new code
    { radius = r;
      height = h; }                         // new code

    double getLength () const
    { return 2 * PI * radius; }             // from class Circle

    double getRadius() const
    { return radius; }                      // from class Circle

    void set(double r)                      // from class Circle
    { radius = r; }

    double getVolume() const                // no getArea()
    { return PI * radius * radius * height; }  // new code
    } ;

const double Cylinder::PI = 3.1415926536;

int main()
{
 Cylinder cyl1(2.5,6.0), cyl2(5.0,7.5);     // initialize data
 double length = cyl1.getLength();          // similar to Circle
 cyl1.set(3.0);
 double diam = 2 * cyl1.getRadius();        // no call to getArea()
 double vol = cyl2.getVolume();             // not in Circle
 cout << " Circumference of first cylinder: " << length << endl;
 cout << " Volume of the second cylinder:   " << vol << endl;
 cout << " Diameter of the first cylinder:  " << diam << endl;
 return 0;
  }
```

```
Circumference of first cylinder: 15.708
Volume of the second cylinder:   589.049
Diameter of the first cylinder:  6
```

Figure 14–1   Output for program in Listing 14.1.

Most of the existing `Circle` code (its data and its methods) are copied verbatim. Unnecessary methods are omitted. New code has to be developed for data and methods missing in `Circle` but that are present in class `Cylinder`. This new code has to be tested. If the existing code is copied using a text editor rather than typed in, testing the `Circle` code should be minimal. Since the interfaces of the `Circle` functions do not change, existing testing sequences for class `Circle` could be reused for class `Cylinder` as well.

Productivity of this method of code reuse is very high. Everybody, including your boss, is stunned by the lightning speed of your code development. If they knew that you were relying on your previous experience, they would be less awed. On the other hand, you were hired to do the job because you had experience in the development of similar systems. This experience is the most valuable asset for the development team.

From the software engineering point of view, there is a serious drawback to this approach. Do you see what it is? These two classes, `Circle` and `Cylinder`, are related to each other. They have common data members and common member functions. This connection between classes `Circle` and `Cylinder` exists only in the mind of the `Cylinder` designer. The maintainer might easily overlook this connection. This could result in errors during maintenance.

Reuse Through Buying Services

It is considered good practice to write C++ programs in such a way that objects that send messages to other objects in the program are related to each other in real life. Sending a message to another object is sometimes called *buying the services* of that object.

Notice that I was careful to say that the objects send messages to other objects in the *program*, not that objects send messages to *each other*. Syntactically, it is quite possible that an object of class A sends a message to an object of class B, and an object of class B sends a message to an object of class A in the same program. C++ does not make such convoluted cooperation illegal. Moreover, in some real-time programs, this architecture might even be useful. Mostly, however, this results in unnecessary complexity of design, that is, in unnecessary complexity of partitioning the job among cooperating classes and in complexity of links among the classes. This is why in most cases of class cooperation, it is one class that plays the role of the client class, and it is another class that plays the role of the server class. When a method of a client class sends a message to an object of the server class, we say that one class "buys the services" of another class.

There are three contexts in which a client method can access a server object and send a message to that object:

- Define a server object as a local variable in the client method.
- Define a server object as a data member in the client class.
- Receive a server object as a parameter to the client method.

The first context is the most beneficial from the point of view of class communications: Only one client function (where the server object is defined) has access to the server object. Given a choice, you should always choose this type of client-server relationship. Often, this is not possible, because the server object has to be accessed by other client class methods or by other classes (or by both).

The second context is the next beneficial: The server object is accessible to all member functions of the client class. Given a choice, you should always prefer to use this type of client-server relationship rather than using the server object as a parameter to the client class method.

The third context is the most complex from the point of view of communications between cooperating classes: The argument object is used as a server both by the function to which it is passed as a parameter and by the functions that call this server function. Given a choice, you should always avoid this type of client-server relationship, reducing it to either the first context (access by one client method only) or to the second context (access by methods of one client class only).

From the point of view of code reuse, it is the second type of the client-server relationship that allows one to create server classes that serve their clients by providing them the services of existing classes.

For an example of the relationship between classes `Circle` and `Cylinder`, this means setting up a client-server relationship between them so that a `Circle` object is a member of class `Cylinder`. Since we try to design data members as private (or protected), the `Circle` services are not available to the `Cylinder` clients directly. To provide such services to its clients (in this case, the getLength() method), the Cylinder class should ask its Circle data member to do the job.

Listing 14.2 shows this design (the output of the program is the same as in Listing 14.1). Class Circle is defined explicitly. Class Cylinder defines a data member of class Circle along with additional data (in this case, data member height). If this data member were made public, it would be accessible to the Cylinder client code.

```
class Cylinder                          // new class Cylinder
{ protected:
    double height;                      // new code
  public:
    Circle c;                           // no PI, no radius
  public:
    Cylinder (double r, double h)       // from Circle plus new code
        : c(r)                          // initializer list (no PI)
    { height = h; }                     // new code
    double getVolume() const            // no getArea()
    { double radius = c.getRadius();    // new code
      return Circle::PI * radius * radius * height; }
  } ;                                   // no getLength(), getRadius(), set()
```

This class Cylinder has very few member functions. It does not have to implement methods getLength(), getRadius(), and set() on behalf of its client code because the client code can send these messages to the Cylinder public data member c.

```
Cylinder cyl1(2.5,6.0), cyl2(5.0,7.5);  // initialize data
double length = cyl1.c.getLength();      // use Circle data member
cyl1.c.set(3.0);
double diam = 2 * cyl1.c.getRadius();    // no call to getArea()
double vol = cyl2.getVolume();           // not in Circle
```

What are the drawbacks of this design? Its data is public. The client uses the name of the class Cylinder data member, c, and develops dependencies on the Cylinder class design. The appropriate way to verbalize your concern about the quality of this design is to notice the division of responsibilities between the class Cylinder and its client code. Here, the designer of class Cylinder has an easy life. All that class Cylinder does is to supply the getVolume() method and duck all other responsibilities. Who knows to what class the methods getLength(), getRadius(), and set() belong? The client code knows about these methods but not its server class Cylinder. How do I know about this distribution of knowledge? Because it is the client code that sends these messages, not class Cylinder.

Notice that I am not complaining about the awkward chain syntax of function calls in the client code. It is awkward, true, but my complaint is about expanding responsibilities of the client code designer. This designer (and the maintainer of this code) is required to learn the services of two classes, class Circle and class Cylinder, instead of learning the services of only one class, Cylinder. In this example, the class definitions are conveniently placed together. In real life, they can be separated. In real life, there might be more than two classes related to each other. In real life, nothing may indicate that these classes (here, Circle and Cylinder) are related to each other.

This is why I think that the design in Listing 14.2 is a better example of buying services. The Circle data member is not public in class Cylinder. (It is protected, but for the client code, this is as much out of reach as private.) As a result, it is class Cylinder, not its client, that knows to what class the methods getLength(), getRadius(), and set() belong. Class Cylinder defines a set of one-liners—the only task of these member functions is to turn around and send the message with the same name to the Cylinder data member c.

Listing 14.2   Example of code reuse through buying data member services (class composition).

```
#include <iostream>
using namespace std;

class Circle                          // original code for reuse
{ protected:                          // inheritance is one of the options
    double radius;                    // internal data
  public:
    static const double PI;           // it must be initialized

  public:
    Circle (double r)                 // conversion constructor
    { radius = r; }

    double getLength () const         // compute circumference
    { return 2 * PI * radius; }

    double getArea () const           // compute area
    { return PI * radius * radius; }

    double getRadius() const
    { return radius; }

    void set(double r)
    { radius = r; } };                // change size
```

```
const double Circle::PI = 3.1415926536;

class Cylinder                               // new class Cylinder
{ protected:
    Circle c;                                // no PI, no radius
    double height;                           // new code

  public:
    Cylinder (double r, double h)            // from Circle plus new code
        : c(r)                               // initializer list (no PI)
    { height = h; }                          // new code

    double getLength () const
    { return c.getLength(); }                // from class Circle

    double getRadius() const                 // from class Circle
    { return c.getRadius(); }

    void set(double r)                       // from class Circle
    { c.set(r); }

    double getVolume() const                 // no getArea()
    { double radius = c.getRadius();         // new code
      return Circle::PI * radius * radius * height; }
  } ;
int main()
{
  Cylinder cyl1(2.5,6.0), cyl2(5.0,7.5);     // initialize data
  double length = cyl1.getLength();          // similar to Circle
  cyl1.set(3.0);
  double diam = 2 * cyl1.getRadius();        // no call to getArea()
  double vol = cyl2.getVolume();             // not in Circle
  cout << " Circumference of first cylinder: " << length << endl;
  cout << " Volume of the second cylinder:   " << vol << endl;
  cout << " Diameter of the first cylinder:  " << diam << endl;
  return 0;
  }
```

In this design, both data encapsulation and separation of concerns are well supported. The designer of the client code only has to know its server Cylinder. There is no need to know the design of class Circle (a server of the server class). The connection between the classes is clear during maintenance.

This method of code reuse might be even faster than rewriting from scratch. Tests are less demanding—the one-liners are easy to test. There is no need for inheritance and its coupling between the base and derived classes.

A potential problem might arise of class Cylinder needing access to Circle data members. It is important that class Circle provide the access

methods needed by class `Cylinder`. Some C++ programmers dislike the proliferation of one-liners. They are simple, but they are too boring. As you are
going to see in the next section, the use of inheritance eliminates this problem.

Code Reuse Through Inheritance

Code reuse through inheritance is the most popular method used today.
Usually, most base services could be inherited "as is," and additions or
changes are relatively few. In such situations, this method works well and
eliminates a lot of one-line methods that are typical for the class composition.

Listing 14.3 shows an example of reusing the code for class `Circle` by making it the base class for the derived class `Cylinder`. Since the client code is
the same as in Listing 14.1 and 14.2, it is small wonder that the program output is the same as the output shown in Figure 14.1.

In the previous version, in Listing 14.2, I assumed that a cylinder "has a"
circle. Hence, class `Cylinder` implemented the method common to both
classes sending messages to its data member of class `Circle`. In this version
of the program, I assume that a cylinder "is a" circle.

The client of the derived class `Cylinder` has easy access to base class services. The client code calls them (e.g., `getLength()`) as if these services were
defined in the class `Cylinder`. The design of class `Cylinder` is easy too. It
defines only the features that are absent in the base class `Circle`. It is as easy
as using composition with public data members of class `Circle`. It is definitely easier than using composition with non-public data members of class
`Circle` as in Listing 14.2. For class composition, class `Cylinder` has to implement a one-liner method for each `Circle` method that has to be made available to the `Cylinder` client code. For inheritance, these one-liners are gone.

The initializer list for the derived class constructor is similar to the initializer list for class composition—the name of the data member in Listing 14.2
is replaced with the name of the base class in Listing 14.3. Do you remember
what the initializer lists are for? Since class `Circle` has no default constructor, it would be a syntax error to create an object of class `Cylinder` (not class
`Cylinder` itself, but an object of class `Cylinder`) without the use of the initializer list, whether you design with composition or with inheritance.

So, the design with inheritance is either just as complex as design with class
composition (e.g., for initializer lists) or is simpler than class composition.
(The one-line data members are gone.) Does it mean that we are getting
something for nothing, that designing with inheritance is so much better than
designing with composition? Of course not.

Listing 14.3   Example of code reuse through inheritance.

```
#include <iostream>
using namespace std;

class Circle                              // original code for reuse
{ protected:                              // inheritance is one of the options
    double radius;                        // internal data
  public:
    static const double PI;               // it must be initialized

  public:
    Circle (double r)                     // conversion constructor
    { radius = r; }

    double getLength () const             // compute circumference
    { return 2 * PI * radius; }

    double getArea () const               // compute area
    { return PI * radius * radius; }

    double getRadius() const
    { return radius; }

    void set(double r)
    { radius = r; } };                    // change size

  const double Circle::PI = 3.1415926536;

class Cylinder : public Circle            // new class Cylinder
{ protected:
    double height;                        // other data is in Circle

  public:
    Cylinder (double r, double h)         // from Circle plus new code
        : Circle(r)                       // initializer list (no PI)
    { height = h; }                       // new code

    double getVolume() const              // no getArea()
    { return height * getArea(); }        // additional capability
    } ;

int main()
{
 Cylinder cyl1(2.5,6.0), cyl2(5.0,7.5);  // initialize data
 double length = cyl1.getLength();        // similar to Circle
 cyl1.set(3.0);
 double diam = 2 * cyl1.getRadius();      // no call to getArea()
 double vol = cyl2.getVolume();           // not in Circle
```

```
cout << " Circumference of first cylinder: " << length << endl;
cout << " Volume of the second cylinder:   " << vol << endl;
cout << " Diameter of the first cylinder:  " << diam << endl;
return 0;
 }
```

The major problem with the use of inheritance is that the client code designer does not have one segment of code that describes the services provided by the server class. In Listing 14.2, where composition was used, this segment of code was the specification of class Cylinder itself. In Listing 14.3, where inheritance is used, the specification of class Cylinder describes only what class Cylinder adds to the capabilities of the base class Circle. The rest of the services available to the client code of class Cylinder are described elsewhere, in the specification of class Circle. It is the responsibility of the programmer of the Cylinder client code to learn the services supplied by the base class. The situation becomes even worse if the inheritance hierarchy is tall.

This is not a problem for the C++ compiler. The compiler searches the inheritance tree to verify the legitimacy of the messages in the client code; so does the human designer (and maintainer). But for a human being this is more difficult than for the compiler.

The second problem with the use of inheritance is that the client code designer might do the job of learning the capabilities of the base class too well and come to use the base services that the derived class should not support. For example, the client code might compute the cylinder surface area this way:

```
double area = cyl1.getArea();    // nonsense - this is not the area!
```

On the surface, this function call looks exactly the same as calls to methods getLength(), getRadius(), and set(). Why are these methods the same for classes Circle and Cylinder, but the method getArea() should be different? These calls look the same to the compiler, they look the same to the Cylinder client code designer, and, yes, they might look the same to the maintainer who might not be very competent in the intricacies of geometry.

It falls to the designer of class Cylinder to make sure that the Cylinder client code can use methods getLength(), getRadius(), and set()—but not the method getArea(). How does one do that? One of the ways to achieve this is to use the private or protected mode of inheritance.

```
class Cylinder : protected Circle        // new class Cylinder
{ protected:
    double height;                       // other data is in Circle
  public:
    Cylinder (double r, double h)        // from Circle plus new code
        : Circle(r)                      // initializer list
    { height = h; }                      // new code
    double getVolume() const             // no getArea()
    { return height * getArea(); }       // additional capability
  } ;
```

But this is too much. True, the Cylinder client code cannot call getArea() because it became protected in class Cylinder, but the methods getLength(), getRadius(), and set() also became protected. There are two remedies. One is to explicitly define the methods getLength(), getRadius(), and set() as public in the derived class Cylinder but not to do that for the method getArea() or whatever other base services should be barred from the derived class clients.

```
class Cylinder : protected Circle        // new class Cylinder
{ protected:
    double height;                       // other data is in Circle
public:
      Circle::getLength;                 // no getArea() here
      Circle::getRadius;
      Circle::set;
  public:
    Cylinder (double r, double h)        // from Circle plus new code
        : Circle(r)                      // initializer list (no PI)
    { height = h; }                      // new code
    double getVolume() const             // no getArea()
    { return height * getArea(); }       // additional capability
  } ;
```

This is not as bad as it looks. Yes, making public base methods protected in the derived class and then making them public again is awkward. From the software engineering point of view, this is excellent. Why? Because we wound up with the explicit list of public services that the class Cylinder provides to its clients! It is a good example of self-documented code.

Another remedy is illustrated in Listing 14.4. The derived class Cylinder makes the inherited methods explicitly available to the Cylinder client code, with the exception of those methods (e.g., getArea()), that should be out of reach of the client code. This is very similar to the version with class composition in Listing 14.2. Notice the use of the class scope operator inside these one-liner functions. With class composition, there is a data member to send a message to. With inheritance, there is no explicit data member; instead, there is the base part of the derived class object. Omitting the scope operator will result in an infinite recursive call.

```
void Cylinder::set(double r)
  { set(r); }                              // implicit recursive call
```

The call to function set() takes place in the scope of the class Cylinder. According to the rule of the function call resolution, the compiler looks first for a name that belongs to the local scope. Since this name is found in class Cylinder, the compiler calls the Cylinder::set() again and never goes up the inheritance chain to call the Circle::set() method. This implementation is equivalent to the following function.

```
void Cylinder::set(double r)
  { Cylinder::set(r); }                    // explicit recursive call
```

To avoid infinite recursion, the use of the Circle scope operation is necessary.

Listing 14.4   Example of code reuse through protected inheritance.

```
#include <iostream>
using namespace std;

class Circle                          // original code for reuse
{ protected:                          // inheritance is one of the options
    double radius;                    // internal data
  public:
    static const double PI;           // it must be initialized

  public:
    Circle (double r)                 // conversion constructor
    { radius = r; }

    double getLength () const         // compute circumference
    { return 2 * PI * radius; }

    double getArea () const           // compute area
    { return PI * radius * radius; }

    double getRadius() const
    { return radius; }

    void set(double r)
    { radius = r; } };                // change size

const double Circle::PI = 3.1415926536;
```

```
class Cylinder : protected Circle          // new class Cylinder
{ protected:
    double height;                         // other data is in Circle

  public:
    Cylinder (double r, double h)          // from Circle plus new code
        : Circle(r)                        // initializer list (no PI)
    { height = h; }                        // new code

    double getLength () const
    { return Circle::getLength(); }        // from class Circle

    double getRadius() const               // from class Circle
    { return Circle::getRadius(); }

    void set(double r)                     // from class Circle
    { Circle::set(r); }

    double getVolume() const               // no getArea()
    { return height * getArea(); }         // additional capability
    } ;
int main()
{
Cylinder cyl1(2.5,6.0), cyl2(5.0,7.5);     // initialize data
double length = cyl1.getLength();          // similar to Circle
cyl1.set(3.0);
double diam = 2 * cyl1.getRadius();        // no call to getArea()
double vol = cyl2.getVolume();             // not in Circle
cout << " Circumference of first cylinder: " << length << endl;
cout << " Volume of the second cylinder:   " << vol << endl;
cout << " Diameter of the first cylinder:  " << diam << endl;
return 0;
  }
```

This solution eliminates both drawbacks of using inheritance. There is an explicit list of the services that the class Cylinder provides to its client code, and there is no danger that the client code will call the base methods whose use is not appropriate for the derived class. On the other hand, the solution with the use of composition presented in Listing 14.2 does not have these two drawbacks either. Given a choice, I would use composition rather than protected inheritance because composition is conceptually simpler, and the links between classes are not as strong as with protected inheritance, although these two solutions are quite similar.

Inheritance with Redefined Functions

The need to suppress some base methods in the derived class objects arises only when inheritance is used inappropriately. The need to do so indicates that an object of the derived class is not an object of the base class. Rather, it has that base object as a data member. This is why I favor the use of composition over the use of protected inheritance.

Often, the relationship between classes is close enough to the inheritance relationship, and there are no methods in the base class that have to be suppressed. There might be, however, methods that should be treated differently in the derived class. The method getArea() is a good example. For an object of the base class Circle, this method should return the area of the circle.

```
double Circle::getArea () const          // compute circle area
{ return PI * radius * radius; }
```

For an object of the derived class Cylinder, this method should return the area of the two circles that the cylinder has (oops! Forgive the slip of the tongue that indicates that the cylinder "has a" circle rather than "is a" circle) plus the side area of the cylinder.

```
double Cylinder::getArea () const         // compute Cylinder area
{ return 2 * Circle::PI * radius * (radius + height); }
```

Often, when the derived class method hides the base class method, the derived class method does the same work as the base class method plus some more. C++ programmers like to "document" this fact by explicitly calling the base class method from the derived class method (using the base class scope operator explicitly).

```
double Cylinder::getArea () const         // compute Cylinder area
{ double area = Circle::getArea();
  return 2 * (area + Circle::PI * radius * height); }
```

Overriding the base methods in the derived class is a very common programming practice. It is rooted in the high premium that C++ programmers put on the use of uniform names. When I was programming in COBOL, my boss would tell me to use different names for each function (or paragraph), for example, COMPUTE-CIRCLE-AREA and COMPUTE-CYLINDER-AREA. In addition, I would be asked to use an elaborate system of numeric prefixes that indicated to what unit in the program each name belonged.

In C++, this practice is frowned on. I am not sure whether the use of uniform names (e.g., getArea()) is driven by a esthetic preferences only. Its technical rationale is the feasibility of using the rules of name resolution for specifying which method (base or derived) should be called. As you saw in the previous chapter, these rules might initially be confusing, but they soon become a part of your programming intuition.

Inheritance with redefinition is usually public. It requires more work than does public inheritance without redefinition: Some design is reused (e.g., radius, and getLength()), some new members are added (e.g., height, and getVolume()), and some methods are redefined e.g., getArea()). This version of the program is shown in Listing 14.5. I changed the Cylinder client code slightly to demonstrate the use of the getArea() method by the client code. The output of the program is shown in Figure 14–2.

Listing 14.5   Example of code reuse through public inheritance with method redefinition.

```cpp
#include <iostream>
using namespace std;

class Circle                         // original code for reuse
{ protected:                         // inheritance is one of the options
    double radius;                   // internal data
  public:
    static const double PI;          // it must be initialized

  public:
    Circle (double r)                // conversion constructor
    { radius = r; }

    double getLength () const        // compute circumference
    { return 2 * PI * radius; }

    double getArea () const          // compute area
    { return PI * radius * radius; }

    double getRadius() const
    { return radius; }

    void set(double r)
    { radius = r; } };               // change size

  const double Circle::PI = 3.1415926536;

class Cylinder : public Circle       // is Cylinder really a Circle?
  { protected:
    double height;                   // other data is in Circle
```

```
public:
    Cylinder (double r, double h)              // from Circle plus new code
        : Circle(r)                            // initializer list (no PI)
    { height = h; }                            // new code

    double getArea () const                    // compute Cylinder area
    { return 2 * Circle::PI * radius * (radius + height); }

    double getVolume() const     { return height * getArea(); }
                                               // additional capability
    } ;

int main()
{
    Cylinder cyl1(2.5,6.0), cyl2(5.0,7.5);     // initialize data
    double length = cyl1.getLength();          // similar to Circle
    cyl1.set(3.0);
    double diam = 2 * cyl1.getRadius();double vol = cyl2.getVolume();
                                               // not in Circle
    cout << " Circumference of first cylinder: " << length << endl;
    cout << " Volume of the second cylinder:    " << vol << endl;
    cout << " Diameter of the first cylinder:   " << diam << endl;
    cout << " Area of first cylinder: " << cyl1.getArea() << endl;
    return 0;
}
```

When the derived class redefines a base class method, it uses the same method name. In this example, both base and derived methods also had the same interface. This happens often because both functions perform similar operations. The objects of the operation are somewhat different, but their general semantics (meaning) is the same. It is only natural that their interfaces be the same.

C++ rules are silent on that. It is okay to overwrite a base function with the same interface but this is not mandatory. For whatever reason, many C++ programmers believe that the interface must be the same. This is not the case. Whether the designer of the derived class changes the method interface or keeps it the same as in the base class, the base method name is hidden from the derived class client code. It is the derived class method that is called

Figure 14–2   Output for program in Listing 14.5.

```
Circumference of first cylinder: 15.708
Volume of the second cylinder:   2945.24
Diameter of the first cylinder:  6
Area of first cylinder: 169.646
```

from the client code. The client code can use the base method if desired, but this requires the base class scope operator to give a command to the compiler and a visual cue to the human reader.

```
Cylinder cyl1(2.5,6.0), cyl2(5.0,7.5);                    // initialize data
   double length = cyl1.getLength();                      // similar to Circle
   cyl1.set(3.0);
   double diam = 2 * cyl1.getRadius();double vol = cyl2.getVolume();
                                                          // not in Circle
   cout << " Circumference of first cylinder: " << length << endl;
   cout << " Volume of the second cylinder:   " << vol << endl;
   cout << " Diameter of the first cylinder:  " << diam << endl;
   cout << " Side area of first cylinder: "
        << cyl1.Circle::getArea() << endl;                // visual cue
```

Pluses and Minuses of Inheritance and Composition

Inheritance is a good abstraction tool. It explicitly stresses conceptual connections among classes when these connections exist. For example, the commonality between classes `Circle` and `Cylinder` is best reflected in the program design by deriving class `Cylinder` from class `Circle`. This inheritance relationship is conspicuous in the `Cylinder` code. For the client programmer and for the maintainer, there is no need to study the classes separately, comparing the code of one class against that of another class, trying to figure out whether these classes are similar.

The use of inheritance helps us to save development effort. It does not always make the source code for class implementation shorter. Often, it is the other way around. Still, many programmers believe that it is easier to develop a complex class in simple stages rather than as a monolithic unit. For example, developing the class `Circle` first allows the designer to concentrate on relatively simple things (like computing circumference) and tackle more complex tasks (like computing the cylinder volume or area) later, when class `Circle` is firmly in place.

However, the use of inheritance introduces extra implicit dependencies between classes, which might not be obvious to the designer (or maintainer) of the client code. Studying the derived class description does not provide the reader with the list of services available to the client. The reader has to study the base class as well.

The use of class composition is good competition for inheritance. The aggregate class provides the reader with the complete list of services that the class supports. Composition also introduces dependencies between classes, but these dependencies are explicit, in the form of one-liner methods, which push the work from the container class to the methods of the component class.

The choice between inheritance and composition depends on the degree of similarity between the related classes. If the number of common methods is relatively small and the number of additional services to be supported is relatively large, composition is the way to go. The aggregate class will have only a few one-liner functions, and the expense of writing them will be offset by the availability of the explicit list of supported services.

If the number of common methods is relatively large and the number of additional services is relatively small, inheritance might be the way to go. Many programmers are annoyed at the need to write "dumb" one-liner methods. The use of inheritance will eliminate these one-liner methods—the base class methods will be inherited by the derived class directly. Redefining base methods in the derived class is aesthetically pleasing and opens the way to the use of polymorphism (to be discussed in the next chapter).

If you use inheritance, use it in the simplest way possible, as public derivation. Avoid protected and private inheritance.

Often, inheritance is used just to speed up work, without a clear conceptual "is a" connection among classes. If you have doubts that a natural "is a" relation exists among classes, do not use inheritance; use composition.

Unified Modeling Language

Traditional programs are written as systems of cooperating functions. Object-oriented programs are written as systems of cooperating classes that include both data and functions. In the first part of this book, I concentrated mainly on techniques of writing functions. The skills of writing processing code and implementing communications between functions are crucial for creating high-quality C++ programs.

In the second part of the book, I concentrated on writing classes. The skills of binding together data and operations and implementing classes as servers and as clients are crucial for creating high-quality C++ programs.

In this part of the book, I concentrate on writing classes that are related to each other. And guess what? I am going to tell you that the skills of implementing relationships among classes, such as inheritance and composition are—what else?—crucial for creating high-quality C++ programs.

When a C++ program becomes sufficiently complex, it becomes difficult to visualize the relationships between classes implemented by the program. Moreover, when a C++ program becomes sufficiently complex, it becomes difficult to visualize the relationships between classes you are going to implement.

The Goals of Using UML

A common approach to this problem is to use graphical notation to describe the relationships among real-life entities whose behavior the application should emulate—circles and cylinders, customers and accounts, inventory items and their suppliers. This is the task of object-oriented analysis, which describes the system activities in the form of cooperation among classes rather than in the form of cooperation among operations (functions).

The next step is to decide which real-life entities should be represented as classes in the C++ program and which relationships between real-life entities should be implemented as relationships among classes in the C++ program. This is the task of object-oriented design, which also uses graphical notation to describe the classes and their relationships within the program.

Unlike object-oriented systems analysis, which concentrates on describing program external interfaces (with users and other systems), object-oriented design concentrates on describing the structural elements of the system: system architecture, allocation of its subsystems to different hardware components, and links between different classes. Most of these links are the same as the links between entities established at the object-oriented analysis phase, but some analysis links might not be implemented in the program, and some additional links between classes (and some additional classes) might be added to improve system performance or user interface.

In the first two parts of the book, I discussed methods of making system components less dependent on each other. This is a very sound approach because dependencies between system components require cooperation between developers, and cooperation between developers is prone to error. But it is not realistic to expect that system components are totally independent from each other. Since they are part of the same system, they have to cooperate with other components. It is important to keep this cooperation to a minimum, but it is also important to describe this cooperation with the appropriate degree of precision.

Enter the UML notation. In the traditional system development process, the analysis, design, and implementation phases all use different techniques of graphical notation to support the diverse interests of the analyst, the designer, and the programmer. In the object-oriented development process, the analyst, the designer, and the programmer use the same notation. This has two important advantages over the traditional approach. First, the cooperating developers—analysts, designers, and programmers—use the same graphical notation and hence there is less opportunity for misunderstanding or for different interpretations of implicit assumption. Second, there is no drastic change of representation between the phases of the development process and hence there is less opportunity for errors creeping in during the course of transformation.

UML is a powerful modeling language that allows the developer to use graphical notation for representing relationships between cooperating system components. "Cooperating" means that the system components know about each other, use each other, and depend on each other. This graphical notation is based on the concept of an object as a system component, with its data members, member functions, and relationships among objects. These object diagrams can be discussed with system users and system implementers to verify that the relationships are reflected correctly. Later, these diagrams are converted to object-oriented implementations.

This is a significant conceptual leap from the object-oriented programming approach I was describing earlier. The essence of object-oriented programming is binding together data and operations. It is the combination of specific data members and the operations over them that characterizes a C++ class. This definition says nothing about relationships. This is unfortunate because it creates a false impression that the combination of data and behavior describes the object sufficiently well.

Object-oriented analysis and object-oriented design take a different approach. They describe objects as a combination of data, behavior, and relationships with other program components. As you will see, the description of data and behavior plays a rather basic role in UML. It is the relationships between classes and objects that most UML notation concentrates on.

The object-oriented programming approach underplays the significance of relationships, or associations, because programmers try to make the program components as independent from each other as possible. As a result of this concentration on component independence, all object-oriented languages give the programmer the specific means for describing data members and for describing member functions. They do not give the programmer the native means for describing associations among program components.

Real life being what it is, program components are always somehow related to each other. Hence, programmers face the task of describing these relationships using ad hoc techniques: data members of programmer-defined types or data members that are pointers or references to other objects.

The major role of every design notation, including UML, is to help developers describe the relationships among objects. When a C++ program is being implemented, it is up to programmers to decide which objects should be related to which objects. It is nice to be able to implement the program so that it can do whatever it is supposed to do without becoming excessively complex. Using the UML notation, the developers can compare different design decisions and choose those relationships that (1) are sufficient for doing the job and (2) minimize the complexity of relationships among program objects.

UML merges three different systems of notation for building graphical models of computer systems. These models help the developers to analyze the requirements for the system. The requirements usually describe system functionality, user interface, interfaces with other systems, performance, and reliability. The graphical methods try to represent these requirements in the form of relationships among system components. This is, of course, an ambitious undertaking.

One system of notation was developed by Grady Booch and his company, Rational Software Corporation. His notation included several views of the system with a separate diagram for each view. The symbols for objects on Booch diagrams were of irregular "cloud" form (very different from the client-server diagrams I used in previous chapters) and were hard to draw by hand. Booch was one of the first to realize that graphical modeling needs the support of computer-based tools. The tool that his company developed, Rational Rose, is one of the most successful tools for object-oriented modeling and is largely responsible for the popularity of the Booch approach. With the introduction of UML, Rational Rose was modified to support the UML notation as well.

Another system of notation was developed by James Rumbaugh and his associates at General Electric. It was called the Object Modeling Technique (OMT). In addition to the object model, which described the relationships among the objects in the system, the OMT notation also included two other models, the dynamic model and the functional model. Even though these two models were not particularly object oriented, they represented the adaptation of two well-known design and analysis notational techniques: state transition diagrams and data flow diagrams. This synthesis smoothed the transition to the object-oriented approach for those developers who had experience in these two graphical notations. This is probably the major reason that OMT was gaining popularity in industry as an emerging standard approach.

The third system was developed in Sweden by Ivar Jacobson and his company, Objective Systems. He marketed his notation under the names Object-

Oriented Software Engineering (OOSE) and Objectory. This notation included so-called "use cases" that describe the interactions between the system and external actors such as the system operator or an interface with other systems.

Each system of notation was described with recommendations on how to use the notation for first, object-oriented analysis, then for object-oriented design, and finally, for object-oriented implementation. Each book tried to explain why the object-oriented approach was better than the traditional approach. I have to be frank: these explanations were not particularly clear. They worked well for people who already wanted to believe in the advantages of the object-oriented approach. Those who did not know where the savings and improvements in quality would come from remained unimpressed.

However, the drawbacks of the traditional approach to system development were so serious that the industry was willing to accept anything that would promise an improvement over the existing state of affairs. But what approach to accept? In addition to the systems of notation developed by Booch, Rumbaugh, and Jacobson, there were similar systems of notation described by Shlaer and Mellor, Yourdon and Coad, Coleman, and others—actually, it is quite a long list. All of these systems of notation are similar, and all are a variation or expansion of the work on entity-relationship diagrams for data base design performed by P. Chen in 1976.

For a number of years, the authors of the different systems of notation devoted significant energy to public argument: which system of notation was better and why. The idea behind this argument was that the choice of method was a very important decision that had to be approached with proper care. Some experts believed that one approach might be better than the others for one kind of software system (e.g., real-time systems), while another approach might be better for another kind of software system (e.g., business systems). Other experts were saying that one method was better than all the others—period. These arguments were called "the method war," although the differences between competing approaches were in notation rather than in methodology; and the differences in notation were not really significant.

Around 1995, Booch, Rumbaugh, and Jacobson, the "three amigos," as they were called, decided to create a unified system of notation that would become the dominant modeling language (another way to describe this is to say that Booch hired both Rumbaugh and Jacobson to work for Rational). The UML is the result of their collaboration. They wrote books that describe the UML and the ways to use it. The Rational Rose tool provides full support to the UML notation.

The bad news is that the UML notation combines diverse ideas and hence is complex. The books that describe it are unwieldy. The learning curve for mastering the modeling language is steep—there is so much to learn. However, when a designer makes a bad modeling decision, there is no compiler to flag the error (unlike the C+ compiler that helps you learn when you make an error). This is why the process of mastering the UML is much slower than, for example, the process of learning C++.

The good news is that you do not have to be an expert in UML to be able to communicate your ideas about the structure of object relationships in your program. In this book, I am describing only the basics of the UML that are sufficient for discussing object relationships in C++ programs.

Basic UML: Notation for Classes

Objects in UML are considered to be instances of classes, and classes are descriptions of object types. The class describes the attributes and behavior of one type of object. The major source of classes that you want to include in your UML model is the analysis of the concepts and entities of the problem domain: the area of the application. For a business system, for example, the classes in the model would be Customer, Item, Shipment, Requisition, Invoice, and so on. For real-time application, the classes would include Sensor, Display, CustomerCard, Button, Motor, and Lock.

Classes included in the model are placed in a class diagram. A class is represented as a rectangle divided into three sections or compartments. The top section contains the class name, the middle section contains class attributes, and the bottom section lists operations. When you implement the class in C++, the attributes become data members, or fields, and the operations become member functions, or methods. Figure 14–3(a) shows a general picture of a class in UML. Figure 14–3(b) shows a specific example of the class Point with attributes x and y, operations set(), get(), and move(), and the

Figure 14–3 UML examples of a generic class template and two specific classes.

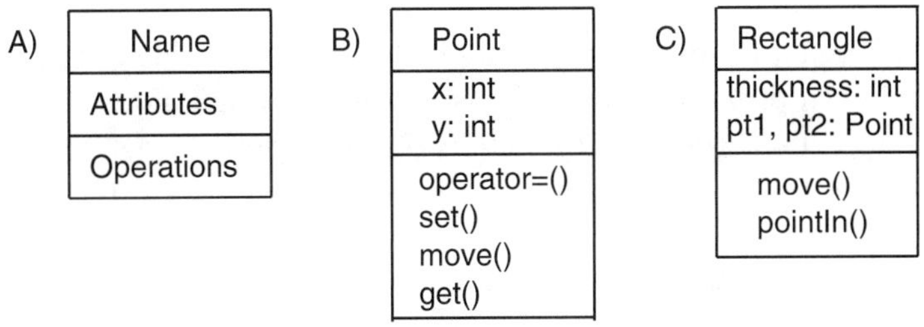

assignment operator. Figure 14–3(c) shows an example of class `Rectangle` with the attributes `thickness`, `pt1`, and `pt2`, and operations `move()` and `pointIn()`.

You see that UML allows you to indicate the type of attributes as either primitive (built-in) types or as a library class (e.g., `String`) or as one of the classes defined in the application (e.g., `Point`). UML allows you to specify much more than just the name and the type of the attribute. You can indicate whether an attribute is static (class scope attribute), the set of allowed values (if the attribute is the enumeration type), the attribute initial value (if it has any), or even the attribute visibility (public, private, or protected). This is optional, because often, especially at the beginning of the analysis and design process, the developers are not sure what the types and other properties of the attributes are. These properties might be clarified later, during the iterative process of refining the design or even during programming.

For operations, UML allows you to specify the operation signature: its name, return type, and the names and types of the parameters. You can also specify the default parameter values (if they are needed), whether the operation is a static operation (class scope operation), and the operation visibility (public, private, or protected).

As you can see, the UML class description can have as many details as does the class specification written in C++. I will spare you the specific details of the UML notation for attributes and operations because it is not necessary for our discussion of relationships among classes. Moreover, to make the class diagram more manageable, the developers often omit the operation section from the class notation and discuss relationships using class diagrams, where classes have only two sections, for the name of the class and for the attributes. For even more complex diagrams (and most class diagrams are complex), you can omit the attribute section as well and represent the class as a rectangle with the class name only. This is the most convenient way of discussing the class relationships.

Basic UML: Notation for Relationships

Real-life entities in the application domain might be related to each other. These relationships are represented on the class diagram using connections between classes. The technical term for a connection between classes is the association. The existence of an association between classes means that objects of these two classes have a link between them. This link might mean that one object knows about another object, or is connected to another, or uses another object to achieve its purposes, or even that for each object of one class there is an object of another class. This is very general and very important: The associations, when implemented, are used to access one object through another object in the C++ program.

Figure 14–4 shows examples of associations. Figure 14–4(a) indicates that each `Circle` object is associated with a `Cylinder` object but does not specify the nature of the association. Notice that it is only the name of the class that is represented in the class rectangle; the attributes and operations are not there. They can be put there, too, but that would only clutter the class diagram; which is worth doing only if the list of attributes and operations somehow clarifies the nature of the relationship between objects.

The association between objects is usually bidirectional—if a `Circle` object is associated with a `Cylinder` object, then the `Cylinder` object is related to the `Circle` object. In the case of these two objects, there is little that can be said about the relationship between the objects. The UML notation allows us to express additional information about the relationship by inventing names for the associations and by assigning roles to the objects associated with each other.

Figure 14–4 UML examples of associations among classes.

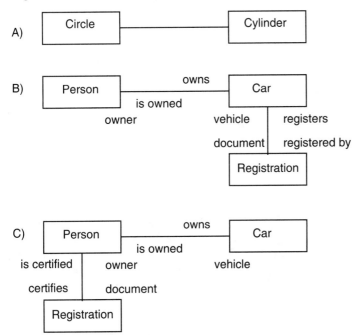

Figure 14–4(b) shows that a Person object can be related to a Car object, and a Car object can be related to a Person object and a Registration object. Each association has two labels, one for traversing the association in one direction and another for traversing the association in the opposite direction. To avoid confusion as to the direction in which the name connects the objects, you can put small arrows next to the name.

In Figure 14–4(a), I was not able to come up with a good name for the association between Circle and Cylinder objects. They are related, and that is it. In Figure 14–4(b), I am saying that a Person object owns a Car object, and a Car object is owned by a Person object. In addition, I am saying that a Car object is registered by a Registration object, and a Registration object registers a Car object. I also specify the role of each object in the relationship. A Person object plays the role of an owner, a Car object plays the role of a vehicle, and a Registration object plays the role of a document.

This probably does not strike you as a very profound method for describing relationships among objects. Rest assured that you are not alone. Indeed, just knowing the names of links between objects and the roles that the objects play does not help much toward understanding how objects cooperate in real life and how program objects cooperate during program execution. If, however, the developer knows very little about the application domain, the names of associations and the roles of objects might be helpful in channeling the analysis in the proper direction.

Often, comparing different names for relationships in a class model feels like describing the theory of relativity in simple terms. The major problem with describing associations is that any solution is indeed relative. Figure 14–4(c) describes the associations between classes Person, Car, and Registration using different relationships. The third alternative is to associate each class with two other classes. Which alternative is better and why? There is no good answer to this question.

Association can be implemented in C++ with pointers (or references) that point from one object to another (associated) object. Another popular technique of implementing association in C++ is the use of an object identifier as an attribute of another class. For example, class `Person` might have an attribute that identifies a `Car` object associated with the `Person` instance. If necessary, class `Car` might include a `Person` identifier as an attribute that associates the `Car` instance and the `Person` instance.

Basic UML: Notation for Aggregation and Generalization

Aggregation is a special case of association. It indicates that two classes are connected through an association, but the association is special. This association indicates that the relationship has the "whole-part" meaning—one object is part of another object, or another object contains the first object (has it) or consists of some objects.

The UML notation for aggregation is the same as for association: a link between classes. To indicate the aggregate object, a hollow diamond is attached to the end of the line between the link and the aggregate object. Obviously, the diamond can be attached to only one end, not to both.

Figure 14–5(a) demonstrates that a `Circle` object is part of a `Cylinder` object. Actually, a hollow diamond indicates that the aggregation is shared, and the part may be in more than one aggregate at the same time. In composition aggregation, sharing is not allowed. The UML notation for the composition aggregation is the same as for the shared aggregation, but the diamond attached to the aggregate is solid rather than hollow. Figure 14–5(b) demonstrates the notation for composition aggregation, where a `Circle` object is part of a `Cylinder` object but it cannot be part of any other object.

Since aggregation is a special case of association, it is always possible to represent the relationship between objects as association rather than as aggregation (shared or composition). See, for example, Figure 14–4(a), where association is used to model the relationship among `Circle` and `Cylinder` objects. However, this model is less precise. It is the task of the designer to represent aggregation as aggregation rather than as just association. This will result in a simpler implementation. Of course, if aggregation does not represent the relationship among objects well, association should be used. The struggle between arguments in favor of general association and specific aggregation is often the source of anguish for the designer.

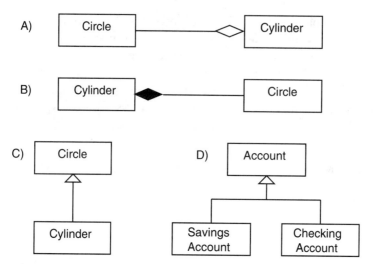

Figure 14–5   UML examples of shared aggregation, composition aggregation, and inheritance.

The shared aggregation can be implemented in C++ similar to an association, with pointers (or references) to the component objects. The composition aggregation can be implemented using the part objects as data members of aggregate objects.

Generalization is the relationship between a more general class and a more specific class. The more specific class contains the same attributes and operations as the more general class and might contain additional information: attributes or operations. Generalization is implemented as inheritance in object-oriented programming languages. A generalization is an "is a" relationship between classes. Notice that this is a relationship between classes, not between object instances. A class can inherit from another class, but an object instance cannot inherit from another object.

The specific class of the generalization relationship (the subclass) inherits all attributes, operations, and associations from the general class of the relationship (the superclass). The UML notation for this relationship uses a solid line as a link between classes on the class diagram. To distinguish between the subclass and the superclass in the relationship, a small hollow triangle is inserted between the link and the superclass in the diagram pointing to the superclass.

Figure 14–5(c) shows the two classes, `Circle` and `Cylinder`, linked with the generalization relationship. In this design, `Circle` is treated as the generalization (superclass), and `Cylinder` is treated as the specialization (subclass).

If a class is used as a superclass for several specializations, each class is represented on the class diagram separately, and each specialization class is linked to the superclass with a separate link with a separate triangle pointing to the superclass. It is common to use only one triangle pointing to the superclass and the link each subclass with this triangle. Figure 14–5 (d) shows class `Account`, which is used as a generalization, and two other classes, `SavingsAccount` and `CheckingAccount`, which represent different specializations of the class `Account`.

If a subclass is used as a generalization for another class, this other class becomes its specialization, and the same notation is used. A class can inherit from one class and be used as a base class for another class. This gives rise to tree-like inheritance hierarchies in UML class diagrams.

Basic UML: Notation for Multiplicity

Most relationships are binary relationships—they link two classes. Well, actually this is not so. Recall the previous discussion between the classes `Person`, `Car`, and `Registration`. It is a ternary relationship: it involves objects of three classes. And the difficulty that I had during the discussion of this relationship stemmed from the fact that I was trying to represent a ternary relationship as a set of binary relationships.

Even though the UML supports notation for the ternary relationship, it does not support notation for relationships between the objects of more than three classes. Even if it did, when it comes to implementation of relationships, the C++ language supports only binary relationships; the link between two objects is established using a physical or a conceptual pointer. So, the relationships we model in the UML class diagram are binary relationships—they link objects of two classes.

There is one exception to this observation. Sometimes, the relationship connects objects that are instances of the same class. For example, an object of class `Person` that plays the role of the supervisor might be associated with an object of class `Person` that plays the role of a team worker. In this case, both objects are of the same class. This is a nice theoretical oddity, and most books on UML have examples of this reflexive (or recursive) relationship. In practice, it is more convenient to model the supervisor with the class `Supervisor` and to model the team member with the class `TeamMember`. It is useful to have two different classes in the model because they implement different responsibilities. And if they have too many features in common, well, you can always introduce class `Person` as their common base.

So, most relationships in UML class diagrams are binary relationships. Each link connects two objects of two different classes—one object at one end of the link and another object at the other end of the link. Each link links two objects, not three or four.

Sometimes, an object of one class might be related to more than one object of another class. For example, an object of the class Supervisor might be associated with several objects of the class TeamMember. On the UML class diagram, you will still have one link between the classes Supervisor and TeamMember, but you will use additional UML notation to indicate multiplicity.

Figure 14–6 shows examples of indicating multiplicity on class diagrams. Figure 14–6(a) demonstrates two classes, Point and Rectangle, in an application where each Rectangle object is associated with exactly two Point objects, no more, no less. UML notation that can be applied to associations can be applied to aggregations as well. Figure 14–6(b) demonstrates the relationship between the same two classes, Point and Rectangle, which is treated as an aggregation rather than as a general association.

Notice that Figure 14–3(c) indicates that class Rectangle has two attributes of class Point, pt1 and pt2. This means that any object of class

Figure 14–6   UML examples indicating multiplicity for relationships.

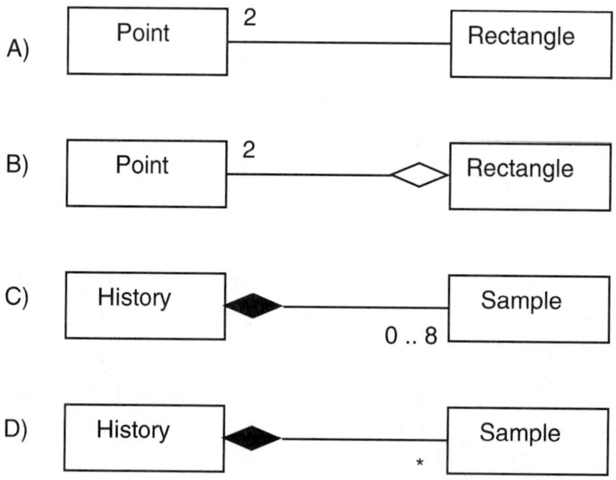

`Rectangle` is associated with exactly two objects of class `Point`. Hence, the link between classes in Figure 14–6(a) or (b) conveys exactly the same analysis and design information as does the class diagram. Some experts are upset by this redundancy and recommend that you use only one way of expressing this information.

The preferred way to do this is to indicate the association and omit the attributes in the class design. The rationale for this approach is that the associations represent the analysis and design point of view and the attributes represent the implementation point of view. So at the stage of analysis you indicate relationships, and during implementation you implement these relationships with appropriate pointers, data members, and so on. I am not sure whether this discussion is important from the practical point of view. To me, it looks like splitting hairs. Since you don't need to worry about the UML compiler, you probably should do whatever your intuition tells you.

If the end of the association or aggregation link is unadorned, this means that exactly one object of this class is required for the relationship to be operational. Figures 14–6(a) and (b) show that the presence of exactly one object of the class `Rectangle` is mandatory.

Sometimes, the relationship between objects is not fixed, and its multiplicity changes during program execution. For example, class `History` in Chapter 12, "Composite Classes: Pitfalls and Advantages," is associated with class `Sample`. Actually, the relationship is the relationship of composition: The object of class `History` contains an array of objects of class `Sample`. As you can see from Listing 12.4, at the beginning of the program execution, there are no valid `Sample` objects in the array. During execution, the measurement samples arrive, and information is stored in the array until either the program terminates or the number of `Sample` objects reaches its maximum—eight objects.

UML allows you to represent this kind of variable multiplicity by indicating the range of the associated objects. Figure 14–6(c) shows an example in which the number of associated objects can change from zero to eight. If the number of objects cannot become less than one, the range starts with 1 rather than with 0, for example, 1…8.

Often, the ranges of objects in relationships are artificial and reflect implementation considerations rather than the nature of the application domain. Why, for example, is the number of `Sample` objects in the measurement history limited to eight? Because C++ does not allow me to define an object without specifying its length, and I had to specify a number. The number 8 looked as good as any other, but there is nothing in the application domain that says that 8 is better than 10, 20, 100, or any other number.

From the conceptual point of view, the number of samples in the history should not be limited. For the same reason, the implementation should not force the designer to commit to a specific number. Listing 12.7 shows the container class with dynamically allocated memory, which implements this conceptual model. Figure 14-6(d) shows the notation for unbounded multiplicity.

Case Study: A Rental Store

Let us consider an application that keeps track of customers borrowing and returning movies at a video rental store.

For simplicity's sake (assuming that the rental store is relatively small and the computer memory is relatively large), the application loads the database of customers and rental items into computer memory at the beginning of the execution. The rental item data includes the item title, quantity on hand, and the item id. The customer data includes the customer name and phone number (with the phone number used as the customer id), the number of movies the customer has borrowed, and their ids.

Even though this example is very simple, it has sufficient details for illustrating the basic issues of designing classes, setting up their relationships, and optimizing the design from the point of view of keeping dependencies between classes to a minimum.

To make it more interesting from the point of view of using inheritance, I will add the following detail: The movie data is stored in a file with a letter indicating the movie category ("f" for feature, "c" for comedy, "h" for horror). When the data is read into memory, the information about the category is stored in numeric form (1 for feature, 2 for comedy, 3 for horror). When the movie information is displayed on the screen, the category is displayed as a word ("feature" for feature, "comedy" for comedy, "horror" for horror). When the data is stored back to the file, the movie category is stored as a letter again.

When a customer brings a movie to the register to check it out, the store clerk enters the customer's phone number for the search of the database. If the customer is not found, a message is displayed. If the customer is found, the customer name and phone number are displayed along with the data about the movies that the customer has on loan. After verifying the customer name, the clerk enters the movie id. The quantity on hand for this movie is decremented by one, and the movie id is added to the list of ids of the movies borrowed by this customer.

If a barcode reader is used to enter the movie id, then the movie will definitely be found in the database. In this prototype, when the movie id is entered manually, an error message is displayed if the movie is not found.

When the customer brings a movie to the register to return it, the store clerk again enters the customer phone number. When the customer record is displayed, the clerk enters the movie id. If the id is found in the list of movies borrowed by the customer, it is deleted from the list, and the quantity on hand for that movie is incremented by one. If the movie id is entered incorrectly, an error message is displayed.

For simplicity of the example, I omitted the monetary aspect of the program (charging rental fees and late fees), the performance part of the program (accumulating the indicators of demand for each movie), and the management part of the program (adding, deleting, and editing customer and movie data).

Classes and Their Associations

The list of classes for an application is often compiled by analysis of the functional specification or another document that describes system user interface and behavior.

Some experts recommend listing all of the nouns from the system description as a good starting point. Other experts ridicule this approach because most of the nouns describe entities that do not rise to the level of a class (phone number, quantity on hand, and so on), and they will later wind up as attributes (data members) rather than classes.

One of the caveats of using the system description for building the model is that the description concentrates on the entities that interface with the system (e.g., customer, store clerk, database). The goal of modeling is to eventually produce the system implementation, which consists of classes that contain data and operate on that data (e.g., `Customer`, `StoreClerk`, and `Database`). The entities from the system description and classes from the system implementation might have the same names, but they are not identical.

Skipping details, let us assume that the class model should include the following classes: `Item` (information about a movie item), `Customer` (information about a customer), `Inventory` (managing the set of items and the set of customers), `File` (managing the database of inventory items and customers), and `Store` (managing the user interface and requesting services from other classes). Figure 14–7 shows each of these classes together with their attributes and operations.

The meaning of most attributes and operations in Figure 14–7 is self-evident. What is not self-evident now will become clearer during further discussion.

Item
title
id, quant
category
set()
getQuant()
getId()
getItem()
printItem()
incrQty()

Customer
name, phone
count, movies
set()
addMovie()
removeMovie()
getCustomer()

Inventory
itemList
itemCount,itemIdx
custList
custCount,custIdx
appendItem()
appendCust()
getItem()
getCustomer()
printRental()
checkOut()
checkIn()

File
f:fstream
getItem()
saveItem()
getCustomer()
saveCustomer()
trim()

Store
loadData()
findcustomer()
processItem()
saveData()

Figure 14–7   UML notation for classes with their attributes and operations.

What classes are associated with what classes here? I have to admit that my system description is not very helpful in figuring that out. On the other hand, I am in no hurry to admit my fault. After all, the description is usually written to help one build and test the program, not to facilitate drawing an UML model of the system.

I think the best way to learn how to create class models is to try to create several alternatives for a simple application, then implement each alternative and evaluate each implementation from the point of view of its complexity. The application of the size of this example is a good tool for this type of learning.

It looks, however, like I am in the minority on this point. Most books on object-oriented analysis and design find it appropriate to give you examples of class diagrams using the system description as the starting point, without further implementation and, most important, without evaluation of how the model affects the complexity of the solution. Meanwhile, the decisions on how to allocate attributes and operations among classes and how to link the classes with relationships affect the complexity of the program and therefore its reusability and maintainability.

Obviously, the classes Item and Customer should play the role of servers for other classes: They provide such services as saving and retrieving the values of data members.

In multifile projects, each class specification is placed in a separate header file. The header files are included in the source files that implement the clients of the class, that is, the source files that use the name of the class to define their variables or parameters. Listing 14.6 shows the header file for the Item class with its data members and member functions. The class provides the data members for the movie title, id, quantity on hand, and category. The methods allow the client code to set the data member values of an Item object and retrieve the object's id, quantity, and all four data members. They also allow the client code to print the item data in the required format (without quantity on hand) and increment (or decrement) the quantity on hand.

Notice the use of conditional compilation directives. According to the rules inherited from C, a header file can be included only once in the source files of your program. If you include the header file in more than one source file, the class type definition will be compiled with each source file. Since each source file can be compiled separately and into a separate object file, the program winds up with several definitions of the same type, and the linker is going to complain about that. Of course, it would be much easier to change the rule and let the linker discard extra definitions when they have the same structure. This is why *every* C++ programmer should put these conditional compilation directives into *every* header file. What a pity.

Listing 14.6   Class specification for the Item class (file item.h).

```
// file item.h

#ifndef ITEM_H
#define ITEM_H

class Item
{
 protected:
      char title[26];
      int id, quant, category;
 public:
      void set (const char *s, int num, int qty, int type);
      int getQuant() const;
      int getId() const;
      void getItem(char* name, int &num, int& qty, int &type) const;
      void printItem() const;
      void incrQty(int qty);
 } ;

#endif
```

Listing 14.7 shows the header file for class Customer. You see the same set of conditional compilation directives to the preprocessor as in Listing 14.6. The Customer class provides data members for storing the customer name, phone number, the count of movies on loan to the customer, and the id for each borrowed movie. Its member functions allow the client code to set the values of customer name and phone number, add a movie id to the list of movies, remove a movie id from the list of movies, and retrieve the customer name, phone number, and list of movies borrowed by the customer.

Listing 14.7   Class specification for the Customer class (file customer.h).

```
// file customer.h

#ifndef CUSTOMER_H
#define CUSTOMER_H

class Customer
{
   char name[20], phone[15];
   int count;
   int movies[10];
public:
   Customer ();
   void set(const char *nm, const char *ph);
   void addMovie(int id);
   int removeMovie(int id);
   void getCustomer(char *nm, char *ph, int &cnt, int m[]) const;
   } ;

#endif
```

Similar to header files, the source C++ code for each class in a multifile project is implemented in a separate source file. Listing 14.8 shows the class implementation for class Item. The header file "item.h" has to be included in this file to make sure that the compiler knows what the scope operator Item:: means.

The implementation indicates that class Item does not need any other classes to support its code. It does need library facilities, and some designers include the library components in their UML diagrams as servers of their classes. I think that this is excessive. You are interested in relationships between components of your program, not in the extent to which your program uses library classes and functions.

To make tracing the links between classes easier for you, I have used line comments to indicate where each Item method is called from. This is a good practice that should make the life of the maintainer easier. The comments say that class Item is a server to classes Inventory and File.

Listing 14.8   Implementation of class Item (file item.cpp).

```
// file item.cpp

#include <iostream>
using namespace std;
#include "item.h"                        // this is a necessity

void Item::set (const char *s, int num, int qty, int type)
{ strcpy(title,s);  id=num;  quant=qty;  category=type; }

int Item::getQuant() const               // used by Inventory::checkOut()
{ return quant; }

int Item::getId() const
{ return id; }                           // in printRental(), checkOut(), checkIn()

void Item::getItem(char* name, int &num, int& qty,
        int &type) const                 // used by File::saveItem()
{ strcpy(name,title);  num = id;
 qty = quant;  type = category; }

void Item::printItem() const             // used by printRental()
{ cout.setf(ios::left,ios::adjustfield);
 cout.width(5);  cout << id;             // it knows its print formats
 cout.width(27);  cout << title;
    switch (category) {                  // different item subtypes
      case 1:  cout << "  feature";  break;
      case 2:  cout << "  comedy";  break;
      case 3:  cout << "  horror";  break; }
    cout << endl; }

    void Item::incrQty(int qty)          // used in checkOut(), checkIn()
      { quant += qty; }
```

Similarly, Listing 14.9 shows the implementation file for class Customer. The header file "customer.h" is included in this file; for any implementation file, the header for this file should be included in addition to the header files for all server classes that this class is using.

You see that the source code file "customer.cpp" does not include any other header files. This means that class Customer does not have server classes—it serves other classes itself. The line comments in each function indicate where the function is used as a server to provide the client code with access to customer data and services.

Listing 14.9   Implementation of class `Customer` (file `customer.cpp`).

```cpp
// file customer.cpp

#include <iostream>
using namespace std;
#include "customer.h"                          // this is a necessity

Customer::Customer ()
{ count = 0; }

void Customer::set(const char *nm, const char *ph)
{ strcpy(name,nm); strcpy(phone,ph); }         // in appendCust()

void Customer::addMovie(int id)
{ movies[count++] = id; }                       // in appendCust(), checkOut()

int Customer::removeMovie(int id)               // used in checkIn()
{ int idx;
  for (idx=0;  idx < count;  idx++)             // find the movie
    if (movies[idx] == id) break;
  if (idx == count) return 0;                   // give up if not found
  while (idx < count - 1)
  { movies[idx] = movies[idx+1];                // shift tail to the left
    idx++; }
  count--;                                       // decrement movie count
  return 1; }                                    // report success

void Customer::getCustomer(char *nm, char *ph,  // saveData()
  int &cnt, int m[]) const                       // Inventory::getCustomer()
{ strcpy(nm,name); strcpy(ph,phone); cnt = count;
  for (int i=0;  i < count;  i++)
    m[i] = movies[i]; }
```

The `Customer` constructor initializes the count of borrowed movies to zero. Method `set()` assigns new values to the customer name and phone number, and method `addMovie()` appends the new id number to the end of the list of movies on loan.

Method `removeMovie()` first checks whether the movie id is found in the list of customer movies. (This is not necessary if a reliable method of data entry is available.) If the id is not found in the list, the function returns zero to indicate its failure. If the id is found in the list, the method shifts remaining id numbers one position to the left, decrements the count of valid movie ids, and returns 1 to indicate success.

Notice that it is the count of ids that is decremented, not the number of values in the array. The number of values in the array does not decrease—the two last array components have the same value of the id after the shift. This is why I say "the count of valid movie ids" rather than "the count of movie ids."

If you feel uncomfortable with the index limits used in the shifting algorithm, you are not alone. Shifting algorithms often contain errors that are hard to find. One way to make this algorithm easier to understand is to decrement the count of movie ids before the shift to the left rather than after the shift.

```
int Customer::removeMovie(int id)          // used in checkIn()
{ int idx;
   for (idx=0;  idx < count;  idx++)        // find the movie
      if (movies[idx] == id) break;
   if (idx == count) return 0;
   count--;                                 // decrement movie count
   while (idx < count)                      // more conventional form
   { movies[idx] = movies[idx+1];           // shift tail to the left
     idx++; }
    return 1; }
```

Many programmers would write the shifting loop in a more concise form by using the increment operator in the shifting statement rather than placing it on a separate line.

```
while (idx < count)
   movies[idx] = movies[idx++];             // concise but risky
```

Recall that assignment in C++ is an expression, and C++ guarantees the order of evaluation of operators in the expressions but not the order of evaluation of operands. This is correct: the order of evaluation of components in an expression is not guaranteed. If the expression is evaluated from left to right, the loop above works fine. If the expression is evaluated from right to left, the loop is in error. It is always better to produce more verbose code that is easy to follow than concise code that confuses the maintainer.

Similar to the file "item.cpp" in Listing 14.7, I have used line comments to indicate clients of Customer methods. These comments show that class Customer is used as a server by class Inventory.

The next class to be discussed is class Inventory. Listing 14.10 shows the header file for class Inventory. Its data members include a list of items and one of customers, the counts of valid components in each list, and the indexes for accessing components in each list. Its member functions allow the client code to append a movie to the item list and append a customer to a customer list, retrieve the current item from the list (pointed to by index itemIdx), retrieve the current customer from the list (pointed to by index custIdx), print out the information describing the movie borrowed by the customer, check the movie out, and check the movie in.

Listing 14.10   Class specification for the `Inventory` class (file `inventory.h`).

```
// file inventory.h

#ifndef INVENTORY_H
#define INVENTORY_H
#include "item.h"
#include "customer.h"

class Inventory {
protected:
    enum { MAXM = 5, MAXC = 4 } ;              // just for the prototype
    Item itemList[MAXM];
    Customer custList[MAXC];
    int itemCount, custCount;
    int itemIdx, custIdx;
public:
  Inventory ();
  void appendItem (const char* ttl, int id, int qty, int cat);
  void appendCust (const char* nm, const char* ph,
                   int cnt, const int *m);
  int getItem(Item& item);
  int getCustomer(char* nm, char* ph, int &cnt, int *m);
  void printRental(int id);
  int checkOut(int id);
  void checkIn(int id);
 } ;

#endif
```

Since class `Inventory` is the client of classes `Item` and `Customer`, the `Inventory` header file should include the header files for classes `Item` and `Customer`.

Some programmers feel insecure about these dependencies, and they include all project header files in every implementation file "just in case." As they say, it is better to be safe than sorry.

This is incorrect. There is no risk of including less than is necessary, but there is harm in including more than is necessary. If you include less than is necessary, the compiler will flag the lines, which use undefined names, as errors. If you include more than is necessary, you will eliminate the risk of reading an error message, but you will make reading more difficult for the maintainer and the client programmer.

The compiler will just ignore redundant `type` definitions. Human readers will also ignore them but only after inspecting class code and finding out that these `type` names are not used in the class. This is a wasted effort and an extra load on human thinking. And this is prone to errors in understanding.

Here, I agree with the risk-takers (especially because there is no risk in excluding unnecessary header files). It is not a good idea to include extra header files "just in case." Instead of avoiding syntax errors, you will confuse the human readers.

Implementation of class `Inventory` is shown in Listing 14.11. You see that it is only the header file "`inventory.h`" that is included. The objects of the type `Item` and `Customer` are used in this file, but the compiler will not complain that these type names are not known. By virtue of the fact that `Item` and `Customer` header files are included in file "`inventory.h`", they are included in the `Inventory` class implementation as well.

Similar to Listing 14.6 and 14.8, I have included line comments that indicate from what part of the server code each method is called. Unlike classes `Item` and `Customer`, class `Inventory` has only one client class—class `Store`.

Listing 14.11 Implementation of class `Inventory` (file inventory.cpp).

```
// file inventory.cpp

#include <iostream>
using namespace std;
#include "inventory.h"                          // this is a necessity

Inventory::Inventory()
  { itemCount = itemIdx = 0;   custCount = custIdx = 0; }

void Inventory::appendItem (const char* ttl, int id,
                            int qty, int cat)
{ if (itemCount == MAXM)                         // used in loadData()
    { cout << "\nNo space to insert item"; }
  else
    { itemList[itemCount++].set(ttl,id,qty,cat); } }
void Inventory::appendCust (const char* nm, const char* ph,
                            int cnt, const int *movie)
{ if (custCount == MAXC)                         // used in loadData()
    { cout << "\nNo space to insert customer";  return; }
  custList[custCount++].set(nm,ph);
  for (int j=0; j < cnt;  j++)
    custList[custCount-1].addMovie(movie[j]); }
```

```
int Inventory::getItem(Item &item)              // used in saveData()
{ if (itemIdx == itemCount)
   {  itemIdx = 0; return 0; }
  item = itemList[itemIdx++];
  return 1; }

int Inventory::getCustomer(char* nm, char* ph, int &cnt, int *m)
{ if (custIdx == custCount)                      // in findCustomer(), saveData()
   {  custIdx = 0; return 0; }
  custList[custIdx++].getCustomer(nm,ph,cnt,m);
  return 1; }

void Inventory::printRental(int id)             // used in findCustomer()
{ for (itemIdx = 0;  itemIdx < itemCount;  itemIdx++)
   { if (itemList[itemIdx].getId() == id)
      { itemList[itemIdx].printItem(); break; } }
  itemIdx = 0;}

int Inventory::checkOut(int id)                 // used in processItem()
{ for (itemIdx = 0; itemIdx < itemCount; itemIdx++)
    if (itemList[itemIdx].getId() == id) break;
  if (itemIdx == itemCount)
  { itemIdx = custIdx = 0; return 0; }
  if (itemList[itemIdx].getQuant() == 0)
  { itemIdx = custIdx = 0; return 1; }
  itemList[itemIdx].incrQty(-1);
  custList[custIdx - 1].addMovie(id);
  itemIdx = custIdx = 0;
  return 2; }

void Inventory::checkIn(int id)                 // used in processItem()
{ if (custList[custIdx - 1].removeMovie(id)==0)
   { cout << " Movie is not found\n";
     itemIdx = custIdx = 0;  return; }
  for (itemIdx = 0;  itemIdx < itemCount;  itemIdx++)
   { if (itemList[itemIdx].getId() == id)
     { itemList[itemIdx].incrQty(1);  break; } }
  itemIdx = custIdx = 0;
  cout << " Movie is returned\n"; }
```

The `Inventory` constructor initializes the indexes and counters of items and customers—initially, both lists are empty. Method `appendItem()` and `appendCust()` are simple: They test for available space (this test is appropriate for the prototype but is redundant when memory is managed dynamically), add the component at the end of the array, and increment the count of valid components.

Methods `getItem()` and `getCustomer()` retrieve the object data from the array at the given index (`itemIdx` for an `Item` object, `custIdx` for a `Customer` object). In one case, I retrieve the whole object; in another case, I retrieve the values of the object data members. Therefore, in one case, it is the client code that cranks out the values of data members, and in another case it is class `Inventory` that does that on behalf of the client code. This is inconsistent—and harmful. It results in different behavior in the client code and makes the client code more difficult to read.

Method `printRental()` uses the movie id to find the movie in the array `itemList[]`. If the movie is found, the `printItem()` message is sent to the object.

Method `checkOut()` with the movie id as the parameter searches for the item in the array `itemList[]`. If the item is not found, it quits and returns 0; if the item is found but the quantity on hand is zero, it quits and returns 1. If the item is available, it decrements the quantity on hand for that item, adds the movie id to the list of movies borrowed by the customer, and returns 2.

Method `checkIn()` also uses the movie id as the parameter. It searches for the item in the list of movies borrowed by the customer by calling the `removeMovie()` method. If the movie is not found, `checkIn()` prints a message and quits. If the movie is found in the customer list (and then removed from the list), `checkIn()` searches for the item in the array of items `itemList[]`, increments quantity on hand, and prints the confirmation message.

The interfaces of methods `checkIn()` and `checkOut()` are inconsistent. The method `checkOut()` is not involved in the user interface dialog. Instead, it returns a value that the client has to analyze and prints the message depending on the return value. The work is pushed to the client. The method `checkIn()` is responsible for the analysis of the error conditions and the corresponding user interface. It hides the error conditions from the client and returns a void value.

The next class to be discussed is class `File`. It is designed to access physical files that contain item and customer data before and after the program run. Figure 14–8 shows a sample input file with movie data. Each line in the file corresponds to one item: movie title (left-aligned), id number, quantity on hand, and category (as a letter).

Figure 14–9 shows a sample input file with customer data. Each customer is allocated two lines. The first line contains the customer name and the customer phone number. The second line contains the number of movies the customer has on loan and the list of movie access numbers.

The format of the output file is the same as that of the input file. Figure 14–10 shows the contents of the output item file after a program run. It shows that one copy of "Splash" was checked in and one copy of "Gone with the Wind" was checked out.

Figure 14–11 shows the contents of the customer file after the program

Figure 14-8   Sample input file with movie data.

```
Splash                      101   11   c
Birds                       102   22   h
Gone with the wind          103   10   f
```

Figure 14-9   Sample input file with customer data.

```
Shtern                      353-2566
2 101 102
Shtern                      358-0008
0
Simons                      277-7506
3 102 101 103
```

Figure 14-10   Sample output file with movie data.

```
Splash                      101   12   c
Birds                       102   22   h
Gone with the wind          103    9   f
```

Figure 14-11   Sample output file with customer data.

```
Shtern                      353-2566
2    102    103
Shtern                      358-0008
0
Simons                      277-7506
3    102    101    103
```

run. It indicates that customer Shtern returned the movie with the id number 101 and checked out the movie with the id number 103.

Listing 14.12 shows the class specification for class `File`. This class encapsulates the `fstream` file object that is capable of both reading and writing data. The class implements public methods `getItem()` and `saveItem()` that perform input/output operations on `Item` data. It also implements public methods `getCustomer()` and `saveCustomer()`, which perform input/output operations on `Customer` data.

Listing 14.12   Class specification for the `File` class (file file.h).

```
// file file.h

#ifndef FILE_H
#define FILE_H
#include "item.h"
#include <fstream>

class File
{ fstream f;
   static void trim(char buffer[]);
   enum { TWIDTH = 27, IWIDTH = 5, QWIDTH = 6,
          NWIDTH = 18, PWIDTH = 16 } ;
public:
   File(const char name[], int mode);
   int getItem(char *ttl, int &id, int &qty, char &type);
   void saveItem(const Item &item);
   int getCustomer(char *name, char *phone, int &count, int *m);
   void saveCustomer(const char *nm, const char *ph,
                     int cnt, int *m);
} ;

#endif
```

Listing 14.13 shows the implementation of class `File`. Its constructor opens the physical file either for reading or for writing and tests the success of the operation by calling the function `fail()`. Another way to test the success or failure is to call the function `is_open()`, which returns true if the file is opened successfully.

The method `getItem()` reads one line of data from the input file into a local array `buffer[]`, trims the trailing blanks away, and copies data into the output array `ttl[]`. It then reads data from the file into other components of the item data—id number, quantity on hand, category. The final call to `getline()` raises the end of file condition if the line just read is the last line in the physical file. When this is the case, the file object becomes null, and `getItem()` returns zero to indicate the end of input data to the caller (class `Store`). Otherwise, it returns one, indicating that there is more data to be read.

The method `saveItem()` saves item data to the physical file. To make sure that the integer category is converted into the corresponding letter correctly, it uses the switch statement.

The method `getCustomer()` reads the customer name, trims the trailing blanks away, reads the customer phone and count of movies on loan, and then reads the ids of the movies on loan.

Method `saveCustomer()` writes to the physical file customer name, phone, count of movies, and the movie ids.

Method `trim()` strips the trailing blanks from the name because `get-line()` does not stop when it finds the end of the word in the input file. It needs either a given number of characters to read or the terminator (carriage return). The string to be trimmed is passed as a parameter. The method `trim()` does not deal with other data members of the class. Hence, the `trim()` function should be declared static. Also, the method trim is called only from `File` methods `getItem()` and `getCustomer()`. Hence the `trim()` function should be declared private.

Listing 14.13   Implementation of class `File` (file `file.cpp`).

```cpp
// file file.cpp

#include <iostream>
using namespace std;
#include "file.h"                          // this is a necessity

File::File(const char name[], int mode)
{ f.open(name,mode);                       // used in loadData(), saveData()
  if (f.fail())                            // if (f.is_open()) is OK, too
    { cout <<" File is not open\n";   exit(1); } }

int File::getItem(char *ttl, int &id, int &qty, char &type)
{ char buffer[200];                        // in loadData()
  f.get(buffer,TWIDTH);
  trim(buffer);
  strcpy(ttl,buffer);                      // it knows file structure
  f >> id;   f >> qty;   f >> type;   f.getline(buffer,4);
  if (!f) return 0;
  return 1; }

void File::saveItem(const Item &item)      // in saveData()
{ char tt[27]; int id, qty, type;
  item.getItem(tt,id,qty,type);
  f.setf(ios::left,ios::adjustfield);
```

```
    f.width(TWIDTH);   f << tt;                     // it knows file format
    f.setf(ios::right,ios::adjustfield);
    f.width(IWIDTH);   f << id ;
    f.width(QWIDTH);   f << qty;
    switch (type) {                          // different for different subtypes
      case 1:  f << "    f\n";   break;
      case 2:  f << "    c\n";   break;
      case 3:  f << "    h\n";   break; } }

int File::getCustomer(char *name,char *phone,int &count,int *m)
{ char buffer[200];                          // in loadData()
  f.get(buffer,NWIDTH);
  trim(buffer);
  strcpy(name,buffer);
  f >> buffer;   f >> count;                  // it knows file structure
  strcpy(phone,buffer);
  for (int i=0;  i < count;  i++)
    f >> m[i];
  f.getline(buffer,2);
  if (!f) return 0;
  return 1; }

void File::saveCustomer(const char *nm, const char *ph,
                        int cnt, int *m)           // in saveData()
{ f.setf(ios::left,ios::adjustfield); f.width(NWIDTH);
  f << nm;
  f.setf(ios::right,ios::adjustfield); f.width(PWIDTH);
  f << ph << endl << cnt;                     // it knows file structure
  for (int i=0;  i < cnt;  i++)
  { f.width(6); f << m[i]; }
  f << endl; }

void File::trim(char buffer[])                     // in getItem(), getCustomer()
{ for (int j = strlen(buffer)-1; j>0; j—)
    if (buffer[j]==' '||buffer[j]=='\n')
      buffer[j] = '\0';
    else
      break; }
```

The top-level class in this design is class `Store`. Listing 14.14 shows its specification. Even though class `Store` is a server to only one program component, global function `main()`, I still go through that dance around the conditional compilation for the sake of uniformity.

This file will not compile without including the "inventory.h" header file—the compiler will not know what the name `Inventory` means. However, it is possible to compile this file without the "file.h" header file because the name of the class `File` is mentioned only in the implementation of class `Store` member functions (see Listing 14.15).

Hence, you can get away with including the "file.h" header file in the implementation file and not in the header file for class Store. The compiler will have no difficulty figuring that out. This is probably not a good idea from the point of view of human comprehension. It is better to keep all server header files in one place, in the header file of the class, to make it easy for the maintenance programmer to immediately see what server classes this class uses.

Some designers go so far that they include the header files for the servers of the servers, for example, "item.h" and "customer.h". This is probably too much—it creates unnecessary clutter in the client header files.

As Listing 14.14 demonstrates, class Store has no data members. This would be the alarm signal for a class in the middle of the hierarchy of classes, but is quite all right for a top-level client class. The methods of class Store are responsible for high-level operations that describe the external interfaces of the system: loading the database at the beginning of system execution, finding the customer in the database, processing requests for renting and returning movies for the customer, and saving the database at program termination.

Listing 14.14   Class specification for the Store class (file store.h).

```
// file store.h

#ifndef STORE_H
#define STORE_H
#include "inventory.h"
#include "file.h"

class Store {
public:
   void loadData(Inventory &inv);
   int findCustomer(Inventory& inv);
   void processItem(Inventory& inv);
   void saveData(Inventory &inv);
} ;
#endif
```

Listing 14.15 shows the implementation of class Store. Method loadData() creates a local File object and sends to it the getItem() messages to read data from the external file. Each set of item data is used as arguments in the call to appendItem(). This message is sent to the Inventory object, which loadData() receives as its parameter. Then loadData() creates another local File object, reads customer data from the file and saves it to the Inventory object. The local File objects disappear when loadData() terminates. This terminates the connection between physical files "Item.dat" and "Cust.dat" and the File objects.

Listing 14.15   Implementation of class `Store` **(file** `store.cpp`**).**

```cpp
// file store.cpp

#include <iostream>
using namespace std;
#include "store.h"                              // this is a necessity

void Store::loadData(Inventory &inv)
{ File itemsIn("Item.dat",ios::in);            // item database
  char ttl[27], category; int id, qty, type;   // item data
  cout << "Loading database ... " << endl;
  while (itemsIn.getItem(ttl,id,qty,category)==1)  // read in
  { switch (category) {                         // set category for the subtype
     case 'f':  type = 1;  break;
     case 'c':  type = 2;  break;
     case 'h':  type = 3;  break; }
    inv.appendItem(ttl,id,qty,type); }
  File custIn("Cust.dat",ios::in);             // customer database
  char name[25], phone[15]; int movies[10], count;
  while (custIn.getCustomer(name,phone,count,movies)==1)
  { inv.appendCust(name,phone,count,movies); } }  // pump data

int Store::findCustomer(Inventory& inv)
{ char buffer[200]; char name[25], phone[13];
  int count, movies[10];
  cout << "Enter customer phone (or press Return to quit) ";
  cin.getline(buffer,15);
  if (strcmp(buffer,"")==0) return 0;          // quit if no data entered
  bool found = false;
  while (inv.getCustomer(name,phone,count,movies) != 0)
   { if (strcmp(buffer,phone) == 0)            // search for the phone
      { found = true;  break; } }              // stop if phone found
  if (!found)
  { cout << "\nCustomer is not found" << endl;
    return 1; }                                // give up if not found
  cout.setf(ios::left,ios::adjustfield);
  cout.width(22);  cout << name << phone << endl;  // print data
  for (int j = 0; j < count;  j++)
   { inv.printRental(movies[j]);}              // print movie Id's
  cout << endl;
  return 2; }                                  // success code

void Store::processItem(Inventory& inv)
 { int cmd, result, id;
   cout << " Enter movie id: ";
   cin >> id;                                  // search attribute
   cout << " Enter 1 to check out, 2 to check in: ";
   cin >> cmd;
```

```
  if (cmd == 1)
  { result = inv.checkOut(id);                    // analyze return value
    if (result == 0)                              // not found
      cout << "Movie is not found " << endl;
    else if (result == 1)                         // out of stock
      cout << "Movie is out of stock" << endl;
    else                                          // it is a success
      cout << " Renting is confirmed\n"; }
  else if (cmd == 2)
      inv.checkIn(id);                            // feedback in checkIn()
  cin.get(); }                                    // eliminate CR from line

void Store::saveData(Inventory &inv)
{ File itemsOut("Item.out",ios::out);  Item item; // item file
  while (inv.getItem(item))                        // no internal structure
    itemsOut.saveItem(item);                       // save each item
  File custOut("Cust.out",ios::out);               // customer output file
  char name[25], phone[13];  int count, movies[10];
  cout << "Saving database ... " << endl;
  while(inv.getCustomer(name,phone,count,movies))  // pump data
    custOut.saveCustomer(name,phone,count,movies); }
```

Method findCustomer() prompts the operator for the customer phone and terminates (returning zero) if the operator just presses the Enter key without entering any data. If the phone number is entered, findCustomer() retrieves each customer data sending the getCustomer() message to the Inventory object, which is passed to findCustomer() as the argument. If the phone number is not found, an error message is printed and findCustomer() returns 1 to notify its client. Otherwise, the customer name, phone number and the movie data are printed and the method returns 2.

Method processItem() also has a parameter of type Inventory. The method prompts the operator for the movie id and for the command (to check in or to check out) and then sends either the checkOut() message or the checkIn() message to its parameter. When checkOut() returns, processItem() analyzes the return value and prints the corresponding message. When checkIn() returns, processItem() just terminates because it is checkIn() that analyzes the results of the operation and prints the messages to the operator.

Method saveData() mirrors the actions of loadData(). It creates local File objects and sends them saveItem() and saveCustomer() messages with information that saveData() extracts from its Inventory parameter by using messages getItem() and getCustomer().

The last element of the program is the client of Store, the function main(). Listing 14.16 shows that main() instantiates two objects, one of class Inventory and one of class Store. It sends messages to the Store object and passes the Inventory object as an argument to these messages.

Listing 14.16   Implementation of function `main()` `Store` (file `video.cpp`).

```
// file video.cpp

#include <iostream>
using namespace std;
#include "store.h"                          // this is a necessity

int main()
{
   Inventory inv;   Store store;            // define objects
   store.loadData(inv);                      // load data
   while(true)
   { int result = store.findCustomer(inv);   // check results
     if (result == 0) break;                 // terminate program
       if (result == 2)                      // 1 if not found
         store.processItem(inv); }           // process the cassette
    store.saveData(inv);                      // save database
    return 0;
   }
```

Figure 14–12 shows the sample of the program execution. It is only a sample; it would be too cumbersome to demonstrate the complete testing sequence. This sample corresponds to the input files shown in Figures 14–8 and 14–9. The output files produced by the execution are shown in Figures 14–10 and 14–11.

Figure 14-12   Example of the execution of the program in Listings 14.6–14.16.

```
Loading database ...

Enter customer phone (or press Return to quit) 353-2566
Shtern                 353-2566
101  Splash                        comedy
102  Birds                         horror

  Enter movie id: 101
  Enter 1 to check out, 2 to check in: 2
  Movie is returned
Enter customer phone (or press Return to quit) 353-2566
Shtern                 353-2566
102  Birds                         horror

  Enter movie id: 103
  Enter 1 to check out, 2 to check in: 1
  Renting is confirmed
Enter customer phone (or press Return to quit)
Saving database ...
```

Presumably, the list of classes that the application implements corresponds to the list of real-life entities that the system has to deal with. This is why these classes are derived from the analysis of the functional specification. Usually, the distribution of responsibilities between classes in the application is quite natural. It is natural that class Item maintains the information about movies but not about customer names or disk files.

This is natural and relatively easy. Things become less certain when it comes to client classes at the top of the hierarchy of classes. Class Store does not have any intuitively clear responsibilities. The division of responsibilities between class Store and main() is completely arbitrary. Some designers feel that main() should have no responsibilities. It should instantiate the top object of the application, and actions should originate from that constructor call.

With such an approach, the contents of main() would be moved to the Store constructor. The Store object would not be needed in the constructor because the Store member functions are available in the constructor immediately, without a target object. Since Store member functions are called from the Store constructor only, these member functions do not have to be public—they can be made private.

```
class Store {
private:
   void loadData(Inventory &inv);
   int findCustomer(Inventory& inv);
   void processItem(Inventory& inv);
   void saveData(Inventory &inv);
public:
   Store(void)
     { Inventory inv;                          // define objects
       loadData(inv);                          // load data
       while(true)
       { int result = findCustomer(inv);       // check results
         if (result == 0) break;               // terminate program
         if (result == 2)                      // 1 if not found
           processItem(inv); }                 // process the cassette
         saveData(inv); }                      // save database
     } ;
```

Function main() becomes very simple.

```
int main()
{ Store store;
  return 0; }
```

From an aesthetic point of view, this is a more elegant solution. From a practical point of view, there are neither advantages nor disadvantages. As I mentioned earlier, the division of responsibilities between top classes in the class hierarchy and the function `main()` is arbitrary and cannot be designed from the analysis of system functionality.

On Class Visibility and Division of Responsibilities

The case study described in Listings 14.6–14.16 presents a good opportunity for a discussion of relationships among classes.

One of the important ideas discussed in the first part of the book was the idea of dividing responsibilities among functions to avoid excessive communication between the functions (and excessive coordination and cooperation among developers). This excessive communication often results from tearing apart what should belong together and from pushing responsibility up to client functions rather than down to server functions.

In this part of the book, this idea takes the form of dividing responsibilities among classes to avoid excessive communication between the classes and excessive communication among developers responsible for different classes.

Excessive communication between classes often results from tearing apart what should belong together: from dividing responsibilities among different functions and different classes so that they have to communicate through function parameters and class data members. The more extensive the communication is between classes, the more details that class designers should keep in mind, and the increased likelihood there is of errors.

Working with classes also involves pushing responsibilities from client classes to server classes. Failure to do so results in simpler server classes but makes client classes more complex and more difficult to understand. This makes the task of the client programmer and the maintainer more complex and error-prone.

An additional concept that is relevant only to design with classes and not to design with functions is the concept of class visibility. The more server classes a client class uses, the broader is the scope of attention of the client class designer and maintainer—they have to study the interfaces of the server classes and understand the constraints on the use of the server classes. Decreasing the number of server classes visible to a client class (that the client designer should know about) makes the program easier to understand and maintain.

Conversely, the larger the number of client classes using the same server class, the more sensitive the program design is to the changes to the server class. Decreasing the number of client classes to which the server class is visible improves the program stability.

Of course, these statements should not be taken to the extreme. After all, any program can be designed using only one class (or no classes at all), and the problems of communication between classes, division of responsibilities among classes, and class visibility to each other happily disappear. Yes, we want to build our program with cooperating classes, but we want the class communication to be minimized.

Using UML class diagrams (similar to the one shown in Figure 14–4) is a good method of analyzing the structure of the program. Class relationships on a class diagram illustrate class visibility: They show which client classes know about a particular server class. Unfortunately, class relationships on UML diagrams cannot illustrate the division of responsibilities among classes, pushing responsibility down to servers, and tearing apart what should belong together. For that, you have to analyze the distribution of data members and member functions among classes. Class diagrams similar to ones shown in Figure 14–3 are more useful for that purpose.

Class Visibility and Class Relationships

Figure 14–13 demonstrates the relationships between classes described in the case study in Listings 14.6–14.16.

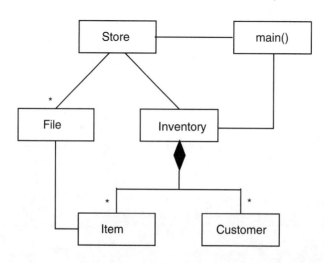

Figure 14–13
The UML class diagram for the program in Listings 14.6–14.16.

The UML class diagram shows that class Inventory "owns" the arbitrary number of objects of classes Item and Customer. In the design of class Inventory, I used the physical limits for array sizes, but these are arbitrary artifacts not related to the conceptual relationships among class Inventory and the objects it contains. From the conceptual point of view, class Inventory can contain any number of Item and Customer objects, and this is what I used in the class diagram in Figure 14–13.

The rest of the class diagram indicates that class Store is the client of classes Inventory and File, and that main() is the client of class Store and class Inventory. It also shows that class File is the client of class Item but not of class Customer.

This is the result of the inconsistency I noticed earlier in the design of classes Item and Customer. The objects of class Item know how to print themselves. The objects of class Customer do not know how to do that. This is why class Customer provides the method getCustomer(), which is used by the client code to retrieve the Customer data member for printing.

This inconsistency was further supported by the design of class Inventory. Its method getItem() provides the client code with the Item object and leaves it to the client code to access the components of the Item object. The Inventory method getCustomer() provides the client code with the Customer components but not with the Customer object. This is why class File sees class Item but does not see class Customer.

The visibility of one class in another class of the same program is an important characteristic that designers can use to minimize dependencies among classes and coordination among developers.

When an object is defined as a local object in a client method, it is only this client method where the object is visible. The amount of coordination is minimal. The example is class File whose objects are defined in Store methods loadData() and saveData() only and are not visible in other classes or in other methods of class Store.

When an object is defined as a data member in a client class, it is visible to all methods of the client class. This is a stronger degree of dependency—the client methods have to coordinate the use of server objects. The example is class Item and class Customer, whose objects are defined as data members of class Inventory, and indices custIdx and itemIdx, which point to these objects. All methods of class Inventory have access to these two arrays and these two indices. This provides greater convenience and flexibility. This also requires greater human coordination.

Consider, for example, Listing 14.11 where class Inventory is implemented. Method getCustomer(), which is called from the Store method findCustomer(), sets the index custIdx that points to the Customer object, which will participate in the checking-in or checking-out operation. Methods checkOut() and checkIn() access the same object using the same index variable custIdx, but they have to subtract 1 to get to the right object. This is an example of coupling, which is created by access to the same computational object from different methods.

When a client object is defined in a method of its own client, its server might be sent to its methods as a parameter—sorry for the complexity of this statement. For example, Figure 14–13 shows that class Store is a client of class Inventory. The client object (Store) is defined as a local variable of its client (function main()), and the server object (Inventory) is sent to Store methods as a parameter.

Listing 14.16 shows the implementation of this relationship. The function main() is the client of both classes, Inventory and Store. It defines Inventory and Store objects and sends the Inventory object to the Store methods as an argument. Both the designer of main() and the designer of Store should know about class Inventory.

This is the familiar issue of information hiding that can now be discussed in terms of object visibility. If the Inventory object is defined as a data member of class Store rather than as a variable in main(), then it is only the methods of class Store that have access to this object.

```
class Store {
   Inventory inv;
public:
   void loadData();
   int findCustomer();
   void processItem();
   void saveData();
} ;
```

The designer of main() in this version knows nothing about class Inventory. His or her scope of attention is reduced. The complexity of programming and maintenance tasks is reduced as well.

Pushing Responsibilities to Server Classes

Pushing responsibilities down to server classes is a good way to streamline code in client methods and to eliminate low-level processing details that make the client code more difficult to read and to grasp the meaning of processing.

For example, in Listing 14.6, class Item provided the methods getId() and getQuant(). These are general methods, which provide the actual item id and item quantity. Because of this generality, this design will satisfy almost any requirements that utilize this data.

This is good in a library class, which you want to sell to the largest number of possible clients. This is not so good for a part of the program that you want to design to satisfy specific requirements of specific client classes that belong to the same program or to the next release of the same program. With a general "library-type" design, the client classes should be flexible to be able to use the services that the server classes provide. Usually, client classes get more information from servers than they really need, and they have to adapt this information to current client needs.

For example, in Listing 14.11, the client function `printRental()` scans each `Item` object in class `Inventory` and retrieves the value of the `Item` object id. Now `printRental()` could do whatever it wants to this value, but it need only compare it with the parameter value.

```
void Inventory::printRental(int id)          // used in findCustomer()
{ for (itemIdx = 0;   itemIdx < itemCount;   itemIdx++)
  { if (itemList[itemIdx].getId() == id)
    { itemList[itemIdx].printItem(); break; } }
  itemIdx = 0;}
```

This information is redundant because the client code only needs to know whether the id inside the next `Item` object is the same as the parameter value. The client code gets more information than it needs (the id value), but it has to work harder using this information. A better division of responsibilities would require the client code to pass the parameter value down to the server function so that the server code can do the work on behalf of the client (compare ids) rather than bringing up information for the client code to process. Then the client code would look this way.

```
void Inventory::printRental(int id)          // used in findCustomer()
{ for (itemIdx = 0;   itemIdx < itemCount;   itemIdx++)
  { if (itemList[itemIdx].sameId(id))        // important difference
    { itemList[itemIdx].printItem(); break; } }
  itemIdx = 0;}
```

Similarly, the client function `checkOut()` in Listing 14.10 calls the server function `getQuant()` to decide whether the current item is available for rental. Now the client function can do with this value whatever it wants, but it only compares this value with zero.

```
int Inventory::checkOut(int id)                 // used in processItem()
{ for (itemIdx = 0; itemIdx < itemCount; itemIdx++)
    if (itemList[itemIdx].getId() == id) break;
  if (itemIdx == itemCount)
  { itemIdx = custIdx = 0; return 0; }
  if (itemList[itemIdx].getQuant()==0)          // what is the meaning?
  { itemIdx = custIdx = 0; return 1; }
  itemList[itemIdx].incrQty(-1);
  custList[custIdx - 1].addMovie(id);
  itemIdx = custIdx = 0;
  return 2; }
```

Again, this information is redundant because the client code only needs to know whether the item is available. The client code gets more information than it needs (the quantity value) but it has to work harder using this information. A better division of responsibilities would require the server function to do the comparison with zero so that the client code would not even know the business rules for item availability. To avoid bringing information from the server up to the client code for processing, the server can provide function inStock(). Then the client code would look this way.

```
int Inventory::checkOut(int id)                 // used in processItem()
{ for (itemIdx = 0; itemIdx < itemCount; itemIdx++)
    if (itemList[itemIdx].sameId(id)) break;
  if (itemIdx == itemCount)
  { itemIdx = custIdx = 0; return 0; }
  if (itemList[itemIdx].inStock())              // meaning is self-evident
  { itemIdx = custIdx = 0; return 1; }
  itemList[itemIdx].incrQty(-1);                // job is pushed to server
  custList[custIdx-1].addMovie(id);             // job is pushed to server
  itemIdx = custIdx = 0;
  return 2; }
```

Notice that the function checkOut() could save the value of the quantity on hand, check whether it is positive, decrement it by 1, and save the new quantity value in the Item object. This would be another example of pulling responsibility up to the client code. Instead, the function checkOut() says to the Item object: "Hey, I do not know how many items are there, and I should not worry about the exact number as long as I know there are items available for rental. So, whatever the quantity is, please decrement it by 1 and let us proceed." This is a good example of pushing responsibility down from a client class to its server class.

Using Inheritance

In the UML diagram in Figure 14–13, inheritance is not used because it is an implementation technique rather than a model of how real-life objects are related to each other.

Inheritance can be used to simplify the design of server classes, simplify the code of the client classes, and reduce the amount of common knowledge shared by classes in the application.

For example, the case study in Listings 14.6–14.16 implements a sort of idiosyncratic behavior for inventory items. In the input file, the kind of movie is denoted by a letter, for example, "f". The same is done in the output file. In the item display, the kind of movie is denoted by a word, for example, "feature." In memory during execution, it is denoted by an integer, for example, 1.

These business requirements are quite common. It is important to make sure that the clients of the server class with such behavior were protected from the need to know about it. The design in Listings 14.6–14.16 does not satisfy this requirement well. Class `Item` knows about it: in its method `printItem()`, it decides which word to display. So does the `Item` client `File`: in its `saveItem()` method, it decides which letter to write to the output file. And so does class `Store`, in its method `loadData()`: `Store` checks which integer it has to save in the item memory for further use. It is only class `Inventory` that is not involved in this issue, which was my error of forgetting to make sure that it does.

If the designer does not try to contain common knowledge among classes, it spreads around the program like cancer. Instead of doing productive work related to the high-level goal of the application, the designers of the client classes are occupied with a host of small details that should be pushed down to server classes.

Inheritance is a good mechanism for containing the knowledge in server classes. By making class `Item` the base class for a set of derived classes, for example, `FeatureItem`, `ComedyItem`, and `HorrorItem`, you can keep the knowledge about specialized item behavior in these classes and prevent the spread of this knowledge throughout the program.

I am not implementing this solution in this chapter because it requires the use of polymorphism, which will be discussed in the next chapter.

Another issue related to the use of inheritance in the case study in Listings 14.6–14.16 is the design of the `File` class. In this program, objects of class `File` are used for four purposes: reading item data, reading customer data, writing item data, and writing customer data. Each object is good for only one purpose. For example, the `File` object `itemsOut` in the method `saveData()` in Listing 14.15 can be used only for writing item data. If the client programmer tries to send the `File` message `getCustomer()` to this object, the compiler will accept this function call. It is only at run-time that the program will be aborted, because the physical file is open for writing.

Notice that if the client programmer uses this `File` object for accepting the message `saveCustomer()`, not only will the compiler accept this code, but the run-time system will have no objection. Wrong data will be written to the output file.

Using inheritance allows you to create specialized classes that can do only one kind of work. For example, class `FileOutItem` can only write data to the file that contains item data. It cannot read data or write customer data.

```
class FileOutItem : public File
{
public:
   FileOutItem(const char name[]);
   void saveItem(const Item &item);
   } ;
```

With this design, an attempt by the client code to send to the `FileOutItem` object the message `getItem()` or `saveCustomer()` will be interpreted by the compiler as a syntax error. This is very good. The tradeoff is that you wind up with a large number of very small classes in the program, and that might make maintenance more complex.

Some programmers say that if a `File` object is opened for writing item data, it is only a person with limited abilities and a narrow span of attention that will try to read data from that file or write customer data instead. I do not know. Theoretically, sure. Errors like this should not happen. But they do. Under pressure, many a programmer who is usually intelligent and alert becomes a less-capable person with a somewhat impaired attention span. (I am trying to be polite.) There is nothing wrong with capable and alert people making mistakes. It is not healthy to deny reality and insist that if the programmer is capable and alert there will be no mistakes. It is much better to face reality and consciously avoid situations that are conducive to making mistakes.

Figure 14–14 shows the UML diagram for the case study. Here, both class `Item` and class `File` are used as base classes for specialized derived classes.

Notice that I am not advocating this design. I am saying that we should consider this type of use of inheritance. The factors to take into account when considering tradeoffs are the number of classes to implement, the protection against misuse of objects, and avoidance of the spread of common knowledge between classes in the application.

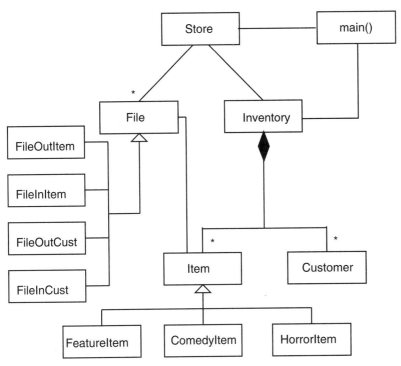

Figure 14-14   The UML class diagram for the program in Listings 14.6–14.16 with inheritance.

Summary

In this chapter, we compared the use of inheritance with other programming techniques, such as aggregation and a general relationship among classes.

I tried to stress the viability of other alternatives because I feel that in general inheritance is used too much. Yes, the job of the server class designer is simpler with the use of inheritance. Formally, the task of the client designer is not more difficult. But it is not more difficult only in the sense of writing code, and this is only a small part of what we do when implementing a program. The use of inheritance forces the client programmer to learn more about the server design than is necessary, especially if the inheritance hierarchy is tall and bushy.

We also looked into examples of using UML diagrams to illustrate the designs. These diagrams are helpful because they allow the designers to look at the big picture discussing the relationships among classes. I used only basic constructs of UML in the examples. The full UML is very complex. Whether you should be in a rush to study UML or concentrate on mastering C++ well first is debatable.

Since I am writing a book on C++ rather than on object-oriented analysis and design, I put a higher premium on C++ skills. It is your ability to write C++ code that pushes responsibilities to server classes that the quality and maintainability of software depend on. As far as your ability to draw complex diagrams is concerned—well, it is useful, but is less useful than the mastery of C++.

Part 4

ADVANCED
USES OF C++

The last part of the book discusses advanced uses of the C++ language: virtual functions, abstract classes, advanced overloaded operators, templates, exceptions, special casts, and run-time identification information.

Chapter 15, "Virtual Functions and Other Advanced Uses of Inheritance," describes the implementation of polymorphism with virtual functions—another jewel of object-oriented programming. First, it introduces the necessary (and often counterintuitive) background material on safe and unsafe type conversions between related and nonrelated classes. Then it applies this material to the task of processing heterogeneous lists of objects that belong to different (but related) classes and perform the same operation in a somewhat different manner. After that, it introduces the syntax of virtual functions and shows the dramatic simplification of the client code that these virtual functions allow.

In addition, Chapter 15 covers pure virtual functions and abstract classes and multiple inheritance. Although virtual functions are very useful for the processing of heterogeneous lists, the importance of this task is often exaggerated. This is even more true of multiple inheritance—its complexity far exceeds its utility from a software engineering point of view.

In Chapter 16, "Advanced Uses of Operator Overloading," I discuss advanced uses of operator overloading: unary operators, subscript and function call operators, and input/output operators. As with other uses of overloaded operators, these operators produce a nice syntax in the client code. Otherwise, the contribution of operator syntax to the quality of a C++ program is limited.

In Chapter 17, "Templates: Yet Another Design Tool," I introduce yet another C++ technique for design reuse: generic templates. The syntax of template definitions is quite complex. Their impact on the size of the object code and on the program execution time is often detrimental, and beginning C++ programmers should exercise restraint in building their own template classes.

However, the template classes that come with the C++ Standard Template Library (STL) are very well designed and should be used for complex data structures whenever possible. These template library classes give an excellent example of design and code reuse.

Chapter 18, "Programming with Exceptions," covers exception processing, yet another new C++ technique. This is a very interesting area of computer programming. You should probably try to use exceptions in a limited way to accumulate your own experience so that you can judge how useful this technique is for you. This chapter also discusses special casts and run-time object identification.

Chapter 19, "What We Have Learned," is a review chapter. In this chapter, I say everything that other authors say in their introductions. I postponed this until the end of the book to make sure that my words do not sound hollow. I hope that you will come to like this wonderful programming language and will be able to use it productively.

VIRTUAL FUNCTIONS AND OTHER ADVANCED USES OF INHERITANCE

Topics in this Chapter

- Conversions Between Nonrelated Classes
- Conversions Between Classes Related Through Inheritance
- Virtual Functions: Yet Another New Idea
- Multiple Inheritance: Several Base Classes
- Summary

Chapter 15

In the previous chapter, we discussed the UML notation for representing client-server relationships and looked at the techniques of implementing these relationships in C++ programs.

The most common relationship is the relationship of containment (composition or aggregation). The most common implementation of this relationship is making an object of the server class a data member of the client class. The server object is operated on exclusively by its client object without sharing with other client objects.

The most general relationship is that of association. If the client class contains a pointer or a reference to an object of the server class, it implements a general association among classes, and the server object can be shared with other client objects.

If the server object has only one client, so that the client object uses the server object exclusively, the server object could be implemented as a data member of the client class even when the objects are related with a general association and not aggregation.

The implementation of the client-server relationship with the server object as a data member of the client object results in a middle degree of visibility. The server object is visible to all member functions of the client class, but it is not visible to other classes in the program. The designers of other classes do not have to learn the details of using this object and coordinate its use with other designers.

A more limited degree of visibility is achieved when the server object is implemented as a local variable in a member function of the client class. In this case, the server object is visible only to this member function and to no other member function of the client class or any other class outside this member function. A broader degree of visibility can be achieved when the server object is passed as a parameter to a member function of the client class. In this case, the server object can be associated with many other objects outside of the client class, and these objects have to cooperate in using the server object.

Implementing associations by defining the server object as a local variable in a server method results in fewer dependencies between parts of the program and hence in less complexity for the implementers and the maintainers. Implementing associations by passing the server object as a parameter to a client method results in greater flexibility but might increase the complexity of the design for the implementers and the maintainers.

Choose whatever is most appropriate—the least degree of visibility that still supports client requirements. The C++ programmer should always think about choosing one of these three alternatives for implementing the association. The UML design notation does not distinguish between these three techniques. Often, the designers do not even know which technique is most appropriate in each case. They just state that the objects are related. So, it rests with the C++ programmer to make the right choice.

We also looked at the implementation of the specialization/generalization relationship between classes. Using inheritance for implementing this relationship between classes allows the programmer to build the server class in stages, implementing part of the server class functionality in the base class and part in the derived class (or classes). Thus, inheritance is a powerful, flexible mechanism for reusing C++ designs.

In this chapter, I will discuss advanced uses of inheritance programming with virtual functions and abstract classes. In its simple form, the goal of utilizing inheritance is making the job of the server class designer easier. In advanced uses, the goal of inheritance is making the job of the client programmer easier by streamlining the client code. This is important when the client code deals with collections of similar objects that undergo similar processing.

"Similar objects" means that they have attributes and operations in common, but some attributes and operations are somewhat different between different kinds of objects. "Similar processing" means that the client code treats these different kinds of objects basically the same way. However, depending on the type of object, some things should be done somewhat differently.

For example, in the case study in the previous chapter, the inventory items of different kinds (feature movies, comedy movies, or horror movies) were treated by the client code in the same way. They were read from the file, linked to the customers that rented them, underwent the checking in and checking out operations, and were saved to the file. In a few stages of processing the items of different kinds were treated differently. For example, when the item data is displayed on the screen, different labels should be displayed, depending on whether the item is a feature movie, comedy movie, or horror movie.

This is why client code in the previous chapter had to use the switch statements to figure out what kind of inventory item it was dealing with and what particular kind of processing should be used. You will see that the use of virtual functions and abstract classes helps you streamline the client code and eliminate this kind of run-time analysis from the client source code.

As the technical foundation for the use of virtual functions and abstract classes, I will first discuss the issues related to using objects of one class where objects of another class are expected. The C++ rules for this substitution with the use of inheritance are quite different from the rules for nonrelated objects. They are also different from what our everyday intuition suggests about the behavior of computational objects, and I will try to explain in what direction you should sharpen your intuition.

And at the end of the chapter, I will discuss how the techniques of using inheritance, virtual functions, and abstract classes can be extended to the case where a derived class has more than one base class.

Programming with virtual functions and abstract classes is often presented as the essence of object-oriented programming. From the practical point of view this is not so. Most of C++ code deals with cooperating objects and does not need virtual functions. Actually, most C++ code is (and should be) written without the use of inheritance. However, programming with virtual functions is definitely fun and is often useful. It is one of the most complex topics in C++, and I hope that you will learn how to use virtual functions correctly and enjoy using them.

Conversions Between Nonrelated Classes

As stated earlier, C++ aspires to support the concept of strong typing. I would like to make sure that you find this principle of modern programming intuitively natural and appealing: If the code context expects an object of a particular type, it is a syntax error to use an object of a different type instead.

What are possible contexts where this rule is important? They include:

- expressions and assignments
- function arguments (including pointers and references)
- objects used as targets of messages

I will call two different classes nonrelated if neither of them serves as a direct or indirect base class for another class. Notice that the classes that are not related to each other through inheritance might be associated with each other through aggregations and general associations. This is fine, but still you cannot use objects of one class instead of objects of another class. If the classes are related through inheritance, this is a different story.

Here is a small example that demonstrates all three contexts where C++ supports strong typing. There are two classes, class Base and class Other, which are not related through inheritance. The member function Base::set() expects an integer argument. The member function Other::setOther() expects an argument of type Base, and the member function Other::getOther() expects a pointer to a Base object. For simplicity, I do not include examples with reference parameters, but everything I am going to say about pointers also holds for references.

```
class Base {                            // one class
    int x;
public:
  void set(int a)                       // modifier
  { x = a; }
  int show() const                      // accessor
  { return x; }
} ;

class Other {                           // another class
    int z;
public:
  void setOther(Base b)                 // modify target
  { z = b.show(); }
  void getOther(Base *b) const          // modify parameter
  { b->set(z); }
} ;
```

In the following client function main(), I define three objects to manipulate, one each of type Base and type Other, and one of a numeric type. The second line is correct and trivial: The parameter is of the correct type, and the message target is of the correct type. The third line is also correct and trivial: The expression operands are compatible with each other, and the assignment target is compatible with the type of the rvalue.

Compatibility here means that the values of two different types (in this case, integer and double floating point) have the same operations defined for them (addition, assignment), and the values can be converted from one type to another (integer to double) and back (double to integer).

The next two statements are also correct. The message names in these statements (setOther() and getOther()) match the member function names described in the target class (class Other), and the message arguments are of the correct type (class Base on the fourth line or class Base pointer on the fifth line). All other statements in the client code are incorrect, and I commented them out. Let us discuss each statement and its problems in turn.

```
int main()
{
   Other a;  Base b;  int x;      // create objects
   b.set(10);                     // OK: correct parameter and target types
   x = 5 + 7.0;                   // OK: right types for expression and lvalue
   a.setOther(b);                 // OK: right type for the target, argument
   a.getOther(&b);                // OK: right type for the target, argument
// b = 5 + 7;                     // not OK: no operator = (int) defined
// x = b + 7;                     // not OK: no operator or conversion to int
// b.set(a);                      // not OK: an object as a numeric argument
// a.setOther(5);                 // not OK: cannot convert number to object
// a.getOther(&a);                // no: no conversion from Other* to Base*
// b.getOther(&b);                // not OK: wrong target type, not a member
// x.getOther(&b);                // not OK: a number as a message target
   return 0; }
```

In the first assignment (see below), the compiler expects an lvalue of a numeric type; instead, I use an object of a programmer-defined type. The compiler would like me to define the assignment operator=(int) with an integer argument for the type Base. This would make the first statement legal. In the second case, I add an object of the programmer-defined type and a numeric variable. These types are incompatible. For this statement to be legal, the compiler would like me to define the operator+(int) for the type Base. In both cases, the C++ attitude is noncompromising: Strong typing weeds out errors at the compilation stage rather than at run time.

```
   b = 5 + 7;   x = b + 7;        // syntax errors
```

The next two statements deal with parameter passing. If a function, for example, Base::set(int), expects an argument of a numeric type, you cannot use an object of a programmer-defined class instead. A conversion operator could help, but we will study it only in the next chapter. Conversely, if a function, for example, `Other::setOther(Base)`, expects an argument of a particular programmer-defined type, you cannot use a numeric value or a value of some other programmer-defined type instead. In all these cases, the compiler refuses to convert the value of one type to the value of another type and labels them as compile-time errors.

```
b.set(a);   a.setOther(5);                // syntax errors
```

C++ also tries to support the principle of strong typing for pointers and references. I lumped together pointers and references because the rules for them are the same. If a function has a parameter that is defined as a pointer (or a reference) to an object of some type it is an error to pass to it a pointer (or a reference) to an object of any other type, built-in or programmer-defined.

```
a.getOther(&a);                           // syntax error
```

It goes without saying that a function that expects a pointer cannot be called with a reference or an object as an actual argument, even if the reference or the object is of the same type as the pointer. Similarly, if a function expects a reference parameter, the actual argument cannot be a pointer, even if it is of the same type (it is fine to pass an object as the actual argument to a function with a reference parameter).

For message targets, the concept of strong typing manifests itself in limiting the set of messages that could be legitimately sent to a given target (an object, pointer, or reference). If the name of the message sent to an object is not found in the class specification, it is an error regardless of whether this function is found in any other class or in no class at all. For the compiler, it is enough that the message is not found in the class to which the message target belongs. And, of course, you cannot send a message to a numeric variable or value because a numeric variable or value does not belong to any class and can respond to no messages. The compiler needs a variable of a programmer-defined type to the left of the dot selector operator.

```
b.setOther(b);   x.setOther(b) ;          // incorrect target types
```

A pointer (and a reference) variable can point to a value of only one type, the type used in its declaration. This is yet another manifestation of strong typing. In this next code snippet, the second line is correct, but the third line is not.

```
Other a;   Base b;
Base &r1 = b;   Base *p1 = &b;            // OK: compatible types
Base &r2 = a;   Base *p2 = &a;            // non-compatible types
```

Strong Typing and Weak Typing

This is the ideal state of affairs. However, C++ allows a number of exceptions to these strict rules. Some of these liberties C++ inherits from C.

For example, all numeric types are considered equivalent from the point of view of type checking. You can mix them freely in an expression, and the compiler will silently convert "smaller" operands to "larger" operands so that all operators are applied to the operands of the same type. On the right-hand side of an assignment or as an argument in a function call, you can use a value of a "larger" numeric type where a value of a "smaller" numeric type is expected. The compiler will again silently convert the "larger" value (e.g., a long integer) into the "smaller" value (e.g., a character). The compiler assumes, so to speak, that you know what you are doing.

If you use a numeric value of a "larger" type where a value of a "smaller" type is expected, some compilers might give you a warning message. This happens, for example, when you try to squeeze a double floating-point value into an integer or into a character variable. But this is just a warning, not a syntax error. Following C, C++ allows you to use explicit casts to indicate to the reader the intent of the designer to convert a value of one numeric type into a value of another numeric type.

But this is just an option for maintenance-conscious programmers. For brevity-starving programmers, again following C, C++ makes all implicit conversions between numeric types legal. This liberal attitude toward a potential loss of precision applies both to assignments and to parameter passing.

From this point of view, C++ is (similar to C) a weakly typed language. In all these cases, the compiler assumes that you know what you are doing and does not try to second-guess you. If you do not know what you are doing or you do not pay attention to this side of your computation, well, let us hope that your computation indeed does not depend on the precision of the truncated values.

C++ also supports other exceptions to the rules of strong typing that cannot be blamed on the backward compatibility with C. These exceptions stem from the use of special member functions that C++ allows you to add to the design of your classes and from the use of casts:

- conversion constructors
- conversion operators
- casts between pointers (or references)

These special functions represent the ways to talk the C++ compiler into accepting the client code that violates the rules of strong typing.

Conversion Constructors

Assume, for example, that class `Base` provides a conversion constructor with a numeric argument.

```
Base::Base(int xInit = 0)    // conversion constructor
{ x = xInit; }
```

With this constructor available, this statement now compiles.

```
a.setOther(5);                   // incorrect type, but no syntax error
```

The compiler interprets this message in the following way.

```
a.setOther(Base(5));             // compiler's point of view
```

A temporary object of class `Base` is created, initialized with a call to the conversion constructor, used as an actual argument of the correct type, and then destroyed. Hence, the requirement of strong typing is satisfied at the compiler level—the function gets a value of the type it needs. This requirement is not satisfied at the programmer level; the programmer passes to `setOther()` an argument of an incorrect type and gets away with it.

Notice that I supplied the default parameter value to this constructor. Why did I do that? Before I added this constructor to class `Base`, it had the system-supplied default constructor, and I was able to define class `Base` objects without arguments. With the conversion constructor in place, the system took away the default constructor, and the definitions of `Base` objects without arguments would become syntactic errors.

As I mentioned earlier, C++ has this exceptional ability to make existing code syntactically incorrect when a new segment of code (in this case, the constructor) is added without removing anything from the code. In other languages, when you add new code, you can make non-related parts of the program run incorrectly, but you cannot make it syntactically incorrect. From one point of view, this is distressing, because adding nonrelated code should not cause problems in existing parts of the program. From another point of view, this is exciting, because the compiler notifies the programmer about problems at compile time, not at run time.

To avoid these problems, I could have added to class `Base` a programmer-defined default constructor that does nothing. This was probably the best solution because I did not need the object to be initialized to any particular value. (I do not have any further use for that value.) But I was lax, and instead of adding yet another constructor, I just added the zero default parameter value to make the existing client code compile. What is the drawback of this solution? I pretend that this zero value is somehow used elsewhere. Meanwhile, it is not used. I know that it is not used, but the maintainer will have to figure that out. Hence, I made a contribution (however small) to increasing the level of difficulty of reading this code.

So, adding the conversion constructor to class Base makes the call to the member function Other::setOther(Base) compile with the actual argument of a numeric type.

```
a.setOther(5);          // the same as a.setOther(Base(5));
```

When the compiler does not find the exact match for the parameter type, it will search for a possible numeric conversion. If there is no appropriate numeric conversion, it will search for a combination of a numeric and programmer-defined conversion. The conversion constructor is one of the possible programmer-defined conversions.

With this constructor in place, the next statement also becomes legitimate because the compiler calls the conversion constructor to satisfy the requirements of strong typing.

```
b = 5 + 7;              // no error: the same as b = Base(5+7);
```

In a sense, the compiler is trying to second-guess the programmer. One of the goals of C++ design was to avoid this and let the programmer explicitly state what the code means. One of the ways to explicitly state what we mean is to use explicit casts. However, according to C/C++ rules of weak typing, explicit casts are not required for conversions among numeric types, and the calls to the conversion constructors can be done implicitly, without explicit calls. What to do? The ISO/ANSI standard comes with a compromise. If the class designer feels that the conversion constructor should be called only explicitly, the keyword explicit is used as the modifier. (See Chapter 10, "Operator Functions: Another Good Idea," for more examples.)

```
explicit Base::Base(int xInit = 0)      // no implicit calls
{ x = xInit; }
```

The use of the keyword explicit is optional. If you use it in the design of the Base class, your code will be harder to write. (You use this extra keyword explicit.) Also, the client code will be harder to write (the client programmer will use explicit casts), but the resulting code will be easier to understand. If you do not use this keyword, you will make everybody's life (including yours) easier, but the quality of the code will suffer. It is hard to strike a good compromise.

C++ allows all kinds of silent conversions, but the explicit keyword prevents you from using them. This statement now is a syntax error again despite the presence of the conversion constructor; it needs an explicit cast.

```
a.getOther(5);       // illegal if constructor is defined as explicit
```

Notice that the implicit conversions apply only to an argument that is passed by value. It does not work with reference and pointer parameters. Adding the conversion constructor would not make a call to `Other::getOther(Base* b)` compile with the numeric argument.

```
int x = 5;
a.getOther(&x);      // is this is still a syntax error
```

Casts Between Pointers (or References)

The rules for implicit conversions (weak typing for values) apply only to values and not to references or to pointers (strong typing for addresses). However, explicit conversions can be applied to arguments of any nature. Can you pass an integer pointer to the place where the `Base` pointer is expected? No; according to the rules of strong typing, this line is an error:

```
a.getOther(&x);          // syntax error
```

However, you can always tell the compiler that you know what you are doing and you want it to accept this code. The C++ way of telling the compiler that you know what you are doing is to use an explicit cast to the correct type.

```
a.getOther((Base*)&x);   // no problem, conversion is OK!!
```

In this function call, a `Base` pointer is created and is initialized to point to the memory location that contains x. Inside `getOther()`, `Base` class messages are sent to the area occupied by x. Since `Base` methods do not know about the data structure of x, they can easily damage it. The whole operation does not make sense at all, but it is legal in C++. If you insist that you know what you are doing, the compiler will not argue with you.

The same is true about pointer (or reference) conversions among pointers (or references) of any type. Implicit conversions among different types are not allowed. For example, this is an error.

```
a.getOther(&a);   // error: no conversion from Other* to Base*
```

The method `getOther()` expects a pointer of type `Base`. Instead, it gets a pointer to an object of type `Other`. According to the principles of strong typing, the compiler flags this line as a syntax error—implicit casts between pointers (or references) of different types are not allowed. However, the function call with an explicit case is acceptable to the compiler.

```
a.getOther((Base*)&a);   // no problem, explicit conversion is OK
```

Here, a pointer to the `Base` class object is created and initialized to point to the `Other` object a. This pointer is passed to the `getOther()` method as an actual argument. Inside the `getOther()` method, this pointer is used to send to the `Other` object messages that belong to class `Base`. The compiler cannot flag these messages as erroneous. The execution of the program might result in a crash or might quietly produce incorrect results. This code is utter nonsense, but it is legal C++.

Conversion Operators

As far as the conversion operators are concerned, they are used as regular C++ casts. When applied to objects of programmer-defined types, they usually return a value of one of the object components. For example, the cast to int applied to an object of type Other might return the value of the data member x. The use of this operator eliminates a syntax error when an object of type Other is used where an integer (or other numeric type) is expected.

```
b.set(a);                    // the same as b.set(int(a));
```

Of course, this does not become legal just because I want it to. This is an example of client code that should be supported by adding appropriate services to the server class Other. I will tell you how to implement this kind of service in Chapter 16, "Advanced Uses of Operating Overloading." But the moral of using conversion operators is clear—this is yet another blow to the C++ system of strong typing.

If you wrote this code because you wanted the conversion from Other to int to happen, fine (using explicit cast would be better). If you used the object a instead of an integer by mistake, the compiler does not stand by to tell you about it. The protection of strong typing is removed, and you have to discover the error through run-time testing and debugging.

In summary, C++ is a weakly typed language as far as numeric types are concerned. You can convert from one numeric type to another freely, and explicit casts are not required. If you made a mistake, beware.

C++ is a strongly typed language as far as programmer-defined types are concerned. The language provides no casts between numeric types and programmer-defined types or between different programmer-defined types. If you made a mistake, it is flagged as a syntax error, and you can correct it before running the program.

Conversion constructors and conversion operators weaken the C++ system of strong typing for programmer-defined types. They allow explicit and even implicit conversions between numeric types and programmer-defined types. If you make a mistake, beware: It is not flagged as a syntax error.

As far as pointers (and references) are concerned, C++ provides a similar mixture of strong typing and weak typing. Pointers (and references) cannot point to objects of types different from their own type. However, they can be freely converted to a pointer (or a reference) of any other type. All that you have to do is to use explicit cast (unlike with numeric values implicit casts are not allowed, even for pointers to numeric types). Be very careful that the memory pointed to by the pointer (or the reference) is used correctly after this cast. Use casts with care.

Conversions Between Classes Related Through Inheritance

The use of inheritance introduces additional possibilities for using an object of one type where an object of another type is expected. Classes related through public inheritance are not totally incompatible because a derived class object has all the operations and data members that a base class object has. As you are going to see, one can assign an object of one class to an object of another type (possibly using an explicit cast). One can pass an object of one class as an argument where a parameter of another class is expected (again, you might need a cast).

The C++ rules for conversions between classes related through inheritance are not very complex. It seems, however, that they run against common programming intuition. If this will be the case for you, make sure that you adjust your intuition accordingly. I will try to help you to do so.

What you should know is that when a derived class publicly inherits from its base class, C++ supports implicit standard conversions from a derived object to its public base class. Conversions from the base object to the derived class are allowed too, but they require explicit casts. This rule applies to class objects, references to class objects, and object pointers.

This is the rule. Why is the rule designed this way? To make this formal rule more intuitive for you, I will consider several examples and offer diagrams that illustrate the conversions from one type to another.

The important concepts that I will use to clarify these conversions are the concepts of safe conversion and unsafe conversion.

Safe and Unsafe Conversions

Let us consider the following code snippet that uses numeric variables and illustrates the handling of variables of different types.

```
int b = 10;   double d;
d = b;                     // from "smaller" to "larger" type: safe move
```

In this example, I am moving a small piece of data (4 bytes on my machine) into a larger piece of data (8 bytes on my machine). Whatever value an integer variable contains, it can be comfortably saved in a double floating-point variable; in the transfer, it can lose neither precision nor value. This is why we think about this conversion as being safe. This is why the C++ compiler does not issue any warning for this type of code.

Now let us consider the movement of data in the opposite direction.

```
int b;   double d = 3.14;
b = d;                    // from "larger" to "smaller" type: unsafe move
```

Here, 8 bytes of the double floating-point value might not fit into a smaller shoe of an integer variable. The fractional part will definitely be lost. If the double value is outside the legal range for integers, the value will be lost as well. This is why we think this conversion is unsafe and this is why C++ compilers might issue a warning for this type of code.

However, C++ does not make this assignment illegal. After all, not all unsafe operations are incorrect operations. The double value might contain a small value that fits into an integer easily. The double value might not have any fractional part at the moment, or the value of the fractional part might not be important for the application.

This is why C++ defers to the programmer in evaluating the situation. If you know what you are doing (what value you are converting and what will happen to this value as the result of the move) and are happy with the results, fine. If not, C++ is not going to be Big Brother and look over your shoulder.

This is the logic behind the C++ rules for conversions between numeric variables. Next we discuss the conversions between variables of different classes. Unlike in the previous section, where I discussed conversions between objects of unrelated classes, I will assume that the classes are related through inheritance.

Let us look at the Base class (which on my machine contains one integer data member and its size is 4 bytes) and the Derived class (which contains two integers and its size is 8 bytes on my machine).

```
class Base {                      // Base class
protected:
    int x;                        // protected data
public:
    Base(int a)                   // to be used in Derived
    { x = a; }
    void set (int a)              // to be inherited
    { x = a; }
    int show () const             // to be inherited
    { return x; }
} ;
```

```
class Derived : public Base {
   int y;                                // in addition to x
public:
   Derived (int a, int b) : Base(a), y(b)    // initialization list
   { }                                   // empty body
  void access (int &a, int &b) const     // additional capability
  { a = Base::x;   b = y; }              // retrieve object data
} ;
```

Let us apply this logic of "fitting into the shoe" to moving data between variables of these two classes.

```
Base b(30);   Derived d(20,40);
d = b;                       // from "smaller" to "larger" type: it fits
```

Similar to the previous example with numeric values, I am moving a "smaller" value (4 bytes on my machine) into a "larger" value (8 bytes on my machine). There is plenty of space in the target object to accommodate the move, and no data is going to be lost.

Now let us move data in the opposite direction.

```
Base b(30);   Derived d(20,40);
b = d;             // from "larger" to "smaller" type: it does not fit
```

Here, I am moving a larger `Derived` value into a smaller `Base` variable. The `Base` variable does not have enough memory to accommodate all data members of a `Derived` value. The big value does not fit into a small shoe. This situation is illustrated in Figure 15–1. It shows the movement of data from a smaller value to a larger value and labels it as being safe. It shows the movement of data from a larger value to a smaller value and labels it as being unsafe.

As you saw earlier, this logic works well for numeric variables but fails for objects of classes related through inheritance. You need to adjust your intuition as quickly as possible. The real issue for class objects is not the existence of sufficient space but rather the availability of data for the consistent state of the object.

When you move data from a derived object to a base object, the derived object has enough data to fill the base object. It has more, but this is not a problem. The extra data will be dropped on the floor—the base object has no use for it. The base object will always be in a consistent state. This is safe.

When you move data from a base object to a derived object, the base object only has enough data to fill the base part of the derived object. The data to set the derived part of the derived object is nowhere to be found, and this is the problem. The derived object winds up in an inconsistent state.

This is not safe, and C++ declares this move a syntax error. Figure 15–2 illustrates this point of view. It shows that for numeric values the issue is the

A) Copying numeric variables

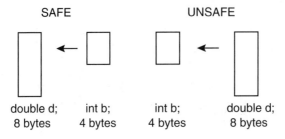

A) Copying object variables

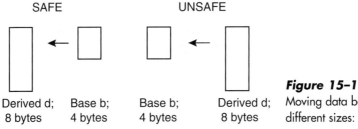

Figure 15-1
Moving data between values of different sizes: incorrect version.

A) Copying numeric variables

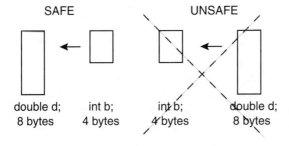

A) Copying object variables

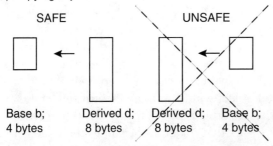

Figure 15-2
Moving data between values of different sizes: correct version.

preservation of value and precision, and for the class values the issue is the availability of data to set all the fields of the target object.

Will the explicit cast help? After all, C++ always gives you the means to tell the compiler that you know what you are doing.

```
Base b(30);   Derived d(20,40);
d = (Derived)b;                       // data has nowhere to come from
```

This is still a syntax error because the base object is not able to supply the missing data. You might want to use zeros to set the derived class data members that cannot be initialized from the base object (data member y in this example). This is fine, but this cannot be done by default—the compiler does not know whether these zeroes are acceptable. To notify the compiler, you can overload the assignment operator for the Derived class: Give this operator a Base parameter, copy the parameter fields and set the remaining fields to whatever you like.

```
void Derived::operator = (const Base &b)       // Base parameter
  { Base::x = b.show();   y = 0; }             // a compromise
```

You can find other examples of class assignment operators in Chapter 11, "Constructors and Destructors: Potential Trouble." In these examples, the assignment operators have the parameter either of the same class as the class of the assignment target or the type of one of the class components. Here you see the assignment operator whose parameter is of the base class. This is fine, because the overloaded assignment operator is just a C++ function, and you can design C++ functions using parameters of any type. And the base class object is one of the components of the derived class object.

Now, two questions. Question number one: why is the body of this assignment operator so complex? Why should I dance around the Base class with such respect as if I am afraid to touch it? Why do I use the scope operator? Why do I use the show() function? After all, the data member x is protected in the Base class, right? You might say that this is more than one question. All right, here is just one question: Can I make the assignment operator simpler and write it this way?

```
void Derived::operator = (const Base &b)       // Base parameter
  { x = b.x;   y = 0; }                        // nice!!
```

The answer to this question will appear later in this chapter.

Question number two: Here are two code lines that try to copy a Base class object into a Derived class object. Which line is supported by this assignment operator? The first line? The second one? Both lines? Neither?

```
d = b;                  // is this the same as d.operator=(b); ??
d = (Derived)b;         // is this the same as d.operator=(b); ??
```

The correct answer is the first line. How do I know that? Because the second line does not *call* the assignment operator; it is the first line that does. I have told you that you should always think about the difference between assignment and initialization because they are different in C++. To support the second line, you need the member function that will be called when the cast operator is compiled. What does the cast mean? The cast means the call to a constructor. To what class does the constructor belong? It belongs to the class of the cast. Hence, to support the second line of code, you should write something like this:

```
Derived::Derived(const ??? &b)      // what type for the parameter?
{ /* what do I do here? */ }
```

All right, now we know the name of the constructor. What is the type of its parameter? It is the type you are going to use to initialize the fields of the Derived class object. According to the code line I want to support, the parameter should be of the type Base.

```
Derived::Derived(const Base &b)     // Base parameter
{ /* what do I do here? */ }
```

Notice how often in this discussion I use the words "the code line that I want to support" in different forms. The reason for this is that it is from the client code to be supported that you decide what the server classes should look like. What I should do is to copy the parameter into the Base part of the Derived class object and do something with the Derived part of the object that leaves the object in the consistent state. Similar to the assignment operator, I can set the Derived data member to zero.

```
Derived::Derived(const Base &b)     // Base parameter
{ Base::x = b.x;   y = 0; }         // Hey, this is incorrect!
```

This is incorrect. I did not heed my own advice to think about the object construction process all the time. I thought that the constructor is called when the object is constructed and not after.

When the object is constructed, its components are allocated memory, and the constructor for each component is called before the next component is allocated memory. For the Derived class object, the Base component is allocated first. Hence, a Base constructor is called. Which constructor? Since I do not pass any data to the Base part, it is the default constructor. Let us go to the Base class definition and check whether this class has the default constructor. No, it has a conversion constructor without a default parameter value. Hence, the attempt to call the `Derived` constructor I am designing will result in a call to a missing `Base` constructor and hence will result in a syntax error. Sound familiar? Good, you should think about these things all the time.

What is the remedy? I should make the default `Base` constructor available. I could add one to the `Base` class or add the default parameter value to the existing `Base` conversion constructor. Another, better way to resolve this problem is not to provide the default constructor in the `Base` class but to use the initialization list for the `Derived` constructor I am designing. Let us use the initialization list.

```
Derived::Derived(const Base &b)         // Base parameter
   : Base(b.x)                          // pass data member?
{ y = 0; }                              // is not this nice?
```

But this is also incorrect. The data member x in class `Base` is not public and hence cannot be accessed from outside of the class scope. Some programmers argue that the constructor code that follows the `Derived::` scope operator is inside the `Derived` class, and the `Derived` class has access to non-private `Base` data members. This is true. However, a `Derived` class object has access to its own non-public data defined in `Base`. But parameter object b is different from the message target, and `Derived` class methods cannot access its non-public data. This is part of the answer to the first question I asked earlier: The `Derived` class assignment operator cannot access the internals of its `Base` parameters. It can access only its own internals defined in `Base`. This is why a `Base` member function should be used.

```
Derived::Derived(const Base &b)         // Base parameter
   : Base(b.show())                     // pass return value
{ y = 0; }                              // is not this nice?
```

This is correct but probably is too exquisite. I am calling the `Base` member function `show()` and passing its return value to the `Base` conversion constructor. It is simpler to call the `Base` copy constructor. This constructor is always available. Since the `Base` class does not manage its memory dynamically, there is no need to write a custom-made copy constructor.

```
Derived::Derived(const Base &b) : Base(b), y(0)    // copy
{ }                                                 // this is really nice
```

Therefore, this is the story about copying a `Derived` object into a `Base` object (no problem, it is always safe) and about copying a `Base` object into a `Derived` object (not safe, this operation is an error unless it is supported by a copy constructor or an assignment operator). The story applies both to using objects in assignment operators and to passing objects to functions by value.

In narrating this story, I used the data integrity analogy. I told you that copying a `Derived` object into a `Base` object is safe because the `Derived` object has all `Base` data (plus more), and the resulting `Base` object would be in a consistent state. I told you that copying a `Base` object into a `Derived` object is not safe because a `Base` object is a small object and it does not have data necessary for initializing a larger `Derived` object. Hence, this operation could leave the `Derived` object in an inconsistent state.

Another possible way to sharpen your intuition is to use the analogy with capabilities to perform operations. The use of an object of one type in the place where an object of another type is expected would be safe only if the object being used can perform all operations that the expected object might be asked to perform. I will illustrate this approach while discussing the use of pointers (or references) of one type where a pointer (or a reference) of another type is expected.

Conversions of Pointers and References to Objects

The next story is about using pointers and references that point to `Derived` and `Base` objects. For the sake of brevity, I will discuss pointers only, but everything I have to say about pointers applies to references as well. I will discuss a hierarchy of only two classes, `Base` and `Derived`, but everything I have to say about these two classes also applies to taller and to wider hierarchies of classes, where the base class has other derived classes, and derived classes are used as bases for other classes.

First, I will create a `Base` object dynamically and will try to call its methods using a `Base` pointer (this is, of course, always possible) and a `Derived` pointer (there will be some problems with that). Next, I will create a `Derived` class object dynamically and then try to call its methods using a `Derived` pointer (this is always possible) and a `Base` pointer (again, there will be some problems). After that, I will generalize the results for passing parameters to functions by pointer and by reference.

Here is an object of the `Base` class, which I allocate on the heap. I can use the `Base` pointer that points to this object to access all `Base` methods (e.g., `show()`) but not methods of any other class. The methods of the `Derive` class (e.g., `access()`) are also out of reach for the `Base` pointer simply because they do not belong to the `Base` class.

In processing these messages, the compiler identifies the name of the pointer (pb) that points to the unnamed target object, uses the pointer declaration to establish the class of the pointer (Base), goes to the class specification, and searches the class specification for the method name. If the name is found (in this case, show()), the object code is generated. If the method name with the appropriate signature is not found (in this case, access()), it is a syntax error.

```
int x, y;   Base *pb = new Base(60);       // base object
cout << " x = " << pb->show() << endl;      // this is OK
pb->access(x,y);                            // this is always impossible
```

Next, I try to set a Derived class pointer to point to the same Base class object. The algorithm for the function name resolution previously described is expanded when the pointer (or, for that matter, a variable) belongs to the Derived class. If the method with the name of the message is found in the Derived class, fine. If not, the compiler goes to the description of the Base class. It is only after the method with the appropriate signature is not found in the Base class description that the compiler flags the function call as a syntax error.

Hence, this Derived class pointer would be able to use any feature of the Derived class. "Any feature" here means the features defined in the Derived class (e.g., access()), and the inherited features (e.g., show()). But no such luck. When I try to set the Derived pointer to point to the Base object, the compiler balks without even getting to the other statements.

```
Derived *pd = pb;                          // point to Base object: not OK
cout << " x = " << pd->show() << endl;      // this would be OK
pd->access(x,y);                            // but this should be prevented
```

The formal explanation is very simple: The conversion from a Base object to a Derived object is not safe. Hence, the conversion from a Base pointer (or reference) to a Derived pointer (reference) is not safe. Period. They all generate syntax errors.

However, the formal explanation does not take you too far in understanding what is going on. You have to develop the appropriate intuition. Unfortunately, programming in traditional programming languages does not develop intuition related to conversions between classes, object substitutions, and allowed and disallowed function calls. Similar to the problem of object conversion, I will try to develop your intuition about pointer and reference conversions using graphics and analogies based on the object size and the ability to do work for the client code.

Figure 15–3 shows a Derived pointer as a larger rectangle than a Base pointer, not because the Derived pointer is allocated more memory (it is

pb

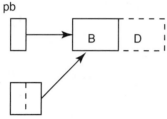

pd = pb; //syntax error
pd = (Derived*) pb; // OK

Figure 15-3
Accessing a Base object through a
pointer of the Derived class: unsafe.

not), but because the Derived pointer can provide more features than the Base pointer can. It is the object's capability to respond to messages and to do the work for the client code that is important in this analysis.

The Base pointer can access the Base class features only, and the Derived pointer can access the Base class features and the Derived class features. I am showing a dynamically allocated Derived class object as a larger rectangle than a Base object not only because it takes more space in memory but because it contains more capabilities. Even if it does not have additional data members (in this example, it does), it always contains additional member functions. I am showing a Base class object with a dashed complement to indicate the capabilities that are present in the Derived class object but are absent in the Base class object. The letters B and D inside the object rectangle denote the Base part and the Derived part of the object, respectively.

As Figure 15-3 shows, copying the contents of pointer pb into pointer pd makes both pointers point to the same Base object. Again, I am not looking into the actual physical addresses or whether the pointers point to the beginning or to the middle of the object—this is not important. What is important is that a pointer that points to an object is capable of invoking object capabilities according to the type of the pointer, not according to the type of the object.

I suggest that you think about base class objects as thin, weak, emasculated objects that can do very little. I suggest you think about derived objects as big, strong, powerful objects capable of doing everything that a base object could do plus much more.

Similarly, you should think about base pointers as thin, weak, myopic pointers that cannot see too far and can fetch only the capabilities defined in the Base class but not the capabilities defined in the Derived class. For example, a Base pointer can fetch the method show() defined in the Base class but not the method access() defined in the Derived class.

And finally, pointers of the Derived type should be thought of as big, strong, farsighted pointers that see far and can fetch a lot of capabilities (both `show()` from `Base` and `access()` from `Derived`).

When you set a powerful pointer of the `Derived` class to point to a weak `Base` class object, this pointer can fetch more than the object can deliver. Of the two lines that follow the pointer assignment `pd = pb` above, the first line (a call to `show()`) would be all right, but the second line (a call to `access()`) would not—there is no `access()` in `Base`. This is why C++ declares the conversion `pd = pb` to be a syntax error: to prevent calls such as `pd->access(x,y)`. This call is syntactically correct (`pd` belongs to class `Derived`) but is semantically meaningless—a `Base` object cannot respond to this message.

Of course, the compiler could see what you see, that is, that the `Derived` pointer `pd` points to a `Base` object and hence the call `pd->show()` should be allowed and the call `pd->access(x,y)` should not be allowed. But that would require too much from the compiler writer. When it comes to choosing between the interests of the compiler writer and a C++ programmer, C++ often favors the compiler writer. The C++ compiler is not required to do data flow analysis. You are required to learn the rules of conversion.

All right, the conversion `pd = pb` is not safe and is flagged as a syntax error. But what if you have only good intentions? What if you are going to call the `Base` functions only (e.g., `show()`), and not the `Derived` functions (e.g., `access()`)? There should be a mechanism for telling the compiler what it does not know but you do, namely, that you will be using the `Base` capabilities only. As you remember from Chapter 6, "Memory Management: The Stack and The Heap," and from the beginning of this chapter, such a mechanism indeed exists. It is called a cast.

Using the cast, you request the compiler to perform the unsafe conversion for you because you want to take the law into your own hands: You want to call `pd->show()` but not `pd->access(x,y)`.

```
Derived *pd = (Derived*)pb;        // hey, compiler, I know what I do
cout <<"x="<<pd->show()<<endl;     // I will do this, this is safe
// pd->access(x,y);                // do not even think about this!
```

Notice that the cast name includes not just the class name, but the pointer as well. It would be incorrect to omit the pointer notation. Also, you cannot use the functional notation; this notation is allowed only when the type name is an identifier, and `Derived*` is not an identifier (recall that asterisks are not allowed in C++ identifiers).

```
Derived *pd = (Derived)pb;         // cannot convert pointer to object
Derived *pd = Derived*(pb);        // illegal name for functional cast
```

If you do want to use the functional notation, use the `typedef` to make up a type name you would like to use, for example, `DerivedPtr`.

```
typedef Derived* DerivedPtr;        // new type name: an identifier
Derived *pd = DerivedPtr(pb);       // identifier: OK for this cast
```

Next, let us create a `Derived` class object on the heap. Using the `Derived` class pointer (big, powerful, far-sighted) that points to this object, you can invoke both the capabilities inherited from the `Base` class and the capabilities defined in the `Derived` class. And this is okay because the `Derived` class object has all these capabilities (big and powerful).

```
Derived *pd = new Derived(50,80);  // Derived object can do all
cout <<" x="<<pd->show()<<endl;    // OK to call a base method
pd->access(x,y);                   // OK to call a derived method
```

Now let us copy the contents of the `Derived` pointer into a `Base` pointer (thin, weak, and shortsighted). This is a type conversion: the `Base` pointer can access only the `Base` capabilities of the object it is pointing to. Trying to access the `Derived` class capabilities through this pointer is futile; these capabilities are not there, and the compiler will generate a syntax error.

```
Base *pb = pd;                     // pointer to the same object
cout <<" x="<<pb->show()<<endl;    // sure, Base method is there
// pb->access(x,y);                // error: not in Base class
```

Figure 15–4 illustrates what is going on. Again, I am showing a `Derived` pointer as a larger rectangle than that of a `Base` pointer. I am showing a dynamically allocated `Derived` class object as a larger rectangle than that of a `Base` object. The letters B and D inside the object rectangle denote the `Base` part and the `Derived` part of the object.

As Figure 15–4 shows, copying the contents of pointer pd into pointer pb makes both pointers point to the same `Derived` object (big, strong, powerful,

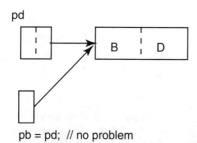

pd

pb = pd; // no problem
pb = (Base*) pd; // OK

Figure 15–4
Accessing a `Derived` object through a pointer of the `Base` class: safe.

capable of doing everything that a `Base` object can do plus much more). But this `Base` pointer `pb` is thin, weak, and myopic, it cannot see too far and can fetch only `Base` capabilities of the object but not `Derived` capabilities. (Even if they are there, in the object pointed to by this pointer.)

When you set a weak pointer of the `Base` class to point to a big `Derived` class object, this weak pointer can do no harm. This pointer can invoke only `Base` capabilities (e.g., `show()`), and they are always present in the powerful `Derived` object. This is why C++ accepts the conversion `pb = pd` as safe, just as it accepts the copying of a large `Derived` class object into a small `Base` object. This conversion cannot result in sending to the unnamed object a message to which the object cannot respond.

If you want to be explicit and tell the maintainer what you know at the time of writing the code (that you are converting a `Derived` pointer into a `Base` pointer), you can use an explicit cast. Since this conversion is safe, the cast is optional.

```
Base *pb = (Base*)pd;               // explicit cast: alert others
cout <<" x="<<pb->show()<<endl;     // sure, Base method is there
// pb->access(x,y);                 // error: not in Base class
```

This conversion is safe, but it is unnecessarily restrictive. The compiler flags the call to the `Derived` method `access(x,y)` in this code snippet as a syntax error. The compiler does this because it knows that the pointer `pb` is of the `Base` class, and the `Base` class does not have any `access()` method. Since the C++ compiler does not do data flow analysis, it has the right not to know what I know, that the pointer `pb`, however weak and myopic, points to a full-fledged `Derived` object that is as capable of responding to the `access()` message as is any other `Derived` object. Again, the C++ compiler writer gets a break, and I am left to search for a method of telling the compiler what I know.

Of course you know how to tell the compiler that this small pointer points to a large object. The way to tell the compiler what you know is to use casting. You have to cast this weak `Base` pointer (the one that cannot fetch `Derived` class capabilities) to the powerful `Derived` pointer so that the `Derived` methods will became reachable.

```
Base *pb = (Base*)pd;               // explicit cast: alert others
cout <<" x="<<pb->show()<<endl;     // sure, Base method is there
(Derived*)pb->access(x,y);          // error: priority of operators
```

This is nice. However, this is not nice enough. The arrow selector operator has a higher priority than the cast operator. As a result, the compiler will try to convert to the derived pointer whatever the method `access()` returns, and it will become confused. So I have to use yet another pair of parentheses.

It looks intimidating, but come to think of it (in steps), there is not much behind this syntax.

```
((Derived*)pb)->access(x,y);               // hey, it works!
```

Yes, it works, but it looks horrible, and all this complexity gets into the code because the compiler cannot recognize that the pointer pb points to the Derived object. It really feels like sanding the floorboards and then putting the boards sanded-side down.

Let us put all of these components together. Listing 15.1 shows the Base and Derived classes, and the client code handles objects of these classes. The output of the program is shown in Figure 15–5.

Listing 15.1   Using pointers to access objects of base and derived classes.

```cpp
#include <iostream>
using namespace std;

class Base {                               // base class
protected:
    int x;
public:
    Base(int a)                            // to be used by Derived
    { x = a; }
    void set (int a)                       // to be inherited
    { x = a; }
    int show () const                      // to be inherited
    { return x; } } ;

class Derived : public Base {              // derived class
    int y;
public:
    Derived (int a, int b) : Base(a), y(b)
    { }                                    // empty constructor body
    void access (int &a, int &b) const     // added in derived class
    { a = Base::x;   b = y; } } ;

int main()
{
    int x, y;
    Derived *pd = new Derived(50,80);      // unnamed derived object
    cout << " 1. Derived pointer, object, and derived method\n";
    pd->access(x,y);                       // no problem: type match
    cout <<" x = " <<x <<" y = " <<y <<endl <<endl;   // x=50 y=80
    cout << " 2. Derived pointer, derived object, base method\n";
    cout << " x = " << pd->show() << endl << endl;   // x = 50
    Base *pb = pd;                         // pointer to same object
    cout << " 3. Base pointer, derived object, base method\n";
```

```
cout << " x = " << pb->show() << endl << endl;         // x = 50
//  pb->access(x,y);                               // error: no access to derived method
   cout << " 4. Converted pointer, derived object and method\n";
   ((Derived*)pb)->access(x,y);                    // we know it is there
   cout <<" x = " <<x <<"  y = " <<y <<endl <<endl;       // x=50 y=80
   pb = new Base(60);                              // unnamed base object
   cout << " 5. Base pointer, base object, base method\n";
   cout << " x = " << pb->show() << endl <<endl;          // x = 60
   cout << " 6. Converted pointer, base object, derived method\n";
   ((Derived*)pb)->access(x,y);                    // pass on your own risk
   cout <<" x = " <<x <<"  y = " <<y <<endl <<endl;       // junk!!
   delete pd;   delete pb;                         // necessary tidiness
   return 0;
}
```

First, client code creates an object of the Derived class and uses the Derived class pointer to access the derived class method access(). This is trivial. The compiler finds the method in the definition of the class to which the pointer belongs and calls it. It prints x=50, y=80, the first output.

Then the client code calls the Base method show() using the same Derived class pointer. This is also trivial. The compiler does not find the definition of the method in the Derived class description, goes to the definition of the Base class, finds the method and generates the call (and prints x=50). No type conversion is involved. The unnamed object pointed to by the Derived pointer is of Derived type and can do everything that might be required from either a Base or a Derived class object (second output).

Figure 15–5   Output for program in Listing 15.1.

1. Derived pointer, object, and derived method
x = 50 y = 80

2. Derived pointer, derived object, base method
x = 50

3. Base pointer, derived object, base method
x = 50

4. Converted pointer, derived object and method
x = 50 y = 80

5. Base pointer, base object, base method
x = 60

6. Converted pointer, base object, derived method
x = 60 y = -33686019

Next, the client code sets the `Base` pointer to point to the `Derived` object. This is not so trivial because these pointers are not of the same type. Normally, implicit conversions between pointers of different types are not allowed. Since these pointers are of a related type, this rule is relaxed for safe conversions.

```
Base *pb = pd;        // different types: safe for related types
```

It is safe because the `Derived` class pointer can do everything a `Base` class pointer can, and there is no danger that the `Base` pointer `pb` will be asked by the client code to do something it cannot do. Still, some programmers believe that the explicit cast is useful because it tells the maintainer (not the compiler—it knows what is going on) about the conversion.

```
Base *pb = (Base*) pd;        // related types: cast is optional
```

In Listing 15.1, the client code does not use this conversion—it is optional. Next, the client code uses this `Base` pointer to call the `Base` method `show()`. Since the unnamed object to which the `Base` pointer is pointing is of type `Derived`, there is no problem with sending the base class message to that object. (It prints `x=50`, third output).

Next, the client code uses the `Base` pointer to call the `access()` method. Here, the issue of safety is irrelevant. It does not matter that the pointer points to a `Derived` class object, which can handle the job. The compiler does not look at the object. The compiler looks at the pointer, searches the definition of the class to which the pointer belongs (`Base`), does not find the match for the method, and declares the call a syntax error. I commented it out.

Next, the client code tells the compiler what the designer knows but the compiler does not, that this `base` pointer points to a `Derived` object. The client code does it by converting the `Base` pointer into a `Derived` pointer. This conversion is not safe and has to be done explicitly. The converted pointer is of class `Derived`, and the compiler has no problem calling a `Derived` method through this pointer.

```
((Derived*)pb)->access(x,y);        // we know it is there
```

Since the object pointed to by this converted pointer is indeed a `Derived` class object, the method call executes correctly and prints `x=50`, `y=80`, the fourth output.

Next, the client code creates a `Base` object and uses the `Base` pointer to call the `Base` method `show()`. This is again trivial. The compiler searches the definition of the class to which the pointer belongs, not the class to which the object belongs (never mind that here it is the same class), matches the message and the method and calls it. (It prints x=60, fifth output.)

Finally, the client code does that horrible thing that the oversight of freedom from the compiler allows it to do. It casts the `Base` pointer into a `Derived` pointer. This conversion is not safe, so the explicit cast is needed to tell the compiler what the compiler does not know, that I know what I am doing. I cast the pointer using all appropriate parentheses and call the `Derived` method `access()`.

```
((Derived*)pb)->access(x,y);        // pass on your own risk
```

Here, telling the compiler that I know what I am doing means that I will not call the `Derived` class methods using this pointer because the object it is pointing to can do only the `Base` class work.

Since I told the compiler that I know what I am doing, the compiler does not try to second-guess me and figure out what kind of object the `Base` pointer is actually pointing to. This is a pity, because the `Derived` method `access()`, being called on a `Base` object, prints whatever it wants (sixth output). This is pretty much like the Soviet Union, which used to have common borders with whatever countries it wanted.

This is a good example of how you can shoot yourself in the foot using perfectly legitimate (if somewhat complex) C++ coding patterns.

Three comments are in order. First, everything I said here about pointers is true about C++ references as well. (The only difference is that a reference cannot be turned to point to another object.) A reference of a base type can point to a derived class object without casting and invoke only methods defined in the base class but not in the derived class. If this base reference is cast to the derived class, it can invoke methods defined both in the base class and in the derived class. A reference of a derived class cannot point to a base class object without an explicit cast. With the cast, it can point to a base class and invoke any method. It is up to the programmer to make sure that a derived class method is not called using a derived class reference that points to the base class object.

Note

Pointers (and references) of a base class can point to a derived class object without an explicit cast. They can do no damage because they can access only the base part of the derived object. Explicit cast is optional. Pointers (and references) of a derived class should not point to a base class object because they might ask this object to respond to derived class messages. If you feel you have to do that, you must use explicit cast.

Second, all that I have told you here about pointers and references holds only for related classes. If classes are not related through inheritance, then pointers (and references) of these classes cannot point to objects of other classes without explicit casts (and these casts usually make no sense). No implicit conversions are allowed because the classes do not have common operations (see the first section of this chapter). The only reason why a base pointer is allowed to point to a derived object is that the base and derived classes have common operations—the operations defined in the base class. It is these operations that the base pointer can invoke.

Alert

Pointers (and references) of a specific class must not point to objects of classes not related to this one by inheritance. This is a syntax error. If you feel that you have to do that, you must use explicit cast. C++ allows this cast—and this is a pity. Trying to treat the same object as an object of two different classes is asking for trouble.

Third, the implicit casts between classes related through inheritance are allowed only if the mode of inheritance is public. If inheritance is private or protected, all conversions require explicit casts. Why is this so? Because with private or protected mode of inheritance, public operations of the base class become private or protected in the derived class. There is no guarantee that the base and the derived classes have any operations in common. Hence, the base pointer should not be allowed to point to a derived class object. The operations of the derived class are not accessible for the base pointer (the major property of C++ classes), and the operations of the base class are not accessible to the derived object (the property of private and protected inheritance).

This is why it is a good idea to only use the public mode of derivation.

Tip

Derive your derived classes using public derivation only. This allows you to point pointers (or references) of one class to an object of another class in the same inheritance hierarchy. With private and protected inheritance, the base and the derived objects do not have public operations (or data) in common. Pointing a pointer of one class to an object of another class in the hierarchy makes as much sense as pointing a pointer of one type to an object of an unrelated class—it is asking for trouble.

Conversions of Pointer and Reference Arguments

Now we have all of the necessary tools to discuss the conversion of arguments in function calls. Here is the class Other, which implements member functions with pointer and reference parameters of classes Base and Derived.

Overloaded methods setB() expect arguments of class Base. They set the value of the Other data member to the value of the data member inside the Base parameter. Overloaded methods setD() expect arguments of class Derived. They set the Other data member to the value of the additional data member inside the Derived parameter object. Method get() returns the internal state of the Other object.

```
class Other {                         // another class
    int z;
public:
    void setB(const Base &b)          // pass by reference
    { z = b.show(); }
    void setB(const Base *b)          // pass by pointer
     { z = b->show(); }
    void setD(const Derived &d)       // pass by reference
    { int a; d.access(a,z); }
    void setD(const Derived *d)       // pass by pointer
    { int a; d->access(a,z); }
    int get() const                   // selector
    { return z; } } ;
```

This is enough to demonstrate the major issues. In the next snippet of code, each function gets an argument of the type specified in the function interface. This is the most natural way of using functions. Since the function expects an argument of a certain type, small wonder that inside the function the argument receives messages that belong to the corresponding type. In the setB() functions, the parameter is sent the Base message show(). In the setD() functions, the parameter is sent the Derived message access().

```
Base b(30);   Derived d(50,80);       // related objects
  Other a1, a2;                       // unrelated objects
  a1.setB(b);   a2.setD(d);           // exact match
  a1.setB(&b);  a2.setD(&d);          // exact match
```

In addition to the messages defined in the Derived class, the functions that expect a Derived class reference as a parameter could send to the parameter messages that are defined in the Base class as well. This is not a problem because the argument of the Derived class can respond to messages inherited from the Base class (provided that inheritance is public and not protected or private).

In functions that expect a Base class parameter (a reference or a pointer), messages of the Derived class cannot be sent to the parameter. How do I know that? Because an argument of the Base class cannot respond to messages defined in the Derived class, and an attempt to send such a message inside the function would not compile.

```
class Other {                       // another class
    int z;
public:
    void setB(const Base &b)        // Base object is expected
    { int a; d.access(a,z); }       // error: Derived message
    . . . } ;                       // the rest of class Other
```

It is these two observations that allow us to decide what happens if a pointer or a reference of a different class is passed as an actual argument of a function. If the parameter and the argument types are not related through inheritance, the answer is simple. If there is no explicit cast, the function call is a syntax error, whether the parameter is passed by reference or by pointer.

```
Account acc1(100), acc2(1000);      // unrelated objects
Other a1, a2;                       // unrelated objects
a1.setB(acc1);   a2.setD(acc2);     // syntax error
a1.setB(&acc1);  a2.setD(&acc2);    // syntax error
```

When parameters are passed by value, implicit casts are possible if the parameter class provides appropriate constructors. No such mechanism exists for reference and pointer parameters. The only way to eliminate syntactic errors is to use an explicit cast.

```
a1.setB((Base&)acc1);               // no syntax error but useless
a1.setB((Base*)&acc1) ;             // no syntax error but useless
```

These function calls are not syntax errors—the compiler accepts my pledge that I know what I am doing. This is too bad, because I do not know what I am doing. Inside these functions, the argument Account objects are going to respond to Base messages, in this case, show(). This is a semantic error: what the program does makes no sense.

When the formal parameter and the actual argument types are related to each other through inheritance, the situation is more complex.

When a function expects a Base pointer (or a Base reference) parameter, you can call this function with a Derived pointer (or reference) as the actual argument. This is fine because the Derived object can do everything that a

`Base` object can. The function that expects a `Base` parameter will ask its parameter to perform only `Base` duties in the body of the function. As I said earlier, `Derived` class messages inside the body of this function would not be tolerated by the compiler.

```
void Other::setB(const Base &b)          // pass by reference
{ int a; b.access(a,z); }                // syntax error
```

This situation is impossible because C++ is a strongly typed language. Hence, the conversion from `Derived` pointer (reference) to `Base` pointer (reference) is safe—bad things will not happen to the `Derived` argument object inside the function that expects a `Base` object.

```
a1.setB(&d);                             // safe conversion
```

Figure 15–6 illustrates this function call. When the space for the pointer parameter `b` is allocated, it is initialized to the contents of the actual argument (the thick arrow). The actual argument is an unnamed pointer to the `Derived` object `d`. I denote this unnamed pointer as `&d`. As a result, both pointers point to the same `Derived` class object (the thin arrows). When the function executes, it sends messages to its parameter `b`. Since this parameter is of the `Base` class, it can fetch messages only from the `Base` part of the object (the dashed line under the object). The parameter pointer cannot fetch messages from the `Derived` part of the object, but these messages are not called inside the function because its parameter is of the `Base` class, not of the `Derived` class.

When a function has a `Derived` pointer (or reference) parameter, you should not call this function with a `Base` pointer (or reference) as the actual argument. Inside this function, the object pointed to by the parameter pointer might be asked to do things that only a mighty `Derived` object could do but a weak `Base` object could not.

Figure 15-6   Conversion from `Derived` to `Base` pointer in parameter passing.

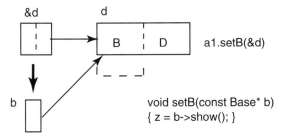

```
a2.setD(&b);                          // syntax error
```

This conversion is not safe and is flagged as a syntax error. Figure 15–7 illustrates this function call. When the space for the parameter d is allocated, it is initialized to the contents of the actual argument, an unnamed pointer to the Base object b. When the function executes, it sends messages to its parameter d. Since this parameter is of class Derived, it can fetch messages both from the Base and the Derived parts of the object (the dashed line).

But this little object does not have any Derived part. A weak Base object does not know how to respond to them. When a message to a nonexistent part of the object is sent at run time, the results are undefined. The program might crash, or it might produce incorrect results.

Let us say the method Derived::setD() is written differently and sends only Base class messages to its parameter.

```
void setD(const Derived *d)           // pass by pointer
{ z = d->show(); }                    // Base services only
```

It is actually safe to send a Base object to this function, but the compiler does not know that. You can insist. I can use our old friend explicit cast to let the compiler know what I know.

```
a2.setD((Derived*)&b);                // explicit conversion
```

This is a common way to tell the compiler that you know what you are doing. When you saw this cast the first time, it probably looked confusing and complex. But it does not contain anything mysterious under the hood. It just says that this Base object will be safe within the setD() function. So this little Base object can pretend that it is a grown-up Derived object; this is all right, because inside this function it will be doing only Base work anyway. But just make sure you know what you are doing!

Figure 15–7   Conversion from Base pointer to Derived pointer in parameter passing.

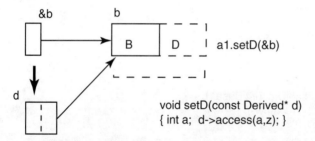

In Listing 15.2, I summarize the results of this discussion. The output of the program is presented in Figure 15–8.

Listing 15.2   Passing pointer and reference arguments of base and derived classes.

```cpp
#include <iostream>
using namespace std;

class Base {                              // base class
protected:
   int x;
public:
   Base(int a)                           // to be used by Derived
   { x = a; }
   void set (int a)                      // to be inherited
   { x = a; }
   int show () const                     // to be inherited
   { return x; } } ;

class Derived : public Base {            // derived class
   int y;
public:
   Derived (int a, int b) : Base(a), y(b)
     { }                                 // empty constructor body
   Derived(const Base &b) : Base(b)      // supports implicit cast
   { y = 0; }                            // explicit initialization
   void access (int &a, int &b) const    // added in derived class
   { a = Base::x;   b = y; } } ;

class Other {                            // another class
   int z;
public:
   void setB(const Base &b)              // pass by reference
   { z = b.show(); }
   void setB(const Base *b)              // pass by pointer
   { z = b->show(); }
   void setD(const Derived &d)           // pass by reference
   { int a; d.access(a,z); }
   void setD(const Derived *d)           // pass by pointer
   { int a; d->access(a,z); }
   int get() const                       // accessor
   { return z; }
} ;

int main()
{
   Base b(30);   Derived d(50,80);       // related objects
   Other a1, a2;                         // unrelated object
   a1.setB(b);   a2.setD(d);             // exact match
```

```
cout << " a1=" << a1.get() << "   a2=" << a2.get() << endl;
a1.setB(d);   a2.setD(b);                            // implicit conversions
cout << " a1=" << a1.get() << "   a2=" << a2.get() << endl;
a1.setB(&b);   a2.setD(&d);                          // exact match
cout << " a1=" << a1.get() << "   a2=" << a2.get() << endl;
a1.setB(&d);                                         // implicit conversion
// a2.setD(&b);                                      // syntax error
a2.setD((Derived*)&b);                               // explicit conversion
cout << " a1=" << a1.get() << "   a2=" << a2.get() << endl;
return 0;
}
```

In this example, I use the same classes Base and Derived as in the previous examples. Class Derived has an additional constructor I will comment on shortly.

Class Other has two overloaded functions setB(), which expect a reference and a pointer parameter of class Base; two overloaded functions setD(), which expect a reference and a pointer parameter of class Derived; and a method get(), which returns the value of the data member z.

The client code defines and initializes a Base object, a Derived object, and two Other objects. The first output line produces a1=30 and a2=80 because the function calls to setB() and setD() use the exact match between the types of actual arguments and formal parameters.

The function call to setB() with a Derived class actual argument does not cause problems. The Base reference can be initialized by a Derived object without a cast because this conversion is safe. The function call to setD() with a Base class argument results in an unsafe conversion. Normally, this function call should be rejected as a syntax error. The call might be made acceptable to the compiler with the use of the explicit cast.

```
a2.setD((Derived&)b);       // syntax for casting references
```

Of course, this cast does not do any good because it just placates the compiler. The Derived reference inside setD() still points to the little Base object (see Figure 15–7), and the function call to Derived::access() in the body of setD() accesses memory that does not belong to the argument object b.

Figure 15–8   Output for program in Listing 15.2.

```
a1=30  a2=80
a1=50  a2=0
a1=30  a2=80
a1=50  a2=7011896
```

To make this call meaningful, the `Derived` parameter pointer in `setD()` should point to a `Derived` object, not to the `Base` object. This `Derived` object has to be initialized to the values that are contained in the fields of the `Base` actual argument. However, the `Derived` object has fields that are not found in the `Base` object. They have to be set to some reasonable values, for example, 0, or whatever suits the application.

What function should the `Derived` class provide to ensure proper initialization of the object fields? Right, this is your old friend the constructor. Which constructor? The name of the constructor depends on the number and type(s) of its parameter(s). Since this constructor initializes the fields of a `Derived` object using data from a `Base` object, it needs only one parameter, and the type of this parameter is `Base` (or a `Base` reference). Hence, the name of this constructor is a conversion constructor.

As you see, this is an apt name. It is well suited for the constructor, which converts a value of the `Base` class into a value of the `Derived` class.

```
Derived::Derived(const Base &b) : Base(b)   // copy constructor
{ y = 0; }                                  // explicit initialization
```

The conversion constructor can be called explicitly, creating a temporary `Derived` class variable, which is initialized by the constructor, is pointed to by the reference parameter inside `setD()`, and is deleted after the call to `setD()`.

```
    a2.setD((Derived)b);           // explicit constructor call
```

This means that this technique can be used for the input parameters only. If it is used for an output parameter, the changes made within the function will be made to a temporary copy, which will be destroyed after the call.

Since I did not define this constructor as `explicit`, implicit calls to it are possible, and this is what the client call does in Listing 15.2. The next output line produces `a1=30` and `a2=0`.

The second part of the client code deals with pointer parameters rather than with reference parameters. The first two calls to `setB()` and `setD()` use an exact match and produce output `a1=30` and `a2=80`. The call to `setB()` with a `Derived` pointer as an actual argument causes no problems—the conversion from `Derived` to `Base` is safe. The call to `setD()` with a `Base` pointer as an argument is problematic. This conversion is not safe and is flagged as a syntax error. (I commented this call out.)

To talk the compiler into accepting this call, I use the explicit cast from a `Base` to `Derived` pointer. This placates the compiler but does not create a `Derived` object. A constructor with the `Base` pointer parameter (similar to one I use for the reference parameter) would resolve this problem. But these constructors are not common, and I decided that I will allow the example to produce junk to illustrate once again that the cast from `Base` to `Derived` is not safe.

Note

It is always safe to pass a derived class pointer (or reference) as an argument to a function with a base class pointer (or reference) parameter (cast is optional). It is a syntax error to pass a base pointer (or reference) as an argument to a function with a derived pointer (or reference) parameter. It is unsafe to coerce the compiler into accepting this function call by casting the base pointer (or reference) to the derived class.

As you can see, I am spending significant time on and paying serious attention to the issues of conversion between objects (or pointers or references) of different classes. For unrelated classes, this topic is not of any practical significance. It is quite rare that one has a legitimate desire to use one type where another unrelated type is expected. In those few cases where this desire seems legitimate, you might try to distract yourself with something entertaining to see whether the desire to do this cast disappears. You will see that there are ways to eliminate the problem without the cast. Conversions between unrelated types are confusing and dangerous.

It is a totally different story for classes related through inheritance. The use of one type from the inheritance hierarchy where another type from the same hierarchy is expected is very popular in C++ programming. Actually, it is very popular in any object-oriented programming. This is why it is important that you understand this technique, its limitations, and its implications.

Conversions between types related by inheritance are also confusing. They can also be dangerous. They do not conform to common programming intuition about conversions among numeric types. I hope that this discussion will help you develop your intuition in terms of what is and is not appropriate. The major yardstick in evaluating conversions is not whether the result of conversion has enough space to accommodate the source but just the other way around. The major criterion is whether conversion is safe, whether the result of conversion will be asked to do something it cannot do.

Conversion from derived type to base type is safe. Conversion from base type to derived class is not safe.

With this approach well understood, let us look at C++ virtual functions.

Virtual Functions: Yet Another New Idea

In C++, each computational object is characterized by the properties that define the type of the object. The object is denoted by its name (identifier), and the type is associated with this identifier. Throughout the book, this association was taking place when I specified the object type in object declarations or definitions. This was true both of program variables and of program functions.

At the declaration or definition of a variable, the source code must make the commitment and specify the type of the computational object. This association between the object name and its type cannot be broken during program execution. The program can define other computational objects using the same identifier and the same (or possibly different) type. This is fine. But these other objects will be other objects. Even if they use the same name, they are different computational objects.

The same is true of program functions. The function declaration (its prototype) or the function definition (its body) includes an identifier for the function name. The function name becomes associated with the object code generated for this function. This is a commitment that cannot be broken or changed during program execution. The program might define some other functions using the same function name. These functions might be in the same class (with a different signature) or in another class or scope (with the same or different signature). But these would be different functions. They would just happen to have the same function name.

Actually, C++ function name overloading did not break the C commitment to unique function names. For a human being, when the name of the function is reused in the same class or in another scope, it is the same name. For the compiler, all these functions would have different names. The name that the compiler knows is a concatenation of the name of the class to which the function belongs, the function identifier, the return type, and the types of its parameters.

So, when the compiler see a function definition, it creates modified names that add the class name, return type, and parameter types to the function identifier. As a result, each function name is actually unique for the compiler. This technique is known as name mangling.

For example, a function `draw()` might be defined in several classes and with different signatures. Each function represents a separate computational entity.

```
class Circle {
   int radius;
public:
   void draw();
    . . . . } ;                     // the rest of class Circle


class Square {
   int side;
public:
   void draw();
    . . . . } ;                     // the rest of class Square


class Rectangle {
   int side1, side2;
public:
   void draw();
    . . . . } ;                     // the rest of class Rectangle
```

What we often take for granted is the time in which the association between the name and the computational object takes place. It takes place at compile time, when the compiler processes the definition or the declaration of the computational object.

Consider, for example, the following client code segment that defines Circle, Square, and Rectangle objects and draws them on the screen.

```
Circle c;  Square s;  Rectangle r;   // name/type are connected
c.draw();  s.draw();  r.draw();      // name/function are coupled
```

The compiler (and the maintainer) knows that the object c is of the type Circle and the object s is of the type Square and the object r is of the type Rectangle. The compiler (and the maintainer) knows that the first call to draw() refers to Circle::draw(), the second call to draw() refers to Square::draw(), and the third call to draw() refers to Rectangle::draw().

In languages like C++, we would not like to change these compile-time associations during program execution. Type of an object in programming describes fixed properties of the object. This is yet another manifestation of strong typing.

Strong typing in expressions and parameter passing is now taken for granted. For each computational object, the set of legal operations over the object is known in advance, both to the compiler and to the designer of client code (and to its maintainer).

Strong typing provides what is known as early binding. The type of the computational object is fixed early, at compile time, and does not change during program execution. Another popular term is static binding. It has the same meaning: The link between the name of the object and the object type is fixed at compile time and cannot be changed dynamically during program execution.

When a message (defined by its name and a list of actual arguments) is sent to an object, the compiler interprets this message according to the class (type) of that object. The class name of the object is known at compile time and cannot change during execution.

Static binding is standard in modern languages such as C++, C, Java, Ada, Pascal (but not Lisp). It was first introduced to improve performance, not the quality of the program. Dynamic binding, the search for the function call meaning at run time, takes time. When the meaning of the function call is fixed at compile time, it increases compilation time; however it speeds up program execution.

Later, it was found that static binding could be successfully used to enforce type checking. If a function is called with the wrong number of or wrong types of arguments, this call is rejected at compile time rather than left to manifest incorrect behavior at run time. If the message name (with the appropriate signature) is not found in the class specification, the call is rejected at compile time rather than at run time.

Strong typing provides compile-time type checking and improves run-time performance. This serves most applications well.

At what other times would we want to establish the association between the identifier and the computational object? And the answer is: later, at run time. What possible advantages might it bring?

Consider the processing of a heterogeneous list of objects or the processing of an external input stream with objects of different types. With file input or interactive user input, the program does not know the exact object type that comes from the environment.

For example, a program might draw a picture on the screen by drawing component shapes one after another. Depending on the actual nature of each shape, the program should call `Circle::draw()`, `Square::draw()`, `Rectangle::draw()`, or whatever other shapes it might know. It would be nice, however, if we could use only one statement in the source code and change its meaning depending on the actual nature of the `shape` object.

```
shape.draw();      // from class Circle, Square, or Rectangle
```

If the object `shape` in the current pass through the loop is a `Circle`, then this statement should call `Circle::draw()`. If it is a `Square`, it should call `Square::draw()`. If it is a `Rectangle`, it should call `Rectangle::draw()`. And so on.

With strong typing, this is impossible. The compiler will find the declaration of the variable shape, identify its class, and inspect the class definition. If a void function draw() with no parameters is not found in this class, the compiler will generate an error message. If the function is found, the compiler will generate object code. But the type of the function draw() will be fixed at compile time. There is no room for searching for the meaning of the function draw() at run time.

What we are looking for here is called run-time, late, or dynamic binding. We do assume that several computational objects exist (functions draw() in different classes). We want one of these computational objects to be bound to the name draw() in a particular function call. We want this function draw() in this function call to mean Circle::draw(), Square::draw(), Rectangle::draw(), and so on. And we want this meaning to be established, not at compile time, but at run time, so that different shapes would be drawn depending on the meaning of the function call.

A few words about terminology. The technical term for establishing the meaning of the function name is binding. The compiler binds the function name to a particular function. We want this binding to take place at run time. This is why it is called run-time binding rather than compile-time binding. We want this binding to take place later than during the compile time. This is why it is called late rather than early binding. We want this binding to allow the same function name to take on different meanings depending on the nature of the object used. This is why it is called dynamic, rather than static, binding.

The ability of the function name in a function call to take different meanings is called polymorphism (from "many forms"). Some authors use the term polymorphism in a much broader sense, including the use of the same function name in different classes but without dynamic binding. I do not want to get into an argument of which definition is more correct (or more useful). And I will not use this term much. But every time I use this term it will mean late or dynamic binding, assigning the meaning to the method call at run time depending on the actual type of the object that is the target of the message.

And this is what C++ virtual functions are set to achieve.

Dynamic Binding: Traditional Approach

Of course, dynamic binding is not an issue specific to object-oriented programming. Processing of heterogeneous lists has always been a common computational task, and programmers used to implement dynamic binding in whatever languages were available. In all the cases, the task was to process similar objects. They are so similar that it makes sense to use the same name for a function in each category of objects (e.g., `draw()`). But the types of objects are not identical—each function does things in its own specific way.

Let us consider an example of processing a list of entries in a university database. For simplicity, let us assume that there are only two types of records: for students and for faculty members. Let us also assume that the program maintains only three pieces of information: university id, name, and either rank (for faculty members) or major (for students). A short sample of data is shown in Figure 15–9.

The length of the id value is the same for each individual (nine characters) and it can be implemented as a fixed-length character array. The name, rank, and major have different lengths for different individuals. It is appropriate to implement them as dynamically allocated arrays. This is how the structure for one individual looks.

```
struct Person {
      int kind;                 // 1 for faculty, 2 for student
      char id[10];              // fixed length
      char* name;               // variable length
      char* rank;               // for faculty only
      char* major; } ;          // for student only
```

Of course, I could have implemented this structure as a class with constructors, the destructor, and member functions, but at this stage of discus-

Figure 15–9   Input data for the dynamic binding example.

```
FACULTY
U12345678
Smith, John
Associate Profesor
STUDENT
U12345611
Jones, Jan
Computer Science
FACULTY
U12345689
Black, Jeanne
Assistant Profesor
STUDENT
U12345622
Green, James
Astronomy
```

sion, this machinery would make the example more obscure. I will introduce these elements later, during the discussion of a more modern approach.

In my first, more traditional approach, I merge characteristics of different kinds of objects (e.g., `rank`, `major`) in one class definition. To process each kind of object differently, I add a field to describe to which kind the specific object belongs. In the client code, I will use either `switch` statements or `if` statements whose branches will implement processing for different kinds of objects.

I could have used the `union` construct instead of defining fields for both kinds of objects. For fixed-size arrays it would make sense. But with dynamic memory management, I decided that memory savings of one pointer per object does not justify the extra complexity that comes with the use of `union`.

Managing memory dynamically saves space and prevents memory overflow. A simple method of keeping data in memory would be defining an array of `Person` objects. Although I use the keyword `struct`, the variables of type `Person` are objects, because in C++ the keywords `struct` and `class` are synonymous (with the exception of default access rights and default inheritance).

```
Person data [1000];              // array of input data
```

Further flexibility can be achieved by keeping data in an array of pointers to objects and not in an array of objects. Allocating a large array of pointers is inexpensive. In case of overflow, the array of pointers can be reallocated without copying existing data (see examples in Chapter 6). The space for each `Person` object will be allocated on the heap after the data for that object is read from the input file.

```
Person* data [1000];             // array of pointers
```

For reading data from the input file, I will define an object of the library class `ifstream`. An object of this class is always open for input. To associate a physical file with the logical file object, the name of the physical file has to be specified as an argument in the constructor call.

```
ifstream from("univ.dat");           // input data file
if (!from) { cout << " Cannot open file\n"; return 0; }
```

For each object in the input file, the program allocates the structure dynamically and then reads four items of data: the string that defines the type of the object, the id, the name, and either the rank (for faculty) or major (for student). To save input data properly, the program checks the value of the string that defines the type of the object ("FACULTY" or "STUDENT") and sets the `kind` field of the object either to 1 or 2.

```
char buf[80];                        // buffer for input data
Person *p = new Person;              // allocate space for new object
from.getline(buf,80);                // recognize the incoming type
if (strcmp(buf, "FACULTY") == 0)
  p->kind = 1;                       // 1 for faculty
else if (strcmp(buf, "STUDENT") == 0)
  p->kind = 2;                       // 2 for student
else
  p->kind = 0;                       // type not known
```

Since the length of the id field is known, it can be read directly into the field of the Person object. The length of the name, rank, and major data are not known in advance, before data is read into memory. Hence, the program should read the data in the fixed-size buffer, measure the length of data, allocate enough heap memory, and copy data from the buffer into the heap memory.

```
from.getline(p->id,10);                    // read id
from.getline(buf,80);                      // read name
p->name = new char[strlen(buf)+1];         // allocate space
strcpy(p->name, buf);                      // copy name
from.getline(buf,80);                      // read rank/major
if (p->kind == 1)
{ p->rank = new char[strlen(buf)+1];       // space for rank
  strcpy(p->rank, buf); }                  // copy rank
else if (p->kind == 2)
{ p->major = new char[strlen(buf)+1];      // space for major
  strcpy(p->major, buf); }                 // copy major
```

Figure 15–10 shows the memory data structure for the example. Array data[] on the left of the picture is a stack array, and all other memory to the right of the array (objects of type Person and their dynamic memory) is allocated from the heap.

It is a good idea to encapsulate the reading algorithm in a function, for example, read(), so that the client code passes to this function the file object and the Person pointer. Function read() should allocate the Person object, read data from the file, and fill the Person object with input data.

```
Person* data[20]; int cnt = 0;       // array of pointers
ifstream from("univ.dat");           // input file: a library object
if (!from) { cout << " Cannot open file\n"; return 0; }
while (!from.eof())                   // read until eof
{ read(from, data[cnt]);             // data[cnt] is of type
Person*
  cnt++; }
cout << " Total records read: " << cnt << endl << endl;
```

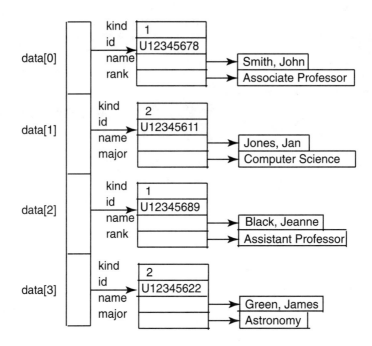

STACK MEMORY   HEAP MEMORY

Figure 15-10 The structure of dynamically allocated memory for input data.

Now I can assemble the read() function from the pieces I have described previously. There are two major flaws in this function, and both are related to parameter passing.

```
void read (ifstream f, Person* person)          // bad interface
{ char buf[80];
  Person* p = new Person;                        // allocate space for new object
  f.getline(buf,80);                             // recognize the incoming type
  if (strcmp(buf, "FACULTY") == 0)
      p->kind = 1;                               // 1 for faculty
  else if (strcmp(buf, "STUDENT") == 0)
      p->kind = 2;                               // 2 for student
  else
      p->kind = 0;                               // type not known
  f.getline(p->id,10);                           // read id
  f.getline(buf,80);                             // read name
  p->name = new char[strlen(buf)+1];             // allocate space
  strcpy(p->name, buf);                          // copy name
  f.getline(buf,80);                             // read rank/major
  if (p->kind == 1)
```

```
{ p->rank = new char[strlen(buf)+1];        // space for rank
  strcpy(p->rank, buf); }                    // copy rank
else if (p->kind == 2)
{ p->major = new char[strlen(buf)+1];        // space for major
  strcpy(p->major, buf); }                   // copy major
person = p; }                                // hook it up to array
```

Be sure you see that I pass parameters to this function by value. It is obvious in the case of the file object. When you read data from the file, you change the internal state of the file object. If the internal state is not changed for some reason, the next time around, the file will read the same data, not the next record. When the file object is passed by value, the internal state of the parameter object will change, but the internal state of the argument file object will remain the same. As I had an opportunity to say earlier, we should not pass objects by value. They should be passed by reference.

```
void read (ifstream& f, Person* person)     // read one record
{ char buf[80];
  Person* p = new Person;                    // allocate space for new object
  . . .                                      // the rest of read()
  person = p; }                              // hook up new object
```

I also insisted that object references be labeled as constant if the function does not change object state during its execution. Here, the const modifier is absent because the file object changes when the information is read from the file. As a client programmer of the server class ifstream, I should be insulated from the details of the server class design. It is enough for me to know that the state of the file object changes to reflect the results of the physical I/O operations.

Now let us look at the pointer parameter. In C++, if a parameter is passed by pointer (or by reference), its value can be changed within the function, and the change will affect the actual argument in the client space. What should be taken seriously in this statement is that it says "a parameter is passed by pointer." It does not say "pointer parameter," and this is where some programmers get confused. In the version of the function read() above, the Person pointer person is not passed by pointer. It is passed by value. Hence, its value cannot be changed in the function call. If before the function call the argument pointer was pointing nowhere, it will be pointing nowhere after the function call, not to the newly allocated Person object.

What is passed by pointer here? Formally, you can say that it is a Person object (not the pointer) that is passed by pointer. Indeed, if you properly pass a Person object to this function it will be filled correctly with incoming file data.

```
Person person;              // Person object, not pointer
read(from, &person);        // object is passed by pointer
```

As you can see, passing "properly" means passing an address of an object. This object exists in the client space. Passing an object by pointer allows the program to change its state during the function call. Even with this interpretation, the function `read()` has a problem: variable person now is of type `Person`, but variable p used in the last line of `read()` is of type `Person*`. As I stressed in Chapter 6, these two types look very similar, but do not discard this little difference. These are two very different types. One is a class with all its members, another is a pointer to a class object. This can be fixed if necessary, but that would leave us with the array of `Person` objects in the client space instead of an array of `Person` pointers.

So, how do you fix this function `read()` to make sure that all this heap memory allocated in `read()` is correctly hooked up to the stack memory depicted in Figure 15–10?

At the time of the function call to `read()`, the `Person` object does not exist yet—it will be allocated within the function. It is a pointer to a `Person` object that exists in the client space (the whole array of pointers). It is a pointer that is passed to the function `read()`.

```
while (!from.eof())         // read until eof
{ read(from, data[cnt]);    // data[cnt] is of type Person*
  cnt++; }
```

Before the call, the actual argument, the `Person` pointer, contains junk, because it is part of a heap array. After the call, the pointer points to the `Person` object allocated within the function `read()`, as Figure 15–10 shows. Hence, it contains a valid address of a chunk of head memory and its contents changed after the call. The pointer should then be passed either by reference or by pointer. This is why the version of `read()` presented above is incorrect.

Make sure that you are not lost in this barrage of terms: pointers to objects, references to pointers, pointers to pointers, or whatever. Just keep in mind that a pointer is an ordinary variable and as such can be passed either by value, by reference, or by pointer. It is just an unfortunate incident of C++ notation (inherited from C) that allows for two interpretations of the function interface.

```
void read (ifstream& f, Person* person)    // read one record
  { char buf[80];
    Person* p = new Person;                 // allocate space for new object
    . . .                                   // the rest of read()
    person = p; }                           // hook up new object
```

Here, `Person* person` can be interpreted either as a `Person` object passed by pointer or as `Person` pointer (of type `Person*`) that is passed by value. To pass this pointer by reference is not at all difficult. The standard C++ rule (described in Chapter 7, "Programming with C++ Functions") says that to switch from pass by value to pass by reference, you should do just one thing, insert the ampersand sign between the type name and the parameter name. No other changes are necessary, neither in the body of the function nor in the syntax of the function call. This is how it should look.

```
void read (ifstream& f, Person* &person)      // read one record
{ char buf[80];
  Person* p = new Person;                      // allocate space for new object
  . . .                                        // the rest of read()
  person = p; }                                // hook up new object
```

It is to make this transition easier that I initially named this parameter `Person* person` and not `Person *person`. But this does not matter. C++ is space blind in this regard, and you can align the asterisk (and the ampersand) between the type name and the parameter name the way you see fit.

What about passing a pointer by pointer? No problem. You have to take care of three places in the program—the function call, the function interface, and the function body. In the function call, you insert the asterisk before the name of the variable (i.e., before the pointer name `data[cnt]`). This is what the function call will look like.

```
while (!from.eof())                 // read until eof
{ read(from, &data[cnt]);           // passing pointer by pointer
  cnt++; }
```

In the function interface, you insert the asterisk before the name of the parameter. That is, instead of `Person* person`, you should say `Person* *person` (or even `Person** person`).

In the function body, and this is the most error-prone moment, you should use the asterisk before the name of the parameter. The name of the parameter is `person`, not `*person` or `**person`. Hence, the last statement in the function `read()` should use dereferencing:

```
void read (ifstream& f, Person** person)      // pointer by pointer
{ char buf[80];
  Person *p = new Person;                      // allocate space for new object
  . . .                                        // the rest of read()
  *person = p; }                               // bingo!
```

This is not difficult after all, but passing a pointer by reference is much simpler than passing a pointer by pointer. But this is true of any type—pass by reference is simpler and less error prone.

So far I have been discussing the technicalities of entering data into the array inside the computer. This discussion has nothing to do with dynamic binding, polymorphism, and other issues. I need to review this only because I want to have a running program at the end. Also, I felt that reviewing the material from Chapters 6 and 7 on dynamic memory management, file I/O, and parameter passing will not do anyone any harm.

Dynamic binding becomes an issue when the program starts processing data that is already in memory. Since different kinds of objects have to be handled differently, the program has to recognize what kind of object it is dealing with in each specific call. This is where the field `kind` of class `Person` comes in handy. In this simple example, "processing data" means going over the array of pointers and printing each `Person` object either as a faculty member (with `rank` displayed) or as a student (with `major` displayed). In real life, there would be a number of functions that have to treat various kinds of objects differently. In this example, I put this processing in `main()`.

```
for (int i=0; i < cnt; i++)                      // go over the array of pointers
{ cout <<" id:      " <<data[i]->id <<endl;      // print id, name
  cout <<" name:    " <<data[i]->name <<endl;
  if (data[i]->kind == 1)
    cout <<" rank:   " <<data[i]->rank <<endl;   // faculty rank
  else if (data[i]->kind == 2)
    cout <<" major: " <<data[i]->major <<endl;   // student major
  cout << endl; }
```

This loop is the center of the program: it processes the heterogeneous list of objects according to the actual type of the object. First, it unconditionally does whatever there is to be done for all types of objects—it prints the university id and the name with appropriate captions. To process each object according to its kind, the loop accesses the `kind` field of the object and prints either the rank or the major.

Listing 15.3 demonstrates the complete program that processes the input file shown in Figure 15–9. In addition to the type `Person` and function `read()` described previously, the program contains function `main()` that plays the role of the client code; it defines the array of pointers and the file object, reads input data in a loop, processes data in a loop, and then returns dynamic memory in a loop. The results of the program execution are shown in Figure 15–11.

Listing 15.3   Heterogeneous list processing—traditional approach.

```
#include <iostream>
#include <fstream>
using namespace std;

struct Person {
      int kind;                               // 1 for faculty, 2 for student
      char id[10];                            // fixed length
      char* name;                             // variable length
      char* rank;                             // for faculty only
      char* major;                            // for student only
   } ;

void read (ifstream& f, Person*& person)      // read one record
{ char buf[80];
  Person* p = new Person;                     // allocate space for new object
  f.getline(buf,80);                          // recognize the incoming type
  if (strcmp(buf, "FACULTY") == 0)
      p->kind = 1;                            // 1 for faculty
  else if (strcmp(buf, "STUDENT") == 0)
      p->kind = 2;                            // 2 for student
  else
      p->kind = 0;                            // type not known
  f.getline(p->id,10);                        // read id
  f.getline(buf,80);                          // read name
  p->name = new char[strlen(buf)+1];          // allocate space
  strcpy(p->name, buf);                       // copy name
  f.getline(buf,80);                          // read rank/major
  if (p->kind == 1)
  { p->rank = new char[strlen(buf)+1];        // space for rank
    strcpy(p->rank, buf); }                   // copy rank
  else if (p->kind == 2)
  { p->major = new char[strlen(buf)+1];       // space for major
    strcpy(p->major, buf); }                  // copy major
  person = p;                                 // hook it up to array
}

int main()
{
  Person* data[20]; int cnt = 0;              // array of pointers
  ifstream from("univ.dat");                  // input data file
  if (!from) { cout << " Cannot open file\n"; return 0; }
  while (!from.eof())
  { read(from, data[cnt]);                    // read until eof
    cnt++; }
  cout << " Total records read: " << cnt << endl << endl;
  for (int i=0;  i < cnt;  i++)
  { cout <<" id:     " <<data[i]->id <<endl;  // print id, name
```

```
    cout <<" name:   " <<data[i]->name <<endl;
    if (data[i]->kind == 1)
      cout <<" rank:   " <<data[i]->rank <<endl;  // faculty rank
    else if (data[i]->kind == 2)
      cout <<" major: " <<data[i]->major <<endl; // student major
    cout << endl; }
for (int j=0;  j < cnt;  j++)
{ delete [] data[j]->name;                      // delete name
  if (data[j]->kind == 1)
    delete [] data[j]->rank;                    // delete rank/major
  else if (data[j]->kind == 1)
    delete [] data[j]->major;
  delete data[j]; }                             // delete the record
return 0;
}
```

There is nothing difficult or confusing about this solution (with the possible exception of pointer notation). Although I am using many nice trappings of the C++ language (e.g., structures, pointers, dynamic memory management with operators new and delete, parameter passing by reference, library file objects), this program could have been written in any language. It achieves the purpose of dynamic binding (each object is processed according to its own kind). However, it does not take advantage of the object-oriented features of the language (e.g., binding together data and operations, constructors and destructors, pushing responsibility to the servers, putting together what should belong together, and, yes, inheritance).

Total records read: 4

id: U12345678
name: Smith, John
rank: Associate Profesor

id: U12345611
name: Jones, Jan
major: Computer Science

id: U12345689
name: Black, Jeanne
rank: Assistant Profesor

id: U12345622
name: Green, James
major: Astronomy

Figure 15-11
Output of processing of a heterogeneous list of objects.

Dynamic Binding: Object-Oriented Approach

In the next version, I will create three classes, `Person`, `Faculty`, and `Student`. All features common to faculty and student processing will go to the base class `Person` – id, name, and the `kind` fields. Instead of using numeric conventions to denote the kind of object (1 for faculty, 2 for student), I introduce the enumeration type with self-explanatory values. This is especially convenient when there are several kinds of objects and when new kinds of objects could be added.

I define data members of the base class `Person` as protected rather than private, so that the derived classes, `Faculty` and `Student`, can access these data members without burdening the designer of class `Person` with the design of trivial access functions.

```
struct Person {
public:
   enum Kind { FACULTY, STUDENT } ;
protected:
   Kind kind;                       // FACULTY or STUDENT
   char id[10];                     // data common to both types
   char* name;                      // variable length
public:
   Person(const char id[], const char nm[], Kind type);
   Kind getKind() const;
   ~Person(); } ;
```

The constructor accepts three parameters for initializing three object data members. It performs the operations that in the previous version were performed in function `read()`: dynamic memory allocation for the name. The destructor performs the operations that in the previous version were performed in function `main()`: deallocation of heap memory. This is a nice, albeit small, example of putting together into the same class what otherwise could have been torn apart and allocated to different parts of code (thus creating the need for coordination).

Yet another member function, `getKind()`, is of auxiliary nature. This message will be sent by the client code (function `read()`), to the objects of derived classes (`Faculty` and `Student`), to figure out who they are. In the previous version, function `read()` accessed the `kind` field directly, thus creating dependencies among different parts of code. In this design, the field `kind` is protected, not public, and the class `Person` must provide the access function to serve the clients of its derived classes. I am not sure this is such a great improvement over direct access to the `kind` field, but it is a common practice (and probably some improvement).

As you see, I treat the client code with more reverence than I do the derived classes. For the derived classes, I allow direct access to the base data members, and I feel no pangs of conscience. For the client code, I provide the functions to access server data members, even though I do that grudgingly.

Derived classes `Faculty` and `Student` inherit from `Person` publicly. Even though I use the keyword `struct` to define them, I specify the mode of inheritance explicitly to avoid confusion. Had I skipped the mode, it would be public by default. The public mode is the most natural and convenient; it does not take away the capabilities of the base class from the clients of the derived classes. In this case, this is not very important: The base class is so small that there is only one capability that the client code uses—the `getKind()` method.

Nevertheless, the use of public inheritance is important here. I am using an array of pointers of type `Person`, but I am going to set these pointers to point to objects of classes `Faculty` and `Student`. This of course involves casting. To make implicit casting possible, C++ requires the mode of inheritance to be public.

This is an issue of convenience—after all, an explicit cast can be used if necessary. But there is another, more important issue. Eventually, I am going to use virtual functions in this design. They allow the client code to call a method of a derived class, for example, `write()`, and let the run-time system figure out to which of the derived classes this function belongs. This behavior is possible only if the mode of derivation is public.

```
struct Faculty : public Person {          // public inheritance
private:
   char* rank;                            // for faculty only
public:
   Faculty(const char id[], const char nm[], const char r[]);
   void write () const;                   // display record
   ~Faculty(); } ;                        // return heap memory

struct Student : public Person {          // public inheritance
private:
   char* major;                           // for student only
public:
   Student(const char id[], const char nm[], const char m[]);
   void write () const;                   // display record
   ~Student(); } ;                        // return heap memory
```

Derived classes `Faculty` and `Student` inherit all the data members from their base class, `Person`, and define their own data, specific to each kind of `Person` (`rank` or `major`).

Constructors for derived classes, `Faculty` and `Student`, accept parameters necessary for initialization of all their fields, whether they are defined in the derived class or inherited from the base class, `Person`. It is the job of the derived class constructor to pass the data to the base class constructor in the initialization list. As you see from the interface of the `Person` constructor, this includes the specification of the kind of object being created, `Faculty` or `Student`. For many programmers, this means that the parameter list for the derived class constructors should include data for initializing the base part (three parameters) and data for initializing the derived part (`major` for `Student`, `rank` for `Faculty`).

```
Faculty(const char id[], const char nm[], Kind k, const char r[])
     : Person(id,nm,k)                      // initialization list
  { rank = new char[strlen(r)+1];
    if (rank == 0) { cout << "Out of memory\n"; exit(0); }
    strcpy(rank,r); }
```

This is a typical example of popping responsibility to the client of the derived class. The client code (function `read()`) will create `Faculty` objects using something like this:

```
person = new Faculty(id,name,FACULTY,buf); }    // object is Faculty
```

But this is an imposition; the client code has already said that it creates a `Faculty` object, so why is it forced to do the useless work of passing an argument that says it is `Faculty`? This responsibility should be pushed down to the `Faculty` object: It knows it is `Faculty`, and it should tell this to its `Person` part without dragging the client `read()` into the loop of cooperation.

```
Faculty(const char id[], const char nm[], const char r[])
        : Person(id,nm,FACULTY)      // this is what OOP is all about
  { rank = new char[strlen(r)+1];
    if (rank == 0) { cout << "Out of memory\n"; exit(0); }
    strcpy(rank,r); }
```

Now the client code has a simpler job to do.

```
person = new Faculty(id,name,buf); }       // object is Faculty
```

Notice that the constructor prototypes in the `Faculty` and `Student` specifications have only three parameters, not four. This is the essence of object-oriented programming: looking for the right way to distribute responsibilities among cooperating classes.

The destructors for derived classes deallocate memory allocated on the heap by the constructors (`rank` for `Faculty`, `major` for `Student`).

The member function `write()` is implemented in both derived classes. They are similar so that they can have the same name. This calls for implementing `write()` in the base class. But the algorithms for different kinds of `Person` are not identical. This is why each class has its separate function but they use the same name. These functions will eventually be called polymorphic.

Functions `write()` represent part of the functionality of the function `main()` of the previous version. Since each derived class, `Faculty` and `Student`, knows its nature, there is no need to look at the kind of target object.

```
void Faculty::write () const                    // display record
{ cout << " id:     " << id << endl;             // print id, name
  cout << " name:   " << name << endl;
  cout << " rank:   " << rank <<endl <<endl; }    // faculty only

void Student::write () const                    // display record
{ cout << " id:     " << id << endl;             // print id, name
  cout << " name:   " << name << endl;
  cout << " major:  " << major <<endl <<endl; }   // student only
```

The global function `read()` represents a streamlined modification of the function from the previous version of the program. It reads data from the input file into local arrays and then checks the `kind[]` array to see what kind of object it has to construct. If it says "FACULTY", `read()` creates a new `Faculty` object (using the operator `new`). If it says "STUDENT", `read()` creates a new `Student` object (again, using the operator `new`). In each case the data is sent as arguments to the class constructor.

```
void read (ifstream& f, . . . ?? person)        // what is its type?
{ char kind[8], id[10], name[80], buf[80];
  f.getline(kind,80);                            // recognize the incoming type
  f.getline(id,10);                              // read id
  f.getline(name,80);                            // read name
  f.getline(buf,80);                             // rank or major?
  if (strcmp(kind, "FACULTY") == 0)
  { person = new Faculty(id,name,buf); }          // object is Faculty
  else if (strcmp(kind, "STUDENT") == 0)
  { person = new Student(id,name,buf); }          // object is Student
  else
  { cout << " Corrupted data: unknown type\n"; exit(0); } }
```

What should be the type of the second parameter to this function? It has to be a pointer; otherwise, it cannot accept the return value of the operator `new`. It should be passed by reference rather than by value; otherwise, the new object will be pointed to by the local pointer `person` only, not by the actual argument, and the new object cannot be accessed from the client code. It cannot be a `Faculty` pointer; this pointer cannot point to a `Student` object. It cannot be a `Student` pointer, as this pointer cannot point to a `Faculty` object.

So, it cannot be a `Faculty` pointer, and it cannot be a `Student` pointer, so what should it be? What should be the type of pointer that is capable of pointing to objects of different classes? Recall from the first section of this chapter that if these different classes are not related through inheritance, no pointer can point to objects of these classes and do any meaningful work. Recall from the second section of this chapter that if these different classes are related through inheritance, a base class pointer can point to objects of any derived class—A, B, or otherwise. A big brother can point to wherever it wants as long as the class of the target is within the limits of the inheritance hierarchy.

So, it has to be a `Person` pointer, just like in the previous version. Inside the function `read()`, objects of different derived classes are created and hooked up to the pointer of the base class.

```
void read (ifstream& f, Person*& person)        // read one record
{ char kind[8], id[10], name[80], buf[80];
  f.getline(kind,80);                           // recognize the incoming type
  f.getline(id,10);                             // read id
  f.getline(name,80);                           // read name
  f.getline(buf,80);                            // rank or major?
  if (strcmp(kind, "FACULTY") == 0)
  { person = new Faculty(id,name,buf); }        // object is Faculty
  else if (strcmp(kind, "STUDENT") == 0)
  { person = new Student(id,name,buf); }        // object is Student
  else
  { cout << " Corrupted data: unknown type\n"; exit(0); } }
```

The function `read()` is called from `main()` in the same way as in the previous version. The difference is that the components of the array `data[]` (of type `Person*`) now point to objects of different derived classes (`Faculty` or `Student`).

```
int main()
{ cout << endl << endl;
  Person* data[20]; int cnt = 0;              // array of pointers
  ifstream from("univ.dat");                  // input data file
  if (!from) { cout << " Cannot open file\n"; return 0; }
  while (!from.eof())
  { read(from, data[cnt]);                    // read until eof
    cnt++; }
  . . . }                                     // the rest of main()
```

The problem, however, is that the base pointer is myopic—it cannot invoke the operations that are defined in derived classes. This is not a difficult problem. As long as the base pointer points to a derived object, there is always a way to tell the compiler what we know, that the base pointer points to a derived object. As you remember, the way to tell that to the compiler is to use the cast to the derived class.

I would like to encapsulate the process of this decision-making in a function, for example, write(). Similar decision-making functions should be designed for each operation that is performed somewhat differently for different kinds of similar objects. The difficulty here again is in deciding on the type of parameter to this function. Here is the outline of this function:

```
void write ( . . . ??  p)                    // display record
{ switch (p.getKind()) {                      // get object type
    case Person::FACULTY:
        . . .;  break;                        // do it Faculty way
    case Person::STUDENT:
        . . .;  break;   } }                  // do it Student way
```

What should be the type of this function parameter? It will get two types of actual arguments, Faculty objects and Student objects. If the type of the object is Faculty, then this function will be able to call Faculty::write() only. If the type of the parameter is Student, then this function will be able to call Student::write() only.

It is here where the material of the previous section on conversions between classes should be used again. I can try to use the parameter of type Person because both Faculty objects and Student objects can be copied into a Person object. (Recall that a derived class object has enough data to initialize a base class object.)

```
void write (Person p)                         // display record
{ switch (p.getKind()) {                      // get object type
    case Person::FACULTY:
        . . .;  break;                        // do it Faculty way
    case Person::STUDENT:
        . . .;  break;   } }                  // do it Student way
```

One problem with this solution is that it passes the parameter by value, and this is definitely not a good idea when objects manage their memory dynamically. The second problem with this solution is that the function body is stuck with a `Person` object, and there is no way to convert a base object back to the derived class object. The original data is stripped away and cannot be restored. Even if I were to add to each derived class a constructor that converts a base object into a derived class object (see Listing 15.2 for an example), this would not be enough. The most this constructor could do is to set default values to derived class fields. What I need, however, is the original values of faculty rank or student major.

This rules out the use of a base object value as the function parameter but does not preclude me from using a base pointer as the function parameter. A derived class pointer (a powerful, farsighted pointer that can perform all operations of the derived class) can be easily converted to a base class pointer—this is a safe conversion, so it needs no cast. No data is stripped away, and conversion back to the derived class pointer is possible. (However, this conversion is not safe and hence it will need a cast.)

```
void write (Person* p)                    // display record
{ switch (p->getKind()) {                 // get object type
    case Person::FACULTY:
        . . .;   break;                   // do it Faculty way
    case Person::STUDENT:
        . . .;   break;  } }              // do it Student way
```

What is lost during this transformation is the ability to perform the operations that are defined for the derived class. All that the weak, shortsighted base pointer can do is to reach the functions that are defined in the base class. But the major advantage of this solution is that this base pointer still points to an object of a derived class. In the switch statement, the function `write()` just found out if the actual argument points to a `Faculty` object or to a `Student` object. So what remains to be done is to call either method `write()` from class `Faculty` or method `write()` from class `Student`.

```
void write (const Person* p)              // display record
{ switch (p->getKind()) {                 // get object type
    case Person::FACULTY:
        p->write();   break;              // do it Faculty way
    case Person::STUDENT:
        p->write();   break;  } }         // do it Student way
```

Since pointer `p` is a base class pointer, it can reach only base class methods. Hence the calls to `write()` in both branches of the switch statement either will reach the `write()` from the base class (if the `Person` class has one) or will result in a syntax error (if the `Person` class does not have a method `write()`).

As you can see, this function `write()` just learned what kind of object its parameter pointer is pointing to. But the compiler does not know that; all the compiler knows is that it is a pointer of class `Person`. So, function `write()` should tell the compiler what it knows: it should cast the base pointer either to class `Faculty` (first switch branch) or to class `Student` (second switch branch).

```
void write (const Person* p)                      // display record
{ switch (p->getKind()) {                         // get object type
    case Person::FACULTY:
        ((Faculty*)p)->write();   break;          // do it Faculty way
    case Person::STUDENT:
        ((Student*)p)->write();   break;          // do it Student way
} }
```

As many casts do, these casts look awful and intimidating. But they do exactly what I said in the previous statement—they cast the pointer p (of class `Person*`) into a pointer of type `Faculty*` (the first branch) or into a pointer of type `Student*`. Parentheses, however unpleasant, should be used because the arrow selector operand is of higher priority than are the cast operands. Should you omit the parentheses and use, for example, `(Faculty*)p->write()`, the compiler will decide that you want to convert the return value of the call to `write()` and not the pointer p. Just keep these parentheses there.

This function `write()` will be called in a loop, receiving as actual arguments `Person` pointers that point to either `Faculty` or `Student` objects.

```
for (int i=0;   i < cnt;   i++)
    { write(data[i]); }                           // display data
```

The complete program is shown in Listing 15.4.

Listing 15.4   Heterogeneous list processing—object-oriented approach.

```
#include <iostream>
#include <fstream>
using namespace std;

struct Person {
public:
        enum Kind { FACULTY, STUDENT } ;
protected:
        Kind kind;                          // FACULTY or STUDENT
        char id[10];                        // data common to both types
        char* name;                         // variable length
```

```
public:
        Person(const char id[], const char nm[], Kind type)
        { strcpy(Person::id,id);                    // copy id
          name = new char[strlen(nm)+1];            // get space for name
          if (name == 0) { cout << "Out of memory\n"; exit(0); }
          strcpy(name,nm);                          // copy name
          kind = type; }                            // remember its type

    Kind getKind() const
        { return kind; }                            // access Person's type

        ~Person()
        { delete [] name; }                         // return heap memory
} ;

struct Faculty : public Person {
private:
        char* rank;                                 // for faculty only

public:
        Faculty(const char id[], const char nm[], const char r[])
            : Person(id,nm,FACULTY)                 // initialization list
        { rank = new char[strlen(r)+1];
          if (rank == 0) { cout << "Out of memory\n"; exit(0); }
          strcpy(rank,r); }

  void write () const                               // display record
  { cout << " id:    " << id << endl;               // print id, name
    cout << " name:  " << name << endl;
    cout << " rank:  " << rank <<endl <<endl; }     // faculty only

        ~Faculty()
        { delete [] rank; }                         // return heap memory
} ;

struct Student : public Person {
private:
        char* major;                                // for student only

public:
        Student(const char id[], const char nm[], const char m[])
            : Person(id,nm,STUDENT)                 // initialization list
        { major = new char[strlen(m)+1];
          if (major == 0) { cout << "Out of memory\n"; exit(0); }
          strcpy(major,m); }

  void write () const                               // display record
  { cout << " id:    " << id << endl;               // print id, name
    cout << " name:  " << name << endl;
    cout << " major: " << major <<endl <<endl; }    // student only
```

```
    ~Student()
    { delete [] major; }                            // return heap memory
} ;

void read (ifstream& f, Person*& person)           // read one record
{ char kind[8], id[10], name[80], buf[80];
  f.getline(kind,80);                              // recognize the incoming type
  f.getline(id,10);                                // read id
  f.getline(name,80);                              // read name
  f.getline(buf,80);                               // rank or major?
  if (strcmp(kind, "FACULTY") == 0)
  { person = new Faculty(id,name,buf); }           // object is Faculty
  else if (strcmp(kind, "STUDENT") == 0)
  { person = new Student(id,name,buf); }           // object is Student
  else
  { cout << " Corrupted data: unknown type\n"; exit(0); }
}

void write (const Person* p)                       // display record
{ switch (p->getKind()) {                          // get object type
    case Person::FACULTY:
        ((Faculty*)p)->write();   break;           // do it Faculty way
    case Person::STUDENT:
        ((Student*)p)->write();   break;           // do it Student way
} }

int main()
{ cout << endl << endl;
  Person* data[20]; int cnt = 0;                   // array of pointers
  ifstream from("univ.dat");                       // input data file
  if (!from) { cout << " Cannot open file\n"; return 0; }
  while (!from.eof())
  { read(from, data[cnt]);                         // read until eof
    cnt++; }
  cout << " Total records read: " << cnt << endl << endl;
  for (int i=0;  i < cnt;  i++)
  { write(data[i]); }                              // display data
  for (int j=0;  j < cnt;  j++)
  { delete data[j]; }                              // delete the record
  return 0;
  }
```

This solution is much nicer than the previous one is. Data and operations are bound together, work is pushed to server classes, tearing apart of related code is eliminated. As in any object-oriented solution, the source code is longer than is the corresponding non-object-oriented solution. Otherwise, the program does exactly what the program in Listing 15.3 does. Its output is the same as for the program in Listing 15.3 (see Figure 15–11).

Our next step is to eliminate the tests for the kind of object that the function `write()` is dealing with. Instead of testing what kind of object the target is, casting the pointer back to that type and then invoking the appropriate derived class function, we want the compiler to do all that. The compiler should generate object code that tests the type of the object, performs casting, and calls the appropriate method. The key to doing this is the use of keyword `virtual` in designating base class member functions.

Dynamic Binding: Virtual Functions

Keyword `virtual` is a syntactic maneuver. It creates the run-time type resolution property for a message sent to an object of a derived type. To use this property, you implement the function with the same name in the base class and in each of the derived classes.

For the example we are discussing this means implementing method `write()` for the base `Person` class and for the derived classes `Faculty` and `Student`. This allows you to write the global `write()` function in the following way:

```
void write (const Person* p)            // display record
{ p->write(); }                         // is not this nice?
```

For compile-time binding, this simply means the call to a method `write()` defined in class `Person`. For run-time binding, the code generated by the compiler will analyze the type of the object pointed to by the base pointer `p`, will decide what type the method to be called belongs to, and will call the method `write()` from that type. Depending on the object pointed to by the pointer, either the `Faculty` method will be called or the `Student` method will be called. All this will be defined at run-time.

However, there are a number of restrictions to satisfy for this approach to work. A virtual function that belongs to a derived class has to be invoked only through a base pointer or a base reference. There is no run-time binding if a message is sent to an object, whether a base object or a derived class object. In both of these cases, the algorithm for static binding is used: Whatever is the type of the object, from that class the message is invoked.

For example, the meaning of `x.write()` depends on the type to which the object `x` belongs, and this type is specified at compilation time, not at execution time.

A virtual function cannot be static. It cannot be called through the class scope operator; it must be called through a base pointer (reference) that points to an object of a derived class.

The inheritance mode of derivation has to be public, not protected nor private. Implicit casts are available for public derivation only.

The member function is designated as virtual in the base class of the inheritance hierarchy. The function with the same name as the base virtual function has to be implemented in each derived class. The function redefinition in a derived class must match the name, signature, and return type of the virtual function from the base class.

If the name in a derived class is different, it is not an issue, but this function cannot be called using run-time binding. Dynamic binding is based on the use of the same function call and interpreting it differently.

If the signature is different, the derived method hides the base method and destroys the virtual function mechanism. If, for example, derived classes define a void function write() with no parameters, and the base class defines a void function write(int), there is no way to call derived class functions using dynamic binding. In this case, p->write() will invoke the function that belongs to the class of pointer p. If this function exists, it will be called. If it does not exist, it is a syntax error.

If the return type of the virtual functions is different in derived classes, it is a syntax error, even if the signature of the functions is the same.

The keyword virtual appears only within the class specification of the base class. There is no need to repeat it in the function definition of the base class. There is no need to repeat it in a derived class specification.

If your hierarchy includes more than two levels of classes, you can define virtual functions at any level of the hierarchy. There is no obligation to implement the function defined, for example, at the top of the hierarchy, at each lower level of the inheritance hierarchy. It can be inherited indirectly.

If all restrictions are satisfied, there is no need to define the kind field in the base class, and there is no need to define a method that returns the value of the kind field. All that it takes to convert the program in Listing 15.3 into a program with virtual functions is to define a function write() in class Person. The function has to have the void return type and have no parameters.

```
struct Person {
protected:
  char id[10];                                // no Kind
  char* name;
public:
  Person(const char id[], const char nm[]);   // no Kind
  virtual void write () const;                // const is part of signature
  ~Person(); } ;
```

As a result, there is no need for the derived classes to push the `kind` information to the base class.

```
struct Faculty : public Person {
private:
        char* rank;                                    // for faculty only
public:
        Faculty(const char id[], const char nm[], const char r[])
            : Person(id,nm)                            // no FACULTY
        { rank = new char[strlen(r)+1];
          if (rank == 0) { cout << "Out of memory\n"; exit(0); }
          strcpy(rank,r); }
   void write () const                                 // it is virtual now
   { cout << " id:     " << id << endl;                // print id, name
      cout << " name:   " << name << endl;
      cout << " rank:   " << rank <<endl <<endl; }     // faculty only
        ~Faculty()
        { delete [] rank; } } ;                        // return heap memory
```

Most important, there is no need to check the kind of object in the client code. Listing 15.5 shows the program from Listing 15.4, which uses the virtual function `write()` to eliminate the subtype analysis from the client code. The output of the program is the same as for the previous version (see Figure 15–11).

Listing 15.5   Heterogeneous list processing using virtual functions.

```
#include <iostream>
#include <fstream>
using namespace std;

struct Person {
protected:
        char id[10];                                   // data common to both types
        char* name;                                    // variable length

public:
        Person(const char id[], const char nm[])  //, Kind type)
        { strcpy(Person::id,id);                       // copy id
          name = new char[strlen(nm)+1];               // get space for name
          if (name == 0) { cout << "Out of memory\n"; exit(0); }
          strcpy(name,nm);                             // copy name
        }

        virtual void write() const                     // not much to do
        { }

        v~Person()                                     // return heap memory
        { delete [] name; }                            // for Person object only
} ;
```

```
struct Faculty : public Person {
private:
        char* rank;                                     // for faculty only

public:
        Faculty(const char id[], const char nm[], const char r[])
          : Person(id,nm)                               // initialization list
        { rank = new char[strlen(r)+1];
          if (rank == 0) { cout << "Out of memory\n"; exit(0); }
          strcpy(rank,r); }

  void write () const                                   // display record
  { cout << " id:     " << id << endl;                  // print id, name
    cout << " name:   " << name << endl;
    cout << " rank:   " << rank <<endl <<endl; } // faculty only

        ~Faculty()
        { delete [] rank; }                             // return heap memory
} ;

struct Student : public Person {
private:
        char* major;                                    // for student only

public:
        Student(const char id[], const char nm[], const char m[])
          : Person(id,nm)                               // initialization list
        { major = new char[strlen(m)+1];
          if (major == 0) { cout << "Out of memory\n"; exit(0); }
          strcpy(major,m); }

  void write () const                                   // display record
  { cout << " id:     " << id << endl;                  // print id, name
    cout << " name:   " << name << endl;
    cout << " major: " << major <<endl <<endl; }// student only

  ~Student()
  { delete [] major; }                                  // return heap memory
} ;

void read (ifstream& f, Person*& person)                // read one record
{ char kind[8], id[10], name[80], buf[80];
  f.getline(kind,80);                                   // recognize the incoming type
  f.getline(id,10);                                     // read id
  f.getline(name,80);                                   // read name
  f.getline(buf,80);                                    // rank or major?
  if (strcmp(kind, "FACULTY") == 0)
  { person = new Faculty(id,name,buf); }                // object is Faculty
  else if (strcmp(kind, "STUDENT") == 0)
  { person = new Student(id,name,buf); }                // object is Student
```

```
    else
    { cout << " Corrupted data: unknown type\n"; exit(0); }
}

void write (const Person* p)                          // display record
{ p->write(); }                                        // Faculty or Student?

int main()
{ cout << endl << endl;
    Person* data[20]; int cnt = 0;                     // array of pointers
    ifstream from("univ.dat");                         // input data file
    if (!from) { cout << " Cannot open file\n"; return 0; }
    while (!from.eof())
    { read(from, data[cnt]);                           // read until eof
      cnt++; }
    cout << " Total records read: " << cnt << endl << endl;
    for (int i=0;  i < cnt;  i++)
    { write(data[i]); }                                // display data
    for (int j=0;  j < cnt;  j++)
    { delete data[j]; }                                // delete the record
    return 0;
    }
```

Polymorphism (run-time interpretation of messages to objects) is based on the legality of implicit casts from derived to base objects: a base pointer (Person in our example) can point to a derived object (Faculty or Student) without an explicit cast.

```
Person *p, *pf, *ps;                    // pointers of type Person
p = new Person("U12345678", "Smith");
pf = new Faculty("U12345689", "Black", "Assistant Professor");
ps = new Student("U12345622", "Green", "Astronomy");
```

The cast is optional. It can be used to attract the maintainer's attention to type transformations between pointers.

```
ps = (Person*) new Student("U12345622", "Green", "Astronomy");
```

Virtual functions make it unnecessary to cast the message back to the type of the object that the derived pointer points to. Notice that pointers to derived objects cannot point to base objects without an explicit cast. A derived pointer cannot call the base method without an explicit cast either.

```
Student* s = (Student*)ps;        // cast is mandatory
s->write();                       // derived class pointer
```

With virtual functions, using the base pointers results in calls to derived class member functions.

```
ps->write();                 // base class pointer
```

However, all of these improvements are cosmetic—they improve the appearance of the client code. Under the hood, the program in Listing 15.5 does the same thing that the program in Listing 15.4 does. The `kind` field is gone from the class `Person`, but actually it is there, accessed by the compiler-generated code and not by the programmer-written source code. The switch statement is gone from the client code, but it too is there, implemented by compiler-generated code and not by programmer-written source code.

The program in Listing 15.4 explicitly allocated extra space to analyze the kind of `Person` objects and spent extra time deciding which `write()` function to call. The program in Listing 15.5 spends the same extra space and extra time.

Some programmers, especially those programmers who write real-time control systems, say that virtual functions are wasteful. This is not fair. It is the polymorphic algorithm that takes extra space and time. Whether it is implemented explicitly, as in Listing 15.4, or with virtual functions as in Listing 15.5, makes little difference.

However, many programmers love virtual functions and make everything in sight virtual. Well, whether or not you use polymorphic algorithms, virtual functions are going to consume some space and execution time. If these resources are scarce in your application, make sure that you make virtual only those functions that contribute to making client code simpler.

Dynamic and Static Binding

Dynamic binding offers the programmer a new and exciting way to structure processing algorithms. You can create a family of related derived classes under a common public base class, equip each derived class with a function that performs processing in the way that is specific for this derived class, make sure that each function has the same name and interface, call this function through a base class pointer, and bingo—the function that is called does not depend on the type of pointer that points to the object; it depends on the type of the object pointed to by the pointer. This is wonderful!

But dynamic binding does not make traditional static binding irrelevant. In most cases of C++ programming, the method being called depends on the type of the pointer that points to the object, not on the type of the object to which the pointer points. This introduces an additional dimension of complexity.

For static binding, when you analyze a function call, you have to consider the type of the target of the message and the signature of the method being called. When dynamic binding is a possibility, you have to consider several additional factors.

First, you have to consider whether the target of the message is an object or a pointer (a reference). If it is an object, only static binding is possible, and you have to consider only the signature of the method to verify that the function call is correct. If the target of the message is a pointer or a reference, dynamic binding remains a possibility.

Next, you should define to which place in the inheritance hierarchy the pointer belongs. If the pointer is of the base type, dynamic binding remains a possibility—it depends on the type of the object pointed to and how the function is defined. If the pointer is of one of the derived types, only static binding is possible. However, the result of the call also depends on the type of the object pointed to and how the function is defined.

This leaves you with two factors to consider: the type of the object pointed to and how the function is defined. The object might be of the base type (no dynamic binding) and of one of the derived types (dynamic binding is possible only if the object is pointed to by the base pointer). The function can be defined either in the base class or in the derived class. Also, the function can be defined both in the base class and in the derived class. For this case, you should distinguish between functions that are redefined in the derived class with the same signature as in the base class and functions with a different signature. Only functions that are redefined with the same signature can support dynamic binding. Other functions only support static binding, and not all of them can be called for a given combination of pointer type and object type. All in all, you should distinguish between four different kinds of member functions:

- defined in the base class and inherited in a derived class without redefinition
- defined in a derived class without a counterpart in the base class
- defined in the base class and redefined in a derived class with the same name and with the same or different signature
- defined in the base class and redefined in a derived class with the same name and the same signature as virtual

Sounds complex? Yes, it is, especially when you are first learning virtual functions. It will become simpler soon.

For the base pointer pointing to a base object, only those methods defined in the base class can be called, regardless of whether they are inherited in derived classes as is or redefined there. An attempt to call a function defined in a derived class without a counterpart in the base class is a syntax error. An attempt to call a function redefined in a derived class is futile—the function defined in the base class will be called anyway.

For a derived pointer pointing to a derived object (of the same class), base functions are not available with the exception of those that are defined in the base class and are inherited as is. This pointer can call those methods that are added in the derived class and those that are redefined in the derived class. Functions redefined in the derived class are called statically no matter how they are redefined—with the same signature or not, as virtual functions or not.

Notice that the base functions that are redefined in the derived class are not accessible to the derived class pointer pointing to the derived class object; they are hidden by the corresponding derived class functions. An attempt to reach a base function will result in a static call to the function defined in the derived class (virtual or non-virtual) if the signatures match or in a syntax error if the signatures do not match.

The base class pointer pointing to an object of a derived class can call base methods that are inherited (and not redefined) by the derived class. It cannot reach the methods defined in the derived class without a counterpart in the base class. If the derived class redefines a base method as a non-virtual function (either with the same or different signature), this derived method also cannot be called through the base pointer—the corresponding base method will be called statically instead. If the derived class redefines a base method as a virtual function, it is the derived class method that is called through the base class pointer, not the base class method. This is the only case where dynamic binding is possible.

The derived class pointer pointing to a base object is an anomaly. It can call methods defined in the base class and inherited in the base class without redefinition. It cannot call base class methods redefined in the derived class; they are hidden from this pointer. It cannot call derived class methods that redefine base class methods (as virtual or non-virtual, with the same or different signature); they are not supported by the base object, and an attempt to do so causes a run-time error: a crash or incorrect results.

This description is lengthy and cumbersome, but it has a very simple foundation. It is based on two principles:

- A derived pointer pointing to a derived object can reach methods defined in the derived class and methods inherited from the base class as is. Methods redefined in the derived class hide methods defined in the base class (with the same or different signature, virtual or not) from the derived class pointer.

- A base pointer pointing to a derived object can reach only those methods defined in the base class with one exception: If the function is redefined in the derived class as virtual, it is the derived class function that the base pointer invokes using dynamic binding, not the base class function.

This is very simple, but it might take some time to digest. When I was writing this, I was struggling with the task of inventing a simple graphical or tabular representation of these rules. The results are in Figure 15–12 and in Table 15.1.

Figure 15–12 shows base class pointers (narrow ones) and derived class pointers (fat one, with two parts) that point to base class objects (the dashed part represents the missing derived part) and to derived class objects (the left part represents the base part, the right part represents the derived part).

The vertical lines inside each part represent member functions of four types. Type 1 is defined in the base class and is inherited in the derived class as is. Type 2 is added to the derived class without a counterpart in the base class. Type 3 is defined in the base class and redefined in the derived class with the same name (with the same or different signatures) Type 4 is defined in the base class (as virtual) and is redefined in the derived class with the same name and the same signature.

The methods that can be called through the pointer are underlined. In case A, functions of types 3 and 4 defined in the base class are hidden by the

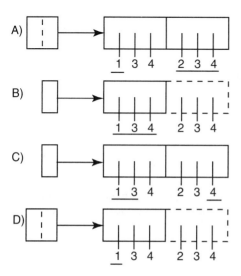

Figure 15–12
Static and dynamic binding for base and derived class pointers.

functions defined in the derived class. In case B, only functions defined in the base class are accessible. In case C, only functions defined in the base class are accessible, but the functions redefined in the derived class as virtual hide their base class counterparts and can be called dynamically. In case D, only functions defined in the base class and not redefined in the derived class can be called.

Table 15.1 summarizes the same rules. The columns describe kinds of objects and kinds of pointers that point to these objects, the rows describe different kinds of member functions.

Table 15.1	Summary of Rules for Static and Dynamic Binding			
Kind of Member Function	*Base Pointers*		*Derived Pointers*	
	Base object	Derived object	Base object	Derived object
Functions defined in the Base class				
Inherited in Derived class as	available	available	available	available
Redefined in Derived (non-virtual)	available	available	not available	hidden
Redefined in Derived (virtual)	available	hidden	not available	hidden
Functions defined in the Derived class				
Defined in Derived class only	syntax error	syntax error	crash	available
Redefined in Derived (non-virtual)	not available	not available	crash	available
Redefined in Derived (virtual)	not available	dynamic binding	crash	available

Pure Virtual Functions

Base virtual functions may have no job to do because they have no meaning within the application. Their job is just to define the interface as a standard for its derived classes. This is why virtual functions are introduced in the first place.

For example, the `write()` method in class `Person` does not contain anything. It has no code. Notice too that it is never called. All calls to the `write()` method in the client code (global function `write()`) are resolved either to a `Faculty` class or to a `Student` class method `write()`.

Actually, class `Person` is a pure generalization with no real role. There are no `Person` objects in the application. All objects are created with the operator new in the global function `read()` and are either of `Student` or `Faculty` class. The description of the problem at the beginning of this section simply says that there are two types of records, one for students and one for faculty members. Class `Person` was first introduced into the application as an abstraction that merges the characteristics of faculty objects and student objects into one generalized class (Listing 15.3). Later, it was used to define a hierarchy of derived classes (Listing 15.4). In the last version of the program (Listing 15.4), class `Person` was used to define the interface of the virtual function `write()`.

In real life, class `Person` might be a very useful class. In addition to the university id and the name, it can contain date of birth, address, phone number, and a host of other characteristics that are common to `Faculty` and `Student` objects. In addition to data, class `Person` can define numerous methods such as change of name, address or phone number, retrieval of the university id, and other data common to `Faculty` and `Student` objects. The derived classes can inherit all these useful functions. The clients of derived classes can use these functions by sending these messages (defined in the `Person` class) to objects of classes `Faculty` and `Student`. Again, I am not saying that class `Person` is useless. I am saying that objects of class `Person` are useless for this application. The application needs only objects of classes derived from `Person`. Please keep this distinction in mind.

The `Person` class designer knows that the application does not create class objects and that class objects have no job to do. It would be nice to pass this knowledge on to the client programmer (and to maintainers), not in comments, but rather in code. C++ allows you to define the base class in such a way that an attempt to create an object of this type would be illegal and would result in a syntax error.

C++ makes it possible through the use of pure virtual functions and abstract classes. I am not sure why two terms, "pure" and "abstract," are used to describe the same idea. A pure virtual function is a virtual function that should not be called (like `write()` in class `Person`). If the program tries to call this function, a syntax error results. An abstract class is a class with at least one pure virtual function (more than one is okay). It is illegal to create objects of this class. If the program tries to create an object of this class either dynamically or on the stack, a syntax error results.

There are no C++ keywords for pure virtual functions and abstract classes. Instead, a pure virtual function is recognized (by the compiler, client programmer, and maintainer) as a member function whose declaration is "initialized" to zero. Here is the class `Person` whose `write()` member function is defined as a pure virtual function.

```
struct Person {                        // abstract class
protected:
  char id[10];                         // data common to both types
  char* name;
public:
  Person(const char id[], const char nm[]);
  virtual void write() const = 0;      // pure virtual function
  ~Person();
} ;
```

Of course, the assignment operator does not denote the assignment here. This is just another example of giving a symbol an additional meaning in yet another context. This is confusing. Adding another keyword, such as pure or abstract, would probably be a better design.

A pure virtual function has no implementation. Actually, it is a syntax error to supply the implementation of the pure virtual function (or to invoke the function). It is the presence of virtual functions that makes a class an abstract (or partial) class.

In addition to the lack of instantiated objects, an abstract class is required to have at least one derived class. If the derived class implements this function, it becomes a regular class. If the derived class does not implement this function, it becomes an abstract class as well. It is illegal to create objects of that derived class, and this class must have at least one derived class.

The derived classes implement the pure virtual functions in the same way they implement regular virtual functions. This means that the derived class should use the same name, the same signature, and the same return type as the pure virtual function should use. The mode of derivation should be public. Here is an example of class `Faculty` that implements the virtual function `write()`. It is a regular non-abstract class.

```
struct Faculty : public Person {       // regular class
private:
  char* rank;                          // for faculty only
public:
  Faculty(const char id[], const char nm[], const char r[]);
  void write () const;                 // regular virtual function
  ~Faculty();
} ;
```

Actually, this is the same derived class I used in Listing 15.5. Looking at the regular non-abstract class, you cannot say whether it is derived from an abstract class or from a regular class. This is perfectly all right, because for the user of the class `Faculty` it does not matter how the base class `Person` is implemented, as long as the client code does not try to instantiate the objects of the abstract class.

For a regular class with virtual functions, the client code can create objects of this class, send messages to these objects, and use polymorphism if needed.

Again, an abstract class is a C++ class in all regards; it can have data members and regular nonpure functions, including virtual functions.

If a class inherits a virtual function as a pure virtual function without defining its body, this derived class is also an abstract class: No objects of that class can be created. If the client code needs objects of that class but is not going to call that function on these objects (because this function has no job yet), an empty body of the function can be used. The class becomes a regular, non-abstract class, and an object of that class can be created.

```
class Base {                    // abstract class
public:
 virtual void member() = 0;     // pure virtual function
 .... } ;                       // the rest of Base class

class Derived : public Base {   // regular class
   public:
    void member()               // virtual function
     { }                        // empty body: noop
 .... } ;                       // the rest of Derived class
```

Here, class `Base` is an abstract class. The objects of this class cannot be created. Class `Derived` is a regular class. Its objects can be instantiated both on the stack (as named variables) and on the heap (as unnamed variables). Function `member()` in the `Base` class is a pure virtual function. It cannot be called. Function `member()` in the `Derived` class is a regular virtual function. However, its call results in no operation.

```
Base *b;  Derived *d;    // Base and Derived pointers
b = new Base;            // syntax error, abstract class
d = new Derived;         // OK, regular class, heap object
b = new Derived;         // OK, implicit pointer conversion
d->member();             // OK, compile time binding, no op
b->member();             // OK, run time binding
d->Base::member();       // linker error: no implementation
```

Redefinition with a different signature makes the function non-virtual in the derived class. Here, class `Derived1` is a class that inherits from the abstract class `Base` but does not redefine the pure function `member()` with no parameters. Instead, it defines a function `member(int)` with one parameter.

```
class Derived1 : public Base {       // also an abstract class
   public:
    void member(int)                 // non-virtual function
      { }                            // empty body: noop
 .... } ;                            // the rest of Derived1 class
```

This means that class `Derived1` is an abstract class. It is a syntax error to create objects of this class. Since this class is not used as a base class to derive other classes, it is quite useless, since there is no way one can use any of its functions.

```
class Derived2 : public Derived1 {   // regular class
   public:
    void member()                            // virtual function
      { }                                    // empty body: noop
 .... } ;                                    // the rest of Derived class
```

Class `Derived2` inherits from class `Derived1`. It implements the virtual member function `member()`, and hence it is legal to create objects of this class. The objects of this class can respond to the message `member()`, both with run-time binding and with static binding. The objects of this class cannot respond to the message `member(int)` because this function is hidden by the member function `member()` defined in class `Derived2`.

```
Derived2 *d2 = new Derived2;      // OK, regular class, heap object
d2->member();                     // OK, static binding
b = new Derived2;                 // OK for virtual functions
b->member();                      // OK, dynamic binding
b->member(0);                     // syntax error
d2->member(0);                    // wrong number of parameters
```

Notice that the base class pointer `b`, when pointing to the derived class object, can invoke only

- non-pure member (virtual or non-virtual) functions defined in the base class
- virtual functions defined in the derived class

It cannot invoke non-virtual member functions defined in the derived class. It is a myopic pointer. It takes a virtual function to extend its scope of vision to the derived part of the object it is pointing to. Otherwise, it can see only the base part of the derived object. It takes the derived class pointer to access both the base part and the derived part of the derived object.

Virtual Functions: Destructors

When the delete operator is invoked, the destructor is called and the object is destroyed. Which destructor is called? The destructor defined in the class of the pointer pointing to the object or the destructor defined in the class to which the object pointed to by the pointer belongs?

When the pointer and the object pointed to by the pointer belong to the same class, the answer is simple: the destructor is of that class.

```
Derived2 *d2 = new Derived2;      // OK, regular class, heap object
d2->member();                     // OK, static binding
b = new Derived2;                 // OK for virtual functions
b->member();                      // OK, dynamic binding
delete d2;                        // class Derived2 destructor
delete b;                         // ??
```

C++ destructors are member functions. They are regular non-virtual member functions. When the `delete` operator is used, the compiler finds the definition of the pointer operand, searches the definition of the class to which the pointer belongs, and calls the destructor that belongs to that class. All this happens at compile time. The compiler pays no attention to the class of object to which the pointer is pointing.

When the pointer and the object are of the same class there is no problem: The dynamic memory (and other resources) allocated to the object are returned as the destructor code executes. When the derived class pointer points to a base object—well, you should not do that. The big and powerful derived class pointer will require the little base object to do things it cannot do.

```
Person p;  Faculty f;                     // base and derived pointers
p = new Person("U12345678", "Smith");
f = p;                                    // syntax error: stay away
f = (Faculty*)p;                          // I insist I know what I do
delete f;                                 // Faculty destructor
```

In this example, the `Faculty` destructor is invoked on a `Person` object. The `delete` operator is called for the data member `rank` that is not in the object. The results are undefined.

When a base pointer points to a derived class object, the base class destructor is called. This might or might not be troublesome. If the dynamic memory is handled in the base class but not in the derived class, there is no problem; the heap memory is returned by the base destructor. If the derived class handles the heap memory, it is not returned by the base destructor. A memory leak results.

```
Person *p;   Faculty* f;                // base and derived pointers
f = new Faculty("U12345689", "Black", "Assistant Professor");
p = f;                                  // or p = (Person*) f;
delete p;                               // memory leak
```

In this example, the `delete` operator invokes the `Person` destructor, which deletes dynamic memory allocated for the name. The `Faculty` destructor is not called, and the heap memory allocated for the `rank` is not returned.

In Listing 15.5, the client code uses a loop to go over the array of base pointers and delete each object allocated dynamically at the beginning of the execution. For each object in the data structure, the `Person` destructor is executed.

```
for (int j=0;  j < cnt;  j++)
{ delete data[j]; }                     // delete Person heap memory
```

As far as `Faculty` and `Student` objects are concerned, their memory is returned completely. The `delete` operator deletes the object no matter what the type of the object. The problem is not with the object memory but with the heap memory allocated to the derived class objects, the right-most part on Figure 15–10. The `Person` destructor deletes the heap memory allocated for name but not the heap memory allocated for `rank` and `major`. When a derived object is destroyed through a base pointer, only the base destructor is called, and the derived class destructor is not called.

C++ offers a way out of this: to declare the base destructor virtual. By convention, it makes every derived class destructor also virtual. When the `delete` operator is applied to a base pointer, the target class destructor is called polymorphically (and then the base class destructor, if any).

```
struct Person {                               // abstract class
protected:
  char id[10];                                // data common to both types
  char* name;
public:
  Person(const char id[], const char nm[]);
  virtual void write() const = 0;             // pure virtual function
  virtual ~Person();                          // this makes the trick
} ;

struct Faculty : public Person {              // regular class
private:
  char* rank;                                 // for faculty only
public:
  Faculty(const char id[], const char nm[], const char r[]);
  void write () const;                        // regular virtual function
  ~Faculty();                                 // now this is virtual, too
} ;
```

This solution is somewhat awkward. After all, the first thing you should remember about virtual functions is that you use exactly the same name everywhere, in the base class and in all derived classes. With destructors, this is not the case because each destructor has the same name as the class name. Hence, destructors violate the rules of virtual functions. This is similar to constructors, and, indeed, there are no virtual constructors in C++.

However, practical considerations are more important that logical beauty. Memory leaks are too dangerous to put up with. This is why C++ allows this inconsistency and supports virtual destructors.

Multiple Inheritance: Several Base Classes

In C++, a derived class might have more than one base class. With single inheritance, the hierarchy of classes is a tree, with the base class on the top of the hierarchy and derived classes below the base class.

With multiple inheritance, the hierarchy of classes might become a graph rather than a tree as with single inheritance. This makes the relationships among classes more complex than with single inheritance. The issues related to multiple inheritance are more difficult to understand than for simple inheritance.

Similar to single inheritance, multiple inheritance is not so much a technique to make the client code simpler or easier to understand; it is a technique that makes the server code easier to produce. Unlike single inheritance, multiple inheritance allows the server class designer to mix the characteristics of diverse classes in one class.

Let us consider a simple example. Let us assume that class B1 provides the clients with a public service f1() and class B2 provides the clients with a public service f2(). This is almost exactly what the client code needs, but in addition to these two services the client code needs a public service f3() to be available. One possible technique to serve the client is to merge characteristics of classes B1 and B2 into one class using multiple inheritance.

```
class B1
  { public:
      void f1();                        // public service f1()
  ... };                                // the rest of class B1


class B2
  { public:
      void f2();                        // public service f2()
  ... };                                // the rest of class B2
```

By inheriting publicly from class B1 and B2, class Derived becomes able to provide its clients with the union of services provided by each of the base classes, in this case, methods f1() and f2(). This means that to provide its clients with all three services (f1(), f2(), f3()), the designer of class Derived has to implement only one function, f3(). This is quite an accomplishment.

```
class Derived : public B1, public B2        // two base classes
  { public:                                 // f1(), f2() are inherited
      void f3();                            // f3() is added to services
  ... };                                    // the rest of class Derived
```

Now the client code can instantiate Derived objects and send to them messages that they inherited from both base classes and messages that are added by the Derived class.

```
Derived d;            // instantiate Derived object
d.f1();   d.f2();     // inherited services (B1, B2)
d.f3();               // the service is added in the Derived class
```

We see that a derived class provides clients with capabilities of all the bases plus its own data and behavior.

Initially, C++ did not have multiple inheritance. But Stroustrup, the designer of C++, complained that programmers "demanded multiple inheritance," and now C++ has it. I am not sure to what extent this was a result of the external pressure. I know of quite a few suggestions that he did not give in to.

Multiple inheritance is good for customizing existing class libraries, for example, for adding or redefining members in existing classes. Derived classes represent a combination of base classes rather than a refinement of a single base class. Each parent class contributes properties to the derived class; the derived class is a union of the base features.

Examples of using multiple inheritance include graphic objects, NOW accounts, and iostream classes in the C++ standard library.

For a graphics package, classes `Shape` and `Position` were used as base classes to produce class `Object`. The objects of class `Object` (sorry for the pun, it was not intended) combined properties of `Shape` objects and `Position` objects. This is an example of unreasonable use of multiple inheritance. Sure, a graphics object is a shape, but it is a stretch to state that a graphics object is a position. It is more natural to say that a graphics object has a position.

For NOW accounts, the classes represent savings accounts and checking accounts. This is a better example of using multiple inheritance because a NOW account indeed combines the properties of savings accounts and checking accounts: It pays interest and allows check writing. However, if you talk to a bank officer, you would hear that yes, basically this is correct, but there are quite a few exceptions that make a NOW account different from both a savings account and a checking account. This means that the benefits of easily merging basic characteristics are offset by the drawbacks of suppressing features that do not fit.

For the C++ iostream class library, the use of multiple inheritance to merge characteristics of input stream classes and output stream classes makes sense. The resulting iostream classes support both input operations and output operations, and there is nothing to suppress in the derived classes.

Notice that C++ does not put a limit on the number of base classes that can participate in forming a derived class. All examples that I cited involve only two base classes. In all examples of multiple inheritance that follow, I will limit myself to two base classes as well. Why not three or four? The answer is simple—it is hard to come up with examples of multiple inheritance with three or four base classes so that they make good sense and do not confuse the user. Why is two better than three or four? I suspect that the examples of multiple inheritance with two base classes are also hard to come by.

This is why I recommend that you use multiple inheritance with caution. The advantages are few and complications are many. There are always ways to adequately support the client code without using multiple inheritance.

Multiple Inheritance: Access Rules

With multiple inheritance, a derived class inherits all data members of all bases and all member functions of all bases. The space that an object of the derived class occupies in memory is the sum of the space that the objects of the base classes occupy in memory (with possible addition for alignment).

Access rules for multiple inheritance are the same as for single inheritance. The methods of the derived class can access public and protected members (data and methods) of all its base classes without any limitations. They cannot access private members of the base classes.

Inheritance links can be public, protected, or private. In either case, all data members and member functions of all base classes are inherited in the derived class, but the access rights can change depending on the mode of derivation.

Modes of derivation for multiple inheritance are the same as for single inheritance. With public derivation, each base member, private, protected, and public, has the same access rights in the derived class object as in the base object. This is the most natural mode of inheritance.

With protected derivation, protected and public base members remain protected and public in the derived class, but public base members (data and functions) become protected in the derived class. Since the derived class has full access to protected base components, protected inheritance does not affect access rights of the derived class. Similar to single inheritance, it does affect access rights of the client code. The client code loses the right to use public base services. The derived class has to provide adequate services to the clients without making the public base services available to the client code.

With private inheritance, all base members become private in the derived class. Similar to single inheritance, the mode of derivation is private by default. The mode of derivation should be specified for each base class separately.

Let us consider the same two base classes B1 and B2 as in the previous example.

```
class B1
  { public:
       void f1();              // public service f1()
   ... };                      // the rest of class B1

class B2
  { public:
       void f2();              // public service f2()
   ... };                      // the rest of class B2
```

Let us combine their characteristics in a derived class `Derived` and add yet another member function in the derived class.

```
class Derived : public B1, B2    // two base classes
  { public:                      // f1(), f2() are inherited
       void f3();                // f3() is added to services
   ... };                        // the rest of class Derived
```

Then the client code can define and use the objects of the `Derived` class.

```
Derived d;          // instantiate Derived object
d.f1();             // inherited from B1
d.f2();             // syntax error: f2() is private
d.f3();             // the service is added in the Derived class
```

This is yet another manifestation of the difference between the keyword `public` used for describing access rights and used for describing the mode of derivation. With access rights, the scope of the keyword `public` includes as many class members as needed, until another access right keyword is found or until the end of the class definition. With mode of derivation, the scope of the keyword `public` is only one identifier.

In the example above, it is only class `B1` from which class `Derived` inherits publicly. For class `B2`, the default (private) mode of derivation is used. This is why method `f2()` becomes private in the `Derived` class, and as such is not available to the client code.

Conversions Between Classes

Conversion rules for multiple inheritance are similar to those for single inheritance. If a base class is inherited from publicly, objects of the derived class can be implicitly converted into objects of that base class; no explicit cast operator is needed for such a conversion.

The concepts behind this rule are the same as those for single inheritance. An object of the derived class has all the capabilities, data, and functions of objects of base classes. Conversion from a derived object to a base object cannot result in the loss of capabilities unless, of course, the mode of derivation is not public.

```
B1 b1;  B2 b2;  Derived d;
b1 = d;  b2 = d;              // OK: extra capabilities are discarded
d = b1;  d = b2;             // error: inconsistent state of object
```

Conversion from a base class to the derived class is not allowed. A base object has only part of the data and capabilities that a derived object has, and the missing capabilities are nowhere to come from. This conversion is not safe.

Similar rules apply to pointers and references. A pointer (reference) of a base class can safely point to an object of the derived class. The derived class object can do everything the base pointer can demand and probably more. This is safe. However, the base pointer can invoke only part of the capabilities of the derived object.

```
B1 *p1; B2 *p2;  Derived *d;
p1 = new Derived;  p2 = new Derived;      // OK: safe
d = new B1;  d = new B2;                   // syntax errors
d = p1;  d = p2;                           // syntax errors
d = (Derived*) p1;                         // OK: explicit cast
```

A pointer of the derived class should not point to a base object (the third line in this example). The base object lacks many capabilities that a derived object has and that are available through the derived class pointer. To avoid run-time errors, the compiler declares this code to be a syntax error.

Similarly, a base pointer (which presumably points to a base object) cannot be copied into a derived class pointer (the fourth line of code in the example). This is not safe: The derived pointer might require services that the base object cannot perform, and the compiler will not be able to catch that. This is why this pointer manipulation is also considered a syntax error.

What do you do if you know that the base pointer indeed points to a derived class object rather than to a base object? The same thing you do with single inheritance—you tell the compiler that you know what you are doing by means of a cast (the last line in the example). Since the compiler cannot check you, it accepts your assurance. You had better be right.

The same rules apply to parameter passing. If a function expects a pointer (or a reference) to one of the base classes, it is safe to call this function, passing to it the address of a derived object instead.

```
void foo1 (B1 *b1)                   // derived objects have additional services
  { b1->f1(); }

void foo2 (B2 *b2)                   // derived objects have additional services
  { b2->f2(); }

void foo(Derived *d)                 // base objects cannot do that
  { d->f3(); }

B1 *b1 = new Derived;  B2 *b2 = new Derived;
Derived d;
foo1(&d);   foo2(&d);                // both are OK: safe conversion
foo(b1);    foo(b2);                 // syntax errors: unsafe conversion
foo((Derived*)b1);  foo((Derived*)b2);     // pass at your own risk
```

In the last example, functions foo1() and foo2() can accept Derived objects as actual arguments because inside these functions their parameters respond to base messages only (f1() and f2()), and derived objects can respond to these services. Function foo() cannot accept base pointers because inside this function the parameter should respond to the derived class message f3(), and base objects cannot do that. On the other hand, pointers b1 and b2 point to Derived class objects that can do the job. To tell the compiler about this, the last line of the code above explicitly casts the base pointer to the Derived pointer.

With the private or protected mode of inheritance, no implicit conversion from objects of the derived class into objects of its base classes is allowed. Even in this "safe" case, an explicit cast by client code is needed (because this case is not "safe" anymore). Conversion from any base class to a derived class requires an explicit cast for any mode of multiple inheritance.

Multiple Inheritance: Constructors and Destructors

A derived class is responsible for the state of its components inherited from the base classes. As with single inheritance, the base class constructors are called when an object of a derived class is constructed.

The mechanism for passing parameters to the base class constructors is similar to single inheritance: The member initialization list should be used. In the next example, the base class B1 has one data member, the base class B2 has another data member, and the derived class has yet another data member (a dynamically allocated character array). The Derived class should provide a constructor with three parameters so that it can pass data to its B1 and B2 components and to its own data member.

```
class B1 {
   int m1;
public:
   B1(int);
   void f1(); ... };

class B2 {
   double m2;
public:
   B2(double);
   void f2(); ... };

class Derived:  public B1, public B2 {
   char* t;
public:
   Derived(const char*, double, int);
   ~Derived();
   void f3(); ... };
```

If the member initialization list is not provided, default base constructors are called. If base classes provide no default constructors, it is a syntax error.

In the member initialization list, the Derived class constructor calls base constructors using class names B1 and B2 (not data member names) in a comma-separated sequence of constructor calls; parameter names for base constructors usually come from the Derived constructor parameter lists (literal values are also okay).

```
Derived::Derived(const char *s, double d, int i) : B1(i),B2(d)
  { if ((t = new char[strlen(s)+1]) == NULL)
     { cout << "\nOut of memory\n";  exit(1); }
    strcpy(t,s); }
```

All base class constructors are called before the derived class constructor is called. They are called in the order in which the base classes are listed in the derived class declaration, not in the order of the initialization list of the derived class constructor.

Similarly to single inheritance, data members of the derived class can be initialized either in the body of the derived class constructor or in the member initialization list.

When a derived class object is destroyed (dynamically or by going out of scope), the derived class destructor is called first.

Then the base class destructors are called in an order that is the reverse of constructor invocations.

Multiple Inheritance: Ambiguities

The use of multiple inheritance might result in name conflicts. If the derived class has a data member or a member function of the same name as one of the base classes, the base class service is hidden by the name defined in the derived class.

In the next example, the `Derived` class has data member x with the same name as a data member in the base class B1; in addition, the `Derived` class has member function f2() with the same name as a member function in the base class B2.

```
class B1 {
protected:
    int x;                          // hidden by Derived::x
public:
    void f1();    ... };

class B2 {
public:
    void f2();    ... };            // hidden by Derived::f2()

class Derived:   public B1, public B2 {
protected:
    float x;                        // hides B1::x
public:
    void f2();                      // it hides B2::f2()
    void f3()
        { x = 0; }   ... };         // Derived::x is used
```

In this example, the object of the `Derived` class has two data members x; the data member inherited from B1 is hidden in `Derived`; the member function f2() inherited from base B2 is hidden by the added function f2().

Both the client code and the `Derived` class code can override the scope rules by using the explicit scope operator.

```
void Derived::f3()
    { B1::x = 0; }                  // disregard Derived::x

Derived d;
d.f2();                             // Der::f2();
d.B2::f2();                         // B2::f2();
```

Clashes between the derived class name and the base class names are not very frequent. Usually, the designer of the derived class has an opportunity to review the design of base classes and avoid conflicts if they are considered harmful.

Base class member names may also clash. This is a more common occurrence and a more difficult one to deal with because base classes are often developed independently from each other and there is little opportunity to coordinate their development to avoid name conflicts.

If two base classes have a data member or a member function with the same name, the derived class object has both copies. The language provides no predefined precedence rules for access to data and functions. If needed, we resolve ambiguities with the use of explicit qualification; the scope operator has to be used both by the client and by the derived class.

In the next example, both base classes have a public member function named f1(). This means that the client code cannot use either of them unless the client code provides an explicit indication of which one to use.

```
class B1 {
public:
   void f1(); ... } ;

class B2 {
public:
   void f1(); ... } ;

class Derived : public B1, public B2 {
public:
   void f3(); ... } ;

Derived d;
d.f1();                                       // ambiguous message
d.B1::f1();   d.B2::f1();   d.f3();            // OK
```

This technique for eliminating ambiguity flies in the face of principles of object-oriented programming. The problem is resolved by adding more responsibility to the client code rather than to its server class. Make sure that you spot these kinds of designs and avoid them.

A better approach would be to ask the Derived class to insulate the client code from ambiguity in member function names.

```
class Derived:  public B1, public B2 {
public:
   void f1() { B1::f1(); }                     // one-liners
   void f2() { B2::f1(); }
   void f3();    ... } ;

Derived d;
d.f1();   d.f2();   d.f3();                     // client is insulated
```

This is a much better solution. It is the server code (class `Derived`) that goes to the trouble of dealing with the problem. The client code is insulated from the problem. After all, when the client code uses class `Derived` as its server, the client code should not be exposed to the details of the server design—what it inherits, from whom it inherits, what conflicts it has to deal with, and so on. All that the client code should know is how to call the services `f1()`, `f2()`, and `f3()` to get the job done.

If two (or more) base classes have a data member with the same name (of the same or different types), the derived class object has both copies, and this results in ambiguity.

```
class B1 {
protected:
   int m;
public:
   B1(int);
   void f(); ... };

class B2 {
protected:
   double m;
public:
   B2(double);
   void f(); ... };

class Derived : public B1, public B2 {
   char* t;
public:
   Derived (char*,double,int);
   void f3() { cout << "m=" << m << endl; }       // ambiguity
   ... };
```

Conflicts between names of data members should be resolved by the derived class to avoid ambiguities and to protect the client code. The scope operator has to be used.

```
void Derived::f3()
{ cout << "m=" << B1::m << endl; }                 // no ambiguity
```

Multiple Inheritance: Directed Graph

This is the most insidious form of ambiguity. It happens when a base class is inherited from more than once. In general, C++ is against that, and a class may explicitly appear only once in a derivation list for a derived class.

```
class B {
public:
   int m;   . . . . } ;

class Derived:  public B, public B        // syntax error
   {  . . . .  } ;
```

This does not make much sense, and it is outlawed as a syntax error. However, the same class can appear multiple times in an inheritance hierarchy. Different base classes may have common parents; such a parent will appear more than once in derivations, and its data will have multiple copies in derived classes.

```
class B1 : public B  {                     // class B is above
   protected:
      int mem;
   public:
      void f1(); ... };

class B2 : public B  {                     // class B is above
   protected:
      int mem;
   public:
      void f2(); ... };

class Derived : public B1, public B2 {     // inherited from B twice
   public:
      void f3();   ... };
```

In this design, class Derived has two data members named mem that are inherited from different base classes. They have the same names, but they refer to different locations in memory. Their roles in the program are also different: They come from different classes. Managing them is a headache, and this headache should not be passed on to the client.

The situation with data member m is worse. Each object of class Derived has two instances of this data member; one is inherited through class B1 and the other through B2. Space required for multiple instances of the same base data member is wasteful. Also, these two data members are functionally the same—they come from the same class, but one of them serves the needs of the B1 part of Derived, and another serves the needs of the B2 part of Derived.

C++ comes with an interesting fix for this problem. It gives the programmer an opportunity to explicitly state that using two (or more) copies of the same data and functions is undesirable. I wish this were the default case, and people who like puzzles would have the right to request that using two copies of the same data and functions is desirable.

You stipulate that by specifying the base classes as virtual base classes. The keyword `virtual` modifies declarations of the derived classes, which are later used in multiple inheritance.

```
class B  {                              // common base class
   int m;
public:
   void f();   ...    } ;

class B1 : virtual public B  {          // virtual base
   protected:
      int mem;
   public:
      void f1(); ... };

class B2 : virtual public B  {          // virtual base
   protected:
      int mem;
   public:
      void f2(); ... };

class Derived : public B1, public B2 {   // works by magic
   public:
      void f3();  ... };
```

Now the `Derived` class has only one copy of data and functions inherited from class `B`. Notice that to eliminate the problems in the `Derived` class, it is the designers of its base classes `B1` and `B2` that have to define these classes as virtual. This flies in the face of the principle that base classes do not know about their derived classes; it is derived classes that know about their bases.

And a final comment: You should not confuse the keyword `virtual` used in this context with the keyword `virtual` used for virtual functions. They are totally different. It would be nice to have two different keywords. It would probably be even nicer not to have multiple inheritance.

Multiple Inheritance: Is It Useful?

I am not sure I can answer this question impartially, but I feel that the complexity of design with multiple inheritance (and I discussed here only part of what exists) outweighs the advantages of its use.

So, what do you do when you feel you have to design a class that provides to its clients the union of services provided by other classes? My answer to this question is: Use composition, or use composition with inheritance.

Consider again the first example of inheritance that I discussed in the beginning of this section. The goal of this design is to provide the client code with the ability to call functions `f1()`, `f2()`, and `f3()`. Functions `f1()` and `f2()` are already implemented in classes B1 and B2. Function `f3()` needs to be implemented. These are two classes that implement required functions `f1()` and `f2()`.

```
class B1
  { public:
       void f1();                    // public service f1()
  ... };                             // the rest of class B1

class B2
  { public:
       void f2();                    // public service f2()
  ... };                             // the rest of class B2
```

When you use multiple inheritance, you implement the required function `f3()` in the new class `Derived`.

```
class Derived : public B1, public B2    // two base classes
  { public:                              // f1(), f2() are inherited
       void f3();                        // f3() is added to services
  ... };                                 // the rest of class Derived
```

Instead, you can create class `Derived` inheriting function `f1()` from class B1. To provide clients of `Derived` with the function `f2()`, you make a field of class B2 a member of class `Derived`.

```
class Derived : public B1 {        // single inheritance
    B2 b2;                         // class composition
public:
    void f2() { b2.f2(); }         // one-liner
    void f3(); ... };
```

Now the client code can instantiate `Derived` objects and send them messages exactly as in the case of multiple inheritance.

```
Derived d;          // instantiate Derived object
d.f1();             // inherited services (B1)
d.f2();             // passed from B2 through Derived
d.f3();             // added in the Derived class
```

It goes without saying that this client code should not go into the details of how its server class Derived is designed. It provides the required services, and this is all that is needed—without the complexity of multiple inheritance.

Summary

In this chapter, we looked at advanced uses of inheritance. They all rotate around the fact that base classes and derived classes have some capabilities in common; hence, objects of one class can be used instead of objects of another class, at least in some circumstances.

You saw that it is always safe to use an object of the derived class where an object of a base class is expected. This conversion is safe, but it is not very interesting. This derived object will be asked to do only things that a base object could do, and the derived class object can do much more.

However, the same is true about pointers (and references), and this is much more interesting. This means that you can use a pointer of the base class where a derived class pointer is expected, that is, you can point to derived class objects using base class pointers.

Why would you want to do that? The most common context for doing that is processing a collection of objects of different classes.

This has always been a problem in programming languages. All of our collections that are supported by modern languages are homogeneous. C++ arrays cannot contain components of different classes. C++ linked lists cannot use nodes of different types. It is only the use of inheritance that allows you to use collections of objects of different classes. These classes are not totally different. The heterogeneous lists discussed in this chapter cannot contain objects of arbitrary classes. But they can contain objects of classes related by inheritance.

When a heterogeneous collection of objects (related by inheritance) is processed, four types of messages are sent to the objects in the collection.

- Messages that every object in the collection can respond to: These are methods defined in the base class of the inheritance hierarchy and are not overwritten in derived classes.

- Messages that only some kinds of objects in the collection can respond to: These are methods defined in derived classes of an inheritance hierarchy without a message with the same name in the base class.

- Messages whose names all kinds of objects in the collection can respond to but which are defined as non-virtual functions in base and derived classes (with the same or different interface).

- Messages that each kind of object in the collection can respond to, which are defined as virtual functions using the same interface in the base and derived classes.

The first type of message can be accessed using the base class pointer; no conversion is necessary when the object in the collection is accessed.

The second kind of message can be sent using only derived class pointers: When the object is taken from the collection, the base pointer has to be converted to the pointer of the class to which the object belongs; only then will the message of the second kind become accessible. This conversion is not safe, and you should know what you are doing (that the object can respond to this message) because the compiler is not able to protect you.

The third kind of message also requires conversion if the object should respond to a message defined in the derived class. The base class message is hidden by the derived class message.

The fourth kind of message does not require conversion. Even though these messages are sent using the base class pointer, they are interpreted by the run-time system according to the type of the object the pointer points to (dynamic binding). The design that uses virtual functions encapsulates the algorithms that are performed differently for different kinds of objects into the functions with the same name.

The use of virtual functions entails some space and performance penalty. Each object of the class that uses virtual functions has a hidden data member that specifies the kind of object or a pointer that points to the table with addresses of available virtual functions. Each time the virtual function is called, this pointer is used to find the required object code, and this extra step of indirection adds to the execution time. This penalty is not large and for most applications is not an issue.

We also took a look at multiple inheritance. I think that the complexity of this topic might equal the complexity of the rest of the language. Meanwhile, its practical utility is small. Everything that can be done with the use of multiple inheritance can be achieved as a combination of inheritance and composition. Use multiple inheritance sparingly if at all.

With virtual functions, it is a different story. They are immensely popular in C++ programming. They are so popular that I am afraid it is not politically correct to argue against their use. Remember, however, that the virtual function mechanism is fragile. You have to use public inheritance. You have to use the same name in all classes in your inheritance hierarchy. You have to use exactly the same parameter list, return value, and even const modifiers. Have a small inconsistency, and your program will call a totally different function just because it has the same name, and you might not notice it.

This being said, use virtual functions everywhere the processing of different kinds of related objects can be reasonably described using the same function name.

ADVANCED USES OF OPERATOR OVERLOADING

Topics in this Chapter

- Operator Overloading: A Brief Overview
- Unary Operators
- Subscript and Function Call Operators
- Input/Output Operators
- Summary

Chapter 16

I already discussed C++ overloaded operators in Chapters 10, "Operator Functions: Another Good Idea," (numeric classes) and 11, "Constructors and Destructors: Potential Trouble," (nonnumeric classes). In this chapter, I am going to extend this coverage and explain more exotic uses of operator overloading in C++. For some, any operator overloading is already quite eccentric. For these programmers, what you will learn in this chapter might appear remote from what most C++ programmers do every day.

This might be true—you do not write advanced overloaded operators often. But this topic is definitely not remote from what many C++ programmers use every day. Advanced operators are an important component of any C++ library, standard or nonstandard, and it is useful to understand how they work. It is certainly not your first priority in studying C++. But these operators are intellectually challenging and aesthetically exciting. You will surely be rewarded for the time and energy spent on studying them.

Operator Overloading: A Brief Overview

An overloaded operator is a programmer-defined function that has a special name (composed of the keyword `operator` and the operator symbol or symbols). Overloaded operators are also known by the names of operator functions, overloaded operator function, or just operators. They provide the convenience of operator syntax for manipulating objects of programmer-defined classes.

The driving force behind the incorporation of overloaded operators into C++ is the desire to treat objects of programmer-defined types in the same way as variables of built-in types are treated. If you can add two numeric values, there is no good reason why you cannot add two `Account` objects. If you can add three numeric values, you should be able to add three `Account` objects, and so on. The overloaded operators enable you to do that.

It is the C++ language that defines the meaning of built-in operators over built-in types. For overloaded operators, the meaning is defined, not by the language, but by the programmer. This meaning should not be arbitrary: it should depend on the nature of objects being added, multiplied and so on. But the programmer has significant freedom in defining the operator meaning, and this can easily lead to abuse—to the design of overloaded operators whose meaning is not intuitively clear. A good example of such abuse is the unary operator plus that I designed in Chapter 10 for displaying the fields of a `Complex` number (see Listing 10.4). Used in the client code, this operator will confuse any maintainer. Very few people could guess correctly that, for example, +x means display the fields of the object x in a specified format.

For the freedom to choose any content of overloaded operators, we pay with the lack of freedom in choosing their names. The name of an operator function should include the keyword `operator` followed by any legal C++ operator (two-symbol operators like == or += are allowed).

There are five exceptions to this rule: operators ".", ".*", "::", "?:" and "sizeof". Overloaded operators can be defined as either class members (and hence used as messages) or top-level global functions (usually, friends of the class whose objects are used as operands of overloaded operators). If an operator is overloaded as a class member, it can have whatever arguments are appropriate.

The target of the message will be used as the first operand. If an operator is overloaded as a global function, it has to have at least one class argument;

it cannot have arguments of built-in types only. This limitation does not apply to memory management operators (`new`, `delete`, and `delete []`).

Operators overloaded in a base class are inherited in derived classes. Obviously, these operators cannot access members defined in derived classes, because the derived class members are outside of the scope of the base class and hence cannot be accessed from the base class methods. The overloaded assignment operator is an anomaly—it is not inherited by the derived classes, or, rather, it can access only the base part of the derived object, not the derived part of the derived object. Hence, each class in the inheritance hierarchy has to define its own assignment operator if needed.

Operator precedence for overloaded operators is the same as for their built-in counterparts. For example, the multiplication operator always has a higher precedence than does the addition operator, whatever their meaning is for the programmer-defined class. The expression syntax for overloaded operators is the same as for corresponding built-in operators. For example, binary operators always occur between their two arguments, whether they are built-in or overloaded. (However, in this chapter you are going to see some exceptions to this rule.)

Arity (the number of operands) for overloaded operators is the same as for corresponding built-in operators. Binary operators remain binary; they require two operands. As global nonmember functions (e.g., friends), binary overloaded operators must have two parameters. As class member functions, binary overloaded operators have only one parameter, because another parameter becomes the target object of the message.

Similarly, unary built-in operators remain unary when they are overloaded. If a unary overloaded operator is implemented as a global nonmember unary operator (e.g., a friend), it will have one parameter. If this overloaded operator is defined as a member function (which is sent as a message to a target object), it will have no parameters.

As a simple example, consider class `Account` similar to one discussed in Chapter 13, "Similar Classes: How to Treat Them." The class maintains information about the owner name and the current balance and supports services that allow the client code to access the values of object data members and carry out deposits and withdrawals.

In addition to four inline member functions, the class has a general constructor. The class does not need a default constructor, since `Account` objects will be created on the heap only when they are needed. The default constructor might be useful only if class objects were created in advance, when the name of the owner and the initial balance are not yet known.

Since the class manages memory dynamically, it would be a good idea to add to it the copy constructor and the assignment operator or, better yet, make the prototypes of these member functions private (see Chapter 11 for more details). For the simplicity of the example, I am not doing that here because I am not passing `Account` objects by value, I do not initialize one `Account` object from the data of another `Account` object, and I do not assign one `Account` object to another `Account` object. In real life, it would be important to protect `Account` objects from accidental abuse.

```
class Account {                                    // base class of hierarchy
protected:
  double balance;                                  // protected data
  char *owner;
public:
  Account(const char* name, double initBalance)    // general
  { owner = new char[strlen(name)+1];              // allocate heap space
    if (owner == 0) { cout << "\nOut of memory\n";  exit(0); }
    strcpy(owner, name);                           // initialize data fields
    balance = initBalance; }
  double getBal() const                            // common for both accounts
  { return balance; }
  const char* getOwner() const                     // protect data from changes
  { return owner; }
  void withdraw(double amount)
  { balance -= amount; }                           // pop responsibility up
  void deposit(double amount)
  { balance += amount; } } ;                       // increment unconditionally
```

I am going to create an array of `Account` pointers, create `Account` objects dynamically, initialize them, search for an account that belongs to a given owner, and deposit and withdraw funds. Again, for simplicity of the example, I will use hardwired data rather than data loaded from an external file.

Listing 16.1 shows the source code for the example. Function `createAccount()` creates an `Account` object dynamically, calls the `Account` constructor with two parameters, and returns the pointer to the newly allocated object. Function `processRequest()` sets up the `ios` flags for printing floating point numbers in the fixed format and with the trailing zeros, searches the customer name within the objects and prints a message if the name is not found. Otherwise, the function prompts the user for the transaction code, requests the transaction amount and performs the transaction (deposit or withdrawal).

The `main()` function defines an array of `Account` pointers and calls `createAccount()` to created `Account` objects. In a loop, it prompts the user to enter the customer name and calls `processRequest()` to process the transaction. An example of the program run is shown in Figure 16–1.

> **Listing 16.1   Example of handling class** `Account` **with programmer-named methods.**

```cpp
#include <iostream>
using namespace std;

class Account {                                    // base class of hierarchy
protected:
  double balance;                                  // protected data
  char *owner;
public:

  Account(const char* name, double initBalance)    // general
  { owner = new char[strlen(name)+1];              // allocate heap space
    if (owner == 0) { cout << "\nOut of memory\n";  exit(0); }
    strcpy(owner, name);                           // initialize data fields
    balance = initBalance; }

  double getBal() const                            // common for both accounts
  { return balance; }

  const char* getOwner() const                     // protect data from changes
  { return owner; }

  void withdraw(double amount)
  { balance -= amount; }                           // pull responsibility up

  void deposit(double amount)
  { balance += amount; }                           // increment unconditionally
} ;

Account* createAccount(const char* name, double bal)
{ Account* a = new Account(name,bal);              // account on the heap
  if (a == 0) { cout << "\nOut of memory\n";  exit(0); }
  return a; }

void processRequest(Account* a[], const char name[])
{ int i;  int choice;  double amount;
  cout.setf(ios::fixed,ios::floatfield);
  cout.precision(2);
  for (i=0; a[i] != 0;  i++)
  { if (strcmp(a[i]->getOwner(),name)==0)          // search for name
      { cout << "Account balance: " << a[i]->getBal() << endl;
        cout <<"Enter 1 to deposit, 2 to withdraw, 3 to cancel: ";
        cin >> choice;                             // transaction type
        if (choice != 1 && choice != 2) break;     // get out
        cout << "Enter amount: ";
        cin >> amount;                             // transaction amount
        switch (choice) {                          // select further path
```

```
      case 1: a[i]->deposit(amount);              // unconditional
              break;
      case 2: if (amount <= a[i]->getBal())       // enough funds?
                 a[i]->withdraw(amount);
              else
                cout << "Insufficient funds\n";
                break; }                          // end of switch scope
      cout << "New balance: "<< a[i]->getBal() << endl;   // OK
      break; } }                                  // end of search loop
   if (a[i] == 0)
      { cout << "Customer is not found\n"; } }

int main()
{
  Account* accounts[100];  char name[80];         // program data
  accounts[0] = createAccount("Jones",5000);      // create objects
  accounts[1] = createAccount("Smith",3000);
  accounts[2] = createAccount("Green",1000);
  accounts[3] = createAccount("Brown",1000);
  accounts[4] = 0;
  while (true) // process requests
  { cout << "Enter customer name ('exit' to exit): ";
    cin >> name;                                  // accept name
    if (strcmp(name,"exit")==0) break;            // test for end
    processRequest(accounts, name);               // next transaction
       }
  return 0;
  }
```

```
Enter customer name ('exit' to exit): Brown
Account balance: 1000.00
Enter 1 to deposit, 2 to withdraw, 3 to cancel: 2
Enter amount: 2000
Insufficient funds
New balance: 1000.00
Enter customer name ('exit' to exit): Brown
Account balance: 1000.00
Enter 1 to deposit, 2 to withdraw, 3 to cancel: 2
Enter amount: 500
New balance: 500.00
Enter customer name ('exit' to exit): Smith
Account balance: 3000.00
Enter 1 to deposit, 2 to withdraw, 3 to cancel: 1
Enter amount: 2000
New balance: 5000.00
Enter customer name ('exit' to exit): Simons
Customer is not found
Enter customer name ('exit' to exit): exit
```

Figure 16–1   Output for program in Listing 16.1.

In this example, class `Account` relies on its client code to check whether the withdrawal transaction is legitimate. The advantage of this approach is that the `Account` member functions are not involved in the user interface; they are responsible for the access to `Account` data members only. The disadvantage of this approach is that the data is popped up to the client code for further handling instead of pushing responsibility down to the server code. The reason why I chose this design is that it lends itself better to using overloaded operators.

The first candidates for becoming overloaded operators are `Account` member functions `deposit()` and `withdraw()`. All that it takes to convert them into operator functions is to cut out their current names (`deposit` and `withdraw`) and move in their new names (`operator+=` and `operator-=`). No other changes are necessary.

```
void operator -= (double amount)
{ balance -= amount; }              // client tests feasibility

void operator += (double amount)
{ balance += amount; }              // increment unconditionally
```

Instead of calling the `deposit()` and `withdraw()` member functions, the client function `processRequest()` will be able to use the expression syntax where the operator is inserted between the left operand (message target) and the right operand (message parameter).

```
switch (choice) {
   case 1: *a[i] += amount;         // a[i]->deposit(amount);
           break;
   case 2: if (amount <= a[i]->getBal())
              *a[i] -= amount;      // a[i]->withdraw(amount);
           else
              cout << "Insufficient funds\n";
           break; }
```

Notice that the target of the message is an `Account` pointer, and hence it has to be dereferenced when used in expressions. This is an inconvenience but is not very serious. At least not more serious than deciding whether you should use the dot selector operator (when the message target is an object or a reference) or the arrow selector operator (when the target is a pointer).

The real meaning of the expression syntax is, of course, a function call, a message sent to the left operand in the expression: `a[i]->operator+=(amount)` and `a[i]->operator-=(amount)`.

Listing 16.2 shows the program that uses the overloaded operator functions instead of programmer-named methods. It is similar to the program in

Listing 16.1. Before starting the interacting stage of processing, the `main()` function calls the function `printList()` that goes over the list of `Account` pointers and prints the contents of the objects pointed to by the pointers (see Figure 16–2). Notice the statements that format the names to be printed left justified and the account balances to be printed right justified.

Similar to `processRequest()`, the function `printList()` iterates through the list until the null pointer (this pointer plays the role of the sentinel value) is found in the array. Notice the difference in the loop headers in these two functions. In `printList()`, the index i is local to the loop. In `processRequest()`, the index is global to the loop. (It is local to the function scope.) The reason for the difference is that the index value is not needed after the loop in `printList()`: Iterations are always from the beginning of the list to the end. In `processRequest()`, the iteration might be stopped before the end of the list is reached (if the name is found), and `processRequest()` needs to know about it.

Listing 16.2   Example of handling class `Account` with overloaded operator methods.

```
#include <iostream>
using namespace std;

class Account {                                    // base class of hierarchy
protected:
  double balance;                                  // protected data
  char *owner;
public:

  Account(const char* name, double initBalance)    // general
  { owner = new char[strlen(name)+1];              // allocate heap space
    if (owner == 0) { cout << "\nOut of memory\n";  exit(0); }
        strcpy(owner, name);                       // initialize data fields
        balance = initBalance; }

  double getBal() const                            // common for both accounts
  { return balance; }

  const char* getOwner() const                     // protect data from changes
  { return owner; }

  void operator -= (double amount)
  { balance -= amount; }                           // pull responsibility up

  void operator += (double amount)
  { balance += amount; }                           // increment unconditionally
} ;
```

```
Account* createAccount(const char* name, double bal)
{ Account* a = new Account(name,bal);                     // account on the heap
  if (a == 0) { cout << "\nOut of memory\n";   exit(0); }
  return a; }

void processRequest(Account* a[], const char name[])
{ int i;   int choice;   double amount;
  cout.setf(ios::fixed,ios::floatfield);
  cout.precision(2);
  for (i=0;   a[i] != 0;   i++)
  { if (strcmp(a[i]->getOwner(),name)==0)                 // search for name
      { cout << "Account balance: " << a[i]->getBal() << endl;
        cout <<"Enter 1 to deposit, 2 to withdraw, 3 to cancel: ";
        cin >> choice;                                    // transaction type
        if (choice != 1 && choice != 2) break;
          cout << "Enter amount: ";
          cin >> amount;                                  // transaction amount
          switch (choice) {
            case 1: *a[i] += amount;                      // a[i]->operator+=(amount);
                    break;
            case 2: if (amount <= a[i]->getBal())
                       *a[i] -= amount;                   // a[i]->operator-=(amount);
                    else
                       cout << "Insufficient funds\n";
                    break; }                              // end of switch scope
          cout << "New balance: "<< a[i]->getBal() << endl;
        break; } }                                        // end of search loop
    if (a[i] == 0)
      { cout << "Customer is not found\n"; } }

void printList (Account* a[])
{ cout << "Customer List:\n\n";
  for (int i=0;   a[i] != 0;   i++)
  { cout.setf(ios::left, ios::adjustfield); cout.width(30);
    cout << a[i]->getOwner();
    cout.setf(ios::right, ios::adjustfield); cout.width(10);
    cout << a[i]->getBal() << endl; }
  cout << endl; }

int main()
{
  Account* accounts[100];   char name[80];                // program data
  accounts[0] = createAccount("Jones",5000);              // create objects
  accounts[1] = createAccount("Smith",3000);
  accounts[2] = createAccount("Green",1000);
  accounts[3] = createAccount("Brown",1000);
  accounts[4] = 0;
  printList(accounts);
  while (true)                                            // process requests
  { cout << "Enter customer name ('exit' to exit): ";
```

```
    cin >> name;                            // accept name
        if (strcmp(name,"exit")==0) break;  // test for end
        processRequest(accounts, name);     // next transaction
        }
    return 0;
    }
```

Implementing overloaded operators as global functions is simple: The target of the message becomes the first function parameter. Instead of data members of the target object, the operators use data members of the first parameter. Here are the two operators implemented as global functions.

```
void operator -= (Account &a, double amount)    // global function
  { a.balance -= amount; }                      // pop responsibility up

void operator += (Account &a, double amount)
  { a.balance += amount; }                      // increment unconditionally
```

Since these two functions access nonpublic members of class Account, they should be declared as friends of class Account. Some programmers view this as an annoyance, as it requires additional work. As I mentioned earlier, the modern approach to programming does not view additional writing as a shortcoming if it results in more understandable code. You write additional declarations only once, but you (and others) read them many times in the course of program development, testing, and maintenance.

In this case, adding friend function declarations to the class clearly indicates that these functions belong to this class. They belong to the class physically; that is, they cannot be used without objects of class Account. They belong to the class conceptually; that is, they are part of operations provided by the class. The

Figure 16–2   Output for program in Listing 16.2.

```
Customer List:

Jones                    5000.00
Smith                    3000.00
Green                    1000.00
Brown                    1000.00

Enter customer name ('exit' to exit): Smith
Account balance: 3000.00
Enter 1 to deposit, 2 to withdraw, 3 to cancel: 1
Enter amount: 1000
New balance: 4000.00
Enter customer name ('exit' to exit): exit
```

syntax of friend functions is different from the syntax of member functions, but this is a minor technical peculiarity. Frequent accusations against using friend functions, breaking of encapsulation and development of extra dependencies between parts of the program, are nonissues for overloaded operator functions.

```
class Account {                                   // base class of hierarchy
protected:
        double balance;                           // protected data
        char *owner;
public:
  Account(const char* name, double initBalance)   // general
  { owner = new char[strlen(name)+1];             // allocate heap space
    if (owner == 0) { cout << "\nOut of memory\n";  exit(0); }
    strcpy(owner, name);                          // initialize data fields
    balance = initBalance; }
  double getBal() const                           // common for both accounts
  { return balance; }
  const char* getOwner() const                    // protect data from changes
  { return owner; }
friend void operator-= (Account &a, double amount);   // operators
friend void operator+= (Account &a, double amount);
} ;
```

The expression syntax in client code does not change with the switch from member function operators to friend operators.

```
switch (choice) {
  case 1: *a[i] += amount;              // operator+=(*a[i],amount);
          break;
  case 2: if (amount <= a[i]->getBal())
              *a[i] -= amount;          // operator-=(*a[i],amount);
          else
            cout << "Insufficient funds\n";
          break; }                      // end of switch scope
```

The meaning of this code changes. The expression syntax is still a syntactic sugar for a function call, but it is a call to a global function. There is no need for the target object in the function call. Instead, the object that participates in the operation is passed as the actual argument to the function. This is how the compiler perceives this client code.

```
switch (choice) {
  case 1: operator+=(*a[i],amount);     // a.k.a. *a[i]+=amount;
          break;
  case 2: if (amount <= a[i]->getBal())
              operator-=(*a[i],amount); // a.k.a. *a[i]-=amount;
          else
            cout << "Insufficient funds\n";
          break; }                      // end of switch scope
```

Notice that the actual argument has to be dereferenced because a[i] is a pointer to an Account object, not an object itself. The reference argument has to be initialized with the value of an object, not with the value of a pointer. This is why this function call needs dereferencing.

The use of overloaded operators offers us a very nice way to write client code, but it does not solve any essential software engineering issues. Everything that can be done with the use of overloaded operators can be done with the use of conventional member functions, as Listing 16.1 clearly attests to.

Unary Operators

Unary operators have only one operand. They include increment and decrement operators, negation operators, logical and bitwise negation, positive and negative sign operators, cast, address, and dereference operators, and operators new, delete, and sizeof. All these operators (with the exception of sizeof) can be overloaded.

Of course, not every operator can have its own special meaning for every class. In Chapter 10, I overloaded the positive sign operator for class Complex as an output operator, and this design is confusing. This is why overloading of unary operators is not very popular. However, there are some situations where these operators can contribute to intuitive understanding of the client code. In this section, I will discuss several examples of overloaded unary operators.

Increment and Decrement Operators

Increment and decrement operators are very popular in C++. They are especially popular in text processing, where incrementing (or decrementing) a pointer can be combined with access to the current character for processing.

```
void printString(const char data[])      // text does not change
{ const char *p = data;                   // point to start of data
  while (*p != 0)                          // go until the end of data
  { cout << *p;                            // print current character
    ++p; }                                 // point to next character
  cout << endl; }
```

In this example, the character array is passed to the global function (as a constant), and each character is displayed in turn. The pointer p is first set to point to the first character of the array data[] and then is incremented until it points to the terminating zero. Even though it looks like a very low-level control construct that increments the memory address, in reality this operation is rather abstract because it does not reveal the real details of storage management—by how much the address is changed and whether it is actually incremented or decremented.

For example, there is no guarantee that an argument array is located in memory from lower addresses to higher addresses. On my machine, physical addresses decrease to the end of the array. Hence, there is no guarantee that the contents of the pointer are actually increased when the increment operator is applied to the pointer. What it implies is that the pointer is set to access the next array component, no matter what size the component is (it can be larger than one) or in what direction the pointer moves.

Nevertheless, this "open" access to array components by the client code is error prone. Accesses to locations outside of array boundaries are not flagged as syntax errors at compile time. These accesses might crash the program at run time, they can quietly produce incorrect results, or they can quietly produce correct results until some later time when the use of memory changes and disaster strikes.

Combining data and operations together in a class protects data from inept access from client programmers and gives client programmers the tools for handling objects that prevent mistakes. Here is an example of class `String` that is similar to one discussed in Chapter 11.

```
class String {
  int size;                          // string size
  char *str;                         // start of internal string
  void set(const char* s);           // private string allocation
public:
  String (const char* s = "")        // default and conversion
    { set(s); }
  String (const String &s)           // copy constructor
    { set(s.str); }
  ~String()                          // destructor
  { delete [ ] str; }
  String& operator = (const String& s);   // assignment
 int getSize() const;                // current string length
 char* reset() const; } ;            // reset to start of string
```

The class data member `str` points to a dynamically allocated array whose size is stored in the data member `size`. The private member function `set()` is used by class constructors and the assignment operator. This function accepts a character array (labeled as constant) as an argument, allocates heap memory dynamically, sets the data member pointers `str` to point to that newly allocated memory, and initializes dynamically allocated memory using the text array supplied as argument.

```
void String::set(const char* s)
  { size = strlen(s);                  // evaluate size
    str = new char[size + 1];          // request heap memory
    if (str == 0) { cout << "Out of memory\n"; exit(0); }
    strcpy(str,s); }                   // copy client data to heap
```

This is a typical design for dynamic memory management. This private function is convenient because it encapsulates the operations common to the constructors and the assignment operator.

As befitting a class that manages its memory dynamically, class String provides a conversion constructor (which doubles as a default constructor because of the default parameter value), a copy constructor, an assignment operator, and a destructor. The default constructor passes to set() an empty string. The conversion constructor passes to set() its own character array parameter. The copy constructor passes to set() the heap memory of its argument object. The destructor returns the heap memory allocated for the String object by a constructor or by an assignment operator.

This complement of member functions supports the use of String objects in a variety of contexts. Client code can define a String object as a noninitialized variable (the default constructor is called), as an object initialized with a character array value (the conversion constructor is used), or as an object initialized with the data from another existing String object (the copy constructor is called).

The assignment operator is intelligent. It supports the assignment of an object to itself (by checking whether the this pointer points to the location of the actual argument). It deletes the existing heap memory and allocates and initializes new heap memory by calling set(). It supports the client code that uses the expression syntax for multiple chain assignments (by returning the reference to the target String object). Notice that even though the body of the assignment returns the whole String object (dereferenced pointer this), it is only a reference to the object that is returned—there is no copying.

```
String& String::operator = (const String& s)
{ if (this == &s) return *this;          // no work if self-assignment
  delete [ ] str;                        // return existing memory
  set(s.str);                            // allocate/set new memory
  return *this; }                        // to support chain assignment
```

Listing 16.3 shows the complete implementation of class String (together with inline member functions getSize() and reset()). The first function returns the maximum number of symbols a `String` object can contain, and the second function returns the pointer to the internal string, so that the client code (functions `printString()` and `modifyString()`) can initialize the external pointer that points to the internal string.

These two client functions use the increment operator to retrieve and replace the symbols inside their parameter `String` objects. The loop in `printString()` continues until the terminating zero is found in the internal string of the `String` parameter. (The pointer `p` to the internal string character has to be dereferenced.) The loop in `modifyString()` continues until all characters in the parameter character array `text[]` have been copied.

The `main()` function creates and initializes a `String` object, prints its contents, modifies its contents, and then prints again. Since the loop in `modifyString()` does not take into account the current size of the heap memory allocated to its `String` parameter, this results in memory corruption. The output of the program is shown in Figure 16–3.

Listing 16.3   Example of using the increment operator with a pointer to internal data.

```
#include <iostream>
using namespace std;

class String {
  int size;                             // string size
  char *str;                            // start of internal string
  void set(const char* s);              // private string allocation
public:
  String (const char* s = "")           // default and conversion
    { set(s); }
  String (const String &s)              // copy constructor
    { set(s.str); }
  ~String()                             // destructor
  { delete [ ] str; }
  String& operator = (const String& s); // assignment
  int getSize() const;                  // current string length
  char* reset() const; } ;              // reset to start of string

void String::set(const char* s)
  { size = strlen(s);                   // evaluate size
    str = new char[size + 1];           // request heap memory
    if (str == 0) { cout << "Out of memory\n"; exit(0); }
    strcpy(str,s); }                    // copy client data to heap

String& String::operator = (const String& s)
{ if (this == &s) return *this;         // no work if self-assignment
  delete [ ] str;                       // return existing memory
```

```
  set(s.str);                                  // allocate/set new memory
  return *this; }                              // to support chain assignment

int String::getSize() const                    // no change to String object
{ return size; }

char* String::reset() const                     // no change to String object
{ return str; }                                 // return pointer to start

void printString(const String& data)            // no change to string
{ char *p = data.reset();                        // point to first character
  while (*p != 0)                                // go until end of characters
  { cout << *p;                                  // print the current character
    ++p; }                                       // point to the next character
  cout << endl; }

void modifyString(const String& data, const char text[])    // bad
{ char *p = data.reset();                        // point to first character
  int len = strlen(text) + 1;                    // set the iteration limit
  for (int i=0;  i < len;  i++)                  // go over each character
  { *p = text[i];                                // copy the current character
    ++p; } }                                     // point to the next character

int main()
{
  String data = "Hello World!";
  printString(data);                             // good output
  modifyString(data,"How is the weather?");
  printString(data);                             // memory is corrupted
  return 0;
  }
```

This problem is not too difficult to correct. The client code, modifyString(), should check for the space available and stop pumping data into the object when the limit is reached.

Figure 16–3   Example of memory corruption by program in Listing 16.3.

> **Hello World!**
> **How is the weather?**

```
void modifyString(const String& data, const char text[])    // ok
{ char *p = data.reset();              // point to first character
  int len = strlen(text) + 1;          // set one the iteration limit
  int size = data.getSize();           // set another iteration limit
  for (int i=0; i<len && i<size; i++)  // go over each character
  { *p = text[i];                      // copy the current character
    ++p; } }                           // point to the next character
```

This `modifyString()` function eliminates the problem of memory corruption. It does not eliminate the design flaw: The responsibility for understanding the details of the server (in this case, `String`) design is popped up to the client code, not pushed down to the server class. Solving this problem by using overloaded operator functions might be useful.

The `String` design should reflect this change of attitude. To be able to protect its object from client abuse, class `String` should maintain the state of its objects. In this case, the state should include a pointer to the current character being printed or being modified.

This is an important technique of design with C++. When you decide what data the class should maintain, always include data members that reflect the state of the object for the client (it is not nice to depend on the kindness of client code designers). This technique will free your objects from this dependency (something I failed to do in Listing 16.3). Here is a better version of class `String`.

```
class String {
  int size;                            // string size
  char *str;                           // start of internal string
  char *ptr;                           // pointer to current symbol
  void set(const char* s);             // private string allocation
public:
  String (const char* s = "")          // default and conversion
    { set(s); }
  String (const String &s)             // copy constructor
    { set(s.str); }
  ~String()                            // destructor
    { delete [ ] str; }
  String& operator = (const String& s);  // assignment
  char* operator++();                  // prefix increment operator
  int getSize() const;                 // current string length
  char* reset(); } ;                   // no const: object changes
```

Here, pointer `ptr` points to the current symbol. This pointer is driven along the heap memory in the increment operator, which returns the address of the current symbol for the client to access or to modify. The increment operator checks whether the client request drives the pointer `ptr` off the heap character array. If it does, the operator does not increment the pointer. Instead, it sets the character pointed to by the pointer to "\0" to make sure that the character array is always properly terminated. Again, I use the expression `ptr-str<size`, but this does not mean that the address value in the data member `ptr` is indeed larger than the address value in the data member `str`. It is just a nice way to express the pointer displacement without getting into any messy details of physical storage management.

```
char* String::operator ++()        // increment then access
{ if (ptr-str < size)              // check if room is available
    return ++ptr;                  // pointer to next character
  else
      { *ptr = 0;                   // set the terminating zero
        return ptr; } }            // do not move it if at end
```

A good place to initialize this pointer is in the member function `reset()`. It can be called by the client code before the start of the next iteration through the text. The important difference between this design and the previous design in Listing 16.3 is that in this version, function `reset()` cannot be labeled as constant—it modifies the state of the object. Always pay attention to the mode of method behavior, and do not neglect to label the member function appropriately. (This issue is not relevant for nonmember functions.)

```
char* String::reset()              // no const: object changes
{ ptr = str;                       // set current pointer to start
  return str; }                    // return pointer to start
```

Some programmers feel uncomfortable when a data member is not initialized to a specific value when the object is created. These programmers would also initialize the data member `ptr` in each constructor call. In this design, where each constructor calls the private function `set()`, it can be done in this function:

```
void String::set(const char* s)
    { size = strlen(s);            // evaluate size
      str = new char[size + 1];    // request heap memory
      if (str == 0) { cout << "Out of memory\n"; exit(0); }
      strcpy(str,s);               // copy client data to heap
      ptr = str;    }              // initialize running pointer
```

What does this design achieve? From the moment the object is born, it is ready for the iteration. There is no need to explicitly send the `reset()` message to it. This is a very good philosophy: the responsibility is shifted from the client code (which should call `reset()` in the previous design) to the object constructor.

This idea works well with the read-only access to the `String` object data. The `printString()` function stops the iteration when the terminating zero is found, and the increment operator could recognize that and set the running pointer back to the beginning of the string.

```
char* String::operator ++()        // increment then access
{ if (ptr-str < size)              // check if room is available
    return ++ptr;                  // pointer to next character
  else
    { *ptr = 0;                    // set the terminating zero
      ptr = str;                   // point to start of data again
      return ptr; } }              // do not move it if at end
```

This eliminates the need for the member function `reset()` and removes the client responsibility to call it. After each scan through the data of the `String` object, the pointer would be reset, and the object would be ready for the next scan.

```
void printString(String& data)     // no const: string changes
{ char *p = data.reset();          // is this call really needed?
  while (*p != 0)                  // go until end of characters
  { cout << *p;                    // print the current character
    p = ++data; }                  // nice syntax: object changes
  cout << endl; }
```

In my design, however, function `reset()` is still needed because the client function `modifyString()` can try to access the string data beyond its legal bound. Since the increment operator has no knowledge of how long the client code will be supplying new data for copying into the string, it cannot move the pointer to the beginning of data.

Of course, all these problems stem from the arrogant nature of the function `modifyString()`, which pumps data into its parameter `String` object without regard for available space.

```
void modifyString(String& data, const char text[])    // no const
{ char *p = data.reset();          // point to first character
  int len = strlen(text) + 1;      // set the iteration limit
  for (int i=0;  i < len;  i++)    // go over each character
  { *p = text[i];                  // copy the current character
    p = ++data; } }                // point to the next character
```

Notice that the parameter object `data` does not have the `const` modifier, but not because the function `modifyString()` writes new contents to its heap memory. In Listing 16.3, the function `modifyString()` does the same thing, but the parameter data is labeled as `const`. C++ is oblivious to the changes to the heap memory of the object but is sensitive to the changes to the data members of the object. The increment operator (and the reset() function) causes changes to the data member ptr and hence prevents the use of the const modifier with the String parameter.

Listing 16.4 shows the complete program that implements the increment operator for the String class. The output of the program is shown in Figure 16–4. As you see, the memory corruption problem went away.

Listing 16.4	Example of using the increment operator as a message to the object.

```
#include <iostream>
using namespace std;

class String {
    int size;                                    // string size
    char *str;                                   // start of internal string
    char *ptr;                                   // pointer to current symbol
    void set(const char* s);                     // private string allocation
public:
    String (const char* s = "")                  // default and conversion
        { set(s); }
    String (const String &s)                     // copy constructor
        { set(s.str); }
    ~String()                                    // destructor
    { delete [ ] str; }
    String& operator = (const String& s);        // assignment
    char* operator++();                          // prefix increment operator
    int getSize() const;                         // current string length
    char* reset(); } ;                           // no const: object changes

void String::set(const char* s)
    { size = strlen(s);                          // evaluate size
      str = new char[size + 1];                  // request heap memory
      if (str == 0) { cout << "Out of memory\n"; exit(0); }
      strcpy(str,s);                             // copy client data to heap
      ptr = str;      }                          // initialize running pointer

String& String::operator = (const String& s)
{ if (this == &s) return *this;                  // no work if self-assignment
    delete [ ] str;                              // return existing memory
    set(s.str);                                  // allocate/set new memory
    return *this; }                              // to support chain assignment

int String::getSize() const                      // no change to String object
{ return size; }
```

```
char* String::reset()                // no const: object changes
{ ptr = str;                         // set current pointer to start
  return str; }                      // return pointer to start

char* String::operator ++()          // increment then access
{ if (ptr-str < size)                // check if room is available
    return ++ptr;                    // pointer to next character
  else
     { *ptr = 0;                      // set the terminating zero
       return ptr; } }               // do not move it if at end

void printString(String& data)       // no const: string changes
{ char *p = data.reset();            // point to first character
  while (*p != 0)                     // go until end of characters
  { cout << *p;                       // print the current character
    p = ++data; }                    // point to the next character
  cout << endl; }

void modifyString(String& data, const char text[])
{ char *p = data.reset();            // point to first character
  int len = strlen(text) + 1;        // set the iteration limit
  for (int i=0;  i < len;  i++)       // go over each character
  { *p = text[i];                     // copy the current character
    p = ++data; } }                  // point to the next character

int main()
{
  String data = "Hello World!";
  printString(data);                 // good output
  modifyString(data,"How is the weather?");
  printString(data);                 // memory is NOT corrupted
  return 0;
  }
```

Of course, the use of the increment operator provides for nice syntax. This is why these operators are so popular. Two side comments about this example are in order. First, the overloaded increment operator checks the index boundary conditions, something that the built-in increment operator cannot do. By doing that in the operator, responsibilities are pushed down to the server class. However, it is the boundary check that makes this example nice, not that it is an increment operator that allows for the nice syntax in

Figure 16–4   Output of program in Listing 16.4.

```
Hello World!
How is the w
```

`printString()` and `modifyString()`. The same boundary check could be performed if the name of the function were `movePointer()` or `next()` rather than `operator++()`.

Second, this implementation of the increment operator returns a pointer to the current character in the heap memory and lets the client do with this pointer whatever the client wants. This is a dangerous and error-prone practice. Later on in this chapter, I will show you less offensive ways to do that.

Decrement operators are built similarly to increment operators. There are no new principles or ideas involved in their implementation.

Postfix Overloaded Operators

In C++, built-in prefix and postfix unary operators are distinguished by their position relative to the operand of the expression. If the expression is written as `++data`, it is a prefix operator. If the expression is written as `data++`, it is a postfix operator. It is important to distinguish between them.

The same is true of overloaded increment and decrement operators. The increment operator was implemented as a prefix operator in Listing 16.4: The state of the target object was changed first, and then the new value (of the current pointer) was returned by the use of the client code.

This is not appropriate for postfix operators. A postfix operator for class `String`, for example, has to first return the current value of the pointer and then increment this value (for future use). Hence, this should be a separate function, different from the increment operator implemented in Listing 16.4.

What is the name of this separate function? Well, according to the C++ rules, it has to be composed out of the keyword `operator` and the symbol(s) that comprise the operator, in this case, either `++` or `--`. It looks as if the name of the postfix overloaded increment operator should be `operator++()`. Similarly, the name of the postfix overloaded decrement operator should be `operator--()`.

But these are exactly the same names that should be used for the prefix overloaded operators! It is illegal to have two functions with the same name in the same scope, unless, of course, these functions have different signatures—a different number or different types of parameters.

As I mentioned earlier, the number of parameters for overloaded operators cannot be chosen arbitrarily, at the whim of the programmer. If a binary operator is implemented as a member function, its first operand plays the role of the target of the message, and its second operand plays the role of the message parameter. If a unary operator is implemented as a member function, its only operand should be used as the target of the message. Such an over-loaded operator cannot have parameters.

So, we would like to implement in the same class two overloaded operators with the same name (e.g., `operator++`) and the same signature (no parame-ters). This is, of course, asking for trouble. The compiler is going to complain that it cannot distinguish between the two.

But, of course, C++ programmers demand that increment and decrement operators could be implemented both in the prefix form and in the postfix form. To resolve this problem, C++ come up with a fix: a dummy integer parameter.

```
char* String::operator ++(int)      // access first then increment
{ if (ptr-str < size)               // check if room is available
    return ptr++;                    // pointer to next character
  else
    { *ptr = 0;                      // set the terminating zero
      return ptr; } }                // do not move it if at end
```

The role of the dummy parameter is very limited: It has to tell the compil-er that this function is a genuinely different function, not a redefinition of the overloaded increment (or decrement) operator with no parameters. On the other hand, this parameter has no role within the function body itself. This is why you can omit the parameter name—the compiler will not indicate that the name is not specified.

With these two functions in place, the compiler finds `++data` in the client code, it is interpreted as `data.operator++()`, and the prefix operation is per-formed. When the compiler finds `++data` in the client code, it is interpreted as `data.operator++(0)`, and the postfix operation is performed. The prefix meaning of `operator++()` and the postfix meaning of `operator++(int)` are not enforced by the language. It is the class designer who is responsible for their contents.

Listing 16.5 shows the program from Listing 16.4 with the postfix over-loaded operator, which is called from `modifyString()`. The postfix operator returns a pointer to the current symbol in heap memory. To change this sym-bol, the client code has to dereference the value returned from the function. This results in neat syntax of the assignment, which is exactly the same as if the variable `data` were a pointer.

```
*data++ = text[i];                  // copy character
```

The output of this version of the program is, of course, the same as for Listing 16.4 (see Figure 16–4).

Listing 16.5   Example of using the prefix and postfix increment operators.

```
#include <iostream>
using namespace std;

class String {
  int size;                              // string size
  char *str;                             // start of internal string
  char *ptr;                             // pointer to current symbol

  void set(const char* s);               // private string allocation
public:
  String (const char* s = "")            // default and conversion
    { set(s); }
  String (const String &s)               // copy constructor
    { set(s.str); }
  ~String()                              // destructor
  { delete [ ] str; }
  String& operator = (const String& s);  // assignment
  char* operator++();                    // prefix increment operator
  char* operator++(int);                 // postfix increment operator
  int getSize() const;                   // current string length
  char* reset(); } ;                     // no const: object changes

void String::set(const char* s)
  { size = strlen(s);                    // evaluate size
    str = new char[size + 1];            // request heap memory
    if (str == 0) { cout << "Out of memory\n"; exit(0); }
    strcpy(str,s);                       // copy client data to heap
    ptr = str;    }                      // initialize running pointer

String& String::operator - (const String& s)
{ if (this == &s) return *this;          // no work if self-assignment
  delete [ ] str;                        // return existing memory
  set(s.str);                            // allocate/set new memory
  return *this; }                        // to support chain assignment

int String::getSize() const             // no change to String object
{ return size; }

char* String::reset()                    // no const: object changes
{ ptr = str;                             // set current pointer to start
  return str; }                          // return pointer to start

char* String::operator ++()              // increment then access
{ if (ptr-str < size)                    // check if room is available
    return ++ptr;                        // pointer to next character
  else
      { *ptr = 0;                         // set the terminating zero
    return ptr; } }                      // do not move it if at end
```

```
char* String::operator ++(int)        // access then increment
{ if (ptr-str < size)                 // check if room is available
     return ptr++;                     // pointer to next character
   else
        { *ptr = 0;                    // set the terminating zero
          return ptr; } }              // do not move it if at end

void printString(String& data)        // no const: string changes
{ char *p = data.reset();              // point to first character
  while (*p != 0)                      // go until end of characters
  { cout << *p;                        // print the current character
    p = ++data; }                      // point to the next character
  cout << endl; }

void modifyString(String& data, const char text[])
{ data.reset();                        // point to first character
  int len = strlen(text) + 1;          // set the iteration limit
  for (int i=0;  i < len;  i++)        // go over each character
     *data++ = text[i]; }              // nice syntax: copy character

int main()
{
   String data = "Hello World!";
   printString(data);                  // good output
   modifyString(data,"How is the weather?");
   printString(data);                  // memory is NOT corrupted
   return 0;
   }
```

As in the case of the prefix increment and decrement operators, the overloaded postfix operators improve the appearance of the program, but they are not very important from a software engineering point of view.

Conversion Operators

Casting a value of one type into a value of another type is achieved by applying the name of the target type to the value (for the name of the variable) of the source type. There are two forms of syntax: traditional syntax and the new function-like syntax. With traditional syntax, the name of the target type (in parentheses) is used in front of the source value (or variable). With the new function-like syntax, the name of the target type is used as if it were a function with one parameter, and the source value (or variable) is used as the actual argument to the function.

```
int x; double y;
x = int ('A');              // function-like syntax; x contains 65
y = (double)x;              // traditional syntax, y contains 65.0
double *p = &y;             // correct pointer type: this is safe
int *q = (int*)p;           // int q points to double y: trouble
```

The only difference between these two forms of casting is that the traditional syntax can be used with any legitimate type name, and the function-like syntax requires an identifier for the type name. This is why in the last example, there are two examples of casts among numeric types and only one example of a cast among pointers. The type name `int*` is a legitimate type name but it is not a legitimate identifier.

C++ allows casts between any numeric types without any restrictions. These casts can be explicit (with the use of cast operator), or implicit (without the use the operator).

```
int x; double y;
x = 'A';   y = x;          // implicit casts: no problem in C++
```

C++ also allows casts between arbitrary pointers (and references), including any programmer-defined types. These conversions can be done employing explicit casts only; implicit casts between pointers are not allowed. Using these casts is almost always asking for trouble. In this segment of code, a `String` pointer points to an integer. The `String` pointer can legally respond to any `String` message. In doing so, it will interpret the memory as if it belonged to a `String` object. Since the first `String` data member is an integer `size`, the message `getSize()` will retrieve the value at the start of the `String` object. Actually, this is the value in the integer variable `z`. If the first data member in the `String` class were not an integer, this code would display gibberish.

```
int z = 42; String *ptr = (String*) &z;   // asking for trouble
cout <<"Size: " <<ptr->getSize() <<endl;  // it prints 42
```

In this segment of code, an integer pointer points to a `String` object. The pointer will interpret the memory of the `String` object as if it were an integer. The value retrieved by the pointer can be used in any expression that requires an integer value. In this example, the `String` object contains an integer data member `size` at its start, and this value is retrieved by the integer pointer. Had the `String` class started with a noninteger data member, this segment of code would print nonsense.

```
int *r; String s("Hello, World!");
r = (int*) &s;
cout << "String: " << 2 + *r << endl;      // it prints 15
```

Figure 16–5 shows the output of the program in Listing 16.5 with the code of these two segments added at the end. As you see, these operations interpret the memory layout for the `String` structure correctly and retrieve the first value in the `String` object that happened to be an integer data member. This is legal C++, but from the software engineering point of view, this is a maintainer's nightmare. If you change the order of data members in the class definition without making any other changes to the code, your output changes drastically.

The permission to cast arbitrary pointers and references is not extended to objects. You cannot convert an integer to an object of a programmer-defined class. You cannot convert an object of a programmer-defined class to an integer or to another numeric value or to an object of another programmer-defined class.

```
String s;   Account a;   int x;
x = s;   a = x;   s = a;                   // this is nonsense
```

C++ allows casts between pointers or references of classes related by inheritance. These casts can be implicit if the cast target (a pointer or a reference) is of the public base class and the cast source (value, pointer, or reference) is of a class publicly derived from the cast target. They are particularly useful when objects of different derived classes are pointed to by an array of pointers of the base class. Insertion of these objects into the array can be done without explicit conversion.

Casts from the base pointer (or reference) to a derived class pointer (or references) must be explicit, similar to casts between unrelated types. They are particularly useful when a derived class object is pointed to by the base class pointer (or reference) but has to perform operations that are defined in the derived class and not in a base class. The explicit cast indicates to what derived class the requested operation belongs.

Casts from a base object to a derived object are not allowed. This is similar to how objects of unrelated types are treated. If necessary, this conversion might be allowed by adding a conversion constructor to the derived class.

Figure 16–5 Output of the program in Listing 16.5 with two segments of code added.

```
Hello World!
How is the w
Size: 42
String: 15
```

This constructor should have a parameter of the base class. You saw examples of such casts and constructors in Chapter 15, "Virtual Functions and Other Advanced Uses of Inheritance."

For classes related by inheritance, C++ allows yet another break in strong typing. While implicit casts from a base object to a derived object are not allowed, the implicit conversions from derived class objects to the base class objects are permitted. The extra data members (and operations) of the derived object are stripped off without explicit cast.

In summary, C++ maintains strong typing only for objects of programmer-derived classes. For other types, conversions are allowed. Some conversions can be done only explicitly, with the cast operator (for pointers and references of any types). Other conversions can be done even implicitly, without explicit cast (between numeric values or from objects, pointers, and references of derived types to objects, pointers, and references of the base type). These conversions give the programmer additional flexibility in implementing algorithms that handle values of different types. Since these conversions break the strong typing, they remove the protection that the syntax checking gives us.

This is not enough, however. C++ allows the programmers to implement additional casts for objects of programmer-defined classes, the only category for which strong typing is maintained. Notice that the protection of syntax checking is not lifted summarily. It is lifted only for designated classes. The programmer designates the classes for which the protection is lifted by using conversion constructors and conversion operators.

I described conversion constructors in Chapter 9, "C++ Classes as a Unit of Modularization." The conversion constructor has one parameter of the type that should be converted to the given class. For example, class `string` has a conversion constructor that converts the value of a character array into a `String` value.

```
String (const char* s)              // conversion constructor
   { set(s); }
```

With this constructor in place, a character array can be used where a `String` object is expected without generating a compile-time syntax error. Since `String` is a programmer-defined class, the situations where a `String` object is expected are not numerous: They are limited to object definition, passing parameters by value (not by pointer or by reference), assignment, and sending messages to an object.

```
printString("Hi there");             // error: pass by reference
printString(String("Hi there"));     // OK: object is created
int sz = String("Hi there").getSize(); // object is created
```

The cast can be implicit (without the use of the cast operator) if the compiler can ascertain the identity of the type required, as in the assignment operator:

```
String s;
s = "Hi there";              // same as s = String("Hi there");
```

In all these cases, an unnamed String object is created on the stack, and the conversion constructor is called. The object is then deleted (with a call to the destructor). C++ does not specify the exact moment when the object is destroyed. The compiler writer has to make sure that the object does exist immediately after its use, and that it disappears before the current scope is terminated.

It is usually assumed that the parameter for the conversion constructor should have a type that belongs to one of a class data member. For example, the conversion constructor for class String has a character array (character pointer) parameter, and the class String has a character pointer data member. This is often true, but it does not have to be so.

The class designer can dream up a conversion from any type the designer sees fit. For example, class Account from Listing 16.1 (or Listing 16.2) can have a conversion constructor with the parameter of the type String even though there is no String data member in class Account. Here is this constructor.

```
Account(String& s)                    // conversion (String changes)
{ char* p = s.reset();                // get pointer to the array
   owner = new char[strlen(p)+1];     // allocate heap memory
   if (owner == 0) { cout << "\nOut of memory\n";   exit(0); }
   strcpy(owner, p);                  // initialize data fields
   balance = 0; }                     // default for new account
```

Now a String object can be used anywhere an Account object is expected. Since a new Account object with zero balance is pretty useless unless it is a target of a series of messages, the most appropriate use of this constructor is to create Account objects when the owner data is represented as a String object rather than as a character array.

```
String owner("Smith");
Account a(owner);                     // create and initialize
a += 500;                             // use the Account object
```

As you can see, conversion constructors allow the class designer to explicitly designate what types can be used where the value of the given class is expected. Notice that these constructors implement casts between objects, not between pointers or references, which are always allowed in C++. The casts implemented by conversion constructors might be explicit (if the compiler cannot define from the context on which class to perform the conversion) or even implicit (if the target of conversion is clear from the context).

Conversion constructors weaken strong typing. They remove compiler protection when conversion is done inadvertently. However, they are very popular in C++ because they allow for greater flexibility in writing C++ code.

The second mechanism for designating which conversions between objects are possible is the use of conversion operators. The conversion operator is an overloaded operator whose name is the name of the target type. As an overloaded operator, the conversion operator is subject to general rules for overloaded operators. However, its syntax is rather unusual.

Similar to constructors and destructors, it should have no return type. Similar to destructors, it should have no parameters. Unlike constructors and destructors, it must return a value. This value should be of the type to which the conversion is made (i.e., the type used in the name of the operator). Here is how an integer conversion operator for class String looks:

```
String::operator int() const        // no change to String object
{ return size; }                    // no return type, just value
```

Usually, the return value is a value of one of the data fields of the class of the appropriate type. If the class has more than one data member of that type, it is up to the class designer to decide which (or no) value is more appropriate to be used in the conversion. If you cannot decide which field to choose, do not anguish over this decision. Recall that all operators are used for convenience and for nicer syntax in the client code, not because they do the job a regular member function cannot do.

Depending on the circumstances, a class can have more than one conversion operator. Here is a character pointer conversion operator for class String that can replace the method reset().

```
String::operator char* () const     // object does not change
{ return str; }                     // return pointer to start
```

Now you can streamline the client code (Account conversion constructor) using these two String conversion operators.

```
Account(const String& s)
{ int len = (int)s;                          // get the size of string
  owner = new char[len+1];                   // allocate heap memory
  if (owner == 0) { cout << "\nOut of memory\n";   exit(0); }
  strcpy(owner, (char*)s);                   // initialize data fields
  balance = 0; }
```

Here, explicit casts help the maintainer understand the flow of values in the function. However, they are not mandatory. If the compiler has no difficulty figuring out what type is required, the explicit casts can be omitted; implicit casts would do.

```
Account(const String& s)
{ int len = s;                        // implicit cast to integer
  owner = new char[len+1];            // allocate heap memory
  if (owner == 0) { cout << "\nOut of memory\n";   exit(0); }
  strcpy(owner, s);                   // implicit cast to char array
  balance = 0; }
```

As you can see, a `String` object can be used everywhere an integer or a character array value is expected. Do not forget that under the hood of the C++ program, the casts, whether implicit or explicit, are messages: function calls to overloaded conversion operators. This is how both versions of the constructor look to the compiler.

```
Account(const String& s)
{ int len = s.operator int();         // call to an operator
  owner = new char[len+1];            // allocate heap memory
  if (owner == 0) { cout << "\nOut of memory\n";   exit(0); }
  strcpy(owner, s.operator char*());  // call to an operator
  balance = 0; }
```

In most cases, conversion operators are employed to extract from an object a value of one of its fields. But this is by no means an inherent limitation. Similar to conversion constructors, conversion operators are used by the class designer to indicate type conversions for the class objects. Whatever the designer designates as a legitimate conversion, goes. For example, class `Account` might support two conversion operators, to `double` and to `String`, even if the class `Account` does not have a `String` data member:

```
Account::operator double () const     // object does not change
{ return balance; }                   // return double value

Account::operator String () const     // create a String object
{ return owner; }                     // implicit conversion
```

Notice that in the second conversion operator, implicit conversion to class `String` is taking place. The `String` object is created and returned for use in the client code. It is destroyed automatically in the client scope. Notice that I am not saying "when the client terminates" because the time of destruction is not defined exactly. Notice also that using a reference in the operator name would be syntactically incorrect because all references must be constant in C++.

```
Account::operator String& () const        // syntax error
{ return owner; }                         // implicit conversion
```

To remedy this problem, you can specify the operator name as a constant String reference. That will placate the compiler.

```
Account::operator const String& () const    // no syntax error
{ return owner; }                           // not a good idea
```

This is fine, but the reference that is returned is a reference to an unnamed temporary object, which can be destroyed whenever the compiler wants it to be destroyed. As a result, the client code might receive an invalid reference. This not a good programming practice.

With these conversions in place, the client program can convert a String object to an integer value and to a character pointer (through conversion operators) and to an Account object (through the Account conversion constructor). It can convert an Account object to a double value and to a String value (through conversion operators). Also, a character array can be converted to a String object (through the String conversion constructor).

Listing 16.6 demonstrates these conversions. A String object is handled by the client code as if it were a character array. An Account object is handled by the client code as if it were a double value and a String value. The results of the execution are shown in Figure 16–6.

Listing 16.6   Examples of using conversion constructors and conversion operators.

```
#include <iostream>
using namespace std;

class String {
  int size;                              // string size
  char *str;                             // start of internal string
  void set(const char* s);               // private string allocation
public:
  String (const char* s = "")            // default and conversion
    { set(s); }
  String (const String &s)               // copy constructor
    { set(s.str); }
  ~String()                              // destructor
  { delete [ ] str; }
  String& operator = (const String& s);  // assignment
  operator int() const;                  // current string length
  operator char* () const;               // return pointer to start
} ;
```

```
void String::set(const char* s)
   { size = strlen(s);                              // evaluate size
     str = new char[size + 1];                      // request heap memory
     if (str == 0) { cout << "Out of memory\n"; exit(0); }
     strcpy(str,s); }                               // copy client data to heap

String& String::operator = (const String& s)
{ if (this == &s) return *this;                     // no work if self-assignment
  delete [ ] str;                                   // return existing memory
  set(s.str);                                       // allocate/set new memory
  return *this; }                                   // to support chain assignment

String::operator int() const                        // no change to String object
{ return size; }

String::operator char* () const                     // object does not change
{ return str; }                                     // return pointer to start

class Account {                                     // base class of hierarchy
protected:
  double balance;                                   // protected data
  char *owner;
public:

  Account(const char* name, double initBalance)     // general
  { owner = new char[strlen(name)+1];               // allocate heap space
    if (owner == 0) { cout << "\nOut of memory\n"; exit(0); }
      strcpy(owner, name);                          // initialize data fields
      balance = initBalance; }

  Account(const String& s)
  { int len = s;                                    // get the size of string
    owner = new char[len+1];                        // allocate heap memory
    if (owner == 0) { cout << "\nOut of memory\n"; exit(0); }
    strcpy(owner, s);                               // initialize data fields
    balance = 0; }

  operator double () const                          // object does not change
  { return balance; }

  operator String () const                          // create a String object
  { return owner; }                                 // implicit conversion

  void operator -= (double amount)
  { balance -= amount; }                            // pop responsibility up

  void operator += (double amount)
  { balance += amount; }                            // increment unconditionally
} ;
```

```
int main()
{
  String owner("Smith");                    // conversion constructor
  Account a(owner);                          // conversion constructor
  a += 500;  a -=200;  a += 400;            // overloaded operators
  String s = a;                              // handle as a String value
  double limit = 2 * a;                      // handle as a double value
  cout << "Name: " << (char *)s << endl;     // explicit conversion
  cout << "Balance: " <<(double)a <<endl;    // explicit conversion
  cout << "Credit limit: " << limit << endl;
  return 0;
  }
```

If several types could be used in the given context, the compiler needs a hint for which type to use. This hint can be made in the form of the cast. In the output statements, a value of any type could be a legitimate output value. The explicit casts are a necessity if more than one type conversion is possible. For example, the String value above could be converted to an integer and a character array. The compiler (and the maintainer) has to be told what the programmer intended.

If the specified conversion is not found, the compiler searches for a built-in conversion (among numeric types) to make the call resolution possible. Consider, for example, the statement:

```
cout << "Balance: " <<(float)a <<endl;     // explicit conversion
```

Class Account does not provide the float conversion operator. This does not mean, however, that the line above is in error. Since the conversion from double to float is available as a built-in conversion, the compiler converts the Account value to double and then converts the double value to float. The compiler cannot add more than one programmer-defined conversion. The compiler cannot chain more than one built-in conversion to the programmer-defined conversion. But chaining of one programmer-defined conversion and one built-in conversion is possible.

Figure 16–6 Output of the program in Listing 16.6.

```
Name: Smith
Balance: 700
Credit limit: 1400
```

Subscript and Function Call Operators

These two operators are binary operators, but they are quite different from other C++ overloaded binary operators in how the client call to the operator is converted to a binary expression. For other overloaded operators, the target of the message is used as the left operand in the expression, with the operator (from the method name) inserted between the right and the left operand and the parameter of the function call used as the right operand of the expression. This is not so with the subscript and function call operators. (You will see the examples soon.)

Another difference is that these overloaded operators can be implemented as class members only—they cannot be implemented as global nonmember functions. The reason for this is to make the context analysis easier for the C++ compiler.

The Subscript Operator

Ideally, the expression form of the overloaded subscript operator should be the same as the syntactic form of the built-in subscript operator: The name of the variable is appended with the subscript surrounded by the left and right brackets. For example, s[i] should be interpreted as the subscript i applied to the object (variable) s.

The meaning of this operation can, of course, be completely arbitrary. Most C++ programmers (and all C++ libraries) interpret this expression as the retrieval of the value of the ith component of the object s. Another popular interpretation is the assignment to the ith component of the object s.

In both cases, the interpretation assumes that the object s is a container that contains an array or a linked list or another appropriate collection of components, and the expression s[i] refers to the value of the ith component in the container. Hence, the overloaded subscript operator is a function that returns the value of a component of a container.

As a simple example of the container class, let us consider a simplified version of the Array class. This is a container class similar to the String class from Listing 16.6. The components of the container are of type int rather than char.

The Array class addresses two drawbacks of built-in C++ array: array overflow and invalid index values. The first problem is addressed by allocating the components on the heap. The solution, as do many solutions, creates other problems to be addressed: To protect the integrity of the program, class `Array` should provide a copy constructor, the destructor, and the overloaded assignment operator.

The second invalid index problem is addressed by providing member functions `getInt()` and `setInt()` that access the internal `Array` memory on behalf of the client code.

```
class Array {
public:
   int size;                                // number of valid components
   int *ptr;                                // pointer to array of components
   void set(const int* a, int n);           // allocate/init heap memory
public:
   Array (const int* a,int n);              // general constructor
   Array (const Array &s);                  // copy constructor
  ~Array();                                 // return heap memory
   Array& operator = (const Array& a);      // copy array to another
   int getSize() const;
   int getInt(int i) const;                 // return the i-th component
   void setInt(int i, int x);               // set int x at position i
 } ;
```

It probably goes without saying, but I would still like to mention that the ith position means in fact the (i+1)th position. That is, the first component is under the index 0, the second component is under the index 1, and so on.

Hence, the member function `getInt()` returns the integer under the index i in the internal heap array. Since `getInt()` is called as a function, I can do some useful things in addition to just retrieving the value from the array. The useful thing to do is to check the validity of the index relative to the string bounds.

```
int Array::getInt (int i) const    // object does not change
{ if (i < 0 || i >= size)          // index is out of bounds
     return ptr[size-1];           // return the last component
  return ptr[i]; }                 // legal index: return value
```

Using this function, the client code can implement iterative algorithms that are very similar to the algorithms used for built-in C++ arrays but are safer because they cannot access memory areas outside the array.

```
void printArray(const Array& a)
{ int size = a.getSize();                   // get array size
   for (int i=0;  i < size;  i++)           // go over each component
   { cout << " " << a.getInt(i); }          // print next component
     cout << endl << endl; }
```

One problem with this additional functionality in getInt() is that it slows down the execution of the program somewhat. It was precisely the desire to avoid this slowdown that was the reason that C and C++ did not introduce index checking initially. However, most modern applications will not suffer much from this slowdown. If this issue turns out to be important, you can always use a faster version of the function that will not spend any time on checking indices and will be implemented inline.

Another problem with this design is that is imposes on the client code the need to check the return value (whether or not the client code needs it). After all, if the client felt that it needed this check, the size of the Array object data could be retrieved using the getSize() member function (as in the function printArray() above or how it is done in Listing 16.6 for similar container, the String class). This allows the client to do the check explicitly. This is a valid objection. However, every design decision is the result of tradeoffs. In general, pushing responsibility to the server code (including the integrity checks) and streamlining the client code so that its algorithm is not burdened by minute details of integrity checks is considered a sound software engineering practice.

Returning the last value in the container when the index is invalid sounds like a good decision. Another alternative is to return a special sentinel value, for example, zero. This will allow the client code to structure the iterations around the Array object to terminate iterations when the zero code is found. But this approach works only when the zero value of the component is illegal from the application point of view—often zero values are legal.

Next, let us look at the setInt() method. It is also a good idea to do some useful things while executing this method, and a useful thing is, of course, boundary checking.

```
void Array::setInt(int i,int x)      // modify Array object
{ if (i < 0 || i >= size)            // check if index is legal
    return;                          // no op if it is out of bounds
  ptr[i] = x; }                      // legal index: set the value
```

One might argue that boundary checking is even more important for this function than for the getInt() method. In getInt(), you risk bringing incorrect data up to the client code, and this can be discovered during debugging and testing. In setInt(), you risk the corruption of memory, and this could elude early detection.

For those of you who are still suffering from the rigid nature of C++ indexing, here are the versions of these two functions that allow the client code to work with indices changing from 1 to the size of the array.

```
int Array::getInt (int i) const    // object does not change
{ if (i < 1 || i > size)           // index is out of bounds
    return ptr[size];              // return the last component
  return ptr[i-1]; }               // legal index: return value

void Array::setInt(int i,int x)    // modify Array object
{ if (i < 1 || i > size)           // check if index is legal
    return;                        // no op if it is out of bounds
  ptr[i-1] = x; }                  // legal index: set the value
```

Here is the version of printArray() that takes advantage of this arrangement. I hope that by now you feel comfortable with the common convention and do not have to write code like this.

```
void printArray(const Array& a)
{ int size = a.getSize();                  // get array size
  for (int i=1;  i <= size;  i++)          // go from 1 to size
  { cout << " " << a.getInt(i); }          // print next component
  cout << endl << endl; }
```

Listing 16.7 shows the implementation of the class Array with the driver client code. The output of the program is shown in Figure 16–7.

Listing 16.7   Using an `Array` class as a container for integer components.

```cpp
#include <iostream>
using namespace std;

class Array {
public:
  int size;                               // number of valid components
  int *ptr;                               // pointer to array of components
  void set(const int* a, int n);         // allocate/init heap memory
public:
  Array (const int* a,int n);             // general constructor
  Array (const Array &s);                 // copy constructor
 ~Array();                                // return heap memory
  Array& operator = (const Array& a);     // copy array to another
  int getSize() const;
  int getInt(int i) const;                // return the i-th component
  void setInt(int i, int x);              // set int x at position i
  } ;

  void Array::set(const int* a, int n)
  { size = n;                             // evaluate array size
    ptr = new int[size];                  // request heap memory
    if (ptr == 0) { cout << "Out of memory\n"; exit(0); }
    for (int i=0;  i < size;  i++)
        ptr[i] = a[i]; }                  // copy client data to heap

Array::Array (const int* a, int n)        // general
  { set(a,n); }

Array::Array (const Array &a)             // copy constructor
  { set(a.ptr,a.size); }

Array::~Array()                           // destructor
  { delete [ ] ptr; }

Array& Array::operator = (const Array& a)
{ if (this == &a) return *this;           // no work if self-assignment
  delete [ ] ptr;                         // return existing memory
  set(a.ptr,a.size);                      // allocate/set new memory
  return *this; }                         // to support chain assignment

int Array::getSize() const                // get array size
{ return size; }

int Array::getInt (int i) const           // object does not change
{ if (i < 0 || i >= size)                 // index is out of bounds
    return ptr[size-1];                   // return the last component
  return ptr[i]; }                        // legal index: return value
```

```
void Array::setInt(int i,int x)            // modify Array object
{ if (i < 0 || i >= size)                  // check if index is legal
    return;                                 // no op if it is out of bounds
  ptr[i] = x; }                            // legal index: set the value

int main()
{
    int arr[] = { 1,3,5,7,11,13,17,19 } ;  // data to process
    Array a(arr, 8);                       // create the object
    int size = a.getSize();               // get array size
    for (int i=0;  i < size;  i++)        // go over each component
    { cout << " " << a.getInt(i); }       // print next component
    cout << endl << endl;
    for (int j=0;  j < size;  j++)        // go over the array again
     { int x = a.getInt(j);               // get next component
       a.setInt(j, 2*x); }                // update the value
    for (int k = 0;  k < size;  k++)
    { cout << " " << a.getInt(k); }       // print updated array
    cout << endl;
    return 0;
    }
```

In this example, the functions set(), the constructors, the destructor, and the assignment operator are similar to the member functions of class String in Listing 16.6. The major difference is that the String functions use the terminating zero in their loops, and the Array functions use the number of components in the container.

A full-fledged Array class should also support adding new components at the end and in the middle of the array, deleting components, comparing components, testing for the presence of valid data, and the like. I have omitted all of that for the sake of brevity of the example.

As I mentioned above, the syntax of using the getInt() method is nice and close to what we do with a built-in C++ array. The syntax of using the setInt() method is more awkward.

```
for (int j=0;  j < size;  j++)      // go over the array again
 { int x = a.getInt(j);             // get next component
   a.setInt(j, 2*x); }              // update the value
```

Figure 16–7   Output of the program in Listing 16.7.

```
1 3 5 7 11 13 17 19

2 6 10 14 22 26 34 38
```

Here, I go over each component of the array and double the value of each component. The syntax of updating here is different from the syntax of access to the components. Meanwhile, the built-in C++ arrays use the same syntax for accessing the elements of the array (e.g., x=a[j]) and for assigning the elements of the array (e.g., a[j]=2*x).

It would be nice to structure the client code for updating the values in the container in the same way as for accessing the values.

```
for (int j=0;  j < size;   j++)          // go over the array again
   { int x = a.getInt(j);                // get next component
//     a.setInt(j, 2*x); }               // update the value
     a.setInt(j) = 2 * x; }              // update the value
```

In traditional programming, this is impossible—the return value of a function cannot be used on the left-hand side of the assignment. C++ makes it possible if the function returns a reference to a value rather than the value itself. Of course, the reference must be a valid reference and should not disappear when the function terminates, but this is another issue.

In Chapter 7, "Programming with C++ Functions," I already discussed the possibilities that returning references from functions opens for writing terse and expressive client code. Here, this opportunity presents itself again. Let us remove the value parameter from the setInt() interface and change the return type of setInt() from an integer value to an integer reference.

```
int& Array::setInt(int i)          // modify Array object
{ if (i < 0 || i >= size)          // check if index is legal
    return ptr[size-1];            // return the last component
  return ptr[i]; }                 // legal index: return reference
```

This function supports the client loop above: It returns a reference to an integer, and the loop assigns a value at the address to which the reference is pointing. The crucial element in this scheme is that the reference is not to a local value that would disappear when the setInt() function terminates. The reference is to the array component that existed before setInt() was called and will exist after setInt() would terminate.

Now let us compare getInt() and the new version of setInt(). You see that their implementations are the same. Does the client code need both functions? There are two differences between these functions, and they are both in the function interface. The return value of getInt() is a value, not a reference. This is not a serious problem. Let us change the return value of getInt() to the reference to an integer.

```
int& Array::getInt(int i) const      // object does not change
{ if (i < 0 || i >= size)            // index is out of bounds
     return ptr[size-1];             // return the last component
  return ptr[i]; }                   // legal index: return reference
```

With this function, the client code in Listing 16.7 (and in any other place too) will work as before.

```
for (int i=0;  i < size;  i++)       // go over each component
{ cout << " " << a.getInt(i); }      // OK if reference is returned
cout << endl << endl;
for (int j=0;  j < size;  j++)       // go over the array again
 { int x = a.getInt(j);              // OK if reference is returned
    a.setInt(j) = 2 * x; }           // OK if reference is returned
```

The second difference is that getInt() does not change the state of the object it operates on and is labeled as constant. On the other hand, setInt() modifies the state of the object it is sent to as a message, and hence it is not labeled as a constant. Do you see that?

This is a typical mistake many C++ programmers make in dealing with the const modifiers. Yes, the function setInt() modifies the state of the heap memory that belongs to the target object. But this memory is not part of the object—it only belongs to it. Data members are part of the object, not the heap memory. The function setInt() does not modify data members of the target object, and this is what counts. This is one of those concepts the C++ programmer has to always remember.

I designed the member function setInt() incorrectly. It has to be labeled as const because it does not change the state of its target object.

```
int& Array::setInt(int i) const      // Array object is not modified
{ if (i < 0 || i >= size)            // check if index is legal
     return ptr[size-1];             // return the last component
  return ptr[i]; }                   // legal index: return reference
```

This is clear from this version of the function. But it has to be clear even from the version of the function in Listing 16.7. Despite the comment that says that the object is modified, setInt() in Listing 16.7 does not modify its target object. Remember that story about the brick that I told you in Chapter 8, "Object-Oriented Programming with Functions"? Make sure you think about the const modifiers all the time.

Now that both functions, getInt() and setInt(), look exactly the same, we can eliminate one of them. Listing 16.8 shows the version of the program from Listing 16.7 where only one function, getInt(), is used. The output of this example is the same as that of Listing 16.7.

Listing 16.8   Using the same member function to get and to set `Array` data.

```
#include <iostream>
using namespace std;

class Array {
public:
  int size;                             // number of valid components
  int *ptr;                             // pointer to array of integers
  void set(const int* a, int n);        // allocate/init heap memory
public:
  Array (const int* a, int n);          // general constructor
  Array (const Array &s);               // copy constructor
 ~Array();                              // return heap memory
  Array& operator = (const Array& a);   // copy array
  int getSize() const;
  int& getInt(int i) const;             // get/set value at position i
} ;

 void Array::set(const int* a, int n)
 { size = n;                            // evaluate array size
   ptr = new int[size];                 // request heap memory
   if (ptr == 0) { cout << "Out of memory\n"; exit(0); }
   for (int i=0;  i < size;  i++)
       ptr[i] = a[i]; }                 // copy client data to heap

Array::Array(const int* a, int n)       // general constructor
 { set(a,n); }

Array::Array (const Array &a)           // copy constructor
 { set(a.ptr,a.size); }

Array::~Array()                         // destructor
 { delete [ ] ptr; }

Array& Array::operator = (const Array& a)
{ if (this == &a) return *this;         // no work if self-assignment
  delete [ ] ptr;                       // return existing memory
  set(a.ptr,a.size);                    // allocate/set new memory
  return *this; }                       // to support chain assignment

int Array::getSize() const              // get array size
{ return size; }

int& Array::getInt(int i) const         // Array object is not modified
{ if (i < 0 || i >= size)               // check if index is legal
    return ptr[size-1];                 // no op if it is out of bounds
  return ptr[i]; }                      // legal index: set the reference
```

```
int main()
{
  int arr[] = { 1,3,5,7,11,13,17,19 } ;    // data to process
  Array a(arr, 8);                          // create an object
  int size = a.getSize();                   // get array size
  for (int i=0;  i < size;  i++)            // go over each component
  { cout << " " << a.getInt(i); }           // print next component
  cout << endl << endl;
  for (int j=0;  j < size;  j++)            // go over the array again
  { int x = a.getInt(j);                    // get next component
    a.getInt(j) = 2*x; }                    // update the value
  for (int k = 0;  k < size;  k++)
  { cout << " " << a.getInt(k); }           // print updated array
  cout << endl;
  return 0;
}
```

The next step is to replace the member function getInt() with an overloaded subscript operator. The change of the function itself is very simple. You take the function, cut out its name getInt, move in the keyword operator, and add the symbol for the operator (in this case, []).

```
//int& Array::getInt(int i) const       // Array object is not modified
int& Array::operator [](int i) const    // operator header
{ if (i < 0 || i >= size)               // check if index is legal
     return ptr[size-1];                // no op if it is out of bounds
   return ptr[i]; }                     // legal index: set the reference
```

Similar changes should be done in the client code—the name of the member function is now operator[], not getInt.

```
int size = a.getSize();                   // get array size
for (int i=0;  i < size;  i++)            // go over each component
{ cout << " " << a.operator[](i); }       // print next component
cout << endl << endl;
for (int j=0;  j < size;  j++)            // go over the array again
{ int x = a.operator[](j);                // get next component
  a.operator[](j) = 2*x; }                // update the value
for (int k = 0;  k < size;  k++)
{ cout << " " << a.operator[](k); }       // print updated array
cout << endl;
```

But of course we did not go all the way from the first implementation in Listing 16.7 only to stop here. The function call syntax should be replaced with the expression syntax. However, treating the operator[] as any other operator results in awkward code. How, for example, do you treat the operator+? You use the message target as the first operand, then the symbol from the operator, for example, +, and then the parameter as the second operand.

```
a.operator+(b);                          // same as a + b;
```

If you do the same thing with the subscript operator, you will arrive at something unreadable.

```
cout << " " << a.operator[](i);          // same as a[]i !
```

To make the subscript operator function consistent with the usage of the built-in subscript operator, C++ cuts a special deal. The compiler is instructed to tolerate the deviation from the general rule. Listing 16.9 shows this example with the use of the overloaded subscript operator.

Listing 16.9   Using the overloaded subscript operator to get and to set `Array` **data.**

```
#include <iostream>
using namespace std;

class Array {
public:
   int size;                             // number of valid components
   int *ptr;                             // pointer to array of integers
   void set(const int* a, int n);        // allocate/init heap memory
public:
   Array (const int* a, int n);          // general constructor
   Array (const Array &s);               // copy constructor
  ~Array();                              // return heap memory
   Array& operator = (const Array& a);   // copy array
   int getSize() const;
   int& operator [ ] (int i);            // get/set value at position i
   } ;

   void Array::set(const int* a, int n)
   { size = n;                           // evaluate array size
     ptr = new int[size];                // request heap memory
     if (ptr == 0) { cout << "Out of memory\n"; exit(0); }
     for (int i=0;  i < size;  i++)
        ptr[i] = a[i]; }                 // copy client data to heap

Array::Array(const int* a, int n)        // general constructor
   { set(a,n); }

Array::Array (const Array &a)            // copy constructor
   { set(a.ptr,a.size); }

Array::~Array()                          // destructor
   { delete [ ] ptr; }
```

```
Array& Array::operator = (const Array& a)
{ if (this == &a) return *this;              // no work if self-assignment
  delete [ ] ptr;                            // return existing memory
  set(a.ptr,a.size);                         // allocate/set new memory
  return *this; }                            // to support chain assignment

int Array::getSize() const                   // get array size
{ return size; }

int& Array::operator [](int i)               // Array object is not modified
{ if (i < 0 || i >= size)                    // check if index is legal
    return ptr[size-1];                      // no op if it is out of bounds
  return ptr[i]; }                           // legal index: set the value

int main()
{
  int arr[] = { 1,3,5,7,11,13,17,19 } ;      // data to process
  Array a(arr, 8);                           // create an object
  int size = a.getSize();                    // get array size
  for (int i=0;  i < size;  i++)             // go over each component
//{ cout <<" "<<a.operator[](i); }           // alternative syntax
  { cout << " " << a[i]; }                    // print next component
  cout << endl << endl;
  for (int j=0;  j < size;  j++)             // go over the array again
   { int x = a[j];                           // special deal
//   { int x = a.operator[](j);              // alternative syntax
     a[j] = 2*x; }                           // special deal
  for (int k = 0;  k < size;  k++)
  { cout << " " << a[k]; }                    // print updated array
  cout << endl;
  return 0;
}
```

It is not clear how much of an improvement this version is over the original one in Listing 16.7. But the operator syntax is nice. And it is definitely useful to review the issues related to returning a reference from a function rather than returning a value and the use of the const modifiers.

Function Call Operator

The function call operator (two parentheses are considered to be an operator in C++) also can be used to access or to set the values of components in a container class object. The operator is often used when the container structures the heap memory as a two-dimensional rather than as a one-dimensional array (as in the previous example).

The reason for the use of the function call operator instead of the subscript operator is that for a two-dimensional array, C++ uses two subscript operators joined together, for example, m[i][j]. Using conventional programming syntax with one subscript operator, for example, m[i,j], would make the subscript a ternary operator. (In this case, its operands are the array m and the indices i and j.) For a multidimensional array, the number of indices might be more than two.

The designers of C and C++ felt that it was all right to allow the plus operator to change its arity—both allow for a unary plus and a binary plus. But a similar dispensation was not made for the subscript operator. It is a binary operator, and it cannot take more than two operands.

Instead of the subscript operator, we can use the function call operator. Its advantage in this situation is that it can have any number of parameters.

As an example, let us consider a class Matrix, which implements a square matrix. The client code manipulates the matrix components by specifying two indices—one for the row and one for the column of the matrix. Matrix objects can be created, passed as function parameters, and assigned to each other. The implementation will be based on a dynamically allocated linear array whose size depends on the size of the square matrix.

Class Matrix uses the private function make(), which is similar to the function set() from the previous example, but it leaves the heap memory noninitialized. The function make() is called by the conversion constructor, copy constructor, and the overloaded assignment operator.

```
class Matrix {
  int *cells;                            // heap array to house the matrix
  int size; // number of rows and of columns
  int* make(int size)                    // private allocator function
  { int* p = new int [size * size];      // total number of elements
    if (p == NULL) { cout << "Matrix too big\n";  exit(0); }
    return p; }                          // return pointer to heap storage
public:
  Matrix (int sz) : size(sz)             // conversion constructor
  { cells = make(size); }                // heap memory is not initialized
  Matrix (const Matrix& m) : size(m.size)
  { cells = make(size); }                // copy constructor: for safety
  Matrix& operator = (const Matrix& m);  // assignment operator
  int getSize() const                    // size of the side
  { return size; }
  int& get (int r, int c) const;         // access or modify a component
  ~Matrix() { delete [] cells; }         // destructor
  } ;
```

The assignment operator disposes of existing heap memory, allocates new memory on the heap and copies data from the parameter `Matrix` object into the target of the assignment.

```
Matrix& Matrix::operator = (const Matrix& m)      // assignment
{ if (this == &m) return *this;                   // no work if self-assignment
  delete [ ] cells;                               // return existing memory
  cells = make(m.size);                           // allocate/set new memory
  size = m.size;                                  // set the matrix size
  for (int i=0;  i<size*size;  i++)               // copy data
        cells[i] = m.cells[i];
  return *this; }                                 // to support chain assignment
```

The function `get()` combines the responsibilities of functions `getInt()` and `setInt()` from the previous example. It uses the row and column coordinates passed from the caller (starting with zero, of course) to compute the position of the matrix cell in the linear array. If the coordinates are illegal, it quietly returns the last element of the array. If the coordinates are legal, it returns the data stored at the given coordinates.

```
int& Matrix::get (int r, int c) const
  { if (r<0 || c<0 || r>=size || c>=size)         // check validity
       return cells[size*size-1];                 // return last matrix cell
    return cells[r*size + c]; }                    // return requested cell
```

Returning the last matrix cell if the row or column coordinate is outside of the matrix is not the best solution. Another possibility is to terminate the execution or to throw exception, but I do not like terminating execution, and we did not discuss exceptions yet. Another possibility is to return some value not otherwise used in the application, for example, the maximum integer value `MAX_INT`. However, the constant value cannot be returned by reference (lest you decide to modify it).

```
int& Matrix::get (int r, int c) const             // not a good version
  { if (r<0 || c<0 || r>=size || c>=size)         // check validity
       return MAX_INT;                            // illegal to return by reference
    return cells[r*size + c]; }                    // return requested cell
```

Listing 16.10 shows the program that implements the class `Matrix` with the function `get()` just described. The client function `printMatrix()` goes over rows and columns of the matrix and prints each row in turn. Notice the use of the `setw()` manipulator. Unfortunately, the `<iostream>` include file is not sufficient for the code that uses manipulators, and you have to include the `<iomanip>` header file.

The `main()` client function creates the square matrix object and initializes each cell by the product of its row number and its column number (in scientific count, not in C++ count—it starts with one). In this loop, `main()` uses the return value of function `get()` as an lvalue. Then `main()` calls `printMatrix()`, which uses the return value of function `get()` as an rvalue. Next, `main()` sets the elements of the main matrix diagonal to zero (using `get()` as an lvalue) and prints the matrix again. Finally, `main()` tries to access the cell outside of the matrix, and function `get()` returns the last cell of the matrix (which has been set to zero). The results of the execution are shown in Figure 16–8.

Listing 16.10 Using a `Matrix` class as a container for a square matrix.

```
#include <iostream>
#include <iomanip>
using namespace std;

class Matrix {
   int *cells;                            // heap array to house the matrix
   int size;                              // number of rows and of columns
   int* make(int size)                    // private allocator function
   { int* p = new int [size * size];      // total number of elements
     if (p == NULL) { cout << "Matrix too big\n";   exit(0); }
     return p; }                          // return pointer to heap storage
public:
   Matrix (int sz) : size(sz)             // conversion constructor
   { cells = make(size); }                // heap memory is not initialized
   Matrix (const Matrix& m)  : size(m.size)
   { cells = make(size); }                // copy constructor: for safety
   Matrix& operator = (const Matrix& m);  // assignment operator
   int getSize() const                    // size of the side
   { return size; }
   int& get (int r, int c) const;         // access or modify a component
   ~Matrix() { delete [] cells; }         // destructor
   } ;

Matrix& Matrix::operator = (const Matrix& m)   // assignment
{ if (this == &m) return *this;          // no work if self-assignment
  delete [ ] cells;                      // return existing memory
  cells = make(m.size);                  // allocate/set new memory
  size = m.size;                         // set the matrix size
  for (int i=0;  i<size*size;  i++)      // copy data
        cells[i] = m.cells[i];
  return *this; }                        // to support chain assignment

  int& Matrix::get (int r, int c) const
   { if (r<0 || c<0 || r>=size || c>=size)  // check validity
        return cells[size*size-1];       // return last matrix cell
      return cells[r*size + c]; }        // return requested cell
```

```
void printMatrix(const Matrix& m)              // client function
{ int size = m.getSize();
  for (int i=0; i < size; i++)                 // go over each row
  { for (int j=0;  j < size;  j++)             // and each column
      cout <<setw(4) <<m.get(i,j);             // print cell at m[i][j]
    cout << endl; }                            // end the current row
  cout << endl; }                              // end the matrix

int main()
{ cout << endl << endl;
  int i, j, n = 5;   Matrix m1(n);             // Matrix object
  for (i=0; i < n; i++)
    for (j=0;  j < n;  j++)
      m1.get(i,j) = (i+1) * (j+1);             // initialize cells
                                               // m1[i][j] = (i+1)*(j+1);
  printMatrix(m1);                             // print matrix state
  for (i=0; i < n; i++)                        // put 0's on main diagonal
    m1.get(i,i) = 0;                           // m1[i][i] = 0
  printMatrix(m1);                             // print new state
  cout <<"m[10][10] = " <<m1.get(10,10) <<endl; // out of range
  return 0;
  }
```

Transforming the function get() into the overloaded function call operator is very simple. You replace the name get with the keyword operator and add the operator symbols: two empty parentheses.

```
int& Matrix::operator() (int r, int c) const
{   if (r<0 || c<0 || r>=size || c>=size)      // check validity
      return cells[size*size-1];               // return last matrix cell
    return cells[r*size + c]; }                // return requested cell
```

You can call this function using the function call syntax, as a synonym for get().

```
    1   2   3   4   5
    2   4   6   8  10
    3   6   9  12  15
    4   8  12  16  20
    5  10  15  20  25

    0   2   3   4   5
    2   0   6   8  10
    3   6   0  12  15
    4   8  12   0  20
    5  10  15  20   0

m[10][10] = 0
```

Figure 16-8
Output of the program in Listing 16.10.

```
void printMatrix(const Matrix& m)          // client function
{ int size = m.getSize();
  for (int i=0; i < size; i++)             // go over each row
  { for (int j=0;  j < size;  j++)         // and each column
      cout <<setw(4) <<m.operator()(i,j);  // cell at m[i][j]
    cout << endl; }                        // end the current row
  cout << endl; }                          // end the matrix
```

It looks strange but is correct. All overloaded operators look strange until you get used to them. Transforming the function call syntax into the expression syntax is unusual as well. The formal application of the C++ rule would yield something like `m()i,j`. Instead, C++ gives you a special dispensation to write it as `m(i,j)`. For some C++ programmers, this syntax does not look like it accesses the matrix component, but for many scientific programmers, this is quite close to what FORTRAN allows you to do.

Listing 16.11 shows the complete version of the program in Listing 16.10, where calls to the function `get()` are replaced with calls to the overloaded function call operator `operator()()`. (I hope you see that the name `operator()()` is formed in the same way as any other function name.) The output of the program is the same as the output of the program in Listing 16.10 (see Figure 16–8).

Listing 16.11 Using a `Matrix` class with the overloaded function call operator.

```
#include <iostream>
#include <iomanip>
using namespace std;

class Matrix {
  int *cells;                              // heap array to house the matrix
  int size;                                // number of rows and of columns
  int* make(int size)                      // private allocator function
  { int* p = new int [size * size];        // total number of elements
    if (p == NULL) { cout << "Matrix too big\n";  exit(0); }
    return p; }                            // return pointer to heap storage
public:
  Matrix (int sz) : size(sz)               // conversion constructor
  { cells = make(size); }                  // heap memory is not initialized
  Matrix (const Matrix& m) : size(m.size)
  { cells = make(size); }                  // copy constructor: for safety
  Matrix& operator = (const Matrix& m);    // assignment operator
  int getSize() const                      // size of the side
  { return size; }
  int& operator () (int r, int c) const;   // access or modify
  ~Matrix() { delete [] cells; }           // destructor
  } ;
```

```
Matrix& Matrix::operator = (const Matrix& m)      // assignment
{ if (this == &m) return *this;                   // no work if self-assignment
  delete [ ] cells;                               // return existing memory
  cells = make(m.size);                           // allocate/set new memory
  size = m.size;                                  // set the matrix size
  for (int i=0;  i<size*size;  i++)               // copy data
       cells[i] = m.cells[i];
  return *this; }                                 // to support chain assignment

int& Matrix::operator () (int r, int c) const
   {  if (r<0 || c<0 || r>=size || c>=size)       // check validity
        return cells[size*size-1];                // return last matrix cell
      return cells[r*size + c]; }                 // return requested cell

void printMatrix(const Matrix& m)                 // client function
{ int size = m.getSize();
  for (int i=0; i < size; i++)                    // go over each row
  { for (int j=0;  j < size;  j++)                // and each column
      cout << setw(4) << m(i,j);                  // print the cell
    cout << endl; }                               // end the current row
  cout << endl; }                                 // end the matrix

int main()
{ cout << endl << endl;
  int i, j, n = 5;   Matrix m1(n);                // Matrix object
  for (i=0; i < n; i++)
     for (j=0;  j < n;  j++)                       // initialize cells
        m1(i,j) = (i+1) * (j+1);                  // m1[i][j] = (i+1)*(j+1);
  printMatrix(m1);                                // print matrix state
  for (i=0; i < n; i++)                           // put 0's on main diagonal
    m1(i,i) = 0;                                  // m1[i][i] = 0
  printMatrix(m1);                                // print new state
  cout << "m[10][10] - " << m1(10,10) << endl;    // out of bounds
  return 0;
  }
```

This design does not support matrix addition, multiplication, comparison, and other useful operations. Its purpose is only to demonstrate the use of a function call operator.

Input/Output Operators

The C++ standard library overloads the input operator >> and the output operator << for all built-in classes. Obviously, these operators do not know anything about programmer-defined classes. This is why when you need to input or output object data, you have to do this individually for each data member of the object.

It would be nice to overload the input/output operators for programmer-defined classes as well. Encapsulating these operations in overloaded operators would contribute to streamlining the client code, to eliminating low-level details of data management from the client code, and to pushing responsibility from client code to server classes.

Overloading operator >>

Consider, for example, class String from Listing 16.6, which manages its memory dynamically and supports the client code's access to its internal data.

```
class String {
  int size; // string size
  char *str;                           // start of internal string
  void set(const char* s);             // private string allocation
public:
  String (const char* s = "")          // default and conversion
    { set(s); }
  String (const String &s)             // copy constructor
    { set(s.str); }
  ~String() // destructor
  { delete [ ] str; }
  String& operator = (const String& s);  // assignment
  operator int() const;                // current string length
  operator char* () const;             // return pointer to start
} ;
```

It would be nice to overload input/output operators for this class so that client code might use something like this:

```
int main ()
{ String s;
  cout << "Enter customer name:   ";
  cin >> s;                            // accept name
  cout << "The customer name is: ";
  cout << s << endl;                   // display name
  return 0; }
```

What should be the interface of the overloaded input operator? It is a binary operator that operates on an object of type `istream` (which supports input from the library object `cin` and from disk files) and on an object of type `String`. Let us overload `operator >>` for class `String`.

```
void String::operator >> (istream& in)
{ char name[80];                        // local storage for data
  in >> name;                           // accept data
  delete [] str;                        // return existing memory
  set(name); }                          // allocate/init new memory
```

Notice that the function parameter is passed by reference, not by value, because it manages its memory dynamically. Notice that this is not a reference to a const object—the input object changes as a result of the input operation. Notice that the function is not labeled as const because it changes the state of the object data members by deleting the existing heap memory and setting the pointer to point to another area of heap memory.

This works. However, this operator provides an awkward interface: According the C++ rules of transforming the function call syntax into expression syntax, it should be called with a `String` object as a target and an `istream` object as an argument.

```
    s.operator >> (cin);                // equivalent to  s >> cin;
```

It would be nice to have a special dispensation similar to one given for the subscript operator and the function call operator, but we do not; and no programmer would use the input operator if the `cin` object were not the left operand.

If this does not work, let us design this operator as a member of the `istream` class. This is easier said than done. The `istream` class is a library class, and we cannot butcher it for the benefit of our programmer-defined `String` class.

So, we cannot overload this operator as a member of the `istream` class, and we can (but do not want to) overload it as a member of the `String` class. What should we do? Remember that story that I told you in Chapter 15 about A & B who were sitting on the chimney? Well, by eliminating all other alternatives, we are left with nothing else but overloading this operator as a global function.

```
void operator >> (String& s, istream& in)   // global function
{ char name[80];                            // local storage for data
  in >> name;                               // accept data
  String temp(name);                        // create/init new object
  s = temp; }                               // copy it into the argument
```

This is not perfect—it is not concise, and is somewhat slow because it first makes a temporary `String` object and then copies it into its argument. But as a part of external input/output, this is not going to affect program performance at all. The execution time for this function is much less than that of human reaction or of reading from a disk file.

This is how you call this function using the function call syntax: the function name, the first parameter, and the second parameter.

```
operator >> (s, cin);                    // same as  s >> cin
```

As you see, this did not buy us much—the problem is that the `String` object is the first operand, not the second. Let us try again by changing the order of the function parameters.

```
void operator >> (istream& in, String& s)   // global function
{ char name[80];                             // local storage for data
  in >> name;                                // accept data
  String temp(name);                         // create/init new object
  s = temp; }                                // copy it into the argument
```

This is much better—with the `String` object as the second parameter, the expression syntax is what we want to see.

```
operator >> (cin, s);              // same as  cin >> s;
```

The next step is to make this function a friend of class `String` so that it will not dance around the target object but will go directly to using its non-public function `set()` and data members.

```
class String {
  int size;                        // string size
  char *str;                       // start of internal string
  void set(const char* s);         // private string allocation
public:
friend void operator >> (istream& in, String& s);
  . . . } ;                        // the rest of class String
```

This is almost perfect. For the purposes of this little example, it is indeed perfect. However, in terms of treating programmer-defined classes similarly to built-in classes, this function does not measure up. For built-in types, the `iostream` library supports chain operations.

```
double x, y;
cin >> x >> y;                     // same as cin >>x; cin >>y;
```

For our example, this client code does not work—it generates a syntax error.

```
String s;   int qty;
cout << "Enter customer name and quantity:   ";
cin >> s >> qty;                                // error: no chain calls
```

What is the meaning of the last line in this last code snippet? Of course, you can always say that this is how it is done in C++ and hence it should compile, but this explanation is not good enough. If you look up the definition of the function `operator >>` (overloaded for all possible types) you will see that its return type is a reference to type `istream`. This is the only reason this chain syntax is possible—no special dispensation would make it possible.

First, you call this operator with objects `cin` and `s` as arguments. When the operator returns an `istream` object reference, you send to it another version of the operator (this time from the library class `istream`) with the variable `qty` as an argument.

```
(operator>>(cin,s)).operator>>(qty);        // same as cin >>s >>qty;
```

But the function that I defined returns `void`, not `istream&`. It is no good for sending to it any messages. The remedy is simple: just redefine the return type to `istream&`.

Listing 16.12 shows the program that implements the class `String` and overloads the `operator >>` as a class friend. Returning an `istream` reference supports chain operations. The output of the program is shown in Figure 16–9.

Listing 16.12   Overloading the input operator for a programmer-defined type.

```
#include <iostream>
using namespace std;

class String {
  int size; // string size
  char *str;                                  // start of internal string
  void set(const char* s);                    // private string allocation
public:
friend istream& operator >> (istream& in, String& s);
  String (const char* s = "")                 // default and conversion
    { set(s); }
  String (const String &s)                    // copy constructor
    { set(s.str); }
  ~String() // destructor
  { delete [ ] str; }
  String& operator = (const String& s);       // assignment
  char* get () const                          // return pointer to start
  { return str; }
} ;
```

```
void String::set(const char* s)
   { size = strlen(s);                                  // evaluate size
     str = new char[size + 1];                          // request heap memory
     if (str == 0) { cout << "Out of memory\n"; exit(0); }
     strcpy(str,s); }                                   // copy client data to heap

String& String::operator = (const String& s)
{ if (this == &s) return *this;                         // no work if self-assignment
  delete [ ] str;                                       // return existing memory
  set(s.str);                                           // allocate/set new memory
  return *this; }                                       // to support chain assignment

istream& operator >> (istream& in, String& s)          // global friend
{ char name[80];                                        // local storage for data
  in >> name;                                           // accept data
  delete [] s.str;                                      // return existing memory
  s.set(name);                                          // allocate/init new memory
  return cin; }                                         // important for chain work

int main ()
{
  String s;  int qty;                                  // local variables
  cout << "Enter customer name and quantity:  ";
  cin >> s >> qty;                                      // accept name, quantity
  cout << "The customer name is: ";
  cout << s.get() << endl;                              // using public methods
  cout << "Quantity ordered is:  ";
  cout << qty << endl;
  return 0;
  }
```

This is a nice example of supporting the idea that programmer-defined types should be treated the same way as built-in C++ types are.

Figure 16-9 Output of the program in Listing 16.12.

```
Enter customer name and quantity:  Simons  25
The customer name is: Simons
Quantity ordered is:  25
```

Overloading operator <<

Similar to the `operator >>`, the output operator `operator <<` can be overloaded for programmer-defined types.

Similar to the overloaded input `operator >>`, it is not a good idea to implement the output operator as a member function of the programmer-defined type, for example, `String`. Doing so will force you to use awkward syntax, where the `String` object is on the left of the operator and the output object `cout` is on the right.

```
String s;
s << cout;                    // same as   s.operator << (cout);
```

Similar to the overloaded `operator >>`, it is not a good idea to implement the output operator as a member function of the library output stream `ostream` class. The only available option is to implement it as a global function. Make sure that the `ostream` object is the first parameter, not the second. Otherwise, you will be trapped in the same syntax where the `String` object has to be on the left of the operator.

```
void operator << (ostream& out, const String& s)
{ out << s.get(); }
```

There is no need to make this function a friend of the programmer-defined type it works with because it has access to all necessary information. Whether or not this function has access to the data, most programmers would make it into a friend.

This function is good for individual output items, but not for chain operations.

```
cout << "The customer name is: ";
cout << s;
cout << endl;
```

This is, of course, quite inconvenient. Similar to the overloaded input operator, the remedy is to return a reference to the object, this time as the object of the output class `ostream`.

```
ostream& operator << (ostream& out, const String& s)
{ return out << s.get(); }
```

Now chaining of output operations becomes possible for programmer-defined types in the same way as it is for built-in types.

```
cout << "The customer name is: " << s << endl;        // nice syntax
```

Listing 16.13 shows the program that implements the class `String` and overloads the `operator >>` as a class friend. Returning an `istream` reference supports chain operations. The output of the program is shown in Figure 16–10.

Listing 16.13   Overloading the input and output operators for a programmer-defined type.

```
#include <iostream>
using namespace std;

class String {
   int size;                                   // string size
   char *str;                                  // start of internal string
   void set(const char* s);                    // private string allocation
public:
friend istream& operator >> (istream& in, String& s);
friend ostream& operator << (ostream& out, const String& s);
   String (const char* s = "")                 // default and conversion
      { set(s); }
   String (const String &s)                    // copy constructor
      { set(s.str); }
   ~String()                                   // destructor
   { delete [ ] str; }
   String& operator = (const String& s);       // assignment
   char* get () const                          // return pointer to start
   { return str; }
} ;

void String::set(const char* s)
   { size = strlen(s);                         // evaluate size
     str = new char[size + 1];                 // request heap memory
     if (str == 0) { cout << "Out of memory\n"; exit(0); }
     strcpy(str,s); }                          // copy client data to heap

String& String::operator = (const String& s)
{ if (this == &s) return *this;                // no work if self-assignment
   delete [ ] str;                             // return existing memory
   set(s.str);                                 // allocate/set new memory
   return *this; }                             // to support chain assignment

istream& operator >> (istream& in, String& s)
{ char name[80];                               // local storage for data
   in >> name;                                 // accept data
   delete [] s.str;                            // return existing memory
   s.set(name);                                // allocate/init new memory
   return cin; }
```

```
ostream& operator << (ostream& out, const String& s)
  { return out << s.str; }                              // it is allowed to a friend

int main ()
{ cout << endl << endl;
   String s;   int qty;                                 // local data
   cout << "Enter customer name and quantity:   ";
   cin >> s >> qty;                                      // accept name and quantity
   cout << "The customer name is: " << s << endl;        // very nice
   cout << "Quantity ordered is:  " << qty << endl;
   return 0;
   }
```

Even though the same purpose could be achieved by writing specialized member functions for input and output of object data, these overloaded operators give a nice elegant touch to C++ programs.

Figure 16–10 Output of the program in Listing 16.13.

```
Enter customer name and quantity:  Smith   42
The customer name is: Smith
Quantity ordered is:  42
```

Summary

This chapter covers a number of topics that are related by one concept: to make it possible to write functions that would allow the client code to treat programmer-defined objects similarly to variables of built-in types.

We looked at unary operators, prefix and postfix increment and decrement operators that give C++ programs a nice touch. We discussed conversion operators—together with conversion constructors, they continue the C++ tendency to weaken strong typing rules in favor of greater flexibility in handling objects.

I also reviewed the subscript and function call operators—a strange breed, they do not follow the common rules of transformation from the function call syntax to the expression syntax. Unlike most C++ operators, they can be overloaded only as member functions and not as global functions. These operators are not very popular, but in cases where they are used, they help create nice effects in client code.

Finally, I examined overloaded input/output operators. This is where operator overloading really shines! These operators allow client code to mix the objects of programmer-defined classes and built-in types. Even though they are not very significant from a software engineering point of view, they streamline the client code.

The overloaded input/output operators are very popular. I hope you will enjoy using them for your classes.

TEMPLATES: YET ANOTHER DESIGN TOOL

Topics in this Chapter

Chapter 17

The remaining two chapters of this book will deal with advanced C++ programming topics: programming with templates and programming with exceptions.

Usually, container classes and processing algorithms (sorting, searching, etc.) should be designed for a specific type of component. If the container contains a set of integers, you cannot use this container to store, for example, account objects. If a function sorts an array of integer values, you cannot use this function to sort inventory items. Often, you cannot use it to sort even double floating-point values. C++ templates allow the programmer to eliminate this limitation. With templates, you can design generic classes and algorithms and then specify what type of component should be handled by a specific container object or by a specific function call.

Programming with exceptions is used to streamline code that implements complex logic. Usually, processing algorithms use C++ `if` or `switch` statements to separate normal processing of data from processing of erroneous or faulty data. For multistep algorithms, the segments of source code for the main algorithm and for the exceptional condition are written in alternative branches of the same source code, and this often makes the source code harder to read—the main line is lost in the multitude of exceptional and rare cases. C++ exceptions allow the programmer to isolate exceptional cases in other, remote, segments of source code and streamline the base processing so that it is easier to understand.

These language features, templates and exceptions, share several common characteristics: They are complex, they increase the size of the executable code of the applications you write, and they introduce additional execution time overhead.

Space and time overhead is the immediate result of the power and complexity of these programming techniques. If you write real-time applications under severe memory and execution speed constraints, you probably should not use templates and exceptions. If your applications are going to be run on computers with plenty of memory and with fast processors, then space and time constraints are not that important.

Still, it might be a good idea to introduce these language features into your programs gradually. If these techniques streamline your source code only marginally, it might not be worth the trouble. As is often the case in programming, the compromise between advantages and disadvantages is in the eye of the beholder. Make sure that in your pursuit of interesting and challenging language features you do not make the life of the maintainer too difficult.

In this chapter, I will discuss programming with C++ templates. In the next chapter, I will cover C++ exceptions and other advanced language features that did not fit into the previous chapters.

A Simple Example of a Class Design Reuse

The strong typing approach of C++ allows the compiler to spot programming errors when the programmer uses one type instead of another. C++ allows a number of exceptions to this rule. Numeric values can be used interchangeably. Programmer-defined types can be used instead of other types provided that conversion constructors and conversion operators are available. Classes related through inheritance also allow limited substitution.

Still, many limitations on the use of typed values remain. Many algorithms are essentially the same regardless of the type of values they operate on. For example, searching for a given account in the array of account objects requires going through each component of the array and comparing the owner name with the given name. Similarly, searching for a given inventory item in the array of items requires going through each component of the array and comparing the item id with the given id. These are the same actions, but you cannot pass an array of inventory items as a parameter to a function that implements the search in the array of accounts. You have to write another function. This function will be almost identical to the account search function. The only difference will be in the comparison operation: One function compares the given name with the owner name in the account object, and another function compares the given id with the id in the item object.

Container classes—stacks, queues, lists, trees, and others—can contain different kinds of components. Often, component classes handle their components in a similar way regardless of the component type. For example, stack operations—pushing the new component on the top of the stack, popping a component from the top of the stack, and checking whether the stack is empty or has any components left—do not depend on the nature of the component. They are done in the same way whether the components are characters, accounts, or inventory items. It would be nice to be able to design a generic stack and use it for any type of component that the application requires. C++ strong typing makes this impossible. A stack of characters contains characters and cannot contain account objects or inventory items. And a stack of accounts contains account objects and cannot contain characters or inventory items.

Let us consider a simple example—a stack of characters. It is a popular data structure. It is used in compilers, calculators, screen managers, and in other applications where the collection of items should support the LIFO (last in, first out) protocol. The example of checking parentheses in the expression in Chapter 8, "Object-Oriented Programming with Functions," was using the stack (I called it temporary storage) as the underlying data structure. The stack in my next example allocates the required number of characters on the heap dynamically and supports the push(), pop() and isEmpty() operations. The pop operation always retrieves the top symbol of the stack, the one that was last pushed on the stack. The next symbol is always pushed on the top of the stack so that it is the first one to be popped out.

```
class Stack {
   char *items;                  // stack of character symbols
   int top, size;               // current top, total size
public:
   Stack(int);                  // conversion constructor
   void push(char);             // push on top of stack
   char pop();                  // pop the top symbol
   bool isEmpty() const;        // is stack empty?
   ~Stack();                    // return heap memory
} ;
```

Listing 17.1 shows the implementation of the stack along with the test driver for the class. The conversion constructor uses the initialization list to initialize class data members: the total size of the character array requested for the stack and the current position of the stack top in the array (the index of the location where the next symbol will be inserted). The constructor allocates the heap memory using the size requested by the client code. If the system is out of memory, the execution is terminated.

The function `push()` inserts its parameter value into the heap array. Since the size of the heap array is requested by the client code, and the client code should know how much stack storage it needs for its algorithm, it is all right to terminate execution in case of array overflow. However, this would pop too much responsibility up to the client code. Meanwhile, the client code should concentrate on its algorithm (e.g., checking whether parentheses match) and not with the user interface for diagnostic messages. It would be more appropriate to push the responsibility for dealing with overflow down to the server class.

One alternative for handling array overflow is to terminate program execution. The advantage of doing this in the server class rather than in the client code is that the client code is streamlined and does not contain error processing related to the implementation details of the server. Another, better alternative is to process the server problem (overflow) in the server and not in the client code. This can be done, for example, by allocating additional memory in the server object in case of array overflow.

How much additional memory to allocate is debatable. In Listing 17.1, I allocate a stack array of double the current size, copy existing stack contents into the newly allocated array, dispose of the existing array, and continue operations using the heap array that is twice as long as its previous version. The client code is totally insulated from these details of memory management.

Function `pop()` is straightforward—it just pops the top character from the stack and updates the index that points to the top of the stack. For a large data structure, it would be appropriate to watch the position of the top and return the existing memory when, for example, half of the existing array is not used. For this simple example, there is no need to do that.

Function `pop()` could check whether the stack is empty and send a message (or a return value) if there is nothing to pop from the stack. I felt that this approach, although possible, would make communications between the stack class and its clients unnecessarily complex. Also, what would a client do if it tries to pop the stack when the stack is empty? In most cases (see, e.g., Chapter 8 and its examples in Listing 8.10–8.13), the empty stack is a signal to the client to stop one phase of processing and to start another phase. Hence, there is no need to involve the server class into this application-related decision. The client code should call the stack method `isEmpty()` before each call to `pop()` and either call the `pop()` method if the stack is not empty or do something else. In Listing 17.1, I terminate the algorithm—the empty stack signals the end of processing.

The last two methods, the method `isEmpty()` and the `Stack` destructor, are trivial. The `isEmpty()` method checks whether the stack index has returned into its initial position. The destructor returns the heap memory allocated to the object during its lifetime.

Class `Stack` objects can only be used to store the elements of given type, not for other operations. These objects are not meant to initialize one another or to be assigned to one another. Formally, you can perform these operations on any C++ variables, including `Stack` objects. Actually, if somebody uses a `Stack` object in initialization or in assignment, this should not be supported. This means that adding the copy constructor and the assignment operator to class `Stack` is overkill. On the other hand, making their prototypes private is helpful. For example, if one wants to pass a `Stack` object by value, this will be a syntax error.

For illustration purposes, Listing 17.1 initially allocates a very small array for the `Stack` object. This is why you can see debugging messages that report the change in the array size. The output of the program is shown in Figure 17–1.

Listing 17.1   Class `Stack` that contains characters.

```
#include <iostream>
using namespace std;

class Stack {
   char *items;                           // stack of character symbols
   int top, size;                         // current top, total size
   Stack(const Stack&);
   operator = (const Stack&);
public:
   Stack(int);                            // conversion constructor
   void push(char);                       // push on top of stack
   char pop();                            // pop the top symbol
   bool isEmpty() const;                  // is stack empty?
   ~Stack();                              // return heap memory
} ;

Stack::Stack(int sz = 100)  : size(sz),top(0)
{ items = new char[sz];                   // allocate heap memory
   if (items==0)
   { cout << "Out of memory\n";   exit(1); } }
```

```
void Stack::push (char c)
  { if (top < size)                              // normal case: push symbol
      items[top++] = c;
    else  // recover from stack overflow
      { char *p = new char[size*2];              // get more heap memory
        if (p == 0)                              // test for success
          { cout << "Out of memory\n";  exit(1); }
        for (int i=0;  i < size;  i++)           // copy existing stack
          p[i] = items[i];
        delete [] items;                         // return heap memory
        items = p;                               // hook up new memory
        size *= 2;                               // update stack size
        cout << "New size: " << size << endl;
        items[top++] = c; } }                    // push symbol on top

char Stack::pop()
{ return items[-top]; }                          // pop unconditionally

bool Stack::isEmpty() const                      // anything to pop?
{ return top == 0; }

Stack::~Stack()
{ delete [] items; }                             // return heap memory

int main()
{
  char data[] = "abcdefghij";                    // pre-canned input data
  Stack s(4);                                    // Stack object
  int n = sizeof(data)/sizeof(char)-1;           // input data count
  cout << "Initial data:  ";
  for (int j = 0;  j < n;  j++)                   // print initial data
  { cout << data[j] << " "; }
  cout << endl;
  for (int i = 0;  i < n;  i++)                   // push data on the stack
    s.push(data[i]);
  cout << "Inversed data: ";
  while (!s.isEmpty())                            // pop until stack is empty
    cout << s.pop() << " ";
  cout << endl;
  return 0;
  }
```

Figure 17-1   Output for program in Listing 17.1.

```
Initial data: a b c d e f g h i j
New size: 8
New size: 16
Inversed data: j i h g f e d c b a
```

The problem with this design is that if you want to have a container for other types of components, the design has to be repeated from scratch. All instances of the previous component type should be replaced by instances of another component type. For example, if you want to have a stack of integers instead of characters, the stack specification should look this way.

```
class Stack {
    int *items;                 // stack of integer symbols
    int top, size;              // current top, total size
    Stack(const Stack&);
    operator = (const Stack&);
public:
    Stack(int);                 // conversion constructor
    void push(int);             // push on top of stack
    int pop();                  // pop the top symbol
    bool isEmpty() const;       // is stack empty?
    ~Stack();                   // return heap memory
} ;
```

For a stack of double floating-point values, the class has to be modified again.

```
class Stack {
    double *items;              // stack of double symbols
    int top, size;             // current top, total size
    Stack(const Stack&);
    operator = (const Stack&);
public:
    Stack(int);                 // conversion constructor
    void push(double);          // push on top of stack
    double pop();               // pop the top symbol
    bool isEmpty() const;       // is stack empty?
    ~Stack();                   // return heap memory
} ;
```

Notice that a global editor is not sufficient to do the job. To arrive at this design, I had to change type `int` to `double` in the pointer definition, in the `push()` parameter list, and in the `pop()` return value. The definition of data members `top` and `size` must not be changed; the type of the constructor parameter does not change either. Hence, the reuse of this design requires attention. This is by no means a no-brainer.

Another method of reusing the container is to design it with a generic "parameter" type. This type corresponds neither to a programmer-defined type nor to a built-in type. For example, class `Stack` can be defined in the following way.

```
class Stack {
   Type *items;                    // stack of symbols of type Type
   int top, size;                  // current top, total size
   Stack(const Stack&);
   operator = (const Stack&);
public:
   Stack(int);                     // conversion constructor
   void push(Type);                // push on top of stack
   Type pop();                     // pop the top symbol
   bool isEmpty() const;           // is stack empty?
   ~Stack();                       // return heap memory
} ;
```

This code does not compile unless the compiler knows what type `Type` is.
Once you have defined it, the code compiles. This is nice because it makes the
job of substitution simpler and less error prone. You should replace the
instances of use of the type `Type` but not others. Moreover, the type `Type` can
be defined using the `typedef` definition, for example:

```
typedef char Type;               // type is equivalent to char
```

This definition has to be seen by the compiler before it processes the `Stack`
definition. The compiler will replace each instance of the identifier `Type` with
the keyword `char` and will compile the resulting class.

With this approach, the reuse of the class design is no longer impaired by
random errors. All that is needed to generate a version of the stack for another type of component is to replace the keyword `char` in the `typedef` statement with the name of another type. There is no danger of accidental errors.
Listing 17.2 shows the version of the class `Stack` where the type `Type` denotes
type `int`. The output of this program is shown in Figure 17–2.

Listing 17.2   Reuse of class design for a `Stack` that contains integers.

```
#include <iostream>
using namespace std;

typedef int Type;                        // portable type definition

class Stack {
   Type *items;                          // stack of items of type Type
   int top, size;                        // current top, total size
   Stack(const Stack&);
   operator = (const Stack&);
public:
   Stack(int);                           // conversion constructor
   void push(const Type&);               // push on top of stack
   Type pop();                           // pop the top symbol
```

```
  bool isEmpty() const;                              // is stack empty?
  ~Stack();                                          // return heap memory
} ;

Stack::Stack(int sz = 100) : size(sz),top(0)
{ items = new Type[sz];                              // allocate heap memory
  if (items==0)
  { cout << "Out of memory\n";   exit(1); } }

void Stack::push (const Type& c)                     // pass by reference
 { if (top < size)                                   // normal case: push symbol
     items[top++] = c;
   else  // recover from stack overflow
     { Type *p = new Type[size*2];                    // get more heap memory
       if (p == 0)                                    // test for success
         { cout << "Out of memory\n";   exit(1); }
       for (int i=0;  i < size;  i++)                 // copy existing stack
          p[i] = items[i];
       delete [] items;                               // return heap memory
       items = p;                                     // hook up new memory
       size *= 2;                                     // update stack size
       cout << "New size: " << size << endl;
       items[top++] = c; } }                          // push symbol on top

Type Stack::pop()
{ return items[-top]; }                               // pop unconditionally

bool Stack::isEmpty() const                           // anything to pop?
{ return top == 0; }

Stack::~Stack()
{ delete [] items; }                                  // return heap memory

int main()
{
  Type data[] = { 1, 2, 3, 4, 5, 6, 7, 8, 9, 0 } ;
  Stack s(4);                                         // stack object
  int n = sizeof(data)/sizeof(Type);                  // input data count
  cout << "Initial data:  ";
  for (int j = 0;  j < n;  j++)
   { cout << data[j] << " "; }                         // print input data
  cout << endl;
  for (int i = 0;  i < n;  i++)
   { s.push(data[i]); }                                // push data on the stack
  cout << "Inversed data: ";
  while (!s.isEmpty())                                 // pop until stack is empty
     cout << s.pop() << " ";
  cout << endl;
  return 0;
  }
```

```
Initial data: 1 2 3 4 5 6 7 8 9 0
New size: 8
New size: 16
Inversed data: 0 9 8 7 6 5 4 3 2 1
```

Figure 17-2   Output for program in Listing 17.2.

The `typedef` approach allows you to reuse the class design, not only for built-in types but for arbitrary programmer-defined types as well—accounts, inventory items, rectangles, and so on. The caveat here is the ability of the component type to support operations that the component objects undergo within the container class. This is not too difficult, but you should make sure you recognize these operations in the container code—they are often implicit.

In the `Stack` example, the container class creates an array of components on the heap. This means that the component class has to provide a default constructor. This is not a problem for built-in types, but might be a problem for a programmer-defined type.

When a component object is inserted into the container in the `push()` method, the assignment is used. If the component class does not handle its memory dynamically, this is not a problem. If it does handle heap memory, the component class has to provide an overloaded assignment operator. Notice that the assignment operator for the container remains private—I am talking about the assignment operator for the component class.

Another reuse issue that requires support from the design of the component class is parameter passing and returning values from container methods. For built-in data types, this issue is trivial. This is why in Listing 17.1, method `push()` had a value parameter, and method `pop()` was returning the value. In Listing 17.2, method `push()` passes the parameter as a constant reference to avoid integrity problem and negative impact on performance (see Chapter 11, "Constructors and Destructors: Potential Trouble," for a detailed discussion of these problems). Method `pop()` still returns the value for compatibility with the first version of the program in Listing 17.1. However, many container designers avoid returning values from container methods and pass reference parameters (non-constant) instead.

This approach allows us to reuse the container design in another program for any type that supports assignment and copying. However, if stacks of different types are used in the same program, this approach does not work. The type `Type` can have only one meaning during compilation.

When the same container is to be used for different types of components in the same program, we are back to the technique of manual editing of design. In the case of the stack, each stack should have a different name, for example, `charStack`, `intStack`, `pointStack`, and so on, and their code and interfaces should be edited.

```
class doubleStack {
   double *items;                      // edit component type
   int top, size;                      // leave the type the same
   Stack(const Stack&);
   operator = (const Stack&);
public:
   Stack(int);                         // leave the type the same
   void push(double);                  // edit parameter type
   double pop();                       // edit return type
   bool isEmpty() const;
   ~Stack();
} ;
```

If source code for each class is edited individually, propagation of future modifications becomes cumbersome and error prone. Unique class names clog the project name space and create the potential for name conflicts.

Use of the macro facility can automate the generation of new class names and code, but this method of reuse is cumbersome and error prone. I do not think that C++ programmers today should learn how to write macros—this is an obsolete approach to design reuse. Just to satisfy your curiosity, this is how the macro for this stack looks.

```
#define MakeName(a,b)  a/**/b

#define DefineStack(Type)        \
class MakeName(Type,Stack) {     \
   Type *items;                  \
   int  top, size;               \
Stack(const Stack&);             \
   operator = (const Stack&);    \
public:                          \
   Stack(int sz = 100)  : size(sz),top(0) \
   { items = new Type[sz];              \
     if (items==0)                      \
        { cout << "Out of memory\n";  exit(1); } }  \
   void push(const Type& c)       \
   { if (top < size)              \
      items[top++] = c;           \
     else                         \
      { Type *p = new Type[size*2];\
        if (p == 0)                \
           { cout << "Out of memory\n";  exit(1); } \
        for (int i=0; i<size; i++) \
```

```
        p[i] = items[i];          \
    delete [] items;              \
    items = p;                    \
    size *= 2;                    \
    cout << "New size: " << size << endl; \
    items[top++] = c; } }         \
Type pop()                        \
{ return items[-top]; }           \
bool isEmpty() const              \
{ return top == 0; }              \
~Stack()                          \
{ delete [] items; }              \
} ;
```

The client must first define stack types using the `DefineStack` name
defined at the start of the macro.

```
DefineStack(int);
```

This will generate the name `intStack` as a concatenation of the type (specified in parentheses) and the name `Stack` (the second argument to the
`MakeName` macro). This will also define code for the stack of integers. Then
the client will be able to declare and use an appropriate stack object.

```
intStack s(4);
```

Since all code fits into one preprocessor-generated line, it is difficult to
debug. Lexical substitution, as is often the case with macros, can generate
incorrect code. This is not a good way to reuse class design.

Syntax of Template Class Definition

C++ supports yet another method to reuse class design. This tool is called a
template class. Instead of the class with a fixed type of component, you create
the class where the type of component is treated as a class parameter.

This parameter has a programmer-defined name, for example, `Type`, `T`, `Tp`,
and so on. (As for any parameter, it is up to the programmer to decide what
to call it.) Its actual value can be any type, built-in or programmer-defined. As
for any parameter, its actual value cannot be known at the time of compiling
the template definition. When the client code instantiates an object of this
class, it specifies the actual type that should be used in the class instead of the
class parameter.

Template Class Specification

Here is how the template class specification for the stack example looks. The type parameter is denoted by the programmer-defined name `Type`.

```
template <class Type>              // Type is given at instantiation
class Stack {
  Type *items;                     // actual type will be used
  int top, size;
  Stack(const Stack&);
  operator = (const Stack&);
public:
  Stack(int);
  void push(const Type&);          // actual type will be used
  Type pop();                      // actual type will be used
  bool isEmpty() const;
  ~Stack();
} ;
```

Theoretically, this is an extension of the concept of function parameters. When a function is written, each parameter is given a name, but this name is just an alias for the name that will be specified later. The function designates all operations to be performed over the value of the actual argument. But the value of the actual argument is not known when the function is written. It is only at the time of the function invocation that the value of the actual argument becomes known. Then all occurrences of the name of the formal parameter within the function are replaced by the name of the actual argument and the computations are performed over this argument value.

The advantage of using functions with parameters is that at the time of the algorithm design, there is no need to make the commitment as to the value over which to perform computations. The computations can be performed over any value, and this value becomes known only at the time of the function call. If the same algorithm is needed in another place in the program and for another value of the argument, it is not necessary to implement it in the source code again. The same function can be called from different places in the program (without any modification) with the names of the actual arguments specified. If necessary, the function can be called again with the same arguments.

Similarly, the template tells the compiler how to generate code when a request for the use of a particular type is made. When the template is written, the type is given a name, but this name is just an alias for the name that will be specified later. The template designates all operations to be performed over the values of this type. But the name of the actual type is not known when the template is written. It is only at the time of the creation of the object that the name of the actual type becomes known, and the computations are performed for this type of value.

The advantage of using template classes is that at the time of the algorithm design, there is no need to make the commitment as to the type over which to perform computations. They can be performed over any type (as long as the type can support these operations), and this type becomes known only at the time of the object instantiation. If the design is needed in another place in the program but for a different type, it is not necessary to implement it in the source code again. The same template class can be instantiated at different places in the program for different types without any modification. Each instantiation is different from another only in the name of the actual type. If necessary, an object can be created with the same actual type as earlier.

This is very good. You design a class only once, and then you use it as a template (this is where the name comes from) to generate any number of specific classes that designate what actual type to use instead of the parameter type you used in the design of the class. Other terms for template classes are generic classes and parameterized classes. They can be used with different actual types of components.

The `template` is a C++ keyword. In the class definition, this keyword is followed by a nonempty parameter list in angle brackets; these angle brackets (rather than parentheses in C++ functions) are used to indicate type parameters. Each template class parameter in the parameter list is a combination of a keyword `class` and a programmer-defined identifier.

Each template parameter in angle brackets is a placeholder for type. A parameterized class (generic class) can have any number of type parameters. Multiple template parameters in the parameter list are separated by commas.

```
template <class T1, class T2, class T3>    // three type parameters
   class Triple;                           // class declaration
```

As in other cases in C++, the keyword `class` in the parameter list does not have the same meaning as in other contexts. Its role here is to denote that the identifier that follows is a placeholder for an actual type. This type does not have to be a class. It can be any built-in type as well. Expression parameters of specific types are also allowed.

```
template <class Type, int size>            // a type and a value
   class Array;
```

This is similar to function parameters—at the time of instantiation of class `Array`, a value of the specified type (here, of the type `int`) should be provided by the client code.

Template Instantiation

Creating an object of a template class is called *instantiation*, similar to creating an object of any class in C++.

When the client code instantiates a specific object from a template class, an actual type argument should be provided by the client code for each template parameter. The `Stack` template described above is not a class, but only a template. It does not support creation of `Stack` objects directly. A `Stack` object without an indication of the actual type is as absurd as a function call, for example, `push()`, without indicating what actual value should be pushed onto the stack.

The actual type is specified at template instantiation as the type name in angle brackets that is appended to the name of the template class. The object name is specified in the same way as for nongeneric classes. Constructor parameters are used as usual where necessary.

```
Stack<int> is(50);          // stack of integers, length 50
Stack<char> cs(200);        // stack of characters, length 200
```

The instantiation resembles a function call where formal parameters are placeholders that receive the values of actual arguments. In the function definition, the formal parameters are listed in parentheses. In the function call, actual arguments are listed in parentheses. In the template definition, the template parameters are listed in angle brackets. In the template object instantiation, the actual types are listed in angle brackets. If the template definition has more than one class parameter, the template instantiation has to specify the same number of actual types (separated by commas) between the left and right angle brackets.

Unlike in a function call, only actual compile time values can be used in the template object instantiation: They are directly hardcoded in the client code. C++ does not implement run-time type variables: You cannot use a variable whose value is a type. Default parameter values cannot be used for template type parameters.

Notice that when the compiler elaborates the template class definition, it does not generate object code for the class. It cannot do that because the actual type of class component is not known yet. So the compiler maintains its internal tables with the information about the template but does not add object code to the object file that corresponds to the source file with the template definition.

When the compiler elaborates a template instantiation, for example, `Stack<int> is(50)`, it first produces an actual class definition (in this case,

Stack<int>) by replacing template formal parameters by the actual template
type arguments. This code should not go to the object code file being generated, because the class might be used in another source file as well. So, the
compiler generates an additional object file for Stack<int>. After that, it
generates the object of the Stack<int> class.

```
template <class Type>
class Stack<int> {                      // type is given at instantiation
    int *items;                         // actual type is used
    int top, size;
    Stack(const Stack&);
    operator = (const Stack&);
public:
    Stack(int);
    void push(const int&);              // actual type is used
    int pop();                          // actual type is used
    bool isEmpty() const;
    ~Stack();
} ;
```

Notice that in defining the generic template, the interface for the push()
function was defined as a reference to a constant. This is why this function is
defined for Stack<int> as push(const int&); this is overkill for built-in
types, but it improves efficiency for actual types when they represent large
complex classes. Function pop(), however, returns a value rather than a reference so that client code does not depend on the life span of the stack object
and its elements.

The object is of type Stack<int> is of the same nature as any other C++
object. There is nothing in this object that says that it is an object of a template class rather than an object of a regular class. This object can be used anywhere a non-template object can; it can be passed as a parameter and respond
to messages defined for the generic class.

```
if (!is.isEmpty())                      // sending a message to object
    DebugPrint(is);                     // passing object as parameter
```

The template class name can be used anywhere where a non-template class
name can, but the parameter list with the actual type names must be specified. For example, function DebugPrint() here should be defined as a function that accepts arguments of a specific type, in this case, Stack<int>.

```
void DebugPrint(Stack<int>& stack);       // function prototype
```

Implementing Template Functions

In the example above, the function `DebugPrint()` is a regular C++ function. The only difference between this function and other C++ functions you saw earlier is that its parameter is an object of a template class. In the body of this function, the parameter stack is treated as a regular C++ object whose class is known.

If the debugging algorithm is the same for stack objects of different types, you might want to specify that in the function interface. The type `Stack<int>` is too specific for such a function: With this type, the function could accept actual argument of this type only, but not of other stack types. To support generality, the function interface should indicate that a stack object of any type is acceptable. C++ supports this with the concept of a template (generic) function.

A template function is specified in the same way as a template class. The keyword `template` is followed with a type parameter list in angle brackets. Each entry in the parameter list is a combination of the keyword `class` and an identifier that is a placeholder for the type name. (Again, it does not have to be a class name—any legal C++ type would do.) The template parameter list is followed by the function header with the function name and the parameter list. In the function parameter list, the notation for instantiated template classes is used. Instead of actual types, the names of type parameters from the template parameter list are specified. This is how a generic `DebugPrint()` function looks, one that is capable of accepting a stack parameter of any type.

```
template <class Type>            // template parameter list
void DebugPrint(Stack<Type>& stack);   // function parameter list
```

The same idea is used when methods of a generic class are implemented outside of the class scope braces. These functions are generic functions—they should work with any type as long as this type is specified as the actual type. (Well, the function might expect some properties in the objects of the actual type, for example, the ability to support the assignment operator; this depends on the algorithm that the function implements.)

```
void push(const Type&);     // no good outside of class braces
```

There are two problems with this function prototype. First, it should indicate that this function belongs to class `Stack`; second, it should indicate that the identifier `Type` is a type parameter to be specified later, not the name of the type specified earlier. If this is not done, the compiler will complain that `Type` is not defined.

C++ treats member functions of template classes as template functions. The definition (or a declaration) of a template function starts with the keyword `template` followed by the template parameter list in angle brackets. Each component of the template parameter list includes the keyword `class` followed by an identifier that specifies the name of the type parameter.

```
template <class Type>            // template parameter list
void Stack::push(const Type&);   // better but not good enough
```

Now the compiler knows that the identifier `Type` is a type parameter name and will wait for the name of the actual type at class object instantiation. Yet another problem with this function definition is the class name. I use the name `Stack`, but there is no such class in the program: the name `Stack` denotes a template class, not a class. For the compiler, the name `Stack` without any qualifier is not defined. It wants to know the components of the type this `Stack` has.

What should I tell the compiler? I do not know what type this `Stack` is going to be because at the time of the class definition, this type can be anything, almost any type. The actual type will become known at the time of instantiation. The only thing that I know is that whatever this type is going to be, it will be the same type as the type specified in the function parameter list. Hence, it is this type that should be specified in the angle brackets following the type name.

```
template <class Type>                  // template parameter list
void Stack<Type>::push(const Type&);   // now it is good enough
```

This is an important concept to keep in mind when you are dealing with template classes. This function prototype is built according to the same rules as any other C++ function prototype. It specifies what the types of function parameters are (in this case, `Type`) and to what class this function belongs to (in this case, `Stack<Type>`).

The template parameter list should be repeated for each member function defined outside the class specification.

```
template <class Type>                        // template parameter list
void Stack<Type>::push (const Type& c)       // template prefix
  { if (top < size)                          // normal case: push symbol
      items[top++] = c;
    else  // recover from stack overflow
      { Type *p = new Type[size*2];          // actual type will be used
        if (p == 0)
          { cout << "Out of memory\n";  exit(1); }
```

```
    for (int i=0;  i < size;  i++)
        p[i] = items[i];                 // copy existing data
    delete [] items;
    items = p;                           // hook up new heap array
    size *= 2;                           // update stack size
    cout << "New size: " << size << endl;
    items[top++] = c; } }                // push symbol on top
```

The scope operator in the name of the member function should specify the identifiers of the template formal parameters; the generic class name is followed by the template parameter list in angle brackets. This is consistent with the requirement to supply the names of generic parameters every time the class name is mentioned outside the class definition.

Notice that the keywords template or class are not used in the template prefix of the scope operator, just the type parameter names. The template prefix makes the formal parameters available to the function that follows. The name of the function itself does not need type parameters.

```
template <class Type>                           // template parameter list
void Stack<Type>::push<Type> (const Type& c);   // overkill
```

Here, the function name push<Type> makes no sense; the name of the function itself is sufficient.

Similarly, when defining template constructors and destructors, template arguments are specified only once, in the template prefix, not in the member function name. You say Stack<Type>::Stack(), not Stack<Type>::Stack<Type>(). Here, the second Stack is a member function name rather than a type specifier.

```
template <class Type>
Stack<Type>::Stack(int sz = 100)  : size(sz),top(0)
{ items = new Type[sz];
  if (items==0)
    { cout << "Out of memory\n";  exit(1); } }
```

The same is true of the destructor: What follows the tilde is the name of the member function, not the name of the class (even though the name is the same) and hence it should not include template parameters. The part that precedes the colon scope operator is the class name and hence should include template parameters.

```
template <class Type>
Stack<Type>::~Stack()            // special destructor syntax
  { delete [] items; }
```

Notice that the destructor does not use the name of the type parameter in the body of the function. However, the type parameter still has to be used both in the template parameter list and in the template prefix. This is a general rule. The keyword `template` with the type parameter list in the function definition has to include all type parameters mentioned in the template parameter list for the class. The same is true of the template prefix that specifies the class name. All template parameters must be mentioned even if not all parameters are used inside the function.

For example, the member function `isEmpty()` checks the value of the integer index. Its body is the same no matter what actual type is used at the object instantiation. Nevertheless, the definition of this member function requires the complete template parameter list and the complete template prefix.

```
template <class T>              // it is not used in the function
bool Stack<T>::isEmpty() const  // return value of type bool
  { return top == 0; }          // same body for any type
```

In this definition, I use the identifier `T` for the type parameter instead of `Type`. This is, of course, allowed—the type name is just a placeholder, and I can use any name as long as I use the same name in other places where the same name should be used. In this example, the requirement of consistency is the requirement to use the same name in the template parameter list and in the template prefix of the same function. For another function, another parameter name could be used.

Listing 17.3 demonstrates the implementation of a stack as a template class. For the sake of the example, I used three different names for the type parameter: `Type`, `T`, and `Tp`. For different member functions, these names are totally independent. After all, these functions could be implemented in totally different source files. From the software engineering point of view, this is not a good idea; C++ classes encourage us to put together what belongs together. But the language syntax allows you to implement different member functions of the same class in different source files.

In this version of the program, the client code instantiates a stack of `Point` objects. Objects of class `Point` have two integer fields for their coordinates: an empty default constructor (to support creation of an array) and a simple copy constructor (to support the return by value from the `pop()` member function). For such a simple class, neither constructor is really necessary. For classes that handle heap memory, both are necessary.

For compatibility with previous examples, the `Point` coordinates are displayed on the screen with the use of the `operator <<`. The operator is overloaded as a global friend of the `Point` class. The output of the program is shown in Figure 17–3.

Listing 17.3   Reuse of class design for a `Stack` that contains `Point` objects.

```
#include <iostream>
using namespace std;

class Point {
      int x, y;
friend ostream& operator << (ostream& out, const Point& p);
public:
      Point() { }                           // default constructor: empty
      Point(const Point &p)                 // copy constructor: for return
      { x = p.x;  y = p.y; }
      void set(int a, int b)                // set Point coordinates
      { x = a;   y = b; }
} ;

ostream& operator << (ostream& out, const Point& p)
{ out << "(" << p.x << "," << p.y << ")";
  return out; }

template <class Type>
class Stack {
  Type *items;                              // stack of items of type Type
  int top, size;                            // current top, total size
  Stack(const Stack&);
  operator = (const Stack&);
public:
  Stack(int);                               // conversion constructor
  void push(const Type&);                   // push on top of stack
  Type pop();                               // pop the top symbol
  bool isEmpty() const;                     // is stack empty?
  ~Stack();                                 // return heap memory
} ;

template <class Type>
Stack<Type>::Stack(int sz = 100) : size(sz),top(0)
{ items = new Type[sz];                     // allocate heap memory
  if (items==0)
  { cout << "Out of memory\n";   exit(1); } }

template <class T>
void Stack<T>::push (const T& c)
  { if (top < size)                         // normal case: push symbol
      items[top++] = c;
    else  // recover from stack overflow
      { T *p = new T[size*2];               // get more heap memory
        if (p == 0)                         // test for success
          { cout << "Out of memory\n";   exit(1); }
```

```
      for (int i=0;  i < size;  i++)                // copy existing stack
        p[i] = items[i];
      delete [] items;                              // return heap memory
      items = p;                                    // hook up new memory
      size *= 2;                                    // update stack size
      cout << "New size: " << size << endl;
      items[top++] = c; } }                         // push symbol on top

template <class Type>
Type Stack<Type>::pop()
{ return items[--top]; }                            // pop unconditionally

template <class Tp>
bool Stack<Tp>::isEmpty() const                     // anything to pop?
{ return top == 0; }

template <class Type>
Stack<Type>::~Stack()
{ delete [] items; }                                // return heap memory

int main()
{
  Point data[5];
  data[0].set(1, 2); data[1].set(3, 4); data[2].set(5, 6);
  data[3].set(7, 8); data[4].set(9, 0);
  Stack<Point> s(4);                                // stack object
  int n = sizeof(data)/sizeof(Point);              // number of components
  cout << "Initial data:  ";
  for (int j = 0;  j < n;  j++)
    { cout << data[j] << " "; }                     // print input data
  cout << endl;
  for (int i = 0;  i < n;  i++)
    { s.push(data[i]); }                            // push data on the stack
  cout << "Inversed data: ";
  while (!s.isEmpty())                              // pop until stack is empty
    cout << s.pop() << " ";
  cout << endl;
  return 0;
  }
```

Figure 17–3   Output for program in Listing 17.3.

```
Initial data: (1,2) (3,4) (5,6) (7,8) (9,0)
New size: 8
Inversed data: (9,0) (7,8) (5,6) (3,4) (1,2)
```

You see that the names of the member functions become available for use in the client code as soon as an object of the class is instantiated with specific values of type arguments. When a member function is sent as a message to an object of the specific class, the function name in the client code is specified without prefixes.

```
Stack<Point> s(4);                    // object is instantiated
. . .
for (int i = 0;  i < n;  i++)
   { s.push(data[i]); }               // no type specifiers here
```

This is true of any client code—nothing indicates that the messages are sent to objects of template classes rather than regular classes. Inside the class definition, the situation is different: The name of the class might or might not be followed by the parameter list in brackets. For example, for a linked list implementation of a container, a node class will be a template that has a pointer to the next node. Hence, the definition of the node class has to use the name of the class for its own data member.

```
template <class T>
struct Node {                         // public data
   T item;
   Node *next;                        // field next points to Node
   Node(const T&);                    // constructor
} ;
```

Here, the name of the parameter is not used on the assumption that the compiler will understand that the next field is of the same type as the class being defined. A more-consistent approach recognizes that there is no such thing as class Node unless the type of the node component is specified.

```
template <class T>
struct Node {                         // public data
   T item;
   Node<T> *next;                     // field next points to Node<T> *next
   Node(const T&);                    // constructor
} ;
```

Again, from the software engineering point of view, the second version of class Node is slightly better than the first one, but the compiler should compile either version without difficulty.

Recall that each class instantiation generates a separate instance of class object code. Depending on the compiler implementation, object code might be placed in a separate object file that is later linked with other object code files. One consequence of this is that the one-to-one correspondence between source files and object files does not exist anymore. There are object files whose origin the developer cannot easily identify.

Proliferation of template instantiations might significantly increase compilation and linking time and the size of the object code. Some compilers might offer possible ways to decrease this negative impact.

When template member functions are implemented inline in the class definition, there is no need to specify the template prefix and the scope operator with parameter names.

```cpp
template <class Type>
class Stack {
  Type *items;                          // stack of items of type Type
  int top, size;                        // current top, total size
  Stack(const Stack&);
  operator = (const Stack&);
public:

  Stack(int sz = 100) : size(sz),top(0)     // conversion constructor
  { items = new Type[sz];                    // allocate heap memory
    if (items==0)
      { cout << "Out of memory\n";  exit(1); } }

  void push(const Type& c)                  // push on top of stack
  { if (top < size)                          // normal case: push symbol
      items[top++] = c;
    else // recover from stack overflow
      { Type *p = new Type[size*2];          // get more heap memory
        if (p == 0)                          // test for success
          { cout << "Out of memory\n";  exit(1); }
        for (int i=0;  i < size;  i++)       // copy existing stack
          p[i] = items[i];
        delete [] items;                     // return heap memory
        items = p;                           // hook up new memory
        size *= 2;                           // update stack size
        cout << "New size: " << size << endl;
        items[top++] = c; } }                // push symbol on top

  Type pop()                                // pop the top symbol
  { return items[-top]; }                    // do it unconditionally

  bool isEmpty() const                      // is stack empty?
  { return top == 0; }

  ~Stack()                                  // return heap memory
  { delete [] items; }
} ;
```

This class definition looks almost like a conventional class definition where the type of the component is specified with the `typedef` statement (see Listing 17.2).

Nested Templates

A template class can use other templates as its data members. For example, a stack template `Stack<T>` with components of class `T` can have a data member of the template type `List<T>`. It is important to make sure that the list components are of the same type as the stack components. Member functions of the stack template can send messages to the list template object to implement stack operations.

Let us assume that the list template provides such operations as `insert_as_first()` and `remove_first()` that add the component as the first element of the list and remove the first list component.

```
template <class T>
class List {
    public:
        void insert_as_first(const T& x);
        T remove_first();
        bool empty();              // is list empty?
    ...} ;                         // the rest of class List
```

Using a list template as a stack data member makes for a simple stack implementation. There is no need to implement dynamic memory management; the list class takes care of this. There is no need to include constructors or destructors or worry about memory overflow. There is still the need to worry about stack underflow, but that is not the job of the stack designer. The client code should structure stack handling algorithms so that underflow is avoided.

```
template <class T>             // same type T for Stack and List
class Stack {
    List<T> lst;               // template data member
public:
    void push(const T&);       // const reference to T
    T pop();                   // return value of type T
    bool isEmpty(); } ;        // no need for a destructor
```

The implementation of stack member functions becomes very simple. The `push()` methods invoke the corresponding list function and rely on the appropriate memory management there.

```
template <class T>
void Stack<T>::push(const T& item)
  { lst.insert_as_first(item); }                // push work down to list
```

Similarly, the `pop()` and `isEmpty()` stack member functions push the work to the list member functions.

```
template <class T>
T Stack<T>::pop()                               // return value of type T
  { return lst.remove_first(); }                // push work down to list

template <class T>
bool Stack<T>::isEmpty()
  { return lst.empty(); }                       // call a similar function
```

When the client code instantiates a `Stack<int>` object, the member functions will be instantiated as

```
void Stack<int>::push(const int& item)
  { lst.insert_as_first(item); }

int Stack<int>::pop()                           // return value of type T
  { return lst.remove_first(); }
```

When the client code declares an instance of a stack object, for example, `Stack<int>`, the instantiation process iterates, and the compiler generates object code for `List<int>`. In turn, the template object of class `List<int>` might need other templates too.

If an object of class `List<int>` cannot be instantiated, the stack instantiation results in an instantiation error. It might be a result of either a bug in the list template or an illegal operation over a template argument (e.g., a comparison might not be defined for a class, or a class operation is applied to a built-in argument). This makes debugging template classes more difficult than debugging regular classes.

Template Classes with Several Parameters

In previous examples, I used a template class with one type parameter only, even though I mentioned that a template class can have several type parameters.

These parameters can be type parameters similar to the previous examples or even parameters that resemble conventional value parameters in functions.

Multiple parameters and the mix of type parameters and expression parameters notably increase the flexibility of C++ templates. At the same time, they introduce additional syntactic complexities.

Several Type Parameters

Let us consider a template class with more than one type parameter. The names of these parameters should be used within the class for its data members, local variables, or method parameters. The client code should supply the names of actual types at object instantiation. C++ uses the positional principle for parameter passing: The first parameter specified by the client code corresponds to the first parameter specified in the template class, and so on.

When specifying the list of type parameters in the template class, you should repeat the keyword `class` for each type parameter (separating the keyword `class` and the type parameter with commas). Here is an example of a template class for dictionary entries. The class has two components: the key component and the information content component. These components can be of arbitrary classes as long as they support assignment and copy constructors.

```
template <class Key, class Data>
class DictEntry {
    Key  key;                          // key field
    Data info;                         // information field
public:
    DictEntry () { }                   // empty default constructor
    DictEntry(const Key& k, const Data& d)
            : key(k),info(d) {}        // initialize data members
    Key getKey() const
    { return key; }                    // return key value
    Data getInfo() const
    { return info; }                   // return information value
    void setKey(const Key& k)
    { key = k; }                       // set key value
    void setInfo(const Data& d)
    { info = d; }                      // set information value
  } ;
```

This is a rather naïve design, because the set of `get()` and `set()` functions for each class data field can be eliminated and data fields made public—the quality of the design would not change. But this is not important; the purpose of this class example is to demonstrate the use of multiple type parameters.

This dictionary entry class implements two objects that can be handled as a pair. For example, an object of this class can be returned from a function call in the client code. This is somewhat faster or simpler than passing a pointer or a reference to an object created by the client code. This is convenient for implementation of associated arrays or dictionaries where the key object serves as an index for finding the associated value of the information field. For the search algorithm to work, the `Key` class has to support the comparison operation in addition to the assignment operator and copy constructor.

There is no need to provide a `DictEntry` destructor because the class itself does not handle its memory (data members `key` and `info`) dynamically. If any of the component classes (`Key` or `Data`) handles additional resources and has a destructor, this destructor will be called automatically in the process of the destruction of the dictionary entry object. This is similar to the last version of the `Stack` class implemented with the `List` data member—the class `List` has a destructor, but this version of class `Stack` does not need one.

To instantiate an object of the class `DictEntry`, the client code has to specify two actual types: one for the key field and another for the data field. One can use built-in and programmer-defined types in any combination, as long as these types support assignment and copying.

```
DictEntry<Point,char*> entry;      // reference semantics for strings
```

Here, the character pointer points to a character array that could be shared with other objects in the program. As a C++ type, the character pointer supports assignment and copying. Of course, the client programmer has to be aware that it is reference semantics that are used in this case and avoid operations appropriate for value semantics only. In addition to providing sharing, reference semantics saves memory (there is no need to maintain multiple copies of the same data) and execution time (there is no need to copy strings from one object to another.

All of the horror stories I was telling you about in Chapter 11 originate from the fact that the destructor forcibly deallocates the heap memory. Since the character pointer is not implemented as a class here, and there is no destructor, the dangers to program integrity that I was describing in Chapter 11 are not relevant here.

Listing 17.4 demonstrates the use of the dictionary entry class for the application that needs to annotate the points on the screen and find the annotation for each given point. The key field in the entry is class `Point` similar to the one I used in Listing 17.3. (I added a general constructor to simplify data initialization and the comparison operator to facilitate the search.) The information field is initialized with pointers to string literals.

After initializing the array of dictionary entries, the `main()` test driver prints each entry in the array. The results of the execution are shown in Figure 17–4.

> **Listing 17.4   Example of a template class with two type parameters.**

```cpp
#include <iostream>
using namespace std;

class Point {
      int x, y;
friend ostream& operator << (ostream& out, const Point& p);
public:
      Point() { }                             // default constructor: empty
      Point(const Point &p)                   // copy constructor: for return
      { x = p.x;  y = p.y; }
      Point(int a, int b)                     // general constructor: set Point
      { x = a;  y = b; }
      void set(int a, int b)                  // set Point coordinates
      { x = a;  y = b; }
      bool operator == (const Point& p) const
      { return x == p.x && y == p.y; }
} ;

ostream& operator << (ostream& out, const Point& p)
{ out << "(" << p.x << "," << p.y << ")";
   return out; }

template <class Key, class Data>
class DictEntry {
   Key  key;
   Data info;
public:
   DictEntry () { }                         // empty default constructor
   DictEntry(const Key& k, const Data& d)
      : key(k),info(d) {}                    // initialize data fields
   Key getKey() const
   { return key; }                          // return key value
   Data getInfo() const
   { return info; }                         // return information value
   void setKey(const Key& k)
   { key = k; }                             // set key value
   void setInfo(const Data& d)
   { info = d; }                            // set information value
 } ;

int main()
{
  DictEntry<Point,char*> data[5];
  data[0].setKey(Point(1,2)); data[0].setInfo("Initial stage");
  data[1].setKey(Point(3,4)); data[1].setInfo("Analysis");
  data[2].setKey(Point(5,6)); data[2].setInfo("Design");
  data[3].setKey(Point(7,8)); data[3].setInfo("Implementation");
  data[4].setKey(Point(9,0)); data[4].setInfo("Testing");
```

```
int n = sizeof(data)/sizeof(DictEntry<Point,char*>);      // risky
cout << "Associated Data:\n";
for (int j = 0;   j < n;   j++)
{ cout << data[j].getKey() << " "
       << data[j].getInfo() << endl; }                     // print input data
cout << endl;
return 0;
}
```

This example demonstrates the use of template classes with more than one type parameter. The use of multiple parameters raises a question about name conflicts. Can you define several template classes that use the same class name? If the class has only one type parameter, the answer is obviously no—the compiler would not be able to decide which class to use when client code instantiates a class object.

And what about multiple parameters? Is it possible to define template classes using the same class name, provided these templates have different numbers of type parameters?

The answer is still no. Class template names cannot be overloaded. A program may contain only one class template with a given name, even if the number of type arguments is different.

Figure 17–4   Output for program in Listing 17.4.

Associated Data:
(1,2) Initial stage
(3,4) Analysis
(5,6) Design
(7,8) Implementation
(9,0) Testing

Templates with Constant Expression Parameters

As I mentioned earlier, template parameters can also be expressions rather than types. These expressions can be of any built-in or programmer-defined type. The type is specified in the template definition explicitly (not as a type parameter); the client code supplies a value of this type at the time of object instantiation.

Here is an example of the Stack template where the initial size of the heap array is specified as a template parameter rather than as a constructor parameter as in previous versions.

```
template <class Type, int sz>        // expression parameter
class Stack {
  Type *items;                       // stack of items of type Type
  int top, size;                     // current top, total size
  Stack(const Stack&);
  operator = (const Stack&);
public:
  Stack();                           // default constructor
  void push(const Type&);            // push on top of stack
  Type pop();                        // pop the top symbol
  bool isEmpty() const;              // is stack empty?
  ~Stack();                          // return heap memory
} ;
```

When an object of this class is instantiated, it is not enough to specify the actual type for the elements of the array. It is also necessary to specify the size of the array.

```
Stack<int,4> s;                      // stack object s
```

Notice that the stack object itself does not have any parameters; the default constructor does not require any. Also notice that the parameter must be passed by value—the information flows in one direction only, from the client code to the template object. Reference parameters are not allowed—a template cannot pass information back to the client code through template parameters; ordinary function parameters can only be used for this purpose.

Template expression parameters are inherently constant even though the const modifier is not used in the parameter definition. They cannot be changed in the code of template functions. Their actual values can be constant expressions only. You cannot use a non-constant variable as an actual argument for template instantiation. Only literal values or identifiers labeled const are acceptable as actual parameters at instantiation.

```
int size = 4;   const int length = 4;
Stack<int,size> s;                // syntax error: non-constant
Stack<int,length> s;              // OK: compile-time constant
```

When template member functions are implemented outside the scope of the class definition, all template parameters must be listed. If the template class has expression parameters, they have to be listed both in the template parameter list and in the class template prefix.

```
template <class Type, int sz>     // expression parameter
Stack<Type,sz>::Stack()           // expression parameter
  : size(sz),top(0)
{ items = new Type[sz];           // use expression parameter
  if (items==0)
  { cout << "Out of memory\n";   exit(1); } }
```

Similar to type parameters (and function parameters), expression parameters are just placeholders; their names are not important as long as they are consistent within the function. They do not have to be consistent across different functions of the template class. Here is another stack function where I use different names for the type parameter and for the expression parameter.

```
template <class T, int s>                 // different names for parameters
void Stack<T,s>::push (const T& c)        // consistent parameter names
  { if (top < size)                       // normal case: push symbol
      items[top++] = c;
    else
      { T *p = new T[size*2];             // get more heap memory
        if (p == 0)
          { cout << "Out of memory\n";   exit(1); }
        for (int i=0;   i < size;   i++)  // copy existing stack
          p[i] = items[i];
        delete [] items;                  // return heap memory
        items = p;
        size *= 2;                        // update stack size
        cout << "New size: " << size << endl;
        items[top++] = c; } }             // push symbol on top
```

Similar to type parameters, expression parameters have to be listed both in the template parameter list and in the class name prefix for all member functions. Even if an expression parameter is not used within the body of the function, it still has to be listed.

```
template <class Type, int sz>
Type Stack<Type,sz>::pop()              // parameters are not used
{ return items[-top]; }

template <class Tp, int s>
bool Stack<Tp,s>::isEmpty() const       // parameters are not used
{ return top == 0; }

template <class Type, int sz>
Stack<Type,sz>::~Stack()
{ delete [] items; }                    // parameters are not used
```

The major characteristic of template classes with expression parameters is that each instantiation represents a different C++ type. As different types, they are not compatible, and an object of one type cannot be used where an object of another type is expected.

```
Stack<int,4> s;              // stack object
Stack<int,8> s1;             // incompatible stack object
```

Consider, for example, a global function DebugPrint(). It has the parameter of class Stack<int,4>. Notice that the parameter object is passed by reference—the private declaration of the Stack<Type,sz> copy constructor prevents passing stack objects by value. Also notice that the parameter is not labeled as const because it changes (even temporarily) during function execution.

```
void DebugPrint(Stack<int,4>& s)        // no const modifier
{ Stack<int,4> temp;
  cout << "Debugging print: ";
  while (!s.isEmpty())                   // pop until stack is empty
  { int x = s.pop();  temp.push(x);      // save in temporary stack
    cout << x << " "; }                  // print each component
  cout << endl;
  while (!temp.isEmpty())                // pop until stack is empty
  { s.push(temp.pop()); } }              // restore initial state
```

The stack objects s and s1, are of different types. Object s can be passed as a parameter to DebugPrint(). An attempt to do so with object s1 causes a syntax error.

```
DebugPrint(s);               // OK
DebugPrint(s1);              // syntax error
```

Actual expressions that evaluate to the same value are equivalent.

```
const int length = 4;
Stack<int,length> s2;        // compatible with Stack<int,4>
```

As far as templates with type parameters only are concerned, all instantiations with the same actual type arguments are of the same type, and one object can be used instead of another object. Here we reconsider the template class with one type parameter.

```
template <class Type>
class Stack {
   Type *items;                    // stack of items of type Type
   int top, size;                  // current top, total size
   Stack(const Stack& = 100);
   operator = (const Stack&);
public:
   Stack(int);                     // conversion constructor
   void push(const Type&);         // push on top of stack
   Type pop();                     // pop the top symbol
   bool isEmpty() const;           // is stack empty?
   ~Stack(); // return heap memory
} ;
```

These two objects, even though they have different initial array lengths, are of the same class, and one object can be used instead of another.

```
Stack<int> stack1(20);      // same type as other Stack<int> objects
Stack<int> stack2(50);
```

This is more flexible and convenient than the implementation with the expression parameter. In general, the template class with type parameters and a constructor parameter can do everything that a template class with the additional expression parameter and no constructor parameter can do, plus the objects of different initial length are compatible. Avoid templates with expression parameters unless their advantages over templates with class parameters only are evident.

Relations Between Instantiations of Template Classes

Template instantiations can be used as actual type arguments to instantiate other template classes. For example, you can create a stack of dictionary entries with the following declaration.

```
Stack<DictEntry<Point,char*> > stackOfEntries;      // 100 entries
```

Notice an extra space between the two "greater than" signs. If you do not insert this space, the compiler will misunderstand the code and will shower you with a deluge of irrelevant error messages. None of these messages indicates that you need an extra space. This is the second place where C++ is not space blind. Another place where space is important is defining the default parameter value for a function parameter of a pointer type where the name of the parameter is not used.

In the declaration above, the `Stack` instantiation prompts the `DictEntry` instantiation. An optimized compiler might cache object code for reuse in future compilations. If the compiler does not do that, compilation and link time can grow significantly.

Template instantiations for different actual types (and expression values) are separate and have no relation or access to each other.

For example, `DictEntry<int,int>` and `DictEntry<float,record>` are two independent distinct classes. So are instantiations for `Stack<int>` and `Stack<float>`. Objects of these types cannot be used one instead of another.

A class can declare all its template instantiations to have a common base non-template class:

```
template <class T>
class Stack : public BaseStack {
.... } ;
```

All instantiations of class `Stack` will have access to `BaseStack` objects according to the rules of inheritance. These instantiations cannot have access to each others non-public components.

Template Classes as Friends

A non-template class (or function) can be declared as a friend of all instantiations of a template class, if the use of instantiated objects does not depend on their type:

```
template <class T>
 class Stack {
    friend class StackUser;
 .... } ;
```

Here, class `StackUser` has access to non-public components of any instantiation of class `Stack`, no matter what type is used as an actual type.

Conversely, a template class (or function) can be declared as a friend of a non-template class even when its type parameter is not bound to any actual value.

```
class Node {
template <class T> friend class Stack;
  int item;
  Node *next;                               // Node *next' is also OK
  Node(const int val) : item(val)
    { next = NULL; }
  } ;
```

Here the `Node` class can support the information field and the link to the next node in the linked list. It does not need any member functions with the exception of the constructor that initializes both data fields.

Each instantiation of the `Stack` class is a friend of the non-template class `Node` and has access to its non-public members. This might be useful if factoring out common code decreases the size (and compile/link time) of the object code. Instead of heap memory allocated at instantiation (or at array overflow), the `Stack` class can allocate a `Node` object every time data is pushed on the stack and deallocate the top `Node` object when the data is popped from the stack.

However, this is not very useful. One type `Node` (e.g., with the integer information field) cannot accommodate different types of objects that the client code wants to push on the stack. This means that class `Node` has to be a template as well.

This also means that class `Node` should be defined as a template class. Then different types of `Stack` objects can instantiate and access different types of the `Node` object with different types of the `item` field.

```
template <class Type>                    // template class
 class Node {
     friend class Stack<T>;              // any type of component
   Type item;
   Node<Type> *next;                     // Node *next'  is also OK
   Node(const Type& val) : item(val)
     { next = NULL; }
 } ;
```

The technical term for this use of templates is *unbounded types*. The parameter `Type` is independent of parameter `T`, and each parameter can accept any actual values independently of each other. Come to think of it, this is more than you need. Here, each instantiation of class `Stack` (e.g., for type `float`) has access to details of each instantiation of class `Node` (e.g., of class `Point`). This code does not implement a realistic model of the real world.

We need to enforce a one-to-one *mapping* between related instantiations, so that a stack of integers becomes a friend of an integer node only, not of a node with other types of the `item` field. To achieve that mapping, we can bind a friend (client) template class (in this case, `Stack`) to the same type(s) as the template class that provides services (in this case, `Node`).

```
template <class Type>                    // template class
  class Node {
       friend class Stack<Type>;         // same type of component
    Type item;
    Node<Type> *next;                    // Node *next'  is also OK
    Node(const Type& val) : item(val)
      { next = NULL; }
  } ;
```

Here, for each instantiation of `Node` to a specific type (e.g., of class `Point`), the `Stack` instantiation to the same type (class `Point`) is made a friend to this instantiation of class `Node`.

Class `Stack` now has a data member of class `Node` pointer that is initialized to zero in the `Stack` constructor. When the next node is pushed on the stack, this pointer points to the new node (and the new node points to the node that used to be the first node in the list). The member function `isEmpty()` checks whether this pointer is NULL or points to a node. This means that function `pop()` has to set this pointer to NULL when the last node is removed from the stack.

```
template <class T>
class Stack {
   Node<T> *top;                         // Node *top;  is illegal here
public:
   Stack()                               // default: no initial length
   { top = NULL; }
   void push(const T&);
   T pop();
   int isEmpty() const
   { return top == NULL; }               // does top point to a node?
   ~Stack();
  } ;
```

As for any template, the use of `Node` outside of `Node` definition must be qualified with the parameter list. This is why the `Stack` data member `top` cannot be of type `Node*`—it should be of type `Node<T>*`, where `T` is the `Stack` type parameter. As a result of this qualification in the `Stack` definition, instantiation of a `Stack` class object results in the automatic instantiation of a `Node` class data field of the same type.

The `Stack` method `push()` allocates a new `Node` object on the heap. The call to the `Node` constructor initializes the item field of the `Node` object to the value of the `push()` parameter. The `next` field of the new `Node` is set to point to the node that the `Stack` field `top` is currently pointing to, and the `top` field is reset to point to the new `Node` object.

```
template <class T>
void Stack<T>::push (const T& val)
  { Node<T> *p = new Node<T>(val);              // type Node<T>, not Node
    if (p == NULL)
      { cout << "Out of memory\n";   exit(1); }
    p->next = top;                              // point it to first node
    top = p; }                                 // point to new node
```

There is no need to test for array overflow in push() because there is no array in this implementation. There is still the need to test whether the allocation of the Node object is successful. Notice the type of the pointer—it is not Node*; it is Node<T>*. Similarly, when the heap space is requested by the operator new, it is of type Node<T>, not of type Node. The type T will be provided at the time of Stack instantiation.

The Stack method pop() sets the local pointer (of type Node<T>, not just Node) to point to the first node of the stack, copies the information field into a local variable (of type T), moves the top field to point to the second node, and deletes the top node because it is not needed anymore.

```
template <class T>
T Stack<T>::pop()                        // return value of type T
  { Node<T> *p = top;                    // Node of type T, not Node
    T val = top->item;                   // get the value of type T
    top = top->next;                     // point to the second node
    delete p;                            // return top node to heap
    return val; }
```

When pop() deletes the last node of the list (and there is no second node for the field top to point to), the top pointer becomes NULL again. Why? Because when the first node was inserted in push(), the statement p->next=top set this field to NULL (because the Stack constructor set the field top to NULL). Make sure you see that the member functions of the same class are tightly coupled to each other through the class data. The source code of the member functions has to be coordinated to make sure the functions cooperate correctly.

The Stack destructor has to scan the linked list of remaining nodes and return them to the heap. The local pointer p of type Node<T> with the component of type T is used again. It is set to point to the first node of the list. Notice that the pointer to the first node of the list, the data member top, is of the same type as pointer p: Node<T>. In a while loop, the top pointer moves to the next node, the node pointed to by the pointer p is deleted, and pointer p moves to point to the next node as well.

```
template <class T>
Stack<T>::~Stack()
  { Node<T> *p = top;                // type Node of type T
    while (top != NULL)              // top is 0 when no nodes
      { top = top->next;             // point to the next node
        delete p;                    // delete the previous node
        p = top; } }                 // traverse to the next node
```

The advantage of this approach is that class Node is independent of class Stack. This means that class Node can be used by other friend classes, for example, Queue, and List. Since all Node members (including the constructor) are private in this design, non-friend clients cannot create or access Node objects.

Another approach is to provide each client with its own private server class. If the Node definition is nested within the private section of the client, then only that client (and its friends) can access class Node. This again raises the issue of coordination (mapping) between template definitions.

Nested Template Classes

With nested design, the definition of the template class Node is nested within the definition of the container class that handles Node objects. Since the Node definition is entirely within the scope of the container class (e.g., Stack), the name Node is not visible to other potential clients (e.g., Queue and List). Hence, Node members can be made public, and there is no need to declare its single client (e.g., Stack) as a friend to class Node.

This is the first attempt on the design with nested classes. Class Node is defined using the keyword struct and all its members are public.

```
template <class T>
class Stack {
    template <class Type>            // Is it legal? Is it needed?
      struct Node {
        Type item;
        Node<Type> *next;            // type depends on instantiation
        Node(const Type& val) : item(val)
        { next = NULL; } } ;
    Node<T> *top;                    // Stack data member
public:
    Stack() // default: no initial length
    { top = NULL; }
    void push(const T&);
    T pop();
    int isEmpty() const
    { return top == NULL; }          // does top point to a node?
    ~Stack();
  } ;
```

There are two problems with this definition. First, some compilers do not accept nested template definitions—they can only process global templates. Second, there is no need to use unbounded template types. In this design, mapping between classes Stack and Node is one-to-many: For any type argument for class Stack, class Node can use any other type. A mapping between Stack and Node should be one-to-one rather than one-to-many: Class Stack needs a Node object that is instantiated to the same actual type as class Stack itself.

A good way to achieve that is to define class Stack as a template and then define class Node as a regular non-template class that uses the Stack type parameter for its data member and for its method parameter types.

```
template <class T>
class Stack {
    struct Node {                        // it depends on parameter type
        T item;                          // same type as in Stack
        Node *next;                      // Node<T> is incorrect here
        Node(const T& val) : item(val)   // same type as in Stack
        { next = NULL; } } ;
    Node *top;                           // it is not a template now
public:
    Stack()                              // default: no initial length
    { top = NULL; }
    void push(const T&);
    T pop();
    int isEmpty() const
    { return top == NULL; }              // does top point to a node?
    ~Stack();
} ;
```

Each instantiation of the Stack templates generates a Node class that uses the same type as the Stack actual type argument. There is no need to qualify the type Node within the Stack definition.

The same is true of Stack member functions. When a local pointer is defined in a member function, it is defined as a pointer to type Node, not a pointer to the type Node<T>. For example, method push() is almost the same as in the previous version, but the pointer p is defined differently. I commented out the previous version of the pointer definition so that you can compare both versions.

```
template <class T>
void Stack<T>::push (const T& val)
// { Node<T> *p = new Node<T>(val);      // type Node<T>, not Node
   { Node *p = new Node(val);            // type Node, not Node<T>
     if (p == NULL)
       { cout << "Out of memory\n";   exit(1); }
     p->next = top;                       // point it to first node
     top = p; }                           // point to new node
```

The same is true of other methods of the container class. Listing 17.5 shows the implementation of the template class `Stack` with a nested class `Node`. The output of the program is shown in Figure 17–5.

Listing 17.5   Example of a template class with a nested server class.

```
#include <iostream>
using namespace std;

template <class T>
class Stack {
    struct Node {                           // it depends on parameter type
        T item;                             // same type as in Stack
        Node *next;                         // Node<T> is incorrect here
        Node(const T& val) : item(val)      // same type as in Stack
        { next = NULL; } } ;
    Node *top;                              // it is not a template now
public:
    Stack()// default: no initial length
    { top = NULL; }
    void push(const T&);
    T pop();
    int isEmpty() const
    { return top == NULL; }                 // does top point to a node?
    ~Stack();
    } ;

template <class T>
void Stack<T>::push (const T& val)
// { Node<T> *p = new Node<T>(val);         // type Node<T>, not Node
  { Node *p = new Node(val);                // type Node, not Node<T>
    if (p == NULL)
      { cout << "Out of memory\n";  exit(1); }
    p->next = top;                          // point it to first node
    top = p; }                              // point it to new node

template <class T>
T Stack<T>::pop()                           // return value of type T
// { Node<T> *p = top;                      // type Node<T>, not Node
  { Node *p = top;                          // type Node, not Node<T>
    T val = top->item;                      // get the value of type T
    top = top->next;                        // point to the second node
    delete p;                               // return top node to heap
    return val; }

template <class T>
Stack<T>::~Stack()
// { Node<T> *p = top;                      // type Node of type T
  { Node *p = top;                          // type Node of type T
```

```
   while (top != NULL)              // top is 0 when no nodes
      { top = top->next;            // point to the next node
        delete p;                   // delete the previous node
        p = top; } }                // traverse to the next node

int main()
{
  int data[] = { 1, 2, 3, 4, 5, 6, 7, 8, 9, 0 } ;
  Stack<int> s;                           // stack object
  int n = sizeof(data)/sizeof(int);       // number of components
  cout << "Initial data:  ";
  for (int j = 0;  j < n;  j++)
     { cout << data[j] << " "; }          // print input data
  cout << endl;
  for (int i = 0;  i < n;  i++)
     { s.push(data[i]); }                 // push data on the stack
  cout << "Inversed data: ";
  while (!s.isEmpty())                     // pop until stack is empty
     cout << s.pop() << " ";
  cout << endl;
  return 0;
  }
```

As you see, binding the component types for coordinated template classes depends on the overall design approach. What is disheartening is that a solution appropriate for one design (e.g., global classes) is not appropriate for another design (e.g., nested classes). In all cases, you should make sure that when one class is instantiated for a specific type, the second class is instantiated to the same type.

Figure 17–5   Output for program in Listing 17.5.

```
Initial data: 1 2 3 4 5 6 7 8 9 0
Inversed data: 0 9 8 7 6 5 4 3 2 1
```

Templates with Static Members

If a template class declares static data, each template instantiation will have a separate set of these static members. All objects that belong to this particular instantiation will share the same static member(s), but they will have no access to static members that belong to an instantiation for a different actual type parameter.

For example, class `Stack` can declare its `top` data member static. This is an interesting design alternative—with the `top` data member static, the data fields `item` and `next` can be moved to the class `Stack` itself as a non-static data member. What is left in class `Node` then? Nothing. It becomes redundant. Hence, this design allows one to get rid of class `Node`.

In this design, class `Stack` combines the roles of the `Stack` in previous examples (calls to `push()`, `pop()`, and `isEmpty()` member functions) and the role of the `Node` class (fields `item` and `next`). This is why it has two constructors: the default constructor and the conversion constructor.

The default constructor is called when a `Stack` object is instantiated in the client code. It does not have to do anything, but it has to be there to eliminate a syntax error. The conversion constructor is called from method `push()`: When a new node has to be allocated, `push()` creates a new `Stack` object rather than a new `Node` object. The constructor initializes the `item` field (to the value to be stored) and the `next` field (to point to the top stack node).

The `pop()` function deletes the top node using a local pointer. The type of pointer is a pointer to `Stack<T>`. Since it is a pointer to an object of type `Stack`, the `Stack` destructor (instead of the `Node` destructor as in previous versions) is called. In the previous versions, the `Stack` destructor deleted remaining stack nodes. Here, this is harmful. This is the reason that class `Stack` does not have a destructor. (It has the default destructor that does nothing.)

```
template <class T>  class Stack {
  static Stack  *top;                      // static data member
  T item;  // from Node
  Stack *next;                             // from Node
public:
  Stack() { }                              // create object in client
  Stack(const T& val)
         : item(val), next(top)            // create new node in push()
    { top = this; }
  void push(const T& val)
    { Stack<T> *p=new Stack<T>(val); }     // no Node<T>, no Node
  T pop()
    { Stack<T> *p = top;
```

```
        T val = top->item;          // no Node<T>, no Node
        top = top->next;            // point to second node
        delete p;                   // delete top node: destructor
        return val; }
    int isEmpty() const
    { return top == NULL; }
    void remove()                   // no call to destructor
    { Stack<T> *p = top;            // trailing pointer
      while (top != NULL)
      { top = top->next;            // go to next node
        delete p;                   // delete previous node
        p = top; } }                // catch up with next node
} ;
```

The absence of the destructor creates the danger of a memory leak. To avoid it, class `Stack` provides the `remove()` method that does the same thing as the `Stack` destructor in the previous versions. The drawback of this design is that the client code has to explicitly call the `remove()` method to dispose of remaining nodes on the stack (if any).

Initialization of the static member of the template class takes place not at the beginning of the program execution (as for static members of regular classes) but when a template object is instantiated, because it is at this moment that the static member for this particular actual type is created.

The syntax of the initialization statement (in a header file) should:

- indicate that the static member belongs to template
- specify the type of the static member
- specify the scope of the static member
- specify its name and the initial value

This is how the initialization statement for the stack static data member `top` looks: Its type is `Stack<T>*`, its scope is `Stack<T>`, its name is `top`, and its initial value is `NULL`.

```
template <class T>                    // it belongs to template
  Stack<T>*  Stack<T>::top = NULL;
```

The client can declare only one object of a given type. For example, for a stack of integers, this is how the template instantiation looks like.

```
Stack<int> s;                          // only one object per type
```

Since all stacks of integers share the same static member pointing to the top of the linked list, it is not a good idea to instantiate more than one object of this type.

Template Specializations

The C++ idea of a template is based on the assumption that the algorithm works in exactly the same way for different data types. Then writing just one class instead of writing a separate class for each type makes sense. Sometimes, however, this assumption does not hold. The algorithm works the same way for different data types, but for some types, some details of the algorithm have to be implemented differently.

Consider, for example, a template class Array that contains a set of data (of a component type) and allows the client code to check whether a given element (of the component type) can be found in the collection.

```cpp
template <class T>
class Array {
  T *data;                                  // heap array of data
  int size;                                 // size of the array
  Array(const Array&);
  operator = (const Array&);
public:
  Array(T items[], int n) : size(n)         // conversion constructor
  { data = new T[n];                        // allocate heap memory
    if (data==0)
      { cout << "Out of memory\n";  exit(1); }
    for (int i=0;  i < n;  i++)             // copy input data
      data[i] = items[i]; }
  int find (const T& val) const
  { for (int i = 0;  i < size;  i++)
    if (val == data[i])  return i;          // return index if found
    return -1; }                            // otherwise return -1
  ~Array()
  { delete [] data; }
} ;
```

This template class contains only a constructor, a method find(), and a destructor. The constructor allocates heap space sufficient for input data and copies the input array into the heap memory. The method find() searches the heap array; if the parameter value is not found, it returns –1; if the value is found, the method returns the index of the value. The destructor returns the heap memory.

The client code instantiates the `Array` object of type `int`, initializes it, and prints the results of the search for the given value.

```
int main()
{ int data1[] = { 1, 2, 3, 4, 5 } ;
   int n1 = sizeof(data1)/sizeof(int);      // number of components
   cout << "Initial data:   ";
   for (int j = 0;  j < n1;  j++)
   { cout << data1[j] << " "; }             // print input data
   cout << endl;
   Array<int> a1(data1,n1);                 // array object
   int item1 = 3;   int idx;
   if ((idx = a1.find(item1)) != -1)
      cout << "Item " << item1 <<" is at index " << idx << endl;
   return 0; }
```

This should work for integers, characters, even `Point` objects in exactly the same way: For each of these types, the `Array` object will contain an independent copy of the input values; and for each of these types, the comparison operation in the `find()` method will do its job well. If, however, the `Array` object is instantiated for the component of the character array type, both the constructor and the `find()` method have a problem.

```
Array<char*> a2(data2,n2);
```

Here, the array `data2[]` is an array of character strings. The constructor of the `Array` template will copy the pointers to strings, not the strings themselves. This creates no problem when the data comes from the hardcoded set (as in the code snippet above). In real life, the data comes from an external source (rather than from hardcoded arrays), and each input value has to be allocated its independent space. The `Array` constructor does not do that: The pointers it will copy into the container will point to the same character array in the client space. Similarly, the `find()` method will compare the string addresses rather than the string contents. You see that for a character array as an `Array` component, the general form of the template class does not work—it needs copying strings in the constructor and comparing strings in `find()`.

C++ supports the concept of *specialization* to deal with the type arguments that need special treatment. For each special class, a separate specialized class template should be provided. The syntax for describing the specialization is a mixture of the syntax for the template class itself (with the template parameter list) and the template initialization in the client code (with the actual type list). You take the type parameter from the template parameter list and move it into the actual type list. If the brackets of the template parameter list become empty as a result, this is fine. For example, the `Array` template class header:

```
template <class T>              // remove class T from brackets
   class Array {                // append <char*> to class name
```

becomes

```
template <>                     // empty template parameter list
   class Array<char*> {         // actual type list
```

In the methods of template specialization, you describe what should be done for this particular type. Notice that the template definition and the specialized template definition should both be present. It is not right to include the specialized template definition without the template itself. The template specialization is instantiated using the same syntax as for the template class object: The actual type, even though it was specified in the template description, is repeated in the type name in the client code.

```
Array<char*> a1(data2,n2);      // specialized template object
```

Listing 17.6 shows the complete program that contains the template `Array` and its specialized template for the components of the character array type. The test driver initializes the template class object a1 and the specialized template object a2 and sends messages to each object. The output of the program is shown in Figure 17–6.

Listing 17.6   Example of a template class specialization.

```cpp
#include <iostream>
using namespace std;

template <class T>
class Array {
   T *data;                              // heap array of data
   int size;                             // size of the array
   Array(const Array&);
   operator = (const Array&);
public:
   Array(T items[], int n) : size(n)     // conversion constructor
   { data = new T[n];                    // allocate heap memory
      if (data==0)
         { cout << "Out of memory\n";  exit(1); }
      for (int i=0;  i < n;  i++)
        data[i] = items[i]; }
   int find (const T& val) const
   { for (int i = 0;  i < size;  i++)
         if (val == data[i])
            return i;
      return -1; }
   ~Array()
```

```
    { delete [] data; }
  } ;

template <>                                  // empty template list
class Array <char *> {                       // type of specialization
  char* *data;                               // heap array of data
  int size;                                  // size of the array
  Array(const Array&);
  operator = (const Array&);
public:
  Array(char* items[], int n) : size(n)      // conversion
  { data = new char*[n];                     // allocate heap memory
    if (data==0)
      { cout << "Out of memory\n";  exit(1); }
    for (int i=0;  i < n;  i++)
      { int len = strlen(items[i]);          // special for strings only
        data[i] = new char[len+1];
      strcpy(data[i],items[i]); } }
  int find (const char*& val) const
  { for (int i = 0;  i < size;  i++)
      if (strcmp(val,data[i])==0)            // special for strings only
        return i;
    return -1; }
  ~Array()
  { delete [] data; }
  } ;

int main()
{
  int data1[] = { 1, 2, 3, 4, 5 } ;
  char* data2[] = { "one", "two", "three", "four", "five" } ;
  int n1 = sizeof(data1)/sizeof(int);        // number of components
  int n2 = sizeof(data2)/sizeof(char*);
  cout << "Initial data:  ";
  for (int j = 0;  j < n1;  j++)
  { cout << data1[j] << " "; }                // print input data
  cout << endl;
  for (int i = 0;  i < n2;  i++)
  { cout << data2[i] << " "; }                // print input data
  cout << endl;
  Array<int> a1(data1,n1);                    // array object
  Array<char*> a2(data2,n2);                  // specialized object
  int item1 = 3;   int idx;
  char* item2 = "three";
  if ((idx = a1.find(item1)) != -1)
      cout << "Item " << item1 <<" is at index " << idx << endl;
  if ((idx = a2.find(item2)) != -1)
      cout << "Item " << item2 <<" is at index " << idx << endl;
  return 0;
  }
```

```
Initial data: 1 2 3 4 5
one two three four five
Item 3 is at index 2
Item three is at index 2
```

Figure 17–6 *Output for program in Listing 17.6.*

C++ also supports partial specializations. They provide specific treatment for only one of several type parameters. For example, the template class `DictEntry` from Listing 17.4 supports two type parameters:

```
template <class Key, class Data>
class DictEntry {
    Key  key;
    Data info;
public:
...} ;                                 // the rest of the class
```

For the `Key` type instantiated to character array, a specialized template is created by moving the `Key` parameter from the template parameter list and appending the specialized type (in angle brackets) to the class name.

```
template <class Data>          // remove the Key type
class DictEntry <char*>{       // append specialized type
    char*  key;                // replace the Key type
    Data info;
public:
...} ;                         // the rest of the class
```

This is not the end of the story. You can specialize as many type parameters as needed. When all parameters are specialized, you wind up with the empty angle brackets in the template parameter list. Here is the example for the `DictEntry` class.

```
template < >                   // remove both parameter types
class DictEntry <char*, char*>{ // append specialized types
    char*  key;                // replace the Key type
    char*  info;               // replace the Data type
public:
...} ;                         // the rest of the class
```

If only the second parameter should be treated in a special way, this is not a problem, but you have to repeat the first type parameter in the list of actual types.

```
template <class Key>
class DictEntry <Key, char*> {
   Key  key;
   char* info;
public:
...} ;                                      // the rest of the class
```

When the compiler processes a template instantiation, it selects the most specialized alternative that fits the bill. If a specialized alternative for the actual type is not found, the compiler uses the general template class to generate the object.

Using specialization is often a necessity (when one component type requires special treatment). Using specializations makes programs larger, more complex, and more difficult to understand. Not all compilers support specializations well. When one of the data types requires special treatment (most often, it is a character array), consider writing a separate class with a separate name, for example, CharArray. The advantage of writing a separate class is that there is no doubt which class is used to instantiate the object. The disadvantage is that there is no guarantee that similar features are treated similarly in different special classes.

Sometimes, this tradeoff is difficult to make. C++ specialized classes give you one way to resolve the problem. Decide for yourself what you want to use.

Template Functions

A stand-alone nonmember function can be defined as a template; the syntax is similar to the syntax of template class member functions.

```
template <class T>
void swap(T& x,  T& y)
{ T a = x;   x = y;   y = a; }
```

When the function needs a prototype, it also contains the template parameter list with each class keyword followed by a parameter.

```
template <class T> void swap(T& x, T& y);
```

Both the definition and the prototype (forward declaration) start with the template keyword followed by the formal parameter list in angle brackets; each formal parameter consists of the keyword class followed by a programmer-defined identifier. The keyword class and the identifier are separated by commas. The identifier must occur only once in the parameter list.

```
template <class T, class T>              // this is illegal
void swap(T& x, T& y)
{ T a = x;   x = y;   y = a; }
```

Each type parameter must be used in the parameter list of the template function. If the type parameter is not present in the parameter list, the compiler flags it as a syntax error

```
template <class T>
   int isEmpty(void);       // compile-time error for global function
```

Similar to non-template functions, template functions can be declared `extern`, `inline`, or `static`; the specifier (if any) follows the template list of formal parameters and precedes the function return type.

```
template <class T>
inline void swap(T& x, T& y)               // inline function
{ T a = x;   x = y;   y = a; }
```

When the compiler processes the definition of a template function, it does not generate object code. Instantiation of a template function takes place at its invocation. Since each actual parameter is mentioned in the parameter list by name, and its type is known to the compiler, there is no need to specify the actual argument type at the template invocation:

```
int a=5, b=10;   double c=3.0, d=4.0;
swap(a,b);                           // instantiation for integers
swap(c,d);                           // instantiation for double
```

Since compiler knows the types of the actual arguments a and b for the first call and c and d for the second call, it generates code for `swap(int&,int&)` and `swap(double&,double&)`.

A return value is not considered for parameter matching; conversions can be done as needed. However, implicit conversions are not used for template arguments. If the compiler cannot decide which function to generate to match arguments exactly, it is a syntax error.

```
   swap(a,c);                       // syntax error: no exact match
```

Overloading of template functions is allowed provided they can be distinguished by the types of the actual arguments or by the number of arguments.

```
template <class T>
inline void swap(T& x, T& y, T& z)        // three parameters
{ T a = x;   x = y;   y = z;   z = a; }
```

This function can be distinguished from the `swap()` function with two parameters.

```
int a=5, b=10, c=20;
swap(a,b);   swap(a,b,c);
```

Template functions can be specialized to adjust their behavior for specific types. For example, character arrays cannot be swapped as integers, and a specialized version must be used. The rules for forming function specializations are the same as for template class specializations. You deplete the template parameter list and move actual types (in angle brackets) between the function name and the parameter list. Here is a specialized function `swap()`.

```
template < >
inline void swap <char*> (char* x, char* y)
{ char* a = new char[strlen(x)+1];
  char* b = new char[strlen(y)+1];
  if (b==NULL) { cout << "Out of memory\n";   exit(1); }
  strcpy(a,x);   strcpy(b,y);               // caller must assure space
  strcpy(x,b);   strcpy(y,a);
  delete a;   delete b; }
```

Client code:

```
char x[20]="Hello!", y[20]="Hi, there!";   int a=5, b=10;
swap(a,b);          // general template function is instantiated
swap(x,y);          // specialized template function is instantiated
```

The compiler first searches for a non-template function; if one is found and parameters match exactly, templates are not considered; if more than one non-template alternative matches, it is a syntax error.

If no matching non-template alternative is found, then templates are examined. If there is an exact match and its instantiation already exists, it is used and no new object code is generated; otherwise, the function is instantiated; if more than one match is found, it is an error.

If no matching template function is found, non-template functions are examined using implicit conversions and promotions of arguments.

A template function cannot be called by or be passed as an argument to a non-template function.

Summary

In this chapter, we looked at a powerful tool for code reuse: C++ templates. The underlying idea is very simple and attractive: If the algorithms should be the same for different types, you should write it only once and later indicate for what actual type you want this algorithm to be used.

This is the ideal, but the practical use of this idea faces a number of difficulties. The syntax of C++ templates is complex. The use of specializations complicates matters even more. Sometimes figuring out which specialization will be called in each case becomes a chore. Sometimes, what works on one machine under one compiler will not work on another machine under a different compiler.

In addition, the use of templates entails space and performance penalty. This is why many C++ programmers try to avoid templates. On the other hand, templates are utilized in the Standard Template Library (STL), and you have to understand the basic principles of using templates to be able to handle the STL library correctly.

It is a powerful tool. Use it with care.

PROGRAMMING WITH EXCEPTIONS

Topics in this Chapter

Chapter 18

In this chapter, I will deal with a relatively new C++ topic: programming with exceptions. Exception is a language mechanism that allows the programmer to separate source code that describes the main case of processing from source code that describes exceptional situations. Exceptional situations are situations that should not occur during normal processing but from time to time do occur. Separating this exception processing from the main case makes the main case easier to read and to maintain. It also makes exceptional cases easier to read and to maintain.

This definition is somewhat vague, is it not? It does leave room for interpretation. Indeed, what some people view as an exceptional or abnormal situation, other people perceive as a genuine part of system operations. For example, when you allocate memory on the heap, the algorithm should describe what happens if the request is satisfied. Since it is possible that the computer runs out of memory, the algorithm should also specify what happens when memory is not available. Is running out of memory an exception? Most people would say yes.

Similarly, when the program reads data interactively from the online user, the algorithm specifies the processing of valid data. What happens if the user makes a mistake and inputs data that is invalid? Is this an exception? Most people would say no, online mistakes are a way of life, and the algorithms for processing these mistakes should be viewed as part of basic system functionality, not something that happens only rarely.

Similarly, when you read data from a file in a loop, the algorithm specifies what happens when the next record is read—how different parts of the record should be processed. Since it is possible that there are no more records in the file, the algorithm should define what happens when there are no more records to read. Is reaching the end-of-file indeed an exception? Most people would say no, this is an event that marks the end of one stage of processing (reading file records in) and the beginning of the next stage of processing (computations on data in memory).

Regardless of whether the programmer perceives the situation as mainline processing with some additional exceptional cases (the first example) or as a set of different cases of approximately equal importance (the second and the third examples), the issue of clogging the source code with diverse computational tasks is both real and important.

To be able to make intelligent decisions on structuring your algorithms, you should have a good understanding of the tools available in the programming language. This is why I will try first and foremost to explain what exceptions (as a C++ programming technique) are, what syntax they impose on the programmer, how to use them correctly, and what incorrect uses you should try to avoid.

Initially, C++ did not support exceptions and relied on C mechanisms for exception processing by using global variables accessible to the whole program (e.g., `errno`) or jumps and calls to special functions whose names are fixed but whose contents might be specified by the programmer (e.g., `setjmp` and `longjmp`).

The C++ exception facility is a relatively new language feature. Similar to C++ templates, the exception mechanism is complex. The experience in using exceptions is rather limited, and the advantages of their use for system design are not demonstrated yet. In addition, the use of C++ exceptions increases the program execution time and the size of the executable program. This is why I do not think you should use exceptions at every opportunity that presents itself. Eventually, however, they should become a legitimate part of your programming toolbox.

A Simple Example of Exception Processing

Usually, processing algorithms use C++ flow control statements, mostly the `if` or `switch` statements, to separate normal processing of data from processing of erroneous or faulty data. For multistep algorithms, the segment of source code for main algorithm and for exceptional conditions are written in alternative branches of the same source code, and this often makes code harder to read—the main line is lost in the multitude of exceptional and rare cases.

When something goes wrong in a function, the function might not know what to do about the error. Aborting the program might be a good solution in many situations, for example, trying to push an item onto a system stack that turns out to be full. On the other hand, aborting the program might not release resources held by the program, such as opened files or database locks.

Another approach is setting an error code or returning an error value for the caller to check and to take a recovery action if this action is possible. For example, when the client code makes an attempt to pop an item from an empty stack, returning an error value might be an attractive alternative. However, this is not always feasible. If any return value of the given type is legal for the pop function, there may be no special value to be returned to signal an exceptional condition to the caller.

When this approach is feasible, it imposes the obligation to always check for possible errors in client code. This increases the overall size of the program, results in awkward client code, and causes slower execution. In general, this approach is error prone. Some functions, such as C++ constructors, do not have returned values, and this approach cannot be used.

Setting a global variable, e.g., `errno`, to indicate an error does not work for concurrent programs. It is also hard to implement consistently for sequential programs because it requires that the client code diligently check the value of the global variable. These checks clog the client code and make it more difficult to understand.

By using library functions such as `setjmp` and `longjmp`, the program can transfer control to an action that would release external resources and perform error recovery, but this would unwind the stack without calling destructors for objects created on the stack before these functions were called. Hence, the resources held by these objects might not be properly released.

Let us consider a simple example and review the issues that exception processing techniques should resolve. Listing 18.1 shows a program that interactively prompts the user for the values of a numerator and denominator of the fraction and computes and prints the fraction's value. To compute the result, the program uses two server functions, `inverse()` and `fraction()`. The first function returns the inverse of its argument. It is called by the second function, `fraction()`, which multiplies its first argument by the value returned by `inverse()`.

This is, of course, a somewhat convoluted design for such a simple computational problem. A simpler design would not let me demonstrate different options of exception processing. A more complex problem would justify a more complex design but would drown me (and you) in a mire of details.

In this problem, the zero value of the denominator is not acceptable and is rejected with a message. A negative value of the denominator is not acceptable either: If the fraction is negative, it is the numerator that should be made negative. The negative denominator value should be rejected with a message that also prints the offending value.

The input loop continues until the user enters a letter instead of numeric input data. The cout statement returns zero, and the break statement terminates the loop. The sample output of the program is shown in Figure 18–1.

Listing 18.1   Example of a program with error processing in the client code.

```
#include <iostream>
using namespace std;

inline void inverse(long value, double& answer)
{ answer = 1.0/value; }                              // answer = 1/value

inline void fraction (long numer,long denom,double& result)
{ inverse(denom, result);                            // result = 1.0 / denom
  result = numer * result; }                         // result = numer/denom

int main()
{
  while (true)                                       // infinite loop
  { long numer, denom; double ans;                   // numerator and denominator
    cout << "Enter numerator and positive\n"
         << "denominator (any letter to quit): ";
    if ((cin >> numer >> denom) == 0) break;         // enter data
    if (denom > 0) {                                 // correct input
      fraction(numer,denom,ans);                     // compute result
      cout << "Value of the fraction:        " << ans <<"\n\n";
      }
    else if (denom == 0)                             // invalid result
      cout << "\nZero denominator is not allowed\n\n";
    else
      cout << "\nNegative denominator: " << denom <<"\n\n"; }
  return 0;
  }
```

```
Enter numerator and positive
denominator (any letter to quit): 21 42
Value of the fraction:      0.5

Enter numerator and positive
denominator (any letter to quit): 21 0

Zero denominator is not allowed

Enter numerator and positive
denominator (any letter to quit): 42 –70

Negative denominator: –70

Enter numerator and positive
denominator (any letter to quit): 42 70
Value of the fraction:      0.6

Enter numerator and positive
denominator (any letter to quit): exit
```

Figure 18–1   Output for program in Listing 18.1.

In this example, both exceptional conditions (the zero denominator and the negative denominator) are discovered in the client code, and the errors are processed immediately in the place where they are discovered. Server functions `inverse()` and `fraction()` do not have a chance to deal with erroneous input data. This is why they compute their output unconditionally, without a test of the validity of input data.

Error recovery here is done by printing an error message and repeating the request for the next input data. The mainline code (a call to the `fraction()` server function) here is not separated from error-processing code, but it does not result in serious problems.

Often, an error can be discovered only after some processing, in the server code, far from the place where the error actually originated. Some of these errors could be processed at the place of their discovery, but some might require additional knowledge that might be absent in the server function that discovered the error. In this case, the information about the error should be passed back to the client code for processing and, if possible, recovery. I will model such a situation by moving the test of input data from client code to the server function `inverse()`.

Listing 18.2 demonstrates this approach to error processing. Function `inverse()` computes the inverse of its argument. If the value of the argument is zero, `inverse()` uses the `DBL_MAX` constant (defined in the header file cfloat or float.h) as the inverse value. Then it checks the answer to determine the validity of the result and tells the caller what happened during the call.

If the answer is DBL_MAX, the inverse() function processes the error by printing an error message and returning the zero value to tell the caller about it. If the argument is negative, the inverse() function returns its value—the client will figure that out and will process the error. Otherwise, inverse() returns 1, and this will tell the caller that the value of the formal argument answer is valid.

Function fraction() evaluates the return value of inverse(). If this value is 1 (the valid result), it computes the value of the fraction. If the returned value is negative (a negative denominator), it passes this value to its own client and sends to the client additional data for error processing (the message to be printed). The client code evaluates the return value of fraction(). If it is 1, the results are valid, and the main function displays the result. If the return value of fraction() is negative, the client code prints this value and the message it received from fraction(). Otherwise, the client code does not do anything because the error (zero denominator) was already processed in inverse(). The result of a sample run of the program in Listing 18.2 is shown in Figure 18–2.

Listing 18.2   Example of a program with errors discovered by the server code.

```
#include <iostream>
#include <cfloat>
using namespace std;

inline long inverse(long value, double& answer)
{ answer = (value) ? 1.0/value : DBL_MAX;
  if (answer==DBL_MAX)
     { cout << "\nZero denominator is not allowed\n\n";
          return 0; }                                  // zero denominator
  else if (value < 0)
       { return value; }                               // negative denominator
  else
     return 1; }                                       // valid denominator

inline long fraction (long n,long d,double& result,char* &msg)
{ long ret = inverse(d, result);                       // result = 1.0 / d
  if (ret == 1)                                        // valid denominator
     { result = n * result; }                          // result = n / d
  if (ret < 0)
        msg = "\nNegative denominator: ";
  return ret; }
```

```
int main()
{
  while (true)
  { long numer, denom;   double ans;               // numerator/denominator
    char *msg;   long ret;                          // error information
    cout << "Enter numerator and positive\n"
         << "denominator (any letter to quit): ";
    if ((cin >> numer >> denom) == 0) break;        // enter data
      ret = fraction(numer,denom,ans,msg);          // compute answer
    if (ret == 1)                                   // valid answer
      cout << "Value of the fraction:   " << ans <<"\n\n";
    else if (ret < 0)
      cout << msg << ret << "\n\n"; }               // negative value
  return 0;
  }
```

You see that the separation between the place of discovery of the error and the place of recovery from the error results in a more complex solution. The server functions have extra return values and extra parameters to deal with—stronger coupling makes different parts of the program more dependent on each other. The client code has to abide by complex conventions on return values (in this example, returning 1 denotes the valid argument value, returning zero or a negative number denotes an invalid argument value) and behave differently for different return values. This makes the client code more complex and requires additional documentation so that client programmers and server programmers use common conventions successfully.

Figure 18-2   Output for program in Listing 18.2.

```
Enter numerator and positive
denominator (any letter to quit): 42 0

Zero denominator is not allowed


Enter numerator and positive
denominator (any letter to quit): 42 -21

Negative denominator: -21

Enter numerator and positive
denominator (any letter to quit): -42 21
Value of the fraction:      -2

Enter numerator and positive
denominator (any letter to quit): exit
```

Another problem with this approach is that the server code, in this example, the `inverse()` and `fraction()` functions, is involved not only in error discovery but also in communications with the user about the causes of the error. For this simple example of three functions this is probably not a grave problem. In more complex programs, it is important to make sure that each function performs one function (pun intended) only. The function that computes the inverse of its argument should know how to compute the inverse of its argument and should not get into the user interface. The function that is responsible for the user interface should know what to tell the user and should not be involved in other computations. These responsibilities have to be separated.

Yet another problem with this approach is that the components of the user interface are spread all over the code of the program. When the program has to be repackaged into French, Spanish, Russian, or another language, there is no specific place in the program that has to be changed—all program source code has to be inspected and modified. This is asking for trouble.

Listing 18.3 represents an attempt to eliminate the last two drawbacks. It also gives you an additional example of using static data members and static member functions. All output strings used by the program are moved into a class, MSG, as a private static array of strings. The class provides a public static function, `msg()`, whose argument indicates the index of the string to be used. If the index is incorrect, an error message is produced instead of the expected information.

You see that the server functions are not involved in the user interface anymore. The code that analyzes the situation, unfortunately, stays, but there was little that could be done about this. If the code is required to discover an error, the code should test some relevant values, and that makes the code more obscure.

You also see that all the components of the user interface are swept into one place. This facilitates not only the adaptation of the program to other languages but also maintenance of the user interface in general. If a prompt to a user has to be changed, it is only class MSG that changes. If a message has to be added or removed, the static array `MSG::data[]` is edited, and the number of array components in the `MSG::msg()` method changes accordingly. To avoid this change, the number of components in the array (defined as local in `msg()`) can be computed as `sizeof(data)/sizeof(char*)`. Since the value of the number of messages is used only once, keeping it as a literal value is not dangerous.

Notice the elements of the utilization of static data and methods: the keyword `static`, initialization of data outside the class boundaries, the use of the class name in the initialization statement and in the calls to the static function, the absence of object class MSG in the application, the lack of name conflict between the function MSG::msg(), and a local variable msg in the client code.

The output of this version of the program is the same as the output for two previous versions of the application. This is why it is not shown again.

Listing 18.3   Example of extensive communications between the client and the server code.

```cpp
#include <iostream>
#include <cfloat>
using namespace std;

class MSG {
      static char* data [];                          // internal static data
public:
      static char* msg(int n)                        // public static method
      { if (n<1 || n > 5)                            // check index validity
         return data[0];
        else
           return data[n]; }                         // return valid string
} ;

char* MSG::data [] = { "\nBad argument to msg()\n",
"\nZero denominator is not allowed\n\n",             // depository of text
"\nNegative denominator: ",
"Enter numerator and positive\n",
"denominator (any letter to quit): ",
"Value of the fraction:        "
 } ;

inline long inverse(long value, double& answer, char* &msg)
{ answer = (value) ? 1.0/value : DBL_MAX;
  if (answer==DBL_MAX)
     { msg = MSG::msg(1);
        return 0; }                                  // zero denominator
  else if (value < 0)
       { msg = MSG::msg(2);
         return value; }                             // negative denominator
  else
       return 1; }                                   // valid denominator

inline long fraction (long n,long d,double& result,char* &msg)
{ long ret = inverse(d, result,msg);                 // result = 1.0 / d
  if (ret == 1)                                      // valid denominator
    { result = n * result; }                         // result = n / d
  return ret; }
```

```
int main()
{
  while (true)
  { long numer, denom;   double ans;          // numerator/denominator
    char *msg;   long ret;                     // error information
    cout << MSG::msg(3) << MSG::msg(4);        // prompt user for data
    if ((cin >> numer >> denom) == 0) break;   // enter data
      ret = fraction(numer,denom,ans,msg);     // compute answer
    if (ret == 1)
      cout << MSG::msg(5) << ans <<"\n\n";     // valid answer
    else if (ret == 0)
      cout << msg;                             // zero denominator
    else
      cout << msg << ret << "\n\n"; }          // negative value
  return 0;
  }
```

You see that limiting the task of the inverse() function to error discovery and moving the task of error recovery (in this case, printing a message with data) increases coupling between clients and their servers. In Listing 18.3, function inverse() has an additional parameter, which is passed by its client fraction() to its own client, main(). In the case of the zero denominator, only this fact has to be reported. This information is passed up by the inverse() parameter msg. In the case of the negative denominator, the value of the denominator has to be reported, and inverse() uses both its parameter msg and its return value to communicate with its caller (and its caller's caller).

It is the use of extra parameters, return values, and complex calling conventions that C++ exceptions help to eliminate.

Syntax of C++ Exceptions

C++ exceptions allow the programmer to change the flow of control when some event occurs, for example, an error. These errors happen at run time (file is not found, index is invalid, etc.); when C++ raises an exception, the program may terminate if it has no handler that knows how to deal with that exception.

Exception handlers are segments of program source code that should be executed when the exception is raised, for example, printing a message to the user, collecting information for the analysis of the causes of the exception, or error recovery.

Organizing error-related source code into exception handlers can make flow of control more logical; instead of doing all the tests in the mainline of the algorithm and thus obscuring its meaning, error handling is coded in a separate place. The tradeoff of this approach is the possibility of obscuring the meaning of server functions that are involved in error discovery.

This separate place for error recovery can be in the same method that caused the exception, in a caller of that method, in a caller of the caller, and so on. This flexibility makes the design with exceptions more difficult. However, the exception mechanism allows the programmer to transfer control to recovery actions in a disciplined way.

Presumably, C++ exceptions allow the programmer to isolate exceptional cases in other, remote segments of source code and streamline the base processing. It should make the program more readable so that it is easier to understand. I am not sure that this is often the case. As I mentioned earlier, the utility of using exceptions is in eliminating extra parameters, return values, and complex calling conventions among the functions that discover the problem and the functions that try to recover from the problem.

When C++ raises or "throws" an exception, it can create an object of a predefined class `Exception` or of a programmer-defined class. This programmer-defined class can be derived from class `Exception`, or it can be an independent class. Again, this flexibility makes designing with exceptions more open ended and hence more difficult to understand.

The exception might be thrown explicitly with the `throw` statement or implicitly as the result of an illegal or invalid action. The exception is caught with the `catch` statement, and control is transferred to the statement that caught the exception. The catch statement (or block of statements) performs the error recovery (if any). The return of control after the error recovery in the catch block depends on the structure of the program. In general, it does not return by itself to the place where the exception occurred. This is why the programmer has to structure the program in a specific way if such return (e.g., to continue processing) is desirable.

There are three operations related to exception handling:

- throwing an exception
- catching an exception
- claiming an exception

Throwing an exception means specifying that certain exceptional (possibly erroneous) conditions are discovered and that they should be processed using the C++ exception mechanism rather than common control flow techniques.

Catching an exception means specifying a segment of code that is designed to respond to a particular exceptional condition but not to other conditions.

Claiming an exception means specifying what exception can be raised within this method; it helps the compiler (and the client programmer and the maintenance programmer) know what to expect from the function and how it should be used.

Throwing an Exception

To raise an exception, the keyword `throw` is used. Its usage indicates that the server code has discovered a condition that it does not know how to handle, and it throws the exception in the hope that someplace (among its client or its client's clients) there will be a segment of code that knows how to handle the situation.

The keyword `throw` is used in a *throw statement*. Its general syntactic form includes the keyword `throw` with an operand that can be a value of any type to be thrown in search of the exception handler.

```
throw value;
```

The `throw` statement is usually executed conditionally after testing some values or relationships in the program and discovering that they do not satisfy requirements. This means that the server code executes the `throw` statement to notify the client of the problem discovered in the server code.

The `throw` statement can take only a single operand of any type. However, some compilers do not flag the `throw` statement as an error if you try to throw more than one value. The value of the `throw` operand is used by the client code (that tries to process the exception) to retrieve information about the context of the error. Often, this information is used to define the client code behavior in error recovery.

Here is a modified example of the function `inverse()`. In Listing 18.3, this function sets up the return values or parameter values to communicate with the client code. In this version, the function `inverse()` throws exceptions in two cases: (1) if it discovers that the denominator is zero and (2) if it discovers that the denominator is negative.

```
inline void inverse(long value,double& answer)      // two parameters
{ answer = (value) ? 1.0/value : DBL_MAX;
  if (answer==DBL_MAX)
        throw MSG::msg(1);                           // zero denominator
  if (value < 0)
        throw value; }                               // negative denominator
```

You see that in the case of a zero denominator, the function throws a value of the character array type, and in the case of a negative denominator, it throws a value of the `long` type. The fact that these types are different is no accident. It would be more difficult to handle the exception handling if both `throw` statements threw the values of the same type. If both exceptions have to be processed the same way, this is not a problem. If the exceptions have to be processed differently, the client code would have to figure out what really occurred in the server code that threw the exception.

If you compare this function `inverse()` with its version in Listing 18.1, you will see that their interfaces are similar: Both functions return a `void` type and have only two parameters. In Listing 18.1, the function `inverse()` did not try to discover any exceptions. Neither did its client `fraction()`. It was the job of the `main()` client code to discover both exceptions (zero denominator, negative denominator) and process them.

In Listing 18.2 and 18.3, functions `inverse()` and `fractions()` were trying to discover exceptions, recover from some of them (zero denominator) and let the `main()` client recover from others (negative denominator). The result was greater coupling and more confusing code. The last version of `inverse()` throws both exceptions. It does have some analysis code (to decide what exception to throw, if any), but its interface is as simple as in the first version in Listing 18.1. This simplicity will be paid for by the additional code I will write to catch and to claim these exceptions.

Catching an Exception

The function `inverse()`, which can throw two exceptions, has a direct client: function `fraction()` that calls `inverse()` and an indirect client: function `main()` that calls `fraction()`. In general, the hierarchy of calls can be arbitrarily high. If a function, in this example `inverse()`, throws an exception and does not process this exception itself, one of its callers (direct or indirect) has to catch this exception.

Catching an exception is a process of finding the code that can handle the error (the exception handler); this is done by searching through a chain of function calls.

One might think that catching an exception requires the keyword `catch`. This is true: C++ does have the keyword `catch`, and this keyword is used in catching the exception. But this is not enough. When a function catches exceptions, it cannot catch them from an arbitrary source of exceptions. The function has to indicate from what segment of its code it will try to catch exceptions. This requires the use of yet another C++ keyword: `try`. This keyword should be followed by a block that can throw exceptions.

The client code that has the responsibility of catching errors encloses the code that can raise the exception in a *try statement*.

```
void foo()                  // function that catches exceptions
{ try                       // the try statement
    { statements; }         // statements that throw exceptions
  ...}                      // the rest of foo() with catch blocks
```

C++ exception handlers are implemented using the keywords `try` and `catch`; the statements (or method calls) that may throw exceptions are put in the try blocks; the exception handlers themselves are put into the catch blocks.

Syntactically, one or more *catch blocks* should follow a try block. Each catch block has a parameter of the type that corresponds to the exception that this catch block handles.

```
void foo()                        // function that catches exceptions
{ try
    { statements; }               // statements that throw exceptions
   catch (Type1 t1)               // catch block for thrown type Type1
    { handler_for_Type1(); }
   catch (Type2 t2)               // catch block for thrown type Type2
    { handler_for_Type2(); }
       . . . . .
   catch (TypeN tN)               // catch block for thrown type TypeN
    { handler_for_TypeN(); }
  statements_executed_after_the_try_or_catch_block; }
```

The try statement must be followed by at least one catch construct (block), which provides exception handling. It is an error to use a catch block that is not preceded by a try statement. (It is all right if there are other catch blocks between this one and the preceding try statement.) It is an error to use a try statement that is not followed by a catch block or blocks.

Recall that the throw statement has an argument of some type—a character array, a long value, or even a value of some programmer-defined class type. The value of the argument usually carries some data about the context of the error. In the case of the `inverse()` function, this data is either a string with the message to be printed or the negative denominator value to be displayed. If the throw statement throws an object of a class type, the constructor for that type should enable the object to carry some information about the problem. This information might be used by the catch construct for diagnostics and error recovery.

If there are several catch constructs after the try block, they have to have arguments of different types. Since catch constructs do not have names, the signatures of these constructs must be unique.

If the exception type thrown in the try block "matches" the argument of a catch construct, the code in the catch construct is executed and the search stops; when the catch block terminates, the statements that follow the catch blocks for this try statement are executed

"Matching the argument" means that the exception object that is thrown by the try block can be assigned to the parameter of the catch block, meaning the exact match, any of the standard conversions, or any of subclasses of the parameter of the catch construct. For example, a `double` value can be caught by a catch block with a `long` parameter, and a `SavingsAccount` object can be caught by a catch block with an `Account` parameter.

After the catch block terminates, the statements that follow the try block and its catch constructs are executed. These statements can have other try blocks (followed by catch constructs) if necessary. If the try statement did not throw any exception, the catch constructs are treated as the null statements—they are skipped.

If the exception was thrown in the middle of the try statement, the execution of the try statement is terminated, the catch construct is found and executed, and so on; the statements in the try block that follow the one that threw the exception are never executed. Usually, this is only logical: The exception was thrown because these statements could not be executed.

What happens if the code in the try block throws an exception that does not have a catch construct of the appropriate type? Too bad—the function is terminated: Not only is the try block not executed in its entirety, but the code that follows the catch constructs is not executed either. This means that the appropriate catch block will be searched for in the client code of the function. If it is found, all is fine and well. If the catch construct capable of handling the exception is not found even in `main()`, the program is terminated.

Let us consider, for example, the following version of the `inverse()` function that throws the exceptions and tries to catch them.

```
inline void inverse(long value,double& answer)       // two parameters
{ try  // start of try block
   { if (value == 0)                                  // zero denominator
        throw MSG::msg(1);
     if (value < 0)                                    // negative denominator
        throw value;
     answer = 1.0 / value; }                           // end of the try block
  catch (char* str)
    { cout << str; }                                   // zero denominator
  catch (long val)
    { cout << MSG::msg(2) << val << "\n\n"; }}         // negative value
```

If the first argument has a legitimate value, the try block is executed completely, and the catch blocks are skipped. There are no statements following the catch blocks, so the function terminates as if it had no exception handling at all.

If the first argument is zero, the character array exception is thrown and the first catch block is executed. Notice that the catch block is a "block"—it has its own scope, and it refers to its parameter str rather than to the variable that has actually been thrown: MSG::msg(1).

Similarly, if the first argument is negative, its value is thrown, and the second catch block is executed. Again, the name of the value to be printed is val rather than value. No matter what exception is thrown, the statement answer = 1.0/value is never executed. This is reasonable because this statement should be executed only if the value passes all the tests.

If the statements in the try block throw an exception that does not have a catch block to handle it in the function inverse(), the search for the exception handler continues in fraction() and then in main().

In this version of the inverse() function, the throw statements and the catch blocks are in the same function scope. Syntactically, this is legal C++. From the software engineering point of view, this is overkill—there is no need to use the exception handling mechanism if the information about exception is not passed across different functions. In this case, a simple if statement within inverse() would give the same results.

Another problem with this version of exception handling is related to the execution of the rest of the program. After the function inverse() terminates, its callers, fraction() and main(), have no idea whether any exceptions were raised. Meanwhile, if any exception was raised, the statement that computes the answer was not executed, and callers of inverse() should know about that.

Next, let us again consider the version of inverse() that throws exceptions but does not catch them.

```
inline void inverse(long value,double& answer)      // two parameters
{ answer = (value) ? 1.0/value : DBL_MAX;
  if (answer==DBL_MAX)
        throw MSG::msg(1);                           // zero denominator
  if (value < 0)
        throw value; }                               // negative denominator
```

Let us try to catch these exceptions in the client function `fraction()`.

```
inline void fraction (long numer, long denom, double& result)
{ try {
    inverse(denom, result);                    // result = 1.0 / denom
    result = numer * result; }                 // result = numer / denom
  catch (char* str)
    { cout << str; }                           // zero denominator
  catch (long val)
    { cout << MSG::msg(2) << val << "\n\n"; }}  // negative value
```

This is not better than the previous version of `inverse()`. The exceptions should be processed in such places in the client code where the information about the exception can be used to change the behavior of the program, in this case, skipping the display of the result of computations.

Listing 18.4 demonstrates this example with exception handling in the `main()` function. As I noted earlier, this example is somewhat artificial because `main()` could discover that the input is invalid itself. Assuming it cannot do that, this scheme of exception handling makes sense: `inverse()` discovers the error and sends information to `main()` so that `main()` could skip the use of invalid results.

In Listing 18.4, function `inverse()` analyzes the situation and throws two expressions for the benefit of its callers. Its immediate caller, `fraction()`, does not have any exception handlers (catch constructs) because it is in the function `main()` where the statement to be skipped is located. Since fraction does not have any catch constructs, it does not have a try statement either because it would be illegal to have a try statement without catch constructs.

If `inverse()` does not throw exceptions, `fraction()` and `main()` continue to compute and to print the result and to request the next set of data. If `inverse()` throws an exception, it is not processed in `inverse()` because it does not have appropriate catch constructs. The search propagates to `fraction()`. Since `fraction()` does not have any exception handlers, the search propagates to `main()`. If `main()` does not have any exception handlers either, the program terminates.

When the search percolates to `main()`, it finds there both the try statement and the catch constructs. From the point of view of `main()`, it is its server function `fraction()` that is the source of trouble. The client `main()` does not care whether `fraction()` received the exception from one of its servers or threw it itself. If `fraction()` throws an exception, the execution of the try block is terminated before the answer is displayed. The corresponding exception handler prints a message that uses the information generated in `inverse()`.

Listing 18.4   Example of throwing and catching exceptions.

```
#include <iostream>
#include <cfloat>
using namespace std;

class MSG {
      static char* data [];                    // internal static data
public:
      static char* msg(int n)                  // public static method
      { if (n<1 || n > 5)                      // check index validity
          return data[0];
        else
          return data[n]; }                    // return valid string
} ;

char* MSG::data [] = { "\nBad argument to msg()\n",
"\nZero denominator is not allowed\n\n",       // depository of text
"\nNegative denominator: ",
"Enter numerator and positive\n",
"denominator (any letter to quit): ",
"Value of the fraction:           "
 } ;

inline void inverse(long value, double& answer)
{ answer = (value) ? 1.0/value : DBL_MAX;
  if (answer==DBL_MAX)
        throw MSG::msg(1);
  if (value < 0)
        throw value; }

inline void fraction (long numer, long denom, double& result)
{ inverse(denom, result);                      // result = 1.0 / denom
  result = numer * result; }                   // result = numer/denom

int main()
{
  while (true)
  { long numer, denom;   double ans;           // numerator/denominator
    cout << MSG::msg(3) << MSG::msg(4);         // prompt user for data
    if ((cin >> numer >> denom) == 0) break;    // enter data
    try {
       fraction(numer,denom,ans);              // compute answer
       cout << MSG::msg(5) << ans <<"\n\n";     // valid answer
       }
    catch (char* str)                          // zero denominator
    { cout << str; }
    catch (long val)                           // negative value
    { cout << MSG::msg(2) << val << "\n\n"; }
  }
  return 0;
  }
```

How large should a try block be? In this example, the try is composed of two statements: a call to `fraction()` and the output statement. What happens if I move the call to `fraction()` outside of the try block?

```
int main()
{ while (true)
  { long numer, denom;  double ans;               // numerator/denominator
    cout << MSG::msg(3) << MSG::msg(4);            // prompt user for data
    if ((cin >> numer >> denom) == 0) break;       // enter data
    fraction(numer,denom,ans);                     // compute answer
    try {
      cout << MSG::msg(5) << ans <<"\n\n"; }        // valid answer
    catch (char* str)                              // zero denominator
    { cout << str; }
    catch (long val)                               // negative value
    { cout << MSG::msg(2) << val << "\n\n"; } }     // end of loop
    return 0; }
```

This design misses the boat. The try statement will not raise any exceptions. And the catch blocks will never intercept any—they can process only exceptions that originate within the preceding try statement. When `inverse()` throws an exception to `fraction()`, and `fraction()` throws this exception to `main()`, no catch block will handle the exception, and the program terminates.

What about putting only the function call in the try block, leaving the output statement outside? The rationale for doing that is that since this statement does not throw any exceptions, it pollutes the precious space in the try block.

```
int main()
{ while (true)
  { long numer, denom;  double ans;               // numerator/denominator
    cout << MSG::msg(3) << MSG::msg(4);            // prompt user for data
    if ((cin >> numer >> denom) == 0) break;       // enter data
    try {
      fraction(numer,denom,ans); }                 // compute answer
    cout << MSG::msg(5) << ans <<"\n\n";            // valid answer
    catch (char* str)                              // zero denominator
    { cout << str; }
    catch (long val)                               // negative value
    { cout << MSG::msg(2) << val << "\n\n"; } }     // end of loop
    return 0; }
```

This results in a syntax error. The output statement is now between the try statement and the catch blocks. Hence, the try statement is not directly followed by the catch constructs. To add insult to injury, the catch blocks are not immediately preceded by the try statement. What exactly the compiler will tell you is anybody's guess, but you are not going to like it.

What about expanding the try statement, including in it more loop statements? The rationale for that might be to combine different sources of exceptions and process them in one cache of catch constructs.

```cpp
int main()
{ while (true)
  { long numer, denom;   double ans;            // numerator/denominator
    try {
      cout << MSG::msg(3) << MSG::msg(4);        // prompt user for data
      if ((cin >> numer >> denom) == 0) break;   // enter data
      fraction(numer,denom,ans);                 // compute answer
      cout << MSG::msg(5) << ans <<"\n\n"; }      // end of try
    catch (char* str)                            // zero denominator
    { cout << str; }
    catch (long val)                             // negative value
    { cout << MSG::msg(2) << val << "\n\n"; } }   // end of loop
  return 0; }
```

This is doable and would be useful if this segment of client code produced additional exceptions. In general, however, it is desirable to keep the scope of the try statement as narrow as possible to make it easier for the maintenance programmer to figure out where the exceptions could come from.

And what about putting the whole `while` loop into the try statement? Well, this depends on how you do it. If you just move the `try` keyword with the opening brace up and leave the closing brace in place, the compiler is not going to like it.

```cpp
int main()
{ try {
  while (true)
  {  long numer, denom;   double ans;            // numerator/denominator
     cout << MSG::msg(3) << MSG::msg(4);          // prompt user for data
     if ((cin >> numer >> denom) == 0) break;     // enter data
     fraction(numer,denom,ans);                   // compute answer
     cout << MSG::msg(5) << ans <<"\n\n"; }        // end of try
  catch (char* str)                              // zero denominator
  { cout << str; }
  catch (long val)                               // negative value
  { cout << MSG::msg(2) << val << "\n\n"; } }     // end of loop
  return 0; }
```

Now the scope of the try statement is not nested within the scope of the `while` loop. Whatever design decision you make, your scopes have to nest correctly; otherwise, the compiler becomes confused. In general, the more narrow the scope of the try statement, the better.

As these examples show, the design with exception handlers has to answer three basic questions:

- where to throw an exception
- where to catch the exception
- what information to send to the exception handler

At the beginning of this chapter, I mentioned the popular rationale for using exceptions—streamlining the client code through separation of the main line of processing from processing of exceptional cases. In this example, this rationale was of secondary importance at best. If anything, the client code became clogged with the try statement and the catch constructs with their parameters and braces.

It is just the other way around in the design with exceptions: You throw the exception in the place where you can discover the error and collect the data necessary for error recovery. You place the catch clauses in the place where the decision how to recover from the error can be made. In this simple example, this decision was just to skip the display of the answer. Still, it required sending data from the place of discovery to the place of recovery.

Claiming an Exception

Claiming exceptions is specifying what exceptions can be thrown within this function without handling it within the function itself, that is, what exceptions the function could pass to its caller. If the function does not catch the exception itself and expects some other function to deal with the problem, it has to declare (claim) the exception.

The keyword throw is used in claiming exceptions. Its general syntactic form combines the conventional function declaration, the keyword throw, and the list of types (in parentheses) whose values are being thrown by the function in search of the exception handler.

```
functionDeclaration throw (Type1, Type2, ... TypeN);
```

Exceptions can be thrown by the function code implicitly, when an illegal condition occurs in a function call to its server function or explicitly by using the keyword throw.

If an exception is thrown by the function code and is caught in the function itself, there is no need to include it in the throw list. If the server function throws an exception and catches it, then this exception should not be included in the list. The list includes only those exceptions that the clients of this function will have to deal with.

For example, function `inverse()` in Listing 18.4 throws (and does not catch) two exceptions explicitly, a character array and a `long`. The definition of this function should include the `throw` keyword with these two types.

```
inline void inverse(long value, double& answer)
                    throw (char*, long)
{ answer = (value) ? 1.0/value : DBL_MAX;
  if (answer==DBL_MAX)
        throw MSG::msg(1);                  // explicit throw
  if (value < 0)
        throw value; }                      // explicit throw
```

Similarly, function `fraction()` in Listing 18.4 does not throw any explicit exceptions, but its server function `inverse()` throws (and does not catch) two exceptions. This means that function `fraction()` throws these two exceptions implicitly and should claim both of them.

```
inline void fraction (long numer, long denom, double& result)
                    throw (char*, long)
{ inverse(denom, result);                   // implicit throw
  result = numer * result; }                // result = numer/denom
```

If a function throws no exceptions at all, it can be declared with the empty throw specification `throw()`. For example,

```
void foo() throw ();                        // expect no exceptions
```

If a function does not define the exception specification, it might throw any exception.

```
void foo();                    // no throw: expect any exception
```

It would be nice if it were an error in C++ to claim an exception that a function actually does not throw. It would also be nice if it were an error not to claim an exception that a function actually throws, either implicitly or explicitly. However, this is not the case, and you can get away with deceiving claims (claiming exceptions that the function does not throw) or inadequate claims (claiming only part of exceptions that the function throws) or blissfully ignoring the issue, as my Listing 18.4 amply illustrates.

Understanding somebody else's design of exception handling in the program could be a daunting adventure, and one might need all the help one could get. Claiming exceptions is a powerful technique for documenting design in code. Make sure that you use it wisely.

When a function processes exceptions only partially, this is reflected in how the function claims exceptions. Listing 18.5 demonstrates claiming of exceptions for a different division of responsibilities between functions inverse() and fraction(). While function inverse() throws (and claims) the same exceptions as in Listing 18.4, function fraction() handles the exception of type long itself. Hence, it claims only one exception in its interface, the character array.

This is why the main() function has to handle only one exception rather than two as in Listing 18.4. The output of a sample run of the program is presented in Figure 18–3.

Listing 18.5   Example of claiming, throwing, and catching exceptions.

```cpp
#include <iostream>
#include <cfloat>
using namespace std;

class MSG {
      static char* data [];                     // internal static data
public:
      static char* msg(int n)                   // public static method
      { if (n<1 || n > 5)                       // check index validity
          return data[0];
        else
          return data[n]; }                     // return valid string
} ;

char* MSG::data [] = { "\nBad argument to msg()\n",
"\nZero denominator is not allowed\n\n",        // depository of text
"\nNegative denominator: ",
"Enter numerator and positive\n",
"denominator (any letter to quit): ",
"Value of the fraction:          "
 } ;

inline void inverse(long value, double& answer)
          throw (char*, long)
{ answer = (value) ? 1.0/value : DBL_MAX;
  if (answer==DBL_MAX)
        throw MSG::msg(1);
  if (value < 0)
        throw value; }

inline void fraction (long numer, long denom, double& result)
          throw (char*)
{ try {
    inverse(denom, result); }                   // result = 1.0 / denom
```

```
  catch (long val)                              // negative value is OK
      { cout << MSG::msg(2) << val << "\n\n"; }
  result = numer * result; }                    // result = numer / denom

int main()
{
  while (true)
  { long numer, denom;   double ans;            // numerator/denominator
    cout << MSG::msg(3) << MSG::msg(4);          // prompt user for data
    if ((cin >> numer >> denom) == 0) break;     // enter data
    try {
       fraction(numer,denom,ans);               // compute answer
       cout << MSG::msg(5) << ans <<"\n\n"; }    // valid answer
    catch (char* str)                           // zero denominator
    { cout << str; }
   }
  return 0;
  }
```

This example shows the advantage of claiming exceptions in function interfaces. When the client programmer wants to know what exceptions the client function should deal with, it is sufficient to inspect the claims of all server functions that this client function calls.

Figure 18–3   Output for program in Listing 18.5.

```
Enter numerator and positive
denominator (any letter to quit): 11 0

Zero denominator is not allowed

Enter numerator and positive
denominator (any letter to quit): 11 –11

Negative denominator: –11

Value of the fraction:      –1

Enter numerator and positive
denominator (any letter to quit): –11 44
Value of the fraction:      –0.25

Enter numerator and positive
denominator (any letter to quit): quit
```

Rethrowing an Exception

Notice that the program behavior shown in Figure 18–3 is different from the behavior shown in Figure 18–2. In Figure 18–2, a negative value of the denominator is rejected, and the new input is requested from the user. In Figure 18–3, a negative value of the denominator is rejected, but the value of the result is printed anyway.

The reason for that is that the function `fraction()` recovers from this exception itself (by printing a message and the value of the denominator), and the `main()` function thinks that the result is valid and does not suppress its output.

This is a quite common situation, where the function can recover from the exception only partially, but some other action should be taken in one of its callers. C++ supports this need by allowing the function to rethrow the exception. This can be done by using the throw statement in the catch construct.

For example, function `inverse()` can avoid fooling `main()` into thinking that it completed the recovery by throwing the exception again.

```
inline void fraction (long numer, long denom, double& result)
          throw (char*, long)              // extra exception claim
{ try {
    inverse(denom, result); }             // result = 1.0 / denom
   catch (long val)
      { cout << MSG::msg(2) << val << "\n\n";
        throw val; }                       // throw it again
   result = numer * result; }
```

Notice that this does not cause an infinite loop. The exception thrown in the catch construct scope cannot enter this scope—to be able to do that, the exception should originate in the try block that precedes the catch construct. Formally, the exception is considered handled on entry into its exception handler. Hence, this throw statement will cause the search for another `long` error handler at a higher level, in the client code that called the function `fraction()`.

Another way to rethrow the exception of the same type (and value) is just to say `throw` in the catch construct, and the exception specified in the parameter of the catch construct will be thrown again.

```
inline void fraction (long numer, long denom, double& result)
          throw (char*, long)              // extra exception claim
{ try {
    inverse(denom, result); }             // result = 1.0 / denom
   catch (long val)
      { cout << MSG::msg(2) << val << "\n\n";
        throw; }                           // same as "throw val"
   result = numer * result; }
```

Listing 18.6 demonstrates this technique. Function `inverse()` is the same as in Listing 18.5. Function `fraction()` does partial processing of the `long` exception, but then it throws this exception again. This means that `fraction()` has to claim this exception in its interface, and `main()` has to provide the catch clause to handle this exception. If `main()` fails to do so, the program will terminate abnormally.

Since the only goal of throwing this exception again is to avoid the display of a result in `main()`, there is no processing that the catch construct for this exception should do in `main()`. This is why the body of the catch block is empty. It still should be there. To avoid generating a warning that the parameter of the catch construct is not used, I omit it from the parameter list, leaving only the type of the value. This is somewhat awkward but legitimate C++ technique.

The output of the program is shown in Figure 18–4. You see that the extraneous output is successfully suppressed.

Listing 18.6   Example of rethrowing of an exception in a catch construct.

```
#include <iostream>
#include <cfloat>
using namespace std;

class MSG {
      static char* data [];                         // internal static data
public:
      static char* msg(int n)                       // public static method
      { if (n<1 || n > 5)                           // check index validity
          return data[0];
        else
          return data[n]; }                         // return valid string
} ;

char* MSG::data [] = { "\nBad argument to msg()\n",
"\nZero denominator is not allowed\n\n",            // depository of text
"\nNegative denominator: ",
"Enter numerator and positive\n",
"denominator (any letter to quit): ",
"Value of the fraction:          "
 } ;

inline void inverse(long value, double& answer)
          throw (char*, long)
{ answer = (value) ? 1.0/value : DBL_MAX;
  if (answer==DBL_MAX)
        throw MSG::msg(1);
  if (value < 0)
        throw value; }
```

```
inline void fraction (long numer, long denom, double& result)
          throw (char*, long)
{ try {
    inverse(denom, result); }                    // result = 1.0 / denom
  catch (long val)                               // negative value is OK
      { cout << MSG::msg(2) << val << "\n\n";
      throw val; }
  result = numer * result; }                     // result = numer / denom

int main()
{ cout << endl << endl;
  while (true)
  { long numer, denom;  double ans;              // numerator/denominator
    cout << MSG::msg(3) << MSG::msg(4);          // prompt user for data
    if ((cin >> numer >> denom) == 0) break;     // enter data
    try {
        fraction(numer,denom,ans);               // compute answer
        cout << MSG::msg(5) << ans <<"\n\n"; }    // valid answer
    catch (char* str)                            // zero denominator
    { cout << str; }
    catch (long)                                 // just type
      { } // empty body
  }
  return 0;
  }
```

Figure 18–4   Output for program in Listing 18.6.

```
Enter numerator and positive
denominator (any letter to quit): 11 0

Zero denominator is not allowed

Enter numerator and positive
denominator (any letter to quit): 11 –11

Negative denominator: –11

Enter numerator and positive
denominator (any letter to quit): –11 44
Value of the fraction:        –0.25

Enter numerator and positive
denominator (any letter to quit): quit
```

This is a powerful technique for making several functions cooperate over processing the same exception. Use it with care, because at the root of this approach is the tearing apart (exception processing) of what probably should belong together. When it becomes difficult to concentrate exception processing in one place, programmers might be tempted to use this technique to make writing programs easier. It will most probably make understanding the code more difficult.

Exceptions with Class Objects

In the examples above, the throw statements not only send control to a catch block, but also pass along a value of the specific type. This value can be accessed in the catch block. This technique is an important means of establishing communications between the place of error discovery and the place of error recovery.

Sending a value of a specific type is both a privilege (communication is established) and a limitation because a function cannot throw the values of the same type so that they would be processed by different catch blocks. For example, if a function throws two different character strings from two different places, these two strings must be processed by the same catch block. If the error recovery is limited to printing the message, this is fine—the same catch block will print two different messages.

```
void foo() throw (char*)
{ if (test1())
    throw "One bad thing happened";          // one problem
  else if (test2())
    throw "Another bad thing happened";      // another problem
  proceed_safely(); }                        // no problem

void client()
{ try
    { foo(); }                               // no problem
  catch(char* msg)
    { cout << msg << endl; } }               // either problem
```

If, however, the program behavior should be different for different sources of trouble, this mechanism of passing data becomes too restrictive—the catch block has to analyze the data sent by the throw statement and take different branches depending on the result. This defeats the goal of processing different errors in different catch blocks.

Another inherent limitation of this exception-handling mechanism is that only one data value can be sent from the try statement to the catch block. When more than one data value needs to be sent, the programmer has to resort to trickery. In the examples shown in Listings 18.1–18.6, exception handling for a negative denominator requires two pieces of information: the fact that the denominator is negative and its value. I sent one piece of information (the value of the denominator) as the parameter to the catch block, and I used a global character array for the error message.

C++ resolves these problems by making it legal to throw composite objects rather than simple values of built-in types.

Syntax of Throwing, Claiming, and Catching Objects

Throwing an object adds a new dimension to C++ programming: The designer has to decide what data items should be sent from the place where the error is discovered to the place where the recovery will take place. For each exception, one has to create a class whose objects can carry necessary data from the place of error. The methods of this class should allow the catch construct to have adequate access to the object data.

For example, class `ZeroDenom` could be designed to carry the data about a zero denominator. At the place of error discovery, an object of this class would be created and thrown. This object needs only one piece of information (the message), and this piece of information is the same for all cases of the error. Hence, the class `ZeroDenom` should have the default constructor. In the catch block, the message has to be printed. Class `ZeroDenom` could provide a method `print()` that would be called by the catch block.

```
class ZeroDenom {
    char *msg;               // data to be carried to error handler
public:
    ZeroDenom ()             // it is called by the throw statement
    { msg = MSG::msg(1); }
    void print () const      // it is called by the catch block
    { cout << msg; }
} ;
```

With class objects used as the carriers of exception information, similar to values of built-in types, you should go through the same three steps of (1) throwing an exception, (2) catching the exception, and (3) claiming the exception.

The function that discovers the exceptional condition, for example, `inverse()`, creates an object of this class and throws it in the search of the catch block.

```
if (answer==DBL_MAX)
    throw ZeroDenom();                    // unusual syntax
```

Notice the syntax of the default constructor call with the class name and two empty parentheses. In other contexts (e.g., creating an object with the operator new), using the parentheses would be a syntax error; in this context, it would be a syntax error to omit the parentheses. If you feel uneasy about this syntax, you can create an object of the required type and then throw this object much the same way as you throw variables of built-in types.

```
if (answer==DBL_MAX)
    { ZeroDenom zd; throw zd; }       // conventional syntax
```

When a nondefault constructor is used, the syntax of throwing the object is the same as it is for other contexts. For example, to carry the information about the negative denominator, I can design class `NegativeDenom` with data members for the error message and the value of the denominator and with the methods that access the object data members.

```
class NegativeDenom {
        long val;                       // private data for exception info
        char* msg;
public:
    NegativeDenom(long value)       // conversion constructor
        : val(value), msg(MSG::msg(2)) { }
    char* getMsg() const
      { return msg; }
    long getVal() const               // public methods to access data
      { return val; }
} ;
```

To throw an object of this type, the argument value has to be specified for the constructor by the method that throws the object, for example, `inverse()`.

```
if (value < 0)                        // analyze the situation
    throw NegativeDenom(value);       // throw an exception
```

Similar to objects without arguments, the object can be created using the conventional syntax and then thrown similarly to a value of a built-in type.

```
if (value < 0)
  {NegativeDenom nd(value); throw nd; }
```

The syntax for claiming exceptions is the same as for built-in values, but the name of the class should be used instead of the name of a built-in type. Here is the function `inverse()` that claims the exceptions of class `ZeroDenom` and class `NegativeDenom`.

```
inline void inverse(long value, double& answer)
            throw (ZeroDenom, NegativeDenom)            // claim exceptions
{ answer = (value) ? 1.0/value : DBL_MAX;
   if (answer==DBL_MAX)
      throw ZeroDenom();                                // throw class object
   if (value < 0)
      throw NegativeDenom(value); }                     // throw class object
```

To catch a class object, the catch construct should define the parameter of this class. Within the scope of the catch construct, the rules of accessing the object are the same as for objects of any other class. Here is how the client `main()` catches these two exceptions.

```
try {
   fraction(numer,denom,ans);                   // compute answer
   cout << MSG::msg(5) << ans <<"\n\n"; }        // valid answer
catch (const ZeroDenom& zd)                      // zero denominator
   { zd.print(); }
catch (const NegativeDenom &nd)                  // negative value
   { cout << nd.getMsg() << nd.getVal() << "\n\n"; }
```

The first catch construct sends a message to the object asking it to print its information, and the second catch construct retrieves the values of the object data members and then prints these values. The first method is, of course, better. With the second method, the data members of the `NegativeDenom` class could just as well be public.

Listing 18.7 shows the same program as in Listings 18.1–18.6. The function `inverse()` throws objects of class `ZeroDenom` and `NegativeDenom`. Since this function is called by the function `fraction()`, and `fraction()` does not know how to handle these exceptions (from the point of view of the caller of the `fraction()`), it is this function that throws these exceptions. This is why the function `fraction()` also claims these two exceptions. This is why `main()` has to put the call to `fraction()` in the try block and supply two catch constructs, one for each exception.

Listing 18.7   Example of throwing class objects rather than built-in values.

```cpp
#include <iostream>
#include <cfloat>
using namespace std;

class MSG {
        static char* data [];                   // internal static data
public:
        static char* msg(int n)                 // public static method
        { if (n<1 || n > 5)                      // check index validity
            return data[0];
          else
            return data[n]; }                    // return valid string
} ;

char* MSG::data [] = { "\nBad argument to msg()\n",
"\nZero denominator is not allowed\n\n",         // depository of text
"\nNegative denominator: ",
"Enter numerator and positive\n",
"denominator (any letter to quit): ",
"Value of the fraction:        "
 } ;

class ZeroDenom {
        char *msg;                               // data to be carried to error handler
public:
        ZeroDenom ()                             // it is called by the throw statement
        { msg = MSG::msg(1); }
        void print () const                      // it is called by the catch block
        { cout << msg; }
} ;

class NegativeDenom {
    long val;                                    // private data for exception info
    char* msg;
public:
    NegativeDenom(long value)                    // conversion constructor
        : val(value), msg(MSG::msg(2)) { }
    char* getMsg() const
        { return msg; }
    long getVal() const                          // public methods to access data
        { return val; }
} ;

inline void inverse(long value, double& answer)
        throw (ZeroDenom, NegativeDenom)
{ answer = (value) ? 1.0/value : DBL_MAX;
  if (answer==DBL_MAX)
    throw ZeroDenom();
```

```
   if (value < 0)
     throw NegativeDenom(value); }

inline void fraction (long numer, long denom, double& result)
          throw (ZeroDenom, NegativeDenom)
{ inverse(denom, result);                          // result = 1.0 / denom
  result = numer * result; }                       // result = numer/denom

int main()
{
  while (true)
  { long numer, denom;   double ans;               // numerator/denominator
     cout << MSG::msg(3) << MSG::msg(4);            // prompt user for data
     if ((cin >> numer >> denom) == 0) break;       // enter data
     try {
        fraction(numer,denom,ans);                  // compute answer
        cout << MSG::msg(5) << ans <<"\n\n"; }       // valid answer
     catch (const ZeroDenom& zd)                    // zero denominator
     { zd.print(); }
     catch (const NegativeDenom &nd)                // negative value
     { cout << nd.getMsg() << nd.getVal() << "\n\n"; }

  }
  return 0;
  }
```

Using Inheritance with Exceptions

Error conditions in the program might be similar to one another. The information that is necessary for error recovery might also have similar structure. For example, in Listing 18.7, each exception carries a pointer to the character array that should be printed as an error message.

As is often the case with similar classes, the designer might organize the program exception classes into an inheritance hierarchy. For example, one might redesign classes ZeroDenom and NegativeDenom so that class NegativeDenom is derived from class ZeroDenom.

```
class ZeroDenom {
protected:
      char *msg;
public:
      ZeroDenom (char* message) : msg(message)
      { }
      void print () const
      { cout << msg; }
} ;
```

In the previous version of this class, I hardcoded the name of the character array in the class constructor. As a result, the client of this class, the function `inverse()` in Listing 18.7, did not have to know which message to send with the exception: It just had to create an exception object using the default constructor. In this version, it is class `ZeroDenom` that does not know what its objects carry, and its clients will have to specify explicitly which message to carry.

I am not sure which approach is better. In general, the first approach (implemented in Listing 18.7) pushes the responsibility down to the server class `ZeroDenom`, and the second approach pops the responsibility to the class clients. However, the overall scheme of distributing knowledge between program classes might make the second approach more attractive. Whatever is better in each particular case, I want to make sure that this difference is not lost on you, that you notice it, and that you are sensitive to the issue of "who knows what" in the program.

```
class NegativeDenom : public ZeroDenom {
      long val;
public:
      NegativeDenom(char *message, long value)
        : ZeroDenom(message), val(value) { }
      void print () const
      { cout << msg << val << "\n\n"; }
} ;
```

I am deriving `NegativeDenom` from `ZeroDenom` rather than the other way around. Is it possible to derive `ZeroDenom` from `NegativeDenom`? In principle, it is possible. From a practical point of view, however, this is not a good idea. Class `NegativeDenom` has more data members than class `ZeroDenom` does.

I am making data in the base class `ZeroDenom` protected rather than private so that the derived class `NegativeDenom` is able to access the base data. If the `ZeroDenom` data were private, the methods in `NegativeDenom` would have to use the `ZeroDenom` methods to access `ZeroDenom` data. For example, class `NegativeDenom` could be designed this way.

```
class NegativeDenom : public ZeroDenom {
      long val;
public:
      NegativeDenom(char *message, long value)
        : ZeroDenom(message), val(value) { }
      void print () const
      { ZeroDenom::print();              // call to the base method
        cout << val << "\n\n"; }
} ;
```

On the one hand, I think that if two algorithms, in the base class and in the derived class, have common elements, it is nice to stress this fact in the code of the derived class (by calling the base class method in the corresponding derived class method). On the other hand, I do not think it is a good use of time and effort to add to the base class access methods that are used only in the derived class.

When exception classes are related through inheritance, claiming exception and throwing exception objects are the same as they are for unrelated exception classes. However, catching exceptions might present additional problems unless you pay attention to the relationships among classes. Listing 18.8 shows the program from Listing 18.7, modified so that the class NegativeDenom is derived from the class ZeroDenom.

Functions inverse() and fraction() claim exceptions in the same way as they do in Listing 18.7. However, it is the function inverse() rather than exception classes ZeroDenom and NegativeDenom that knows which message is generated for each exception.

The sample output of the program is shown in Figure 18–5. I am using approximately the same sequence of input data as for the previous versions of the program.

Listing 18.8   Example of using exception classes related through inheritance.

```
#include <iostream>
#include <cfloat>
using namespace std;

class MSG {
      static char* data [];                       // internal static data
public:
      static char* msg(int n)                     // public static method
      { if (n<1 || n > 5)                          // check index validity
          return data[0];
        else
          return data[n]; }                        // return valid string
} ;

char* MSG::data [] = { "\nBad argument to msg()\n",
"\nZero denominator is not allowed\n\n",            // depository of text
"\nNegative denominator: ",
"Enter numerator and positive\n",
"denominator (any letter to quit): ",
"Value of the fraction:         "
  } ;
```

```
class ZeroDenom {
protected:
      char *msg;
public:
      ZeroDenom (char* message) : msg(message)
      { }
      void print () const
      { cout << msg; }
} ;

class NegativeDenom : public ZeroDenom {
      long val;
public:
      NegativeDenom(char *message, long value)
        : ZeroDenom(message), val(value) { }
      void print () const
      { cout << msg << val << "\n\n"; }
} ;

inline void inverse(long value, double& answer)
         throw (ZeroDenom, NegativeDenom)
{ answer = (value) ? 1.0/value : DBL_MAX;
  if (answer==DBL_MAX)
       throw ZeroDenom(MSG::msg(1));
    if (value < 0)
       throw NegativeDenom(MSG::msg(2), value); }

inline void fraction (long numer, long denom, double& result)
         throw (ZeroDenom, NegativeDenom)
{ inverse(denom, result);                        // result = 1.0 / denom
  result - numer * result; }                     // result = numer / denom

int main()
{
  while (true)
  { long numer, denom;  double ans;              // numerator/denominator
    cout << MSG::msg(3) << MSG::msg(4);           // prompt user for data
    if ((cin >> numer >> denom) == 0) break;      // enter data
    try {
      fraction(numer,denom,ans);                  // compute answer
      cout << MSG::msg(5) << ans <<"\n\n"; }       // valid answer
    catch (const ZeroDenom &zd)                   // zero denominator
    { zd.print(); }
    catch (const NegativeDenom &nd)               // negative value
    { nd.print(); } }                             // end of loop
  return 0;
  }
```

Enter numerator and positive
denominator (any letter to quit): 11 0

Zero denominator is not allowed

Enter numerator and positive
denominator (any letter to quit): 11 –42

Negative denominator: Enter numerator and positive
denominator (any letter to quit): –11 44
Value of the fraction: –0.25

Enter numerator and positive
denominator (any letter to quit): exit

Figure 18–5   Output for program in Listing 18.8.

As you see, the program output is incorrect. When the denominator is neg-ative, the program prints the appropriate error message but does not display the value of the negative denominator. Instead, it goes on to request the next set of input data. What went wrong?

Recall that an exception can be thrown in two contexts: within a try block and outside of any try block. When the exception is thrown outside a try block, the function terminates immediately, and the test is repeated in the caller space: The call to the function that threw the exception might be either within a try block or outside of any try block.

For example, function `inverse()` throws its exceptions outside of any try block. When any of these exceptions is thrown, `inverse()` terminates imme-diately and control is passed to its caller, `fraction()`. In `fraction()`, the call to `inverse()` that threw an exception is outside of any try block. This is why `fraction()` also terminates immediately, and control is passed to `main()`.

When an exception is thrown within a try block, control is transferred to the end of the try block that contains the throw statement. The try block must be followed by one or several catch constructs. The parameters of these catch constructs are inspected strictly one after another. If no match is found, the situation is treated exactly as if the exception is thrown outside of the try block—the function terminates immediately, and control is passed to its caller. If a match is found, the search is terminated, and control transfers to the matching catch construct. After this catch construct terminates, all fol-lowing catch constructs (if any) are skipped and execution continues by exe-cuting the statements that follow the catch constructs.

The types match if they are the same. They also match if the thrown object is derived from the caught type or if the thrown object points to a derived class object, while the caught type points to an object of a base class. Sound complex? Make sure that you recognize here the rule we discussed in Chapter 15, "Virtual Functions and Other Advanced Uses of Inheritance:" A derived class object can be used where a base class object is expected.

In Listing 18.8, when a `NegativeDenom` exception is processed, functions `inverse()` and `fraction()` terminate because they do not have a try block. When function `fraction()` terminates, it throws the exception (received from `inverse()`) to function `main()`. Since `main()` calls `fraction()` within the try block, the catch constructs are inspected one after another. The catch with the `ZeroDenom` parameter is inspected first. Since the `NegativeDenom` object thrown by `fraction()` can be used where a `ZeroDenom` object is expected, the search terminates, and the `ZeroDenom` catch block is executed. It sends the base class `ZeroDenom::print()` message to its argument object, and it prints only the message, not the value that a `NegativeDenom` object has, but `ZeroDenom::print()` does not know how to print because the value is a data member of the derived class.

Some compilers could produce a warning about the problem, but no compiler will flag this design as a syntax error because it is the programmer's inalienable right to place the catch blocks in the order the programmer sees fit.

The remedy is relatively simple—you do not put the catch block for the base class first, you put it last in the series of catch blocks. But you have to remember this. Here is how the `main()` function in Listing 18.8 looks in eliminating this problem.

```
int main()
{ while (true)
  { long numer, denom;   double ans;
    cout << MSG::msg(3) << MSG::msg(4);          // prompt user for data
    if ((cin >> numer >> denom) == 0) break;     // enter data
    try {
      fraction(numer,denom,ans);                 // compute answer
      cout << MSG::msg(5) << ans <<"\n\n"; }      // valid answer
    catch (const NegativeDenom &nd)              // derived class
    { nd.print(); }
    catch (const ZeroDenom &zd)                  // base class
    { zd.print(); } }                            // end of loop
  return 0; }
```

Standard Library Exceptions

The C++ standard library defines several standard exception classes organized in an inheritance hierarchy. The most important classes are class exception (all in lowercase) that is the base class of the hierarchy and bad_alloc that is derived from class exception.

The exception class is defined in the header file <exception>, <except.h>, or <exception.h>. The exception class has a virtual function what() that returns a character pointer, similar to the method getMsg() in class NegativeDenom in Listing 18.7 above. The contents of the string are not defined, but you can design a class that inherits from class exception, and you can redefine what() in that class.

```cpp
class NegativeDenom {
    long val;                               // private data for exception info
    char* msg;
public:
    NegativeDenom(long value)               // conversion constructor
            : val(value), msg(MSG::msg(2)) { }
    const char* what() const                // can return an arbitrary string
        { return msg; }
    long getVal() const
        { return val; }
} ;
```

Class bad_alloc is defined in the header file <new> or <new.h>. Its object is thrown when the operator new fails to allocate the required amount of memory from the heap. Not all compilers support this exception yet. Here is a small example that builds a long linked list of blocks of memory. It uses both the bad_alloc exception and the test of whether the new operator returns the null pointer.

```cpp
#include <iostream>                         // include files
#include <exception>
#include <new>
using namespace std;

struct Block
{ char a[1000];                             // memory block
  Block* next;
Block (Block* ptr)                          // hook up before ptr
  { next = ptr; } } ;

int main()
{ Block *list = 0, *p;   int cnt = 1;
  while (true)                              // go until it crashes
```

```
{ try {
    p = new Block(list); }                          // this can fail
  catch (bad_alloc &bad)
  { cout << bad.what() << endl;                      // message as recovery
    exit(0); }
  if (p == 0)                                        // message as recovery
    { cout << "Out of memory\n\n";  exit(0); }
  list = p;                                          // success: top of list
  if (++cnt%100 == 0)
    cout << "Block #" << cnt << endl; }              // watch progress
while (p != 0)
  { p = p->next; delete list; list = p; }            // return memory
return 0; }
```

The exception mechanism does not support asynchronous exceptions such as interrupts. It handles synchronous exceptions that arise in the course of sequential execution, such as overflow, out-of-range errors, resource allocation errors, and bad input data. Exceptions should not be used for conditions that are normal for the flow of execution, for example, to terminate one stage of normal processing (end-of-list iteration) and start another. This is slower and more complex than necessary.

There are two major advantages in using C++ exceptions. One advantage is that they provide communications between the place of the discovery of the error and the place where the recovery can be done. Another advantage is that unwinding the stack in the process of terminating the called function and returning control to the calling function is safe. If any of the called functions allocate objects on the stack, the destructors for these objects are called in exactly the same way as if each of these functions returned normally. This ensures the orderly return of system resources, and prevents deadlocks and depletion of resources.

Type Cast Operators

This material does not actually belong to this chapter. However, it could not be discussed earlier in the book because it is based on advanced concepts of inheritance, templates, and exceptions.

Actually, I had doubts about discussing these cast operators at all. They are relatively new to the C++ language, and the experience of using them in industry is rather limited. There is no strong evidence that these operators are better than the standard simple casts we used on so many occasions before.

However, these cast operators represent a set of interesting software engineering ideas, and it is definitely worth becoming familiar with them. As far as using them in your practice—see for yourself.

As you have seen on many previous occasions, cast operators and conversion constructors weaken the strong typing system of C++. They add to possible type conversions. Client programmers and maintenance programmers might become confused as to what conversions are possible and what conversions are in fact taking place.

To help the programmers to deal with this situation, C++ introduces a number of additional cast operators. They are more verbose than standard casts discussed earlier. Actually, this is viewed as one of their advantages because these cast operators are easier to spot in the source code than standard casts are.

The `static_cast` *Operator*

The `static_cast` operator can be applied everywhere a standard cast can. Well, this is an exaggeration. It can be applied everywhere a standard cast makes sense, but it cannot be applied where the standard cast is considered too dangerous. You will see a few examples in a moment.

The `static_cast` is a unary operator that is applied to the operand of one type to receive a value of another type. The programmer has to specify the operand (an object or an expression of the type being converted) in regular parentheses. In addition, the programmer has to specify the target type as a parameter in angle brackets similar to the syntax that is used in templates.

```
valueOfTargetType = static_cast<TargetType>(valueOfSourceType);
```

As you can see, this cast is not really a unary operator because it needs both the value of the source type (one operand) and the name of the target type (another operand). However, it is not really a binary operator because the name of the cast does not appear between operands as is common for binary operators.

The use of this cast is not limited to the assignment as in the example above. It can be used anywhere a value of the target type `TargetType` (assuming it is defined) can be used. Here is a simple example.

```
double d;  int i = 20;
d = static_cast<double>(i);          // ok: d is 20.0
```

You might ask how it is better than your old and reliable friend cast `double`. It does exactly the same thing.

```
double d;   int i = 20;
d = double(i);                              // ok: d is 20.0
```

Here is a more-complex example. Class `Account` provides several conversion operators that retrieve the values of its components. For simplicity, I use the fixed-size array for the owner name.

```
class Account {                             // base class of hierarchy
protected:
  double balance;                           // protected data
  int pin;                                  // identification number
  char owner[40];
public:
  Account(const char* name, int id, double bal)  // general
  { strcpy(owner, name);                    // initialize data fields
      balance = bal; pin = id; }
  operator double () const                  // common for both accounts
  { return balance; }
  operator int () const
  { return pin; }
  operator const char* () const
  { return owner; }
  void operator -= (double amount)
  { balance -= amount; }
  void operator += (double amount)
  { balance += amount; }                    // increment unconditionally
} ;
```

As I told you in Chapter 15, these overloaded operator functions can be called using the same syntax as standard casts.

```
Account a1("Jones",1122,5000);             // create object
int pin = (int)a1;
double bal = (double) a1;                   // legitimate casts
const char *c = (const char*) a1;
```

The `static_cast` operator is also available in this context. It does exactly the same job as the standard casts.

```
Account a1("Jones",1122,5000);             // create object
int pin = static_cast<int>(a1);            // ok
double bal = static_cast<double>(a1);
const char *c = static_cast<const char*>(a1);
```

Make no mistake: These `static_cast` operators work for only one reason: because the class `Account` supports overloaded conversion operators `int`, `double`, and `const char*`. Otherwise, an attempt to apply the `static_cast` operator to `Account` objects would be as futile as an attempt to apply the standard casts.

The major difference between standard casts and `static_cast` is in how they convert pointers. Standard casts rely on the common sense of the programmer. If you want to point a double pointer to an int variable, this means that you have a good reason to do so, and nobody is going to look over your shoulder telling you what to do and what not to do.

Listing 18.9 shows a simple example of using pointer conversions. The results of the program execution are shown in Figure 18–6.

At the start of `main()`, two pointers, `pd` and `pi`, are set to point to an integer variable `i`. Then these pointers are dereferenced to print the value of `i`. As you see, the integer pointer `pi` retrieves the value of `i` correctly, and the `double` pointer `pd` retrieves junk.

Then the `double` pointer `pd` is set to point to an `Account` object `a1`. Dereferencing this pointer, the program not only retrieves the value of the object's data member `balance` but also changes it to whatever it wants.

Listing 18.9   Examples of pointer conversions using standard casts.

```
#include <iostream>
using namespace std;

class Account {                                      // base class of hierarchy
protected:
  double balance;                                    // protected data
  int pin;  // identification number
  char owner[40];
public:
  Account(const char* name, int id, double bal)      // general
  { strcpy(owner, name);                             // initialize data fields
    balance = bal; pin = id; }
  operator double () const                           // common for both accounts
  { return balance; }
  operator int () const
  { return pin; }
  operator const char* () const
  { return owner; }
  void operator -= (double amount)
  { balance -= amount; }
  void operator += (double amount)
  { balance += amount; }                             // increment unconditionally
} ;
```

```
int main()
{
  double *pd, d=20.0; int i = 20, *pi = &i;
  pd = (double*) pi;
  cout << "i=" << *pd << "  i=" << *pi <<endl;
  Account a1("Jones",1122,5000);              // create objects
  pd = (double*)(&a1);
  cout << "balance = " << *pd << endl;
  *pd = 10000;                                // change data member
  cout << "balance = " << *pd << endl;
  return 0;
}
```

Here, the behavior of static_cast is different from the behavior of standard casts. The double pointer is able to misrepresent the value of variable i because the integer address can be used as an operand for the (double*) cast. This is impossible to do using the static_cast operator.

```
pd = (double*) pi;                    // ok
pd = static_cast<double*> (pi);       // syntax error
```

Similarly, the double pointer pd is able to access and modify an Account object data member only because the Account address could be used as an operand to a standard cast. This is impossible to do if the static_cast operator is used.

```
Account a1("Jones",1122,5000);        // create object
pd = (double*)(&a1);                  // ok
*pd = 10000;                          // ok
pd = static_cast<double*>(&a1);       // syntax error
```

This does not mean that the static_cast operator cannot be used with pointers. It can. It cannot be used with pointers where conversion does not make software engineering sense. When pointer conversion makes sense, the static_cast operator can be used even if it is not particularly safe to do. Consider, for example, class SavingsAccount: it is publicly derived from class Account.

Figure 18–6   Output for program in Listing 18.9.

```
i=9.881 31 e−323  i=20
balance = 5000
balance = 10000
```

```
class SavingsAccount : public Account {
       double rate;                              // fixed interest rate
public:
       SavingsAccount(const char* name, int id, double bal)
          : Account(name, id, bal), rate (6.0) { }
       void payInterest()                        // pay once a month
       { balance += balance * rate / 12 / 100; }
} ;
```

SavingsAccount objects can do everything that Account objects can, plus they have more data members and more member functions. Hence, an Account pointer can point to a SavingsAccount object without any difficulty. This is safe and does not require any cast, standard or otherwise.

```
Account a1("Jones",1122,5000);           // create objects
SavingsAccount a2("Smith",1133,3000);
Account *pa = &a2;                        // save conversion, no cast is needed
```

A SavingsAccount pointer should not point to an Account object because this pointer could send to the object a message that a base object would not be able to respond to.

```
SavingsAccount *psa = pa;                 // syntax error
```

Of course, if that Account pointer actually points to a SavingsAccount object, this assignment (conversion) makes sense, but you should tell that to the compiler using a cast. A standard cast would do.

```
psa = (SavingsAccount *)pa;               // explicit cast is ok
```

It is in this situation that the static_cast operator uses its aversion to pointers. It can be used for this conversion instead of a standard cast.

```
psa = static_cast<SavingsAccount*>(pa);  // this is perfectly ok
```

And, of course, the static_cast operator can be used in situations where the conversion is not safe. Here, for example, I point the SavingsAccount pointer to an Account object, and the static_cast operator has as few objections to that as does a standard cast operator.

```
psa = static_cast<SavingsAccount*>(&a1); // this is perfectly ok
```

To summarize, the answer to the question how is this cast better than standard casts is twofold. First, it is verbose: this cast is easier to notice in code. Second, it is less permissive than standard casts. If you think that these advantages are somewhat offset by the increase in typing, I will have to correct you: On many occasions, Bjarne Stroustrup, the creator of C++, has said that the less we use casts the better, and everything that discourages us to use casts is beneficial.

The `reinterpret_cast` *Operator*

The `reinterpret_cast` operator is designed to do everything that standard casts could do, without limitations that the `static_cast` operator imposes.

The `reinterpret_cast` operator can be applied when the programmer knows what the compiler does not know about the actual types pointed to by pointers. In the example below, an integer pointer p points to a `double` value. In the last line, the `double` pointer q is assigned the value of p. The compiler does not know that the pointer p in fact points to a `double` value. The programmer tells this to the compiler by using the `reinterpret_cast` operator.

```
double y = 42;
int *p = reinterpret_cast<int*>(&y);          // potential trouble
double *q = reinterpret_cast<double*>(p);     // p points to double
cout << "The answer is " << *q << endl;       // it prints 42!
```

The same result could be achieved by using the standard casts `int*` and `double*`.

```
double y = 42;
int *p = (int*)&y;                     // integer p points to double: trouble
double *q = (double*)(p);              // ok because p points to double
cout << "The answer is " << *q << endl;    // it prints 42!
```

The `reinterpret_cast` operator is considered better than standard casts because it is more conspicuous.

Notice that `static_cast` cannot be used here: It can convert values of different types but not pointers. Notice also that the `static_cast` operator is portable because the compiler checks whether the types are related (as numeric types) or whether the appropriate conversion operator or conversion constructor exists.

The `reinterpret_cast` operator is not guaranteed to be portable. It simply picks up the set of bits in the source expression and interprets it according to the rule of the target type. There is no guarantee whatsoever that what happens on one machine will happen on another machine. The results are indeed machine dependent.

This cast should be used as little as possible. Still, if you have to use a cast (remember that story about traveling abroad?), use the `reinterpret_cast` operator rather than a standard cast.

The const_cast *Operator*

The const_cast operator has the power to eliminate the constant property of a constant value or object. Its syntax is the same as that of other C++ modern casts, including the target type in angle brackets and the source expression in parentheses. (The parentheses are mandatory.)

```
nonConstValue = const_cast<TypeName>(constValue);
```

Its syntax and semantics are more rigid than for other casts. All that it can do is remove the const property of the source value constValue, so that the assignment from a constant value constValue to a nonconstant value nonConstValue becomes possible. The type of nonConstValue should be exactly TypeName. The type of constValue should be const TypeName.

Consider the following simple example. Since the variable d is defined as const, a regular pointer cannot point to it (to avoid the change in value through the dereferenced pointer).

```
const double d = 42;
double *pd = &d;          // error: to prevent *pd = 21
```

A pointer to constant value can point to the variable d, but this pointer cannot be used to change the value of its target.

```
const double d = 42;
const double *pd = &d;    // ok but not very useful
*pd = 21;                 // syntax error: a pointer to const
```

The const_cast operator does the trick: It removes the constant requirement and opens the possibility for changing the value that is defined as const.

```
const double d = 42;
double *pd = const_cast<double*>(&d);       // remove const
*pd = 21;                                   // now it is ok
cout << "The answer is " << *pd << endl;    // it prints 21
```

This is a trick that even standard C-type casts cannot do. Obviously, you should not do it very often. One situation where it might be necessary is maintenance of code where a variable was defined as const, but new conditions require changing it. Rather than changing the existing definition, you might prefer to add new code where the variable is changed with the use of the const_cast operator.

Using the const_cast operator removes the protection. The pointer does not have to be a pointer to a constant, and it can be dereferenced while changing the object it is pointing to. This is a very offensive technique.

Consider again, for example, the class `Account`.

```
class Account {                                 // base class of hierarchy
protected:
  double balance;                               // protected data
  int pin;                                      // identification number
  char owner[40];
public:
  Account(const char* name, int id, double bal) // general
  { strcpy(owner, name);                        // initialize data fields
    balance = bal; pin = id; }
  operator double () const                      // common for both accounts
  { return balance; }
  operator int () const
  { return pin; }
  operator const char* () const
  { return owner; }
  void operator -= (double amount)
  { balance -= amount; }
  void operator += (double amount)
  { balance += amount; }                        // increment unconditionally
} ;
```

If you try to call a non-const member function (e.g., `operator+=()`) on a const object of class `Account`, the compiler will reject the code.

```
const Account a1("Jones",1122,5000.0);    // create object
a1 += 1000.0;                             // syntax error
```

If you try to set a regular `Account` pointer to point to a const object, the compiler will also reject this code for fear that the object can be changed through the dereferenced pointer.

```
const Account a1("Jones",1122,5000.0);    // create object
Account *pa = &a1;                        // syntax error
```

If the pointer points to a constant object, it has to be defined as a pointer to a const object. This is permitted, but this pointer cannot be used to change the state of the object.

```
const Account a1("Jones",1122,5000.0);    // create object
const Account *pa = &a1;                  // ok
*pa += 1000.0;                            // syntax error
```

However, a regular pointer can be set to point to a const object using the const_cast operator.

```
const Account a1("Jones",1122,5000.0);        // create object
Account *pa = const_cast<Account*>(&a1);      // ok
*pa += 1000.0;                                 // this is permitted
```

As a result, the state of a constant object changes—its balance now is $6,000, but no explicit operation over the object was performed directly.

The only job that the const_cast operator can do is to remove the const protection. It cannot do any additional type conversions. If the nonConstValue (the result of the cast) is not of the same type as constValue (the value being cast) and a type conversion is needed, it has to be done as a separate additional step.

For example, the const char*() conversion operator of class Account returns a character pointer that cannot (and should not) be used to change the contents of the character array within an Account object.

```
const Account a1("Jones",1122,5000.0);    // create object
char *c2 = static_cast<const char*>(a1);  // syntax error
```

This pointer can be assigned to a pointer to a constant only, and this pointer cannot be used to change the state of the Account object.

```
const Account a1("Jones",1122,5000.0);           // create object
const char *c2 = static_cast<const char*>(a1);   // this is ok
strcpy(c2,"Jones");                               // syntax error
```

Using the const_cast operator on the Account object does not help because the target value and the source value are of different types.

```
const Account a1("Jones",1122,5000.0);           // create object
char *c2 = const_cast<char*>(a1);                 // syntax error
```

Since the const_cast operator can do only one job, it is perfectly all right to convert a constant Account object to a pointer to a constant first (using a static_cast or a standard cast) and then convert the pointer to a constant to a regular pointer (using const_cast).

```
const Account a1("Jones",1122,5000.0);           // create object
const char *c1 = static_cast<const char*>(a1);   // this is ok
char *c2 = const_cast<char*>(c1);                 // and this is ok
strcpy(c2,"Jones");                               // not a syntax error
```

Again, the name of the owner is changed without explicit processing of the constant Account object.

The `dynamic_cast` *Operator*

The `dynamic_cast` operator is an element of a set of C++ components that supports run-time-type information (RTTI). Other elements of this set of components are the `typeid` operator and the `type_info` structure.

The `dynamic_cast` operator is used to convert pointers (or references) of the base class into pointers (or references) of one of the derived classes. As you saw earlier, the `static_cast` operator (or a standard cast) could be used too, but the program must know the type of the object to make sure it converts the pointer to the correct class.

The `dynamic_cast` operator uses the same syntax as do other cast operators: The argument pointer (or reference) is in parentheses, and the target type to convert the argument to is in angle brackets. If the argument pointer does indeed belong to the target type requested, then the operator returns the argument pointer to the object unchanged. It also returns the pointer to the object if the argument pointer points to an object of a class derived (directly or indirectly) from the target type. Otherwise, it returns null, and the program can check the value.

For this technique to work, the hierarchy of classes has to contain both virtual and nonvirtual functions. It does not work for inheritance without virtual functions.

Consider, for example, a simplified `Account` class that has a virtual function `display()`. It displays the contents of the `Account` object.

```
class Account {                                  // base class of hierarchy
protected:
  double balance;                                // protected data
  int pin;                                       // identification number
  char owner[40];
public:
  Account(const char* name, int id, double bal)  // general
  { strcpy(owner, name);                         // initialize data fields
    balance = bal; pin = id;}
  virtual void display()                         // virtual function for RTTI
  { cout.setf(ios::fixed,ios::floatfield); cout.precision(2);
    cout <<setw(6) << pin << setw(20) << balance
         << "  " << owner <<endl; }
  void operator -= (double amount)
  { balance -= amount; }
  void operator += (double amount)
  { balance += amount; }                         // increment unconditionally
} ;
```

The derived class `SavingsAccount` adds an additional method `payInterest()` and redefines the base method `display()` so that the additional data member `interest` is also displayed.

```
class SavingsAccount : public Account {
      double rate, interest;                    // accumulated interest
public:
   SavingsAccount(const char* name, int id, double bal)
      : Account(name, id, bal), rate (6.0), interest(0) { }
   void payInterest()                           // pay once a month
   { double pay = balance * rate / 12 / 100;
     balance += pay;  interest += pay; }
   virtual void display()
   { cout.setf(ios::fixed,ios::floatfield); cout.precision(2);
     cout <<setw(6) << pin << setw(8) << interest << setw(12)
          << balance << "   " << owner << endl; }
} ;
```

Here, I am defining two objects, one of the base class and another of the derived class. I also define an `Account` pointer and use the `dynamic_cast` operator to set this pointer to point to the base object first and then to the derived object. As is common when using the `dynamic_cast` operator, I check whether the pointer is null. If it is, then the question is answered in the negative. If the pointer is not null, the answer is affirmative—yes, the object pointed to by the pointer can be used as an object of the class specified in the `dynamic_cast` operator.

```
Account a1("Jones",1122,5000);                  // create objects
SavingsAccount a2("Smith",1133,3000);
Account *pa = dynamic_cast<Account *>(&a1);      // ok
if (pa == 0)
   cout << "Null pointer\n";
else
   pa->display();                               // Jones
pa = dynamic_cast<SavingsAccount *>(&a2);        // ok
   if (pa == 0) cout << "Null pointer\n";
else
   pa->display();                               // Smith
```

In this example, the answers to this question are not very important because the pointer I use as the target of the assignment is a base pointer—it cannot do much damage, whether it points to a base class object or to a derived class object. Indeed, the first cast returns a pointer to object a1, and the second cast returns a pointer to object a2, which is converted to the base pointer. Since the function `display()` is polymorphic, it displays data in the base format in the first case and in derived format in the second case. This code snippet demonstrates the behavior of the dynamic_cast operator when the object pointed to by the pointer is of the same type as the type specified in the operator.

In the next code snippet, I use the base pointer as the target again. First, I point it to the base object and ask whether it can perform Account operations. The answer is yes; that is, the operator returns a base pointer pointing to the object in question. Nevertheless, the display() message sent through this pointer points data in the derived class format because the function is virtual, and the object is of the derived class. Next, I check whether the object a1 can perform the duties of the SavingsAccount object. The answer is no, it is a base class object, and the operator returns null.

```
pa = dynamic_cast<Account *>(&a2);                    // ok
if (pa == 0)
    cout << "Null pointer\n";
else
    pa->display();                                   // Smith
pa = dynamic_cast<SavingsAccount *>(&a1);            // null
    if (pa == 0) cout << "Null pointer\n";
else
    pa->display();
```

The next code snippet is more interesting because it uses the derived class pointer. First, I check whether the object a1 can perform the derived class duties. As in the previous case, the answer is no: It does not matter whether the target of the assignment is a base pointer (as in the previous case) or a derived pointer (as in this case)—the null is the null. Next, I check whether the object a2 can perform the duties of the derived class. The answer, as in the very first code snippet, is yes, it can. In the first snippet, I converted the result to the base pointer and hence could call only Account methods and virtual methods of the derived class. Here, there is no conversion. The target of the assignment is a derived pointer, and it can access the base functions, virtual functions, and functions defined in the derived class.

```
SavingsAccount *psa = dynamic_cast<SavingsAccount *>(&a1);    // 0
if (psa == 0)
    cout << "Null pointer\n";                                 // null pointer
else
    psa->display();                                          // no display
psa = dynamic_cast<SavingsAccount *>(&a2);                   // ok
if (psa == 0)
    cout << "Null pointer\n";
else
    { psa->payInterest();                                    // derived method
      psa->display(); }                                      // Smith
```

You see that the `dynamic_cast` operator provides a powerful method of checking whether a given object can perform the required operation. Since it is a relatively new language feature, not all compilers support it. Those that support it might not do it by default. To use the feature, you have to set up the compiler flags or choices to explicitly support RTTI features.

Similar to operator `new`, C++ supports another method of checking whether the cast was successful: throwing an exception. If the pointer does not point to an object of the class specified in the operator, the `bad_cast` exception is thrown. This is especially important for references. C++ pointers might or might not point to an object, but C++ references always do—they cannot have a null value. For references, the use of `dynamic_cast` is not asking a question (as for pointers) but is making an assertion that it indeed points to an object of the class specified in the cast. When the assertion fails, throwing an exception is appropriate.

The `typeid` *Operator*

Another technique for deciding into what class to cast the base pointer is based on using the operator `typeid`. The operator `typeid` allows you to do one of two things: check what the name of the argument class is or check whether the object pointed to belongs to a given class.

Unlike cast operators, the `typeid` operator works with an object argument, not with a pointer argument. It returns a reference to an object of the library class `type_info`. The implementation of this call is compiler dependent. However, it always includes a member function `name()` among its class members. This function returns a character array that is, again, implementation dependent; most often, it is the name of the class to which the argument of the operator belongs or the name of the class preceded by the keyword `class`.

Some compiler implementations make the `type_info` constructors private. In this case, the C++ program cannot create an object of class `type_info`. Instead, it has to send a message to a return value of the `type-id` operator.

```
Account a1("Jones",1122,5000);          // create objects
SavingsAccount a2("Smith",1133,3000);
const char *c1 = typeid(a1).name();     // get class name
const char *c2 = typeid(a2).name();
cout << c1 << endl;                      // prints "class Account"
cout << c2 << endl;                      // prints "class SavingsAccount"
```

This is, of course, not very useful unless it is used for debugging. The real utility of the `typeid` operator is based on the fact that its operator cannot only be an expression of some class but also a class name spelled as an identifier (no quotes). This allows you to compare the results of applying the `typeid` operator to the class name and to the object. If the equality operator returns true, the object belongs to the specified class.

```
if (typeid(Account) == typeid(a1))              // true
    cout << "a1 is Account\n";
if (typeid(SavingsAccount) == typeid(a2))       // true
    cout << "a2 is SavingsAccount\n";
if (typeid(Account) == typeid(a2))              // false
    cout << "a2 is Account\n";
if (typeid(SavingsAccount) == typeid(a1))       // false
    cout << "a1 is SavingsAccount\n";
```

When dealing with a collection of heterogeneous objects pointed to by base pointers, the pointers have to be dereferenced when used as typeid arguments.

```
pa = &a2;
if (typeid(Account) == typeid(*pa))             // false
    cout << "pa points to Account\n";
if (typeid(SavingsAccount) == typeid(*pa))      // true
    cout << "pa points to SavingsAccount\n";
```

Notice that these comparisons do not compare objects—the operation of comparison is not defined for C++ structures. It does not compare pointers: Unlike other special casts, the `typeid` operator returns an object, not a pointer. It applies the overloaded comparison operator to the `type_info` object, which is returned by the `typeid` operator.

The `typeid` operator is a very powerful tool and can easily be abused. It is an unstructured competition to the use of virtual functions. Make sure you do not use it too much.

Summary

The topics discussed in this chapter are relatively new. Not all compiler and library implementations support them. The industry has not accumulated much experience in using them. This is why you should use these C++ features with caution.

Exceptions come with significant memory and execution time penalty. This might be important for some applications. For most applications, this is not very important. What is important, however, is how to use exceptions to structure and simplify the flow of control in the application.

It seems that exceptions that throw values of built-in types are not very useful, because the exception handlers cannot distinguish between values of the same type thrown from different places in the source code. Designing classes for passing exception information from the place of error discovery to the place of error recovery is more useful and interesting, even though it increases the number of classes in the application and the number of lines to write.

Many people say the exceptions streamline the flow of control in the application and allow the designer to separate mainline processing from processing of confusing exceptional cases. Perhaps. The use of `if` and `switch` control constructs is indeed confusing—the source code is complex and hard to understand. But this complexity reflects the complexity of the task performed by the program, and it is foolish to blame the control constructs for the complexity of the code. The definite advantage of using standard control constructs for processing different cases is that the code is all in the same place; it is not broken into separate pieces.

When exceptions are used, the maintainer has to perform an additional task: the analysis of the decisions made by the designer as to how to break processing into separate pieces. These decisions are often complex and arbitrary; what has to be kept together is sometimes broken into separate pieces. All this adds to the complexity of the program.

I think that the use of exceptions is definitely justified in one case only—when the program is designed in such a way that the part of the program that does error recovery does not have information that is known only to the part of the program that discovers the error; in this case, using exceptions to pass necessary data from one part of the program to another part of the program. This is fine, but keep in mind that the cause of the need to pass information from one part of the program to another is the previous design decision to break processing into separate pieces. Reconsidering this decision might eliminate the need for excessive exception handling.

When you use C++ exceptions, make sure that you do not make the life of the maintainer too difficult. Claim all exceptions that each function throws or passes through from its servers, and do not claim exceptions that the function cannot throw. Document exception processing in the source code and in separate documentation as much as possible (that is, as much as your boss will let you). Make sure that you test every exception handler, even when testing exceptions is not easy.

The type cast operations that I discussed at the end of this chapter are rather new, and industry does not have much experience in their use. I have to admit that I also do not have much experience using them—I use C-style standard casts and feel that they are quite adequate.

Yes, standard casts can be easily abused. Yes, standard casts allow me to make conversions between pointers that do not make sense, and the `static_cast` operator would prevent me from doing that. But I do not make conversions that do not make sense. Also, if I wanted to make such a conversion, the `reinterpret_cast` operator would allow me to do that as easily as a standard cast would.

However, most experts agree that these cast operators add to code readability: They are conspicuous and easily attract the maintainer's attention. This is true, and I recommend that you try to use them. With more experience, you might come to love them.

WHAT WE HAVE LEARNED

Topics in this Chapter

- C++ as a Traditional Programming Language
- C++ as a Modular Language
- C++ as an Object-Oriented Language
- C++ and Competition
- Summary

Chapter 19

All right, it was a long way to go. I have to admit that this book took so much work that sometimes I thought that I would never get to write this last chapter. I am glad that I was wrong. The time came to stop plowing ahead. Now we can look back at the starting point and at the road that has led us here.

In this chapter, there will be no new syntax to study. Instead, I will try to summarize the basic characteristics of this great, wonderful, confusing—and dangerous—language: C++ as we know it. Now that you have grasped the entire subject and understand how different components fit together, you can appreciate how much thought went into its design and how careful one has to be in using it.

In earlier chapters, I had to constrain myself as to what I could and could not discuss with you, because some of the things that were relevant for the discussion were not yet familiar to you. Now that we have discussed everything, this limitation no longer applies. That is why this last chapter is great fun for me.

C++ was designed as a software engineering language for building large computer programs. It pursued several goals, and these goals were sometimes conflicting. On the one hand, C++ tries to be a performance-oriented systems programming language: It provides low-level operators (e.g., shifts and bitwise logic operators) and supports access to machine resources (e.g., the register and volatile data types and arithmetic operations over pointers). On the other hand, C++ tries to facilitate the breaking up of programs into relatively independent pieces that can be developed by different programmers, who communicate with one another as little as possible.

C++ is a tool for achieving several conflicting goals. It was designed:

- as a high-level language for readability (data aggregation, flow of control, scope of names)
- as a language for sharp and quick minds (unique shorthand operators, concise expressions)
- to use character strings and dynamic memory management
- to use libraries that are provided (defacto standard)

C++ as a Traditional Programming Language

Unlike many high-level languages, C++ is case sensitive. Similar to many modern high-level languages, C++ is space blind (with two or three exceptions). It uses end-of-line comments but does not use nested block comments.

Similar to most other programming languages, C++ provides basic built-in data types with operations over the values of these types. The C++ built-in data types are rather limited—just simple integers and floating point values.

C++ Built-in Data Types

To achieve maximum performance, the C++ integer type is always the fastest type on any platform. Its size is 16 bits on 16-bit machines and 32 bits on 32-bit machines. This results in a portability problem, so typical for C++: There is no guarantee that a program running on one machine will produce exactly the same results on another machine.

To aid flexibility (i.e., to save memory where possible) and to add computational power (i.e., to expand ranges where necessary) for complex computations, C++ provides size modifiers (short, long, unsigned) for finer use of memory. C++ does not standardize the sizes of different types. It just requires that a short value is not longer than an integer value; it also requires that a long value is not shorter than an integer value.

As a result, on modern machines, short values are always 16 bits, and long values are always 32 bits. Programmers who strive for portability avoid using plain integers and instead use either short or long modifiers. Programmers who strive for speed use plain integers and avoid using short and long modifiers.

Use of unsigned values supports even finer memory use and is even more controversial. On the one hand, defining a value as unsigned indicates to the maintainer that the value is inherently positive and cannot be negative. Also, the use of the unsigned qualifier doubles the maximum integer value on the given architecture (for the same number of bits). On the other hand, the mixture of signed and unsigned values might result in incorrect results in computations. To avoid these errors, many programmers give up the potential benefits of unsigned values by not using them.

To simplify the choices for the programmer, C++ supports defaults. If the programmer does not specify whether the value is signed or unsigned, the default is signed; if the programmer does not specify whether the value is a short integer, a long integer, or just an integer, the default is just an integer.

Striving for maximum performance, C++ tests computational results neither for underflow nor for overflow. Everything that should be tested in the program should be tested explicitly in the source code of the program on the program's own time. If the program does not want to spend time checking the legitimacy of the results, C++ does not provide any default tests or warnings.

C++ treats characters as just another kind of integer. Their size varies from one byte per character to two bytes per character (expanded character set). Arithmetic operations over character values are legal in C++. They are popular, but they could create portability problems when different machines use different character sets.

The language allows the programmer to specify both signed and unsigned characters. There is no standard for default type—on some machines it is unsigned, on others it is signed. It is a good idea to assume that a character cannot contain a negative value and to use an integer instead of a character if a negative value (e.g., end-of-file code) is possible.

Character literals are enclosed in single quotes. They should not be confused with string literals that are enclosed in double quotes. C++ does not store the string length with the string contents. It uses the 0 code to mark the end of the string. This is why the length of a string literal is one more than the number of characters in the literal.

For floating point types, C++ supports three different sizes: float, double, and long double. Their sizes range from 4 to 8 to 10 bytes, their precision ranges from 7 to 15 to 19 digits. These characteristics are machine dependent. C++ floating-point constants are always double, not float or long double. In most cases, this is not important. When it is necessary to specify that the literal is, for example, float, the appropriate suffix should be used. C++ supports both the fixed decimal point notation and scientific notation (with the exponent).

Boolean types have two values, true and false. They are also treated as small integers. The size of a Boolean value of type `bool` is one byte rather than one bit. C++ does not pack Boolean values one per bit because addressing individual bits in C++ requires logical operations and shifts. In this tradeoff between space efficiency and time efficiency, C++ favors time efficiency, since the byte is the least segment of memory that can be addressed directly.

Symbolic names for literal values of any built-in type can be specified using the preprocessor `#define` directive. The preprocessor will replace each occurrence of the symbolic name in the source code with the literal value. Since this is done before the compiler sees the source code, the errors in the preprocessor directives are often hard to find. Using the `const` modifier is better because the names defined with the `const` modifier follow the scope rules (the names defined in the `#define` directive are global).

For each data type, C++ supports two derived data types, a pointer type and a reference type. Both these types contain an address of the value, but the syntax of their use is different.

C++ allows any conversions between numeric values of different types: the value of one type can be used where the value of another type is expected. Boolean values and numeric values are also interchangeable—no syntax error is generated. For numeric values, C++ is a weakly typed language.

The values of pointers (or references) to different types cannot be converted to each other (or to the value of the type). For addresses, C++ is a strongly typed language—a syntax error is generated even when the pointers of different types contain the same address.

An explicit cast can be used for conversions between pointers (and references), but the integrity of results remains the responsibility of the programmer—no syntax error is generated by the compiler if the results do not have reasonable meaning or are not portable between different computer architectures.

C++ Expressions

C++ contains a conventional set of operations over numeric values, such as sign operators, arithmetic operations, relational operators, equality operators, and logical operators. It has no exponentiation operator. Similar to most other programming languages, it has no implied multiplication—the asterisk should be used as an explicit operator.

C++ treats statements as expressions. To achieve this uniformity, C++ treats the assignment and the comma as operators (although their priority is the lowest). As a result, erroneous constructs can be accepted by C++ compilers as valid code.

Since the number of operators is large, C++ uses two-symbol operators and even one three-symbol operator (the conditional operator). In C++, the meaning of an operator (and of a keyword) is often reused for different purposes and thus depends on the context.

Since the sizes of built-in data types are machine dependent, C++ allows the programmer to evaluate the size of a given variable (given the name of the variable) or the size of any variable of a given type (given the type name).

Logical, relational, and equality operators return Boolean values true and false, but these values can be freely converted to numerical values 1 (true) and zero (false). Moreover, any numerical value can be used where a Boolean value is expected—no syntax error is generated. The zero value is converted to false, and any other numeric value is interpreted as true. This leniency sometimes forces C++ compilers to accept code that is semantically incorrect.

Another source of error is the equality operator, which is written as two consecutive equal signs: omitting one equal sign does not generate a syntax error but quietly changes the meaning of the source code. This is a common source of error that causes waste of time, frustration, and anxiety.

Logical operators && and || are of different priority—the operator && binds tighter than ||. This allows avoiding extra parentheses. Both logical operators are short-circuit operators: In the compound logical expression, the first operand is evaluated first, and the second one is not evaluated if the result of the operation is known from the evaluation of the first operator.

C++ has a number of unique operators that provide access to the underlying representation of information in computer memory. Bitwise logical operators are these operators along with, inclusive or, exclusive or, negation (complement). They operate on each bit of the operand(s) individually, creating the result bit by bit.

Bitwise shifts shift the given bit pattern to the left and to the right. When the pattern is shifted to the left, or a positive value is shifted to the right, zeroes are shifted in—these operations are portable. When a negative value is shifted to the right, the result depends on the implementation: Either zeroes are shifted in (logical shift), or ones are shifted in (arithmetic shift). This operation is not portable.

Another set of unique operators includes the increment and decrement operators. They emulate assembly language type processing by providing a side effect (increment or decrement by 1) on the single lvalue operand. These operators can be prefix or postfix. The prefix operator is applied first, then the value is used in other expressions; the postfix operator is applied after the value is used in other expressions.

C++ does specify the order of evaluation of operators in an expression. However, it does not specify the order of evaluation of operands. Hence, a C++ program is not allowed to rely on a specific order of evaluation of operands in an expression. In particular, the operands with side effects (increment and decrement operators) are a common source of portability problems. It is a good idea to only use increment and decrement operators in stand-alone expressions to avoid portability issues.

Another unique operator is the conditional operator: Depending on the value of its first operand, it evaluates either its second operand (the first operand is true) or its third operand (the second operand is false).

Yet another set of unique C++ operators includes arithmetic assignments and the comma operator. These operators help to write succinct and expressive C++ code.

C++ binary operators are always applied to operands of exactly the same type. When the source code specifies operands of different types, C++ applies widening conversions: A shorter operand is converted to the widest type in the expression. In the assignment operator, the value on the right-hand side is converted to the type of the left-hand side, even if this might cause a possible loss of precision.

C++ Control Flow

As in other languages, C++ statements are executed sequentially. Each statement is terminated by a semicolon. Blocks (compound statements) are allowed; they are delimited by braces and can have local variables. No semicolon is used after the closing brace of the block.

Compound statements can be nested; they can serve as a function body or as a control statement body. Local variables defined in a nested block are not visible outside the block.

C++ has a standard set of control constructs. The `if-else` statement does not use the `then` keyword; it executes the true branch when the statement's expression has a nonzero value of any type; it executes the false branch when the statement's expression has a zero (false) value.

It implements repeated actions. C++ supports three forms of iterative statements: the `while` loop (it allows for zero repetitions), the `do-while` loop (it enforces at least one repetition), and the `for` loop (mostly for a fixed number of repetitions).

A popular C++ programming idiom is to combine a test for continued iteration with the assignment. Using this idiom, one has to be careful with parentheses: Omitting parentheses might change the meaning of the expression because C++ comparison has a higher precedence than C++ assignment has.

C++ does not support unrestricted jumps. The `goto` statement cannot leave its scope and cannot jump over definitions of variables. The `break` statement exits from a loop so that control flow jumps to the statement after the loop. The `break` statement can be used with all three loop constructs and is usually executed in a conditional statement. The `continue` statement skips the rest of the loop body and returns to the loop top for the test of further iterations.

The C++ `switch` statement supports multiway decisions in the program: It provides alternative execution paths based on the value of an integral expression. (Floating point cannot be used.) The default case is executed if no match is found. Unlike in other languages, the default statement is optional; if it is absent and the match is not found, the next statement is executed. To create a construct with multiple branches, `break` statements should be used at the end of each branch.

C++ as a Modular Language

Similar to most modern high-level languages, C++ supports hierarchies of building blocks for program data and for program operations. From a software engineering point of view, the benefits of modularization for large projects include division of labor, simpler programming tasks, reusable and maintainable program elements, and the opportunity to study the program at different levels, either in general (disregarding details), or in detail (disregarding high-level issues).

When used correctly, these benefits result in higher productivity both for development and for maintenance and in fewer errors.

C++ supports programmer-defined aggregate data types: arrays, structures, unions, and enumerations. Their components can be either of built-in data types or of other C++ aggregate types (arrays, structures, etc.).

C++ supports programmer-defined functions. The hierarchies of functions model the hierarchies of actions of real-life objects that the program maintains information about. C++ supports the use of standard libraries. Standard libraries implement a variety of common tasks. Library functions are optimized, well tested, and have broad applicability.

The need to specify header files with function prototypes makes using library functions more difficult than necessary, but one can learn to live with it.

C++ Aggregate Types: Arrays

C++ arrays can only contain elements of the same type. The greatest limitation of C++ arrays is that the array size must be known at compile time. If the array contains more elements than necessary, memory is wasted. If the array contains less elements than necessary, memory is corrupted.

Another common source of errors in using C++ arrays is that the index of the first element is always 0. This cannot be changed. Hence, the index of the last element is 1 less than the array range. C++ does not support the compile time index check: This is often impossible, but the compiler would not do that even if it were possible. Neither does C++ support the run-time test of index validity: It would affect execution time.

C++ philosophy assumes that you do not want to waste time at any access to the array; when you want to check index validity, you can write your own code to do that; when you do not check index validity, C++ assumes that you know what you are doing. On memory-rich machines, index errors might not result in incorrect run-time results (until the memory usage changes). This is a serious problem with no good solution.

C++ allows the programmer to implement array processing algorithms using either indices to access array components or pointers. This is based on the fact that the increment (or decrement) operator applied to a pointer increments the address not by 1 but by the size of the array element. This operation points the pointer to the next element of the array. The use of pointers allows one to write concise and expressive array processing code. However, there are no performance advantages in using this technique. Some programmers find this kind of code somewhat difficult to verify.

C++ supports arrays of any dimension. Under the hood, they are implemented as one-dimensional arrays with the row-major order. (The right subscript varies the fastest.) Similar to one-dimensional arrays, C++ multidimensional arrays support no checks of index validity.

C++ represents text as arrays of characters. These arrays have to have an extra element to accommodate the zero sentinel value that is used to mark the end of valid data in the array. When the compiler processes the program text literals, it also appends the terminating zero to the symbols of the string; hence, the literals have an extra element as well. All library functions that deal with arrays of characters expect the terminating zero at the end of valid data. When these library functions change the contents of the array, they append the terminating zero to the end of valid data to keep the string in the valid state.

C++ supports neither array assignments nor array comparisons. For arrays of arbitrary types, it is the responsibility of the programmer to make sure that these operations are performed correctly. For text strings, library functions are used for assignment, comparisons, concatenation, and other standard operations.

Most library functions do not work well when strings overlap in memory. When writing to a character array, no C++ library function checks for available space. If the string does not have enough available space, the computer memory is silently corrupted. This is a serious integrity problem.

C++ Aggregate Types: Structures, Unions, Enumerations

C++ structures combine related components. What components are related and what are not is often a matter of judgment. C++ leaves this to the discretion of the programmer and does not impose any limitations on the types of the components.

The structure definition is a blueprint for creation of structure variables. For each structure field, the programmer supplies the type and the name of the field. The scope of the structure definition is delimited by the opening and the closing brace that is followed by the semicolon.

Structure variables can be initialized using the syntax similar to the syntax of array initialization (a comma-separated list of values delimited by the braces).

The dot selector operator selects a structure object's fields (both as an lvalue and as an rvalue). When the structure variable is referred through a pointer, the dot selector operator does not work; instead, the arrow selector operator should be used.

C++ supports assignment for structure variables of the same type. The value semantics is implemented: The fields of the rvalue structure variable are copied bitwise into the fields of the lvalue structure variables.

Assignments between structure variables of different types are not allowed, even when they have the same composition and even when the fields in both structure definitions have the same names. It is the type name that has to be the same. Notice that using the `typedef` facility would not make the type name the same: It would only create a synonym for the type name.

Assignments between structure variables and numeric variables (or pointer or reference variables) are not allowed: For programmer-defined types, C++ behaves as a strongly typed language, and these assignments are marked as syntax errors by the compiler.

C++ supports no structure comparisons or any other operations over structures; you should write your own code to implement structure operations.

Union is a type definition that syntactically is similar to the structure definition: Several fields of different types can be listed between the scope braces (followed by a semicolon). However, these fields exist in the memory of the computer, not simultaneously (as in structure variables), but sequentially.

This design allows the program to save space: A union variable can contain information of one of the mutually exclusive types specified in the union type definition. This is, of course, error prone because the programmer should make sure that the value retrieved from the union variable is of the same type as the value saved in this variable earlier, and the union itself has no means to keep the type information.

If the program makes a mistake and retrieves a value of a different type, there is no compile-time error, and there is no run-time error; a useless bit pattern is retrieved silently. To avoid these errors, union variables can be used as fields of structures; a tag field can be added to the structure to keep information on how the union field value was initialized. When the union value is retrieved, the program consults this tag field and acts accordingly. This is how polymorphism used to be implemented before virtual functions were invented.

Enumeration types define variables that accept values from a predefined set of symbolic identifiers. The syntax of the enumeration type definition is similar to the syntax of the structure definition: A set of comma-separated symbolic names is specified within the scope of the braces (followed by the semicolon). This is a popular way to define symbolic constants for the program.

C++ defines no operations over enumeration values. Under the hood, they are implemented as integer (starting, naturally, with zero), and the program might try to use this knowledge, but this is not a good idea.

C++ Functions as Modularization Tools

C++ supports hiding operation complexity in functions. The client code uses server functions as single units of code. This streamlines the caller code toward its goal: The client code is expressed in terms of function calls to the server functions rather than in terms of lower-level details of operations over data.

In the latter case, when the client code implements data processing without calling server functions, the maintenance programmer should figure out what the meaning of the sequence of statements is. In the case of using server functions, the goal of each operation is expressed by the name of the function (provided that the function name is sufficiently descriptive).

C++ functions cooperate with each other working toward a common program goal. They cooperate by working on common data. The values of data can be set in one function and used in another function. The exchange of data can be implemented using global variables, parameters, and return values. Coupling through global variables is implicit: It is not immediately evident to the maintainer and hence should be used as little as possible.

Coupling through parameters is better because it is explicit: It is immediately evident to the maintainer (and to the client programmer) what values participate in the data flow between the function and its client functions.

Coupling (the number of parameters) should be minimized by dividing responsibilities between functions so that what belongs together is not torn apart between different functions. It is the tearing apart of what should belong together that causes the need for communication between functions.

When calling a function, the client code has to supply an actual argument for every formal parameter in the function definition. It is possible to define default values of the arguments so that they will be used when the client code does not specify the values of actual arguments.

In parameter passing, C++ is designed as a strongly typed language: the number of arguments should match the number of formal parameters; the type of each argument has to match the type of the corresponding formal parameter. The deviations from this rule are flagged as syntax errors by the compiler.

The exception to this rule is made for numeric types only. If there is a type mismatch between a formal parameter and its actual argument, promotions and conversions can be applied: small arguments (`enum`, `char`, `unsigned char`, `short`) are promoted to integers, `unsigned short` are promoted either to `int` or to `unsigned int` (depending on the machine architecture), and `float` arguments are promoted to type `double`. If after promotion the actual argument type still does not match the formal parameter type, conversions are applied: Any numeric type can be converted to any other numeric type, even if it results in loss of accuracy (e.g., from double to integer).

Promotions and conversions do not apply to programmer-defined types, pointers, and references (even when they are pointers or references to numeric types). They are applied to numeric types only.

C++ is a language for separate compilations. To assist the compiler, the function interface must be known to the compiler before a function call is processed. Unless the function definition precedes the function call in the source file (not a common occurrence), a function prototype should be used, with the types of parameters and return value specified. Parameter names in a function prototype are useful but optional.

A C++ function may be defined only once. It can be declared (as a proto-type) as many times as needed. If the function is used in several files, it has to be declared in each one. Function prototypes are often put in `#include` header files.

A C++ global function is defined by its name and by the sequence of types of its parameters. When the function is defined as a class member, the class name is also a part of the function definition. This combination (the function signature)—the class name (if any), the function name, and the list of para-meter types—has to be unique. This means that the function name can be overloaded: A function with the same name but with a different set of para-meters will be considered a different function. The return type of the func-tion is not a part of the function signature.

A C++ function can be defined as an inline function. Instead of the func-tion call, the compiler generates object code for such a function and inserts it into the client code. When this function is called, time is not spent on the con-text switch. For applications that are concerned with the speed of execution, this is important.

C++ has functions only: There are no procedures. If the application needs a procedure, a void function can be used.

If a function returns a value, C++ allows the caller to ignore a return value in a call and use a function as a statement. Many C++ library functions have return values that are rarely used. It is a good idea, however, not to ignore return values.

C++ Functions: Parameter Passing

C++ passes parameters by value. At the time of the call, the space for para-meters and local variables is allocated from the stack, and the argument values (variables, expressions, or literals) are copied into the space allocated for parameters. These values are used in the function during its execution. When function terminates, the stack space is returned.

In parameter passing, the values move in one direction only, from actual arguments to formal parameters; changed parameter values are not passed back, and the actual arguments in the client scope do not change.

For side effects in the client space, C++ supports pass by pointer: instead of the value of a given type, a pointer to the value of a given type is passed as an actual argument. C++ pointers are variables in all respects. They are passed by value: The value of the pointer is copied into the formal parameter. When the pointer is used during function execution, it contains the address of the variable in the client space. The value of this variable can be changed through the pointer if necessary.

When the function execution reaches the closing brace, the pointer is destroyed along with other formal parameters (if any). Hence, the function cannot change the value of the pointer. But this is not a problem, because there is no need to change the address. The goal of parameter passing by pointer is to change the variable in the client space whose address is passed as the actual parameter.

Passing parameters by pointer is complex: The programmer has to coordinate the code in three places: (1) the pointer notation (*) is used in the function header and in the prototype, (2) the dereferencing operator (*) is used in the function body, and (3) the address-of operator (&) is used in the function call.

To simplify parameter passing, C++ adds yet another mode of parameter passing that supports side effects in the caller space. In pass by reference, the coordination between different places in code is simpler: (1) the name of the variable without operators is used in the function header, (2) the reference operator (&) is used in the function body, and (3) the name of the variable without operators is used in the function call.

Since this mode of passing parameters supports side effects, it could be used for output parameters (modified by the function) of built-in types instead of passing by pointer.

C++ passes arrays the same way whether its components change in the body of the function or not. Again, there are three places where the code should be coordinated: (1) array name with empty brackets in the function header, (2) index notation (or array name without brackets) in the function body, and (3) array name without brackets in the function call.

C++ structure objects can be passed by value, by pointer, and by reference. Passing parameters by value is simple: The name of the variable without modifiers is used in all three places (in the function header, in the function body, and in the function call). However, it does not support side effects in the client space. Even when the side effects in the client space are not needed, passing by value might be detrimental when large structure variables are passed: Copying them could slow the program down.

Passing parameters by pointer is complex, but it supports side effects in the client space, and it does not require copying the data even for large structures. Passing structure parameters by reference combines the advantages of pass by value and pass by pointer.

This mode of passing parameters should be used for both input and output parameters of programmer-defined types. To tell the maintenance programmer which parameters are modified by the function and which are not (without the need to inspect the function in detail), the designer should use the const modifier for the input parameters (not modified by the function). This is a powerful technique for expressing the intent of the designer directly in code and not in comments.

Scope and Storage Class in C++

Lexical scope in C+ is conventional: Objects (variables) are defined at the beginning (or in the middle) of a scope denoted by the braces; names defined within the scope can be reused in independent scopes; if the same name is reused in nested scopes, the inner scope object hides the object in the outer scope.

Storage class (extent) is a span of run time when the storage is allocated for the object, and its name is associated with its location in memory. Most C++ variables belong to the automatic storage class; these are variables that are defined as local variables in the scope of a function or a block. The storage for an automatic variable is allocated from the system stack when execution enters the opening brace of the block.

Automatic variables exist (and can be referenced by name) from the place of declaration to the closing brace. Automatic variables can be initialized at definition. If they are not initialized, they have no default initial values: When they are allocated on the stack, they contain a random set of bits left from the previous use of this memory.

Memory used for another call to the function (or another iteration through the block) might not be at the same location. Hence, an automatic variable cannot pass data between consecutive calls to the same function.

The advantage of using automatic variables is that the name can be reused in different functions without any coordination among development teams.

Global (or extern) variables are declared outside any function, at the start of a file (or elsewhere in the file scope). Their scope is from the place of declaration until the end of the file. The space for global variables is allocated before the start of program execution (the opening brace of main) and is returned at program termination, when the execution reaches the closing brace of main.

Global variables can be initialized at definition. If a global variable has no initialization, it is initialized to zero by default.

A global variable can be redeclared as a local variable in any file or function. The local name hides the global name in the scope of the block where the local name is defined. The local name uses a different location in memory and does not affect the memory allocated for the global variable.

Global variables can be made visible in other files with the use of an extern declaration. This is a popular technique for communications between functions implemented in different files.

C++ static storage class represents a design compromise: This is the keyword that can be used in several contexts.

When a global object is defined as static, its space is allocated before the start of main and is destroyed at program termination, similar to a regular global variable. Unlike a regular global variable, a static global variable cannot be made external in other files: It is visible to functions in one file only. In a sense, it is a crude way to support private data.

When a local object is defined as static, its space is also allocated before the start of main and is destroyed at program termination. A static local variable is private in a scope—it cannot be accessed by other functions. However, the variable (and its value) exists when it is not in scope. It becomes available when the function is called again.

If the function initializes a local static variable, this initialization is performed only once (at the start of the program). When the function terminates, the static local variable retains its value, and this value can be used in another invocation of the function. It is a tool for communications between different invocations of the same function.

Dynamic storage class gives control over allocation and deallocation of the variable to the programmer. There are two dangers that the programmer should avoid when the program uses dynamic memory management: not returning the memory that the program has and using the memory that the program does not have.

Not returning memory that the program has results in memory leak. Memory leaks deplete the program of memory, especially when the program works around the clock. The program crashes or produces incorrect results.

Using memory that the program does not have results in memory corruption. The program crashes or produces incorrect results or produces correct results until the memory use on the computer changes. The program suddenly crashes or produces incorrect results (quietly).

C++ as an Object-Oriented Language

Even without its object-oriented features, C++ provides a number of improvements over C. Such features as end-of-line comments, flexible definitions of variables in the middle of a scope, symbolic constants for variables and pointers, the scope operator, function-like casts between types, the new and delete operators, default parameters, reference parameters, function and operator overloading, inline functions, the iostream library of I/O objects, and operations (this is quite a long list) contribute to the program quality.

But the major contribution of C++ to software engineering is the implementation of object-oriented features—classes, data members and member functions, constructors and destructors, class composition and inheritance, virtual functions, templates, and exceptions.

C++ Classes

The major goal of C++ classes is to give the programmer the tool for binding together related data and operations. This eliminates the drawbacks of using stand-alone global functions for implementing operations over values of programmer-defined data types.

The data is specified as class data members. The operations are specified as class member functions. The syntax of the class definition specifies data members and member functions within the class scope that is delimited by the opening and closing braces (followed by a semicolon).

C++ allows the class designer to specify the rights that other parts of the program (client code) have for accessing the class components. Public members can be referenced from everywhere where a class object can be defined. Protected members can be referenced from class member functions and from member functions of the classes for which this class is a base class (directly or indirectly). Private members can be referenced from class member functions only.

Hence, parts of the program that do not belong to the given class can access class public members only. This rule can be relaxed with the use of friend classes and functions: They have the same access rights as do the class member functions.

Usually, data members are defined as private, and member functions are defined as public. This not only binds together data and operations in the eyes of the maintenance programmer, but it also hides data implementation from the client code. With data private and operations public, the class is viewed by the client code as the combination of its function interfaces. This supports such modern programming concepts as data encapsulation and information hiding.

Programming with data encapsulation prevents the client code from using the names of class private (or protected) data members. This in turn protects the client code from ripple effects when the data implementation changes. The client code is also protected from ripple effects of changes in the member function implementation as long as the function interfaces remain the same.

Of course, the benefits of object-oriented programming do not come automatically just because C++ classes are used. If member functions just save the values of class data members and retrieve them for use in the client code, the use of these functions in the client code does not make the client code easier to read or to modify. The class designer has to push responsibility down to the server class instead of popping it up to the client code. This is done by adding to class member functions that implement operations significant to achieving client code goals.

Expressing the client code in terms of calls to these server class member functions (rather then in terms of retrieving and manipulating class data members) makes class code self-explanatory, facilitates both design and maintenance, decreases the number of errors, and does all kinds of good things to the quality of the program.

Constructors, Destructors, and Overloaded Operators

Constructors and destructors are special member functions that cannot have arbitrary programmer-defined names. Their names must be derived from the name of the class to which they belong. In return, the client programmer is freed from the duty of calling this function explicitly. Instead, they are called automatically at specific moments in the life of a class object.

A constructor is automatically called immediately after a new class object is created (on the stack or on the heap). A class can have several constructors: They all have the same name (class name), but they should have different parameter lists. Which constructor is called depends on the number and type of arguments that the client code specifies when the object is created.

In the constructor, the class designer specifies how the class data members are initialized and how additional resources (e.g., heap memory) should be allocated.

Constructors should not have return types, and they cannot return values. If the constructor should communicate with the caller and provide information that something went wrong when the object was initialized, the constructor could throw an exception.

Important constructors include a default constructor, a copy constructor, and conversion constructors. The default constructor is called when an object is created without passing any arguments to it. A conversion constructor is called when only one parameter (usually of the type of one of the class data members) is specified.

The copy constructor is called when another object of the same class is used to supply initialization data to the target object. It is also called when a class object is passed to a function by value.

When the class objects allocate heap memory (or other resources) dynamically, passing these objects by value creates integrity problems: The program crashes or behaves erratically (or produces correct results until the memory usage of the computer changes). To prevent integrity problems, the copy constructor can be used to implement value semantics. However, this slows the program down. It is better to pass class objects by reference, not by value. To make passing class objects by value impossible, the copy constructor can be declared private (or protected).

A destructor is called automatically, immediately before the object is destroyed (because of the scope rules or as a result of the delete operator). In the destructor, the class designer specifies how the resources that the object acquired during its lifetime are returned to the system.

Destructors cannot have return types, they cannot return values; in addition, they cannot have parameters. This means that the destructors cannot be overloaded.

Using constructors and destructors requires an adjustment in how we think about program execution. In C++ (unlike in other languages) there is no such thing as merely creating or destroying an object of a programmer-defined type. It is always a constructor call that follows the object creation, and it is always the destructor call that precedes the object destruction.

The usefulness of constructors and destructors for dynamic memory management cannot be overestimated. Instead of dealing with complex and confusing linked data structures that consist of many diverse components, the programmer manages a narrow and well-defined task of handling only one or two components. As a result, the complexity of the programmer's task decreases, and the likelihood of errors becomes less.

C++ is designed to treat objects of programmer-defined types and the variables of built-in types in the same way. This is why, in addition to function overloading, C++ supports operator overloading. This unique feature allows the client code to apply C++ operators to class objects. In most cases, this is a cosmetic, but nice, improvement.

Some overloaded operators provide more than just cosmetic improvement. For example, the subscript operator can be designed to enforce index checking and avoid memory corruption that is a common threat when standard C++ arrays are used. The assignment operator can be designed to enforce value semantics and avoid memory corruption and memory leaks. If the value semantic is not necessary (one object should not be assigned from another object), the assignment operator should be made private (or protected).

Class Composition and Inheritance

Using classes gives the greatest flexibility when class objects work together. C++ supports implementation of associations among objects using pointers and references: Data members of one class point to objects of another type.

C++ also supports class composition where objects of one class are used as data members of another class. Another important relationship between classes that can be implemented in C++ is class inheritance, where one class is used as a base class and another class is used as a class derived from the base class.

With class composition, C++ breaks the process of object creation at run time into stages: First the component objects are created, and then the container object is created. Since object creation is always accompanied by a function call to a constructor, creation of composite objects often becomes a long series of function calls that might affect program performance. Another possible complication is that creating an object results in constructor calls to constructors that are not implemented by the class (resulting in a syntax error).

C++ provides the initialization list technique that resolves both of these problems. Its syntax is unusual (it gives yet another job to the colon operator), but the result is superior to the simple-minded approach. It specifies the names of data members whose nondefault constructors should be called instead of default constructors and specifies the arguments for these constructor calls. It is important to master this technique of object initialization and use it well.

With inheritance, C++ allows the programmer to link two classes with a conceptual link. As a result, everything that is defined for the base class also becomes defined for the derived class. The derived class can define some additional data members and member functions and also redefine some member functions, using the same name and replacing the function body with more appropriate contents.

From the client code point of view, an object of the derived class is the combination of capabilities defined in the base class and in the derived class. Using inheritance is a great way to reuse software design, because the capabilities defined in the base class are immediately reused in the derived class without writing any code.

As the result, a derived class object's data members are defined in the base class and in the derived class. It also has member functions defined in the base class and in the derived class. The client code has access to all public members (data members and member functions) of the derived class object, both inherited from the base class and added in the derived class. The derived class code has access to public and protected members of the base class (both data members and member functions) but not to private base class members.

The syntax of inheritance reuses the keywords public, protected, private (and the colon operator) with different meaning. With the public mode of inheritance, the public, protected, and private data members and member functions defined in the base class remain public, protected, and private in the derived class object. With protected inheritance, public base members become protected in the derived class object and hence are not available to the client code. With private inheritance, public and protected base members become private in the derived class object and hence are not available for further derivation.

This is a rather complex system of changing access rights, and it is a good idea to use public inheritance that maintains the most natural relationships between classes: An object of the derived class is also an object of the base class. This means that a derived class object has all the data members and member functions of the derived class.

When an object of the derived class is instantiated, its base part is created first. This involves a call to the base class constructor; the absence of the default constructor could present syntactic problems. C++ provides the initialization list technique that resolves this problem. Its syntax is similar to the initialization list for class composition, but the base class name is used instead of the names of the component data members. It is important to master this technique of object initialization and use it well.

When a message is sent to an object of the derived class, the compiler searches the definition of the derived class for a match. If no match is found, the compiler searches the base class (or the base of the base class, etc.); if a match is found there, the appropriate function call to the base method is generated; if no match is found, it is a syntax error. If the function name is found in the derived class, the search is terminated. If the arguments match the parameter list, the function call to a derived class method is generated. If the arguments do not match, the search is not resumed: It is a syntax error even when the base class has a function with the same name that matches the arguments.

This means that the derived class method hides the base class method of the same name, no matter what the signatures of these two methods are: There is no function overloading between functions in different scopes with different signatures. This is often a source of subtle errors, when a function that is actually called is different from the function the client programmer (or the maintainer) thinks should be called.

Since an object of the publicly derived class has all the properties of a base class object, the derived object can be used anywhere a base class object is expected—in assignment, parameter passing, and pointer manipulation. The conversion from derived objects (pointers, references) to base objects (pointers, references) is safe. It can always be done and does not even need an explicit cast.

The conversion from a base object to a derived object is not safe. It can be performed only if an explicit assignment operator or conversion constructor is available.

The conversion from a base class pointer (reference) to a derived class pointer (reference) is not safe. It cannot be done implicitly: An attempt to do so is flagged as a syntax error. If the base pointer points to a derived class object, the conversion to the derived class pointer makes sense. To talk the compiler into accepting such a conversion, the explicit cast should be used. If the programmer makes a mistake (the base pointer does not point to a derived class object) a run-time error results.

Virtual Functions and Abstract Classes

Virtual functions extend the concept of hiding base functions in derived class objects. These functions are used when the program has to process a heterogeneous collection of objects that belong to a family of similar classes.

Each class defines a function (they use the same name, e.g., update; and the same signature) that performs a similar operation (again, update) on objects of these classes but does it somewhat differently for objects of different classes (e.g., SavingsAccount and CheckingAccount).

The goal of the design is to achieve a polymorphic effect, that is, send the update() message to each object in the list and invoke either the update() message of the SavingsAccount class or the update() message of the CheckingAccount class. To achieve that goal, you derive these similar classes from the same class (e.g., Account).

There are several restrictions to abide by. The derivation should be public. The base class should have the method with the same name and the same signature (e.g., update) as in the derived classes. This method should be defined as virtual. The heterogeneous collection of objects should be implemented as a list of pointers of the base class pointing to dynamically allocated objects of derived classes.

As the reward for complying with these limitations, the message sent to the base pointer does not invoke the base class method, but rather invokes the method of the derived class to which the object pointed to by the pointer belongs. For example, if the base pointer points to a SavingsAccount object, it will call the update() method from the SavingsAccount class. If it points to a CheckingAccount object, it will call the update() method of the CheckingAccount class.

Many C++ programmers are excited about this technique. This is small wonder because this technique is very nice and very elegant. However, it is not terribly important because the processing of heterogeneous lists is not the most frequent programming task.

Often, the base objects for such a family of classes have no job in the application (e.g., the application deals with savings accounts and checking accounts, but not with unidentified accounts). The further extension of this technique is making the base class into an abstract class.

In an abstract class, the virtual function is defined as a pure virtual function, that is, as a function that has no implementation. Instead, its prototype in the class specification is "assigned" to zero. This is the syntax that defines the virtual function as a pure function and the base class as an abstract class. The application cannot create objects of the abstract class. If the programmer creates an object of the abstract class by mistake, it will be flagged as a syntax error.

Templates

Templates represent yet another tool for design reuse. When the application needs container classes that contain components of different types, it would be nice to avoid repeating the design for each component type—these classes would be almost identical.

C++ templates allow the programmer to create a class where the type of components is defined as a class parameter. When an object of this type is instantiated, the client code supplies the name of the actual type, and the compiler generates class object code where each instance of the class parameter is replaced by the name of the actual type specified by the client code.

The template syntax is rather complex: It involves using parameter lists in angle brackets. The syntax of object instantiation is also complex: The client code specifies actual types also by using angle brackets. Implementation of member functions requires angle brackets for the formal parameter lists and for the class name in the scope operator.

It is not clear to what extent individual applications can benefit from using templates. This is a relatively new feature that is not supported by all compilers yet and the experience of using this feature is limited. However, the C++ Standard Template Library uses templates to implement data structures such as lists, queues, vectors, hash tables, and the like. These classes are well designed and optimized. Their use in individual applications is definitely beneficial. This is why it is important to understand the syntax of instantiating and using template objects.

Exceptions

Exceptions also represent a new C++ feature, designed to support separation between the processing of the main algorithm and the processing of exceptional and rare cases. Presumably, this untangles convoluted code, contributes to streamlining the main processing algorithm, and reduces the complexity of the entire program.

When exception is thrown, an object of a built-in or programmer-defined type is created and sent from the place where the exceptional condition occurred to the place where the exception should be processed. This value (or object) carries the information that is useful for exception processing, for example, a string with an error message.

The syntax of using exceptions requires the programmer to write statements for claiming exceptions, throwing exceptions, and catching exceptions.

When claiming exceptions, the programmer uses the keyword `throw` between the function header and the function body followed by the list of types that this function could throw (in parentheses, comma separated). If the function prototype is specified, the keyword and the list are inserted between the closing parenthesis of the parameter list and the final semicolon.

When throwing an exception, the programmer uses the same keyword `throw` with the single argument (a value of a built-in type or an object of a programmer-defined type). This statement is usually used within a conditional: Some condition is tested, and if it turns out to be true, the exception is thrown to notify the exception handler that the condition turns out to be true.

If the throw statement throws an exception of a programmer-defined class, and the data should be passed with the object, the exception class should define a constructor that accepts necessary values and initializes object data members. If the object does not need any data, the default constructor is called: Unlike in all other cases of creating an object with a default constructor, the empty parentheses must be used after the name of the object.

When catching an exception, a complex syntactic construct should be used—the try block with a statement that could throw an exception and the set of catch blocks that follow the try block. Each catch block is designed to process an exception of only one type.

The try block is just an unnamed block that is preceded by the keyword `try`. A catch block is just a block that is preceded by the keyword `catch` and a parameter list with only one parameter. The type of the catch parameter is of the type (built-in or programmer defined) that this catch block is designed to process.

If the statements in the try block throw no exception, the try block terminates, the catch blocks are skipped, and the next statement (if any) is executed. If one of the statements in the try block throws an exception, the segment of code from this place until the end of the try block is skipped; it will not be executed even if the exception is caught and processed.

Then the catch blocks are examined in sequence for a match between the type in the parameter list and the type of the value thrown in the exception. If the value does not match, the next catch block is examined. If the value matches the parameter type, this catch block is executed and does whatever it takes to process this exception. After that, the rest of the catch blocks are skipped, and the statement following the last catch block is executed.

If no match is found, the statements following the try-catch sequence are skipped, and the function that contains this try-catch sequence is terminated. Before termination, it throws the exception that has not been caught, and the search continues in the caller of this function. If the catch block that handles the exception is found, all is well and the program continues. If not, the search propagates to `main()` and the program is terminated.

This technique can result in complex coding patterns because the programmer can place the try-catch sequences in any function and in any combination. Often, it is hard to figure out in what place the exception is processed and how the program continues the execution. It is not clear whether the use of exceptions indeed results in streamlining of the main line of processing and in easy-to-understand exception processing.

The advantage of this technique is that the place of error discovery can be quite separated from the place of error recovery, and all the necessary information can be sent from the place of discovery to the place of recovery inside the exception object thrown by the throw statement. Another advantage is that the destructors are called for all the objects that are removed from the stack in the process of terminating the functions that do not have the appropriate catch block. This means that if the program recovers from the error and continues execution, it will not suffer from the memory leak.

C++ and Competition

In a sense, C++ competes with every programming language in use today, from FORTRAN and COBOL to PL/I and Ada.

C++ and Older Languages

Of course, even older languages have their own strengths. For example, FORTRAN is superior for implementing scientific algorithms. Its libraries make the job of a scientific programmer much easier.

COBOL and PL/I are superior to C++ when it comes to flexible formatting of output: a C++ programmer has to work much harder to achieve similar results, especially if the iostream library is used. If the older standard library is used, formatting code can be more concise. Still, it is error prone and complicated.

Ada has such features as tasks for concurrent programming and packages for implementing simple objects. These features allow the programmer to implement basic object-oriented designs.

However, none of these languages supports composition, inheritance, and virtual functions. Object-oriented features of C++ make it superior to these languages for writing large applications.

C++ and Virtual Basic

One interesting competitor to C++ that is becoming more and more important is Visual Basic. Over the years, Visual Basic has evolved from a very simple language into a powerful and flexible language.

The output formatting facilities that Visual Basic supports rival those of COBOL and PL/I and are much better than those supported by C++. Visual Basic gives the programmer quick and easy access to building interactive input and output with Graphical User Interfaces (GUIs). For C++ programmer to achieve a similar effect, one has to learn a window library, and all libraries available on the market today are extremely difficult to learn and to use.

Visual Basic also supports some object-oriented features, even though its object-oriented features do not rival those of C++. The learning curve for Visual Basic is easier than for C++: One can learn to produce meaningful applications in Visual Basic much faster than in C++.

However, object-oriented features of C++ are integrated into the language better than in Visual Basic, where they remain a nice but alien addition.

C++ and C

Another language with which C++ has to compete now is its own predecessor, the C programming language.

C remains a language of choice for those programmers who develop real-time and embedded systems. These programmers are apprehensive of such complex C++ features as virtual functions, templates, iostream library, and exceptions. They have a point—all of these features affect program performance and increase the size of the executable code. For real-time and embedded systems, both performance and the size of executables are of primary importance. This is why acceptance of C++ for these kinds of applications has been relatively slow.

I think this was a mistake. C is a language designed for quick and sharp minds, and it is conducive to using concise and expressive coding patterns. These coding patterns sometimes become quite confusing for the reader, especially when the programmer tries to optimize performance and minimize the size of the object code.

As a result, the organizations that use C for real-time and embedded systems wind up with complex schemes of using memory, complex global data structures with dynamic memory management, and convoluted calling conventions. The design of these systems is so complex that they cannot be properly documented given the pressure of tight release schedules. Training new hires takes a long time and negatively affects the productivity of existing staff. Misconceptions and incomplete understanding of decisions made for other parts of the system lead to design errors and mistakes in maintenance that are costly to correct.

I am not sure whether what I am describing is universal, but this is what I saw in several companies that were struggling with the issue of switching from C to C++.

It is obvious that using C++ classes with private data members and public member functions will result in better modularization of code with no effect on program performance and on the size of the object code. Using constructors and destructors properly will eliminate mistakes in memory management and will make the search for errors easier. Also, limited use of virtual functions will not have a significant impact on program size and performance.

After all, polymorphic algorithms can be implemented in any language, and when you implement them, say, in C, you do allocate additional memory to store information about the kind of object the program is dealing with, and the program spends some time figuring out how to treat this object. Using C++ encapsulates this complexity for the programmer and does not waste additional resources.

Unfortunately, many C++ compilers produce bloated object code regardless of whether the programmers use templates, iostream libraries, exceptions, or run-time identification. The limited use of advanced C++ facilities requires cooperation from compiler vendors, so that the programmers could choose what should be included in each build. I think that eventually all C programmers will switch to C++, even if not all C++ features will be used in each application.

C++ and Java

Java is probably the most formidable competition to C++ today. Java is a C++ cousin—similar to C++, it was designed as a superset of C. Most of Java object-oriented syntax is borrowed from C++ (with some changes).

Similar to C++, Java was designed to support classes with data members, member functions, constructors, virtual functions, and exceptions. Java code is a collection of cooperating objects that provide services to each other. Java supports class composition, class inheritance, and polymorphism. Java encourages reuse of programmer-defined classes and reuse of the library classes for graphical visual user interface.

Unlike C++, the goal of backward compatibility with C was not a Java design goal. As a result, Java avoided a significant number of error-prone features that C++ inherited from C. In addition, Java does not include a number of C++ features that either result in the increase in size of object code or encourage inferior software engineering techniques.

Some people say that Java does not have pointers, and hence Java source code is much simpler that comparable C++ code. These people just do not know what they are talking about. Java does have pointers; those who do not believe me are invited to run a simple program and see the message "Null pointer exception" appear on the screen before the program aborts.

Java has an explicit new operator similar to C++. However, Java does not have an explicit delete operator. Instead, Java uses garbage collection. This is a major break from C/C++ ideology: Less time is spent on debugging of memory management; more time is left for other algorithms.

The use of the garbage collector, along with the use of the interpreter during run time, makes Java significantly slower than C++. A few years ago, this conclusion would have meant the death of the language: Nobody would touch it with a ten-foot pole. Not so today. Performance, however important, is not the most important criteria in evaluating a programming language anymore. Portability, robustness, and simplicity are much more important (provided that the language does support a modern object-oriented software engineering approach).

Java is portable: All Java data types are of standard sizes on all machines. An integer is always four bytes; it is not necessarily the fastest type on a given platform, but the program executes the same way on all machines. One cannot choose between signed and unsigned data types: Numeric types are always signed, and boolean and characters are always unsigned. Java identifiers can be of any length.

Java is robust: Implicit casts between numeric types are not allowed; explicit casts are allowed between numeric types but not between numeric types and boolean types. Unlike in C/C++, the relational and logical operators return boolean "true" or "false", and not int 1 or 0; hence, misspelling the comparison operator == as an assignment operator = is flagged as a syntax error—a major source of programming errors disappears without a trace.

Java is simple: It lacks many error-prone C++ features: overloading operator functions, generic templates, multiple inheritance, parameter passing by pointer, pointer-related unprotected array operations, friend classes and functions, global functions, and variables with project-wide names. (Each Java function, including main, must be a member of some class.)

Java has no preprocessor with its macros, include files, and conditional compilations. There is no need for function prototypes—a major source of headache in C++. The Java compiler knows where libraries are located and does not expect the programmer to specify the location.

Java implements object-oriented features that C++ does not have: All functions are virtual functions by default, inheritance supports both hiding the base functions in the derived class and overloading if the signatures are different; classes can be combined into packages. Java has the interface construct that governs the use of objects of one class where the object of another class is expected better than inheritance. Java supports threads that help implement concurrency.

Instead of producing machine-dependent object code, the Java compiler generates so-called bytecode that requires the interpreter to be run. This looks like a liability, right? No, this means that Java bytecode can run on any platform equipped with a Java interpreter: A program compiled on a Solaris machine can run on any UNIX, PC, or Mac machine without any changes. C++ programmers cannot even dream about this kind of portability.

This is why Java is such a success as an Internet language: The bytecode produced on one platform can be downloaded from another platform and executed without even asking what the server platform is. Java programs can be used on heterogeneous networks as easily as on homogeneous networks.

Java comes with a huge library of GUI classes. It is true that learning these classes is no piece of cake. However, a novice programmer can produce a meaningful Java application almost as easily as producing a Visual Basic application and much more easily and faster than producing a similar C++ application.

On the Internet, Java is a clear winner. For backend processing, C++ is a clear winner, mostly because of its performance superiority. But the situation today is not as clear cut as it was several years ago.

Summary

How do you like it? You have seen it all by now. I have tried to be honest with you about the advantages and disadvantages of C++. Those features that are great, I told you are great. Those features that are not so great, I told you are not so great. Those features that are dangerous, I told you are dangerous.

But first and foremost, I tried to show you that using C++ effectively requires a change in programming thinking. You should think about the division of responsibilities between different parts of a program and about pushing these responsibilities down to server classes. You should think about making design decisions clear to the maintenance programmer in code, without comments. You should think about using objects of one class where an object of another class is expected.

Using these software engineering principles, you will be able to create robust, portable, reusable, and maintainable C++ applications. And you will be able to do that while having fun, because C++ is a fun language to use.

I wish you well!

Index